Connecting Researc

As a master teacher, John Santrock connects current research with real-world application, helping students see how developmental psychology plays a role in their own lives and future careers. Through an integrated, personalized digital learning program, students gain the insight they need to study smarter, stay focused, and improve their performance.

Better Data, Smarter Revision, Improved Results

McGraw-Hill Education's SmartBook® is an adaptive learning program designed to help students stay focused and maximize their study time. Based on metacognition, and powered by McGraw-Hill LearnSmart®, SmartBook's adaptive capabilities provide students with a personalized reading and learning experience that helps them identify the concepts they know, and more importantly, the concepts they *don't* know.

Make It Effective.
Unlike other eBooks, SmartBook is adaptive. SmartBook creates a personalized reading experience by highlighting the most impactful concepts a student needs to learn at that moment in time. This ensures that every minute spent with SmartBook is returned to the student as the most value-added minute possible.

Make It Informed.
SmartBook continuously adapts, highlighting content based on what the student knows and doesn't know. Real-time reports quickly identify the concepts that require more attention from individual students—or the entire class. Because SmartBook is personalized, it detects the content individual students are most likely to forget and refreshes them, helping improve retention.

THE HEAT MAP STORY

STEP 1. Over the course of three years, data points showing concepts that caused students the most difficulty were anonymously collected from McGraw-Hill Connect® for Lifespan Development's LearnSmart.

STEP 2. The author was provided with data from LearnSmart that graphically illustrated "hot spots" in the text impacting student learning.

STEP 3. The author used this "heat map" data to refine content and reinforce student comprehension in the new edition. Additional quiz questions and assignable activities were created for use in Connect to further support student success.

RESULT: With empirically based feedback at the paragraph and even sentence level, the author developed the new edition using precise student data to pinpoint concepts that caused students to struggle.

D1567004

Real People, Real World, Real Life

The McGraw-Hill Education Milestones video series is a powerful tool that allows students to experience life as it unfolds, from infancy to late adulthood. This ground-breaking, longitudinal video series tracks the development of real children as they progress through the early stages of physical, social, and emotional development in their first few weeks, months, and years of life. Assignable and assessable within McGraw-Hill Connect, Milestones also includes interviews with adolescents and adults to reflect development throughout the entire lifespan.

Personalized Grading, On the Go, Made Easier

Connect Insight® is a one-of-kind visual analytics dashboard—now available for both instructors and students—that provides at-a-glance information regarding student performance.

Designed for mobile devices, Connect Insight travels from office to classroom, available on demand wherever or whenever it's needed.

A TOPICAL APPROACH TO LIFE-SPAN DEVELOPMENT

Eighth Edition

JOHN W. SANTROCK

University of Texas at Dallas

A TOPICAL APPROACH TO LIFE-SPAN DEVELOPMENT, EIGHTH EDITION

Published by McGraw-Hill Education, 2 Penn Plaza, New York, NY 10121. Copyright © 2016 by McGraw-Hill Education. All rights reserved. Printed in the United States of America. Previous editions © 2014, 2012, and 2010. No part of this publication may be reproduced or distributed in any form or by any means, or stored in a database or retrieval system, without the prior written consent of McGraw-Hill Education, including, but not limited to, in any network or other electronic storage or transmission, or broadcast for distance learning.

Some ancillaries, including electronic and print components, may not be available to customers outside the United States.

This book is printed on acid-free paper.

5 6 7 8 9 10 LWI 21 20 19 18 17

ISBN   978-0-07-786199-5
MHID   0-07-786199-X

Senior Vice President, Products & Markets: *Kurt L. Strand*
Vice President, General Manager, Products & Markets: *Michael Ryan*
Vice President, Content Design & Delivery: *Kimberly Meriwether David*
Managing Director: *William Glass*
Executive Director: *Krista Bettino*
Director, Product Development: *Meghan Campbell*
Product Developer: *Vicki Malinee, Van Brien & Associates*
Marketing Manager: *Christina Yu*
Lead Product Developer: *Dawn Groundwater*
Senior Product Developer: *Sarah Colwell*
Director, Content Design & Delivery: *Terri Schiesl*
Program Manager: *Debra Hash*
Content Project Managers: *Sheila M. Frank, Jodi Banowetz*
Buyer: *Sandy Ludovissy*
Design: *Matt Backhaus*
Content Licensing Specialists: *Carrie Burger, Ann Marie Jannette*
Cover Image: © GettyImages/Isabelle Limbach
Compositor: *Aptara®, Inc.*
Printer: *LSC Communications*

All credits appearing on page are considered to be an extension of the copyright page.

Library of Congress Cataloging-in-Publication Data

Santrock, John W., author.
    A topical approach to life-span development / John W. Santrock. — Eighth edition.
        pages cm
    ISBN 978-0-07-786199-5 (alk. paper) — ISBN 0-07-786199-X
1. Developmental psychology. I. Title.
    BF713.S257 2016
    305.2—dc23

                                                                    2015023443

The Internet addresses listed in the text were accurate at the time of publication. The inclusion of a website does not indicate an endorsement by the authors or McGraw-Hill Education, and McGraw-Hill Education does not guarantee the accuracy of the information presented at these sites.

brief contents

contents

SECTION 1   THE LIFE-SPAN PERSPECTIVE   1

© Randy M. Ury/Corbis

SECTION 2   BIOLOGICAL PROCESSES, PHYSICAL DEVELOPMENT, AND HEALTH   41

© MedicalRF.com/Getty Images RF

© JGI/Jamie Grill/Getty Images RF

CHAPTER 6

Cognitive Developmental Approaches   174

Piaget's Theory of Cognitive Development   175
  Processes of Development   175
  Sensorimotor Stage   176

  CONNECTING WITH RESEARCH   *How Do Researchers Study Infants' Understanding of Object Permanence and Causality?   180*
  Preoperational Stage   182
  Concrete Operational Stage   185
  Formal Operational Stage   186

  CONNECTING DEVELOPMENT TO LIFE   *Are Social Media an Amplification Tool for Adolescent Egocentrism?   188*

Applying and Evaluating Piaget's Theory   189
  Piaget and Education   189
  Evaluating Piaget's Theory   190

Vygotsky's Theory of Cognitive Development   191
  The Zone of Proximal Development   192
  Scaffolding   192
  Language and Thought   192
  Teaching Strategies   193
  Evaluating Vygotsky's Theory   194

Cognitive Changes in Adulthood   196
  Piaget's View   196
  Realistic and Pragmatic Thinking   196
  Reflective and Relativistic Thinking   197
  Cognition and Emotion   197
  Is There a Fifth, Postformal Stage?   197
  Are There Cognitive Stages in Middle and Late Adulthood?   199

Reach Your Learning Goals   200

CHAPTER 7

Information Processing   203

The Information-Processing Approach   204
  The Information-Processing Approach and Its Application to Development   204
  Speed of Processing Information   206

Attention   207
  What Is Attention?   207
  Infancy   207
  Childhood and Adolescence   209
  Adulthood   210

Memory   211
  What Is Memory?   211
  Infancy   212

  Childhood   213
  Adulthood   217

  CONNECTING WITH RESEARCH   *How Well Do Adults Remember What They Learned in High School and College Spanish?   219*

Thinking   220
  What Is Thinking?   220
  Infancy and Childhood   220

  CONNECTING WITH CAREERS   *Helen Hadani, Ph.D., Developmental Psychologist, Toy Designer, and Associate Director of Research for the Center for Childhood Creativity   223*
  Adolescence   225
  Adulthood   227

  CONNECTING DEVELOPMENT TO LIFE   *The Remarkable Helen Small   232*

Metacognition   234
  What Is Metacognition?   234
  Theory of Mind   235
  Metacognition in Adolescence and Adulthood   237

Reach Your Learning Goals   238

CHAPTER 8

Intelligence   242

The Concept of Intelligence   243
  What Is Intelligence?   243
  Intelligence Tests   243
  Theories of Multiple Intelligences   245
  The Neuroscience of Intelligence   248

Controversies and Group Comparisons   249
  The Influence of Heredity and Environment   249
  Group Comparisons and Issues   252

  CONNECTING WITH RESEARCH   *Can Early Intervention in the Lives of Children Growing Up in Impoverished Circumstances Improve Their Intelligence?   251*

The Development of Intelligence   253
  Tests of Infant Intelligence   253

  CONNECTING WITH CAREERS   *Toosje Thyssen Van Beveren, Infant Assessment Specialist   254*
  Stability and Change in Intelligence Through Adolescence   255
  Intelligence in Adulthood   255

The Extremes of Intelligence and Creativity   259
  Intellectual Disability   259
  Giftedness   260
  Creativity   263

  CONNECTING DEVELOPMENT TO LIFE   *Living a More Creative Life   266*

Reach Your Learning Goals   267

SECTION 4 · SOCIOEMOTIONAL PROCESSES AND DEVELOPMENT 293

© David P. Hall/Corbis

SECTION 6   **ENDINGS   563**

© Russell Underwood/Corbis

about the author

John W. Santrock

John Santrock received his Ph.D. from the University of Minnesota in 1973. He taught at the University of Charleston and the University of Georgia before joining the program in Psychology in the School of Behavioral and Brain Sciences at the University of Texas at Dallas, where he currently teaches a number of undergraduate courses and was recently given the University's Effective Teaching Award.

John Santrock (back row middle) with the 2015 recipients of the Santrock Travel Scholarship Award in developmental psychology. Created by Dr. Santrock, this annual award (now in its sixth year) provides undergraduate students with the opportunity to attend a professional meeting. A number of the students shown here attended the 2015 meeting of the Society for Research in Child Development.
Courtesy of Jessica Serna

John has been a member of the editorial boards of *Child Development* and *Developmental Psychology.* His research on father custody is widely cited and used in expert witness testimony to promote flexibility and alternative considerations in custody disputes. John also has authored these exceptional McGraw-Hill texts: *Psychology* (7th edition), *Children* (13th edition), *Child Development* (14th edition), *Adolescence* (16th edition), *Life-Span Development* (15th edition), and *Educational Psychology* (5th edition).

For many years, John was involved in tennis as a player, teaching professional, and a coach of professional tennis players. As an undergraduate, he was a member of the University of Miami (FL) tennis team that still holds the record for most consecutive wins (137) in any NCAA Division I sport. John has been married for four decades to his wife, Mary Jo, who is a Realtor. He has two daughters—Tracy and Jennifer—both of whom are Realtors after long careers in technology marketing and medical sales, respectively. He has one granddaughter, Jordan, age 23, who recently completed her Master's degree from the Cox School of Business at SMU and currently works for Ernst & Young, and two grandsons—the Belluci brothers: Alex, age 10, and Luke, age 9. In the last decade, John also has spent time painting expressionist art.

Dedication:

**With special appreciation to my mother,
Ruth Santrock, and my father, John Santrock.**

expert consultants

Life-span development has become an enormous, complex field, and no single author, or even several authors, can possibly keep up with all of the rapidly changing content in the many periods and different areas in this field. To solve this problem, author John Santrock has sought the input of leading experts about content in a number of areas of life-span development. These experts have provided detailed evaluations and recommendations in their area(s) of expertise.

The following individuals were among those who served as expert consultants for one or more of the previous editions of this text:

Karen Adolph	Elena Grigorenko	Charles Nelson
David Almeida	Scott Hofer	Crystal Park
Karlene Ball	William Hoyer	Denise Park
Martha Ann Bell	Janet Shibley Hyde	Ross Parke
Jay Belsky	Rachel Keen	Glenn Roisman
James Birren	James Marcia	Carolyn Saarni
Kirby Deater-Deckard	Linda Mayes	Robert J. Sternberg
Susanne Denham	Patricia Miller	Elizabeth Stine-Morrow
James Garbarino	David Moore	Ross Thompson
Linda George	Daniel Mroczek	Doug Wahlsten
Gilbert Gottlieb	Darcia Narváez	Allan Wigfield

Following are the expert consultants for the eighth edition, who (like those of previous editions) literally represent a *Who's Who* in the field of life-span development.

Ross Thompson Dr. Thompson is one of the world's leading experts on children's socioemotional development. He currently is Distinguished Professor of Psychology at the University of California–Davis, where he directs the Social and Emotional Development Lab. A developmental psychologist, Dr. Thompson studies early parent-child relationships, the development of emotion understanding and emotion regulation, early moral development, and the growth of self-understanding in young children. He also works on the applications of developmental research to public policy concerns, including school readiness and its development, early childhood investments, and early mental health. Dr. Thompson has published five books, several best-selling textbooks, and over 200 papers related to his work. He is a founding member of the National Scientific Council on the Developing Child, has twice been Associate Editor of *Child Development*, and has received the Boyd McCandless Young Scientist Award for Early Distinguished Achievement from the American Psychological Association. Dr. Thompson also recently was given the Ann Brown Award for Excellence in Developmental Research and the University of California–Davis Distinguished Scholarly Public Service Award.

"It was once again a pleasure to read chapters that are so effectively constructed to provide students with a state-of-the-art, engaging, comprehensive overview of developmental issues. The writing enlists student interest into topics that reflect the current state of knowledge in developmental science but which are also relevant to students' experience and well-being." —**Ross Thompson** *University of California—Davis*
Photo courtesy of Dr. Ross Thompson, photo by V.I.P Studios Photography, Davis, CA

Patricia Miller Dr. Miller is a leading expert in the cognitive development of children. She obtained her Ph.D. from the University of Minnesota and currently is Professor of Psychology at San Francisco State University, having previously been a professor at the University of Michigan, University of Georgia, and University of Florida. Her research focuses on children's executive function, memory, attention, and learning strategies. Topics of current projects include the development of executive function in preschoolers, the effects of exercise on children's executive function and academic achievement, and the development and transfer of strategies. Dr. Miller is a recent president of the developmental psychology division of the American Psychological Association and is a Fellow of that organization as well as the Association for Psychological Science. She also has been an Associate Editor of *Child Development* and has served on the editorial boards of several major developmental journals. Her book, *Theories of Developmental Psychology*, is in its fifth edition, and she is co-author or co-editor of three other volumes. Dr. Miller's work has been published in top journals such as *Child Development*, *Developmental Psychology*, and *Cognitive Development*.

"This book continues to have the qualities that led me to adopt it several years ago: It is clear, interesting, and up to date. Moreover, it captures the current controversies in the field. The applications, especially to education, are strong. The new material strengthens the book. I certainly will continue to use it in my courses." —**Patricia Miller** *San Francisco State University*
Photo courtesy of Dr. Patricia Miller

William J. Hoyer Dr. Hoyer is a leading expert on cognitive aging and life-span development. He obtained his Ph.D. from West Virginia University and is currently Professor of Psychology at Syracuse University. Dr. Hoyer is also a faculty affiliate of the Aging Studies Institute at Syracuse University. His research focuses on age-related changes in memory, attention, and learning. His research appears in journals such as *Psychology of Aging*; *Aging, Neuropsychology, and Cognition*; and *Journal of Gerontology: Psychological Sciences*. He is co-author of *Adult*

Development and Aging. Dr. Hoyer is a Fellow in the American Psychological Association, the Association for Psychological Science, and The Gerontological Society of America.

"Importantly, Dr. Santrock presents the essential information that students need to know about physical development and biological aging. Further, in the revised material, he adds new material that is solid and intriguing, and that reflects the emerging state of the field. . . Clearly, Dr. Santrock stays abreast of the latest work by leading researchers that comprise the field of life-span development. . . This new edition effectively represents the field in his choice of core topics, and provides a solid across-the-board background requisite to advanced, specialized study of topics in psychological science that have implications for human development, or its course and outcomes." —**William Hoyer** *Syracuse University*

Mandy Maguire Dr. Maguire is a leading expert in language development. She obtained her Ph.D. from Temple University and completed a postdoctoral fellowship in the Developmental Neuroscience Lab at the University of Louisville. She is currently an Associate Professor in the School of Behavioral and Brain Sciences at the University of Texas at Dallas. Her research focuses on the behavioral and neurological aspects of how typically developing children acquire language. Topics of current projects include using EEG to identify individual differences in word learning across children, specifically why some children struggle more than others in this task, and the impact of poverty on language and the neural correlates of language in school-aged children. Dr. Maguire's work has been published in journals such as *Brain and Language, Developmental Science, Developmental Psychology, Cognition,* and *Developmental Cognitive Neuroscience.*

". . . I really liked the chapter (Language Development). It is well laid out and includes a great deal of the information that I believe is necessary for students at this level of education. . . I'm impressed by how much of this work is very new and how the chapter highlights exactly where the field of language development is today. . . The book also provides a lot of the 'why' for important findings in the field. . . There also is a good deal of practical information. . . The linking of topics across chapters is also very important." —**Mandy McGuire** *University of Texas–Dallas*

John Bates Dr. Bates is one of the world's leading experts on temperament and socioemotional development in infants and young children. He currently is Professor of Psychological and Brain Sciences at Indiana University. Dr. Bates obtained his Ph.D. in clinical psychology at UCLA. A major focus of his research is the development of behavior problems versus positive adjustment. Dr. Bates has especially been interested in children's temperament characteristics, in combination with parenting. Most of his research has been longitudinal in nature, including one study conducted from 6 months to 17 years of age, another from 5 to 25 years of age (which includes analyses of temperament-environment and gene-environment interactions), and yet another study from 30 to 42 months of age.

"Largely the chapter (Emotional Development and Attachment) is highly current. It is clear that Dr. Santrock systematically reviews

the literature as it emerges. Overall, the scholarship is impressive. . . I expect that the students who work through this chapter and the others will end up with a relatively deep and broad understanding of development. . . I really like how the book sets up a new topic by reviewing some previously presented ideas and putting them in a new context. I also like how it presents a lot of advanced concepts for understanding the current literature in an accessible way. The writing is almost always quite clear and easy to read, even if it is talking about fairly complex topics." —**John Bates** *Indiana University*

Kristen M. Kennedy Dr. Kennedy is an expert in the cognitive neuroscience of aging. She obtained her Ph.D. from Wayne State University and currently is a professor in the School of Behavioral and Brain Sciences at The University of Texas at Dallas and the Center for Vital Longevity, as well as Adjunct Assistant Professor of Advanced Imaging Research at The University of Texas Southwestern Medical Center. Her research focuses on adult life-span (ages 20 to 90+) differences and changes in brain structure and function, and associated cognitive consequences. Current projects include studying the role of differences in brain structure on brain function using a variety of neuroimaging techniques (such as functional magnetic resonance imaging and diffusion tensor imaging). She is also currently investigating the modifying influence of genetics and gene × environment interaction on the brain and cognitive aging. Dr. Kennedy was recently named a Rising Star by the Association for Psychological Science. She currently serves on the Editorial Board of *NeuroImage.* Dr. Kennedy's work has been published in journals such as *Cerebral Cortex, NeuroImage, Neuropsychologia,* and *Journal of Neuroscience.*

"There is a strong framework for the chapter (Physical Development and Biological Aging). . . I like the discussion of major theories of biological aging. . . The Information Processing chapter is a great chapter. . . I like the organization of different types of information processing and the epochs of life-span subsections. It works very well." —**Kristen Kennedy** *University of Texas–Dallas*

Jennifer E. Lansford Dr. Lansford is a developmental psychologist who studies the development of aggression and other behavior problems in children and adolescents. She earned her Ph.D. from the University of Michigan and is currently Research Professor at Duke University in the Center for Child and Family Policy and Social Science Research Institute. Dr. Lansford's research focuses on understanding how contexts (such as culture and schools) affect socializing agents (such as parents and peers) on trajectories of social and behavioral development from childhood to adulthood. She leads the Parenting Across Cultures project, a longitudinal study of mothers, fathers, and children in nine countries that investigates biological, familial, and cultural processes in development. Dr. Lansford has been Associate Editor of *Aggressive Behavior* and currently serves on the Editorial Boards of several journals. She has over 150 publications in journals such as *Child Development* and *Development and Psychopathology.*

" . . . from the preface, the textbook appears to offer well-organized, up-to-date overviews on key topics of importance in

development over the life course. The 'Connect,' 'Reflect on Your Own Personal Journey' and 'Review' sections appear to be strengths in terms of promoting student learning." —**Jennifer Lansford** *Duke University*

Crystal Park Dr. Park is Professor of Clinical Psychology at the University of Connecticut–Storrs and an affiliate professor of the University of Connecticut Center for Health, Intervention, and Prevention. Her research focuses on multiple aspects of coping with stressful events, including the roles of religious beliefs and religious coping, stress-related growth, and the making of meaning in the context of traumatic events and life-threatening illnesses, especially cancer and congestive heart failure. She is currently Principal Investigator of NIH and foundation-funded studies of yoga interventions, breast cancer survivors' health behaviors, and college student self-regulation and success. She is co-author of *Empathic Counseling: Meaning, Context, Ethics, and Skill* and co-editor of *The Handbook of the Psychology of Religion and Spirituality* (first and second editions) and *Medical Illness and Positive Life Change: Can Crisis Lead to Personal Transformation?*

"I think there is a strong framework for this chapter (Death, Dying, and Grieving). . . I like the interweaving of previous chapters with this one. . . The narrative is quite up-to-date. . . I think the coverage is fine." —**Crystal Park** *University of Connecticut–Storrs*

Santrock—connecting *research* and *results!*

As a master teacher, John Santrock connects current research and real-world applications. Through an integrated, personalized digital learning program, students gain the insight they need to study smarter and improve performance.

Real People, Real World, Real Life

The McGraw-Hill Education Milestones video series is a powerful tool that allows students to experience life as it unfolds, from infancy to late adulthood. This ground-breaking, longitudinal video series tracks the development of real children as they progress through the early stages of physical, social, and emotional development in their first few weeks, months, and years of life. Assignable and assessable within Connect Psychology, Milestones also includes interviews with adolescents and adults to reflect development throughout the entire lifespan.

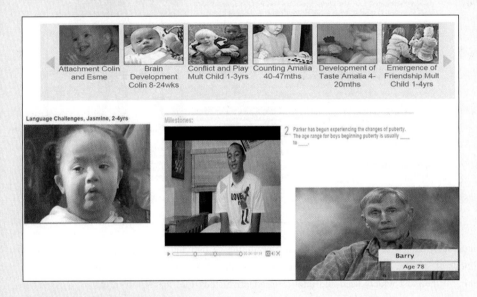

Better Data, Smarter Revision, Improved Results

Students helped inform the revision strategy of *A Topical Approach to Life-Span Development.*

STEP 1. Over the course of three years, data points showing concepts that caused students the most difficulty were anonymously collected from Connect Lifespan Development's LearnSmart®.

STEP 2. The data from LearnSmart was provided to the author in the form of a *Heat Map*, which graphically illustrates "hot spots" in the text that impacts student learning (see image below).

STEP 3. The author used the *Heat Map* data to refine the content and reinforce student comprehension in the new edition. Additional quiz questions and assignable activities were created for use in Connect Lifespan Development to further support student success.

RESULT: Because the *Heat Map* gave the author empirically based feedback at the paragraph and even sentence level, he was able to develop the new edition using precise student data that pinpointed concepts that gave students the most difficulty.

LearnSmart is an adaptive learning program designed to help students learn faster, study smarter, and retain more knowledge for greater success. Distinguishing what students know from what they don't, and focusing on concepts they are most likely to forget, LearnSmart

FIGURE **3.1**

CHANGES IN PROPORTIONS OF THE HUMAN BODY DURING GROWTH. As individuals develop from infancy through adulthood, one of the most noticeable physical changes is that the head becomes smaller in relation to the rest of the body. The fractions listed refer to head size as a proportion of total body length at different ages.

Infancy The average North American newborn is 20 inches long and weighs 7½ pounds. Ninety-five percent of full-term newborns are 18 to 22 inches long and weigh between 5½ and 10 pounds.

In the first several days of life, most newborns lose 5 to 7 percent of their body weight. Once infants adjust to sucking, swallowing, and digesting, they grow rapidly, gaining an average of 5 to 6 ounces per week during the first month. Typically they have doubled their birth weight by the age of 4 months and have nearly tripled it by their first birthday. Infants grow about ¾ inch per month during the first year, increasing their birth length by about 40 percent by their first birthday.

Infants' rate of growth slows considerably in the second year of life (Burns & others, 2013). By 2 years of age, infants weigh approximately 26 to 32 pounds, having gained a quarter to half a pound per month during the second year; at age 2 they have reached about one-fifth of their adult weight. The average 2-year-old is 32 to 35 inches tall, which is nearly one-half of adult height.

Early Childhood As the preschool child grows older, the percentage of increase in height and weight decreases with each additional year (Leifer, 2011). Girls are only slightly smaller and lighter than boys during these years. Both boys and girls slim down as the trunks of their bodies lengthen. Although their heads are still somewhat large for their bodies, by the end of the preschool years most children have lost their top-heavy look. Body fat also shows a slow, steady decline during the preschool years. Girls have more fatty tissue than boys; boys have more muscle tissue (McMahon & Stryjewski, 2012).

Growth patterns vary individually (Wilson & Hockenberry, 2012). Think back to your preschool years. This was probably the first time you noticed that some children were taller than you, some shorter; some were fatter, some thinner; some were stronger, some weaker. Much of the variation is due to heredity, but environmental experiences are also involved. A review of the height and weight of children around the world concluded that two important contributors to height differences are ethnic origin and nutrition (Meredith, 1978).

Why are some children unusually short? The culprits may be congenital factors (a prenatal problem), growth hormone deficiency, a physical problem that develops in childhood, maternal smoking during pregnancy, or an emotional difficulty (Wit, Kiess, & Mullis, 2011).

Middle and Late Childhood The period of middle and late childhood involves slow, consistent growth. This is a period of calm before the rapid growth spurt of adolescence.

The bodies of 5-year-olds and 2-year-olds are different from one another. The 5-year-old not only is taller and heavier, but also has a longer trunk and legs than the 2-year-old. *What might be some other physical differences between 2- and 5-year-olds?*

---

continuously adapts to each student's needs by building an individual learning path. Millions of students have answered over a billion questions in LearnSmart since 2009, making it the most widely used and intelligent adaptive study tool that's proven to strengthen memory recall, keep students in class, and boost grades.

Fueled by LearnSmart, SmartBook is the first and only adaptive reading experience currently available.

- **Make It Effective.** SmartBook creates a personalized reading experience by highlighting the most impactful concepts a student needs to learn at that moment in time. This ensures that every minute spent with SmartBook is returned to the student as the most value-added minute possible.

- **Make It Informed.** The reading experience continuously adapts by highlighting content based on what the student knows and doesn't know. Real-time reports quickly identify the concepts that require more attention from individual students—or the entire class. SmartBook detects the content a student is most likely to forget and brings it back to improve long-term knowledge retention.

Personalized Grading, on the Go, Made Easier

Connect Insight is a one-of-kind visual analytics dashboard—now available for both instructors and students—that provides at-a-glance information regarding student performance. The immediate analysis from Connect Insight empowers students and helps instructors improve class performance efficiently and effectively.

- **Make It Intuitive.** Instructors and students receive instant, at-a-glance views of performance matched with student activity.

- **Make It Dynamic.** Connect Insight puts real-time analytics in the user's hands for a just-in-time approach to teaching and learning.

- **Make It Mobile.** Connect Insight is available on demand wherever and whenever needed.

preface

Making Connections . . . From My Classroom to *A Topical Approach to Life-Span Development* to You

Having taught life-span development every semester for three decades now, I'm always looking for ways to improve my course and *A Topical Approach to Life-Span Development*. Just as McGraw-Hill looks to those who teach the life-span development course for input, each year I ask the approximately 200 students in my life-span development course to tell me what they like about the course and the text, and what they think could be improved. What have my students told me lately about my course and text? Students said that highlighting connections among the different aspects of life-span development would help them to better understand the concepts. As I thought about this, it became clear that a *connections* theme would provide a systematic, integrative approach to the course material. I used this theme to shape my current goals for my life-span development course, which, in turn, I've incorporated into *A Topical Approach to Life-Span Development*:

1. **Connecting with today's students** To help students learn about life-span development more effectively.

2. **Connecting research to what we know about development** To provide students with the best and most recent theory and research in the world today about each of the periods of the human life span.

3. **Connecting topical processes in development** To guide students in making *topical connections* across different aspects of development through the life span.

4. **Connecting development to the real world** To help students understand ways to *apply* content about the human life span to the real world and improve people's lives; and to motivate them to think deeply about *their own personal journey through life* and better understand who they were, are, and will be.

Connecting with Today's Students

In *A Topical Approach to Life-Span Development,* I recognize that today's students are as different in some ways from the learners of the last generation as today's discipline of life-span development is different from the field 30 years ago. Students now learn in multiple modalities; rather than sitting down and reading traditional printed chapters in linear fashion from beginning to end, their work preferences tend to be more visual and more interactive, and their reading and study often occur in short bursts. For many students, a traditionally formatted printed textbook is no longer enough when they have instant, 24/7 access to news and information from around the globe. Two features that specifically support today's students are the adaptive ebook, Smartbook (see pages xv–xvii) and the learning goals system.

The Learning Goals System

My students often report that the life-span development course is challenging because of the amount of material covered. To help today's students focus on the key ideas, the Learning Goals System I developed for *A Topical Approach to Life-Span Development*

1 Body Growth and Change · **LG1** Discuss major changes in the body through the life span

Patterns of Growth | Height and Weight in Infancy and Childhood | Puberty | Early Adulthood | Middle Adulthood | Late Adulthood provides extensive learning connections throughout the chapters. The learning system connects the chapter opening outline, learning goals for the chapter, mini-chapter maps that open each main section of the chapter, *Review, Connect, Reflect* questions at the end of each main section, and the chapter summary at the end of each chapter.

The learning system keeps the key ideas in front of the student from the beginning to the end of the chapter. The main headings of each chapter correspond to the learning goals that are presented in the chapter-opening spread. Mini-chapter maps that link up with the learning goals are presented at the beginning of each major section in the chapter.

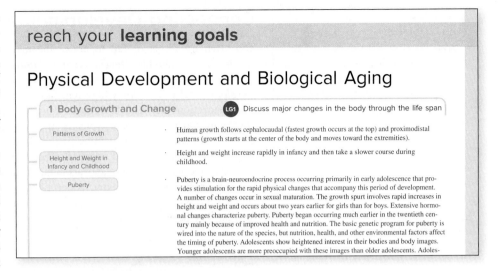

Then, at the end of each main section of a chapter, the learning goal is repeated in *Review, Connect, Reflect,* which prompts students to review the key topics in the section, connect to existing knowledge, and relate what they learned to their own personal journey through life. *Reach Your Learning Goals,* at the end of the chapter, guides students through the bulleted chapter review, connecting with the chapter outline/learning goals at the beginning of the chapter and the *Review, Connect, Reflect* questions at the end of major chapter sections.

Connecting Research to What We Know about Development

Over the years, it has been important for me to include the most up-to-date research available. I continue that tradition in this edition by looking closely at specific areas of research, involving experts in related fields, and updating research throughout. **Connecting with Research** describes a study or program to illustrate how research in life-span development is conducted and how it influences our understanding of the discipline. Topics range from *How Are Preterm Infants Affected by Touch?* (Chapter 2) to *Does Intervention Reduce Juvenile Delinquency?* (Chapter 13) to *Parenting and Children's Achievement: My Child Is My Report Card, Tiger Moms, and Tiger Babies Strike Back* (Chapter 16).

The tradition of obtaining detailed, extensive input from a number of leading experts in different areas of life-span development also continues in this edition. Biographies and photographs of the leading experts in the field of life-span development appear on pages xii to xiv, and the chapter-by-chapter highlights of new research content are listed on pages xxii to xxxix. Finally, the research discussions have been updated in every area and topic. I expended every effort to make this edition of *A Topical Approach to Life-Span Development* as contemporary and up-to-date as possible. To that end, there are more than 1,500 citations from 2014, 2015, and 2016 in the text.

developmental **connection**

Peers

How is adult friendship different among female friends, male friends, and cross-gender friends? Connect to "Peers and the Sociocultural World."

Connecting Developmental Processes

Too often we forget or fail to notice the many connections from one point or topic in development to another. *Developmental Connections,* which appear multiple times in each chapter, point readers to where the topic is discussed in a previous or subsequent chapter. *Developmental Connections* highlight links across topics and age periods of development *and* connections between biological, cognitive, and socioemotional processes. These key developmental processes are typically discussed in isolation from each other, and students often fail to see their connections. Included in the *Developmental Connections* is a brief description of the backward or forward connection.

Also, a *Connect* question appears in the section self-reviews—*Review, Connect, Reflect*—so students can practice making connections between topics. For example, in Chapter 12, students are asked to connect the chapter's discussion of the gender-intensification hypothesis to what they have already read about identity development in adolescence.

Connecting Development to the Real World

In addition to helping students make research and developmental connections, *A Topical Approach to Life-Span Development* shows the important connections between the concepts discussed and the real world. In recent years, students in my life-span development course have increasingly told me that they want more of this type of information. In this edition, real-life connections are explicitly made through *Connecting Development to Life,* the *Milestones* program that helps students watch life as it unfolds, and *Connecting with Careers.*

Connecting Development to Life, along with a variety of life-span connecting boxed features, describes the influence of development in a real-world context on topics including *Helping Overweight Children Lose Weight* (Chapter 4), *Working During College* (Chapter 16), and *Communicating with a Dying Person* (Chapter 17).

The *Milestones* program, described on page xv, shows students what developmental concepts look like by letting them watch actual humans develop. Starting from infancy, students track several individuals, seeing them achieve major developmental milestones, both

---

connecting development to life

Are Social Media an Amplification Tool for Adolescent Egocentrism?

Earlier generations of adolescents did not have social media to connect with large numbers of people; instead, they connected with fewer people, either in person or via telephone. Might today's teens be drawn to social media and its virtually unlimited friend base to express their imaginary audience and sense of uniqueness? A recent analysis concluded that amassing a large number of friends (audience) may help to validate adolescents' perception that their life is on stage and everyone is watching them (Psychster Inc, 2010). A look at a teen's home Twitter comments may suggest to many adults that what teens are reporting is often rather mundane and uninteresting as they update to the world at large what they are doing and having, such as: "Studying heavy. Not happy tonight." or "At Starbucks with Jesse. Lattes are great." Possibly for adolescents, though, such tweets are not trivial but rather an expression of the personal fable's sense of uniqueness. (Source: Psychster Inc, 2010).

A recent study of social networking sites found that the indiscriminate monologue communication from one to many, in which the diverse interests of others are not considered, that often occurs on such sites as Facebook may produce an egocentric tendency that undermines prosocial behavior (Chiou, Chen, & Liao, 2014).

In what ways might frequent use of social media, such as Facebook®, influence adolescents' cognitive development?
© Brendan O'Sullivan/Getty Images

What do you think? Are social media, such as Facebook and Twitter, amplifying the expression of adolescents' imaginary audience and personal fable sense of uniqueness?

physically and cognitively. Clips continue through adolescence and adulthood, capturing attitudes toward issues such as family, sexuality, and death and dying.

Connecting with Careers profiles careers ranging from an educational psychologist (Chapter 1) to a toy designer (Chapter 7) to a marriage and family therapist (Chapter 14) to a teacher of English language learners (Chapter 9) to a home hospice nurse (Chapter 17), each of which requires knowledge about human development.

The careers highlighted extend from the Careers Appendix in Chapter 1 that provides a comprehensive overview of careers in life-span development to show students where knowledge of human development could lead them.

Part of applying development to the real world is understanding its impact on

connecting with careers

Helen Hadani, Ph.D., Developmental Psychologist, Toy Designer, and Associate Director of Research for the Center for Childhood Creativity

Helen Hadani obtained a Ph.D. from Stanford University in developmental psychology. As a graduate student at Stanford, she worked part-time for Hasbro Toys and Apple testing children's software and computer products for young children. Her first job after graduate school was with Zowie Intertainment, which was subsequently bought by LEGO. In her work as a toy designer there, Helen conducted experiments and focus groups at different stages of a toy's development, and she also studied the age-effectiveness of each toy. In Helen's words, "Even in a toy's most primitive stage of development . . . you see children's creativity in responding to challenges, their satisfaction when a problem is solved or simply their delight in having fun" (Schlegel, 2000, p. 50).

More recently, she began working with the Bay Area Discovery Museum's Center for Childhood Creativity (CCC) in Sausalito, California, an education-focused think tank that pioneers new research, thought-leadership, and teacher training programs that advance creative thinking in all children. Helen is currently the Associate Director of Research for the CCC.

Helen Hadani has worked as both a toy designer and in a museum position that involves thinking of ways to increase children's creative thinking.
Courtesy of Helen Hadani

oneself. An important goal I have established for my life-span development course and this text is to motivate students to think deeply about their own journey of life. To further encourage students to make personal connections to content in the text, *Reflect: Your Own Personal Journey of Life* appears in the end-of-section review in each chapter. This feature involves a question that asks students to reflect on some aspect of the discussion in the section they have just read and connect it to their own life. For example, in Chapter 1, students are asked:

Imagine what your development would have been like in a culture that offered fewer or distinctly different choices. How might your development have been different if your family had been significantly richer or poorer than it was when you were growing up?

In addition, students are asked a number of personal connections questions in the photograph captions.

Content Revisions

A significant reason why *A Topical Approach to Life-Span Development* has been successfully used by instructors for eight editions now is the painstaking effort and review that goes into making sure the text provides the latest research on all topic areas discussed in the classroom. This new edition is no exception, with more than 1,500 citations from 2014, 2015, and 2016.

New research highlights include very recent studies on outcomes of adoption; links of infant attachment (including attachment to both parents) to developmental outcomes; whether delay of gratification in early childhood can predict physical and mental health in adulthood; more precise discoveries about the adolescent's changing brain; cohabitation contexts that are or are not linked to divorce; the far-reaching benefits of exercise in the lives of older adults; and genetic, cellular, and lifestyle factors that characterize individuals with Alzheimer disease. **New techniques** are described, such as neurofeedback and mindfulness training to reduce ADHD symptoms; and **ongoing debates** are explored, such as whether supportive or tiger parenting is better for Chinese American children, and if adolescence is taking too long.

Below is a sample of the many chapter-by-chapter changes that were made in this new edition of *A Topical Approach to Life-Span Development*. A more extensive, detailed list of chapter-by-chapter changes can be obtained by contacting your McGraw-Hill sales representative.

Chapter 1: Introduction

- Update on life expectancy in the United States (U.S. Census Bureau, 2014)

- Updated statistics on the increasing percentage of U.S. children under 18 years of age living in poverty, especially in African American and Latino families (U.S. Census Bureau, 2014)

- New discussion of the recently created large-scale two-generation intervention, *Ascend*, by the Aspen Institute that is designed to help children escape from poverty through three avenues: education, economic support, and social capital (Aspen Institute, 2013)

- Expanded content on ethnic minority children, including concern about the discrimination and prejudice they experience (Renzetti & Kennedy-Bergen, 2015)

- Inclusion of recent research on individuals from 22 to 93 years of age that found older adults reported having more positive emotional experiences than did young adults (English & Carstensen, 2014)

- Expanded content on the early-later experience issue regarding sensitive parenting to include the importance of positive close relationships later in childhood, in adolescence, and in adulthood (Luong, Rauers, & Fingerman, 2015; Mikulincer & Shaver, 2015; Wentzel, 2015)

- New coverage of Robert Siegler's microgenetic approach to the study of information processing (Siegler, 2006; Siegler & Lortie-Forgues, 2015; Siegler & others, 2015; Siegler & Thompson, 2014)

Chapter 2: Biological Beginnings

- Editing and updating of chapter based on detailed reviews by leading experts Kirby Deater-Deckard and David Moore

- Updated content on the number of genes that humans have and a recent prediction that humans likely have less than 20,000 genes (Abyzov & others, 2013; Flicek & others, 2013)

- New description of recent research on how exercise and nutrition can modify the behavior of genes (Lindholm & others, 2014; Ma & others, 2015)

- New content on how sleep deprivation can influence gene expression in negative ways such as increased inflammation, expression of stress-related genes, and impairment of protein functioning (Da Costa Souza & Ribeiro, 2015)

- New coverage of Cynthia Kenyon's important research on the search for longevity genes and interventions that might involve the use of drugs that mimic gene mutations linked to increased longevity

- Expanded discussion of how the process from genotype to phenotype works

- Coverage of a recent research review that concluded the young scientific area of gene × environment (G × E) interaction is plagued by difficulties in replicating results, inflated claims, and other weaknesses (Manuck & McCaffery, 2014)

- New research indicating that the stress hormone cortisol can cross the placenta (Parrott & others, 2014)

- New organizing commentary that describes four important phases of brain development during the prenatal period

- New commentary on the conclusions reached by Great Britain's National Institutes of Care and Health Excellence that consumption of one to two drinks not more than twice a week during pregnancy is safe (O'Keeffe, Greene, & Kearney, 2014)

- Description of a recent study that found no differences in the presence of developmental problems in 7-year-olds whose mothers either were light drinkers (no more than two drinks per week) and mothers who did not drink (Kelly & others, 2013)

- Discussion of a recent research review that concluded maternal smoking during pregnancy is linked to altered neurotransmitter effects in offspring, and to elevated blood pressure in offspring when they are adults (Suter & others, 2015)

- New coverage of research indicating that prenatal smoking has been implicated in as many as 25 percent of infants being born with low birth weight (Brown & Graves, 2013)

- Inclusion of recent research indicating that smoking during pregnancy was associated with increased risk of asthma and wheezing in adolescence (Hollams & others, 2014)

- Coverage of a recent study that indicated marijuana use by pregnant women and environmental tobacco smoke during prenatal development were linked to stillbirth (Varner & others, 2014)

- Inclusion of information from a recent research review that concluded maternal obesity during pregnancy is associated with an increased likelihood of offspring becoming obese in childhood and adulthood (Santangeli, Sattar, & Huda, 2015)
- New description of a study that found stressful events prior to conception were linked with very low birth weight (Witt & others, 2014)
- Discussion of recent research that revealed maternal depression during pregnancy was linked to low birth weight (Chang & others, 2014)
- Discussion of a recent Norwegian study that found that maternal of age of 30 years and older was linked to the same elevated risk for fetal deaths as 25- to 29-year-old pregnant women who were smokers or overweight/obese (Waldenstrom & others, 2014)
- Update on the continuing decline in preterm births in the United States in 2013 (March of Dimes, 2014)
- Update on the percentage of U.S. births that take place in hospitals, at home, and in birthing centers and the percentage of babies born through caesarean delivery (Martin & others, 2013)
- Coverage of a recent study that found doula-assisted mothers were four times less likely to have a low birth weight baby (Gruber, Cupito, & Dobson, 2013)
- Updated statistics on the percentage of babies born preterm and low birth weight in the United States, including ethnic variations (Martin & others, 2013)
- Inclusion of autism spectrum disorders as among the outcomes associated with low birth weight (Dudova & others, 2014; Maramara, He, & Ming, 2014)
- Discussion of a recent study that found long-term positive benefits for maternal-newborn kangaroo care through 10 years of age for respiratory and cardiovascular functioning, sleep, and cognitive functioning (Feldman, Rosenthal, & Eidelman, 2014)
- Inclusion of recent research in which kangaroo care led to better physical development in low birth weight infants (Bera & others, 2014)
- Description of a recent research review that concluded mother kangaroo care was associated with a lower incidence of mortality in low birth weight babies (Conde-Agudelo & Diaz-Rossello, 2014)
- Expanded discussion of kangaroo care including recent concerns that many NICU nurses are not using kangaroo care with high-risk newborns (Kymre, 2014) and recommendations for the use of kangaroo care with all newborns (Rodgers, 2013)
- Description of a recent study in which both massage (moderate-pressure stroking) and exercise (flexion and extension of the limbs) led to weight gain in preterm infants (Diego, Field, & Hernandez-Reif, 2014)
- Description of a recent study that found depression during pregnancy, a history of physical abuse, migrant status, and postpartum physical complications were major risk factors for postpartum depression (Gaillard & others, 2014)

Chapter 3: Physical Development and Biological Aging

- Writing revisions were made in the chapter that involve the most difficult concepts for students on tests based on feedback from LearnSmart and Heat Maps. These changes include editing of paragraphs, addition of topical sentences, and inclusion of bullets. Examples of topics where these changes were made include the following: Key patterns of growth, factors involved in being unusually short, overall rate of growth in early childhood, main factors in height worldwide, roles of testosterone and estradiol, development of the brain in adolescence, and key aspects of brain adaption in late adulthood.
- Content changes on physical development and biological aging based on feedback from leading experts Elizabeth Susman, Bonnie Halpern Fletcher, William Hoyer, and Kristen Kennedy
- Revised definition of puberty to include brain-neuroendocrine processes (Susman & Dorn, 2013)
- Description of a recent study of 9- to 17-year-old boys that found testosterone level peaked at 17 years of age (Khairullah & others, 2014)
- Inclusion of recent research that documented the growth of the pituitary gland during adolescence and linked its volume to circulating blood levels of estradiol and testosterone (Wong & others, 2014)
- Description of a recent research review that concluded there is insufficient quality research to confirm that changing testosterone levels in puberty are linked to adolescent males' mood and behavior (Duke, Balzer, & Steinbeck, 2014)
- New content indicating that early-maturing girls engage in sexual intercourse at younger ages and have more unstable sexual relationships (Moore, Harden, & Mendle, 2014)
- Coverage of a recent study that revealed later-maturing boys had a more negative body image in the early high school years than early-maturing boys (De Guzman & Nishina, 2014)
- Discussion of recent research in which the longer adults had smoked the more likely they were to have facial sagging and wrinkles (Okada & others, 2013)
- Description of the increasing use of the term "sarcopenic obesity" and its link to hypertension (Park & others, 2013)
- Coverage of a recent study in which hypertension in middle age was linked to lower cognitive functioning 23 years later (Virta & others, 2013)
- Discussion of recent research that found obesity was linked to mobility limitations in older adults (Murphy & others, 2014)
- Inclusion of changes in the coverage of the development of the brain based on comments by leading expert consultants Martha Ann Bell and Philip David Zelazo
- New introductory content indicating that the brain's developmental trajectory occurs in a bottom-up, top-down sequence (Zelazo, 2013)
- New Figure 8: Measuring the Activity of an Infant's Brain with Magnetoencephalography (MEG) that shows an infant in a Meg brain imaging device while listening to spoken words in Dr. Patricia Kuhl's laboratory

- Expanded and updated description of research conducted by leading experts—Martha Ann Bell, Charles Nelson, and John Richard—on the development of the brain in infancy
- Updated and expanded coverage of the development of the brain in adolescence to emphasize changes in the limbic system and its link to rewards (Casey, 2015; Steinberg, 2015b)
- New discussion of neurotransmitter changes in adolescence, particularly increased dopamine production (Leyton & Vezina, 2014; Steinberg, 2015a, b)
- New closing statement for the section on brain development in adolescence underscoring the correlational nature of research on the development of the brain, which means caution should be used in making causal statements about the brain's influence
- New commentary about the sensory regions of the brain being less vulnerable to decline than the prefrontal cortex in older adults (Rodrique & Kennedy, 2011)
- Main new section to open the coverage of sleep that focuses on different views of the functions of sleep and why we sleep, including an evolutionary perspective on its importance for survival, its restorative function in protein production and removal of neural waste (Picchioni & others, 2014; Xie & others, 2013), and its role in brain plasticity and synaptic connection (Barnes & Wilson, 2014; Pace-Schott & Spencer, 2015)
- New commentary that after prone sleeping position, the two most critical factors in predicting SIDS are (1) maternal smoking, and (2) bed sharing (Mitchell & Krous, 2015)
- New section, Sleep and Cognitive Development, including recent research that linked sleep quality in infancy with higher cognitive functioning in early childhood (Bernier & others, 2013)
- Coverage of a recent study that found poor sleep consolidation in infancy was associated with language delays in early childhood (Dionne & others, 2011)
- Discussion of a recent study of preschool children that found longer sleep duration was linked to better peer acceptance, social skills, and receptive vocabulary (Vaughn & others, 2015)
- Inclusion of recent research indicating that inadequate sleep duration at 4 years of age was linked to inadequate sleep duration at 6 years of age (Koulouglioti & others, 2014)
- Coverage of a large-scale study of more than 270,000 adolescents from 1991 to 2012 that found adolescents have been decreasing the amount of sleep they get in recent years (Keyes & others, 2015)
- New research that found when adolescents get less than average sleep per night they have more emotional and peer-related problems, higher anxiety, and higher levels of suicidal ideation (Sarchiapone & others, 2014)
- Description of a recent Swedish study of 16- to 19-year-olds in which shorter sleep duration was associated with a greater likelihood of school absence (Hysing & others, 2015)
- New discussion citing electronic media usage and caffeine intake, along with changes in the brain coupled with early school starting times, as possible reasons for adolescents' sleep debt (Owens, 2014)
- Coverage of a recent study of fourth- and seventh-graders in which sleeping near small screens, sleeping with a TV in the room, and having more screen time were associated with shorter sleep duration (Falbe & others, 2015)
- Discussion of a recent study that revealed early school start times were linked to a higher vehicle crash rate by adolescent drivers (Vorona & others, 2014)
- Inclusion of the recent recommendation by the American Academy of Pediatrics that schools institute start times from 8:30 to 9:30 a.m. to improve students' academic performance and quality of life (Adolescent Sleep Working Group, AAP, 2014)
- Coverage of a study of individuals from 20 to 90 years of age in which total sleep decreased about 8 minutes per decade for males and about 10 minutes per decade for females (Dorffner, Vitr, & Anderer, 2015). In this study, as people aged they spent more time in light sleep and less time in deep sleep.
- Description of a recent study that found engaging in regular aerobic exercise improved the sleep profiles of older men (Melancon, Lorrain, & Dionne, 2015)
- Expanded content on the New England Centenarian Study, including recent research indicating increased support for the compression of morbidity, which involves chronic high-mortality diseases being markedly delayed in centenarians (Sebastiani & Perls, 2012)
- New commentary about ethnic differences in longevity widening and a suggestion that the powerful influence of education may make it impossible to bridge the gap (Olshansky & others, 2012)
- New coverage of the oldest person in the world in 2015 (Misao Okawo, 117 years of age) and the oldest person in the United States (Gertrude Weaver, 116 years of age) and their comments about why they were able to live so long
- Description of recent research indicating the shorter telomere length was linked to having worse social relationships, being less optimistic, and showing greater hostility (Uchino & others, 2012; Zalli & others, 2014)
- New discussion of the increased emphasis on changes in myelination and neural networks in the aging brain (Callaghan & others, 2014; Rodrique & Kennedy, 2011)

Chapter 4: Health

- Coverage of a longitudinal study that found adolescents who had more friends who drank alcohol were more likely to binge drink in adolescence and early adulthood (Soloski, Kale Monk, & Durtschi, 2015)
- Inclusion of recent information that because of dramatic declines in smoking and increased effectiveness in treating cardiovascular disease, rates for dementia and Alzheimer disease may not increase as much in the future as was previously envisioned and might even decline (Rocca & others, 2011)
- New discussion of the current research interest in the roles that amyloid and tau play in Alzheimer disease (Avila & others, 2014; Tian & others, 2014)

- Discussion of a recent study that highlighted several key factors involved in the change from mild cognitive impairment to Alzheimer disease (Alegret & others, 2014)
- Coverage of a recent study in which cognitively impaired older adults receiving home-based care had better cognitive function, were less depressed, and reported better social connectedness than their counterparts living in institutionalized care (Nikmat, Al-Mashoor, & Hashim, 2015)
- Description of recent research indicating that chronic stress increased pancreatic cancer growth (Kim-Fuchs & others, 2014)
- New discussion of a recent study of middle-aged adults that found a high level of allostatic load (wearing down of bodily systems in response to high stress levels) was linked to lower levels of episodic memory and executive function (Karlamangia & others, 2013)
- Expanded and updated content on links between chronic stress and a downturn in immune system functioning in a number of contexts, including living next to a nuclear reactor, failures in close relationships, loneliness, depression, and burdensome caregiving for a family member with a progressive illness (Fagundes & others, 2013; Jaremka & others, 2014)
- New coverage of recent data (2011–2012) indicating a substantial drop in obesity for U.S. preschool children, possibly due to parents' increased purchasing of low-calorie foods (Ogden & others, 2014). Also in this study, obese preschool children were five times more likely than normal-weight children to be overweight or obese as adults.
- Inclusion of a recent large-scale study of U.S. children that found overweight 5-year-olds were four times more likely to be obese at 14 years of age than their 5-year-old counterparts who began kindergarten at a normal weight (Cunningham & others, 2014)
- Description of recent research indicating that 17.5 percent of U.S. 6- to 11-year-olds were obese in 2011–2012, essentially unchanged from 2009–2010 (Ogden & others, 2014)
- Updated data on the increasing percentage of U.S. adolescents who are obese (Ogden & others, 2014) and developmental changes in obesity from kindergarten to early adolescence (Cunningham, Kramer, & Narayan, 2014)
- Updated information about the continuing drop in vegetable and fruit consumption by U.S. adolescents through 2013 (Kann & others, 2014)
- Inclusion of a recent international study of adolescents in 56 countries that found fast food consumption was linked to higher body mass index (Braithwaite & others, 2014)
- Description of a recent study in which participation in family meals during adolescence protected against overweight or obesity in adulthood (Berge & others, 2015)
- New discussion of the likely brain changes in adolescents who are anorexic (Fuglset & others, 2014)
- Coverage of a recent study that found bulimics have difficulty controlling their emotions (Lavender & others, 2014)
- Description of a recent study that revealed rates of overweight or obesity increased from 25.6 percent for college freshmen to 32 percent for college seniors (Nicoteri & Miskovsky, 2014)

- Inclusion of information from a recent Gallup (2013a) survey on the increase in obesity in 2013 in 30- to 44-year-olds
- Expanded and updated coverage of links between children's exercise and their physical well-being (McCormack & others, 2014; Shin & others, 2014)
- Coverage of a recent study in which in-class high-intensity exercise improved the selective attention of 9- to 11-year-olds (Ma, Le Mare, & Gurd, 2015)
- New content on research that strongly supports the positive effects of exercise on children's bone strength and even on the prevention of osteoporosis in aging adults (Janz & others, 2015)
- Description of recent research that found moderate-intensity aerobic exercise improved children's cognitive inhibitory control (Drollette & others, 2014)
- Discussion of recent research that found adolescents who were high in physical fitness had better connectivity between brain regions than adolescents who were less fit (Herting & others, 2014)
- New information about recent survey data on the percentage of U.S. adults who exercise regularly (Gallup, 2013b)
- Coverage of a study in Copenhagen, Denmark, in which engaging in light or moderate jogging on a regular basis was linked to increased longevity (Schnohr & others, 2015)
- Description of a recent study in which a brief water-based exercise program improved the attention, memory, and executive function of older adults (Fedor, Garcia, & Gunstad, 2015)
- Discussion of a recent research review that concluded more active and physically fit older adults can allocate more attentional resources in interacting with the environment than their less physically fit counterparts (Gomez-Pinilla & Hillman, 2013). This review also concluded that exercise's influence on cognition occurs through changes in molecular events associated with the management of energy metabolism and synaptic plasticity.
- Updated coverage of the Monitoring the Future study's assessment of drug use by secondary school students with 2014 data on U.S. eighth-, tenth-, and twelfth-graders (Johnston & others, 2015)
- Updated data from the Monitoring the Future indicating that the peak of binge drinking occurs at 21 to 22 years of age in 2012 (Johnston & others, 2013)
- Description of recent research on adolescents indicating that neighborhood disadvantage was linked to a higher level of alcohol use two years later, mainly through a pathway that included exposure to delinquent peers (Trucco & others, 2014)
- Coverage of a recent study in which low parental knowledge of adolescents' peer relations and behavior, coupled with friends' delinquency, predicted adolescent substance abuse (McAdams & others, 2014)
- Discussion of a recent study that found early onset of drinking and a quick progression to drinking to intoxication were linked to drinking problems in high school (Morean & others, 2014)

- New research that revealed early- and rapid-onset trajectories of alcohol, marijuana, and substance use were associated with substance use in early adulthood (Nelson, Van Ryzin, & Dishion, 2015)

Chapter 5: Motor, Sensory, and Perceptual Development

- A number of changes made in the content on motor development based on feedback from leading experts Karen Adolph and Scott Johnson
- New description of how the development of sitting skills in infancy might produce a developmental cascade of changes (Adolph & Robinson, 2015)
- New discussion of how advances in walking skills might produce a developmental cascade of changes in infancy, including increased language skills (Adolph & Robinson, 2015; Walle & Campos, 2014)
- Coverage of a recent study indicating that children, especially girls, who participate in sports have a higher quality of life than children who do not participate (Vella & others, 2014)
- New commentary about the increasing concern about the risk of concussions when children play football or soccer (Purcell & others, 2014)
- Expanded and updated coverage of the dramatic increase in the use of sophisticated eye-tracking equipment in the study of infant perception (Guimard-Brunault & others, 2013; Kretch, Franchak, & Adolph, 2014; Righi & others, 2014; Sasson & Touchstone, 2014)
- New commentary noting that most studies of infant eye-tracking use remote optics eye trackers in which the camera is not attached to the infant's head
- Coverage of a recent meta-analysis that found exercise reduced the rate of falls in adults 60 years of age and older (Stubbs, Brefka, & Denkinger, 2015)
- Description of a recent study that revealed walking was more effective than balance training in reducing falls in older adults (Okubo & others, 2015)
- Expanded and updated discussion of pain in older adults, including the frequency of persistent pain, most frequent pain complaints, and lower tolerance of pain (Farrell, 2012; Molton & Terrill, 2014)

Chapter 6: Cognitive Developmental Approaches

- New discussion of a recent study of 10-month-olds that found a wide variation in search behaviors on the A-not-B task, possibly due to temperament, maturity of short-term/long-term memory, inhibition, and cognitive flexibility (Johansson, Forssman, & Bohlin, 2014)
- Discussion of recent research indicating that preverbal infants might have an inborn sense of morality, which supports the core knowledge approach (Hamlin, 2013, 2014)
- Added criticism of the nativist approach for ignoring the immersion of the infant in a social world and instead focusing only on what happens within the infant's head (Nelson, 2013)

- New commentary noting that some critics argue that the Baillargeon and Spelke experiments mainly demonstrate perceptual competencies or detection of consistencies in the environment, therefore reflecting only rudimentary understanding that likely differs from older children's understanding (Heyes, 2014; Ruffman, 2014)
- New description of a recent study of social networking sites that found the indiscriminate monologue involving communication from one to many that often occurs on such sites as Facebook may produce an egocentric tendency that undermines prosocial behavior (Chiou, Chen, & Liao, 2014)
- New coverage of factors that influence the effectiveness of the zone of proximal development in advancing young children's learning and development (Gauvain, 2013)
- New discussion of a recent study that found the following scaffolding techniques improved 4- to 5-year-olds' geometric knowledge: heightened engagement, direct exploration, and facilitation of "sense making" through techniques such as guided play (Fisher & others, 2013)

Chapter 7: Information Processing

- Inclusion of changes based on feedback from leading experts Patricia Miller, William Hoyer, and Kristen Kennedy
- Inclusion of information from a recent meta-analysis of research indicating that processing speed increases through the childhood and adolescent years, begins to decline during the latter part of early adulthood, and then declines further through the remainder of the adult years (Verhaeghen, 2013).
- Description of recent research that found older adults especially have difficulty in processing the change from green to yellow at traffic intersections and that a cue 1.5 seconds prior to the light change reduces their accident likelihood (Mischel, 2014)
- Discussion of a recent study in which slow processing speed at baseline was linked to the emergence of dementia over the next 6 years (Welmer & others, 2014)
- Coverage of a recent study that found infants visually attend to events that are of intermediate complexity and are more likely to look away from events that are overly simple or complex (Kidd, Piantadosi, & Aslin, 2012)
- Description of recent research indicating that individual differences in attention at 5 months of age that involve efficiency in processing information were linked to executive function in the preschool years (Cuevas & Bell, 2014)
- Coverage of recent research that revealed problems in joint attention as early as 8 months of age were linked to a child being diagnosed with autism by 7 years of age (Veness & others, 2014)
- Expanded description of sustained attention and vigilance with research indicating that the greatest increase in vigilance occurs during early childhood (Rueda & Posner, 2013)
- Inclusion of recent research indicating that the ability to focus attention better at age 5 was linked to a higher level of academic achievement at age 9 (Razza, Martin, & Brooks-Gunn, 2012)

- Discussion of recent research indicating that 10 weeks of training in speed of processing resulted in improved selective attention in older adults (O'Brien & others, 2013)
- Inclusion of recent research in which older adults who participated in a video game training session showed a significant reduction in distraction and increased alertness (Mayas & others, 2014)
- Discussion of recent research indicating that infantile amnesia begins to especially become stronger by the time children are 8 to 9 years of age (Bauer & Larkina, 2014)
- New research indicating that children with learning disabilities in reading and math have working memory deficits (Peng & Fuchs, 2015)
- Description of the early onset of explicit memory deficits, but not implicit memory deficits, in individuals with Alzheimer disease (Boccia, Silveri, & Guariglia, 2014)
- Coverage of recent research that found visually encoded working memory was linked to older adults' mobility (Kawagoe & Sekiyama, 2014)
- Discussion of a recent study in which strategy training improved older adults' working memory (Borella & others, 2013)
- Description of a recent experimental study that linked moderate exercise in older adults to faster reaction times on a working memory task (Hogan, Mata, & Carstensen, 2013)
- New coverage of classic research by Walter Mischel and his colleagues (Mischel, Cantor, & Feldman, 1996; Mischel & Moore, 1980) on the role of "hot thoughts" and "cool thoughts" in influencing young children's delay of gratification and recent research indicating a link between this delay of gratification and body mass index (BMI) three decades later (Schlam & others, 2013)
- Inclusion of recent research that found executive function skills predicted math gains in kindergarten (Fuhs & others, 2014)
- Description of recent research in which sensitive parenting at 3 years of age predicted fewer problems with executive function at 4 years of age (Kok & others, 2014)
- New discussion of the importance of adolescents quickly getting the gist of a dangerous situation, which can cue personal values that will reduce the likelihood adolescents will engage in risky decision making (Reyna & Zayas, 2014)
- Inclusion of recent research that revealed more physically fit older adults were more cognitively flexible than their less physically fit counterparts (Berryman & others, 2013)
- New description of increasing research evidence that aerobic exercise improves executive function in older adults (Guiney & Machado, 2013)
- Inclusion of a recent meta-analysis that found tai chi participation was associated with better executive function in older adults (Wayne & others, 2014)
- Coverage of a recent study in which various executive functions predicted mobility function over a one-year period (Gothe & others, 2014)
- Discussion of a recent study that revealed a higher level of education was linked to better cognitive functioning in older adults (Rapp & others, 2013)
- Coverage of recent research that found working in an occupation with a high level of cognitive demands was linked to higher levels of cognitive functioning before retirement and a slower rate of cognitive decline after retirement (Fisher & others, 2014)
- Description of a recent study in which sustained engagement in cognitively demanding activities for three months improved the episodic memory of older adults (Park & others, 2014)
- Inclusion of recent research that found iPad training improved the episodic memory and processing speed of 60- to 90-year-olds (Chan & others, 2015)
- Coverage of recent research on older adults that revealed fish oil had beneficial effects on executive function and a number of areas of brain functioning (Witte & others, 2014)
- Discussion of a recent study that found playing a multitasking video game improved the cognitive skills of older adults (Anguera & others, 2013)
- New commentary noting that some critics argue that the research evidence for the effectiveness of brain training games is weak or unfounded (Hambrick, 2014; Redick & others, 2013)
- New content indicating that some experts conclude that, in most cases, cognitive training of older adults is effective only when it involves extensive effortful practice over a long period of time (Lovden & others, 2012; Nyberg & others, 2012)
- Various changes made in the discussion of cognitive functioning in older adults based on feedback from leading experts K. Warner Schaie and Patricia Reuter-Lorenz
- New coverage of the influence of symbolic thinking skills on the development of theory of mind (Lillard & Kavanaugh, 2014)
- New discussion of a recent study of young children in which their metacognitive ability in the numerical domain predicted their school-based math knowledge (Vo & others, 2014)

Chapter 8: Intelligence

- Discussion of Robert Sternberg's (2015b) recent definition of intelligence as the ability to adapt to, shape, and select environments
- Inclusion of the most recent version of the WPPSI—Fourth Edition (revised in 2012 for young children) (Syeda & Climie, 2014)
- Coverage of a recent study that found children who are gifted engage in faster processing speed and more accurate processing of information than do children who are not gifted (Duan, Dan, & Shi, 2014)
- Inclusion of Robert Sternberg's (2014b) commentary about how research on the brain's role in intelligence has been more productive in producing answers to some questions than to others
- Discussion of a recent study in which emotional intelligence abilities were linked to academic achievement above and beyond cognitive and personality factors (Lanciano & Curci, 2014)
- Description of a recent meta-analysis of 53 studies since 1972 that found IQ scores have been rising about 3 points

per decade since that year and that the increase in IQ scores does not seem to be diminishing (Trahan & others, 2014)

· New discussion of the increase in intelligence test scores even for the brightest individuals in recent years (Wai, Putallaz, & Makel, 2012)

· Inclusion of a recent study using the Stanford Binet Scales that found no differences between non-Latino White and African American preschool children when they were matched for age, gender, and level of parent education (Dale & others, 2014)

· Description of a recent analysis that concluded the under-representation of African Americans in STEM subjects and careers is linked to practitioners' expectations that they have less innate talent than non-Latino Whites (Leslie & others, 2015)

· Coverage of a longitudinal study in which children identified before 13 years of age as having profound math and verbal reasoning skills (top 1 in 10,000 children) had achieved considerable success in their various careers by the time they were 38 years of age (Kell, Lubinski, & Benbow, 2013)

· Inclusion of recent research in which parents and teachers rated elementary school children who are not gifted as having more emotional and behavioral problems than children who are gifted (Eklund & others, 2015). Also in this study, when children who are gifted have emotional and behavioral problems, they are more likely to be internalized rather than externalized problems.

· Description of a recent experimental study that compared individuals after they had participated in four activities and found that the most creative thinking occurred following the activity of walking (Oppezzo & Schwartz, 2014)

Chapter 9: Language Development

· Inclusion of changes recommended by leading expert Mandy Maguire

· New discussion of how infants in the second half of their first year rely on statistical information such as the co-occurrence of phonemes and syllables to help them extract potential word forms (Werker & Gervain, 2013; Willits, Seidenberg, & Saffran, 2014; Zamuner, Fais, & Werker, 2014)

· New coverage of cross-linguistic differences in word learning

· Revised and updated content on bilingualism, including information about whether parents of infants and young children should teach them two languages simultaneously (Bialystok, 2014, 2015)

· Discussion of a recent study that revealed 18- to 24-month-old infants in low-SES families already had a smaller vocabulary and less efficient language processing than their infant counterparts in middle-SES families (Fernald, Marchman, & Weisleder, 2013)

· Description of a recent study in which child-directed speech in a one-to-one context at 11 to 14 months of age was linked to greater word production at two years of age than standard speech and speech in a group setting (Ramirez-Esparza, Garcia-Sierra, & Kuhl, 2014)

· Coverage of a recent study of low-SES Spanish-speaking families that found infants who experienced more child-directed speech were better at processing words in real time and had larger vocabularies at 2 years of age (Weisleder & Fernald, 2013)

· New discussion of the possibility that bilingualism may delay the onset of Alzheimer disease, including recent research on this topic (Alladi & others, 2013; Bialystok & others, 2014; Fischer & Schweizer, 2014)

· Inclusion of recent research that found Japanese mothers who used more elaborative information-seeking responses during joint picture-book reading at 20 months had children with a better productive vocabulary at 27 months (Murase, 2014)

· New content on whether infants learn language effectively through television and videos

· Discussion of a recent study of toddlers in which frequent TV exposure increased the risk of delayed language development (Lin & others, 2015)

· Coverage of a recent study that found use of Skype technology provides some improvement in children's language learning over television and videos (Roseberry & others, 2014)

Chapter 10: Emotional Development and Attachment

· Changes in chapter based on feedback from leading experts John Bates and Ross Thompson

· New discussion of biological factors involved in the temperament dimension of negative emotionality

· New description of how some leading researchers have recently argued that empathy can be expressed before the infant's first birthday (Davidov & others, 2013)

· Inclusion of information about the Emotion-Based Prevention Program (EBP) that is designed to improve young children's understanding of emotions and a recent study that found EBP was effective in improving Head Start children's emotional understanding and decreasing their negative emotions (Finion & others, 2015)

· Coverage of a recent study of 10- to 12-year-olds in which mothers of anxious children were more likely to engage in more psychologically controlling behavior intended to manipulate the children's emotional state, showed less interest in the children, and elaborated less during conversations about an emotionally negative event (Brumariu & Kerns, 2015)

· Description of a recent study of 9- to 15-year-olds in which those who had a higher level of emotion regulation were less likely to be depressed in stressful environments even though they had a short version of the serotonin transporter gene (Ford & others, 2014)

· Inclusion of recent research showing that babies quickly pick up on their mothers' stress and negative emotions when they are reunited with them after the mothers have experienced a negative, stressful circumstance (Waters, West, & Mendes, 2014)

· Discussion of a recent research study indicating that 9-month-old infants displayed jealousy-related behavior and

EEG patterns characteristic of jealousy when their mothers gave attention to a social rival (Mize & others, 2014)

· Coverage of recent research indicating that smiling and laughing at 7 months of age was associated with self-regulation at 7 years of age (Posner & others, 2014)

· Description of recent research indicating that a higher level of positive emotionality predicted more initial infant smiling and laughter, while a higher level of parenting stress predicted a lower trajectory of infant smiling and laughter (Bridgett & others, 2013)

· Description of recent research indicating that understanding others' emotions was linked to children's emotion regulation (Hudson & Jacques, 2014)

· Coverage of a recent study that revealed fathers' internalizing problems were linked to a higher level of negative affectivity in 6-year-olds (Potapova, Gartstein, & Bridgett, 2014)

· New content on how during middle and late childhood, as part of their understanding of emotions, children can engage in "mental time travel" in which they anticipate and recall the cognitive and emotional aspects of events (Lagattuta, 2014b)

· New discussion of describing temperament in terms of its reactivity and self-regulation (Bates & Pettit, 2015)

· Description of recent research that found an inhibited temperament at 2 to 3 years of age was related to symptoms of social phobia at 7 years of age (Lahat & others, 2014)

· Inclusion of recent findings indicating that an inhibited temperament in infants and young children is linked to the development of social anxiety disorder in adolescence and adulthood (Rapee, 2014; Perez-Edgar & Guyer, 2014)

· Discussion of recent research that found preschool children with high levels of surgency and negative affectivity were more likely to engage in a number of obesity-related eating behaviors (Leung & others, 2014)

· New research that revealed effortful control was a strong predictor of academic success skills in kindergarten children from low-income families (Morris & others, 2014)

· Description of a recent study in which maternal negativity and child behavior problems were most strongly linked for children who were low in effortful control and living in chaotic homes (Chen, Deater-Deckard, & Bell, 2014)

· New discussion of the recent interest in the differential susceptibility and biological sensitivity to context models emphasizing that certain characteristics—such as a difficult temperament—may render children more vulnerable to difficulty in adverse contexts but also make them more susceptible to optimal growth in very supportive conditions (Belsky & others, 2015; Belsky & van Izjendoorn, 2015; Ellis & others, 2011; Hartman & Belsky, 2015; Simpson & Belsky, 2016)

· Coverage of a recent study in which parent sensitivity during the still-face paradigm when infants were 3, 5, and 7 months old was linked to infants' emotional and behavioral trajectories, which in turn predicted secure and insecure attachment at 12 and 14 months of age (Braungart-Rieker & others, 2014)

· Inclusion of recent research in which infant attachment insecurity (especially insecure resistant attachment) and

early childhood behavioral inhibition predicted adolescent social anxiety symptoms (Lewis-Morrarty & others, 2015)

· Description of a meta-analysis in which secure attachment in infancy was related to social competence with peers in early childhood (Groh & others, 2014)

· Discussion of a recent study that found fathers with lower testosterone levels engaged in more optimal parenting with their infants and that fathers who were given oxytocin showed improved parenting behavior with their infants (Weisman, Zagoory-Sharon, & Feldman, 2014)

· Description of a recent national poll that estimated there are 2 million stay-at-home dads in the United States, a significant increase from 1.6 million in 2004 and 1.1 million in 1989 (Livingston, 2014)

· Inclusion of recent research that found high-quality child care during the infant/toddler years was linked to better memory skills at the end of the preschool years (Li & others, 2013)

· Coverage of recent research indicating that insecure disorganized children (Type D) are most at risk for developing anxiety problems (Kerns & Brumariu, 2014)

· Added commentary noting that infants and toddlers are more likely to receive care in family child care and informal care settings while older children are more likely to be enrolled in child care centers and preschool and early education programs

· Coverage of recent research that revealed early daters have more externalized problems throughout adolescence than on-time and late daters (Connolly & others, 2013)

· Coverage of a recent meta-analysis that found a lower percentage of U.S. college students are securely attached and a higher percentage are insecurely attached than in the past (Konrath & others, 2014)

· New discussion of two longitudinal studies of newly married couples in which spouses were more likely to engage in infidelity when either they or their partner had a highly anxious attachment style (Russell, Baker, & McNulty, 2013)

· Description of a recent Australian study that found higher child care quality that included positive child-caregiver relationship at 2 to 3 years of age was linked to children's better self-regulation of attention and emotion at ages 4 to 5 and 6 to 7 (Gialamas & others, 2014)

· Inclusion of recent research with adults in which secure attachment was linked to fewer sleep disruptions than insecure avoidant or anxious attachment (Adams & McWilliams, 2015)

· New research in which oxytocin was associated with diminished stress among securely attached older adults (Emeny & others, 2015)

· Discussion of a recent study that revealed a heightened state of romantic love in young adults was linked to stronger depression and anxiety symptoms but better sleep quality (Bajoghli & others, 2014)

· New discussion of a recent national study of more than 19,000 individuals that found more than one-third of marriages now begin with online contact and that these marriages are slightly less likely to break up and are characterized by slightly higher marital satisfaction than marriages that begin in offline contexts (Cacioppo & others, 2013)

- Description of a recent study of individuals from 22 to 93 years of age that found older adults experienced more positive emotions than younger adults both in the morning and in the evening (English & Carstensen, 2014a)
- Coverage of a recent study of individuals from 18 to 94 years of age that found older adults had fewer peripheral social contacts but retained close relationships with people who provided them with emotional support (English & Carstensen, 2014b)

Chapter 11: The Self, Identity, and Personality

- Writing revisions were made in this chapter that focus on the most difficult concepts for students on tests based on feedback from LearnSmart and Heat Maps. The changes made include editing of a number of paragraphs, addition of new topical sentences, and use of bullets to alert students to key ideas. Among the topic discussions that were improved include reorganization of the content on selective optimization with compensation, developmental changes in self-esteem, assessment of self-understanding, children's self-awareness, why adolescence is a unique time for identity development, parenting influences on identity development, bicultural identity, and the contemporary life events approach.
- Changes made based on recommendations from leading experts Kate McLean and Ross Thompson
- New commentary about recent evidence of infants' understanding of others (Rhodes & others, 2015), including research indicating that infants as young as 13 months of age seem to consider another's perspective when predicting their actions (Choi & Luo, 2015)
- Description of a recent study of 6- to 9-year-olds that revealed older children were less trusting and more skeptical of others' distorted claims than were younger children (Mills & Elashi, 2014)
- Inclusion of recent research on Hong Kong adolescents in which those reporting pragmatic support from parents were more likely to believe they could attain their hoped-for possible selves and avoid their feared possible selves (Zhu & others, 2014)
- Discussion of a recent study of elderly institutionalized adults in which 8 weeks of group reminiscence therapy resulted in a number of positive outcomes (Melendez-Moral & others, 2013)
- Expanded and updated coverage of the consequences of low self-esteem (O'Brien, Bartoletti, & Leitzel, 2013; Zeigler-Hill, 2013)
- Description of a recent study that found low and decreasing self-esteem during adolescence was linked with adult depression two decades later (Steiger & others, 2014)
- Discussion of a recent longitudinal study in which self-esteem predicted subsequent changes in social support but not the reverse (Marshall & others, 2014)
- Coverage of recent research indicating that inflated praise, although well intended, may cause children with low self-esteem to avoid important learning experiences such as tackling challenging tasks (Brummelman & others, 2014)
- New discussion of effortful control as a key aspect of self-regulation and a recent study that found effortful control at

17 years of age predicted academic persistence and educational attainment at 23 to 25 years of age (Veronneau & others, 2014)
- Coverage of some factors that might help individuals develop better self-regulation and some factors that might inhibit their development of self-regulation (McClelland & others, 2015)
- New description of child and adolescent precursors to adult health and longevity, including the view of Nancy Eisenberg and her colleagues (2014) that early development of self-regulation fosters conscientiousness later in life, both directly and through its link to academic motivation/success and internalized compliance with norms
- Inclusion of recent research with older adults who had dementia that found reminiscence therapy reduced their depressive symptoms and improved their self-acceptance and positive relations with others (Gonzalez & others, 2015)
- Description of a recent study in which a variation of reminiscence therapy called instrumental reminiscence therapy improved the adaptive coping and resilience of older adults in adverse situations (Melendez & others, 2015)
- Coverage of a recent study which another variation of reminiscence therapy called attachment-focused reminiscence therapy reduced the depressive symptoms, perceived stress, and emergency room visits of older African Americans (Sabir & others, 2015)
- Inclusion of recent research that revealed narcissistic parents especially overvalue their children's talents (Brummelman & others, 2015)
- Discussion of recent research indicating that self-regulation was a protective factor in helping children in low-income circumstances to avoid developing emotional problems (Flouri, Midouhas, & Joshi, 2014)
- Inclusion of recent research in which higher levels of self-control at 4 years of age were linked to improvements in math and reading achievement in the early elementary school years for children living predominantly in rural and low-income contexts (Blair & others, 2015)
- Description of recent research that found self-control played important roles in older adults' quality of life, including lower levels of depression and obesity (Levasseur & Couture, 2015; Privitera & others, 2015)
- New coverage of the narrative approach to identity, in which individuals tell their life stories and evaluate the extent to which the stories are meaningful and integrated (McAdams & McLean, 2013; Pasupathi, 2015; Singer & Kasmark, 2015)
- Expanded description of why college often produces some key changes in an individual's identity (Arnett & Fischel, 2013)
- Description of recent analysis of Vaillant's longitudinal data that found that men who achieved generativity in later life had better physical health and adjustment to aging (Landes & others, 2014)
- Coverage of a recent study in which stressful life events were associated with cardiovascular disease in middle-aged women (Kershaw & others, 2014)

- Discussion of a recent study that found stressful daily hassles were linked to increased anxiety and decreased physical well-being (Falconier & others, 2015)
- Revised organization of the discussion of the Big Five factors of personality so that research involving each of the five factors is covered separately
- Description of recent research on the link between neuroticism and a variety of outcomes, including individuals who are high in neuroticism being more drug dependent (Valero & others, 2014) and having a lower sense of well-being 40 years later (Gale & others, 2013)
- Coverage of recent research indicating that individuals high in extraversion had a more positive sense of well-being later in life (Soto, 2015)
- Description of recent research that found individuals high in openness to experience have superior cognitive functioning across the life span (Briley, Domiteaux, & Tucker-Drob, 2014)
- Inclusion of recent research in which perceived social support predicted increased conscientiousness in older adults (Hill & others, 2014)
- Inclusion of recent research that found conscientiousness was linked to college students' grade point averages but the other four Big Five factors were not (McAbee & Oswald, 2013)
- New conceptual and research content on the increasing interest in the role of conscientiousness in health and longevity (English & Carstensen, 2014; Friedman & others, 2014; Roberts & others, 2014)
- New coverage of a recent study of 66- to 102-year-olds that revealed the self-discipline component of conscientiousness was a strong predictor of living longer, with individuals having high self-discipline showing a 34 percent increase in survival time (Costa & others, 2014)
- Inclusion of recent research in which conscientiousness was linked to better cognitive status and less cognitive decline in older adults (Luchetti & others, 2015)
- New section on optimism and its links to a number of positive outcomes, including recent studies that link optimism with better health and living longer (Engberg & others, 2013; Kim, Chopik, & Smith, 2014; Wurm & Benyamini, 2014)

Chapter 12: Gender and Sex

- Description of the most recent National Assessment of Educational Progress report (2014) in which girls continue to have higher reading achievement scores than boys
- New commentary about the multiple factors that may contribute to gender differences in academic achievement in areas such as reading and math (Eccles, 2014; Wigfield & others, 2015)
- Updated research on the lack of benefits when students attend same-sex schools (Pahlke, Hyde, & Allison, 2014)
- Coverage of a longitudinal study in which preschool relational aggression predicted adolescent relational aggression for girls but not for boys (Nelson & others, 2014)
- Inclusion of information from a meta-analysis indicating that females are better than males at recognizing nonverbal displays of emotion (Thompson & Voyer, 2014)

- New content on the special concern about sexting, including recent data on the percentage of adolescents who send and receive sexual pictures (Ybarra & Mitchell, 2014)
- New coverage of a recent study that identified two main sexual scripts in young adult men: (1) a traditional masculine "player" script, and (2) a script that emphasized mutual sexual pleasure (Morrison & others, 2014)
- Updated national data (including updated Figure 6) on the percentages of adolescents at different age levels who have engaged in sexual intercourse, including gender and ethnic variations (Kann & others, 2014)
- Description of a recent Swedish study of more than 3,000 adolescents indicating that sexual intercourse prior to age 14 was linked to a number of risky sexual behaviors at age 18 (Kastbom & others, 2015)
- Coverage of recent research indicating that 40 percent of 22-year-olds reported recently having had a casual sex partner (Lyons & others, 2015)
- Inclusion of recent research of more than 3,900 18- to 25-year-olds that found having casual sex was negatively linked to well-being and positively related to psychological distress (Bersamin & others, 2014)
- Coverage of a recent study that found difficulties and disagreements between Latino adolescents and their parents were linked to the adolescents' early sexual initiation (Cordova & others, 2014)
- Discussion of a recent study that revealed adolescent females who skipped school or failed a test were more likely to have frequent sexual intercourse and less likely to use contraceptives (Hensel & Sorge, 2014)
- New research indicating that adolescent males who play sports engage in more risky sexual behavior while adolescent females who play sports engage in less risky sexual behavior (Lipowski & others, 2015)
- Inclusion of recent research indicating that a greater age difference between sexual partners in adolescence was associated with less consistent condom use (Volpe & others, 2013)
- Updated data on the percentage of adolescents who use contraceptives when they have sexual intercourse (Kann & others, 2014)
- Inclusion of a recent cross-cultural study of adolescent pregnancy rates in 21 countries (Sedgh & others, 2015)
- Updated statistics (including updated Figure 7) on the continuing decline in overall adolescent pregnancy rates in the United States and the decline in all ethnic groups (Martin & others, 2015)
- New coverage of recent research on the negative interactions of adolescent mothers with their infants and an intervention program that improved the mothers' parenting behavior and the children's outcomes (Guttentag & others, 2014; Riva Crugnola & others, 2014)
- Description of recent research that indicated higher levels of maternal education were linked to children's reading and math achievement through the eighth grade but that the achievement of adolescent mothers' children never reached the levels of non-adolescent mothers' children (Tang & others, 2015)

- Coverage of a recent study of African American teen versus nonteen mothers and fathers comparing long-term life outcomes in a number of areas (Assini-Meytin & Green, 2015)
- New description of the U.S. government's Teen Pregnancy Prevention (TPP) program that is under the direction of the recently created Office of Adolescent Health (Koh, 2014)
- Description of the following recent study that reflects the uncertainty in the sexual relationships of emerging adults: More than half of daters and cohabitors reported a breakup followed by a reunion (Halpern-Meekin & others, 2013)
- Coverage of a recent study of 18- to 26-year-olds that revealed perceived relationship commitment was associated with sexual enjoyment (Galinsky & Sonenstein, 2013)
- New discussion of a recent study of almost 8,000 emerging adults that found males had more permissive sexual attitudes, especially regarding casual sexual encounters, than did females (Sprecher, Treger, & Sakaluk, 2013)
- Inclusion of a recent meta-analysis that revealed 60 percent of rape victims do not acknowledge their rape, with an especially high percent not acknowledging rape in the college years (Wilson & Miller, 2015)
- Inclusion of a recent study that revealed 20 percent of first-year college women students engaged in hooking up at least once during the school year and that certain characteristics were linked with a likelihood of hooking up (Fielder & others, 2013)
- New commentary about "friends with benefits" and the high level of casual sex that is now common among emerging adults (Owen, Fincham, & Manthos, 2013)
- Expanded content on bisexuality, including recent evidence indicating that it is not merely a stepping stone to homosexuality but rather is a stable sexual orientation that involves being sexually attracted to people of both sexes (King, 2014)
- New content indicating that women are more likely than men to change their sexual patterns and desires and that women are more likely to be bisexual (King, 2014; Mock & Eibach, 2012)
- Discussion of a recent study of sedentary women that found 6 months of aerobic training decreased their menopausal symptoms (Moilanen & others, 2012)
- Coverage of a recent study that found yoga improved the quality of life of menopausal women (Reed & others, 2014)
- Description of recent research indicating that when women start HRT in their fifties and continue its use for 5 to 30 years, there is an increase of 1.5 quality years of life (Hodis & Mack, 2014)
- Coverage of a recent meta-analysis that found hormone replacement therapy was linked to decreased rates of lung cancer in females, especially nonsmoking females and females with BMIs lower than 25kg/m (Yao & others, 2013)
- Significantly revised discussion of the role of testosterone in the lives of middle-aged men and the dramatic increase in the use of testosterone replacement therapy (TRT) to increase the level of testosterone (Khera & others, 2014; Rahnema & others, 2014)
- Coverage of two recent studies that found TRT improved older men's sexual function as well as their mood (Miner & others, 2013; Okada & others, 2014)
- Discussion of a recent study that found a higher testosterone level was linked to better episodic memory in middle-aged males (Panizzon & others, 2014)
- Description of a recent study of adults 55 years and older indicating that levels of sexual activity were associated with their physical and mental health (Bach & others, 2013)
- New commentary noting that the benefit-risk ratio for testosterone replacement therapy in older adults is uncertain (Isidori & others, 2014)

Chapter 13: Moral Development, Values, and Religion

- Changes based on feedback from leading expert Sam Hardy
- New section on Jonathan Haidt's (2013) criticism of Kohlberg's view of moral reasoning as always conscious and deliberate, and his lack of attention to the automatic, intuitive precursors of moral reasoning
- New section on the criticism that Kohlberg's moral development theory ignores the importance of emotion in moral thinking
- Added conclusion to criticisms of Kohlberg's theory noting that although it is an important theory of moral development it is no longer as influential and dominant as it once was
- Inclusion of recent research in which young children's sympathy predicted whether they would share with others (Ongley & Malti, 2014)
- Coverage of a recent study of 18- to 30-month-olds indicating that those whose parents more frequently labeled emotions and mental states during joint play and who elicited this type of talk during book reading were more likely to quickly engage in empathic helping when the experimenter was in distress (Drummond & others, 2014)
- Expanded discussion of contemporary views of conscience to include its roots in close relationships, connection with advances in self-understanding and understanding of others, and links to affective feelings (Thompson, 2014)
- Expanded and updated discussion of the view of Sam Hardy and his colleagues (Hardy & others, 2014) about the importance of morality as part of one's identity
- Added commentary noting that the point of conducting research on moral exemplars is to study the ideal end point of moral development
- Inclusion of recent research with college students in which moral identity predicted all five health outcomes assessed (anxiety, depression, hazardous alcohol use, sexual risk taking, and self-esteem) (Hardy & others, 2013)
- Description of a recent study in which a higher level of moral identity was found to possibly reduce the negative effects of moral disengagement and low self-regulation (Hardy, Bean, & Olsen, 2015)
- Expanded description of domain theory based on the views of Judith Smetana (2013) and Eliot Turiel (2014, 2015) and addition of Smetana and Turiel as key people involved in content related to this chapter

- Coverage of a recent study exploring how extensively children cheat and factors involved in whether they cheat (Ding & others, 2014)
- Important new section on whether infants engage in prosocial behavior and have moral awareness, including recent research describing how these qualities can be assessed in preverbal infants and the outcomes of the research (Hamlin, 2013, 2014; Hamlin & others, 2011, 2015)
- Expanded discussion regarding why adolescents are more likely to engage in prosocial behavior than children are (Eisenberg, Spinrad, & Morris, 2013)
- Discussion of a recent study that found even 5-year-olds were inclined to give more to poor than wealthy individuals (Paulus, 2014)
- Description of a recent study in which 8-year-olds were more likely to donate resources to needy peers than were 4-year-olds (Ongley, Nola, & Malti, 2014)
- Inclusion of recent research involving a series of studies that found older adults engaged in altruistic behavior more than younger adults (Freund & Blanchard-Fields, 2014)
- Updated description of the controversy regarding whether adolescents should be tried as adults for certain criminal acts (Cauffman & others, 2015; Shulman & Steinberg, 2015)
- Inclusion of research on a recent intervention study that found a combination of a parenting program and a teacher development program led to a reduction in the incidence of conduct disorder in African American boys from low-income backgrounds (Dawson-McClure & others, 2015)
- Discussion of a recent study in which youth with conduct disorder that had begun in childhood had more cognitive impairment, psychiatric problems, and serious violent offenses than youth with conduct disorder characterized by the onset of antisocial behavior in adolescence (Johnson & others, 2015)
- Coverage of a recent study that found low rates of delinquency among adolescents and emerging adults from 14 to 23 years of age were associated with an authoritative parenting style (Murphy & others, 2012)
- Discussion of a recent research review indicating that prevention programs focused on the family context were more effective in reducing persistent delinquency than were individual and group-focused programs (de Vries & others, 2015)
- Inclusion of recent research in which mothers' reports of their sons' impulsiveness at 15 years of age predicted the sons' arrest records up to 6 years later (Bechtold & others, 2014)
- Description of a recent study involving the Fast Track program that revealed adolescents' delinquent behavior was linked to three social cognitive processes: reducing hostile-attribution biases, improving responses to social problems, and devaluing aggression (Dodge, Godwin, & The Conduct Problems Prevention Research Group, 2013)
- Updates on Jewel Cash's and Nina Vasan's careers and work
- Updated information about the goals of first-year college students in relation to the relative importance they place on developing a meaningful philosophy of life versus becoming well-off financially (Eagan & others, 2014)

- Description of a recent study that found when youth attend religious services with their parents, this activity enhances the positive influence of parenting on their psychological well-being (Petts, 2014)
- Inclusion of data from a recent Pew Research Center (2012) survey on age variations in the percentage of U.S. adults who have a religious affiliation
- Coverage of a recent study that found highly religious individuals were less likely than their moderately religious, somewhat religious, and nonreligious counterparts to be psychologically distressed (Park, 2013)
- Updated information about Gabriel Dy-Liacco in the *Connecting with Careers* box
- Coverage of a longitudinal study that found religious service attendance was stable in middle adulthood, increased in late adulthood, then declined in the older adult years (Hayward & Krause, 2013a)
- Inclusion of a recent study in which older adults who had a higher level of religious identification were less likely to be depressed (Ysseldyk, Haslam, & Haslam, 2013)
- Coverage of a recent study that revealed older adults who attended church regularly over a period of seven years increased the amount of emotional support they gave and received but decreased the amount of tangible support they gave and received (Hayward & Krause, 2013b)
- Description of a recent study in which religious attendance was linked to increased longevity (Kim, Smith, & Kang, 2015)

Chapter 14: Families

- Some changes based on feedback from leading expert Jennifer Lansford
- Coverage of a recent study that found maternal scaffolding was associated with higher verbal IQ scores in preschool children born with a very low birth weight (Lowe & others, 2014)
- New research that found the increased risk of marital dissolution in cohabitors compared with those who married without previously cohabiting was much smaller when the couples had cohabited in their mid-twenties or later (Kuperberg, 2014)
- Updated information indicating that marriage and divorce rates in the United States are continuing to decline (National Center for Vital Statistics, 2013; U.S. Census Bureau, 2013)
- Discussion of recent research that found newlyweds who had a high level of general disposition optimism had higher marital satisfaction across the first year of the marriage while newlyweds who had a high level of specific relationship optimism had more marital problems across this time frame (Neff & Geers, 2013)
- Coverage of a recent study indicating that couples who participated in premarital education had higher marital quality (Rhoades & Stanley, 2014)
- Coverage of a recent study in which low levels of agreeableness and conscientiousness and high levels of

- neuroticism and openness to experience were linked to daily experiences over time that reduced relationship quality and eventually led to a breakup (Solomon & Jackson, 2014)
- Inclusion of content from a recent Pew Research Center (2015) poll of 40- to 50-year-old U.S. women that found those with a master's degree or higher first became mothers at age 30 but their counterparts with lower levels of education became parents at age 24
- Discussion of recent research indicating that an increasing number of children are growing up in homes in which their parents have never been married and that this is far more likely to occur when the mother has a low level of education (Gibson-Davis & Rackin, 2014)
- Updated statistics on the marriage and divorce rates of older adults (U.S. Census Bureau, 2013)
- Description of recent research that revealed older adult men were more satisfied with their marriages than were older adult women (Boerner & others, 2014)
- New commentary about Russia having the highest divorce rate in the world (UNSTAT, 2011)
- Description of a recent study in Finland that found divorce rates peak approximately 5 to 7 years into a marriage and then gradually decline (Kulu, 2014)
- Description of recent research that found women who became divorced from 40 to 59 years of age reported becoming more lonely following the divorce than men who became divorced in this age period (Nicolaisen & Thorsen, 2014)
- Inclusion of recent research in which middle-aged women in very low-quality marriages were found to gain life satisfaction following divorce (Bourassa, Sbarra, & Whisman, 2015)
- Discussion of a recent study that revealed a positive attitude about divorce, low marital quality, and divorce proneness were more common in remarried individuals than their counterparts in first marriages (Whitton & others, 2013)
- Updated data indicating that the remarriage rate in the United States had declined in recent years, with one reason for the decline involving the dramatic increase in cohabitation (U.S. Census Bureau, 2013)
- New coverage of the higher rates of divorce in second and third marriages compared with first marriages (Banschick & Tabatsky, 2011)
- New discussion of a recent survey indicating that fathers and mothers wish they could spend more time with their children but that both mothers and fathers are spending more time with their children today than parents did a generation ago (Pew Research Center, 2013)
- Description of a recent research review that concluded parents are unhappy when they experience more negative emotions, more financial problems, more sleep problems, and have a troubled marriage (Nelson, Kushlev, & Lyubomirsky, 2014). In this study, parents were happy when they experienced meaning in life, satisfied basic needs, and had positive social roles.
- Inclusion of recent research indicating that maternal scaffolding, sensitivity, and support for autonomy were

linked to better executive function in preschool children (Blair, Raver, & Berry, 2014)
- New coverage of the increasing number of countries (41) that are banning physical punishment as part of an effort to promote children's rights related to abuse and exploitation (Committee on Rights of the Child, 2014)
- Discussion of a recent study in which 80 percent of U.S. parents reported spanking their children by the time they reached kindergarten (Gershoff & others, 2012)
- New commentary based on a research review by Elizabeth Gershoff (2013) noting that the defenders of spanking have not produced any evidence that spanking is linked to positive outcomes for children and that negative outcomes of spanking have been replicated in many studies
- New content on the correlational nature of research on punishment, as well as bidirectional, reciprocal socialization influences that take into account child characteristics and problems (Laible, Thompson, & Froimson, 2015; Sheehan & Watson, 2008)
- Coverage of a recent study in which unmarried African American parents who were instructed in coparenting techniques during the prenatal period and also one month after the baby was born improved their rapport, communication, and problem-solving skills when the baby was 3 months old (McHale, Salman-Engin, & Coovert, 2015)
- Discussion of recent research indicating that child maltreatment at 3 to 5 years of age was more strongly associated with depression in early adulthood than maltreatment in other age periods (Dunn & others, 2013)
- Inclusion of a 30-year longitudinal study that found offspring of parents who engaged in child maltreatment and neglect are at risk for engaging in child neglect and sexual maltreatment themselves (Widom, Czaja, & DuMont, 2015)
- Description of a recent study that revealed low parental monitoring was associated with adolescent depression (Yap & others, 2014)
- Inclusion of recent research indicating that low parental monitoring was a key factor in predicting a developmental trajectory of delinquency and substance use in adolescence (Wang & others, 2014)
- Coverage of recent research on differing expectations of Mexican immigrant mothers and their U.S.-born 13- and 14-year-old daughters regarding the daughters' autonomy at 15 years of age (Romo, Mireles-Rios, & Lopez-Tello, 2014)
- Inclusion of recent research that found avoidant attachment predicted suicidal behavior in adolescents (Sheftall, Schoppe-Sullivan, & Bridge, 2014)
- Description of a recent study in which a higher level of parent-adolescent conflict was associated with higher adolescent anxiety, depression, and aggression, and lower self-esteem (Smokowski & others, 2015)
- New research indicating that childhood divorce was linked to worse cohabiting/marital relationships from 16 to 30 years of age, but that these associations were influenced by a variety of factors, such as childhood sexual abuse and lower SES status of the child at birth (Fergusson, McLeod, & Horwood, 2014)

- Inclusion of recent research in which children were more likely to have behavior problems if the post-divorce home environment was less supportive and stimulating, their mother was less sensitive and more depressed, and the household income was lower (Weaver & Schofield, 2015). Also in this study, higher levels of predivorce maternal sensitivity and child IQ served as protective factors in reducing child problems after the divorce.
- Description of recent research on almost 3,000 adolescents that revealed a negative association of the father's, but not the mother's, unemployment with the adolescents' health (Bacikov-Sleskova, Benka, & Orosova, 2014)
- Discussion of a recent study that found spillover effects from the mother's work on adolescents' health (Lawson & others, 2014)
- Inclusion of recent research that found more positive parenting in adoptive gay father families and fewer child externalizing problems in these families than in heterosexual families (Golombok & others, 2014)
- New content on how an increasing number of adoptions in the next decade will come from the child welfare system (Grotevant & McDermott, 2014)
- Coverage of a recent research review that concluded children who are adopted are more likely than those growing up with biological parents to have problems in three areas: externalized, internalized, and attentional (Grotevant & McDermott, 2014)
- New coverage of a longitudinal study on the positive outcomes of contact for birth mothers, adoptive parents, and birth children (Grotevant & others, 2013)
- Update on the continued increase in the age at which women have their first child (U.S. Census Bureau, 2013)
- Discussion of a recent review that concluded grandparents who raise grandchildren are especially at risk for developing depression (Hadfield, 2014)
- Coverage of a recent study that found middle-aged adults positively supported family responsibility to emerging adult children but were more ambivalent about providing care for aging parents, viewing it as both a joy and a burden (Igarashi & others, 2013)

Chapter 15: Peers and the Sociocultural World

- Coverage of a recent study in which having friends who engage in delinquency is associated with earlier onset of delinquent behavior and more persistent delinquency (Evans, Simons, & Simons, 2015)
- Description of a recent study that compared the effects of parent, teacher, and peer events and found that negative peer events (fighting or arguing with a peer, for example) were most likely to account for maintaining depressive symptoms across a two-year period in early adolescence (Herres & Kobak, 2015)
- Discussion of a longitudinal study of adolescents 13 to 23 years of age in which adolescents' autonomy from peer influences predicted long-term success in avoiding

problematic behavior but also more difficulty in establishing strong friendships in emerging adulthood (Allen, Chango, & Swedo, 2014)
- Discussion of a recent study in which adolescents' dating popularity was associated with their peer popularity (Houser, Mayeux, & Cross, 2014)
- Description of a recent study of 13- to 23-year-olds that revealed early adolescent pseudomature behavior was associated with a desire to be popular with peers (Allen & others, 2014). In this study, pseudomature behavior was linked to long-term problems in close relationships, substance abuse, and a higher level of criminal behavior.
- Inclusion of recent research in which college students with risky social networks (friends who drink, for example) were ten times more likely to engage in alcohol abuse (Mason, Zaharakis, & Benotsch, 2014)
- Coverage of a recent study that indicated low peer status in childhood was linked to an increased probability of being unemployed and having mental health problems in adulthood (Almquist & Brannstrom, 2014)
- Discussion of recent research revealing higher levels of depression and suicide in children who are the victims of bullying (Yen & others, 2014)
- Description of a recent study that found peer victimization in the fifth grade was linked to worse physical and mental health in the tenth grade (Bogart & others, 2014)
- Inclusion of information from a recent meta-analysis that found both negative and positive parenting practices were linked to bullying and victimization (Lereya, Samara, & Wolke, 2013)
- Discussion of a recent analysis that concluded bullying can have long-term effects, including difficulty establishing long-term relationships and problems at work (Wolke & Lereya, 2015)
- Coverage of a longitudinal study in which adolescents experiencing social and emotional difficulties were more likely to be both cyberbullied and traditionally bullied than to be traditionally bullied only (Cross, Lester, & Barnes, 2015)
- Expanded and updated discussion of the costs and benefits of bullying in the context of the peer group, including a longitudinal study that revealed short-term benefits for bullies (Reijntjes & others, 2013)
- Description of a recent study that indicated peer victimization during the elementary school years was a leading predictor of internalizing problems in adolescence (Schwartz & others, 2015)
- Discussion of a recent meta-analysis that revealed being the victim of cyberbullying was linked to stress and suicidal ideation (Kowalski & others, 2014)
- Inclusion of information from a recent meta-analysis in which traditional bullying occurred twice as much as cyberbullying and that those who engaged in cyberbullying were often likely to have also engaged in traditional bullying (Modecki & others, 2014)
- Coverage of recent research that found cyberbullying was more strongly associated with suicidal ideation than traditional bullying was (van Geel, Vedder, & Tanilon, 2014)

- New research review in which antibullying interventions that focused on the whole school, such as Olweus', were more effective than interventions involving classroom curricula or social skills training (Cantone & others, 2015)
- Discussion of a recent study of older adults that found that activities with friends increased positive affect and life satisfaction (Huxhold, Miche, & Schüz, 2014)
- Inclusion of recent research on 60- to 80-year-olds indicating that the partner's death was more strongly associated with loneliness in men than in women (Nicolaisen & Thorsen, 2014)
- Inclusion of recent research on elderly adults that revealed both loneliness and social isolation were associated with decreased cognitive functioning four years later (Shankar & others, 2013)
- Coverage of a recent study in which the most consistent factor associated with loneliness in older adults at 70, 78, and 85 years of age was not being married (Stessman & others, 2014)
- Inclusion of recent research in which older adults with higher levels of social integration were less depressed (Ivan Santini & others, 2015)
- Description of a recent study of Canadian older adults in which those who were more physically active had higher life satisfaction and greater social interaction than their physically inactive counterparts (Azagba & Sharaf, 2014)
- Coverage of a recent study in which having multiple chronic diseases was linked to a lower level of successful aging (Hsu, 2015)
- Inclusion of recent research on 90- to 91-year-olds that found living circumstances, independence, health, and a good death were associated with successful aging (Nosraty & others, 2015)
- Discussion of a recent Canadian study on the self-rated predictability of successful aging at different age levels and factors that influenced successful aging (Meng & D'Arcy, 2014)
- Description of a study from 1990 to 2007 of 18- to 65-year-old Chinese that found individuals increasingly have been including individualistic characteristics in their descriptions of what constitutes happiness and well-being (Steele & Lynch, 2013)
- Coverage of a longitudinal study from 1970 to 2008 which found that although China is still characterized by collectivistic values, Chinese people increasingly use words that index individualistic values (Zeng & Greenfield, 2015)
- Coverage of a recent study in which playing action video games improved attentional control (Chisholm & Kingstone, 2015)
- Discussion of a recent study that found video game consumption was linked to rape myth acceptance through connections with interpersonal aggression and hostile sexism (Fox & Potocki, 2015)
- Inclusion of recent research with 9- to 11-year-olds that revealed a higher number of screens in the child's bedroom was associated with higher risk of obesity (Chaput & others, 2014)
- Description of a recent research review that found when children's and adolescents' screen time exceeded two hours a day, they were more likely to be overweight or obese (Atkin & others, 2015)
- Coverage of a recent research review that concluded more extensive screen time was linked to negative sleep outcomes, especially for computer use, video games, and mobile devices (Hale & Guan, 2015)
- Discussion of a recent study in which parental reduction in their own screen time was associated with decreased child screen time (Xu, Wen, & Rissel, 2015)
- Inclusion of recent research in which duration of screen time was linked to depression and anxiety (Maras & others, 2015)
- New description of a recent meta-analysis of studies in 14 countries that found positive outcomes of *Sesame Street* viewing on children's development in three areas: (1) cognitive, (2) learning about the world, and (3) social reasoning and attitudes toward outgroups (Mares & Pan, 2013)
- Inclusion of recent research in which a higher degree of parental monitoring of media use was linked to a number of positive outcomes (more sleep, better school performance, less aggressive behavior, and more prosocial behavior) (Gentile & others, 2014)
- Inclusion of recent data from a national study on various aspects of Internet use by older adults (Smith, 2014)
- Discussion of a longitudinal study that revealed Internet use by older adults reduced their likelihood of becoming depressed by one-third (Cotten & others, 2014)
- Discussion of a recent study of older adults that revealed increased use of the Internet was associated with greater ease in meeting new people, reduced isolation, and stronger connections with friends and family (Cotten, Anderson, & McCullough, 2013)
- Updated statistics on poverty levels in U.S. families with children and adolescents, including data for ethnic groups and single-mother-headed households (De Navas-Walt & Proctor, 2014)
- Inclusion of recent research with youth that revealed living in neighborhoods where poverty increased from the time they were 11 to 19 years of age was associated with an increased allostatic load, except when the youth experienced high emotional support (Brody & others, 2014)
- Coverage of a recent intervention program (the Positive Action program) that assessed youth from the third to eighth grades in 14 schools in low-income areas of Chicago (Lewis & others, 2013). Compared to a control group, students in the intervention program engaged in lower rates of violence-related behavior and received fewer disciplinary referrals and school suspensions.
- Discussion of a recent study of more than 500 high school students living in low-income areas of Los Angeles who were selected through a random admissions lottery to attend high-performing charter schools, which resulted in the students doing better on standardized tests of math and Eng-

lish and being less likely to drop out of school (Wong & others, 2014)

- Description of a recent study in which processing speed was slower in older adults living in poverty (Zhang & others, 2015)

Chapter 16: Schools, Achievement, and Work

- New coverage of the recently developed Common Core Standards Initiative to provide more detailed guidelines and milestones for students to achieve at each level, and a discussion of the controversy the Standards have generated (Common Core State Standards Initiative, 2014)
- Description of a recent study in which one year of Head Start participation was linked to higher levels of performance in early math, early reading, and receptive vocabulary (Miller & others, 2014)
- Updated data on school dropout rates indicating a continuing decline in dropouts among various ethnic groups (Child Trends, 2014; National Center for Education Statistics, 2014)
- Updated and expanded coverage of differing incomes of high school and college graduates in a year and in a lifetime (Daly & Bengali, 2014)
- Updated content on how overwhelmed U.S. college students are feeling with all they have to do (Eagan & others, 2014)
- Updated data from the 2011–2012 school year (including updated Figure 3) on the percentage of students who receive special education services and the areas in which they receive those services (Condition of Education, 2014)
- New coverage of recent research interest in the possibility that neurofeedback may reduce the level of ADHD symptoms in children (Gevensleben & others, 2014; Steiner & others, 2014a, b)
- New information about how neurofeedback works, including links between EEG patterns and the main brain region involved in using neurofeedback with children who have ADHD
- Description of a recent experimental study that found biofeedback was effective in reducing ADHD symptoms and also improved children's academic performance (Meisel & others, 2013)
- New description of the use of mindfulness in treating ADHD children (Cassone, 2015; Converse & others, 2014), and discussion of recent research indicating that mindfulness training can be effective in improving the attention of adolescents who have ADHD at least in the short term (van de Weijer-Bergsma & others, 2012)
- New coverage of the possibility that exercise might improve the functioning of children with ADHD, including recent research indicating that a single 20-minute bout of moderately intense aerobic exercise improved the neurocognitive functioning and inhibitory control of children with ADHD (Pontifex & others, 2013)
- New description of reasons that aerobic exercise might reduce negative symptoms in children with ADHD (Chang & others, 2012)

- New coverage of the proposed change in the DSM-V psychiatric classification system that involves having an overarching single category called autism spectrum disorder (Autism Research Institute, 2015)
- Updated data on the percentage of time students with disabilities spend in the general classroom, revealing that the percentage has reached the highest level (61 percent) since it was first assessed (Condition of Education, 2014)
- New discussion of recent research indicating that underachieving high school students who read online modules about how the brain changes when you learn and study improved their grade point averages (Paunesku & others, 2015)
- Description of a longitudinal study of university students in which a nonlimited theory of mind predicted better self-regulation and higher grades (Job & others, 2015)
- Inclusion of recent research indicating that the superior academic performance of Asian American children was due to their greater effort and not to advantages in tested cognitive abilities or sociodemographic factors (Hsin & Xie, 2014)
- New coverage of Eva Pomerantz' (2014) parenting recommendations related to students' motivation in school
- New *Connecting with Research* box that describes the research of Eva Pomerantz and her colleagues (Cheung & Pomerantz, 2012; Ng, Pomerantz, & Lam, 2013; Pomerantz, Cheung, & Qin, 2012; Pomerantz, Kim, & Cheung, 2012; Qu & Pomerantz, 2015) focusing on the role of parenting in children's learning and achievement. Details about three studies are discussed in the Research box, one indicating that Chinese parents are more involved in their children's learning than are U.S. parents (Cheung & Pomerantz, 2012), the second that Chinese parents use more psychological control with their children than do U.S. parents (Ng, Pomerantz, & Deng, 2014), and the third that young Chinese adolescents have a greater sense of responsibility to parents than do their U.S. counterparts, with the U.S. students' sense of responsibility, but not the Chinese students', declining across two years (Qu & Pomerantz, 2015)
- New discussion of recent research on some negative outcomes of authoritarian parenting on Chinese-American immigrant children (Zhou & others, 2012)
- New coverage of two recent books on the strong disciplinary orientation of Chinese parents: *Battle Hymn of the Tiger Mom* (2011) and *Tiger Babies Strike Back* (2013)
- Updated data on the percentage of full-time and part-time college students who work while attending college (National Center for Education Statistics, 2013)
- Description of a recent study in which high school students who held part-time jobs were more likely to drink alcohol, binge drink, and use marijuana (Leeman & others, 2014)
- New coverage of the unemployment rate of recent college graduates and the high percentage who must take jobs that do not require a college degree (Center for Economic and Policy Research, 2014; Gabor, 2014)
- Discussion of a recent study in which stressors at work were linked to arterial hypertension in employees (Lamy & others, 2015)

- Coverage of a recent study in which 90 or more days of unemployment was associated with subsequent cardiovascular disease across an 8-year follow-up period (Lundin & others, 2014)

- Expanded outcomes of unemployment to include research on an increase in substance abuse (Compton & others, 2014)

- Description of recent studies that found unemployment was linked to an increase in cardiovascular disease (Lundin & others, 2014) and suicide (Milner & others, 2014; Phillips & Nugent, 2014)

- Discussion of a recent study in which unemployment was associated with higher mortality but the link was stronger for those who were unmarried (Van Hedel & others, 2015)

- Coverage of longitudinal data that revealed low self-control in childhood was linked to the emergence and persistence of self-control from 21 to 50 years of age (Daly & others, 2015)

- Updated information about fastest-growing job categories through 2022 in the United States (Occupational Outlook Handbook, 2014)

- Description of recent research in which women reported more family interference from work than did men (Allen & Finkelstein, 2014)

- Inclusion of recent research in which partner coping, having a positive attitude about multiple roles, using planning and management skills, and not having to cut back on professional responsibilities were linked to better relationships between dual earners (Matias & Fontaine, 2015)

- Coverage of a recent study of middle-aged adults that found difficulty managing different job demands was associated with poor health (Nabe-Nielsen & others, 2014)

- New discussion of research by leading Finnish expert Clas-Haken Nygard (2013) indicating that the ability to work effectively peaks in middle age, including coverage of factors related to quality of work in middle age, and links between various aspects of work in middle age and health and well-being in late adulthood

- Description of research indicating that work performance in middle age was associated with mortality and disability 28 years later (von Bonsdorff & others, 2011, 2012)

- Updated data on the dramatic increase in the percentage of older adults who are in the work force and projections to 2020, including gender differences (Short, 2015)

Chapter 17: Death, Dying, and Grieving

- Some changes based on feedback from leading expert Crystal Park

- New commentary that while the color black is associated with death in the United States, white is associated with death in China

- Discussion of a recent study in which advance care planning decreased life-sustaining treatment, increased hospice use, and decreased hospital use (Brinkman-Stoppelenburg, Rietjens, & van der Heide, 2014)

- Description of a recent study that revealed physicians have a positive view of advance directives (Coleman, 2013)

- Updated content on the increasing number of countries and U.S. states in which assisted suicide is legal

- Commentary that although Canada has yet to legalize assisted suicide, a recent survey indicated that a majority of Canadians favored legalization (Schafer, 2013)

- Inclusion of information from a recent research review indicating that the percentage of physician-assisted deaths range from 0.1 to 0.2 percent in the United States compared with 1.8 to 2.9 percent in the Netherlands (Steck & others, 2013). This review found that the percentage of assisted suicides has increased in recent years and the individuals who die through assisted suicide are most likely to be males from 60 to 75 years of age.

- New content on why euthanasia is such a controversial issue

- Updated data on the percentage of U.S. adolescents who seriously consider suicide each year (Kann & others, 2014)

- Inclusion of recent research in which both depression and hopelessness were predictors of whether adolescents would repeat a suicide attempt across a six-month period (Consoli & others, 2015)

- Updated data on the countries with the highest suicide rates for males and females, including data for the United States (Centers for Disease Control and Prevention, 2013) and new data on the age ranges in which suicide happens most often

- New discussion of the lack of a national study of suicide rates in sexual minority adolescents and inclusion of recent research in Boston indicating that suicidal ideation and attempts were higher in adolescents living in neighborhoods with higher rates of crimes against gay, lesbian, and bisexual adolescents (Duncan & Hatzenbuehler, 2014)

- Coverage of recent research that found peer victimization was linked to suicidal ideation and suicide attempts, with cyberbullying more strongly associated with suicidal ideation than traditional bullying (van Geel, Vedder, & Tanilon, 2014)

- Description of a recent study that revealed playing sports predicted lower suicidal ideation in boys and that venting by talking to others was associated with lower suicidal ideation in girls (Kim & others, 2014)

- Inclusion of recent research indicating that authoritative parenting was linked to fewer adolescent suicide attempts while rejecting/neglecting parenting was associated with a higher likelihood of adolescent suicide attempts (Donath & others, 2014)

- New Figure 5 on what to do and what not to do when someone is likely to attempt suicide

- Coverage of recent research that identified four meaning-making processes (sense making, benefit finding, continuing bonds, and identity reconstruction) in parent-physician bereavement meetings following a child's death (Meert & others, 2015)

- Description of a recent study in which older adults who were bereaved had more dysregulated cortisol patterns, indicative of the intensity of their stress (Holland & others, 2014)

- Discussion of recent research that found college students who had lost someone close to them in college shootings and had severe posttraumatic stress symptoms four months later were more likely to have severe grief one year after the shootings (Smith & others, 2015)

· In a study of individuals diagnosed with complicated grief, 40 percent reported at least one full or limited-symptom grief-related panic attack in the past week (Bui & others, 2015)

· Inclusion of recent data indicating that approximately 7 to 10 percent of bereaved individuals experience prolonged or complicated grief (Maccalum & Bryant, 2013; Shear, Ghesquiere, & Glickman, 2013)

· Description of a recent study in which widowed individuals in 2011, especially women, reported fewer social and financial difficulties than their counterparts in 1979 (Perrig-Chiello & others, 2015). Nonetheless, there were no differences in the widowed individuals' depression and psychological difficulties across the two time frames.

· New commentary noting that becoming widowed is especially difficult for individuals who have been happily married for a number of decades

· Coverage of a recent study that found individuals in the early stages of spousal bereavement are at increased risk of distress in situations with special significance for the couple, such as the late spouse's birthday or a wedding anniversary (Carr & others, 2014)

· Updated discussion of complicated or prolonged grief disorder and DSM-5, including the recent decision by the American Psychiatric Association (2013) not to include it as a psychiatric disorder but to relegate a description of the condition to an appendix. The main reason complicated or prolonged grief was not included as a psychiatric disorder was the concern that a normal grieving process would be turned into a medical condition.

· New description of what to say and do versus what not to say and do when a person is grieving

· Updated data on the dramatic increase in the percentage of people in the United States who choose cremation (45 percent in 2013, 27 percent in 2000, and 14 percent in 1985) (Cremation Association of North America, 2015)

· Description of a recent study in which becoming widowed was associated with a 48 percent increase in risk of mortality (Sullivan & Fenelon, 2014). In this study, mortality risk increased for men if their wives' deaths were unexpected, but unexpected death of a husband mattered less for women in terms of mortality risk.

· Coverage of a recent study in which widowed individuals, especially those in age-heterogamous unions (between partners of significantly different ages), had worse mental health than married persons but not worse physical health (Choi & Vasunilashorn, 2014)

· Description of a recent study that found widowed persons who did not expect to be reunited with their loved ones in the afterlife reported more depression, anger, and intrusive thoughts 6 and 18 months after their loss (Carr & Sharp, 2014)

Online Instructor Resources

The resources listed here accompany *A Topical Approach to Life-Span Development,* 8th edition. Please contact your McGraw-Hill representative for details concerning the availability of these and other valuable materials that can help you design and enhance your course.

Instructor's Manual   Broken down by chapter, these include chapter outlines, suggested lecture topics, classroom activities and demonstrations, suggested student research projects, essay questions, and critical thinking questions.

Test Bank and Computerized Test Bank   This comprehensive Test Bank includes more than 1,500 multiple-choice and approximately 75 essay questions. Organized by chapter, the questions are designed to test factual, applied, and conceptual understanding. All test questions are compatible with EZ Test, McGraw-Hill's Computerized Test Bank program.

PowerPoint Slides   These presentations cover the key points of each chapter and include charts and graphs from the text. They can be used as is, or you may modify them to meet your specific needs.

Acknowledgments

I very much appreciate the support and guidance provided to me by many people at McGraw-Hill. Krista Bettino, Executive Director, Products and Markets, has provided excellent guidance, vision, and direction for this book. Vicki Malinee provided considerable expertise in coordinating many aspects of the editorial process for this text. Janet Tilden again did an outstanding job as the book's copy editor. Sheila Frank did a terrific job in coordinating the book's production. Dawn Groundwater, Lead Product Developer, did excellent work on various aspects of the book's development, technology, and learning systems. Thanks also to Ann Helgerson and A.J. Laferrera for their extensive and outstanding work in marketing *A Topical Approach to Life-Span Development*. And Jennifer Blankenship provided me with excellent choices of new photographs for this edition of the book.

I also want to thank my parents, John and Ruth Santrock, my wife, Mary Jo, our children, Tracy and Jennifer, and our grandchildren, Jordan, Alex, and Luke, for their wonderful contributions to my life and for helping me to better understand the marvels and mysteries of life-span development.

EXPERT CONSULTANTS

As I develop a new edition of this text, I consult with leading experts in their respective areas of life-span development. Their invaluable feedback ensures that the latest research, knowledge, and perspectives are presented throughout the text. Their willingness to devote their time and expertise to this endeavor is greatly appreciated. The Expert Consultants who contributed to this edition, along with their biographies and commentary, can be found on pages xii-xiv.

REVIEWERS

I owe a special debt of gratitude to the reviewers who have provided detailed feedback on *A Topical Approach to Life-Span Development* over the years.

Anora Ackerson, *Kalamazoo Community College;* **Katherine Adams,** *Valdosta State University;* **Randy Allen,** *Barton Community College;* **Denise M. Arehart,** *University of Colorado—Denver;* **Harriet Bachner,** *Northeastern State University;* **Andrea Backschneider,** *University of Houston;* **Catherine E. Barnard,** *Kalamazoo Valley Community College;* **Terra Bartee,** *Cisco Community College;* **Sheri Bauman,** *University of Arizona;* **Jay Belsky,** *Birkbeck College, University of London;* **James E. Birren,** *University of California—Los Angeles;* **Tracie L. Blumentritt,** *University of Wisconsin—La Crosse;* **John Bonvillian,** *University of Virginia;* **Janet Boseovski,** *University of North Carolina—Greensboro;* **Brenda Butterfield,** *University of Minnesota—Duluth;* **Ann Calhoun-Sauls,** *Belmont Abbey College;* **Silvia Canetto,** *Colorado State University;* **Rick Chandler,** *Itawamba Community College;* **Andrea D. Clements,** *East Tennessee State University;* **Sunshine Corwan,** *University of Central Oklahoma;* **Gregory Cutler,** *Bay de Noc Community College;* **Scott Delys,** *North Central Texas College;* **Susanne Denham,** *George Mason University;* **Kimberly DuVall,** *James Madison University;* **Jerri Edwards,** *University of South Florida—Tampa;* **Marion A. Eppler,** *East Carolina University;* **Carolyn Fallahi,** *Central Connecticut State University;* **Dan P. Fawaz,** *Georgia Perimeter College;* **E. Richard Ferraro,** *University of North Dakota;* **Fan Flovell,** *Eastern Kentucky University;* **James Forbes,** *Angelo State University;* **Tom Frangicetto,** *Northampton Community College;* **James Garbarino,** *Cornell University;* **Janet Gebelt,** *University of Portland;* **Suzanne Gibson,** *Meridian Community College;* **Gilbert Gottlieb,** *University of North Carolina–Chapel Hill;* **Trione Grayson,** *Florida Community College at Jacksonville, South Campus;* **Elena Grigorenko,** *Yale University;* **James Guinee,** *University of Central Arkansas;* **Jim Hanson,** *Grand View University;* **Yvette Harris,** *Miami (Ohio) University;* **Carol H. Hoare,** *George Washington University;* **Scott Hofer,** *Pennsylvania State University;* **La Tishia Horrell,** *Ivy Tech Community College;* **William Hoyer,** *Syracuse University;* **Fergus Hughes,** *University of Wisconsin;* **Mary P. Hughes Stone,** *San Francisco State University;* **Janet Shibley Hyde,** *University of Wisconsin—Madison;* **Alisah Janowsky,** *University of Central Florida;* **Emily J. Johnson,** *University of Wisconsin—La Crosse;* **Seth Kalichman,** *University of Connecticut;* **Robert Kastenbaum,** *Emeritus, Arizona State University;* **Kevin Keating,** *Broward Community College;* **Rachel Keen,** *University of Virginia;* **Sue Kelley,**

Lycoming College; **Melanie Killian,** *University of Maryland;* **Larry Kollman,** *North Area Iowa Community College—Mason City;* **Suzanne G. Krinsky,** *University of Southern Colorado;* **Richard P. Lanthier,** *George Washington University;* **Kathleen Lawler,** *University of Tennessee;* **Gary Leka,** *University of Texas—Pan American;* **Gloria Lopez,** *Sacramento City College;* **Salvador Macias III,** *University of South Carolina;* **James Marcia,** *Simon Fraser University;* **Carole Martin,** *Colorado College;* **Gabriela Martorell,** *Portland State University;* **Linda Mayes,** *Yale University;* **Lara Mayeux,** *University of Oklahoma—Norman;* **Monica McCoy,** *Converse College;* **Katrina McDaniel,** *Barton College;* **Sharon McNeely,** *Northeastern Illinois University;* **Gigliana Meltzi,** *New York University;* **Patricia A. Mills,** *Miami University;* **Daniel K. Mroczek,** *Fordham University;* **Winnie Mucherah,** *Ball State University;* **Bridget Murphy-Kelsey,** *University of Oklahoma;* **Charles Nelson,** *Harvard University;* **Margaret M. Norwood,** *Thomas Nelson Community College;* **Lois Oestreich,** *Salt Lake Community College;* **Pamela Balls Organista,** *University of San Francisco;* **Rob Palkovitz,** *University of Delaware;* **Debbie Palmer,** *University of Wisconsin—Stevens Point;* **Laura Pannell,** *Itawamba Community College;* **Crystal Park,** *University of Connecticut;* **Denise Park,** *University of Texas at Dallas;* **Ross Parke,** *University of California—Riverside;* **Scott Peterson,** *Cameron University;* **Warren Phillips,** *Iowa State University;* **Peter Phipps,** *Dutchess Community College;* **Janet Polivy,** *University of Toronto;* **James S. Previte,** *Victor Valley College;* **Mary Kay Reed,** *York College of Pennsylvania;* **Janet Reis,** *University of Illinois—Champaign;* **Madeline Rex-Lear,** *University of Texas—Arlington;* **Elizabeth Rodriguez,** *Salt Lake City Community College;* **Theresa Sawyer,** *Carroll Community College;* **Kim Schrenk,** *Montana State University;* **Pamela Schuetze,** *Buffalo State College;* **Matthew Scullin,** *West Virginia University;* **Rebecca Shiner,** *Colgate University;* **Jerry Snead,** *Coastal Carolina Community College;* **Karina Sokol,** *Glendale Community College;* **Thomas D. Spencer,** *San Francisco State University;* **Robert J. Sternberg,** *University of Colorado;* **Robert B. Stewart, Jr.,** *Oakland University;* **Pam Terry,** *Gordon College;* **Ross Thompson,** *University of California—Davis;* **Jonathan Tudge,** *University of North Carolina—Greensboro;* **Robin Valeri,** *St. Bonaventure University;* **Kay Walsh,** *James Madison University;* **Allan Wigfield,** *University of Maryland;* **Clarissa Willis,** *Arkansas Technical University;* **Linda M. Woolf,** *Webster University;* **Dawn Young,** *Boissier Parish Community College*

section one

All the world's a stage,
And all the men and women merely players;
They have their exits and their entrances,
And one man in his time plays many parts.

—WILLIAM SHAKESPEARE
English playwright, 17th century

The Life-Span Perspective

This book is about human development—its universal features, its individual variations, its nature. Every life is distinct, a new biography in the world. Examining the shape of life-span development allows us to understand it better. *A Topical Approach to Life-Span Development* is about the rhythm and meaning of people's lives, about turning mystery into understanding, and about weaving a portrait of who each of us was, is, and will be. In Section 1, you will read one chapter titled "Introduction."

chapter 1

INTRODUCTION

chapter outline

1 The Life-Span Perspective

Learning Goal 1 Discuss the distinctive features of a life-span perspective on development

The Importance of Studying Life-Span Development
Characteristics of the Life-Span Perspective
Some Contemporary Concerns

2 The Nature of Development

Learning Goal 2 Identify the most important processes, periods, and issues in development

Biological, Cognitive, and Socioemotional Processes
Periods of Development
The Significance of Age
Developmental Issues

3 Theories of Development

Learning Goal 3 Describe the main theories of human development

Psychoanalytic Theories
Cognitive Theories
Behavioral and Social Cognitive Theories
Ethological Theory
Ecological Theory
An Eclectic Theoretical Orientation

4 Research on Life-Span Development

Learning Goal 4 Explain how research on life-span development is conducted

Methods for Collecting Data
Research Designs
Time Span of Research
Conducting Ethical Research
Minimizing Bias

preview

This book is a window into the journey of human development—your own and that of every other member of the human species. Every life is distinct, a new biography in the world. Examining the shape of life-span development helps us to understand it better. In this first chapter, we explore what it means to take a life-span perspective on development, examine the nature of development, discuss theories of development, and outline how science helps us to understand it.

1 The Life-Span Perspective

LG1 Discuss the distinctive features of a life-span perspective on development

The Importance of Studying Life-Span Development

Characteristics of the Life-Span Perspective

Some Contemporary Concerns

Each of us develops partly like all other individuals, partly like some other individuals, and partly like no other individuals. Most of the time, our attention is directed to an individual's uniqueness. But as humans, we have all traveled some common paths. Each of us—Leonardo da Vinci, Joan of Arc, George Washington, Martin Luther King, Jr., and you—walked at about 1 year, engaged in fantasy play as a young child, and became more independent as a youth. Each of us, if we live long enough, will experience hearing problems and the death of family members and friends. This is the general course of our **development**—the pattern of movement or change that begins at conception and continues through the human life span.

In this section, we explore what is meant by the concept of development and why the study of life-span development is important. We outline the main characteristics of the life-span perspective and discuss various sources of contextual influences. In addition, we examine some contemporary concerns in life-span development.

THE IMPORTANCE OF STUDYING LIFE-SPAN DEVELOPMENT

How might people benefit from examining life-span development? Perhaps you are, or will be, a parent or a teacher. If so, responsibility for children is, or will be, a part of your everyday life. The more you learn about them, the better you can deal with them. Perhaps you hope to gain some insight about your own history—as an infant, a child, an adolescent, or an adult. Perhaps you want to know more about what your life will be like as you move through the adult years—as a middle-aged adult or as an adult in old age, for example. Or perhaps you have just stumbled upon this course, thinking that it sounded intriguing and that the study of the human life span might raise some provocative issues. Whatever your reasons, you will discover that the study of life-span development is filled with intriguing information about who we are, how we came to be this way, and where our future will take us.

Most development involves growth, but it also includes decline and dying. In exploring development, we examine the life span from the point of conception until the time when life—at least, life as we know it—ends. You will see yourself as an infant, as a child, and as an adolescent, and be stimulated to think about how those years influenced the kind of individual you are today. And you will see yourself as a young adult, as a middle-aged adult, and as an adult in old age, and be motivated to think about how your experiences today will influence your development through the remainder of your adult years.

CHARACTERISTICS OF THE LIFE-SPAN PERSPECTIVE

Although growth and development are dramatic during the first two decades of life, development is not something that happens only to children and adolescents (Park & others, 2014;

development The pattern of movement or change that begins at conception and continues through the human life span.

Willis, 2015). The traditional approach to the study of development emphasizes extensive change from birth to adolescence (especially during infancy), little or no change during adulthood, and decline in old age. But a great deal of change does occur in the five or six decades after adolescence. The life-span perspective emphasizes developmental change throughout adulthood as well as during childhood (Kennedy & Raz, 2015).

The recent increase in human life expectancy has contributed to the popularity of the life-span approach to development. The upper boundary of the human life span (based on the oldest age documented) is 122 years, as indicated in Figure 1; this maximum life span of humans has not changed since the beginning of recorded history. What has changed is *life expectancy:* the average number of years that a person born in a particular year can expect to live. During the twentieth century alone, life expectancy in the United States increased by 30 years, thanks to improvements in sanitation, nutrition, and medicine (see Figure 2). For individuals born today in the United States, their life expectancy is 79 years of age (U.S. Census Bureau, 2014).

The belief that development occurs throughout life is central to the **life-span perspective** on human development, but this perspective has other characteristics as well. According to life-span development expert Paul Baltes (1939–2006), the life-span perspective views development as lifelong, multidimensional, multidirectional, plastic, multidisciplinary, and contextual, and as a process that involves growth, maintenance, and regulation of loss (Baltes, 1987, 2003; Baltes, Lindenberger, & Staudinger, 2006). In Baltes' view, it is important to understand that development is constructed through biological, sociocultural, and individual factors working together. Let's look at each of these characteristics.

Development Is Lifelong   In the life-span perspective, early adulthood is not the endpoint of development; rather, no age period dominates development. Researchers increasingly study the experiences and psychological orientations of adults at different points in their lives. Later in this chapter, we consider the age periods of development and their characteristics.

Development Is Multidimensional   At every age, your body, your mind, your emotions, and your relationships change and affect each other. Development has biological, cognitive, and socioemotional dimensions. Within each of these dimensions are many components—for example, attention, memory, abstract thinking, speed of processing information, and social intelligence are just a few of the components of the cognitive dimension.

Development Is Multidirectional   Throughout life, some dimensions or components of a dimension expand and others shrink. For example, when one language (such as English) is acquired early in development, the capacity for acquiring second and third languages (such as Spanish and Chinese) decreases later in development, especially after early childhood (Levelt, 1989). During adolescence, as individuals establish romantic relationships, their time spent with friends may decrease. During late adulthood, older adults might become wiser by calling on past experience to guide their intellectual decision making (Maynard & others, 2014; Thomas & Kunzmann, 2014), but they perform more poorly on tasks that require speed in processing information (Hoogendam & others, 2014; Kennedy & others, 2015).

Development Has Plasticity   Developmentalists debate how much *plasticity* people have in various dimensions at different points in their development. Plasticity means the capacity for change. For example, can you still improve your intellectual skills when you are in your seventies or eighties? Or might these intellectual skills be fixed by the time you are in your thirties, so that further improvement is impossible? Researchers have found that the cognitive skills of older adults can be improved through training and development of better strategies (Rebok & others, 2014). However, possibly we possess less capacity for change when we become old (Salthouse, 2015). The search for plasticity and its constraints is a key element on the contemporary agenda for developmental research (de Frias & Dixon, 2014; Luchetti & others, 2015).

Developmental Science Is Multidisciplinary   Psychologists, sociologists, anthropologists, neuroscientists, and medical researchers all share an interest in unlocking

Life expectancy has
Hasn't Changed

Species (common name)	Maximum Life Span (years)
Human	122
Galápagos turtle	100+
Indian elephant	70
Chinese alligator	52
Golden eagle	46
Gorilla	39
Common toad	36
Domestic cat	27
Domestic dog	20
Vampire bat	13
House mouse	3

FIGURE 1

MAXIMUM RECORDED LIFE SPAN FOR DIFFERENT SPECIES. Our only competitor for the maximum recorded life span is the Galápagos turtle.
(tortoise): © MedioImages/SuperStock RF;
(mouse): © Redmond Durrell/Alamy RF

What characterizes the life-span perspective on development?
© Walter Hodges/Corbis

Average Life Expectancy (years)	Time Period
79	2014, USA
70	1954, USA
54	1915, USA
47	1900, USA
41	19th century, England
35	1620, Massachusetts Bay Colony
33	Middle Ages, England
20	Ancient Greece
18	Prehistoric times

FIGURE 2

HUMAN LIFE EXPECTANCY AT BIRTH FROM PREHISTORIC TO CONTEMPORARY TIMES. It took 5,000 years to extend human life expectancy from 18 to 41 years of age.
© Eliza Snow/iStockPhoto.com

Paul Baltes, a leading architect of the life-span perspective on development, converses with one of the long-time research participants in the Berlin Aging Study that he directs. She joined the study in the early 1990s and has participated six times in extensive physical, medical, psychological, and social assessments. In her professional life, she was a practicing physician.
Margaret M. and Paul B. Baltes Foundation

the mysteries of development through the life span. How do your heredity and health limit your intelligence? Do intelligence and social relationships change with age in the same way around the world? How do families and schools influence intellectual development? These are examples of research questions that cut across disciplines.

Development Is Contextual All development occurs within a context, or setting. Contexts include families, neighborhoods, schools, peer groups, work settings, churches, university laboratories, cities, countries, and so on. Each of these settings is influenced by historical, economic, social, and cultural factors (Cushner, McClelland, & Safford, 2015).

Contexts, like individuals, change (Clarke-Stewart & Parke, 2014). Thus, individuals are changing beings in a changing world. As a result of these changes, contexts exert three types of influences (Baltes, 2003): (1) normative age-graded influences, (2) normative history-graded influences, and (3) nonnormative or highly individualized life events. Each type of influence can have a biological or an environmental impact on development.

Normative age-graded influences are similar for individuals in a particular age group. These influences include biological processes such as puberty and menopause. They also include sociocultural or environmental processes such as beginning formal education (usually at about age 6 in most cultures) and retirement (which takes place during the fifties and sixties in most cultures).

Normative history-graded influences are common to people of a particular generation because of historical circumstances (Karlsson & others, 2015). For example, in their youth, American baby boomers shared experiences that included the Cuban missile crisis, the assassination of John F. Kennedy, and the Beatles invasion. Other examples of normative history-graded influences include economic, political, and social upheavals such as the Great Depression of the 1930s, World War II during the 1940s, the civil rights and women's rights movements of the 1960s and 1970s, the terrorist attacks of 9/11/2001, as well as the integration of computers, cell phones, and iPods into everyday life in recent

[handwritten margin note:] Family Friends Church groups Group Projects

life-span perspective View of development as being lifelong, multidimensional, multidirectional, plastic, multidisciplinary, and contextual; involving growth, maintenance, and regulation of loss; and constructed through biological, sociocultural, and individual factors working together.

normative age-graded influences Influences that are similar for individuals in a particular age group.

normative history-graded influences Influences that are common to people of a particular generation because of historical circumstances.

Nonnormative life events, such as Hurricane Sandy in October 2012, are unusual circumstances that have a major impact on a person's life.
© Adam Hunger/Reuters/Landov Images

nonnormative life events Unusual occurrences that have a major impact on an individual's life.

- - - - - - - - ->
developmental **connection**

Parenting

Which parenting style is most often linked with positive child outcomes? Connect to "Families, Lifestyles, and Parenting."

Children learn to love when they are loved

© Robert Maust/Photo Agora

decades (Schaie & Zanjani, 2014). Long-term changes in the genetic and cultural makeup of a population (due to immigration or changes in fertility rates) are also part of normative historical change.

Nonnormative life events are unusual occurrences that have a major impact on an individual's life. These events do not happen to all people, and when they do occur they can influence people in different ways. Examples include experiencing the death of a parent when one is still a child, becoming pregnant in early adolescence, surviving a fire that destroys one's home, winning the lottery, or getting an unexpected career opportunity.

Development Involves Growth, Maintenance, and Regulation of Loss

Baltes and his colleagues (2006) assert that achieving mastery of life often involves conflicts and competition among three goals of human development: growth, maintenance, and regulation of loss. As individuals age into middle and late adulthood, the maintenance and regulation of loss in their capacities shift their attention away from growth. Thus, a 75-year-old man might aim not to improve his memory or his golf swing but to maintain his independence and merely to continue playing golf.

Development Is a Co-construction of Biology, Culture, and the Individual

Development is a co-construction of biological, cultural, and individual factors working together (Baltes, Reuter-Lorenz, & Rösler, 2012). For example, the brain shapes culture, but it is also shaped by culture and the experiences that individuals have or pursue. In terms of individual factors, we can go beyond what our genetic inheritance and environment have given us. We can author a unique developmental path by actively choosing from the environment the things that optimize our lives (Rathunde & Csikszentmihalyi, 2006).

SOME CONTEMPORARY CONCERNS

Pick up a newspaper or magazine and you might see headlines like these: "Political Leanings May Be Written in the Genes," "Mother Accused of Tossing Children into Bay," "Gender Gap Widens," "FDA Warns About ADHD Drug," "Heart Attack Deaths Higher in African American Patients," "Test May Predict Alzheimer Disease." Researchers using the life-span perspective are examining these and many other topics of contemporary concern. The roles that health and well-being, parenting, education, and sociocultural contexts play in life-span development, as well as how social policy is related to these issues, are a particular focus of *A Topical Approach to Life-Span Development*.

Health and Well-Being   Health professionals today recognize the power of lifestyles and psychological states in health and well-being (Donatelle, 2015; Schiff, 2015). Does a pregnant woman endanger her fetus if she drinks a few beers per week? How does a poor diet affect a child's ability to learn? Are children getting less exercise today than in the past? What roles do parents and peers play in whether adolescents abuse drugs? What health-enhancing and health-compromising behaviors do college students engage in? What factors are causing the obesity epidemic in the United States and around the world? How can older adults cope with declining health? We will discuss many questions like these regarding health and well-being. In every chapter, issues of health and well-being are integrated into our discussion.

Parenting and Education   Can two gay men raise a healthy family? Are children harmed if both parents work outside the home? Are U.S. schools failing to teach children how to read and write and calculate adequately? We hear many questions like these related to pressures on the contemporary family and the problems of U.S. schools (Cicchetti & Toth, 2015; Powell, 2015). In other chapters, we analyze child care, the effects of divorce, parenting styles, intergenerational relationships, early childhood education, relationships between childhood poverty and education, dual-language learning, new educational efforts to improve lifelong learning, and many other issues related to parenting and education (Fergusson, McLeod, & Horwood, 2014; Morrison, 2015).

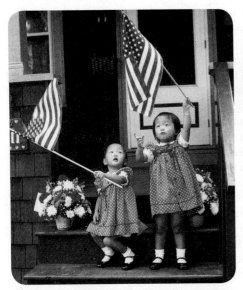

Two Korean-born children on the day they became United States citizens. Asian American and Latino children are the fastest-growing immigrant groups in the United States. *How diverse are the students in your life-span development class? How are their experiences in growing up likely to be similar to or different from yours?*
© Nancy Agostini

Around the world women too often are treated as burdens rather than assets in the political process. *What can be done to strengthen women's roles in the political process?*
© Andy Nelson/The Christian Science Monitor/Getty Images

Doly Akter, age 17, lives in a slum in Dhaka, Bangladesh, where sewers overflow, garbage rots in the streets, and children are undernourished. Nearly two-thirds of young women in Bangladesh marry before they are 18. Doly organized a club supported by UNICEF in which girls go door-to-door monitoring the hygiene habits of households in their neighborhood, leading to improved hygiene and health in the families. Also, her group has stopped several child marriages by meeting with parents and convincing them that it is not in their daughter's best interests. When talking with parents, the girls in the club emphasize the importance of staying in school and how this will improve their daughters' future. Doly says that the girls in her UNICEF group are far more aware of their rights than their mothers ever were (UNICEF, 2007).
Naser Siddique/UNICEF Bangladesh

Sociocultural Contexts and Diversity

Health, parenting, and education—like development itself—are shaped by their sociocultural context. In analyzing this context, four concepts are especially useful: culture, ethnicity, socioeconomic status, and gender.

Culture encompasses the behavior patterns, beliefs, and all other products of a particular group of people that are passed on from generation to generation. Culture results from the interaction of people over many years. A cultural group can be as large as the United States or as small as an isolated Appalachian town. Whatever its size, the group's culture influences the behavior of its members (Berry, 2015; Cole & Tan, 2015). **Cross-cultural studies** compare aspects of two or more cultures. The comparison provides information about the degree to which development is similar, or universal, across cultures, or instead is culture-specific (Polanczyk & others, 2015; Putnick & others, 2015; Sonuga-Barke, 2014).

Ethnicity (the word *ethnic* comes from the Greek word for "nation") is rooted in cultural heritage, nationality, race, religion, and language. African Americans, Latinos, Asian Americans, Native Americans, European Americans, and Arab Americans are examples of broad ethnic groups in the United States. Diversity exists within each ethnic group (Banks, 2014). A special concern is the discrimination and prejudice experienced by ethnic minority children (Cheng, Cohen, & Goodman, 2015; Koppelman, 2014; Renzetti & Kennedy-Bergen, 2015).

The sociocultural context of the United States has become increasingly diverse in recent years. Its population includes a greater variety of cultures and ethnic groups than ever before. This changing demographic tapestry promises not only the richness that diversity produces but also difficult challenges in extending the American dream to all individuals (Marks & others, 2015; Murry & others, 2015.

Socioeconomic status (SES) refers to a person's position within society based on occupational, educational, and economic characteristics. Socioeconomic status implies certain inequalities. Differences in the ability to control resources and to participate in society's rewards produce unequal opportunities (Parillo, 2014).

Gender refers to the characteristics of people as males and females. Few aspects of our development are more central to our identity and social relationships than gender (Bigler, 2015; Hyde, 2014; Leaper, 2015; Liben, Bigler, & Hilliard, 2014).

Social Policy

Social policy is a government's course of action designed to promote the welfare of its citizens. Values, economics, and politics all shape a nation's social policy. Out of

culture The behavior, patterns, beliefs, and all other products of a group of people that are passed on from generation to generation.

cross-cultural studies Comparisons of one culture with one or more other cultures. These provide information about the degree to which development is similar, or universal, across cultures, and the degree to which it is culture-specific.

ethnicity A characteristic based on cultural heritage, nationality characteristics, race, religion, and language.

socioeconomic status (SES) Classification of a person's position in society based on occupational, educational, and economic characteristics.

gender The characteristics of people as females or males.

social policy A government's course of action designed to promote the welfare of its citizens.

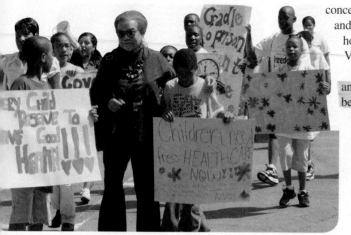

Marian Wright Edelman, president of the Children's Defense Fund, has been a tireless advocate of children's rights and instrumental in calling attention to the needs of children. *What are some of these needs?*
Courtesy of the Children's Defense Fund and Marian Wright Edelman

- - - - - - - - - - - ▸

developmental **connection**

Environment

An increasing number of studies are showing that positive outcomes can be achieved through intervention in the lives of children living in poverty. Connect to "Peers and the Sociocultural World."

concern that policy makers are doing too little to protect the well-being of children and older adults, life-span researchers are increasingly undertaking studies that they hope will lead to the enactment of effective social policy (Duncan, Magnuson & Votruba-Drzal, 2015; Lerner & others, 2015; McLoyd, Mistry, & Hardaway, 2014). Statistics such as infant mortality rates, mortality among children under age 5, and the percentage of children who are malnourished or living in poverty provide benchmarks for evaluating how well children are doing in a particular society. For many years, Marian Wright Edelman, a tireless advocate of children's rights, has pointed out that indicators like these place the United States at or near the lowest rank among industrialized nations in the treatment of children.

Children who grow up in poverty represent a special concern (Duncan & Magnuson, 2015; McCartney & Yoshikawa, 2015). In 2012, 21.8 percent of U.S. children were living in families with incomes below the poverty line, with African American and Latino families with children having especially high rates of poverty (more than 30 percent) (U.S. Census Bureau, 2014). The overall rate is an increase from 2001 (16.2 percent) but a slight decrease from a peak of 22.7 percent in 1993. As indicated in Figure 3, one study found that a higher percentage of U.S. children in poor families than in middle-income families were exposed to family turmoil, separation from a parent, violence, crowding, excessive noise, and poor housing (Evans & English, 2002). Another study revealed that the more years children spent living in poverty, the higher were their physiological indices of stress (Evans & Kim, 2007).

The U.S. figure of 21.8 percent of children living in poverty is much higher than child poverty rates in other industrialized nations. For example, Canada has a child poverty rate of 9 percent and Sweden has a rate of 2 percent.

Edelman says that parenting and nurturing the next generation of children are our society's most important functions and that we need to take them more seriously than we have in the past. To read about efforts to improve the lives of children through social policies, see *Connecting Development to Life.*

Some children triumph over poverty or other adversities. They show resilience. Are there certain characteristics that make children resilient? Ann Masten (2001, 2006, 2009, 2011, 2013, 2014a, b, c, d; Masten & others, 2015) concludes that individual factors, especially good intellectual functioning, and social contexts, especially positive parenting, are key aspects of children showing resilience in the face of adversity. Figure 4 shows the individual factors and social contexts that tend to characterize resilient children.

Risk factor (stressor) / **Pecent of children exposed**

Family turmoil: 45 / 12
Child separation: 45 / 14
Exposure to violence: 73 / 49
Crowding: 16 / 7
Excessive noise: 32 / 21
Poor housing quality: 24 / 3

Poor children
Middle-income children

FIGURE **3**

EXPOSURE TO SIX STRESSORS AMONG POOR AND MIDDLE-INCOME CHILDREN. One study analyzed the exposure to six stressors among poor children and middle-income children (Evans & English, 2002). Poor children were much more likely to face each of these stressors.

Source	Characteristic
Individual	Good intellectual functioning
	Appealing, sociable, easygoing disposition
	Self-confidence, high self-esteem
	Talents
	Faith
Family	Close relationship to caring parent figure
	Authoritative parenting: warmth, structure, high expectations
	Socioeconomic advantages
	Connections to extended supportive family networks
Extrafamilial Context	Bonds to caring adults outside the family
	Connections to positive organizations
	Attending effective schools

FIGURE **4**

CHARACTERISTICS OF RESILIENT CHILDREN: INDIVIDUAL FACTORS AND SOCIAL CONTEXTS

connecting development to life

Improving Family Policy

In the United States, the national government, state governments, and city governments all play a role in influencing the well-being of children. When families neglect or seriously endanger a child's well-being, governments often step in to help. At the national and state levels, policy makers have debated for decades whether helping poor parents will benefit their children. Researchers are providing some answers by examining the effects of specific policies (Duncan, Magnuson, & Votruba-Drzal, 2015; McLoyd, Purtell, & Hardaway, 2015; Murry & others, 2015; White & others, 2014).

For example, the Minnesota Family Investment Program (MFIP) was designed in the 1990s primarily to influence the behavior of adults—specifically, to move adults off the welfare rolls and into paid employment. A key element of the program was its guarantee that adults participating in the program would receive more income if they worked than if they did not. When the adults' income rose, how did that affect their children? A study of the effects of MFIP found that increases in the incomes of working poor parents were linked with benefits for their children (Gennetian & Miller, 2002). The children's achievement in school improved, and their behavior problems decreased. A current MFIP study is examining the influence of specific services on low-income families at

risk for child maltreatment and other negative outcomes for children (Minnesota Family Investment Program, 2009).

A recent large-scale effort to help children escape from poverty is the *Ascend* two-generation educational intervention being conducted by the Aspen Institute (2013). The intervention emphasizes education (increasing postsecondary education for mothers and improving the quality of their children's early childhood education), economic support (housing, transportation, financial education, health insurance, and food assistance), and social capital (peer support including friends and neighbors; participation in community and faith-based organizations; school and work contacts).

Developmental psychologists and other researchers have examined the effects of many other government policies. They are seeking ways to help families living in poverty improve their well-being, and they have offered many suggestions for improving government policies (Duncan & Magnuson, 2015; Leventhal, Dupere, & Shuey, 2015; McCartney & Yoshikawa, 2015).

How does the life-span perspective support this and other research on the role government should play in improving the well-being of children?

At the other end of the life span, efforts to promote the well-being of older adults also create policy issues (Hooyman, Kiyak, & Kawamoto, 2015; Pillas & others, 2014). Key concerns are controlling health-care costs and ensuring that older adults have access to adequate health care (Lynch, Elmore, & Kotecki, 2015; Milte & others, 2014). One study found that the health-care system fails older adults in many ways (Wenger & others, 2003). For example, older adults received the recommended care for general medical conditions such as heart disease only 52 percent of the time; they received appropriate care for undernourishment and Alzheimer disease only 31 percent of the time.

These concerns about the well-being of older adults are heightened by two facts. First, the number of older adults in the United States is growing dramatically, as Figure 5 shows.

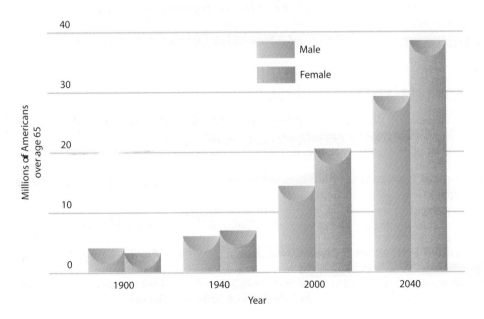

FIGURE 5

THE AGING OF AMERICA. The number of Americans over 65 has grown dramatically since 1900 and is projected to continue increasing until 2040. A significant increase will also occur in the number of individuals in the 85-and-over age group.

SECTION 1   The Life-Span Perspective   **9**

Second, many of these older Americans are likely to need society's help (Hsuan & Rodriguez, 2014; Leung & others, 2015). Compared with earlier decades, U.S. adults today are less likely to be married, more likely to be childless, and more likely to live alone (Dahlberg & McKee, 2014; Machielse, 2015). As the older population continues to expand, an increasing number of older adults will be without either a spouse or children—traditionally the main sources of support for older adults. These individuals will need social relationships, networks, and supports (Antonucci, Ajrouch, & Birditt, 2014; Fingerman & Tennant, 2015; Kim & others, 2015; Luo & Waite, 2014).

Review Connect Reflect

 LG1 Discuss the distinctive features of a life-span perspective on development

Review

- What is meant by the concept of development? Why is the study of life-span development important?
- What are eight main characteristics of the life-span perspective? What are three sources of contextual influences?
- What are some contemporary concerns in life-span development?

Connect

- In other courses and throughout your life you have learned that no two

people are exactly alike. How might the life-span perspective explain this observation?

Reflect *Your Own Personal Journey of Life*

- Imagine what your development would have been like in a culture that offered fewer or distinctly different choices. How might your development have been different if your family had been significantly richer or poorer than it was when you were growing up?

2 The Nature of Development

 LG2 Identify the most important processes, periods, and issues in development

Biological, Cognitive, and Socioemotional Processes | Periods of Development | The Significance of Age | Developmental Issues

In this section, we explore what is meant by developmental processes and periods, as well as variations in the way age is conceptualized. We examine key developmental concepts, explore how they describe development, and discuss strategies we can use to evaluate them.

A chronicle of the events in any person's life can quickly become a confusing and tedious array of details. Two concepts help provide a framework for describing and understanding an individual's development: developmental processes and periods of development.

BIOLOGICAL, COGNITIVE, AND SOCIOEMOTIONAL PROCESSES

At the beginning of this chapter, we defined development as the pattern of change that begins at conception and continues throughout the life span. The pattern is complex because it is the product of biological, cognitive, and socioemotional processes.

Biological Processes   **Biological processes** produce changes in an individual's physical nature. Genes inherited from parents, the development of the brain, height and weight gains, changes in motor skills, nutrition, exercise, the hormonal changes of puberty, and cardiovascular decline are all examples of biological processes that affect development.

Cognitive Processes   **Cognitive processes** refer to changes in the individual's thought process, intelligence, and language. Watching a colorful mobile swinging above the crib, putting together a two-word sentence, memorizing a poem, imagining what it would be like to be a movie star, and solving a crossword puzzle all involve cognitive processes.

biological processes Processes that produce changes in an individual's physical nature.

cognitive processes Processes that involve changes in an individual's thought, intelligence, and language.

Socioemotional Processes Socioemotional processes involve changes in the individual's relationships with other people, changes in emotions, and changes in personality. An infant's smile in response to a parent's touch, a toddler's aggressive attack on a playmate, a school-age child's development of assertiveness, an adolescent's joy at the senior prom, and the affection of an elderly couple all reflect the influence of socioemotional processes on development.

Connecting Biological, Cognitive, and Socioemotional Processes Biological, cognitive, and socioemotional processes are inextricably intertwined (Diamond, 2013). Consider a baby smiling in response to a parent's touch. This response depends on biological processes (the physical nature of touch and responsiveness to it), cognitive processes (the ability to understand intentional acts), and socioemotional processes (the act of smiling often reflects a positive emotional feeling, and smiling helps to connect us in positive ways with other human beings). Nowhere is the connection across biological, cognitive, and socioemotional processes more obvious than in two rapidly emerging fields:

- *Developmental cognitive neuroscience,* which explores links between development, cognitive processes, and the brain (Callaghan & others, 2014; Casey, 2015)
- *Developmental social neuroscience,* which examines connections between socioemotional processes, development, and the brain (Frenkel & Fox, 2015; Reyna & Zayas, 2014; Steinberg, 2015a, b)

In many instances, biological, cognitive, and socioemotional processes are bidirectional. For example, biological processes can influence cognitive processes and vice versa. Thus, although usually we study the different processes of development (biological, cognitive, and socioemotional) in separate locations, keep in mind that we are talking about the development of an integrated individual with a mind and body that are interdependent.

PERIODS OF DEVELOPMENT

The interplay of biological, cognitive, and socioemotional processes produces the periods of the human life span (see Figure 6). A *developmental period* refers to a time frame in a person's life that is characterized by certain features. For the purposes of organization and understanding, we commonly describe development in terms of these periods. The most widely used classification of developmental periods involves the eight-period sequence shown in Figure 7. Approximate age ranges are listed for the periods to provide a general idea of when each period begins and ends.

The prenatal period is the time from conception to birth. It involves tremendous growth—from a single cell to an organism complete with brain and behavioral capabilities—and takes place within approximately a nine-month period.

Infancy is the developmental period from birth to 18 or 24 months. Infancy is a time of extreme dependence upon adults. During this period, many psychological activities—language, symbolic thought, sensorimotor coordination, and social learning, for example—are just beginning.

Early childhood is the developmental period from the end of infancy to age 5 or 6. This period is sometimes called the "preschool years." During this time, young children learn to become more self-sufficient and to care for themselves, develop school readiness skills (following instructions, identifying letters), and spend many hours in play with peers. First grade typically marks the end of early childhood.

Middle and late childhood is the developmental period from about 6 to 11 years of age, approximately corresponding to the elementary school years. During this period, the fundamental skills of reading, writing, and arithmetic are mastered. The child is formally exposed to the larger world and its culture. Achievement becomes a more central theme of the child's world, and self-control increases.

Adolescence is the developmental period of transition from childhood to early adulthood, entered at approximately 10 to 12 years of age and ending at 18 to 21 years of age. Adolescence begins with rapid physical changes—dramatic gains in height and weight, changes in body contour, and the development of sexual characteristics such as enlargement of the breasts, growth of pubic and facial hair, and deepening of the voice. At this point in development, the pursuit

socioemotional processes Processes that involve changes in an individual's relationships with other people, emotions, and personality.

developmental **connection**

Brain Development

Might changes that take place during the development of the adolescent brain be related to teens' mood swings and increased risk taking? Connect to "Physical Development and Biological Aging."

FIGURE 6

PROCESSES INVOLVED IN DEVELOPMENTAL CHANGES. Biological, cognitive, and socioemotional processes interact as individuals develop.

We reach backward to our parents and forward to our children, and through their children to a future we will never see, but about which we need to care.

—CARL JUNG
Swiss psychiatrist, 20th century

© Ieva/iStockPhoto.com

Prenatal period (conception to birth)	Infancy (birth to 18–24 months)	Early childhood (3–5 years)	Middle and late childhood (6–10/11 years)	Adolescence (10–12 to 18–21 years)	Early adulthood (20s and 30s)	Middle adulthood (40s and 50s)	Late adulthood (60s–70s to death)

Biological Processes

Cognitive Processes

Socioemotional Processes

Processes of Development

FIGURE 7

PROCESSES AND PERIODS OF DEVELOPMENT. The unfolding of life's periods of development is influenced by the interaction of biological, cognitive, and socioemotional processes.

(left to right): © Brand X Pictures/PunchStock RF; Courtesy of John Santrock; © Laurence Mouton/Photoalto/PictureQuest RF; © Digital Vision/Getty Images RF; © SW Productions/Getty Images RF; © Blue Moon Stock/Alamy Images RF; © Kristi J. Black/Corbis RF; © Ronnie Kaufman/Blend Images LLC RF.

"This is the path to adulthood. You're here."

© Robert Weber/The New Yorker Collection/ www.cartoonbank.com

emerging adulthood The developmental time frame occurring from approximately 18 to 25 years of age; this transitional period between adolescence and adulthood is characterized by experimentation and exploration.

of independence and an identity are prominent. Thought is more logical, abstract, and idealistic. More time is spent outside the family.

Recently, considerable interest has been directed toward the transition from adolescence to adulthood now referred to as **emerging adulthood,** which lasts from approximately 18 to 25 years of age. Experimentation and exploration characterize the emerging adult (Arnett, 2006, 2012, 2014a, b). At this point in their development, many individuals are still exploring which career path they want to follow, what they want their identity to be, and which lifestyle they want to adopt (for example, single, cohabiting, or married).

Jeffrey Arnett (2006) described five key features that characterize emerging adulthood:

- *Identity exploration,* especially in love and work. Emerging adulthood is the time during which key changes in identity take place for many individuals (Schwartz & others, 2013).
- *Instability.* Residential changes peak during emerging adulthood, a time during which there also is often instability in love, work, and education.
- *Self-focused.* According to Arnett (2006, p. 10), emerging adults "are self-focused in the sense that they have little in the way of social obligations, little in the way of duties and commitments to others, which leaves them with a great deal of autonomy in running their own lives."
- *Feeling in-between.* Many emerging adults don't consider themselves adolescents or full-fledged adults.
- *The age of possibilities, a time when individuals have an opportunity to transform their lives.* Arnett (2006) describes two ways in which emerging adulthood is the age of possibilities: (1) many emerging adults are optimistic about their future; and (2) for emerging adults who have experienced difficult times while growing up, emerging adulthood presents an opportunity to direct their lives in a more positive way.

Recent research indicates that these five aspects characterize not only individuals in the United States as they make the transition from adolescence to early adulthood, but also their counterparts in European countries and Australia (Arnett, 2012, 2014a, b; Sirsch & others, 2009). Although emerging adulthood does not characterize development in all cultures, it does appear to occur in those where assuming adult roles and responsibilities is postponed (Kins & Beyers, 2010).

connecting with research

Is There a Best Time of Day to Conduct Research?

Laura Helmuth (2003) described how researchers are finding that certain testing conditions exaggerate the severity of age-related declines in older adults' performance. Optimum testing conditions are not the same for young adults as they are for older adults. Most researchers conduct their studies in the afternoon, a convenient time for researchers and undergraduate participants. Traditional-aged college students in their late teens and early twenties are often more alert and function optimally in the afternoon, but about 75 percent of older adults are "morning people," performing at their best early in the day (Helmuth, 2003).

Lynn Hasher and her colleagues (2001) tested the memory of college students 18 to 32 years of age and community volunteers 58 to 78 years of age in the late afternoon (about 4 to 5 P.M.) and in the morning (about 8 to 9 A.M.). Regardless of the time of day, the younger college students performed better than the older adults on the memory tests, which involved recognizing sentences from a story and memorizing a list of words. However, when the participants took the memory tests in the morning rather than in the late afternoon, the age difference in performance decreased considerably (see Figure 8).

The relevance of information also affects memory. Thomas Hess and his colleagues (2003) asked younger adults (18 to 30 years of age) and older adults (62 to 84 years of age) to listen to a drawn-out description that was identified as either someone's experiences on a first job or their experiences while searching for a retirement home. The younger adults remembered the details of both circumstances. However, the older adults showed a keen memory for the retirement-home search but not for the first-job experience.

In short, researchers have found that age differences in memory are robust when researchers ask for information that doesn't matter much, but when older adults are asked about information that is relevant to their lives, differences in the memory capacity of younger

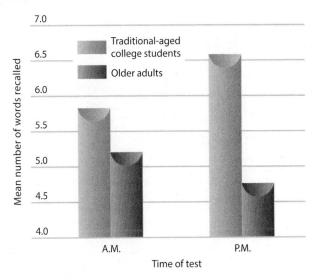

FIGURE 8

MEMORY, AGE, AND TIME OF DAY TESTED (A.M. OR P.M.). In one study, traditional-aged college students performed better than older adults in both the morning and the afternoon. Note, however, that the memory of the older adults was better when they were tested in the morning than in the afternoon, whereas the memory of the traditional-aged college students was not as good in the morning as it was in the afternoon (Hasher & others, 2001).

and older adults often decline considerably (Hasher, 2003). Thus, the type of information selected by researchers may produce an exaggerated view of age-related declines in memory.

What other factors besides time of day or types of information retained do you think might affect research results in a study of cognitive differences between two age groups?

Early adulthood is the developmental period that begins in the late teens or early twenties and lasts through the thirties. It is a time of establishing personal and economic independence, pursuing career development, and, for many, selecting a mate, learning to live with someone in an intimate way, starting a family, and rearing children.

Middle adulthood is the developmental period from approximately 40 years of age to about 60. It is a time of expanding personal and social involvement and responsibility; of assisting the next generation in becoming competent, mature individuals; and of reaching and maintaining satisfaction in a career.

Late adulthood is the developmental period that begins during the sixties or seventies and lasts until death. It is a time of life review, retirement from paid employment, and adjustment to new social roles involving decreasing strength and health. Late adulthood has the longest span of any period of development, and—as noted earlier—the number of people in this age group has been increasing dramatically. As a result, life-span developmentalists have been paying more attention to differences within late adulthood. Paul Baltes and Jacqui Smith (2003) argue that a major change takes place in older adults' lives as they become the "oldest old," on average at about 85 years of age. For example, the "young old" (classified as 65 through 84 in this analysis) have substantial potential for physical and cognitive fitness, retain much of their cognitive capacity, and can develop strategies to cope with the gains and

One's children's children's children: Look back to us as we look to you; we are related by our imaginations. If we are able to touch, it is because we have imagined each other's existence, our dreams running back and forth along a cable from age to age.

—ROGER ROSENBLATT
American writer, 20th century

Below are five statements that you may agree or disagree with. Using the 1–7 scale below, indicate your agreement with each item by placing the appropriate number on the line preceding that item. Please be open and honest in your responding.

Response	Statement
_____	In most ways my life is close to my ideal.
_____	The conditions of my life are excellent.
_____	I am satisfied with my life.
_____	So far I have gotten the important things I want in life.
_____	If I could live my life over, I would change almost nothing.
	Total score

Scale

7 Strongly agree
6 Agree
5 Slightly agree
4 Neither agree nor disagree
3 Slightly disagree
2 Disagree
1 Strongly disagree

Scoring

31–35 Extremely satisfied
26–30 Satisfied
21–25 Slightly satisfied
   20 Neutral
15–19 Slightly dissatisfied
10–14 Dissatisfied
 5–9 Extremely dissatisfied

FIGURE 9

HOW SATISFIED AM I WITH MY LIFE?

Source: Diener, E., Emmons, R.A., Larson, R.J., & Griffin, S. (1985). The Satisfaction with Life Scale, *Journal of Personality Assessment, 49,* 71–75.

losses of aging. In contrast, the oldest old (85 and older) show considerable loss in cognitive skills, experience an increase in chronic stress, and are more frail (Baltes & Smith, 2003). Nonetheless, as we see in other chapters, considerable variation exists in the degree to which the oldest old retain their capabilities (Elisa & others, 2014; Stevenson & others, 2015; Wilhelmsen & others, 2015). As you saw in the *Connecting with Research* interlude, situational contexts, including time of day, play an important role in how well older adults perform.

THE SIGNIFICANCE OF AGE

In the earlier description of developmental periods, an approximate age range was linked with each period. But there are also variations in the capabilities of individuals who are the same age, and we have seen how changes with age can be exaggerated. How important is age when we try to understand an individual?

Age and Happiness Is one age in life better than another? An increasing number of studies indicate that at least in the United States adults are happier as they age. For example, a study of more than 300,000 U.S. adults revealed that psychological well-being increased after the age of 50 years (Stone & others, 2010). In a recent study of individuals from 22 to 93 years of age, older adults reported having more positive emotional experiences than younger adults (English & Carstensen, 2014).

Consider also a U.S. study of approximately 28,000 individuals from age 18 to 88 that revealed happiness increased with age (Yang, 2008). For example, about 33 percent were very happy at 88 years of age compared with only about 24 percent in their late teens and early twenties. Why might older people report being happier and more satisfied with their lives than younger people? Despite the increase in physical problems and losses older adults experience, they are more content with what they have in their lives, have better relationships with the people who matter to them, are less pressured to achieve, have more time for leisurely pursuits, and have many years of experience that may help them use their accrued wisdom to adapt better to their circumstances than younger adults do (Cornwell, Schumm, & Laumann, 2008; Ram & others, 2008). Also in the study, baby boomers (those born between 1946 and 1964) reported being less happy than individuals born earlier—possibly because they are not lowering their aspirations and idealistic hopes as they age as did earlier generations. Because growing older is a certain outcome of living, it is good to know that we are likely to be happier as older adults than when we were younger.

Now that you have read about age variations in life satisfaction, think about how satisfied you are with your life. To help you answer this question, complete the items in Figure 9, which presents the most widely used measure in research on life satisfaction (Diener, 2015).

Conceptions of Age *Chronological age*—the number of years that have elapsed since birth—is not the only way of measuring age. Age has been conceptualized not just as chronological age but also as biological age, psychological age, and social age (Hoyer & Roodin, 2009). *Biological age* is a person's age in terms of biological health. Determining biological age involves knowing the functional capacities of a person's vital organs. One person's vital capacities may be better or worse than those of others of comparable age (Borrell & Samuel, 2014; Richards & others, 2015). The younger the person's biological age, the longer the person is expected to live, regardless of chronological age.

(*Left*) Pam McSwain, competing in the high jump in the Senior Olympics in Memphis; (*right*) a sedentary, overweight middle-aged man. *Even though Pam McSwain's chronological age is older, might her biological age be younger than the middle-aged man's?*
Left: © Karen Pulfer Focht/The Commercial Appeal/Landov Images; Right: © Owaki-Kulla/Corbis

Psychological age reflects an individual's adaptive capacities compared with those of other individuals of the same chronological age. Thus, older adults who continue to learn, are flexible, cope effectively with stress, and think clearly are engaging in more adaptive behaviors than their chronological age-mates who don't engage in these behaviors (Kandler & others, 2015; Neupert & others, 2015; Schaie, 2013). Reflecting the importance of psychological age, a longitudinal study of more than 1,200 individuals across seven decades revealed that the personality trait of conscientiousness (being organized, careful, and disciplined, for example) predicted lower mortality risk from childhood through late adulthood (Martin, Friedman, & Schwartz, 2007).

Social age refers to connectedness with others and the social roles individuals adopt. Individuals who have better social relationships with others are happier with their lives and are likely to live longer than those who are lonely (Antonucci, Ajrouch, & Birditt, 2014; Chui & others, 2014; Hsu & others, 2015).

From a life-span perspective, an overall age profile of an individual involves not just chronological age but also biological age, psychological age, and social age. For example, a 70-year-old man (chronological age) might be in good physical health (biological age), be experiencing memory problems and not be coping well with the demands placed on him by his wife's recent hospitalization (psychological age), and have a number of friends with whom he regularly plays golf (social age).

DEVELOPMENTAL ISSUES

Is your own journey through life marked out ahead of time, or can your experiences change your path? Are the experiences that take place early in your journey more important than later ones? Is your journey more like taking an elevator up a skyscraper with distinct stops along the way, or more like cruising down a river with smoother ebbs and flows? These questions point to three issues about the nature of development: the roles played by nature and nurture, by stability and change, and by continuity and discontinuity.

Nature and Nurture   The **nature-nurture issue** involves the extent to which development is influenced by nature and by nurture. Nature refers to an organism's biological inheritance, nurture to its environmental experiences.

According to those who emphasize the role of nature, just as a sunflower grows in an orderly way—unless flattened by an unfriendly environment—so too a human grows in an orderly way. An evolutionary and genetic foundation produces commonalities in growth and development (Brooker, 2015; Bugenthal, Corpuz, & Beaulieu, 2015; Cowan, 2015). We walk before we talk, speak one word before two words, grow rapidly in infancy and less so in early childhood, experience a rush of sex hormones in puberty, reach the

- - - - - - - ➤
developmental connection
Nature Versus Nurture
Can specific genes be linked to specific environmental experiences? Connect to "Biological Beginnings."

What is the nature of the early- and later-experience issue in development?
© Rubberball/PictureQuest RF

nature-nurture issue Debate about whether development is primarily influenced by nature or nurture. Nature refers to an organism's biological inheritance, nurture to its environmental experiences. The "nature proponents" claim biological inheritance is the more important influence on development; the "nurture proponents" claim that environmental experiences are more important.

developmental **connection**

Personality

Is personality more stable at some points in adult development than at others? Connect to "The Self, Identity, and Personality."

Continuity

Discontinuity

FIGURE **10**

CONTINUITY AND DISCONTINUITY IN DEVELOPMENT. *Is our development like that of a seedling gradually growing into a giant oak tree? Or is it more like that of a caterpillar suddenly becoming a butterfly?*

stability-change issue Debate as to whether and to what degree we become older renditions of our earlier selves (stability) or whether we develop into someone different from who we were at an earlier point in development (change).

continuity-discontinuity issue Debate that focuses on the extent to which development involves gradual, cumulative change (continuity) or distinct stages (discontinuity).

theory An interrelated, coherent set of ideas that helps to explain phenomena and make predictions.

hypotheses Specific assumptions and predictions that can be tested to determine their accuracy.

peak of our physical strength in late adolescence and early adulthood, and then decline physically. Proponents of the developmental influence of nature acknowledge that extreme environments—those that are psychologically barren or hostile—can depress development. However, they believe that basic growth tendencies are genetically programmed into humans (Mader, 2014).

By contrast, others emphasize the impact of nurture, or environmental experiences, on development (Leventhal, Dupere, & Shuey, 2015; Thompson, 2015). Experiences run the gamut from the individual's biological environment (nutrition, medical care, drugs, and physical accidents) to the social environment (family, peers, schools, community, media, and culture).

Stability and Change   Is the shy child who hides behind the sofa when visitors arrive destined to become a wallflower at college dances, or might the child become a sociable, talkative individual? Is the fun-loving, carefree adolescent bound to have difficulty holding down a 9-to-5 job as an adult? These questions reflect the **stability-change issue,** which involves the degree to which early traits and characteristics persist or change as a person matures.

Many developmentalists who emphasize stability in development argue that stability is the result of heredity and possibly early experiences in life. Developmentalists who emphasize change take the more optimistic view that later experiences can produce change. Recall that in the life-span perspective, plasticity—the potential for change—exists throughout the life span.

The roles of early and later experience are an aspect of the stability-change issue that has long been hotly debated (Fraley & Roisman, 2015; Yu & others, 2014). Some argue that unless infants experience warm, nurturant caregiving in the first year or so of life, their development will never be optimal (Cassidy & others, 2011). The later-experience advocates see children as malleable throughout development, with sensitive caregiving and positive close relationships playing important roles later in child development, adolescence, and adulthood just as they do in infancy (Luong, Rauers, & Fingerman, 2015; Mikulincer & Shaver, 2015; Wentzel, 2015).

Continuity and Discontinuity   When developmental change occurs, is it gradual or abrupt? Think about your own development for a moment. Did you gradually become the person you are? Or did you experience sudden, distinct changes in your growth? For the most part, developmentalists who emphasize nurture describe development as a gradual, continuous process. Those who emphasize nature often describe development as a series of distinct stages.

The **continuity-discontinuity issue** focuses on the degree to which development involves either gradual, cumulative change (continuity) or distinct stages (discontinuity). In terms of continuity, as the oak grows from seedling to giant tree, it becomes more and more an oak—its development is continuous (see Figure 10). Similarly, a child's first word, though seemingly an abrupt, discontinuous event, is actually the result of weeks and months of growth and practice. Puberty might seem abrupt, but it is a gradual process that occurs over several years.

In terms of discontinuity, as an insect grows from a caterpillar to a chrysalis to a butterfly, it passes through a sequence of stages in which change differs qualitatively rather than quantitatively. Similarly, at some point a child moves from not being able to think abstractly about the world to being able to do so. This is a qualitative, discontinuous change in development rather than a quantitative, continuous change.

Evaluating the Developmental Issues   Most life-span developmentalists acknowledge that development is not all nature or all nurture, not all stability or all change, and not all continuity or all discontinuity. Nature and nurture, stability and change, continuity and discontinuity characterize development throughout the human life span.

Although most developmentalists do not take extreme positions on these three important issues, there is spirited debate regarding how strongly development is influenced by each of them (Lamb, 2015; Magdon-Maksymowicz & Maksymowicz, 2015; Thompson, 2015).

Review Connect Reflect

LG2 Identify the most important processes, periods, and issues in development

Review

- What are three key developmental processes?
- What are eight main developmental periods?
- How is age related to development?
- What are three main developmental issues?

Connect

- In this chapter, you learned about the importance of the life-span perspective

on development. Do you think this view provides more support for a focus on nature, on nurture, or on both? Why?

Reflect *Your Own Personal Journey of Life*

- Think about your own development in the adolescent, early adulthood, middle adulthood, and late adulthood periods. During which age period do you think you are likely to be happiest? Why?

---

3 Theories of Development   **LG3**   Describe the main theories of human development

| Psychoanalytic Theories | Cognitive Theories | Behavioral and Social Cognitive Theories | Ethological Theory | Ecological Theory | An Eclectic Theoretical Orientation |

How can we answer questions about the roles of nature and nurture, stability and change, and continuity and discontinuity in development? How can we determine, for example, whether special care can repair the harm inflicted by child neglect or whether memory loss in older adults can be prevented? The scientific method is the best tool we have to answer such questions (Smith & Davis, 2013).

The *scientific method* is essentially a four-step process: (1) conceptualize a process or problem to be studied, (2) collect research information (data), (3) analyze data, and (4) draw conclusions.

In step 1, when researchers are formulating a problem to study, they often draw on theories and develop hypotheses. A **theory** is an interrelated, coherent set of ideas that helps to explain phenomena and make predictions. It may suggest **hypotheses,** which are specific assertions and predictions that can be tested. For example, a theory on mentoring might state that sustained support and guidance from an adult improve the lives of children from impoverished backgrounds because the mentor gives the children opportunities to observe and imitate the behavior and strategies of the mentor.

This section outlines key aspects of five theoretical orientations to development: psychoanalytic, cognitive, behavioral and social cognitive, ethological, and ecological. Each contributes an important piece to the life-span development puzzle. Although the theories disagree about certain aspects of development, many of their ideas are complementary rather than contradictory. Together they let us see the total landscape of life-span development in all its richness.

PSYCHOANALYTIC THEORIES

Psychoanalytic theories describe development as primarily unconscious (beyond awareness) and heavily colored by emotion. Psychoanalytic theorists emphasize that behavior is merely a surface characteristic and that a true understanding of development requires analyzing the symbolic meanings of behavior and the deep inner workings of the mind. Psychoanalytic theorists also stress that early experiences with parents extensively shape development. These characteristics are highlighted in the main psychoanalytic theory, that of Sigmund Freud (1856–1939).

Freud's Theory As Freud listened to, probed, and analyzed his patients, he became convinced that their problems were the result of experiences early in life. He thought that as children grow up, their focus of pleasure and sexual impulses shifts from the mouth to the anus and eventually to the genitals. As a result, we go through five stages of psychosexual

Science refines everyday thinking.

—Albert Einstein
German-born American physicist, 20th century

Sigmund Freud, the pioneering architect of psychoanalytic theory. *How did Freud portray the organization of an individual's personality?*
© Bettmann/Corbis

psychoanalytic theories Theories that describe development as primarily unconscious and heavily colored by emotion. Behavior is merely a surface characteristic, and the symbolic workings of the mind must be analyzed to understand behavior. Early experiences with parents are emphasized.

Oral Stage	Anal Stage	Phallic Stage	Latency Stage	Genital Stage
Infant's pleasure centers on the mouth.	Child's pleasure focuses on the anus.	Child's pleasure focuses on the genitals.	Child represses sexual interest and develops social and intellectual skills.	A time of sexual reawakening; source of sexual pleasure becomes someone outside the family.
Birth to 1½ Years	1½ to 3 Years	3 to 6 Years	6 Years to Puberty	Puberty Onward

FIGURE 11

FREUDIAN STAGES. Because Freud emphasized sexual motivation, his stages of development are known as psychosexual stages. In his view, if the need for pleasure at any stage is either undergratified or overgratified, an individual may become fixated, or locked in, at that stage of development.

development: oral, anal, phallic, latency, and genital (see Figure 11). Our adult personality, Freud (1917) claimed, is determined by the way we resolve conflicts between sources of pleasure at each stage and the demands of reality.

Freud's theory has been significantly revised by a number of psychoanalytic theorists. Many of today's psychoanalytic theorists argue that Freud overemphasized sexual instincts; they place more emphasis on cultural experiences as determinants of an individual's development. Unconscious thought remains a central theme, but thought plays a greater role than Freud envisioned. Next, you will read about the ideas of an important revisionist of Freud's ideas—Erik Erikson.

Erikson's Psychosocial Theory Erik Erikson recognized Freud's contributions but stressed that Freud misjudged some important dimensions of human development. For one thing, Erikson (1950, 1968) said we develop in psychosocial stages, rather than in psychosexual stages as Freud maintained. According to Freud, the primary motivation for human behavior is sexual in nature; according to Erikson, it is social and reflects a desire to affiliate with other people. According to Freud, our basic personality is shaped in the first five years of life; according to Erikson, developmental change occurs throughout the life span. Thus, in terms of the early-versus-later-experience issue described earlier in the chapter, Freud viewed early experiences as far more important than later experiences, whereas Erikson emphasized the importance of both early and later experiences.

In **Erikson's theory,** eight stages of development unfold as we go through life (see Figure 12). At each stage, a unique developmental task confronts individuals with a crisis that must be resolved. According to Erikson, this crisis is not a catastrophe but a turning point marked by both increased vulnerability and enhanced potential. The more successfully individuals resolve these crises, the healthier their development will be.

Trust versus mistrust is Erikson's first psychosocial stage, which is experienced in the first year of life. Trust in infancy sets the stage for a lifelong expectation that the world will be a good and pleasant place to live.

Autonomy versus shame and doubt is Erikson's second stage. This stage occurs in late infancy and toddlerhood (1 to 3 years). After gaining trust in their caregivers, infants begin to discover that their behavior is their own. They start to assert their sense of independence or autonomy. They realize their will. If infants and toddlers are restrained too much or punished too harshly, they are likely to develop a sense of shame and doubt.

Initiative versus guilt, Erikson's third stage of development, occurs during the preschool years. As preschool children encounter a widening social world, they face new challenges that require active, purposeful, responsible behavior. Feelings of guilt may arise, though, if the child is irresponsible and is made to feel too anxious.

Industry versus inferiority is Erikson's fourth developmental stage, occurring approximately in the elementary school years. Children now need to direct their energy toward mastering knowledge and intellectual skills. The negative outcome is that the child may develop a sense of inferiority—feeling incompetent and unproductive.

Erik Erikson with his wife, Joan, an artist. Erikson generated one of the most important developmental theories of the twentieth century. *Which stage of Erikson's theory are you in? Does Erikson's description of this stage characterize you?*
© Jon Erikson/The Image Works

Erikson's theory Theory that proposes eight stages of human development. Each stage consists of a unique developmental task that confronts individuals with a crisis that must be resolved.

During the adolescent years individuals face finding out who they are, what they are all about, and where they are going in life. This is Erikson's fifth developmental stage, *identity versus identity confusion*. If adolescents explore roles in a healthy manner and arrive at a positive path to follow in life, they achieve a positive identity; if they do not, identity confusion reigns.

Intimacy versus isolation is Erikson's sixth developmental stage, which individuals experience during early adulthood. At this time, individuals face the developmental task of forming intimate relationships. If young adults form healthy friendships and an intimate relationship with another, intimacy will be achieved; if not, isolation will result.

Generativity versus stagnation, Erikson's seventh developmental stage, occurs during middle adulthood. By generativity Erikson means primarily a concern for helping the younger generation to develop and lead useful lives. The feeling of having done nothing to help the next generation is stagnation.

Integrity versus despair is Erikson's eighth and final stage of development, which individuals experience in late adulthood. During this stage, a person reflects on the past. If the person's life review reveals a life well spent, integrity will be achieved; if not, the retrospective glances likely will yield doubt or gloom—the despair Erikson described.

We examine Erikson's theory in more detail in the chapter on "The Self, Identity, and Personality."

Evaluating Psychoanalytic Theories Contributions of psychoanalytic theories include an emphasis on a developmental framework, family relationships, and unconscious aspects of the mind. These theories have been criticized, however, for a lack of scientific support, too much emphasis on sexual underpinnings, and an image of people that is viewed as too negative.

COGNITIVE THEORIES

Whereas psychoanalytic theories stress the importance of the unconscious, cognitive theories emphasize conscious thoughts. Three important cognitive theories are Piaget's cognitive developmental theory, Vygotsky's sociocultural cognitive theory, and information-processing theory.

Piaget's Cognitive Developmental Theory Piaget's theory states that children go through four stages of cognitive development as they actively construct their understanding of the world. Two processes underlie this cognitive construction of the world: organization and adaptation. To make sense of our world, we organize our experiences. For example, we separate important ideas from less important ideas, and we connect one idea to another. In addition to organizing our observations and experiences, we adapt in response to new environmental demands (Miller, 2011).

Jean Piaget (1954) also proposed that we go through four stages in understanding the world (see Figure 13). Each age-related stage consists of a distinct way of thinking, a *different way* of understanding the world. Thus, according to Piaget, the child's cognition is *qualitatively different* in one stage compared with another. What are Piaget's four stages of cognitive development?

The *sensorimotor stage,* which lasts from birth to about 2 years of age, is the first Piagetian stage. In this stage, infants construct an understanding of the world by coordinating sensory experiences (such as seeing and hearing) with physical, motoric actions—hence the term *sensorimotor*.

The *preoperational stage,* which lasts from approximately 2 to 7 years of age, is Piaget's second stage. In this stage, children begin to go beyond simply connecting sensory information with physical action and represent the world with

Erikson's Stages	Developmental Period
Integrity versus despair	Late adulthood (60s onward)
Generativity versus stagnation	Middle adulthood (40s, 50s)
Intimacy versus isolation	Early adulthood (20s, 30s)
Identity versus identity confusion	Adolescence (10 to 20 years)
Industry versus inferiority	Middle and late childhood (elementary school years, 6 years to puberty)
Initiative versus guilt	Early childhood (preschool years, 3 to 5 years)
Autonomy versus shame and doubt	Infancy (1 to 3 years)
Trust versus mistrust	Infancy (first year)

FIGURE 12

ERIKSON'S EIGHT LIFE-SPAN STAGES. Like Freud, Erikson proposed that individuals go through distinct, universal stages of development. Thus, in terms of the continuity-discontinuity issue discussed in this chapter, both favor the discontinuity side of the debate. Notice that the timing of Erikson's first four stages is similar to that of Freud's stages. *What are the implications of saying that people go through stages of development?*

Jean Piaget, the famous Swiss developmental psychologist, changed the way we think about the development of children's minds. *What are some key ideas in Piaget's theory?*
© Yves de Braine/Black Star/Stock Photo

Piaget's theory Theory stating that children actively construct their understanding of the world and go through four stages of cognitive development.

Sensorimotor Stage

The infant constructs an understanding of the world by coordinating sensory experiences with physical actions. An infant progresses from reflexive, instinctual action at birth to the beginning of symbolic thought toward the end of the stage.

Birth to 2 Years of Age

Preoperational Stage

The child begins to represent the world with words and images. These words and images reflect increased symbolic thinking and go beyond the connection of sensory information and physical action.

2 to 7 Years of Age

Concrete Operational Stage

The child can now reason logically about concrete events and classify objects into different sets.

7 to 11 Years of Age

Formal Operational Stage

The adolescent reasons in more abstract, idealistic, and logical ways.

11 Years of Age Through Adulthood

FIGURE 13

PIAGET'S FOUR STAGES OF COGNITIVE DEVELOPMENT. According to Piaget, how a child thinks—not how much the child knows—determines the child's stage of cognitive development.

(left to right): © Stockbyte/Getty Images RF; © BananaStock/PunchStock RF; © image100/Corbis RF; © Jose Pelaez/Corbis RF

Lev Vygotsky was born the same year as Piaget, but he died much earlier, at the age of 37. There is considerable interest today in Vygotsky's sociocultural cognitive theory of child development. *What are some key characteristics of Vygotsky's theory?*
A.R. Lauria/Dr. Michael Cole, Laboratory of Human Cognition, University of California, San Diego

Vygotsky's theory Sociocultural cognitive theory that emphasizes how culture and social interaction guide cognitive development.

words, images, and drawings. However, according to Piaget, preschool children still lack the ability to perform what he calls operations, which are internalized mental actions that allow children to do mentally what they previously could only do physically. For example, if you imagine putting two sticks together to see whether they would be as long as another stick, without actually moving the sticks, you are performing a concrete operation.

The *concrete operational stage,* which lasts from approximately 7 to 11 years of age, is the third Piagetian stage. In this stage, children can perform operations that involve objects, and they can reason logically when the reasoning can be applied to specific or concrete examples. For instance, concrete operational thinkers cannot imagine the steps necessary to complete an algebraic equation, which is too abstract for thinking at this stage of development.

The *formal operational stage,* which appears between the ages of 11 and 15 and continues through adulthood, is Piaget's fourth and final stage. In this stage, individuals move beyond concrete experiences and think in abstract and more logical terms. As part of thinking more abstractly, adolescents develop images of ideal circumstances. They might think about what an ideal parent is like and compare their parents to this ideal standard. They begin to entertain possibilities for the future and are fascinated with what they can become. In solving problems, they become more systematic, developing hypotheses about why something is happening the way it is and then testing these hypotheses. We examine Piaget's cognitive developmental theory in more detail in the chapter entitled "Cognitive Developmental Approaches."

Vygotsky's Sociocultural Cognitive Theory   Like Piaget, the Russian developmentalist Lev Vygotsky (1896–1934) maintained that children actively construct their knowledge. However, Vygotsky (1962) gave social interaction and culture far more important roles in cognitive development than Piaget did. **Vygotsky's theory** is a sociocultural cognitive theory that emphasizes how culture and social interaction guide cognitive development.

Vygotsky portrayed the child's development as inseparable from social and cultural activities (Gauvain & Perez, 2015). He argued that cognitive development involves learning to use the inventions of society, such as language, mathematical systems, and memory strategies. Thus, in one culture, children might learn to count with the help of a computer; in another, they might learn by using beads. According to Vygotsky, children's social interaction with more-skilled adults and peers is indispensable to their cognitive development (Mahn & John Steiner, 2013). Through this interaction, they learn to use the tools that will help them adapt and be successful in their culture (Rogoff & others, 2015). In the chapter entitled "Cognitive Developmental Approaches," we examine ideas about learning and teaching that are based on Vygotsky's theory.

© David Cook/www.blueshiftstudios.co.uk/Alamy RF

The Information-Processing Theory   Information-processing theory emphasizes that individuals manipulate information, monitor it, and strategize about it. Unlike Piaget's theory, but like Vygotsky's theory, information-processing theory does not describe development as stage-like. Instead, according to this theory, individuals develop a gradually increasing capacity for processing information, which allows them to acquire increasingly complex knowledge and skills (Carlson, White, & Davis-Unger, 2014; Muller & Kerns, 2015).

Robert Siegler (2006, 2013), a leading expert on children's information processing, states that thinking is information processing. In other words, when individuals perceive, encode, represent, store, and retrieve information, they are thinking. Siegler emphasizes that an important aspect of development is learning good strategies for processing information (Ramani & Siegler, 2014; Siegler & others, 2015). For example, becoming a better reader might involve learning to monitor the key themes of the material being read. In the chapter on "Information Processing," we explore the information-processing approach in greater depth.

Siegler (2006) also argues that the best way to understand how children learn is to observe them while they are learning. He emphasizes the importance of using the *microgenetic method* to obtain detailed information about processing mechanisms as they are occurring moment to moment. Siegler concludes that most research methods indirectly assess cognitive change, being more like snapshots than movies. The microgenetic method seeks to discover not just what children know but the cognitive processes involved in how they acquired the knowledge (Miller, 2010). A number of microgenetic studies have focused on a specific aspect of academic learning, such as how children learn whole number arithmetic, fractions, and other areas of math (Siegler & Lortie-Forgues, 2015; Siegler & Thompson, 2014).

Evaluating Cognitive Theories   Contributions of cognitive theories include a positive view of development and an emphasis on the active construction of understanding. Criticisms include skepticism about the pureness of Piaget's stages and insufficient attention given to individual variations.

BEHAVIORAL AND SOCIAL COGNITIVE THEORIES

Behaviorism essentially holds that we can study scientifically only what we can directly observe and measure. Out of the behavioral tradition grew the belief that development is observable behavior that we can learn through experience with the environment (Chance, 2014; Spiegler, 2016). In terms of the continuity-discontinuity issue discussed earlier in this chapter, the behavioral and social cognitive theories emphasize continuity in development and argue that development does not occur in stage-like fashion. Let's explore two versions of behaviorism: Skinner's operant conditioning and Bandura's social cognitive theory.

B. F. Skinner was a tinkerer who liked to make new gadgets. From birth to age 2 his younger daughter, Deborah, slept and played in Skinner's enclosed Air-Crib, which he invented because he wanted to control her environment completely. The Air-Crib was sound-proofed and temperature controlled. Debbie, shown here as a child with her parents, is currently a successful artist, married and living in London. *What do you think about Skinner's Air-Crib?*
© AP Images

Skinner's Operant Conditioning   According to B.F. Skinner (1904–1990), through *operant conditioning* the consequences of a behavior produce changes in the probability of the behavior's occurrence. A behavior followed by a rewarding stimulus is more likely to recur, whereas a behavior followed by a punishing stimulus is less likely to recur. For example, when an adult smiles at a child after the child has done something, the child is more likely to engage in that behavior again than if the adult gives the child a disapproving look.

information-processing theory Theory emphasizing that individuals manipulate information, monitor it, and strategize about it. Central to this theory are the processes of memory and thinking.

In Skinner's (1938) view, such rewards and punishments shape development. For Skinner the key aspect of development is behavior, not thoughts and feelings. He emphasized that development consists of the pattern of behavioral changes that are brought about by rewards and punishments. For example, Skinner would say that shy people learned to be shy as a result of experiences they had while growing up. It follows that modifications in an environment can help a shy person become more socially oriented.

Bandura's Social Cognitive Theory   Some psychologists agree with the behaviorists' notion that development is learned and is influenced strongly by environmental interactions. However, unlike Skinner, they also see cognition as important in understanding development. **Social cognitive theory** holds that behavior, environment, and cognition are the key factors in development.

American psychologist Albert Bandura (1925–) is the leading architect of social cognitive theory. Bandura (2001, 2010a, b, 2012) emphasizes that cognitive processes have important links with the environment and behavior. His early research program focused heavily on *observational learning* (also called *imitation,* or *modeling*), which is learning that occurs through observing what others do. For example, a young boy might observe his father yelling in anger and treating other people with hostility; with his peers, the young boy later acts very aggressively, showing the same characteristics as his father's behavior. Social cognitive theorists stress that people acquire a wide range of behaviors, thoughts, and feelings through observing others' behavior and that these observations form an important part of life-span development.

What is *cognitive* about observational learning in Bandura's view? He proposes that people cognitively represent the behavior of others and then sometimes adopt this behavior themselves.

Bandura's (2001, 2010a, b, 2012) model of learning and development includes three elements: behavior, the person/cognition, and the environment. An individual's confidence that he or she can control his or her success is an example of a person factor; strategies are an example of a cognitive factor. As shown in Figure 14, behavior, person/cognition, and environmental factors operate interactively.

Discussion of Bandura's social cognitive theory appears in the chapter entitled "Schools, Achievement, and Work."

Evaluating Behavioral and Social Cognitive Theories   Contributions of the behavioral and social cognitive theories include an emphasis on scientific research and environmental determinants of behavior. These theories have been criticized for deemphasizing the role of cognition (Skinner) and giving inadequate attention to developmental changes.

ETHOLOGICAL THEORY

Ethology stresses that behavior is strongly influenced by biology, is tied to evolution, and is characterized by critical or sensitive periods. These are specific time frames during which, according to ethologists, the presence or absence of certain experiences has a long-lasting influence on individuals.

European zoologist Konrad Lorenz (1903–1989) helped bring ethology to prominence. In his best-known research, Lorenz (1965) studied the behavior of greylag geese, which will follow their mothers as soon as they hatch. Lorenz separated the eggs laid by one goose into two groups. One group he returned to the goose to be hatched by her. The other group was hatched in an incubator. The goslings in the first group performed as predicted. They followed their mother as soon as they hatched. However, those in the second group, which saw Lorenz when they first hatched, followed him everywhere as though he were their mother. Lorenz marked the goslings and then placed both groups under a box. Mother goose and "mother" Lorenz stood aside as the box lifted. Each group of goslings went directly to its "mother." Lorenz called this process *imprinting,* the rapid, innate learning that involves attachment to the first moving object that is seen.

John Bowlby (1969, 1989) illustrated an important application of ethological theory to human development. Bowlby stressed that attachment to a caregiver over the first year of life has important consequences throughout the life span. In his view, if this attachment is positive and secure, the individual will likely develop positively in childhood and adulthood. If the

Albert Bandura has been one of the leading architects of social cognitive theory. *How does Bandura's theory differ from Skinner's? Courtesy of Dr. Albert Bandura*

FIGURE 14

BANDURA'S SOCIAL COGNITIVE MODEL. The arrows illustrate how relations between behavior, person/cognition, and environment are reciprocal rather than one-way. Person/cognition refers to cognitive processes (for example, thinking and planning) and personal characteristics (for example, believing that you can control your experiences).

- - - - - - - >

developmental **connection**

Achievement

Bandura emphasizes that self-efficacy is a key person/cognitive factor in achievement. Connect to "Schools, Achievement, and Work."

social cognitive theory Theoretical view that behavior, environment, and cognition are the key factors in development.

ethology Theory stressing that behavior is strongly influenced by biology, is tied to evolution, and is characterized by critical or sensitive periods.

Konrad Lorenz, a pioneering student of animal behavior, is followed through the water by three imprinted greylag geese. Describe Lorenz's experiment with the geese. *Do you think his experiment would have the same results with human babies? Explain.*

© Nina Leen/The Life Picture Collection/Getty Images

attachment is negative and insecure, life-span development will likely not be optimal. In the chapter entitled "Emotional Development," we explore the concept of infant attachment in much greater detail.

In Lorenz's view, imprinting needs to take place at a certain, very early time in the life of the animal, or else it will not take place. This point in time is called a *critical period.* A related concept is that of a *sensitive period,* and an example of this is the time during infancy when, according to Bowlby, attachment should occur in order to promote optimal development of social relationships.

Another theory that emphasizes biological foundations of development—evolutionary psychology—is presented in the chapter entitled "Biological Beginnings," along with views on the role of heredity in development. In addition, we examine a number of biological theories of aging in the chapter entitled "Physical Development and Biological Aging."

Contributions of ethological theory include its focus on the biological and evolutionary basis of development and its use of careful observations in naturalistic settings. Ethological theory has been criticized for its overemphasis on biological foundations and lack of flexibility regarding the concepts of critical and sensitive periods.

ECOLOGICAL THEORY

While ethological theory stresses biological factors, ecological theory emphasizes environmental factors. One ecological theory that has important implications for understanding life-span development was created by Urie Bronfenbrenner (1917–2005).

Bronfenbrenner's ecological theory (1986, 2004; Bronfenbrenner & Morris, 1998, 2006) holds that development reflects the influence of several environmental systems. The theory identifies five environmental systems: microsystem, mesosystem, exosystem, macrosystem, and chronosystem (see Figure 15).

The *microsystem* is the setting in which the individual lives. Contexts within it include the person's family, peers, school, and neighborhood. It is in the microsystem that the most direct interactions with social agents take place—with parents, friends, and teachers, for example. The individual is not a passive recipient of experiences in these settings, but someone who helps to construct the settings.

The *mesosystem* involves relations between microsystems or connections between contexts. Examples are the relationship of family experiences to school experiences, school experiences to church experiences, and family experiences to peer experiences. For example, children whose parents have rejected them may have difficulty developing positive relations with teachers.

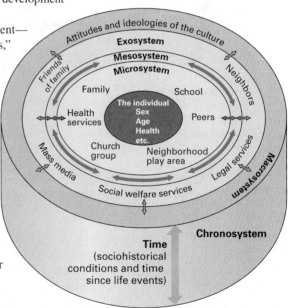

FIGURE 15

BRONFENBRENNER'S ECOLOGICAL THEORY OF DEVELOPMENT. Bronfenbrenner's ecological theory consists of five environmental systems: microsystem, mesosystem, exosystem, macrosystem, and chronosystem.

Bronfenbrenner's ecological theory
Bronfenbrenner's environmental systems theory that focuses on five environmental systems: microsystem, mesosystem, exosystem, macrosystem, and chronosystem.

Urie Bronfenbrenner developed ecological theory, a perspective that is receiving increased attention today. His theory emphasizes the importance of both micro and macro dimensions of the environment in which the child lives.
Cornell University Photography

The *exosystem* consists of links between the individual's immediate context and a social setting in which the individual does not play an active role. For example, a husband's or child's experience at home may be influenced by a mother's experiences at work. The mother might receive a promotion that requires more travel, which might increase conflict with the husband and change patterns of interaction with the child.

The *macrosystem* involves the culture in which individuals live. Remember from earlier in the chapter that culture refers to the behavior patterns, beliefs, and all other products of a group of people that are passed on from generation to generation. Remember also that cross-cultural studies—the comparison of one culture with one or more other cultures—provide information about the generality of development.

The *chronosystem* consists of the patterning of environmental events and transitions over the life course, as well as sociohistorical circumstances. For example, divorce is one transition. Researchers have found that the negative effects of divorce on children often peak during the first year after the divorce (Hetherington, 1993, 2006). By two years after the divorce, family interaction is more stable. As an example of sociohistorical circumstances, consider how the opportunities for women to pursue a career have increased since the 1960s.

Bronfenbrenner (2004; Bronfenbrenner & Morris, 2006) subsequently added biological influences to his theory, describing it as a bioecological theory. Nonetheless, it is still dominated by ecological, environmental contexts (Ceci, 2000).

Contributions of the theory include its systematic examination of micro and macro dimensions of environmental systems, and its attention to connections between environmental systems. A further contribution of Bronfenbrenner's theory is an emphasis on a range of social contexts beyond the family, such as neighborhood, religious community, school, and workplace, as influential in children's development (Gauvain & Perez, 2015). The theory has been criticized for giving inadequate attention to the influence of biological and cognitive factors.

AN ECLECTIC THEORETICAL ORIENTATION

eclectic theoretical orientation An orientation that does not follow any one theoretical approach but rather selects from each theory whatever is considered best in it.

No single theory described in this chapter can explain entirely the rich complexity of life-span development, but each has contributed to our understanding of development. Psychoanalytic theory best explains the workings of the unconscious mind. Erikson's theory best describes the changes that occur in adult development. Piaget's, Vygotsky's, and the information-processing views provide the most complete description of cognitive development. The behavioral and social cognitive and ecological theories have been the most adept at examining the

THEORY	ISSUES	
	Continuity/discontinuity, early versus later experiences	**Biological and environmental factors**
Psychoanalytic	Discontinuity between stages—continuity between early experiences and later development; early experiences very important; later changes in development emphasized in Erikson's theory	Freud's biological determination interacting with early family experiences; Erikson's more balanced biological-cultural interaction perspective
Cognitive	Discontinuity between stages in Piaget's theory; continuity between early experiences and later development in Piaget's and Vygotsky's theories; no stages in Vygotsky's theory or information-processing theory	Piaget's emphasis on interaction and adaptation; environment provides the setting for cognitive structures to develop; information-processing view has not addressed this issue extensively but mainly emphasizes biological-environmental interaction
Behavioral and social cognitive	Continuity (no stages); experience at all points of development important	Environment viewed as the cause of behavior in both views
Ethological	Discontinuity but no stages; critical or sensitive periods emphasized; early experiences very important	Strong biological view
Ecological	Little attention to continuity/discontinuity; change emphasized more than stability	Strong environmental view

FIGURE **16**

A COMPARISON OF THEORIES AND ISSUES IN LIFE-SPAN DEVELOPMENT

environmental determinants of development. The ethological theories have highlighted biology's role and the importance of sensitive periods in development.

In short, although theories can be helpful guides, relying on a single theory to explain development probably would be a mistake. This book instead takes an **eclectic theoretical orientation**—rather than following a single theoretical approach, it selects from each theory whatever is considered its best features. Figure 16 compares the main theoretical perspectives in terms of how they view important issues in human development.

Review *Connect* Reflect

 LG3 Describe the main theories of human development

Review

- How can theory and hypotheses be defined? What are the four steps of the scientific method?
- What are two main psychoanalytic theories? What are some contributions and criticisms of the psychoanalytic theories?
- What are three main cognitive theories? What are some contributions and criticisms of the cognitive theories?
- What are two main behavioral and social cognitive theories? What are some contributions and criticisms of the behavioral and social cognitive theories?
- What is the nature of ethological theory? What are some contributions and criticisms of this theory?

- What characterizes ecological theory? What are some contributions and criticisms of this theory?
- What is an eclectic theoretical orientation?

Connect

- In this section you learned about cognitive theories and social cognitive theories. What do these theories have in common? How are they different?

Reflect *Your Own Personal Journey of Life*

- Which of the life-span theories do you think best explains your own development? Why?

4 Research on Life-Span Development

LG4 Explain how research on life-span development is conducted

Methods for Collecting Data | Research Designs | Time Span of Research | Conducting Ethical Research | Minimizing Bias

If they follow an eclectic orientation, how do scholars and researchers determine that one feature of a theory is somehow better than another? The scientific method discussed earlier in this chapter provides the guide. Through scientific research, they can test and refine the features of theories (Trochim, Donnelly, & Arora, 2016).

Generally, research in life-span development is designed to test hypotheses, which in some cases are derived from the theories just described. Through research, theories are modified to reflect new data, and occasionally new theories arise.

METHODS FOR COLLECTING DATA

Whether we are interested in studying attachment in infants, the cognitive skills of children, or social relationships in older adults, we can choose from several ways of collecting data. Here we consider the measures most often used, beginning with observation.

Observation Scientific observation requires an important set of skills (Stangor, 2015). For observations to be effective, they have to be systematic. We need to have some

What are some important strategies in conducting observational research with children?
© Charles Fox/Philadelphia Inquirer/MCT/Landov Images

FIGURE 17

PARENTS' EXPLANATIONS OF SCIENCE TO SONS AND DAUGHTERS AT A SCIENCE MUSEUM. In a naturalistic observation study at a children's science museum, parents were three times more likely to explain science to boys than to girls (Crowley & others, 2001). The gender difference occurred regardless of whether the father, the mother, or both parents were with the child, although the gender difference was greatest for fathers' science explanations to sons and daughters.

laboratory A controlled setting from which many of the complex factors of the "real world" have been removed.

naturalistic observation Observing behavior in real-world settings.

idea of what we are looking for. We have to know whom we are observing, when and where we will observe, how we will make our observations, and how we will record them.

Where should we make our observations? We have two choices: the laboratory and the everyday world.

When we observe scientifically, we often need to control certain factors that determine behavior but are not the focus of our inquiry (Jackson, 2016). For this reason, some research in life-span development is conducted in a **laboratory,** a controlled setting where many of the complex factors of the "real world" are absent. For example, suppose you want to observe how children react when they see other people act aggressively. If you observe children in their homes or schools, you have no control over how much aggression the children observe, what kind of aggression they see, which people they see acting aggressively, or how other people treat the children. In contrast, if you observe the children in a laboratory, you can control these and other factors and therefore have more confidence about how to interpret your observations.

Laboratory research does have some drawbacks, however, including the following:

· It is almost impossible to conduct research without the participants knowing they are being studied.

· The laboratory setting is unnatural and therefore can cause the participants to behave unnaturally.

· People who are willing to come to a university laboratory may not fairly represent groups from diverse cultural backgrounds.

· People who are unfamiliar with university settings may be intimidated by the laboratory atmosphere.

Naturalistic observation provides insights that sometimes cannot be obtained in the laboratory. **Naturalistic observation** means observing behavior in real-world settings, making no effort to manipulate or control the situation. Life-span researchers conduct naturalistic observations at sporting events, child-care centers, schools, work settings, malls, and other places people live in and frequent.

Naturalistic observation was used in one study that focused on conversations in a children's science museum (Crowley & others, 2001). When visiting exhibits at the science museum, parents were three times as likely to engage boys as girls in explanatory talk. This finding suggests a gender bias that encourages boys more than girls to be interested in science (see Figure 17).

Survey and Interview   Sometimes the best and quickest way to get information about people is to ask them for it. One technique is to *interview* them directly. A related method is the survey—sometimes referred to as a *questionnaire*—which is especially useful when information from many people is needed (Madill, 2012). A standard set of questions is used to obtain people's self-reported attitudes or beliefs about a particular topic. In a good survey, the questions are clear and unbiased, allowing respondents to answer unambiguously.

Surveys and interviews can be used to study a wide range of topics from religious beliefs to sexual habits to attitudes about gun control to beliefs about how to improve schools. Surveys and interviews may be conducted in person, over the telephone, and over the Internet.

One problem with surveys and interviews is the tendency of participants to answer questions in a way that they think is socially acceptable or desirable rather than to say what they truly think or feel. For example, on a survey or in an interview some individuals might say that they do not take drugs even though they do.

Standardized Test A **standardized test** has uniform procedures for administration and scoring. Many standardized tests allow a person's performance to be compared with that of other individuals; thus, they provide information about individual differences among people (Gregory, 2014). One example is the Stanford-Binet intelligence test, which is described in the chapter entitled "Intelligence." Your score on the Stanford-Binet test tells you how your performance compares with that of thousands of other people who have taken the test.

One criticism of standardized tests is that they assume a person's behavior is consistent and stable, although personality and intelligence—two primary targets of standardized testing—can vary with the situation. For example, a person may perform poorly on a standardized intelligence test in an office setting but score much higher at home, where he or she is less anxious.

Case Study A **case study** is an in-depth look at a single individual. Case studies are performed mainly by mental health professionals when, for either practical or ethical reasons, the unique aspects of an individual's life cannot be duplicated and tested in other individuals. A case study provides information about one person's experiences; it may focus on nearly any aspect of the subject's life that helps the researcher understand the person's mind, behavior, or other attributes. In other chapters, we discuss vivid case studies, such as that of Michael Rehbein, who had much of the left side of his brain removed at 7 years of age to end severe epileptic seizures.

A case study can provide a dramatic, in-depth portrayal of an individual's life, but we must be cautious when generalizing from this information. The subject of a case study is unique, with a genetic makeup and personal history that no one else shares. In addition, case studies involve judgments of unknown reliability. Researchers who conduct case studies rarely check to see if other professionals agree with their observations or findings (Yin, 2012).

Mahatma Gandhi was the spiritual leader of India in the middle of the twentieth century. Erik Erikson conducted an extensive case study of Gandhi's life to determine what contributed to his identity development. *What are some limitations of the case study approach?*
© Bettmann/Corbis

standardized test A test with uniform procedures for administration and scoring. Many standardized tests allow a person's performance to be compared with the performance of other individuals.

case study An in-depth look at a single individual.

Physiological Measures Researchers are increasingly using physiological measures when they study development at different points in the life span (Chuang & others, 2014; Kennedy & others, 2015). Hormone levels are increasingly examined in developmental research. Cortisol is a hormone produced by the adrenal gland that is linked to the body's stress level and has been measured in studies of temperament, emotional reactivity, and peer relations (Gunnar & Herrera, 2013). Also, as puberty unfolds, the blood levels of certain hormones increase. To determine the nature of these hormonal changes, researchers analyze blood samples from adolescent volunteers (Susman & Dorn, 2013).

Another physiological measure that is increasingly being used is neuroimaging, especially *functional magnetic resonance imaging* (fMRI), in which electromagnetic waves are used to construct images of a person's brain tissue and biochemical activity (Casey, 2015; Leshikar & others, 2014). Figure 18 compares the brain images of two adolescents—one a non-drinker and the other a heavy drinker—while they are engaged in a memory task. Electroencephalography (EEG)

FIGURE **18**

BRAIN IMAGING OF 15-YEAR-OLD ADOLESCENTS. These two brain images indicate how alcohol can influence the functioning of an adolescent's brain. Notice the pink and red coloring (which indicates effective brain functioning involving memory) in the brain of the 15-year-old nondrinker (*left*) while engaging in a memory task, and compare it with the lack of those colors in the brain of the 15-year-old heavy drinker (*right*) under the influence of alcohol.
Dr. Susan Tapert, University of California, San Diego

is a physiological measure that has been used for many decades to monitor overall electrical charges in the brain (Reznick, 2013). Recent electroencephalography research includes studies of infants' attention and memory (Rajan & Bell, 2015; Xiao & others, 2014).

Heart rate has been used as an indicator of infants' and children's development of perception, attention, and memory (Columbo, Brez, & Curtindale, 2013). Further, heart rate has been used as an index of different aspects of emotional development, such as inhibition and anxiety (Reznick, 2013).

Eye movement also is increasingly being assessed to learn more about perceptual development and other developmental topics. Sophisticated eye-tracking equipment is used to provide more detailed information about infants' perception, attention, and the development of autism (Bulf & Valenza, 2014; Johnson & Hannon, 2015).

RESEARCH DESIGNS

In conducting research on life-span development, in addition to having a method for collecting data, you also need a research design. There are three main types of research designs: descriptive, correlational, and experimental.

Descriptive Research   All of the data-collection methods that we have discussed can be used in **descriptive research,** which aims to observe and record behavior. For example, a researcher might observe the extent to which people are altruistic or aggressive toward each other. By itself, descriptive research cannot prove what causes some phenomenon, but it can reveal important information about people's behavior (Leedy & Ormrod, 2016).

Correlational Research   In contrast with descriptive research, correlational research goes beyond describing phenomena to provide information that will help us to predict how people will behave (Howell, 2014; Levin, Fox, & Forde, 2015). In **correlational research,** the goal is to describe the strength of the relationship between two or more events or characteristics. The more strongly the two events are correlated (or related or associated), the more effectively we can predict one event from the other.

For example, to find out whether children of permissive parents have less self-control than other children, you would need to carefully record observations of parents' permissiveness and their children's self-control. You might observe that the higher a parent was in permissiveness, the lower the child was in self-control. You would then analyze these data statistically to yield a numerical measure, called a **correlation coefficient,** a number based on a statistical analysis that is used to describe the degree of association between two variables. The correlation coefficient ranges from +1.00 to −1.00. A negative number means an inverse (reversed) relation. In the example just given, you might find an inverse correlation between permissive parenting and children's self-control, with a coefficient of, say, −.30. By contrast, you might find a positive correlation of +.30 between parental monitoring of children and children's self-control.

The higher the correlation coefficient (whether positive or negative), the stronger the association between the two factors. A correlation of 0 means that there is no association between the factors. A correlation of −.40 is stronger than a correlation of +.20 because we disregard whether the correlation is positive or negative in determining the strength of the correlation.

A caution is in order, however. Correlation does not equal causation (Heiman, 2014, 2015). The correlational finding just mentioned does not mean that permissive parenting necessarily causes low self-control in children. It could mean that, but it also could mean that a child's lack of self-control caused the parents to throw up their arms in despair and give up trying to control the child. It also could mean that other factors, such as heredity or poverty, caused the correlation between permissive parenting and low self-control in children. Figure 19 illustrates these possible interpretations of correlational data.

Experimental Research   To study causality, researchers turn to experimental research. An **experiment** is a carefully regulated procedure in which one or more factors believed to influence the behavior being studied are manipulated while all other factors are held constant. If the behavior under study changes when a factor is manipulated, the manipulated

descriptive research A type of research that aims to observe and record behavior.

correlational research A type of research that strives to describe the strength of the relationship between two or more events or characteristics.

correlation coefficient A number based on a statistical analysis that is used to describe the degree of association between two variables.

experiment Carefully regulated procedure in which one or more factors believed to influence the behavior being studied are manipulated while all other factors are held constant.

Observed Correlation: As permissive parenting increases, children's self-control decreases.

Possible explanations for this observed correlation

Permissive parenting	causes →	Children's lack of self-control
Children's lack of self-control	causes →	Permissive parenting
A third factor such as genetic tendencies or poverty	causes both →	Permissive parenting and children's lack of self-control

An observed correlation between two events cannot be used to conclude that one event causes the second event. Other possibilities are that the second event causes the first event or that a third event causes the correlation between the first two events.

FIGURE 19

POSSIBLE EXPLANATIONS OF CORRELATIONAL DATA
© Digital Vision/PunchStock RF

factor has caused the behavior to change (Christensen, Johnson, & Turner, 2015). In other words, the experiment has demonstrated cause and effect. The cause is the factor that was manipulated. The effect is the behavior that changed because of the manipulation. Nonexperimental research methods (descriptive and correlational research) cannot establish cause and effect because they do not involve manipulating factors in a controlled way (Kantowitz, Roediger, & Elmes, 2015).

Independent and Dependent Variables Experiments include two types of changeable factors, or variables: independent and dependent. An *independent variable* is a manipulated, influential, experimental factor. It is a potential cause. The label "independent" is used because this variable can be manipulated independently of other factors to determine its effect. An experiment may include one independent variable or several of them.

A *dependent variable* is a factor that can change in an experiment, in response to changes in the independent variable. As researchers manipulate the independent variable, they measure the dependent variable for any resulting effect.

For example, suppose that you are conducting a study to determine whether pregnant women could change the breathing and sleeping patterns of their newborn babies by engaging in aerobic exercise during pregnancy. You might require one group of pregnant women to engage in a certain amount and type of aerobic exercise each day while another group would not exercise; the aerobic exercise is thus the independent variable. When the infants are born, you would observe and measure their breathing and sleeping patterns. These patterns are the dependent variable, the factor that changes as the result of your manipulation.

Experimental and Control Groups Experiments can involve one or more experimental groups and one or more control groups. An experimental group is a group whose experience is manipulated. A *control group* is a comparison group that resembles the experimental group as closely as possible and is treated in every way like the experimental group except for the manipulated factor (independent variable). The control group serves as a baseline against which the effects of the manipulated condition can be compared.

Random assignment is an important principle for deciding whether each participant will be placed in the experimental group or in the control group. Random assignment means that researchers assign participants to experimental and control groups by chance. It reduces the likelihood that the experiment's results will be due to any preexisting differences between groups (Gravetter & Forzano, 2016). In the example of the effects of aerobic exercise by pregnant women on the breathing and sleeping patterns of their newborns, you would randomly assign half of the pregnant women to engage in aerobic exercise over a period of weeks (the experimental group) and the other half not to exercise during the same number of weeks (the control group). Figure 20 illustrates the nature of experimental research.

FIGURE 20

PRINCIPLES OF EXPERIMENTAL RESEARCH. Imagine that you decide to conduct an experimental study of the effects of aerobic exercise by pregnant women on their newborns' breathing and sleeping patterns. You would randomly assign pregnant women to experimental and control groups. The experimental-group women would engage in aerobic exercise over a specified number of sessions and weeks. The control group would not. Then, when the infants are born, you would assess their breathing and sleeping patterns. If the breathing and sleeping patterns of newborns whose mothers were in the experimental group are more positive than those of the control group, you would conclude that aerobic exercise caused the positive effects.

TIME SPAN OF RESEARCH

Researchers in life-span development have a special concern with studies that focus on the relation of age to some other variable (Reznick, 2013). They have several options: Researchers can study different individuals of varying ages and compare them, or they can study the same individuals as they age over time.

Cross-Sectional Approach   The **cross-sectional approach** is a research strategy that simultaneously compares individuals of different ages. A typical cross-sectional study might include three groups of children: 5-year-olds, 8-year-olds, and 11-year-olds. Another study might include groups of 15-year-olds, 25-year-olds, and 45-year-olds. The groups can be compared with respect to a variety of dependent variables: IQ, memory, peer relations, attachment to parents, hormonal changes, and so on. All of these comparisons can be accomplished in a short time. In some studies, data are collected in a single day. Even in large-scale cross-sectional studies with hundreds of subjects, data collection does not usually take longer than several months to complete.

The main advantage of the cross-sectional study is that the researcher does not have to wait for the individuals to grow up or become older. Despite its efficiency, though, the cross-sectional approach has its drawbacks. It gives no information about how individuals change or about the stability of their characteristics. It can obscure the increases and decreases of development—the hills and valleys of growth and development. For example, a cross-sectional study of life satisfaction might reveal average increases and decreases, but it would not show how the life satisfaction of individual adults waxed and waned over the years. It also would not tell us whether the same adults who had positive or negative perceptions of life satisfaction in early adulthood maintained their relative degree of life satisfaction as they became middle-aged or older adults.

Longitudinal Approach   The **longitudinal approach** is a research strategy in which the same individuals are studied over a period of time, usually several years or more. For example, in a longitudinal study of life satisfaction, the same adults might be assessed periodically over a 70-year time span—at the ages of 20, 35, 45, 65, and 90, for example.

Longitudinal studies provide a wealth of information about vital issues such as stability and change in development and the importance of early experience for later development, but they do have drawbacks (Cicchetti & Toth, 2015). They are expensive and time consuming. The longer the study lasts, the more participants drop out—they move, get sick, lose interest, and so forth. The participants who remain may be dissimilar to those who drop out, biasing the outcome of the study. Those individuals who remain in a longitudinal study over a number of years may be more responsible and conformity-oriented, for example, or they might have more stable lives.

Cohort Effects   A *cohort* is a group of people who are born at a similar point in history and share similar experiences as a result, such as living through the Vietnam War or growing up in the same city around the same time. These shared experiences may produce a range of differences among cohorts (Hofer, Rast, & Piccinin, 2012; Kadlecova & others, 2015). For example, people who were teenagers during World War II are likely to differ from people who were teenagers during the booming 1990s in their educational opportunities and economic status, in how they were raised, and in their attitudes toward sex and religion. In life-span development research, **cohort effects** are due to a person's time of birth, era, or generation but not to actual age.

Cohort effects are important because they can powerfully affect the dependent measures in a study ostensibly concerned with age (Schaie, 2013). Researchers have shown it is especially important to be aware of cohort effects when assessing adult intelligence (Schaie, 2007). Individuals born at different points in time—such as 1930, 1960, and 1990—have had varying opportunities for education. Individuals born in earlier years had less access to education, and this fact may have a significant effect on how this cohort performs on intelligence tests.

Cross-sectional studies can show how different cohorts respond, but they can confuse age changes and cohort effects. Longitudinal studies are effective in studying age changes but only within one cohort.

Various generations have been given labels by the popular culture. Figure 21 describes the labels of various generations, their historical period, and the reasons for their labels.

cross-sectional approach A research strategy in which individuals of different ages are compared at one time.

longitudinal approach A research strategy in which the same individuals are studied over a period of time, usually several years or more.

cohort effects Characteristics attributable to a person's time of birth, era, or generation but not to actual age.

Cohort effects are due to a person's time of birth or generation but not actually to age. Think for a moment about growing up in (a) the Great Depression and (b) today. *How might your development be different depending on which of these time frames has dominated your life? your parents' lives? your grandparents' lives?*

Consider the following description of the current generation of youth, the Millennials, and think about how this group differs from earlier youth generations:

> They are history's first "always connected" generation. Steeped in digital technology and social media, they treat their multi-tasking hand-held gadgets almost like a body part—for better or worse. More than 8-in-10 say they sleep with a cell phone glowing by the bed, poised to disgorge texts, phone calls, e-mails, songs, news, videos, games, and wake-up jingles. But sometimes convenience yields to temptation. Nearly two-thirds admit to texting while driving (Pew Research Center, 2010, p. 1).

CONDUCTING ETHICAL RESEARCH

Ethics in research may affect you personally if you ever serve as a participant in a study. In that event, you need to know your rights as a participant and the responsibilities of researchers to assure that these rights are safeguarded.

If you ever become a researcher in life-span development yourself, you will need an even deeper understanding of ethics. Even if you only carry out experimental projects in psychology courses, you must consider the rights of the participants in those projects. A student might

How are today's Millennials experiencing youth differently from earlier generations?

FIGURE **21**

GENERATIONS, THEIR HISTORICAL PERIODS, AND CHARACTERISTICS.

Generation	Historical Period	Reasons for Label
Millennials	Individuals born in 1980 and later	First generation to come of age and enter emerging adulthood (18 to 25 years of age) in the twenty-first century (the new millennium). Two main characteristics: (1) connection to technology, and (2) ethnic diversity.
Generation X	Individuals born between 1965 and 1980	Described as lacking an identity and savvy loners.
Baby Boomers	Individuals born between 1946 and 1964	Label used because this generation represents the spike in the number of babies born after World War II; the largest generation ever to enter late adulthood in the United States.
Silent Generation	Individuals born between 1928 and 1945	Children of the Great Depression and World War II; described as conformists and civic minded.

think, "I volunteer in a home for individuals with an intellectual disability several hours per week. I can use the residents of the home in my study to see if a particular treatment helps improve their memory for everyday tasks." But without proper permissions, the most well-meaning and considerate studies still violate the rights of the participants (Jackson, 2016).

Today, proposed research at colleges and universities must pass the scrutiny of a research ethics committee before the research can begin. In addition, the American Psychological Association (APA) has developed ethics guidelines for its members. The code of ethics instructs psychologists to protect their participants from mental and physical harm. The participants' best interests need to be kept foremost in the researcher's mind. APA's guidelines address four important issues:

1. *Informed consent.* All participants must know what their research participation will involve and what risks might develop. Even after informed consent is given, participants must retain the right to withdraw from the study at any time and for any reason.

2. *Confidentiality.* Researchers are responsible for keeping all of the data they gather on individuals completely confidential and, when possible, completely anonymous.

3. *Debriefing.* After the study has been completed, participants should be informed of its purpose and the methods that were used. In most cases, the experimenter also can inform participants in a general manner beforehand about the purpose of the research without leading participants to behave in a way they think the experimenter is expecting.

4. *Deception.* In some circumstances, telling the participants beforehand what the research study is about substantially alters the participants' behavior and invalidates the researcher's data. Thus, researchers may deceive the participants about the details of the study. In all cases of deception, however, the psychologist must ensure that the deception will not harm the participants and that the participants will be *debriefed* (told the actual nature of the study) as soon as possible after the study is completed.

MINIMIZING BIAS

Studies of life-span development are most useful when they are conducted without bias or prejudice toward any group of people. Of special concern is bias based on gender and bias based on culture or ethnicity.

Gender Bias   For most of its existence, our society has had a strong gender bias, a preconceived notion about the abilities of women and men that prevented individuals from pursuing their own interests and achieving their potential. Gender bias also has had a less obvious effect within the field of life-span development. For example, it is not unusual for conclusions to be drawn about females' attitudes and behaviors from research conducted with males as the only participants (Hyde, 2014).

Furthermore, when researchers find gender differences, their reports sometimes magnify those differences (Denmark & others, 1988). For example, a researcher might report that 74 percent of the men in a study had high achievement expectations versus only 67 percent of the women and go on to talk about the differences in some detail. In reality, this might be a rather small difference. It also might disappear if the study were repeated, or the study might have methodological problems that don't allow such strong interpretations.

Pam Reid is a leading researcher who studies gender and ethnic bias in development. To read about Pam's interests, see the *Connecting with Careers* profile.

Cultural and Ethnic Bias   There is a growing awareness that research on life-span development needs to include more people from diverse ethnic groups. Historically, people from ethnic minority groups (African American, Latino, Asian American, and Native American) were excluded from most research in the United States and simply thought of as variations from the norm or average. If minority individuals were included in samples and their scores didn't fit the norm, they were viewed as confounds or "noise" in data and discounted (Schaefer, 2015). Given the fact that individuals from diverse ethnic groups were excluded from research on life-span development for so long, we might reasonably conclude that people's real lives are perhaps more varied than research data have indicated in the past.

Researchers also have tended to overgeneralize about ethnic groups. **Ethnic gloss** involves using an ethnic label such as African American or Latino in a superficial way that

ethnic gloss Use of an ethnic label such as African American or Latino in a superficial way that portrays an ethnic group as being more homogeneous than it really is.

connecting with careers

Pam Reid, Educational and Development Psychologist

When she was a child, Pam Reid liked to play with chemistry sets. Reid majored in chemistry during college and wanted to become a doctor. However, when some of her friends signed up for a psychology class as an elective she also decided to take the course. She was intrigued by learning about how people think, behave, and develop—so much so that she changed her major to psychology. Reid went on to obtain her Ph.D. in psychology (American Psychological Association, 2003, p. 16).

For a number of years, Reid was professor of education and psychology at the University of Michigan, where she also was a research scientist at the Institute for Research on Women and Gender. Her main focus has been on how children and adolescents develop social skills, with a special interest in the development of African American girls (Reid & Zalk, 2001). In 2004, Reid became Provost and Executive Vice-President at Roosevelt University in Chicago, and in 2007 she became president of Saint Joseph College in Hartford, Connecticut.

Pam Reid (*center*), with students at Saint Joseph College in Hartford, Connecticut, where she is the president of the college.
Courtesy of Dr. Pam Reid

For more information about what educational psychologists do, see the Careers in Life-Span Development appendix.

portrays an ethnic group as being more homogeneous than it really is (Trimble, 1988). For example, a researcher might describe a research sample like this: "The participants were 60 Latinos." A more complete description of the Latino group might be something like this: "The 60 Latino participants were Mexican Americans from low-income neighborhoods in the southwestern area of Los Angeles. Thirty-six were from homes in which Spanish is the dominant spoken language, 24 from homes in which English is the main spoken language. Thirty were born in the United States, 30 in Mexico. Twenty-eight described themselves as Mexican American, 14 as Mexican, 9 as American, 6 as Chicano, and 3 as Latino." Ethnic gloss can cause researchers to obtain samples of ethnic groups that are not representative of the group's diversity, which can lead to overgeneralization and stereotyping.

The growing proportion of minority families in the U.S. population in approaching decades will mainly be due to the immigration of Latino and Asian families. Researchers need "to take into account their acculturation level and generational status of parents and children" and

Look at these two photographs, one of all non-Latino White males, the other of a diverse group of females and males from different ethnic groups, including some non-Latino White males. Consider a topic in life-span development, such as parenting, love, or cultural values. *If you were conducting research on this topic, might the results of the study be different depending on whether the participants in your study were the individuals in the photograph on the left or the right?*
(left): © Anthony Cassidy/The Image Bank/Getty Images; (right): © Punchstock/Digital Vision RF

consider how these factors influence family processes and child outcomes (Parke & Buriel, 2006, p. 487). More attention also needs to be given to biculturalism, because the complexity of diversity means that some children of color identify with two or more ethnic groups (Schwartz & others, 2015a, b; Umana-Taylor & others, 2014). And language development research needs to focus more on dual-language acquisition and how it is linked to school achievement (Echevarria, Richards-Tutor, & Vogt, 2015; Haley & Austin, 2014).

Review Connect Reflect

 LG4 Explain how research on life-span development is conducted

Review
- What methods do researchers use to collect data on life-span development?
- What research designs are used to study human development?
- How are cross-sectional and longitudinal research designs different?
- What are researchers' ethical responsibilities to the people they study?
- How can gender, cultural, and ethnic bias affect the outcome of a research study?

Connect
- Earlier in this chapter you read about research on age-related memory

decline that revealed some potential biases based on the type of information involved and the time of day when the testing was done. How might researchers study memory decline while accounting for such possible biases?

Reflect Your Own Personal Journey of Life
- Imagine that you are conducting a research study on the sexual attitudes and behaviors of adolescents. What ethical safeguards should you use in conducting the study?

reach your learning goals

Introduction

1 The Life-Span Perspective

 LG1 Discuss the distinctive features of a life-span perspective on development

The Importance of Studying Life-Span Development

- Development is the pattern of change that begins at conception and continues through the human life span. It includes both growth and decline. Studying life-span development helps prepare us to take responsibility for children, gives us insight about our own lives, and gives us knowledge about what our lives will be like as we age.

Characteristics of the Life-Span Perspective

- The life-span perspective includes the following basic concepts: development is lifelong, multidimensional, multidirectional, and plastic; its study is multidisciplinary; it is embedded in contexts; it involves growth, maintenance, and regulation; and it is a co-construction of biological, sociocultural, and individual factors. Three important sources of contextual influences are (1) normative age-graded influences, (2) normative history-graded influences, and (3) nonnormative life events.

Some Contemporary Concerns

- Health and well-being, parenting, education, sociocultural contexts and diversity, and social policy are all areas of contemporary concern that are closely tied to life-span development. Important dimensions of the sociocultural context include culture, ethnicity, socioeconomic status, and gender. There is increasing interest in social policy issues related to children and to older adults, as well as the importance of resiliency in development.

2 The Nature of Development

 LG2 Identify the most important processes, periods, and issues in development

Biological, Cognitive, and Socioemotional Processes

- Three key developmental processes are biological, cognitive, and socioemotional. Development is influenced by an interplay of these processes.

Periods of Development

- The life span is commonly divided into the following periods of development: prenatal, infancy, early childhood, middle and late childhood, adolescence, early adulthood, middle adulthood, and late adulthood. Attention is increasingly being directed to age differences in functioning within the late adulthood period, especially between the young old (65 through 84) and oldest old (85 and older).

The Significance of Age

- An increasing number of studies have found that as adults get older they are happier. We often think of age only in terms of chronological age, but a full evaluation of age requires consideration of chronological, biological, psychological, and social age.

Developmental Issues

- The nature-nurture issue focuses on the extent to which development is mainly influenced by nature (biological inheritance) or nurture (experience). The stability-change issue focuses on the degree to which we become older renditions of our early experience or develop into someone different from who we were earlier in development. A special aspect of the stability-change issue is the extent to which development is determined by early versus later experiences. Developmentalists describe development as continuous (gradual, a cumulative change) or as discontinuous (abrupt, a sequence of stages). Most developmentalists recognize that extreme positions on the nature-nurture, stability-change, and continuity-discontinuity issues are unwise. Despite this consensus, there is still spirited debate on these issues.

3 Theories of Development   Describe the main theories of human development

Psychoanalytic Theories

- The scientific method involves four main steps: (1) conceptualize a problem, (2) collect data, (3) analyze data, and (4) draw conclusions. Theory is often involved in conceptualizing a problem. A theory is an interrelated, coherent set of ideas that helps to explain phenomena and to make predictions. Hypotheses are specific assertions and predictions, often derived from theory, that can be tested. According to psychoanalytic theories, development primarily depends on the unconscious mind and is heavily couched in emotion. Freud also argued that individuals go through five psychosexual stages. Erikson's theory emphasizes eight psychosocial stages of development: trust versus mistrust, autonomy versus shame and doubt, initiative versus guilt, industry versus inferiority, identity versus identity confusion, intimacy versus isolation, generativity versus stagnation, and integrity versus despair. Contributions of psychoanalytic theories include an emphasis on a developmental framework, family relationships, and unconscious aspects of the mind. Criticisms include a lack of scientific support for psychoanalytic theories, too much emphasis on sexual underpinnings, and an image of people that is too negative.

Cognitive Theories

- Three main cognitive theories are Piaget's, Vygotsky's, and information processing. Cognitive theories emphasize thinking, reasoning, language, and other cognitive processes. Piaget proposed a cognitive developmental theory in which children use their cognition to adapt to their world. In Piaget's theory, children go through four cognitive stages: sensorimotor, preoperational, concrete operational, and formal operational. Vygotsky's sociocultural cognitive theory emphasizes how culture and social interaction guide cognitive development. The information-processing approach emphasizes that individuals manipulate information, monitor it, and strategize about it. Contributions of cognitive theories include an emphasis on the active construction of understanding and developmental changes in thinking. Criticisms include giving too little attention to individual variations and underrating the unconscious aspects of thought.

Behavioral and Social Cognitive Theories

- Two main behavioral and social cognitive theories are Skinner's operant conditioning and social cognitive theory. In Skinner's operant conditioning, the consequences of a behavior produce changes in the probability of the behavior's occurrence. In social cognitive theory, observational learning is a key aspect of life-span development. Bandura emphasizes reciprocal interactions among person/cognition, behavior, and environment. Contributions of the behavioral and social cognitive theories include an emphasis on scientific research, a focus on environmental factors, and recognition of the importance of person and cognitive factors in social cognitive theory. Criticisms include inadequate attention to developmental changes, too much emphasis on environmental determinants, and (in Skinner's behaviorism) too little attention to cognition.

Ethological Theory

- Ethology stresses that behavior is strongly influenced by biology, is tied to evolution, and is characterized by critical or sensitive periods. Contributions of ethological theory include its focus on the biological and evolutionary basis of development. Criticisms include inflexibility regarding the concepts of critical and sensitive periods.

Ecological Theory

- Ecological theory emphasizes environmental contexts. Bronfenbrenner's environmental systems view of development proposes five environmental systems: microsystem, mesosystem, exosystem, macrosystem, and chronosystem. Contributions of the theory include a systematic examination of micro- and macro dimensions of environmental systems and consideration of sociohistorical influences. Criticisms include inadequate attention to biological factors, as well as a lack of emphasis on cognitive factors.

An Eclectic Theoretical Orientation

· An eclectic theoretical orientation does not follow any one theoretical approach but rather selects from each theory whatever is considered the best in it.

4 Research on Life-Span Development

 LG4 Explain how research on life-span development is conducted

Methods for Collecting Data

· Methods for collecting data about life-span development include observation (in a laboratory or a naturalistic setting), survey (questionnaire) or interview, standardized test, case study, and physiological measures.

Research Designs

· Three main research designs are descriptive, correlational, and experimental. Descriptive research aims to observe and record behavior. The goal of correlational research is to describe the strength of the relationship between two or more events or characteristics. Experimental research involves conducting an experiment, which can determine cause and effect. An independent variable is the manipulated, influential, experimental factor. A dependent variable is a factor that can change in an experiment, in response to changes in the independent variable. Experiments can involve one or more experimental groups and control groups. In random assignment, researchers assign participants to experimental and control groups by chance.

Time Span of Research

· When researchers decide about the time span of their research, they can conduct cross-sectional or longitudinal studies. Life-span researchers are especially concerned about cohort effects.

Conducting Ethical Research

· Researchers' ethical responsibilities include seeking participants' informed consent, ensuring their confidentiality, debriefing them about the purpose and potential personal consequences of participating, and avoiding unnecessary deception of participants.

Minimizing Bias

· Researchers need to guard against gender, cultural, and ethnic bias in research. Every effort should be made to make research equitable for both females and males. Individuals from varied ethnic backgrounds need to be included as participants in life-span research, and overgeneralization about diverse members within a group must be avoided.

key **terms**

biological processes
Bronfenbrenner's ecological theory
case study
cognitive processes
cohort effects
continuity-discontinuity issue
correlation coefficient
correlational research
cross-cultural studies
cross-sectional approach

culture
descriptive research
development
eclectic theoretical orientation
emerging adulthood
Erikson's theory
ethnic gloss
ethnicity
ethology
experiment
gender

hypotheses
information-processing theory
laboratory
life-span perspective
longitudinal approach
naturalistic observation
nature-nurture issue
nonnormative life events
normative age-graded influences
normative history-graded influences

Piaget's theory
psychoanalytic theories
social cognitive theory
social policy
socioeconomic status (SES)
socioemotional processes
stability-change issue
standardized test
theory
Vygotsky's theory

key **people**

Jeffrey Arnett
Paul Baltes
Albert Bandura
Urie Bronfenbrenner

Marian Wright Edelman
Erik Erikson
Sigmund Freud
Konrad Lorenz

Ann Masten
Jean Piaget
Robert Siegler

B. F. Skinner
Lev Vygotsky

appendix

Careers in Life-Span Development

The field of life-span development offers an amazing breadth of careers that can provide extremely satisfying work. College and university professors teach courses in many areas of life-span development. Teachers impart knowledge, understanding, and skills to children and adolescents. Counselors, clinical psychologists, nurses, and physicians help people of different ages to cope more effectively with their lives and improve their well-being.

These and many other careers related to life-span development offer many rewards. By working in the field of life-span development, you can help people to improve their lives, understand yourself and others better, possibly advance the state of knowledge in the field, and have an enjoyable time while you are doing these things. Many careers in life-span development pay reasonably well. For example, psychologists earn well above the median salary in the United States.

If you are considering a career in life-span development, would you prefer to work with infants? children? adolescents? older adults? As you go through this term, try to spend some time with people of different ages. Observe their behavior. Talk with them about their lives. Think about whether you would like to work with people of this age in your life's work.

In addition, to find out about careers in life-span development you might talk with people who work in various jobs. For example, if you have some interest in becoming a school counselor, call a school, ask to speak with a counselor, and set up an appointment to discuss the counselor's career and work. If you have an interest in becoming a nurse, call the nursing department at a hospital and set up an appointment to speak with the nursing coordinator about a nursing career.

Another way of exploring careers in life-span development is to work in a related job while you are in college. Many colleges and universities offer internships or other work experiences for students who major in specific fields. Course credit or pay is given for some of these jobs. Take advantage of these opportunities. They can help you decide if this is the right career for you, and they can help you get into graduate school, if you decide you want to go.

An advanced degree is not absolutely necessary for some careers in life-span development, but usually you can considerably expand your opportunities (and income) by obtaining a graduate degree. If you think you might want to go to

graduate school, talk with one or more professors about your interests, keep a high grade-point average, take appropriate courses, and realize that you likely will need to take the Graduate Record Examination at some point.

We will profile a number of careers in four areas: education/research; clinical/counseling; medical/nursing/physical development; and families/relationships. These are not the only career options in life-span development, but the profiles should give you an idea of the range of opportunities available. For each career, we describe the work and address the amount of education required and the nature of the training. We have provided chapter titles after some entries telling you where to find *Connecting with Careers*, the career profiles of people who hold some of these positions.

Education/Research

Numerous careers in life-span development involve education or research. The opportunities range from college professor to preschool teacher to school psychologist.

College/University Professor

Professors teach courses in life-span development at many types of institutions, including research universities with master's or Ph.D. programs in life-span development, four-year colleges with no graduate programs, and community colleges. The courses in life-span development are offered in many different programs and schools, including psychology, education, nursing, child and family studies, social work, and medicine. In addition to teaching at the undergraduate or graduate level (or both), professors may conduct research, advise students or direct their research, and serve on college or university committees. Research is part of a professor's job description at most universities with master's and Ph.D. programs, but some college professors do not conduct research and focus instead on teaching.

Teaching life-span development at a college or university almost always requires a Ph.D. or master's degree. Obtaining a Ph.D. usually takes four to six years of graduate work; a master's degree requires approximately two years. The training involves taking graduate courses, learning to conduct research, and attending and presenting papers at professional meetings. Many graduate students work as teaching or research assistants for professors in an apprenticeship relationship that helps them to become competent teachers

and researchers. **Read the profiles of professors in "Gender and Sexuality" and "Peers and the Sociocultural World."**

Researcher

Some individuals in the field of life-span development work in research positions. They might work for a university, a government agency such as the National Institute of Mental Health, or private industry. They generate research ideas, plan studies, carry out the research, and usually attempt to publish the research in a scientific journal. A researcher often works in collaboration with other researchers. One researcher might spend much of his or her time in a laboratory; another researcher might work in the field, such as in schools, hospitals, and so on. Most researchers in life-span development have either a master's or a Ph.D.

Elementary or Secondary School Teacher

Elementary and secondary school teachers teach one or more subject areas, preparing the curriculum, giving tests, assigning grades, monitoring students' progress, conducting parent-teacher conferences, and attending workshops. Becoming an elementary or secondary school teacher requires a minimum of an undergraduate degree. The training involves taking a wide range of courses with a major or concentration in education as well as completing supervised practice teaching.

Exceptional Children (Special Education) Teacher

Teachers of exceptional children spend concentrated time with children who have a disability such as ADHD, mental retardation, or cerebral palsy, or with children who are gifted. Usually some of their work occurs outside of the students' regular classroom and some of it inside the students' regular classroom. A teacher of exceptional children works closely with the student's regular classroom teacher and parents to create the best educational program for the student. Teachers of exceptional children often continue their education after obtaining their undergraduate degree and attain a master's degree.

Early Childhood Educator

Early childhood educators work on college faculties and usually teach in community colleges that award an associate degree in early childhood education. They have a minimum of a master's degree in their field. In graduate school, they take courses in early childhood education and receive supervisory training in child-care or early childhood programs.

Preschool/Kindergarten Teacher

Preschool teachers teach mainly 4-year-old children, and kindergarten teachers primarily teach 5-year-old children. They usually have an undergraduate degree in education, specializing in early childhood education. State certification to become a preschool or kindergarten teacher usually is required.

Family and Consumer Science Educator

Family and consumer science educators may specialize in early childhood education or instruct middle and high school students about such matters as nutrition, interpersonal relationships, human sexuality, parenting, and human development. Hundreds of colleges and universities throughout the United States offer two- and four-year degree programs in family and consumer science. These programs usually require an internship. Additional education courses may be needed to obtain a teaching certificate. Some family and consumer educators go on to graduate school for further training, which provides a background for possible jobs in college teaching or research. **Read a profile of a family and consumer science educator in "Gender and Sexuality."**

Educational Psychologist

Educational psychologists most often teach in a college or university and conduct research in various areas of educational psychology such as learning, motivation, classroom management, and assessment. They help train students for positions in educational psychology, school psychology, and teaching. Most educational psychologists have a doctorate in education, which takes four to six years of graduate work. **Read a profile of an educational psychologist in "Introduction."**

School Psychologist

School psychologists focus on improving the psychological and intellectual well-being of elementary, middle/junior, and high school students. They give psychological tests, interview students and their parents, consult with teachers, and may provide counseling to students and their families. They may work in a centralized office in a school district or in one or more schools.

School psychologists usually have a master's or doctoral degree in school psychology. In graduate school, they take courses in counseling, assessment, learning, and other areas of education and psychology.

Gerontologist

Gerontologists usually work in research in some branch of the federal or state government. They specialize in the study of aging with a particular focus on government programs for older adults, social policy, and delivery of services to older adults. In their research, gerontologists define problems to be studied, collect data, interpret the results, and make recommendations for social policy. Most gerontologists have a master's or doctoral degree and have taken a concentration of coursework in adult development and aging.

Clinical/Counseling

There are a wide variety of clinical and counseling jobs that are linked with life-span development. These range from child clinical psychologist to adolescent drug counselor to geriatric psychiatrist.

Clinical Psychologist

Clinical psychologists seek to help people with psychological problems. They work in a variety of settings, including colleges and universities, clinics, medical schools, and private practice. Some clinical psychologists only conduct psychotherapy; others do psychological assessment and psychotherapy; some also do research. Clinical psychologists may specialize in a particular age group, such as children (child clinical psychologist) or older adults (geropsychologist).

Clinical psychologists have either a Ph.D. (which involves clinical and research training) or a Psy.D. degree (which only involves clinical training). This graduate training usually takes five to seven years and includes courses in clinical psychology and a one-year supervised internship in an accredited setting toward the end of the training. Many geropsychologists pursue a year or two of postdoctoral training. Most states require clinical psychologists to pass a test in order to become licensed in the state and to call themselves clinical psychologists.

Psychiatrist

Psychiatrists obtain a medical degree and then do a residency in psychiatry. Medical school takes approximately four years and the psychiatry residency another three to four years. Unlike most psychologists (who do not go to medical school), psychiatrists can administer drugs to clients. (Recently, several states gave clinical psychologists the right to prescribe drugs.)

Like clinical psychologists, psychiatrists might specialize in working with children (child psychiatry) or with older adults (geriatric psychiatry). Psychiatrists might work in medical schools in teaching and research roles, in a medical clinic or hospital, or in private practice. In addition to administering drugs to help improve the lives of people with psychological problems, psychiatrists also may conduct psychotherapy. **Read a profile of a child psychiatrist in "Schools, Achievement, and Work."**

Counseling Psychologist

Counseling psychologists work in the same settings as clinical psychologists and may do psychotherapy, teach, or conduct research. Many counseling psychologists do not do therapy with individuals who have severe mental disorders, such as schizophrenia.

Counseling psychologists go through much the same training as clinical psychologists, although in a graduate program in counseling rather than clinical psychology. Counseling psychologists have either a master's degree or a doctoral degree. They also must go through a licensing procedure. One type of master's degree in counseling leads to the designation of licensed professional counselor.

School Counselor

School counselors help students cope with adjustment problems, identify their abilities and interests, develop academic plans, and explore career options. The focus of the job depends on the age of the children. High school counselors advise students about vocational and technical training and admissions requirements for college, as well as about taking entrance exams, applying for financial aid, and choosing a major. Elementary school counselors mainly counsel students about social and personal problems. They may observe children in the classroom and at play as part of their work. School counselors may work with students individually, in small groups, or even in a classroom. They often consult with parents, teachers, and school administrators when trying to help students. School counselors usually have a master's degree in counseling. **Read a profile of a high school counselor in "The Self, Identity, and Personality."**

Career Counselor

Career counselors help individuals to identify their best career options and guide them in applying for jobs. They may work in private industry or at a college or university. They usually interview individuals and give them vocational and/or psychological tests to identify appropriate careers that fit their interests and abilities. Sometimes they help individuals to create résumés or conduct mock interviews to help them feel comfortable in a job interview. They might arrange and promote job fairs or other recruiting events to help individuals obtain jobs.

Rehabilitation Counselor

Rehabilitation counselors work with individuals to identify career options, develop adjustment and coping skills to maximize independence, and resolve problems created by a disability. A master's degree in rehabilitation counseling or guidance or counseling psychology is generally considered the minimum educational requirement.

Social Worker

Many social workers are involved in helping people with social or economic problems. They may investigate, evaluate, and attempt to rectify reported cases of abuse, neglect, endangerment, or domestic disputes. They may intervene in families and provide counseling and referral services to individuals and families. Some social workers specialize in a certain area. For example, a medical social worker might coordinate support services to people with a long-term disability; family-care social workers often work with families with children or an older adult who needs support services. Social workers often work for publicly funded agencies at the city, state, or national level, although increasingly they work in the private sector in areas such as drug rehabilitation and family counseling.

Social workers have a minimum of an undergraduate degree from a school of social work that includes coursework in sociology and psychology. Some social workers also have a master's or doctoral degree. For example, medical social workers have a master's degree in social work (M.S.W.) and complete graduate coursework and supervised clinical experiences in medical settings.

Drug Counselor
Drug counselors provide counseling to individuals with drug-abuse problems. Some drug counselors specialize in working with adolescents or older adults. They may work on an individual basis with a substance abuser or conduct group therapy. They may work in private practice, with a state or federal government agency, for a company, or in a hospital.

At a minimum, drug counselors complete an associate's or certificate program. Many have an undergraduate degree in substance-abuse counseling, and some have master's and doctoral degrees. Most states provide a certification procedure for obtaining a license to practice drug counseling.

Medical/Nursing/Physical Development
This third main area of careers in life-span development includes a wide range of choices in the medical and nursing areas, as well as jobs pertaining to improving some aspect of a person's physical development.

Obstetrician/Gynecologist
An obstetrician/gynecologist prescribes prenatal and postnatal care, performs deliveries in maternity cases, and treats diseases and injuries of the female reproductive system. Becoming an obstetrician/gynecologist requires a medical degree plus three to five years of residency in obstetrics/gynecology. Obstetricians may work in private practice, a medical clinic, a hospital, or a medical school.

Pediatrician
A pediatrician monitors infants' and children's health, works to prevent disease or injury, helps children attain optimal health, and treats children with health problems. Pediatricians have earned a medical degree and completed a three- to five-year residency in pediatrics.

Pediatricians may work in private practice or at a medical clinic, a hospital, or a medical school. Many pediatricians on the faculty of medical schools also teach and conduct research on children's health and diseases.

Geriatric Physician
Geriatric physicians diagnose medical problems of older adults, evaluate treatment options, and make recommendations for nursing care or other arrangements. They have a medical degree and specialized in geriatric medicine by doing a three-to five-year residency. Like other doctors, geriatric physicians may work in private practice or at a medical clinic, a hospital, or a medical school. Those in medical school settings may not only treat older adults but also teach future physicians and conduct research.

Neonatal Nurse
Neonatal nurses deliver care to newborn infants. They may work with infants born under normal circumstances or premature and critically ill neonates. A minimum of an undergraduate degree in nursing with a specialization in the newborn is required. This training involves coursework in nursing and the biological sciences, as well as supervised clinical experiences.

Nurse-Midwife
A nurse-midwife formulates and provides comprehensive care to expectant mothers as they prepare to give birth, guides them through the birth process, and cares for them after the birth. The nurse-midwife also may provide care to the newborn, counsel parents on the infant's development and parenting, and provide guidance about health practices. Becoming a nurse-midwife generally requires an undergraduate degree from a school of nursing. A nurse-midwife most often works in a hospital setting. **Read a profile of a perinatal nurse in "Biological Beginnings."**

Pediatric Nurse
Pediatric nurses monitor infants' and children's health, work to prevent disease or injury, and help children attain optimal health. They may work in hospitals, schools of nursing, or with pediatricians in private practice or at a medical clinic.

Pediatric nurses have a degree in nursing that takes two to five years to complete. They take courses in biological sciences, nursing care, and pediatrics, usually in a school of nursing. They also undergo supervised clinical experiences in medical settings. Some pediatric nurses go on to earn a master's or doctoral degree in pediatric nursing. **Read a profile of a pediatric nurse in "Health."**

Geriatric Nurse
Geriatric nurses seek to prevent or intervene in the chronic or acute health problems of older adults. They may work in hospitals, nursing homes, schools of nursing, or with geriatric medical specialists or psychiatrists in a medical clinic or in private practice. Like pediatric nurses, geriatric nurses take courses in a school of nursing and obtain a degree in nursing, which takes from two to five years. They complete courses in biological sciences, nursing care, and mental health as well as supervised clinical training in geriatric settings. They also may obtain a master's or doctoral degree in their specialty. **Read a profile of a geriatric nurse in "Physical Development and Biological Aging."**

Physical Therapist
Physical therapists work with individuals who have a physical problem due to disease or injury to help them function as competently as possible. They may consult with other professionals and coordinate services for the individual. Many physical therapists work with people of all ages, although some specialize in working with a specific age group, such as children or older adults.

Physical therapists usually have an undergraduate degree in physical therapy and are licensed by a state. They take courses and undergo supervised training in physical therapy.

Occupational Therapist
Occupational therapists initiate the evaluation of clients with various impairments and manage their treatment. They help people regain, develop, and build skills that are important for independent functioning, health, well-being, security, and happiness. An "Occupational Therapist Registered" (OTR) must have a master's and/or doctoral degree with education ranging from two to six years. Training includes occupational therapy courses in a specialized program. National certification is required and licensing/registration is required in some states.

Therapeutic/Recreation Therapist
Therapeutic/recreation therapists maintain or improve the quality of life for people with special needs through intervention, leisure education, and recreation. They work in hospitals, rehabilitation centers, local government agencies, at-risk youth programs, and other settings. Becoming a therapeutic/recreation therapist requires an undergraduate degree with coursework in leisure studies and a concentration in therapeutic recreation. National certification is usually required. Coursework in anatomy, special education, and psychology is beneficial.

Audiologist
Audiologists assess and identify the presence and severity of hearing loss, as well as problems in balance. They may work in a medical clinic, with a physician in private practice, in a hospital, or in a medical school.

An audiologist completes coursework and supervised training to earn a minimum of an undergraduate degree in hearing science. Some audiologists also go on to obtain a master's or doctoral degree.

Speech Therapist

Speech therapists identify, assess, and treat speech and language problems. They may work with physicians, psychologists, social workers, and other health care professionals in a team approach to help individuals with physical or psychological problems that involve speech and language. Some speech therapists specialize in working with individuals of a particular age or people with a particular type of speech disorder. Speech therapists have a minimum of an undergraduate degree in speech and hearing science or in a type of communication disorder. They may work in private practice, hospitals and medical schools, and government agencies. **Read a profile of a speech therapist in "Language Development."**

Genetic Counselor

Genetic counselors identify and counsel families at risk for genetic disorders. They work as members of a health care team, providing information and support to families who have members who have genetic defects or disorders or are at risk for a variety of inherited conditions. They also serve as educators and resource people for other health care professionals and the public. Almost one-half of genetic counselors work in university medical centers; one-fourth work in private hospital settings.

Genetic counselors have specialized graduate degrees and experience in medical genetics and counseling. Most enter the field after majoring in undergraduate school in such disciplines as biology, genetics, psychology, nursing, public health, or social work. **Read a profile of a genetic counselor in "Biological Beginnings."**

Families/Relationships

A number of careers and jobs related to life-span development focus on working with families and addressing relationship problems. These range from home health aide to marriage and family therapist.

Home Health Aide

A home health aide provides services to older adults in the older adults' homes, helping them with basic self-care tasks. No higher education is required for this position. There is brief training by an agency.

Child Welfare Worker

Child protective services in each state employ child welfare workers. They protect children's rights, evaluate any maltreatment, and may have children removed from their homes if necessary. A child social worker has a minimum of an undergraduate degree in social work.

Child Life Specialist

Child life specialists work with children and their families when the child needs to be hospitalized. They monitor the child's activities, seek to reduce the child's stress, and help the child to cope and to enjoy the hospital experience as much as possible. Child life specialists may provide parent education and develop individualized treatment plans based on an assessment of the child's development, temperament, medical plan, and available social supports. Child life specialists have an undergraduate degree. They have taken courses in child development and education and usually completed additional courses in a child life program.

Marriage and Family Therapist

Marriage and family therapists work on the principle that many individuals who have psychological problems benefit when psychotherapy is provided in the context of a marital or family relationship. Marriage and family therapists may provide marital therapy, couple therapy to individuals in a relationship who are not married, and family therapy to two or more members of a family.

Marriage and family therapists have a master's or a doctoral degree. They complete a training program in graduate school similar to a clinical psychologist's but with the focus on marital and family relationships. In most states, it is necessary to go through a licensing procedure to practice marital and family therapy. **Read a profile of a marriage and family therapist in "Families, Lifestyles, and Parenting."**

Further Careers

These are only a handful of careers that knowledge of developmental psychology can prepare you for. The *Connecting with Careers* profiles highlight additional careers, including an infant assessment specialist, child care director, toy designer, health psychologist, teacher of English language learners, college/career counselor, parent educator, pastoral counselor, and home hospice nurse. *What other careers can you think of that require a knowledge of human development?*

Babies are such a nice way to start people.

—**Don Herold**
American writer, 20th century

Biological Processes, Physical Development, and Health

The rhythm and meaning of life involve biological foundations. How, from so simple a beginning, can endless forms develop and grow and mature? What was this organism, what is it, and what will it be? In Section 2, you will read and study four chapters: "Biological Beginnings," "Physical Development and Biological Aging," "Health," and "Motor, Sensory, and Perceptual Development."

chapter 2

BIOLOGICAL BEGINNINGS

chapter **outline**

1 The Evolutionary Perspective

Learning Goal 1 Discuss the evolutionary perspective on life-span development

Natural Selection and Adaptive Behavior
Evolutionary Psychology

2 Genetic Foundations of Development

Learning Goal 2 Describe what genes are and how they influence human development

The Collaborative Gene
Genes and Chromosomes
Genetic Principles
Chromosomal and Gene-Linked Abnormalities

3 Heredity and Environment Interaction: The Nature-Nurture Debate

Learning Goal 3 Explain some of the ways that heredity and environment interact to produce individual differences in development

Behavior Genetics
Heredity-Environment Correlations
Shared and Nonshared Environmental Influences
The Epigenetic View and Gene x Environment (G x E) Interaction
Conclusions About Heredity-Environment Interaction

4 Prenatal Development

Learning Goal 4 Characterize the course of prenatal development and its hazards

The Course of Prenatal Development
Prenatal Diagnostic Tests
Hazards to Prenatal Development
Prenatal Care

5 Birth and the Postpartum Period

Learning Goal 5 Summarize how birth takes place and describe the nature of the postpartum period

The Birth Process
The Transition from Fetus to Newborn
Low Birth Weight and Preterm Infants
Bonding
The Postpartum Period

preview

Organisms are not like billiard balls, moved by simple external forces to predictable positions on life's table. Environmental experiences and biological foundations work together to make us who we are. In this chapter, we explore life's biological beginnings and experiences, charting growth from conception through the prenatal period and examining the birth process itself. We will begin our exploration of biological foundations by considering possible evolutionary influences.

1 The Evolutionary Perspective

 LG1 Discuss the evolutionary perspective on life-span development

Natural Selection and Adaptive Behavior

Evolutionary Psychology

From the perspective of evolutionary time, humans are relative newcomers to Earth. As our earliest ancestors left the forest to feed on the savannahs and then to form hunting societies on the open plains, their minds and behaviors changed, and humans eventually became the dominant species on Earth. How did this evolution come about?

NATURAL SELECTION AND ADAPTIVE BEHAVIOR

Charles Darwin (1859) described *natural selection* as the evolutionary process by which those individuals of a species that are best adapted to their environment are the ones that are most likely to survive and reproduce. He reasoned that an intense, constant struggle for food, water, and resources must occur among the young of each generation, because many of them do not survive. Those that do survive and reproduce pass on their characteristics to the next generation (Hoefnagels, 2015; Johnson, 2015). Darwin concluded that these survivors are better adapted to their world than are the nonsurvivors. The best-adapted individuals survive and leave the most offspring. Over the course of many generations, organisms with the characteristics needed for survival make up an increased percentage of the population (Mader & Windelspecht, 2016; Starr, Evers, & Starr, 2015).

EVOLUTIONARY PSYCHOLOGY

Although Darwin introduced the theory of evolution by natural selection in 1859, his ideas have only recently become a popular framework for explaining behavior. Psychology's newest approach, **evolutionary psychology,** emphasizes the importance of adaptation, reproduction, and "survival of the fittest" in shaping behavior. ("Fit" in this sense refers to the ability to bear offspring that survive long enough to bear offspring of their own.) In this view, natural selection favors behaviors that increase reproductive success— that is, the ability to pass your genes to the next generation (Bateson, 2015; Durrant & Ellis, 2013; Fetterman, Kruger, & Robinson, 2015; Hooper & others, 2015).

David Buss (2008, 2012, 2015) argues that just as evolution shapes our physical features, such as body shape and height, it also pervasively influences how we make decisions, how aggressive we are, our fears, and our mating patterns. For example, assume that our ancestors were hunters and gatherers on the plains and that men did most of the hunting and women stayed close to home, gathering seeds and plants for food. If you had to walk some distance from your home in an effort to track and slay a fleeing animal, you would need not only certain physical traits but also the ability to perform certain types of spatial thinking. Men with these traits would be more likely than men without them to survive, to bring home lots of food, and to be considered attractive mates—and thus to reproduce and potentially pass on these characteristics to their children. In other words, if these assumptions were correct, these traits would provide a reproductive advantage for males, and over many generations, men with good spatial thinking skills might become more numerous in the population. Critics point out that this scenario might or might not have actually happened.

How does the attachment of this Vietnamese baby to its mother reflect the evolutionary process of adaptive behavior?
© Frans Lemmens/Corbis

evolutionary psychology A branch of psychology that emphasizes the importance of adaptation, reproduction, and "survival of the fittest" in shaping behavior.

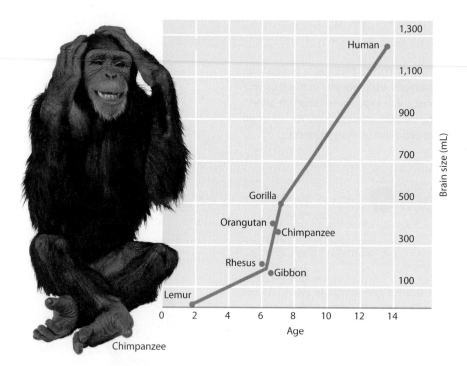

FIGURE 1

THE BRAIN SIZES OF VARIOUS PRIMATES AND HUMANS IN RELATION TO THE LENGTH OF THE CHILDHOOD PERIOD. Compared with other primates, humans have both a larger brain and a longer childhood period. *What conclusions can you draw from the relationship indicated by this graph?*
© Photodisc/Getty Images RF

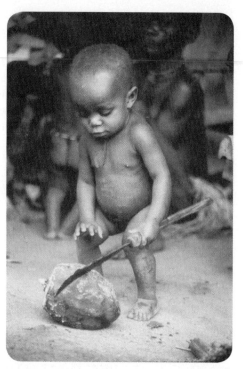

Children in all cultures are interested in the tools that adults in their cultures use. For example, this 11-month-old boy from the Efe culture in the Democratic Republic of the Congo in Africa is trying to cut a papaya with an *apopau* (a smaller version of a machete). *Might the infant's behavior be evolutionary-based or be due to both biological and environmental conditions?*
Courtesy of Dr. Gilda Morelli

Evolutionary Developmental Psychology There is growing interest in using the concepts of evolutionary psychology to understand human development (Anderson & Finlay, 2014; Bjorklund, 2012; Bugenthal, Corpuz, & Beaulieu, 2015). Following are some ideas proposed by evolutionary developmental psychologists (Bjorklund & Pellegrini, 2002).

One important concept is that an extended childhood period might have evolved because humans require time to develop a large brain and learn the complexity of human societies. Humans take longer to become reproductively mature than any other mammal (see Figure 1). During this extended childhood period, they develop a large brain and have the experiences needed to become competent adults in a complex society.

Evolved characteristics are not always adaptive in contemporary society. Some behaviors that were adaptive for our prehistoric ancestors may not serve us well today. For example, the food-scarce environment of our ancestors likely led to humans' propensity to gorge when food is available and to crave high-caloric foods, a trait that might lead to an epidemic of obesity when food is plentiful.

Evolution and Life-Span Development In evolutionary theory, what matters is that individuals live long enough to reproduce and pass on their characteristics (Brooker & others, 2014; Starr, Evers, & Starr, 2016). So why do humans live so long after reproduction? Perhaps evolution favored longevity because having older people around improves the survival rates of babies. Possibly having grandparents alive to care for the young while parents were out hunting and gathering food created an evolutionary advantage.

According to life-span developmentalist Paul Baltes (2003), the benefits conferred by evolutionary selection decrease with age. Natural selection has not weeded out many harmful conditions and nonadaptive characteristics that appear among older adults. Why? Natural

developmental **connection**

Life-Span Perspective

Baltes described eight main characteristics of the life-span perspective. Connect to "Introduction."

selection operates primarily on characteristics that are tied to reproductive fitness, which extends through the earlier part of adulthood. Thus, says Baltes, selection primarily operates during the first half of life.

As an example, consider Alzheimer disease, an irreversible brain disorder characterized by gradual deterioration. This disease typically does not appear until age 70 or later. If it were a disease that struck 20-year-olds, perhaps natural selection would have eliminated it eons ago.

Thus, unaided by evolutionary pressures against nonadaptive conditions, we suffer the aches, pains, and infirmities of aging. And, as the benefits of evolutionary selection decrease with age, argues Baltes, the need for culture increases (see Figure 2). That is, as older adults weaken biologically, they need culture-based resources such as cognitive skills, literacy, medical technology, and social support. For example, older adults may need help and training from other people to maintain their cognitive skills (Dixon & others, 2013; Jak, 2012).

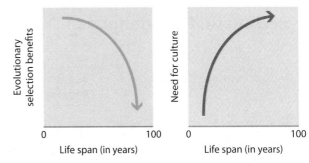

FIGURE 2

BALTES' VIEW OF EVOLUTION AND CULTURE ACROSS THE LIFE SPAN. Benefits derived from evolutionary selection decrease as we age, whereas the need for culture increases with age.

Evaluating Evolutionary Psychology Evolutionary psychology has its critics (Hyde, 2014). Common criticisms are that much of evolutionary psychology cannot be tested scientifically and that it relies mainly on *post hoc* (after the fact) explanations. Another criticism was offered by Albert Bandura (1998), the leading architect of social cognitive theory. He acknowledges the influence of evolution on human adaptation but rejects what he calls "one-sided evolutionism," which views social behavior as strictly the product of evolved biology. An alternative is a bidirectional view, in which environmental and biological conditions influence each other. In this view, evolutionary pressures created changes in biological structures that allowed the use of tools, which enabled our ancestors to manipulate the environment, constructing new environmental conditions. In turn, environmental innovations produced new selection pressures that led to the evolution of specialized biological systems for consciousness, thought, and language.

In other words, evolution has given us body structures and biological potentialities, but it does not dictate behavior. People have used their biological capacities to produce diverse cultures—aggressive and peaceful; egalitarian and autocratic.

The "big picture" idea of natural selection leading to the development of human traits and behaviors is difficult to refute or test because evolution occurs on a time scale that does not lend itself to empirical study. Thus, studying specific genes in humans and other species—and their links to traits and behaviors—may be the best approach for testing ideas coming out of the evolutionary psychology perspective.

Review *Connect* Reflect

 Discuss the evolutionary perspective on life-span development

Review

- How can natural selection and adaptive behavior be defined?
- What is evolutionary psychology? What basic ideas about human development are proposed by evolutionary psychologists? How might evolutionary influences have different effects at different points in the life span? How can evolutionary psychology be evaluated?

Connect

- In the section on ethological theory in "Introduction," the concept of critical time period is explored. How does this concept relate to what you learned about older adults and aging in this section?

Reflect: *Your Own Personal Journey of Life*

- Which is more persuasive to you as an explanation of your development: the views of evolutionary psychologists or those of their critics? Why?

The Collaborative Gene | Genes and Chromosomes | Genetic Principles | Chromosomal and Gene-Linked Abnormalities

Genetic influences on behavior evolved over time and across many species. Our many traits and characteristics that are genetically influenced have a long evolutionary history that is retained in our DNA. In other words, our DNA is not just inherited from our parents; it's also what we've inherited as a species from the species that were our ancestors. Let's take a closer look at DNA and its role in human development.

How are characteristics that suit a species for survival transmitted from one generation to the next? Darwin could not answer this question because genes and the principles of genetics had not yet been discovered. Each of us carries a "genetic code" that we inherited from our parents. Because a fertilized egg carries this human code, a fertilized human egg cannot grow into an egret, eagle, or elephant.

THE COLLABORATIVE GENE

Each of us began life as a single cell weighing about one twenty-millionth of an ounce! This tiny piece of matter housed our entire genetic code—information that helps us grow from that single cell to a person made of trillions of cells, each containing a replica of the original code. That code is carried by our genes. What are genes and what do they do? For the answer, we need to look into our cells.

The nucleus of each human cell contains **chromosomes,** which are threadlike structures made up of deoxyribonucleic acid, or DNA. **DNA** is a complex molecule that has a double helix shape, like a spiral staircase, and it contains genetic information. **Genes,** the units of hereditary information, are short segments of DNA, as you can see in Figure 3. They help cells to reproduce themselves and to assemble proteins. Proteins, in turn, are the building blocks of cells as well as the regulators that direct the body's processes (Brooker, 2016; Cowan, 2015).

Each gene has its own location, its own designated place on a particular chromosome. Today, there is a great deal of enthusiasm about efforts to discover the specific locations of genes that are linked to certain functions and developmental outcomes (Mason & others, 2015; Starr & others, 2016). An important step in this direction was accomplished in 2003 when the Human Genome Project completed a preliminary map of the human *genome*—the complete set of developmental information for creating proteins that initiate the making of a human organism (Brooker, 2015; Cummings, 2014).

---

developmental **connection**

Biological Processes

A current biological theory of aging emphasizes that changes in the tips of chromosomes play a key role in aging. Connect to "Physical Development and Biological Aging."

chromosomes Threadlike structures made up of deoxyribonucleic acid, or DNA.

DNA A complex molecule that has a double helix shape and contains genetic information.

genes Units of hereditary information composed of DNA. Genes help cells to reproduce themselves and assemble proteins that direct body processes.

Cell | Nucleus | Chromosome | DNA

FIGURE **3**

CELLS, CHROMOSOMES, DNA, AND GENES. (*Left*) The body contains trillions of cells. Each cell contains a central structure, the nucleus. (*Middle*) Chromosomes are threadlike structures located in the nucleus of the cell. Chromosomes are composed of DNA. (*Right*) DNA has the structure of a spiral staircase. A gene is a segment of DNA.

Among the major approaches to gene identification and discovery that are being used today are the genome-wide association method, linkage analysis, next-generation sequencing, and the Thousand Genomes Project:

· Completion of the Human Genome Project has led to use of the *genome-wide association method* to identify genetic variations linked to a particular disorder, such as obesity, cancer, cardiovascular disease, or Alzheimer disease (Brown & others, 2014; Locke & others, 2015). To conduct a genome-wide association study, researchers obtain DNA from individuals who have the disease and those who don't have it. Then, each participant's complete set of DNA, or genome, is purified from the blood or cells and scanned on machines to determine markers of genetic variation. If the genetic variations occur more frequently in people who have the disease, the variations point to the region in the human genome where the disease-causing problem exists. Genome-wide association studies have recently been conducted for cancer (Stegeman & others, 2015), obesity (Apalasamy & Mohamed, 2015; Zhao & others, 2014), cardiovascular disease (Malik & others, 2014; Smith, Humphries, & Talmud, 2015), depression (He & others, 2014; Nho & others, 2015), and Alzheimer disease (Chauhan & others, 2015).

· *Linkage analysis*, in which the goal is to discover the location of one or more genes in relation to a marker gene (whose position is already known), is often used in the search for disease genes (Lyon & Wang, 2012). Genes transmitted to offspring tend to be in close proximity to each other so that the gene(s) involved in the disease are usually located near the marker gene. Gene linkage studies are now being conducted on a wide variety of disorders, including attention deficit hyperactivity disorder (Hawi & others, 2015; Li & others, 2014), autism (Warrier, Baron-Cohen, & Chakrabarti, 2013; Pan & others, 2015), depression (Cohen-Woods, Craig, & McGuffin, 2013), and Alzheimer disease (D'Aoust & others, 2015; Roussotte & others, 2014).

· *Next-generation sequencing* is a term used to describe the vast increase in genetic data generated at a much reduced cost and in a much shorter period of time. Next-generation sequencing has considerably increased knowledge about genetic influences on development in recent years (Hegele & others, 2015; Lango Allen & others, 2014; Oleksiewicz & others, 2015; Steinhilber & others, 2015).

· The human genome varies between individuals in small but very important ways. Understanding these variations will require examination of the whole genomes of many individuals. A current project that began in 2008, the Thousand Genomes Project, is the most detailed study of human genetic variation to date. This project has the goal of determining the genomic sequences of at least 1,000 individuals from different ethnic groups around the world (Abyzov & others, 2013; Shibata & others, 2012). By compiling complete descriptions of the genetic variations of many people, the project will make it possible for genetic variations in disease to be studied in greater detail.

One of the big surprises of the Human Genome Project was a report indicating that humans have only about 30,000 genes (U.S. Department of Energy, 2001). In subsequent analyses, the number of human genes was revised downward to approximately 20,500 (Ensembl Human, 2008; Flicek & others, 2013). Further recent analysis proposes that humans may actually have fewer than 20,000 protein-producing genes (Ezkurdia & others, 2014). Scientists had thought that humans had as many as 100,000 or more genes. They had also maintained that each gene programmed just one protein. In fact, because humans appear to have far more proteins than they have genes, there cannot be a one-to-one correspondence between genes and proteins (Commoner, 2002). Each gene is not translated, in automaton-like fashion, into one and only one protein. A gene does not act independently, as developmental psychologist David Moore (2001) emphasized by titling his book *The Dependent Gene*.

Rather than being a group of independent genes, the human genome consists of many genes that collaborate both with each other and with nongenetic factors inside and outside the body. The collaboration operates at many points. For example, the cellular machinery mixes, matches, and links small pieces of DNA to reproduce the genes, and that machinery is influenced by what is going on around it (Moore, 2013, 2015).

Whether a gene is turned "on," working to assemble proteins, is also a matter of collaboration. The activity of genes (*genetic expression*) is affected by their environment (Gottlieb, 2007; Moore, 2013, 2015). For example, hormones that circulate in the blood make their way into the cell where they can turn genes "on" and "off." And the flow of hormones can be affected by

FIGURE 4
A SINGLE SPERM PENETRATING AN EGG AT THE POINT OF FERTILIZATION
© Don W. Fawcett/Science Source

environmental conditions such as light, day length, nutrition, and behavior. Numerous studies have shown that external events outside of the original cell and the person, as well as events inside the cell, can excite or inhibit gene expression (Gottlieb, 2007; Moore, 2013, 2015). Recent research has documented that factors such as stress, exercise, nutrition, respiration, radiation, temperature, and sleep can influence gene expression (Craft & others, 2014; Dedon & Begley, 2014; Donnelly & Storchova, 2015; McInnis & others, 2015). For example, one study revealed that an increase in the concentration of stress hormones such as cortisol produced a fivefold increase in DNA damage (Flint & others, 2007). Another study also found that exposure to radiation changed the rate of DNA synthesis in cells (Lee & others, 2011). And recent research indicates that sleep deprivation can affect gene expression in negative ways, causing increased inflammation, expression of stress-related genes, and impairment of protein functioning (da Costa Souza & Ribeiro, 2015).

Scientists have found that certain genes are turned on or off as a result of exercise, mainly through a process called *methylation*, in which tiny atoms attach themselves to the outside of a gene (Lindholm & others, 2014). This process makes the gene more or less capable of receiving and responding to biochemical signals from the body (Reynolds, 2014). In this way the behavior of the gene, but not its structure, is changed. Researchers also have found that diet may also affect gene behavior through the process of methylation (Ma & others, 2015; Taylor, Jones, & Henagan, 2014).

GENES AND CHROMOSOMES

Genes are not only collaborative, they are enduring. How do genes manage to get passed from generation to generation and end up in all of the trillion cells in the body? The answer lies in three processes that happen at the cellular level: mitosis, meiosis, and fertilization.

Mitosis, Meiosis, and Fertilization   All of the cells in your body, except your sperm or eggs, have 46 chromosomes arranged in 23 pairs. These cells reproduce by a process called **mitosis.** During mitosis, the cell's nucleus—including the chromosomes—duplicates itself and the cell divides. Two new cells are formed, each containing the same DNA as the original cell, arranged in the same 23 pairs of chromosomes (Mader & Windelspecht, 2015).

However, a different type of cell division—**meiosis**—forms eggs and sperm (which also are called *gametes*). During meiosis, a cell of the testes (in men) or ovaries (in women) duplicates its chromosomes but then divides twice, thus forming four cells, each of which has only half of the genetic material of the parent cell (Colbert & Gonzalez, 2016; Johnson, 2015). By the end of meiosis, each egg or sperm has 23 *unpaired* chromosomes.

During **fertilization,** an egg and a sperm fuse to create a single cell, called a **zygote** (see Figure 4). In the zygote, the 23 unpaired chromosomes from the egg and the 23 unpaired chromosomes from the sperm combine to form one set of 23 paired chromosomes—one chromosome of each pair from the mother's egg and the other from the father's sperm. In this manner, each parent contributes half of the offspring's genetic material.

Figure 5 shows 23 paired chromosomes of a male and a female. The members of each pair of chromosomes are both similar and different: Each chromosome in the pair contains varying forms of the same genes, at the same location on the chromosome. A gene that influences hair color, for example, is located on both members of one pair of chromosomes, in the same location on each. However, one of those chromosomes might carry a gene associated with blond hair, and the other chromosome in the pair might carry a gene associated with brown hair.

Do you notice any obvious differences between the chromosomes of the male and the chromosomes of the female in Figure 5? The difference lies in the 23rd pair. Ordinarily, in females this pair consists of two chromosomes called X chromosomes; in males the 23rd pair consists of an X and a Y chromosome. The presence of a Y chromosome is one factor that makes a person male rather than female.

Sources of Variability   Combining the genes of two parents in offspring increases genetic variability in the population, which is valuable for a species because it provides more characteristics on which natural selection can operate (Belk & Borden Maier, 2016). In fact, the human genetic process includes several important sources of variability (Simon, 2015).

First, the chromosomes in the zygote are not exact copies of those in the mother's ovaries or the father's testes. During the formation of the sperm and egg in meiosis, the members of each pair of chromosomes are separated, but which chromosome in the pair goes to the gamete

mitosis Cellular reproduction in which the cell's nucleus duplicates itself; two new cells are formed, each containing the same DNA as the original cell, arranged in the same 23 pairs of chromosomes.

meiosis A specialized form of cell division that occurs to form eggs and sperm (or gametes).

fertilization A stage in reproduction when an egg and a sperm fuse to create a single cell, called a zygote.

zygote A single cell formed through fertilization.

(a)   (b)

is a matter of chance. In addition, before the pairs separate, pieces of the two chromosomes in each pair are exchanged, creating a new combination of genes on each chromosome (Lewis, 2015). Thus, when chromosomes from the mother's egg and the father's sperm are brought together in the zygote, the result is a truly unique combination of genes.

Another source of variability comes from DNA (Bauman, 2015). Chance, a mistake by cellular machinery, or damage from an environmental agent such as radiation may produce a *mutated gene*, which is a permanently altered segment of DNA.

Even when their genes are identical, however, people vary. The difference between genotypes and phenotypes helps us to understand this source of variability. All of a person's genetic material makes up his or her **genotype.**

There is increasing interest in studying *susceptibility genes*, those that make an individual more vulnerable to specific diseases or acceleration of aging, and *longevity genes*, those that make an individual less vulnerable to certain diseases and more likely to live to an older age (Dong & others, 2015; Howard & Rogers, 2014; Wei & others, 2014). These are aspects of the individual's genotype.

In the search for longevity genes, Cynthia Kenyon (2010) has extensively studied *C. elegans,* a roundworm, the first animal to have its entire genome sequenced. In early research, Kenyon found that modifying a single gene, *daf-2,* which is linked to hormones, slows aging in the roundworm. She also discovered that another gene, *daf-16,* is necessary for the roundworm to live longer. *Daf-16* encodes a gene switch that turns on a number of genes related to stress resistance, immunity, and metabolism (Mendler & others, 2015). These genes possibly may extend life by protecting and repairing body tissues (Patti & others, 2014). Other researchers have found that genetic variants in a human *daf-16* version labeled *FOXO3A* are linked to increased longevity in a wide range of people, including Americans, Europeans, and Chinese (Bao & others, 2014; Soerensen & others, 2010). Further, *daf-2*-type mutations extend life and slow aging not only in roundworms but also in flies and mice, resulting in delayed onset and severity of many diseases related to aging, including cancer, cardiovascular disease, and Alzheimer disease (Kenyon, 2010). Recently, Cynthia Kenyon joined a think tank of scientists at Google's Calico (short for California Life Company) division, which seeks to understand the aging process and discover how to modify it. Kenyon believes that interventions to extend the human life span might be possible through the development of drugs that mimic the action of gene mutations that are linked to greater longevity.

However, not all of the genetic material is apparent in an individual's observed and measurable characteristics. A **phenotype** consists of observable characteristics, including physical characteristics (such as height, weight, and hair color) and psychological characteristics (such as personality and intelligence). For each genotype, a range of phenotypes can be expressed, providing another source of variability. An individual can inherit the genetic potential to grow very large, for example, but good nutrition, among other things, will be essential for achieving that potential.

How does the process from genotype to phenotype work? It's highly complex. but at a very basic level DNA information in a cell is transcribed to RNA (ribonucleic acid), which in turn is translated into amino acids that will become proteins (Brooker, 2015). Once proteins have been assembled, they become capable of producing phenotype traits and characteristics. Also, environments interact with genotypes to produce phenotypes.

Researcher Cynthia Kenyon found that modifying a gene called *daf-16* slows the aging in *C. elegans* (shown above). This type of roundworm was the first animal to have its entire genome sequenced.
© PA-HO/AP Images

genotype All of a person's actual genetic material.

phenotype Observable and measurable characteristics of an individual, such as height, hair color, and intelligence.

GENETIC PRINCIPLES

What determines how a genotype is expressed to create a particular phenotype? Much is still unknown about the answer to this question. However, a number of genetic principles have been discovered, such as those involving dominant-recessive genes, sex-linked genes, genetic imprinting, and polygenically determined characteristics.

Dominant-Recessive Genes   In some cases, one gene of a pair always exerts its effects; it is *dominant*, overriding the potential influence of the other gene, called the *recessive* gene. This is the principle of *dominant-recessive* genes. A recessive gene exerts its influence only if the two genes of a pair are both recessive. If you inherit a recessive gene for a trait from each of your parents, you will show the trait. If you inherit a recessive gene from only one parent, you may never know you carry the gene. Brown hair, farsightedness, and dimples rule over blond hair, nearsightedness, and freckles in the world of dominant-recessive genes.

Can two brown-haired parents have a blond-haired child? Yes, they can. Suppose that each parent has a dominant gene for brown hair and a recessive gene for blond hair. Since dominant genes override recessive genes, the parents have brown hair, but both are *carriers* of blondness and pass on their recessive genes for blond hair. With no dominant gene to override them, the recessive genes can make the child's hair blond.

Sex-Linked Genes   Most mutated genes are recessive. When a mutated gene is carried on the X chromosome, the result is called *X-linked inheritance*. It may have very different implications for males and females (Simon & others, 2016). Remember that males have only one X chromosome. Thus, if there is an absent or altered disease-relevant gene on the X chromosome, males have no "backup" copy to counter the harmful gene and therefore may develop an X-linked disease. However, females have a second X chromosome, which is likely to be unchanged. As a result, they are not likely to have the X-linked disease. Thus, most individuals who have X-linked diseases are males. Females who have one abnormal copy of the gene on the X chromosome are known as "carriers," and they usually do not show any signs of the X-linked disease. Hemophilia and fragile X syndrome, which we discuss later in this chapter, are examples of X-linked inheritance diseases (Bartel, Weinstein, & Schaffer, 2012).

Genetic Imprinting   *Genetic imprinting* occurs when genes have differing effects depending on whether they are inherited from the mother or the father (Moore & others, 2015; Schneider & others, 2014). A chemical process "silences" one member of the gene pair. For example, as a result of imprinting, only the maternally derived copy of a gene might be active, while the paternally derived copy of the same gene is silenced—or vice versa (Court & others, 2014). Only a small percentage of human genes appear to undergo imprinting, but it is a normal and important aspect of development. When imprinting goes awry, development is disturbed, as in the case of Beckwith-Wiedemann syndrome, a growth disorder, and Wilms tumor, a type of cancer (Okun & others, 2014; Royer-Pokora, 2013).

Polygenic Inheritance   Genetic transmission is usually more complex than the simple examples we have examined thus far (Moore, 2013). Few characteristics reflect the influence of only a single gene or pair of genes. Most are determined by the interaction of many different genes; they are said to be *polygenically determined* (Lu, Yu, & Deng, 2012). Even a simple characteristic such as height, for example, reflects the interaction of many genes as well as the influence of the environment.

The term *gene-gene interaction* is increasingly used to describe studies that focus on the interdependence of two or more genes in influencing characteristics, behavior, diseases, and development (Hu, Wang, & Wang, 2014; Sarlos & others, 2014). For example, recent studies have documented gene-gene interaction in immune system functioning (Reijmerink & others, 2011), asthma (Lee & others, 2014; Lee & Park, 2014), cancer (Jin & Lee, 2015; Mandal, Abebe, & Chaudhary, 2014), cardiovascular disease (Musameh & others, 2015; Kumar & others, 2014), and alcoholism (Yokoyama & others, 2013).

These athletes, several of whom have Down syndrome, are participating in a Special Olympics competition. Notice the distinctive facial features of the individuals with Down syndrome, such as a round face and a flattened skull. *What causes Down syndrome?*
© James Shaffer/PhotoEdit

Name	Description	Treatment	Incidence
Down syndrome	An extra chromosome causes mild to severe intellectual disability and physical abnormalities.	Surgery, early intervention, infant stimulation, and special learning programs	1 in 1,900 births at age 20 1 in 300 births at age 35 1 in 30 births at age 45
Klinefelter syndrome (XXY)	An extra X chromosome causes physical abnormalities.	Hormone therapy can be effective	1 in 1000 male births
Fragile X syndrome	An abnormality in the X chromosome can cause intellectual disability, learning disabilities, or short attention span.	Special education, speech and language therapy	More common in males than in females
Turner syndrome (XO)	A missing X chromosome in females can cause intellectual disability and sexual underdevelopment.	Hormone therapy in childhood and puberty	1 in 2,500 female births
XYY syndrome	An extra Y chromosome can cause above-average height.	No special treatment required	1 in 1,000 male births

FIGURE 6

SOME CHROMOSOMAL ABNORMALITIES. The treatments for these abnormalities do not necessarily erase the problem but may improve the individual's adaptive behavior and quality of life.

CHROMOSOMAL AND GENE-LINKED ABNORMALITIES

Sometimes abnormalities characterize the genetic process. Some of these abnormalities involve whole chromosomes that do not separate properly during meiosis. Other abnormalities are produced by harmful genes.

Chromosomal Abnormalities When a gamete is formed, sometimes the sperm or ovum does not have its normal set of 23 chromosomes. The most notable examples involve Down syndrome and abnormalities of the sex chromosomes (see Figure 6).

Down Syndrome An individual with **Down syndrome** has a round face, a flattened skull, an extra fold of skin over the eyelids, a protruding tongue, short limbs, and intellectual and motor disabilities. It is not known why the extra chromosome is present, but the health of the male sperm or the female ovum may be involved.

Down syndrome appears approximately once in every 700 live births. Women between the ages of 16 and 34 are less likely to give birth to a child with Down syndrome than are younger or older women. African American children are rarely born with Down syndrome.

Sex-Linked Chromosomal Abnormalities Recall that a newborn normally has either an X and a Y chromosome or two X chromosomes. Human embryos must possess at least one X chromosome to be viable. The most common sex-linked chromosomal abnormalities involve the presence of an extra chromosome (either an X or Y) or the absence of one X chromosome in females.

Klinefelter syndrome is a chromosomal disorder in which males have an extra X chromosome, making them XXY instead of XY. Males with this disorder have undeveloped testes, and they usually have enlarged breasts and become tall (Lunenfeld & others, 2015; Ross & others, 2012). Klinefelter syndrome occurs approximately once in every 1000 live male births. Only 10 percent of individuals with Klinefelter syndrome are diagnosed before puberty, with the majority not identified until adulthood (Aksglaede & others, 2013).

Fragile X syndrome is a chromosomal disorder that results from an abnormality in the X chromosome, which becomes constricted and often breaks (Yudkin & others, 2014). Mental deficiency frequently is an outcome, but it may take the form of an intellectual disability, autism, a learning disability, or a short attention span (Dan & others, 2015; Hall & others, 2014; Lipton & Sahin, 2013). This disorder occurs more frequently in males than in females, possibly because the second X chromosome in females negates the effects of the abnormal X chromosome (Bonaccorso & others, 2015; McDuffie & others, 2015).

Turner syndrome is a chromosomal disorder in females in which either an X chromosome is missing, making the person XO instead of XX, or part of one X chromosome is deleted (Vlatkovic & others, 2014). Females with Turner syndrome are short in stature and

Down syndrome A chromosomally transmitted form of intellectual disability caused by the presence of an extra copy of chromosome 21.

Klinefelter syndrome A chromosomal disorder in which males have an extra X chromosome, making them XXY instead of XY.

fragile X syndrome A chromosomal disorder involving an abnormality in the X chromosome, which becomes constricted and often breaks.

Turner syndrome A chromosomal disorder in females in which either an X chromosome is missing, making the person XO instead of XX, or part of one X chromosome is deleted.

A boy with fragile X syndrome.
From R. Simensen and R. Curtis Rogers, "Fragile X Syndrome" in American Family Physician, 39(5): 186, May 1989 © American Academy of Family Physicians

Name	Description	Treatment	Incidence
Cystic fibrosis	Glandular dysfunction that interferes with mucus production; breathing and digestion are hampered, resulting in a shortened life span.	Physical and oxygen therapy, synthetic enzymes, and antibiotics; most individuals live to middle age.	1 in 2,000 births
Diabetes	Body does not produce enough insulin, which causes abnormal metabolism of sugar.	Early onset can be fatal unless treated with insulin.	1 in 2,500 births
Hemophilia	Delayed blood clotting causes internal and external bleeding.	Blood transfusions/injections can reduce or prevent damage due to internal bleeding.	1 in 10,000 males
Huntington's disease	Central nervous system deteriorates, producing problems in muscle coordination and mental deterioration.	Does not usually appear until age 35 or older; death likely 10 to 20 years after symptoms appear.	1 in 20,000 births
Phenylketonuria (PKU)	Metabolic disorder that, left untreated, causes intellectual disability.	Special diet can result in average intelligence and normal life span.	1 in 10,000 to 1 in 20,000 births
Sickle-cell anemia	Blood disorder that limits the body's oxygen supply; it can cause joint swelling, as well as heart and kidney failure.	Penicillin, medication for pain, antibiotics, and blood transfusions.	1 in 400 African American children (lower among other groups)
Spina bifida	Neural tube disorder that causes brain and spine abnormalities.	Corrective surgery at birth, orthopedic devices, and physical/medical therapy.	2 in 1,000 births
Tay-Sachs disease	Deceleration of mental and physical development caused by an accumulation of lipids in the nervous system.	Medication and special diet are used, but death is likely by 5 years of age.	1 in 30 American Jews is a carrier.

FIGURE 7
SOME GENE-LINKED ABNORMALITIES

XYY syndrome A chromosomal disorder in which males have an extra Y chromosome.

phenylketonuria (PKU) A genetic disorder in which an individual cannot properly metabolize phenylalanine, an amino acid; PKU is now easily detected—but, if left untreated, results in intellectual disability and hyperactivity.

sickle-cell anemia A genetic disorder that affects the red blood cells and occurs most often in African Americans.

have a webbed neck (Kaur & Phadke, 2012). They might be infertile and have difficulty in mathematics, but their verbal ability is often quite good. Turner syndrome occurs in approximately 1 of every 2,500 live female births (Pinsker, 2012).

The **XYY syndrome** is a chromosomal disorder in which the male has an extra Y chromosome (Lepage & others, 2014). Early interest in this syndrome focused on the belief that the extra Y chromosome found in some males contributed to aggression and violence. However, researchers subsequently found that XYY males are no more likely to commit crimes than are XY males (Witkin & others, 1976).

Gene-Linked Abnormalities Abnormalities can be produced not only by an abnormal number of chromosomes but also by harmful genes. More than 7,000 such genetic disorders have been identified, although most of them are rare.

Phenylketonuria (PKU) is a genetic disorder in which the individual cannot properly metabolize phenylalanine, an amino acid. It results from a recessive gene and occurs about once in every 10,000 to 20,000 live births. Today, phenylketonuria is easily detected, and it is treated by a diet that prevents an excess accumulation of phenylalanine. If phenylketonuria is left untreated, however, excess phenylalanine builds up in the child, producing intellectual disability and hyperactivity. Phenylketonuria accounts for approximately 1 percent of institutionalized individuals who have an intellectual disability, and it occurs primarily in non-Latino Whites.

Sickle-cell anemia, which occurs most often in African Americans, is a genetic disorder that impairs the body's red blood cells. Red blood cells carry oxygen to the body's other cells and are usually shaped like a disk. In sickle-cell anemia, a recessive gene causes the red blood cell to become a hook-shaped "sickle" that cannot carry oxygen properly and dies quickly. As a result, the body's cells do not receive adequate oxygen, causing anemia and often early death (Derebail & others, 2014). About 1 in 400 African American babies is affected by sickle-cell anemia. One in 10 African Americans is a carrier, as is 1 in 20 Latin Americans.

Other diseases that result from genetic abnormalities include cystic fibrosis, some forms of diabetes, hemophilia, Alzheimer disease, Huntington disease, spina bifida, and Tay-Sachs disease (Capurro & others, 2015; Cruchaga & others, 2014; Huang & others, 2014; Tai & others, 2015). Figure 7 provides further information about these diseases. Someday, scientists may identify the origins of these and other genetic abnormalities and discover how to cure them.

Holly Ishmael, Genetic Counselor

Holly Ishmael is a genetic counselor at Children's Mercy Hospital in Kansas City. She obtained an undergraduate degree in psychology from Sarah Lawrence College and a master's degree in genetic counseling from the same college. She uses many of the principles discussed in this chapter in her genetic counseling work.

Ishmael says, "Genetic counseling is a perfect combination for people who want to do something science-oriented, but need human contact and don't want to spend all of their time in a lab or have their nose in a book" (Rizzo, 1999, p. 3).

There are approximately 30 graduate genetic counseling programs in the United States. If you are interested in this profession, you can obtain further information from the National Society of Genetic Counselors at www.nsgc.org.

Holly Ishmael (*left*) in a genetic counseling session.
Courtesy of Holly Ishmael Welsh

Genetic counselors, usually physicians or biologists who are well versed in the field of medical genetics, provide their clients with information regarding the kinds of problems just described, the odds of encountering them, and helpful strategies for offsetting some of their effects (Paneque, Sequeiros, & Skirton, 2015; Rohde & others, 2014). To read about the career and work of a genetic counselor, see the *Connecting with Careers* profile.

Review Connect Reflect

 Describe what genes are and how they influence human development

Review
- What are genes?
- How are genes passed on?
- What basic principles describe how genes interact?
- What are some chromosomal and gene-linked abnormalities?

Connect
- Would you want to be able to access a full genome analysis of your offspring? Why or why not?

Reflect *Your Own Personal Journey of Life*
- Imagine that you are considering having a child. Would you want to see a genetic counselor to find out about possible genetic risks that might be transmitted to your offspring? Explain.

3 Heredity and Environment Interaction: The Nature-Nurture Debate

 Explain some of the ways that heredity and environment interact to produce individual differences in development

| Behavior Genetics | Heredity-Environment Correlations | Shared and Nonshared Environmental Influences | The Epigenetic View and Gene x Environment (G x E) Interaction | Conclusions about Heredity-Environment Interaction |

Is it possible to untangle the influence of heredity from that of environment and discover the role of each in producing individual differences in development? When heredity and environment interact, how does heredity influence the environment, and vice versa?

Twin studies compare identical twins with fraternal twins. Identical twins develop from a single fertilized egg that splits into two genetically identical organisms. Fraternal twins develop from separate eggs, making them genetically no more similar than nontwin siblings. *What is the nature of the twin study method?*
© Jack Hollingsworth/Getty Images RF

BEHAVIOR GENETICS

Behavior genetics is the field that seeks to discover the influence of heredity and environment on individual differences in human traits and development. To study the influence of heredity on behavior, behavior geneticists often use either twins or adoption situations (Krushkal & others, 2014; Lickliter & Honeycutt, 2015; Maxson, 2013).

In the most common **twin study,** the behavioral similarity of identical twins (who are genetically identical) is compared with the behavioral similarity of fraternal twins. Recall that although fraternal twins share the same womb, they are no more genetically alike than nontwin siblings. Thus, by comparing groups of identical and fraternal twins, behavior geneticists capitalize on the basic knowledge that identical twins are more similar genetically than are fraternal twins (Chen & others, 2014b; Jansen & others, 2015; Tan & others, 2015). For example, one study found that conduct problems were more prevalent in identical twins than in fraternal twins; the researchers concluded that the study demonstrated an important role for heredity in conduct problems (Scourfield & others, 2004).

However, several issues complicate interpretation of twin studies. For example, perhaps the environments of identical twins are more similar than the environments of fraternal twins. Parents and other caregivers might stress the similarities of identical twins more than those of fraternal twins, and identical twins might perceive themselves as a "set" and play together more than fraternal twins do. If so, the influence of the environment on the observed similarities between identical and fraternal twins might be highly significant. To read more about identical twins, see *Connecting Development to Life.*

In an **adoption study,** investigators seek to discover whether the behavior and psychological characteristics of adopted children are more like those of their adoptive parents, who have provided a home environment, or more like those of their biological parents, who have contributed their heredity (Cvijetic & others, 2014; Kendler & others, 2012). Another form of the adoption study compares adoptive and biological siblings.

HEREDITY-ENVIRONMENT CORRELATIONS

The difficulties that researchers encounter when they interpret the results of twin studies and adoption studies reflect the complexities of heredity-environment interaction. Some of these interactions are *heredity-environment correlations,* which means that individuals' genes may be systematically related to the types of environments to which they are exposed (Klahr & Burt, 2014). In a sense, individuals "inherit," seek out, or "construct" environments that may be related or linked to genetic "propensities." Behavior geneticist Sandra Scarr (1993) described three ways that heredity and environment can be correlated. Behavior geneticist Sandra Scarr (1993) described three ways that heredity and environment are correlated (see Figure 8):

- **Passive genotype-environment correlations** occur because biological parents, who are genetically related to the child, provide a rearing environment for the child. For example, the parents might have a genetic predisposition to be intelligent and read skillfully. Because they read well and enjoy reading, they provide their children with books to read. The likely outcome is that their children, because of both their own inherited predispositions and their book-filled environment, will become skilled readers.
- **Evocative genotype-environment correlations** occur because a child's genetically influenced characteristics elicit certain types of environments. For example, active, smiling children receive more social stimulation than passive, quiet children do. Cooperative, attentive children evoke more pleasant and instructional responses from the adults around them than uncooperative, distractible children do.
- **Active (niche-picking) genotype-environment correlations** occur when children seek out environments that they find compatible and stimulating. *Niche-picking* refers to

behavior genetics The field that seeks to discover the influence of heredity and environment on individual differences in human traits and development.

twin study A study in which the behavioral similarity of identical twins is compared with the behavioral similarity of fraternal twins.

adoption study A study in which investigators seek to discover whether, in behavior and psychological characteristics, adopted children are more like their adoptive parents, who provided a home environment, or more like their biological parents, who contributed their heredity. Another form of the adoption study compares adoptive and biological siblings.

passive genotype-environment correlations Correlations that exist when the biological parents, who are genetically related to the child, provide a rearing environment for the child.

evocative genotype-environment correlations Correlations that exist when the child's characteristics elicit certain types of environments.

active (niche-picking) genotype-environment correlations Correlations that exist when children seek out environments they find compatible and stimulating.

Am I an "I" or "We"?

College freshman Colin Kunzweiler (2007) wrote about his thoughts and experiences related to being an identical twin:

> As a monozygotic individual, I am used to certain things. "Which one are you?" happens to be the most popular question I'm asked, which is almost always followed by "You're Colin. No, wait, you're Andy!"
>
> I have two names: one was given to me at birth, the other thrust on me in a random, haphazard way. . . . My twin brother and I are as different from each other as caramel sauce is from gravy. We have different personalities, we enjoy different kinds of music, and I am even taller than he is (by a quarter of an inch). We are different, separate, and individual. I have always been taught that I should maintain my own individuality; that I should be my own person. But if people keep constantly mistaking me for my twin, how can I be my own person with my own identity?

"Am I an 'I' or 'We'?" was the title of an article written by Lynn Perlman (2008) about the struggle twins have in developing a sense of being an individual. Of course, triplets have the same issue, possibly even more strongly so. One set of triplets entered a beauty contest as one person and won the contest!

Perlman, an identical twin herself, is a psychologist who works with twins (her identical twin also is a psychologist). She says that how twins move from a sense of "we" to "I" is a critical task for them as children and sometimes even as adults. For non-

twins, separating oneself from a primary caregiver—mother and/or father—is an important developmental task in childhood, adolescence, and emerging adulthood. When a child has a twin, the separation process is likely to be more difficult because of the constant comparison with a twin. Since they are virtually identical in their physical appearance, identical twins are likely to have more problems in distinguishing themselves from their twin than are fraternal twins.

The twin separation process often accelerates in adolescence when one twin is likely to mature earlier than the other (Perlman, 2013). However, for some twins it may not occur until emerging adulthood when they may go to different colleges and/or live apart for the first time. And for some twins, even as adults twin separation can be emotionally painful. One 28-year-old identical twin female got a new boyfriend but the relationship caused a great deal of stress and conflict with her twin sister (Friedman, 2013).

In Lynn Perlman's (2008) view, helping twins develop their own identities needs to be done on a child-by-child basis, taking into account their preferences and what is in their best interests. She commented that most of the twins she has counseled consider having a twin a positive experience, and while they also are usually strongly attached to each other they are intensely motivated to be considered unique persons.

---

finding a setting that is suited to one's genetically influenced abilities. Children select from their surrounding environment some aspects that they respond to, learn about, or ignore. Their active selections of environments are related to their particular genotype. For example, outgoing children tend to seek out social contexts in which to interact with people, whereas shy children don't. Children who are musically inclined are likely to

Heredity-Environment Correlation	Description	Examples
Passive	Children inherit genetic tendencies from their parents, and parents also provide an environment that matches their own genetic tendencies.	Musically inclined parents usually have musically inclined children and they are likely to provide an environment rich in music for their children.
Evocative	The child's genetic tendencies elicit stimulation from the environment that supports a particular trait. Thus genes evoke environmental support.	A happy, outgoing child elicits smiles and friendly responses from others.
Active (niche-picking)	Children actively seek out "niches" in their environment that reflect their own interests and talents and are thus in accord with their genotype.	Libraries, sports fields, and a store with musical instruments are examples of environmental niches children might seek out if they have intellectual interests in books, talent in sports, or musical talents, respectively.

FIGURE 8

EXPLORING HEREDITY-ENVIRONMENT CORRELATIONS

select musical environments in which they can successfully perform their skills. How these "tendencies" come about will be discussed shortly under the topic of the epigenetic view.

Scarr notes that the relative importance of the three genotype-environment correlations changes as children develop from infancy through adolescence. In infancy, much of the environment that children experience is provided by adults. Thus, passive genotype-environment correlations are more common in the lives of infants and young children than they are for older children and adolescents who can extend their experiences beyond the family's influence and create and select their environments to a greater degree.

SHARED AND NONSHARED ENVIRONMENTAL INFLUENCES

Behavior geneticists have argued that to understand the environment's role in differences among people, we should distinguish between shared and nonshared environments. That is, we should consider experiences that children have in common with other children living in the same home, and experiences that are not shared (Burt, 2014; Waszczuk & others, 2015; White & others, 2014).

Shared environmental experiences are siblings' common experiences, such as their parents' personalities or intellectual orientation, the family's socioeconomic status, and the neighborhood in which they live. By contrast, **nonshared environmental experiences** are a child's unique experiences, both within the family and outside the family, that are not shared with a sibling. For example, siblings often have different peer groups, different friends, and different teachers at school, all of which contribute to their nonshared environment.

Behavior geneticist Robert Plomin (2004, 2011) has found that shared environment accounts for little of the variation in children's personality or interests. In other words, even though two children live under the same roof with the same parents, their personalities are often very different. Further, Plomin argues that heredity influences the nonshared environments of siblings through the heredity-environment correlations we described earlier. For example, a child who has inherited a tendency to be athletic is likely to spend more time in environments related to sports, whereas a child who has inherited a tendency to be musically inclined is more likely to spend time in environments related to music.

THE EPIGENETIC VIEW AND GENE × ENVIRONMENT (G × E) INTERACTION

In line with the concept of a collaborative gene, Gilbert Gottlieb (2007) proposed an **epigenetic view** which states that development is the result of an ongoing, bidirectional interchange between heredity and the environment. Figure 9 compares the heredity-environment correlation and epigenetic views of development.

Let's look at an example that reflects the epigenetic view. A baby inherits genes from both parents at conception. During prenatal development, toxins, nutrition, and stress can influence some genes to stop functioning while others become more active or less active. During infancy, environmental experiences, such as exposure to toxins, nutrition, stress, learning, and encouragement, continue to modify genetic activity and the activity of the nervous system that directly underlies behavior. Heredity and environment thus operate together—or collaborate—to produce a person's intelligence, temperament, health, ability to pitch a baseball, ability to read, and so on (Gottlieb, 2007; Lickliter, 2013; Lickliter & Honeycutt, 2015; Moore, 2013, 2015).

An increasing number of studies are exploring how the interaction between heredity and environment influences development, including interactions that involve specific DNA

Tennis stars Venus and Serena Williams. What might be some shared and nonshared environmental experiences they had while they were growing up that contributed to their tennis stardom?
© Greg Wood/AFP/Getty Images

FIGURE 9

COMPARISON OF THE HEREDITY-ENVIRONMENT CORRELATION AND EPIGENETIC VIEWS

shared environmental experiences Siblings' common experiences, such as their parents' personalities or intellectual orientation, the family's socioeconomic status, and the neighborhood in which they live.

nonshared environmental experiences The child's own unique experiences, both within the family and outside the family, that are not shared by another sibling; thus, experiences occurring within the family can be part of the "nonshared environment."

epigenetic view Perspective that emphasizes that development is the result of an ongoing, bidirectional interchange between heredity and environment.

sequences (Manuck & McCaffery, 2014). The epigenetic mechanisms involve the actual molecular modification of the DNA strand as a result of environmental inputs in ways that alter gene functioning (Davies & Cicchetti, 2014; Moore, 2013, 2015).

One study found that individuals who have a short version of a gene labeled 5-HTTLPR (a gene involving the neurotransmitter serotonin) have an elevated risk of developing depression only if they *also* lead stressful lives (Caspi & others, 2003). Thus, the specific gene did not directly cause the development of depression; rather the gene interacted with a stressful environment in a way that allowed the researchers to predict whether individuals would develop depression. A recent meta-analysis indicated that the short version of 5-HTTLPR was linked with higher cortisol stress reactivity (Miller & others, 2013). Recent studies also have found support for the interaction between the 5-HTTLPR gene and stress levels in predicting depression in adolescents and older adults (Petersen & others, 2012; Zannas & others, 2012).

The type of research just described is referred to as studies of **gene × environment (G × E) interaction**—the interaction of a specific measured variation in DNA and a specific measured aspect of the environment. Although there is considerable enthusiasm about the concept of gene × environment interaction (G × E), a recent research review concluded that the area is plagued by difficulties in replicating results, inflated claims, and other weaknesses (Manuck & McCaffery, 2014). The science of G × E interaction is very young and in the next several decades it will likely produce more precise findings.

gene × environment (G × E) interaction The interaction of a specific measured variation in the DNA and a specific measured aspect of the environment.

CONCLUSIONS ABOUT HEREDITY-ENVIRONMENT INTERACTION

If an attractive, popular, intelligent girl is elected president of her high school senior class, is her success due to heredity or to environment? Of course, the answer is "both."

The relative contributions of heredity and environment are not additive. That is, we can't say that such-and-such a percentage of nature and such-and-such a percentage of experience make us who we are. Nor is it accurate to say that full genetic expression happens once, at the time of conception or birth, after which we carry our genetic legacy into the world to see how far it takes us. Genes produce proteins throughout the life span, in many different environments. Or they don't produce these proteins, depending in part on how harsh or nourishing those environments are.

The emerging view is that complex behaviors are influenced by genes in ways that give people a propensity for a particular developmental trajectory (Lewis, Haworth, & Plomin, 2014). However, the individual's actual development also involves a specific environment. And that environment is complex, just like the mixture of genes we inherit (Cicchetti & Toth, 2015; Thompson, 2015). Environmental influences range from the things we lump together under "nurture" (such as parenting, family dynamics, schooling, and neighborhood quality) to biological encounters (such as viruses, birth complications, and even biological events in cells).

In developmental psychologist David Moore's (2013, 2015) view, the biological systems that generate behaviors are extremely complex but too often these systems have been described in overly simplified ways that can be misleading. Thus, although genetic factors clearly contribute to behavior and psychological processes, they don't determine these phenotypes independently from the contexts in which they develop. From Moore's (2013, 2015) perspective, it is misleading to talk about "genes for" eye color, intelligence, personality, or other characteristics. Moore commented that in retrospect we should not have expected to be able to make the giant leap from analyzing the molecules in DNA to achieving a complete understanding of human behavior, any more than we should anticipate being able to make the leap from understanding how sound waves move molecules in a concert hall to attaining a full-blown appreciation of a symphony's wondrous experience.

Imagine for a moment that there is a cluster of genes that are somehow associated with youth violence. (This example is hypothetical because we don't know of any such combination.) The adolescent who carries this genetic mixture might experience a world of loving parents, regular nutritious meals, lots of books, and a series of competent teachers. Or the adolescent's world might include parental neglect, a neighborhood in which gunshots and crime are everyday occurrences, and inadequate schooling. In which of these environments are the adolescent's genes likely to manufacture the biological underpinnings of criminality?

If heredity and environment interact to determine the course of development, is that all there is to answering the question of what causes development? Are humans completely at

To what extent are this young girl's piano skills likely due to heredity, environment, or both?
© Francisco Romero/Getty Images RF

The interaction of heredity and environment is so extensive that to ask which is more important, nature or nurture, is like asking which is more important to a rectangle, height or width.

—WILLIAM GREENOUGH
Contemporary developmental psychologist, University of Illinois at Urbana

developmental **connection**
Life-Span Perspective
An important aspect of the life-span perspective is the co-construction of biology, culture, and the individual. Connect to "Introduction."

the mercy of their genes and their environment as they develop through the life span? Genetic heritage and environmental experiences are pervasive influences on development. But in thinking about what causes development, consider that development is the co-construction of biology, culture, and the individual. Not only are we the outcomes of our heredity and the environment we experience, but we also can author a unique developmental path by changing our environment. As one psychologist concluded:

> In reality, we are both the creatures and creators of our worlds. We are . . . the products of our genes and environments. Nevertheless, . . . the stream of causation that shapes the future runs through our present choices. . . . Mind matters. . . . Our hopes, goals, and expectations influence our future. (Myers, 2010, p. 168)

Review Connect Reflect

LG3 Explain some of the ways that heredity and environment interact to produce individual differences in development

Review

- What is behavior genetics?
- What are three types of heredity-environment correlations?
- What is meant by the concepts of shared and nonshared environmental experiences?
- What is the epigenetic view of development?
- What conclusions can be reached about heredity-environment interaction?

Connect

- Of passive, evocative, and active genotype-environment correlations, which is the best explanation for the similarities discovered between the many sets of adult twins who share characteristics and experiences despite being raised apart?

Reflect Your Own Personal Journey of Life

- A friend tells you that she has analyzed her genetic background and environmental experiences and reached the conclusion that environment definitely has had little influence on her intelligence. What would you say to this person about her ability to make this self-diagnosis?

4 Prenatal Development

LG4 Characterize the course of prenatal development and its hazards

The Course of Prenatal Development   Prenatal Diagnostic Tests   Hazards to Prenatal Development   Prenatal Care

We turn now to a description of how the process of development unfolds from its earliest moment—the moment of *conception*—when two parental cells, with their unique genetic contributions, meet to create a new individual.

Conception occurs when a single sperm cell from a male unites with an ovum (egg) in a female's fallopian tube in a process called fertilization. Over the next few months the genetic code discussed earlier directs a series of changes in the fertilized egg, but many events and hazards will influence how that egg develops and becomes a person.

THE COURSE OF PRENATAL DEVELOPMENT

Prenatal development lasts approximately 266 days, beginning with fertilization and ending with birth. It can be divided into three periods: germinal, embryonic, and fetal.

The Germinal Period   The **germinal period** is the period of prenatal development that takes place in the first two weeks after conception. It includes the creation of the fertilized egg (the *zygote*), cell division, and the attachment of the zygote to the uterine wall.

Rapid cell division by the zygote begins the germinal period. (Recall from earlier in the chapter that this cell division occurs through a process called *mitosis*.) By approximately one

germinal period The period of prenatal development that takes place during the first two weeks after conception; it includes the creation of the zygote, continued cell division, and the attachment of the zygote to the wall of the uterus.

week after conception, the differentiation of these cells—their specialization for different tasks—has already begun. At this stage the group of cells, now called the *blastocyst*, consists of an inner mass of cells that will eventually develop into the embryo, and the *trophoblast*, an outer layer of cells that later provides nutrition and support for the embryo. *Implantation*, the attachment of the zygote to the uterine wall, takes place about 10 to 14 days after conception.

The Embryonic Period

The **embryonic period** is the period of prenatal development that occurs from two to eight weeks after conception. During the embryonic period, the rate of cell differentiation intensifies, support systems for cells form, and organs appear.

This period begins as the blastocyst attaches to the uterine wall. The mass of cells is now called an *embryo*, and three layers of cells form. The embryo's *endoderm* is the inner layer of cells, which will develop into the digestive and respiratory systems. The *ectoderm* is the outermost layer, which will become the nervous system, sensory receptors (ears, nose, and eyes, for example), and skin parts (hair and nails, for example). The *mesoderm* is the middle layer, which will become the circulatory system, bones, muscles, excretory system, and reproductive system. Every body part eventually develops from these three layers. The endoderm primarily produces internal body parts, the mesoderm primarily produces parts that surround the internal areas, and the ectoderm primarily produces surface parts. **Organogenesis** is the name given to the process of organ formation during the first two months of prenatal development. While they are being formed, the organs are especially vulnerable to environmental influences (Halt & Vainio, 2014).

As the embryo's three layers form, life-support systems for the embryo develop rapidly. These systems include the amnion, the umbilical cord (both of which develop from the fertilized egg, not the mother's body), and the placenta. The amnion is like a bag or an envelope; it contains a clear fluid in which the developing embryo floats. The amniotic fluid provides an environment that is temperature- and humidity-controlled, as well as shockproof. The *umbilical cord*, which contains two arteries and one vein, connects the baby to the placenta. The *placenta* consists of a disk-shaped group of tissues in which small blood vessels from the mother and the offspring intertwine but do not join.

Very small molecules—oxygen, water, salt, and nutrients from the mother's blood, as well as carbon dioxide and digestive wastes from the baby's blood—pass back and forth between the mother and the embryo or fetus. Virtually any drug or chemical substance the pregnant woman ingests can cross the placenta to some degree, unless it is metabolized or altered during passage, or is too large (Holme & others, 2015; Hutson & others, 2013). A recent study confirmed that ethanol crosses the human placenta and primarily reflects maternal alcohol use (Matlow & others, 2013). Another recent study revealed that cigarette smoke weakened and increased the oxidative stress of fetal membranes from which the placenta develops (Menon & others, 2011). The stress hormone cortisol also can cross the placenta (Parrott & others, 2014). Large molecules that cannot pass through the placental wall include red blood cells and harmful substances such as most bacteria, maternal wastes, and hormones. The complex mechanisms that govern the transfer of substances across the placental barrier are still not entirely understood (Mandelbrot & others, 2015; Yuen & others, 2013).

The Fetal Period

The **fetal period,** which lasts about seven months, is the prenatal period that extends from two months after conception until birth in typical pregnancies. Growth and development continue their dramatic course during this time.

Three months after conception, the fetus is about 3 inches long and weighs about 3 ounces. It has become active, moving its arms and legs, opening and closing its mouth, and moving its head. The face, forehead, eyelids, nose, and chin are distinguishable, as are the upper arms, lower arms, hands, and lower limbs. In most cases, the genitals can be identified as male or female. By the end of the fourth month of pregnancy, the fetus has grown to 6 inches in length and weighs 4 to 7 ounces. At this time, a growth spurt occurs in the body's lower parts. For the first time, the mother can feel arm and leg movements.

By the end of the fifth month, the fetus is about 12 inches long and weighs close to a pound. Structures of the skin have formed—toenails and fingernails, for example. The fetus is more active, showing a preference for a particular position in the womb. By the end of the sixth month, the fetus is about 14 inches long and has gained another 6 to 12 ounces. The eyes and eyelids are completely formed, and a fine layer of hair covers the head. A grasping reflex is present and irregular breathing movements occur.

embryonic period The period of prenatal development that occurs from two to eight weeks after conception. During the embryonic period, the rate of cell differentiation intensifies, support systems for the cells form, and organs appear.

organogenesis Process of organ formation that takes place during the first two months of prenatal development.

fetal period The prenatal period of development that begins two months after conception and lasts for seven months, on average.

First trimester (first 3 months)

Conception to 4 weeks

- Is less than $1/10$ inch long
- Beginning development of spinal cord, nervous system, gastrointestinal system, heart, and lungs
- Amniotic sac envelops the preliminary tissues of entire body
- Is called a "zygote"

8 weeks

- Is just over 1 inch long
- Face is forming with rudimentary eyes, ears, mouth, and tooth buds
- Arms and legs are moving
- Brain is forming
- Fetal heartbeat is detectable with ultrasound
- Is called an "embryo"

12 weeks

- Is about 3 inches long and weighs about 1 ounce
- Can move arms, legs, fingers, and toes
- Fingerprints are present
- Can smile, frown, suck, and swallow
- Sex is distinguishable
- Can urinate
- Is called a "fetus"

Second trimester (middle 3 months)

16 weeks

- Is about 6 inches long and weighs about 4 to 7 ounces
- Heartbeat is strong
- Skin is thin, transparent
- Downy hair (lanugo) covers body
- Fingernails and toenails are forming
- Has coordinated movements; is able to roll over in amniotic fluid

20 weeks

- Is about 12 inches long and weighs close to 1 pound
- Heartbeat is audible with ordinary stethoscope
- Sucks thumb
- Hiccups
- Hair, eyelashes, eyebrows are present

24 weeks

- Is about 14 inches long and weighs 1 to $1\frac{1}{2}$ pounds
- Skin is wrinkled and covered with protective coating (vernix caseosa)
- Eyes are open
- Waste matter is collected in bowel
- Has strong grip

Third trimester (last 3 months)

28 weeks

- Is about 16 inches long and weighs about 3 pounds
- Is adding body fat
- Is very active
- Rudimentary breathing movements are present

32 weeks

- Is $16\frac{1}{2}$ to 18 inches long and weighs 4 to 5 pounds
- Has periods of sleep and wakefulness
- Responds to sounds
- May assume the birth position
- Bones of head are soft and flexible
- Iron is being stored in liver

36 to 38 weeks

- Is 19 to 20 inches long and weighs 6 to $7\frac{1}{2}$ pounds
- Skin is less wrinkled
- Vernix caseosa is thick
- Lanugo is mostly gone
- Is less active
- Is gaining immunities from mother

FIGURE **10**

THE THREE TRIMESTERS OF PRENATAL DEVELOPMENT. Both the germinal and embryonic periods occur during the first trimester. The end of the first trimester as well as the second and third trimesters are part of the fetal period.
(top to bottom): © David Spears/PhotoTake, Inc.; © Neil Bromhall/Science Source; © Brand X Pictures/PunchStock RF

As early as six months of pregnancy (about 24 to 25 weeks after conception), the fetus for the first time has a chance of surviving outside the womb—that is, it is *viable.* Infants that are born early, or between 24 and 37 weeks of pregnancy, usually need help breathing because their lungs are not yet fully mature. By the end of the seventh month, the fetus is about 16 inches long and now weighs about 3 pounds.

During the last two months of prenatal development, fatty tissues develop and the functioning of various organ systems—heart and kidneys, for example—steps up. During the eighth and ninth months, the fetus grows longer and gains substantial weight—about 4 more pounds. At birth, the average American baby weighs 7½ pounds and is about 20 inches long.

In addition to describing prenatal development in terms of germinal, embryonic, and fetal periods, prenatal development also can be divided into equal three-month periods, called *trimesters* (see Figure 10). Remember that the three trimesters are not the same as the three prenatal periods we have discussed. The germinal and embryonic periods occur in the first trimester. The fetal period begins toward the end of the first trimester and continues through the second and third trimesters.

The Brain   One of the most remarkable aspects of the prenatal period is the development of the brain (Dubois & others, 2014). By the time babies are born, they have approximately 100 billion **neurons,** or nerve cells, which handle information processing at the cellular level in the brain. During prenatal development, neurons move to specific locations and start to become connected. The basic architecture of the human brain is assembled during the first two trimesters of prenatal development. Typically, the third trimester of prenatal development and the first two years of postnatal life are characterized by connectivity and functioning of neurons (Nelson, 2013).

As the human embryo develops inside its mother's womb, the nervous system begins forming as a long, hollow tube located on the embryo's back. This pear-shaped *neural tube,* which forms at about 18 to 24 days after conception, develops out of the ecto- derm. The tube closes at the top and bottom at about 24 days after conception. Figure 11 shows that the nervous system still has a tubular appearance six weeks after conception.

Two birth defects related to a failure of the neural tube to close are anenceph- aly and spina bifida. When fetuses have *anencephaly* (that is, when the head end of the neural tube fails to close), the high- est regions of the brain fail to develop and death occurs in the womb, during childbirth, or shortly after birth (Reynolds, 2014). *Spina bifida*, an incomplete devel- opment of the spinal cord, results in varying degrees of paralysis of the lower limbs (Grivell, Andersen, & Dodd, 2014). Individuals with spina bifida usually need assistive devices such as crutches, braces, or wheelchairs. A strategy that can help to prevent neural tube defects is for women to take adequate amounts of the B vitamin folic acid, a topic we will discuss later in this chapter (Branum,

Yelyi Nordone, 12, of New York City, casts her line out into the pond during Camp Spifida at Camp Victory, near Millville, Pennsylvania, in July 2008. Camp Spifida is a weeklong residential camp for children with spina bifida.
© Bill Hughes/AP Images

FIGURE **11**

EARLY FORMATION OF THE NERVOUS SYSTEM. The photograph shows the primitive, tubular appearance of the nervous system at six weeks in the human embryo.
© Claude Edelmann/Science Source

Bailey, & Singer, 2013). Both maternal diabetes and obesity place the fetus at risk for developing neural tube defects (McMahon & others, 2013). Researchers also have found that a high level of maternal stress is linked to neural tube defects (Li & others, 2013).

Four important phases of the brain's development during the prenatal period involve (1) the neural tube, (2) neurogenesis, (3) neural migration, and (4) neural connectivity.

In a normal pregnancy, once the neural tube has closed, a massive proliferation of new immature neurons begins to take place at about the fifth prenatal week and continues through- out the remainder of the prenatal period. The generation of new neurons is called *neurogen esis* (Yang & others, 2015). At the peak of neurogenesis, it is estimated that as many as 200,000 neurons are being generated every minute.

At approximately 6 to 24 weeks after conception, *neuronal migration* occurs (Nelson, 2013). Cells begin moving outward from their point of origin to their appropriate locations and creating the different levels, structures, and regions of the brain. Once a cell has migrated to its target destination, it must mature and develop a more complex structure.

At about the 23rd prenatal week, connections between neurons begin to form, a process that continues postnatally (Kostovic, Judas, & Sedmak, 2011). We will have much more to say about the structure of neurons, their connectivity, and the development of the infant brain in the chapter on "Physical Development and Biological Aging."

developmental **connection**

Brain Development

At birth, infants' brains weigh approxi- mately 25 percent of what they will weigh in adulthood. Connect to "Physical Develop- ment and Biological Aging."

neurons Nerve cells that handle information processing at the cellular level.

PRENATAL DIAGNOSTIC TESTS

Together with her doctor, a pregnant woman will decide the extent to which she should undergo prenatal testing. A number of tests can indicate whether a fetus is developing normally; these include ultrasound sonography, fetal MRI, chorionic villus sampling, amniocentesis, and maternal blood screening. The decision to have a given test depends on several criteria, such as the mother's age, medical history, and genetic risk factors.

Ultrasound Sonography An ultrasound test is generally performed 7 weeks into a pregnancy and at various times later in pregnancy. *Ultrasound sonography* is a noninvasive prenatal medical procedure in which high-frequency sound waves are directed into the pregnant woman's abdomen (Ekin & others, 2014; Li & others, 2015). The echo from the sounds is transformed into a visual representation of the fetus's inner structures. This technique can detect many structural abnormalities in the fetus, including microencephaly, a form of intellectual disability involving an abnormally small brain; it can also give clues to the baby's sex and indicate whether there is more than one fetus (Chen & others, 2014a). Ultrasound results are available as soon as the images are read by a radiologist.

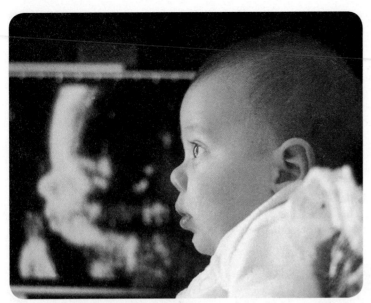

A 6-month-old infant poses with the ultrasound sonography record taken four months into the baby's prenatal development. *What is ultrasound sonography?*
© Jacques Pavlovsky/Sygma/Corbis

Fetal MRI The development of brain-imaging techniques has led to increasing use of *fetal MRI* to diagnose fetal malformations (Sanz-Cortes & others, 2015; Wu & others, 2014) (see Figure 12). MRI (magnetic resonance imaging) uses a powerful magnet and radio waves to generate detailed images of the body's organs and structures. Currently, ultrasound is still the first choice in fetal screening, but fetal MRI can provide more detailed images than ultrasound. In many instances, ultrasound will indicate a possible abnormality and fetal MRI will then be used to obtain a clearer, more detailed image (Koelblinger & others, 2013; Milani & others, 2015). Among the fetal malformations that fetal MRI may be able to detect better than ultrasound sonography are certain abnormalities of the central nervous system, chest, gastrointestinal tract, genital/urinary tract, and placenta (Malinger & Lerman-Sagie, 2015; Milesi & others, 2014; Mlczoch & others, 2014).

FIGURE **12**

A FETAL MRI, WHICH IS INCREASINGLY BEING USED IN PRENATAL DIAGNOSIS OF FETAL MALFORMATIONS
© Du Cane Medical Imaging Ltd./Science Source

Chorionic Villus Sampling At some point between the 10th and 12th weeks of pregnancy, chorionic villus sampling may be used to screen for genetic defects and chromosome abnormalities. *Chorionic villus sampling* (*CVS*) is a prenatal medical procedure in which a tiny tissue sample from the placenta is removed and analyzed (Gimovsky & others, 2014; Lankford & others, 2015). The results are available in about 10 days.

Amniocentesis Between the 15th and 18th weeks of pregnancy, *amniocentesis* may be performed. In this procedure, a sample of amniotic fluid is withdrawn by syringe and tested for chromosome or metabolic disorders (Ekblad & others, 2015; Menon & others, 2014). The later in the pregnancy amniocentesis is performed, the better its diagnostic potential. However, the earlier it is performed, the more useful it is in deciding how to handle a pregnancy when the fetus is found to have a disorder. It may take two weeks for enough cells to grow so that amniocentesis test results can be obtained. Amniocentesis brings a small risk of miscarriage: about 1 woman in every 200 to 300 miscarries after amniocentesis.

Maternal Blood Screening During the 16th to 18th weeks of pregnancy, maternal blood screening may be performed. *Maternal blood screening* identifies pregnancies that have an elevated risk for birth defects such as spina bifida and Down syndrome (Bernard & others, 2013; Sun & others, 2015). The current blood test is called the *triple screen* because it measures three substances in the mother's blood. After an abnormal triple screen result, the next step is usually an ultrasound examination. If an ultrasound does not explain the abnormal triple screen results, amniocentesis typically is used.

Fetal Sex Determination   Chorionic villus sampling has often been used to determine the sex of the fetus at some point between 11 and 13 weeks of gestation. Recently, though, some noninvasive techniques have been able to detect the sex of the fetus at an earlier point (Kolialexi, 2012; Moise & others, 2013; Wright & others, 2012). A recent meta-analysis of studies confirmed that a baby's sex can be detected as early as 7 weeks into pregnancy (Devaney & others, 2011). Being able to detect an offspring's sex as well as the presence of various diseases and defects at such an early stage raises ethical concerns about couples' motivation to terminate a pregnancy (Dickens, 2014).

HAZARDS TO PRENATAL DEVELOPMENT

For most babies, the course of prenatal development goes smoothly. Their mother's womb protects them as they develop. Despite this protection, however, the environment can affect the embryo or fetus in many well-documented ways.

General Principles   A **teratogen** is any agent that can potentially cause a birth defect or negatively alter cognitive and behavioral outcomes. The field of study that investigates the causes of birth defects is called *teratology* (Kancherla, Oakley, & Brent, 2014). Teratogens include drugs, incompatible blood types, environmental pollutants, infectious diseases, nutritional deficiencies, maternal stress, advanced maternal and paternal age, and environmental pollutants.

> **teratogen** Any agent that can potentially cause a birth defect or negatively alter cognitive and behavioral outcomes.

The dose, the genetic susceptibility, and the time of exposure to a particular teratogen influence both the severity of the damage to an embryo or fetus and the type of defect:

· *Dose* The dose effect is obvious—the greater the dose of an agent, such as a drug, the greater the effect.
· *Genetic Susceptibility* The type or severity of abnormalities caused by a teratogen is linked to the genotype of the pregnant woman and the genotype of the embryo or fetus. For example, how a mother metabolizes a particular drug can influence the degree to which the drug effects are transmitted to the embryo or fetus. Differences in placental membranes and placental transport also affect exposure. The extent to which an embryo or fetus is vulnerable to a teratogen may also depend on its genotype (de Planell-Saguer, Lovinsky-Desir, & Miller, 2014). Also, for unknown reasons, male fetuses are far more likely to be affected by teratogens than female fetuses are.
· *Time of Exposure* Teratogens do more damage at some points in development than at others. Damage during the germinal period may even prevent implantation. In general, the embryonic period is more vulnerable than the fetal period (Ortigosa Gomez & others, 2011).

Figure 13 summarizes additional information about the effects of time of exposure to a teratogen. The probability of a structural defect is greatest early in the embryonic period, when organs are being formed. Each body structure has its own critical period of formation (a fixed time period very early in development during which certain experiences or events can have a long-lasting effect on development). The critical period for the nervous system (week 3) is earlier than that for arms and legs (weeks 4 and 5).

After organogenesis is complete, teratogens are less likely to cause anatomical defects. Instead, exposure during the fetal period is more likely to stunt growth or to create problems in the way organs function. To examine some key teratogens and their effects, let's begin with drugs.

Prescription and Nonprescription Drugs   Prescription drugs that can function as teratogens include antibiotics, such as streptomycin and tetracycline; some antidepressants; certain hormones, such as progestin and synthetic estrogen; and Accutane (often prescribed for acne) (Gonzalez-Echavarri & others, 2015; Koren & Nordeng, 2012). Nonprescription

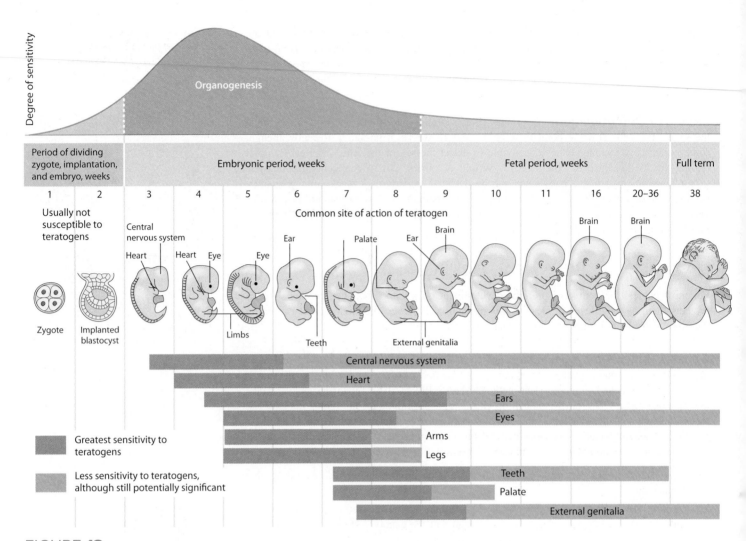

FIGURE 13

TERATOGENS AND THE TIMING OF THEIR EFFECTS ON PRENATAL DEVELOPMENT. The danger of structural defects caused by teratogens is greatest early in embryonic development. The period of organogenesis (red color) lasts for about six weeks. Later assaults by teratogens (blue color) mainly occur in the fetal period and instead of causing structural damage are more likely to stunt growth or cause problems of organ function.

drugs that can be harmful include diet pills and aspirin. Recent research revealed that low doses of aspirin pose no harm to the fetus but that high doses can contribute to maternal and fetal bleeding (Bennett, Bagot, & Arya, 2012).

Psychoactive Drugs *Psychoactive drugs* are drugs that act on the nervous system to alter states of consciousness, modify perceptions, and change moods. Examples include caffeine, alcohol, and nicotine, as well as illegal drugs such as cocaine and marijuana.

Caffeine People often consume caffeine by drinking coffee, tea, or colas, or by eating chocolate. A recent research review found that high amounts of caffeine consumption by pregnant women do not increase the risk of miscarriage, congenital malformations, or growth retardation (Brent, Christian, & Diener, 2011). However, the increased consumption of energy drinks that typically have extremely high levels of caffeine has not yet been studied. The U.S. Food and Drug Administration recommends that pregnant women either not consume caffeine or consume it only sparingly.

Alcohol Heavy drinking by pregnant women can be devastating to offspring. **Fetal alcohol spectrum disorders (FASD)** are a cluster of abnormalities and problems that appear in the offspring of mothers who drink alcohol heavily during pregnancy. The abnormalities include facial deformities and defective limbs, face, and heart. Most children with FASD have

fetal alcohol spectrum disorders (FASD) A cluster of abnormalities that may appear in the offspring of mothers who drink alcohol heavily during pregnancy.

learning problems, and many are below average in intelligence; some have an intellectual disability (Glass, Ware, & Mattson, 2014; Harper & others, 2014). Although mothers of FASD infants are heavy drinkers, many mothers who are heavy drinkers may not have children with FASD or may have one child with FASD and other children who do not have it.

What are some guidelines for alcohol use during pregnancy? Even drinking just one or two servings of beer or wine or one serving of hard liquor a few days a week can have negative effects on the fetus, although it is generally agreed that this level of alcohol use will not cause fetal alcohol spectrum disorders (Valenzuela & others, 2012). The U.S. Surgeon General recommends that no alcohol be consumed during pregnancy.

However, in Great Britain, the National Institutes of Care and Health Excellence have concluded that consuming one to two alcoholic drinks not more than twice a week is safe during pregnancy (O'Keeffe, Greene, & Kearney, 2014). A recent study of more than 7,000 7-year-olds found that children born to mothers who were light drinkers during pregnancy (up to two drinks per week) did not show more developmental problems than children born to non-drinking mothers (Kelly & others, 2013).

Nicotine   Cigarette smoking by pregnant women can adversely influence prenatal development, birth, and postnatal development. Preterm births and low birth weights, fetal and neonatal deaths, respiratory problems, sudden infant death syndrome (SIDS, also known as crib death), and cardiovascular problems are all more common among the offspring of mothers who smoked during pregnancy (Grabenhenrich & others, 2014; Ortigosa & others, 2012). Prenatal smoking has been implicated in as many as 25 percent of infants being born with a low birth weight (Brown & Graves, 2013). Researchers also have found that maternal smoking during pregnancy is a risk factor for the development of attention deficit hyperactivity disorder in children (Sagiv & others, 2012). Also, a recent study found that maternal smoking during pregnancy was associated with increased risk of asthma and wheezing in adolescence (Hollams & others, 2014). Further, in a recent research review, it was concluded that maternal use of electronic cigarettes during pregnancy is linked to alterations in a number of neurotransmitters in offspring, including serotonin and dopamine, and also elevated blood pressure in offspring when they are adults (Suter & others, 2015).

Smoking by pregnant women is not the only source of prenatal risk posed by tobacco use. Maternal exposure to environmental tobacco smoke, or secondhand smoke, has been linked to an increased risk of low birth weight in offspring (Salama & others, 2013) and to diminished ovarian functioning in female offspring (Kilic & others, 2012). And one study revealed that environmental tobacco smoke was associated with 114 deregulations of gene expression, especially those involving immune functioning, in the fetal cells of offspring (Votavova & others, 2012). Also, a recent study found that environmental tobacco smoke during prenatal development increased the risk of stillbirth (Varner & others, 2014).

Cocaine   Does cocaine use during pregnancy harm the developing embryo and fetus? A recent research study found that cocaine quickly crossed the placenta to reach the fetus (De Giovanni & Marchetti, 2012). The most consistent finding is that cocaine exposure during prenatal development is associated with reduced birth weight, length, and head circumference (Gouin & others, 2011; Ortigosa & others, 2012). In other studies, prenatal cocaine exposure has been linked to lower arousal, less effective self-regulation, higher excitability, and lower quality of reflexes at 1 month of age (Ackerman, Riggins, & Black, 2010; Lester & others, 2002); impaired motor development at 2 years of age and a slower rate of growth through 10 years of age (Richardson, Goldschmidt, & Williford, 2008); elevated blood pressure at 9 years of age (Shankaran & others, 2010); impaired language development and information processing (Beeghly & others, 2006) and attention deficits (especially in sustained attention) in preschool and elementary school children (Accornero & others, 2007; Ackerman, Riggins, & Black, 2010); increased likelihood of being in a special education program that offers support services (Levine & others, 2008); and increased

Fetal alcohol spectrum disorders (FASD) are characterized by a number of physical abnormalities and learning problems. Notice the wide-set eyes, flat cheekbones, and thin upper lip in this child with FASD.
Streissguth, AP, Landesman-Dwyer S, Martin, JC, & Smith, DW (1980). Teratogenic effects of alcohol in humans and laboratory animals. Science, 209, 353-361

In what ways are expectant mothers' alcohol and nicotine intake linked to outcomes for their offspring?
© Bubbles Photolibrary/Alamy

This baby was exposed to cocaine prenatally. *What are some of the possible effects on development of being exposed to cocaine prenatally?*
© Chuck Nacke/Alamy

developmental **connection**

Conditions, Diseases, Disorders

The greatest incidence of HIV/AIDS occurs in sub-Saharan Africa, where in some areas as many as 30 percent of mothers have HIV; many are unaware that they are infected with the virus. Connect to "Gender and Sexuality."

behavioral problems, especially externalizing problems such as high rates of aggression and delinquency (Minnes & others, 2010; Richardson & others, 2011).

Some researchers argue that these findings should be interpreted cautiously (Accornero & others, 2007). Why? Because other factors in the lives of pregnant women who use cocaine (such as poverty, malnutrition, and other substance abuse) often cannot be ruled out as possible contributors to the problems found in their children (Hurt & others, 2005; Messiah & others, 2011). For example, cocaine users are more likely than nonusers to smoke cigarettes, use marijuana, drink alcohol, and take amphetamines.

Despite these cautions, the weight of research evidence indicates that children born to mothers who use cocaine are likely to have neurological, medical, and cognitive deficits (Cain, Bornick, & Whiteman, 2013; Field, 2007; Mayer & Zhang, 2009; Richardson & others, 2011). Cocaine use by pregnant women is never recommended.

Marijuana An increasing number of studies find that marijuana use by pregnant women also has negative outcomes for their offspring. For example, one study found that prenatal marijuana exposure was related to lower intelligence in children (Goldschmidt & others, 2008). Another study indicated that prenatal exposure to marijuana was linked to marijuana use at 14 years of age (Day, Goldschmidt, & Thomas, 2006). And a recent study discovered that marijuana use by pregnant women was associated with stillbirth (Varner & others, 2014). In sum, marijuana use is not recommended for pregnant women.

Maternal Diseases Maternal diseases and infections can produce defects in offspring by crossing the placental barrier, or they can cause damage during birth (Brunell, 2014). Rubella (German measles) is one disease that can cause prenatal defects. Women who plan to have children should have a blood test before they become pregnant to determine whether they are immune to the disease (Ogbuanu & others, 2014).

Syphilis (a sexually transmitted infection) is more damaging later in prenatal development—four months or more after conception. When syphilis is present at birth, problems can develop in the central nervous system and gastrointestinal tract (Qin & others, 2014). Most states require that pregnant women be given a blood test to detect the presence of syphilis.

Another infection that has received widespread attention recently is genital herpes. Newborns contract this virus when they are delivered through the birth canal of a mother with genital herpes (Sudfeld & others, 2013). If an active case of genital herpes is detected in a pregnant woman close to her delivery date, a cesarean section (in which the infant is delivered through an incision in the mother's abdomen) can be performed to keep the virus from infecting the newborn.

AIDS is a sexually transmitted infection that is caused by the human immunodeficiency virus (HIV), which destroys the body's immune system. A mother can infect her offspring with HIV/AIDS in three ways: (1) across the placenta during gestation, (2) through contact with maternal blood or fluids during delivery, and (3) through breast feeding. The transmission of AIDS through breast feeding is a particular problem in many developing countries (UNICEF, 2014). Babies born to HIV-infected mothers can be (1) infected and symptomatic (show HIV symptoms), (2) infected but asymptomatic (not show HIV symptoms), or (3) not infected at all. An infant who is infected and asymptomatic may still develop HIV symptoms up to 15 months of age.

Maternal Diet and Nutrition A developing embryo or fetus depends completely on its mother for nutrition, which comes from the mother's blood. The nutritional status of the embryo or fetus is determined by the mother's total caloric intake as well as her intake of proteins, vitamins, and minerals. Children born to malnourished mothers are more likely than other children to be malformed.

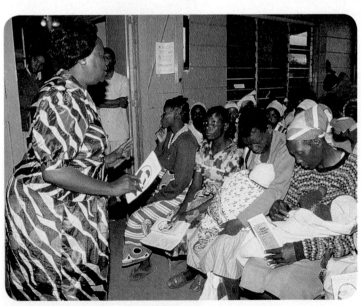

Because the fetus depends entirely on its mother for nutrition, it is important for the pregnant woman to have good nutritional habits. In Kenya, this government clinic provides pregnant women with information about how their diet can influence the health of their fetus and offspring. *What might the information about diet be like?*
© Betty Press/Woodfin Camp & Associates

Being overweight before and during pregnancy can also put the embryo or fetus at risk, and an increasing number of pregnant women in the United States are overweight (Finer & others, 2015; Murray & McKinney, 2014). Maternal obesity adversely affects pregnancy outcomes through elevated rates of hypertension, diabetes, respiratory complications, and infections in the mother (Nodine & Hastings-Tolsma, 2012). Recent research studies have found that maternal obesity is linked to an increase in stillbirth (Gardosi & others, 2013) and an increased likelihood that the newborn will be placed in a neonatal intensive care unit (Minsart & others, 2013). Further, a recent research review concluded that maternal obesity during pregnancy is associated with an increased likelihood of offspring being obese in childhood and adulthood (Santangeli, Sattar, & Huda, 2015). Management of obesity that includes weight loss and increased exercise prior to pregnancy is likely to benefit the mother and the baby (Vesco & others, 2012).

One aspect of maternal nutrition that is important for normal prenatal development is folic acid, a B-complex vitamin (Kancherla, Oakley, & Brent, 2014). Also, as indicated earlier, lack of folic acid is related to neural tube defects in offspring (Reynolds, 2014). The U.S. Department of Health and Human Services (2014) recommends that pregnant women consume a minimum of 400 micrograms of folic acid per day (about twice the amount the average woman gets in one day). Orange juice and spinach are examples of foods that are rich in folic acid.

Emotional States and Stress

When a pregnant woman experiences intense fears, anxieties, and other emotions or negative mood states, physiological changes occur that may affect her fetus (Howerton & Bale, 2012). A mother's stress may also influence the fetus indirectly by increasing the likelihood that the mother will engage in unhealthy behaviors such as taking drugs and receiving poor prenatal care.

High maternal anxiety and stress during pregnancy can have long-term consequences for the offspring (Brunton, 2015; Schuurmans & Kurrasch, 2013; Rash & others, 2015). A recent study found that high levels of depression, anxiety, and stress during pregnancy were linked to internalizing problems in adolescence (Betts & others, 2014). A research review indicated that pregnant women with high levels of stress are at increased risk for having a child with emotional or cognitive problems, attention deficit hyperactivity disorder (ADHD), and language delay (Taige & others, 2007). Another study revealed that maternal stressful life events prior to conception increased the risk of having a very low birth weight infant (Witt & others, 2014).

Might maternal depression also have an adverse effect on birth outcomes? Recent research indicates that maternal depression during pregnancy is linked to preterm birth and low birth weight (Mparmpakas & others, 2013). And a recent study discovered that maternal depression during pregnancy was associated with low birth weight in full-term offspring (Chang & others, 2014).

Maternal Age

When possible harmful effects on the fetus and infant are considered, two maternal age groups are of special interest: adolescents and women 35 years and older (de Jongh & others, 2015; Rudang & others, 2012). The mortality rate of infants born to adolescent mothers is double that of infants born to mothers in their twenties. Adequate prenatal care decreases the probability that a

What are some of the risks for infants born to adolescent mothers?
© Barbara Penoyar/Getty Images RF

- - - - - - - - - ->
developmental **connection**

Health

What are some key factors that influence whether individuals will become obese? Connect to "Health."

How do pregnant women's emotional states and stress levels affect prenatal development and birth?
© Rafal Strzechowski/age fotostock

- - - - - - - - - ->
developmental **connection**

Sexuality

Adolescent pregnancy creates negative developmental trajectories for mothers and their offspring. Connect to "Gender and Sexuality."

An explosion at the Chernobyl nuclear power plant in Ukraine produced radioactive contamination that spread to surrounding areas. Thousands of infants were born with health problems and deformities as a result of the nuclear contamination, including this boy whose right arm did not form. *Other than radioactive contamination, what are some other types of environmental hazards to prenatal development?*
© Sergey Guneev/RIA Novosti

child born to an adolescent girl will have physical problems. However, adolescents are the least likely age group to obtain prenatal assistance from clinics and health services.

Maternal age is also linked to the risk that a child will have Down syndrome (Ghosh & others, 2010). A baby with Down syndrome rarely is born to a mother 16 to 34 years of age. However, when the mother reaches 40 years of age, the probability is slightly over 1 in 100 that a baby born to her will have Down syndrome, and by age 50 it is almost 1 in 10. When mothers are 35 years and older, risks also increase for low birth weight, preterm delivery, and fetal death (Koo & others, 2012). A recent Norwegian study found that maternal age of 30 years or older was linked to the same level of increased risk for fetal deaths as that of 25- to 29-year-old pregnant women who were overweight/obese or were smokers (Waldenstrom & others, 2014).

We still have much to learn about the effects of the mother's age on pregnancy and childbirth. As women remain active, exercise regularly, and are careful about their nutrition, their reproductive systems may remain healthier at older ages than was thought possible in the past.

Environmental Hazards   Many aspects of our modern industrial world can endanger the embryo or fetus (Lin & others, 2013). Some specific hazards to the embryo or fetus include radiation, toxic wastes, and other chemical pollutants.

Women and their physicians should weigh the risk of an X-ray when the woman is or might be pregnant (Baysinger, 2010). However, a routine diagnostic X-ray of a body area other than the abdomen, with the woman's abdomen protected by a lead apron, is generally considered safe (Brent, 2009, 2011).

Paternal Factors   So far, we have discussed how characteristics of the mother—such as drug use, disease, diet and nutrition, age, and emotional states—can influence prenatal development and the development of the child. Might there also be some paternal risk factors? Indeed, there are several (Pedersen & others, 2014). Men's exposure to lead, radiation, certain pesticides, and petrochemicals may cause abnormalities in sperm that lead to miscarriage or diseases such as childhood cancer (Cordier, 2008). The father's smoking during the mother's pregnancy also can cause problems for the offspring. In one study, heavy paternal smoking was associated with the risk of early miscarriage (Venners & others, 2004). This negative outcome may be related to maternal exposure to secondhand smoke. And in a recent study, paternal smoking around the time of the child's conception was linked to an increased risk of the child developing leukemia (Milne & others, 2012). Also, a recent research review concluded that there is an increased risk of spontaneous abortion (miscarriage), autism, and schizophrenic disorders when the father is 40 years of age or older (Liu & others, 2012). And a recent research study revealed that children born to fathers who were 40 years of age or older had increased risk of developing autism because of an increase in random gene mutations in older fathers (Kong & others, 2012). However, the age of the offspring's mother was not linked to development of autism in children.

The father may contribute to positive outcomes for the fetus by providing support and having a positive attitude toward the pregnancy. Earlier you read about how maternal stress and depression have negative developmental outcomes for offspring. Fathers can play an important role in helping mothers keep their stress and depression levels lower by contributing to a positive marital relationship, not engaging in spousal abuse, sharing more in household tasks, and participating in childbirth classes.

PRENATAL CARE

Although prenatal care varies enormously from one woman to another, it usually involves a defined schedule of visits for medical care, which typically includes screening for manageable conditions and treatable diseases that can affect the baby or the mother. In addition to medical care, prenatal programs often include comprehensive educational, social, and nutritional services. Information about pregnancy, labor, delivery, and caring for the newborn can be especially valuable for first-time mothers (Yun & others, 2014).

In one study in China, the longer fathers smoked, the greater the risk that their children would develop cancer (Ji and others, 1997). *What are some other paternal factors that can influence the development of the fetus and the child?*
© David Butow/Corbis

Prenatal care is also very important for women in poverty and immigrant women because it links them with other social services (Lyberg & others, 2012).

An innovative program that is rapidly expanding in the United States is CenteringPregnancy (Foster & others, 2012; Hale & others, 2014). This program is relationship-centered and provides complete prenatal care in a group setting. It replaces traditional 15-minute physician visits with 90-minute peer group support sessions and self-examination led by a physician or certified nurse-midwife. Groups of up to 10 women (and often their partners) meet regularly beginning at 12 to 16 weeks of pregnancy. The sessions emphasize empowering women to play an active role in experiencing a positive pregnancy. A recent study revealed that participants in CenteringPregnancy groups made more prenatal visits, had higher breast-feeding rates, and were more satisfied with their prenatal care than were women in individual care (Klima & others, 2009). In another recent study, high-stress women were randomly assigned to a CenteringPregnancy Plus group, group prenatal care, or standard individual care from 18 weeks gestation to birth (Ickovics & others, 2011). The most stressed women in the CenteringPregnancy Plus group showed increased self-esteem and decreased stress and social conflict in their third trimester of pregnancy; their social conflict and depression also were lower at one year postpartum.

A CenteringPregnancy program. This increasing popular program alters routine prenatal care by bringing women out of exam rooms and into relationship-oriented groups.
© Jose Luis Pelaez Inc./Blend Images/Getty Images RF

Review Connect Reflect

 LG4 Characterize the course of prenatal development and its hazards

Review

- What is the course of prenatal development? How does the brain develop during the prenatal period?
- What are some prenatal diagnostic tests?
- What are some of the main hazards to prenatal development?
- What types of resources do prenatal care programs provide?

Connect

- In a previous section of this chapter we discussed chromosomal and gene-linked abnormalities that can affect prenatal development. How are the symptoms of the related conditions or risks similar to or different from those caused by prenatal exposure to teratogens or other hazards?

Reflect *Your Own Personal Journey of Life*

- If you are a woman, imagine that you have just found out that you are pregnant. What health-enhancing strategies will you follow during the prenatal period? For others, imagine that you are the partner of a woman who has just found out she is pregnant. What will be your role in increasing the likelihood that the prenatal period will go smoothly?

5 Birth and the Postpartum Period

LG5 Summarize how birth takes place and describe the nature of the postpartum period

| The Birth Process | The Transition from Fetus to Newborn | Low Birth Weight and Preterm Infants | Bonding | The Postpartum Period |

The long wait for the moment of birth is over, and the infant is about to appear. What happens during childbirth, and what can be done to make the experience a positive one? Nature writes the basic script for how birth occurs, but parents make important choices about the conditions surrounding birth. We will look first at the sequence of physical steps through which a child is born.

There was a star danced, and under that I was born.

—**WILLIAM SHAKESPEARE**
English playwright, 17th century

After the long journey of prenatal development, birth takes place. During birth the baby is on a threshold between two worlds. *What is the fetus/newborn transition like?*
© Jonathan Nourok/Getty Images

In India, a midwife checks on the size, position, and heartbeat of a fetus. Midwives deliver babies in many cultures around the world. *What are some cultural variations in prenatal care?*
© Viviane Moos/Corbis

doula A caregiver who provides continuous physical, emotional, and educational support for the mother before, during, and after childbirth.

natural childbirth A childbirth method that attempts to reduce the mother's pain by decreasing her fear through education about childbirth stages and relaxation techniques during delivery.

THE BIRTH PROCESS

The birth process occurs in three stages. It may take place in different contexts and in most cases involves one or more attendants.

Stages of Birth   The first stage of the birth process is the longest. Uterine contractions are 15 to 20 minutes apart at the beginning and last up to a minute each. These contractions cause the woman's cervix to stretch and open. As the first stage progresses, the contractions come closer together, occurring every two to five minutes. Their intensity increases. By the end of the first stage, contractions dilate the cervix to an opening of about 10 centimeters (4 inches), so that the baby can move from the uterus to the birth canal. For a woman having her first child, the first stage lasts an average of 6 to 12 hours; for subsequent children, this stage typically is much shorter.

The second birth stage begins when the baby's head starts to move through the cervix and the birth canal. It terminates when the baby completely emerges from the mother's body. With each contraction, the mother bears down hard to push the baby out of her body. By the time the baby's head is out of the mother's body, the contractions come almost every minute and last for about a minute each. This stage typically lasts approximately 45 minutes to an hour.

Afterbirth is the third stage, during which the placenta, umbilical cord, and other membranes are detached and expelled from the uterus. This final stage is the shortest of the three birth stages, lasting only a few minutes.

Childbirth Setting and Attendants   In 2011 in the United States, 98.7 percent of births took place in hospitals (Martin & others, 2013). Of the 1.3 percent of births occurring outside of a hospital, approximately two-thirds took place in homes and almost 30 percent in free-standing birthing centers. The percentage of U.S. births at home is the highest since reporting of this context began in 1989. An increase in home births has occurred mainly among non-Latino White women, especially those who were older and married. For these non-Latino White women, two-thirds of their home births are attended by a midwife.

In U.S. hospitals, it has become the norm for the baby's father or a birth coach to be with the mother throughout labor and delivery. In the East African Nigoni culture, men are completely excluded from the childbirth process. When a woman is ready to give birth, female relatives move into the woman's hut and the husband leaves, taking his belongings (clothes, tools, weapons, and so on) with him. He is not permitted to return until after the baby is born. In some cultures, childbirth is an open, community affair. For example, in the Pukapukan culture in the Pacific Islands, women give birth in a shelter that is open to villagers, who may observe the birth.

Midwives   *Midwifery* is practiced in most countries throughout the world (Moulton, 2014). In Holland, more than 40 percent of babies are delivered by midwives rather than by doctors. However, in 2010 only 8 percent of women who delivered a baby in the United States were attended by a midwife, a figure that is unchanged since 2000 (Martin & others, 2012). Nevertheless, the 8 percent figure for 2010 represents a substantial increase from less than 1 percent in 1975.

Doulas   In some countries, a doula attends a childbearing woman. *Doula* is a Greek word that means "a woman who helps." A **doula** is a caregiver who provides continuous physical, emotional, and educational support for the mother before, during, and after childbirth. Doulas remain with the parents throughout labor, assessing and responding to their needs. Researchers have found positive effects when a doula is present at the birth of a child (Kang, 2014; Torres,

2013). A recent study found that doula-assisted mothers were four times less likely to have a low birth weight baby and two times less likely to experience a birth complication involving themselves or their baby (Gruber, Cupito, & Dobson, 2013).

In the United States, most doulas work as independent service providers hired by the expectant parents. Doulas typically function as part of a "birthing team," serving as an adjunct to the midwife or the hospital's obstetric staff.

Methods of Childbirth   U.S. hospitals often allow the mother and her obstetrician a range of options regarding their method of delivery. Key choices involve the use of medication, whether to use any of a number of nonmedicated techniques to reduce pain, and when to have a cesarean delivery.

Medication   Three basic kinds of drugs that are used for labor are analgesia, anesthesia, and oxytocin/Pitocin. *Analgesia* is used to relieve pain. Analgesics include tranquilizers, barbiturates, and narcotics such as Demerol.

Predicting how a drug will affect an individual woman and her fetus is difficult (Lowdermilk, Cashion, & Perry, 2014). A particular drug might have only a minimal effect on one fetus yet have a much stronger effect on another. The drug's dosage is also a factor. Higher doses of tranquilizers and narcotics given to decrease the mother's pain potentially have a more negative effect on the fetus than do lower doses. It is important for the mother to assess her level of pain and have a voice in the decision as to whether or not she should receive medication.

Natural and Prepared Childbirth   For a brief time not long ago, the idea of avoiding all medication during childbirth gained favor in the United States. Instead, many women chose to reduce the pain of childbirth through techniques known as natural childbirth and prepared childbirth. Today, at least some medication is used in the typical childbirth, but elements of natural childbirth and prepared childbirth remain popular (Oates & Abraham, 2010).

A doula assisting a birth. *What types of support do doulas provide?*
© 13/Andersen Ross/Ocean/Corbis RF

Natural childbirth is a childbirth method in which no drugs are given to relieve pain or assist in the birth process. The mother and her partner are taught to use breathing methods and relaxation techniques during delivery. French obstetrician Ferdinand Lamaze developed a method similar to natural childbirth that is known as **prepared childbirth,** or the Lamaze method. It includes a special breathing technique to control pushing in the final stages of labor, as well as detailed education about anatomy and physiology. The Lamaze method has become very popular in the United States.

prepared childbirth Developed by French obstetrician Ferdinand Lamaze, a childbirth strategy similar to natural childbirth but one that teaches a special breathing technique to control pushing in the final stages of labor and provides details about anatomy and physiology.

The pregnant woman's partner usually serves as her labor coach; he attends childbirth classes with her and guides her breathing and relaxation during labor and delivery. In sum, proponents of current prepared childbirth methods conclude that when information and support are provided, women know how to give birth.

Other Nonmedicated Techniques to Reduce Pain   The effort to reduce stress and control pain during labor has recently led to an increase in the use of some older and some newer nonmedicated techniques (Henderson & others, 2014; Simkin & Bolding, 2004). These include waterbirth, massage, and acupuncture.

Waterbirth involves giving birth in a tub of warm water. Some women go through labor in the water and get out for delivery; others remain in the water for delivery. The

An instructor conducting a Lamaze class. *What characterizes the Lamaze method of prepared childbirth?*
© Barros & Barros/Getty Images RF

What characterizes the use of waterbirth in delivering a baby?
© Eddie Lawrence/Science Source

rationale for waterbirth is that the baby has been in an amniotic sac for many months and therefore delivery in a similar environment is likely to be less stressful for the baby and the mother. Mothers get into the warm water when contractions become closer together and more intense. Getting into the water too soon can cause labor to slow or stop. Reviews of research have indicated mixed results for waterbirths (Cluett & Burns, 2009; Dahlen & others, 2013; Pinette, Wax, & Wilson, 2004; Nutter & others, 2014). One study did find that waterbirth was linked with a shorter second stage of labor (Cortes, Basra, & Kelleher, 2011). Waterbirth has been practiced more often in European countries such as Switzerland and Sweden than in the United States in recent decades, but it is increasingly being included in U.S. birth plans.

Massage is increasingly used as a procedure prior to and during delivery (Beckmann & Stock, 2013). Two recent research reviews concluded that massage therapy reduced pain during labor (Jones & others, 2012; Smith & others, 2012).

Acupuncture, the insertion of very fine needles into specific locations in the body, is used as a standard procedure to reduce the pain of childbirth in China, although it only recently has begun to be used for this purpose in the United States and Europe (Betts, Smith, & Hannah, 2012). Recent research indicates that acupuncture can have positive effects on labor and delivery (Citkovitz, Schnyer, & Hoskins, 2011).

Cesarean Delivery   Normally, the baby's head comes through the vagina first. But if the baby is in a *breech position,* its buttocks are the first part to emerge from the vagina. In 1 of every 25 deliveries, the baby's head is still in the uterus when the rest of the body is out. Because breech births can cause respiratory problems, if the baby is in a breech position a surgical procedure known as a cesarean delivery is usually performed. In a *cesarean* delivery (or cesarean section), the baby is removed from the uterus through an incision made in the mother's abdomen (Glavind & Uldbjerg, 2015). More cesarean sections are performed in the United States than in any other country in the world. In 2011, 32.8% of births in the United States were cesarean deliveries, unchanged from 2010 (Martin & others, 2013). The benefits and risks of cesarean deliveries continue to be debated in the United States and around the world (Furukawa, Sameshima, & Ikenoue, 2014; O'Neill & others, 2013).

THE TRANSITION FROM FETUS TO NEWBORN

Much of our discussion of birth so far has focused on the mother. However, birth also involves considerable stress for the baby. If the delivery takes too long, the baby can develop *anoxia*, a condition in which the fetus or newborn has an insufficient supply of oxygen. Anoxia can cause brain damage.

What characterizes the transition from fetus to newborn?
© ERproductions Ltd/Blend Images LLC RF

Apgar Scale A widely used method to assess the health of newborns at one and five minutes after birth; it evaluates an infant's heart rate, respiratory effort, muscle tone, body color, and reflex irritability.

The baby has considerable capacity to withstand the stress of birth. Large quantities of adrenaline and noradrenaline, hormones that protect the fetus in the event of oxygen deficiency, are secreted in the newborn's body during the birth process (Van Beveren, 2011).

Immediately after birth, the umbilical cord is cut and the baby begins to breathe on its own. Before birth, oxygen came from the mother via the umbilical cord, but a full-term baby's lungs are sufficiently developed to support independent breathing.

Almost immediately after birth, a newborn is weighed, cleaned up, and tested for signs of developmental problems that might require urgent attention. The **Apgar Scale** is widely used to assess the health of newborns at one and five minutes after birth. The Apgar Scale evaluates infants' heart rate, respiratory effort, muscle tone, body color, and reflex irritability (see Figure 14). An obstetrician or nurse does the evaluation and gives the newborn a score, or reading, of 0, 1, or 2 on each of these five health signs. A total score of 7 to 10 indicates that the newborn's condition is good. A score of 5 indicates that there may be developmental difficulties. A score of 3 or below signals an emergency and warns that the baby might not survive. The Apgar Scale is especially good at assessing the newborn's ability to respond to the stress of delivery and to adapt to its new environment (Miyakoshi & others, 2013). It also

Score	0	1	2
Heart rate	Absent	Slow—less than 100 beats per minute	Fast—100–140 beats per minute
Respiratory effort	No breathing for more than one minute	Irregular and slow	Good breathing with normal crying
Muscle tone	Limp and flaccid	Weak, inactive, but some flexion of extremities	Strong, active motion
Body color	Blue and pale	Body pink, but extremities blue	Entire body pink
Reflex irritability	No response	Grimace	Coughing, sneezing and crying

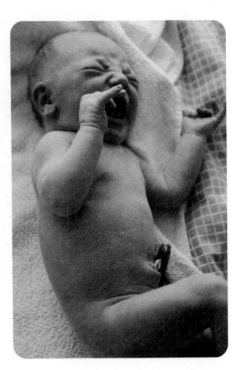

FIGURE 14

THE APGAR SCALE. A newborn's score on the Apgar Scale indicates whether the baby has urgent medical problems.
© altrendo images/Getty Images RF

identifies high-risk infants who need resuscitation. A recent study revealed that in comparison with children who had a high Apgar score (9 to 10), the risk of developing attention deficit hyperactivity disorder (ADHD) in childhood was 75 percent higher for newborns with a low Apgar score (1 to 4) and 63 percent higher for those with an Apgar score of 5 or 6 (Li & others, 2011).

Nurses often play important roles in the birth of a baby. To read about the work of a nurse who specializes in caring for women during labor and delivery, see *Connecting with Careers.*

connecting with careers

Linda Pugh, Perinatal Nurse

Perinatal nurses work with childbearing women to support health and growth during the childbearing experience. Linda Pugh, Ph.D., R.N.C., is a perinatal nurse on the faculty at The Johns Hopkins University School of Nursing. She is certified as an inpatient obstetric nurse and specializes in the care of women during labor and delivery. She teaches undergraduate and graduate students, educates professional nurses, and conducts research. In addition, Pugh consults with hospitals and organizations about women's health issues and many of the topics we discuss in this chapter. Her research interests include implementing nursing interventions with low-income breast-feeding women, discovering ways to prevent and ameliorate fatigue during childbearing, and using breathing exercises during labor.

Linda Pugh (*right*), assisting a mother and her newborn infant.
Courtesy of Linda Pugh

A "kilogram kid," weighing less than 2.3 pounds at birth. *What are some long-term outcomes for infants who weigh so little at birth?*
© Diether Endlicher/AP Images

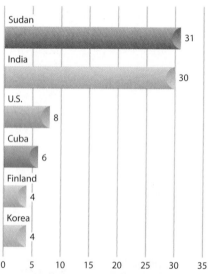

Percentage of infants born with low birth weight

FIGURE 15

PERCENTAGE OF INFANTS BORN WITH LOW BIRTH WEIGHT IN SELECTED COUNTRIES

low birth weight infants Infants who weigh less than 5½ pounds at birth.

preterm infants Infants born three weeks or more before the pregnancy has reached its full term.

small for date infants Infants whose birth weights are below normal when the length of pregnancy is considered; also called small for gestational age infants. Small for date infants may be preterm or full-term.

LOW BIRTH WEIGHT AND PRETERM INFANTS

Three related conditions pose threats to many newborns: low birth weight, preterm birth, and being small for date. **Low birth weight infants** weigh less than 5½ pounds at birth. *Very low birth weight* newborns weigh less than 3 pounds, and *extremely low birth weight* newborns weigh less than 2 pounds. **Preterm infants** are born three weeks or more before the pregnancy has reached its full term—in other words, 35 or fewer weeks after conception. **Small for date infants** (also called *small for gestational age infants*) have a birth weight that is below normal when the length of the pregnancy is considered. They weigh less than 90 percent of all babies of the same gestational age. Small for date infants may be preterm or full term. One study found that small for date infants have a 400 percent greater risk of death (Regev & others, 2003).

In 2013, 11.4 percent of U.S. infants were born preterm—a 34 percent increase since the 1980s but a decrease of 1.4 percent since 2008 (Lynch, Dezen, & Brown, 2012; March of Dimes, 2014). The increase in preterm births is likely due to such factors as the increasing number of births to women 35 years of age or older, increasing rates of multiple births, increased management of maternal and fetal conditions (for example, inducing labor preterm if medical technology indicates that it will increase the likelihood of survival), increased rates of substance abuse (including tobacco and alcohol), and increased stress. Ethnic variations characterize preterm birth. For example, in 2013, the likelihood of being born preterm was 11.4 percent for all U.S. infants and 10.4 percent for non-Latino White infants, but the rate was 16.8 percent for African American infants and 11.7 for Latino infants (March of Dimes, 2014).

Most, but not all, preterm babies are also low birth weight babies. The incidence of low birth weight varies considerably from country to country. In some countries, such as India and Sudan, where poverty is rampant and the health and nutrition of mothers are poor, the percentage of low birth weight babies reaches as high as 31 percent (See Figure 15). In the United States, there has been an increase in low birth weight infants in the last two decades, and the U.S. low birth weight rate of 8.1 percent in 2011 is considerably higher than that of many other developed countries (Martin & others, 2013). For example, only 4 percent of the infants born in Sweden, Finland, Norway, and Korea are low birth weight, and only 5 percent of those born in New Zealand, Australia, and France are low birth weight.

Consequences of Low Birth Weight Although most preterm and low birth weight infants are healthy, as a group they have more health and developmental problems than do infants of normal birth weight (Bassil & others, 2014). For preterm birth, the terms *extremely preterm* and *very preterm* are increasingly used (Webb & others, 2014). *Extremely preterm infants* are those born at less than 28 weeks gestation, and *very preterm infants* are those born between 28 and 33 weeks of gestational age.

The number and severity of these problems increase when infants are born very early and as their birth weight decreases (Castrodale & Rinehart, 2014; Griffin & others, 2015). Survival rates for infants who are born very early and very small have risen, but with this improved survival rate have come increased rates of severe brain damage (McNicholas & others, 2014). A recent study revealed that very preterm, low birth weight infants had abnormal axon development in their brains and impaired cognitive development at 9 years of age (Iwata & others, 2012). Low birth weight children are more likely than their normal birth weight counterparts to develop a learning disability, attention deficit hyperactivity disorder, autism spectrum disorders, or breathing problems such as asthma (Anderson & others, 2011; Dudova & others, 2014; Maramara, He, & Ming, 2014). Approximately 50 percent of all low birth weight children are enrolled in special education programs. And a recent study in four Asian countries revealed that very low birth weight infants were likely to have a much higher mortality rate as neonates (Wariki & others, 2013).

Nurturing Low Birth Weight and Preterm Infants

Two increasingly used interventions in the neonatal intensive care unit (NICU) are kangaroo care and massage therapy. **Kangaroo care** involves skin-to-skin contact in which the baby, wearing only a diaper, is held upright against the parent's bare chest, much as a baby kangaroo is carried by its mother. Kangaroo care is typically practiced for two to three hours per day over an extended time in early infancy.

A new mother practicing kangaroo care. *What is kangaroo care?*
© iStockPhoto.com/casenbina RF

Why use kangaroo care with preterm infants? Preterm infants often have difficulty coordinating their breathing and heart rate, and the close physical contact with the parent provided by kangaroo care can help stabilize the preterm infant's heartbeat, temperature, and breathing (Mitchell & others, 2013). Preterm infants who experience kangaroo care also gain more weight than their counterparts who are not given this care (Ahmed & others, 2011). Recent research also revealed that kangaroo care decreased pain responses in preterm infants (Cong, Ludington-Hoe, & Walsh, 2011). Also, a recent study found that preterm infants who experienced kangaroo care for 16 weeks had more complex electroencephalogram (EEG) patterns (which reflects neurological maturation) at 40 weeks of age than did preterm infants who had not received kangaroo care (Kaffashi & others, 2013). A recent study revealed that kangaroo care led to better physical development in low birth weight infants (Bera & others, 2014). And a recent research review concluded that kangaroo mother care with low birth weight babies was associated with a reduction in the risk of the babies' mortality (Conde-Agudelo & Diaz-Rossello, 2014). Further, a recent study demonstrated the positive long-term benefits of kangaroo care (Feldman, Rosenthal, & Eidelman, 2014). In this study, maternal-newborn kangaroo care with preterm infants was linked to better respiratory and cardiovascular functioning, sleep patterns, and cognitive functioning from 6 months to 10 years of age.

A recent U.S. survey found that mothers had a much more positive view of kangaroo care than did neonatal intensive care nurses and that the mothers were more likely to think it should be provided daily (Hendricks-Munoz & others, 2013). There is concern that kangaroo care is not used as often as it could be used in neonatal intensive care units (Davanzo & others, 2013; Kymre, 2014; Stikes & Barbier, 2013). Increasingly, kangaroo care is recommended as standard practice for all newborns (Rodgers, 2013).

In addition to kangaroo care, another technique to improve the development of preterm infants is massage therapy. To read about research on massage therapy, see the *Connecting with Research* interlude.

---

developmental **connection**

Attachment

A classic study with surrogate cloth and wire monkeys demonstrates the important role that touch plays in infant attachment. Connect to "Emotional Development and Attachment."

BONDING

A special component of the parent-infant relationship is **bonding,** the formation of a connection, especially a physical bond, between parents and their newborn infant during the period shortly after birth. In the mid-twentieth century, U.S. hospitals seemed almost determined to deter bonding. Anesthesia given to the mother during delivery would make the mother drowsy, interfering with her ability to respond to and stimulate the newborn. Mothers and newborns were often separated shortly after delivery, and preterm infants were isolated from their mothers even more than full-term infants were. In recent decades these practices have changed, but to some extent they are still followed in many hospitals.

Do these practices do any harm? Some physicians believe that during the "critical period" shortly after birth the parents and newborn need to form an emotional attachment as a foundation for optimal development in the years to come (Kennell, 2006; Kennell & McGrath, 1999). Although some research supports this bonding hypothesis (Klaus & Kennell, 1976), a body of research challenges the significance of the first few days of life as a critical period (Bakeman & Brown, 1980; Rode & others, 1981). Indeed, the extreme form of the bonding

developmental **connection**

Attachment

Lorenz demonstrated the importance of early bonding in greylag geese, but the first few days of life are unlikely to be a critical period for bonding in human infants. Connect to "Introduction."

kangaroo care A way of holding a preterm infant so that there is skin-to-skin contact.

bonding The formation of a close connection, especially a physical bond between parents and their newborn in the period shortly after birth.

How Are Preterm Infants Affected by Touch?

Many preterm infants experience less touch than full-term infants do because they are isolated in temperature-controlled incubators. Research by Tiffany Field and her colleagues (2001, 2007; Diego, Field, & Hernandez-Reif, 2008, 2014; Field, Diego, & Hernandez-Reif, 2008, 2011). has led to a surge of interest in the role that massage might play in improving developmental outcomes for preterm infants. In Field's first study in this area, massage therapy that consisted of firm stroking with the palms of the hands was given three times per day for 15-minute periods to preterm infants (Field & others, 1986). The massage therapy led to 47 percent greater weight gain than did standard medical treatment. The massaged infants also were more active and alert than preterm infants who were not massaged, and they performed better on developmental tests.

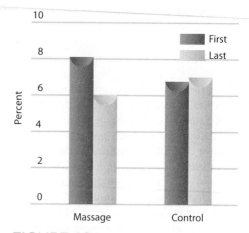

FIGURE 16

PRETERM INFANTS SHOW REDUCED STRESS BEHAVIORS AND ACTIVITY AFTER FIVE DAYS OF MASSAGE THERAPY

Shown here is Tiffany Field massaging a newborn infant. *What types of infants has massage therapy been shown to help?*
Courtesy of Dr. Tiffany Field

In later studies, Field demonstrated the benefits of massage therapy for infants who faced a variety of problems. For example, preterm infants exposed to cocaine in utero who received massage therapy gained weight and improved their scores on developmental tests (Field, 2001). In one study, preterm infants in a neonatal intensive care unit (NICU) were randomly assigned to a massage therapy group or a control group (Hernandez-Reif, Diego, & Field, 2007). For five consecutive days, the preterm infants in the massage group were

given three 15-minute moderate-pressure massages. Behavioral observations of the following stress behaviors were made on the first and last days of the study: crying, grimacing, yawning, sneezing, jerky arm and leg movements, startles, and finger flaring. The various stress behaviors were summarized in a composite stress behavior index. As indicated in Figure 16, massage had a stress-reducing effect on the preterm infants, which is especially important because they encounter numerous stressors while they are hospitalized.

In a review of the use of massage therapy with preterm infants, Field and her colleagues (2010) concluded that the most consistent findings were two positive results: (1) increased weight gain and (2) discharge from the hospital three to six days earlier. A recent study revealed that the mechanisms responsible for increased weight gain as a result of massage therapy were stimulation of the vagus nerve (one of 12 cranial nerves leading to the brain) and in turn the release of insulin (a food absorption hormone) (Field, Diego, & Hernandez-Reif, 2011). Another recent study found that both massage therapy (moderate-pressure stroking) and exercise (flexion and extension of the limbs) led to weight gain in preterm infants (Diego, Field, & Hernandez-Reif, 2014). In this study, massage was linked to increased vagal activity while exercise was associated with increased calorie consumption.

What results do you think researchers might expect to find if they investigate the effects of massage on full-term infants?

hypothesis—the insistence that the newborn *must* have close contact with the mother in the first few days of life to develop optimally—simply is not true.

Nevertheless, the weakness of the bonding hypothesis should not be used as an excuse to keep motivated mothers from interacting with their newborns. Such contact brings pleasure to many mothers and may dispel maternal anxiety about the baby's health and safety. In some cases—including preterm infants, adolescent mothers, and mothers from disadvantaged circumstances—early close contact is key to establishing a climate for improved interaction after the mother and infant leave the hospital.

Many hospitals now offer a *rooming-in* arrangement, in which the baby remains in the mother's room most of the time during its hospital stay. However, if parents choose not to use this rooming-in arrangement, the weight of the research suggests that this decision will not harm the infant emotionally (Lamb, 1994).

THE POSTPARTUM PERIOD

The weeks after childbirth present challenges for many new parents and their offspring. This is the **postpartum period,** the period after childbirth or delivery that lasts for about six weeks or until the mother's body has completed its adjustment and has returned to a nearly prepregnant state. It is a time when the woman adjusts, both physically and psychologically, to the process of childbearing.

Physical Adjustments A woman's body makes numerous physical adjustments in the first days and weeks after childbirth (Durham & Chapman, 2014). She may have a great deal of energy or feel exhausted and let down. Though these changes are normal, the fatigue can undermine the new mother's sense of well-being and confidence in her ability to cope with a new baby and a new family life.

A concern is the loss of sleep that the primary caregiver experiences during the postpartum period (Dorheim, Bjorvatn, & Eberhard-Gran, 2014; Ko & others, 2014). In the 2007 Sleep in America survey, a substantial percentage of women reported loss of sleep during pregnancy and in the postpartum period (National Sleep Foundation, 2007) (see Figure 17). The loss of sleep can contribute to stress, marital conflict, and impaired decision making (Meerlo, Sgoifo, & Suchecki, 2008).

After delivery, the mother's body undergoes sudden and dramatic changes in hormone production. When the placenta is delivered, estrogen and progesterone levels drop steeply and remain low until the ovaries start producing hormones again.

Involution is the process by which the uterus returns to its prepregnant size five or six weeks after birth. Immediately following birth, the uterus weighs 2 to 3 pounds. By the end of five or six weeks, the uterus weighs 2 to 3½ ounces. Nursing the baby helps contract the uterus at a rapid rate.

Emotional and Psychological Adjustments Emotional fluctuations are common for mothers in the postpartum period. For some women, emotional fluctuations decrease within several weeks after the delivery, but other women experience more long-lasting emotional swings (Haran & others, 2014).

As shown in Figure 18, about 70 percent of new mothers in the United States have what are called the *postpartum blues*. About two to three days after birth, they begin to feel depressed, anxious, and upset. These feelings may come and go for several months after the birth, often peaking about three to five days after birth. Even without treatment, these feelings usually go away after one or two weeks.

However, some women develop **postpartum depression,** which involves a major depressive episode that typically occurs about four weeks after delivery. Women with postpartum depression have such strong feelings of sadness, anxiety, or despair that for at least

FIGURE 17

SLEEP DEPRIVATION IN PREGNANT AND POSTPARTUM WOMEN

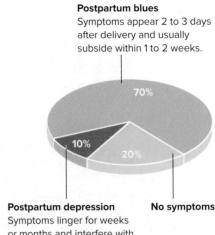

Postpartum blues
Symptoms appear 2 to 3 days after delivery and usually subside within 1 to 2 weeks.

Postpartum depression
Symptoms linger for weeks or months and interfere with daily functioning.

No symptoms

FIGURE 18

POSTPARTUM BLUES AND POSTPARTUM DEPRESSION AMONG U.S. WOMEN. Some health professionals refer to the postpartum period as the "fourth trimester." Though the time span of the postpartum period does not necessarily cover three months, the term "fourth trimester" suggests continuity and the importance of the first several months after birth for the mother.

postpartum period The period after childbirth when the mother adjusts, both physically and psychologically, to the process of childbirth. This period lasts for about six weeks or until her body has completed its adjustment and returned to a near prepregnant state.

postpartum depression A major depressive episode that typically occurs about four weeks after delivery; women with this condition have such strong feelings of sadness, anxiety, or despair that they have trouble coping with daily tasks during the postpartum period.

The postpartum period is a time of considerable adjustment and adaptation for both the mother and the father. Fathers can provide an important support system for mothers, especially in helping mothers care for young infants. *What kinds of tasks might the father of a newborn do to support the mother?*
© Howard Grey/Getty Images RF

a two-week period they have trouble coping with their daily tasks. Without treatment, postpartum depression may become worse and last for many months (Di Florio & others, 2014). And many women with postpartum depression don't seek help. For example, one study found that 15 percent of the women surveyed had experienced postpartum depression symptoms but less than half had sought help (McGarry & others, 2009). Estimates indicate that 10 to 14 percent of new mothers experience postpartum depression. Also, a recent study found that depression during pregnancy, a history of physical abuse, migrant status, and postpartum physical complications were major risk factors for postpartum depression (Gaillard & others, 2014).

Several antidepressant drugs are effective in treating postpartum depression and appear to be safe for breast-feeding women and their infants (O'Hara & McCabe, 2013). Psychotherapy, especially cognitive therapy, also is an effective treatment of postpartum depression for many women (Bevan, Wittkowski, & Wells, 2013; Milgrom & others, 2015). Also, engaging in regular exercise may help to relieve postpartum depression (Ko & others, 2013).

A mother's postpartum depression affects the way she interacts with her infant (Giallo & others, 2015). A research review concluded that the interaction difficulties of depressed mothers and their infants occur across cultures and socioeconomic status groups, comprising reduced sensitivity of the mothers and decreased responsiveness on the part of infants (Field, 2010). Several caregiving activities also are compromised, including feeding, sleep routines, and safety practices.

Fathers also undergo considerable adjustment during the postpartum period, even when they work away from home all day. When the mother develops postpartum depression, many fathers also experience depressed feelings (Gawlik & others, 2014; Serhan & others, 2013). Many fathers feel that the baby comes first and gets all of the mother's attention; some feel that they have been replaced by the baby.

The father's support and caring can influence whether the mother develops postpartum depression (Flanagan & others, 2015; Persson & others, 2011). One study revealed that higher support by fathers was related to a lower incidence of postpartum depression in women (Smith & Howard, 2008).

Review Connect Reflect

 Summarize how birth takes place and describe the nature of the postpartum period

Review

- What are the three main stages of birth? What are some different birth strategies?
- What is the transition from fetus to newborn like?
- What are the outcomes for children if they are born preterm or with a low birth weight?
- What is bonding? How is it linked to child outcomes?
- What are some characteristics of the postpartum period?

Connect

- Compare and contrast what you learned about kangaroo care and breast feeding of preterm infants with what you learned about bonding and breast feeding when the mother is suffering from postpartum depression.

Reflect *Your Own Personal Journey of Life*

- If you are a female, which birth strategy would you prefer? Why? If you are a male, how involved would you want to be in helping your partner through pregnancy and the birth of your baby?

reach your **learning goals**

Biological Beginnings

1 The Evolutionary Perspective

 Discuss the evolutionary perspective on life-span development

Natural Selection and Adaptive Behavior

Evolutionary Psychology

- Natural selection is the process by which those individuals of a species that are best adapted to their environment are more likely to survive and reproduce. Darwin proposed that natural selection fuels evolution. In evolutionary theory, adaptive behavior is behavior that promotes the organism's survival in a natural habitat.

- Evolutionary psychology holds that adaptation, reproduction, and "survival of the fittest" are important in shaping behavior. Ideas proposed by evolutionary developmental psychologists include the view that an extended childhood period is needed for humans to develop a large brain and learn the complexity of social communities. According to Baltes, the benefits resulting from evolutionary selection decrease with age, mainly because of a decline in reproductive fitness. At the same time, cultural needs increase. Like other theoretical approaches to development, evolutionary psychology has limitations. Bandura rejects "one-sided evolutionism" and argues for a bidirectional link between biology and environment.

2 Genetic Foundations of Development

 Describe what genes are and how they influence human development

The Collaborative Gene

Genes and Chromosomes

Genetic Principles

Chromosomal and Gene-Linked Abnormalities

- Short segments of DNA constitute genes, the units of hereditary information that help cells to reproduce and manufacture proteins. Genes act collaboratively, not independently.

- Genes are passed on to new cells when chromosomes are duplicated during the processes of mitosis and meiosis, which are two ways in which new cells are formed. When an egg and a sperm unite in the fertilization process, the resulting zygote contains the genes from the chromosomes in the father's sperm and the mother's egg. Despite this transmission of genes from generation to generation, variability is created in several ways, including the exchange of chromosomal segments during meiosis, mutations, and the distinction between a genotype and a phenotype.

- Genetic principles include those involving dominant-recessive genes, sex-linked genes, genetic imprinting, and polygenic inheritance.

- Chromosomal abnormalities produce Down syndrome, which is caused by the presence of an extra copy of chromosome 21. Other sex-linked chromosomal abnormalities include Klinefelter syndrome, fragile X syndrome, Turner syndrome, and XYY syndrome. Gene-linked abnormalities involve absent or harmful genes. Gene-linked disorders include phenylketonuria (PKU) and sickle-cell anemia.

3 Heredity and Environment Interaction: The Nature-Nurture Debate

 Explain some of the ways that heredity and environment interact to produce individual differences in development

Behavior Genetics

- Behavior genetics is the field that seeks to discover the influence of heredity and environment on individual differences in human traits and development. Methods used by behavior geneticists include twin studies and adoption studies.

Heredity-Environment Correlations	· In Scarr's heredity-environment correlations view, heredity may influence the types of environments that children experience. She describes three genotype-environment correlations: passive, evocative, and active (niche-picking). Scarr notes that the relative importance of these three genotype-environment correlations changes as children develop.
Shared and Nonshared Environmental Influences	· Shared environmental experiences refer to siblings' common experiences, such as their parents' personalities and intellectual orientation, the family's socioeconomic status, and the neighborhood in which they live. Nonshared environmental experiences involve the child's unique experiences, both within the family and outside the family, that are not shared with a sibling. Many behavior geneticists argue that differences in the development of siblings are due to nonshared environmental experiences (and heredity) rather than shared environmental experiences.
The Epigenetic View and Gene x Environment (G x E) Interaction	· The epigenetic view emphasizes that development is the result of an ongoing, bidirectional interchange between heredity and environment. Gene x environment (G x E) interaction involves the interaction of a specific measured variation in DNA and a specific measured aspect of the environment.
Conclusions About Heredity-Environment Interaction	· Complex behaviors have some genetic loading that gives people a propensity for a particular developmental trajectory. However, actual development also requires an environment, and that environment is complex. The interaction of heredity and environment is extensive. Much remains to be discovered about the specific ways that heredity and environment interact to influence development.

4 Prenatal Development

 Characterize the course of prenatal development and its hazards

The Course of Prenatal Development	· Prenatal development is divided into three periods: germinal (conception until 10 to 14 days later), which ends when the zygote (a fertilized egg) attaches to the uterine wall; embryonic (two to eight weeks after conception), during which the embryo differentiates into three layers, life-support systems develop, and organ systems begin to form (organogenesis); and fetal (lasting from two months after conception until about nine months, or when the infant is born), a time when organ systems have matured to the point at which life can be sustained outside of the womb. By the time babies are born they have approximately 100 billion neurons, or nerve cells. The nervous system begins with the formation of a neural tube at 18 to 24 days after conception. Neurogenesis, proliferation, and migration are three processes that characterize brain development in the prenatal period. The basic architecture of the brain is formed in the first two trimesters of prenatal development.
Prenatal Diagnostic Tests	· Amniocentesis, ultrasound sonography, fetal MRI, chorionic villus sampling, and maternal blood screening are used to determine whether a fetus is developing normally. The sex of the fetus can be determined as early as seven weeks into pregnancy.
Hazards to Prenatal Development	· A teratogen is any agent that can potentially cause a birth defect or negatively alter cognitive and behavioral outcomes. The dose, time of exposure, and genetic susceptibility influence the severity of the damage to an unborn child and the type of defect that occurs. Prescription drugs that can be harmful include antibiotics, some depressants, and certain hormones; nonprescription drugs that can be harmful include diet pills and aspirin. The psychoactive drugs caffeine, alcohol, nicotine, cocaine, and marijuana are potentially harmful to offspring. Cigarette smoking by pregnant women also has serious adverse effects on prenatal and child development (such as low birth weight). Problems may also result if a pregnant woman has rubella (German measles), syphilis, genital herpes, or AIDS. A developing fetus depends entirely on its mother for nutrition, and it may be harmed if the mother is malnourished, is overweight, or has a diet deficient in folic acid. High anxiety and stress in the mother are linked with less than optimal prenatal and birth outcomes. Maternal age can negatively affect the offspring's development if the mother is an adolescent or if she is 35 or older. Radiation is a potential environmental hazard. Paternal factors also can affect the developing fetus.
Prenatal Care	· Prenatal care programs provide information about teratogens and other prenatal hazards. In addition, various medical conditions are screened for and medical care is given in a defined schedule of visits. Prenatal classes often give information on nutrition, sexuality during pregnancy, and types of birth.

5 Birth and the Postpartum Period Summarize how birth takes place and describe the nature of the postpartum period

The Birth Process

· Childbirth occurs in three stages. Childbirth strategies involve the childbirth setting and attendants. Methods of delivery include medicated, natural and prepared, and cesarean. An increasing number of nonmedicated techniques, such as waterbirth, are being used to reduce childbirth pain.

The Transition from Fetus to Newborn

· Being born involves considerable stress for the baby, but the baby is well prepared and adapted to handle the stress. For many years, the Apgar Scale has been used to assess the newborn's health.

Low Birth Weight and Preterm Infants

· Low birth weight infants weigh less than 5½ pounds, and they may be preterm or small for date. Although most low birth weight infants are normal and healthy, as a group they have more health and developmental problems than infants of normal birth weight. Kangaroo care and massage therapy have been shown to provide benefits to preterm infants.

Bonding

· Bonding is the formation of a close connection, especially a physical bond between parents and the newborn shortly after birth. Early bonding has not been found to be critical in the development of a competent infant.

The Postpartum Period

· The postpartum period lasts from childbirth until about six weeks after the delivery or until the mother's body has completed its adjustment to a nonpregnant state. The development of postpartum depression is a concern during this period.

key terms

active (niche-picking) genotype-environment correlations
adoption study
Apgar Scale
behavior genetics
bonding
chromosomes
DNA
doula
Down syndrome
embryonic period
epigenetic view
evocative genotype-environment correlations

evolutionary psychology
fertilization
fetal alcohol spectrum disorders (FASD)
fetal period
fragile X syndrome
gene × environment (G × E) interaction
genes
genotype
germinal period
kangaroo care
Klinefelter syndrome
low birth weight infants

meiosis
mitosis
natural childbirth
neurons
nonshared environmental experiences
organogenesis
passive genotype-environment correlations
phenotype
phenylketonuria (PKU)
postpartum depression
postpartum period
prepared childbirth

preterm infants
shared environmental experiences
sickle-cell anemia
small for date infants
teratogen
Turner syndrome
twin study
XYY syndrome
zygote

key people

Paul Baltes
Albert Bandura
David Buss

Charles Darwin
Tiffany Field
Gilbert Gottlieb

Ferdinand Lamaze
David Moore

Robert Plomin
Sandra Scarr

chapter 3

PHYSICAL DEVELOPMENT AND BIOLOGICAL AGING

chapter outline

preview

Think about how much you have changed physically and will continue to change as you age. We come into this life as small beings. But we grow very rapidly in infancy, more slowly in childhood, and once again more rapidly during puberty, and then experience another slowdown. Eventually we decline, but many older adults are still physically robust. In this chapter, we explore changes in body growth, the brain, and sleep across the life span. We also examine longevity and evaluate some fascinating theories about why we age.

1 Body Growth and Change **LG1** Discuss major changes in the body through the life span

Patterns of Growth | Height and Weight in Infancy and Childhood | Puberty | Early Adulthood | Middle Adulthood | Late Adulthood

In life's long journey, we go through many bodily changes. We grow up, we grow out, we shrink. The very visible changes in height and weight are accompanied by less visible ones in bones, lungs, and every other organ of the body. These changes will help shape how we think about ourselves, how other people think about us, and what we are capable of thinking, doing, and feeling. Are there strict timelines for these changes? Are they set in our genes? Let's begin by studying some basic patterns of growth and then trace bodily changes from the time we are infants through the time we are older adults.

PATTERNS OF GROWTH

Two key patterns of growth are the cephalocaudal and proximodistal patterns. The **cephalocaudal pattern** is the sequence in which the fastest growth in the human body occurs at the top, with the head. Physical growth in size, weight, and feature differentiation gradually works its way down from the top to the bottom (for example, neck, shoulders, middle trunk, and so on). This same pattern occurs in the head area, because the top parts of the head—the eyes and brain—grow faster than the lower parts, such as the jaw. During prenatal development and early infancy, the head constitutes an extraordinarily large proportion of the total body (see Figure 1).

In most cases, sensory and motor development proceeds according to the cephalocaudal pattern. For example, infants see objects before they can control their torso, and they can use their hands long before they can crawl or walk. However, one study contradicted the cephalocaudal pattern by finding that infants reached for toys with their feet before using their hands (Galloway & Thelen, 2004). In this study, infants on average first contacted the toy with their feet when they were 12 weeks old and with their hands when they were 16 weeks old. Thus, contrary to long-standing beliefs, early leg movements can be precisely controlled, some aspects of development that involve reaching do not involve lengthy practice, and early motor behaviors don't always develop in a strict cephalocaudal pattern.

The **proximodistal pattern** is the growth sequence that starts at the center of the body and moves toward the extremities. An example is the early maturation of muscular control of the trunk and arms, compared with that of the hands and fingers. Further, infants use the whole hand as a unit before they can control several fingers.

HEIGHT AND WEIGHT IN INFANCY AND CHILDHOOD

Height and weight increase rapidly in infancy, then take a slower course during the childhood years.

cephalocaudal pattern The sequence in which the fastest growth occurs at the top of the body—the head—with physical growth in size, weight, and feature differentiation gradually working from top to bottom.

proximodistal pattern The sequence in which growth starts at the center of the body and moves toward the extremities.

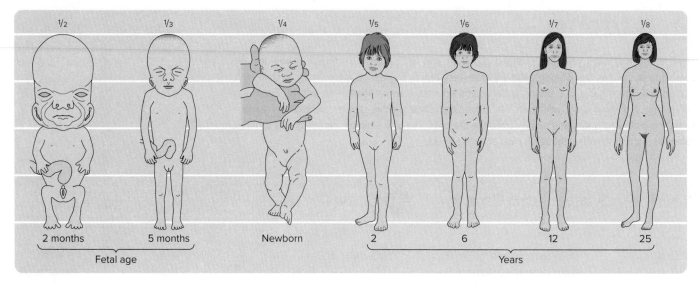

FIGURE 1

CHANGES IN PROPORTIONS OF THE HUMAN BODY DURING GROWTH. As individuals develop from infancy through adulthood, one of the most noticeable physical changes is that the head becomes smaller in relation to the rest of the body. The fractions listed refer to head size as a proportion of total body length at different ages.

The bodies of 5-year-olds and 2-year-olds are different from one another. The 5-year-old not only is taller and heavier, but also has a longer trunk and legs than the 2-year-old. *What might be some other physical differences between 2- and 5-year-olds?*
© Michael Hitoshi/Getty Images RF

Infancy   The average North American newborn is 20 inches long and weighs 7½ pounds. Ninety-five percent of full-term newborns are 18 to 22 inches long and weigh between 5½ and 10 pounds.

In the first several days of life, most newborns lose 5 to 7 percent of their body weight. Once infants adjust to sucking, swallowing, and digesting, they grow rapidly, gaining an average of 5 to 6 ounces per week during the first month. Typically they have doubled their birth weight by the age of 4 months and have nearly tripled it by their first birthday. Infants grow about 3/4 inch per month during the first year, increasing their birth length by about 40 percent by their first birthday.

Infants' rate of growth slows considerably in the second year of life (Burns & others, 2013; Marcdante & Kliegman, 2014). By 2 years of age, infants weigh approximately 26 to 32 pounds, having gained a quarter to half a pound per month during the second year; at age 2 they have reached about one-fifth of their adult weight. The average 2-year-old is 32 to 35 inches tall, which is nearly one-half of adult height.

Early Childhood   What is the overall growth rate like in early childhood? As the preschool child grows older, the percentage of increase in height and weight decreases with each additional year (Goldstone & Reynolds, 2014). Girls are only slightly smaller and lighter than boys during these years. Both boys and girls slim down as the trunks of their bodies lengthen. Although their heads are still somewhat large for their bodies, by the end of the preschool years most children have lost their top-heavy look. Body fat also shows a slow, steady decline during the preschool years. Girls have more fatty tissue than boys; boys have more muscle tissue (McMahon & Stryjewski, 2012).

Growth patterns vary individually (Goldstone & Reynolds, 2014). Think back to your preschool years. This was probably the first time you noticed that some children were taller than you, some shorter; some were fatter, some thinner; some were stronger, some weaker. Much of the variation is due to heredity, but environmental experiences are also involved. A review of the height and weight of children around the world concluded that two important contributors to height differences are ethnic origin and nutrition (Meredith, 1978).

Why are some children unusually short? The culprits are congenital factors (genetic or prenatal problems), growth hormone deficiency, a physical problem that develops in childhood, maternal smoking during pregnancy, or an emotional difficulty (Wit, Kiess, & Mullis, 2011). In sum. the main factors that contribute to children's height are genetic influences, ethnic origin, and nutrition.

Middle and Late Childhood   The period of middle and late childhood involves slow, consistent growth. This is a period of calm before the rapid growth spurt of adolescence.

During the elementary school years, children grow an average of 2 to 3 inches a year. At the age of 8, the average girl and the average boy are 4 feet 2 inches tall. During the middle and late childhood years, children gain about 5 to 7 pounds a year. The average 8-year-old girl and the average 8-year-old boy weigh 56 pounds. The weight increase is due mainly to increases in the size of the skeletal and muscular systems, as well as the size of some body organs. Muscle mass and strength gradually increase as "baby fat" decreases in middle and late childhood (Burns & others, 2013).

Changes in proportions are among the most pronounced physical changes in middle and late childhood. Head circumference, waist circumference, and leg length decrease in relation to body height.

What characterizes children's physical growth in middle and late childhood?
© RubberBall Productions/Getty Images RF

PUBERTY

Puberty is a brain-neuroendocrine process occurring primarily in early adolescence that provides stimulation for the rapid physical changes that take place during this period of development (Susman & Dorn, 2013). In this section, we explore a number of puberty's physical changes and its psychological accompaniments.

Sexual Maturation, Height, and Weight   Think back to the onset of your puberty. Of the striking changes that were taking place in your body, what was the first to occur? Researchers have found that male pubertal characteristics typically develop in this order: increase in penis and testicle size, appearance of straight pubic hair, minor voice change, first ejaculation (which usually occurs through masturbation or a wet dream), appearance of curly pubic hair, onset of maximum growth in height and weight, growth of hair in armpits, more detectable voice changes, and, finally, growth of facial hair.

What is the order of appearance of physical changes in females? First, for most girls, their breasts enlarge or pubic hair appears. Later, hair appears in the armpits. As these changes occur, the female grows in height and her hips become wider than her shoulders.

Menarche—a girl's first menstruation—comes rather late in the pubertal cycle. Initially, her menstrual cycles may be highly irregular. For the first several years, she may not ovulate every menstrual cycle; some girls do not ovulate at all until a year or two after menstruation begins.

Marked weight gains coincide with the onset of puberty. During early adolescence, girls tend to outweigh boys, but by about age 14 boys begin to surpass girls. Similarly, at the beginning of the adolescent period, girls tend to be as tall as or taller than boys of their age, but by the end of the middle school years most boys have caught up or, in many cases, surpassed girls in height.

As indicated in Figure 2, the growth spurt occurs approximately two years earlier for girls than for boys. The mean age at the beginning of the growth spurt in girls is 9; for boys, it is 11. The peak rate of pubertal change occurs at 11½ years for girls and 13½ years for boys. During their growth spurt, girls increase in height about 3½ inches per year, boys about 4 inches.

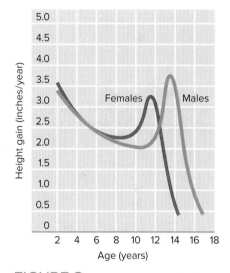

FIGURE **2**

PUBERTAL GROWTH SPURT. On average, the peak of the growth spurt during puberty occurs two years earlier for girls (11½) than for boys (13½). *How are hormones related to the growth spurt and to the difference between the average height of adolescent boys and that of girls?*

From J.M. Tanner et al., "Standards from Birth to Maturity for Height, Weight, Height Velocity: British Children in 1965" in Archives of Diseases in Childhood 41(219), pp. 454–471, 1966. With permission from BMJ Publishing Group Ltd.

puberty A brain-neuroendocrine process occurring primarily in early adolescence that provides stimulation for the rapid physical changes that occur in this period of development.

menarche A girl's first menstrual period.

Hypothalamus: A structure in the brain that interacts with the pituitary gland to monitor the bodily regulation of hormones.

Pituitary: This master gland produces hormones that stimulate other glands. It also influences growth by producing growth hormones; it sends gonadotropins to the testes and ovaries and a thyroid-stimulating hormone to the thyroid gland. It sends a hormone to the adrenal gland as well.

Thyroid gland: It interacts with the pituitary gland to influence growth.

Adrenal gland: It interacts with the pituitary gland and likely plays a role in pubertal development, but less is known about its function than about sex glands. Recent research, however, suggests it may be involved in adolescent behavior, particularly for boys.

The gonads, or sex glands: These consist of the testes in males and the ovaries in females. The sex glands are strongly involved in the appearance of secondary sex characteristics, such as facial hair in males and breast development in females. The general class of hormones called estrogens is dominant in females, while androgens are dominant in males. More specifically, testosterone in males and estradiol in females are key hormones in pubertal development.

FIGURE 3

THE MAJOR ENDOCRINE GLANDS INVOLVED IN PUBERTAL CHANGE

hormones Powerful chemical substances secreted by the endocrine glands and carried through the body by the bloodstream.

hypothalamus A structure in the brain that is involved with eating and sexual behavior.

pituitary gland An important endocrine gland that controls growth and regulates the activity of other glands.

gonads The sex glands, which are the testes in males and the ovaries in females.

gonadotropins Hormones that stimulate the testes or ovaries.

testosterone A hormone associated in boys with the development of the genitals, increased height, and voice changes.

estradiol A hormone associated in girls with breast, uterine, and skeletal development.

Hormonal Changes   Behind the first whisker in boys and the widening of hips in girls is a flood of **hormones,** powerful chemical substances secreted by the endocrine glands and carried through the body by the bloodstream. The endocrine system's role in puberty involves the interaction of the hypothalamus, the pituitary gland, and the gonads (see Figure 3). The **hypothalamus,** a structure in the brain, is involved with eating and sexual behavior. The **pituitary gland,** an important endocrine gland, controls growth and regulates other glands; among these, the **gonads**—the testes in males, the ovaries in females—are particularly important in giving rise to pubertal changes in the body.

How do the gonads, or sex glands, work? The pituitary gland sends a signal via **gonadotropins** (hormones that stimulate the testes or ovaries) to the appropriate gland to manufacture hormones. These hormones give rise to such changes as the production of sperm in males and menstruation and the release of eggs from the ovaries in females. The pituitary gland, through interaction with the hypothalamus, detects when the optimal level of hormones is reached and maintains it with additional gonadotropin secretion (Susman & Dorn, 2013). Not only does the pituitary gland release gonadotropins that stimulate the testes and ovaries, but through interaction with the hypothalamus the pituitary gland also secretes hormones that either directly lead to growth and skeletal maturation or produce growth effects through interaction with the thyroid gland, located at the base of the throat.

The concentrations of certain hormones increase dramatically during adolescence (Koolschijn, Peper & Crone, 2014). The concentrations of two key hormones increase in puberty, and the changes are very different in boys and girls:

· **Testosterone** is a hormone associated in boys with the development of genitals, increased height, and deepening of the voice.

· **Estradiol** is a type of estrogen associated in girls with breast, uterine, and skeletal development.

A recent study documented the growth of the pituitary gland in adolescence and found that its volume was linked to circulating blood levels of estradiol and testosterone (Wong & others, 2014). In one study, testosterone levels increased eighteenfold in boys but only twofold in girls during puberty; estradiol increased eightfold in girls but only twofold in boys (Nottelmann & others, 1987). Thus, both testosterone and estradiol are present in the hormonal makeup of both boys and girls, but testosterone dominates in male pubertal development, estradiol in female pubertal development (Richmond & Rogol, 2007). A recent study of 9- to 17-year-old boys found that testosterone levels peaked at 17 years of age (Khairullah & others, 2014).

The same influx of hormones that grows hair on a male's chest and increases the fatty tissue in a female's breasts may also contribute to psychological development in adolescence (Susman & Dorn, 2013). In one study of boys and girls ranging in age from 9 to 14, a higher concentration of testosterone was present in boys who rated themselves as more socially competent (Nottelmann & others, 1987). However, a recent research review concluded that there is insufficient quality research to confirm that changing testosterone levels during puberty are linked to mood and behavior in adolescent males (Duke, Balzer, & Steinbeck, 2014).

Hormonal effects by themselves do not account for adolescent psychological development (Graber, 2008). For example, in one study, social factors were much better predictors of young adolescent girls' depression and anger than hormonal factors (Brooks-Gunn & Warren, 1989). Behavior and moods also can affect hormones. Stress, eating patterns, exercise, sexual activity, tension, and depression can activate or suppress various aspects of the hormonal system. In sum, the hormone-behavior link is complex (Susman & Dorn, 2013).

Timing and Variations in Puberty   In the United States—where children mature up to a year earlier than children in European countries—the average age of menarche has declined significantly since the mid-nineteenth century. Fortunately, however, we are unlikely to see pubescent toddlers, since what has happened in the past century is likely the result of improved nutrition and health, and the rate of decline in age of onset of puberty has slowed considerably in the last several decades. However, some researchers recently have found that the onset of puberty is still occurring earlier in girls and boys (Herman-Giddens & others, 2012; McBride, 2013).

Is age of pubertal onset linked to how tall boys and girls will be toward the end of adolescence? A recent study found that for girls, earlier onset of menarche, breast development, and growth spurt were linked to shorter height at 18 years of age; however, for boys, earlier age of growth spurt and slower progression through puberty were associated with being taller at 18 years of age (Yousefi & others, 2013).

Why do the changes of puberty occur when they do, and how can variations in their timing be explained? The basic genetic program for puberty is wired into the species (Dvornyk & Waqar-ul-Haq, 2012). However, nutrition, health, family stress, and other environmental factors also affect puberty's timing (Susman & Dorn, 2013). A recent cross-cultural study of 48,000 girls in 29 countries found that childhood obesity was linked to early puberty (Currie & others, 2012). Another study found that early onset of menarche was associated with severe child sexual abuse (Boynton-Jarrett & others 2013).

For most boys, the pubertal sequence may begin as early as age 10 or as late as 13½, and it may end as early as age 13 or as late as 17. Thus, the normal range is wide enough that, given two boys of the same chronological age, one might complete the pubertal sequence before the other one has begun it. For girls, menarche is considered within the normal range if it appears between the ages of 9 and 15.

Psychological Accompaniments of Puberty   What are some links between puberty and psychological characteristics? How do early and late maturation influence adolescents' psychological development?

Body Image   One psychological aspect of puberty is certain for both boys and girls: Adolescents are preoccupied with their bodies (Leone & others, 2014; Park & Epstein, 2013). At this age you may have looked in the mirror on a daily, and sometimes even hourly, basis to see if you could detect anything different about your changing body. Preoccupation with one's body image is strong throughout adolescence but it is especially acute during puberty, a time when adolescents are more dissatisfied with their bodies than in late adolescence.

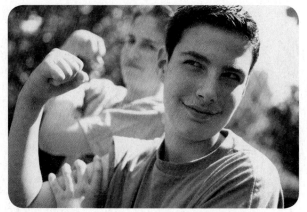

Adolescents show a strong preoccupation with their changing bodies and develop images of what their bodies are like. *Why might adolescent males have more positive body images than adolescent females?*
© age fotostock/SuperStock

What are some outcomes of early and late maturation in adolescence?
© Corbis RF

- - - - - - - - - - ➤
developmental **connection**

Sexuality

Early sexual experience is one of a number of risk factors in adolescent development. Connect to "Gender and Sexuality."

Gender Differences Gender differences characterize adolescents' perceptions of their bodies (Calzo & others, 2012). Girls tend to have more negative body images, which to some extent may be due to media portrayals of the attractiveness of being thin while the percentage of girls' body fat is increasing during puberty (Benowitz-Fredericks & others, 2012). A recent study found that both boys' and girls' body images became more positive as they moved from the beginning to the end of adolescence (Holsen, Carlson Jones, & Skogbrott Birkeland, 2012).

Early and Late Maturation Did you enter puberty early, late, or on time? When adolescents mature earlier or later than their peers, they often perceive themselves differently (Susman & Dorn, 2013). A recent study found that in the early high school years, late-maturing boys had a more negative body image than early-maturing boys (de Guzman & Nishina, 2014). Similarly, in the Berkeley Longitudinal Study conducted half a century ago, early-maturing boys perceived themselves more positively and had more successful peer relations than did late-maturing boys (Jones, 1965). The findings for early-maturing girls were similar but not as strong as for boys. When the late-maturing boys were in their thirties, however, they had developed a more positive identity than the early-maturing boys had (Peskin, 1967). Perhaps the late-maturing boys had had more time to explore life's options, or perhaps the early-maturing boys continued to focus on their physical status instead of paying attention to career development and achievement.

An increasing number of researchers have found that early maturation increases girls' vulnerability to a number of problems (Graber, 2013; Hamilton & others, 2014). Early-maturing girls are more likely to smoke, drink, be depressed, have an eating disorder, struggle for earlier independence from their parents, and have older friends (Negriff, Susman, & Trickett, 2011; Verhoef & others, 2014). Researchers have found that early-maturing girls tend to engage in sexual intercourse earlier and have more unstable sexual relationships (Moore, Harden, & Mendle, 2014). Another study found that early-maturing girls' higher level of internalizing problems (depression, for example) was linked to their heightened sensitivity to interpersonal stress (Natsuaki & others, 2010). And early-maturing girls are more likely to drop out of high school and to cohabit and marry at younger ages (Cavanagh, 2009). Apparently as a result of their social and cognitive immaturity, combined with early physical development, early-maturing girls are easily lured into problem behaviors, not recognizing how these behaviors might affect their development. Thus, early-maturing adolescents, especially girls, require earlier risk education efforts related to sexual development, risky behaviors, relationships, and Internet safety than their on-time peers (Susman & Dorn, 2013).

In sum, early maturation often has more favorable outcomes for boys than for girls, especially in early adolescence. However, late maturation may be more favorable for boys, especially in terms of identity and career development. Research increasingly has found that early-maturing girls are vulnerable to a number of problems.

EARLY ADULTHOOD

After the dramatic physical changes of puberty, the years of early adulthood might seem to be an uneventful time in the body's history. Physical changes during these years may be subtle, but they do continue.

Height remains rather constant during early adulthood. Peak functioning of the body's joints usually occurs in the twenties. Many individuals also reach a peak of muscle tone and strength in their late teens and twenties (Candow & Chilibeck, 2005). However, these attributes may begin to decline in the thirties. Sagging chins and protruding abdomens may also appear for the first time. Muscles start to have less elasticity, and aches may appear in places not felt before.

Most of us reach our peak levels of physical performance before the age of 30, often between the ages of 19 and 26. This peak of physical performance occurs not only for the average young adult, but for outstanding athletes as well. Different types of athletes, however, reach their peak performances at different ages. Most swimmers and gymnasts peak in their late teens. Golfers and marathon runners tend to peak in their late twenties. In other areas of athletics, peak performance often occurs in the early to mid-twenties. However, in recent years, some highly conditioned athletes—such as Dana Torres (Olympic swimming) and Tom Watson (golf)—have stretched the upper age limits of award-winning performances.

MIDDLE ADULTHOOD

Like the changes of early adulthood, midlife physical changes are usually gradual. Although everyone experiences some physical change due to aging in middle adulthood, the rates of aging vary considerably from one individual to another. Genetic makeup and lifestyle factors play important roles in whether and when chronic diseases will appear. Middle age is a window through which we can glimpse later life while there is still time to engage in preventive behaviors and influence the course of aging (Bertrand, Graham, & Lachman, 2013; Lachman, 2004).

Physical Appearance   Individuals lose height in middle age, and many gain weight (Winett & others, 2014). On average, from 30 to 50 years of age, men lose about ½ inch in height, then lose another ¾ inch from 50 to 70 years of age (Hoyer & Roodin, 2009). The height loss for women can be as much as 2 inches from 25 to 75 years of age. Note that there are large variations in the extent to which individuals become shorter with aging. The decrease in height is due to bone loss in the vertebrae. On average, body fat accounts for about 10 percent of body weight in adolescence; it makes up 20 percent or more in middle age.

Noticeable signs of aging usually are apparent by the forties or fifties. The skin begins to wrinkle and sag because of a loss of fat and collagen in underlying tissues (Pageon & others, 2014). Small, localized areas of pigmentation in the skin produce aging spots, especially in areas that are exposed to sunlight, such as the hands and face. A recent twin study found that twins who had been smoking longer were more likely to have more sagging facial skin and wrinkles, especially in the middle and lower portion of the face (Okada & others, 2013). The hair thins and grays because of a lower replacement rate and a decline in melanin production.

Since a youthful appearance is valued in many cultures, many Americans strive to make themselves look younger. Undergoing cosmetic surgery, dyeing hair, purchasing wigs, enrolling in weight reduction programs, participating in exercise regimens, and taking heavy doses of vitamins are common in middle age. Baby boomers have shown a strong interest in plastic surgery and Botox, which may reflect their desire to take control of the aging process (Jiang & others, 2014).

Strength, Joints, and Bones   The term *sarcopenia* is given to age-related loss of lean muscle mass and strength (Sayer & others, 2013; Spira & others, 2015). After age 50, muscle loss occurs at a rate of approximately 1 to 2 percent per year. A loss of strength especially occurs in the back and legs. Obesity is a risk factor for sarcopenia (Meng & others, 2015; Parr, Coffey, & Hawley, 2013). Recently, researchers began using the term "sarcopenic obesity" in reference to individuals who have sarcopenia and are obese (Scott & others, 2014). A recent study found that sarcopenic obesity was linked to hypertension (Park & others, 2013). And a research review concluded that weight management and resistance training were the best strategies for slowing down sarcopenia (Rolland & others, 2011)

Maximum bone density occurs by the mid- to late thirties. From this point on, there is a progressive loss of bone. The rate of bone loss begins slowly but accelerates during the fifties (Baron, 2012). Women's rate of bone loss is about twice that of men. By the end of midlife, bones break more easily and heal more slowly (Rachner, Khosia, & Hofbauer, 2011).

Cardiovascular System   Cardiovascular disease increases considerably in middle age (Hwang & others, 2014; Wang & others, 2014). The level of cholesterol in the blood increases through the adult years. Cholesterol comes in two forms: LDL (low-density lipoprotein) and HDL (high-density lipoprotein). LDL is often referred to as "bad" cholesterol because when the level of LDL is too high, it sticks to the lining of blood vessels, a condition that can lead to atherosclerosis (hardening of the arteries). HDL is often referred to as "good" cholesterol because when it is high and LDL is low, the risk of cardiovascular disease is lessened (Tzourio, Laurent, & Debette, 2014). A recent study revealed that a higher level of HDL was linked to a higher probability of being alive at 85 years of age (Rahilly-Tierney & others, 2011). In middle age, cholesterol begins to accumulate on the artery walls, which are thickening. The result is an increased risk of cardiovascular disease.

Famous actor Sean Connery as a young adult in his twenties (*top*) and as a middle-aged adult in his fifties (*bottom*). *What are some of the most outwardly noticeable signs of aging in middle adulthood?*
(top): © Bettmann/Corbis; *(bottom):* © Matthew Mendelsohn/Corbis

------------------------→

developmental **connection**

Cardiovascular Disease and Alzheimer Disease

Cardiovascular disease in increasingly recognized as a risk factor in Alzheimer disease. Connect to "Health."

Members of the Masai tribe in Kenya, Africa, can stay on a treadmill for a long time because of their active lives. Incidence of heart disease is extremely low in the Masai tribe, which also can be attributed to their energetic lifestyle.
Courtesy of the family of Dr. George V. Mann

Researchers have found that almost 50 percent of Canadian and American menopausal women have occasional hot flashes, but only one in seven Japanese women do (Lock, 1998). *What factors might account for these variations?*
© Blue Moon Stock/PunchStock RF

climacteric The midlife transition during which fertility declines.

menopause The time in middle age, usually in the late forties or early fifties, when a woman's menstrual periods have ceased for one year.

Blood pressure, too, usually rises in the forties and fifties, and high blood pressure (hypertension) is linked with an increased rate of mortality as well as lower cognitive functioning (Shavelle, 2014). For example, a recent study revealed that hypertension in middle age was linked to an increased risk of cognitive impairment in late adulthood (23 years later) (Virta & others, 2013). At menopause, a woman's blood pressure rises sharply and usually remains above that of a man through life's later years (Taler, 2009). The health benefits of cholesterol-lowering and hypertension-lowering drugs are a major factor in improving the health of many middle-aged adults and increasing their life expectancy (Hwang & others, 2015; Wenger, 2014). Regular exercise and healthy eating habits also have considerable benefits in preventing cardiovascular disease (Aatashak, Stannard, & Azizbeigi, 2015; Cuenca-Garcia & others, 2014).

Lungs There is little change in lung capacity through most of middle adulthood. However, at about the age of 55, the proteins in lung tissue become less elastic. This change, combined with a gradual stiffening of the chest wall, decreases the lungs' capacity to shuttle oxygen from the air people breathe to the blood in their veins.

For smokers, however, the picture is different and bleaker (Tomiyama & others, 2010). The lung capacity of smokers drops precipitously in middle age. However, if the individuals quit smoking their lung capacity improves, although not to the level of individuals who have never smoked (Williams, 1995). Also, a recent study found that lung cancer diagnoses were 68 percent lower among men who were the most physically fit compared than among those who were the least physically fit (Lakoski & others, 2013).

Sexuality **Climacteric** is a term used to describe the midlife transition in which fertility declines. **Menopause** is the time in middle age, usually in the late forties or early fifties, when a woman has not had a menstrual period for a full year. The average age at which women have their last period is 52. A small percentage of women—10 percent—go through menopause before age 40. Just as puberty has been coming earlier, however, menopause has been coming later (Birren, 2002). Specific causes of the later incidence of menopause have not been documented, but improved nutrition and lower incidence of infectious diseases may be the reasons.

In menopause, production of estrogen by the ovaries declines dramatically, and this decline produces uncomfortable symptoms in some women—"hot flashes," nausea, fatigue, and rapid heartbeat, for example (Avis & others, 2015; Brockie & others, 2014). However, cross-cultural studies reveal wide variations in the menopause experience (Sievert & Obermeyer, 2012). For example, hot flashes are uncommon in Mayan women (Beyene, 1986), and Asian women report fewer hot flashes than women in Western societies (Payer, 1991). It is difficult to determine the extent to which these cross-cultural variations are due to genetic, dietary, reproductive, or cultural factors.

Menopause is not the negative experience for most women that it was once thought to be. One study in Taiwan found no significant effect of menopausal transition on women's quality of life (Cheng & others, 2007). However, the loss of fertility is an important marker for women.

Do men go through anything like the menopause that women experience? In other words, is there a male menopause? During middle adulthood, most men do not lose their capacity to father children, although there usually is a modest decline in their sexual hormone level and activity (Blumel & others, 2014). Testosterone production begins to decline about 1 percent a year during middle adulthood, and this decline can reduce sexual drive (Hyde & others, 2012). Sperm count usually shows a slow decline, but men do not lose their fertility altogether.

We will have more to say about the climacteric and the sexual attitudes and behaviors of middle-aged women and men in the chapter on "Gender and Sexuality."

connecting with careers

Sarah Kagan, Geriatric Nurse

Sarah Kagan is a professor of nursing at the University of Pennsylvania School of Nursing. She provides nursing consultation to patients, their families, nurses, and physicians regarding the complex needs of older adults related to their hospitalization. She also consults on research and the management of patients who have head and neck cancers. Kagan teaches in the undergraduate nursing program, where she directs a course on "Nursing Care in the Older Adult." In 2003, she was awarded a MacArthur Fellowship for her work in the field of nursing.

In Kagan's own words:

I'm lucky to be doing what I love—caring for older adults and families—and learning from them so that I can share this knowledge and develop or investigate better ways of caring. My special interests in the care of older adults who have cancer allow me the intimate privilege of being with patients at the best and worst times of their lives. That intimacy acts as a beacon—it reminds me of the value I and nursing as a profession contribute to society and the rewards offered in return (Kagan, 2008, p. 1).

Sarah Kagan with a patient.
© Jacqueline Larma/AP Images

For more information about what geriatric nurses do, see the Careers in Life-Span Development *appendix.*

LATE ADULTHOOD

Late adulthood brings an increased risk of physical disability, but there is considerable variability in rates of decline in functioning. Let's explore changes in physical appearance and the cardiovascular system in older adults.

Physical Appearance   The changes in physical appearance that take place in middle adulthood become more pronounced in late adulthood. Most noticeable are facial wrinkles and age spots. Our weight usually drops after we reach 60 years of age, likely because we lose muscle, which also gives our bodies a more "sagging" look. Recent research indicates that obesity was linked to mobility limitation in older adults (Murphy & others, 2014). The good news is that exercise and weight lifting can help slow the decrease in muscle mass and improve the older adult's body appearance (Fragala, Kenny, & Kuchel, 2015; Fragala & others, 2014; Zhang & others, 2015). A recent study found that long-term aerobic exercise was linked with greater muscle strength in 65- to 86-year-olds (Crane, Macneil, & Tarnopsolsky, 2013).

Circulatory System   Significant changes also take place in the circulatory system of older adults (Krakoff & others, 2014). In late adulthood, hypertension becomes even more problematic and the likelihood of a stroke increases. In one analysis, 57 percent of 80-year-old men and 60 percent of 81-year-old women had hypertension, and 32 percent of the men and 31 percent of the women had experienced a stroke (Aronow, 2007). Today, most experts on aging recommend that consistent blood pressure above 120/80 should be treated to reduce the risk of heart attack, stroke, or kidney disease. A rise in blood pressure with age can be linked to illness, obesity, stiffening of blood vessels, stress, or lack of exercise (Kramer, 2015). The longer any of these factors persist, the higher the individual's blood pressure gets. Various drugs, a healthy diet, and exercise can reduce the risk of cardiovascular disease in older adults (Tselepis, 2014).

Geriatric nurses can be especially helpful to older adults who experience acute or chronic illness. To read about the work of one geriatric nurse, see the *Connecting with Careers* profile.

Review

- What are cephalocaudal and proximodistal patterns?
- How do height and weight change in infancy and childhood?
- What changes characterize puberty?
- What physical changes occur in early adulthood?
- How do people develop physically during middle adulthood?
- What is the nature of physical changes in late adulthood?

Connect

- In this section, you learned that growth spurts in puberty differ for boys and girls. What research methods probably were used to collect such data?

Reflect *Your Own Personal Journey of Life*

- How old were you when you started puberty? How do you think this timing affected your social relationships and development?

2 The Brain **LG2** Describe how the brain changes through the life span

The Neuroconstructivist View · Brain Physiology · Infancy · Childhood · Adolescence · Adulthood and Aging

Until recently, little was known for certain about how the brain changes as we grow and age. Today, dramatic progress is being made in understanding these changes (Casey, 2015; de Haan, 2015; Gao & others, 2015; Johnson, Jones, & Gliga, 2015; Luna, Marek, & Larsen, 2015). The study of age-related changes in the brain is one of the most exciting frontiers in science. As we saw in "Biological Beginnings," remarkable changes occur in the brain during prenatal development. Here we consider the changes in the brain from infancy through late adulthood. Before exploring these developmental changes, let's first explore what is meant by the neuroconstructivist view and examine some key structures of the brain and see how they function.

THE NEUROCONSTRUCTIVIST VIEW

Not long ago, scientists thought that our genes exclusively determine how our brains are "wired" and that the cells in the brain responsible for processing information just maturationally unfold with little or no input from environmental experiences. In that view, your genes provide the blueprint for your brain and you are essentially stuck with it. This view, however, has turned out to be wrong. Instead, researchers have found that the brain has plasticity and its development depends on context (Berardi, Sale, & Maffei, 2015; Dennis & others, 2014; Johnson, Jones, & Gliga, 2015; Sale, Berardi, & Maffei, 2014).

The brain depends on experiences to determine how connections are made (Holman & de Villers-Sidani, 2014). Before birth, it appears that genes mainly direct basic wiring patterns. Neurons grow and travel to distant places awaiting further instructions (Nelson, 2013). After birth, the inflowing stream of sights, sounds, smells, touches, language, and eye contact help shape the brain's neural connections.

Thus, the dogma of the unchanging brain has been discarded and researchers are mainly focused on context-induced plasticity of the brain over time (Johnson, Jones, & Gliga, 2015; Zelazo, 2013). The development of the brain mainly changes in a bottom-up, top-down sequence with sensory, appetitive (eating, drinking), sexual, sensation-seeking, and risk-taking brain linkages maturing first and higher-level brain linkages such as self-control, planning, and reasoning maturing later (Zelazo, 2013).

In the increasingly popular **neuroconstructivist view,** (a) biological processes (genes, for example) and environmental experiences (enriched or impoverished, for example) influence the brain's development; (b) the brain has plasticity and is context dependent; and

neuroconstructivist view Developmental perspective in which biological processes and environmental conditions influence the brain's development; the brain has plasticity and is context dependent; and cognitive development is closely linked with brain development.

(c) development of the brain and cognitive development are closely linked. These factors constrain or advance the construction of cognitive skills (Westermann, Thomas, & Karmiloff-Smith, 2011). The neuroconstructivist view emphasizes the importance of interactions between experiences and gene expression in the brain's development, much as the epigenetic view proposes (Dennis & others, 2014).

BRAIN PHYSIOLOGY

The brain includes a number of major structures. The key components of these structures are *neurons*—nerve cells that handle information processing.

FIGURE 4

THE HUMAN BRAIN'S HEMISPHERES.
The two hemispheres of the human brain are clearly seen in this photograph. It is a myth that the left hemisphere is the exclusive location of language and logical thinking or that the right hemisphere is the exclusive location of emotion and creative thinking.
© A.Glauberman/Science Source

Structure and Function Looked at from above, the brain has two halves, or hemispheres (see Figure 4). The top portion of the brain, farthest from the spinal cord, is known as the forebrain. Its outer layer of cells, the cerebral cortex, covers it like a thin cap. The cerebral cortex is responsible for about 80 percent of the brain's volume and is critical in perception, thinking, language, and other important functions.

Each hemisphere of the cortex has four major areas, called lobes. Although the lobes usually work together, each has somewhat different primary functions (see Figure 5):

· *Frontal lobes* are involved in voluntary movement, thinking, personality, emotion, memory, sustained attention, and intentionality or purpose.
· *Occipital lobes* function in vision.
· *Temporal lobes* have an active role in hearing, language processing, and memory.
· *Parietal lobes* play important roles in registering spatial location, focusing attention, and maintaining motor control.

Deeper in the brain, beneath the cortex, lie other key structures. These include the hypothalamus and the pituitary gland as well as the amygdala, which plays an important role in emotions, and the hippocampus, which is especially important in memory and emotion.

Neurons As we discussed earlier, neurons process information. Figure 6 shows some important parts of the neuron, including the axon and dendrites. Basically, an axon sends electrical signals away from the central part of the neuron. At tiny gaps called synapses, the axon communicates with the dendrites of other neurons, which then pass the signals on. The communication in the synapse occurs through the release of chemical substances known as *neurotransmitters* (Emes & Grant, 2013; Zanella & others, 2014).

As Figure 6 shows, most axons are covered by a myelin sheath, which is a layer of fat cells. Development of this sheath through a process called **myelination** helps impulses travel faster along the axon, increasing the speed and efficiency with which information travels from neuron to neuron (Buttermore, Thaxton, & Bhat, 2013). Myelination also is involved in providing energy to neurons and in facilitating communication (White & Kramer-Albers, 2014).

To some extent, the type of information handled by neurons depends on whether they are in the left or the right hemisphere of the cortex (Griffiths & others, 2013; McAvoy & others, 2015). Speech and grammar, for example, depend on activity in the left hemisphere in most people; humor and the use of metaphors depend on activity in the right hemisphere (Moore, Brendel, & Fiez, 2014). This specialization of function in one hemisphere of the cerebral cortex or the other is called **lateralization.** However, most neuroscientists agree that complex functions such as reading or performing music involve both hemispheres. Labeling people as "left-brained" because they are logical thinkers or "right-brained" because they are creative thinkers does not reflect the way the brain's hemispheres work. For the most part, complex thinking is the outcome of communication between the hemispheres of the brain (Ibrahim & Eviatar, 2012).

The degree of lateralization may change as people develop through the human life span. Let's now explore a number of age-related changes in the brain.

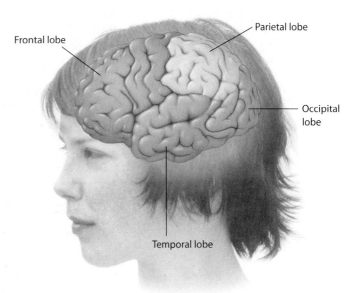

Frontal lobe

Parietal lobe

Occipital lobe

Temporal lobe

FIGURE 5

THE BRAIN'S FOUR LOBES. Shown here are the locations of the brain's four lobes: frontal, occipital, temporal, and parietal.

myelination The process of encasing axons with a myelin sheath, which helps increase the speed and efficiency of information processing.

lateralization Specialization of function in one hemisphere or the other of the cerebral cortex.

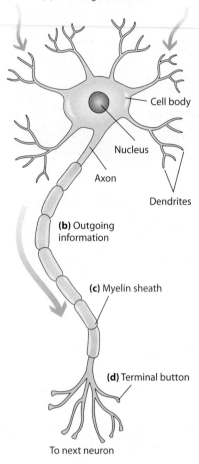

(a) Incoming information

Cell body

Nucleus

Axon

Dendrites

(b) Outgoing information

(c) Myelin sheath

(d) Terminal button

To next neuron

FIGURE **6**

THE NEURON. (*a*) The dendrites of the cell body receive information from other neurons, muscles, or glands through the axon. (*b*) Axons transmit information away from the cell body. (*c*) A myelin sheath covers most axons and speeds information transmission. (*d*) As the axon ends, it branches out into terminal buttons.

INFANCY

Brain development occurs extensively during the prenatal period. The brain's development is also substantial during infancy and later (Alcauter & others, 2014; Steinberg, 2015a, b).

Conducting Research and Measuring the Infant's Brain Activity Among the researchers who are making strides in finding out more about the brain's development in infancy are:

- Martha Ann Bell and her colleagues (Bell, 2015; Bell & Cuevas, 2012, 2014, 2015; Bell, Kraybill, & Diaz, 2014; Morasch, Raj, & Bell, 2013) who are studying brain-behavior links, emotion regulation, and the integration of cognition and emotion
- Charles Nelson and his colleagues (Berens & Nelson, 2015; Bick & others, 2015; McLaughlin & others, 2014; Moulson & Nelson, 2008; Nelson, 2007, 2013; Nelson, Fox, & Zeanah, 2014; Righi & others, 2014) who are exploring various aspects of memory development, face recognition and facial emotion, and the role of experience in influencing the course of brain development
- John Richards and his colleagues (Lloyd-Fox & others, 2015; Richards, 2009, 2010, 2013; Richards, Reynolds, & Courage, 2010; Richards & others, 2015; Sanchez, Richards, & Almi, 2012) who are examining sustained attention, perception of TV programs, and eye movements

Researchers have been successful in using the electroencephalogram (EEG), a measure of the brain's electrical activity, to learn about the brain's development in infancy (Bell, 2015; Lusby & others, 2014) (see Figure 7). Recently Patricia Kuhl and her colleagues at the Institute for Learning and Brain Sciences at the University of Washington have been using magnetoencephalography, or MEG, brain imaging machines to assess infants' brain activity. MEG maps brain activity by recording magnetic fields produced by electrical currents and is being used with infants to assess such perceptual and cognitive activities such as vision, hearing, and language in infants (see Figure 8).

FIGURE **7**

MEASURING THE ACTIVITY OF AN INFANT'S BRAIN WITH AN ELECTROENCEPHALOGRAM (EEG). By attaching up to 128 electrodes to a baby's scalp to measure the brain's activity, researchers have found that newborns produce distinctive brain waves that reveal they can distinguish their mother's voice from another woman's, even while they are asleep.
Courtesy of Vanessa Vogel Farley

FIGURE **8**

MEASURING THE ACTIVITY OF AN INFANT'S BRAIN WITH MAGNETOENCEPHALOGRAPHY (MEG). This baby's brain activity is being assessed with a MEG brain imaging device while the baby is listening to spoken words in a study at the Institute of Learning and Brain Sciences at the University of Washington. The infant sits under the machine and when he or she experiences a word, touch, sight, or emotion, the neurons working together in the infant's brain generate magnetic fields and MEG pinpoints the location of the fields in the brain.
© Dr. Patricia Kuhl, Institute for Learning and Brain Sciences, University of Washington

Changing Neurons

At birth, the newborn's brain is about 25 percent of its adult weight. By the second birthday, the brain is about 75 percent of its adult weight. Two key developments during these first two years involve the myelin sheath (the layer of fat cells that speeds up movement of electrical impulses along the axons) and connections between dendrites.

Myelination, the process of encasing axons with a myelin sheath, begins prenatally and continues after birth (see Figure 9). Myelination for visual pathways occurs rapidly after birth, reaching completion in the first six months. Auditory myelination is not completed until 4 or 5 years of age. Some aspects of myelination continue even into emerging adulthood and possibly beyond. Indeed, the most extensive changes in myelination in the frontal lobes occur during adolescence (Casey, 2015; Steinberg, 2015a, b).

Dramatic increases in dendrites and synapses (the tiny gaps between neurons across which neurotransmitters carry information) also characterize the development of the brain in the first two years of life (see Figure 10). Nearly twice as many of these connections are made as will ever be used (Huttenlocher & Dabholkar, 1997). The connections that are used become stronger and survive, while the unused ones are replaced by other pathways or disappear. In the language of neuroscience, these connections are "pruned" (Campbell & others, 2012). Figure 11 vividly illustrates the growth and later pruning of synapses in the visual, auditory, and prefrontal cortex areas of the brain (Huttenlocher & Dabholkar, 1997). As shown in Figure 11, "blooming and pruning" vary considerably by brain region in humans (Gogtay & Thompson, 2010).

Changing Structures

The areas of the brain do not mature uniformly (Blakemore & Mills, 2014; Casey, 2015). The frontal lobe is immature in the newborn. As neurons in the frontal lobe become myelinated and interconnected during the first year of life, infants develop an ability to regulate their physiological states (such as sleep) and gain more control over their reflexes. Cognitive skills that require deliberate thinking do not emerge until later (Bell, 2015; Bell & Fox, 1992). At about 2 months of age, the motor control centers of the brain develop to the point at which infants can suddenly reach out and grab a nearby object. At about 4 months, the neural connections necessary for depth perception begin to form. And at about 12 months, the brain's speech centers are poised to produce one of infancy's magical moments: when the infant utters its first word.

Early Experience and the Brain

Children who grow up in a deprived environment may have depressed brain activity (Berens & Nelson, 2015; Narvaez & others, 2013; Nelson,

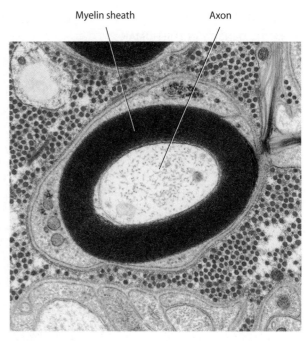

Myelin sheath   Axon

FIGURE 9

A MYELINATED NERVE FIBER. The myelin sheath, shown in brown, encases the axon (white). This image was produced by an electron microscope that magnified the nerve fiber 12,000 times. *What role does myelination play in the brain's development and children's cognition?*
© Steve Gschmeissner/Science Source

| At birth | 1 month | 3 months | 15 months | 24 months |

FIGURE 10

THE DEVELOPMENT OF DENDRITIC SPREADING. Note the increase in connectedness between neurons over the course of the first two years of life.
Source: Reprinted by permission of the publisher from The Postnatal Development of the Human Cerebral Cortex, Vols. I-VIII, *by J. LeRoy Conel, Cambridge, MA: Harvard University Press, Copyright © 1939, 1941, 1947, 1951, 1955, 1959, 1963, 1967 by the President and Fellows of Harvard College. Copyright © renewed 1967, 1969, 1975, 1979, 1983, 1987, 1991.*

FIGURE 11

SYNAPTIC DENSITY IN THE HUMAN BRAIN FROM INFANCY TO ADULTHOOD.
The graph shows the dramatic increase followed by pruning in synaptic density for three regions of the brain: visual cortex, auditory cortex, and prefrontal cortex. Synaptic density is believed to be an important indication of the extent of connectivity between neurons.

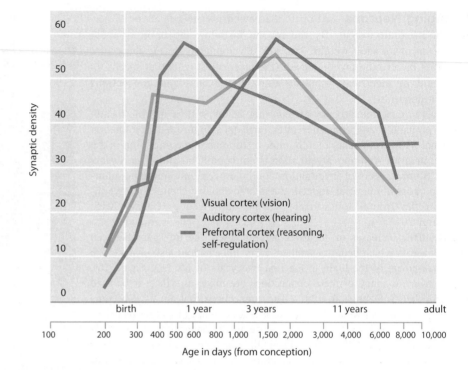

developmental **connection**

Brain Development

Might some regions of the brain be more closely linked with children's intelligence than others? Connect to "Intelligence."

Fox, & Zeanah, 2014). As shown in Figure 12, a child who grew up in the unresponsive and unstimulating environment of a Romanian orphanage showed considerably depressed brain activity compared with a normal child.

Are the effects of deprived environments reversible? There is reason to think that at least for some individuals the answer is yes (Dennis & others, 2014). The brain demonstrates both

(a)　　　　　　　　　　　　　　　(b)

FIGURE **12**

EARLY DEPRIVATION AND BRAIN ACTIVITY. These two photographs are PET (positron emission tomography) scans—which use radioactive tracers to image and analyze blood flow and metabolic activity in the body's organs. These scans show the brains of (*a*) a normal child and (*b*) an institutionalized Romanian orphan who experienced substantial deprivation since birth. In PET scans, the highest to lowest brain activity is reflected in the colors of red, yellow, green, blue, and black, respectively. As can be seen, red and yellow show up to a much greater degree in the PET scan of the normal child than that of the deprived Romanian orphan.

Courtesy of Dr. Harry T. Chugani, Children's Hospital of Michigan flexibility and resilience. Consider 14-year-old Michael Rehbein. At age 7, he began to experience uncontrollable seizures—as many as 400 a day. Doctors said the only solution was to remove the left hemisphere of his brain where the seizures were occurring. Recovery was slow, but his right hemisphere began to reorganize and take over functions that normally occur in the brain's left hemisphere, including speech (see Figure 13).

Neuroscientists note that what wires the brain—or rewires it, in the case of Michael Rehbein—is repeated experience (Nash, 1997). Each time a baby tries to touch an attractive object or gazes intently at a face, tiny bursts of electricity shoot through the brain, knitting together neurons into circuits. The results are some of the behavioral milestones we discuss in this and other chapters.

CHILDHOOD

The brain and other parts of the nervous system continue developing through childhood (Diamond, 2013). These changes enable children to plan their actions, to attend to stimuli more effectively, and to make considerable strides in language development.

During early childhood, the brain and head grow more rapidly than any other part of the body. Figure 14 shows how the growth curve for the head and brain advances more rapidly than the growth curve for height and weight. Some of the brain's increase in size is due to myelination and some is due to an increase in the number and size of dendrites. Some developmentalists conclude that myelination is important in the maturation of a number of abilities in children (Markant & Thomas, 2013). For example, myelination in the areas of the brain related to hand-eye coordination is not complete until about 4 years of age. Myelination in the areas of the brain related to focusing attention is not complete until the end of middle or late childhood.

The brain in early childhood is not growing as rapidly as it did in infancy, yet the anatomical changes in the child's brain between the ages of 3 and 15 are dramatic. By repeatedly obtaining brain scans of the same children for up to four years, scientists have found that children's brains experience rapid, distinct growth spurts (Gogtay & Thompson, 2010). The amount of brain material in some areas can nearly double in as little as one year, followed by a drastic loss of tissue as unneeded cells are purged and the brain continues to reorganize itself.

Significant changes in various structures and regions of the brain continue to occur during middle and late childhood (Johnson, Jones, & Gliga, 2015). In particular, the brain pathways and circuitry involving the **prefrontal cortex,** the highest level in the brain, continue to increase in middle and late childhood (Diamond, 2013). The brain is hierarchically organized and mainly develops from the bottom up, with sensory areas reaching maturity before the higher-level association areas such as the prefrontal cortex.

In one study, researchers found less diffusion and more focal activation in the prefrontal cortex from 7 to 30 years of age (Durston & others, 2006). The activation change was accompanied by increased efficiency in cognitive performance, especially in *cognitive control,* which involves flexible and effective control in a number of areas. These areas include controlling attention, reducing interfering thoughts, inhibiting motor actions, and being cognitively flexible in switching between competing choices (Diamond, 2013).

Developmental neuroscientist Mark Johnson and his colleagues (Johnson, Grossmann, & Cohen-Kadosh, 2009; Johnston, Jones, & Gliga, 2015) have proposed that the prefrontal cortex likely orchestrates the functions of many other brain regions during development. As part of this neural leadership and organizational role, the prefrontal cortex may provide an advantage to neural connections and networks that include the prefrontal cortex. In their view, the prefrontal cortex likely coordinates the best neural connections for solving a problem.

ADOLESCENCE

Until recently, little research has been conducted on developmental changes in the brain during adolescence. Although research in this area is still in its infancy, an increasing number of studies are under way (Blakemore & Mills, 2014; Casey, 2015; Monahan &

FIGURE **13**

PLASTICITY IN THE BRAIN'S HEMISPHERES. Michael Rehbein at 14 years of age. Following removal of the left hemisphere of Michael's brain because of uncontrollable seizures, his right hemisphere reorganized to take over the language functions normally carried out by corresponding areas in the left hemisphere of an intact brain.
Courtesy of The Rehbein Family

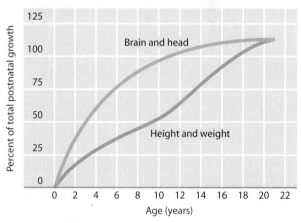

FIGURE **14**

GROWTH CURVES FOR THE HEAD AND BRAIN AND FOR HEIGHT AND WEIGHT. The more rapid growth of the brain and head can easily be seen. Height and weight advance more gradually over the first two decades of life.

prefrontal cortex The highest level of the frontal lobes that is involved in reasoning, decision making, and self-control.

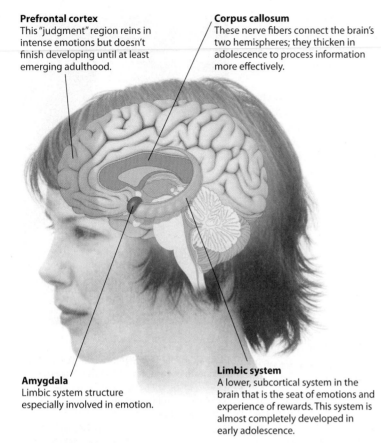

Prefrontal cortex
This "judgment" region reins in intense emotions but doesn't finish developing until at least emerging adulthood.

Corpus callosum
These nerve fibers connect the brain's two hemispheres; they thicken in adolescence to process information more effectively.

Amygdala
Limbic system structure especially involved in emotion.

Limbic system
A lower, subcortical system in the brain that is the seat of emotions and experience of rewards. This system is almost completely developed in early adolescence.

FIGURE 15

THE CHANGING ADOLESCENT BRAIN: PREFRONTAL CORTEX, LIMBIC SYSTEM, AND CORPUS CALLOSUM

corpus callosum A large bundle of axon fibers that connects the brain's left and right hemispheres.

limbic system The region of the brain where emotions and rewards are experienced.

amygdala A part of the brain's limbic system that is the seat of emotions such as anger.

others, 2015). Scientists now note that the adolescent's brain is different from the child's brain, and that in adolescence the brain is still growing (Reyna & Zayas, 2014; Steinberg, 2015a, b).

Earlier we indicated that connections between neurons become "pruned" as children and adolescents develop. Because of this pruning, by the end of adolescence individuals have "fewer, more selective, more effective neuronal connections than they did as children" (Kuhn, 2009, p. 153). And this pruning indicates that the activities adolescents choose to engage in or not to engage in influence which neural connections will be strengthened and which will disappear.

Using fMRI brain scans, scientists have discovered that adolescents' brains undergo significant structural changes (Casey, 2015; Raznahan & others, 2014; Reyna & Zayas, 2014). These structural changes occur in the corpus callosum, the prefrontal cortex, and the limbic system. The **corpus callosum,** where fibers connect the brain's left and right hemispheres, thickens in adolescence, which improves adolescents' ability to process information (Chavarria & others, 2014). We described advances in the development of the prefrontal cortex—the highest level of the frontal lobes involved in reasoning, decision making, and self-control—earlier. The prefrontal cortex doesn't finish maturing until the emerging adult years (18 to 25 years old) or later.

At a lower, subcortical level, the **limbic system,** which is the seat of emotions and where rewards are experienced, matures much earlier than the prefrontal cortex and is almost completely developed by early adolescence (Blakemore & Mills, 2014; Casey, 2015; Luna, Padmanabman, & Geier, 2014; Steinberg, 2015a, b). The limbic system structure that is especially involved in emotion is the **amygdala.** Figure 15 shows the locations of the corpus callosum, prefrontal cortex, and the limbic system.

With the onset of puberty, the levels of neurotransmitters change (McEwen, 2013). For example, an increase in the neurotransmitter dopamine occurs in both the prefrontal cortex and the limbic system during adolescence (Ernst & Spear, 2009). Increases in dopamine have been linked to increased risk taking and the use of addictive drugs (Steinberg, 2015a, b). Researchers have found that dopamine plays an important role in reward seeking during adolescence (Leyton & Vezina, 2014).

Let's further consider the developmental disjunction between the early development of the limbic system and the later development of the prefrontal cortex. This disjunction may account for an increase in risk taking and other problems in adolescence. To read further about risk-taking behavior in adolescence, see the *Connecting Development to Life* interlude.

Many of the changes in the adolescent brain that have been described involve the rapidly emerging field of *developmental social neuroscience* (which involves connections between development, the brain, and socioemotional processes) and *developmental cognitive neuroscience* (which involves links between development, cognition, and neuroscience) (Blakemore & Mills, 2014; Monahan & others, 2015). For example, consider leading researcher Charles Nelson's (2003) view that, although adolescents are capable of very strong emotions, their prefrontal cortex hasn't adequately developed to the point at which they can control these passions. It is as if their brain doesn't have the brakes to slow down their emotions. Or consider this interpretation of the development of emotion and cognition in adolescents: "early activation of strong 'turbo-charged' feelings with a relatively un-skilled set of 'driving skills' or cognitive abilities to modulate strong emotions and motivations" (Dahl, 2004, p. 18). And in the view of leading expert Jay Giedd (2007), biology doesn't make teens rebellious or have purple hair and it does not mean that they are going to do drugs, but it increases their chances of doing that.

Strategies for Helping Adolescents Reduce Their Risk-Taking Behavior

Beginning in early adolescence, individuals seek experiences that create high-intensity feelings. Adolescents like intensity, excitement, and arousal. They are drawn to music videos that shock and bombard the senses. Teenagers flock to horror and slasher movies. They dominate queues waiting to ride high-adrenaline rides at amusement parks. Adolescence is a time when sex, drugs, very loud music, and other high-stimulation experiences take on great appeal. It is a developmental period when an appetite for adventure, a predilection for risks, and desire for novelty and thrills seem to reach naturally high levels. While these patterns of emotional changes are present to some degree in most adolescents, it is important to recognize the wide range of individual differences during this period of development (Dahl, 2004, p. 6).

The self-regulatory skills necessary to inhibit risk taking often don't develop fully until later in adolescence or emerging adulthood (Casey, 2015). And, as we just saw, this gap between the increase in risk-taking behavior and the delay in self-regulation is linked to brain development in the limbic system (involved in pleasure seeking and emotion) taking place earlier than development of the frontal lobes (involved in self-regulation) (Steinberg, 2015a, b).

It is important for parents, teachers, mentors, and other responsible adults to effectively monitor adolescents' behavior. In many cases, adults decrease their monitoring of adolescents too early, leaving them to cope with tempting situations alone or with friends and peers. When adolescents are in tempting and dangerous situations with minimal adult supervision, their inclination to engage in risk-taking behavior combined with their immature self-regulatory

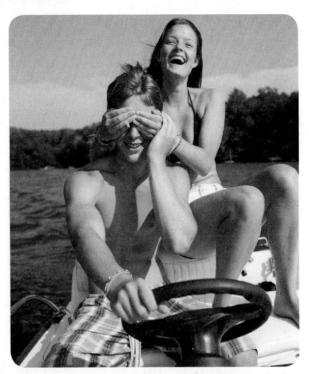

How might developmental changes in the brain be involved in adolescent risk taking? What are some strategies for reducing adolescent risk taking?
© Chris Garrett/Getty Images

skills can make them vulnerable to a host of negative outcomes (Steinberg, 2015a, b).

What does the nature-nurture debate suggest about the influence of adults who monitor adolescents' lives?

Of course, a major issue is which comes first, biological changes in the brain or experiences that stimulate these changes (Lerner, Boyd, & Du, 2008; Steinberg, 2015a, b). Consider a study in which the prefrontal cortex thickened and more brain connections formed when adolescents resisted peer pressure (Paus & others, 2008). Scientists have yet to determine whether the brain changes come first or whether the brain changes are the result of experiences with peers, parents, and others (Monahan & others, 2015). Once again, we encounter the nature/nurture issue that is so prominent in an examination of development through the life span. Nonetheless, there is adequate evidence that environmental experiences make important contributions to the brain's development (Steinberg, 2015a, b; Zelazo, 2013).

In closing this section on the development of the brain in adolescence, a further caution is in order. Much of the research on neuroscience and the development of the brain in adolescence is correlational in nature, and thus causal statements need to be scrutinized. This caution, of course, applies to any period in the human life span.

developmental **connection**

Brain Development

Developmental social neuroscience and developmental cognitive neuroscience are recent developed fields. Connect to "Introduction."

ADULTHOOD AND AGING

Changes in the brain continue during adulthood. Most of the research on the brains of adults, however, has focused on the aging brains of older adults. What are some of the general findings about the aging brain? How much plasticity and adaptability does it retain?

The Shrinking, Slowing Brain On average, the brain loses 5 to 10 percent of its weight between the ages of 20 and 90. Brain volume also decreases (Sala & others, 2012). A study found a decrease in total brain volume and volume in key brain structures such as the frontal lobes and hippocampus from 22 to 88 years of age (Sherwood & others, 2011). Another study found that the volume of the brain was 15 percent less in older adults than younger adults (Shan & others, 2005). In one analysis, it was concluded that in healthy aging the decrease in brain volume is due mainly to shrinkage of neurons, lower numbers of synapses, and reduced length of axons but only to a minor extent attributable to neuron loss (Fjell & Walhovd, 2010).

Some areas shrink more than others. The prefrontal cortex is one area that shrinks with aging, and recent research has linked this shrinkage with a decrease in working memory and other cognitive activities in older adults (Hoyer, 2015; Rosano & others, 2012). The sensory regions of the brain—such as the primary visual cortex, primary motor cortex, and somatosensory cortex—are less vulnerable to the aging process (Rodrique & Kennedy, 2011).

A general slowing of function in the brain and spinal cord begins in middle adulthood and accelerates in late adulthood (Rosano & others, 2012; Yang & others, 2015). Both physical coordination and intellectual performance are affected. For example, after age 70, many adults no longer show a knee jerk reflex and by age 90 most reflexes are much slower (Spence, 1989). The slowing of the brain can impair the performance of older adults on intelligence tests and various cognitive tasks, especially those that are timed (Lu & others, 2011).

Aging also has been linked to a decline in the production of some neurotransmitters. Reduction in acetylcholine is linked to memory loss, especially in people with Alzheimer disease (Jensen & others, 2015; Merad & others, 2014). Severe reductions in dopamine are involved in a reduction in motor control in Parkinson disease (Park & others, 2014; Ruitenberg & others, 2015).

Historically, as in the research just discussed, much of the focus on links between brain functioning and aging has been on volume of brain structures and regions. Recently, increased emphasis is being given to changes in myelination and neural networks. Research indicates that demyelination (a deterioration in the myelin sheath that encases axons, which is associated with information processing) of the brain occurs with aging in older adults (Callaghan & others, 2014; Rodrique & Kennedy, 2011).

The Adapting Brain The human brain has remarkable repair capability (Cai & others, 2014). Even in late adulthood, the brain loses only a portion of its ability to function, and the activities older adults engage in can influence the brain's development (Ansado & others, 2013). For example, an fMRI study found that higher levels of aerobic fitness were linked with greater volume in the hippocampus, which translates into better memory (Erickson & others, 2011).

Three areas reflect the adaptiveness of the human brain in older adults: (1) the capacity to generate new neurons, (2) dendritic growth, and (3) delateralization. Researchers have found that **neurogenesis,** the generation of new neurons, does occur in lower mammalian species such as mice (Berry & others, 2012; Kask & others, 2015). Also, research indicates that exercise and an enriched, complex environment can generate new brain cells in mice and that stress reduces the cells' survival rate (Lee & others, 2013; Ramirez-Rodriquez & others, 2014; Shin & others, 2013) (see Figure 16). And one study revealed that coping with stress stimulated hippocampal neurogenesis in adult monkeys (Lyons & others, 2010). Researchers also recently have discovered that if rats are cognitively challenged to learn something, new brain cells survive longer (Shors, 2009).

It also is now accepted that neurogenesis can occur in humans (Kazanis, 2013; Peretto & Bonfanti, 2014). However, researchers have documented neurogenesis only in two brain regions: the hippocampus (Stolp & Molnar, 2015), which is involved in memory, and the olfactory bulb (Brann & Firestein, 2014), which is involved in smell (Brann & Firestein, 2014). It also is not known what functions these new brain cells perform, and at this point researchers have documented that they last only a few weeks (Nelson, 2006). Researchers currently are studying factors that might inhibit and promote neurogenesis, including various drugs, stress, and exercise (Gregoire & others, 2014; Hoeijmakers, Lucassen, & Korosi, 2015; Niwa & others, 2015; Schoenfeld & Gould, 2013). They also are examining how the grafting of neural stem cells to various regions of the brain, such as the hippocampus, might increase

neurogenesis The generation of new neurons.

Exercise   Enriched Environment

FIGURE 16

GENERATING NEW NERVE CELLS IN ADULT MICE. Researchers have found that exercise (running) and an enriched environment (a larger cage and many toys) can cause brain cells to divide and form new brain cells (Kempermann, van Praag, & Gage, 2000). Cells were labeled with a chemical marker that becomes integrated into the DNA of dividing cells (red). Four weeks later, they were also labeled to mark neurons (nerve cells). As shown here, both the running mice and the mice in an enriched environment had many cells that were still dividing (red) and others that had differentiated into new nerve cells (orange).
Courtesy of Dr. Fred Gage, The Salk Institute for Biological Studies

neurogenesis (Farioli-Vecchioli & others, 2014; Noguchi & others, 2015). And increasing attention is being given to the possible role neurogenesis might play in reversing the course of neurodegenerative diseases such as Alzheimer disease, Parkinson disease, and Huntington disease (Foltynie, 2015; Sarlak & Vincent, 2015; Wang & Jin, 2015).

Dendritic growth can occur in human adults, possibly even in older adults (Eliasieh, Liets, & Chalupa, 2007). One study compared the brains of adults at various ages (Coleman, 1986). From the forties through the seventies, the growth of dendrites increased. However, in people in their nineties, dendritic growth no longer occurred. This dendritic growth might compensate for the possible loss of neurons through the seventies but not in the nineties. Lack of dendritic growth in older adults could be due to a lack of environmental stimulation and activity.

Changes in lateralization may provide one type of adaptation in aging adults (Cabeza & Dennis, 2013; Davis & others, 2012; Hong & others, 2015). Recall that lateralization is the specialization of function in one hemisphere of the brain or the other. Using neuroimaging techniques, researchers have found that brain activity in the prefrontal cortex is lateralized less in older adults than in younger adults when they are engaging in cognitive tasks (Cabeza, 2002; Rossi & others, 2005). For example, Figure 17 shows that when younger adults are given the task of recognizing words they have previously seen, they process the information primarily in the right hemisphere, while older adults doing the same task are more likely to use both hemispheres (Madden & others, 1999).

The decrease in lateralization in older adults might play a compensatory role in the aging brain (Hong & others, 2015). That is, using both hemispheres may improve the cognitive functioning of older adults. Support for this view comes from another study in which older adults who used both brain hemispheres were faster at completing a working memory task than their counterparts who primarily used only one hemisphere (Reuter-Lorenz & others, 2000). However, the decrease in lateralization may be a mere by-product of aging; it may reflect an age-related decline in the brain's ability to specialize functions. In this view, during childhood the brain becomes increasingly differentiated in terms of its functions; as adults become older, this process may reverse. Support for the dedifferentiation view is found in the higher intercorrelations of performance on cognitive tasks in older adults than in younger adults (Baltes & Lindenberger, 1997).

What kinds of mental activities can slow the changes in the brain that occur with age? To read about how one group of researchers is seeking to answer this question, see the *Connecting with Research* interlude.

FIGURE 17

THE DECREASE IN BRAIN LATERALIZATION IN OLDER ADULTS. Younger adults primarily used the right prefrontal region of the brain (*top left photo*) during a recall memory task, whereas older adults used both the left and right prefrontal regions (*bottom two photos*).
Courtesy of Dr. Roberto Cabeza

The Nun Study

The Nun Study, directed by David Snowdon, is an intriguing, ongoing investigation of aging in 678 nuns, many of whom have lived in a convent in Mankato, Minnesota (Pakhomov & Hemmy, 2014; Snowdon, 1997, 2002, 2003; Tyas & others, 2007). Each of the 678 nuns agreed to participate in annual assessments of their cognitive and physical functioning. They also agreed to donate their brains for scientific research when they die, and they are the largest group of brain donors in the world. Examination of the nuns' donated brains, as well as others, has led neuroscientists to believe that the brain has a remarkable capacity to change and grow, even in old age. The Sisters of Notre Dame in Mankato lead an intellectually challenging life, and brain researchers believe this contributes to their quality of life as older adults and possibly to their longevity.

(a)

Findings from the Nun Study so far include the following:

- Positive emotions early in adulthood were linked to longevity (Danner, Snowdon, & Friesen, 2001). Handwritten autobiographies from 180 nuns, composed when they were 22 years of age, were scored for emotional content. The nuns whose early writings had higher scores for positive emotional content were more likely to still be alive at 75 to 95 years of age than their counterparts whose early writings were characterized by negative emotional content.

- Sisters who had taught for most of their lives showed more moderate declines in intellectual skills than those who had spent most of their lives in service-based tasks, a finding supporting the notion that stimulating the brain with intellectual activity keeps neurons healthy and alive (Snowdon, 2002).

This study and other research provide hope that scientists will discover ways to tap into the brain's capacity to adapt in order to prevent and treat brain diseases (Zhao & others, 2014a). For example, scientists might learn more effective ways to improve older adults' cognitive functioning, reduce Alzheimer disease, and help older adults recover from strokes (Adriaanse & others, 2014; Vinters, 2015). Even when areas of the brain are permanently damaged by stroke, new message routes can be created to get around the blockage or to resume the function of the damaged area, indicating that the brain does adapt.

(b)

(*a*) Sister Marcella Zachman (*left*) finally stopped teaching at age 97. Now, at 99, she helps ailing nuns exercise their brains by quizzing them on vocabulary or playing a card game called Skip-Bo, at which she deliberately loses. Sister Mary Esther Boor (*right*), also 99 years of age, is a former teacher who stays alert by doing puzzles and volunteering to work the front desk. (*b*) A technician holds the brain of a deceased Mankato nun. The nuns donate their brains for research that explores the effects of stimulation on brain growth.
© James Balog

Although the Nun Study's results are intriguing, an order of nuns is in some ways a self-selected group whose members may come to share many social and environmental characteristics through long years of living together. How might future researchers account for any potential biases in such studies?

Review Connect Reflect

LG2 Describe how the brain changes through the life span

Review

- What are the major areas of the brain, and how does it process information?
- How does the brain change during infancy?
- What characterizes the development of the brain in childhood?
- How can the changes in the brain during adolescence be summarized?
- What is the aging brain like?

Connect

- What types of brain research technology can be used to study infants that cannot be used to study them before they are born? Which types can be used on adults but not infants? How might these differences in research tools affect our understanding of how the human brain functions across the life span?

Reflect *Your Own Personal Journey of Life*

- If you could interview the Mankato nuns, what questions would you want to ask them?

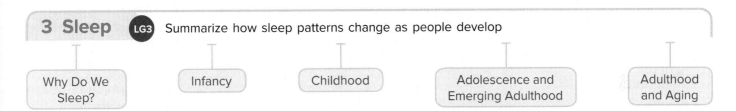

3 Sleep
LG3 Summarize how sleep patterns change as people develop

Why Do We Sleep?	Infancy	Childhood	Adolescence and Emerging Adulthood	Adulthood and Aging

Sleep restores, replenishes, and rebuilds our brains and bodies. What function does sleep have in people's lives? How do sleep patterns change across the life span?

WHY DO WE SLEEP?

A number of theories have been proposed about why we sleep. From an evolutionary perspective, all animals sleep, and this sleep likely is necessary for survival. Thus, sleep may have developed because animals needed to protect themselves at night. A second perspective is that sleep is restorative, with sleep replenishing and rebuilding the brain and body after the day's activities. In support of this restorative function, many of the body's cells show increased production and reduced breakdowns of proteins during sleep (Picchioni & others, 2014). Further, a current hypothesis is that sleep is essential to clearing out waste in neural tissues, such as metabolites and cerebrospinal fluid (Xie & others, 2013). A third perspective is that sleep is critical for brain plasticity (Barnes & Wilson, 2014). For example, neuroscientists recently have argued that sleep increases synaptic connections between neurons (Gronli, Soule, & Bramham, 2014). These increased synaptic connections during sleep have been linked to improved consolidation of memories (Pace-Schott & Spencer, 2015). Further, a recent research review concluded that not only can sleep improve memory, but losing just a few hours of sleep a night has negative effects on attention, reasoning, and decision making (Diekelmann, 2014).

In sum, sleep likely serves a number of important functions, with no one theory accounting for all of these functions. Let's now turn our attention to how sleep functions at different points in the human life span.

INFANCY

How much do infants sleep? Can any special problems develop regarding infants' sleep?

The Sleep/Wake Cycle   When we were infants, sleep consumed more of our time than it does now (Lushington & others, 2014). Newborns sleep 16 to 17 hours a day, although some sleep more and others less—the range is from a low of about 10 hours to a high of about 21 hours per day. A recent research review concluded that infants 0 to 2 years of age slept an average of 12.8 hours out of the 24, within a range of 9.7 to 15.9 hours (Galland & others, 2012). A recent study also revealed that by 6 months of age the majority of infants slept through the night, awakening their parents only one or two nights per week (Weinraub & others, 2012).

Although total sleep remains somewhat consistent for young infants, their sleep during the day does not always follow a rhythmic pattern. An infant might change from sleeping several long bouts of 7 or 8 hours to three or four shorter sessions only several hours in duration. By about 1 month of age, most infants have begun to sleep longer at night. By 6 months of age, they usually have moved closer to adult-like sleep patterns, spending their longest span of sleep at night and their longest span of waking during the day (Sadeh, 2008).

The most common infant sleep-related problem reported by parents is nighttime waking (Hospital for Sick Children & others, 2010). Surveys indicate that 20 to 30 percent of infants have difficulty going to sleep and staying asleep at night (Sadeh, 2008). One study revealed that maternal depression during pregnancy, early introduction of solid foods, infant TV viewing, and child-care attendance were related to shorter duration of infant sleep (Nevarez & others, 2010). And a recent study found that nighttime wakings at 1 year of age predicted lower sleep efficiency at 4 years of age (Tikotzky & Shaashua, 2012).

REM Sleep   A much greater amount of time is taken up by *REM (rapid eye movement)* sleep in infancy than at any other point in the life span. Figure 18 shows developmental changes in the average number of total hours spent in REM and non-REM sleep. Unlike adults, who spend about one-fifth of their night in REM sleep, infants spend about half of their sleep time in REM sleep, and they often begin their sleep cycle with REM sleep rather than non-REM sleep. By the time infants reach 3 months of age, the percentage of time they spend in REM sleep decreases to about 40 percent, and REM sleep no longer begins their sleep cycle.

Why do infants spend so much time in REM sleep? Researchers are not certain. The large amount of REM sleep may provide infants with added self-stimulation, since they spend less time awake than do older children. REM sleep also might promote the brain's development in infancy (Graven, 2006).

When adults are awakened during REM sleep, they frequently report that they have been dreaming, but when they are awakened during non-REM sleep they are much less likely to report they have been dreaming (Cartwright & others, 2006). Since infants spend more time

FIGURE **18**

SLEEP ACROSS THE HUMAN LIFE SPAN

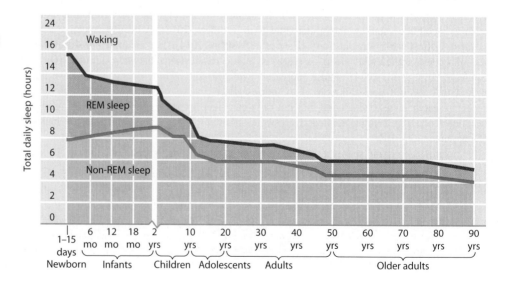

than adults in REM sleep, can we conclude that they dream a lot? We don't know whether infants dream or not, because they don't have any way of reporting dreams.

SIDS   Sudden infant death syndrome (SIDS) is a condition that occurs when infants stop breathing, usually during the night, and die suddenly without an apparent cause. SIDS remains the highest cause of infant death in the United States, with nearly 3,000 infant deaths attributed to it annually (Montagna & Chokroverty, 2011). Risk of SIDS is highest at 2 to 4 months of age (NICHD, 2014).

Since 1992, the American Academy of Pediatrics (AAP) has recommended that infants be placed to sleep on their backs to reduce the risk of SIDS, and the frequency of prone (stomach) sleeping among U.S. infants and infants in many other countries has dropped dramatically (AAPTFIPS, 2000; Elder, 2015; Wennergren & others, 2015). Researchers have found that the rate of SIDS does indeed decrease when infants sleep on their backs rather than their stomachs or sides (Liebenthal & others, 2015; Wong & others, 2013). Why? Because sleeping on their backs increases their access to fresh air and reduces their chances of getting overheated.

In addition to sleeping in a prone position (stomach down), researchers have found that the following are risk factors for SIDS:

- Heart arrhythmias are estimated to occur in as many as 15 percent of SIDS cases, and two recent studies found that gene mutations were linked to the occurrence of these arrhythmias (Brion & others, 2012).
- SIDS occurs more often in infants with abnormal brain stem functioning involving the neurotransmitter serotonin (Rognum & others, 2014).
- Six percent of infants with sleep apnea, a temporary cessation of breathing in which the airway is completely blocked, usually for 10 seconds or longer, die of SIDS (Ednick & others, 2010).
- Low birth weight infants are 5 to 10 times more likely to die of SIDS than are their normal-weight counterparts (Horne & others, 2002).
- Infants whose siblings have died of SIDS are two to four times as likely to die of it (Lenoir, Mallet, & Calenda, 2000).
- African American and Eskimo infants are four to six times as likely as all others to die of SIDS (Ige & Shelton, 2004; Kitsantas & Gaffney, 2010).
- Breast feeding is linked to a lower incidence of SIDS (Byard, 2013).
- SIDS is more common in lower socioeconomic groups (Hogan, 2014).
- SIDS occurs more often in infants who are passively exposed to cigarette smoke (Cerpa & others, 2015; Jarosinska & others, 2014).
- SIDS is more common when infants and parents share the same bed (Senter & others, 2010).
- SIDS is more common if infants sleep in soft bedding (McGarvey & others, 2006).
- SIDS is more likely to occur in infants who do not use a pacifier when they go to sleep than in those who do use a pacifier (Moon & others, 2012; Walsh & others, 2014).
- SIDS is less common when infants sleep in a bedroom with a fan. One study revealed that sleeping in a bedroom with a fan lowers the risk of SIDS by 70 percent (Coleman-Phox, Odouli, & Li, 2008).

It is generally now accepted that the most critical factor in predicting whether an infant will develop SIDS is prone sleeping. In a recent research review, it was concluded that the two other factors that place infants at the highest risk for SIDS are (1) maternal smoking, and (2) bed sharing (Mitchell & Krous, 2015).

Sleep and Cognitive Development   Might infant sleep be linked to children's cognitive development? A recent study revealed that infants who did most of their sleeping at night (rather than during the daytime) engaged in a higher level of executive function at age 4 (Bernier & others, 2013). The link between infant sleep and children's cognitive functioning likely occurs because of sleep's role in brain maturation and memory consolidation, which may improve daytime alertness and learning (Sadeh, 2007). Another recent study found that poor sleep consolidation in infancy as associated with language delays in early childhood (Dionne & others, 2011).

Is this a good sleep position for this 3-month-old infant? Why or why not?
© Maria Teijeiro/Getty Images RF

sudden infant death syndrome (SIDS)
Condition that occurs when an infant stops breathing, usually during the night, and suddenly dies without an apparent cause.

What characterizes children's sleep?
© Sigrid Olsson/PhotoAlto/Corbis RF

CHILDHOOD

A good night's sleep is an important aspect of a child's development (El-Sheikh & Buckhalt, 2015; El-Sheikh & others, 2013; Kouros & El-Sheikh, 2015; Lushington & others, 2014). Experts recommend that young children get 11 to 13 hours of sleep each night and that first- to fifth-graders get 10 to 11 hours of sleep each night (National Sleep Foundation, 2014). Most young children sleep through the night and have one daytime nap (Moore, 2012).

Following is a sampling of recent research on factors linked to children's sleep problems:

· Preschool children who had a longer sleep duration were more likely to have better peer acceptance, social skills, and receptive vocabulary (Vaughn & others, 2015).

· A national survey indicated that children who do not get adequate sleep are more likely to show depressive symptoms, have problems at school, have a father in poor health, live in a family characterized by frequent disagreements and heated arguments, and live in an unsafe neighborhood than are children who get adequate sleep (Smaldone, Honig, & Byrne, 2007).

· Children who had trouble sleeping in childhood were more likely to have alcohol use problems in adolescence and early adulthood (Wong & others, 2010).

· Sleep problems in early childhood were a subsequent indicator of attention problems that in some cases persisted into early adolescence (O'Callaghan & others, 2010).

· Inadequate sleep duration at 4 years of age predicted inadequate sleep duration at 6 years of age (Koulouglioti & others, 2014).

Children can experience a number of sleep problems (Caldwell & Redeker, 2015). One estimate indicates that more than 40 percent of children experience a sleep problem at some point in their development (Boyle & Cropley, 2004). One analysis concluded that chronic sleep disorders that deprive children of adequate sleep may result in impaired brain development (Jan & others, 2010).

Child sleep expert Mona El-Sheikh (2013) recommends controlling the following aspects of the child's environment to improve the child's sleep: making sure the bedroom is cool, dark, and comfortable; maintaining consistent bedtimes and wake times; and creating positive family relationships. Also, helping the child slow down before bedtime often contributes to less resistance in going to bed. Reading the child a story, playing quietly with the child in the bath, and letting the child sit on the caregiver's lap while listening to music are calming activities.

ADOLESCENCE AND EMERGING ADULTHOOD

Might changing sleep patterns in adolescence contribute to adolescents' health-compromising behaviors? Recently there has been a surge of interest in adolescent sleep patterns (Doane & Thurston, 2014; Fuligni & others, 2015; Hysing & others, 2015; Orzech & others, 2014; Telzer & others, 2013).

In a national survey of youth, only 31 percent of U.S. adolescents got eight or more hours of sleep on an average school night (Eaton & others, 2008). In this study, the percentage of adolescents getting this much sleep on an average school night decreased as they got older (see Figure 19). Adolescents who got inadequate sleep (eight hours or less) on school nights were more likely to feel tired or sleepy, act cranky and irritable, fall asleep in school, be in a depressed mood, and drink caffeinated beverages than their counterparts who got optimal sleep (nine or more hours). Also, one study of more than 270,000 U.S. adolescents from 1991–2012 found that they have been decreasing the amount of sleep they get in recent years (Keyes & others, 2015).

Studies recently have confirmed that adolescents in other countries also are not getting adequate sleep (Leger & others, 2012; Short & others, 2012). In one study, Asian adolescents had later bedtimes and were getting less sleep than U.S. adolescents (Gradisar, Gardner, & Dohnt, 2011).

FIGURE 19

DEVELOPMENTAL CHANGES IN U.S. ADOLESCENTS' SLEEP PATTERNS ON AN AVERAGE SCHOOL NIGHT

Percentage of students who got 8 hours of sleep or more on an average school night

Grade	Percentage
9th	42.3
10th	32.4
11th	24.9
12th	21.8

Getting too little sleep in adolescence is linked to a number of problems, including various illnesses (Orzech & others, 2014), delinquency (Clinkinbeard & others, 2011), sleep disturbances in emerging and early adulthood (Dregan & Armstrong, 2010), and less effective attention (Beebe, Rose, & Amin, 2010). A longitudinal study in which adolescents completed daily diaries every 14 days in ninth, tenth, and twelfth grades found that regardless of how much students studied each day, when the students sacrificed sleep time to study more than usual, they had difficulty understanding what was taught in class and were more likely to struggle with class assignments the next day (Gillen-O'Neel, Huynh, & Fuligni, 2013). A recent Swedish study of 16- to 19-year-olds revealed short sleep duration was linked to a higher incidence of school absence (Hysing & others, 2015). Another recent study found that adolescents who got less than 7.7 hours of sleep per night on average had more emotional and peer-related problems, higher anxiety, and a higher level of suicidal ideation (Sarchiapone & others, 2014).

Why are adolescents getting too little sleep? Among the reasons given are the use of electronic media, caffeine intake, and changes in the brain coupled with early school start times (Owens, 2014). In one study, adolescents averaged four electronic activities (in some cases, simultaneous use of different devices) after 9 p.m. (Calamaro & others, 2009). Engaging is these electronic activities in the evening can replace sleep time, and such media use may increase sleep-disrupting arousal (Cain & Gradisar, 2010). Also, a recent study of fourth- and seventh-graders found that those sleeping near small screens (smartphones, for example), sleeping with a TV in their room, and engaging in more screen time had shorter sleep duration (Falbe & others, 2015).

Caffeine intake also is likely to be associated with adolescents not getting adequate sleep (Owens, 2014). Greater caffeine intake as early as 12 years of age is linked to later sleep onset, shorter sleep duration, and increased daytime sleepiness (Bryant Ludden & Wolfson, 2010; Carskadon & Tarokh, 2014; Orbeta & others, 2006). The association of caffeine consumption and daytime sleepiness is also related to lower academic achievement (James, Kristjansson, & Sigfusdottir, 2011). Further, researchers have yet to study the effects on adolescent sleep patterns of very high levels of caffeine intake involving high-energy drinks.

Mary Carskadon (2002, 2004, 2005, 2006, 2011a, b) has conducted a number of research studies on adolescent sleep patterns. She has found that adolescents sleep an average of 9 hours and 25 minutes when given the opportunity to sleep as long as they like. Most adolescents get considerably less sleep than this, especially during the week. This creates a sleep debt, which adolescents often try to make up on the weekend. Carskadon also has found that older adolescents are often more sleepy during the day than are younger adolescents. She concludes that this is not because of factors such as academic work and social pressures. Rather, her research suggests that adolescents' biological clocks undergo a hormonal phase shift as they get older. This pushes the time of wakefulness to an hour later than when they were young adolescents. Carskadon has found that the shift was caused by a delay in the nightly presence of the hormone melatonin, which is produced by the brain's pineal gland in preparing the body for sleep. Melatonin is secreted at about 9:30 p.m. in younger adolescents but is produced approximately an hour later in older adolescents, which delays the onset of sleep.

What are some developmental changes in sleep patterns during adolescence? How might these changes influence alertness at school?
© Gareth Brown/Corbis

Carskadon determined that early school starting times can result in grogginess and lack of attention in class and poor performance on tests. Based on this research, some schools are now starting later (Cassoff & others, 2013). For example, school officials in Edina, Minnesota, made the decision to start classes at 8:30 a.m. instead of 7:25 a.m. Discipline problems dropped, and so did the number of students reporting illness or depression. Test scores in Edina improved for high school students but not for middle school students—results that support Carskadon's theory that older adolescents are more affected by earlier school start times than younger adolescents are. Also, a recent study found that just a 30-minute delay in school start time was linked to improvements in adolescents' sleep, alertness, mood, and health (Owens, Belon, & Moss, 2010). In another study, early school start times were linked to a higher vehicle crash rate in adolescent drivers (Vorona & others, 2014). Recently, the

In Mary Carskadon's sleep laboratory at Brown University, an adolescent girl's brain activity is being monitored. Carskadon (2005) says that in the morning, sleep-deprived adolescents' "brains are telling them it's nighttime . . . and the rest of the world is saying it's time to go to school" (p. 19).
© Courtesy of Jim LoScalzo

American Academy of Pediatrics recommended that schools institute start times from 8:30 to 9:30 a.m. to improve adolescents' academic performance and quality of life (Adolescent Sleep Working Group, AAP, 2014).

Do sleep patterns change in emerging adulthood? Research indicates that they do (Galambos, Howard, & Maggs, 2011). A recent study revealed that more than 60 percent of college students were categorized as poor-quality sleepers (Lund & others, 2010). In this study, the weekday bedtimes and rise times of first-year college students were approximately 1 hour and 15 minutes later than those of seniors in high school (Lund & others, 2010). However, the first-year college students had later bedtimes and rise times than third- and fourth-year college students, indicating that at about 20 to 22 years of age, a reverse in the timing of bedtimes and rise times occurs. In this study, poor-quality sleep was linked to worse physical and mental health, and the students reported that emotional and academic stress negatively affected their sleep. In another study, the sleep quality of first-year college students was poorer during the months when they experienced the most stress (Galambos, Howard, & Maggs, 2011).

ADULTHOOD AND AGING

Young people are not the only ones who are getting inadequate sleep. Many adults don't get enough either. A recent statement by the American Academy of Sleep Medicine and Sleep Research Society (Luyster & others, 2012) emphasized that chronic sleep deprivation may contribute to cardiovascular disease and a shortened life span, and also result in cognitive and motor impairment that increase the risk of motor vehicle crashes and work-related accidents.

The average American adult gets just under seven hours of sleep a night. How much sleep do adults need to function optimally the next day? An increasing number of experts note that eight hours of sleep or more per night are necessary for optimal performance the next day. These experts argue that many adults have become sleep deprived (Banks & Dinges, 2008). Work pressures, school pressures, family obligations, and social obligations often lead to long hours of wakefulness and irregular sleep/wake schedules (Soderstrom & others, 2012).

Some aspects of sleep become more problematic in middle age (Green & others, 2012). In a recent analysis of sleep patterns from 20 to 90 years of age, total sleep for males decreased about 8 minutes per decade for males and about 10 minutes per decade for females as they got older (Dorffner, Vitr, & Anderer, 2015). Also in this study, as individuals aged, they engaged in more light sleep and less deep sleep. Beginning in the forties, wakeful periods are more frequent and there is less of the deepest type of sleep. The amount of time spent lying awake in bed at night begins to increase in middle age, which can produce a feeling of being less rested in the mornings (Abbott, 2003). Sleep problems in middle-aged adults are more common among individuals who take a higher number of prescription drugs, are obese, have cardiovascular disease, or are depressed (Miller & Cappuccio, 2007).

Beginning in middle adulthood and continuing through late adulthood, the timing of sleep also changes. Many older adults go to bed earlier at night and wake up earlier in the morning (Liu & Liu, 2005). Many older adults also take a nap in the afternoon.

Approximately 50 percent of older adults complain of having difficulty sleeping (Neikrug & Ancoli-Israel, 2010). Poor sleep can result in earlier death and is linked to a lower level of cognitive functioning. For example, a recent study of healthy older adults revealed that daytime napping and getting 6½ hours of sleep or more were associated with a lower risk of cognitive decline over a 10-year period (Keage & others, 2012).

Many of the sleep problems of older adults are associated with health problems (Rothman & Mattson, 2012). For example, a recent study found that middle-aged adults who sleep less than six hours a night on average had an increased risk of developing stroke symptoms (Ruiter & others, 2012). Here are some strategies to help older adults sleep better at night: avoid caffeine, avoid over-the-counter sleep remedies, stay physically active during the day, stay mentally active, and limit naps. A recent study found that engaging in regular aerobic exercise improved the sleep profiles of older men (Melancon, Lorrain, & Dionne, 2015).

Review *Connect* Reflect

LG3 Summarize how sleep patterns change as people develop

Review
- Why do people sleep?
- How can sleep be characterized in infancy?
- What changes occur in sleep during childhood?
- How does sleep change in adolescence and emerging adulthood?
- What changes in sleep take place during adulthood and aging?

Connect
- How might behavioral theory be applied to help older adults avoid difficulty in sleeping?

Reflect *Your Own Personal Journey of Life*
- How much sleep do you get on a typical night? Do you get enough sleep to function optimally the next day? Explain.

4 Longevity and Biological Aging

LG4 Explain longevity and the biological aspects of aging

Life Expectancy and Life Span · Centenarians · Biological Theories of Aging

How long do most people live, and what distinguishes people who live a very long time? What is it like to live to a very ripe old age, and why do we age in the first place?

LIFE EXPECTANCY AND LIFE SPAN

We are no longer a youthful society. As more individuals live to older ages, the proportion of individuals at different ages has become increasingly similar. Indeed, the concept of a period called "late adulthood" is a recent one—until the twentieth century, most individuals died before they reached 65. A much greater percentage of persons live to older ages today. However, the life span has remained virtually unchanged since the beginning of recorded history. **Life span** is the upper boundary of life, the maximum number of years an individual can live. The maximum life span of humans is approximately 120 to 125 years of age.

Life expectancy is the number of years that the average person born in a particular year will probably live. The average life expectancy of individuals born today in the United States is 78.3 years (U.S. Census Bureau, 2011). Sixty-five-year-olds in the United States today can expect to live an average of 18.6 more years (19.9 for females, 17.2 for males) (U.S. Census Bureau, 2011). Older adults who are 100 years of age can only expect to live an average of 2.3 years longer (U.S. Census Bureau, 2011). Keep in mind that it is not just improvements in the health and well-being of adults that has contributed to increased longevity but also the substantial reduction in infant deaths in recent decades.

How does the United States fare in life expectancy, compared with other countries around the world? We do considerably better than some and somewhat worse than others. In 2011, Monaco had the highest estimated life expectancy at birth (90 years), followed by Macau (a region of China near Hong Kong), Japan, and Singapore (84 years) (Central Intelligence Agency, 2012). Of 221 countries, the United States ranked fiftieth at 78 years. The lowest estimated life expectancy in 2011 occurred in the African countries of Chad, Guinea-Bissau, South Africa, and Swaziland (49 years). Differences in life expectancies across countries are due to factors such as health conditions and the availability of medical care throughout the life span.

Life expectancy also differs for various ethnic groups within the United States and for men and women (Centers for Disease Control and Prevention, 2012). For example, the life expectancy of African Americans (74) in the United States is five years lower than the life expectancy for non-Latino Whites (79) (Centers for Disease Control and Prevention, 2012).

© Comstock/PunchStock RF

To me old age is always fifteen years older than I am.

—**Bernard Baruch**
American statesman, 20th century

life span The upper boundary of life, which is the maximum number of years an individual can live. The maximum life span of humans is about 120 years of age.

Non-Latino White women have a life expectancy of 80.8, followed by African American women (76.8), non-Latino White men (75.9 years), and African American men (70.0 years). The ethnicity difference in life expectancy has been widening in recent years, likely because of the powerful influence of education. Some experts argue that catch-up may not be possible (Olshansky & others, 2012).

In 2010 the overall life expectancy for women was 80.8 years of age, and for men it was 75.7 years of age (Centers for Disease Control and Prevention, 2012). Beginning in the mid-thirties, females outnumber males; this gap widens during the remainder of the adult years. By the time adults are 75 years of age, more than 61 percent of the population is female; for those 85 and over, the figure is almost 70 percent female. Why can women expect to live longer than men? Social factors such as health attitudes, habits, lifestyles, and occupation are probably important (Saint Onge, 2009). For example, men are more likely than women to die from the leading causes of death in the United States, such as cancer of the respiratory system, motor vehicle accidents, cirrhosis of the liver, emphysema, and coronary heart disease (Yoshida & others, 2006). These causes of death are associated with lifestyle. For example, the sex difference in deaths due to lung cancer and emphysema occurs because men tend to be heavier smokers than women.

The sex difference in longevity also is influenced by biological factors (Gems, 2014; Regan & Partridge, 2013). In virtually all species, females outlive males. Women have more resistance to infections and degenerative diseases (Pan & Chang, 2012). For example, the female's estrogen production helps to protect her from arteriosclerosis (hardening of the arteries). And the additional X chromosome that women carry in comparison with men may be associated with the production of more antibodies to fight off disease. The sex difference in mortality is still present but less pronounced in late adulthood than earlier in adulthood and is especially linked to the higher level of cardiovascular disease in men than women (Yang & Kozloski, 2011).

CENTENARIANS

In industrialized countries, the number of centenarians (individuals 100 years and older) is increasing at a rate of approximately 7 percent each year (Perls, 2007). In the United States, there were only 15,000 centenarians in 1980, a number that rose to 72,000 in 2010 and is projected to reach 600,000 by 2050 (U.S. Census Bureau, 2011). The United States has the most centenarians, followed by Japan, China, and England/Wales (Hall, 2008). It is estimated that there are 75 to 100 supercentenarians (individuals 110 years or older) in the United States and about 300 to 450 worldwide (Perls, 2007).

  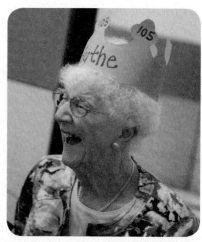

Three participants in the New England Centenarian Study: (*Left*) Agnes Fenton of Englewood, New Jersey, is 107 years of age and says she doesn't feel any older than when she was 15. She still cooks her own meals and her only health complaint is arthritis in her hand. (*Center*) Louis Carpenter, who lives in the Boston area, is 99 and every day carves wooden figures in his basement shop. Louis says his memory is still terrific. (*Right*) Edythe Kirchmaier of the New York City area is Facebook's oldest user at 105 years of age. As of July 2014, Edythe had more than 51,000 Facebook followers! She volunteers every week at her favorite charity, still drives her car, and frequently uses the Internet to look up information.
(left to right): © Carmine Galasso/The Record/MCT/Newscom; Courtesy of the New England Centenarian Study, Boston University; © Isaac Hernandez

Many people expect that "the older you get, the sicker you get." However, researchers are finding that this is not true for some centenarians (Willcox, Scapagnini, & Willcox, 2014). The researchers have found that chronic high-mortality diseases are markedly delayed for many years in centenarians, with many not experiencing disability until near the end of their lives (Sebastiani & Perls, 2012). And a recent study of centenarians from 100 to 119 years of age found that the older the age group (110 to 119 compared with 100 to 104, for example), the later the onset of diseases such as cancer and cardiovascular disease, as well as functional decline (Andersen & others, 2012). The research just described was conducted as part of the ongoing New England Centenarian Study.

In addition to the New England Centenarian study, another major ongoing study is the Georgia Centenarian study conducted by Leonard Poon and his colleagues (da Rosa & others, 2014; Martin & others, 2014; Mitchell & others, 2013; Poon & others, 2010, 2012). In a review, Poon and his colleagues (2010) concluded that social dynamics involving life events (experiencing a higher number of negative life events is linked to lower self-rated health), personality (conscientiousness is positively associated with higher levels of physical and mental health), cognition (cognitive measures are better predictors of mental health than physical health), and socioeconomic resources and support systems (social, economic, and personal resources are related to mental and physical health) contribute to the health and quality of life of older adults, including centenarians.

Yet another major study is the Chinese Longitudinal Healthy Longevity Survey, which includes older adults, some of whom are centenarians (Feng & others, 2012a, b; Zeng & Shen, 2010). In one investigation involving this sample, Chinese centenarians showed better coping and adjustment (greater personal tenacity, optimism, coping with negative moods, secure relationships, and personal control) than their Chinese counterparts in their nineties, eighties, or seventies (Zeng & Shen, 2010). In this study, 94- to 98-year-olds with better resilience had a 43 percent higher likelihood of becoming a centenarian than their same-aged counterparts who were less resilient.

How do centenarians view their lives? What are their explanations for being able to live so long?

Elza Winn concluded that he has been able to live so long because he made up his mind to do so. He says he was thinking about dying when he was 77 but decided to wait awhile (Segerberg, 1982).

Ruth Climer was a physical education teacher for many years and later competed in the Senior Olympics. To live to be 100, she says it is important to stay focused on what is good now and not give in to negative thoughts. Ruth also thinks staying busy and continually moving forward are keys to longevity as well (O'Dell, 2013).

Misao Okawo, at 117 years of age, was the oldest person in the world in 2015. A resident of Osaka, Japan, she attributes her longevity to eating sushi, getting eight hours of sleep per night, and being able to relax.

Gertrude Weaver, who at 116 years of age was the oldest person in the United States in 2015, lives in Arkansas and says her faith is what keeps her alive. She has been a wheelchair-dancing enthusiast for many years.

Simo Radulovich thinks living to an old age requires having a sense of humor, living moderately, and sleeping well. He still engages in exercise games with his friends every day and says he never has been afraid of anything, always having the confidence to get through the tough times (O'Dell, 2013).

Mary Butler says that finding something to laugh about every day helps you live longer. She thinks a good laugh is better than a dose of medicine anytime (Segerberg, 1982).

Duran Baez remarried at 50 and went on to have 15 more children. At 100 years of age, he was asked if he had any ambitions he had not yet realized. Duran replied, "No" (Segerberg, 1982).

Jeanne Louise Calment, a Frenchwoman, was the world's longest-living person. She died at 122 years of age in 1997 and attributed her longevity to a number of things. Among her comments as to why she was able to live so long are the following:

· Don't worry about things you can't do anything about.

· Have an occasional glass of Port wine and a diet rich in olive oil.

· Keep a sense of humor. Regarding her ability to live so long, she once said that God must have forgotten about her. On her 120th birthday, an interviewer asked her what kind of future she anticipated. She replied, "A very short one."

(*Top*) Frenchwoman Jeanne Louise Calment, shown here celebrating her 117th birthday. Calment was the oldest documented person. She lived to be 122 years of age. (Bottom) Japanese centenarian Misao Okawo was the oldest person in the world at 117 years of age in 2015, but died soon after her 117th birthday.
(top): © *Jean-Pierre Fizet/Sygma/Corbis; bottom:* © *Buddhika Weerasinghe/ Getty Images*

Life Expectancy

This test gives you a rough guide for predicting your longevity. The basic life expectancy for men is age 75, and for women it is 81. Write down your basic life expectancy. If you are in your fifties or sixties, you should add ten years to the basic figure because you have already proved yourself to be a durable individual. If you are over age 60 and active, you can even add another two years.

Decide how each item applies to you and add or subtract the appropriate number of years from your basic life expectancy.

1. Family history

____ Add five years if two or more of your grandparents lived to 80 or beyond.

____ Subtract four years if any parent, grandparent, sister, or brother died of a heart attack or stroke before 50.

____ Subtract two years if anyone died from these diseases before 60.

____ Subtract three years for each case of diabetes, thyroid disorder, breast cancer, cancer of the digestive system, asthma, or chronic bronchitis among parents or grandparents.

2. Marital status

____ If you are married, add four years.

____ If you are over 25 and not married, subtract one year for every unmarried decade.

3. Economic status

____ Add two years if your family income is over $60,000 per year.

____ Subtract three years if you have been poor for the greater part of your life.

4. Physique

____ Subtract one year for every 10 pounds you are overweight.

____ For each inch your girth measurement exceeds your chest measurement deduct two years.

____ Add three years if you are over 40 and not overweight.

5. Exercise

____ Add three years if you exercise regularly and moderately (jogging three times a week).

____ Add five years if you exercise regularly and vigorously (long-distance running three times a week).

____ Subtract three years if your job is sedentary.

____ Add three years if your job is active.

6. Alcohol

____ Add two years if you are a light drinker (one to three drinks a day).

____ Subtract five to ten years if you are a heavy drinker (more than four drinks per day).

____ Subtract one year if you are a teetotaler.

7. Smoking

____ Subtract eight years if you smoke two or more packs of cigarettes per day.

____ Subtract two years if you smoke one to two packs per day.

____ Subtract two years if you smoke less than one pack.

____ Subtract two years if you regularly smoke a pipe or cigars.

8. Disposition

____ Add two years if you are a reasoned, practical person.

____ Subtract two years if you are aggressive, intense, and competitive.

____ Add one to five years if you are basically happy and content with life.

____ Subtract one to five years if you are often unhappy, worried, and often feel guilty.

9. Education

____ Subtract two years if you have less than a high school education.

____ Add one year if you attended four years of school beyond high school.

____ Add three years if you attended five or more years beyond high school.

10. Environment

____ Add four years if you have lived most of your life in a rural environment.

____ Subtract two years if you have lived most of your life in an urban environment.

11. Sleep

____ Subtract five years if you sleep more than nine hours a day.

12. Temperature

____ Add two years if your home's thermostat is set at no more than 68° F.

13. Health care

____ Add three years if you have regular medical checkups and regular dental care.

____ Subtract two years if you are frequently ill.

____ **Your Life Expectancy Total**

FIGURE 20

CAN YOU LIVE TO BE 100?

· Becoming accustomed to the media attention she got, at 117 she stated, "I wait for death . . . and journalists."

· She walked, biked, and exercised a lot. Jeanne Louise began taking fencing lessons at 85 and rode a bicycle until she was 100.

What chance do you have of living to be 100? Genes play an important role in surviving to an extreme old age (Bihlmeyer & others, 2015; Robert & Fulop, 2014). There is increasing interest in studying *susceptibility genes,* which make an individual more vulnerable to specific diseases or acceleration of aging, and *longevity genes,* which make an individual less vulnerable to certain diseases and more likely to live to an older age (Crocco & others, 2015; Howard & Rogers, 2014; Wei & others, 2014). But as indicated in Figure 20, there are also other factors at work, such as family history, health (weight, diet, smoking, and exercise), education, personality, and lifestyle (Stevenson & others, 2015; Vigorito & Giallauria, 2014). The epigenetic approach focuses increasing interest on determining gene × environment (G × E) interactions that influence development (Davies & Cicchetti, 2014). Nonetheless, most people are not biologically capable of living to be 100 (Carnes, Olshansky, & Hayflick, 2013).

BIOLOGICAL THEORIES OF AGING

Even if we stay remarkably healthy, we begin to age at some point. In fact, life-span experts argue that biological aging begins at birth (Schaie, 2000). What are the biological explanations of aging? Intriguing explanations of why we age are provided by five biological theories: evolutionary, cellular clock, free-radical, mitochondrial, and hormonal stress.

Evolutionary Theory   In the evolutionary theory of aging, natural selection has not eliminated many harmful conditions and nonadaptive characteristics in older adults (Gems, 2014; Metcalf & Jones, 2015; Shokhirev & Johnson, 2014). Why? Because natural selection is linked to reproductive fitness, which is present only in the earlier part of adulthood. For example, consider Alzheimer disease, an irreversible brain disorder that does not appear until late middle adulthood or beyond. In evolutionary theory, if Alzheimer disease had occurred earlier in development, it might have been eliminated many centuries ago.

Cellular Clock Theory   **Cellular clock theory** is Leonard Hayflick's (1977) theory that cells can divide a maximum of about 75 to 80 times and that, as we age, our cells become less capable of dividing. Hayflick found that cells extracted from adults in their fifties to seventies divided fewer than 75 to 80 times. Based on the ways cells divide, Hayflick places the upper limit of the human life-span potential at about 120 to 125 years of age.

In the last decade, scientists have tried to fill in a gap in cellular clock theory (Boccardi & others, 2015; Ding & others, 2014; Zhao & others, 2014b). Hayflick did not know why cells die. The answer may lie at the tips of chromosomes, at telomeres, which are DNA sequences that cap chromosomes (Rizvi, Raza, & Mahdi, 2015; Zhang & others, 2014).

Each time a cell divides, the telomeres become shorter and shorter (see Figure 21). After about 70 or 80 replications, the telomeres are dramatically reduced and the cell no longer can reproduce. One study revealed that healthy centenarians had longer telomeres than unhealthy centenarians (Terry, Nolan, & others, 2008). And recent studies even have found that shorter telomere length is linked to having worse social relationships, being less optimistic, and showing greater hostility (Uchino & others, 2012; Zalli & others, 2014).

Injecting the enzyme *telomerase* into human cells grown in the laboratory can substantially extend the life of the cells beyond the approximately 70 to 80 normal cell divisions (Harrison, 2012). However, telomerase is present in approximately 85 percent of cancerous cells and thus may not produce healthy life extension of cells (Bertorelle & others, 2014). To capitalize on the high presence of telomerase in cancerous cells, researchers currently are investigating gene therapies that inhibit telomerase and lead to the death of cancerous cells while keeping healthy cells alive (Christodoulidou, 2013; Pandita & others, 2015; Verma & others, 2015). A recent focus of these gene therapies is on stem cells and their renewal (Hoffmeyer & others, 2012). Telomeres and telomerase are increasingly thought to be key components of the stem cell regeneration process, providing a possible avenue to restrain cancer and delay aging (Koziel & Herbert, 2015; Ozturk, 2015; Samsonraj & others, 2013; Shay, Reddel, & Wright, 2012).

Free-Radical Theory   A second microbiological theory of aging is **free-radical theory,** which states that people age because when cells metabolize energy, the by-products include unstable oxygen molecules known as free radicals. The free radicals ricochet around the cells, damaging DNA and other cellular structures (da Cruz & others, 2014). The damage can lead to a range of disorders, including cancer and arthritis (Kolovou & others, 2014; Phaniendra, Jestadi, & Periyasamy, 2015). Overeating is linked with an increase in free radicals, and researchers recently have found that calorie restriction—a diet restricted in calories although adequate in proteins, vitamins, and minerals—reduces the oxidative damage created by free radicals (Brandes & others, 2013; Cerqueira & others, 2012). In addition to diet, researchers also are exploring the role that exercise might play in reducing oxidative damage in cells (Muthusamy & others, 2012).

Mitochondrial Theory   There is increasing interest in the role that mitochondria—tiny bodies within cells that supply energy for function, growth, and repair—might play in aging

To be seventy years young is sometimes far more cheerful and hopeful than to be forty years old.

—OLIVER WENDELL HOLMES, SR.
American physician, 19th century

developmental connection

Culture

In Baltes' view, the benefits of evolutionary selection decrease with age and the need for culture increases with age. Connect to "Biological Beginnings."

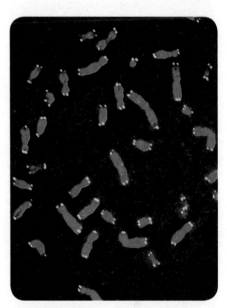

FIGURE 21

TELOMERES AND AGING. The photograph shows actual telomeres lighting up the tips of chromosomes.
Courtesy of Dr. Jerry Shay

cellular clock theory Leonard Hayflick's theory that the number of times human cells can divide is about 75 to 80. As we age, our cells become less able to divide.

free-radical theory A microbiological theory of aging stating that people age because when their cells metabolize energy, they generate waste that includes unstable oxygen molecules, known as free radicals, that damage DNA and other structures.

FIGURE 22

MITOCHONDRIA. This color-coded illustration of a typical cell shows mitochondria in green. The illustration also includes the nucleus (pink) with its DNA (brown). *How might changes in mitochondria be involved in aging?*
© J. Bavosi/Science Source

mitochondrial theory The theory that aging is caused by the decay of the mitochondria, which are tiny cellular bodies that supply energy for cell function, growth, and repair.

hormonal stress theory The theory that aging in the body's hormonal system can lower resistance to stress and increase the likelihood of disease.

(Romano & others, 2014; Valcarcel-Ares & others, 2014). (See Figure 22.) **Mitochondrial theory** states that aging is due to the decay of mitochondria. It appears that this decay is primarily due to oxidative damage and loss of critical micronutrients supplied by the cell (Eckert, Lipka, & Muller, 2012; Venditti, Di Stefano, & Di Meo, 2013; Ziegler, Wiley, & Velarde, 2015).

How do oxidative damage and loss of nutrients occur? Among the by-products of mitochondrial energy production are the free radicals just described. According to the mitochondrial theory, the damage caused by free radicals initiates a self-perpetuating cycle in which oxidative damage causes impairment of mitochondrial function, which results in the generation of even greater amounts of free radicals. The mitochondrial damage may lead to a range of disorders, including cancer, arthritis, and Alzheimer disease (Mastroeni & others, 2015; Romano & others, 2014)

Hormonal Stress Theory   The three theories of aging that we have discussed so far—cellular clock, free-radical, and mitochondrial—attempt to explain aging at the cellular level. In contrast, **hormonal stress theory** argues that aging in the body's hormonal system can lower resistance to stress and increase the likelihood of disease.

When faced with external challenges such as stressful situations, the human body adapts by altering internal physiological processes (Almeida & others, 2011). This process of adaptation and adjustment is referred to as *allostasis*. Allostasis is adaptive in the short term; however, continuous accommodation of physiological systems in response to stressors may result in *allostatic load*, a wearing down of body systems due to constant activity (McEwen, 1998).

Normally, when people experience stressors, the body responds by releasing certain hormones. As people age, the hormones stimulated by stress remain at elevated levels longer than when they were younger (Finch, 2011). These prolonged, elevated levels of stress-related hormones are associated with increased risks for many diseases, including cardiovascular disease, cancer, diabetes, and hypertension (Gems & Partridge, 2013; Steptoe & Kivimaki, 2012).

A variation of hormonal stress theory has emphasized the contribution of a decline in immune system functioning with aging (Mate, Madrid, & la Fuente, 2014; Muller & Pawelec, 2015). Aging contributes to immune system deficits that give rise to infectious diseases in older adults (Badowski & others, 2014). The extended duration of stress and diminished restorative processes in older adults may accelerate the effects of aging on immunity. Researchers are exploring stress buffering strategies, including exercise, in an effort to find ways to attenuate some of the negative effects of stress on the aging process (Bauer & others, 2013).

Which of these biological theories best explains aging? That question has not yet been answered. It might turn out that all of these biological processes contribute to aging.

Review *Connect* Reflect

 LG4 Explain longevity and the biological aspects of aging

Review

- What is the difference between life span and life expectancy? What sex differences exist in longevity?
- What do centenarians have in common?
- What are the four main biological theories of aging?

Connect

- There are differences among biological, psychological, and social age. How do biological theories of aging inform these three different conceptions of age?

Reflect *Your Own Personal Journey of Life*

- To what age do you think you will live? Why? To what age would you like to live?

reach your learning goals

Physical Development and Biological Aging

1 Body Growth and Change

LG1 Discuss major changes in the body through the life span

- Patterns of Growth
- Height and Weight in Infancy and Childhood
- Puberty

- · Human growth follows cephalocaudal (fastest growth occurs at the top) and proximodistal patterns (growth starts at the center of the body and moves toward the extremities).

- · Height and weight increase rapidly in infancy and then take a slower course during childhood.

- · Puberty is a brain-neuroendocrine process occurring primarily in early adolescence that provides stimulation for the rapid physical changes that accompany this period of development. A number of changes occur in sexual maturation. The growth spurt involves rapid increases in height and weight and occurs about two years earlier for girls than for boys. Extensive hormonal changes characterize puberty. Puberty began occurring much earlier in the twentieth century mainly because of improved health and nutrition. The basic genetic program for puberty is wired into the nature of the species, but nutrition, health, and other environmental factors affect the timing of puberty. Adolescents show heightened interest in their bodies and body images. Younger adolescents are more preoccupied with these images than older adolescents. Adolescent girls often have a more negative body image than do adolescent boys. Early maturation often favors boys, at least during early adolescence, but as adults, late-maturing boys have a more positive identity than do early-maturing boys. Early-maturing girls are at risk for a number of developmental problems.

- Early Adulthood
- Middle Adulthood

- · In early adulthood, height remains rather constant. Many individuals reach their peak of muscle tone and strength in their late teens and twenties; however, these can decline in the thirties.

- · In middle adulthood, changes usually are gradual. Visible signs of aging, such as the wrinkling of skin, appear in the forties and fifties. Middle-aged individuals also tend to lose height and gain weight. Strength, joints, and bones show declines in middle age. The cardiovascular system declines in functioning, and lung capacity begins to decline, more so in smokers than nonsmokers. The climacteric is a term used to describe the midlife transition in which fertility declines. Menopause is the time in middle age, usually in the late forties or early fifties, when a woman has not had a menstrual period for a year. Men do not experience an inability to father children in middle age, although their testosterone level declines.

- Late Adulthood

- · In late adulthood, outwardly noticeable physical changes become more prominent, individuals get shorter, and weight often decreases because of muscle loss. The circulatory system declines further.

2 The Brain

LG2 Describe how the brain changes through the life span

- The Neuroconstructivist View
- Brain Physiology

- · This increasingly popular view of brain development states that biological processes and environmental conditions influence the brain's development; the brain has plasticity; and cognitive development is closely linked with brain development.

- · The brain has two hemispheres, each of which has four lobes (frontal, occipital, temporal, and parietal). Throughout the brain, nerve cells called neurons process information. Communication among neurons involves the axon, dendrites, synapses, neurotransmitters, and the myelin sheath. Clusters of neurons, known as neural circuits, work together to handle specific types of information.

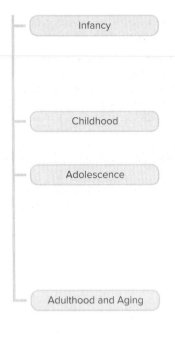

Infancy

· Researchers have found that early experience influences the brain's development. Myelination begins prenatally and continues after birth. In infancy, one of the most impressive changes in the brain is the enormous increase in dendrites and synapses. These connections between neurons are overproduced and pruned. Specialization of functioning does occur in the brain's hemispheres, as in language, but for the most part both hemispheres are at work in most complex functions.

Childhood

· During early childhood, the brain and head grow more rapidly than any other part of the body. Researchers have found that dramatic anatomical changes in brain patterns occur from 3 to 15 years of age, often involving spurts of brain activity and growth.

Adolescence

· The corpus callosum, a large bundle of axon fibers that connects the brain's left and right hemispheres, thickens in adolescence, and this thickening improves the adolescent's ability to process information. The prefrontal cortex, the highest level of the frontal lobes that are involved in reasoning, decision making, and self-control, continues to mature through emerging adulthood or later. The amygdala, the part of the limbic system that is the seat of emotions such as anger, matures earlier than the prefrontal cortex. The later development of the prefrontal cortex combined with the earlier maturity of the amygdala may explain the difficulty adolescents have in putting the brakes on their emotional intensity.

Adulthood and Aging

· On average, the brain loses 5 to 10 percent of its weight between the ages of 20 and 90. Brain volume also decreases with aging. Shrinking occurs in some areas of the brain, such as the prefrontal cortex, more than in other areas. A general slowing of function of the central nervous system begins in middle adulthood and increases in late adulthood. A decline in the production of some neurotransmitters is related to aging. Neurogenesis has been demonstrated in lower mammals, but whether it occurs in human adults is still controversial. It appears that dendritic growth can occur in adults. The brain has the capacity to virtually rewire itself to compensate for loss in late adulthood. Brain lateralization usually decreases in older adults.

3 Sleep
 LG3 Summarize how sleep patterns change as people develop

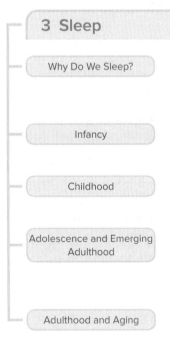

Why Do We Sleep?

· A number of theories have been proposed about the functions of sleep, including evolutionary theory and sleep's role in survival; the role of sleep as a restorative function involving protein production and neural waste removal; and the role of sleep in brain plasticity. Sleep likely serves a number of important functions.

Infancy

· Newborns sleep about 16 to 17 hours a day. By about 4 months of age, most infants have sleep patterns similar to those of adults. REM sleep occurs more in infancy than in childhood and adulthood. A special concern is sudden infant death syndrome.

Childhood

· Most experts recommend that young children get 11 to 13 hours of sleep each night. Most young children sleep through the night and have one daytime nap. Inadequate sleep is linked to children's depression and attention problems. Children can experience a number of sleep problems.

Adolescence and Emerging Adulthood

· Many adolescents stay up later and sleep longer in the morning than they did when they were children. Recent interest focuses on biological explanations of these developmental changes in sleep during adolescence and their link to school success. Recent research indicates that a majority of first-year college students have sleep difficulties and that they go to bed even later and get up later than adolescents do. However, by the end of college they have begun to reverse this trend.

Adulthood and Aging

· An increasing concern is that adults do not get enough sleep. In middle age, wakeful periods may interrupt nightly sleep more often. Many older adults go to bed earlier and wake up earlier the next morning. Almost half of older adults report having some insomnia.

4 Longevity and Biological Aging
LG4 Explain longevity and the biological aspects of aging

Life Expectancy and Life Span

· Life expectancy is the number of years an individual is expected to live when he or she is born. Life span is the maximum number of years any member of a species has been known to live. On average, females live about five years longer than males do. The sex difference is likely due to biological and social factors. An increasing number of individuals live to be 100 or older.

Centenarians

Biological Theories of
Aging

• Heredity, family history, health, education, personality, and lifestyle are important factors in living to be a centenarian. The ability to cope with stress also is important.

• Five biological theories of the causes of aging are evolutionary, cellular clock, free-radical, mitochondrial, and hormonal stress. The evolutionary theory of aging proposes that natural selection has not eliminated many harmful conditions and nonadaptive characteristics in older adults; thus, the benefits conferred by evolution decline with age because natural selection is linked to reproductive fitness. Hayflick proposed the cellular clock theory, which states that cells can divide a maximum of about 75 to 80 times and that as we age, our cells become less capable of dividing. Telomeres are likely involved in explaining why cells lose their capacity to divide. According to free-radical theory, people age because unstable oxygen molecules called free radicals are produced in the cells. According to mitochondrial theory, aging is due to the decay of mitochondria, tiny cellular bodies that supply energy for function, growth, and repair. According to hormonal stress theory, aging in the body's hormonal system can lower resistance to stress and increase the likelihood of disease.

key **terms**

amygdala	gonadotropins	limbic system	pituitary gland
cellular clock theory	gonads	menarche	prefrontal cortex
cephalocaudal pattern	hormonal stress theory	menopause	proximodistal pattern
climacteric	hormones	mitochondrial theory	puberty
corpus callosum	hypothalamus	myelination	sudden infant death syndrome
estradiol	lateralization	neuroconstructivist view	(SIDS)
free-radical theory	life span	neurogenesis	testosterone

key **people**

Martha Ann Bell	Monah El-Sheikh	Mark Johnson	John Richards
Mary Carskadon	Leonard Hayflick	Charles Nelson	

chapter 4

HEALTH

chapter **outline**

1 Health, Illness, and Disease

Learning Goal 1 Describe developmental changes in health

Children's Health
Adolescents' Health
Emerging and Young Adults' Health
Health and Aging

2 Nutrition and Eating Behavior

Learning Goal 2 Characterize developmental changes in nutrition and eating behavior

Infancy
Childhood
Adolescence
Adult Development and Aging

3 Exercise

Learning Goal 3 Summarize the roles of exercise in child and adult health

Childhood and Adolescence
Adulthood
Aging and Longevity

4 Substance Use

Learning Goal 4 Evaluate substance use in adolescence and adulthood

Adolescence and Emerging Adulthood
Substance Use in Older Adults

© Fuse/Getty Images RF

preview

Life is more than just existing. It is important to lead a healthy life. As we grow and develop through the life span, we have many opportunities to engage in health-enhancing or health-compromising behaviors, either by our choosing or because of the contexts provided by our caregivers. In this chapter, we will explore many aspects of health, including illness and disease, nutrition and eating behavior, exercise, and substance use.

1 Health, Illness, and Disease   LG1   Describe developmental changes in health

- Children's Health
- Adolescents' Health
- Emerging and Young Adults' Health
- Health and Aging

Changing patterns of illness have fueled an interest in searching not just for biological causes of health, illness, and disease, but for psychological and sociocultural causes as well. With these multiple causes in mind, let's now examine changes in health through the life span.

Nothing can be changed until it is faced.

—JAMES BALDWIN
American novelist, 20th century

CHILDREN'S HEALTH

Many factors affect children's health. In this chapter, we focus on two of the most important influences: prevention and poverty. We will also consider the health impact of immunization, accidents, and access to health care.

Prevention   Although the dangers of many diseases for children have greatly diminished, it is still important for parents to keep their children on a timely immunization schedule (Hollan, 2012; Kempe & others, 2015). The recommended ages for various immunizations are shown in Figure 1.

In addition to immunization, another important way to prevent health problems in children is to avoid accidents, which are the leading cause of death during childhood (Gururaj, 2013; Holland & Cawthon, 2015). Infants need close monitoring as they gain locomotor and manipulative skills along with a strong curiosity to explore their environment. Aspiration of foreign objects, suffocation, falls, poisoning, burns, and motor vehicle accidents are among the most common accidents in infancy (Alonge & Hyder, 2014; Duke & others, 2011).

The status of children's motor, cognitive, and socioemotional development makes their health-care needs unique. For example, think about how the infant's and young child's motor skills are inadequate to ensure their personal safety while riding in an automobile. Adults must take preventive measures to restrain infants and young children in car seats (Macy & others, 2014; Oliveira & others, 2012). Young children also lack the cognitive skills, including reading ability, to discriminate between safe and unsafe household substances. And they may lack the impulse control to keep from running out into a busy street while chasing a ball or toy.

Caregivers play an important role in promoting children's health (Sorte, Daeschel, & Amador, 2014). An increasing number of studies reach the conclusion that children are at risk for health problems when they live in homes where a parent smokes (Jarosinksa & others, 2014). For example, children exposed to tobacco smoke in the home are more likely to develop wheezing symptoms and asthma than are children in homes where nobody smokes (Hur, Liang, & Lin, 2014). By driving at safe speeds, decreasing or eliminating drinking—especially before driving—and not smoking around children, caregivers can enhance their children's health.

Poverty   Of special concern in the United States is the poor health of many young children from low-income families. An estimated 7 percent of U.S. children have no usual source of health care. Approximately 11 million preschool children in the United States are malnourished.

Age	Immunization
Birth	Hepatitis B
2 months	Diphtheria Polio Influenza
4 months	Diphtheria Polio Influenza
6 months	Diphtheria Influenza
1 year	TB test
15 months	Measles Mumps Rubella Influenza
18 months	Diphtheria Polio
4 to 6 years	Diphtheria Polio
11 to 12 years	Measles Mumps Rubella
14 to 16 years	Tetanus-diphtheria

FIGURE 1

RECOMMENDED IMMUNIZATION SCHEDULE FOR INFANTS AND CHILDREN

developmental **connection**

Environment

Poverty is linked to many environmental inequities in childhood. Connect to "Peers and the Sociocultural World."

Their malnutrition places their health at risk. Many have poor resistance to diseases—including minor ones, such as colds, and major ones, such as influenza.

What is the best way to improve the health of children who live in poverty? Some experts argue that offering medical care is not enough. If you give an antibiotic to a child with a sore throat who then returns to a home where she will be cold and hungry, have you provided good health care? One approach to children's health aims to treat not only medical problems of the individual child but also the conditions of the entire family. In fact, some programs seek to identify children who are at risk for problems and then try to alter the risk factors in an effort to prevent illness and disease (Miller & others, 2011).

ADOLESCENTS' HEALTH

Adolescence is a critical juncture for adopting behaviors that affect health (Chisholm & others, 2014). Many of the factors linked to poor health habits and early death in the adult years begin during adolescence (Levy & others, 2014; Van Horn & others, 2014).

developmental **connection**

Brain Development

Developmental changes in the adolescent's brain may be related to increased risk taking. Connect to "Physical Development and Biological Aging."

Social contexts, including families, peers, schools, neighborhoods, and culture, influence adolescent health (Espie & Eisler, 2015; Trucco & others, 2014). Parents and older siblings can serve as important models of health-enhancing behaviors (Fuligni & others, 2015). In the National Longitudinal Study of Health, which was based on data collected from more than 12,000 seventh- through twelfth-graders, youth who did not eat dinner with a parent five or more days a week had dramatically higher rates of smoking cigarettes, using marijuana, getting into fights, and initiating sexual activity (Council of Economic Advisors, 2000). Parental caring and monitoring often combine to reduce risk taking in youth.

Peers also can influence adolescents' health (Wang & others, 2014). Adolescents who have a limited capacity to resist dares often engage in risk taking at the urging of their peers. Peer pressure can instigate health-compromising behaviors such as cigarette smoking, substance abuse, early sexual activity, and violence (Trucco & others, 2014). A recent study found that adolescents whose friends drank alcohol were more likely to binge drink in adolescence and early adulthood (Solosky, Kale Monk, & Durtschi, 2015).

What are some influences on adolescents' health?
© Tom Stewart/Corbis

Because adolescents spend so much time in school, it is not surprising that what goes on there can influence their health behavior. Teachers, like parents, can serve as important health role models.

Health experts increasingly recognize that whether adolescents will develop a health problem or be healthy depends primarily on their own behavior (Thompson & Manore, 2015). Improving adolescent health involves (1) reducing adolescents' health-compromising behaviors, such as drug abuse, violence, unprotected sexual intercourse, and dangerous driving; and (2) increasing health-enhancing behaviors, such as eating nutritious foods, exercising, and wearing seat belts.

EMERGING AND YOUNG ADULTS' HEALTH

Emerging adults have more than twice the mortality rate of adolescents (Park & others, 2008) (see Figure 2). As indicated in Figure 2, males are mainly responsible for the higher mortality rate of emerging adults. Also, compared with adolescents, emerging adults engage in more health-compromising behaviors, have higher rates of chronic health problems, are more likely to be obese, and are more likely to have a mental health disorder (Irwin, 2010).

Although emerging adults may know what it takes to be healthy, they often don't apply this information to their own behavior (Furstenberg, 2006). In many cases, emerging adults are not as healthy as they seem (Fatusi & Hindin, 2010).

In emerging and early adulthood, few individuals stop to think about how their personal lifestyles will affect their health later in their adult lives. As young adults, many of us develop a pattern of not eating breakfast, not eating regular meals and relying on snacks as our main food source during the day, eating excessively to the point where we exceed the normal weight for our height, smoking moderately or excessively, drinking moderately or excessively, failing to exercise, and getting by with only a few hours of sleep at night

(Blake, 2015). These lifestyles are associated with poor health, which in turn impairs life satisfaction (Donatelle, 2013; Meeks, Heit, & Page, 2016). In some cases, unhealthy behavior increases as individuals go through college. For example, a recent study found that rates of being overweight or obese increased from 25.6 percent for college freshmen to 32 percent for college seniors (Nicoteri & Miskovsky, 2014). Also, in the Berkeley Longitudinal Study—in which individuals were evaluated over a period of 40 years—physical health at age 30 predicted life satisfaction at age 70, more so for men than for women (Mussen, Honzik, & Eichorn, 1982).

HEALTH AND AGING

Aging can bring new health problems, such as Alzheimer disease. Keep in mind, though, that many older adults are healthy. For example, only 17 percent of U.S. adults from 65 to 74 years of age have a disability. As shown in Figure 3, the percentage of Americans without a disability remains above 50 percent until they reach 85 years and older.

Chronic Disorders **Chronic disorders** are characterized by a slow onset and long duration. Chronic disorders are rare in early adulthood, increase in middle adulthood, and become common in late adulthood.

The most common chronic disorders in middle age differ for females and males (Austad, 2011). The most common chronic disorders in middle adulthood for U.S. women, in order of prevalence, are arthritis, hypertension, and sinus problems; the most common ones for U.S. men are hypertension, arthritis, hearing impairments, and heart disease. Men have a higher incidence of fatal chronic conditions (such as coronary heart disease, cancer, and stroke); women have a higher incidence of nonfatal ones (such as sinus problems, varicose veins, and bursitis). Older women have higher incidences of arthritis and hypertension and are more likely to have visual problems, but they are less likely to have hearing problems than older men are.

Nearly 60 percent of U.S. adults 65 to 74 years of age die of cancer or cardiovascular disease (Murphy, Xu, & Kochanek, 2012). Cancer recently replaced cardiovascular disease as the leading cause of death in U.S. middle-aged adults (Heron, 2013). The same realignment of causes of death has also occurred in 65- to 74-year-olds, with cancer now the leading cause of death in this age group (Hoyert & Xu, 2012). The decline in cardiovascular disease in middle-aged and older adults has been attributed to improved drugs, decreased rates of smoking, improved diets, and increased exercise (Anthony, George, & Eaton, 2014; Caetano & Delgado Alves, 2015; Cuenca-Garcia & others, 2014; Franklin, Lavie, & Arena, 2015).

However, in the 75-to-84 and 85-and-over age groups, cardiovascular disease still is the leading cause of death (Hoyert & Xu, 2012). As individuals age through the late adult years, the older they are the more likely it becomes that they will die of cardiovascular disease rather than cancer (Hoyert & Xu, 2012).

Even when adults over the age of 65 have a physical impairment, many of them can still carry on their everyday activities or work. Chronic conditions associated with the greatest limitation on work are heart conditions (52 percent), diabetes (34 percent), asthma (27 percent), and arthritis (27 percent).

Arthritis—an inflammation of the joints accompanied by pain, stiffness, and movement problems—is the most common chronic disorder in older adults (Davis, Burke, & others, 2013). There is no known cure for arthritis, but the symptoms can be treated with drugs such as aspirin, range-of-motion exercises, weight reduction, and in extreme cases, replacement of

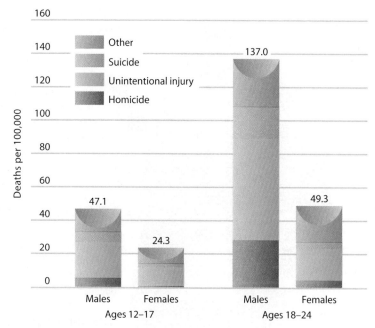

FIGURE 2
MORTALITY RATES OF U.S. ADOLESCENTS AND EMERGING ADULTS

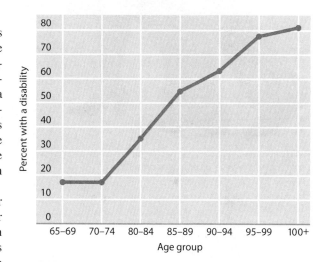

Note: Data for the 75 to 79 age group were unavailable.

FIGURE 3
PERCENTAGE OF U.S. OLDER ADULTS OF DIFFERENT AGES WHO HAVE A DISABILITY

chronic disorders Disorders characterized by slow onset and long duration.

the crippled joint with a prosthesis (Jinesh, 2015; Peeters, Brown, & Burton, 2014). Recent research has documented the benefits of exercise for older adults with arthritis (Semanik, Chang, & Dunlop, 2012; White & others, 2015).

Normal aging involves some loss of bone tissue from the skeleton. However, in some instances loss of bone tissue can become severe. **Osteoporosis** involves an extensive loss of bone tissue. Osteoporosis is the main reason many older adults walk with a marked stoop (Rothman & others, 2014). Women are especially vulnerable to osteoporosis, the leading cause of broken bones in women (Davis, Burke, & others, 2013). Approximately 80 percent of osteoporosis cases in the United States occur in females, 20 percent in males. Almost two-thirds of all women over the age of 60 are affected by osteoporosis. This aging disorder is most common in non-Latina White, thin, and small-framed women.

Osteoporosis is related to deficiencies in calcium, vitamin D, and estrogen, as well as lack of exercise (Welch & Hardcastle, 2014). To prevent osteoporosis, young and middle-aged women should eat foods rich in calcium, exercise regularly, and avoid smoking (Giangregorio & others, 2015; Nadler & others, 2013).

Health problems that accompany aging also can involve neurological disorders. Next, we examine a neurological disorder in aging that has dramatically increased in recent decades—Alzheimer disease.

Alzheimer Disease **Dementia** is a global term for any neurological disorder in which the primary symptoms involve a deterioration of mental functioning. Individuals with dementia often lose the ability to care for themselves and can become unable to recognize familiar surroundings and people, including family members (McMillan & others, 2014; Plassman & Grafman, 2015; Valkanova & Ebmeier, 2014). It is estimated that 23 percent of women and 17 percent of men 85 years and older are at risk for developing dementia (Alzheimer's Association, 2014). However, these estimates may be high because of the Alzheimer's Association's lobbying efforts to increase funding for research and treatment facilities. Dementia is a broad category, and it is important to identify the specific cause of a person's deteriorating mental functioning (Brodaty & others, 2015; Velayudhan & others, 2014).

One form of dementia is **Alzheimer disease**—a progressive, irreversible brain disorder that is characterized by a gradual deterioration of memory, reasoning, language, and eventually, physical function. In 2012, an estimated 5.4 million adults in the United States had Alzheimer disease, and it has been projected that 10 million baby boomers will develop Alzheimer disease in their lifetime (Alzheimer's Association, 2014). Figure 4 shows the estimated risks for developing Alzheimer disease at different ages for women and men (Alzheimer's Association, 2010). Women are likely to develop Alzheimer disease because they live longer than men and their longer life expectancy increases the number of years during which they can develop it. It is estimated that Alzheimer disease triples the health-care costs of Americans 65 years of age and older (Alzheimer's Association, 2014). Because of the increasing prevalence of Alzheimer disease, researchers have stepped up their efforts to discover the causes of the disease and find more effective ways to treat it. However, some experts on dementia and Alzheimer disease argue that these diseases may not increase as much as envisioned in the future and may even decline (Rocca & others, 2011). They especially highlight the dramatic reduction in smoking and increasingly effective treatment of cardiovascular disease (two health factors that are linked to Alzheimer disease) as reasons for a possible decline.

Causes Alzheimer disease involves a deficiency in the brain messenger chemical acetylcholine, which plays an important role in memory (Jensen & others, 2015; Nardone & others, 2014). Also, as Alzheimer disease progresses, the brain shrinks and deteriorates (see Figure 5). This deterioration is characterized by the formation of *amyloid plaques* (dense deposits of protein that accumulate in the blood vessels) and *neurofibrillary tangles* (twisted fibers that build up in neurons) (Mather & others,

What characterizes osteoporosis? What are some strategies for reducing the severity of osteoporosis?
© George Gardner/The Image Works

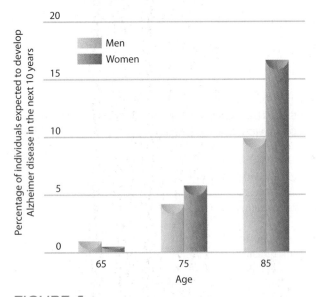

FIGURE 4

ESTIMATED RISKS FOR DEVELOPING ALZHEIMER DISEASE AT DIFFERENT AGES FOR WOMEN AND MEN. *Source:* Alzheimer's Association (2010). 2010 Alzheimer's facts and figures. *Alzheimer's & Dementia, 6,* 158–194.

FIGURE **5**

**TWO BRAINS: NORMAL AGING AND
ALZHEIMER DISEASE.** The computer
graphic on the left shows a slice of a normal
aging brain, while the photograph on the right
shows a slice of a brain ravaged by Alzheimer
disease. Notice the deterioration and shrinking
in the diseased brain.
© *Alfred Pasieka/Science Source*

2015; Mungas & others, 2014; Wisnewski & Goni, 2014; Zhang & Jiang, 2015). Neurofi-brillary tangles consist mainly of a protein called *tau* (Avila & others, 2014; Hoglund & others, 2015; Pooler, Noble, & Hanger, 2014). Currently, there is considerable research interest in the roles that amyloid and tau play in Alzheimer disease (Beduer & others, 2015; Krstic & Knuesel, 2013; Li & others, 2015; Tian & others, 2014).

There is increasing interest in the role that oxidative stress might play in the development of Alzheimer disease (Gaspar & others, 2015; Hritcu & others, 2015; Luque-Contreras & others, 2014; Meraz-Rios & others, 2014). Oxidative stress occurs when the body's antioxi-dant defenses are unable to cope with free-radical attacks and oxidation in the body. Recall from earlier in the chapter that free-radical theory is one of the major explanations of the aging process.

Although scientists have not identified the specific causes of Alzheimer disease, age is an important risk factor and genes also are likely to play an important role (Tang & others, 2014). The number of individuals with Alzheimer disease doubles every five years after the age of 65. A gene called *apolipoprotein E (ApoE)* is linked to increasing presence of plaques and tangles in the brain (Osorio & others, 2014). Special attention has focused on the presence of an allele (an alternative form of a gene) labeled ApoE4 that has been identified as a strong risk factor for Alzheimer disease (Argyri & others, 2014; Dorey & others, 2014). In K. Warner Schaie's (2013) recent research, individuals who had the ApoE4 allele showed more rapid cognitive decline beginning in middle age. A recent study found that the ApoE4 allele creates a cascade of molecular signaling that causes blood vessels to become more porous, allowing toxic substances to leak into the brain and damage neurons (Bell & others, 2012).

Despite links between the presence of the ApoE4 allele and Alzheimer disease, less than 50 percent of the individuals who are carriers of the ApoE4 allele develop dementia in old age. Knowledge gained from the Human Genome Project has recently resulted in identification of additional genes that are risk factors for Alzheimer disease, although they are not as strongly linked to the disease as the ApoE4 allele (Chen & others, 2015; Ferencz & Gerritsen, 2015).

Although individuals with a family history of Alzheimer disease are at greater risk than the general population, the disease is complex and likely to be caused by a number

osteoporosis A disorder that involves an extensive loss of bone tissue and is the main reason many older adults walk with a marked stoop. Women are especially vulnerable to osteoporosis.

dementia A global term for any neurological disorder in which the primary symptom is deterioration of mental functioning.

Alzheimer disease A progressive, irreversible brain disorder characterized by a gradual deterioration of memory, reasoning, language, and eventually, physical function.

Memory loss is a common characteristic of Alzheimer disease. Written reminders can help individuals with Alzheimer remember daily tasks.
© Ingram Publishing RF

A wife feeding her husband who has Alzheimer disease. *What are some concerns about the family caregivers of individuals with Alzheimer disease?*
© Ray Chavez/MCT/Landov

of factors, including lifestyle choices (Argyri & others, 2014). Researchers are finding that healthy lifestyle factors may lower the risk of Alzheimer disease or delay the onset of the disease (Suehs & others, 2014). For example, older adults with Alzheimer disease are more likely to have cardiovascular disease than are individuals who do not have Alzheimer disease (Murr & others, 2014; Sery & others, 2015). Recently, many cardiac risk factors have been implicated in Alzheimer disease—obesity, smoking, atherosclerosis, high cholesterol, and lipids (Dublin & others, 2014; Grammas & others, 2014; Lista, Dubois, & Hampel, 2015). One of the best strategies for preventing or delaying the onset of Alzheimer disease in people who are at risk is to improve their cardiac functioning through diet, drugs, and exercise (Hall & others, 2013).

Early Detection and Drug Treatment   Mild cognitive impairment (MCI) represents a transitional state between the cognitive changes of normal aging and very early Alzheimer disease and other dementias. MCI is increasingly recognized as a risk factor for Alzheimer disease. Estimates indicate that as many as 10 to 20 percent of individuals 65 years of age and older have MCI (Alzheimer's Association, 2014). Some individuals with MCI do not go on to develop Alzheimer disease, but MCI is a risk factor for Alzheimer disease.

Distinguishing between individuals who merely have age-associated declines in memory and those with MCI is difficult, as is predicting which individuals with MCI will subsequently develop Alzheimer disease (Richens & others, 2014; Vos & others, 2015). A recent study revealed that individuals with mild cognitive impairment who developed Alzheimer disease had at least one copy of the ApoE4 allele (Alegret & others, 2014). In this study, the extent of memory impairment was the key factor that was linked to the speed of decline from mild cognitive impairment to Alzheimer disease.

Drug Treatment of Alzheimer Disease   Several drugs called cholinesterase inhibitors have been approved by the U.S. Food and Drug Administration to treat Alzheimer disease. They are designed to improve memory and other cognitive functions by increasing levels of acetylcholine in the brain (Reale & others, 2014). Keep in mind, though, that the drugs used to treat Alzheimer disease only slow the downward progression of the disease; they do not treat its cause (Gu, Chen, & Gao, 2015). Also, no drugs have yet been approved by the Federal Drug Administration for the treatment of MCI (Alzheimer's Association, 2014).

Caring for Individuals with Alzheimer Disease   A special concern is the stress involved in caring for Alzheimer patients (Kamiya & others, 2014). Health-care professionals emphasize that the family can be an important support system for the

developmental **connection**

Memory

A number of changes in memory occur in late adulthood. Connect to "Information Processing."

How Stressful Is Caring for an Alzheimer Patient at Home?

Researchers have recently found that the stress of caring for an Alzheimer patient at home can prematurely age the immune system, putting caregivers at risk for developing age-related diseases (Chiu, Wesson, & Sadavoy, 2014; Glaser & Kiecolt-Glaser, 2005). In one study, 119 older adults who were caring for a spouse with Alzheimer disease or another form of dementia (which can require up to 100 hours a week of time) were compared with 106 older adults who did not have to care for a chronically ill spouse (Kiecolt-Glazer & others, 2003). The age of the older adults upon entry into the study ranged from 55 to 89, with an average age of 70.

Periodically during the six-year study, blood samples were taken and the levels of a naturally produced immune chemical called interleukin-6, or IL-6, were measured. IL-6 increases with age and can place people at risk for a number of illnesses, including cardiovascular disease, type 2 diabetes, frailty, and certain cancers. The researchers found that the levels of IL-6 increased much faster in the Alzheimer caregivers than in the older adults who did not have to care for a critically ill spouse (see Figure 6).

Each time IL-6 was assessed by drawing blood, the participants also completed a 10-item perceived stress scale to assess the extent to which they perceived their daily life during the prior week as being "unpredictable, uncontrollable, and overloading" (Kiecolt-Glazer & others, 2003, p. 9091). Participants rated each item from 0 (never) to 4 (very often). Alzheimer caregivers reported greater stress than the noncaregiver controls across each of the six annual assessments.

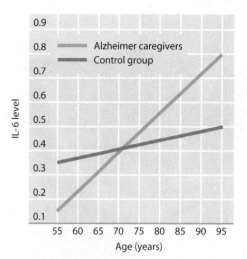

FIGURE 6

COMPARISON OF IL-6 LEVELS IN ALZHEIMER CAREGIVERS AND A CONTROL GROUP OF NONCAREGIVERS. Notice that IL-6 (an immune chemical that places individuals at risk for a number of diseases) increased for both the Alzheimer caregivers and a control group of noncaregivers. However, also note that IL-6 increased significantly more in the Alzheimer caregivers. A higher score for IL-6 reflects a higher level of the immune chemical.

Since family members are especially important in helping Alzheimer patients cope, an important research agenda is to assess the benefits of respite care and to find other ways to relieve the stress the disease can impose on others. What kinds of studies might help provide some answers? What challenges will researchers face in collecting data?

Alzheimer patient, but this support can have costs for family members who become emotionally and physically drained from providing the extensive care required for a person with Alzheimer disease (Ornstein & others, 2013) A recent study compared family members' perceptions of caring for someone with Alzheimer disease, cancer, or schizophrenia (Papastavrou & others, 2012). In this study, the highest perceived burden was reported for Alzheimer disease.

Respite care (services that provide temporary relief for those who are caring for individuals with disabilities or illnesses) can ease the stress experienced by people who have to meet the day-to-day needs of Alzheimer patients. This type of care provides an important break from the burden of providing chronic care (de la Cuesta-Benjumea, 2011; Neville & others, 2015). To read further about individuals who care for Alzheimer patients, see the *Connecting with Research* interlude.

Parkinson Disease Another type of dementia is **Parkinson disease,** a chronic, progressive disorder characterized by muscle tremors, slowing of movement, and partial

Parkinson disease A chronic, progressive disease characterized by muscle tremors, slowing of movement, and partial facial paralysis.

facial paralysis. Parkinson disease is triggered by degeneration of dopamine-producing neurons in the brain (da Luz & others, 2015; Shimizu & Ohno, 2013). Dopamine is a neurotransmitter that is necessary for normal brain functioning. Why these neurons degenerate is not known.

The main treatment for Parkinson disease involves administering drugs that enhance the effect of dopamine (dopamine agonists) in the disease's earlier stages and later administering the drug L-dopa, which is converted by the brain into dopamine (Enomoto & others, 2015; Mestre & others, 2014). However, it is difficult to determine the correct dosage of L-dopa, and it loses its efficacy over time. Another treatment for advanced Parkinson disease is deep brain stimulation (DBS), which involves implanting electrodes in the brain (Kim & others, 2014; Pulliam & others, 2015). The electrodes are then stimulated by a pacemaker-like device. Stem cell transplantation and gene therapy offer hope for the future in treating Parkinson disease (Badger & others, 2014; Yeh & others, 2015).

Stress and Disease   Stress is increasingly being identified as a factor in many diseases (Evers & others, 2014; Jaremka & others, 2014). The cumulative effect of chronic stress often takes a toll on the health of individuals by the time they reach middle age. A recent study of middle-aged adults found that when they had a high level of allostatic load (wearing down of the body's systems in response to high stress levels), their episodic memory and executive function were harmed (Karlamangia & others, 2013). And a recent study of occupationally active 44- to 58-year-olds revealed that perceived stress symptoms in midlife were linked to self-care disability and mobility limitations 28 years later (Kulmala & others, 2013). Margie Lachman and her colleagues (2011) argue that having a sense of control is one of the most important modifiable factors in reducing stress and delaying the onset of diseases in middle adulthood and reducing the frequency of diseases in late adulthood.

Chronic stressors have been linked to a downturn in immune system functioning in a number of contexts, including worries about living next to a damaged nuclear reactor, failures in close relationships (divorce, separation, and marital distress), depression, loneliness, and burdensome caregiving for a family member with progressive illness (Fagundes, Glaser, & Kiecolt-Glaser, 2013; Fagundes & others, 2013; Jaremka & others, 2014; Prenderville & others, 2015). A recent study discovered that chronic stress accelerated pancreatic cancer growth (Kim-Fuchs & others, 2014).

Health Treatment for Older Adults   The development of alternative forms of home and community-based care has decreased the percentage of older adults who are living in nursing homes (Katz & others, 2009). Still, as older adults age, their probability of being in a nursing home increases (see Figure 7). What is the quality of nursing homes and extended-care facilities for older adults? What is the relationship between older adults and health-care providers?

The quality of nursing homes and other extended-care facilities for older adults varies enormously and is a source of ongoing national concern (Winsvold Prang & Jelsness-Jorgensen, 2014). More than one-third of these facilities are seriously deficient. They fail federally mandated inspections because they do not meet the minimum standards for physicians, pharmacists, and various rehabilitation specialists (occupational and physical therapists). Further concerns focus on protecting the patient's right to privacy, providing access to medical information, preventing inappropriate prescriptions, ensuring safety, and preserving lifestyle freedom within the individual's range of mental and physical capabilities (Stafford, Alswayan, & Tenni, 2010).

Because of the inadequate quality of many nursing homes and the escalating costs for nursing home care, many specialists in the health problems of the aged stress that home health care, elder-care centers,

Muhammad Ali, one of the world's leading sports figures, has Parkinson disease.
© AP Images

developmental **connection**

Stress

A variation of hormonal stress theory identifies a decline in immune system functioning as an important contributor to lower resistance to stress in older adults. Connect to "Physical Development and Biological Aging."

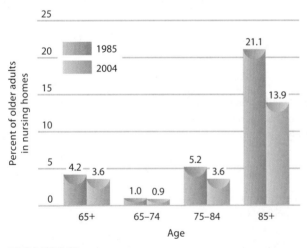

FIGURE **7**

PERCENT OF U.S. OLDER ADULTS LIVING IN NURSING HOMES: 1985 TO 2004. Note: The Lewin Group calculations are based on the 1985 and 2004 National Nursing Home Survey (NNHS), National Center for Health Statistics.

and preventive medicine clinics are good alternatives (Hunt, Corazzini, & Anderson, 2014). They are potentially less expensive than hospitals and nursing homes. They also are less likely to engender the feelings of depersonalization and dependency that occur so often in residents of institutions. Currently, there is an increased demand for home-care workers because of the expanding population of older adults and their preference to stay in their own homes (Bardach & Rowles, 2012). In a recent study of elderly adults with cognitive impairment, those being cared for at home were less depressed, had better cognitive functioning, and reported a higher level of social connectedness than their counterparts experiencing formal institutional care (Nikmat, Al-Mashoor, & Hashim, 2015).

In a classic study that focused on the way older adults are cared for in nursing homes, Judith Rodin and Ellen Langer (1977) found that an important factor related to health, and even survival, in a nursing home is the patient's feelings of control and self-determination. A group of elderly nursing home residents were encouraged to make more day-to-day choices and thus feel they had greater control over their lives. They began to decide such matters as what they ate, when their visitors could come, what movies they saw, and who could come to their rooms. A similar group in the same nursing home was told by the administrator how caring the nursing home was and how much the staff wanted to help, but these elderly nursing home residents were given no opportunities to take more control over their lives. Eighteen months later, the residents who had been given responsibility and control were more alert and active, and said they were happier, than the residents who had been encouraged only to feel that the staff would try to satisfy their needs. And the "responsible" or "self-control" group had significantly better improvement in their health than did the "dependent" group. Even more important was the finding that after 18 months only half as many nursing home residents in the "responsibility" group had died as in the "dependent" group (see Figure 8). Perceived control over one's environment, then, can literally be a matter of life or death.

developmental **connection**

Self and Identity

Perceived self-control changes as individuals age. Connect to "The Self, Identity, and Personality."

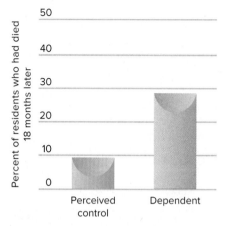

FIGURE **8**

PERCEIVED CONTROL AND MORTALITY. In the study by Rodin and Langer (1977), nursing home residents who were encouraged to feel more in control of their lives were more likely to be alive 18 months later than those who were treated as being more dependent on the nursing home staff.

Review *Connect* Reflect

LG1 Describe developmental changes in health

Review

- How can children's health be characterized?
- What is the nature of adolescents' health?
- What characterizes the health of emerging and young adults?
- How extensively does health decline in old age?

Connect

- What have you learned in earlier chapters about risk-taking behavior

that might help explain the attitudes that many young adults have toward their own health?

Reflect *Your Own Personal Journey of Life*

- What changes in your lifestyle right now might help you to age more successfully when you get older?

2 Nutrition and Eating Behavior

LG2 Characterize developmental changes in nutrition and eating behavior

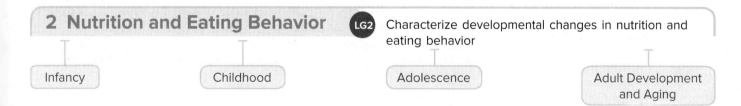

Infancy · Childhood · Adolescence · Adult Development and Aging

Nutritional needs, eating behavior, and related issues vary to some extent across the life span. Let's begin by exploring what takes place with infants.

INFANCY

For infants, the importance of receiving adequate energy intake and nutrients in a loving and supportive environment cannot be overstated (Schiff, 2015). From birth to 1 year of age, human infants triple their weight and increase their length by 50 percent. Because infants vary in their nutrient reserves, body composition, growth rates, and activity patterns, their nutrient needs vary as well. However, because parents need guidelines, nutritionists recommend that infants consume approximately 50 calories per day for each pound they weigh—more than twice an adult's requirement per pound.

Caregivers play very important roles in infants' early development of eating patterns (Birch & Doub, 2014; Montano & others, 2015). Caregivers who are not sensitive to developmental changes in infants' nutritional needs, neglectful caregivers, and conditions of poverty can contribute to the development of eating problems in infants (Black & Dewey, 2014). A recent study found that low maternal sensitivity when infants were 15 and 24 months of age was linked to a higher risk of obesity in adolescence (Anderson & others, 2012).

Breast Versus Bottle Feeding For the first four to six months of life, human milk or an alternative formula is the baby's source of nutrients and energy. For years, debate has focused on whether breast feeding is better for the infant than bottle feeding. The growing consensus is that breast feeding is better for the baby's health (Schiff, 2015). Since the 1970s, breast feeding by U.S. mothers has soared (see Figure 9). In 2008 more than 75 percent of U.S. mothers breast fed their newborns, and 44 percent breast fed their 6-month-olds (Centers for Disease Control and Prevention, 2012a). The American Academy of Pediatrics Section on Breastfeeding (2012) recently reconfirmed its recommendation of exclusive breast feeding in the first six months followed by continued breast feeding as complementary foods are introduced, with further breast feeding for one year or longer as mutually desired by the mother and infant.

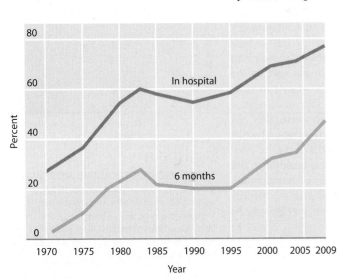

FIGURE 9
TRENDS IN BREAST FEEDING IN THE UNITED STATES: 1970–2009

Outcomes of Breast Feeding for the Child What are some of the benefits of breast feeding? The following conclusions are based on current research:

- *Gastrointestinal infections.* Breast fed infants have fewer gastrointestinal infections (Garofalo, 2010; Pfluger & others, 2010).
- *Lower respiratory tract infections.* Breast fed infants have fewer infections of the lower respiratory tract (Prameela, 2011).
- *Allergies.* There is no evidence that breast feeding reduces the risk of allergies in children (Greer & others, 2008). Modest evidence exists for feeding hypoallergenic formulas to susceptible babies if they are not solely breast fed (Greer & others, 2008).
- *Asthma.* Exclusive breast feeding for three months protects against wheezing in babies, but whether it prevents asthma in older children is unclear (Greer & others, 2008).
- *Otitis media.* Breast fed infants are less likely to develop this middle ear infection (Pelton & Leibovitz, 2009).
- *Overweight and obesity.* Consistent evidence indicates that breast fed infants are less likely to become overweight or obese in childhood, adolescence, and adulthood (Khuc & others, 2012; Scott, Ng, & Cobiac, 2012).
- *Diabetes.* Breast fed infants are less likely to develop type 1 diabetes in childhood (Ping & Hagopian, 2006) and type 2 diabetes in adulthood (Villegas & others, 2008).
- *SIDS.* Breast fed infants are less likely to experience SIDS (Zotter & Pichler, 2012).

In a large-scale research review, no conclusive evidence for the benefits of breast feeding was found for children's cognitive development and cardiovascular functioning (Agency for Healthcare Research and Quality, 2007; Ip & others, 2009).

developmental **connection**

Conditions, Diseases, and Disorders

What characterizes SIDS? Connect to "Physical Development and Biological Aging."

Outcomes of Breast Feeding for the Mother

- *Breast cancer.* Consistent evidence indicates a lower incidence of breast cancer in women who breast feed their infants (Akbari & others, 2011).
- *Ovarian cancer.* Evidence also reveals a reduction in ovarian cancer in women who breast feed their infants (Stuebe & Schwarz, 2010).
- *Type 2 diabetes.* Some evidence suggests a small reduction in type 2 diabetes in women who breast feed their infants (Stuebe & Schwarz, 2010).

In recent large-scale research reviews, no conclusive evidence could be found for the maternal benefits of breast feeding on return to prepregnancy weight, prevention of osteoporosis, and avoidance of postpartum depression (Agency for Healthcare Research and Quality, 2007; Ip & others, 2009).

As mentioned previously, the American Academy of Pediatrics Section on Breastfeeding (2012) strongly endorses exclusive breast feeding through six months and further recommends breast feeding for another year. Are there circumstances when mothers should not breast feed? Yes, a mother should not breast feed (1) if the mother is infected with HIV or some other infectious disease that can be transmitted through her milk, (2) if she has active tuberculosis, or (3) if she is taking any drug that may not be safe for the infant (D'Apolito, 2013; Goga & others, 2012).

Some women cannot breast feed their infants because of physical difficulties; others feel guilty if they terminate breast feeding early. Mothers may also worry that they are depriving their infants of important emotional and psychological benefits if they bottle feed rather than breast feed. Some researchers have found, however, that there are no psychological differences between breast fed and bottle fed infants (Fergusson, Horwood, & Shannon, 1987; Young, 1990).

A further issue in interpreting the benefits of breast feeding was underscored in a large-scale research review (Ip & others, 2009). While highlighting a number of breast feeding benefits for children and mothers, the report issued a caution about breast feeding research: None of the findings implies causality. Breast versus bottle feeding studies are correlational, not experimental, and women who breast feed are wealthier, older, more educated, and likely more health-conscious than their bottle feeding counterparts—characteristics that could explain why breast fed children are healthier.

Pediatric nurses can play an important role in improving the lives of children and advising parents on feeding practices. To read about the work of one pediatric nurse, see the *Connecting with Careers* profile.

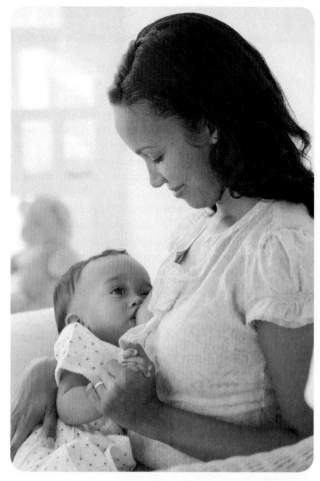

Human milk or an alternative formula is a baby's sole source of nutrients for the first four to six months. The growing consensus is that breast feeding is better than bottle feeding for the baby's health, although controversy still surrounds the issue of breast feeding versus bottle feeding. *Why is breast feeding strongly recommended by pediatricians?*
© Blend Images/Getty Images RF

developmental **connection**
Research Methods
How does a correlational study differ from an experimental study? Connect to "Introduction."

CHILDHOOD

Malnutrition continues to be a major threat to millions during the childhood years (Wardlaw, Smith, & Collene, 2015). Malnutrition and starvation are a daily fact of life for children in many developing countries (UNICEF, 2014). One study revealed that two food-assisted maternal and child health programs (both of which emphasized food provision, communication about behavior change, and preventive health services) helped to reduce the impact of economic hardship on stunting of children's growth in Haiti (Donegan & others, 2010).

Poor nutrition also is a special concern in the lives of infants from low-income families in the United States. To address this problem, the WIC (Women, Infants, and Children) program provides federal grants to states for healthy supplemental foods, health-care referrals, and nutrition education for women from low-income families beginning in pregnancy, and to infants and young children up to 5 years of age who are at nutritional risk (Jackson, 2015; Kong & others, 2013; Marshall & others, 2013). WIC serves approximately 7,500,000 participants in the United States.

Barbara Deloian, Pediatric Nurse

Barbara Deloian is a pediatric nurse in Denver, Colorado. She practices nursing in the Pediatric Oral Feeding Clinic and is involved in research as part of an irritable infant study for the Children's Hospital in Denver. She also is on the faculty of nursing at the Colorado Health Sciences Center. Deloin previously worked in San Diego, where she was coordinator of the Child Health Program for the County of San Diego.

Deloian's research interests focus on children with special health-care needs, especially high-risk infants and children, and promoting positive parent-child experiences. She is a former president of the National Association of Pediatric Nurse Associates and Practitioners.

For more information about what pediatric nurses do, see the Careers in Life-Span Development appendix.

Barbara Deloian, working with a child with special health-care needs.
Courtesy of Barbara Deloian

Overweight Children   Being overweight has become a serious health problem in childhood (Thompson & Manore 2015). Exemplifying the eating habits of young children that contribute to being overweight, a study of U.S. 2- and 3-year-olds found that French fries and other fried potatoes were the vegetable they were most likely to consume (Fox & others, 2010). A comparison of 34 countries revealed that the United States had the second highest rate of child obesity (Janssen & others, 2005).

The Centers for Disease Control and Prevention (2014a) has established categories for obesity, overweight, and at risk for being overweight. These categories are determined by body mass index (BMI), which is computed by a formula that takes into account height and weight. Children and adolescents whose BMI is at or above the 97th percentile are classified as obese; those whose BMI is at or above the 95th percentile are overweight; and those whose BMI is at or above the 85th percentile are at risk of becoming overweight.

The percentages of young children who are overweight or at risk of being overweight in the United States have increased dramatically in recent decades, but in the last several years there are indications that fewer preschool children are obese (Wardlaw, Smith, & Collene, 2015). In 2009–2010, 12.1 percent of U.S. 2- to 5-year-olds were classified as obese, compared with 5 percent in 1976–1980 and 10.4 percent in 2007–2008 (Ogden & others, 2012). However, in 2011–2012, a substantial drop (43 percent) in the obesity rate of 2- to 5-year-old children occurred in comparison with their counterparts in 2003–2004 (Ogden & others, 2012). In 2011–2012, 8 percent of 2- to 5-year-olds were obese, compared with 14 percent in 2004. It is not clear why this drop occurred, but among the possibilities are families buying lower-calorie foods and receiving help from the Special Supplementation Program for Women, Infants, and Children that subsidizes food for women in low-income families that emphasizes consuming less fruit juice, cheese, and eggs and more whole fruits and vegetables.

The risk that overweight children will continue to be overweight when they are older was documented in a recent U.S. study of nearly 8,000 children (Cunningham, Kramer, & Narayan, 2014). In this study, overweight 5-year-olds were four times more likely to be obese at 14 years of age than

What are some trends in the eating habits and weight of young children?
© Lilian Perez/Corbis

Helping Overweight Children Lose Weight

Most parents with an overweight child want to help the child lose weight but aren't sure of the best things to do to accomplish this goal. Since overweight children are likely to become overweight adolescents and adults, it is important for parents to help their children attain a healthy weight and maintain it. Following are some ways parents can help their overweight children lose weight (DiLeonardo, 2015; Matthiessen, 2015; Moninger, 2015):

- *Work on a healthy project together and involve the child in the decision-making process.* Get the child involved in an activity that helps him or her lose weight, such as purchasing pedometers for all family members and developing goals for how many steps to take each day. When children are involved in making decisions about the family's health, they may begin to take responsibility for their own health.
- *Be a healthy model for your child.* In many aspects of life, what people do is more influential than what they say. If parents are overweight and engaging in unhealthy behaviors such as eating unhealthy fast food and being inactive, then telling their overweight children to lose weight is unlikely to be effective.
- *Engage in physical activities with children.* Parents and children can engage in activities like bicycling, jogging, hiking, and swimming together. A parent might say something like "Let's take a bike ride after dinner this evening. It would be fun and could help us both get in better shape."
- *Give children opportunities to decide what they want to do to lose weight.* Take them to the grocery store and let them select the fruits and vegetables they are willing to eat. Let them choose which sport or type of exercise they would like to do.
- *Eat healthy family meals together on a regular basis.* Children who eat meals with their family are less likely to be overweight.
- *Reduce screen time.* Children who spend large numbers of hours per day in screen time are more likely to be overweight than their counterparts who are physically active.

their counterparts who began kindergarten at a normal weight. Also, in a recent study, preschool children who were obese were five times more likely to be overweight or obese as adults (Ogden & others, 2014).

Consequences of Obesity   The increasing number of overweight children in recent decades is cause for great concern because being overweight raises the risk for many medical and psychological problems (Buttitta & others, 2014; Lobstein & others, 2015; Sypniewska, 2015). Overweight children are at risk for developing pulmonary problems such as sleep apnea (which involves upper-airway obstruction), and for having hip problems (Tauman & Gozal, 2006). Type 2 diabetes, hypertension (high blood pressure), and elevated blood cholesterol levels also are common in children who are overweight (Prendergast & Gidding, 2014; Zhang, Zhang, & Xie, 2014). Social and psychological consequences of being overweight in childhood include low self-esteem, depression, and exclusion from peer groups (Danielson & others, 2012; Gomes & others, 2011; Hampl & Campbell, 2015).

© Brand X Pictures/PunchStock RF

Treatment of Obesity   A combination of diet, exercise, and behavior modification is often recommended to help children lose weight (Kaiser & others, 2015; Lumpkin, 2014; Rauner, Mess, & Woll, 2013). Intervention programs that emphasize getting parents to engage in more healthful life styles themselves, as well as to feed their children nutrient-dense food and get them to exercise more, can produce weight reduction in overweight and obese children (Jurkowski & others, 2014). For example, one study found that family participation in a child-centered activity program and a parent-centered dietary modification program helped overweight children lose pounds over a two-year period (Collins & others, 2011). To read further about ways to help children lose weight, see the *Connecting Development to Life* interlude.

ADOLESCENCE

Nutrition and being overweight are also key problems among adolescents (Lynch, Elmore, & Kotecki, 2015). National data indicated that the percentage of overweight U.S. 12- to 19-year-olds increased from 11 percent in the early 1990s to nearly 21 percent in 2011–2012 (Ogden & others, 2014). In another recent study, 12.4 percent of U.S. kindergarten children were obese and by 14 years of age, 20.8 percent were obese (Cunningham, Kramer, & Narayan, 2014).

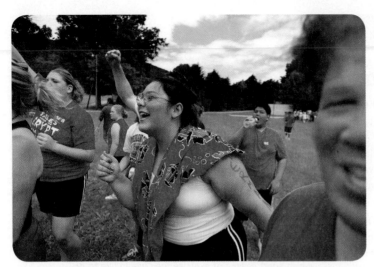

These overweight girls and boys are attending a weight-management camp. *What are some trends in the frequency of obesity in U.S. adolescents?*
© Mark Richards/Corbis

An international study of adolescents in 56 countries found fast food consumption is high in childhood and continues to increase in adolescence (Braithwaite & others, 2014). In this study, adolescents who ate fast food frequently or very frequently had higher body mass indices than adolescents in the lower frequency categories. A comparison of adolescents in 28 countries found that U.S. adolescents ate more junk food than teenagers ate in most other countries (World Health Organization, 2000). The National Youth Risk Survey found that U.S. high school students showed a linear decrease in their intake of fruits and vegetables from 1999 through 2013 (Kann & others, 2014).

What are some other aspects of adolescents' lives that are linked to being overweight or obese? A recent study revealed that playing on a sports team was an important factor in adolescents' weight (Drake & others, 2012). In this study, among a wide range of activities (other physical activity, physical education, screen time, and diet quality, for example), team sports participation was the strongest predictor of lower risk for being overweight or obese. A recent study revealed that family meals during adolescence protected against the development of being overweight or obese in adulthood (Berge & others, 2015).

What types of interventions have been successful in reducing overweight in adolescents? One review indicated that a combination of calorie restriction, exercise (such as walking or biking to school and participating in a regular exercise program), reduction of sedentary activity (such as watching TV or playing video games), and behavioral therapy (such as keeping weight-loss diaries and receiving rewards for meeting goals) have been moderately effective in helping overweight adolescents lose weight (Fowler-Brown & Kahwati, 2004).

Anorexia Nervosa Although most U.S. girls have been on a diet at some point, slightly less than 1 percent ever develop anorexia nervosa. **Anorexia nervosa** is an eating disorder that involves the relentless pursuit of thinness through starvation. It is a serious disorder that can lead to death. Four main characteristics apply to people suffering from anorexia nervosa: (1) weight less than 85 percent of what is considered normal for their age and height; (2) an intense fear of gaining weight that does not decrease with weight loss; (3) a distorted perception of their body shape (Stewart & others, 2012), and (4) *amenorrhea* (lack of menstruation) in girls who have reached puberty. Obsessive thinking about weight and compulsive exercise also are linked to anorexia nervosa (Simpson & others, 2013). Even when they are extremely thin, they see themselves as too fat (Cornelissen & others, 2015). They never think they are thin enough, especially in the abdomen, buttocks, and thighs. They usually weigh themselves frequently, often take their body measurements, and gaze critically at themselves in mirrors.

Anorexia nervosa typically begins in the early to middle adolescent years, often following an episode of dieting and some type of life stress (Fitzpatrick, 2012). It is about 10 times more likely to occur in females than males. When anorexia nervosa does occur in males, the symptoms and other characteristics (such as a distorted body image and family conflict) are usually similar to those reported by females who have the disorder (Ariceli & others, 2005).

Most individuals with anorexia are non-Latina White adolescent or young adult females from well-educated, middle- and upper-income families and are competitive and high-achieving (Darcy, 2012). They set high standards, become stressed about not being able to reach the standards, and are intensely concerned about how others perceive them (Woelders & others, 2010). Unable to meet these unrealistic expectations, they turn to something they can control—their weight. Offspring of mothers with anorexia nervosa are at increased risk for becoming anorexic themselves (Striegel-Moore & Bulik, 2007). Problems in family functioning are increasingly being found to be linked to anorexia nervosa in adolescent girls (Machado & others, 2014), and family therapy is often recommended as a treatment for adolescent girls with anorexia nervosa (Dimitropoulos & others, 2015; Espie & Eisler, 2015).

Biology and culture are involved in anorexia nervosa. Genes play an important role in the development of this disorder (Boraska & others, 2014). Also, the physical effects of dieting may change brain functioning and neural networks and thus sustain the disordered

Anorexia nervosa has become an increasing problem for adolescent girls and young adult women. *What are some possible causes of anorexia nervosa?*
© Ian Thraves/Alamy

anorexia nervosa An eating disorder that involves the relentless pursuit of thinness through starvation.

pattern (Fuglset & others, 2015). The fashion image in U.S. culture likely contributes to the incidence of anorexia nervosa (Benowitz-Fredericks & others, 2012). The media portray thin as beautiful in their choice of fashion models, whom many adolescent girls strive to emulate (Carr & Peebles, 2012). And many adolescent girls who strive to be thin hang out together.

Bulimia Nervosa Although anorexics control their eating by restricting it, most bulimics cannot. **Bulimia nervosa** is an eating disorder in which the individual consistently follows a binge-and-purge eating pattern. The bulimic goes on an eating binge and then purges by self-induced vomiting or use of a laxative. Although some people binge and purge occasionally and some experiment with it, a person is considered to have a serious bulimic disorder only if the episodes occur at least twice a week for three months (Cuzzolaro, 2014).

As with anorexics, most bulimics are preoccupied with food, have a strong fear of becoming overweight, and are depressed or anxious. Like anorexics, bulimics are highly perfectionistic (Lampard & others, 2012). A recent study found that bulimics have difficulty controlling their emotions (Lavender & others, 2014). Unlike anorexics, people who binge and purge typically fall within a normal weight range, a characteristic that makes bulimia more difficult to detect.

Bulimia nervosa typically begins in late adolescence or early adulthood. About 90 percent of the cases are women. Approximately 1 to 2 percent of women are estimated to develop bulimia nervosa. Many women who develop bulimia nervosa were somewhat overweight before the onset of the disorder, and the binge eating often began during an episode of dieting. One study of adolescent girls found that increased dieting, pressure to be thin, exaggerated importance placed on appearance, body dissatisfaction, depression symptoms, low self-esteem, and low social support predicted binge eating two years later (Stice, Presnell, & Spangler, 2002). Drug therapy and psychotherapy have been effective in treating anorexia nervosa and bulimia nervosa (Hagman & Frank, 2012; Harrington & others, 2015).

ADULT DEVELOPMENT AND AGING

Nutrition and eating behavior continue to play important roles in adult physical development and health. Among the topics we discuss in this section are obesity, exercising and dieting to lose weight, and links between aging, weight, and nutrition.

Obesity Obesity is a serious and pervasive health problem for many individuals (Donatelle, 2015; Smith & Collene, 2016). A recent national survey found that 27 percent of U.S. 20- to 39-year-olds were obese (National Center for Health Statistics, 2011). A recent Gallup poll (2013a) reported that 29.1 percent of 30- to 44-year-olds are obese, the highest in the poll's history. Also, a recent analysis predicted that by 2030, 42 percent of U.S. adults will be obese (Finkelstein & others, 2012).

In an international comparison of 33 developed countries, the United States had the highest percentage of obese adults (OECD, 2010). Figure 10 shows the developed countries with the highest and lowest percentages of obese adults.

Overweight and obesity are linked to increased risk of hypertension, diabetes, and cardiovascular disease (Schiff, 2016; Wenger, 2014). For individuals who are 30 percent overweight, the probability of dying in middle adulthood increases by about 40 percent. Overweight and obesity also are associated with mental health problems. For example, a meta-analysis revealed that overweight women were more likely to be depressed than women who were not overweight, but no significant difference was found for men (de Wit & others, 2010).

What causes obesity? Some individuals do inherit a tendency to be overweight (Apalasamy & Mohamed, 2015; Li & others, 2015; Tutone & others, 2014). Only 10 percent of

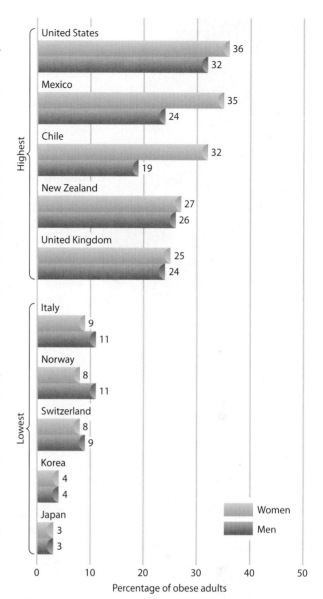

FIGURE 10

HIGHEST AND LOWEST PERCENTAGES OF OBESE ADULTS AMONG 33 DEVELOPED COUNTRIES. *Source:* OECD (2010). *Obesity and the Economics of Prevention—Fit Not Fat.* Paris, France: OECD.

bulimia nervosa An eating disorder in which the individual consistently follows a binge-and-purge eating pattern.

How effective are diet programs?
© BananaStock/PunchStock RF

developmental **connection**

Theories

Evolutionary theory proposes explanations of development and aging. Connect to "Biological Beginnings."

children who do not have obese parents become obese themselves, whereas 40 percent of children who become obese have one obese parent. Further, 70 percent of children who become obese have two obese parents. Researchers also have documented that animals can be inbred to have a propensity for obesity (Mathes & others, 2010).

Environmental factors play an important role in obesity (Larsen & others, 2015; Willett, 2013). Strong evidence of the environment's influence on weight is the doubling of the rate of obesity in the United States since 1900. This dramatic increase in obesity likely is due to greater availability of food (especially food high in fat), energy-saving devices, and declining physical activity (Li & others, 2007).

Losing Weight   What we do know about losing weight is that the most effective programs include exercise (Ryan & others, 2014; Stephenson & Schiff, 2016; Thompson & Manore, 2015). A research review concluded that adults who engaged in diet-plus-exercise programs lost more weight than those who relied on diet-only programs (Wu & others, 2009). A study of approximately 2,000 U.S. adults found that exercising 30 minutes a day, planning meals, and weighing themselves daily were the main strategies used by successful dieters compared with unsuccessful dieters (Kruger, Blanck, & Gillespie, 2006) (see Figure 11). Another study also revealed that obese adults in a diet program who kept a food diary for six or seven days a week had double the weight loss of obese adults who did not keep a food diary (Hollis & others, 2008).

Calorie Restriction and Longevity   Some studies have shown that calorie restriction in laboratory animals (such as rats and roundworms) can increase the animals' longevity (Fontana & Hu, 2014; Xu & others, 2015). And researchers have found that chronic problems such as cardiovascular, kidney, and liver disease appear at a later age when calories are restricted (Robertson & Mitchell, 2013). In addition, some recent research indicates that calorie restriction may provide neuroprotection for an aging central nervous system (Willette & others, 2012). One study revealed that after older adults engaged in calorie restriction for three months, their verbal memory improved (Witte & others, 2009).

No one knows for certain how calorie restriction works to increase the life span of animals. Some scientists note that it might lower the level of free radicals and reduce oxidative stress in cells (Bloomer & others, 2011). For example, one study found that calorie restriction slowed the age-related increase in oxidative stress (Ward & others, 2005). Others argue that calorie restriction might trigger a state of emergency called "survival mode" in which the body eliminates all unnecessary functions to focus only on staying alive. This survival mode likely is the result of evolution in which calorie restriction allowed animals to survive periods of famine, and thus the genes remain in the genomes of animal and human species today (Chen & Guarente, 2007).

However, a 25-year longitudinal study conducted by the National Institute of Aging casts some doubt on whether a calorie-restricted diet will increase longevity (Mattison & others, 2012). In this study, monkeys that were fed 30 percent fewer calories did not live longer than a control group of monkeys. The researchers concluded that genes and diet composition are likely better predictors of longevity than calorie restriction per se. The results in the National Institute of Aging study contrast with an ongoing study at the Wisconsin National Primate Research Center, which has reported a 30 percent improved survival rate for calorie-restricted monkeys (Colman & others, 2009). Thus, an appropriate conclusion at this time is that further research is needed to determine whether calorie restriction increases longevity, especially in humans. Whether very low-calorie diets can stretch the human life span is not known (Stein & others, 2012). In some instances, the animals in these studies ate 40 percent less than normal. In humans, a typical level of calorie restriction involves a 30 percent decrease, resulting in about 1,120 calories a day for the average woman and 1,540 for the average man.

Do underweight women and men live longer lives? One study revealed that women who were 20 pounds or more underweight lived longer even after controlling for smoking, hypertension, alcohol intake, and other factors (Wandell, Carlsson, & Theobald, 2009). In this study, underweight men did not live longer when various factors were controlled.

Successful | Unsuccessful

Exercised 30 minutes a day
47
38

Planned meals
36
25

Weighed themselves daily
20
11

50   40   30   20   10   0
Percent

FIGURE 11

COMPARISON OF STRATEGIES USED BY SUCCESSFUL AND UNSUCCESSFUL DIETERS
© iStock.com/Ljupco

The Controversy Over Vitamins and Aging For years, most experts on aging and health argued that a balanced diet was all that was needed for successful aging; vitamin supplements were not recommended. However, researchers recently began exploring the possibility that some vitamin supplements—mainly a group called "antioxidants" consisting of vitamin C, vitamin E, and beta-carotene—help to slow the aging process and improve the health of older adults (Sadowski-Bartosz & Bartosz, 2014).

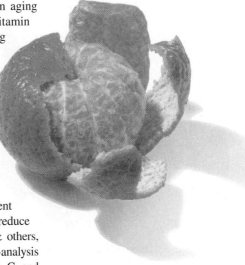

The theory is that antioxidants counteract the cell damage caused by free radicals, which are produced both by the body's own metabolism and by environmental factors such as smoking, pollution, and bad chemicals in the diet (Gandhi & Abramov, 2012). When free radicals cause damage (oxidation) in one cell, a chain reaction of damage follows. Antioxidants act much like a fire extinguisher, helping to neutralize free-radical activity.

What have research studies found about the role of antioxidants in health? Recent research reviews have not supported the belief that antioxidant vitamin supplements can reduce the incidence of cancer and cardiovascular disease (Moyer, 2013; Otaegui-Arrazola & others, 2014; Paganini-Hill, Kawas, & Corrada, 2015; Potter, 2014). However, a recent meta-analysis of seven studies concluded that dietary intakes (not vitamin supplements) of vitamin E, C, and beta-carotene were linked to a reduced risk of Alzheimer disease (Li, Shen, & Ji, 2012).

© Imagestate Media (John Foxx)/Imagestate RF

Review Connect Reflect

LG2 Characterize developmental changes in nutrition and eating behavior

Review
- What are some important aspects of nutrition and eating behavior in infancy?
- What are some key nutritional problems in American children?
- How can eating behavior and disorders in adolescence be characterized?
- What are some controversies and issues involving nutrition and eating behavior in the adult years?

Connect
- What does the nature versus nurture debate suggest about children's risk of becoming obese?

Reflect *Your Own Personal Journey of Life*
- How good are you at choosing nutritious foods? Have your lifestyle and behavior in this area affected your health? Might your food choices affect your health in the future?

3 Exercise **LG3** Summarize the roles of exercise in child and adult health

Childhood and Adolescence | Adulthood | Aging and Longevity

We have seen the important role exercise plays in losing weight. Exercise is linked with many aspects of being physically and mentally healthy. Let's explore the impact of exercise throughout the life span.

CHILDHOOD AND ADOLESCENCE

American children and adolescents are not getting enough exercise (Wuest & Fisette, 2015). Educators and policy makers in the United States and numerous countries around the world, including China, Finland, and Great Britain, have become very concerned about the sedentary lifestyles of many children and adolescents in their countries (Dowda & others, 2009; Janssen, 2014).

How much physical activity should preschool children engage in per day?
© RubberBall Productions/Getty Images RF

Childhood   Because of their activity level and the development of large muscles, especially in the arms and legs, children need daily exercise (Graham, Holt-Hale, & Parker, 2013; Wuest & Fisette, 2015). Screen time is linked with low activity levels in children. A recent research review concluded that a higher level of screen time (watching TV, using a computer) at 4 to 6 years of age was linked to a lower activity level and being overweight from preschool through adolescence (te Velde & others, 2012).

An increasing number of studies document the importance of exercise in children's physical development (McCormack & others, 2014; Myer & others, 2015; Shin & others, 2014). A recent experimental study found that 13 weeks of aerobic training had significant benefits for insulin resistance and body fat levels of overweight/obese elementary school children, regardless of gender or ethnicity (Davis & others, 2012). A recent research review concluded that exercise programs with a frequency of three weekly sessions lasting longer than 60 minutes was effective in lowering both systolic and diastolic blood pressure (Garcia-Hermoso, Saavedra, & Escalante, 2013). Also, research strongly supports the positive effects of exercise on children's bone strength and even on the prevention of osteoporosis in aging adults (Janz & others, 2015).

Aerobic exercise also is linked to children's cognitive skills (Best, 2010). Researchers have found that aerobic exercise benefits children's attention, memory, effortful and goal-directed thinking and behavior, and creativity (Davis & Cooper, 2011; Davis & others, 2011; Ma, Le Mare, & Gurd, 2015; Monti, Hillman, & Cohen, 2012). For example, in a recent fMRI study of physically unfit 8- to 11-year-old overweight children, a daily instructor-led aerobic exercise program that lasted eight months was effective in improving the efficiency or flexible modulation of neural circuits that support better cognitive functioning (Kraftt & others, 2014). Further, a recent study found that moderately intensive aerobic exercise improved children's cognitive inhibitory control (Drollette & others, 2014). And a recent study found that in-class, high-intensity exercise improved the selective attention of 9- to 11-year-olds (Ma, Le Mare, & Gurd, 2015).

Parents and schools strongly influence children's exercise habits (Gilbertson & Graves, 2015; Meyer & others, 2014). Growing up with parents who regularly exercise provides positive models of exercise for children. A study found that school-based physical activity was successful in improving children's fitness and lowering their fat content (Kriemler & others, 2011).

In 2007, Texas became the first state to test students' physical fitness. The student shown here is performing the trunk lift. Other assessments include aerobic exercise, muscle strength, and body fat. Assessments will be done annually.
© Dallas Morning News, Vernon Bryant Photographer

Adolescence   Researchers have found that individuals become less active as they reach and progress through adolescence (Kwan & others, 2012). A national study of U.S. 9- to 15-year-olds revealed that almost all 9- and 11-year-olds met the federal government's moderate to vigorous exercise recommendations per day (a minimum of 60 minutes daily), but only 31 percent of 15-year-olds met the recommendations on weekdays, and on weekends only 17 percent met the recommendations (Nader & others, 2008). The recent national study also found that adolescent boys were more likely than girls to engage in moderate to vigorous exercise. Figure 12 shows the average amount of exercise engaged in by U.S. boys and girls from 9 to 15 years of age on weekdays and weekends.

Ethnic differences in exercise participation rates of U.S. adolescents also occur, and these rates vary by gender. As indicated in Figure 13, in the National Youth Risk Survey, non-Latino White boys exercised the most, African American girls the least (Eaton & others, 2012).

Exercise is linked to a number of positive outcomes in adolescence. One important outcome is that exercise helps adolescents maintain an appropriate weight (Alberga & others, 2012; Todd & others, 2015). Higher levels of exercise in adolescence are associated with reduced triglyceride levels, lower blood pressure, and a lower incidence of type II diabetes (Anyaegbu & Dharnidharka, 2014). Also, recent study found that adolescents with high levels of physical fitness had better connectivity between brain regions than adolescents with lower levels of fitness (Herting & others, 2014). Another study revealed that a daily morning running program for three weeks improved the sleep quality, mood, and concentration capacity of adolescents (Kalak & others, 2012). And a study of young adolescents found that regular exercise was associated with higher academic achievement (Hashim, Freddy, & Rosmatunisah, 2012).

As with children, parents play an important role in influencing adolescents' exercise patterns. A research review also found that peers play an especially important role in adolescents' physical activity (Fitzgerald, Fitzgerald, & Aherne, 2012). In this review, among the peer factors that were linked to adolescents' exercise levels were peer/friend support of exercise and friendship quality and acceptance.

ADULTHOOD

The benefits of exercise continue in adulthood. Both moderate and intense exercise produce important physical and psychological gains (Powers & Howley, 2015; Thompson & Manore, 2015). The enjoyment and pleasure we derive from exercise added to its physical benefits make exercise one of life's most important activities (Donatelle, 2015). A national poll in the United States found that 51.6 percent of individuals 18 years and older exercised for 30 or more minutes three or more days a week (Gallup, 2013b). In this survey, young adults 18 to 29 years of age (56.8 percent) were the most likely age group to exercise. Also in this survey, men were more likely to exercise than women.

Among the most important health benefits of exercise are reduced risks for obesity, cardiovascular disease, and diabetes (Nagamatsu & others, 2014; Park, Han, & Kang, 2014; Phillips & others, 2015). Even getting hogs to jog has documented the cardiovascular benefits of exercise (see Figure 14).

Although exercise designed to strengthen muscles and bones or to improve flexibility is important to fitness, many health experts stress the benefits of aerobic exercise. **Aerobic exercise** is sustained activity—jogging, swimming, or cycling, for example—that stimulates heart and lung functioning.

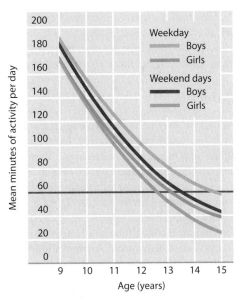

FIGURE 12

AVERAGE AMOUNT OF MODERATE TO VIGOROUS EXERCISE ENGAGED IN BY U.S. 9- TO 15-YEAR-OLDS ON WEEKDAYS AND WEEKENDS. *Note:* The federal government recommends 60 minutes of moderate to vigorous physical activity per day.

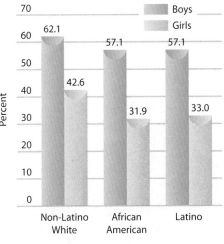

FIGURE 13

EXERCISE RATES OF U.S. HIGH SCHOOL STUDENTS: GENDER AND ETHNICITY. *Note:* Data are for high school students who were physically active doing any kind of physical activity that increased their heart rate and made them breathe hard some of the time for a total of at least 60 minutes a day on five or more of the seven days preceding the survey. *Source:* After Eaton & others, 2012, Table 91.

FIGURE 14

THE JOGGING HOG EXPERIMENT. Jogging hogs reveal the dramatic effects of exercise on health. In one investigation, a group of hogs was trained to run approximately 100 miles per week (Bloor & White, 1983). Then the researchers narrowed the arteries that supplied blood to the hogs' hearts. The hearts of the jogging hogs developed extensive alternate pathways for blood supply, and 42 percent of the threatened heart tissue was salvaged compared with only 17 percent in a control group of nonjogging hogs.
Courtesy of Maxine Bloor

aerobic exercise Sustained activity that stimulates heart and lung functioning.

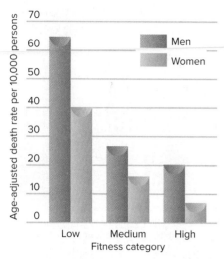

FIGURE **15**

PHYSICAL FITNESS AND MORTALITY. In
a study of middle-aged and older adults,
being moderately fit or highly fit meant that
individuals were less likely to die over a
period of eight years than their less fit
(sedentary) counterparts (Blair & others, 1989).

developmental **connection**

Research Methods

What differentiates a longitudinal study
from a cross-sectional study? Connect to
"Introduction."

Many health experts recommend that adults engage in 45 minutes or more of moderate
physical activity on most, preferably all, days of the week. Most recommend trying to raise
your heart rate to at least 60 percent of your maximum heart rate. However, only about one-
fifth of adults achieve these recommended levels of physical activity.

AGING AND LONGEVITY

Although we may be in the evening of our lives in late adulthood, we are not meant to live
out our remaining years passively. Everything we know about older adults suggests they are
healthier and happier the more active they are (Bielak & others, 2014; Morrow-Howell &
others, 2014). Can regular exercise lead to a healthier late adulthood and increased longevity?
Let's examine several research studies on exercise and aging.

In one study, exercise literally meant a difference between life and death for middle-aged
and older adults (Blair, 1990). More than 10,000 men and women were divided into categories
of low fitness, medium fitness, and high fitness (Blair & others, 1989). Then they were studied
over a period of eight years. As shown in Figure 15, sedentary participants (low fitness) were
more than twice as likely to die during the eight-year time span of the study as those who were
moderately fit and more than three times as likely to die as those who were highly fit. The
positive effects of being physically fit occurred for both men and women in this study. Also, a
longitudinal study found that men who exercised regularly at 72 years of age had a 30 percent
higher probability of still being alive at 90 years of age than their sedentary counterparts (Yates
& others, 2008). And a study of more than 11,000 women found that low cardiorespiratory
fitness was a significant predictor of all-cause mortality (Farrell & others, 2010). Also, a study
of joggers in Copenhagen, Denmark, revealed that engaging in light or moderate jogging on a
regular basis was linked to increased longevity (Schnohr & others, 2015).

Exercise is an excellent way to maintain health (Stensvold & others, 2015; Vrantsidis &
others, 2014). The current recommendations for older adults' physical activity are 2 hours
and 30 minutes of moderate intensity aerobic activity (brisk walking, for example) per week
and muscle strengthening activities on two or more days a week (Centers for Disease Control
and Prevention, 2014c). In the recent recommendations, even greater benefits can be attained
with 5 hours of moderate-intensity aerobic activity per week.

Gerontologists increasingly recommend strength training in addition to aerobic activity
and stretching for older adults (Lima & others, 2015; Nascimento Dda & others, 2014). The
average person's lean body mass declines with age—about 6.6 pounds of lean muscle are lost
each decade during the adult years. The rate of muscle loss accelerates after age 45. Resistance exercise can preserve and possibly increase muscle mass in older adults (Kennis &
others, 2013; Lima & others, 2015).

Exercise is an excellent way to maintain health and live longer (Coombs, Stamatakis, &
Lee, 2015; Katzel & Steinbrenner, 2012). The current recommended level of aerobic activity
for adults 60 years of age and older is 30 minutes of moderately intense activity, such as
brisk walking or riding a stationary bicycle, five or more days a week, and strength training
two or more days a week (Der Ananian & Prohaska, 2007).

Researchers continue to document the positive effects of exercise in older adults:

· *Exercise is linked to increased longevity.* A recent study of older adults found that
total daily physical activity was linked to increased longevity across a four-year
period (Buchman & others, 2012). In a longitudinal study of Chinese women, those
who exercised regularly were less likely to die over approximately a six-year time
period (Matthews & others, 2007). In one analysis, energy expenditure by older
adults during exercise that burns up at least 1,000 calories a week was estimated to
increase life expectancy by about 30 percent, and burning up 2,000 calories a week
in exercise was estimated to increase life expectancy by about 50 percent (Lee &
Skerrett, 2001).

· *Exercise is related to prevention of common chronic diseases.* Exercise can reduce the
risk of developing cardiovascular disease, type 2 diabetes, osteoporosis, stroke, and
breast cancer (Vigorito & Giallauria, 2014).

· *Exercise is associated with improved outcomes for many diseases.* When exercise is
used as part of the treatment, individuals with the following disorders show improvement in symptoms: arthritis, pulmonary disease, congestive heart failure, coronary

artery disease, hypertension, type 2 diabetes, obesity, and Alzheimer disease (Grace & others, 2015; Hernandez & others, 2015; O'Keefe, Schnohr, & Lavie, 2013).

· *Exercise improves older adults' cellular functioning.* Researchers increasingly are finding that exercise improves cellular functioning in older adults (Gielen & others, 2011). For example, researchers have recently discovered that aerobic exercise is linked to greater telomere length in older adults (Du & others, 2012).

· *Exercise improves immune system functioning in older adults* (Apostolopoulos & others, 2014; Simpson & others, 2012). One study found that following exercise, a number of components of immune system functioning in older adult women improved (Sakamoto & others, 2009).

· *Exercise can optimize body composition and reduce the decline in motor skills as aging occurs.* Exercise can increase muscle mass and bone mass, as well as decrease bone fragility (Perry & Downey, 2012). A recent study found that an exercise program reduced the number of falls in older adults with dementia (Burton & others, 2015).

· *Exercise reduces the likelihood that older adults will develop mental health problems and can be effective as part of the treatment of mental health problems.* For example, exercise reduces the likelihood that older adults will develop depression and can be effective in treating depression in older adults (Villaverde & others, 2012).

· *Exercise is linked to improved brain and cognitive functioning in older adults.* Older adults who exercise show better brain functioning and process information more effectively than older adults who don't exercise (Kirk-Sanchez & McGough, 2014; Nagamatsu & others, 2014). For example, a study of older adults revealed that exercise increased the size of the hippocampus and improved memory (Erickson & others, 2011). In another study, a brief water-based exercise program improved the attention, memory, and executive function of older adults (Fedor, Garcia, & Gunstad, 2015). Also, a recent research review concluded that more active and physically fit older adults can allocate more attentional resources in interacting with the environment and process information more quickly (Gomez-Pinilla & Hillman, 2013). This review also concluded that exercise's influence on cognition occurs through changes in molecular events associated with the management of energy metabolism and synaptic plasticity.

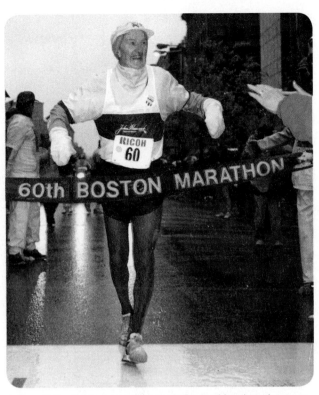

Johnny Kelley finishes one of the many Boston Marathons he ran as an older adult. In 1991 he ran his sixteenth Boston Marathon, and in 2000 he was named "Runner of the Century" by *Runner's World* magazine. At 70 years of age, Kelley was still running 50 miles a week. At that point in his life, Kelley said, "I'm afraid to stop running. I feel so good. I want to stay alive." He lived 27 more years and died at age 97 in 2004.
© *Charles Krupa/AP Images*

developmental **connection**

Aging

What are telomeres, and how are they being investigated in the search for an explanation of why people age? Connect to "Physical Development and Biological Aging."

Despite the extensive documentation of exercise's power to improve older adults' health and quality of life, a national survey revealed that older adults have increased their exercise levels only slightly in recent years (Centers for Disease Control and Prevention, 2008) (see Figure 16). Possible explanations of older adults' failure to substantially increase their exercise focus on factors such as chronic illnesses, life crises (such as a spouse's death) that disrupt exercise schedules, embarrassment at being around others who are in better shape (especially if they haven't exercised much earlier in life), and a "why bother?" perspective (not believing that exercise will improve their lives much) (Painter, 2008). But it is never too late to start exercising, and older adults can significantly benefit from regular exercise (Guirado & others, 2012; Hernandez & others, 2015).

FIGURE **16**

REGULAR EXERCISE BY U.S. OLDER ADULTS: 1997 TO 2006

Review Connect Reflect

LG3 Summarize the roles of exercise in child and adult health

Review

- How extensively do U.S. children and adolescents exercise?
- What roles does exercise play in adult health?
- How does exercise influence development in aging adults?

Connect

- Consider what you have learned so far about parents' potential influence on children's health. Do active

parents send a different message to their children than sedentary parents do?

Reflect *Your Own Personal Journey of Life*

- Imagine that you have become middle-aged and someone asks you this question: "What would give you the greater advantage: exercising more or eating less?" What would your answer be?

---

4 Substance Use

LG4 Evaluate substance use in adolescence and adulthood

- Adolescence and Emerging Adulthood

- Substance Use in Older Adults

Besides exercising, another important way to preserve health is not to engage in substance abuse (Fields, 2013). For example, in one longitudinal study, individuals who did not abuse alcohol at age 50 were more likely to still be alive and healthy at 75 to 80 years of age than their counterparts who abused alcohol at age 50 (Vaillant, 2002). In the chapter titled "Biological Beginnings," we described the negative effects on the fetus and developing child that can result from substance use by the pregnant mother. Here we examine the effects of substance use on adolescents, emerging adults, and older adults.

ADOLESCENCE AND EMERGING ADULTHOOD

Adolescence is a critical time for the onset of substance abuse. Many individuals who abuse drugs begin to do so during the adolescent years. Let's explore some trends in adolescent drug use and then examine drug use in emerging adulthood.

Trends in Adolescent Drug Use Each year since 1975, Lloyd Johnston and his colleagues at the Institute of Social Research at the University of Michigan have monitored the drug use of America's high school seniors in a wide range of public and private high schools. Since 1991, they also have surveyed drug use by eighth- and tenth-graders. In 2014, the study surveyed more than 41,000 secondary school students in more than 400 public and private schools (Johnston & others, 2015).

According to this study, the proportions of eighth-, tenth-, and twelfth-grade U.S. students who used any illicit drug declined in the late 1990s and the first decade of the twenty-first century (Johnston & others, 2015) (see Figure 17). The use of drugs among U.S. secondary school students declined in the 1980s but began to increase in the early 1990s (Johnston & others, 2015). In the late 1990s and the early part of the twenty-first century, the proportion of secondary school students reporting the use of any illicit drug has been declining. The overall decline in the use of illicit drugs by adolescents during this time frame is approximately one-third for eighth-graders, one-fourth for tenth-graders, and one-eighth for twelfth-graders. The most notable declines in drug use by U.S. adolescents in the twenty-first century have occurred for LSD, cocaine, cigarettes, sedatives, tranquilizers, and Ecstasy. Marijuana is the illicit drug most widely used in the United States and Europe (Hibell & others, 2004; Johnston & others, 2015). Even with the recent decline in use, the United States still has one of the highest rates of adolescent drug use of any industrialized nation.

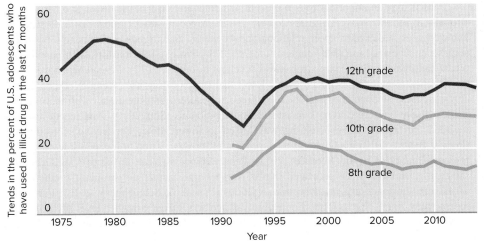

FIGURE **17**

TRENDS IN DRUG USE BY U.S. EIGHTH-, TENTH-, AND TWELFTH-GRADE STUDENTS. This graph shows the percentage of U.S. eighth-, tenth-, and twelfth-grade students who reported having taken an illicit drug in the last 12 months from 1991 to 2014 (for eighth- and tenth-graders) and from 1975 to 2014 (for twelfth-graders) (Johnston & others, 2015).

As shown in Figure 17, in which marijuana is included, an increase in illicit drug use by U.S. adolescents occurred from 2008 to 2014. However, when marijuana use is subtracted from the illicit drug index, no increase in U.S. adolescent drug use occurred in this time frame (Johnston & others, 2015).

How extensive is alcohol use by U.S. adolescents? Sizable declines in adolescent alcohol use have occurred in recent years (Johnston & others, 2015). The percentage of U.S. eighth-graders who reported having any alcohol to drink in the past 30 days fell from a 1996 high of 26 percent to 9 percent in 2014. The 30-day prevalence fell among tenth-graders from 39 percent in 2001 to 23.5 percent in 2014 and among high school seniors from 72 percent in 1980 to 37 percent in 2014. Binge drinking (defined in the University of Michigan surveys as having five or more drinks in a row in the last two weeks) by high school seniors declined from 41 percent in 1980 to 23.5 percent in 2014. However, the 23.5 percent figure represents an increase of 3 percent from 2011. Binge drinking by eighth- and tenth-graders also has dropped in recent years. A consistent gender difference occurs in binge drinking, with males engaging in this behavior more than females do (Johnston & others, 2015).

Cigarette smoking is decreasing among adolescents. Cigarette smoking among U.S. adolescents peaked in 1996 and 1997 and has gradually declined since then (Johnston & others, 2015). Following peak use in 1996, smoking rates for U.S. eighth-graders have fallen by 50 percent. In 2014, the percentages of twelfth-graders who said they had smoked cigarettes in the last 30 days was 13.6 percent (a 5 percent decrease from 2011), 7 percent (tenth grade), and 4 percent (eighth grade). Since the mid-1990s an increasing percentage of adolescents have reported that they perceive cigarette smoking as dangerous, that they disapprove of it, that they are less accepting of being around smokers, and that they prefer to date nonsmokers (Johnston & others, 2015).

Cigarette smoking (in which the active drug is nicotine) is one of the most serious yet preventable health problems. Smoking is likely to begin in grades 7 through 9, although sizable percentages of youth are still establishing regular smoking habits during high school and college. Risk factors for becoming a regular smoker in adolescence include having a friend who smokes, a weak academic orientation, and low parental support (Tucker, Ellickson, & Klein, 2003).

The Roles of Development, Parents, Peers, and Educational Success

A special concern involves adolescents who begin to use drugs early in adolescence or even in childhood (Fields, 2013). A longitudinal study of individuals from 8 to 42 years of age also found that early onset of drinking was linked to increased risk of heavy drinking in middle age (Pitkanen, Lyrra, & Pulkkinen, 2005). And a recent study revealed that the onset of alcohol use before age 11 was linked to a higher risk of alcohol dependence in early adulthood (Guttmannova & others, 2012). Also, a recent study found that early onset of drinking and a quick progression to drinking to intoxication were linked to drinking problems in high school (Morean & others, 2014). And another recent study indicated that early- and rapid-onset trajectories of alcohol, marijuana, and substance use were associated with substance abuse in early adulthood (Nelson, Van Ryzin, & Dishion, 2015).

developmental **connection**

Biological Processes

Early maturation in adolescence is linked with an increased likelihood of substance abuse problems in adolescent girls. Connect to "Physical Development and Biological Aging."

Parents play an important role in preventing adolescent drug abuse (Abar & others, 2015; Broning & others, 2014; Zehe & Colder, 2014). A recent study found that low parental knowledge of adolescents' peer relations and behavior, and friends' delinquency, predicted adolescent substance use (McAdams & others, 2014). Positive relationships with parents and others can reduce adolescents' drug use (Cleveland & others, 2012). Researchers have found that parental monitoring is linked with a lower incidence of drug use (Wang & others, 2014). A research review concluded that the more frequently adolescents ate dinner with their family, the less likely they were to have substance abuse problems (Sen, 2010). And recent research revealed that authoritative parenting was linked to lower adolescent alcohol consumption (Piko & Balazs, 2012) while parent-adolescent conflict was related to higher adolescent alcohol consumption (Chaplin & others, 2012). Peer relations also are linked to adolescent substance use, and one study indicated that of various risk factors the strongest predictors of adolescent substance use involved peer relations (Patrick & Schulenberg, 2010). Further, a recent study found that neighborhood disadvantage was linked a higher level of adolescent alcohol use two years later, mainly through a pathway that included exposure to delinquent peers (Trucco & others, 2014).

Educational success is also a strong buffer for the emergence of drug problems in adolescence. An analysis by Jerald Bachman and his colleagues (2008) revealed that early educational achievement considerably reduced the likelihood that adolescents would develop drug problems, including those involving alcohol abuse, smoking, and abuse of various illicit drugs.

Emerging Adults' Drug Use   The transition from high school to college may be a critical risk period for alcohol abuse. The large majority of emerging adults recognize that drinking is common among individuals their age and is largely acceptable, even expected by their peers. They also perceive that they get some social and coping benefits from alcohol use and even occasional heavy drinking. One study revealed that only 20 percent of college students reported that they abstain from drinking alcohol (Huang & others, 2009).

In 2012, 37.4 percent of U.S. college students reported having had five or more drinks in a row at least once in the last two weeks (Johnston & others, 2013). The term *extreme binge drinking* describes individuals who had 10 or more drinks in a row. In 2010 approximately 13 percent of college students reported drinking this heavily (Johnston & others, 2011). While drinking rates among college students have remained high, drinking, including binge drinking, has declined in recent years. For example, binge drinking declined by 4 percent from 2007 to 2012 (Johnston & others, 2013).

The effects of heavy drinking take a toll. In a national survey of drinking patterns on 140 campuses, almost half of the binge drinkers reported problems that included missed classes, physical injuries, troubles with police, and unprotected sex (Wechsler & others, 1994). This survey also found that binge-drinking college students were eleven times more likely to drive after drinking and twice as likely to have unprotected sex as college students who did not binge drink.

Drinking alcohol before going out—called *pregaming*—has become common among college students (Ahmed & others, 2014). A recent study revealed that almost two-thirds of students on one campus had pregamed at least once in a two-week period (DeJong, DeRicco, & Schneider, 2010). Drinking games, in which the goal is to become intoxicated, also have become common on college campuses (LaBrie & others, 2011). Higher levels of alcohol use have been consistently linked to higher rates of sexual risk taking, such as engaging in casual sex, sex without contraceptives, and sexual assaults (Khan & others, 2012).

Fortunately, by the time individuals reach their mid-twenties, many have reduced their use of alcohol and drugs. That is the conclusion reached by Gerald Bachman and his colleagues (2002) in a longitudinal analysis of more than 38,000 individuals (see Figure 18). They were evaluated from the time they were high school seniors through their twenties.

What kinds of problems are associated with binge drinking in college?
© Nathaniel Welch/Redux

- - - - - - - - - ->
developmental **connection**

Sexuality

When emerging adults drink alcohol, they are most likely to have casual sex. Connect to "Gender and Sexuality."

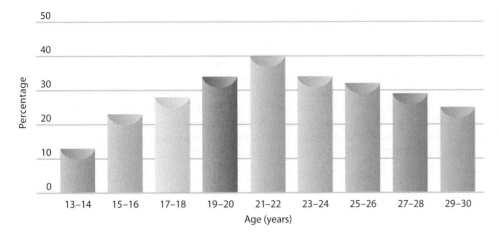

50

40

30

Percentage

20

10

0

13–14   15–16   17–18   19–20   21–22   23–24   25–26   27–28   29–30

Age (years)

FIGURE **18**

**BINGE DRINKING IN THE ADOLESCENCE–
EARLY ADULTHOOD TRANSITION.** Note
that the percentage of individuals engaging in
binge drinking peaked at 21 or 22 years of age
and then began to gradually decline through
the remainder of the twenties. Binge drinking
was defined as having five or more alcoholic
drinks in a row in the past two weeks.

Do individuals smoke cigarettes more in emerging adulthood than adolescence? According to a U.S. survey, 18- to 25-year-olds reported a smoking rate that was substantially higher than the rate of 12- to 17-year-olds and higher than the rate of individuals who were 26 years and older (Substance Abuse and Mental Health Services Administration, 2005). Thus, cigarette smoking peaks in emerging adulthood (Park & others, 2006).

SUBSTANCE USE IN OLDER ADULTS

As indicated earlier, alcohol and substance abuse peak in emerging adulthood and then decline somewhat by the mid-twenties. Of course, alcohol and substance abuse continue to raise serious health concerns for many people in early and middle adulthood. How extensive is substance abuse in older adults? A national survey found that in 2010 the percentage of individuals who engaged in binge drinking (defined as four or more drinks for women and five more drinks for men on an occasion in the past 30 days) declined considerably in middle and late adulthood compared with early adulthood (Centers for Disease Control and Prevention, 2012b) (see Figure 19). However, the frequency of binge drinking in the past 30 days was highest in older adults (5.5 episodes).

Despite the decline in the percentage of individuals who engage in binge drinking in late adulthood, the Substance Abuse and Mental Health Services Administration (2005) has identified substance abuse among older adults as the "invisible epidemic" in the United States. The belief is that substance abuse often goes undetected in older adults, and there is concern about older adults who abuse not only illicit drugs but prescription drugs as well (Wu & Blazer, 2011). The consequences of abuse—such as depression, inadequate nutrition, congestive heart failure, and frequent falls—may erroneously be attributed to other medical or psychological conditions (Hoyer & Roodin, 2009). As the number of older adults rises, substance abuse is likely to characterize an increasing number of older adults. For older adults who are taking multiple medications, the dangers of substance abuse rise. For example, when combined with tranquilizers or sedatives, alcohol use can impair breathing, produce excessive sedation, and even be fatal.

Despite the concerns about substance abuse in later adulthood, researchers have found a protective effect of moderate alcohol use in older adults (Holahan & others, 2012; O'Keefe & others, 2014). One study of older adults revealed that those who drank moderately (compared with those who drank heavily or did not drink at all) had better physical and mental health, and increased longevity (Rozzini, Ranhoff, & Trabucchi, 2007).

Age Group	Percent	Drinks Per Occasion	Frequency
18–24	28	9	4.2
25–34	28	8	4.2
35–44	19	8	4.1
45–64	13	7	4.7
65 & over	4	5	5.5

FIGURE **19**

BINGE DRINKING THROUGH THE LIFE SPAN. *Note:* Percent
refers to percent of individuals in a particular age group who
engaged in binge drinking on at least one occasion in the past
30 days (4 or more drinks for women, 5 or more for men). Drinks
per occasion reflects the intensity of the binge drinking. Frequency
indicates the number of occasions in which binge drinking occurred
in the past 30 days. *Source:* After data presented by the Centers for Disease Control
and Prevention, 2012, Table 1.

*What might explain the finding that drinking red wine in moderation is linked
to better health and increased longevity?*
© Arthur Tilley/Getty Images RF

The explanation of moderate drinking's benefits involves better physical and mental performance, being more open to social contacts, and being able to assert mastery over one's life.

Researchers have especially found that moderate drinking of red wine is linked to better health and increased longevity (Khurana & others, 2013). Explanations of the benefits of red wine involve its connection to lowering stress and reducing the risk of coronary heart disease (Carrizzo & others, 2013). Evidence is increasing that a chemical in the skin of red wine grapes—resveratrol—plays a key role in red wine's health benefits (Artero & others, 2015; Tome-Carneiro & others, 2012). One study found that red wine, but not white, killed several lines of cancer cells (Wallenborg & others, 2009). Scientists are exploring how resveratrol might activate SIRT1, an enzyme that is involved in DNA repair and aging (Barger, 2013).

Review *Connect* Reflect

 LG4 Evaluate substance use in adolescence and adulthood

Review
- How extensively do adolescents take drugs? What factors are linked with drug abuse by adolescents? What is the nature of substance use in college students and young adults?
- How can substance use in older adults be described?

Connect
- Research has shown that older adults fare better when they are given more responsibility and control over their lives. In what other age periods is giving individuals more responsibility and control especially important for their development? In what ways is this helpful?

Reflect *Your Own Personal Journey of Life*
- Do you know someone who has a drug problem? If so, describe the nature of the problem. Is the person willing to admit to having a problem?

reach your **learning goals**

Health

1 Health, Illness, and Disease   **LG1** Describe developmental changes in health

Children's Health

Adolescents' Health

Emerging and Young Adults' Health

Health and Aging

- Prevention and poverty are important factors in children's health. Children need timely immunizations. Accident prevention is a key aspect of children's health. Of special concern are children living in poverty, who often are malnourished.

- Adolescence is a critical juncture in health because many health habits—good or bad—still are being formed. Social contexts, including family, peers, and schools, influence the health of adolescents.

- Few emerging and young adults have chronic health problems. Many emerging and young adults don't stop to think about how their personal lifestyles will affect their health later in life. Emerging adults have double the mortality rate of adolescents.

- Chronic disorders increase in middle-aged adults and are common in older adults. Osteoporosis is a concern, especially among older women. Various forms of dementia, especially Alzheimer disease, are a major health problem. Another type of brain disorder is Parkinson disease. Stress increasingly is recognized as a key factor in disease, especially in its connection to the immune system. A special concern is the quality of nursing homes for older adults and the treatment of older adults in nursing homes.

2 Nutrition and Eating Behavior

 LG2 Characterize developmental changes in nutrition and eating behavior

Infancy

· The importance of adequate energy intake consumed in a loving and supportive environment in infancy cannot be overstated. The growing consensus is that breast feeding is better for the baby's health than bottle feeding. Nutritional supplements can improve infants' cognitive development.

Childhood

· Concerns about nutrition in childhood focus on fat content in diet and obesity. Thirty percent of U.S. children are at risk for being overweight. Obesity increases a child's risk of developing many medical and psychological problems. Poor nutrition in children from low-income families is a special concern.

Adolescence

· Nutrition and being overweight are also key problems among adolescents. Anorexia nervosa and bulimia nervosa can develop in adolescence; most anorexics and bulimics are women.

Adult Development and Aging

· Obesity is a major concern in adulthood, and dieting is pervasive. Calorie restriction is associated with longevity in many animal studies, but a recent longitudinal study did not find greater longevity for calorie-restricted monkeys. A balanced diet is usually recommended for older adults. Recent research views have found that antioxidant supplements do not reduce the risk for many diseases, such as cancer and cardiovascular disease.

3 Exercise

 LG3 Summarize the roles of exercise in child and adult health

Childhood and Adolescence

Adulthood

· Most children and adolescents are not getting nearly enough exercise.

· Both moderate and intense exercise produce physical and psychological advantages, such as lowered risk of heart disease and lowered anxiety.

Aging and Longevity

· Regular exercise in middle-aged and older adults can promote health and increase longevity.

4 Substance Use

LG4 Evaluate substance use in adolescence and adulthood

Adolescence and Emerging Adulthood

· The United States has one of the highest adolescent drug use rates of any industrialized country. Alcohol and cigarette smoking are special concerns. Development, parents, peers, and educational success play important roles in preventing drug abuse in adolescents. Forty percent of U.S. college students say they drink heavily. Substance use peaks in emerging adulthood and then often decreases by the mid-twenties.

Substance Use in Older Adults

· Alcohol use declines in older adults, although abuse is more difficult to detect in older adults than in younger adults. There is concern about older adults who abuse prescription drugs and illicit drugs.

key **terms**

aerobic exercise	anorexia nervosa	chronic disorders	osteoporosis
Alzheimer disease	bulimia nervosa	dementia	Parkinson disease

key **people**

Lloyd Johnston	Ellen Langer	K. Warner Schaie
Margie Lachman	Judith Rodin	

chapter 5

MOTOR, SENSORY, AND PERCEPTUAL DEVELOPMENT

chapter outline

1 Motor Development

Learning Goal 1 Describe how motor skills develop

The Dynamic Systems View
Reflexes
Gross Motor Skills
Fine Motor Skills

2 Sensory and Perceptual Development

Learning Goal 2 Outline the course of sensory and perceptual development

What Are Sensation and Perception?
The Ecological View
Visual Perception
Hearing
Other Senses
Intermodal Perception
Nature/Nurture and Perceptual Development

3 Perceptual-Motor Coupling

Learning Goal 3 Discuss the connection between perception and action

preview

Think about what is required for us to find our way around our environment, to play sports, or to create art. These activities require both active perception and precisely timed motor actions. Neither innate, automatic movements nor simple sensations are enough to let us do the things we take for granted every day. How do we develop perceptual and motor abilities, and what happens to them as we age? In this chapter, we will focus first on the development of motor skills, then on sensory and perceptual development, and finally on the coupling of perceptual-motor skills.

1 Motor Development   **LG1** Describe how motor skills develop

| The Dynamic Systems View | Reflexes | Gross Motor Skills | Fine Motor Skills |

Most adults are capable of coordinated, purposive actions of considerable skill, including driving a car, playing golf, and typing accurately on a computer keyboard. Some adults have extraordinary motor skills, such as those involved in winning an Olympic pole vault competition, painting a masterpiece, or performing heart surgery. Look all you want at a newborn infant, and you will observe nothing even remotely approaching these skilled actions. How, then, do the motor behaviors of adults come about?

THE DYNAMIC SYSTEMS VIEW

Developmentalist Arnold Gesell (1934) thought his painstaking observations had revealed how people develop their motor skills. He had discovered that infants and children develop rolling, sitting, standing, and other motor skills in a fixed order and within specific time frames. These observations, said Gesell, show that motor development comes about through the unfolding of a genetic plan, or maturation.

Later studies, however, demonstrated that the sequence of developmental milestones is not as fixed as Gesell indicated and not due as much to heredity as Gesell argued (Adolph & Berger, 2016; Adolph & Robinson, 2013, 2015; Berger, Chan, & Adolph, 2014). In the past two decades, the study of motor development experienced a renaissance as psychologists developed new insights about *how* motor skills develop (Gerson & Woodward, 2014; Kretch, Franchak, & Adolph, 2014). One increasingly influential perspective is dynamic systems theory, proposed by Esther Thelen (Thelen & Smith, 1998, 2006).

According to **dynamic systems theory,** infants assemble motor skills for perceiving and acting (Thelen & Smith, 2006). To develop motor skills, infants must perceive something in the environment that motivates them to act and then use their perceptions to fine-tune their movements. Motor skills represent pathways to the infant's goals (Keen, 2011).

How is a motor skill developed, according to this theory? When infants are motivated to do something, they might create a new motor behavior. The new behavior is the result of many converging factors: the development of the nervous system, the body's physical properties and its possibilities for movement, the goal the child is motivated to reach, and the environmental support for the skill. For example, babies learn to walk only when maturation of the nervous system allows them to control certain leg muscles, when their legs have grown enough to support their weight, and when they want to move.

Mastering a motor skill requires the infant's active efforts to coordinate several components of the skill. Infants explore and select possible solutions to the demands of a new task; they assemble adaptive patterns by modifying their current movement patterns. The first step occurs when the infant is motivated by a new challenge—such as the desire to cross a room—and gets into the "ballpark" of the task demands by taking a couple of stumbling steps. Then, the infant "tunes" these movements to make them smoother and more effective. The tuning

Esther Thelen is shown conducting an experiment to discover how infants learn to control their arms to reach and grasp for objects. A computer device is used to monitor the infant's arm movements and to track muscle patterns. Thelen's research is conducted from a dynamic systems perspective. *What is the nature of this perspective?*
Courtesy of Dr. David Thelen

The experiences of the first three years of life are almost entirely lost to us, and when we attempt to enter into a small child's world, we come as foreigners who have forgotten the landscape and no longer speak the native tongue.

—Selma Fraiberg
Developmentalist and child advocate, 20th century

dynamic systems theory A theory proposed by Esther Thelen that seeks to explain how infants assemble motor skills for perceiving and acting.

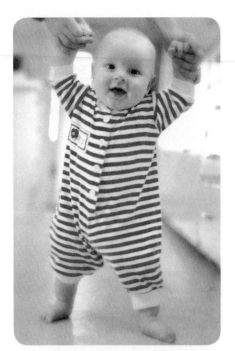

How might dynamic systems theory explain the development of learning to walk?
© Harry Bartlett/Taxi/Getty Images

developmental **connection**

Nature and Nurture

The epigenetic view states that development is an ongoing, bidirectional interchange between heredity and the environment. Connect to "Biological Beginnings."

rooting reflex A newborn's built-in reaction that occurs when the infant's cheek is stroked or the side of the mouth is touched. In response, the infant turns its head toward the side that was touched, in an apparent effort to find something to suck.

sucking reflex A newborn's reaction of sucking an object placed in its mouth. The sucking reflex enables the infant to get nourishment before it has begun to associate a nipple with food.

Moro reflex A startle response that occurs in reaction to a sudden, intense noise or movement. When startled, the newborn arches its back, throws its head back, and flings out its arms and legs. Then the newborn rapidly closes its arms and legs to the center of the body.

grasping reflex A reflex that occurs when something touches an infant's palms. The infant responds by grasping tightly.

gross motor skills Motor skills that involve large-muscle activities, such as walking.

is achieved through repeated cycles of action and perception of the consequences of that action. According to the dynamic systems view, even universal milestones, such as crawling, reaching, and walking, are learned through this process of adaptation: Infants modulate their movement patterns to fit a new task by exploring and selecting possible configurations (Adolph & Berger, 2016; Thelen & Smith, 2006).

To see how dynamic systems theory explains motor behavior, imagine that you offer a new toy to a baby named Gabriel (Thelen & others, 1993). There is no exact program that can tell Gabriel ahead of time how to move his arm and hand and fingers to grasp the toy. Gabriel must adapt to his goal—grasping the toy—and the context. From his sitting position, he must make split-second adjustments to extend his arm, holding his body steady so that his arm and torso don't plow into the toy. Muscles in his arm and shoulder contract and stretch in a host of combinations, exerting a variety of forces. He improvises a way to reach out with one arm and wrap his fingers around the toy.

Thus, according to dynamic systems theory, motor development is not a passive process in which genes dictate the unfolding of a sequence of skills over time. Rather, the infant actively puts together a skill to achieve a goal within the constraints set by the infant's body and environment (Adoph & Tamis-Lemonda, 2015). Nature and nurture, the infant and the environment, are all working together as part of an ever-changing system.

As you read about the course of motor development, you will see how dynamic systems theory applies to some specific skills. First, though, let's examine how the story of motor development begins with reflexes.

REFLEXES

Newborn infants are not completely helpless. Among other things, they have some basic reflexes. For example, when they are submerged, they will hold their breath and contract their throat to keep water out. Reflexes allow infants to respond adaptively to their environment before they have had the opportunity to learn.

The rooting and sucking reflexes are important examples. Both have survival value for newborn mammals, who must find a mother's breast to obtain nourishment. The **rooting reflex** occurs when an infant's cheek is stroked or the side of the mouth is touched. In response, the infant turns its head toward the side that was touched in an apparent effort to find something to suck. The **sucking reflex** occurs when newborns suck an object placed in their mouth. This reflex enables newborns to get nourishment before they have associated a nipple with food; it also serves as a self-soothing or self-regulating mechanism.

Another example is the **Moro reflex,** which occurs in response to a sudden, intense noise or movement (see Figure 1). When startled, newborns arch their back, throw back their head, and fling out their arms and legs. Then they rapidly close their arms and legs. The Moro reflex is believed to be a way of grabbing for support while falling, because it would have had survival value for our primate ancestors.

Some reflexes—coughing, sneezing, blinking, shivering, and yawning, for example—persist throughout life. They are as important for the adult as they are for the infant. Other reflexes, though, disappear several months following birth, as the infant's brain matures and voluntary control over many behaviors develops. The rooting and Moro reflexes, for example, tend to disappear when the infant is 3 to 4 months old.

The movements of some reflexes eventually become incorporated into more complex, voluntary actions. One important example is the **grasping reflex,** which occurs when something touches the infant's palms (see Figure 1). The infant responds by grasping tightly. By the end of the third month, the grasping reflex diminishes, and the infant shows a more voluntary grasp. As its motor development becomes smoother, the infant will grasp objects, carefully manipulate them, and explore their qualities.

Individual differences in reflexive behavior appear soon after birth. For example, the sucking capabilities of newborns vary considerably. Some newborns are efficient at sucking forcefully and obtaining milk; others are not as adept and get tired before they are full. Most infants take several weeks to establish a sucking style that is coordinated with the way the mother is holding the infant, the way milk is coming out of the bottle or breast, and the infant's temperament (Blass, 2008).

The old view of reflexes portrayed them as exclusively genetic, built-in mechanisms that govern the infant's movements. The new perspective on infant reflexes is that they are not automatic or completely beyond the infant's control. For example, infants can deliberately control such movements as alternating their legs to make a mobile jiggle or change their sucking rate to listen to a recording (Adolph & Robinson, 2015).

GROSS MOTOR SKILLS

Ask any parents about their baby, and sooner or later you are likely to hear about one or more advances in motor skills, such as "Cassandra just learned to crawl," "Jesse is finally sitting alone," or "Angela took her first step last week." Parents proudly announce such milestones as their children transform themselves from babies unable to lift their heads to toddlers who grab things off the grocery store shelf, chase a cat, and participate actively in the family's social life (Thelen, 2000). These milestones are examples of **gross motor skills,** skills that involve large-muscle activities such as moving one's arms and walking.

The Development of Posture   How do gross motor skills develop? As a foundation, these skills require postural control (Adolph & Joh, 2009). For example, to track moving objects, you must be able to control your head in order to stabilize your gaze; before you can walk, you must be able to balance on one leg.

Posture is more than just holding still and straight. Posture is a dynamic process that is linked with sensory information in the skin, joints, and muscles, which tell us where we are in space; in vestibular organs in the inner ear that regulate balance and equilibrium; and in vision and hearing (Thelen & Smith, 2006).

Newborn infants cannot voluntarily control their posture. Within a few weeks, though, they can hold their heads erect, and soon they can lift their heads while prone. By 2 months of age, babies can sit while supported on a lap or an infant seat, but they cannot sit independently until they are 6 or 7 months of age. Standing also develops gradually during the first year of life. By about 8 to 9 months of age, infants usually learn to pull themselves up and hold onto a chair, and they often can stand alone by about 10 to 12 months of age.

Learning to Walk   Locomotion and postural control are closely linked, especially in walking upright (Soska, Robinson, & Adolph, 2015).

Even young infants can make the alternating leg movements that are needed for walking. The neural pathways that control leg alternation are in place from a very early age, even at birth or before. Indeed, researchers have found that alternating leg movements occur during the fetal period and at birth (Adolph & Robinson, 2015).

If infants can produce forward stepping movements so early, why does it take them so long to learn to walk? The key skills in learning to walk appear to be stabilizing balance on one leg long enough to swing the other forward and shifting the weight without falling. This is a difficult biomechanical problem to solve, and it takes infants about a year to do it.

In learning to locomote, infants must discover what kinds of places and surfaces are safe for crawling or walking (Adolph & Kretch, 2015; Adolph & Robinson, 2015; Ishak, Franchak, & Adolph, 2014). Karen Adolph (1997) investigated how experienced and inexperienced crawling and walking infants go down steep slopes (see Figure 2). Newly crawling infants, who averaged about 8 months in age, rather indiscriminately went down the steep slopes, often falling in the process (with their mothers standing next to the slope to catch them). After weeks of practice, the crawling babies became more adept at judging which slopes were too steep to crawl down and which ones they could navigate safely.

Thus, practice and learning are very important in the development of new motor skills (Adolph & Berger, 2016). In one study, Adolph and her colleagues (2012) observed 12- to 19-month-olds during free play. Locomotor experience was extensive, with the infants averaging 2,368 steps and 17 falls per hour.

Might the development of walking be linked to advances in other aspects of development? Walking experience leads to being able to gain contact with objects that were previously out of reach and to initiate interaction with parents and other adults, thereby promoting

Moro reflex

Grasping reflex

FIGURE 1

NEWBORN REFLEXES
(top): © Petit Format/Science Source;
(bottom): © Stockbyte/PunchStock RF

What are some developmental changes in posture during infancy?
© Fabio Cardoso/Corbis

Newly crawling infant

Experienced walker

FIGURE 2

THE ROLE OF EXPERIENCE AND LEARNING IN CRAWLING AND WALKING INFANTS' JUDGMENTS OF WHETHER TO GO DOWN A SLOPE. Karen Adolph (1997) found that locomotor experience rather than age was the primary predictor of adaptive responding on slopes of varying steepness. Newly crawling and walking infants could not judge the safety of the various slopes. With experience, they learned to avoid slopes where they would fall. When expert crawlers began to walk, they again made mistakes and fell, even though they had judged the same slope accurately when crawling. Adolph referred to this as the specificity of learning because it does not transfer across crawling and walking.
© Dr. Karen Adolph, New York University

A baby is an angel whose wings decrease as his legs increase.

—French Proverb

language development (Adolph & Robinson, 2015; Walle & Campos, 2014). Thus, just as with advances in postural skills, walking skills can produce a cascade of changes in the infant's development.

The First Year: Motor Development Milestones and Variations Figure 3 summarizes important accomplishments in gross motor skills during the first year, culminating in the ability to walk easily. The timing of these milestones, especially the later ones, may vary by as much as two to four months, and experiences can modify the onset of these accomplishments (Adolph & Berger, 2016). For example, in the early 1990s, pediatricians began recommending that parents place their babies on their backs to sleep. Following that instruction, babies who back-sleep began crawling later, typically several weeks later than babies who sleep prone (Davis & others, 1998). Also, some infants do not follow the standard sequence of motor accomplishments (Eaton, 2008). For example, many American infants never crawl on their belly or on their hands and knees. They might discover an idiosyncratic form of locomotion before walking, such as rolling, or they might never locomote until they get upright (Adolph & Robinson, 2015). In Jamaica, approximately one-fourth of babies skip crawling (Hopkins, 1991).

According to Karen Adolph and Sarah Berger (2005), the early view that growth and motor development simply reflect the age-related output of maturation is, at best, incomplete. Rather, infants develop new skills with the guidance of their caregivers in a real-world environment of objects, surfaces, and planes.

Development in the Second Year The motor accomplishments of the first year bring increasing independence, allowing infants to explore their environment more extensively and to initiate interaction with others more readily. In the second year of life, toddlers become more motorically skilled and mobile (Marcdante & Kliegman, 2014). Motor activity during the second year is vital to the child's competent development and few restrictions, except for safety, should be placed on their adventures.

By 13 to 18 months, toddlers can pull a toy attached to a string and use their hands and legs to climb up a number of steps. By 18 to 24 months, toddlers can walk quickly or run stiffly for a short distance, balance on their feet in a squatting position while playing with objects on the floor, walk backward without losing their balance, stand and kick a ball without falling, stand and throw a ball, and jump in place.

Can parents give their babies a head start on becoming physically fit and physically talented through structured exercise classes? Most infancy experts recommend against structured exercise classes for babies. But there are other ways to guide infants' motor development. Caregivers in some cultures do handle babies vigorously, and such treatment might advance motor development, as we discuss next.

Cultural Variations in Guiding Infants' Motor Development Mothers in developing countries tend to stimulate their infants' motor skills more than mothers in more developed countries (Hopkins, 1991). In many African, Indian, and Caribbean cultures, mothers massage and stretch their infants during daily baths (Adolph, Karasik, & Tamis-LeMonda, 2010). Mothers in the Gusii culture of Kenya also encourage vigorous movement in their babies.

Do these cultural variations make a difference in motor development? When caregivers provide babies with physical guidance by physically handling them in special ways (such as stroking, massaging, or stretching) or by giving them opportunities for exercise, the infants often reach motor milestones earlier than infants whose caregivers have not provided these activities (Adolph, Cole, & Vereijken, 2015; Adolph, Karasik, & Tamis-LeMonda, 2010). For example, Jamaican mothers expect their infants to sit and walk alone two to three months earlier than English mothers do (Hopkins & Westra, 1990). And in sub-Saharan Africa, traditional practices in many villages involve mothers and siblings engaging babies in exercises, such as frequent exercise for trunk and pelvic muscles (Super & Harkness, 2010).

Practices that restrain infants' movement—such as Chinese sandbags, orphanage restrictions, and failure of caregivers to encourage movement in Budapest—have been found to produce substantial delays in motor development (Adolph, Karasik, & Tamis-LeMonda,

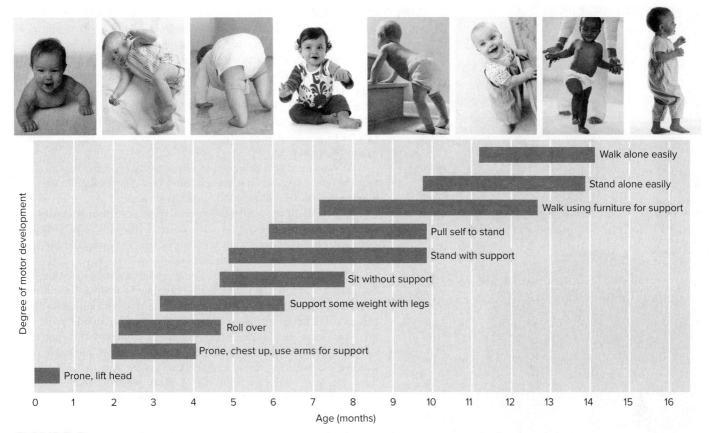

FIGURE 3

MILESTONES IN GROSS MOTOR DEVELOPMENT. The horizontal red bars indicate the range in which most infants reach various milestones in gross motor development.

(left to right): © Barbara Penoyar/Getty Images RF; © Digital Vision/Getty Images RF; © Image Source/Alamy RF; © Titus/Getty Images RF; © Digital Vision RF; © BananaStock/PictureQuest RF; © Corbis/PictureQuest RF; © Brand X Pictures/PunchStock RF

2010). In some rural Chinese provinces, for example, babies are placed in a bag of fine sand, which acts as a diaper and is changed once a day. The baby is left alone, face up, and is visited only when being fed by the mother (Xie & Young, 1999). Some studies of swaddling show slight delays in motor development, but other studies show no delays. Cultures that swaddle infants usually do so before the infant is mobile. When the infant becomes more mobile, swaddling decreases.

(*Left*) In the Algonquin culture in Quebec, Canada, babies are strapped to a cradle board for much of their infancy. (*Right*) In Jamaica, mothers massage and stretch their infants' arms and legs. *To what extent do cultural variations in the activity infants engage in influence the time at which they reach motor milestones?*
(left): © Michael Greenlar/The Image Works;
(right): © Pippa Hetherington/Earthstock/Newscom

What are some developmental changes in children's motor development in early childhood and middle and late childhood?
© F1online digitale Bildagentur GmbH/Alamy

Childhood The preschool child no longer has to make an effort to stay upright and to move around. As children move their legs with more confidence and carry themselves more purposefully, moving around in the environment becomes more automatic.

At 3 years of age, children enjoy simple movements, such as hopping, jumping, and running back and forth, just for the sheer delight of performing these activities. They take considerable pride in showing how they can run across a room and jump all of 6 inches. For the 3-year-old, such activity is a source of considerable pride in accomplishment.

At 4 years of age, children are still enjoying the same kind of activities, but they have become more adventurous. They scramble over low jungle gyms as they display their athletic prowess.

At 5 years of age, children are even more adventuresome than they were at 4. It is not unusual for self-assured 5-year-olds to perform hair-raising stunts on practically any climbing object. They run hard and enjoy racing with each other and their parents.

During middle and late childhood, children's motor development becomes much smoother and more coordinated than it was in early childhood. For example, only one child in a thousand can hit a tennis ball over the net at the age of 3, yet by the age of 10 or 11 most children can learn to play the sport. Running, climbing, skipping rope, swimming, bicycle riding, and skating are just a few of the many physical skills elementary school children can master. And, when mastered, these physical skills are a source of great pleasure and a sense of accomplishment. In gross motor skills involving large-muscle activity, boys usually outperform girls.

Organized sports are one way of encouraging children to be active and to develop their motor skills. Schools and community agencies offer programs for children that involve baseball, soccer, football, basketball, swimming, gymnastics, and other sports. For children who participate in them, these programs may play a central role in their lives.

Participation in sports can have both positive and negative consequences for children (Vest & Simpkins, 2013). Participation can provide exercise, opportunities to learn how to compete, enhanced self-esteem, persistence, and a setting for developing peer relations and friendships (Theokas, 2009). A recent study found that 8-year-old children who continued to participate in sports over the next 24 months were rated by their parents as having a higher health-related quality of life than children who did not participate in sports (Vella & others, 2014). In this study, the positive effects of sports participation were stronger for girls than boys. Further, recent research indicates that participating in sports reduces the likelihood that children will become obese (Basterfield & others, 2015).

However, sports also can bring pressure to achieve and win, physical injuries, a distraction from academic work, and unrealistic expectations for success as an athlete (Bastos & others, 2013; Launay, 2015; Stracciolini & others, 2014). There is increasing concern about the occurrence of concussions in youth football and soccer (Purcell & others, 2014; Rivera & others, 2015). The *Connecting Development to Life* interlude examines the roles of parents and coaches in children's sports.

Adolescence and Adulthood Gross motor skills typically improve during adolescence. Most of us reach our peak physical performance before the age of 30, often between the ages of 19 and 26. This peak occurs both for the average young adult and for outstanding athletes. Even though athletes keep getting better than their predecessors—running faster, jumping higher, and lifting more weight—the age at which they reach their peak performance has remained virtually the same (Schultz & Curnow, 1988). Most swimmers and gymnasts reach their peak in their late teens. Many athletes, including track performers in sprint races (100- and 200-yard dashes), peak in their early to mid-twenties. Golfers and marathon runners tend to peak in their late twenties or even early thirties.

developmental **connection**

Health

Exercise is linked to prevention and effective treatment of many diseases. Connect to "Health."

Parents, Coaches, and Children's Sports

Most sports psychologists stress that it is important for parents to show an interest in their children's sports participation. Most children want their parents to watch them perform in sports. Many children whose parents do not come to watch them play in sporting events feel that their parents do not adequately support them. However, some children become extremely nervous when their parents watch them perform, or they get embarrassed when their parents cheer too loudly or make a fuss. If children request that their parents not watch them perform, parents should respect their children's wishes (Schreiber, 1990).

Parents should praise their children for their sports performance, and if they don't become overinvolved, they can help their children build their physical skills and guide them emotionally by discussing with them how to deal with a difficult coach, how to cope with a tough loss, and how to put in perspective a poorly played game. The following guidelines provided by the Women's Sports Foundation (2001) in its booklet *Parents' Guide to Girls' Sports* can benefit both parents and coaches of all children in sports.

What are some of the possible positive and negative aspects of children's participation in sports?
(top): © SW Productions/Brand X Pictures/Getty Images RF;
(bottom): © BananaStock/Alamy RF

The Dos

- Make sports fun; the more children enjoy sports, the more they will want to play.
- Remember that it is okay for children to make mistakes; it means they are trying.
- Allow children to ask questions about the sport and discuss the sport in a calm, supportive manner.
- Show respect for the child's sports participation.
- Be positive and convince the child that he or she is making a good effort.
- Be a positive role model for the child in sports.

The Don'ts

- Yell or scream at the child.
- Condemn the child for poor play or continue to bring up failures long after they happen.
- Point out the child's errors in front of others.
- Expect the child to learn something immediately.
- Expect the child to become a pro.
- Ridicule or make fun of the child.
- Compare the child to siblings or to more talented children.
- Make sports all work and no fun.

What developmental theories offer support for the Women's Sports Foundation's assertion that parents should strive to be positive role models for their children in sports?

After an individual reaches the age of 30, most biological functions begin to decline, although the decline of specific organs can vary considerably. The decline in general biological functioning that begins at about age 30 occurs at a rate of about 0.75 to 1 percent a year. Declines often occur in cardiovascular functioning, muscle strength, bone density (especially for females), neural function, balance, and flexibility.

Older adults move more slowly than young adults, and this slowing occurs for movements with a wide range of difficulty (Sakuma & Yamaguchi, 2010) (see Figure 4). Even when they perform everyday tasks such as reaching and grasping, moving from one place to another, and continuous movement, older adults tend to move more slowly than they did when they were young (Mollenkopf, 2007).

Recent research connects obesity with mobility limitation in older adults (Murphy & others, 2014). Also, a recent study found that a combined program of physical activity and weight loss helped to preserve mobility in older, obese adults in poor cardiovascular health

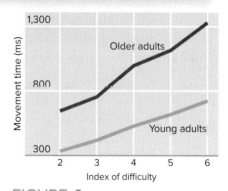

FIGURE 4

MOVEMENT AND AGING. Older adults take longer to move than young adults, and this change occurs across a range of movement difficulty (Ketcham & Stelmach, 2001).

Motor skills decline less in older adults who are active and biologically healthy. *What is the difference between chronological age and biological age?*
© David Zurick RF

(Rejeski & others, 2011). And another study revealed that it's not just physical exercise and weight loss that are linked to preserving older adults' motor functions; in this study, engaging in social activities protected against loss of motor abilities (Buchman & others, 2009).

The risk of falling in older adults increases with age and is greater for women than for men. Two-thirds of older adults who experience a fall are likely to fall again in the next six months. Falls are the leading cause of injury deaths among adults who are 65 years and older (National Center for Health Statistics, 2014). Each year, approximately 200,000 adults over the age of 65 (many of them women) fracture a hip in a fall. Half of these older adults die within 12 months, frequently from pneumonia. A recent meta-analysis found that exercise reduces falls in adults 60 years of age and older (Stubbs, Brefka, & Denkinger, 2015). One study revealed that participation in an exercise class once a week for three years reduced the fall risk and the number of falling incidents in older adults who were at high risk for falling (Yokoya, Demura, & Sato, 2009). In another study, walking was more effective than balance training in older adults (Okubo & others, 2015).

FINE MOTOR SKILLS

Whereas gross motor skills involve large-muscle activity, **fine motor skills** involve finely tuned movements. Buttoning a shirt, typing, or doing any task that requires finger dexterity demonstrates fine motor skills.

A young girl using a pincer grip to pick up puzzle pieces.
© Newstockimages/SuperStock RF

fine motor skills Motor skills that involve finely tuned movements, such as any activity that requires finger dexterity.

Infancy Infants have hardly any control over fine motor skills at birth, but newborns do have many components of what will become finely coordinated arm, hand, and finger movements. The onset of reaching and grasping marks a significant milestone in infants' increasing ability to interact with their surroundings (Greif & Needham, 2012; Ziemer, Plumert, & Pick, 2012). During the first two years of life, infants refine how they reach and grasp (Keen, 2011). Initially, infants reach by moving their shoulders and elbows crudely, swinging toward an object. Later, when infants reach for an object they move their wrists, rotate their hands, and coordinate their thumb and forefinger. Infants do not have to see their own hands in order to reach for an object (Clifton & others, 1993). Cues from muscles, tendons, and joints, not sight of the limb, guide reaching by 4-month-old infants.

Infants refine their ability to grasp objects by developing two types of grasps. Initially, infants grip with the whole hand, which is called the *palmer grasp*. Later, toward the end of the first year, infants also grasp small objects with their thumb and forefinger, which is called the *pincer grip*. Their grasping system is very flexible. They vary their grip on an object depending on its size, shape, and texture, as well as the size of their own hands relative to the object's size. Infants grip small objects with their thumb and forefinger (and sometimes their middle finger too), whereas they grip large objects with all of the fingers of one hand or both hands.

Perceptual-motor coupling is necessary for the infant to coordinate grasping (Keen, 2011). Which perceptual system the infant is most likely to use in coordinating grasping varies with age. Four-month-old infants rely greatly on touch to determine how they will grip an object; 8-month-olds are more likely to use vision as a guide (Newell & others, 1989). This developmental change is efficient because vision lets infants preshape their hands as they reach for an object.

Experience plays a role in reaching and grasping (Sacrey & others, 2014). In one study, 3-month-old infants participated in play sessions wearing "sticky mittens"—"mittens with palms that stuck to the edges of toys and allowed the infants to pick up the toys" (Needham, Barrett, & Peterman, 2002, p. 279) (see Figure 5). Infants who participated in sessions with the mittens grasped and manipulated objects earlier in their development than a control group of infants who did not receive the "mitten" experience. The experienced infants looked at the objects longer, swatted at them more during visual contact, and were more likely to mouth the objects. In a recent study, 5-month-old infants whose parents trained them to use the sticky mittens for 10 minutes a day over a two-week period showed advances in their reaching behavior at the end of the two weeks (Libertus & Needham, 2010).

Just as infants need to exercise their gross motor skills, they also need to exercise their fine motor skills (Keen, 2011). Especially when they can manage a pincer grip, infants delight in picking up small objects. Many develop the pincer grip and begin to crawl at about the same time, and infants at this time pick up virtually everything in sight, especially on the floor, and put the objects in their mouth. Thus, parents need to be vigilant in regularly monitoring what objects are within the infant's reach (Keen, 2005).

Rachel Keen (2011; Keen, Lee, & Adolph, 2014) emphasizes that tool use is an excellent context for studying problem solving in infants because tool use provides information about how infants plan to reach a goal. Researchers in this area have studied infants' intentional actions that range from picking up a spoon in different orientations to retrieving rakes placed inside tubes. A recent study explored motor origins of tool use by assessing developmental changes in banging movements in 6- to 15-month-olds (Kahrs, Jung, & Lockman, 2013). In this study, younger infants were inefficient and variable when banging an object but by one year of age infants showed consistent straight up-and-down hand movements that resulted in precise aiming and consistent levels of force.

FIGURE 5

INFANTS' USE OF "STICKY MITTENS" TO EXPLORE OBJECTS. Amy Needham and her colleagues (2002) found that "sticky mittens" enhanced young infants' object exploration skills.
Courtesy of Dr. Amy Needham

Childhood and Adolescence As children get older, their fine motor skills improve (Sveistrup & others, 2008). At 3 years of age, children have had the ability to pick up the tiniest objects between their thumb and forefinger for some time, but they are still somewhat clumsy at it. Three-year-olds can build surprisingly high block towers, each block placed with intense concentration but often not in a completely straight line. When 3-year-olds play with a form board or a simple puzzle, they are rather rough in placing the pieces. Even when they recognize the hole that a piece fits into, they are not very precise in positioning the piece. They often try to force the piece into the hole or pat it vigorously.

By 4 years of age, children's fine motor coordination has become much more precise. Sometimes 4-year-old children have trouble building high towers with blocks because, in their desire to place each of the blocks perfectly, they may upset those already stacked. By age 5, children's fine motor coordination has improved further. Hand, arm, and fingers all move together under better command of the eye. Mere towers no longer interest the 5-year-old, who now wants to build a house or a church, complete with steeple, though adults may still need to be told what each finished project is meant to be.

Increased myelination of the central nervous system is reflected in the improvement of fine motor skills during middle and late childhood. Children use their hands more adroitly as tools. Six-year-olds can hammer, paste, tie shoes, and fasten clothes. By 7 years of age, children's hands have become steadier. At this age, children prefer a pencil to a crayon for printing, and reversal of letters is less common. Printing becomes smaller. At 8 to 10 years of age, children can use their hands independently with more ease and precision; children can now write rather than print words. Letter size becomes smaller and more even. At 10 to 12 years of age, children begin to show manipulative skills similar to the abilities of adults. The complex, intricate, and rapid movements needed to produce fine-quality crafts or to play a difficult piece on a musical instrument can be mastered. Girls usually outperform boys in fine motor skills.

Adult Development Fine motor skills may undergo some decline in middle and late adulthood as dexterity decreases, although for most healthy individuals, fine motor skills, such as reaching and grasping, continue to be performed in functional ways (Hoogendam & others, 2014). However, pathological conditions may result in weakness or paralysis of an individual's hands, in which case performance of fine motor skills may be impossible.

Review Connect Reflect

 LG1 Describe how motor skills develop

Review

- What is the dynamic systems view of motor development?
- What are reflexes? What are some reflexes of infants?
- What are gross motor skills, and how do they develop?
- What are fine motor skills? How do fine motor skills develop?

Connect

- How does the development of infants' gross motor skills differ from the development of fine motor skills?

Reflect *Your Own Personal Journey of Life*

- Imagine that you are the parent of a 7-year-old child. How would you evaluate the benefits and drawbacks of allowing him or her to participate in organized competitive sports such as soccer, basketball, or tennis?

2 Sensory and Perceptual Development   **LG2** Outline the course of sensory and perceptual development

| What Are Sensation and Perception? | The Ecological View | Visual Perception | Hearing | Other Senses | Intermodal Perception | Nature/Nurture and Perceptual Development |

How do sensations and perceptions develop? Can newborn infants see? If so, what can they perceive? What about the other senses—hearing, smell, taste, touch, and pain? What are they like in the newborn, and how do they develop? How do sensation and perception change when adults become older? These are among the intriguing questions that we explore in this section.

WHAT ARE SENSATION AND PERCEPTION?

How does a newborn know that her mother's skin is soft rather than rough? How does a 5-year-old know what color his hair is? How does a 10-year-old know that a firecracker is louder than a cat's meow? Infants and children "know" these things because of information that comes through the senses. Without vision, hearing, touch, taste, smell, and other senses, we would be isolated from the world; we would live in dark silence, a tasteless, colorless, feelingless void.

Sensation occurs when information interacts with sensory *receptors*—the eyes, ears, tongue, nostrils, and skin. The sensation of hearing occurs when waves of pulsating air are collected by the outer ear and conducted through the bones of the inner ear and the *cochlea*, where mechanical vibrations are converted into electrical impulses. Then the electrical impulses move to the *auditory nerve*, which transmits them to the brain. The sensation of vision occurs as rays of light contact the eyes and become focused on the *retina*, where light is converted into electrical impulses. Then the electrical impulses are transmitted by the *optic nerve* to the visual centers of the brain.

sensation Reaction that occurs when information interacts with sensory receptors—the eyes, ears, tongue, nostrils, and skin.

Perception is the interpretation of what is sensed. The air waves that contact the ears might be interpreted as noise or as musical sounds, for example. The physical energy transmitted to the retina of the eye might be interpreted as a particular color, pattern, or shape, depending on how it is perceived.

THE ECOLOGICAL VIEW

In recent decades, much of the research on perceptual development in infancy has been guided by the ecological view of Eleanor and James J. Gibson (E. Gibson, 1969, 1989, 2001; J. Gibson, 1966, 1979). They argue that we do not have to take bits and pieces of data from sensations and build up representations of the world in our minds. Instead, our perceptual system can select from the rich information that the environment itself provides.

According to the Gibsons' **ecological view,** we directly perceive information that exists in the world around us. Perception brings us into contact with the environment in order to interact with and adapt to it. Perception is designed for action. Perception gives people such information as when to duck, when to turn their bodies to get through a narrow passageway, and when to put up their hands to catch something.

How would you use the Gibsons' ecological theory of perception and the concept of affordance to explain the role that perception is playing in this baby's activity?
© Dorling Kindersley/Getty Images

In the Gibsons' view, all objects and surfaces have **affordances,** which are opportunities for interaction offered by objects that fit within our capabilities to perform activities. A pot may afford you something to cook with, and it may afford a toddler something to bang. Adults immediately know when a chair is appropriate for sitting, when a surface is safe for walking, or when an object is within reach. We directly and accurately perceive these affordances by sensing information from the environment—the light or sound reflecting from the surfaces of the world—and from our own bodies through muscle receptors, joint receptors, and skin receptors (Adolph & Kretch, 2015; Ziemer, Plumert, & Pick, 2012).

An important developmental question is "What affordances can infants or children detect and use?" In one study, for example, when babies who could walk were faced with a squishy waterbed, they stopped and explored it, then chose to crawl rather than walk across it (Gibson & others, 1987). They combined perception and action to adapt to the demands of the task.

Studying infants' perception has not been an easy task. What do you think some of the research challenges might be? The *Connecting with Research* interlude describes some of the ingenious ways researchers study infants' perception.

VISUAL PERCEPTION

Some important changes in visual perception as we age can be traced to differences in how the eye itself functions over time. These changes in the eye's functioning influence, for example, how clearly we can see an object, whether we can differentiate its colors, at what distances, and in what light. But the differences between what a newborn sees and what a toddler or an adult sees go far beyond those that can be explained by changes in the eye's functioning, as we discuss in this section.

Infancy   Psychologist William James (1890/1950) called the newborn's perceptual world a "blooming, buzzing confusion." More than a century later, we can safely say that he was wrong (Johnson & Hannon, 2015; Shirai & Imura, 2014). Even the newborn perceives a world with some order. That world, however, is far different from the one perceived by the toddler or the adult.

Visual Acuity   Just how well can infants see? At birth, the nerves and muscles and lens of the eye are still developing. As a result, newborns cannot see small things that are far away. The newborn's vision is estimated to be 20/240 on the well-known Snellen chart used for eye examinations, which means an object 20 feet away is only as clear to the newborn as it would be if it were 240 feet away from an adult with normal vision (20/20). By 6 months of age, though, average visual acuity is 20/40 (Aslin & Lathrop, 2008).

perception The interpretation of sensation.

ecological view The view proposed by the Gibsons that people directly perceive information in the world around them. Perception brings people in contact with the environment in order to interact with it and adapt to it.

affordances Opportunities for interaction offered by objects that fit within our capabilities to perform activities.

How Do Scientists Study the Newborn's Perception?

Scientists have developed a number of research methods and tools sophisticated enough to examine the subtle abilities of infants and to interpret their complex actions (Bendersky & Sullivan, 2007).

Visual Preference Method

Robert Fantz (1963) was a pioneer in this effort. Fantz made an important discovery that advanced the ability of researchers to investigate infants' visual perception: Infants look at different things for different lengths of time. Fantz placed infants in a "looking chamber," which had two visual displays on the ceiling above the infant's head. An experimenter viewed the infant's eyes by looking through a peephole. If the infant was fixating on one of the displays, the experimenter could see the display's reflection in the infant's eyes. This arrangement allowed the experimenter to determine how long the infant looked at each display. Fantz (1963) found that infants only 2 days old look longer at patterned stimuli, such as faces and concentric circles, than at red, white, or yellow discs. Infants 2 to 3 weeks old preferred to look at patterns—a face, a piece of printed matter, or a bull's-eye—longer than at red, yellow, or white discs (see Figure 6). Fantz's research method—studying whether infants can distinguish one stimulus from another by measuring the length of time they attend to different stimuli—is referred to as the **visual preference method.**

Habituation and Dishabituation

Another way that researchers have studied infant perception is to present a stimulus (such as a sight or a sound) a number of times. If the infant decreases its response to the stimulus after several presentations, this change indicates that the infant is no longer interested in looking at the stimulus. If the researcher now presents a new stimulus, the infant's response will recover—an indication that the infant can discriminate between the old and new stimulus (Snyder & Torrence, 2008).

Habituation is the name given to decreased responsiveness to a stimulus after repeated presentations of the stimulus. **Dishabituation** is the recovery of a habituated response after a change in stimulation. Newborn infants can habituate to repeated sights, sounds, smells, or touches (Rovee-Collier, 2004). Among the measures researchers use in habituation studies are sucking behavior (sucking stops when the young infant attends to a novel object), heart and respiration rates, and the length of time the infant looks at an object. Figure 7 shows the results of one study of habituation and dishabituation with newborns (Slater, Morison, & Somers, 1988).

High-Amplitude Sucking

To assess an infant's attention to sound, researchers often use a method called *high-amplitude sucking.* In this method, infants are given a nonnutritive nipple to suck, and the nipple is connected to a sound-generating system. The researcher computes a baseline high-amplitude sucking rate in a one-minute silent period. Following the baseline, presentation of a sound is made contingent on the rate of high-amplitude sucking. Initially babies suck frequently so the sound occurs often. Gradually, they lose interest in hearing the same sound

FIGURE 6

FANTZ'S EXPERIMENT ON INFANTS' VISUAL PERCEPTION.
(*a*) Infants 2 to 3 weeks old preferred to look at some stimuli more than others. In Fantz's experiment, infants preferred to look at patterns rather than at color or brightness. For example, they looked longer at a face, a piece of printed matter, or a bull's-eye than at red, yellow, or white discs. (*b*) Fantz used a "looking chamber" to study infants' perception of stimuli.
© David Linton, Courtesy of the Linton Family

Habituation

(a)

Dishabituation

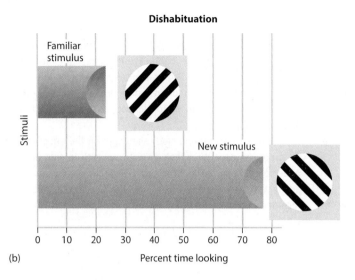

(b)

FIGURE 7

HABITUATION AND DISHABITUATION. In the first part of one study (*a*), 7-hour-old newborns were shown a stimulus. As indicated, the newborns looked at it an average of 41 seconds when it was first presented to them (Slater, Morison, & Somers, 1988). Over seven more presentations of the stimulus, they looked at it less and less. In the second part of the study (*b*), infants were presented with both the familiar stimulus to which they had just become habituated and a new stimulus (which was rotated 90 degrees). The newborns looked at the new stimulus three times as much as the familiar stimulus.

so they begin to suck less often. Then the researcher changes the sound that is being presented. If the babies renew their vigorous sucking, the inference is that they have noticed the sound change and are sucking more because they want to hear the interesting new sound (Menn & Stoel-Gammon, 2009).

The Orienting Response

A technique that can be used to determine whether an infant can see or hear is the *orienting response,* which involves turning one's head toward a sight or sound. Another technique, *tracking,* measures eye movements that follow (track) a moving object; it can be used to evaluate an infant's early visual ability. A startle response can be used to determine an infant's reaction to a noise (Bendersky & Sullivan, 2007).

Equipment

Technology can facilitate the use of most methods for investigating infants' perceptual abilities. Videotape equipment allows researchers to investigate elusive behaviors. High-speed computers make it possible to perform complex

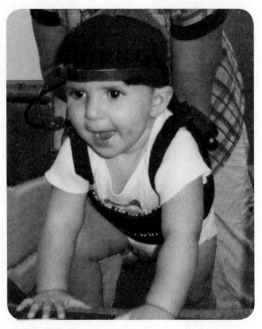

FIGURE 8

AN INFANT WEARING EYE-TRACKING HEADGEAR. Using the ultralight, wireless, head-mounted eye-tracking equipment shown here, researchers can record where infants look while the infants freely locomote. Most studies of infant eye-tracking now use remote optics eye trackers that have a camera that is not attached to the infant's head.

© *Dr. Karen Adolph, New York University*

data analysis in minutes. Other equipment records respiration, heart rate, body movement, visual fixation, and sucking behavior, which provide clues to what the infant is perceiving.

The most important recent advance in measuring infant perception is the development of sophisticated eye-tracking equipment (Kretch, Franchak, & Adolph, 2014; Valenza, Franchin, & Bulf, 2014). Figure 8 shows an infant wearing an eye-tracking headgear in a recent study on visually guided motor behavior and social interaction.

One of the main reasons that infant perception researchers are so enthusiastic about the recent availability of sophisticated eye-tracking equipment is that looking time is among the most important measures of infant perceptual and cognitive development (Aslin, 2012). The new eye-tracking equipment allows for much greater precision than human observation in assessing various aspects of infant looking and gaze (Oakes, 2012). Among the areas of infant perception in which eye-tracking

(continued)

(continued)

equipment is being used are memory, joint attention, and face processing (Righi & others, 2014). Eye-tracking equipment also is improving our understanding of atypically developing infants, such as those who have autism or were born preterm (Guimard-Brunault & others, 2013; Sasson & Touchstone, 2014; Stagg, Linnell, & Heaton, 2014).

A recent eye-tracking study shed light on the effectiveness of TV programs and DVDs that claim to educate infants (Kirkorian, Anderson, & Keen, 2012). In this study, 1-year-olds, 4-year-olds, and adults watched *Sesame Street* and the eye-tracking equipment recorded precisely what they looked at on the screen. The 1-year-

olds were far less likely to consistently look at the same part of the screen as their older counterparts, suggesting that the 1-year-olds showed little understanding of the *Sesame Street* video but instead were more likely to be attracted by what was salient than by what was relevant.

Scientists have become ingenious at assessing the development of infants, discovering ways to "interview" them even though they cannot yet talk. How might researchers account for any individual differences in infant development in their studies?

FIGURE 9

VISUAL ACUITY DURING THE FIRST MONTHS OF LIFE. The four photographs represent a computer estimation of what a picture of a face looks like to a 1-month-old, 2-month-old, 3-month-old, and 1-year-old (whose visual acuity approximates that of an adult).
© Kevin Peterson/Getty Images RF, Simulation by Vischeck

visual preference method A method developed by Fantz to determine whether infants can distinguish one stimulus from another by measuring the length of time they attend to different stimuli.

habituation Decreased responsiveness to a stimulus after repeated presentations of the stimulus.

dishabituation The recovery of a habituated response after a change in stimulation.

size constancy Recognition that an object remains the same even though the retinal image of the object changes as the viewer moves toward or away from the object.

shape constancy Recognition that an object remains the same even though its orientation to the viewer changes.

Infants show an interest in human faces soon after birth (Lee & others, 2013). Figure 9 shows a computer estimation of what a picture of a face looks like to an infant at different ages from a distance of about 6 inches. Infants spend more time looking at their mother's face than a stranger's face as early as 12 hours after being born (Bushnell, 2003). By 3 months of age, infants match voices to faces, distinguish between male and female faces, and discriminate between faces of their own ethnic group and those of other ethnic groups (Gaither & others, 2012; Kelly & others, 2007, 2009).

Also, as we discussed in the *Connecting with Research* interlude, young infants can perceive certain patterns. With the help of his "looking chamber," Robert Fantz (1963) found that even 2- to 3-week-old infants prefer to look at patterned displays rather than nonpatterned displays. For example, they prefer to look at a normal human face rather than one with scrambled features, and prefer to look at a bull's-eye target or black and white stripes rather than a plain circle.

Color Vision   The infant's color vision also improves over time (Atkinson & Braddick, 2013). By 8 weeks, and possibly as early as 4 weeks, infants can discriminate some colors (Kelly, Borchert, & Teller, 1997). By 4 months of age, they have color preferences that mirror those of adults in some cases, preferring saturated colors such as royal blue over pale blue, for example (Bornstein, 1975). A recent study of the reactions to blue, yellow, red, and green hues by 4- to 5-month-old infants revealed that they looked longest at reddish hues and shortest at greenish hues (Franklin & others, 2010). In part, the changes in vision described here reflect maturation. Experience, however, is also necessary for color vision to develop normally (Sugita, 2004).

Perceptual Constancy   Some perceptual accomplishments are especially intriguing because they indicate that the infant's perception goes beyond the information provided by the senses (Johnson, 2013; Slater & others, 2011). This is the case in perceptual constancy, in which sensory stimulation is changing but perception of the physical world remains constant. If infants did not develop perceptual constancy, each time they saw an object at a different distance or in a different orientation, they would perceive it as a different object. Thus, the development of perceptual constancy allows infants to perceive their world as stable. Two types of perceptual constancy are size constancy and shape constancy.

Size constancy is the recognition that an object remains the same even though the retinal image of the object changes as you move toward or away from the object. The farther away from us an object is, the smaller its image is on our eyes. Thus, the size of an object on the retina is not sufficient to tell us its actual size. For example, you perceive a bicycle standing right in front of you as smaller than the car parked across the street, even though the bicycle casts a larger image on your eyes than the car does. When you move away from the bicycle, you do not perceive it to be shrinking even though its image on your retinas shrinks; you perceive its size as constant. But what about babies? Do they have size constancy? Researchers have found that babies as young as 3 months of age show size constancy (Bower, 1966; Day & McKenzie, 1973). However, at 3 months of age, a baby's ability is not full-blown. It continues to develop until 10 or 11 years of age (Kellman & Banks, 1998).

Shape constancy is the recognition that an object remains the same shape even though its orientation to us changes. Look around the room you are in right now. You likely see objects of varying shapes, such as tables and chairs. If you get up and walk around the room, you will see these objects from different sides and angles. Even though your retinal image of the objects changes as you walk and look, you will still perceive the objects as the same shape.

Do babies have shape constancy? As with size constancy, researchers have found that babies as young as 3 months of age have shape constancy (Bower, 1966; Day & McKenzie, 1973). Three-month-old infants, however, do not have shape constancy for irregularly shaped objects such as tilted planes (Cook & Birch, 1984).

Perception of Occluded Objects Look again at the objects surrounding you. You likely see that some objects are partly occluded (hidden) by other objects that are in front of them—possibly a desk behind a chair, some books behind a computer, or a car parked behind a tree. Do infants perceive an object as complete when it is partly occluded by an object in front of it?

In the first two months of postnatal development, infants don't perceive occluded objects as complete, but instead perceive only what is visible (Johnson, 2013; Johnson & Hannon, 2015). Beginning at about 2 months of age, infants develop the ability to perceive that occluded objects are whole (Slater & others, 2011). How does perceptual completion develop? In Scott Johnson's (2004, 2011, 2013) research, learning, experience, and self-directed exploration via eye movements play key roles in the development of perceptual completion in young infants.

Many of the objects in the world that are occluded appear and disappear behind closer objects, as when you are walking down the street and see cars appear and disappear behind buildings as they move or you move. Can infants predictively track briefly occluded moving objects? They develop the ability to track briefly occluded moving objects at about 3 to 5 months of age (Bertenthal, 2008). One study explored 5- to 9-month-old infants' ability to track moving objects that disappeared gradually behind an occluded partition, disappeared abruptly, or imploded (shrank quickly in size) (see Figure 10) (Bertenthal, Longo, & Kenny, 2007). In this study, the infants were more likely to accurately predict the reappearance of the moving object when it disappeared gradually rather than disappearing abruptly or imploding.

Depth Perception Might infants even perceive depth? To investigate this question, Eleanor Gibson and Richard Walk (1960) constructed a miniature cliff with a drop-off covered by glass. They placed infants on the edge of this visual cliff and had their mothers coax them to crawl onto the glass (see Figure 11). Most infants would not crawl out on the glass, choosing instead to remain on

(a) Gradual occlusion

(b) Abrupt occlusion

(c) Implosion

FIGURE 10

INFANTS' PREDICTIVE TRACKING OF A BRIEFLY OCCLUDED MOVING BALL

FIGURE 11

EXAMINING INFANTS' DEPTH PERCEPTION ON THE VISUAL CLIFF. Eleanor Gibson and Richard Walk (1960) found that most infants would not crawl out on the glass, which, according to Gibson and Walk, indicated that they had depth perception. However, critics suggest that the visual cliff may be a better indication of the infant's social referencing and fear of heights than of the infant's perception of depth.
© Mark Richards/PhotoEdit

FIGURE 12

VISUAL EXPECTATIONS ABOUT THE PHYSICAL WORLD. When young children see the ball dropped into the tube, many of them will search for it immediately below the dropping point.
Courtesy of Dr. Bruce Hood, University of Bristol

the shallow side, an indication that they could perceive depth. However, critics point out that the visual cliff likely is a better test of social referencing and fear of heights than of depth perception.

The 6- to 12-month-old infants in the visual cliff experiment had extensive visual experience. Do younger infants without this experience still perceive depth? Since younger infants do not crawl, this question is difficult to answer. Infants 2 to 4 months old show differences in heart rate when they are placed directly on the deep side of the visual cliff instead of on the shallow side (Campos, Langer, & Krowitz, 1970). However, these differences might mean that young infants respond to differences in some visual characteristics of the deep and shallow cliffs, with no actual knowledge of depth (Adolph & Kretch, 2012; Ishak, Franchak, & Adolph, 2014). Although researchers do not know exactly how early in life infants can perceive depth, we do know that infants develop the ability to use binocular cues to depth by about 3 to 4 months of age.

Childhood Changes in children's perceptual development continue in childhood (Atkinson & Braddick, 2013; Lee & others, 2013). Children become increasingly efficient at detecting the boundaries between colors (such as red and orange) at 3 to 4 years of age (Gibson, 1969). When children are about 4 or 5 years old, their eye muscles usually are developed enough that they can move their eyes efficiently across a series of letters. Many preschool children are farsighted, unable to see close up as well as they can see far away. By the time they enter the first grade, though, most children can focus their eyes and sustain their attention effectively on close-up objects.

What are the signs of vision problems in children? They include rubbing the eyes, blinking or squinting excessively, appearing irritable when playing games that require good distance vision, shutting or covering one eye, and tilting the head or thrusting it forward when looking at something. A child who shows any of these behaviors should be examined by an ophthalmologist.

After infancy, children's visual expectations about the physical world continue to develop. In one study, 2- to 4½-year-old children were given a task in which the goal was to find a ball that had been dropped through an opaque tube (Hood, 1995). As shown in Figure 12, if the ball is dropped into the tube at the top right, it will land in the box at the bottom left. However, in this task, most of the 2-year-olds, and even some of the 4-year-olds, persisted in searching in the box immediately beneath the dropping point. For them, gravity ruled and they had failed to perceive the end location of the curved tube. In two studies involving the task in Figure 12, 3-year-olds were able to overcome the gravity bias and their impulsive tendencies when they were given verbal instructions from a knowledgeable adult (Bascandziev & Harris, 2011; Joh, Jaswal, & Keen, 2011).

How do children learn to deal with situations like that in Figure 12, and how do they come to understand other laws of the physical world? These questions are addressed by studies of cognitive development, which we discuss in the chapters on "Cognitive Developmental Approaches" and "Information Processing."

Adulthood Vision changes little after childhood until the effects of aging emerge (Hochberg & others, 2012). With aging, declines in visual acuity, color vision, and depth perception occur. Several diseases of the eye also may emerge in aging adults.

Visual Acuity **Accommodation of the eye**—the eye's ability to focus and maintain an image on the retina—declines most sharply between 40 and 59 years of age. This loss of accommodation is what is commonly known as *presbyopia*. In particular, middle-aged individuals begin to have difficulty viewing close objects. The eye's blood supply also diminishes, although usually not until the fifties or sixties. The reduced blood supply may decrease the visual field's size and account for an increase in the eye's *blind spot*, the location where the retina does not register any light. And there is some evidence that the retina becomes less sensitive to low levels of illumination (Hughes, 1978). As a result, middle-aged adults begin to have difficulty reading or working in dim light. Presbyopia is correctable with bifocals, reading glasses, laser surgery, or implantation of intraocular lenses. Indeed, laser surgery and implantation of intraocular lenses have become routine procedures for correcting vision in middle-aged adults (Ang, Evans, & Mehta, 2012).

In late adulthood, the decline in vision that began for most adults in early or middle adulthood becomes more pronounced (Polat & others, 2012). Visual processing speed declines in older adults (Owsley, 2011). Night driving is especially difficult, to some extent because of diminishing sensitivity to contrasts and reduced tolerance for glare (van Rijn & others,

---

developmental connection

Information Processing

Perceptual speed declines in middle adulthood and late adulthood. Connect to "Intelligence."

---

accommodation of the eye The eye's ability to focus and maintain an image on the retina.

2011). *Dark adaptation* is slower—that is, older individuals take longer to recover their vision when going from a well-lighted room to semidarkness. The area of the visual field becomes smaller, an indication that the intensity of a stimulus in the peripheral area of the visual field needs to be increased if the stimulus is to be seen. Events taking place away from the center of the visual field might not be detected (West & others, 2010).

This visual decline often can be traced to a reduction in the quality or intensity of light reaching the retina. At 60 years of age, the retina receives only about one-third as much light as it did at 20 years of age (Scialfa & Kline, 2007). In extreme old age, these changes might be accompanied by degenerative changes in the retina, causing severe difficulty in seeing. Large-print books and magnifiers might be needed in such cases.

Older adults also show a decline in motion sensitivity (Mateus & others, 2013). In terms of practical applications of this decline, researchers have found that compared with younger drivers, older drivers overestimate the time needed for an approaching vehicle to reach their location (Staplin, Lococo, & Sim, 1993). This decline in the accuracy of effortless perceptual guidance means that older adult drivers need to expend cognitive effort when driving, especially when approaching intersections.

Recent research has shown that sensory decline in older adults is linked to a decline in cognitive functioning. One study of individuals in their seventies revealed that visual decline was related to slower speed of processing information, which in turn was associated with greater cognitive decline (Clay & others, 2009).

Color Vision   Color vision also may decline with age in older adults as a result of the yellowing of the lens of the eye (Scialfa & Kline, 2007). This decline is most likely to occur in the green-blue-violet part of the color spectrum. As a result, older adults may have trouble accurately distinguishing between objects that are closely related in color, such as navy socks and black socks.

Depth Perception   As with many areas of perception, depth perception changes little after infancy until adults become older. Depth perception typically declines in late adulthood, which can make it difficult for the older adult to determine how close or far away or how high or low something is (Bian & Andersen, 2008). A decline in depth perception can make steps or street curbs difficult to manage.

Diseases of the Eye   Three diseases that can impair the vision of older adults are cataracts, glaucoma, and macular degeneration:

· **Cataracts** are a thickening of the lens of the eye that causes vision to become cloudy, opaque, and distorted (Huang & others, 2013). By age 70, approximately 30 percent of individuals experience a partial loss of vision due to cataracts. Initially, vision impairment from cataracts can be minimized by wearing glasses; if they worsen, a simple surgical procedure can remove the cloudy lens and replace it with an artificial one (Chung & others, 2009). Diabetes is a risk factor for the development of cataracts (Olafsdottir, Andersson, & Stefansson, 2012).

· **Glaucoma** damages the optic nerve because of the pressure created by a buildup of fluid in the eye (Kokotas & others, 2012). Approximately 1 percent of individuals in their seventies and 10 percent of those in their nineties have glaucoma, which can be treated with eye drops. If left untreated, glaucoma can ultimately destroy a person's vision.

· **Macular degeneration** is a disease that causes deterioration of the macula of the retina, which corresponds to the focal center of the visual field (see Figure 13). Individuals with macular degeneration may have relatively normal peripheral vision but be unable to see clearly what is directly in front of them (Miller, 2013). Macular degeneration affects 1 in 25 individuals from 66 to 74 years of age and 1 in 6 of those 75 years old and older. If the disease is detected early, it can be treated with laser surgery (Sorensen & Kemp, 2010). However, macular degeneration is difficult to treat and thus a leading cause of blindness in older adults (Lucifero, 2010). A recent study found that macular degeneration was linked to increased risk of falls in adults 77 years and older (Wood & others, 2011).

HEARING

Can the fetus hear? What kind of changes in hearing take place in infancy? When does hearing begin to decline in adulthood?

What are some concerns about older adults' driving based on changes in visual perception?
© Steve Prezant/Corbis

FIGURE **13**

MACULAR DEGENERATION. This simulation of the effect of macular degeneration shows how individuals with this eye disease can see their peripheral field of vision but can't clearly see what is in their central visual field.
© Cordelia Molloy/Science Source

cataracts A thickening of the lens of the eye that causes vision to become cloudy, opaque, and distorted.

glaucoma Damage to the optic nerve because of pressure created by a buildup of fluid in the eye.

macular degeneration A vision problem in the elderly that involves deterioration of the macula of the retina.

FIGURE 14

HEARING IN THE WOMB. (a) Pregnant mothers read *The Cat in the Hat* to their fetuses during the last few months of pregnancy. (b) When they were born, the babies preferred listening to a recording of their mothers reading *The Cat in the Hat,* as evidenced by their sucking on a nipple that produced this recording, rather than another story, *The King, the Mice and the Cheese.*
(a): © McGraw-Hill Companies, Inc./Jill Braaten, photographer; (b): Courtesy of Dr. Melanie J. Spence

(a)   (b)

The Fetus, Infant, and Child During the last two months of pregnancy, as the fetus nestles in its mother's womb, it can hear sounds such as the mother's voice, music, and so on (Kisilevsky & others, 2009; Morokuma & others, 2008). Two psychologists wanted to find out whether a fetus who heard Dr. Seuss' classic story *The Cat in the Hat* while still in the mother's womb would prefer hearing the story after birth (DeCasper & Spence, 1986). During the last months of pregnancy, 16 women read *The Cat in the Hat* to their fetuses. Then, shortly after the infants were born, the mothers read aloud either *The Cat in the Hat* or a story with a different rhyme and pace, *The King, the Mice and the Cheese* (which they had not read aloud during pregnancy). The infants sucked on a nipple in a different way when the mothers read the two stories, suggesting that they recognized the pattern and tone of *The Cat in the Hat* (see Figure 14). This study illustrates not only that a fetus can hear but also that it has a remarkable ability to learn even before birth. A recent fMRI study confirmed that the fetus can hear at 33 to 34 weeks by assessing fetal brain response to auditory stimuli (Jardri & others, 2012).

Infancy What changes in hearing take place during infancy? They involve perception of a sound's loudness, pitch, and localization.

Immediately after birth, infants cannot hear soft sounds quite as well as adults can; a stimulus must be louder for the newborn to hear it (Trehub & others, 1991). By three months of age, infants' perception of sounds improves, although some aspects of loudness perception do not reach adult levels until 5 to 10 years of age (Trainor & He, 2013). Infants are also less sensitive to the pitch of a sound than adults are. *Pitch* is the frequency of a sound; a soprano voice sounds high-pitched, a bass voice low-pitched. Infants are less sensitive to low-pitched sounds and are more likely to hear high-pitched sounds (Aslin, Jusczyk, & Pisoni, 1998). By 2 years of age, infants have considerably improved their ability to distinguish sounds with different pitches.

Even newborns can determine the general location from which a sound is coming, but by 6 months they are more proficient at localizing sounds, detecting their origins. The ability to localize sounds continues to improve during the second year (Saffran, Werker, & Warner, 2006).

Although young infants can process variations in sound loudness, pitch, and localization, these aspects of hearing continue to improve through the childhood years (Trainor & He, 2013).

Most children's hearing is adequate, but early hearing screening tests should be conducted during infancy (Russ & others, 2010). About 1 in 1,000 newborns is deaf and 6 in 1,000 have some degree of hearing loss. Hearing aids or surgery can improve hearing for many of these infants (Halpin & others, 2010).

Adolescence Most adolescents' hearing is excellent. However, anyone who listens to loud sounds for sustained periods of time is at risk for hearing problems. H.E.A.R. (Hearing Education and Awareness for Rockers) was

What are some concerns about adolescents who listen to loud music?
© Stockbyte/Getty Images RF

Perceptual System	Young-Old (65 to 74 years)	Old-Old (75 years and older)
Vision	There is a loss of acuity even with corrective lenses. Less transmission of light occurs through the retina (half as much as in young adults). Greater susceptibility to glare occurs. Color discrimination ability decreases.	There is a significant loss of visual acuity and color discrimination, and a decrease in the size of the perceived visual field. In late old age, people are at significant risk for visual dysfunction from cataracts and glaucoma.
Hearing	There is a significant loss of hearing at high frequencies and some loss at middle frequencies. These losses can be helped by a hearing aid. There is greater susceptibility to masking of what is heard by noise.	There is a significant loss at high and middle frequencies. A hearing aid is more likely to be needed than in young-old age.

FIGURE 15

VISION AND HEARING DECLINE IN THE YOUNG-OLD AND THE OLD-OLD

founded by rock musicians whose hearing has been damaged by exposure to high-volume rock music. Increasingly, rock groups wear earplugs when they are playing loud music. Listening to loud music on iPods and MP3 players also can produce hearing problems.

Adulthood and Aging Few changes in hearing are believed to take place during the adult years until middle adulthood (Feeney & Sanford, 2004). Hearing can start to decline by the age of 40. Sensitivity to high pitches usually declines first. The ability to hear low-pitched sounds does not seem to decline much in middle adulthood, however. Men usually lose their sensitivity to high-pitched sounds sooner than women do, but this sex difference might be due to men's greater exposure to noise in occupations such as mining and automobile work.

Hearing impairment usually does not become much of an impediment until late adulthood (Pacala & Yeuh, 2012). A national survey revealed that 63 percent of adults 70 years and older had a hearing loss, defined as inability to hear sounds at amplitudes below 25 dB with their better ear (Lin & others, 2011). In this study, hearing aids were used by 40 percent of those with moderate hearing loss. One study also found that hearing loss was associated with a reduction in cognitive functioning in older adults (Lin, 2011). Fifteen percent of the population over the age of 65 is estimated to be legally deaf, usually due to degeneration of the cochlea, the primary neural receptor for hearing in the inner ear (Adams, 2009).

Earlier, in discussing changes in vision, we considered research on the importance of the age of older adults in determining the degree of their visual decline. Age also is a factor in the degree of hearing decline in older adults (Li-Korotky, 2012). As indicated in Figure 15, the declines in vision and hearing are much greater in individuals 75 years and older than in individuals 65 to 74 years of age (Charness & Bosman, 1992).

Older adults often don't recognize that they have a hearing problem, deny that they have one, or accept it as a part of growing old (Pacala & Yeuh, 2012). A recent study found that severe age-related hearing loss was linked to impaired ability to perform activities of daily living (Gopinath & others, 2012).

Two devices can be used to minimize problems created by hearing loss: (1) hearing aids that amplify sound to reduce middle-ear-based conductive hearing loss, and (2) cochlear implants that restore some hearing following neurosensory hearing loss (Di Nardo & others, 2014). Currently, researchers are exploring the use of stem cells as an alternative to cochlear implants (Parker, 2011).

OTHER SENSES

As we develop, we not only obtain information about the world from our eyes and our ears but also through sensory receptors in our skin, nose, and tongue.

Touch and Pain Do newborns respond to touch (called tactile stimulation)? Can they feel pain? How does the perception of touch and pain change with age?

Infancy Newborns do respond to touch. A touch to the cheek produces a turning of the head; a touch to the lips produces sucking movements.

Newborns can also feel pain (von Ganzewinkel & others, 2014). If and when you have a son and consider whether he should be circumcised, the issue of an infant's pain perception probably will become important to you. When circumcision is performed during infancy, it usually takes place between the third and eighth days after birth. Will your young son experience pain if he is circumcised when he is 3 days old? An investigation by Megan Gunnar and her colleagues (1987) found that infant males cried intensely during circumcision. The circumcised infants also displayed amazing resiliency. Within several minutes after the surgery, they could nurse and interact in a normal manner with their mothers. And, if allowed to, the newly circumcised infants drifted into a deep sleep, which seemed to serve as a coping mechanism. Also, once researchers discovered that newborns feel pain, the practice of operating on newborns without anesthesia began to be reconsidered. Anesthesia is now used in some circumcisions (Morris & others, 2012).

Adulthood　There has been little research on developmental changes in touch and pain after infancy until the middle and late adulthood years. Changes in touch and pain are associated with aging (Lenz & others, 2012). One study found that older adults could detect touch much less in the lower extremities (ankles, knees, and so on) than in the upper extremities (wrists, shoulders, and so on) (Corso, 1977). For most older adults, though, a decline in touch sensitivity is not problematic (Hoyer & Roodin, 2009).

An estimated 60 to 75 percent of older adults report at least some persistent pain (Molton & Terrill, 2014). The most frequent pain complaints of older adults are back pain (40 percent), peripheral neuropathic pain (35 percent), and chronic joint pain (15 to 25 percent) (Denard & others, 2010). The presence of pain increases with age in older adults, and women are more likely to report having pain than are men (Tsang & others, 2008). Older adults are less sensitive to pain than are younger adults (Harkins, Price, & Martinelli, 1986). However, once older adults experience pain they may be less tolerant of it than are younger adults (Farrell, 2012).

Smell　Newborns can differentiate odors (Doty & Shah, 2008). The expressions on their faces seem to indicate that they like the way vanilla and strawberry smell but do not like the way rotten eggs and fish smell (Steiner, 1979). In one investigation, 6-day-old infants who were breast fed showed a clear preference for smelling their mother's breast pad rather than a clean breast pad (MacFarlane, 1975) (see Figure 16). However, when they were 2 days old, they did not show this preference, an indication that they require several days of experience to recognize this odor.

A decline in sensitivity to odors may occur as early as the twenties, with declines continuing through each subsequent decade of life into the nineties (Margran & Boulton, 2005). Beginning in the sixties, the decrease in sensitivity to smells becomes more noticeable to most people (Hawkes, 2006). A majority of individuals 80 years of age and older experience a significant reduction in smell (Lafreniere & Mann, 2009). A decline in the sense of smell can reduce the ability to detect smoke from a fire.

The decline in the olfactory system can reduce older adults' enjoyment of food and their life satisfaction. If elderly individuals need to be encouraged to eat more, compounds that stimulate the olfactory nerve are sometimes added to food.

Taste　Sensitivity to taste is present even before birth (Doty & Shah, 2008). Human newborns learn tastes prenatally through the amniotic fluid and in breast milk after birth (Beauchamp & Mennella, 2009; Mennella, 2009). In one study, even at only 2 hours of age, babies made different facial expressions when they tasted sweet, sour, and bitter solutions (Rosenstein & Oster, 1988) (see Figure 17). At about 4 months of age, infants begin to prefer salty tastes, which as newborns they had found to be aversive (Doty & Shah, 2008).

One study found a significant reduction in the ability of older adults to recognize sweet, salty, sour, and bitter tastes (Fukunaga, Uematsu, & Sugimoto, 2005). As with smell, there is less decline in taste in healthy older adults than in unhealthy older adults. However, when even relatively healthy older adults take medications, their taste sensitivity declines (Roberts & Rosenberg, 2006). Many older adults prefer highly seasoned foods (sweeter, spicier, saltier) to compensate for their diminished taste and smell (Hoyer & Roodin, 2009). This preference can lead to increased eating of nonnutritious, highly seasoned "junk food."

Researchers have found that older adults show a greater decline in their sense of smell than in their taste (Schiffman, 2007). Smell, too, declines less in healthy older adults than in their less healthy counterparts.

FIGURE **16**

NEWBORNS' PREFERENCE FOR THE SMELL OF THEIR MOTHER'S BREAST PAD. In the experiment by MacFarlane (1975), 6-day-old infants preferred to smell their mother's breast pad rather than a clean one that had never been used, but 2-day-old infants did not show the preference, indicating that this odor preference requires several days of experience to develop.
© Jean Guichard/Sygma/Corbis

(a) (b) (c)

FIGURE 17

NEWBORNS' FACIAL RESPONSES TO BASIC TASTES. Facial expressions elicited by (*a*) a sweet solution, (*b*) a sour solution, and (*c*) a bitter solution.
Rosenstein, D. & Oster, H. (1988). Differential facial responses to four basic tastes in newborns. *Child Development, 59, p. 1561*

INTERMODAL PERCEPTION

Imagine that you are playing basketball or tennis. You are experiencing many visual inputs—the ball is coming and going, other players are moving around, and so on. However, you are experiencing many auditory inputs as well: the sound of the ball bouncing or being hit, the grunts and groans of the other players, and so on. There is good correspondence between much of the visual and auditory information: When you see the ball bounce, you hear a bouncing sound; when a player stretches to hit a ball, you hear a groan. When you look at and listen to what is going on, you do not experience just the sounds or just the sights; you put all of these things together. You experience a unitary episode. This is **intermodal perception,** which involves integrating information from two or more sensory modalities, such as vision and hearing (Bremner & others, 2012). Most perception is intermodal (Bahrick, 2010; Kirkham & others, 2012).

How is intermodal perception involved in this context in which a boy is listening to headphones while working on a computer?
© Özgür Donmaz/Getty Images RF

Early, exploratory forms of intermodal perception exist even in newborns (Bahrick & Hollich, 2008). For example, newborns turn their eyes and their head toward the sound of a voice or rattle when the sound is maintained for several seconds (Clifton & others, 1981), but the newborn can localize a sound and look at an object only in a crude way (Bechtold, Bushnell, & Salapatek, 1979). These early forms of intermodal perception become sharpened with experience in the first year of life (Kirkham & others, 2012). In one study, infants as young as 3½ months old looked more at their mother when they also heard her voice and longer at their father when they also heard his voice (Spelke & Owsley, 1979). Thus, even young infants can coordinate visual-auditory information about people.

Can young infants put vision and sound together as precisely as adults do? In the first six months, infants have difficulty connecting sensory input from different modes, but in the second half of the first year they show an increased ability to make this connection mentally.

NATURE/NURTURE AND PERCEPTUAL DEVELOPMENT

Now that we have discussed many aspects of perceptual development, let's explore one of developmental psychology's key issues as it relates to perceptual development: the nature-nurture issue. There has been a long-standing interest in how strongly infants' perception is influenced by nature or nurture (Johnson & Hannon, 2015; Slater & others, 2011). In the field of perceptual development, nature proponents are referred to as *nativists* and those who emphasize learning and experience are called *empiricists*.

In the nativist view, the ability to perceive the world in a competent, organized way is inborn or innate. At the beginning of our discussion of perceptual development, we examined the ecological view of the Gibsons because it has played such a pivotal role in guiding research in perceptual development. In some quarters, the Gibsons' ecological view has been described

intermodal perception The ability to integrate information about two or more sensory modalities, such as vision and hearing.

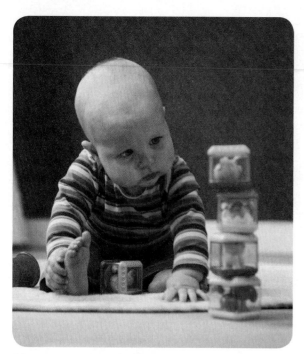

What roles do nature and nurture play in the infant's perceptual development?
© altrendo images/Getty Images

as leaning toward a nativist explanation of perceptual development because it holds that perception is direct and evolved over time to allow the detection of size and shape constancy, a three-dimensional world, intermodal perception, and so on early in infancy. However, the Gibsons' view is not entirely nativist because they emphasized that perceptual development involves distinctive features that are detected at different ages (Johnson & Hannon, 2015; Slater & others, 2011). Further, the Gibsons argued that a key question in infant perception is what information is available in the environment and how infants learn to generate, differentiate, and discriminate the information—certainly not a nativist view.

The Gibsons' ecological view is quite different from Piaget's constructivist view, which reflects an empiricist approach to explaining perceptual development. According to Piaget, much of perceptual development in infancy reflects a sequence of cognitive stages during which infants can accomplish more complex perceptual tasks. Thus, in Piaget's view, the ability to perceive size and shape constancy, a three-dimensional world, intermodal perception, and so on develops later in infancy than the Gibsons envision.

The longitudinal research of Daphne Maurer and her colleagues (Lewis & Maurer, 2005, 2009; Maurer & Lewis, 2013; Maurer & others, 1999) has focused on infants born with cataracts—a thickening of the lens of the eye that causes vision to become cloudy, opaque, and distorted and thus severely restricts infants' ability to experience their visual world. Studying infants whose cataracts were removed at different points in development, they discovered that those whose cataracts were removed and new lenses placed in their eyes in the first several months after birth showed a normal pattern of visual development. However, the longer the delay in removing the cataracts, the more their visual development was impaired. In their research, Maurer and her colleagues (2007) have found that experiencing patterned visual input early in infancy is important for holistic and detailed face processing after infancy. Maurer's research program illustrates how deprivation and experience influence visual development, identifying an early sensitive period in which visual input is necessary for normal visual development (Maurer & Lewis, 2013).

Today, it is clear that an extreme empiricist position on perceptual development is unwarranted. Much of early perception develops from innate (nature) foundations, and the basic foundation of many perceptual abilities can be detected in newborns, whereas other abilities unfold maturationally (Arterberry, 2008). However, as infants develop, environmental experiences (nurture) refine or calibrate many perceptual functions, and they may be the driving force behind some functions. The accumulation of experience with and knowledge about their perceptual world contributes to infants' ability to perceive coherent impressions of people and things (Johnson & Hannon, 2015; Slater & others, 2011). Thus, a full portrait of perceptual development acknowledges the influence of nature, nurture, and a developing sensitivity to information (Arterberry, 2008).

developmental **connection**

Theories

Piaget's theory states that children construct their understanding of the world through four stages of cognitive development. Connect to "Introduction" and "Cognitive Developmental Approaches."

Review Connect Reflect

LG2 Outline the course of sensory and perceptual development

Review

- What are sensation and perception?
- What is the ecological view of perception? What are some research methods used to study infant perception?
- How does vision develop?
- How does hearing develop?
- How do sensitivity to touch and pain develop? How does smell develop? How does taste develop?
- What is intermodal perception, and how does it develop?
- What roles do nature and nurture play in perceptual development?

Connect

- How might the development of vision and hearing contribute to infants' gross motor development?

Reflect *Your Own Personal Journey of Life*

- Imagine that you are the parent of a 1-year-old infant. How would you stimulate your 1-year-old's vision and hearing?

As we come to the end of this chapter, we return to the important theme of perceptual-motor coupling. The distinction between perceiving and doing has been a time-honored tradition in psychology. However, a number of experts on perceptual and motor development question whether this distinction makes sense (Adolph & Robinson, 2015; Thelen & Smith, 2006). The main thrust of research in Esther Thelen's dynamic systems approach is to explore how people assemble motor behaviors for perceiving and acting. The main theme of the ecological approach of Eleanor and James J. Gibson is to discover how perception guides action. Action can guide perception, and perception can guide action. Only by moving one's eyes, head, hands, and arms and by moving from one location to another can an individual fully experience his or her environment and learn how to adapt to it. Perception and action are coupled.

Babies, for example, continually coordinate their movements with perceptual information to learn how to maintain balance, reach for objects in space, and move across various surfaces and terrains (Adolph & Robinson, 2015; Thelen & Smith, 2006). They are motivated to move by what they perceive. Consider the sight of an attractive toy across the room. In this situation, infants must perceive the current state of their bodies and learn how to use their limbs to reach the toy. Although their movements at first are awkward and uncoordinated, babies soon learn to select patterns that are appropriate for reaching their goals.

Equally important is the other part of the perception-action coupling. That is, action educates perception (Adolph & Berger, 2016). For example, watching an object while exploring it manually helps infants to discriminate its texture, size, and hardness. Locomoting in the environment teaches babies about how objects and people look from different perspectives, or whether surfaces will support their weight. Individuals perceive in order to move and move in order to perceive. Perceptual and motor development do not occur in isolation from each other but instead are coupled.

How do infants develop new perceptual-motor couplings? Recall from our discussion earlier in this chapter that in the traditional view of Gesell, infants' perceptual-motor development is prescribed by a genetic plan to follow a fixed and sequential progression of stages in development. The genetic determination view has been replaced by the dynamic systems

> The infant is by no means as helpless as it looks and is quite capable of some very complex and important actions.
>
> —**HERB PICK**
> *Developmental psychologist, University of Minnesota*

Perception and action are coupled throughout the human life span.
(left): © Anthony Cain/Flickr/Getty Images RF; (right): © Corbis RF

view that infants learn new perceptual-motor couplings by assembling skills for perceiving and acting. New perceptual-motor coupling is not passively accomplished; rather, the infant actively develops a skill to achieve a goal within the constraints set by the infant's body and the environment (Adolph & Kretch, 2015).

Driving a car illustrates the coupling of perceptual and motor skills. The decline in perceptual-motor skills in late adulthood makes driving a car difficult for many older adults (Stavrinos & others, 2013). Drivers over the age of 65 are involved in more traffic accidents than middle-aged adults because of mistakes such as improper turns, not yielding the right of way, and not obeying traffic signs; their younger counterparts are more likely to have accidents because they are speeding (Lavalliere & others, 2011). Older adults can compensate for declines in perceptual-motor skills by driving shorter distances, choosing less congested routes, and driving only in daylight.

Cognitive training programs have shown some success in older adults, including improving their driving safety and making driving less difficult. In one study conducted by Karlene Ball and her colleagues (2010), training designed to enhance speed of processing produced more than a 40 percent reduction in at-fault crashes over a six-year period.

Review *Connect* **Reflect**

 LG3 Discuss the connection between perception and action

Review
- How are perception and action coupled in development?

Connect
- If perception and action are closely linked, can parents enhance their infants' motor development or must it follow its own course?

Reflect *Your Own Personal Journey of Life*
- Describe two examples not given in the text in which perception guides action. Then describe two examples not given in the text in which action guides perception.

---

reach your **learning goals**

Motor, Sensory, and Perceptual Development

1 Motor Development

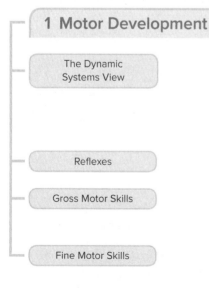

LG1 Describe how motor skills develop

- The Dynamic Systems View

  · Thelen's dynamic systems theory seeks to explain how motor behaviors are assembled by infants for perceiving and acting. Perception and action are coupled. According to this theory, motor skills are the result of many converging factors, such as the development of the nervous system, the body's physical properties and its movement possibilities, the goal the child is motivated to reach, and environmental support for the skill. In the dynamic systems view, motor development involves far greater complexity than the unfolding of a genetic blueprint.

- Reflexes

  · Reflexes govern the newborn's movements. They include the sucking, rooting, and Moro reflexes.

- Gross Motor Skills

  · Gross motor skills involve large-muscle activities. Key skills developed during infancy include control of posture and walking. Gross motor skills improve dramatically during childhood. Peak levels of physical performance often occur between 19 and 26 years of age. In general, older adults show a slowing of movement.

- Fine Motor Skills

  · Fine motor skills involve finely tuned motor actions. The onset of reaching and grasping marks a significant accomplishment. Fine motor skills continue to develop during childhood and then decline somewhat with aging.

2 Sensory and Perceptual Development Outline the course of sensory and perceptual development

What Are Sensation and Perception?

- Sensation occurs when information interacts with sensory receptors. Perception is the interpretation of sensation.

The Ecological View

- Created by the Gibsons, the ecological view states that people directly perceive information that exists in the world. Perception brings people in contact with the environment so that they can interact with and adapt to it. Affordances provide opportunities for interaction offered by objects that fit within our capabilities to perform activities. Researchers have developed a number of methods to assess the infant's perception, including the visual preference method (which Fantz used to determine young infants' interest in looking at patterned over nonpatterned displays), habituation and dishabituation, and tracking.

Visual Perception

- The infant's visual acuity increases dramatically during the first year of life. Infants can distinguish some colors by 8 weeks of age and possibly by as early as 4 weeks. Young infants systematically scan human faces. By 3 months of age, infants show size and shape constancy. As visual perception develops, infants develop visual expectations. In Gibson and Walk's classic study, infants as young as 6 months of age had depth perception. Much of vision develops from biological foundations, but environmental experiences can contribute to the development of visual perception. During the preschool years, children become better at differentiating colors and scanning the visual world. After the early adult years, visual acuity declines. Eye accommodation decreases the most from 40 to 59 years of age. In older adults, the yellowing of the eye's lens reduces color differentiation, and the ability to see the periphery of a visual field declines. Significant declines in visual functioning related to glare characterize adults 75 years and older and are even more severe among those who are 85 years and older. Three diseases that can impair the vision of older adults are cataracts, glaucoma, and macular degeneration.

Hearing

- The fetus can hear sounds such as the mother's voice and music during the last two months of pregnancy. Immediately after birth newborns can hear, but their sensory threshold is higher than that of adults. Developmental changes in the perception of loudness, pitch, and localization of sound occur during infancy. Hearing can start to decline by the age of 40, especially sensitivity to high-pitched sounds. However, hearing impairment usually doesn't become much of an impediment until late adulthood. Hearing aids can diminish hearing problems for many older adults.

Other Senses

- Newborns can respond to touch and feel pain. Sensitivity to pain decreases in late adulthood. Newborns can differentiate odors, and sensitivity to taste is present before birth. Smell and taste may decline in late adulthood, although in healthy individuals the decline is minimal.

Intermodal Perception

- Crude, exploratory forms of intermodal perception—the ability to relate and integrate information from two or more sensory modalities—are present in newborns and become sharpened over the first year of life.

Nature/Nurture and Perceptual Development

- In theorizing about perception, nature advocates are referred to as nativists and nurture proponents are called empiricists. The Gibsons' ecological view that has guided much of perceptual development research leans toward a nativist approach but still allows for developmental changes in distinctive features. Piaget's constructivist view leans toward an empiricist approach, emphasizing that many perceptual accomplishments must await the development of cognitive stages in infancy. A strong empiricist approach is unwarranted. A full account of perceptual development acknowledges the roles of nature, nurture, and the developing sensitivity to information.

3 Perceptual-Motor Coupling Discuss the connection between perception and action

- Perception and action often are not isolated but rather are coupled. Action can guide perception and perception can guide action. Individuals perceive in order to move and move in order to perceive.

key terms

accommodation of the eye	fine motor skills	intermodal perception	sensation
affordances	glaucoma	macular degeneration	shape constancy
cataracts	grasping reflex	Moro reflex	size constancy
dishabituation	gross motor skills	perception	sucking reflex
dynamic systems theory	habituation	rooting reflex	visual preference method
ecological view			

key people

Karen Adolph	Eleanor Gibson	William James	Daphne Maurer
Karlene Ball	James J. Gibson	Scott Johnson	Esther Thelen
Robert Fantz	Megan Gunnar	Rachel Keen	Richard Walk

section three

Learning is an ornament in prosperity, a refuge in adversity.

—ARISTOTLE
Greek philosopher, 4th century B.C.

Cognitive Processes and Development

Children thirst to know and understand. They construct their own ideas about the world around them and are remarkable for their curiosity, intelligence, and language. And it is always in season for the old to learn. In Section 3, you will read four chapters: "Cognitive Developmental Approaches," "Information Processing," "Intelligence," and "Language Development."

chapter 6

COGNITIVE DEVELOPMENTAL APPROACHES

chapter **outline**

preview

Cognitive developmental approaches place a special emphasis on how individuals actively construct their thinking. They also focus heavily on how thinking changes from one point in development to another. In this chapter, we will focus on the cognitive developmental approaches of Jean Piaget and Lev Vygotsky. We also will explore the possibility that adults think in a qualitatively more advanced way than adolescents do.

1 Piaget's Theory of Cognitive Development

LG1 Discuss the key processes and four stages in Piaget's theory

Processes of Development	Sensorimotor Stage	Preoperational Stage	Concrete Operational Stage	Formal Operational Stage

Poet Nora Perry asks, "Who knows the thoughts of a child?" As much as anyone, Piaget knew. Through careful observations of his own three children—Laurent, Lucienne, and Jacqueline— and observations of and interviews with other children, Piaget reached groundbreaking conclusions regarding the ways children think about the world.

Piaget's theory is a general, unifying story of how biology and experience sculpt cognitive development. Piaget thought that, just as our physical bodies have structures that enable us to adapt to the world, we build mental structures that help us adapt to the world. Adaptation involves adjusting to new environmental demands. Piaget stressed that children actively construct their own cognitive worlds; information is not just poured into their minds from the environment. He sought to discover how children at different points in their development think about the world and how systematic changes in their thinking occur.

PROCESSES OF DEVELOPMENT

What processes do children use as they construct their knowledge of the world? Piaget developed several concepts to answer this question; especially important among them are schemes, assimilation, accommodation, organization, equilibrium, and equilibration.

Schemes   As the infant or child seeks to construct an understanding of the world, said Piaget (1954), the developing brain creates **schemes.** These are actions or mental representations that organize knowledge. In Piaget's theory, behavioral schemes (physical activities) characterize infancy and mental schemes (cognitive activities) develop in childhood (Lamb, Bornstein, & Teti, 2002). A baby's schemes are structured by simple actions that can be performed on objects, such as sucking, looking, and grasping. Older children have schemes that include strategies and plans for solving problems. By the time we have reached adulthood, we have constructed an enormous number of diverse schemes, ranging from driving a car to balancing a budget to the concept of fairness.

Next, we will look at other important cognitive processes—assimilation, accommodation, organization, and equilibration—that individuals use throughout the life span in actively constructing their knowledge.

Assimilation and Accommodation   To explain how children use and adapt their schemes, Piaget offered two concepts: assimilation and accommodation. **Assimilation** occurs when children use their existing schemes to deal with new information or experiences. Think about a toddler who has learned to use the word *car* to identify the family's car. The toddler might call all moving vehicles on roads "cars," including motorcycles and trucks; the child has assimilated these objects to his or her existing scheme. **Accommodation** occurs when children adjust their schemes to take account of new information and experiences. The child soon learns that motorcycles and trucks are not cars and fine-tunes the category to exclude motorcycles and trucks, accommodating the scheme.

Jean Piaget, the famous Swiss developmental psychologist.
© Corbis

We are born capable of learning.

—JEAN-JACQUES ROUSSEAU
Swiss-born French philosopher, 18th century

schemes In Piaget's theory, actions or mental representations that organize knowledge.

assimilation Piagetian concept in which children use existing schemes to incorporate new information.

accommodation Piagetian concept of adjusting schemes to fit new information and experiences.

In Piaget's view, what is a scheme? What schemes might this young infant be displaying?
© Laura Dwight/Corbis

Assimilation and accommodation operate even in very young infants. Newborns reflexively suck everything that touches their lips; they assimilate all sorts of objects into their sucking scheme. By sucking different objects, they learn about their taste, texture, shape, and so on. After several months of experience, though, they construct their understanding of the world differently. Some objects, such as fingers and the mother's breast, can be sucked, and others, such as fuzzy blankets, should not be sucked. In other words, they accommodate their sucking scheme.

Organization   To make sense of their world, said Piaget, children cognitively organize their experiences. **Organization** in Piaget's theory is the grouping of isolated behaviors and thoughts into a higher-order system. Continual refinement of this organization is an inherent part of development. A child who has only a vague idea about how to use a hammer may also have a vague idea about how to use other tools. After learning how to use each one, the child relates these uses, organizing his knowledge.

Equilibration and Stages of Development   Assimilation and accommodation always take the child to a higher ground, according to Piaget. In trying to understand the world, the child inevitably experiences cognitive conflict, or *disequilibrium*. That is, the child constantly encounters inconsistencies and counterexamples to his or her existing schemes. For example, if a child believes that pouring water from a short and wide container into a tall and narrow container changes the amount of water, then the child might be puzzled by where the "extra" water came from and whether there is actually more water to drink. The puzzle creates disequilibrium; for Piaget, an internal search for equilibrium creates motivation for change. The child assimilates and accommodates, adjusting old schemes, developing new schemes, and organizing and reorganizing the old and new schemes. Eventually, the organization is fundamentally different from the old organization; it is a new way of thinking.

In short, according to Piaget, children constantly assimilate and accommodate as they seek equilibrium. There is considerable movement between states of cognitive equilibrium and disequilibrium as assimilation and accommodation work in concert to produce cognitive change. **Equilibration** is the name Piaget gave to this mechanism by which children shift from one stage of thought to the next.

The result of these processes, according to Piaget, is that individuals go through four stages of development. A different way of understanding the world makes each stage more advanced than the previous one. Cognition is *qualitatively* different in one stage compared with another. In other words, the way children reason at one stage is different from the way they reason at another stage. Figure 1 provides a brief description of the four Piagetian stages.

SENSORIMOTOR STAGE

The **sensorimotor stage** lasts from birth to about 2 years of age. In this stage, infants construct an understanding of the world by coordinating sensory experiences (such as seeing and hearing) with physical, motoric actions—hence the term "sensorimotor." At the beginning of this stage, newborns have little more than reflexes with which to work. By the end of the sensorimotor stage, 2-year-olds can produce complex sensorimotor patterns and use primitive symbols.

Substages   Piaget divided the sensorimotor stage into six substages: (1) simple reflexes; (2) first habits and primary circular reactions; (3) secondary circular reactions; (4) coordination of secondary circular reactions; (5) tertiary circular reactions, novelty, and curiosity; and (6) internalization of schemes.

Simple reflexes, the first sensorimotor substage, corresponds to the first month after birth. In this substage, sensation and action are coordinated primarily through reflexive behaviors, such as rooting and sucking. Soon the infant produces behaviors that resemble reflexes in the absence of the usual stimulus for the reflex. For example, a newborn will suck a nipple or bottle only when it is placed directly in the baby's mouth or touched to the lips. But soon the infant might suck when a bottle or nipple is only nearby. Even in the first month of life, the infant is initiating action and actively structuring experiences.

organization Piagetian concept of grouping isolated behaviors and thoughts into a higher-order, more smoothly functioning cognitive system.

equilibration A mechanism that Piaget proposed to explain how children shift from one stage of thought to the next.

sensorimotor stage The first of Piaget's stages, which lasts from birth to about 2 years of age, during which infants construct an understanding of the world by coordinating sensory experiences (such as seeing and hearing) with physical, motoric actions.

Sensorimotor Stage	**Preoperational Stage**	**Concrete Operational Stage**	**Formal Operational Stage**
The infant constructs an understanding of the world by coordinating sensory experiences with physical actions. An infant progresses from reflexive, instinctual action at birth to the beginning of symbolic thought toward the end of the stage.	The child begins to represent the world with words and images. These words and images reflect increased symbolic thinking and go beyond the connection of sensory information and physical action.	The child can now reason logically about concrete events and classify objects into different sets.	The adolescent reasons in more abstract, idealistic, and logical ways.
Birth to 2 Years of Age	**2 to 7 Years of Age**	**7 to 11 Years of Age**	**11 Years of Age Through Adulthood**

FIGURE 1

PIAGET'S FOUR STAGES OF COGNITIVE DEVELOPMENT
(left to right): © Stockbyte/Getty Images RF; © BananaStock/PunchStock RF; © image100/Corbis RF; © Jose Pelaez/Corbis RF

First habits and primary circular reactions is the second sensorimotor substage, which develops between 1 and 4 months of age. In this substage, the infant coordinates sensation and two types of schemes: habits and primary circular reactions. A *habit* is a scheme based on a reflex that has become completely separated from its eliciting stimulus. For example, infants in substage 1 suck when bottles are put to their lips or when they see a bottle. Infants in substage 2 might suck even when no bottle is present. A *circular reaction* is a repetitive action.

A *primary circular reaction* is a scheme based on the attempt to reproduce an event that initially occurred by chance. For example, suppose an infant accidentally sucks his fingers when they are placed near his mouth. Later, he searches for his fingers to suck them again, but the fingers do not cooperate because the infant cannot coordinate visual and manual actions.

Habits and circular reactions are stereotyped—that is, the infant repeats them the same way each time. During this substage, the infant's own body remains the infant's center of attention. There is no outward pull by environmental events.

Secondary circular reactions is the third sensorimotor substage, which develops between 4 and 8 months of age. In this substage, the infant becomes more object oriented, moving beyond preoccupation with the self. The infant's schemes are not intentional or goal-directed, but they are repeated because of their consequences. By chance, an infant might shake a rattle. The infant repeats this action for the sake of its fascination. This is a *secondary circular reaction:* an action repeated because of its consequences. The infant also imitates some simple actions, such as the baby talk or burbling of adults, and some physical gestures. However, the baby imitates only actions that she is already able to produce.

Coordination of secondary circular reactions is Piaget's fourth sensorimotor substage, which develops between 8 and 12 months of age. To progress into this substage, the infant must coordinate vision and touch, hand and eye. Actions become more outwardly directed. Significant changes during this substage involve the coordination of schemes and intentionality. Infants readily combine and recombine previously learned schemes in a coordinated

I wish I could travel by the road that crosses the baby's mind, and out beyond all bounds; where messengers run errands for no cause between the kingdoms of kings of no history; where reason makes kites of her laws and flies them, and truth sets facts free from its fetters.

—Rabindranath Tagore
Bengali poet and essayist, 20th century

This 17-month-old is in Piaget's stage of tertiary circular reactions. *What might the infant do to suggest that she is in this stage?* © Corbis/PunchStock RF

way. They might look at an object and grasp it simultaneously, or they might visually inspect a toy, such as a rattle, and finger it simultaneously, exploring it tactilely. Actions are even more outwardly directed than before. Related to this coordination is the second achievement—the presence of intentionality. For example, infants might manipulate a stick in order to bring a desired toy within reach, or they might knock over one block to reach and play with another one.

Tertiary circular reactions, novelty, and curiosity is Piaget's fifth sensorimotor substage, which develops between 12 and 18 months of age. In this substage, infants become intrigued by the many properties of objects and by the many things that they can make happen to objects. A block can be made to fall, spin, hit another object, and slide across the ground. *Tertiary circular reactions* are schemes in which the infant purposely explores new possibilities with objects, continually doing new things to them and exploring the results. Piaget says that this stage marks the starting point for human curiosity and interest in novelty.

Internalization of schemes is Piaget's sixth and final sensorimotor substage, which develops between 18 and 24 months of age. In this substage, the infant develops the ability to use primitive symbols. For Piaget, a symbol is an internalized sensory image or word that represents an event. Primitive symbols permit the infant to think about concrete events without directly acting them out or perceiving them. Moreover, symbols allow the infant to manipulate and transform the represented events in simple ways. In a favorite Piagetian example, Piaget's young daughter saw a matchbox being opened and closed. Later, she mimicked the event by opening and closing her mouth. This was an obvious expression of her image of the event. A summary of Piaget's six substages of sensorimotor development is shown in Figure 2.

Object Permanence   Imagine how chaotic and unpredictable your life would be if you could not distinguish between yourself and your world. This is what the life of a newborn must be like, according to Piaget. There is no differentiation between the self and world; objects have no separate, permanent existence.

By the end of the sensorimotor period, objects are both separate from the self and permanent. **Object permanence** is the understanding that objects continue to exist even when they cannot be seen, heard, or touched. Acquiring the sense of object permanence is one of the infant's most important accomplishments, according to Piaget.

FIGURE 2
PIAGET'S SIX SUBSTAGES OF SENSORIMOTOR DEVELOPMENT

Substage	Age	Description	Example
1 Simple reflexes	Birth to 1 month	Coordination of sensation and action through reflexive behaviors.	Rooting, sucking, and grasping reflexes; newborns suck reflexively when their lips are touched.
2 First habits and primary circular reactions	1 to 4 months	Coordination of sensation and two types of schemes: habits (reflex) and primary circular reactions (reproduction of an event that initially occurred by chance). Main focus is still on the infant's body.	Repeating a body sensation first experienced by chance (sucking thumb, for example); then infants might accommodate actions by sucking their thumb differently from how they suck on a nipple.
3 Secondary circular reactions	4 to 8 months	Infants become more object-oriented, moving beyond self-preoccupation; they repeat actions that bring interesting or pleasurable results.	An infant coos to make a person stay near; as the person starts to leave, the infant coos again.
4 Coordination of secondary circular reactions	8 to 12 months	Coordination of vision and touch—hand-eye coordination; coordination of schemes and intentionality.	Infant manipulates a stick in order to bring an attractive toy within reach.
5 Tertiary circular reactions, novelty, and curiosity	12 to 18 months	Infants become intrigued by the many properties of objects and by the many things they can make happen to objects; they experiment with new behavior.	A block can be made to fall, spin, hit another object, and slide across the ground.
6 Internalization of schemes	18 to 24 months	Infants develop the ability to use primitive symbols and form enduring mental representations.	An infant who has never thrown a temper tantrum before sees a playmate throw a tantrum; the infant retains a memory of the event, then throws one himself the next day.

FIGURE 3

OBJECT PERMANENCE. Piaget argued that object permanence is one of infancy's landmark cognitive accomplishments. For this 5-month-old boy, "out of sight" is literally out of mind. The infant looks at the toy monkey (*left*), but when his view of the toy is blocked (*right*), he does not search for it. Several months later, he will search for the hidden toy monkey, an action reflecting the presence of object permanence.
© Doug Goodman/Science Source

How can anyone know whether an infant has a sense of object permanence? The principal way that object permanence is studied is by watching an infant's reaction when an interesting object disappears (see Figure 3). If infants search for the object, it is assumed that they believe it continues to exist.

Object permanence is just one of the basic concepts about the physical world developed by babies. To Piaget, children, even infants, are much like little scientists, examining the world to see how it works. How can the accuracy of this view of children's development be assessed? The *Connecting with Research* interlude describes some of the ways in which adult scientists try to discover what these "baby scientists" are finding out about the world.

Evaluating Piaget's Sensorimotor Stage Piaget opened up a new way of looking at infants with his view that their main task is to coordinate their sensory impressions with their motor activity. However, the infant's cognitive world is not as neatly packaged as Piaget portrayed it, and some of Piaget's explanations for the cause of change are debated. In the past several decades, sophisticated experimental techniques have been devised to study infants, and there have been a large number of research studies on infant development. Much of the new research suggests that Piaget's view of sensorimotor development needs to be modified (Baillargeon, 2014; Diamond, 2013).

The A-Not-B Error One modification concerns Piaget's claim that certain processes are crucial in transitions from one stage to the next. The data do not always support his explanations. For example, in Piaget's theory, an important feature in the progression into substage 4, *coordination of secondary circular reactions*, is an infant's inclination to search for a hidden object in a familiar location rather than to look for the object in a new location. For example, if a toy is hidden twice, initially at location A and subsequently at location B, 8- to 12-month-old infants search initially and correctly at location A. But when the toy is subsequently hidden at location B while the infants watch, they make the mistake of continuing to search for it at location A. **A-not-B error** is the term used to describe this common mistake. Older infants are less likely to make the A-not-B error because their concept of object permanence is more complete. Researchers have found, however, that the A-not-B error does not show up consistently (Sophian, 1985). The evidence indicates that A-not-B errors are sensitive to the delay between hiding the object at B and the infant's attempt to find it (Diamond, 1985). Thus, the A-not-B error might be due to a failure in memory. Another explanation is that infants tend to repeat a previous motor behavior (Clearfield & others, 2006). Also, a recent study involving 10-month-olds found a wide variation in search behaviors on the A-not-B task, producing individual differences in performance, possibly due to temperament, maturation of short-term/long-term memory, inhibition, and cognitive flexibility (Johansson, Forssman, & Bohlin, 2014).

object permanence The Piagetian term for one of an infant's most important accomplishments: understanding that objects continue to exist even when they cannot directly be seen, heard, or touched.

A-not-B error This error occurs when infants make the mistake of selecting the familiar hiding place (A) of an object rather than its new hiding place (B) as they progress into substage 4 in Piaget's sensorimotor stage.

How Do Researchers Study Infants' Understanding of Object Permanence and Causality?

Two accomplishments of infants that Piaget examined were the development of object permanence and the child's understanding of causality. Let's examine two research studies that address these topics.

In both studies, Renée Baillargeon and her colleagues used a research method that involves violation of expectations. In this method, infants see an event happen as it normally would. Then the event is changed, often in a way that creates a physically impossible event. If infants look longer at the changed event, their reaction indicates they are surprised by it. In other words, this reaction is interpreted to indicate that the infant had certain expectations about the world that were violated.

In one study that focused on object permanence, researchers showed infants a toy car that moved down an inclined track, disappeared behind a screen, and then reemerged at the other end, still on the track (Baillargeon & DeVos, 1991). After this sequence was repeated several times, something different occurred: A toy mouse was placed behind the track but was hidden by the screen while the car rolled by. This was the "possible" event. Then, the researchers created an "impossible event": The toy mouse was placed on the track but was secretly removed after the screen was lowered so that the car seemed to go through the mouse. In this study, infants as young as 3½ months of age looked longer at the impos-

sible event than at the possible event, an indication that they were surprised by it. Their surprise suggested that they remembered not only that the toy mouse still existed (object permanence) but where it was located.

Another study focused on the infant's understanding of causality (Kotovsky & Baillargeon, 1994). In this research, a cylinder rolls down a ramp and hits a toy bug at the bottom of the ramp. By 5½ and 6½ months of age, after infants have seen how far the bug will be pushed by a medium-sized cylinder, their reactions indicate that they understand that the bug will roll farther if it is hit by a large cylinder than if it is hit by a small cylinder. Thus, by the middle of the first year of life, these infants understood that the size of a moving object determines how far it will move a stationary object that it collides with.

In Baillargeon's (2008, 2014; Baillargeon & others, 2012) view, infants have a pre-adapted, innate bias called the *principle of persistence* that explains their assumption that objects don't change their properties—including how solid they are, their location, their color, and their form—unless some external factor intervenes (a person moves the object, for example). Shortly, we will revisit the extent to which nature and nurture are at work in the changes that take place in the infant's cognitive development.

Research discussed in this interlude and elsewhere indicates that infants develop object permanence earlier than Piaget proposed (Baillargeon & others, 2011, 2012). Indeed, as you will see in the next section, a major theme of infant cognitive development today is that infants are more cognitively competent than Piaget envisioned. What methods might researchers use to arrive at this conclusion?

Perceptual Development and Expectations A number of theorists, such as Eleanor Gibson (2001) and Elizabeth Spelke (2011), argue that infants' perceptual abilities are highly developed very early in life. Spelke argues that young infants interpret the world as having predictable occurrences. For example, in the chapter on "Motor, Sensory, and Perceptual Development," you read about research that demonstrated the presence of intermodal perception—the ability to coordinate information from two or more sensory modalities, such as vision and hearing—by 3½ months of age, much earlier than Piaget would have predicted (Spelke & Owsley, 1979).

Research also suggests that infants develop the ability to understand how the world works at a very early age (Baillargeon, 2014; Baillargeon & Carey, 2012; Scott & Baillargeon, 2013; Spelke. Bernier, & Snedeker, 2013). For example, what kinds of expectations do infants form? Are infants born expecting the world to obey basic physical laws, such as gravity, or if not, then when do they learn about how the world works? Experiments by Elizabeth Spelke (1991, 2000; Spelke & Hespos, 2001) have addressed these questions. She placed babies before a puppet stage and showed them a series of actions that are unexpected if you know how the physical world works—for example, one ball seemed to roll through a solid barrier, another seemed to leap between two platforms, and a third appeared to hang in midair (Spelke, 1979). Spelke measured and compared the

developmental **connection**

Theories

Eleanor Gibson was a pioneer in crafting the ecological view of development. Connect to "Motor, Sensory, and Perceptual Development."

babies' looking times for unexpected and expected actions. She concluded that by 4 months of age, even though infants do not yet have the ability to talk about objects, move around objects, manipulate objects, or even see objects with high resolution, they expect objects to be solid and continuous. However, at 4 months of age, infants do not expect an object to obey gravitational constraints (Spelke & others, 1992). Similarly, research by Renée Baillargeon (1995, 2004, 2014; Baillargeon & others, 2011, 2012) documents that infants as young as 3 to 4 months expect objects to be *substantial* (in the sense that other objects cannot move through them) and *permanent* (in the sense that objects continue to exist when they are hidden).

In sum, researchers such as Baillargeon and Spelke conclude that infants see objects as bounded, unitary, solid, and separate from their background, possibly at birth or shortly thereafter, but definitely by 3 to 4 months of age—much earlier than Piaget envisioned. Young infants still have much to learn about objects, but the world appears both stable and orderly to them.

However, some critics argue that the Baillargeon and Spelke experiments mainly demonstrate perceptual competencies or detection of regularities in the environment (Heyes, 2014; Ruffman, 2014). The critics stress that the infants' responses in their studies reflect a very rudimentary understanding that likely differs greatly from the understanding of older children.

The Nature-Nurture Issue   In considering the big issue of whether nature or nurture plays the more important role in infant development, Elizabeth Spelke (Huang & Spelke, 2014; Spelke, 2003, 2011; Spelke, Bernier, & Snedeker, 2013) comes down clearly on the side of nature. Spelke endorses a **core knowledge approach,** which states that infants are born with domain-specific innate knowledge systems. Among these domain-specific knowledge systems are those involving space, number sense, object permanence, and language. Strongly influenced by evolution, the core knowledge domains are theorized to be prewired to allow infants to make sense of their world (Coubart & others, 2014). After all, Spelke concludes, how could infants possibly grasp the complex world in which they live if they didn't come into the world equipped with core sets of knowledge? In this approach, the innate core knowledge domains form a foundation around which more mature cognitive functioning and learning develop. The core knowledge approach argues that Piaget greatly underestimated the cognitive abilities of infants, especially young infants (Huang & Spelke, 2014).

Recently, researchers also have explored whether preverbal infants might have a built-in innate sense of morality. In this research, infants as young as 4 months of age are more likely to make visually guided reaches toward a puppet who has acted as a helper (such as helping someone get up a hill, assisting in opening a box, or giving a ball back) rather than toward a puppet who has hindered others' efforts to achieve such goals (Hamlin, 2013, 2014).

In criticizing the core knowledge approach, British developmental psychologist Mark Johnson (2008) says that the infants Spelke assesses in her research already have accumulated hundreds, and in some cases even thousands, of hours of experience in grasping what the world is about, which gives considerable room for the environment's role in the development of infant cognition (Highfield, 2008). According to Johnson (2008), infants likely come into the world with "soft biases to perceive and attend to different aspects of the environment, and to learn about the world in particular ways." In line with Johnson's view, one major criticism is that nativists completely neglect the infant's social immersion in the world and instead focus only on what happens inside the infant's head apart from the environment (Nelson, 2013).

Although debate about the cause and course of infant cognitive development continues, most developmentalists today agree that Piaget underestimated the early cognitive accomplishments of infants and that both nature and nurture are involved in infants' cognitive development (Baillargeon, 2014; Johnson & Hannon, 2015).

Conclusions   In sum, many researchers conclude that Piaget wasn't specific enough about how infants learn about their world and that infants, especially young infants, are more competent than Piaget thought (Ristic & Enns, 2015; Sloutsky, 2015). As they have examined the

developmental **connection**

Nature Versus Nurture

The nature-nurture issue involves the debate about whether development is primarily influenced by nature (biological inheritance) or nurture (environmental experiences). Connect to "Introduction" and "Biological Beginnings."

core knowledge approach States that infants are born with domain-specific innate knowledge systems. Among these domain-specific knowledge systems are those involving space, number sense, object permanence, and language.

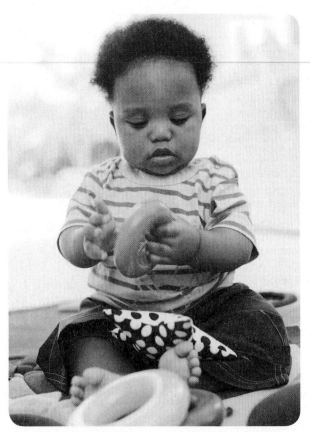

According to contemporary researchers, what revisions in Piaget's theory of sensorimotor development need to be made?
© BananaStock/PictureQuest RF

specific ways that infants learn, the field of infant cognition has become very specialized. There are many researchers working on different questions, with no general theory emerging that can connect all of the different findings. Their theories often are local theories, focused on specific research questions, rather than grand theories like Piaget's (Kuhn, 1998). Among the unifying themes in the study of infant cognition are seeking to understand more precisely how developmental changes in cognition take place, to answer questions about the relative importance of nature and nurture, and to examine the brain's role in cognitive development (Aslin, 2012). Exploring connections between brain, cognition, and development is a central focus in the recently emerging field of *developmental cognitive neuroscience* (Marshall, 2015; Stiles & others, 2015).

PREOPERATIONAL STAGE

The cognitive world of the preschool child is creative, free, and fanciful. The imaginations of preschool children work overtime, and their mental grasp of the world improves. Piaget described the preschool child's cognition as preoperational. What did he mean?

The **preoperational stage,** which lasts from approximately 2 to 7 years of age, is the second Piagetian stage. In this stage, children begin to represent the world with words, images, and drawings. They form stable concepts and begin to reason. At the same time, the young child's cognitive world is dominated by egocentrism and magical beliefs.

Because Piaget called this stage "preoperational," it might sound like an unimportant waiting period. Not so. However, the label *preoperational* emphasizes that the child does not yet perform **operations,** which are reversible mental actions that allow children to do mentally what before they could do only physically. Mentally adding and subtracting numbers are examples of operations. *Preoperational thought* is the beginning of the ability to reconstruct in thought what has been established in behavior. It can be divided into two substages: the symbolic function substage and the intuitive thought substage.

preoperational stage The second Piagetian developmental stage, which lasts from about 2 to 7 years of age; children begin to represent the world with words, images, and drawings.

operations Reversible mental actions that allow children to do mentally what before they had done only physically.

symbolic function substage The first substage of preoperational thought, occurring roughly between the ages of 2 and 4. In this substage, the young child gains the ability to represent mentally an object that is not present.

egocentrism The inability to distinguish between one's own and someone else's perspective; an important feature of preoperational thought.

animism A facet of preoperational thought— the belief that inanimate objects have lifelike qualities and are capable of action.

The Symbolic Function Substage   The **symbolic function substage** is the first substage of preoperational thought, occurring roughly between the ages of 2 and 4. In this substage, the young child gains the ability to mentally represent an object that is not present. This ability vastly expands the child's mental world (Callaghan & Corbit, 2015; Mandler & DeLoache, 2013). Young children use scribble designs to represent people, houses, cars, clouds, and so on; they begin to use language and engage in pretend play. However, although young children make distinct progress during this substage, their thinking still has important limitations, two of which are egocentrism and animism.

Egocentrism is the inability to distinguish between one's own perspective and someone else's perspective. Piaget and Barbel Inhelder (1969) initially studied young children's egocentrism by devising the three mountains task (see Figure 4). The child walks around the model of the mountains and becomes familiar with what the mountains look like from different perspectives and can see that there are different objects on the mountains. The child is then seated on one side of the table on which the mountains are placed. The experimenter moves a doll to different locations around the table, at each location asking the child to select from a series of photos the one photo that most accurately reflects the view that the doll is seeing. Children in the preoperational stage often pick their own view rather than the doll's view. Preschool children frequently show the ability to take another's perspective on some tasks but not others.

Animism, another limitation of preoperational thought, is the belief that inanimate objects have lifelike qualities and are capable of action (Gelman & Opfer, 2004). A young child might show animism by saying, "That tree pushed the leaf off, and it fell down" or "The sidewalk made me mad; it made me fall down." A young child who uses animism fails

Model of Mountains

Photo 1
(View from A)

Photo 2
(View from B)

Photo 3
(View from C)

Photo 4
(View from D)

FIGURE 4

THE THREE MOUNTAINS TASK. Photo 1 shows the child's perspective from where he or she is sitting. Photos 2, 3, and 4 were taken from different perspectives. For example, Photo 2 shows what the mountains look like to a person sitting at spot B. When asked what a view of the mountains looks like from spot B, the child selects Photo 1, taken from spot A (the child's own view at the time) instead of Photo 2, the correct view.

(a)

(b)

to distinguish the appropriate occasions for using human and nonhuman perspectives (Opfer & Gelman, 2011).

Possibly because young children are not very concerned about reality, their drawings are fanciful and inventive. Suns are blue, skies are yellow, and cars float on clouds in their symbolic, imaginative world. One 3½-year-old looked at a scribble he had just drawn and described it as a pelican kissing a seal (see Figure 5a). The symbolism is simple but strong, like abstractions found in some modern art. Twentieth-century Spanish artist Pablo Picasso commented, "I used to draw like Raphael but it has taken me a lifetime to draw like young children." In the elementary school years, a child's drawings become more realistic, neat, and precise (see Figure 5b). Suns are yellow, skies are blue, and cars travel on roads (Winner, 1986).

The Intuitive Thought Substage

The **intuitive thought substage** is the second substage of preoperational thought, occurring between approximately 4 and 7 years of age. In this substage, children begin to use primitive reasoning and want to know the answers to all sorts of questions. Consider 4-year-old Tommy, who is at the beginning of the intuitive thought substage. Although he is starting to develop his own ideas about the world he lives in, his ideas are still simple, and he is not very good at thinking things out. He has difficulty understanding events that he knows are taking place but that he cannot see. His fantasized thoughts bear little resemblance to reality. He cannot yet answer the question "What if?" in any reliable way. For example, he has only a vague idea of what would happen if a car were to hit him. He also has difficulty negotiating traffic because he cannot do the mental calculations necessary to estimate whether an approaching car will hit him when he crosses the road.

By the age of 5, children have just about exhausted the adults around them with "why" questions. The child's questions signal the emergence of interest in reasoning and in figuring out why things are the way they are. Following are some samples of the questions children ask during the questioning period of 4 to 6 years of age (Elkind, 1976):

What makes you grow up?

Who was the mother when everybody was a baby?

Why do leaves fall?

Why does the sun shine?

Piaget called this substage *intuitive* because young children seem so sure about their knowledge and understanding yet are unaware of how they know what they know. That is, they know something but know it without the use of rational thinking.

FIGURE 5

THE SYMBOLIC DRAWINGS OF YOUNG CHILDREN. (a) A 3½-year old's symbolic drawing. Halfway into his drawing, the 3½-year-old artist said it was a "pelican kissing a seal." (b) This 11-year-old's drawing is neater and more realistic but also less inventive.

intuitive thought substage The second substage of preoperational thought, occurring between approximately 4 and 7 years of age. Children begin to use primitive reasoning and want to know the answers to all sorts of questions.

"I still don't have all the answers, but I'm beginning to ask the right questions."

Centration and the Limits of Preoperational Thought One limitation of preoperational thought is **centration,** a centering of attention on one characteristic to the exclusion of all others. Centration is most clearly evidenced in young children's lack of **conservation,** the awareness that altering an object's or a substance's appearance does not change its basic properties. For example, to adults, it is obvious that a certain amount of liquid stays the same, regardless of a container's shape. But this is not at all obvious to young children. Instead, they are struck by the height of the liquid in the container; they focus on that characteristic to the exclusion of others.

The situation that Piaget devised to study conservation is his most famous task. In the conservation task, children are presented with two identical beakers, each filled to the same level with liquid (see Figure 6). They are asked if these beakers have the same amount of liquid, and they usually say yes. Then the liquid from one beaker is poured into a third beaker, which is taller and thinner than the first two. The children are then asked if the amount of liquid in the tall, thin beaker is equal to that which remains in one of the original beakers. Children who are younger than 7 or 8 years old usually say no and justify their answers in terms of the differing height or width of the beakers. Older children usually answer yes and justify their answers appropriately ("If you poured the water back, the amount would still be the same").

In Piaget's theory, failing the conservation-of-liquid task is a sign that children are at the preoperational stage of cognitive development. The failure demonstrates not only centration but also an inability to mentally reverse actions. To understand this concept, see the conservation-of-matter example shown in Figure 7. In the row labeled "matter" you'll see that preoperational children say the longer shape has more clay because they assume that "longer is more." Preoperational children cannot mentally reverse the clay-rolling process to see that the amount of clay is the same in both the shorter ball shape and the longer stick shape.

In Figure 7 you can see that, in addition to failing the conservation-of-liquid task, preoperational children also fail to conserve number, matter, and length. However, children often vary in their performance on different conservation tasks. Thus, a child might be able to conserve volume but not number. A recent fMRI brain-imaging study of conservation of number revealed that advances in a network in the parietal and frontal lobes were linked to

FIGURE **6**

PIAGET'S CONSERVATION TASK. The beaker test is a well-known Piagetian test to determine whether a child can think operationally—that is, can mentally reverse actions and show conservation of the substance. (*a*) Two identical beakers are presented to the child. Then the experimenter pours the liquid from B into C, which is taller and thinner than A or B. (*b*) The child is asked if these beakers (A and C) have the same amount of liquid. The preoperational child says "no." When asked to point to the beaker that has more liquid, the preoperational child points to the tall, thin beaker.
© Paul Fusco/Magnum Photos

centration Focusing attention on one characteristic to the exclusion of all others.

conservation The awareness that altering the appearance of an object or a substance does not change its basic properties.

Type of Conservation	Initial Presentation	Manipulation	Preoperational Child's Answer
Number	Two identical rows of objects are shown to the child, who agrees they have the same number.	One row is lengthened and the child is asked whether one row now has more objects.	Yes, the longer row.
Matter	Two identical balls of clay are shown to the child. The child agrees that they are equal.	The experimenter changes the shape of one of the balls and asks the child whether they still contain equal amounts of clay.	No, the longer one has more.
Length	Two sticks are aligned in front of the child. The child agrees that they are the same length.	The experimenter moves one stick to the right, then asks the child if they are equal in length.	No, the one on the top is longer.

FIGURE 7

SOME DIMENSIONS OF CONSERVATION: NUMBER, MATTER, AND LENGTH. *What characteristics of preoperational thought do children demonstrate when they fail these conservation tasks?*

9- and 10-year-olds' conservation success in comparison with non-conserving 5- and 6-year-olds (Houde & others, 2011).

Some developmentalists do not believe Piaget was entirely correct in his estimate of when children's conservation skills emerge. For example, Rochel Gelman (1969) showed that when the child's attention to relevant aspects of the conservation task is improved, the child is more likely to conserve. Gelman has also demonstrated that attentional training on one dimension, such as number, improves the preschool child's performance on another dimension, such as mass. Thus, Gelman noted that conservation appears earlier than Piaget thought and that attention is especially important in explaining conservation.

CONCRETE OPERATIONAL STAGE

Piaget proposed that the **concrete operational stage** lasts from approximately 7 to 11 years of age. In this stage, children can perform concrete operations, and they can reason logically as long as reasoning can be applied to specific or concrete examples. Remember that *operations* are mental actions that are reversible, and *concrete operations* are operations that are applied to real, concrete objects. When a child adds two apples together with four apples and concludes that there are now six apples, she is performing a concrete operation.

The conservation tasks described earlier indicate whether children are capable of concrete operations. Concrete operations allow the child to consider several characteristics rather than to focus on a single property of an object. In the clay example, the preoperational child is likely to focus on height or width. The concrete operational child coordinates information about both dimensions.

What other abilities are characteristic of children who have reached the concrete operational stage? One important skill is the ability to classify or divide things into different sets or subsets and to consider their interrelationships. Consider the family tree of four generations that is shown in Figure 8 (Furth & Wachs, 1975). This family tree suggests that the grandfather (A) has three children (B, C, and D), each of whom has two children (E through J), and that one of these children (J) has three children (K, L, and M). A child who comprehends the classification system can move up and down a level, across a level, and up and down and across within the system. The concrete operational child understands that person J can at the same time be father, brother, and grandson, for example.

Children who have reached the concrete operational stage are also capable of **seriation**, which is the ability to order stimuli along a quantitative dimension (such as length). To see if students can serialize, a teacher might haphazardly place eight sticks of different lengths

concrete operational stage The third Piagetian stage, which lasts from approximately 7 to 11 years of age; children can perform concrete operations, and logical reasoning replaces intuitive reasoning as long as the reasoning can be applied to specific or concrete examples.

seriation The concrete operation that involves ordering stimuli along a quantitative dimension (such as length).

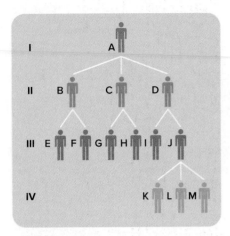

FIGURE 8

CLASSIFICATION: AN IMPORTANT ABILITY IN CONCRETE OPERATIONAL THOUGHT. A family tree of four generations (*I to IV*): The preoperational child has trouble classifying the members of the four generations; the concrete operational child can classify the members vertically, horizontally, and obliquely (up and down and across). For example, the concrete operational child understands that a family member can be a son, a brother, and a father, all at the same time.

transitivity The ability to logically combine relations to understand certain conclusions. Piaget argued that an understanding of transitivity is characteristic of concrete operational thought.

formal operational stage The fourth and final Piagetian stage, which appears between the ages of 11 and 15; individuals move beyond concrete experiences and think in more abstract and logical ways.

hypothetical-deductive reasoning Piaget's formal operational concept that adolescents have the cognitive ability to develop hypotheses about ways to solve problems and can systematically deduce which is the best path to follow in solving the problem.

adolescent egocentrism The heightened self-consciousness of adolescents, which is reflected in adolescents' beliefs that others are as interested in them as they are themselves, and in adolescents' sense of personal uniqueness and invincibility.

imaginary audience That aspect of adolescent egocentrism that involves feeling that one is the center of attention and sensing that one is on stage.

personal fable The part of adolescent egocentrism that involves an adolescent's sense of personal uniqueness and invincibility.

on a table. The teacher then asks the students to order the sticks by length. Many young children end up with two or three small groups of "big" sticks or "little" sticks, rather than a correct ordering of all eight sticks. Another mistaken strategy they use is to evenly line up the tops of the sticks but ignore the bottoms. The concrete operational thinker who is capable of seriation simultaneously understands that each stick must be longer than the one that precedes it and shorter than the one that follows it.

Another aspect of reasoning about the relations between classes is **transitivity,** which is the ability to logically combine relations to reach certain conclusions. In this case, consider three sticks (A, B, and C) of differing lengths. A is the longest, B is intermediate in length, and C is the shortest. Does the child understand that, if A is longer than B and B is longer than C, then A is longer than C? In Piaget's theory, concrete operational thinkers who are capable of transitivity do; preoperational thinkers do not.

FORMAL OPERATIONAL STAGE

So far we have studied the first three of Piaget's stages of cognitive development: sensorimotor, preoperational, and concrete operational. What are the characteristics of the fourth and final stage?

The **formal operational stage,** which appears between 11 and 15 years of age, is the fourth and final Piagetian stage. In this stage, individuals move beyond concrete experiences and think in abstract and more logical ways. As part of thinking more abstractly, adolescents develop images of ideal circumstances. They might think about what an ideal parent is like and compare their parents to their ideal standards. They begin to entertain possibilities for the future and are fascinated with what they can become. In solving problems, formal operational thinkers are more systematic and use logical reasoning.

Abstract, Idealistic, and Logical Thinking   The abstract quality of the adolescent's thought at the formal operational level is evident in the adolescent's verbal problem-solving ability. Whereas the concrete operational thinker needs to see the concrete elements A, B, and C to be able to make the logical inference that if A = B and B = C, then A = C, the formal operational thinker can solve this problem merely through verbal presentation.

Another indication of the abstract quality of adolescents' thought is their increased tendency to think about thought itself. One adolescent commented, "I began thinking about why I was thinking about what I was. Then I began thinking about why I was thinking about what I was thinking about what I was." If this sounds abstract, it is, and it characterizes the adolescent's enhanced focus on thought and its abstract qualities.

Accompanying the abstract nature of formal operational thought in adolescence is thought full of idealism and possibilities. Although children frequently think in concrete ways, or in terms of what is real and limited, adolescents begin to engage in extended speculation about ideal characteristics—qualities they desire in themselves and in others. Such thoughts often lead adolescents to compare themselves with others in regard to such ideal standards. And the thoughts of adolescents are often fantasy flights into future possibilities. It is not unusual for the adolescent to become impatient with these newfound ideal standards and to become perplexed over which of many ideal standards to adopt.

As adolescents are learning to think more abstractly and idealistically, they are also learning to think more logically. Children are more likely to solve problems in a trial-and-error fashion. Adolescents begin to think more as a scientist thinks, devising plans to solve problems and systematically testing solutions. They use **hypothetical-deductive reasoning**—that is, they develop hypotheses, or best guesses, and systematically deduce (or conclude) which is the best path to follow in solving the problem.

Assimilation (incorporating new information into existing knowledge) dominates the initial development of formal operational thought, and these thinkers perceive the world subjectively and idealistically. Later in adolescence, as intellectual balance is restored, these individuals accommodate to the cognitive upheaval that has occurred (they adjust to the new information).

Some of Piaget's ideas on formal operational thought are being challenged, however (Byrnes, 2012; Reyna & Zayas, 2014). There is much more individual variation in formal operational thought than Piaget envisioned (Kuhn, 2009). Only about one in three young adolescents is a formal operational thinker. Many American adults never become formal operational thinkers, and neither do many adults in other cultures.

Adolescent Egocentrism

In addition to thinking more logically, abstractly, and idealistically—characteristics of Piaget's formal operational thought stage—in what other ways do adolescents change cognitively? David Elkind (1978) described how adolescent egocentrism governs the way that adolescents think about social matters. **Adolescent egocentrism** is the heightened self-consciousness of adolescents, which is reflected in their belief that others are as interested in them as they are themselves, and in their sense of personal uniqueness and invincibility. Elkind argued that adolescent egocentrism can be dissected into two types of social thinking—imaginary audience and personal fable.

The **imaginary audience** refers to the aspect of adolescent egocentrism that involves feeling that one is the center of everyone's attention and sensing that one is on stage. An adolescent boy might think that others are as aware as he is of a few hairs that are out of place. An adolescent girl walks into her classroom and thinks that all eyes are riveted on her complexion. Adolescents especially sense that they are "on stage" in early adolescence, believing they are the main actors and all others are the audience.

Might adolescents' ability to reason hypothetically and to evaluate what is ideal versus what is real lead them to engage in demonstrations such as this protest related to financial support for public education? What other causes might be attractive to adolescents' newfound cognitive abilities of hypothetical-deductive reasoning and idealistic thinking?
© Jim West/Alamy

According to Elkind, the **personal fable** is the part of adolescent egocentrism that involves an adolescent's sense of personal uniqueness and invincibility. Adolescents' sense of personal uniqueness makes them believe that no one can understand how they really feel. For example, an adolescent girl thinks that her mother cannot possibly sense the hurt she feels because her boyfriend has broken up with her. As part of their effort to retain a sense of personal uniqueness, adolescents might craft stories about themselves that are filled with fantasy, immersing themselves in a world that is far removed from reality. Personal fables frequently show up in adolescent diaries.

I check my look in the mirror. I wanna change my clothes, my hair, my face.

—Bruce Springsteen
Contemporary American rock star

One study of sixth- through twelfth-graders revealed that a sense of invincibility was linked to risky behaviors such as smoking cigarettes, drinking alcohol, and engaging in juvenile delinquency, whereas a sense of personal uniqueness was related to depression and suicidal thoughts (Aalsma, Lapsley, & Flannery, 2006). However, some research studies suggest that, rather than perceiving themselves to be invulnerable, many adolescents view themselves as vulnerable (Reyna & Rivers, 2008). For example, in a recent study, 12- to 18-year-olds were asked about their chances of dying in the next year and prior to age 20 (Fischoff & others, 2010). The adolescents greatly overestimated their chances of dying.

Some researchers have questioned the view that invulnerability is a unitary concept and argued rather that it consists of two dimensions (Duggan, Lapsley, & Norman, 2000; Lapsley & Hill, 2010):

· *Danger invulnerability,* which involves adolescents' sense of indestructibility and tendency to take on physical risks (driving recklessly at high speeds, for example)

· *Psychological invulnerability*, which captures an adolescent's felt invulnerability related to personal or psychological distress (getting one's feelings hurt, for example)

One study revealed that adolescents who scored high on a danger invulnerability scale were more likely to engage in juvenile delinquency or substance abuse, or to be depressed (Lapsley & Hill, 2010). In this study, adolescents who scored high on psychological invulnerability were less likely to be depressed, had higher self-esteem, and maintained better interpersonal relationships. In terms of psychological invulnerability, adolescents often benefit from the normal developmental challenges of exploring identity options, making new friends, asking someone to go out on a date, and learning a new skill. All of these important adolescent tasks involve risk and failure as an option but, if successful, result in enhanced self-image.

Many adolescent girls spend long hours in front of the mirror, depleting bottles of hair spray, tubes of lipstick, and jars of cosmetics. *How might this behavior be related to changes in adolescent cognitive and physical development?*
© Image Source/JupiterImages RF

Are Social Media an Amplification Tool for Adolescent Egocentrism?

Earlier generations of adolescents did not have social media to connect with large numbers of people; instead, they connected with fewer people, either in person or via telephone. Might today's teens be drawn to social media and its virtually unlimited friend base to express their imaginary audience and sense of uniqueness? A recent analysis concluded that amassing a large number of friends (audience) may help to validate adolescents' perception that their life is on stage and everyone is watching them (Psychster Inc, 2010). A look at a teen's home Twitter comments may suggest to many adults that what teens are reporting is often rather mundane and uninteresting as they update to the world at large what they are doing and having, such as: "Studying heavy. Not happy tonight." or "At Starbucks with Jesse. Lattes are great." Possibly for adolescents, though, such tweets are not trivial but rather an expression of the personal fable's sense of uniqueness. (Source: Psychster Inc, 2010).

A recent study of social networking sites found that the indiscriminate monologue communication from one to many, in which the diverse interests of others are not considered, that often occurs on such sites as Facebook may produce an egocentric tendency that undermines prosocial behavior (Chiou, Chen, & Liao, 2014).

What do you think? Are social media, such as Facebook and Twitter, amplifying the expression of adolescents' imaginary audience and personal fable sense of uniqueness?

In what ways might frequent use of social media, such as Facebook®, influence adolescents' cognitive development?
© Brendan O'Sullivan/Getty Images

Review Connect Reflect

 Discuss the key processes and four stages in Piaget's theory

Review

- What are the key processes in Piaget's theory of cognitive development? What are Piaget's four stages of cognitive development?
- What are the main characteristics of the sensorimotor stage?
- What are the main characteristics of the preoperational stage?
- What are the main characteristics of the concrete operational stage?
- What are the main characteristics of the formal operational stage?

Connect

- In this section, you read that by the age of 6 to 8 months infants have learned to perceive gravity and support. What aspects of physical development and perceptual/motor development occurring around this time frame might contribute to infants' exploration and understanding of these concepts?

Reflect *Your Own Personal Journey of Life*

- Do you consider yourself to be a formal operational thinker? Do you still sometimes feel like a concrete operational thinker? Give examples.

Piaget and Education

Evaluating Piaget's Theory

What are some applications of Piaget's theory to education? What are the main contributions and criticisms of Piaget's theory?

PIAGET AND EDUCATION

Piaget was not an educator, but he provided a sound conceptual framework for viewing learning and education. Here are some ideas in Piaget's theory that can be applied to teaching children (Elkind, 1976; Heuwinkel, 1996):

1. *Take a constructivist approach.* Piaget emphasized that children learn best when they are active and seek solutions for themselves. Piaget opposed teaching methods that treat children as passive receptacles for knowledge. The educational implication of Piaget's view is that, in all subjects, students learn best by making discoveries, reflecting on them, and discussing them, rather than by blindly imitating the teacher or doing things by rote.

2. *Facilitate rather than direct learning.* Effective teachers design situations that allow students to learn by doing. These situations promote students' thinking and discovery. Teachers listen, watch, and question students, to help them gain better understanding.

3. *Consider the child's knowledge and level of thinking.* Students do not come to class with empty minds. They have concepts of space, time, quantity, and causality. These ideas differ from the ideas of adults. Teachers need to interpret what a student is saying and respond in a way that is not too far from the student's level. Also, Piaget suggested that it is important to examine children's mistakes in thinking, not just what they get correct, to help guide them to a higher level of understanding.

4. *Promote the student's intellectual health.* When Piaget came to lecture in the United States, he was asked, "What can I do to get my child to a higher cognitive stage sooner?" He was asked this question so often here compared with other countries that he called it the American question. Piaget emphasized that children's learning should occur naturally. Children should not be pushed and pressured into achieving too much too early in their development, before they are maturationally ready. Some parents spend long hours every day holding up large flash cards with words on them to improve their baby's vocabulary. In the Piagetian view, this is not an effective way for infants to learn. It places too much emphasis on speeding up intellectual development, involves passive learning, and will not lead to positive outcomes.

5. *Turn the classroom into a setting of exploration and discovery.* What do actual classrooms look like when the teachers adopt Piaget's views? Several first- and second-grade math classrooms provide some good examples (Kamii, 1985, 1989). The teachers emphasize students' own exploration and discovery. The classrooms are less structured than we would expect in a typical classroom. Workbooks and predetermined assignments are not used. Rather, the teachers observe the students' interests and natural participation in activities to determine what the

What are some educational strategies that can be derived from Piaget's theory?
© Corbis RF

course of learning will be. For example, a math lesson might be constructed around counting the day's lunch money or dividing supplies among students. Often, games are prominently used in the classroom to stimulate mathematical thinking. For example, a version of dominoes teaches children about even-numbered combinations. A variation on tic-tac-toe involves replacing Xs and Os with numbers. Teachers encourage peer interaction during the lessons and games because students' different viewpoints can contribute to advances in thinking.

EVALUATING PIAGET'S THEORY

What were Piaget's main contributions? Has his theory withstood the test of time?

Piaget's Contributions   Piaget, the founder of the study of children's cognitive development, was a giant in the field of developmental psychology (Miller, 2011). Psychologists are indebted to him for devising a long list of masterful concepts of enduring power and fascination: assimilation, accommodation, object permanence, egocentrism, conservation, and others. Psychologists also owe him for instilling the current vision of children as active, constructive thinkers. And they have a debt to him for creating a theory that has generated a huge volume of research on children's cognitive development.

Piaget also was a genius when it came to observing children. His careful observations showed us inventive ways to discover how children act on and adapt to their world. Piaget pointed out some important things to look for in cognitive development, such as the shift from preoperational to concrete operational thinking. He also showed us how children need to make their experiences fit their schemes (cognitive frameworks) yet simultaneously adapt their schemes to fit their experiences. Piaget revealed that cognitive change is more likely to occur if the context is structured to allow gradual movement to the next higher level. Concepts do not emerge suddenly, full-blown, but instead develop through a series of partial accomplishments that lead to increasingly comprehensive understanding.

Criticisms of Piaget's Theory   Piaget's theory has not gone unchallenged (Miller, 2011). Questions are raised about estimates of children's competence at different developmental levels, stages, the training of children to reason at higher levels, and culture and education.

Estimates of Children's Competence   Researchers have found that some cognitive abilities emerge earlier than Piaget thought (Johnson & Hannon, 2015; Stiles & others, 2015). For example, as previously noted, some aspects of object permanence emerge earlier than he believed. Even 2-year-olds are nonegocentric in some contexts. When they realize that another person will not see an object, they investigate whether the person is blindfolded or looking in a different direction. Some understanding of the conservation of number has been demonstrated as early as age 3, although Piaget did not think it emerged until 7. Young children are not as uniformly "pre" this and "pre" that (precausal, preoperational) as Piaget thought.

Other cognitive abilities also can emerge later than Piaget thought (Kuhn, 2009, 2011). Many adolescents still think in concrete operational ways or are just beginning to master formal operations. Even many adults are not formal operational thinkers. In sum, recent theoretical revisions highlight more cognitive competencies of infants and young children and more cognitive shortcomings of adolescents and adults (Johnson & Hannon, 2015; Casey, 2015; Reyna & Zayas, 2014).

neo-Piagetians Developmentalists who have elaborated on Piaget's theory, emphasizing attention to children's strategies; information-processing speed; the task involved; and division of the problem into more precise, smaller steps.

Stages   Children's cognitive development is not as stage-like as Piaget envisioned (Muller & Kerns, 2015; Ricco, 2015). Because some cognitive abilities have been found to emerge earlier than Piaget thought, and others later, children do not appear to move cleanly from one stage to another. Other evidence casting doubt on the stage notion is that children often show more understanding on one task than on another similar task.

Effects of Training Some children who are at one cognitive stage (such as pre-operational) can be trained to reason at a higher cognitive stage (such as concrete operational). This discovery poses a problem for Piaget's theory. He argued that such training is only superficial and ineffective unless the child is at a maturational transition point between the stages (Gelman & Williams, 1998).

Culture and Education Culture and education exert stronger influences on children's development than Piaget maintained (Gauvain & Perez, 2015; Goodnow & Lawrence, 2015; Gonzalez Rey, 2014). For example, the age at which children acquire conservation skills is related to how much practice their culture provides in these skills. An outstanding teacher who provides instruction in the logic of math and science can promote concrete and formal operational thought.

An Alternative View **Neo-Piagetians** argue that Piaget got some things right but that his theory needs considerable revision. They give more emphasis to how children use attention, memory, and strategies to process information (Case, 1987, 1999). They especially stress that a more accurate portrayal of children's thinking requires attention to children's strategies and other cognitive skills, such as inhibition; the speed at which children process information; the specific task involved; and the division of problems into smaller, more precise steps (Borst & others, 2013; Siegler, 2015). In the chapter on "Information Processing," we further discuss these aspects of children's thought.

An outstanding teacher and education in the logic of science and mathematics are important cultural experiences that promote the development of operational thought. *Might Piaget have underestimated the roles of culture and schooling in children's cognitive development?*
© M & E Bernheim/Woodfin Camp & Associates

Review Connect Reflect

 LG2 Apply Piaget's theory to education, and evaluate Piaget's theory

Review
- How can Piaget's theory be applied to educating children?
- What are some key contributions and criticisms of Piaget's theory?

Connect
- When Piaget developed his theory, research on the development of the child's brain had not yet occurred. Based on the content in the chapter "Physical Development and Biological Aging," describe developmental changes in the brain that might serve as a foundation for the development of Piaget's stages.

Reflect *Your Own Personal Journey of Life*
- How might thinking in formal operational ways rather than concrete operational ways help students to develop better study skills?

3 Vygotsky's Theory of Cognitive Development

LG3 Identify the main concepts in Vygotsky's theory, and compare it with Piaget's theory

| The Zone of Proximal Development | Scaffolding | Language and Thought | Teaching Strategies | Evaluating Vygotsky's Theory |

Piaget's theory is a major developmental theory. Another developmental theory that focuses on children's cognition is Vygotsky's theory. Like Piaget, Lev Vygotsky emphasized that children actively construct their knowledge and understanding. In Piaget's theory, children develop ways of thinking and understanding by their actions and interactions with the physical world. In Vygotsky's theory, children are more often described as social creatures than

↑
Upper limit

Level of additional responsibility
child can accept with assistance
of an able instructor

**Zone of proximal
development (ZPD)**

Lower limit

Level of problem solving
reached on these tasks by
child working alone
↓

FIGURE 9

**VYGOTSKY'S ZONE OF PROXIMAL
DEVELOPMENT.** Vygotsky's zone of proximal
development has a lower limit and an upper
limit. Tasks in the ZPD are too difficult for the
child to perform alone. They require assistance
from an adult or a more-skilled child. As
children experience the verbal instruction or
demonstration, they organize the information
in their existing mental structures so they can
eventually perform the skill or task alone.
© Jose Luis Pelaez Inc./Blend Images/Getty Images RF

zone of proximal development (ZPD)
Vygotsky's term for tasks that are too difficult
for children to master alone but can be
mastered with guidance and assistance from
adults or more-skilled children.

scaffolding In cognitive development, a term
Vygotsky used to describe the changing
level of support over the course of a teaching
session, with the more-skilled person adjusting
guidance to fit the child's current performance
level.

in Piaget's theory. They develop their ways of thinking and understanding primarily through social interaction (Gonzalez Rey, 2014; Mahn & John-Steiner, 2013). Their cognitive development depends on the tools provided by society, and their minds are shaped by the cultural context in which they live (Gauvain & Perez, 2015).

We briefly described Vygotsky's theory in the chapter titled "Introduction." Here we take a closer look at his ideas about how children learn and his view of the role of language in cognitive development.

THE ZONE OF PROXIMAL DEVELOPMENT

Vygotsky's belief in the importance of social influences, especially instruction, to children's cognitive development is reflected in his concept of the zone of proximal development. **Zone of proximal development (ZPD)** is Vygotsky's term for the range of tasks that are too difficult for the child to master alone but that can be learned with guidance and assistance from adults or more-skilled children. Thus, the lower limit of the ZPD is the level of skill reached by the child working independently. The upper limit is the level of additional responsibility the child can accept with the assistance of an able instructor (see Figure 9). The ZPD captures the child's cognitive skills that are in the process of maturing and can be accomplished only with the assistance of a more-skilled person (Petrick-Steward, 2012). Vygotsky (1962) called these the "buds" or "flowers" of development, to distinguish them from the "fruits" of development, which the child already can accomplish independently.

What are some factors that can influence the effectiveness of the ZPD in children's learning and development? Factors that researchers have found that can enhance the ZPD's effectiveness include better emotion regulation, secure attachment, absence of maternal depression, and child compliance (Gauvain, 2013).

SCAFFOLDING

Closely linked to the idea of the ZPD is the concept of scaffolding. **Scaffolding** means changing the level of support. Over the course of a teaching session, a more-skilled person (a teacher or advanced peer) adjusts the amount of guidance to fit the child's current performance (Daniels, 2011). When the student is learning a new task, the skilled person may use direct instruction. As the student's competence increases, the person gives less guidance. A recent study found that scaffolding techniques that heightened engagement, encouraged direct exploration, and facilitated "sense-making," such as guided play, improved 4- to 5-year-old children's acquisition of geometric knowledge (Fisher & others, 2013).

Dialogue is an important tool of scaffolding in the zone of proximal development. Vygotsky viewed children as having rich but unsystematic, disorganized, and spontaneous concepts. In a dialogue, these concepts meet with the skilled helper's more systematic, logical, and rational concepts. As a result, the child's concepts become more systematic, logical, and rational. For example, a dialogue might take place between a teacher and a child when the teacher uses scaffolding to help a child understand a concept like "transportation."

LANGUAGE AND THOUGHT

The use of dialogue as a tool for scaffolding is only one example of the important role of language in a child's development. According to Vygotsky, children use speech not only for social communication but also to help them solve tasks. Vygotsky (1962) further believed that young children use language to plan, guide, and monitor their behavior. This use of language for self-regulation is called private speech (Alderson-Day & Fernyhough, 2014). For Piaget, private speech is egocentric and immature—but for Vygotsky, it is an important tool of thought during the early childhood years.

Vygotsky said that language and thought initially develop independently of each other and then merge. He emphasized that all mental functions have external, or social, origins. Children must use language to communicate with others before they can focus inward on their own thoughts. Children also must communicate externally and use language for a long period of time before they can make the transition from external to internal speech. This transition period occurs between 3 and 7 years of age and involves talking to oneself. After a while, the self-talk becomes second nature to children, and they can act without verbalizing; at this point, children have internalized their egocentric speech in the form of *inner speech*, which becomes their thoughts (Mercer, 2008).

Vygotsky held that children who use a lot of private speech are more socially competent than those who don't. He argued that private speech represents an early transition in becoming more socially communicative. For Vygotsky, when young children talk to themselves, they are using language to govern their behavior and guide themselves. For example, a child working on a puzzle might say to herself, "Which pieces should I put together first? I'll try those green ones first. Now I need some blue ones. No, that blue one doesn't fit there. I'll try it over here."

Piaget argued that self-talk is egocentric and reflects immaturity. However, researchers have found support for Vygotsky's view that private speech plays a positive role in children's development (Alderson-Day & Fernyhough, 2014). Researchers have found that children use private speech more often when tasks are difficult, when they have made errors, and when they are not sure how to proceed (Berk, 1994). They also have discovered that children who use private speech are more attentive and improve their performance more than children who do not use private speech (Berk & Spuhl, 1995).

Lev Vygotsky (1896–1934), shown here with his daughter, reasoned that children's cognitive development is advanced through social interaction with more-skilled individuals embedded in a sociocultural backdrop. *How is Vygotsky's theory different from Piaget's?*
Courtesy of James V. Wertsch, Washington University

TEACHING STRATEGIES

Vygotsky's theory has been embraced by many teachers and has been successfully applied to education (Costley, 2012; Gauvain, 2013; Gauvain & Perez, 2015). Here are some ways Vygotsky's theory can be incorporated in classrooms:

1. *Use the child's ZPD in teaching.* Teaching should begin near the zone's upper limit, so that the child can reach the goal with help and move to a higher level of skill and knowledge. Offer just enough assistance. You might ask, "What can I do to help you?" Or simply observe the child's intentions and attempts and provide support when needed. When the child hesitates, offer encouragement. And encourage the child to practice the skill. You may watch and appreciate the child's practice or offer support when the child forgets what to do.

2. *Use more-skilled peers as teachers.* Remember that it is not just adults who are important in helping children learn. Children also benefit from the support and guidance of more-skilled children.

3. *Monitor and encourage children's use of private speech.* Be aware of the developmental change from externally talking to oneself when solving a problem during the preschool years, to privately talking to oneself in the early elementary school years (Mercer, 2008). In the elementary school years, encourage children to internalize and self-regulate their talk to themselves.

4. *Place instruction in a meaningful context.* Educators today are moving away from abstract presentations of material, instead providing students with opportunities to experience learning in real-world settings. For example, instead of just memorizing math formulas, students work on math problems with real-world implications.

5. *Transform the classroom with Vygotskian ideas. Tools of the Mind* is an early childhood education curriculum that emphasizes children's development of self-regulation and the cognitive foundations of literacy (Shaheen, 2014). The curriculum was created by Elena Bodrova and Deborah Leong (2007) and has been implemented in more than 200 classrooms. Most of the children in the Tools of the Mind programs are at risk because of their living circumstances, which in many instances involve poverty and other difficult conditions such as being homeless and having parents with drug problems.

Tools of the Mind is grounded in Vygotsky's (1962) theory with special attention given to cultural tools and developing self-regulation, the zone of proximal development, scaffolding, private speech, shared activity,

How can Vygotsky's ideas be applied to educating children?
© BananaStock/PunchStock RF

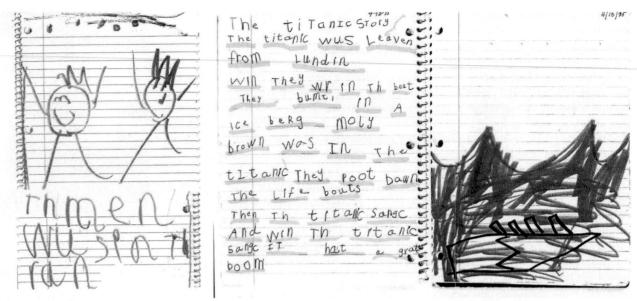

(a) Five-year-old Aaron's independent journal writing prior to using the scaffolded writing technique.

(b) Aaron's journal two months after using the scaffolded writing technique.

FIGURE 10

WRITING PROGRESS OF A 5-YEAR-OLD BOY OVER TWO MONTHS USING THE SCAFFOLDING WRITING PROCESS IN TOOLS OF THE MIND.

and play as important activity. In a Tools of the Mind classroom, dramatic play has a central role. Teachers guide children in creating themes that are based on the children's interests, such as treasure hunt, store, hospital, and restaurant. Teachers also incorporate field trips, visitor presentations, videos, and books in the development of children's play. In addition, they help children develop a play plan, which increases the maturity of their play. Play plans describe what the children expect to do in the play period, including the imaginary context, roles, and props to be used. The play plans increase the quality of children's play and self-regulation.

Scaffolding writing is another important theme in the Tools of the Mind classroom. Teachers guide children in planning their own message by drawing a line to stand for each word the child says. Children then repeat the message, pointing to each line as they say the word. Then, a child writes on the lines, trying to represent each word with some letters or symbols. Figure 10 shows how the scaffolding writing process improved a 5-year-old child's writing over the course of two months.

Research assessments of children's writing in Tools of the Mind classrooms revealed that children in the program have more advanced writing skills than children in other early childhood programs (Bodrova & Leong, 2007) (see Figure 10). For example, they write more complex messages, use more words, spell more accurately, show better letter recognition, and have a better understanding of the concept of a sentence.

Research also indicates that a Tools of the Mind early childhood curriculum improves children's executive function, such as their cognitive control (Diamond & others, 2007). In such interventions, children who are the most behind, including children from disadvantaged backgrounds, benefit the most from interventions, such as the Tools of the Mind curriculum (Diamond, 2013; Diamond & Lee, 2011).

EVALUATING VYGOTSKY'S THEORY

Even though their theories were proposed at about the same time, most of the world learned about Vygotsky's theory later than they learned about Piaget's theory, so Vygotsky's theory has not yet been evaluated as thoroughly. Vygotsky's view of the importance of sociocultural influences on children's development fits with the current belief that it is important to evaluate

	Vygotsky	**Piaget**
Sociocultural Context	Strong emphasis	Little emphasis
Constructivism	Social constructivist	Cognitive constructivist
Stages	No general stages of development proposed	Strong emphasis on stages (sensorimotor, preoperational, concrete operational, and formal operational)
Key Processes	Zone of proximal development, language, dialogue, tools of the culture	Schema, assimilation, accommodation, operations, conservation, classification
Role of Language	A major role; language plays a powerful role in shaping thought	Language has a minimal role; cognition primarily directs language
View on Education	Education plays a central role, helping children learn the tools of the culture	Education merely refines the child's cognitive skills that have already emerged
Teaching Implications	Teacher is a facilitator and guide, not a director; establish many opportunities for children to learn with the teacher and more-skilled peers	Also views teacher as a facilitator and guide, not a director; provide support for children to explore their world and discover knowledge

FIGURE **11**

COMPARISON OF VYGOTSKY'S AND PIAGET'S THEORIES

(Vygotsky): A.R. Lauria / Dr. Michael Cole, Laboratory of Human Cognition, University of California, San Diego; (Piaget): © Bettmann/Corbis

the contextual factors in learning (Gauvain & Perez, 2015; Elder, Shanahan, & Jennings, 2015; McBride Murry & others, 2015).

We already have considered several contrasts between Vygotsky's and Piaget's theories, such as Vygotsky's emphasis on the importance of private speech in development and Piaget's view that such speech is immature. Although both theories are constructivist, Vygotsky's is a **social constructivist approach,** which emphasizes the social contexts of learning and the construction of knowledge through social interaction (Shaheen, 2014; Van Hoorn & others, 2015).

In moving from Piaget to Vygotsky, the conceptual shift is from the individual to collaboration, social interaction, and sociocultural activity (Van Hoorn & others, 2015). The endpoint of cognitive development for Piaget is formal operational thought. For Vygotsky, the endpoint can differ, depending on which skills are considered to be the most important in a particular culture. For Piaget, children construct knowledge by transforming, organizing, and reorganizing previous knowledge. For Vygotsky, children construct knowledge through social interaction (Mahn & John-Steiner, 2013). The implication of Piaget's theory for teaching is that children need support to explore their world and discover knowledge. The main implication of Vygotsky's theory for teaching is that students need many opportunities to learn with the teacher and more-skilled peers. In both Piaget's and Vygotsky's theories, teachers serve as facilitators and guides, rather than as directors and molders of learning. Figure 11 compares Vygotsky's and Piaget's theories.

Criticisms of Vygotsky's theory also have surfaced. Some critics point out that Vygotsky was not specific enough about age-related changes. Another criticism focuses on Vygotsky not adequately describing how changes in socioemotional capabilities contribute to cognitive development (Goncu & Gauvain, 2012). Yet another criticism is that he overemphasized the role of language in thinking. Also, his emphasis on collaboration and guidance has potential pitfalls. Might facilitators be too helpful in some cases, as when a parent becomes overbearing and controlling? Further, some children might become lazy and expect help when they could have done something on their own.

developmental **connection**

Education

Whether to follow a constructivist or direct instruction approach is a major educational issue. Connect to "Schools, Achievement, and Work."

social constructivist approach An emphasis on the social contexts of learning and construction of knowledge through social interaction. Vygotsky's theory reflects this approach.

4 Cognitive Changes in Adulthood   **LG4** Describe cognitive changes in adulthood

| Piaget's View | Realistic and Pragmatic Thinking | Reflective and Relativistic Thinking | Cognition and Emotion | Is There a Fifth, Postformal Stage? | Are There Cognitive Stages in Middle and Late Adulthood? |

We have discussed the theories that Piaget and Vygotsky proposed to account for how the cognitive development of children proceeds. Neither, however, had much to say about cognitive development in adulthood. What do developmentalists know about changes in the way that adults think?

PIAGET'S VIEW

Recall that, according to Piaget, the formal operational stage of thought begins at 11 to 15 years of age. During this stage, the final one in Piaget's theory, thinking becomes more abstract, idealistic, and logical than the concrete operational thinking of 7- to 11-year-olds. Of course, young adults have more knowledge than adolescents. But, according to Piaget, adults and adolescents use the same type of reasoning. Adolescents and adults think in qualitatively the same way.

Many individuals don't reach the highest level of their formal operational thinking until adulthood. That is, though many individuals begin to plan and hypothesize about intellectual problems as adolescents, they become more systematic and sophisticated in applying these skills as young adults. Also, many adults do not think in formal operational ways (Keating, 2004).

REALISTIC AND PRAGMATIC THINKING

Some developmentalists propose that as young adults move into the world of work, their way of thinking does change. One idea is that as they face the constraints of reality that work promotes, their idealism decreases (Labouvie-Vief, 1986).

A related change in thinking was proposed by K. Warner Schaie (1977). He concluded that it is unlikely that adults go beyond the powerful methods of scientific thinking characteristic of the formal operational stage. However, Schaie argued that adults do progress beyond adolescents in their use of intellect. For example, in early adulthood individuals often switch from acquiring knowledge to applying knowledge as they pursue success in their work.

REFLECTIVE AND RELATIVISTIC THINKING

William Perry (1970) also described changes in cognition that take place in early adulthood. He said that adolescents often view the world in terms of polarities—right/wrong, we/they, or good/bad. As youth age into adulthood, they gradually move away from this type of absolutist thinking as they become aware of the diverse opinions and multiple perspectives of others. Thus, in Perry's view, the absolutist, dualistic thinking of adolescence gives way to the reflective, relativistic thinking of adulthood. Other developmentalists also argue that reflective thinking is an important indicator of cognitive change in young adults (Mascalo & Fischer, 2010).

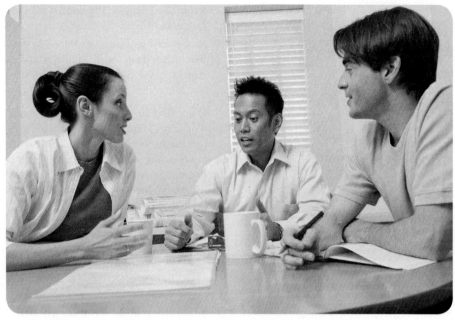

How might emerging and young adults think differently from adolescents?
© Circlestock/Corbis RF

COGNITION AND EMOTION

Gisela Labouvie-Vief and her colleagues (Labouvie-Vief, 2009; Labouvie-Vief, Gruhn, & Studer, 2010) also argue that to understand cognitive changes in adulthood it is necessary to consider how emotional maturity might affect cognitive development. They conclude that although emerging and young adults become more aware that emotions influence their thinking, at this point thinking is often swayed too strongly by negative emotions that can produce distorted and self-serving conclusions. In their research, a subset of emerging adults who are high in empathy, flexibility, and autonomy are more likely to engage in complex, integrated cognitive-emotional thinking. Labouvie-Vief and her colleagues have found that the ability to think in this cognitively and emotionally balanced, advanced manner increases during middle adulthood. Further, they emphasize that in middle age, individuals become more inwardly reflective and less context-dependent in their thinking than they were as young adults. In the work of Labouvie-Vief and her colleagues, we see the effort to discover connections between cognitive and socioemotional development that is an increasing trend in the field of life-span development.

developmental **connection**
Cognitive Theory
Links between cognition and emotion are increasingly being studied. Connect to "Introduction" and "Emotional Development and Attachment."

IS THERE A FIFTH, POSTFORMAL STAGE?

Some theorists have pieced together these descriptions of adult thinking and have proposed that young adults move into a new qualitative stage of cognitive development, postformal thought (Sinnott, 2003). **Postformal thought** is described as follows:

· *Reflective, relativistic, and contextual.* As young adults engage in solving problems, they might think deeply about many aspects of work, politics, relationships, and other areas of life (Labouvie-Vief, 1986). They find that what might be the best solution to a problem at work (with a boss or co-worker) might not be the best solution at home (with a romantic partner). Thus, postformal thought holds that the correct answer to a problem requires reflective thinking and may vary from one situation to another. Some psychologists argue that reflective thinking continues to increase and becomes more internal and less contextual in middle age (Labouvie-Vief, Gruhn, & Studer, 2010; Mascalo & Fischer, 2010).

· *Provisional.* Many young adults also become more skeptical about what is presented as absolute truth and seem unwilling to accept an answer as final. Thus, they come to see the search for truth as an ongoing and perhaps never-ending process.

postformal thought Thinking that is reflective, relativistic, and contextual; provisional; realistic; and influenced by emotions.

What characterizes a possible fifth stage of cognitive development called postformal thought?
© Yuri Arcurs/Alamy RF

- *Realistic.* Young adults understand that thinking can't always be abstract. In many instances, it must be realistic and pragmatic.
- *Recognized as being influenced by emotion.* Emerging and young adults are more likely than adolescents to understand that their thinking is influenced by emotions. However, too often negative emotions produce thinking that is distorted and self-serving at this point in development.

One effort to assess postformal thinking is the 10-item Complex Postformal Thought Questionnaire (Sinnott & Johnson, 1997). Figure 12 presents the questionnaire and gives you an opportunity to evaluate your thinking at the postformal level. A recent study found that the questionnaire items reflect three main categories of postformal thinking: (1) taking into account multiple aspects of a problem or situation; (2) making a subjective choice regarding a particular problem or situation; and (3) perceiving underlying complexities in a situation (Cartwright & others, 2009).

A study using the Complex Postformal Thought Questionnaire revealed that college students who had more cross-category friends (based on categories of gender, age, ethnicity, socioeconomic status, and sexual orientation) scored higher on the postformal thought measure than their counterparts who had fewer cross-category friends (Galupo, Cartwright, & Savage, 2010). Cross-category friendships likely stimulate individuals to move beyond either/or thinking, critically evaluate stereotypical thinking, and consider alternative explanations.

How strong is the evidence for a fifth, postformal stage of cognitive development? Researchers have found that young adults are more likely to engage in postformal thinking than adolescents are (Commons & Richards, 2003; Commons & others, 1989). But critics argue that research has yet to document that postformal thought is a qualitatively more advanced stage than formal operational thought.

Respond to each of the items below in terms of how well they characterize your thinking from 1 = Not True (of Self) to 7 = Very True (of Self).	Not True						Very True
	1	2	3	4	5	6	7
1. I see the paradoxes in life.							
2. I see more than one method that can be used to reach a goal.							
3. I am aware that I can decide which reality to experience at a particular time; but I know that reality is really multi-level and more complicated.							
4. There are many "right" ways to define any life experience; I must make a final decision on how I define the problems of life.							
5. I am aware that sometimes "succeeding" in the everyday world means finding a concrete answer to one of life's problems; but sometimes it means finding a correct path that would carry me through any problems of this type.							
6. Almost all problems can be solved by logic, but this may require different types of "logics."							
7. I tend to see several causes connected with any event.							
8. I see that a given dilemma always has several good solutions.							
9. I realize that I often have several goals in mind, or that life seems to have several goals in mind for me. So I go toward more than one in following my path in life.							
10. I can see the hidden logic in others' solutions to the problems of life, even if I don't agree with their solutions and follow my own path.							

FIGURE 12

COMPLEX POSTFORMAL THOUGHT QUESTIONNAIRE. After you have responded to the items, total your score, which can range from 10 to 70. The higher your score, the more likely you are to engage in postformal thinking.

ARE THERE COGNITIVE STAGES IN MIDDLE AND LATE ADULTHOOD?

Adult cognitive stages per se have not been proposed beyond the postformal fifth stage we just discussed. And for the middle and late adulthood periods of development there has been little discussion of what the contents of those stages might be like.

What are some changes in cognitive development that would provide some of the content of a stage-like description of what takes place during middle and late adulthood? Rather than qualitative stage descriptions of cognitive changes in middle and late adulthood, some gradual, quantitative cognitive changes have been proposed and studied. These include fluid and crystallized intelligence, and cognitive mechanics and cognitive pragmatics.

- *Fluid and Crystallized Intelligence. Fluid intelligence,* the person's ability to reason abstractly, has been theorized to decrease in middle and late adulthood (Horn & Donaldson, 1980). *Crystallized intelligence,* the individual's accumulated information and verbal skills, has been proposed to increase during middle and late adulthood.
- *Cognitive Mechanics and Cognitive Pragmatics. Cognitive mechanics,* linked to biological foundations and brain development, have been hypothesized to decline in middle and late adulthood. Cognitive processes that are components of cognitive mechanics include processing speed, attention, and some aspects of memory. *Cognitive pragmatics,* which are associated with experience and culture, have been proposed to increase during middle and late adulthood. Components of cognitive pragmatics include reading and writing skills, language comprehension, professional skills, and wisdom.

The overlap between fluid intelligence and cognitive mechanics, and the similarities between crystallized intelligence and cognitive pragmatics, have been recognized with the creation of the labels *fluid mechanics* and *crystallized pragmatics* (Lovden & Lindenberger, 2007).

The combination of multiple cognitive processes and abilities in an age-related manner takes on the characteristics of a stage-like description. However, as indicated earlier, at this point a stage of fluid mechanics and crystallized intelligence has not been proposed. Further discussion of these aspects of cognitive development is highlighted in the chapter on "Intelligence."

Current theory and research on changes in adult cognitive development mainly focuses on specific aspects of information processing, such as attention, memory, and thinking, but not on stages of development (Bailey, Dunlosky, & Hertzog, 2014; Borges, Radanovic, & Forienza, 2015; Pierce & Andersen, 2014; Pulopulos & others, 2015). In the chapter on "Information Processing" you will read about these specific cognitive processes and how they change during various stages of development.

developmental **connection**

Life-Span Perspective

How might wisdom change as individuals go through the adult years? Connect to "Intelligence."

developmental **connection**

Memory

How does memory change in middle and late adulthood? Connect to "Information Processing."

Review *Connect* Reflect

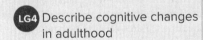 Describe cognitive changes in adulthood

Review

- What is Piaget's view of adult cognitive development?
- Do young adults retain the idealism of the formal operational stage?
- What is Perry's view on cognitive changes from adolescence to adulthood?
- What role does emotion play in cognitive changes in emerging and early adulthood?
- What characteristics have been proposed for a fifth, postformal stage of cognitive development?
- Are there cognitive stages in middle and late adulthood?

Connect

- What does Piaget's view of adult cognitive development have in common with his views about cognitive development in adolescence?

Reflect *Your Own Personal Journey of Life*

- If you are an emerging adult (18 to 25 years of age), what do you think are the most important cognitive changes that have taken place so far in this transition period in your life between adolescence and early adulthood? If you are older, reflect on your emerging adult years and describe what cognitive changes occurred during this time.

Cognitive Developmental Approaches

1 Piaget's Theory of Cognitive Development

LG1 Discuss the key processes and four stages in Piaget's theory

Processes of Development

- In Piaget's theory, children construct their own cognitive worlds, building mental structures to adapt to their world. Schemes are actions or mental representations that organize knowledge. Behavioral schemes (physical activities) characterize infancy, whereas mental schemes (cognitive activities) develop in childhood. Adaptation involves assimilation and accommodation. Assimilation occurs when children use existing schemes to deal with new information. Accommodation happens when children adjust their schemes to account for new information and experiences. Through organization, children group isolated behaviors into a higher-order, more smoothly functioning cognitive system. Equilibration is a mechanism Piaget proposed to explain how children shift from one cognitive stage to the next. As children experience cognitive conflict in trying to understand the world, they seek equilibrium. The result is equilibration, which brings the child to a new stage of thought. According to Piaget, there are four qualitatively different stages of thought: sensorimotor, preoperational, concrete operational, and formal operational.

Sensorimotor Stage

- In sensorimotor thought, the first of Piaget's four stages, the infant organizes and coordinates sensations with physical movements. The stage lasts from birth to about 2 years of age. Sensorimotor thought has six substages: simple reflexes; first habits and primary circular reactions; secondary circular reactions; coordination of secondary circular reactions; tertiary circular reactions, novelty, and curiosity; and internalization of schemes. One key aspect of this stage is object permanence, the ability of infants to understand that objects continue to exist even though they are no longer observing them. Another aspect involves infants' understanding of cause and effect. In the past several decades, revisions of Piaget's view have been proposed based on research. For example, researchers have found that a stable and differentiated perceptual world is established earlier than Piaget envisioned.

Preoperational Stage

- Preoperational thought is the beginning of the ability to reconstruct at the level of thought what has been established in behavior. It involves a transition from a primitive to a more sophisticated use of symbols. In preoperational thought, the child does not yet think in an operational way. The symbolic function substage occurs roughly from 2 to 4 years of age and is characterized by symbolic thought, egocentrism, and animism. The intuitive thought substage stretches from about 4 to 7 years of age. It is called intuitive because children seem sure about their knowledge yet are unaware of how they know what they know. The preoperational child lacks conservation and asks a barrage of questions.

Concrete Operational Stage

- Concrete operational thought occurs roughly from 7 to 11 years of age. During this stage, children can perform concrete operations, think logically about concrete objects, classify things, and reason about relationships among classes of things. Concrete thought is not as abstract as formal operational thought.

Formal Operational Stage

- Formal operational thought appears between 11 and 15 years of age. Formal operational thought is more abstract, idealistic, and logical than concrete operational thought. Piaget argues that adolescents become capable of engaging in hypothetical-deductive reasoning. But Piaget did not give adequate attention to individual variation in adolescent thinking. Many young adolescents do not think in hypothetical-deductive ways but rather are consolidating their concrete operational thinking. In addition, adolescents develop a special kind of egocentrism that involves an imaginary audience and a personal fable about being unique and invulnerable.

2 Applying and Evaluating Piaget's Theory

 Apply Piaget's theory to education, and evaluate Piaget's theory

Piaget and Education

- Piaget was not an educator, but his constructivist views have been applied to teaching. These applications include an emphasis on facilitating rather than directing learning, considering the child's level of knowledge, using ongoing assessment, promoting the student's intellectual health, and turning the classroom into a setting for exploration and discovery.

Evaluating Piaget's Theory

- We are indebted to Piaget for establishing the field of cognitive development. He was a genius at observing children, and he gave us a number of masterful concepts. Critics, however, question his estimates of competence at different developmental levels, his stage concept, and other ideas. Neo-Piagetians emphasize the importance of information processing.

3 Vygotsky's Theory of Cognitive Development

 Identify the main concepts in Vygotsky's theory, and compare it with Piaget's theory

The Zone of Proximal Development

- Zone of proximal development (ZPD) is Vygotsky's term for the range of tasks that are too difficult for children to master alone but that can be learned with the guidance and assistance of more-skilled adults and peers.

Scaffolding

- Scaffolding is a teaching technique in which a more-skilled person adjusts the level of guidance to fit the child's current performance level. Dialogue is an important aspect of scaffolding.

Language and Thought

- Vygotsky argued that language plays a key role in cognition. Language and thought initially develop independently, but then children internalize their egocentric speech in the form of inner speech, which becomes their thoughts. This transition to inner speech occurs between 3 and 7 years of age. Vygotsky's view contrasts with Piaget's view that young children's self-talk is immature and egocentric.

Teaching Strategies

- Applications of Vygotsky's ideas to education include using the child's zone of proximal development and scaffolding, using more-skilled peers as teachers, monitoring and encouraging children's use of private speech, and accurately assessing the zone of proximal development. The *Tools of the Mind* curriculum reflects the Vygotskian approach. These practices can transform the classroom and establish a meaningful context for instruction.

Evaluating Vygotsky's Theory

- Like Piaget, Vygotsky emphasized that children actively construct their understanding of the world. Unlike Piaget, he did not propose stages of cognitive development, and he emphasized that children construct knowledge through social interaction. In Vygotsky's theory, children depend on tools provided by the culture, which determines which skills they will develop. Some critics say that Vygotsky overemphasized the role of language in thinking.

4 Cognitive Changes in Adulthood

 Describe cognitive changes in adulthood

Piaget's View

- Piaget said that formal operational thought, entered at 11 to 15 years of age, is the final cognitive stage, although adults are more knowledgeable than adolescents.

Realistic and Pragmatic Thinking

- Some experts argue that the idealism of Piaget's formal operational stage declines in young adults, being replaced by more realistic, pragmatic thinking.

Reflective and Relativistic Thinking

- Perry said that adolescents often engage in dualistic, absolutist thinking, whereas young adults are more likely to think reflectively and relativistically.

Cognition and Emotion

- Emerging and young adults become more aware that emotions influence their thinking. However, at this point in development, negative emotions often produce distorted and self-serving thinking that interferes with achieving an integrated, complex understanding of the link between cognition and emotion. Nonetheless, a subset of emotionally mature emerging and young adults achieve this understanding.

Is There a Fifth, Postformal Stage?

Are There Cognitive Stages in Middle and Late Adulthood?

· A fifth, postformal stage that has been proposed is postformal thought, which is reflective, relativistic, and contextual; provisional; realistic; and influenced by emotions.

· No cognitive stages per se have been proposed for middle and late adulthood, although the concepts of fluid mechanics and crystallized pragmatics take on stage-like characteristics. Theory and research today in adult cognitive development focuses mainly on specific aspects of information processing rather than on cognitive stages.

Key terms

A-not-B error
accommodation
adolescent egocentrism
animism
assimilation
centration
concrete operational stage
conservation

core knowledge approach
egocentrism
equilibration
formal operational stage
hypothetical-deductive reasoning
imaginary audience
intuitive thought substage
neo-Piagetians

object permanence
operations
organization
personal fable
postformal thought
preoperational stage
scaffolding
schemes

sensorimotor stage
seriation
social constructivist approach
symbolic function substage
transitivity
zone of proximal development (ZPD)

key people

Renée Baillargeon
Elena Bodrova
David Elkind
Rochel Gelman

Eleanor Gibson
Barbel Inhelder
Mark Johnson
Gisela Labouvie-Vief

Deborah Leong
William Perry
Jean Piaget
K. Warner Schaie

Elizabeth Spelke
Lev Vygotsky

INFORMATION PROCESSING

chapter **outline**

preview

What do people notice in their environment? What do they remember? And how do they think about it? Questions like these characterize the information-processing approach. Researchers who take this approach usually do not describe individuals as being in one stage of cognitive development or another. But they do describe and analyze how the speed of processing information, attention, memory, thinking, and metacognition change over time.

1 The Information-Processing Approach

LG1 Explain the information-processing approach and its application to development

The Information-Processing Approach and Its Application to Development

Speed of Processing Information

What are some of the basic ideas of the information-processing approach? How does information processing change as individuals develop? How important is speed of processing at various points in development?

THE INFORMATION-PROCESSING APPROACH AND ITS APPLICATION TO DEVELOPMENT

The *information-processing approach* analyzes how individuals encode information, manipulate it, monitor it, and create strategies for handling it (Siegler, 2006, 2012, 2013, 2015; Siegler & Lortie-Forgues, 2015; Siegler & others, 2015; Siegler & Thompson, 2014). This approach shares some characteristics with the theories of cognitive development discussed in the chapter on "Cognitive Developmental Approaches." Both those theories and the information-processing approach rejected the behavioral approach that dominated psychology during the first half of the twentieth century. The behaviorists argued that to explain behavior it is important to examine associations between stimuli and behavior. In contrast, the information-processing approach—like the theories of Piaget and Vygotsky—focuses on how people think.

Effective information processing involves attention, memory, and thinking (Howe, 2015; Ristic & Enns, 2015). Figure 1 is a basic, simplified representation of how information processing works; it omits a great deal and does not indicate the many routes that the flow of information takes. For example, the processes may overlap and not always go in the left-to-right direction indicated in the figure. A number of different processes may be involved in the way memory functions in processing information. The purpose of the model is to get you to begin thinking in a general way about how people process information. In subsequent sections, we consider details about the way people process information and how information processing changes throughout the life span.

Robert Siegler (2006, 2009, 2012, 2013, 2015) emphasizes that *mechanisms of change* play especially important roles in the advances children make in cognitive development. According to Siegler, three mechanisms work together to create changes in children's cognitive skills: encoding, automaticity, and strategy construction.

Encoding is the process by which information gets into memory. Changes in children's cognitive skills depend on increased skill at encoding relevant information and ignoring irrelevant information. For example, to a 4-year-old, an *s* in cursive writing has a shape very

developmental connection

Cognitive Theory

Piaget theorized that cognitive development occurs in four stages: sensorimotor, preoperational, concrete operational, and formal operational. Connect to "Cognitive Developmental Approaches."

developmental connection

Theories

In Skinner's behavioral view, it is external rewards and punishment that determine behavior, not thoughts. Connect to "Introduction."

encoding The process by which information gets into memory.

FIGURE 1

A BASIC, SIMPLIFIED MODEL OF INFORMATION PROCESSING

different from an *s* that is printed. But a 10-year-old has learned to encode the relevant fact that both are the letter *s* and to ignore the irrelevant differences in shape.

Automaticity refers to the ability to process information with little or no effort. Practice allows children to encode increasing amounts of information automatically. For example, once children have learned to read well, they do not think about each letter in a word as a letter; instead, they encode whole words. Once a task is automatic, it does not require conscious effort. As a result, as information processing becomes more automatic, we can complete tasks more quickly and handle more than one task at a time. If you did not encode words automatically but instead read this page by focusing your attention on each letter in each word, imagine how long it would take you to read it.

Strategy construction is the creation of new procedures for processing information. For example, children become more proficient readers when they develop the strategy of stopping periodically to take stock of what they have read so far.

In addition, Siegler (2006, 2012, 2013, 2015) argues that children's information processing is characterized by *self-modification*. That is, children learn to apply what they have learned in previous circumstances to adapt their responses to a new situation. Part of this self-modification draws on **metacognition,** which means "thinking about thinking or knowing about knowing" (Flavell, 2004; Jankowski & Holas, 2014). One example of metacognition is what children know about the best ways to remember what they have read. Do they know that they will be better able to remember what they have read if they can relate it to their own lives in some way? Thus, in Siegler's application of information processing to development, children play an active role in their own cognitive development.

Siegler (2006, 2015) also argues that the best way to understand how children learn is to observe them while they are learning. He emphasizes the importance of using the *microgenetic method* to obtain detailed information about processing mechanisms as they are occurring moment to moment. Siegler concludes that most research methods assess cognitive change indirectly, being more like snapshots than movies. The microgenetic method seeks to discover not just what children know but the cognitive processes involved in how they acquired the knowledge. A typical microgenetic study will be conducted across a number of trials assessed at various times over weeks or months (Miller, 2010). A number of microgenetic studies have focused on a specific aspect of academic learning, such as how children learn whole number arithmetic, fractions, and other areas of math (Siegler & others, 2013, 2015). Microgenetic studies also have been used to discover how children learn a particular issue in science or a key aspect of learning to read.

Strategies also have been the focus of a number of microgenetic investigations (Kuhn, 2013; Siegler, 2015). Using the microgenetic approach, researchers have shown that developing effective strategies doesn't occur abruptly but rather gradually. This research has found considerable variability in children's use of strategies, even revealing that they may use an incorrect strategy in solving a math problem for which they had used a correct strategy several trials earlier.

I think, therefore I am.

—RENÉ DESCARTES
Philosopher, 17th century

SPEED OF PROCESSING INFORMATION

A limitation on processing information is the speed at which it takes place. How quickly we process information often influences what we can do with that information. If you are trying to add up in your mind the cost of items you are buying at the grocery store, you need to be able to rapidly compute the sum before you have forgotten the prices of the individual items. Even in infancy, processing speed is important. For example, a longitudinal study found that 5-month-olds who were more efficient in processing information quickly had better higher-level cognitive functioning in the preschool years (Cuevas & Bell, 2014).

Researchers have devised a number of ways to assess processing speed. For example, processing speed can be assessed using a reaction-time task in which individuals are asked to push a button as soon as they see a stimulus such as a light. Or individuals might be asked to match numbers with symbols on a computer screen.

automaticity The ability to process information with little or no effort.

strategy construction Creation of new procedures for processing information.

metacognition Cognition about cognition, or "knowing about knowing."

Changes in Speed of Processing There is abundant evidence that the speed with which cognitive tasks are completed improves dramatically across the childhood years (Ferrer & others, 2013). Processing speed continues to improve in early adolescence (Kuhn, 2009). For example, in one study, 10-year-olds were approximately 1.8 times slower at processing

FIGURE 2

THE RELATION OF AGE TO REACTION TIME. In one study, the average reaction time began to slow in the forties, and this decline accelerated in the sixties and seventies (Salthouse, 1994). The task used to assess reaction time required individuals to match numbers with symbols on a computer screen.

information than young adults on such tasks as reaction time, letter matching, mental rotation, and abstract matching (Hale, 1990). Twelve-year-olds were approximately 1.5 times slower than young adults, but 15-year-olds processed information on the tasks as quickly as the young adults. Also, a study of 8- to 13-year-old children revealed that processing speed increased with age and, further, that the developmental change in processing speed preceded an increase in working memory capacity (Kail, 2007). A recent study of 9- to 14-year-olds also revealed that faster processing speed was linked to a higher level of oral reading fluency (Jacobson & others, 2011).

Does processing speed decline in adulthood? In K. Warner Schaie's (1996, 2012) Seattle Longitudinal Study, processing speed began declining in middle adulthood. As Figure 2 shows, the slowdown in processing speed continues into late adulthood (Salthouse, 2007, 2012). A recent meta-analysis was generally consistent with the graph shown in Figure 2 (Verhaeghen, 2013). The recent meta-analysis included data from childhood and adolescent studies of processing speed, which showed that processing speed improved from childhood through adolescence. Then processing speed began to slow down in the latter part of early adulthood, as indicated in Figure 2, and continued to decline thereafter through the remainder of the life span. In this analysis, age-related losses in processing speed were explained by a decline in neural connectivity or indirectly through changing levels of dopamine, or both (Verhaeghen, 2013). Also, a recent study revealed that age-related slowing of processing speed was linked to a breakdown in myelin in the brain (Lu & others, 2013).

Recent research indicates that processing speed is an important indicator of the ability of older adults to continue to effectively drive a vehicle (Edwards & others, 2010). A recent analysis of driving accidents revealed that approximately 50 percent of accidents in people over 50 years of age occur at intersections, compared with only about 23 percent for those under 50 years of age (Mischel, 2014). Intersections with yellow traffic lights posed difficulty for older adults, but when given advanced warning 1.5 seconds before the traffic light was about to change from green to yellow, they were less likely to have an accident. Further, one study revealed that older drivers who went through speed of processing training were less likely to stop driving (Edwards, Delahunt, & Mahncke, 2009).

In other research, a slowing of processing speed at baseline was linked to the emergence of dementia over the next 6 years (Welmer & others, 2014). Health and exercise can influence the extent to which processing speed declines (Hillman, Erickson, & Kramer, 2008; Leon & others, 2015). And a recent study found that 10 weeks of processing speed training improved the selective attention of older adults (O'Brien & others, 2013).

Does Processing Speed Matter?   How quickly individuals can process information through the life span is linked with their competence in many aspects of cognition (Hoyer, 2015; Tam & others, 2015). For example, how quickly children can articulate a series of words affects how many words they can remember.

For some tasks in everyday life, though, speed of processing information may not be important. In addition, the strategies that people learn through experience may compensate for some decline in processing speed with age. In general, however, speed is a very important aspect of processing information (Hoyer, 2015; Salthouse, 2012).

Review Connect Reflect

LG1 Explain the information-processing approach and its application to development

Review

- What is the information-processing approach, and how can it be applied to development?
- How does processing speed change developmentally?

Connect

- How are Piaget's theory and Vygotsky's theory similar to or different from the information-processing approach in explaining how individuals learn and think?

Reflect *Your Own Personal Journey of Life*

- The importance of strategies in processing information was discussed in the section you have just read. What strategies do you use to process information?

2 Attention LG2 Define attention and outline its developmental changes

What Is Attention?   Infancy   Childhood and Adolescence   Adulthood

The world holds a lot of information to perceive. Right now, you are perceiving the letters and words that make up this sentence. Now look at your surroundings and focus on something other than this book. After that, curl up the toes on your right foot. In each of these circumstances, you engaged in the process of paying attention. What is attention and what effect does it have? How does it change with age?

WHAT IS ATTENTION?

Attention is the focusing of mental resources. Attention improves cognitive processing for many tasks. At any one time, though, people can pay attention to only a limited amount of information.

Individuals can allocate their attention in different ways (Ellison & others, 2014; Ristic & Enns, 2015). Psychologists have labeled these types of allocation as selective attention, divided attention, sustained attention, and executive attention.

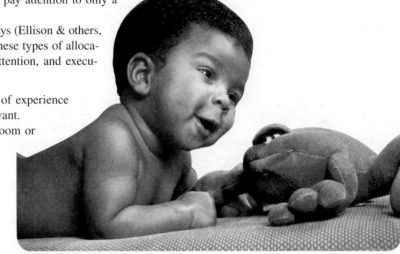

- **Selective attention** is focusing on a specific aspect of experience that is relevant while ignoring others that are irrelevant. Focusing on one voice among many in a crowded room or a noisy restaurant is an example of selective attention. When you switched your attention to the toes on your right foot, you were engaging in selective attention.
- **Divided attention** involves concentrating on more than one activity at the same time. If you are listening to music or the television while you are reading this chapter, you are engaging in divided attention.
- **Sustained attention** is the ability to maintain attention to a selected stimulus for a prolonged period of time. Sustained attention, which is also called vigilance, involves being on high alert for opportunity or danger as well as paying attention for a length of time.
- **Executive attention** involves planning actions, allocating attention to goals, detecting and compensating for errors, monitoring progress on tasks, and dealing with novel or difficult circumstances.

This young infant's attention is riveted on the blue toy frog that has just been placed in front of him. *What are some different types of attention?*
© Myrleen Pearson/PhotoEdit

INFANCY

How effectively can infants attend to something? Even newborns can detect a contour and fixate on it. Older infants scan patterns more thoroughly. By 4 months, infants can selectively attend to an object. Also, a recent study examined 7- and 8-month-old infants' visual attention to sequences of events that varied in complexity (Kidd, Piantadosi, & Aslin, 2012). The infants tended to look away from events that were overly simple or complex, preferring instead to attend to events of intermediate complexity. As the baby gets older, the preferred level of complexity likely would be greater, insuring that they are learning to process more complex information as they get older.

Orienting/Investigative Process   Attention in the first year of life is dominated by an *orienting/investigative process* (Columbo, Brez, & Curtindale, 2013). This process involves directing attention to potentially important locations in the environment (that is, *where*) and recognizing objects and their features (such as color and form) (that is, *what*). From 3 to 9 months of age, infants can deploy their attention more flexibly and quickly.

attention Focusing of mental resources.

selective attention Focusing on a specific aspect of experience that is relevant while ignoring others that are irrelevant.

divided attention Concentrating on more than one activity at the same time.

sustained attention The ability to maintain attention to a selected stimulus for a prolonged period of time.

executive attention Cognitive process involving planning actions, allocating attention to goals, detecting and compensating for errors, monitoring progress on tasks, and dealing with novel or difficult circumstances.

Habituation and Dishabituation   Closely linked with attention are the processes of habituation and dishabituation (Kavsek, 2013). If you say the same word or show the same toy to a baby several times in a row, the baby usually pays less attention to it each time. This is *habituation*—decreased responsiveness to a stimulus after repeated presentations of the stimulus. *Dishabituation* is the recovery of responsiveness after a change in stimulation.

Infants' attention is often linked to novelty and habituation (Columbo, Brez, & Curtindale, 2013). When an object becomes familiar, attention becomes shorter, making infants more vulnerable to distraction.

Knowing about habituation and dishabituation can help parents interact effectively with infants. Infants respond to changes in stimulation. Wise parents sense when an infant shows an interest and realize that they may have to repeat something many times for the infant to process information. But if the stimulation is repeated often, the infant stops responding to the parent. In parent-infant interaction, it is important for parents to do novel things and to repeat them often until the infant stops responding. The parent stops or changes behaviors when the infant redirects his or her attention (Rosenblith, 1992).

A mother and her infant daughter engaging in joint attention. *What about this photograph tells you that joint attention is occurring? Why is joint attention an important aspect of infant development?*
© XiXinXing/age fotostock RF

joint attention Focus by individuals on the same object or event; requires an ability to track another's behavior, one individual to direct another's attention, and reciprocal interaction.

Joint Attention   Another type of attention that is an important aspect of infant development is **joint attention,** in which two or more individuals focus on the same object or event. Joint attention requires (1) an ability to track another's behavior, such as following the gaze of someone; (2) one person directing another's attention; and (3) reciprocal interaction. Early in infancy, joint attention usually involves a caregiver pointing or using words to direct an infant's attention. Emerging forms of joint attention may occur as early as midway through the first year, but it is not until toward the end of the first year that joint attention skills are frequently observed (Kawai & others, 2010). In a study conducted by Rechele Brooks and Andrew Meltzoff (2005), at 10 to 11 months of age infants first began engaging in "gaze following," looking where another person has just looked (see Figure 3). And by their first birthday, infants have begun to direct adults' attention to objects that capture their interest (Heimann & others, 2006). A recent study also revealed that the extent to which 9-month-old infants engaged in joint attention was linked to their long-term memory (a one-week delay), possibly because joint attention enhances the relevance of attended items and improves encoding (Kopp & Lindenberger, 2012). And a recent study found that problems in joint attention as early as 8 months of age were linked to a child having been diagnosed with autism by 7 years of age (Veness & others, 2014).

Joint attention plays important roles in many aspects of infant development and considerably increases infants' ability to learn from other people (Brooks & Meltzoff, 2014;

(a)

(b)

FIGURE 3

GAZE FOLLOWING IN INFANCY. Researcher Rechele Brooks shifts her eyes from the infant to a toy in the foreground (*a*). The infant then follows her eye movement to the toy (*b*). Brooks and colleague Andrew Meltzoff (2005) found that infants begin to engage in this kind of behavior called "gaze following" at 10 to 11 months of age. *Why might gaze following be an important accomplishment for an infant?*
Courtesy of Dr. Andrew Meltzoff

Dunphy-Lelii & others, 2014). Nowhere is this more apparent than in observations of interchanges between caregivers and infants as infants are learning language (Tomasello, 2011). For example, a parent might point to a toy and say "ball." When caregivers and infants frequently engage in joint attention, infants say their first word earlier and develop a larger vocabulary (Beuker & others, 2013; Flom & Pick, 2003).

Joint attention skills in infancy also are associated with the development of self-regulation later in childhood. For example, a recent study revealed that responding to joint attention at 12 months of age was linked to self-regulation skills at 3 years of age that involved delaying gratification for an attractive object (Van Hecke & others, 2012).

CHILDHOOD AND ADOLESCENCE

The child's ability to pay attention improves significantly during the preschool years (Bell & Cuevas, 2014). Toddlers wander around, shift attention from one activity to another, and seem to spend little time focused on any one object or event. By comparison, the preschool child might be observed watching television for a half hour. However, one research study revealed that television watching and video game playing were both linked to attention problems in children (Swing & others, 2010). Young children especially make advances in two aspects of attention—executive attention and sustained attention. Also, research indicates that although older children and adolescents show increases in vigilance, it is during the preschool years that individuals show the greatest increase in vigilance (Rueda & Posner, 2013).

Mary Rothbart and Maria Gartstein (2008, p. 332) described why advances in executive and sustained attention are so important in early childhood:

> The development of the . . . executive attention system supports the rapid increases in effortful control in the toddler and preschool years. Increases in attention are due, in part, to advances in comprehension and language development. As children are better able to understand their environment, this increased appreciation of their surroundings helps them to sustain attention for longer periods of time.

In at least two ways, however, the preschool child's control of attention is still deficient:

· *Salient versus relevant dimensions.* Preschool children are likely to pay attention to stimuli that stand out, or are salient, even when those stimuli are not relevant to solving a problem or performing a task. For example, if a flashy, attractive clown presents the directions for solving a problem, preschool children are likely to pay more attention to the clown than to the directions. After the age of 6 or 7, children attend more efficiently to the dimensions of the task that are relevant, such as the directions for solving a problem. This change reflects a shift to cognitive control of attention, so that children act less impulsively and reflect more.

· *Planfulness.* Although in general young children's planning improves as part of advances in executive attention, when experimenters ask children to judge whether two complex pictures are the same, preschool children tend to use a haphazard comparison strategy, not examining all of the details before making a judgment. By comparison, elementary-school-age children are more likely to systematically compare the details across the pictures, one detail at a time (Vurpillot, 1968) (see Figure 4).

In Central European countries such as Hungary, kindergarten children participate in exercises designed to improve their attention (Mills & Mills, 2000; Posner & Rothbart, 2007a, b). For example, in one eye-contact exercise, the teacher sits in the center of a circle of children, and each child is required to catch the teacher's eye before being permitted to leave the group. In other exercises created to improve attention, teachers have children participate in stop-go activities during which they have to listen for a specific signal, such as a drumbeat or an exact number of rhythmic beats, before stopping the activity.

Computer exercises also recently have been developed to improve children's attention (Rueda & Posner, 2013; Stevens & Bavelier, 2012). For example, one study revealed that five days of computer exercises that involved learning how to use a joystick, draw upon working memory, and resolve conflicts improved the attention of 4- to 6-year-old children (Rueda, Posner, & Rothbart, 2005). In one of the computer games, young children have to move a joystick to keep a cat on the grass and out of the mud, and in another they help a cat find a duck in a pond. Although these games are not commercially available, further information

developmental **connection**

Brain Development

One shift in activation of the brain in middle and late childhood is from diffuse, large areas to more focused, smaller areas, which especially involves more focal activation in the prefrontal cortex. Connect to "Physical Development and Biological Aging."

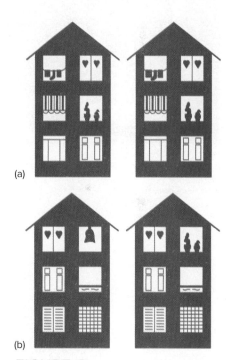

(a)

(b)

FIGURE 4

THE PLANFULNESS OF ATTENTION. In one study, children were given pairs of houses to examine, like the ones shown here (Vurpillot, 1968). For three pairs of houses, what was in the windows was identical (*a*). For the other three pairs, some of the windows had different items in them (*b*). By filming the reflection in the children's eyes, it could be determined what they were looking at, how long they looked, and the sequence of their eye movements. Children under 6 examined only a fragmentary portion of each display and made their judgments on the basis of insufficient information.

about computer exercises for improving children's attention is available at www.teach-the-brain.org/learn/attention/index.

How might good attentional skills benefit children's development? Preschool children's ability to control and sustain their attention is related to school readiness (Rothbart, 2011). For example, a study of more than 1,000 children revealed that their ability to sustain their attention at 54 months of age was linked to their school readiness (which included achievement and language skills) (NICHD Early Child Care Research Network, 2005). And in another study, the ability to focus attention better at age 5 was linked to a higher level of school achievement at age 9 (Razza, Martin, & Brooks-Gunn, 2012). Attention to relevant information increases steadily during the elementary and secondary school years (Davidson, 1996). Processing of irrelevant information decreases in adolescence.

Another important aspect of attention is the ability to shift it from one activity to another as needed. For example, writing a good story requires shifting attention among the competing tasks of forming letters, composing grammar, structuring paragraphs, and conveying the story as a whole. Older children and adolescents are better than younger children at tasks that require shifting attention.

developmental **connection**

Culture

In a recent survey, when media multitasking was taken into account, 11- to 14-year-olds spent nearly 12 hours a day using media. Connect to "Peers and the Sociocultural World."

Is multitasking, which involves divided attention, beneficial or distracting?
© Tim Hawley/Getty Images

One trend involving divided attention is adolescents' multitasking, which in some cases involves not just dividing attention between two activities, but even three or more (Bauerlein, 2008). A major factor that encourages multitasking is the availability of multiple electronic media. Many adolescents have a range of electronic media at their disposal. It is not unusual for adolescents to divide their attention by working on homework while engaging in an instant messaging conversation, surfing the Web, and listening to an iTunes playlist. And a national survey revealed that 50 percent of adolescents made and answered phone calls while driving, and 13 percent (approximately 1.7 million) wrote and/or read text messages while driving (Allstate Foundation, 2005).

Is this multitasking beneficial or distracting? If the key task is at all complex and challenging, such as trying to figure out how to solve a homework problem, multitasking considerably reduces attention to the key task (Myers, 2008).

Controlling attention is a key aspect of learning and thinking in adolescence and emerging adulthood (Rueda & Posner, 2013). Later in this chapter, we will further discuss some of the difficulties many adolescents encounter when faced with distractions that harm their attention.

ADULTHOOD

What happens to attention in adulthood? Attentional skills are often excellent in early adulthood and, of course, the discussion of divided attention and multitasking applies to many adults as well as adolescents. However, in many contexts older adults may not be able to focus on relevant information as effectively as younger adults (Gordon & others, 2015; Pierce & Andersen, 2014; Sylvain-Roy, Lungu, & Belleville, 2015). Older adults have more difficulty in attention that involves various aspects of driving, distraction, selective attention, and complex vigilance tasks. Let's examine research that documents declines in older adults' attention in these areas.

Consider a study that examined the role that visual attention, involving search, selection, and switching, played in the performance of older adult drivers (Richardson & Marottoli, 2003). Thirty-five community-dwelling drivers aged 72 and older (mean age, 80) underwent an on-road driving evaluation involving parking lot maneuvers and urban, suburban, and highway driving. They were also given tests of visual attention. The worse their driving, the lower their visual attention score was. Yielding right of way and negotiating safe turns or merges were especially related to visual attention.

developmental **connection**

Perception

Researchers study declines in the perceptual skills involved in older adults' driving performance. Connect to "Motor, Sensory, and Perceptual Development."

Might training sessions to improve older adults' attention be beneficial? A recent study revealed that older adults who participated in 20 one-hour video game training sessions with a commercially available program (Lumosity) showed a significant reduction in distraction and increased alertness (Mayas & others, 2014). The Lumosity program sessions focus on problem solving, mental calculation, working memory, and attention.

Older adults tend to be less adept at exercising selective attention—focusing on a specific aspect of experience while ignoring others—than younger adults are (Quigley & Muller, 2014). These age differences are minimal if the task involves a simple search (such as determining whether a target item is present on a computer screen) or if individuals have practiced the task (Kramer & Madden, 2008). As the demands on attention increase, however, the performance of older adults declines (Kramer & Madden, 2008). As long as two competing tasks are reasonably easy, age differences among adults are minimal or nonexistent. However, as competing tasks become more difficult, older adults divide attention less effectively than younger adults do (Maciokas & Crognale, 2003).

How well do older adults function on tasks that involve vigilance? On tests of simple vigilance and sustained attention, older adults usually perform as well as younger adults. For example, one study revealed that sustained attention increased in early adulthood but remained unchanged thereafter through 77 years of age (Carriere & others, 2010). However, on complex vigilance tasks, older adults' performance usually drops (Bucur & Madden, 2007).

Possibly, though, older adults' experience and wisdom might be able to offset some of their declines in vigilance. For example, consider how many young people intensely focus on their smartphone rather than looking at traffic when crossing a dangerous intersection.

What are some developmental changes in attention in adulthood?
© Digital Vision/PunchStock RF

Review Connect Reflect

 Define attention and outline its developmental changes

Review

- What is attention? What are three ways that people allocate their attention?
- How does attention develop in infancy?
- How does attention develop in childhood and adolescence?

Connect

- Relate the characteristics of the life-span perspective to what you have learned about attention and its developmental changes.

Reflect *Your Own Personal Journey of Life*

- Imagine that you are an elementary school teacher. Devise some strategies to help your students pay attention in class.

---

3 Memory   LG3 Describe what memory is and how it changes through the life span

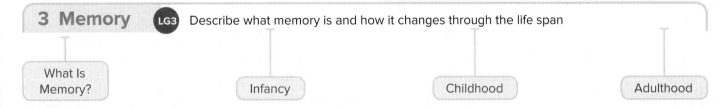

| What Is Memory? | Infancy | Childhood | Adulthood |

Twentieth-century American playwright Tennessee Williams once commented that life is all memory except for that one present moment that goes by so quickly that you can hardly catch it going. But just what is memory?

WHAT IS MEMORY?

Memory is the retention of information over time. Without memory you would not be able to connect what happened to you yesterday with what is going on in your life today. Human memory is truly remarkable when you think of how much information we put into our

memory Retention of information over time.

FIGURE **5**

PROCESSING INFORMATION IN
MEMORY. As you read about the many
aspects of memory in this chapter, think about
the organization of memory in terms of these
three main activities.

Encoding	Storage	Retrieval
Getting information into memory	Retaining information over time	Taking information out of storage

developmental **connection**

Gender

Gender schema theory emphasizes children's gender schemas that organize the
world in terms of male and female.
Connect to "Gender and Sexuality."

schema theory Theory stating that people
mold memories to fit information that already
exists in their minds.

schemas Mental frameworks that organize
concepts and information.

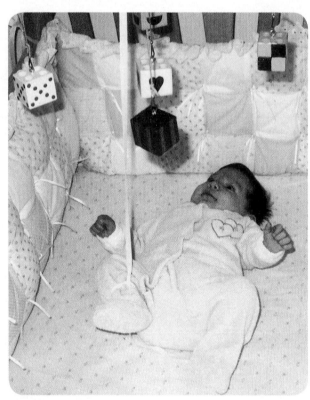

FIGURE **6**

THE TECHNIQUE USED IN ROVEE-COLLIER'S
INVESTIGATION OF INFANT MEMORY. In Rovee-Collier's
experiment, operant conditioning was used to demonstrate that
infants as young as 2½ months of age can retain information from
the experience of being conditioned.
Courtesy of Dr. Carolyn Rovee-Collier

memories and how much we must retrieve to perform all of life's activities. However, human
memory has imperfections that will be discussed shortly.

Processes of Memory   Researchers study how information is initially placed in or
encoded into memory, how it is retained or stored after being encoded, and how it is found
or retrieved for a certain purpose later (see Figure 5). Encoding, storage, and retrieval are the
basic processes required for memory. Failures can occur in any of these processes. Some part
of an event might not be encoded, the mental representation of the event might not be stored,
or even if the memory exists, the information may not be retrievable.

Constructing Memory   Memories may be inaccurate for a number of reasons. Memory
is not like a tape recorder or a camera or computer flash drive. People construct and reconstruct
their memories (Bauer, 2013; Howe, 2015). According to **schema theory,** people mold memories to fit information that already exists in their minds. This process is guided by **schemas,**
which are mental frameworks that organize concepts and information. Schemas influence the
way people encode, make inferences about, and retrieve information. Often when we retrieve
information, we fill in gaps.

We have schemas for all sorts of information. If a teacher tells your
class a story about two men and two women who were involved in a train
crash in France, students won't remember every detail of the story and will
reconstruct the story with their own particular stamp on it. One student might
reconstruct the story by saying that the people died in a plane crash, another
might describe three men and three women, another might say the crash was
in Germany, and so on. Such reconstruction and distortion are nowhere more
apparent than in clashing testimony given by eyewitnesses at trials.

In sum, schema theory accurately predicts that people don't store and
retrieve bits of data in computer-like fashion (van Kesteren & others,
2014). We reconstruct the past rather than take an exact photograph of it,
and the mind can distort an event as it encodes and stores impressions of
it (O'Neill & Csicsvari, 2014).

INFANCY

Popular child-rearing expert Penelope Leach (1990) told parents that 6- to
8-month-old babies cannot hold a picture of their mother or father in their
mind. However, child development researchers have revealed that newborns
and even fetuses show a limited type of memory.

First Memories   Carolyn Rovee-Collier (1987, 2007) has conducted
research that demonstrates infants can remember perceptual-motor information. In a characteristic experiment, she places a baby in a crib underneath
an elaborate mobile and ties one end of a ribbon to the baby's ankle and
the other end to the mobile. The baby kicks and makes the mobile move
(see Figure 6). Weeks later, the baby is returned to the crib, but its foot is
not tied to the mobile. The baby kicks, apparently trying to make the mobile
move. However, if the mobile's makeup is changed even slightly, the baby
doesn't kick. If the mobile is then restored to being exactly as it was when
the baby's ankle was tied to it, the baby will begin kicking again. According to Rovee-Collier, even at 2½ months the baby's memory is detailed.

How well can infants remember? Some researchers such as Rovee-Collier (2007; Rovee-Collier & Barr, 2010) have concluded that infants as young as 2 to 6 months of age can remember some experiences until they are 1½ to 2 years of age. However, critics such as Jean Mandler (2000), a leading expert on infant cognition, argue that the infants in Rovee-Collier's experiments are displaying only implicit memory. **Implicit memory** refers to memory without conscious recollection—memories of skills and routine procedures that are performed automatically. In contrast, **explicit memory** refers to the conscious recollection of facts and experiences.

When people think about memory, they are usually referring to explicit memory. Most researchers find that babies do not show explicit memory until the second half of the first year (Bauer & Fivush, 2014). Then explicit memory improves substantially during the second year of life (Lukowski & Bauer, 2014). In one longitudinal study, infants were assessed several times during their second year (Bauer & others, 2000). Older infants showed more accurate memory and required fewer prompts to demonstrate their memory than younger infants. Researchers have documented that 6-month-olds can remember information for 24 hours but by 20 months of age infants can remember information they encountered 12 months earlier.

In sum, most of young infants' conscious memories are fragile and short-lived, except for memory of perceptual-motor actions, which can be substantial (Mandler, 2000). Conscious memories improve across the second year of life (Bauer & Fivush, 2014).

What changes in the brain are linked to infants' memory development? From about 6 to 12 months of age, the maturation of the hippocampus and the surrounding cerebral cortex, especially the frontal lobes, makes the emergence of explicit memory possible (Mullally & Maguire, 2014; Nelson, 2013) (see Figure 7). Explicit memory continues to improve during the second year as these brain structures further mature and connections between them increase. Less is known about the areas of the brain involved in implicit memory in infancy.

Infantile Amnesia Do you remember your third birthday party? Probably not. Most adults can remember little if anything from their first three years of life (Callaghan, Li, & Richardson, 2014; Riggins, 2012). This is called infantile, or childhood, amnesia. The few reported adult memories of life at age 2 or 3 are at best very sketchy (Li, Callaghan, & Richardson, 2014).

Patrica Bauer and her colleagues (Bauer & Larkina, 2015; Pathman, Doydum, & Bauer, 2015) have been recently studying when infantile amnesia begins to occur. In one study, children's memory for events that occurred at 3 years of age was periodically assessed through age 9 (Bauer & Larkina, 2014). By 8 to 9 years of age, children's memory of events that occurred at 3 years of age began to significantly fade away.

What causes infantile amnesia? One reason for the difficulty older children and adults have in recalling events from their infancy is the immaturity of the hippocampus and prefrontal cortex—brain regions that play key roles in memory for events (Josselyn & Frankland, 2012).

CHILDHOOD

Children's memory improves considerably after infancy (Bauer & Fivush, 2014; Howe, 2015). What are some of the significant strides in memory as children grow older? The progress includes improvements in short-term and long-term memory, as well as the use of strategies.

Short-Term and Working Memory When people talk about memory, they are usually referring to **long-term memory,** which is relatively permanent and unlimited. When you remember the types of games you enjoyed playing as a child, details of your first date, or characteristics of the life-span perspective, you are drawing on your long-term memory. But when you remember the word you just read, you are using short-term memory.

Short-term memory involves retaining information for up to 30 seconds without rehearsal of the information. Using rehearsal, individuals can keep information in short-term memory longer (Yen, 2008).

Memory Span Unlike long-term memory, short-term memory has a very limited capacity. One method of assessing that capacity is the memory-span task. You simply hear a short

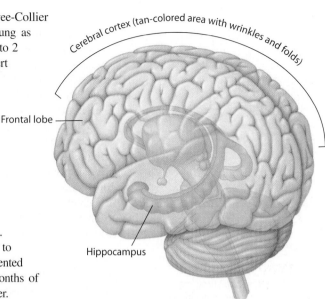

Cerebral cortex (tan-colored area with wrinkles and folds)

Frontal lobe

Hippocampus

FIGURE **7**

KEY BRAIN STRUCTURES INVOLVED IN EXPLICIT MEMORY DEVELOPMENT IN INFANCY

implicit memory Memory without conscious recollection—memory of skills and routine procedures that are performed automatically.

explicit memory Conscious memory of facts and experiences.

long-term memory A relatively permanent and unlimited type of memory.

short-term memory Retention of information for up to 15 to 30 seconds, without rehearsal of the information. Using rehearsal, individuals can keep the information in short-term memory longer.

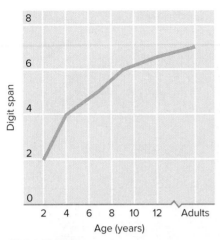

FIGURE 8

DEVELOPMENTAL CHANGES IN MEMORY SPAN. In one study, memory span increased by about three digits from 2 years to 7 years of age (Dempster, 1981). By 12 years of age, memory span had increased on average another one and a half digits.

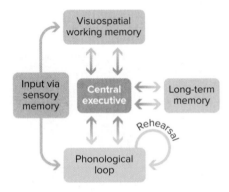

FIGURE 9

WORKING MEMORY. In Baddeley's working memory model, working memory is like a mental workbench where a great deal of information processing is carried out. Working memory consists of three main components. The phonological loop and visuospatial working memory serve as assistants, helping the central executive do its work. Input from sensory memory goes to the phonological loop, where information about speech is stored and rehearsal takes place, and visuospatial working memory, where visual and spatial information, including imagery, are stored. Working memory is a limited-capacity system, and information is stored there for only a brief time. Working memory interacts with long-term memory, using information from long-term memory in its work and transmitting information to long-term memory for longer storage.

working memory A mental "workbench" where individuals manipulate and assemble information when making decisions, solving problems, and comprehending written and spoken language.

list of stimuli—usually digits—presented at a rapid pace (one per second, for example). Then you are asked to repeat the digits.

Research with the memory-span task suggests that short-term memory increases during childhood. For example, in one investigation, memory span increased from about two digits in 2- to 3-year-old children to about five digits in 7-year-old children. Between 7 and 13 years of age, memory span increased only by one and a half digits (Dempster, 1981) (see Figure 8). Keep in mind, though, that individuals have different memory spans.

Why does memory span change with age? Rehearsal of information is important; older children rehearse the digits more than younger children do. Speed of processing information is important, too, especially the speed with which memory items can be identified. For example, one study tested children on their speed at repeating words presented orally (Case, Kurland, & Goldberg, 1982). Speed of repetition was a powerful predictor of memory span. The children who were able to quickly repeat the presented words were also far more likely to have greater memory spans. Indeed, when the speed of repetition was controlled, the 6-year-olds' memory spans were equal to those of young adults.

Working Memory   Short-term memory is like a passive storehouse with shelves to store information until it is moved to long-term memory. Alan Baddeley (1990, 2001, 2007, 2010a, b, 2012, 2013) defines **working memory** as a kind of mental "workbench" where individuals manipulate and assemble information when they make decisions, solve problems, and comprehend written and spoken language (see Figure 9). Working memory is described as more active and powerful in modifying information than short-term memory.

Working memory is linked to many aspects of children's development (Baddeley, 2013; Cowan, 2014; Mella & others, 2015; Reznick, 2014). For example, children who have better working memory are more advanced in reading comprehension, math skills, and problem solving than their counterparts with less effective working memory (Kroesbergen, van't Noordende, & Kolkman, 2014; Kudo, Lussier, & Swanson, 2015; Nevo & Breznitz, 2013).

The following three studies illustrate the importance of working memory in children's cognitive and language development:

·   A recent research review concluded that children with learning difficulties in reading and math have working memory deficits (Peng & Fuchs, 2015).
·   A computerized working memory intervention with 9- to 11-year-old children improved their reading performance (Loosli & others, 2012).
·   Assessment of working memory in kindergarten was a key process in predicting math achievement at the end of the first grade (Monette, Bigras, & Guay, 2011).
·   Working memory capacity at 9 to 10 years of age predicted foreign language comprehension two years later at 11 to 12 years of age (Andersson, 2010).

Children's Long-Term Memory   In contrast to short-term and working memory, *long-term memory* is relatively permanent type of memory that stores huge amounts of information for a long time. One aspect of long-term memory that has been extensively studied in children's development is autobiographical memory. Also, there has been considerable interest in children's memory in the courtroom when they are asked about eyewitness testimony.

Autobiograhical memory involves memory of significant events and experiences in one's life (Bauer & Larkina, 2015; Pathman, Doydum, & Bauer, 2015; Valentino & others, 2014). You are engaging in autobiographical memory when you answer questions such as: Who was your first grade teacher and what was s/he like? What is the most traumatic event that happened to you as a child?

Earlier we described the phenomenon of infantile amnesia, in which individuals can't remember anything from their first three years of life, and recent research indicating that these memories especially begin to fade by 8 to 9 years of age.

During the preschool years, young children's memories increasingly take on more autobiographical characteristics (Bauer, 2013; Miller, 2014). In some areas, such as remembering a story, a movie, a song, or an interesting event or experience, young children have been shown to have reasonably good memories. From 3 to 5 years of age, they (1) increasingly remember events as occurring at a specific time and location, such as "on my birthday at Chuck E. Cheese's last year" and (2) include more elements that are rich in detail in their narratives (Bauer, 2013). In one study, children went from using four descriptive items per event at 3½ years of age to 12 such items at 6 years of age (Fivush & Haden, 1997). Although the long-term memories of preschoolers can seem to be erratic at times, they can remember a great deal of information if they are given appropriate cues and prompts.

As children go through middle and late childhood, and through adolescence, their autobiographical narratives broaden and become more elaborated (Bauer, 2013). Researchers have found that children develop more detailed, coherent, and evaluative autobiographical memories when their mothers reminisce with them in elaborated and evaluative ways (Fivush, 2010).

Culture influences children's autobiographical memories (Nelson, 2014). American children, especially American girls, describe autobiographical narratives that are longer, more detailed, more specific, and more personal than narratives by children from China and Korea (Bauer, 2006, 2013). The pattern is consistent with their conversations about past events, in which American mothers and their children are more elaborative and more focused on themes related to being independent while Korean mothers and their children less often engage in detailed conversations about the past. Possibly the more elaborated content of American children's narratives contributes to the earlier first memories researchers have found in American adults (Han, Leichtman, & Wang, 1998).

Eyewitness Testimony One area in which children's long-term memory is being examined extensively relates to whether young children should be allowed to testify in court (Bruck & Ceci, 2013; Goodman, 2014). Increasingly, young children are being allowed to testify, especially if they are the only witnesses to abuse, a crime, and so forth (Bruck & Ceci, 2012, 2013; Goodman, 2014; Lamb & others, 2015).

Several factors influence the accuracy of a young child's memory (Bruck & Ceci, 1999):

- *There are age differences in children's susceptibility to suggestion.* Preschoolers are the most suggestible age group in comparison with older children and adults (Ceci, Papierno, & Kulkofsky, 2007). For example, preschool children are more susceptible to absorbing misleading or incorrect post-event information (Ghetti & Alexander, 2004). Despite these age differences, there is still concern about older children when they are subjected to suggestive interviews (Ahern & Lamb, 2015).

- *There are individual differences in susceptibility.* Some preschoolers are highly resistant to interviewers' suggestions, whereas others immediately succumb to the slightest suggestion (Sim & Lamb, 2015). A research review concluded that suggestibility is linked to low self-concept, low support from parents, and mothers' insecure attachment in romantic relationships (Bruck & Melnyk, 2004).

- *Interviewing techniques can produce substantial distortions in children's reports about highly salient events.* Children are suggestible not just about peripheral details but also about the central aspects of an event (Malloy & others, 2012). Their false claims have been found to persist for at least three months (Ornstein, Gordon, & Larus, 1992). Nonetheless, young children are capable of recalling much that is relevant about an event (Goodman, Batterman-Faunce, & Kenney, 1992). When children do accurately recall an event, the interviewer often has a neutral tone, there is limited use of misleading questions, and there is an absence of any motivation for the child to make a false report (Bruck & Ceci, 2013).

In sum, whether a young child's eyewitness testimony is accurate or not may depend on a number of factors such as the type, number, and intensity of the suggestive techniques the child has experienced (Goodman, 2014; Lamb & others, 2015). It appears that the reliability of young children's reports has as much to do with the skills and motivation of the interviewer as with any natural limitations on young children's memory (Bruck & Ceci, 2013).

Children's long-term memory improves even more as they move into the middle and late childhood years. This advance is especially true when they use the strategies that we describe next.

Strategies *Strategies* involve the use of mental activities to improve the processing of information (Friedman, 2014). For memory, rehearsing information and organizing are two typical strategies that older children (and adults) use to remember information more effectively. Rehearsal (repetition) works better for short-term memory. Strategies such as organization, elaborating on the information to be remembered, and making it personally relevant can make long-term memory more effective. Preschool children usually do not use strategies such as rehearsal and organization to remember (Flavell, Miller, & Miller, 2002).

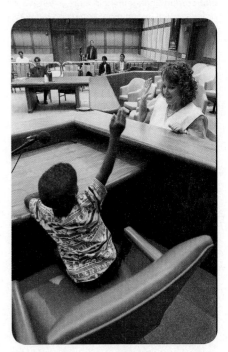

What are some conclusions from research on young children's ability to provide accurate eyewitness testimony?
© Buddy Norris/KRT/Newscom

Imagery Creating mental images is another strategy for improving memory. However, using imagery to remember verbal information works better for older children than for younger children (Schneider, 2011).

Elaboration One important strategy is **elaboration,** which involves engaging in more extensive processing of information. When individuals engage in elaboration, their memory benefits. Thinking of examples, especially those related to yourself, is an effective way to elaborate information. Thinking about personal associations with information makes the information more meaningful and helps children to remember it. For example, if the word *win* is on a list of words a child is asked to remember, the child might think of the last time she won a bicycle race.

The use of elaboration changes developmentally (Schneider, 2011). Adolescents are more likely than children to use elaboration spontaneously. Elementary school children can be taught to use elaboration strategies on a learning task, but they will be less likely than adolescents to use the strategies on other learning tasks in the future. Nonetheless, verbal elaboration can be an effective strategy even for young elementary school children.

Fuzzy Trace Theory One theory that emphasizes the reconstructive aspects of memory provides an alternative to strategies in explaining developmental changes in children's memory. Proposed by Charles Brainerd and Valerie Reyna (1993, 2004, 2014), **fuzzy trace theory** states that memory is best understood by considering two types of memory representations: (1) verbatim memory trace and (2) gist. The verbatim memory trace consists of the precise details of the information, whereas gist refers to the central idea of the information. When gist is used, fuzzy traces are built up. Although individuals of all ages extract gist, young children tend to store and retrieve verbatim traces. At some point during the early elementary school years, children begin to use gist more and, according to the theory, its use contributes to the improved memory and reasoning of older children because fuzzy traces are more enduring and less likely to be forgotten than verbatim traces (Brainerd & Reyna, 2014).

Knowledge An especially important influence on memory is the knowledge that individuals possess about a specific topic or skill (Staszewski, 2013). Knowledge influences what people notice and how they organize, represent, and interpret information. This skill, in turn, affects their ability to remember, reason, and solve problems.

One study found that 10- and 11-year-olds who were experienced chess players were able to remember more information about chess pieces than college students who were not chess players (Chi, 1978) (see Figure 10). In contrast, the college students were able to remember other stimuli better than the children were. Thus, the children's expertise in chess gave them superior memories, but only in chess. A key reason the child chess experts did better at this activity was their ability to organize (chunk) the chess pieces into meaningful subgroups based on their understanding of chess.

Teaching Strategies So far we have described several important strategies adults can adopt when guiding children to remember information more effectively over the long term. These

elaboration Engagement in more extensive processing of information, benefiting memory.

fuzzy trace theory Theory stating that memory is best understood by considering two types of memory representations: verbatim memory trace and gist. In this theory, older children's better memory is attributed to the fuzzy traces created by extracting the gist of information.

FIGURE 10
MEMORY FOR NUMBERS AND CHESS PIECES
© Tetra Images/Alamy RF

strategies include showing children how to organize information, how to elaborate the information, and how to develop images of the information. Another good strategy is to encourage children to understand the material that needs to be remembered rather than rotely memorizing it. Two other strategies adults can use to guide children's retention of memory were recently proposed:

- *Repeat with variation on the instructional information and link early and often.* These are memory development research expert Patricia Bauer's (2009) recommendations to improve children's consolidation and reconsolidation of the information they are learning. Variations on a lesson theme increase the number of associations in memory storage, and linking expands the network of associations in memory storage; both strategies expand the routes for retrieving information from storage.

- *Embed memory-relevant language when instructing children.* Teachers vary considerably in how much they use memory-relevant language that encourages students to remember information. In recent research that involved extensive observations of a number of first-grade teachers in the classroom, Peter Ornstein and his colleagues (Ornstein, Coffman, & Grammer, 2007; Ornstein, Grammer. & Coffman, 2010; Ornstein, Haden, & Coffman, 2010; Ornstein & others, 2010) found that in the time segments observed, the teachers rarely used strategy suggestions or metacognitive (thinking about thinking) questions. In this research, when lower-achieving students were placed in classrooms in which teachers were categorized as "high-mnemonic teachers" who frequently embedded memory-relevant information in their teaching, the students' achievement increased (Ornstein, Coffman, & Grammer, 2007).

ADULTHOOD

Memory changes during the adult years, but different aspects of memory are affected differently as adults age (Friedman, 2013; Kremen & others, 2014). Let's look first at working memory and processing speed.

Working Memory and Processing Speed   Two important cognitive resources that are linked with aging are working memory and processing speed (Nilsson & others, 2014). Remember that working memory is like a mental "workbench" that allows us to manipulate and assemble information (Baddeley, 2010a, b, 2012). Researchers have consistently found declines in working memory during late adulthood (Brockmole & Logie, 2013; Nyberg & others, 2012). A recent study revealed that working memory continued to decline from 65 to 89 years of age (Elliott & others, 2011). Another recent study found that visually encoded working memory was linked to older adults' mobility (Kawagoe & Sekiyama, 2014).

Is plasticity part of the working memory of older adults? A recent experimental study revealed that moderate exercise resulted in faster reaction time on a working memory task in older adults (Hogan, Mata, & Carstensen, 2013). Another study found that cognitive training improved older adults' working memory (Borella & others, 2013). Also, in a recent study, strategy training improved the working memory of older adults (Bailey, Dunlosky, & Hertzog, 2014). Thus, there appears to be some plasticity in the working memory of older adults.

Explanations of the decline in working memory in older adults focus on their less efficient inhibition in preventing irrelevant information from entering working memory and their increased distractibility (Healey & others, 2010). Declines in processing speed in middle and late adulthood may play a role in working memory decline as well (Hoogendam & others, 2014; Salthouse, 2013).

Explicit and Implicit Memory   Long-term memory systems include explicit and implicit memory. Recall that *explicit memory* refers to the conscious memory of facts and experiences. Explicit memory is also sometimes called *declarative memory*. Examples of explicit memory include being at a grocery store and remembering that you want to buy something or being able to recall the plot of a movie you have seen.

Recall that *implicit memory* refers to memory of skills and routine procedures that are performed automatically. (Implicit memory is sometimes referred to as procedural memory.) Examples of implicit memory include unconsciously remembering how to drive a car, swing a golf club, or type on a computer keyboard.

Explicit memory can be subdivided into episodic memory and semantic memory. **Episodic memory** is retention of information about the where and when of life's happenings.

episodic memory Retention of information about the where and when of life's happenings.

semantic memory A person's knowledge about the world, including fields of expertise, general academic knowledge, and "everyday knowledge" about meanings of words, names of famous individuals, important places, and common things.

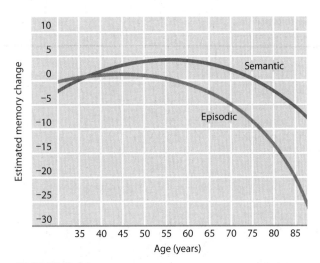

FIGURE 11

CHANGES IN EPISODIC AND SEMANTIC MEMORY IN ADULTHOOD

Prospective memory involves remembering to do something in the future. The older adult woman here is keeping track of what she plans to buy when she goes to a grocery store the next day.
© Image Source/Getty Images RF

source memory The ability to remember where something was learned.

For example, what color were the walls in your bedroom when you were a child? What did you eat for breakfast this morning? What were you doing when you heard that the World Trade Center had been destroyed on 9/11/2001?

Autobiographical memories are stored as episodic memories. A robust finding in autobiographical memory is called the *reminiscence bump,* in which adults remember more events from the second and third decades of their lives than from other decades (Berntsen & Rubin, 2002; Koppel & Bernsten, 2014; Steiner & others, 2014). The "bump" is found more for positive than negative life events. One study revealed support for the reminiscence bump and indicated that these memories were more distinct and more important for identity development (Demiray, Gulgoz, & Bluck, 2009).

Semantic memory is a person's knowledge about the world. It includes a person's fields of expertise (such as knowledge of chess, for a skilled chess player); general academic knowledge of the sort learned in school (such as knowledge of geometry); and "everyday knowledge" about meanings of words, famous individuals, important places, and common things (such as who Nelson Mandela and Mahatma Gandhi are).

Aging and Explicit Memory Younger adults have better episodic memory than older adults have (Ward, Berry, & Shanks, 2014). Does semantic memory decline with age? Older adults often take longer to retrieve semantic information, but usually they can ultimately retrieve it. As shown in Figure 11, semantic memory continues to increase through the fifties, showing little decline even through the sixties (Rönnlund & others, 2005). Figure 11 also shows how the gap between semantic and episodic memory widens during the middle and late adulthood years. In one study, after almost five decades adults identified pictures of their high school classmates with better than 70 percent accuracy (Bahrick, Bahrick, & Wittlinger, 1975). How well do most adults remember the actual subjects they learned in high school, however? In the *Connecting with Research* interlude, we focus on another study that examined the developmental aspects of semantic memory.

Although many aspects of semantic memory are reasonably well preserved in late adulthood, a common memory problem for older adults is the *tip-of-the-tongue (TOT) phenomenon,* in which individuals can't quite retrieve familiar information but have the feeling that they should be able to retrieve it (Salthouse & Mandell, 2013). Researchers have found that older adults are more likely to experience TOT states than younger adults (Bucur & Madden, 2007). A recent study of older adults found that the errors in memory they most commonly reported having had in the last 24 hours were those involving tip-of-the-tongue (Ossher, Flegal, & Lustig, 2012).

Aging and Implicit Memory Implicit memory is less likely than explicit memory to be adversely affected by aging (Kuo & others, 2014). Thus, older adults are more likely to forget which items they wanted to buy at the grocery store (unless they wrote them down on a list and took it with them) than they are to forget how to drive a car. Their processing speed may be slower when driving the car, but they can remember how to do it.

Further, Alzheimer's disease is characterized by the early onset of explicit memory deficits, while implicit memory is not affected until later stages of the disease (Boccia, Silveri, & Guariglia, 2014).

Source Memory **Source memory** is the ability to remember where one learned something. The contexts of source memory might be the physical setting, the emotional context, or the identity of the speaker. Failures of source memory increase with age in the adult years (Dulas & Duarte, 2014). Such failures can be embarrassing, as when an older adult forgets who told a joke and retells it to the source (El Haj & Allain, 2012). However, researchers have found that when information is more relevant to older adults, age differences in source memory are less robust (Hasher, 2003).

How Well Do Adults Remember What They Learned in High School and College Spanish?

When older adults are assessed for what they learned in high school or college, researchers find neither great durability in memory nor huge deterioration (Salthouse, 1991). In one study, non-Latino adults of various ages in the United States were studied to determine how much Spanish they remembered from classes they had taken in high school or college (Bahrick, 1984). The individuals chosen for the study had used Spanish very little since they initially learned it in high school or college. Not surprisingly, young adults who had taken Spanish classes within the last three years remembered their Spanish best. After that, the deterioration in memory was very gradual (see Figure 12). For example, older adults who had studied Spanish 50 years earlier remembered about 80 percent of what young adults did who had studied it in the last three years! The most important factor in the adults' memory of Spanish was not how long ago they had studied it but how well they initially learned it—those who got an A in Spanish 50 years earlier remembered more Spanish than those who got a C when taking Spanish only one year earlier.

What are some of the implications of the research on what adults remember from high school for improving teaching methods in U.S. schools?

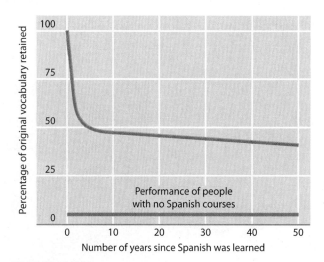

FIGURE 12

MEMORY FOR SPANISH AS A FUNCTION OF AGE SINCE SPANISH WAS LEARNED. An initial steep drop over about a three-year period in remembering the vocabulary learned in Spanish classes occurred. However, there was little drop-off in memory for Spanish vocabulary from three years after taking Spanish classes to 50 years after taking them. Even 50 years after taking Spanish classes, individuals still remembered almost 50 percent of the vocabulary they had learned.

Prospective Memory   **Prospective memory** involves remembering to do something in the future, such as remembering to take your medicine or remembering to do an errand (Mioni & others, 2015). Some researchers have found a decline in prospective memory with age (Kelly & others, 2012; Kennedy & others, 2015). However, a number of studies show that the cause of the decline is complex and involves factors such as the nature of the task and what is being assessed (Scullin, Bugg, & McDaniel, 2012). For example, age-related deficits occur more often in time-based tasks (such as remembering to call someone next Friday) than in event-based tasks (remembering to tell your friend to read a particular book the next time you see her).

prospective memory Remembering to do something in the future.

Review Connect Reflect

 Describe what memory is and how it changes through the life span

Review
- What is memory? What are memory's processes? What is involved in constructing memory? Can new information alter memories?
- How does memory develop in infancy?
- How does memory change in childhood?
- What are some changes in memory during the adult years?

Connect
- How might the changes in the brain during late adulthood be linked to the changes in memory in older adults that were just discussed?

Reflect *Your Own Personal Journey of Life*
- What is your earliest memory? Why do you think this particular situation was so memorable?

FIGURE 13

CATEGORIZATION IN 9- TO 11-MONTH-OLDS. These are the type of stimuli used in the study that indicated 9- to 11-month-old infants categorized birds as animals and airplanes as vehicles even though the objects were perceptually similar (Mandler & McDonough, 1993).

Infants are creating concepts and organizing their world into conceptual domains that will form the backbone of their thought throughout life.

—JEAN MANDLER

Contemporary developmental psychologist, University of California—San Diego

thinking Manipulating and transforming information in memory, in order to reason, reflect, think critically, evaluate ideas and solve problems, and make decisions.

concepts Cognitive groupings of similar objects, events, people, or ideas.

Attention and memory are often steps toward another level of information processing—thinking. What is thinking? How does it change developmentally? What is children's scientific thinking like? Let's explore these questions.

WHAT IS THINKING?

Thinking involves manipulating and transforming information in memory. We think in order to reason, reflect, evaluate ideas, solve problems, and make decisions.

INFANCY AND CHILDHOOD

To explore thinking in infancy and childhood, we ask questions like the following: To what extent do infants form concepts and engage in categorization? What is critical thinking and how can it be encouraged in schools? What is executive function and how does it change developmentally? What is children's scientific thinking like? How do children solve problems?

Concept Formation and Categorization in Infancy

Along with attention, memory, and imitation, concepts are key aspects of infants' cognitive development (Sloutsky, 2015). **Concepts** are cognitive groupings of similar objects, events, people, or ideas. Without concepts, you would see each object and event as unique and you would not be able to make any generalizations.

Do infants have concepts? Yes, they do, although we do not know just how early concept formation begins (Quinn, 2015). Using habituation experiments like those described earlier in the chapter, some researchers have found that infants as young as 3 to 4 months of age can group together objects with similar appearances, such as animals (Rakison & Lawson, 2013).

Jean Mandler (2010) argues that these early categorizations are best described as *perceptual categorization*. That is, the categorizations are based on similar perceptual features of objects, such as size, color, and movement, as well as parts of objects, such as legs for animals. Mandler (2004) concludes that it is not until about 7 to 9 months of age that infants form *conceptual* categories rather than just making perceptual discriminations between different categories. In one study of 9- to 11-month-olds, infants classified birds as animals and airplanes as vehicles even though the objects were perceptually similar—airplanes and birds with their wings spread (Mandler & McDonough, 1993) (see Figure 13).

In addition to infants categorizing items on the basis of external, perceptual features such as shape, color, and parts, they also may categorize items on the basis of prototypes, or averages, that they extract from the structural regularities of items (Rakison & Lawson, 2013).

Further advances in categorization occur during the second year of life (Rakison & Lawson, 2013). Many infants' "first concepts are broad and global in nature, such as 'animal' or 'indoor thing.' Gradually, over the first two years these broad concepts become more differentiated into concepts such as 'land animal,' then 'dog,' or to 'furniture,' then 'chair'" (Mandler, 2006, p. 1).

Learning to put things into the correct categories—knowing what makes something one kind of thing rather than another kind of thing, such as what makes a bird a bird, or a fish a fish—is an important aspect of learning. As infant development researcher Alison Gopnik (2010, p. 159) recently pointed out, "If you can sort the world into the right categories—put things in the right boxes—then you've got a big advance on understanding the world."

Do some very young children develop an intense, passionate interest in a specific category of objects or activities? A study of 11-month-old to 6-year-old children confirmed that they do (DeLoache, Simcock, & Macari, 2007). A striking finding was the large gender difference in categories—with an extremely intense interest in particular categories stronger for boys than girls. Categorization of boys' intense interests focused on vehicles, trains, machines, dinosaurs, and balls; girls' intense interests were more likely to involve dress-ups and books/reading (see Figure 14). By the time your author's grandson Alex was 2 years old, he already had developed an intense, passionate interest in the category of vehicles. He categorized vehicles into such subcategories as cars, trucks, earthmoving equipment, and buses. In addition to common classifications of cars into police cars, jeeps, taxis, and such, and trucks into fire trucks, dump trucks, and the like, his categorical knowledge of earthmoving equipment included bulldozers and excavators, and he categorized buses into school buses, London buses, and funky Malta buses (retro buses on the island of Malta). By 2½ years of age, Alex developed an intense, passionate interest in categorizing dinosaurs.

The author's grandson Alex at 2 years of age showing his intense, passionate interest in the category of vehicles while playing with a London taxi and a funky Malta bus.
Courtesy of Dr. John Santrock

In sum, the infant's advances in processing information—through attention, memory, and concept formation—is much richer, more gradual, and less stage-like, and occurs earlier than was envisioned by earlier theorists, such as Piaget (Bauer & Fivush, 2014; Johnson & Hannon, 2015; Ristic & Enns, 2015; Sloutsky, 2015). As leading infant researcher Jean Mandler (2004) concluded, "The human infant shows a remarkable degree of learning power and complexity in what is being learned and in the way it is represented" (p. 304).

Executive Function   Recently, increasing interest has surrounded the development of children's **executive function**, an umbrella-like concept that encompasses a number of higher-level cognitive processes linked to the development of the brain's prefrontal cortex. Executive function involves managing one's thoughts to engage in goal-directed behavior and exercise self-control (Carlson, Zelazo, & Faja, 2013). Earlier in this chapter, we described the recent interest in *executive attention*, which comes under the umbrella of executive function.

In early childhood, executive function especially involves developmental advances in cognitive inhibition (such as inhibiting a strong tendency that is incorrect), cognitive flexibility (such as shifting attention to another item or topic), goal-setting (such as sharing a toy or mastering a skill like catching a ball), and delay of gratification (the ability to forego an immediate pleasure or reward for a more desirable one later) (Bell & Cuevas, 2014; Carlson, Claxton, & Moses, 2015; Carlson & White, 2013). During early childhood, the relatively stimulus-driven toddler is transformed into a child capable of flexible, goal-directed problem solving that characterizes executive function (Zelazo & Muller, 2011). Figure 15 describes a research study on young children's executive function (Carlson & White, 2011).

Walter Mischel and his colleagues (Berman & others, 2013; Mischel, 2014; Mischel, Cantor, & Feldman, 1996; Mischel & Moore, 1980; Mischel & others, 2011; Schlam & others, 2013; Zayas, Mischel, & Pandey, 2014) have conducted a number of studies of delay of gratification with young children. The main way they assess delay of gratification is to place a young child alone in a room with an alluring marshmallow that is within their reach. The children are told that they either can ring a bell at any time and eat the marshmallow or they can wait until the experimenter returns and then get two marshmallows. For the young children who waited for the experimenter to return, what did they do to help them wait? They engaged in a number of strategies to distract their attention from the marshmallow, including singing songs, picking their noses—anything to keep from looking at the marshmallow. Mischel and his colleagues labeled these strategies "cool thoughts" (that is, doing non-marshmallow-related thoughts and activities), whereas they said the young children who looked at the marshmallow were engaging in "hot thoughts." The young children who engaged in cool thoughts were more

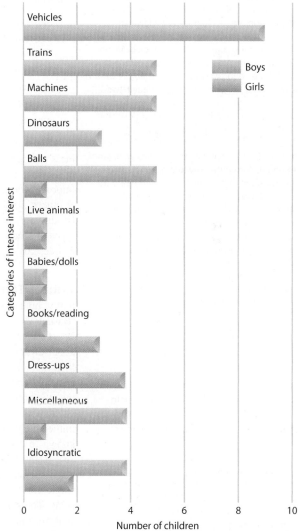

FIGURE 14

CATEGORIZATION OF BOYS' AND GIRLS' INTENSE INTERESTS

FIGURE 15

STUDYING EXECUTIVE FUNCTION IN YOUNG CHILDREN. Researcher Stephanie Carlson has conducted a number of research studies on young children's executive function. In one study, young children were read either *Planet Opposite*—a fantasy book in which everything is turned upside down—or *Fun Town*—a reality-oriented fiction book (Carlson & White, 2011). After being read one of the books, the young children completed the Less Is More Task, in which they were shown two trays of candy—one with 5 pieces, the other with 2—and told that the tray they pick will be given to the stuffed animal seated at the table. This task is difficult for 3-year-olds, who tend to pick up the tray that they themselves want (and so end up losing the tray to the stuffed animal). Sixty percent of the 3-year-olds who heard the *Planet Opposite* story selected the smaller number of candies (hence keeping the five pieces of candy) compared with only 20 percent of their counterparts who heard the more straightforward story. The results indicated that learning about a topsy-turvy imaginary world likely helped the young children become more flexible in their thinking.
© Dawn Villella Photography

- - - - - - - - - - ➤

developmental connection

Education

A criticism of the No Child Left Behind legislation is that it does not give adequate attention to the development of critical thinking skills. Connect to "Schools, Achievement, and Work."

executive function An umbrella-like concept that encompasses a number of higher-level cognitive processes linked to the development of the brain's prefrontal cortex. Executive function involves managing one's thoughts to engage in goal-directed behavior and to exercise self-control.

critical thinking Thinking reflectively and productively, and evaluating the evidence.

likely to eat the marshmallow later or wait until the experimenter returned to the room. In one study using the delay of gratification task just described, longer delay of gratification at 4 years of age was linked to a lower body mass index (BMI) three decades later (Schlam & others, 2013).

Parents and teachers play important roles in the development of executive function. A recent study revealed that sensitive parenting at 3 years of age predicted fewer executive function problems at 4 years of age (Kok & others, 2014). Ann Masten and her colleagues (Cuevas & others, 2014; Herbers & others, 2011; Masten, 2013, 2014a, b; Masten & others, 2008) have found that executive function and parenting skills are linked to homeless children's success in school. Masten believes that executive function and good parenting skills are related. In her words, "When we see kids with good executive function, we often see adults around them that are good self-regulators. . . . Parents model, they support, and they scaffold these skills" (Masten, 2012, p. 11).

Researchers have discovered that advances in executive function in the preschool years are linked with school readiness (Ursache, Blair, & Raver, 2012). A recent study revealed that executive function skills predicted mathematical gains in kindergarten (Fuhs & others, 2014).

How might executive function change in the middle and late childhood years and be linked to children's success in school? Adele Diamond and Kathleen Lee (2011) recently highlighted the following dimensions of executive function that they conclude are the most important for 4- to 11-year-old children's cognitive development and school success:

- *Self-control/inhibition.* Children need to develop self-control that will allow them to concentrate and persist on learning tasks, to inhibit their tendencies to repeat incorrect responses, and to resist the impulse to do something now that they later would regret.
- *Working memory.* Children need an effective working memory to effectively process the masses of information they will encounter as they go through school and beyond.
- *Flexibility.* Children need to be flexible in their thinking to consider different strategies and perspectives.

Some researchers have found that executive function is a better predictor of school readiness than general IQ (Blair & Razza, 2007). A number of diverse activities have been found to increase children's executive function, such as computerized training that uses games to improve working memory (CogMed, 2013), aerobic exercise (Chang & others, 2012; Hillman & others, 2014), scaffolding of self-regulation (the Tools of the Mind program is an example) (Bodrova, Leong, & Akhutina, 2011), mindfulness training (Zelazo & Lyons, 2012), and some types of school curricula (the Montessori curriculum, for example) (Diamond, 2013; Diamond & Lee, 2011).

Critical Thinking Executive function also involves being able to think critically. Currently, both psychologists and educators have shown considerable interest in critical thinking (Barnett & Francis, 2012; Sternberg & Sternberg, 2013).

Critical thinking involves grasping the deeper meaning of ideas, keeping an open mind about different approaches and perspectives, and deciding for oneself what to believe or do. In this book, the third part of the Review *Connect* Reflect sections challenges you to think critically about a topic or an issue related to the discussion. Thinking critically includes asking not only what happened, but how and why; examining supposed "facts" to determine whether there is evidence to support them; evaluating what other people say rather than immediately accepting it as the truth; and asking questions and speculating beyond what is known to create new ideas and acquire new information.

In the view of critics such as Jacqueline and Martin Brooks (1993, 2001), few schools teach students to think critically. Schools spend much more time getting students to give a single correct answer than encouraging them to come up with new ideas and rethink conclusions. Too often teachers ask students to recite, define, describe, state, and list rather than to analyze, infer, connect, synthesize, criticize, create, evaluate, think, and rethink. As a result, many schools graduate students who think superficially, staying on the surface of problems rather than becoming deeply engaged in meaningful thinking.

According to Ellen Langer (2005), *mindfulness*—being alert, mentally present, and cognitively flexible while going through life's everyday activities and tasks—is an important

Helen Hadani, Ph.D., Developmental Psychologist, Toy Designer, and Associate Director of Research for the Center for Childhood Creativity

Helen Hadani obtained a Ph.D. from Stanford University in developmental psychology. As a graduate student at Stanford, she worked part-time for Hasbro Toys and Apple testing children's software and computer products for young children. Her first job after graduate school was with Zowie Intertainment, which was subsequently bought by LEGO. In her work as a toy designer there, Helen conducted experiments and focus groups at different stages of a toy's development, and she also studied the age-effectiveness of each toy. In Helen's words, "Even in a toy's most primitive stage of development . . . you see children's creativity in responding to challenges, their satisfaction when a problem is solved or simply their delight in having fun" (Schlegel, 2000, p. 50).

More recently, she began working with the Bay Area Discovery Museum's Center for Childhood Creativity (CCC) in Sausalito, California, an education-focused think tank that pioneers new research, thought-leadership, and teacher training programs that advance creative thinking in all children. Helen is currently the Associate Director of Research for the CCC.

Helen Hadani has worked as both a toy designer and in a museum position that involves thinking of ways to increase children's creative thinking.
Courtesy of Helen Hadani

---

aspect of thinking critically. Mindful children and adults maintain an active awareness of the circumstances in their life and are motivated to find the best solutions to tasks. Mindful individuals create new ideas, are open to new information, and operate from multiple perspectives. By contrast, mindless individuals are entrapped in old ideas, engage in automatic behavior, and operate from a single perspective.

Recently, Robert Roeser and Philip Zelazo (2012) have emphasized that mindfulness is an important mental process that children can engage in to improve a number of cognitive and socioemotional skills, such as executive function, focused attention, emotion regulation, and empathy (Roeser & Zelazo, 2012). It has been proposed that mindfulness training could be implemented in schools through practices such as using age-appropriate activities that increase children's reflection on moment-to-moment experiences and result in improved self-regulation (Zelazo & Lyons, 2012).

In addition to mindfulness, activities such as yoga, meditation, and tai chi have been recently suggested as candidates for improving children's cognitive and socioemotional development (Roeser & Pinela, 2014). Together these activities are being grouped under the topic of *contemplative science*, a cross-disciplinary term that involves the study of how various types of mental and physical training might enhance children's development (Roeser & Zelazo, 2012).

To read about one developmental psychologist who used her training in cognitive development to pursue a career in an applied area, see the *Connecting with Careers* profile.

Scientific Thinking
Some aspects of thinking are specific to a particular domain, such as mathematics, science, or reading. We explore reading in the "Language Development" chapter. Here we examine scientific thinking by children.

Like scientists, children ask fundamental questions about reality and seek answers to problems that seem utterly trivial or unanswerable to other people (such as "Why is the sky blue?"). Do children generate hypotheses, perform experiments, and reach conclusions about their data in ways resembling those of scientists?

S. GROSS

"For God's sake, think!
Why is he being so nice to you?"
© Sam Gross/The New Yorker Collection/
www.cartoonbank.com.

developmental **connection**
Exercise

Recent research indicates that children who are more physically fit have better thinking skills, including those involving executive function, than less physically fit children. Connect to "Health."

Scientific reasoning often is aimed at identifying causal relations. Like scientists, children place a great deal of emphasis on causal mechanisms. Their understanding of how events are caused weighs more heavily in their causal inferences than even such strong influences as whether the cause happened immediately before the effect.

There also are important differences between the reasoning of children and the reasoning of scientists (Kuhn, 2011, 2013). Children are more influenced by happenstance events than by an overall pattern (Kuhn, 2011, 2013). Often, children maintain their old theories regardless of the evidence (Kuhn, Schauble, & Garcia-Mila, 1992).

Children might go through mental gymnastics trying to reconcile seemingly contradictory new information with their existing beliefs. For example, after learning about the solar system, children sometimes conclude that there are two earths—the seemingly flat world in which they live and the round ball floating in space that their teacher described.

Children also have difficulty designing experiments that can distinguish among alternative causes. Instead, they tend to bias the experiments in favor of whatever hypothesis they began with. Sometimes they see the results as supporting their original hypothesis even when the results directly contradict it. Thus, although there are important similarities between children and scientists in their basic curiosity and in the kinds of questions they ask, there are also important differences in the degree to which they can separate theory and evidence and in their ability to design conclusive experiments (Lehrer & Schauble, 2006).

Too often, the skills scientists use, such as careful observation, graphing, self-regulatory thinking, and knowing when and how to apply one's knowledge to solve problems, are not routinely taught in schools (Zembal-Saul, McNeill, & Hershberger, 2013). Children hold many concepts that are incompatible with science and reality. Good teachers perceive and understand a child's underlying scientific concepts, then use the concepts as a scaffold for learning. Effective science teaching helps children distinguish between fruitful errors and misconceptions, and detect plainly wrong ideas that need to be replaced by more accurate conceptions (Contant, Bass, & Carin, 2015).

It is important for teachers to at a minimum initially scaffold students' science learning, extensively monitor their progress, and ensure that they are learning science content (DeRosa & Abruscato, 2015). Thus, in pursuing science investigations, students need to "learn inquiry skills and science content" (Lehrer & Schauble, 2006).

Solving Problems   Children face many problems that they must solve in order to adapt effectively, both in school and out of school. Problem solving involves finding an appropriate way to attain a goal. Developing effective strategies is a key aspect of problem solving (McCormick, Dimmitt, & Sullivan, 2013).

In Michael Pressley's view (Pressley, 2003, 2007), the key to education is helping students learn a rich repertoire of strategies for solving problems. Good thinkers routinely use strategies and effective planning to solve problems. Pressley argues that when children are given instruction about effective strategies, they often can apply strategies that they had not used on their own. Pressley emphasizes that children benefit when their teacher models the appropriate strategy, verbalizes the steps in the strategy, and then guides the children to practice the strategy. Their practice is supported by the teacher's feedback until the children can effectively execute the strategy autonomously.

When instructing children about employing the strategy, the teacher also should explain how using the strategy will benefit them. Children need to be motivated to learn and to use the strategies. Just having children learn a new strategy is usually not enough for them to continue to use it and to transfer the strategy to new situations. For effective maintenance and transfer, children should be encouraged to monitor the effectiveness of the new strategy by comparing their performance on tests and other assessments.

Learning to use strategies effectively often takes time (Schneider, 2011). Initially, it takes time to execute the strategies and to practice them. "Practice" means that children use the effective strategy over and over again until they perform it automatically. To execute the strategies effectively, they need to have the strategies in long-term memory, and extensive practice makes this possible.

Most children benefit from generating a variety of alternative strategies and experimenting with different approaches to a problem, discovering what works well, when, and where.

This approach is especially true for children from the middle elementary school grades on, although some cognitive psychologists believe that even young children should be encouraged to practice varying strategies (Siegler, 2012, 2013).

Pressley and his colleagues (Pressley, 2007; Pressley & others, 2001, 2003, 2004) observed the use of strategy instruction by teachers and strategy use by students in elementary and secondary school classrooms. They concluded that teachers' use of strategy instruction is far less complete and intense than what is needed for students to learn how to use strategies effectively. They argue that education needs to be restructured so that students are provided with more opportunities to become competent strategic learners.

A final point about strategies is that many strategies depend on prior knowledge (Pressley, 2007). For example, students can't apply organizational strategies to a list of items unless they know the correct categories into which the items fall.

ADOLESCENCE

Deanna Kuhn (2009) discussed some important characteristics of adolescents' information processing and thinking. In her view, during the later years of childhood and continuing into adolescence, individuals approach cognitive levels that may or may not be achieved, in contrast with the largely universal cognitive levels that young children attain. By adolescence, considerable variation in cognitive functioning is present across individuals. This variability supports the argument that adolescents are producers of their own development to a greater extent than are children.

Kuhn (2009) further argues that the most important cognitive change in adolescence is improvement in executive function, which we discussed earlier in this chapter. A very important aspect of executive function in adolescence is cognitive control. Indeed, for most purposes, executive function and cognitive control can be thought of as synonyms.

The mind is an enchanting thing.

—MARIANNE MOORE
American poet, 20th century

Cognitive Control   Cognitive control involves exercising effective control in a number of areas, including focusing attention, reducing interfering thoughts, and being cognitively flexible (Diamond, 2013). Cognitive control increases in adolescence and emerging adulthood (Casey, Jones, & Somerville, 2011).

Think about all the times adolescents need to engage in cognitive control, such as the following situations (Galinsky, 2010):

- Making a real effort to stick with a task, avoiding interfering thoughts or environmental events, and instead doing what is most effective.
- Stopping and thinking before acting to avoid blurting out something that a minute or two later they wished they hadn't said.
- Continuing to work on something that is important but boring when there is something a lot more fun to do, inhibiting their behavior and doing the boring but important task, saying to themselves, "I have to show the self-discipline to finish this."

Controlling attention is a key aspect of cognition in adolescence and emerging adulthood (Rueda & Posner, 2013). Distractions that can interfere with attention in adolescence and emerging adulthood come from the external environment (other students talking while the student is trying to listen to a lecture, or the student turning on a laptop or tablet PC during a lecture and looking at a new friend request on Facebook, for example) or intrusive distractions from competing thoughts in the individual's mind. Self-oriented thoughts, such as worrying, self-doubt, and intense emotionally laden thoughts may especially interfere with focusing attention on thinking tasks (Walsh, 2011).

Cognitive flexibility involves being aware that options and alternatives are available and adapting to the situation. Before adolescents and emerging adults adapt their behavior in a situation, they must be aware that they need

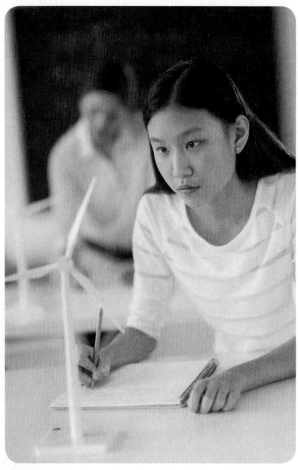

How might information processing and thinking skills change in adolescence?
© Tetra Images/Getty Images RF

to change their way of thinking and be motivated to do so. Having confidence in their ability to adapt their thinking to a particular situation, an aspect of *self-efficacy*, also is important in being cognitively flexible (Bandura, 2012).

Decision Making   Adolescence is a time of increased decision making—deciding which friends to choose, which person to date, whether to have sex, buy a car, go to college, and so on (Stanovich, West, & Toplak, 2013; Steinberg, 2015a, b). How competent are adolescents at making decisions? In some reviews, older adolescents are described as more competent than younger adolescents, who in turn are more competent than children (Keating, 2004). Compared with children, young adolescents are more likely to generate different options, examine a situation from a variety of perspectives, anticipate the consequences of decisions, and consider the credibility of sources.

However, older adolescents' (as well as adults') decision-making skills are far from perfect, and having the capacity to make competent decisions does not guarantee that such decisions will be made in everyday life, where breadth of experience often comes into play (Kuhn, 2009). Most people make better decisions when they are calm rather than emotionally aroused, and intense emotional arousal is a common state for adolescents (Steinberg, 2015a, b). Thus, the same adolescent who makes a wise decision when calm may make an unwise decision when emotionally aroused. In the heat of the moment, then, adolescents' emotions may be more likely to overwhelm their decision-making ability.

The social context plays a key role in adolescent decision making (Steinberg, 2015a, b). For example, adolescents' willingness to make risky decisions is more likely to occur in contexts where alcohol, drugs, and other temptations are readily available. Recent research reveals that the presence of peers in risk-taking situations increases the likelihood that adolescents will make risky decisions (Albert & Steinberg, 2011a, b). In one study of risk taking involving a simulated driving task, the presence of peers increased an adolescent's decision to engage in risky driving by 50 percent but had no effect on adults (Gardner & Steinberg, 2005). One possible explanation is that the presence of peers activates the brain's reward system, especially its dopamine pathways (Steinberg, 2015a, b).

To better understand adolescent decision making, Valerie Reyna and her colleagues (Reyna & Brainerd, 2011; Reyna & Farley, 2006; Reyna & Zayas, 2014; Reyna & others, 2010, 2011) have proposed the **dual-process model,** which states that decision making is influenced by two cognitive systems—one analytical and one experiential, which compete

dual-process model Theory stating that decision making is influenced by two cognitive systems—one analytical and one experiential—that compete with each other.

How do emotions and social contexts influence adolescents' decision making?
© Scott Houston/Corbis

with each other. The dual-process model emphasizes that it is the experiential system—monitoring and managing actual experiences—that benefits adolescents' decision making, not the analytical system. In this view, adolescents don't benefit from engaging in reflective, detailed, higher-level cognitive analysis about a decision, especially in high-risk, real-world contexts. In such contexts, adolescents just need to know that there are some circumstances that are so dangerous that they need to be avoided at all costs.

In the experiential system, in risky situations, it is important for an adolescent to quickly get the *gist,* or meaning, of what is happening and glean that the situation is a dangerous context, which can cue personal values that will protect the adolescent from making a risky decision (Reyna & Zayas, 2014). Further, adolescents who have a higher level of trait inhibition (self-control that helps them to manage their impulses effectively) and find themselves in risky contexts are less likely to engage in risk-taking behavior than their adolescent counterparts who a lower level of trait inhibition (Chick & Reyna, 2012).

However, some experts on adolescent cognition argue that in many cases adolescents benefit from both analytical and experiential systems (Kuhn, 2009).

Critical Thinking   Among the factors that provide a basis for improvement in critical thinking during adolescence are the following (Keating, 1990):

·   Increased speed, automaticity, and capacity of information processing, which free cognitive resources for other purposes;
·   Greater breadth of content knowledge in a variety of domains;
·   Increased ability to construct new combinations of knowledge;
·   A greater range and more spontaneous use of strategies and procedures for obtaining and applying knowledge, such as planning, considering the alternatives, and cognitive monitoring.

ADULTHOOD

Earlier in the chapter, we examined the changes that take place in speed of processing information, attention, and memory during adulthood. Here we continue to focus on changes in executive function, including some gains in thinking in the middle adulthood years and some of the challenges that older adults face.

Practical Problem Solving and Expertise   Nancy Denney (1986, 1990) observed circumstances such as how young and middle-aged adults handled a landlord who would not fix their stove and what they did if a bank failed to deposit a check. She found that the ability to solve such practical problems improved through the forties and fifties as individuals accumulated practical experience. However, since Denney's research, other studies on everyday problem-solving and decision-making effectiveness across the adult years have been conducted; a meta-analysis of these studies indicated that both qualities remained stable in early and middle adulthood, then declined in late adulthood (Thornton & Dumke, 2005). However, in late adulthood, older adults' everyday problem-solving and decision-making effectiveness benefited when individuals were highly educated and the content of the problems involved interpersonal matters. Further, a study revealed that older adults are better than younger adults at solving emotionally-laden and interpersonal problems (Blanchard-Fields, 2007). However, a more recent study revealed that older adults showed less effective decision making on a complex laboratory task that required sustained attention than did younger adults (Isella & others, 2008).

Experience as well as years of learning and effort may bring the rewards of **expertise,** or extensive, highly organized knowledge and understanding of a particular domain. Because it takes so long to attain, expertise often shows up more among middle-aged or older adults than among younger adults (Clancy & Hoyer, 1994; Kim & Hasher, 2005). Individuals may be experts in areas as diverse as physics, art, or knowledge of wine.

Stephen J. Hawking is a world-renowned expert in physics. Hawking authored the best-selling book *A Brief History of Time.* Hawking has a neurological disorder that prevents him from walking or talking. He communicates with the aid of a voice-equipped computer. *What distinguishes experts from novices?*
© Mackenzie Stroh/Contour/Getty Images

expertise Having extensive, highly organized knowledge and understanding of a particular domain.

Whatever their area of expertise, within that domain experts tend to process information differently from the way novices do (Bransford & others, 2006). Here are some of the characteristics that distinguish experts from novices:

- Experts are more likely to rely on their accumulated experience to solve problems.
- Experts often process information automatically and analyze it more efficiently when solving a problem in their domain than novices do.
- Experts have better strategies and shortcuts for solving problems in their domain than novices do.
- Experts are more creative and flexible in solving problems in their domain than novices are.

Decision Making   Despite declines in many aspects of memory, such as working memory and long-term memory, many older adults preserve decision-making skills reasonably well (Healey & Hasher, 2009). In some cases, though, age-related decreases in memory will impair decision making (Brand & Markowitsch, 2010). One study revealed that a reduction in effective decision making in risky situations during late adulthood was linked to declines in memory and processing speed (Henninger, Madden, & Huettel, 2010). However, older adults especially perform well when decision making is not constrained by time pressures and when the decision is meaningful for them (Boyle & others, 2012).

Executive Function   How does executive function change in late adulthood? Older adults are less effective at engaging in cognitive control than when they were younger (Campbell & others, 2012). For example, in terms of cognitive flexibility, older adults don't perform as well as younger adults at switching back and forth between tasks or mental sets (Luszcz, 2011). And in terms of cognitive inhibition, older adults are less effective than younger adults at inhibiting dominant or automatic responses (Coxon & others, 2012).

Although in general aspects of executive function decline in late adulthood, there is considerable variability in executive function among older adults. For example, some older adults have a better working memory and are more cognitively flexible than other older adults (Peltz, Gratton, & Fabiani, 2011). And there is increasing research evidence that aerobic exercise improves executive function in older adults (Guiney & Machado, 2013). For example, a recent study found that more physically fit older adults were more cognitively flexible than their less physically fit counterparts (Berryman & others, 2013). Further, a recent study found that 10 hours of visual speed of processing training was effective in improving older adults' speed of processing, attention, and executive function (Wolinsky & others, 2013). Also, in a recent meta-analysis, tai chi participation was associated with better executive function in older adults (Wayne & others, 2014). And in a recent study, executive functions of inhibitory control, mental set shifting, and attentional flexibility predicted functional mobility over a one-year period in older adults (Gothe & others, 2014).

Some critics argue that not much benefit is derived from placing various cognitive processes under the broader concept of executive function. Although we have described a number of components of executive function here—working memory, cognitive inhibition, cognitive flexibility, and so on—a consensus has not been reached on what the components are, how they are connected, and how they develop. That said, the concept of executive function is not likely to go away any time soon, and further research, especially meta-analyses, should provide a clearer picture of executive function and how it develops through the human life span (Luszcz, 2011).

Education, Work, and Health   Education, work, and health are three important influences on the cognitive functioning of older adults (Hofer, Rast, & Piccinin, 2012). They are also three of the most important factors involved in understanding why cohort effects need to be taken into account in studying the cognitive functioning of older adults. Indeed, cohort effects are very important to consider in the study of cognitive aging (Schaie, 2012). For

How are education, work, and health linked to cognitive functioning in older adults?
(left to right): © Silverstock/Getty Images RF; © Dorgie Productions/Getty Images; © Tom Grill/Corbis RF

example, one study of two cohorts tested 16 years apart revealed that at age 74, the average performance on a wide range of cognitive tasks for older adults from the more recent cohort was equal to those of the older adults from the earlier cohort when they were 15 years younger (Zelinski & Kennison, 2007).

Education Successive generations in America's twentieth century were better educated, and this trend continues in the twenty-first century (Schaie, 2012). Educational experiences are positively correlated with scores on intelligence tests and information-processing tasks, such as memory exercises (Steffener & others, 2014). Also, a recent study found that older adults with a higher level of education had better cognitive functioning (Rapp & others, 2013).

Not only were today's older adults more likely to go to college when they were young adults than were their parents or grandparents, but more older adults are returning to college today to further their education than in past generations. Educational experiences are positively correlated with scores on intelligence tests and information-processing tasks, such as memory exercises (Aiken Morgan, Sims, & Whitfield, 2010). One study revealed that older adults with less education had lower cognitive abilities than those with more education (Lachman & others, 2010). However, for older adults with less education, frequently engaging in cognitive activities improved their episodic memory.

Work Successive generations have also had work experiences that include a stronger emphasis on cognitively oriented labor. Our great-grandfathers and grandfathers were more likely to be manual laborers than were our fathers, who are more likely to be involved in cognitively oriented occupations. As the industrial society continues to be replaced by the information society, younger generations will have more experience in jobs that require considerable cognitive investment. The increased emphasis on complex information processing in jobs likely enhances an individual's intellectual abilities (Kristjuhan & Taidre, 2010; Schooler, 2007). In one study, substantive complex work was linked with higher intellectual functioning in older adults (Schooler, Mulatu, & Oates, 1999). Further, a recent study found that working in an occupation with a high level of mental demands was linked to higher levels of cognitive functioning before retirement and a slower rate of cognitive decline after retirement (Fisher & others, 2014).

developmental **connection**

Work

Cognitive ability is one of the best predictors of job performance in older adults. Connect to "Schools, Achievement, and Work."

Health   Successive generations have also been healthier in late adulthood as better treatments for a variety of illnesses (such as hypertension) have been developed. Many of these illnesses, such as stroke and heart disease, have a negative impact on intellectual performance (Chuang & others, 2014; de Frias, Schaie, & Willis, 2014; Ganguli & others, 2014). Researchers also have found age-related cognitive decline in adults with mood disorders such as depression (Mackin & others, 2014). Thus, some of the decline in intellectual performance found for older adults is likely due to health-related factors rather than to age per se (Korten & others, 2014).

A number of research studies have found that exercise is linked to improved cognitive functioning (Kirk-Sanchez & McGough, 2014; Leon & others, 2014). Walking or any other aerobic exercise appears to get blood and oxygen pumping to the brain, which can help people think more clearly.

Cognitive Neuroscience and Aging   Certain regions of the brain are involved in links between aging, brain health, and cognitive functioning (Prakash & others, 2015). In this section, we further explore the substantial increase in interest in the brain's role in aging and cognitive functioning. The field of *developmental cognitive neuroscience* has emerged as the major discipline that studies links between development, the brain, and cognitive functioning (Banuelos & others, 2014; Yuan & Raz, 2014). This field especially relies on brain-imaging techniques, such as functional magnetic resonance imaging (fMRI) and positron-emission tomography (PET), to reveal the areas of the brain that are activated when individuals are engaging in certain cognitive activities (Leshikar & others, 2014). For example, as an older adult is asked to encode and then retrieve verbal materials or images of scenes, the older adult's brain activity will be monitored by an fMRI brain scan.

Changes in the brain can influence cognitive functioning, and changes in cognitive functioning can influence the brain. For example, aging of the brain's prefrontal cortex may produce a decline in working memory. And when older adults do not regularly use their working memory, neural connections in the prefrontal lobe may atrophy. Further, cognitive interventions that activate older adults' working memory may increase these neural connections.

Although it is in its infancy as a field, the cognitive neuroscience of aging is beginning to uncover some important links between aging, the brain, and cognitive functioning (Prakash & others, 2015). These include the following:

FIGURE 16

THE PREFRONTAL CORTEX. Advances in neuroimaging are allowing researchers to make significant progress in connecting changes in the brain with cognitive development. Shown here is an fMRI of the brain's prefrontal cortex. *What links have been found between the prefrontal cortex, aging, and cognitive development?*

Courtesy of Dr. Sam Gilbert, Institute of Cognitive Neuroscience, UK

- Neural circuits in specific regions of the brain's prefrontal cortex decline, and this decline is linked to poorer performance by older adults on complex reasoning tasks, working memory, and episodic memory tasks (Fandakova, Lindenberger, & Shing, 2013; Toepper & others, 2014) (see Figure 16).

- Older adults are more likely than younger adults to use both hemispheres of the brain to compensate for age-related declines in attention, memory, and language (Davis & others, 2012; Dennis & Cabeza, 2008). Two recent neuroimaging studies revealed that better memory performance in older adults was linked to higher levels of activity in both hemispheres of the brain in processing information (Angel & others, 2011; Manenti, Cotelli, & Miniussi, 2011).

- Functioning of the hippocampus declines but to a lesser degree than the functioning of the frontal lobes in older adults (Antonenko & Floel, 2014). In K. Warner Schaie's (2013) recent research, individuals whose memory and executive function declined in middle age had more hippocampal atrophy in late adulthood, while those whose memory and executive function improved in middle age did not show a decline in hippocampal functioning in late adulthood.

- Patterns of neural decline with aging are larger for retrieval than encoding (Gutchess & others, 2005).
- Compared with younger adults, older adults often show greater activity in the frontal and parietal lobes of the brain on simple tasks, but as attentional demands increase, older adults display less effective functioning in the frontal and parietal lobes of the brain that involve cognitive control (Campbell & others, 2012).
- Younger adults have better connectivity between brain regions than older adults do (Antonenko & Floel, 2014).
- An increasing number of cognitive and fitness training studies include brain-imaging techniques such as fMRI to assess the results of such training on brain functioning (Erickson, Gildengers, & Butters, 2013; Kirk-Sanchez & McGough, 2014; Prakash & others, 2015; Voss & others, 2013). In one study, older adults who walked one hour a day three days a week for six months showed increased volume in the frontal and temporal lobes of the brain (Colcombe & others, 2006).

Denise Park and Patricia Reuter-Lorenz (2009; Reuter-Lorenz & Park, 2014) proposed a neurocognitive scaffolding view of connections between the aging brain and cognition. In this view, increased activation in the prefrontal cortex with aging reflects an adaptive brain that is compensating for the challenges of declining neural structures and function, as well as declines in various aspects of cognition, including working memory and long-term memory. Scaffolding involves the use of complementary neural circuits to protect cognitive functioning in an aging brain. Among the factors that can strengthen brain scaffolding are cognitive engagement and exercise.

Use It or Lose It Changes in cognitive activity patterns might result in disuse and consequent atrophy of cognitive skills (de Frias & Dixon, 2014). This concept is captured in the expression "use it or lose it." Mental activities that are likely to benefit the maintenance of cognitive skills in older adults include reading books, doing crossword puzzles, and attending lectures and concerts (Park & others, 2014). "Use it or lose it" also is a significant component of the engagement model of cognitive optimization that emphasizes how intellectual and social engagement can buffer age-related declines in intellectual development (Reuter-Lorenz & Park, 2014). The following studies support the "use it or lose it" concept and the engagement model of cognitive optimization:

- When middle-aged and older adults participated in intellectually engaging activities, it served to buffer them against cognitive decline (Hultsch & others, 1999).
- Catholic priests 65 years and older who regularly read books, did crossword puzzles, or otherwise exercised their minds were 47 percent less likely to develop Alzheimer disease than priests who rarely engaged in these activities (Wilson & others, 2002).
- Reading daily was linked to reduced mortality in men in their seventies (Jacobs & others, 2008).
- Older adults indicated how often they participated in six activities—reading, writing, doing crossword puzzles, playing card or board games, having group discussions, and playing music—on a daily basis (Hall & others, 2009). Across the five years of the study, the point at which memory loss accelerated was assessed and it was found that for each additional activity the older adult engaged in, the onset of rapid memory loss was delayed by 0.18 years. For older adults who participated in 11 activities per week compared with their counterparts who engaged in only 4 activities per week, for example, the point at which accelerated memory decline occurred was delayed by 1.29 years.
- A recent study of older adults over a 12-year period found that those who reduced their cognitive lifestyle activities (such as using a computer, playing bridge) subsequently showed declining cognitive functioning in verbal speed, episodic memory, and semantic memory (Small & others, 2012). The decline in cognitive functioning was linked to subsequent lower engagement in social activities.

To read further about "use it or lose it," see *Connecting Development to Life.*

developmental **connection**

Brain Development

A decrease in brain lateralization occurs in older adults when they engage in complex cognitive activities. Connect to "Physical Development and Biological Aging."

The Young@Heart chorus—whose average age is 80. Young@Heart became a hit documentary in 2008. The documentary displays the singing talents, energy, and optimism of a remarkable group of older adults, who clearly are on the "use it" side of "use it or lose it."
© Fox Searchlight/Photofest

The Remarkable Helen Small

In 2010, 90-year-old Helen Small completed her master's degree at the University of Texas at Dallas (UT-Dallas). The topic of her master's degree research project was romantic relationships in late adulthood. Helen said that she only interviewed one individual who was older than she was—a 92-year-old man.

I (your author, John Santrock) first met Helen when she took my undergraduate course in life-span development in 2006. After the first test, Helen stopped showing up and I wondered what had happened to her. It turns out that she had broken her shoulder when she tripped over a curb while hurrying to class. The next semester, she took my class again and did a great job in it, even though the first several months she had to take notes with her left hand (she's right-handed) because of her lingering shoulder problem.

Helen grew up in the Great Depression and first went to college in 1938 at the University of Akron, where she only attended for one year. She got married and her marriage lasted 62 years. After her husband's death, Helen went back to college. When I interviewed her recently, she told me that she had promised her mother that she would finish college. Her most important advice for college students, "Finish college and be persistent. When you make a commitment, always see it through. Don't quit. Go after what you want in life."

Helen not only is cognitively fit, she also is physically fit. She works out three times a week for about an hour each time—aerobically on a treadmill for about 30 minutes and then on six different weight machines.

What struck me most about Helen when she took my undergraduate course in life-span development was how appreciative she was of the opportunity to learn and how tenaciously she pursued studying and doing well in the course. Helen was quite popular with

Helen Small with the author of your text, John Santrock, in his undergraduate course on life-span development at the University of Texas at Dallas in spring 2012. Helen now returns each semester to talk with students in the class about cognitive aging. This past semester, the author had to reschedule the date of the topic because Helen had other work commitments on the day it was originally scheduled.
Courtesy of Dr. John Santrock

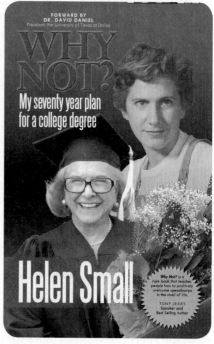

Helen Small published her first book, *Why Not? My Seventy Year Plan for a College Degree,* in 2011 at the age of 91.
Courtesy of Helen Small

the younger students in the course and she was a terrific role model for them.

After her graduation, I asked her what she planned to do during the next few years and she responded, "I've got to figure out what I'm going to do with the rest of my life." Helen now comes each semester to my course in life-span development when we are discussing cognitive aging. She wows the class and has been an inspiration to all who come in contact with her.

What has Helen done during the last several years to stay cognitively fit? She has worked as a public ambassador for Dr. Denise Park's Center for Vital Longevity at UT-Dallas and wrote her first book: *Why Not? My Seventy Year Plan for a College Degree* (Small, 2011). It's a wonderful, motivating invitation to live your life fully and reach your potential no matter what your age.

Cognitive Training If older adults are losing cognitive skills, can these skills be regained through training? An increasing number of research studies indicate that they can be restored to some extent (Bailey, Dunlosky, & Hertzog, 2014; Boron, Willis, & Schaie, 2007; Mayas & others, 2014; Willis & Caskie, 2013).

Consider a recent study of 60- to 90-year-olds which found that sustained engagement in cognitively demanding, novel activities improved the older adults' episodic memory

(Park & others, 2014). To produce this result, the older adults spent an average of 16.5 hours a week for three months learning to quilt or how to use digital photography. Consider also a recent study of 60- to 90-year-olds in which iPAD training 15 hours a week for 3 months improved their episodic memory and processing speed relative to engaging in social or non-challenging activities (Chan & others, 2015).

Researchers are also finding that improving the physical fitness of older adults can improve their cognitive functioning (Prakash & others, 2015). A review of studies revealed that aerobic fitness training for older adults improved their performance in the areas of planning, scheduling, working memory, resistance to distraction, and processing involving multiple tasks (Colcombe & Kramer, 2003).

Recent meta-examinations of four longitudinal observational studies (Long Beach Longitudinal Study; Origins of Variance in the Oldest-old (Octo-Twin) Study in Sweden; Seattle Longitudinal Study; and Victoria Longitudinal Study in Canada) of older adults' naturalistic cognitive activities found that changes in cognitive activity predicted cognitive outcomes as long as two decades later (Brown & others, 2012; Lindwall & others, 2012; Mitchell & others, 2012; Rebok & others, 2014). However, the concept that engaging in cognitive activity at an earlier point in development would improve older adults' ability to later withstand cognitive decline was not supported. On a positive note, when older adults continued to increase their engagement in cognitive and physical activities, they were better able to maintain their cognitive functioning in late adulthood.

To what extent can training improve the cognitive functioning of older adults?
© Blend Images/Alamy RF

The Stanford Center for Longevity (2011) recently reported on a consensus reached by leading scientists in the field of aging. One of their concerns is the misinformation given to the public touting products to improve the functioning of the mind for which there is no scientific evidence. Nutritional supplements, games, and software products have all been advertised as "magic bullets" to slow the decline of mental functioning and improve the mental ability of older adults. Some of the claims are reasonable but not scientifically tested, and others are unrealistic and implausible. A recent research review of dietary supplements and cognitive aging linked Ginkgo biloba to improvements in some aspects of attention in older adults and omega-3 polyunsaturated fatty acids to a reduced risk of age-related cognitive decline (Gorby, Brownell, & Falk, 2010). In this research review, there was no evidence of cognitive improvements in aging adults who consumed ginseng and glucose. However, a recent experimental study with 50- to 75-year-old females found that those who took fish oil for 26 weeks had improved executive function and beneficial effects in a number of areas of brain functioning compared with their female counterparts who took a placebo pill (Witte & others, 2014). Overall, though, research has not provided consistent plausible evidence that dietary supplements can accomplish major cognitive goals in aging adults over a number of years.

By contrast, some software-based cognitive training games have been found to improve older adults' cognitive functioning (Hertzog & others, 2009; Lange & others, 2010; Nouchi & others, 2013). For example, a recent study of 60- to 85-year-olds found that a multitasking video game that simulates day-to-day driving experiences (NeuroRacer) improved the cognitive control skills, such as sustained attention and working memory, after training on the video game and six months later (Anguera & others, 2013). Nonetheless, the training games may improve cognitive skills in a laboratory setting but not generalize to gains in the real world. And some critics argue that the effectiveness of brain games has been exaggerated and the research evidence is often weak or unfounded (Hambrick, 2014; Redick & others, 2013).

In sum, some improvements in the cognitive vitality of older adults can be accomplished through cognitive and fitness training (Prakash & others, 2015; Rebok & others, 2014). However, the resulting cognitive improvements often occur only when there is a substantial amount of effortful practice over a long period of time (Hambrick, 2014; Lovden & others, 2012; Nyberg & others, 2012; Redick & others, 2013). And, although sustained effortful training can improve the cognitive skills of many older adults, there is some loss in plasticity in late adulthood, especially in those who are 85 and older (Baltes, Lindenberger, & Staudinger, 2006).

LG4 Characterize thinking and its developmental changes

Review

- What is thinking?
- What characterizes concept formation and categorization in infancy? What is critical thinking? Do children and scientists think in the same ways? What are two important aspects of problem solving?
- What are some changes in thinking during adolescence?
- What are some changes in thinking in adulthood?

Connect

- You've learned that the nature-nurture debate examines the extent to which development is influenced by nature and by nurture. Which side of the debate would be reflected in the dual-process model that attempts to explain adolescent decision making and the "use it or lose it" view of cognitive aging?

Reflect *Your Own Personal Journey of Life*

- Choose an area in which you consider yourself at least somewhat of an expert. Compare your ability to learn in this field with the ability of a novice.

5 Metacognition

 LG5 Define metacognition and summarize its developmental changes

| What Is Metacognition? | Theory of Mind | Metacognition in Adolescence and Adulthood |

Cognitive developmentalist John Flavell is a pioneer in providing insights about children's thinking. Among his many contributions are establishing the field of metacognition and conducting numerous studies in this area, including metamemory and theory of mind studies.
Courtesy of Dr. John Flavell

As mentioned at the beginning of this chapter, metacognition is "thinking about thinking or knowing about knowing." John Flavell (1971, 1976) pioneered theory and research on metacognition, which has developed into a major research field in the study of cognitive development. In this section, we examine the role of metacognition in performing cognitive tasks, theory of mind, children's memory abilities, and metacognition in adolescents and adults.

WHAT IS METACOGNITION?

Metacognition can take many forms. It includes thinking about and knowing when and where to use particular strategies for learning or for solving problems (Carretti & others, 2014; Destan & others, 2014). Conceptualization of metacognition includes several dimensions of executive function, such as planning (deciding how much time to spend focusing on a task, for example), evaluation (monitoring progress toward task completion, for example), and self-regulation (modifying strategies as the task progresses, for example) (Dimmitt & McCormick, 2012).

Metacognition helps people to perform many cognitive tasks more effectively (Flavell, 2004). A recent study of young children found that their metacognitive ability in the numerical domain predicted their school-based math knowledge (Vo & others, 2014). Also, a study of college students revealed that metacognition was a key factor in their ability to engage effectively in critical thinking (Magno, 2010). Another study found that metacognition played an important role in adolescents' ability to generate effective hypotheses about solving problems (Kim & Pedersen, 2010).

Metamemory, individuals' knowledge about memory, is an especially important form of metacognition. Metamemory includes general knowledge about memory, such as knowing that recognition tests (for example, multiple-choice questions) are easier than recall tests (for example, essay questions). It also encompasses knowledge about one's own memory, such as knowing whether you have studied enough for an upcoming test.

By 5 or 6 years of age, children usually know that familiar items are easier to learn than unfamiliar ones, that short lists are easier to remember than long ones, that recognition is easier than recall, and that forgetting becomes more likely over time (Lyon & Flavell, 1993). However,

metamemory Knowledge about memory.

in other ways young children's metamemory is limited. They don't understand that related items are easier to remember than unrelated ones or that remembering the gist of a story is easier than remembering information verbatim (Kreutzer, Leonard, & Flavell, 1975). By fifth grade, students understand that gist recall is easier than verbatim recall.

Preschool children also have an inflated opinion of their memory abilities. For example, in one study, a majority of preschool children predicted that they would be able to recall all ten items of a list of ten items. When tested, none of the young children managed this feat (Flavell, Friedrichs, & Hoyt, 1970). As they move through the elementary school years, children give more realistic evaluations of their memory skills (Schneider, 2011).

Preschool children also have little appreciation for the importance of cues for memory, such as "It helps when you can think of an example of it." By 7 or 8 years of age, children better appreciate the importance of cueing for memory.

In general, children's understanding of their memory abilities and their skill in evaluating their performance on memory tasks are relatively poor at the beginning of the elementary school years but improve considerably by 11 to 12 years of age (Bjorklund & Rosenbaum, 2000).

© Joe Baker/Illustration Source

THEORY OF MIND

Even young children are curious about the nature of the human mind (Buttelmann & others, 2014; Hughes & Devine, 2015; Mahy, Moses, & Pfeifer, 2014). They have a **theory of mind,** which refers to awareness of one's own mental processes and the mental processes of others. Studies of theory of mind view the child as "a thinker who is trying to explain, predict, and understand people's thoughts, feelings, and utterances" (Harris, 2006, p. 847). Researchers are increasingly discovering that children's theory of mind is linked to cognitive processes (Wellman, 2011). For example, one study found that theory of mind competence at age 3 is related to a higher level of metamemory at age 5 (Lockl & Schneider, 2007).

Developmental Changes   Although whether infants have a theory of mind continues to be questioned by some (Rakoczy, 2012), the consensus is that some changes occur quite early in development, as we see next. From 18 months to 3 years of age, children begin to understand three mental states:

· *Perceptions.* By 2 years of age, children recognize that another person will see what's in front of her own eyes instead of what's in front of the child's eyes (Lempers, Flavell, & Flavell, 1977), and by 3 years of age, they realize that looking leads to knowing what's inside a container (Pratt & Bryant, 1990).
· *Emotions.* The child can distinguish between positive (for example, happy) and negative (for example, sad) emotions. A child might say, "Tommy feels bad."
· *Desires.* All humans have some sort of desires. But when do children begin to recognize that someone else's desires may differ from their own? Toddlers recognize that if people want something, they will try to get it. For instance, a child might say, "I want my mommy."

Two- to three-year-olds understand the way that desires are related to actions and to simple emotions. For example, they understand that people will search for what they want and that if they obtain it, they are likely to feel happy, but if they don't get it they will keep searching for it and are likely to feel sad or angry (Wellman & Woolley, 1990). Children also refer to desires earlier and more frequently than they refer to cognitive states such as thinking and knowing (Bartsch & Wellman, 1995).

One of the landmark developments in understanding others' desires is recognizing that someone else may have different desires from one's own (Wellman, 2011). Eighteen-month-olds understand that their own food preferences may not match the preferences of others— they will give an adult the food to which she says "Yummy!" even if the food is something that the infants detest (Repacholi & Gopnik, 1997). As they get older, they can verbalize that they themselves do not like something but an adult might (Flavell & others, 1992).

Between the ages of 3 and 5, children come to understand that the mind can represent objects and events accurately or inaccurately (Rhodes & Brandone, 2014). The realization that people can have *false beliefs*—beliefs that are not true—develops in a majority of children by the time they are 5 years old (Wellman, Cross, & Watson, 2001) (see Figure 17). This

FIGURE **17**

DEVELOPMENTAL CHANGES IN FALSE-BELIEF PERFORMANCE. False-belief performance—the child's understanding that a person has a false belief that contradicts reality—dramatically increases from 2½ years of age through the middle of the elementary school years. In a summary of the results of many studies, 2½-year-olds gave incorrect responses about 80 percent of the time (Wellman, Cross, & Watson, 2001). At 3 years 8 months, they were correct about 50 percent of the time and, after that, they gave increasingly correct responses.

theory of mind Thoughts about how one's own mental processes work and the mental processes of others.

FIGURE 18

THE SALLY AND ANNE FALSE-BELIEF TASK. In the false-belief task, the skit above in which Sally has a basket and Anne has a box is shown to children. Sally places a toy in her basket and then leaves. While Sally is gone and can't watch, Anne removes the toy from Sally's basket and places it in her box. Sally then comes back and the children are asked where they think Sally will look for her toy. Children are said to "pass" the false-belief task if they understand that Sally looks in her basket first before realizing the toy isn't there.

FIGURE 19

AMBIGUOUS LINE DRAWING

point is often described as a pivotal one in understanding the mind—recognizing that beliefs are not just mapped directly into the mind from the surrounding world, but also that different people can have different, and sometimes incorrect, beliefs (Liu & others, 2008). In a classic false-belief task, young children were shown a Band-Aids box and asked what was inside it (Jenkins & Astington, 1996). To the children's surprise, the box actually contained pencils. When asked what a child who had never seen the box would think was inside it, 3-year-olds typically responded, "Pencils." However, the 4- and 5-year-olds, grinning at the anticipation of the false beliefs of other children who had not seen what was inside the box, were more likely to say "Band-Aids."

In a similar task, children are told a story about Sally and Anne: Sally places a toy in a basket and then leaves the room (see Figure 18). In her absence, Anne takes the toy from the basket and places it in a box. Children are asked where Sally will look for the toy when she returns. The major finding is that 3-year-olds tend to fail false-belief tasks, saying that Sally will look in the box (even though Sally could not know that the toy had been moved to this new location). Four-year-olds and older children tend to pass the task, correctly saying that Sally will have a "false belief"—she will think the object is in the basket, even though that belief is now false. The conclusion from these studies is that children younger than 4 years old do not understand that it is possible to have a false belief.

However, there are reasons to question the focus on this one supposedly pivotal moment in the development of a theory of mind. For example, the false-belief task is a complicated one that involves a number of factors such as the characters in the story and all of their individual actions (Bloom & German, 2000). Children also have to disregard their own knowledge in making predictions about what others would think, which is difficult for young children (Birch & Bloom, 2003). Another important issue is that there is more to understanding the minds of others than this false-belief task would indicate.

One example of a limitation in 3- to 5-year-olds' understanding the mind is how they think about thinking. Preschoolers often underestimate when mental activity is likely to take place. For example, they sometimes think that a person who is sitting quietly or reading is not actually thinking very much (Flavell, Green, & Flavell, 1995). Their understanding of their own thinking is also limited. One study revealed that even 5-year-olds have difficulty reporting their thoughts (Flavell, Green, & Flavell, 1995). Children were asked to think quietly about the room in their home where they kept their toothbrushes. Shortly after this direction, many children denied they had been thinking at all and failed to mention either a toothbrush or a bathroom. In another study, when 5-year-olds were asked to try to have no thoughts at all for about 20 seconds, they reported that they were successful at doing this (Flavell, Green, & Flavell, 2000). By contrast, most of the 8-year-olds said they had engaged in mental activity during the 20 seconds and reported specific thoughts.

It is only beyond the preschool years—at approximately 5 to 7 years of age—that children have a deepening appreciation of the mind itself rather than just an understanding of mental states. For example, they begin to recognize that people's behaviors do not necessarily reflect their thoughts and feelings (Flavell, Green, & Flavell, 1993). Not until middle and late childhood do children see the mind as an active constructor of knowledge or a processing center (Flavell, Green, & Flavell, 1998) and move from understanding that beliefs can be false to realizing that the same event can be open to multiple interpretations (Carpendale & Chandler, 1996). For example, in one study, children saw an ambiguous line drawing (for example, a drawing that could be seen as either a duck or a rabbit); one puppet told the child she believed the drawing was a duck while another puppet told the child he believed the drawing was a rabbit (see Figure 19). Before the age of 7, children said that there was one right answer, and it was not okay for the two puppets to have different opinions.

Although most research on children's theory of mind focuses on children around or before their preschool years, at 7 years of age and beyond there are important developments in the ability to understand the beliefs and thoughts of others. While understanding that people may have different interpretations is important, it is also important to recognize that some interpretations and beliefs may still be evaluated on the basis of the merits of arguments and evidence (Kuhn, Cheney, & Weinstock, 2000). In early adolescence, children begin to understand that people can have ambivalent feelings (Harter, 2006). They start to recognize that the same person can feel both happy and sad about the same event. They also engage in more recursive thinking: thinking about what other people are thinking about.

Individual Differences As in other developmental research, there are individual differences in the ages when children reach certain milestones in their theory of mind (Hughes & Devine, 2015). For example, preschoolers who have more siblings perform better on theory of mind tasks than preschoolers with fewer siblings, especially if they have older siblings (McAlister & Peterson, 2007, 2013). Children who talk with their parents about feelings frequently as 2-year-olds show better performance on theory of mind tasks (Ruffman, Slade, & Crowe, 2002), as do children who frequently engage in pretend play (Harris, 2000).

Executive function, which involves goal-directed behavior and self-control, and which was discussed earlier in the chapter, is linked to the development of a theory of mind (Fizke & others, 2014; Muller & Kerns, 2015). For example, in one executive function task, children are asked to say the word *night* when they see a picture of a sun, and the word *day* when they see a picture of a moon and stars. Children who perform better at executive function tasks seem also to have a better understanding of theory of mind (Sabbagh & others, 2006).

Young children's symbolic skills also contribute to the development of theory of mind. A recent study found that young children's symbolic understanding provided a foundation for their theory of mind and also for language, pretend play, and representational understanding (Lillard & Kavanaugh, 2014).

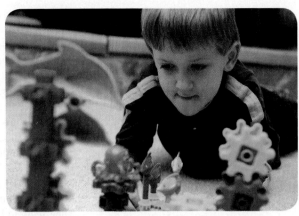

A young boy with autism. *What are some characteristics of autistic children? What are some deficits in autistic children's theory of mind?*
© Robin Nelson/PhotoEdit

Theory of Mind and Autism Another individual difference in understanding the mind involves autism (Fletcher-Watson & others, 2014). Approximately 1 in 150 children are estimated to have some type of autism (National Autism Association, 2010). Autism can usually be diagnosed by the age of 3 years and sometimes earlier. Children with autism show a number of behaviors different from other children their age, including deficits in social interaction and communication as well as repetitive behaviors or interests. However, children with autism might have difficulty understanding others' beliefs and emotions not solely due to theory of mind deficits but to other aspects of cognition such as problems in focusing attention, eye gaze, face recognition, memory, language impairment, or some general intellectual impairment (Boucher, Mayes, & Bigham, 2012; Siller & others, 2014).

Children and adults with autism have difficulty in social interactions, often described as huge deficits in theory of mind (Adler & others, 2010). These deficits are generally greater than deficits in children the same mental age with developmental disabilities (Baron-Cohen, 2009, 2011). Researchers have found that autistic children have difficulty in developing a theory of mind, especially in understanding others' beliefs and emotions (Bertoglio & Hendren, 2009). Although children with autism tend to do poorly on reasoning in false-belief tasks, they can perform much better on reasoning tasks requiring an understanding of physical causality (Peterson, 2005).

developmental connection

Conditions, Diseases, and Disorders

The current consensus is that autism is a brain dysfunction involving abnormalities in brain structure and neurotransmitters, and that genetic factors play an important role in its occurrence. Connect to "Schools, Achievement, and Work."

METACOGNITION IN ADOLESCENCE AND ADULTHOOD

Metacognition is increasingly recognized as a very important cognitive skill not only in adolescence but also in emerging adulthood. Compared with children, adolescents have an increased capacity to monitor and manage cognitive resources to effectively meet the demands of a learning task (Kuhn, 2009). This increased metacognitive ability results in improved cognitive functioning and learning. A recent longitudinal study revealed that from 12 to 14 years of age, young adolescents increasingly used metacognitive skills and used them more effectively in math and history classes than in other subjects (van der Stel & Veenman, 2010). For example, 14-year-olds monitored their own text comprehension more frequently and did so more effectively than their younger counterparts. Another recent study documented the importance of metacognitive skills, such as planning, strategizing, and monitoring, in college students' ability to think critically (Magno, 2010).

An important aspect of cognitive functioning and learning is determining how much attention will be allocated to an available resource. Evidence is accumulating that adolescents have a better understanding of how to effectively deploy their attention to different aspects of a task than children do (Kuhn, 2008, 2009). Further, adolescents have a better meta-level understanding of strategies—that is, knowing the best strategy to use and when to use it in performing a learning task.

Keep in mind, though, that there is considerable individual variation in adolescents' metacognition. Indeed, some experts argue that individual variation in metacognition becomes much more pronounced in adolescence than in childhood (Kuhn & Franklin, 2006). Thus, some adolescents are quite good at using metacognition to improve their learning, while others are far less effective.

By middle age, adults have accumulated a great deal of metacognitive knowledge. They can draw on this metacognitive knowledge to help them combat a decline in memory skills. For example, they are likely to understand that they need to have good organizational skills and reminders to help combat the decline in memory skills they face.

Older adults tend to overestimate the memory problems they experience on a daily basis. They seem to be more aware of their memory failures than younger adults and become more anxious about minor forgetfulness than younger adults do (Hoyer & Roodin, 2009). Researchers have found that in general older adults are as accurate as younger adults in monitoring the encoding and retrieval of information (Hertzog & Dixon, 2005). However, some aspects of monitoring information, such as source memory (discussed earlier in the chapter), decline in older adults (Hertzog & Dixon, 2005; Isingrini, Perrotin, & Souchay, 2008).

Review Connect Reflect

 LG5 Define metacognition and summarize its developmental changes

Review

- What is metacognition? How does metamemory typically change during childhood?
- How does the child's theory of mind change during the preschool years?
- How does metacognition change in adolescence and adulthood?

Connect

- How is metacognition in children different from metacognition in adolescents?

Reflect *Your Own Personal Journey of Life*

- Take an inventory of your study skills. How might you improve your metacognitive study skills?

---

reach your **learning goals**

Information Processing

1 The Information-Processing Approach

 LG1 Explain the information-processing approach and its application to development

The Information-Processing Approach and Its Application to Development

The information-processing approach analyzes how individuals encode information, manipulate it, monitor it, and create strategies for handling it. Attention, memory, and thinking are involved in effective information processing. The computer has served as a model for how humans process information. In the information-processing approach, children's cognitive development results from their ability to overcome processing limitations by increasingly executing basic operations, expanding information-processing capacity, and acquiring new knowledge and strategies. According to Siegler, three important mechanisms of change are encoding (how information gets into memory), automaticity (ability to process information with little or no effort), and strategy construction (creation of new procedures for processing information). Children's information processing is characterized by self-modification, and an important aspect of this self-modification involves metacognition—that is, knowing about knowing.

Speed of Processing Information

· Processing speed increases across childhood and adolescence. Processing speed slows in middle and late adulthood. However, strategies that people learn through experience can compensate for age-related decline in processing speed to some degree.

2 Attention

 Define attention and outline its developmental changes

What Is Attention?

· Attention is the focusing of mental resources. Four ways that people can allocate their attention are selective attention (focusing on a specific aspect of experience that is relevant while ignoring others that are irrelevant); divided attention (concentrating on more than one activity at the same time); sustained attention (maintaining attention to a selected stimulus for a prolonged period of time; also referred to as vigilance); and executive attention (involving action planning, allocating attention to goals, error detection and compensation, monitoring progress on tasks, and dealing with novel or difficult tasks).

Infancy

· Even newborns can fixate on a contour, but as they get older they scan a pattern more thoroughly. Attention in the first year of life is dominated by the orienting/investigative process. Attention in infancy often occurs through habituation and dishabituation. Joint attention plays an important role in infant development, especially in the infant's acquisition of language.

Childhood and Adolescence

· Salient stimuli tend to capture the attention of the preschooler. After 6 or 7 years of age, there is a shift to more cognitive control of attention. Selective attention improves through childhood and adolescence. Multitasking is an example of divided attention, and it can harm adolescents' attention when they are engaging in a challenging task.

Adulthood

· Attentional skills often are excellent in early adulthood. Older adults are generally less adept than younger adults at selective and divided attention.

3 Memory

 Describe what memory is and how it changes through the life span

What Is Memory?

· Memory is the retention of information over time. Psychologists study the processes of memory: how information is initially placed or encoded into memory, how it is retained or stored, and how it is found or retrieved for a certain purpose later. People construct and reconstruct their memories. Schema theory states that people mold memories to fit the information that already exists in their minds.

Infancy

· Infants as young as 2 to 6 months of age display implicit memory, which is memory without conscious recollection, as in memory of perceptual-motor skills. However, many experts believe that explicit memory, which is the conscious memory of facts and experiences, does not emerge until the second half of the first year of life. The hippocampus and frontal lobes of the brain are involved in development of memory in infancy. Older children and adults remember little if anything from the first three years of their lives.

Childhood

· One method of assessing short-term memory (the retention of information for up to 15 to 30 seconds, assuming there is no repetition of the information) is with a memory-span task, on which there are substantial developmental changes through the childhood years. Working memory (a kind of "mental workbench" where individuals manipulate and assemble information when they make decisions, solve problems, and comprehend language) is linked to children's reading comprehension and problem solving. Increasing interest has been shown in children's autobiographical memories, and these memories change developmentally. Young children can remember a great deal of information if they are given appropriate cues and prompts. Strategies can improve children's memory, and older children are more likely to use these than younger children. Imagery and elaboration are two important strategies. Knowledge is an important influence on memory.

| Adulthood | | Younger adults have better episodic memory than older adults do. Older adults have more difficulty retrieving semantic information. Working memory and processing speed decrease in older adults. Explicit memory is more likely to decline in older adults than is implicit memory. Source memory—remembering where one learned something—declines with age. Controversy characterizes whether prospective memory, which is remembering to do something in the future, declines as adults age. |

4 Thinking

LG4 Characterize thinking and its developmental changes

- **What Is Thinking?**
- **Infancy and Childhood**

· Thinking involves manipulating and transforming information in memory.

· Mandler argues that it is not until about 7 to 9 months of age that infants form conceptual categories, although we do not know precisely when concept formation begins. Infants' first concepts are broad. Over the first two years of life, these broad concepts gradually become more differentiated. Many infants and young children develop an intense interest in a particular category (or categories) of things. Advances in executive function, an umbrella-like concept that encompasses a number of higher-level cognitive processes linked to the development of the prefrontal cortex, occur in early childhood. Executive function involves managing one's thoughts to engage in goal-directed behavior and to exercise self-control. Critical thinking involves thinking reflectively and productively, and evaluating evidence. Children and scientists think alike in some ways but differently in others. Children are less influenced by an overall pattern than by happenstance events, and they often cling to old theories despite new evidence. Two important ways of solving problems involve using strategies and using analogies.

- **Adolescence**

· Key changes in information processing occur during adolescence, particularly advances in executive function. These changes focus on monitoring and managing cognitive resources, controlling attention and reducing interfering thoughts, making decisions, and exercising critical thinking.

- **Adulthood**

· Everyday problem-solving and decision-making effectiveness remain stable in early and middle adulthood, and then some aspects decline in late adulthood while others may increase. One aspect of cognition that may improve with aging is expertise. Many aspects of executive function decline in late adulthood, but individual differences occur as well. In the twentieth and twenty-first centuries, successive generations of older adults have been better educated, have had work experiences that included a stronger emphasis on cognitively oriented labor, and have been healthier. These cohort effects are linked to higher cognitive functioning. There has been increased interest in the cognitive neuroscience of aging that focuses on links between aging, the brain, and cognitive functioning. This field especially relies on fMRI and PET scans to assess brain functioning while individuals are engaging in cognitive tasks. One of the most consistent findings in this field is a decline in the functioning of specific regions in the prefrontal cortex in older adults and links between this decline and poorer performance on complex reasoning, working memory, and episodic memory tasks. Some improvements in the cognitive vitality of older adults can be accomplished through cognitive and fitness training. However, such benefits have not been observed in all studies.

5 Metacognition

 LG5 Define metacognition and summarize its developmental changes

- **What Is Metacognition?**

· Metacognition is thinking about thinking, or knowing about knowing. Metamemory is one aspect of metacognition that has been studied developmentally. By 5 to 6 years of age, children usually know that familiar items are easier to learn than unfamiliar ones and that short lists are easier to remember than long ones. By 7 to 8 years of age, children better appreciate the importance of cues for memory.

- **Theory of Mind**

· Theory of mind is the awareness of one's own mental processes and the mental processes of others. Children begin to understand mental states involving perceptions, desires, and emotions at 2 to 3 years of age, and at 4 to 5 years of age they realize that people can have false beliefs. It is only beyond the early childhood years that children have a deepening appreciation of the mind itself rather than just understanding mental states. Autistic children have difficulty developing a theory of mind.

> **Metacognition in Adolescence and Adulthood**

Adolescents have an increased capacity to monitor and manage resources to effectively meet the demands of a learning task, although there is considerable individual variation in metacognition during adolescence. Metacognition continues to improve in early adulthood, and many middle-aged individuals have accumulated considerable metacognitive knowledge. Older adults tend to overestimate their everyday memory problems.

key **terms**

attention	episodic memory	long-term memory	semantic memory
automaticity	executive attention	memory	short-term memory
concepts	executive function	metacognition	source memory
critical thinking	expertise	metamemory	strategy construction
divided attention	explicit memory	prospective memory	sustained attention
dual-process model	fuzzy trace theory	schemas	theory of mind
elaboration	implicit memory	schema theory	thinking
encoding	joint attention	selective attention	working memory

key **people**

Alan Baddeley	John Flavell	Walter Mischel	Carolyn Rovee-Collier
Patricia Bauer	Maria Gartstein	Michael Pressley	K. Warner Schaie
Charles Brainerd	Kathleen Lee	Valerie Reyna	Robert Siegler
Nancy Denney	Jean Mandler	Robert Roeser	Philip Zelazo
Adele Diamond	Ann Masten	Mary Rothbart	

chapter 8

INTELLIGENCE

chapter **outline**

© Jonathan Kim/Riser/Getty Images

preview

The concept of intelligence has generated many controversies, including debates about whether intelligence is more strongly influenced by heredity or by environment, whether there is cultural bias in intelligence testing, and whether intelligence tests are misused. We will explore these controversies, as well as the extent to which we have a single intelligence or multiple intelligences, the development of intelligence across the life span, and the extremes of intelligence and creativity.

1 The Concept of Intelligence — LG1 Explain the nature of intelligence

| What Is Intelligence? | Intelligence Tests | Theories of Multiple Intelligences | The Neuroscience of Intelligence |

Intelligence is one of our most prized possessions. However, even the most intelligent people have not been able to agree on how to define and measure the concept of intelligence.

WHAT IS INTELLIGENCE?

What does the term *intelligence* mean to psychologists? Some experts describe intelligence as the ability to solve problems. Others describe it as the capacity to adapt and learn from experience. Still others argue that intelligence includes characteristics such as creativity and interpersonal skills.

The problem with intelligence is that, unlike height, weight, and age, intelligence cannot be directly measured. We can't peel back a person's scalp and see how much intelligence he or she has. We can evaluate intelligence only *indirectly* by studying and comparing the intelligent acts that people perform.

The primary components of intelligence are similar to the cognitive processes of thinking and memory that we discussed in the chapter on "Information Processing." The differences in how we described these cognitive processes in that chapter, and how we discuss intelligence, lie in the concepts of *individual differences* and assessment (Kehle & Bray, 2014). Individual differences are the stable, consistent ways in which people differ from one another. Individual differences in intelligence generally have been measured by intelligence tests designed to tell us whether a person can reason better than others who have taken the test (Williams & others, 2014).

How can intelligence be defined? **Intelligence** is the ability to solve problems and to adapt and learn from experiences. But even this broad definition doesn't satisfy everyone. As you will see shortly, Robert J. Sternberg (2014a, 2015a,b,c) proposes that practical know-how should be considered part of intelligence. In his view, intelligence involves weighing options carefully and acting judiciously, as well as developing strategies to improve shortcomings. Sternberg (2014b) also recently described intelligence as the ability to adapt to, shape, and select environments. In adapting to the environment, if individuals find the environment suboptimal, they can change it to make it more suitable for their skills and desires.

Also, a definition of intelligence based on a theory such as Vygotsky's would have to include the ability to use the tools of the culture with help from more-skilled individuals. Because intelligence is such an abstract, broad concept, it is not surprising that there are so many different ways to define it.

INTELLIGENCE TESTS

What types of intelligence tests are given to children and adults? What are some contributions and criticisms of intelligence tests?

What a piece of work is a man! How noble in reason! How infinite in faculty! In form, in moving, how express and admirable! In action how like an angel! In apprehension how like a god!

—WILLIAM SHAKESPEARE
English playwright, 17th century

developmental connection

Information Processing

The information-processing approach emphasizes how individuals manipulate information, monitor it, and create strategies for handling it. Connect to "Information Processing."

developmental connection

Social Contexts

Vygotsky's theory emphasizes the social contexts of learning and constructing knowledge through social interaction. Connect to "Cognitive Developmental Approaches."

intelligence The ability to solve problems and to adapt to and learn from experiences.

Alfred Binet constructed the first intelligence test after being asked to create a measure to determine which children could benefit from instruction in France's schools and which could not.
© Bettmann/Corbis

The Binet Tests   In 1904, the French Ministry of Education asked psychologist Alfred Binet to devise a method to determine which students would not profit from typical school instruction. Binet and his student Théophile Simon developed an intelligence test to fulfill this request. The test consisted of 30 items ranging from the ability to touch one's nose or ear when asked to the ability to draw designs from memory and to define abstract concepts.

Binet stressed that the core of intelligence consists of complex cognitive processes such as memory, imagery, comprehension, and judgment. In addition, he noted that a developmental approach was crucial for understanding intelligence. He proposed that a child's intellectual ability increases with age. Therefore, he tested potential items and determined the age at which a typical child could answer them correctly. Thus, Binet developed the concept of **mental age (MA),** which is an individual's level of mental development relative to others. For an average child, MA scores correspond to *chronological age (CA)*, which is age from birth. A bright child has an MA considerably above CA; a child with a low level of intelligence has an MA considerably below CA.

The Binet test has been revised many times to incorporate advances in the understanding of intelligence and intelligence testing. Many revisions were carried out by Lewis Terman, who developed extensive norms and provided detailed, clear instructions for each problem on the test. Terman also applied a concept introduced by William Stern (1912), who coined the term **intelligence quotient (IQ)** to refer to an individual's mental age divided by chronological age, multiplied by 100: IQ = MA/CA × 100.

If a child's mental age, as measured by the Binet test, was the same as the child's chronological age, then the child's IQ score was 100. If the measured mental age was above chronological age, then the IQ score was greater than 100. If mental age was below chronological age, the IQ score was less than 100. Although this scoring system is no longer used, the term IQ is often still used to refer to a score on a standardized intelligence test.

In 2004, the test, now called the Stanford-Binet 5 (Stanford University is where the revisions have been done), was revised to analyze an individual's responses in five content areas: fluid reasoning, knowledge, quantitative reasoning, visual-spatial reasoning, and working memory. A general composite score also is obtained. Today the test is scored by comparing the test-taker's performance with the results achieved by other people of the same age. The average score is set at 100.

The current Stanford-Binet is given to individuals from age 2 through adulthood. It includes a wide variety of items, some requiring verbal responses, and others, nonverbal responses. For example, a 6-year-old is expected to complete the verbal task of defining at least six words, such as *orange* and *envelope*, and the nonverbal task of tracing a path through a maze. An adult with average intelligence is expected to define such words as *disproportionate* and *regard*, explain a proverb, and compare the concepts of idleness and laziness.

Over the years, the Stanford-Binet has been given to thousands of children and adults of different ages. By administering the test to large numbers of individuals selected at random from different parts of the United States, researchers have found that the scores approximate a normal distribution (see Figure 1). A **normal distribution** is a symmetrical, bell-shaped curve with a majority of the cases falling in the middle of the range of possible scores and

mental age (MA) An individual's level of mental development relative to that of others.

intelligence quotient (IQ) An individual's mental age divided by chronological age, multiplied by 100; devised in 1912 by William Stern.

normal distribution A symmetrical, bell-shaped curve with a majority of the cases falling in the middle of the possible range of scores and few scores appearing toward the extremes of the range.

FIGURE 1

THE NORMAL CURVE AND STANFORD-BINET IQ SCORES. The distribution of IQ scores approximates a normal curve. Most of the population falls in the middle range of scores. Notice that extremely high and extremely low scores are very rare. Slightly more than two-thirds of the scores fall between 85 and 115. Only about 1 in 50 individuals has an IQ higher than 130, and only about 1 in 50 individuals has an IQ lower than 70.

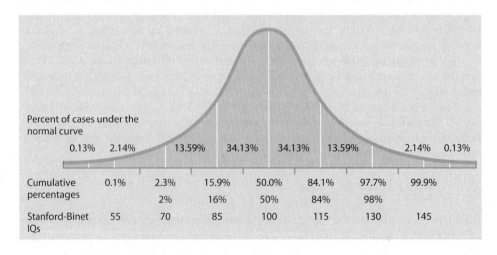

Percent of cases under the normal curve								
0.13%	2.14%	13.59%	34.13%	34.13%	13.59%	2.14%	0.13%

Cumulative percentages							
0.1%	2.3%	15.9%	50.0%	84.1%	97.7%	99.9%
	2%	16%	50%	84%	98%	

Stanford-Binet IQs							
55	70	85	100	115	130	145

few scores appearing toward the extremes of the range. The Stanford-Binet continues to be one of the most widely used individual tests of intelligence.

The Wechsler Scales   Besides the Stanford-Binet, the other most widely used intelligence tests are the Wechsler scales (Carlozzi & others, 2015). In 1939, David Wechsler introduced the first of his scales, designed for use with adults (Wechsler, 1939); the current edition is the Wechsler Adult Intelligence Scale—Fourth Edition (WAIS-IV). The Wechsler Intelligence Scale for Children—Fourth Edition (WISC-IV) is designed for children and adolescents between the ages of 6 and 16. The Wechsler Preschool and Primary Scale of Intelligence—Fourth Edition (WPPSI-IV) was published in 2012 and is appropriate for children from age 2 years 6 months to 7 years 7 months (Syeda & Climie, 2014).

The Wechsler scales not only provide an overall IQ score but also yield several composite scores (for example, the Verbal Comprehension Index, the Working Memory Index, and the Processing Speed Index). These allow the examiner to quickly see whether the individual is strong or weak in different areas of intelligence. Three of the Wechsler subscales (two verbal, one nonverbal) are shown in Figure 2.

The Use and Misuse of Intelligence Tests   Psychological tests are tools. As with all tools, their effectiveness depends on the knowledge, skill, and integrity of the user. A hammer can be used to build a beautiful kitchen cabinet or it can be used as a weapon of assault. Like a hammer, psychological tests can be used for positive purposes or they can be abused.

Intelligence tests have real-world applications as predictors of school and job success (Kuncel & others, 2014). For example, scores on tests of general intelligence are substantially correlated with school grades and achievement test performance, both at the time of the test and years later (Brody, 2007). IQ in the sixth grade correlates about .60 with the number of years of education the individual will eventually obtain (Jencks, 1979).

Intelligence tests are moderately correlated with work performance (Lubinski, 2000). Individuals with higher scores on tests designed to measure general intelligence tend to get higher-paying, more prestigious jobs, and are more intrinsically satisfied with their jobs (Ganzach & Fried, 2012; Zagorsky, 2007). However, general IQ tests predict only 10 to 30 percent of the variation in job success, with the majority of job success due to motivation, education, and other factors (Sternberg, 2014b). Further, the correlations between IQ and achievement decrease the longer people work at a job, presumably because as they gain more job experience they perform better (Hunt, 1995).

Thus, although there are correlations between IQ scores and academic achievement and occupational success, many other factors contribute to success in school and at work. These include the motivation to succeed, physical and mental health, and social skills (Sternberg, 2003).

The single number provided by many IQ tests can easily lead to false expectations about an individual (Rosnow & Rosenthal, 1996). Sweeping generalizations are too often made on the basis of an IQ score and can become self-fulfilling prophecies (Weinstein, 2004).

Even though they have limitations, tests of intelligence are among psychology's most widely used tools (Dale & others, 2014). To be effective, they should be used in conjunction with other information about an individual. For example, an intelligence test alone should not determine whether a child is placed in a special education or gifted class. The child's developmental history, medical background, performance in school, social competencies, and family experiences should be taken into account as well.

THEORIES OF MULTIPLE INTELLIGENCES

The use of a single score to describe how people perform on intelligence tests implies that intelligence is a general ability, a single trait. Wechsler scales provide scores for a number of intellectual skills, as well as an overall score. Do people have some general mental ability

Verbal Subscales

Similarities

A child must think logically and abstractly to answer a number of questions about how things might be similar.

Example: "In what way are a lion and a tiger alike?"

Comprehension

This subscale is designed to measure an individual's judgment and common sense.

Example: "What is the advantage of keeping money in a bank?"

Nonverbal Subscales

Block Design

A child must assemble a set of multicolored blocks to match designs that the examiner shows.
Visual-motor coordination, perceptual organization, and the ability to visualize spatially are assessed.

Example: "Use the four blocks on the left to make the pattern on the right."

FIGURE 2

SAMPLE SUBSCALES OF THE WECHSLER INTELLIGENCE SCALE FOR CHILDREN—FOURTH EDITION (WISC-IV). The Wechsler includes 11 subscales—6 verbal and 5 nonverbal. Three of the subscales are shown here. Sample subscales from the Wechsler Intelligence Scale for Children–Fourth Edition (WISC–IV). Copyright © 2004 NCS Pearson, Inc. Reproduced with permission. All rights reserved. "Wechsler Intelligence Scale for Children" and "WISC" are trademarks, in the US and/or other countries, of Pearson Education, Inc. or its affiliates(s).

that determines how they perform on all of these tests? Or is intelligence a label for a combination of several distinct abilities? And do conventional intelligence tests measure everything that should be considered part of intelligence? Psychologists disagree about the answers to these questions.

Sternberg's Triarchic Theory

Robert J. Sternberg (1986, 2004, 2010, 2011, 2012, 2013, 2014a, b, 2015a, b, c) notes that traditional IQ tests fail to measure some important dimensions of intelligence. Sternberg proposes a triarchic theory of intelligence involving three main types of intelligence: analytical, creative, and practical.

Sternberg developed the **triarchic theory of intelligence,** which states that intelligence comes in three forms: (1) *analytical intelligence,* which refers to the ability to analyze, judge, evaluate, compare, and contrast; (2) *creative intelligence,* which consists of the ability to create, design, invent, originate, and imagine; and (3) *practical intelligence,* which involves the ability to use, apply, implement, and put ideas into practice.

Sternberg (2014a, b, 2015a, b, c) says that children with different triarchic patterns "look different" in school. Students with high analytical ability tend to be favored in conventional schooling. They often do well under direct instruction, in which the teacher lectures and gives students objective tests. They often are considered to be "smart" students who get good grades, show up in high-level tracks, do well on traditional tests of intelligence and the SAT, and later get admitted to competitive colleges.

In contrast, children who are high in creative intelligence often are not on the top rung of their class. Many teachers have specific expectations about how assignments should be done, and creatively intelligent students may not conform to those expectations. Instead of giving conformist answers, they give unique answers, for which they might get reprimanded or marked down. No teacher wants to discourage creativity, but Sternberg stresses that too often a teacher's desire to increase students' knowledge suppresses creative thinking.

Like children high in creative intelligence, children who are high in practical intelligence often do not relate well to the demands of school. However, many of these children do well outside the classroom's walls. They may have excellent social skills and good common sense. As adults, some become successful managers, entrepreneurs, or politicians in spite of having undistinguished school records.

Gardner's Theory of Multiple Intelligences

According to Howard Gardner (1983, 1993, 2002, 2014), people have multiple intelligences, and IQ tests measure only a few of these. He argues that IQ tests measure verbal, math, and spatial aspects of intelligence while overlooking a number of other abilities. For evidence of the existence of multiple intelligences, Gardner uses information about the ways in which certain cognitive abilities survive particular types of brain damage. He also points to child prodigies and to some individuals with intellectual disability or autism who have an extraordinary skill in a particular domain. An example was portrayed by Dustin Hoffman in the movie *Rain Man.* Hoffman's character was autistic but had a remarkable computing ability. In one scene, he helped his brother successfully gamble in Las Vegas by keeping track of all the cards that had been played.

Gardner has proposed eight types of intelligence. They are described here, along with examples of the occupations in which they are regarded as strengths (Campbell, Campbell, & Dickinson, 2004):

- *Verbal.* The ability to think in words and use language to express meaning (occupations: authors, journalists, speakers)
- *Mathematical.* The ability to carry out mathematical operations (occupations: scientists, engineers, accountants)
- *Spatial.* The ability to think three-dimensionally (occupations: architects, artists, sailors)
- *Bodily-kinesthetic.* The ability to manipulate objects and be physically adept (occupations: surgeons, craftspeople, dancers, athletes)
- *Musical.* A sensitivity to pitch, melody, rhythm, and tone (occupations: composers, musicians, and sensitive listeners)
- *Interpersonal.* The ability to understand and effectively interact with others (occupations: successful teachers, mental health professionals)

Robert J. Sternberg, who developed the triarchic theory of intelligence.
Courtesy of Dr. Robert Sternberg

"You're wise, but you lack tree smarts."
© Donald Reilly/The New Yorker Collection/
www.cartoonbank.com

triarchic theory of intelligence Sternberg's theory that intelligence consists of analytical intelligence, creative intelligence, and practical intelligence.

- *Intrapersonal.* The ability to understand oneself (occupations: theologians, psychologists)
- *Naturalist.* The ability to observe patterns in nature and understand natural and human-made systems (occupations: farmers, botanists, ecologists, landscapers)

Recently, Gardner has considered adding a ninth type of intelligence to his list of multiple intelligences—existentialist, which involves exploring and finding meaning in life, especially regarding questions about life, death, and existence.

Gardner notes that each of the eight intelligences can be destroyed by brain damage, that each involves unique cognitive skills, and that each shows up in exaggerated fashion in the gifted and in individuals with intellectual disability or autism. According to Gardner, everyone has all of these intelligences but to varying degrees. As a result, we prefer to learn and process information in different ways. People perform best when they can apply their strong intelligences to the task.

Howard Gardner, working with a child. *How many intelligences does Gardner believe there are and what are they?*
© Steve Hansen/The Life Collection/Getty Images

Emotional Intelligence   Both Sternberg's and Gardner's theories include one or more categories related to social intelligence. In Sternberg's theory, the category is practical intelligence; in Gardner's theory, they are interpersonal intelligence and intrapersonal intelligence. Another theory that emphasizes interpersonal, intrapersonal, and practical aspects of intelligence is called **emotional intelligence,** which has been popularized by Daniel Goleman (1995) in his book *Emotional Intelligence.* The concept of emotional intelligence was initially developed by Peter Salovey and John Mayer (1990), who define it as the ability to perceive and express emotion accurately and adaptively (such as taking the perspective of others), to understand emotion and emotional knowledge (such as understanding the roles that emotions play in friendship and marriage), to use feelings to facilitate thought (such as being in a positive mood, which is linked to creative thinking), and to manage emotions in oneself and others (such as being able to control one's anger).

There continues to be considerable interest in the concept of emotional intelligence (Bhullar, Schutte, & Malouff, 2013; Boyatzis & others, 2015; Brouzos, Misailidi, & Hadjimattheou, 2014; Fiori & others, 2014; Schermer, Petrides, & Vernon, 2015). One study of college students revealed that both a general mental abilities test and an emotional intelligence assessment were linked to academic performance, although the general mental abilities test was a better predictor (Song & others, 2010). And a recent study revealed that emotional intelligence abilities were linked to academic achievement above and beyond cognitive and personality factors (Lanciano & Curci, 2014).

Critics argue that emotional intelligence broadens the concept of intelligence too far to be useful and has not been adequately assessed and researched.

Do People Have One or Many Intelligences?   Figure 3 compares Sternberg's, Gardner's, and Salovey/Mayer's views of intelligence. Notice that Sternberg's view is unique in emphasizing creative intelligence and that Gardner's includes a number of types of intelligence that are not addressed by the other views. These theories of multiple intelligence have much to offer. They have stimulated us to think more broadly about what makes up people's intelligence and competence (Sternberg, 2014a, b, 2015a, b, c), and they have motivated educators to develop programs that instruct students in different domains.

Theories of multiple intelligences have their critics (Haier & others, 2014). Some argue that the research base to support these theories has not yet been developed. In particular, some critics say that Gardner's classification seems arbitrary. For example, if musical skills represent a type of intelligence, why don't we also refer to chess intelligence, prize-fighter intelligence, and so on?

A number of psychologists continue to support the concept of general intelligence (Haier & others, 2014; te Nijenhuis, Jongeneel-Grimen, & Kirkegaard, 2014; Trzaskowski & others, 2014). For example, one expert on intelligence, Nathan Brody (2007), argues that people who excel at one type of intellectual task are likely to excel in other intellectual tasks. Thus, individuals who do well at memorizing lists of digits are also likely to be good at solving verbal problems and spatial layout problems. This general intelligence includes abstract reasoning or thinking, the capacity to acquire

emotional intelligence The ability to perceive and express emotions accurately and adaptively, to understand emotion and emotional knowledge, to use feelings to facilitate thought, and to manage emotions in oneself and others.

Gardner	Sternberg	Salovey/Mayer
Verbal Mathematical	Analytical	
Spatial Movement Musical	Creative	
Interpersonal Intrapersonal	Practical	Emotional
Naturalistic		

FIGURE **3**

COMPARING STERNBERG'S, GARDNER'S, AND SALOVEY/MAYER'S INTELLIGENCES

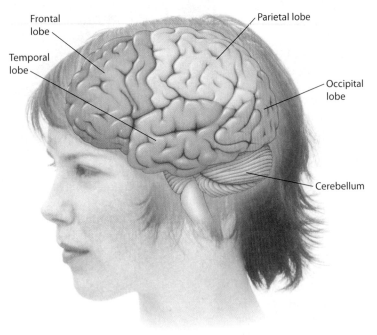

FIGURE 4

INTELLIGENCE AND THE BRAIN. Researchers recently have found that a higher level of intelligence is linked to a distributed neural network in the frontal and parietal lobes. To a lesser extent than the frontal/parietal network, the temporal and occipital lobes, as well as the cerebellum, also have been found to have links to intelligence. The current consensus is that intelligence is likely to be distributed across brain regions rather than being localized in a specific region, such as the frontal lobes.

Frontal lobe
Temporal lobe
Parietal lobe
Occipital lobe
Cerebellum

developmental **connection**

Information Processing

Speed of processing information declines in middle adulthood and then declines further in late adulthood. Connect to "Information Processing."

knowledge, and problem-solving ability (Brody, 2000). Some experts who argue for the existence of general intelligence conclude that individuals also have specific intellectual abilities (Brody, 2007).

In sum, controversy still surrounds the issue of whether it is more accurate to conceptualize intelligence as a general ability, as specific abilities, or as both (Gardner, 2014; Haier & others, 2014). Sternberg (2014b) accepts that there is evidence to support the concept of general intelligence in the kinds of analytical tasks that traditional IQ tests assess, but he thinks that the range of intellectual tasks those tests measure is too narrow.

THE NEUROSCIENCE OF INTELLIGENCE

In the current era of extensive research on the brain, interest in the neurological underpinnings of intelligence has increased (Deary, 2012; Santarnecchi, Rossi, & Rossi, 2015). Among the questions about the brain's role in intelligence that are being explored are these: Is having a bigger brain linked to higher intelligence? Is intelligence located in certain brain regions? Is the speed at which the brain processes information linked to intelligence?

Are individuals with bigger brains more intelligent than those with smaller brains? Studies using MRI scans to assess total brain volume indicate a moderate correlation (about 1.3 to 1.4) between brain size and intelligence (Carey, 2007; Luders & others, 2009).

Might intelligence be linked to specific regions of the brain? Early consensus was that the frontal lobes are the likely location of intelligence. Today, some experts continue to emphasize that high-level thinking skills involved in intelligence are linked to the prefrontal cortex (Santarnecchi, Rossi, & Rossi, 2015; Sternberg & Sternberg, 2012, 2016). However, other researchers recently have found that intelligence is distributed more widely across brain regions (da Rocha, Rocha, & Massad, 2011; Lee & others, 2012; Sepulcre & others, 2012). The most prominent finding from brain-imaging studies is that a distributed neural network involving the frontal and parietal lobes is related to higher intelligence (Colom & others, 2009, 2010; Margolis & others, 2013) (see Figure 4). A recent study revealed that the frontoparietal network is responsible for cognitive control and connectivity to brain regions outside the network (Cole & others, 2012). Albert Einstein's total brain size was average, but a region of his brain's parietal lobe that is very active in processing math and spatial information was 15 percent larger than average (Witelson, Kigar, & Harvey, 1999). Other brain regions that have been linked to higher intelligence (although at a lower level of significance than the frontal/parietal lobe network) include the temporal and occipital lobes, as well as the cerebellum (Luders & others, 2009).

Examining the neuroscience of intelligence has also led to study of the role that neurological speed might play in intelligence (Waiter & others, 2009). Research results have not been consistent for this possible link, although a recent study found that children who are gifted show faster processing speed and more accurate processing of information than children who are not gifted (Duan, Dan, & Shi, 2013).

As technological advances allow closer study of the brain's functioning in coming decades, we are likely to see more specific conclusions about the brain's role in intelligence. As this research proceeds, keep in mind that both heredity and environment likely contribute to links between the brain and intelligence, including the connections we discussed between brain size and intelligence. Also, Robert Sternberg (2014) recently concluded that research on the brain's role in intelligence has been more effective in answering some questions (such as "What aspects of the brain are involved in learning a list of words?") than in answering others (such as "Why do some individuals consider shaking hands socially intelligent but others do not?").

Review *Connect* Reflect

LG1 Explain the nature of intelligence

Review

- What is intelligence?
- What are the main individual tests of intelligence? What are some issues regarding the use and misuse of intelligence tests?
- What theories of multiple intelligences have been developed? Do people have one intelligence or many intelligences? What are some criticisms of the multiple intelligences concept?
- What are some links between the brain and intelligence?

Connect

- What do Sternberg's triarchic theory and Gardner's theory of multiple intelligences have in common that could be applied in elementary school classrooms?

Reflect *Your Own Personal Journey of Life*

- A DVD is being sold to parents for testing their child's IQ. Several parents tell you that they purchased the DVD and assessed their children's IQ. Why might you feel skeptical about giving your children an IQ test and interpreting the results yourself?

---

2 Controversies and Group Comparisons

LG2 Outline key controversies about differences in IQ scores

```
The Influence of Heredity
and Environment

Group Comparisons
and Issues
```

We have seen that intelligence is a slippery concept with competing definitions, tests, and theories. It is not surprising, therefore, that attempts to understand the concept of intelligence are filled with controversy. In some cases, the controversies arise over comparisons of the intelligence of different groups, such as people from different cultural or ethnic backgrounds.

THE INFLUENCE OF HEREDITY AND ENVIRONMENT

An area of considerable debate in the study of intelligence centers on the extent to which intelligence is influenced by genetics (nature) versus the extent to which it is influenced by environment (nurture) (Bagshaw & others, 2013; Marioni & others, 2014). It is difficult to tease apart these influences, but psychologists keep trying to unravel them.

Genetic Influences To what degree do our genes make us smart? Researchers have attempted to answer this question by comparing the IQ similarity of identical twins (who have the same genes) with that of fraternal twins (who do not have matching genes). A research review found that the difference in the average correlations for identical and fraternal twins was not very high—only .15 (Grigorenko, 2000) (see Figure 5).

Have scientists been able to pinpoint specific genes that are linked to intelligence? A recent research review concluded that there may be more than 1,000 genes that affect intelligence, each possibly having a small influence on an individual's intelligence (Davies & others, 2011). However, researchers have not been able to identify the specific genes that contribute to intelligence (Deary, 2012; Zhao, Kong, & Qu, 2014).

The concept of **heritability** attempts to distinguish between the effects of heredity and environment in a population. Heritability is the portion of the variance in a population that is attributed to genes. The heritability index is computed using correlational techniques. Thus, the highest possible degree of heritability is 1.00, and correlations of .70 and above suggest a strong genetic influence. A committee of respected researchers convened by the American Psychological Association concluded that by late adolescence, the heritability of intelligence is about .75, which reflects a strong genetic influence (Neisser & others, 1996).

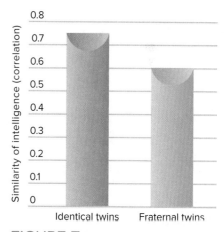

FIGURE 5

CORRELATION BETWEEN INTELLIGENCE TEST SCORES AND TWIN STATUS. The graph represents a summary of research findings that have compared the intelligence test scores of identical and fraternal twins. An approximate .15 difference has been found, with a higher correlation for identical twins (.75) and a lower correlation for fraternal twins (.60).

heritability The portion of the variance in a population that is attributed to genes.

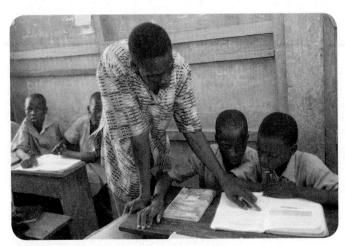

Students in an elementary school in South Africa. *How might schooling influence the development of children's intelligence?*
© Owen Franken/Corbis

developmental **connection**

Nature and Nurture

The epigenetic approach emphasizes the ongoing, bidirectional interaction of heredity and environment. Connect to "Biological Beginnings."

An important point to keep in mind about heritability is that it refers to a specific group (population) rather than to individuals. Researchers use the concept of heritability to try to describe why people differ. Heritability says nothing about why a single individual, like yourself, has a certain intelligence—nor does it say anything about differences between groups.

Most research on heredity and environment does not include environments that differ radically. Thus, it is not surprising that many genetic studies show environment to be a fairly weak influence on intelligence (Fraser, 1995).

The heritability index has several limitations. It is only as good as the data that are entered into its analysis and the interpretations made from it. The data are virtually all from traditional IQ tests, which some experts believe are not always the best indicator of intelligence (Gardner, 2014; Sternberg, 2014a, b, 2015a, b, c). Also, the heritability index assumes that researchers can treat genetic and environmental influences as factors that can be separated, with each part contributing a distinct amount of influence. In reality, genes and the environment always work together: genes always exist in an environment, and the environment shapes their activity.

Environmental Influences   Although genetic endowment influences a person's intellectual ability, the environmental experiences of children and adults do make a difference (Ritchie, 2014; Sternberg, 2014a, b, 2015a, b, c). In one study, researchers found that how much parents communicated with their children during the first three years of their lives was correlated with the children's Stanford-Binet IQ scores at age 3 (Hart & Risley, 1995). The more parents communicated with their children, the higher the children's IQs were. And a recent research analysis by Richard Nisbett and his colleagues (2012) supported the importance of environmental influences on intelligence: A 12- to 18-point increase in IQ was found when children are adopted from low-income families into middle- and upper-income families.

Schooling also influences intelligence (Ceci & Gilstrap, 2000; Cliffordson & Gustafsson, 2008). The biggest effects have been found when large groups of children received no formal education for an extended period, resulting in lower intelligence.

Another possible effect of education can be seen in rapidly increasing IQ test scores around the world (Flynn, 1999, 2007, 2011, 2013). IQ scores have been rising so quickly that a high percentage of people regarded as having average intelligence in the early 1900s would be considered below average in intelligence today (see Figure 6). If a representative sample of today's children took the Stanford-Binet test used in 1932, about one-fourth would be defined as very superior, a label usually accorded to less than 3 percent of the population. A recent meta-analysis of 53 studies since 1972 found that IQ scores have been rising about 3 points per decade since that year and that the increase in IQ scores does not seem to be diminishing (Trahan & others, 2014). This worldwide increase in intelligence test scores over a short time frame is called the *Flynn effect* after the researcher who discovered it—James Flynn (1999, 2007, 2011, 2013).

Recent research indicates that even the IQ scores of individuals at the highest level of intelligence are also getting higher (Wai, Putallaz, & Makel, 2012). Responding to this development, some test makers have begun to include more challenging items that allow very bright individuals more room to express their ability,

FIGURE **6**

THE INCREASE IN IQ SCORES FROM 1932 TO 1997. As measured by the Stanford-Binet test, American children seem to be getting smarter. Scores of a group tested in 1932 fell along a bell-shaped curve with half below 100 and half above. Studies show that if children took that same test today, half would score above 120 on the 1932 scale. Very few of them would score in the "intellectually deficient" end, on the left side, and about one-fourth would rank in the "very superior" range.

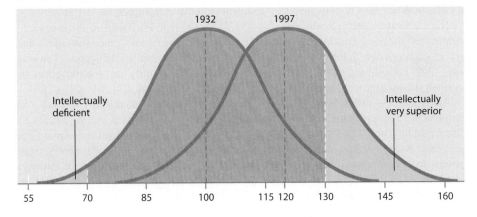

Can Early Intervention in the Lives of Children Growing Up in Impoverished Circumstances Improve Their Intelligence?

Each morning a young mother waited with her child for the bus that would take the child to school. The child was only 2 months old, and "school" was an experimental program at the University of North Carolina at Chapel Hill. There the child experienced a number of interventions designed to improve her intellectual development—everything from bright objects dangled in front of her eyes while she was a baby to language instruction and counting activities when she was a toddler (Wickelgren, 1999). The child's mother had an IQ of 40 and could not read signs or determine how much change she should receive from a cashier. Her grandmother had a similarly low IQ.

Today, at age 20, the child's IQ measures 80 points higher than her mother's did when the child was 2 months old. Not everyone agrees that IQ can be affected this extensively, but it is clear that environment can make a substantial difference in a child's intelligence. As behavior geneticist Robert Plomin (1999) has said, even something that is highly heritable (like intelligence) may be malleable through interventions.

The child we just described was part of the Abecedarian Intervention program at the University of North Carolina at Chapel Hill conducted by Craig Ramey and his associates (Campbell, 2007; Campbell & others, 2012; Ramey & Campbell, 1984; Ramey & Ramey, 1998). They randomly assigned 111 young children from low-income, poorly educated families to either an intervention group, which received full-time, year-round child care along with medical and social work services, or a control group, which received medical and social benefits but no child care. The child-care program included gamelike learning activities aimed at improving language, motor, social, and cognitive skills.

The success of the program in improving IQ was evident by the time the children were 3 years of age. At that age, the experimental group showed normal IQs averaging 101, a 17-point advantage over the control group. Recent follow-up results suggest that the effects are long-lasting. More than a decade later, at 15, children from the intervention group still maintained an IQ advantage of 5 points over the control-group children (97.7 to 92.6) (Campbell, 2007; Campbell & others, 2001; Ramey, Ramey, & Lanzi, 2001). They also did better on standardized tests of reading and math, and were less likely to be held back a year in school. Also, the greatest IQ gains were made by the children whose mothers had especially low IQs—below 70. At age 15, these children showed a 10-point IQ advantage over a group of children whose mothers' IQs were below 70 but who had not experienced the child-care intervention. In a recent analysis of the Abecedarian intervention project, at age 30 the children who experienced the early intervention had attained more years of education but the intervention had not led to any benefits involving social adjustment and criminal activity (Campbell & others, 2012).

The Abecedarian intervention study supports other research that has found prevention/intervention to be more effective than later remediation in improving the lives of children growing up in impoverished circumstances (Phillips & Lowenstein, 2011). Thus, it is important to consider the types of environments children experience as they develop, both in the general population and in especially challenging contexts.

Because the change in test scores has taken place in a relatively short period of time, it can't be due to heredity. Rather, it might result from environmental factors such as the exploding quantities of information to which people are exposed and the much higher percentage of the population who receive education (Flynn & Rossi-Case, 2012).

Keep in mind that environmental influences are complex. Growing up with all the "advantages," for example, does not guarantee success. Children from wealthy families may have easy access to excellent schools, books, travel, and tutoring, but they may take such opportunities for granted and fail to develop the motivation to learn and to achieve. In the same way, "poor" or "disadvantaged" does not automatically equal "doomed." Researchers increasingly are exploring ways to improve the early environments of children who are at risk for impoverished intelligence (Duncan & Magnuson, 2014; Duncan, Magnuson, & Votruba-Drzal, 2015). The emphasis is on prevention rather than remediation. Many low-income parents have difficulty providing an intellectually stimulating environment for their children. Programs that educate parents to be more sensitive caregivers and better teachers, while providing support services such as quality child-care programs, can make a difference in a child's intellectual development (Follari, 2015).

A review of the research on early interventions concluded that (1) high-quality center-based interventions improve children's intelligence and school achievement; (2) the effects are strongest for poor children and for children whose parents have little education; (3) the positive benefits continue into adolescence, although the effects are smaller than in early childhood or the beginning of elementary school; and (4) the programs that are continued into elementary school have the most sustained long-term effects (Brooks-Gunn, 2003). Can we actually measure environmental influences on intelligence? To read more, see the *Connecting with Research* interlude.

The highest-risk children often benefit the most cognitively when they experience early interventions.

—CRAIG RAMEY
Contemporary psychologist, Georgetown University

In sum, there is a consensus among psychologists that both heredity and environment influence intelligence (Sternberg, 2014b, 2015a, b, c). This consensus reflects the nature-nurture issue, which was highlighted in the chapter titled "Introduction." Recall that the nature-nurture issue focuses on the extent to which development is influenced by nature (heredity) and nurture (environment). Although psychologists agree that intelligence is the product of both nature and nurture, there is still disagreement about how strongly each factor influences intelligence.

GROUP COMPARISONS AND ISSUES

Group comparisons in intelligence can involve cultures and ethnic groups. We begin by examining cross-cultural comparisons and exploring cultural bias in testing.

Cross-Cultural Comparisons   Cultures vary in the way they describe what it means to be intelligent (Zhang & Sternberg, 2012; Sternberg, 2014b). People in Western cultures tend to view intelligence in terms of reasoning and thinking skills, whereas people in Eastern cultures see intelligence as a way for members of a community to successfully engage in social roles (Nisbett, 2003).

In a study of the Luo culture in rural Kenya, children who scored highly on a test of knowledge about medicinal herbs—a measure of practical intelligence—tended to score poorly on tests of academic intelligence (Sternberg & others, 2001). These results indicated that practical and academic intelligence can develop independently and may even conflict with each other. They also suggest that the values of a culture may influence the direction in which a child develops. In a cross-cultural context, then, intelligence depends a great deal on environment (Zhang & Sternberg, 2012).

Cultural Bias in Testing   Many of the early intelligence tests were culturally biased, favoring people who were from urban rather than rural environments, middle socioeconomic status rather than low socioeconomic status, and non-Latino White rather than African American ethnicity (Provenzo, 2002). Also, members of minority groups who do not speak English or who speak nonstandard English are at a disadvantage in trying to understand questions framed in standard English.

Researchers have developed **culture-fair tests,** which are intelligence tests that are designed to avoid cultural bias. Two types of culture-fair tests have been developed. The first includes questions that are familiar to people from all socioeconomic and ethnic backgrounds. For example, a child might be asked how a bird and a dog are different, on the assumption that virtually all children are familiar with birds and dogs. The second type of culture-fair test contains no verbal questions.

Why is it so hard to create culture-fair tests? Most tests tend to reflect what the dominant culture thinks is important (Zhang & Sternberg, 2012). If tests have time limits, these will bias the test against groups not concerned with time. If languages differ, the same words might have different meanings for different language groups. Even pictures can produce bias because some cultures have less experience than others with drawings and photographs (Anastasi & Urbina, 1996). Within the same culture, different groups could have different attitudes, values, and motivation, and this could affect their performance on intelligence tests. Items that ask why buildings should be made of brick are biased against children who have little or no experience with brick houses. Questions about railroads, furnaces, seasons of the year, distances between cities, and so on can be biased against groups who have less experience than others with these contexts. Because of such difficulties, Robert Sternberg (2012) concludes that there are no culture-fair tests, but only culture-reduced tests.

Ethnic Comparisons   In the United States, children from African American and Latino families score below children from non-Latino White families on standardized intelligence tests (Yeung, 2012). On average, African American schoolchildren score 10 to 15 points lower on standardized intelligence tests than non-Latino White schoolchildren do (Brody, 2000). These are *average scores*, however. About 15 to 25 percent of African American schoolchildren score higher than half of non-Latino White schoolchildren do. The reason is that the distribution of scores for African Americans and non-Latino Whites overlap.

"You can't build a hut, you don't know how to find edible roots and you know nothing about predicting the weather. In other words, you do terribly on our I.Q. test."
Cartoon by Sidney Harris Copyright © ScienceCartoonsPlus.com.

culture-fair tests Intelligence tests that are designed to avoid cultural bias.

As African Americans have gained social, economic, and educational opportunities, the gap between African Americans and non-Latino Whites on standardized intelligence tests has begun to narrow (Ogbu & Stern, 2001). A recent research review concluded that the IQ gap between African Americans and non-Latino Whites has been reduced considerably in recent years (Nisbett & others, 2012). This gap especially narrows in college, where African American and non-Latino White students often experience more similar environments than during the elementary and high school years (Myerson & others, 1998). Also, when children from disadvantaged African American families are adopted into more advantaged middle-socioeconomic-status families, their scores on intelligence tests more closely resemble national averages for middle-socioeconomic-status children than for lower-socioeconomic-status children (Scarr & Weinberg, 1983). Further, a recent study using the Stanford Binet Intelligence Scales found no differences in overall intellectual ability between non-Latino White and African American preschool children when the children were matched on age, gender, and parental education level (Dale & others, 2014). Nonetheless, a recent analysis concluded that the underrepresentation of African Americans in STEM (science, technology, engineering, and math) subjects and careers is linked to practitioners' expectations that they have less innate talent than non-Latino Whites (Leslie & others, 2015).

Review Connect Reflect

 Outline key controversies about differences in IQ scores

Review

- What evidence suggests genetic influences on IQ scores?
- What evidence suggests environmental influences on IQ scores?
- What do IQ tests tell us about intelligence among people in different cultures and ethnic groups?

Connect

- Apply what you have learned about the nature-nurture debate to discuss possible gender similarities and differences in intelligence.

Reflect *Your Own Personal Journey of Life*

- Do you think your performance on standardized tests accurately reflects your intelligence?

3 The Development of Intelligence

 Discuss the development of intelligence across the life span

Tests of Infant Intelligence

Stability and Change in Intelligence Through Adolescence

Intelligence in Adulthood

How can the intelligence of infants be assessed? Is intelligence stable throughout childhood? Does intelligence decline in older adults, and if so, when and by how much? These are some of the questions we will explore as we examine the development of intelligence.

TESTS OF INFANT INTELLIGENCE

The infant-testing movement grew out of the tradition of IQ testing. However, tests that assess infants are necessarily less verbal than IQ tests for older children. Tests for infants contain far more items related to perceptual-motor development. They also include measures of social interaction. To read about the work of one infant assessment specialist, see the *Connecting with Careers* profile.

Toosje Thyssen Van Beveren, Infant Assessment Specialist

Toosje Thyssen Van Beveren is a developmental psychologist at the University of Texas Medical Center in Dallas. She has a master's degree in child clinical psychology and a Ph.D. in human development. Currently, Van Beveren is involved in a 12-week program called New Connections, which is a comprehensive intervention for young children who were affected by substance abuse prenatally and for their caregivers.

In the New Connections program, Van Beveren assesses infants' developmental status and progress. She might refer the infants to a speech, physical, or occupational therapist and monitor the infants' services and progress. Van Beveren trains the program staff and encourages them to use the exercises she recommends. She also discusses the child's problems with the primary caregivers, suggests activities, and assists them in enrolling infants in appropriate programs.

During her graduate work at the University of Texas at Dallas, Van Beveren was author John Santrock's teaching assistant in his undergraduate course on life-span development for four years. As a teaching assistant, she attended classes, graded exams, counseled students, and occasionally gave lectures. Each semester, Van Beveren

Toosje Thyssen Van Beveren conducts an infant assessment.
Courtesy of Dr. John Santrock

returns to give a lecture on prenatal development and infancy. She also teaches several courses each semester in the psychology department at UT–Dallas. In Van Beveren's words, "My days are busy and full. The work is often challenging. There are some disappointments, but mostly the work is enormously gratifying."

Items in the Bayley-III Scales of Infant Development.
Bayley Scales of Infant and Toddler Development-Third Edition (Bayley-III). Copyright © 2006 by NCS Pearson, Inc. Reproduced with permission. All rights reserved.

Bayley Scales of Infant Development
Widely used scales, developed by Nancy Bayley, for assessing infant development. The current version, the Bayley-III, has five scales: cognitive, language, motor, socio-emotional, and adaptive; the first three are administered to the infant, the latter two to the caregiver.

The widely used **Bayley Scales of Infant Development** were developed by Nancy Bayley (1969) to assess infant behavior and predict later development. The current version, Bayley-III, has five scales: cognitive, language, motor, socio-emotional, and adaptive (Bayley, 2006). The first three scales are administered directly to the infant, while the latter two are questionnaires given to the caregiver. The Bayley-III also is more appropriate for use in clinical settings than the two previous editions (Lennon & others, 2008).

How should a 6-month-old perform on the Bayley cognitive scale? The 6-month-old infant should be able to vocalize pleasure and displeasure, persistently search for objects that are just outside immediate reach, and approach a mirror that is placed in front of the infant by the examiner. By 12 months of age, the infant should be able to inhibit behavior when commanded to do so, imitate words the examiner says (such as *Mama*), and respond to simple requests (such as "Take a drink").

The increasing interest in infant development has produced many new measures, especially tasks that evaluate the ways infants process information (Fagan, 2011). The Fagan Test of Infant Intelligence is increasingly being used (Fagan, 1992). This test focuses on the infant's ability to process information in ways such as encoding the attributes of objects, detecting similarities and differences between objects, forming mental representations, and retrieving these representations. For example, it measures the amount of time babies look at a new object compared with the amount of time they spend looking at a familiar object.

Unlike the Bayley scales, the Fagan test is correlated with measures of intelligence in older children. In fact, evidence is accumulating that measures of habituation and dishabituation are linked to intelligence in childhood, adolescence, and even adulthood. For example, one study revealed that habituation assessed at 3 or 6 months of age was linked to verbal skills and intelligence assessed at 32 months of age (Domsch, Lohaus, & Thomas, 2009).

Another study found that selective attention to novelty at 6 to 12 months was positively correlated with intelligence at 21 years of age (Fagan, Holland, & Wheeler, 2007). And a longitudinal study revealed that scores in four information-processing domains (attention, processing speed, memory, and representational competence) assessed in infancy and early childhood were linked to general intelligence scores on the Wechsler Intelligence Scale for Children–III assessed at 11 years of age (Rose & others, 2012).

It is important, however, not to go too far and think that connections between cognitive development in early infancy and later cognitive development are so strong that no discontinuity takes place. Significant changes in cognitive development occur after infancy.

STABILITY AND CHANGE IN INTELLIGENCE THROUGH ADOLESCENCE

A longitudinal study examined the intelligence of 200 children from 12 months (using the Bayley scales) to 4 years old (using the Stanford-Binet test) (Blaga & others, 2009). The results indicated considerable stability from late infancy through the preschool years.

An early study examined correlations between IQ at a number of different ages (Honzik, MacFarlane, & Allen, 1948). There was a strong relation between IQ scores obtained at the ages of 6, 8, and 9 and IQ scores obtained at the age of 10. For example, the correlation between IQ at the age of 8 and IQ at the age of 10 was .88. The correlation between IQ at the age of 9 and IQ at the age of 10 was .90. These figures show a very high relation between IQ scores obtained in these years. The correlation between IQ in the preadolescent years and IQ at the age of 18 was slightly lower but still statistically significant. For example, the correlation between IQ at the age of 10 and IQ at the age of 18 was .70.

What has been said so far about the stability of intelligence has been based on measures of groups of individuals. The stability of intelligence also can be evaluated through studies of individuals. Robert McCall and his associates (McCall, Applebaum, & Hogarty, 1973) studied 140 children between the ages of 2½ and 17. They found that the average range of IQ scores was more than 28 points. The scores of one out of three children changed by as much as 40 points.

What can we conclude about stability and changes in intelligence during childhood? Intelligence test scores can fluctuate dramatically across the childhood years. Intelligence is not as stable as the original intelligence theorists envisioned. Children are adaptive beings. They have the capacity for intellectual change, but they do not become entirely new intelligent beings. In a sense, children's intelligence changes but remains connected with earlier points in development.

INTELLIGENCE IN ADULTHOOD

Does intelligence increase or decrease in adulthood? Might older adults have greater wisdom than younger adults? These are among the questions that we will explore in this section.

Fluid and Crystallized Intelligence John Horn emphasizes that some abilities increase throughout the life span, whereas others steadily decline from middle adulthood onward (Horn, 2007; Horn & Donaldson, 1980). Horn argues that **crystallized intelligence,** an individual's accumulated information and verbal skills, continues to increase throughout the life span. However, he notes that **fluid intelligence,** the ability to reason abstractly, begins to decline in middle adulthood (see Figure 7).

Horn's data were collected in a cross-sectional manner. A *cross-sectional study* assesses individuals of different ages at the same point in time. For example, a cross-sectional study might assess the intelligence of groups of 40-, 50-, and 60-year-olds in one evaluation, such as in 1990. The average 40-year-old and the average 60-year-old were born in eras that offered different economic and educational opportunities. For example, as the 60-year-olds grew up they likely had fewer educational opportunities, which probably

developmental **connection**

Life-Span Perspective

The stability-change issue is a major focus of study in the field of life-span development. Connect to "Introduction."

crystallized intelligence An individual's accumulated information and verbal skills, which continues to increase with age.

fluid intelligence The ability to reason abstractly, which begins to decline in middle adulthood.

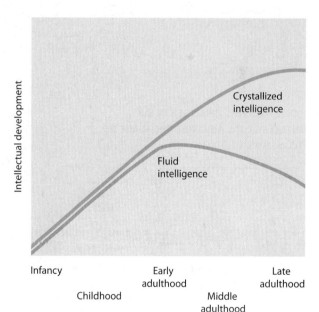

FIGURE 7

FLUID AND CRYSTALLIZED INTELLECTUAL DEVELOPMENT ACROSS THE LIFE SPAN. According to Horn, crystallized intelligence (based on cumulative learning experiences) increases throughout the life span, but fluid intelligence (the ability to perceive and manipulate information) steadily declines from middle adulthood.

influenced their scores on intelligence tests. Thus, if we find differences between 40- and 60-year-olds on intelligence tests when they are assessed cross-sectionally, these differences might be due to cohort effects (attributes reflecting an individual's time of birth or generation rather than his or her age) such as educational differences rather than the person's age.

In contrast, in a *longitudinal study*, the same individuals are studied over a period of time. Thus, a longitudinal study of intelligence in middle adulthood might consist of giving the same intelligence test to the same individuals when they are 40, when they are 50, and when they are 60 years of age. Whether data are collected cross-sectionally or longitudinally makes a difference in what is found about intellectual decline.

The Seattle Longitudinal Study K. Warner Schaie (1983, 1996, 2000, 2005, 2010, 2011, 2013) has conducted an extensive study of intellectual abilities during adulthood. Five hundred individuals initially were tested in 1956, and new waves of participants are added periodically. The main mental abilities tested in the Seattle Longitudinal Study are as follows:

· *Verbal comprehension* (ability to understand ideas expressed in words)
· *Verbal memory* (ability to encode and recall meaningful language units, such as a list of words)
· *Numeric ability* (ability to perform simple mathematical computations such as addition, subtraction, and multiplication)
· *Spatial orientation* (ability to visualize and mentally rotate stimuli in two- and three-dimensional space)
· *Inductive reasoning* (ability to recognize and understand patterns and relationships in a problem and use this understanding to solve other instances of the problem)
· *Perceptual speed* (ability to quickly and accurately make simple discriminations in visual stimuli)

As shown in Figure 8, the highest level of functioning for four of the six intellectual abilities occurred during middle adulthood (Schaie, 2013). For both women and men, performance on verbal ability, verbal memory, inductive reasoning, and spatial orientation peaked in middle age. Only two of the six abilities—numeric ability and perceptual speed—declined in middle age. Perceptual speed showed the earliest decline, beginning in early adulthood.

Notice in Figure 8 that the declines in functioning for most cognitive abilities began to steepen in the sixties, although the decline in verbal ability did not steepen until the mid-seventies. From the mid-seventies through the mid-nineties, all cognitive abilities showed

FIGURE 8

LONGITUDINAL CHANGES IN SIX INTELLECTUAL ABILITIES FROM AGE 25 TO AGE 95. *Source:* K.W. Schaie: "Longitudinal Changes in Six Intellectual Abilities from Age 25 to Age 95" Figure 5.7a, in *Developmental Influences on Intelligence: The Seattle Longitudinal Study* (2nd rev edit.), 2013, p. 162.

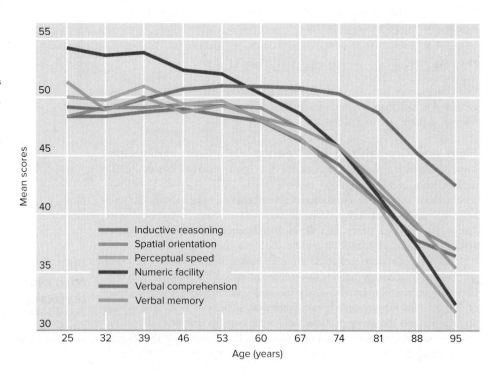

considerable decline. When Schaie (1994) assessed intellectual abilities both cross-sectionally and longitudinally, he found that decline was more likely to occur in the cross-sectional than in the longitudinal assessments. For example, as shown in Figure 9, when assessed longitudinally, inductive reasoning increased until toward the end of middle adulthood and then began to show a slight decline. In contrast, when assessed cross-sectionally, inductive reasoning showed a consistent decline during middle adulthood. For the participants in the Seattle Longitudinal Study, middle age was a time of peak performance for both some aspects of crystallized intelligence (verbal comprehension) and fluid intelligence (spatial orientation and inductive reasoning).

Some researchers disagree with Schaie that middle adulthood is the time when the level of functioning in a number of cognitive domains is maintained or even increases (Finch, 2009). For example, Timothy Salthouse (2009, 2012, 2015a, b) recently has argued that cross-sectional research on aging and cognitive functioning should not be dismissed and that this research indicates reasoning, memory, spatial visualization, and processing speed begin declining in early adulthood and show further decline in the fifties. Salthouse (2009, 2012) does agree that cognitive functioning involving accumulated knowledge, such as vocabulary and general information, does not show early age-related decline but rather continues to increase at least until 60 years of age. Salthouse (2009, 2012) has emphasized that a lower level of cognitive functioning in middle adulthood is likely due to age-related neurobiological decline.

Schaie (2013) continues to emphasize that longitudinal studies hold the key to determining age-related changes in cognitive functioning and that middle age is the time during which many cognitive skills actually peak. In the next decade, expanding research on age-related neurobiological changes and their possible links to cognitive skills should further refine our knowledge about age-related cognitive functioning in the adult years (Fletcher & Rapp, 2013; Merrill & others, 2012).

Cognitive Mechanics and Cognitive Pragmatics

Paul Baltes (1993, 2000, 2003; Baltes, Lindenberger, & Staudinger, 2006) clarified the distinction between those aspects of the aging mind that decline and those that remain stable or even improve. He makes a distinction between "cognitive mechanics" and "cognitive pragmatics," that extends the fluid/crystallized intelligence conceptualization described earlier:

- **Cognitive mechanics** are the "hardware" of the mind and reflect the neurophysiological architecture of the brain developed through evolution. Cognitive mechanics consist of the speed and accuracy of the processes involved in sensory input, attention, visual and motor memory, discrimination, comparison, and categorization. Because of the strong influence of biology, heredity, and health on cognitive mechanics, a decline with aging is likely.
- **Cognitive pragmatics** are the culture-based "software programs" of the mind. Cognitive pragmatics include reading and writing skills, language comprehension, educational qualifications, professional skills, and also the type of knowledge about the self and life skills that help us to master or cope with life. Because of the strong influence of culture on cognitive pragmatics, their improvement into old age is possible. Thus, although cognitive mechanics may decline in old age, cognitive pragmatics may actually improve (see Figure 10).

The distinction between cognitive mechanics and cognitive pragmatics is similar to the one between fluid (mechanics) and crystallized (pragmatics) intelligence that was described earlier. Indeed, the similarity is so strong that some experts now use the terms *fluid mechanics* and *crystallized pragmatics* to describe cognitive aging patterns (Lovden & Lindenberger, 2007).

K. Warner Schaie (*right*) is one of the leading pioneers in the field of life-span development. He is shown here with two older adults who are actively using their cognitive skills. Schaie's research represents one of the most thorough examinations of how individuals develop and change as they go through the adult years.
Courtesy of Dr. K. Warner Schaie

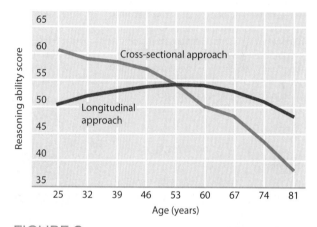

FIGURE 9

CROSS-SECTIONAL AND LONGITUDINAL COMPARISONS OF INDUCTIVE REASONING ABILITY ACROSS ADULTHOOD. In Schaie's research, the cross-sectional approach revealed declining scores with age; the longitudinal approach showed a slight rise of scores in middle adulthood and only a slight decline beginning in the early part of late adulthood.

cognitive mechanics The "hardware" of the mind, reflecting the neurophysiological architecture of the brain as developed through evolution. Cognitive mechanics involves the speed and accuracy of the processes involving sensory input, visual and motor memory, discrimination, comparison, and categorization.

cognitive pragmatics The culture-based "software" of the mind. Cognitive pragmatics include reading and writing skills, language comprehension, educational qualifications, professional skills, and also the type of self-knowledge and life skills that helps us to master or cope with life.

FIGURE **10**

THEORIZED AGE CHANGES IN COGNITIVE MECHANICS AND COGNITIVE PRAGMATICS. Baltes argues that cognitive mechanics decline during aging, whereas cognitive pragmatics do not, at least for many people until they become very old. Cognitive mechanics have a biological/genetic foundation; cognitive pragmatics have an experiential/cultural foundation. The broken lines from 75 to 100 years of age indicate possible individual variations in cognitive pragmatics.

developmental **connection**

Culture

In Baltes' view, for older adults the benefits of evolutionary selection decrease while the need for culture increases. Connect to "Biological Beginnings."

wisdom Expert knowledge about the practical aspects of life that permits excellent judgment about important matters.

intellectual disability A condition of limited mental ability in which an individual has a low IQ, usually below 70 on a traditional test of intelligence, and has difficulty adapting to the demands of everyday life.

Wisdom   As you just saw, Baltes stresses that wisdom is an important aspect of cognitive pragmatics. Baltes and his colleagues (2006) define **wisdom** as expert knowledge about the practical aspects of life that permits excellent judgment about important matters. This practical knowledge involves exceptional insight about human development and life matters, good judgment, and understanding of how to cope with difficult life problems. Thus, wisdom, more than standard conceptions of intelligence, focuses on life's pragmatic concerns and human conditions (Karelitz, Jarvin, & Sternberg, 2010; Staudinger & Gluck, 2011; Sternberg, 2013).

In regard to wisdom, Baltes and his colleagues (Baltes & Kunzmann, 2004; Baltes, Lindenberger, & Staudinger, 2006; Baltes & Smith, 2008) have reached the following conclusions:

· High levels of wisdom are rare. Few people, including older adults, attain a high level of wisdom. That only a small percentage of adults show wisdom supports the contention that it requires experience, practice, or complex skills.

· Factors other than age are critical for wisdom to develop to a high level. For example, certain life experiences, such as being trained and working in a field concerned with difficult life problems and having wisdom-enhancing mentors, contribute to higher levels of wisdom. Also, people higher in wisdom have values that are more likely to consider the welfare of others than their own happiness.

· Personality-related factors, such as openness to experience, generativity, and creativity, are better predictors of wisdom than cognitive factors such as intelligence.

A recent study compared college students and older adults on a wisdom scale, which consisted of three dimensions: cognitive, reflective, and affective (Ardelt, 2010, p. 199):

· *Cognitive* scale items measured the absence of cognitive wisdom and included items on not having the ability or being unwilling to understand something thoroughly ("ignorance is bliss," for example), and tending to perceive the world as either/or instead of more complex ("People are either good or bad," for example), and being unaware of ambiguity and uncertainty in life ("There is only one right way to do anything," for example).

· *Reflective* scale items evaluated having the ability and being willing to examine circumstances and issues from different perspectives ("I always try to look at all sides of

Older adults might not be as quick with their thoughts or behavior as younger people, but wisdom may be an entirely different matter. This older man shares the wisdom of his experience with children at an elementary school. *How is wisdom described by life-span developmentalists?*
© Michael J. Doolittle/The Image Works

a problem," for example) and the lack of self-examination and self-insight ("Things often go wrong for me through no fault of my own," for example).

· *Affective* scale items assessed positive and caring emotions ("Sometimes I feel a real compassion for everyone," for example) and the lack of those characteristics ("It's not really my problem if others are in trouble and need help," for example).

On the overall wisdom scale that included an assessment of all three dimensions combined, no differences were found between the two age groups. However, older adults who were college educated scored higher on the reflective and affective, but not the cognitive, dimensions of wisdom than the college students.

Review Connect Reflect

 LG3 Discuss the development of intelligence across the life span

Review
- How is intelligence assessed during infancy?
- How much does intelligence change through childhood and adolescence?
- To what extent does intelligence change as adults age? What is wisdom, and how can it be characterized?

Connect
- In this section, you read about longitudinal and cross-sectional studies of intelligence. What are the potential advantages and disadvantages of these research approaches?

Reflect *Your Own Personal Journey of Life*
- Think about your parents' and grandparents' intelligence. How might their intelligence have been influenced by cohort effects?

---

4 The Extremes of Intelligence and Creativity

 LG4 Describe the characteristics of intellectual disability, giftedness, and creativity

Intellectual Disability

Giftedness

Creativity

Intellectual disability and intellectual giftedness are the extremes of intelligence. Often intelligence tests are used to identify exceptional individuals. We will explore the nature of intellectual disability and giftedness, then examine how creativity differs from intelligence.

INTELLECTUAL DISABILITY

The most distinctive feature of intellectual disability (formerly called mental retardation) is inadequate intellectual functioning. Long before formal tests were developed to assess intelligence, individuals with an intellectual disability were identified by a lack of age-appropriate skills in learning and caring for themselves. Once intelligence tests were developed, they were used to identify the degree of intellectual disability. But of two individuals with an intellectual disability who have the same low IQ, one might be married, employed, and involved in the community and the other might require constant supervision in an institution. Such differences in social competence led psychologists to include deficits in adaptive behavior in their definition of intellectual disability.

Intellectual disability is a condition of limited mental ability in which the individual (1) has a low IQ, usually below 70 on a traditional intelligence test; (2) has difficulty adapting to the demands of everyday life; and (3) first exhibits these characteristics by age 18 (Hodapp & others, 2011). The age limit is included in the definition of intellectual disability because, for example, we don't usually think of a college student who suffers massive brain damage in a car accident, resulting in an IQ of 60, as having an "intellectual disability." The

What causes a child to develop Down syndrome? In which major classification of intellectual disability does Down syndrome fall?
© Stockbyte/Veer RF

Type of Intellectual Disability	IQ Range	Percentage of Individuals with an Intellectual Disability
Mild	55 to 70	89
Moderate	40 to 54	6
Severe	25 to 39	4
Profound	Below 25	1

FIGURE 11

CLASSIFICATION OF INTELLECTUAL DISABILITY BASED ON IQ

Classification of Intellectual Disability	Level of Support Needed
Intermittent	Supports are provided "as needed." The individual may need episodic or short-term support during life-span transitions (such as job loss or acute medical crisis). Intermittent supports may be low or high intensity when provided.
Limited	Supports are intense and relatively consistent over time. They are time-limited but not intermittent, require fewer staff members, and cost less than more intense supports. These supports likely will be needed for adaptation to the changes involved in the school-to-adult period.
Extensive	Supports are characterized by regular involvement (for example, daily) in at least some setting (such as home or work) and are not time-limited (for example, extended home-living support).
Pervasive	Supports are constant, very intense, and are provided across settings. They may be of a life-sustaining nature. These supports typically involve more staff members and intrusiveness than the other support categories.

FIGURE 12

CLASSIFICATION OF INTELLECTUAL DISABILITY BASED ON LEVELS OF SUPPORT NEEDED

developmental connection

Conditions, Diseases, and Disorders

Down syndrome is caused by the presence of an extra copy of chromosome 21. Connect to "Biological Beginnings."

giftedness Having above-average intelligence (an IQ of 130 or higher) and/or superior talent for something.

low IQ and low adaptiveness should be evident in childhood, not after normal functioning is interrupted by damage of some form. About 5 million Americans fit this definition of intellectual disability.

There are several ways to define degrees of intellectual disability (Hallahan, Kaufmann, & Pullen, 2015). Most school systems use the classifications shown in Figure 11, in which IQ scores categorize intellectual disability as mild, moderate, severe, or profound.

Note that a large majority of individuals diagnosed with an intellectual disability fit into the mild category. However, these categories are not perfect predictors of functioning. A different classification is based on the degree of support required for a person with an intellectual disability to function at the highest level. As shown in Figure 12, these categories of support are intermittent, limited, extensive, and pervasive.

Some cases of intellectual disability have an organic cause. *Organic intellectual disability* describes a genetic disorder or a lower level of intellectual functioning caused by brain damage. Down syndrome is one form of organic intellectual disability, and it occurs when an extra chromosome is present. Other causes of organic intellectual disability include fragile X syndrome, an abnormality in the X chromosome; prenatal malformation; metabolic disorders; and diseases that affect the brain. Most people who suffer from organic intellectual disability have IQs between 0 and 50.

When no evidence of organic brain damage can be found, cases are labeled *cultural-familial intellectual disability*. Individuals with this type of disability have IQs between 55 and 70. Psychologists suspect that this type of disability is often the result from growing up in a below-average intellectual environment. Children with this type of disability can be identified in schools, where they often fail, need tangible rewards (candy rather than praise), and are highly sensitive to what others expect of them. However, as adults, they are usually not noticeable, perhaps because adult settings don't tax their cognitive skills as sorely. It may also be that they increase their intelligence as they move toward adulthood.

GIFTEDNESS

There have always been people whose abilities and accomplishments outshine those of others—the whiz kid in class, the star athlete, the natural musician. People who are **gifted** have high intelligence or superior talent of some kind. An IQ of 130 is often used as the low threshold for giftedness, although this figure is arbitrary. Programs for the gifted in most school systems select children who have intellectual superiority and academic aptitude. They tend to overlook children who are talented in the arts or athletics or who have other special aptitudes, including their passion and sense of destiny (Olszewski-Kubilius & Thomson, 2013; Sternberg, 2014b; Sternberg & Bridges, 2014). Estimates vary but indicate that approximately 3 to 5 percent of U.S. students are gifted (National Association for Gifted Children, 2009). This percentage is likely conservative because it focuses more on children who are gifted intellectually and academically, often failing to include those who are gifted in creative thinking or the visual and performing arts (Ford, 2012).

Until recently, giftedness and emotional distress were thought to go hand-in-hand. Virginia Woolf, Sir Isaac Newton, Vincent van Gogh, Anne Sexton, Socrates, and Sylvia Plath all had emotional problems. However, these individuals are the exception rather than the rule. In general, no relation between giftedness and mental disorder has been found. Research supports the conclusion that gifted people tend to be more mature, to have fewer emotional problems than others, and to grow up in a positive family climate (Feldhusen, 1999). A recent study revealed that parents and teachers identified elementary school children who are not gifted as having more emotional and behavioral risks than children who are gifted (Eklund & others, 2015). In this study, when children who are gifted did have problems, they were more likely to be internalized problems, such as anxiety and depression, than externalized problems, such as acting out and high levels of aggression.

Characteristics of Children Who Are Gifted   Aside from their abilities, do children who are gifted have distinctive characteristics? Lewis Terman (1925) conducted an extensive study of 1,500 children whose Stanford-Binet IQs averaged 150. Contrary to the popular myth that children who are gifted are maladjusted, Terman found that they were socially well adjusted.

Ellen Winner (1996) described three criteria that characterize gifted children, whether in art, music, or academic domains:

1. *Precocity*. Gifted children are precocious. They begin to master an area earlier than their peers. Learning in their domain is more effortless for them than for ordinary children. In most instances, these gifted children are precocious because they have an inborn high ability.

2. *Marching to their own drummer*. Gifted children learn in a qualitatively different way from ordinary children. For one thing, they need minimal help from adults to learn. In many cases, they resist explicit instruction. They also often make discoveries on their own and solve problems in unique ways.

3. *A passion to master*. Gifted children are driven to understand the domain in which they have high ability. They display an intense, obsessive interest and an ability to focus. They do not need to be pushed by their parents. They motivate themselves, says Winner.

Art prodigy Alexandra Nechita. *What are some characteristics of gifted children?*
© Koichi Kamoshida/Newsmakers/Getty Images

Life Course of the Gifted   As a 10-year-old, Alexandra Nechita (born in 1985) was described as a child prodigy. She paints quickly and impulsively on large canvases, some as large as 5 feet by 9 feet. It is not unusual for her to complete several of these large paintings in a week's time. Her paintings sell for up to $100,000 apiece. When she was only 2 years of age, Alexandra colored in coloring books for hours. She had no interest in dolls or friends. Once she started school, she would start painting as soon as she got home. And she continues to paint as an adult—relentlessly and passionately. It is, she says, what she loves to do. Recently, Alexandra completed a degree in Fine Arts at UCLA. Also, a longitudinal study of children identified before 13 years of age as having profound math or verbal reasoning skills (top 1 in 10,000) found that they had achieved considerable success in their careers in various domains by the time they were 38 years of age (Kell, Lubinski, & Benbow, 2013).

Is giftedness, like Alexandra Nechita's artistic talent and the children with profound math and verbal skills just described, a product of heredity or of environment? Likely both (Duggan & Friedman, 2014; Johnson & Bouchard, 2014). Individuals who are gifted recall that they had signs of high ability in a specific area at a very young age, prior to or at the beginning of formal training (Howe & others, 1995). This suggests the importance of innate ability in giftedness. However, researchers also have found that individuals with world-class status in the arts, mathematics, science, and sports all report strong family support and years of training and practice (Bloom, 1985). Deliberate practice is an important characteristic of individuals who become experts in a specific domain. For example, in one study, the best musicians engaged in twice as much deliberate practice over their lives as the least successful ones did (Ericsson, Krampe, & Tesch-Römer, 1993).

Do gifted children become gifted and highly creative adults? In Terman's research on children with superior IQs, the children typically became experts in a well-established domain, such as medicine, law, or business. However, they did not become major creators (Winner, 2000). That is, they did not create a new domain or revolutionize an old domain.

Margaret (Peg) Cagle with some of the gifted seventh- and eighth-grade math students she teaches at Lawrence Middle School in Chatsworth, California. Cagle especially advocates challenging gifted students to take intellectual risks. To encourage collaboration, she often has students work together in groups of four, and frequently tutors students during lunch hour. As 13-year-old Madeline Lewis commented, "If I don't get it one way, she'll explain it another and talk to you about it and show you until you do get it." Cagle says it is important to be passionate about teaching math and open up a world for students that shows them how beautiful learning math can be (Wong Briggs, 2007, p. 6D).
© Scott Buschman

One reason that some gifted children do not become gifted adults is that they often have been pushed too hard by overzealous parents and teachers. As a result, they lose their intrinsic (internal) motivation (Winner, 1996, 2006). As adolescents, they may ask themselves, "Who am I doing this for?" If they are achieving in an effort to please others rather than themselves, they may not want to do it anymore. Another reason that gifted children do not become gifted adults is that the criteria for giftedness change—as an adult, an individual has to actually do something special to be labeled gifted.

Domain-Specific Giftedness Individuals who are highly gifted are typically not gifted in many domains, and research on giftedness increasingly focuses on domain-specific developmental trajectories (Kell & Lubinski, 2014; Sternberg & Bridges, 2014). During the childhood years, the domains in which individuals are gifted usually emerge. Thus, at some point in childhood, a person who is to become a gifted artist or a gifted mathematician begins to show expertise in that domain. Regarding domain-specific giftedness, software genius Bill Gates (1998), the founder of Microsoft and one of the world's richest persons, commented that sometimes you have to be careful when you are good at something and resist the urge to think that you will be good at everything. Gates says that because he has been so successful at software development, people expect him to be brilliant in other domains where he is far from being a genius.

A young Bill Gates. Like many highly gifted students, Gates was not especially fond of school. He hacked a computer security system when he was 13, and as a high school student he was allowed to take some college math classes. He dropped out of Harvard University and began developing a plan for what was to become Microsoft Corporation. *What are some ways that schools can enrich the education of such highly talented students as Gates to make it a more challenging, interesting, and meaningful experience?*
© Doug Wilson/Corbis

Education of Children Who Are Gifted An increasing number of experts argue that the education of gifted children in the United States requires a significant overhaul (Olszewski-Kubilius & Thomson, 2013; Reis & Renzulli, 2014). Consider the titles of the following books and reports: *Genius Denied: How to Stop Wasting Our Brightest Young Minds* (Davidson & Davidson, 2004) and *A Nation Deceived: How Schools Hold Back America's Brightest Students* (Colangelo, Assouline, & Gross, 2004).

Underchallenged gifted children can become disruptive, skip classes, and lose interest in achieving. Sometimes these children just disappear into the woodwork, becoming passive and apathetic toward school. It is extremely important for teachers to challenge children who are gifted to establish high expectations (Olszewski-Kubilius & Thomson, 2013; Sternberg, Jarvin, & Grigorenko, 2011).

Some educators conclude that the inadequate education of children who are gifted has been compounded by the federal government's No Child Left Behind policy, which seeks to raise the achievement level of students who are not doing well in school at the expense of enriching the education of children who are gifted (Clark, 2008). A number of experts argue that too often children who are gifted are socially isolated and underchallenged in the classroom (Karnes & Stephens, 2008; Sternberg, Jarvin, & Grigorenko, 2011). It is not unusual for them to be ostracized and labeled "nerds" or "geeks." Ellen Winner (1996, 2006) concludes that a child who is truly gifted often is the only child in the room who does not have the opportunity to learn with students of like ability.

Many eminent adults report that school was a negative experience for them, that they were bored and sometimes knew more than their teachers (Bloom, 1985). Winner stresses that American education will benefit when standards are raised for all children. When some children are still underchallenged, she recommends that they be allowed to attend advanced classes in their domain of exceptional ability, such as allowing some especially precocious middle school students to take college classes in their area of expertise. For example, Bill Gates took college math classes and hacked a computer security system at 13; Yo-Yo Ma, a famous cellist, graduated from high school at 15 and attended Juilliard School of Music in New York City.

A final concern is that African American, Latino, and Native American children are underrepresented in gifted programs (Ford, 2012). Much of the underrepresentation involves the lower test scores for these children compared with non-Latino White and Asian American children, which may be due to a number of reasons such as test bias and fewer opportunities to develop language skills such as vocabulary and comprehension (Ford, 2012).

- - - - - - - - - ➤
developmental **connection**

Education

A number of criticisms of the No Child Left Behind policy have been made. Connect to "Schools, Achievement, and Work."

CREATIVITY

We have encountered the term "creative" on several occasions in our discussion of giftedness. What does it mean to be creative? **Creativity** is the ability to think about something in novel and unusual ways and to come up with unique, good solutions to problems.

Intelligence and creativity are not the same thing (Barbot & Tinio, 2015; Sternberg & Sternberg, 2016). Most creative people are quite intelligent, but the reverse is not necessarily true. Many highly intelligent people (as measured by high scores on conventional tests of intelligence) are not very creative. Many highly intelligent people produce large numbers of products, but their output is not necessarily novel.

Why don't IQ scores predict creativity? Creativity requires divergent thinking (Guilford, 1967). **Divergent thinking** produces many answers to the same question. In contrast, conventional intelligence tests require **convergent thinking.** For example, a typical question on a conventional intelligence test is "How many quarters will you get in return for 60 dimes?" There is only one correct answer to this question. In contrast, a question such as "What image comes to mind when you hear the phrase 'sitting alone in a dark room'?" has many possible answers; it calls for divergent thinking.

What do you mean, "What is it"? It's the spontaneous, unfettered expression of a young mind not yet bound by the restraints of narrative or pictorial representation.
Cartoon by Sidney Harris Copyright © ScienceCartoonsPlus.com.

Steps in the Creative Process   The creative process has often been described as a five-step sequence:

1. *Preparation.* You become immersed in a problem or an issue that interests you and arouses your curiosity.
2. *Incubation.* You churn ideas around in your head. This is the point at which you are likely to make some unusual connections in your thinking.
3. *Insight.* You experience the "Aha!" moment when all pieces of the puzzle seem to fit together.
4. *Evaluation.* Now you must decide whether the idea is valuable and worth pursuing. Is the idea really novel or is it obvious?
5. *Elaboration.* This final step often covers the longest span of time and requires the hardest work. This is what the famous twentieth-century American inventor Thomas Edison was talking about when he said that creativity is 1 percent inspiration and 99 percent perspiration. Elaboration may require a great deal of perspiration.

Mihaly Csikszentmihalyi (pronounced ME-high CHICK-sent-me-high-ee) (1996) notes that this five-step sequence provides a helpful framework for thinking about how creative ideas are developed. However, he argues that creative people don't always go through the steps in a linear sequence. For example, elaboration is often interrupted by periods of incubation. Fresh insights may appear during incubation, evaluation, and elaboration. And insight might take years or only a few hours. Sometimes the creative idea consists of one deep insight. Other times it's a series of small ones.

Characteristics of Creative Thinkers   Creative thinkers tend to have the following characteristics (Perkins, 1994):

· *Flexibility and playful thinking.* Creative thinkers are flexible and play with problems, which gives rise to a paradox. Although creativity takes hard work, the work goes more smoothly if you take it lightly (Goleman, Kaufman, & Ray, 1993). When you are joking around, you are more likely to consider any possibility.
· *Inner motivation.* Creative people often are motivated by the joy of creating. They tend to be less inspired by grades, money, or favorable feedback from others. Thus, creative people are motivated more internally than externally.
· *Willingness to risk.* Creative people make more mistakes than their less imaginative counterparts. It's not that they are less proficient but that they come up with more ideas, more possibilities (Lubart, 2003). They win some, they lose some. For example, the twentieth-century Spanish artist Pablo Picasso created more than 20,000 paintings. Not all of them were masterpieces. Creative thinkers learn to cope with unsuccessful projects and see failure as an opportunity to learn.

creativity The ability to think in novel and unusual ways and to come up with unique solutions to problems.

divergent thinking Thinking that produces many answers to the same question; characteristic of creativity.

convergent thinking Thinking that produces one correct answer; characteristic of the kind of thinking required on conventional intelligence tests.

What are some good strategies for guiding children to think more creatively?
© Ariel Skelley/Blend Images/Corbis RF

· *Objective evaluation of work.* Contrary to the stereotype that creative people are eccentric and highly subjective, most creative thinkers strive to evaluate their work objectively. They may use established criteria to make this judgment or rely on the judgments of people they respect. In this manner, they can determine whether further creative thinking will improve their work.

Creativity in Schools   A special concern is that children's creative thinking appears to be declining. A study of approximately 300,000 U.S. children and adults found that creativity scores rose until 1990, but since then have been steadily declining (Kim, 2010). Among the likely causes of the creativity decline are the number of hours U.S. children watch TV and play video games instead of engaging in creative activities, as well as the lack of emphasis on creative thinking skills in schools (Gregorson, Kaufman, & Snyder, 2013; Kaufman & Sternberg, 2013). Some countries, though, are placing increasing emphasis on creative thinking in schools. For example, historically, creative thinking has typically been discouraged in Chinese schools. However, Chinese educators are now encouraging teachers to spend more classroom time on creative activities (Plucker, 2010).

An important teaching goal is to help students become more creative (Hennessey, 2011). Teachers need to recognize that students will show more creativity in some domains than in others (Kaufman & Sternberg, 2013). A student who shows creative thinking skills in mathematics may not exhibit these skills in art, for example.

School environments that encourage independent work, are stimulating but not distracting, and make resources readily available are likely to encourage students' creativity. There is mounting concern that the U.S. government's No Child Left Behind legislation has harmed the development of students' creative thinking by focusing attention on memorizing information to ensure high performance on standardized tests (Burke-Adams, 2007; Kaufman & Sternberg, 2013).

Strategies for increasing children's creative thinking include the following:

· *Encourage brainstorming.* **Brainstorming** is a technique in which people are encouraged to come up with creative ideas in a group, play off each other's ideas, and say practically whatever comes to mind that seems relevant to a particular issue. Participants are usually told to hold off from criticizing others' ideas at least until the end of the brainstorming session.

· *Provide environments that stimulate creativity.* Some environments nourish creativity, while others inhibit it. Parents and teachers who encourage creativity often rely on children's natural curiosity. They provide exercises and activities that stimulate children to find insightful solutions to problems, rather than ask a lot of questions that require rote

brainstorming Technique in which individuals are encouraged to come up with creative ideas in a group, play off each other's ideas, and say practically whatever comes to mind that is relevant to a particular issue.

answers (Baer & Kaufman, 2013). Teachers also encourage creativity by taking students on field trips to locations where creativity is valued. Science, discovery, and children's museums offer rich opportunities to stimulate creativity.

· *Don't overcontrol students.* Teresa Amabile (1993) says that telling children exactly how to do things leaves them feeling that originality is a mistake and exploration is a waste of time. If, instead of dictating which activities they should engage in, you let children select their interests and you support their inclinations, you will be less likely to destroy their natural curiosity (Hennessey, 2011).

· *Encourage internal motivation.* Excessive use of prizes, such as gold stars, money, or toys, can stifle creativity by undermining the intrinsic pleasure students derive from creative activities. Creative children's motivation is the satisfaction generated by the work itself. Competition for prizes and formal evaluations often undermine intrinsic motivation and creativity (Amabile & Hennessey, 1992). However, material rewards should not be eliminated altogether.

· *Build children's confidence.* To expand children's creativity, encourage them to believe in their own ability to create something innovative and worthwhile. Building children's confidence in their creative skills aligns with Bandura's (2010, 2012) concept of self-efficacy—the belief that one can master a situation and produce positive outcomes.

· *Guide children to be persistent and delay gratification.* Most highly successful creative products take years to develop. Most creative individuals work on ideas and projects for months and years without being rewarded for their efforts (Sternberg & Williams, 1996).

· *Encourage children to take intellectual risks.* Creative individuals take intellectual risks and seek to discover or invent something that has never before been discovered or invented (Sternberg & Williams, 1996). They risk spending extensive time on an idea or project that may not work. Creative people are not afraid of failing or getting something wrong.

· *Introduce children to creative people.* Teachers can invite creative people to their classrooms and ask them to describe what helps them become creative or to demonstrate their creative skills. Writers, poets, musicians, scientists, and many others can bring their props and productions to the class, turning it into a theater for stimulating students' creativity.

You can find out about steps you can take to live a more creative life in the *Connecting Development to Life* interlude.

Changes in Adulthood   At the age of 30, Thomas Edison invented the phonograph, Hans Christian Andersen wrote his first volume of fairy tales, and Mozart composed *The Marriage of Figaro*. One early study of creativity found that individuals' most creative products were generated in their thirties and that 80 percent of the most important creative contributions were completed by age 50 (Lehman, 1960). More recently, researchers have found that creativity often peaks in the forties before declining (Simonton, 1996). However, any generalization about a relationship between age and creative accomplishments must be qualified by consideration of (1) the size of the decline and (2) differences across domains (Jones, Reedy, & Weinberg, 2014; McKay & Kaufman, 2014).

Even though a decline in creative contributions is often found in the fifties and later, the decline is often not great. And a study of artists from 53 to 75 years of age found no age differences in the artists' perceptions of their creativity (Reed, 2005). An impressive array of creative accomplishments have occurred in late adulthood (Tahir & Gruber, 2003). Benjamin Franklin invented the bifocal lens when he was 78 years old; Wolfgang von Goethe completed *Faust* when he was in his eighties. After a distinguished career as a physicist, Henri Chevreul switched fields in his nineties to become a pioneer in gerontological research. He published his last research paper just a year prior to his death at the age of 103!

Furthermore, the age at which creativity typically declines varies with the domain involved. In philosophy and history, for example, older adults often show as much creativity as they did when they were in their thirties and forties. In contrast, in lyric poetry, abstract mathematics, and theoretical physics, the peak of creativity is often reached in the twenties or thirties.

developmental **connection**

Achievement

Intrinsic motivation requires the internal motivation to do something for its own sake (the activity is an end in itself). Connect to "Schools, Achievement, and Work."

developmental **connection**

Achievement

Self-efficacy is the belief that "I can"; helplessness is the belief that "I cannot." Connect to "Schools, Achievement, and Work."

Living a More Creative Life

Leading expert on creativity Mihaly Csikszentmihalyi (1996) interviewed 90 leading figures in art, business, government, education, and science to learn how creativity works. He discovered that creative people regularly engage in challenges that absorb them. Based on his interviews with some of the most creative people in the world, he concluded that the first step toward a more creative life is to cultivate your curiosity and interest. Here are his recommendations for doing this:

1. *Try to be surprised by something every day.* Maybe it is something you see, hear, or read about. Become absorbed in a lecture or a book. Be open to what the world is telling you. Life is a stream of experiences. Swim widely and deeply in it, and your life will be richer.

2. *Try to surprise at least one person every day.* In a lot of things you do, you have to be predictable and patterned. Do something different for a change. Ask a question you normally would not ask. Invite someone to go to a show or a museum you never have visited.

3. *Write down each day what surprised you and how you surprised others.* Most creative people keep a diary, notes, or lab records to ensure that their experience is not forgotten. Start with a specific task. Each evening, record the most surprising event that occurred that day and your most surprising action. After a few days, reread your notes and reflect on your experiences. After a few weeks, you might see a pattern emerging, one that suggests an area you can explore in greater depth.

4. *When something sparks your interest, follow it.* Usually when something captures your attention, it is short-lived—an idea, a song, a flower. Too often we are too busy to explore the idea, song, or flower further. Or we think these areas are none of our business because we are not experts about them. Yet the world is our business. We can't know which part of it is best suited to our interests until we make a serious effort to learn as much about as many aspects of it as possible.

5. *Wake up in the morning with a specific goal to look forward to.* Creative people wake up eager to start the day. Why? Not necessarily because they are cheerful, enthusiastic types but because they know that there is something meaningful to accomplish each day, and they can't wait to get started.

6. *Take charge of your schedule.* Figure out which time of the day is your most creative time. Some of us are more creative late at night, others early in the morning. Carve out some time for yourself when your creative energy is at its best.

Leading creativity theorist Mihaly Csikszentmihalyi, in the setting where he gets his most creative ideas.
Courtesy of Dr. Mihaly Csiksentmihalyi

7. *Spend time in settings that stimulate your creativity.* In Csikszentmihalyi's (1996) research, he gave people an electronic pager and beeped them randomly at different times of the day. When he asked them how they felt, they reported the highest levels of creativity when walking, driving, or swimming. For example, one person said, "I do my most creative thinking when I'm jogging." A recent experimental study compared the creative thinking skills of individuals after they had experienced one of four conditions: sitting inside, walking on a treadmill inside, walking outside, or being rolled outside in a wheelchair (Oppezzo & Schwartz, 2014). In this study, walking was more likely to produce the most creative thinking. These activities, such as walking, jogging, and swimming are semiautomatic in that they take a certain amount of attention while leaving some time free to make connections among ideas. Another setting in which highly creative people report coming up with novel ideas is the half-asleep, half-awake state we are in when we are deeply relaxed or barely awake.

Can the strategies for stimulating creative thinking in children found earlier in this chapter also be used by adults? How do those strategies compare to those discussed here?

Review Connect Reflect

LG4 Describe the characteristics of intellectual disability, giftedness, and creativity

Review

- What is intellectual disability and what are its causes?
- What makes people gifted?
- What makes people creative?

Connect

- Regarding children's critical-thinking skills and problem-solving strategies, what role, if any, might these play in determining whether or not children become creative thinkers?

Reflect *Your Own Personal Journey of Life*

- How many of the tips in the *Connecting Development to Life* interlude, "Living a More Creative Life," do you practice? In what ways might you benefit from these suggestions, in addition to becoming more creative?

reach your **learning goals**

Intelligence

1 The Concept of Intelligence

LG1 Explain the nature of intelligence

- What Is Intelligence?

- Intelligence Tests

- Theories of Multiple Intelligences

- The Neuroscience of Intelligence

- Intelligence consists of the ability to solve problems and to adapt and learn from experiences. A key aspect of intelligence focuses on its individual variations. Traditionally, intelligence has been measured by tests designed to compare people's performance on cognitive tasks.

- Sir Francis Galton is considered the father of mental tests. Alfred Binet developed the first intelligence test and created the concept of mental age. William Stern developed the concept of IQ for use with the Binet test. Revisions of the Binet test are called the Stanford-Binet. The test scores on the Stanford-Binet approximate a normal distribution. The Wechsler scales, created by David Wechsler, are the other main intelligence assessment tool. These tests provide an overall IQ and yield several composite scores, allowing the examiner to identify strengths and weaknesses in different areas of intelligence. Test scores should be only one type of information used to evaluate an individual, not the only criterion. IQ scores can produce unfortunate stereotypes and expectations.

- Sternberg's triarchic theory states that there are three main types of intelligence: analytical, creative, and practical. Gardner identifies eight types of intelligence: verbal skills, mathematical skills, spatial skills, bodily-kinesthetic skills, musical skills, interpersonal skills, intrapersonal skills, and naturalist skills. Emotional intelligence is the ability to perceive and express emotion accurately and adaptively, to understand emotion and emotional knowledge, to use feelings to facilitate thought, and to manage emotions in oneself and others. The multiple intelligences approaches have broadened the definition of intelligence and motivated educators to develop programs that instruct students in different domains. Critics maintain that the multiple intelligences theories include factors that really aren't part of intelligence, such as musical skills and creativity. Critics also say that not enough research has been done to support the concept of multiple intelligences.

- Interest in discovering links between the brain and intelligence have been stimulated by advances in brain imaging. A moderate correlation has been found between brain size and intelligence. Some experts emphasize that the highest level of intelligence that involves reasoning is linked to the prefrontal cortex. However, other researchers recently have found a link between a distributed neural network in the frontal and parietal lobes and intelligence. The search for a connection between neural processing speed and intelligence has produced mixed results.

2 Controversies and Group Comparisons

 Outline key controversies about differences in IQ scores

The Influence of Heredity and Environment

· Genetic similarity might explain why identical twins show stronger correlations on intelligence tests than fraternal twins do. Many studies show that intelligence has a reasonably strong heritability component, but criticisms of the heritability concept have been made. In recent decades there has been a considerable rise in intelligence test scores around the world—called the Flynn effect—and this supports the role of environment in intelligence. Researchers have found that how much parents talk with their children in the first three years of life is correlated with the children's IQs and that being deprived of formal education lowers IQ scores. Ramey's research revealed the positive effects of educational child care on intelligence.

Group Comparisons and Issues

· Cultures vary in the way they define intelligence. Early intelligence tests favored non-Latino White, middle-socioeconomic-status, urban individuals. Tests may be biased against certain groups that are not familiar with a standard form of English, with the content tested, or with the testing situation. Tests are likely to reflect the values and experience of the dominant culture. In the United States, the average score of African American children is below the average score of non-Latino White children on standardized intelligence tests, but as African Americans have gained economic, social, and educational opportunities, the gap between these average scores has begun to narrow.

3 The Development of Intelligence

 Discuss the development of intelligence across the life span

Tests of Infant Intelligence

· The Bayley scales are widely used to assess infant intelligence. The Fagan Test of Infant Intelligence, which assesses how effectively infants process information, is increasingly being used.

Stability and Change in Intelligence Through Adolescence

· Although intelligence is more stable across childhood and adolescence than are many other attributes, many children's and adolescents' scores on intelligence tests fluctuate considerably.

Intelligence in Adulthood

· Horn argued that crystallized intelligence continues to increase in middle adulthood, whereas fluid intelligence begins to decline. Schaie found that when assessed longitudinally, inductive reasoning is less likely to decline and more likely to improve than when assessed cross-sectionally in middle adulthood. The highest level of four intellectual abilities (vocabulary, verbal memory, inductive reasoning, and spatial orientation) occurs in middle adulthood. Baltes emphasizes a distinction between cognitive mechanics (the "hardware" of the mind, reflecting the neurophysiological architecture of the brain) and cognitive pragmatics (the culture-based "software" of the mind). Cognitive mechanics are more likely to decline in older adults than are cognitive pragmatics. Wisdom is expert knowledge about the practical aspects of life that permits excellent judgment about important matters. Baltes and his colleagues have found that high levels of wisdom are rare, factors other than age are critical for a high level of wisdom to develop, and personality-related factors are better predictors of wisdom than cognitive factors such as intelligence.

4 The Extremes of Intelligence and Creativity

 Describe the characteristics of intellectual disability, giftedness, and creativity

Intellectual Disability

· Intellectual disability is a condition of limited mental ability in which the individual (1) has a low IQ, usually below 70; (2) has difficulty adapting to the demands of everyday life; and (3) has an onset of these characteristics by age 18. Most affected individuals have an IQ in the 55 to 70 range (mild intellectual disability). Intellectual disability can have an organic cause or a cultural/familial cause.

Giftedness

· People who are gifted have high intelligence (an IQ of 130 or higher) or some type of superior talent. Three characteristics of gifted children are precocity, marching to their own drummer, and a passion to achieve mastery in their domain. Giftedness is likely a consequence of both heredity and environment. A current concern is the education of children who are gifted.

Creativity

Creativity is the ability to think about something in novel and unusual ways and come up with unique solutions to problems. Although most creative people are intelligent, individuals with high IQs are not necessarily creative. Creative people tend to be divergent thinkers, but traditional intelligence tests measure convergent thinking. Creativity has often been described as occurring in a five-step process: preparation, incubation, insight, evaluation, and elaboration. Characteristics of creative thinkers include flexibility and playful thinking, inner motivation, a willingness to take risks, and interest in objective evaluation. Creativity often peaks in the forties and then declines, but the decline may be slight and the peak age varies across domains. Csikszentmihalyi notes that cultivating curiosity and interest is the first step toward leading a more creative life.

key **terms**

Bayley Scales of Infant Development
brainstorming
cognitive mechanics
cognitive pragmatics
convergent thinking

creativity
crystallized intelligence
culture-fair tests
divergent thinking
emotional intelligence
fluid intelligence

giftedness
heritability
intellectual disability
intelligence
intelligence quotient (IQ)

mental age (MA)
normal distribution
triarchic theory of intelligence
wisdom

key **people**

Paul Baltes
Nancy Bayley
Alfred Binet
Mihaly Csikszentmihalyi
James Flynn

Howard Gardner
Daniel Goleman
John Horn
John Mayer
Robert McCall

Robert Plomin
Craig Ramey
Peter Salovey
K. Warner Schaie
Théophile Simon

Robert J. Sternberg
Lewis Terman
David Wechsler
Ellen Winner

Chapter 9

LANGUAGE DEVELOPMENT

chapter outline

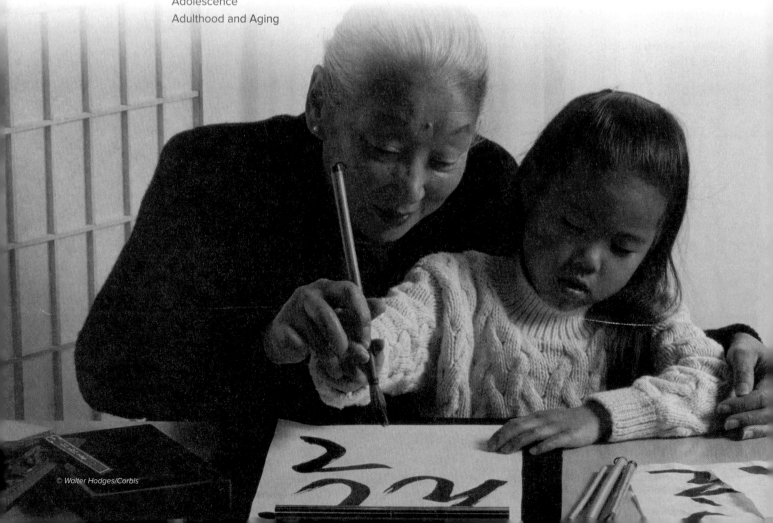

© Walter Hodges/Corbis

preview

In this chapter, we will tell the remarkable story of language and how it develops. The questions we will explore include these: What is language? What is the course of language development across the life span? What does biology contribute to language? How do different experiences influence language?

1 What Is Language? LG1 Define language and describe its rule systems

> Defining Language

> Language's Rule Systems

In 1799, a nude boy was observed running through the woods in France. The boy was captured when he was 11 years old. He was called the Wild Boy of Aveyron and was believed to have lived in the woods alone for six years (Lane, 1976). When found, he made no effort to communicate. He never learned to communicate effectively. A modern-day wild child named Genie was discovered in Los Angeles in 1970. Genie had been locked away in almost complete social isolation during her childhood. At age 13, Genie could not speak or stand erect. Sadly, despite intensive intervention, Genie never acquired more than a primitive form of language. Both cases—the Wild Boy of Aveyron and Genie—raise questions about the biological and environmental determinants of language, topics that we will examine later in the chapter. First, though, we need to define language.

> Words not only affect us temporarily; they change us, they socialize us, and they unsocialize us.
>
> **—DAVID REISMAN**
> *American social scientist, 20th century*

DEFINING LANGUAGE

Language is a form of communication—whether spoken, written, or signed—that is based on a system of symbols. Language consists of the words used by a community and the rules for varying and combining them.

Think how important language is in our everyday lives. We need language to speak with others, listen to others, read, and write. Our language enables us to describe past events in detail and to plan for the future. Language lets us pass down information from one generation to the next and create a rich cultural heritage.

All human languages have some common characteristics (MacWhinney, 2015; Waxman & others, 2013). These include infinite generativity and organizational rules. **Infinite generativity** is the ability to produce an endless number of meaningful sentences using a finite set of words and rules. Rules describe the way language works. Let's explore what these rules involve.

Language allows us to communicate with others. *What are some important characteristics of language?*
© Graeme Montgomery/Getty Images

LANGUAGE'S RULE SYSTEMS

When nineteenth-century American writer Ralph Waldo Emerson said, "The world was built in order and the atoms march in tune," he must have had language in mind. Language is highly ordered and organized (MacWhinney, 2015). The organization involves five systems of rules: phonology, morphology, syntax, semantics, and pragmatics.

Phonology Every language is made up of basic sounds. **Phonology** is the sound system of the language, including the sounds that are used and how they may be combined (Vihman, 2014). For example, English has the initial consonant cluster *spr* as in *spring*, but no words begin with the cluster *rsp*.

language A form of communication, whether spoken, written, or signed, that is based on a system of symbols.

infinite generativity The ability to produce an endless number of meaningful sentences using a finite set of words and rules.

phonology The sound system of a language—includes the sounds used and how they may be combined.

Phonology provides a basis for constructing a large and expandable set of words out of two or three dozen phonemes (Del Campo & others, 2015). A *phoneme* is the basic unit of sound in a language; it is the smallest unit of sound that affects meaning. For example, in English the sound represented by the letter *p*, as in the words *pot* and *spot*, is a phoneme. The /p/ sound is slightly different in the two words, but this variation is not distinguished in English, and therefore the /p/ sound is a single phoneme. In some languages, such as Hindi, the variations of the /p/ sound represent separate phonemes.

Morphology   **Morphology** refers to the units of meaning involved in word formation. A morpheme is a minimal unit of meaning; it is a word or a part of a word that cannot be broken into smaller meaningful parts (Booij, 2013). Every word in the English language is made up of one or more morphemes. Some words consist of a single morpheme (for example, *help*), whereas others are made up of more than one morpheme (for example, *helper* has two morphemes, *help* and *er*, with the morpheme *-er* meaning "one who"—in this case "one who helps"). Thus, not all morphemes are words by themselves—for example, *pre-*, *tion*, and *-ing* are morphemes.

Just as the rules that govern phonology describe the sound sequences that can occur in a language, the rules of morphology describe the way meaningful units (morphemes) can be combined in words (Brown, 2013). Morphemes have many jobs in grammar, such as marking tense (for example, "she walks" versus "she walked") and number ("she walks" versus "they walk").

Syntax   **Syntax** involves the way words are combined to form acceptable phrases and sentences (Culicover, 2013; Los, 2015; Tallerman, 2013). If someone says to you, "Bob slugged Tom" or "Bob was slugged by Tom," you know who did the slugging and who was slugged in each case because you have a syntactic understanding of these sentence structures. You also understand that the sentence "You didn't stay, did you?" is a grammatical sentence but that "You didn't stay, didn't you?" is unacceptable and ambiguous.

If you learn another language, English syntax will not get you very far. For example, in English an adjective usually precedes a noun (as in *blue sky*), whereas in Spanish the adjective usually follows the noun (*cielo azul*). Despite the differences in their syntactic structures, however, syntactic systems in all of the world's languages have some common ground (Brown, Chumakina, & Corbett, 2013; Whaley, 2013). For example, no language we know of permits sentences like the following one:

> *The mouse the cat the farmer chased killed ate the cheese.*

It appears that language users cannot process subjects and objects arranged in too complex a fashion in a sentence.

Semantics   **Semantics** refers to the meaning of words and sentences. Every word has a set of semantic features, which are required attributes related to meaning (Harris, Golinkoff, & Hirsh-Pasek, 2012; Parrish-Morris, Golinkoff, & Hirsh-Pasek, 2013). *Girl* and *woman*, for example, share many semantic features, but they differ semantically in regard to age.

Words have semantic restrictions on how they can be used in sentences (Crain & Zhou, 2013; Duff, Tomblin, & Catts, 2015). The sentence *The bicycle talked the boy into buying a candy bar* is syntactically correct but semantically incorrect. The sentence violates our semantic knowledge that bicycles don't talk.

Pragmatics   A final set of language rules involves **pragmatics,** the appropriate use of language in different contexts. Pragmatics covers a lot of territory (Clark, 2014; Elbourne, 2012). When you take turns speaking in a discussion or use a question to convey a command ("Why is it so noisy in here? What is this, Grand Central Station?"), you are demonstrating knowledge of pragmatics. You also apply the pragmatics of English when you use polite language in appropriate situations (for example, when talking to your teacher) or tell stories that are interesting, jokes that are funny, and lies that are convincing. In each of these cases, you are demonstrating that you understand the rules of your culture for adjusting language to suit the context.

Pragmatic rules can be complex and differ from one culture to another (Bryant, 2012). Consider the pragmatics of saying "thank you." Even preschoolers' use of the phrase *thank you* varies with sex, socioeconomic status, and the age of the individual they are addressing. If you were to study the Japanese language, you would come face-to-face with countless

morphology Units of meaning involved in word formation.

syntax The ways words are combined to form acceptable phrases and sentences.

semantics The meanings of words and sentences.

pragmatics The appropriate use of language in different contexts.

Rule System	Description	Examples
Phonology	The sound system of a language. A phoneme is the smallest sound unit in a language.	The word *chat* has three phonemes or sounds: /ch/ /ā/ /t/. An example of a phonological rule in the English language is while the phoneme /r/ can follow the phonemes /t/ or /d/ in an English consonant cluster (such as *track* or *drab*), the phoneme /l/ cannot follow these letters.
Morphology	The system of meaningful units involved in word formation.	The smallest sound units that have a meaning are called morphemes, or meaning units. The word *girl* is one morpheme, or meaning unit; it cannot be broken down any further and still have meaning. When the suffix *s* is added, the word becomes *girls* and has two morphemes because the *s* changed the meaning of the word, indicating that there is more than one girl.
Syntax	The system that involves the way words are combined to form acceptable phrases and sentences.	Word order is very important in determining meaning in the English language. For example, the sentence "Sebastian pushed the bike" has a different meaning from "The bike pushed Sebastian."
Semantics	The system that involves the meaning of words and sentences.	Semantics involves knowing the meaning of individual words—that is, vocabulary. For example, semantics includes knowing the meaning of such words as *orange*, *transportation*, and *intelligent*.
Pragmatics	The system of using appropriate conversation and knowledge of how to effectively use language in context.	An example is using polite language in appropriate situations, such as being mannerly when talking with one's teacher. Taking turns in a conversation involves pragmatics.

FIGURE **1**

THE RULE SYSTEMS OF LANGUAGE

pragmatic rules about how to say "thank you" to individuals of various social levels and with various relationships to you.

In this section, we have discussed five important rule systems involved in language. An overview of these rule systems is presented in Figure 1.

Review *Connect* Reflect

 LG1 Define language and describe its rule systems

Review
- What is language?
- What are language's five main rule systems?

Connect
- What have you learned about thinking in childhood that might help explain why Genie and the Wild Boy of Aveyron never learned effective verbal communication skills?

Reflect *Your Own Personal Journey of Life*
- How good are your family members and friends at the pragmatics of language? Describe a situation in which an individual showed pragmatic skills and another in which a person did not.

2 How Language Develops   **LG2** Describe how language develops through the life span

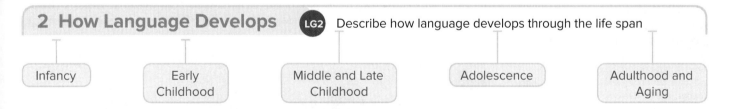

Infancy · Early Childhood · Middle and Late Childhood · Adolescence · Adulthood and Aging

In the thirteenth century, Emperor Frederick II of Germany had a cruel idea. He wanted to know what language children would speak if no one talked to them. He selected several newborns and threatened their caregivers with death if they ever talked to the infants. Frederick never found out what language the children spoke because they all died. As we move forward in the twenty-first century, we are still curious about infants' development of language, although our experiments and observations are, to say the least, far more humane than the evil Frederick's.

INFANCY

Whatever language they learn, infants all over the world follow a similar path in language development. What are some key milestones in this development?

developmental **connection**

Emotional Development

Three basic cries that infants display are the basic cry, anger cry, and pain cry. Connect to "Emotional Development and Attachment."

Babbling and Other Vocalizations   Long before infants speak recognizable words, they produce a number of vocalizations (Masapollo, Polka, & Ménard, 2015). The functions of these early vocalizations are to practice making sounds, to communicate, and to attract attention (Ramsdell & others, 2012). Babies' sounds go through the following sequence during the first year:

· *Crying.* Babies cry even at birth. Crying can signal distress, but different types of cries signal different things.

· *Cooing.* Babies first coo at about 2 to 4 months. These gurgling sounds that are made in the back of the throat usually express pleasure during interaction with the caregiver.

· *Babbling.* In the middle of the first year, babies babble—that is, they produce strings of consonant-vowel combinations, such as *ba, ba, ba, ba.*

Gestures   Infants start using gestures, such as showing and pointing, at about 8 to 12 months of age. They may wave bye-bye, nod to mean "yes," show an empty cup to ask for more milk, and point to a dog to draw attention to it. Some early gestures are symbolic, as when an infant smacks her lips to indicate food or drink. Pointing is considered by language experts to be an important index of the social aspects of language, and it follows a specific developmental sequence: from pointing without checking on adult gaze to pointing while looking back and forth between an object and the adult (Begus & Southgate, 2012).

Lack of pointing is a significant indicator of problems in the infant's communication system (Goldin-Meadow, 2014a, b, 2015). Pointing is a key aspect of the development of joint attention and an important index of the social aspects of language (Begus & Southgate, 2012). Failure to engage in pointing also characterizes many autistic children. The ability to use the pointing gesture effectively improves in the second year of life as advances in other aspects of language communication occur.

One study found that parents in families with high socioeconomic status (SES) were more likely to use gestures when communicating with their 14-month-old infants (Rowe & Goldin-Meadow, 2009). Further, the infants' use of gestures at 14 months of age in high-SES families was linked to a larger vocabulary at 54 months of age.

Long before infants speak recognizable words, they communicate by producing a number of vocalizations and gestures. *At approximately what ages do infants begin to produce different types of vocalizations and gestures?*
© Don Hammond/Design Pics RF

Recognizing Language Sounds   Long before they begin to learn words, infants can make fine distinctions among the sounds of the language. In Patricia Kuhl's (1993, 2000, 2007, 2009, 2011) research, phonemes from languages all over the world are piped through a speaker for infants to hear (see Figure 2). A box with a toy bear in it is placed where the infant can see it. A string of identical syllables is played, and then the syllables are changed (for example, *ba ba ba ba*, and then *pa pa pa pa*). If the infant turns its head when the syllables change, the box lights up and the bear dances and drums, rewarding the infant for noticing the change.

FIGURE 2

FROM UNIVERSAL LINGUIST TO LANGUAGE-SPECIFIC LISTENER. In Patricia Kuhl's research laboratory, babies listen to tape-recorded voices that repeat syllables. When the sounds of the syllables change, the babies quickly learn to look at the bear. Using this technique, Kuhl has demonstrated that babies are universal linguists until about 6 months of age, but in the next six months become language-specific listeners. *Does Kuhl's research give support to the view that either "nature" or "nurture" is the source of language acquisition?*
Courtesy of Dr. Patricia Kuhl, Institute for Learning and Brain Sciences, University of Washington

Kuhl's research (2007, 2009, 2011) has demonstrated that from birth to about 6 months of age, infants are "citizens of the world": They recognize when sounds change most of the time, no matter what language the syllables come from. But over the next six months, infants get even better at perceiving the changes in sounds from their "own" language, the one their parents speak, and they gradually lose the ability to recognize differences that are not important in their own language.

Also, in the second half of the first year, infants begin to segment the continuous stream of speech they encounter into words (Werker & Gervain, 2013). Initially, they likely rely on statistical information such as the co-occurrence patterns of phonemes and syllables, which allows them to extract potential word forms (Willits, Seidenberg, & Saffran, 2014). For example, discovering that the sequence *br* occurs more often at the beginning of words while *nt* is more common at the end of words helps infants detect word boundaries. And as infants extract an increasing number of potential word forms from the speech stream they hear, they begin to associate these with concrete, perceptually available objects in their world (Zamuner, Fais, & Werker, 2014).

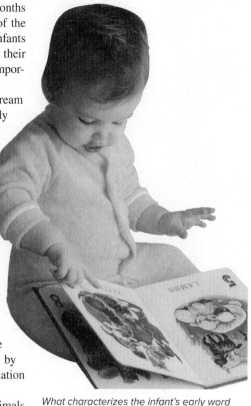

What characterizes the infant's early word learning?
© Niki Mareschal/Photographer's Choice/Getty Images

First Words Infants understand words before they can produce or speak them (Harris, Golinkoff, & Hirsh-Pasek, 2011). Between about 5 and 12 months of age, infants often indicate their first understanding of words. The infant's first spoken word is a milestone eagerly anticipated by every parent. This event usually occurs between 10 and 15 months of age and at an average age of about 13 months. However, long before babies say their first words, they have been communicating with their parents, often by gesturing and using their own special sounds. The appearance of first words is a continuation of this communication process.

A child's first words include those that name important people (*dada*), familiar animals (*kitty*), vehicles (*car*), toys (*ball*), food (*milk*), body parts (*eye*), clothes (*hat*), household items (*clock*), and greeting terms (*bye*). Children often express various intentions with their single words, so that *cookie* might mean "That's a cookie" or "I want a cookie." Nouns are easier to learn because the majority of words in this class are more perceptually accessible than other types of words (Parish-Morris, Golinkoff, & Hirsh-Pasek, 2013). Think how the noun "car" is so much more concrete and imaginable than the verb "goes," making the word "car" much easier to acquire than the word "goes."

The first words of infants can vary across languages. The first words of English-speaking and Romance-language-speaking infants usually are nouns. However, because of the structure of the Korean language, the first words of Korean infants are most often verbs (Choi & Gopnik, 1995).

On average, infants understand about 50 words by 13 months of age, but they can't say that many words until about 18 months (Menyuk, Liebergott, & Schultz, 1995). Thus, in infancy *receptive vocabulary* (words the child understands) considerably exceeds *spoken vocabulary* (words the child uses).

The infant's spoken vocabulary rapidly increases once the first word is spoken (Waxman & Goswami, 2012). The average 18-month-old can speak about 50 words, but by the age of 2 years can speak about 200 words. This rapid increase in vocabulary that begins at approximately 18 months is called the vocabulary spurt (Bloom, Lifter, & Broughton, 1985).

Like the timing of a child's first word, the timing of the vocabulary spurt varies. Figure 3 shows the range for these two language milestones in 14 children (Bloom, 1998). On average, these children said their first word at 13 months and had a vocabulary spurt at 19 months. However, the ages for the first word of individual children varied from 10 to 17 months and for their vocabulary spurt from 13 to 25 months.

Cross-linguistic differences occur in word learning (Waxman & others, 2013). Children learning Mandarin Chinese, Korean, and Japanese acquire more verbs earlier in their development than do children learning English. This cross-linguistic difference reflects the greater use of verbs in the language input to children in these Asian languages.

Children sometimes overextend or underextend the meanings of the words they use (Woodward & Markman, 1998). *Overextension* is the tendency to apply a word to objects that are inappropriate for the word's meaning. For example, children at first may say "*dada*"

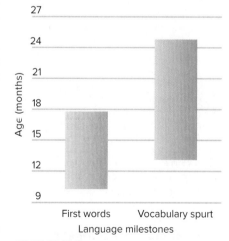

FIGURE 3

VARIATION IN LANGUAGE MILESTONES.
What are some possible explanations for variations in the timing of these milestones?

Around the world, most young children learn to speak in two-word utterances, in most cases at about 18 to 24 months of age. *What implications does this have for the biological basis of language?*
© McPhoto/age fotostock

Typical Age	Language Milestones
Birth	Crying
2 to 4 months	Cooing begins
5 months	Understands first word
6 months	Babbling begins
7 to 11 months	Change from universal linguist to language-specific listener
8 to 12 months	Uses gestures, such as showing and pointing; Comprehension of words appears
13 months	First word spoken
18 months	Vocabulary spurt starts
18 to 24 months	Uses two-word utterances; Rapid expansion of understanding of words

FIGURE 4

SOME LANGUAGE MILESTONES IN INFANCY. Despite great variations in the language input received by infants, around the world they follow a similar path in learning to speak.

not only for "father" but also for other men, strangers, or boys. With time, overextensions decrease and eventually disappear. *Underextension* is the tendency to apply a word too narrowly; it occurs when children fail to use a word to name a relevant event or object. For example, a child might use the word *boy* to describe a 5-year-old neighbor but not apply the word to a male infant or to a 9-year-old male.

Two-Word Utterances   By the time children are 18 to 24 months of age, they usually vocalize two-word utterances (Tomasello, 2011). To convey meaning with just two words, the child relies heavily on gesture, tone, and context. Children can communicate a wealth of meaning with a two-word utterance, as illustrated below (Slobin, 1972):

- Identification: "See doggie."
- Location: "Book there."
- Repetition: "More milk."
- Nonexistence: "All gone."
- Possession: "My candy."
- Attribution: "Big car."
- Agent-action: "Mama walk."
- Question: "Where ball?"

These examples are from children whose first language is English, German, Russian, Finnish, Turkish, or Samoan.

Notice that the two-word utterances omit many parts of speech and are remarkably succinct. In fact, in every language, a child's first combinations of words have this economical quality; they are telegraphic. **Telegraphic speech** is the use of short and precise words without grammatical markers such as articles, auxiliary verbs, and other connectives. Telegraphic speech is not limited to two words. "Mommy give ice cream" and "Mommy give Tommy ice cream" also are examples of telegraphic speech.

We have discussed a number of language milestones in infancy. Figure 4 summarizes the time at which infants typically reach these milestones.

EARLY CHILDHOOD

Toddlers move rather quickly from producing two-word utterances to creating three-, four-, and five-word combinations. Between 2 and 3 years of age, they begin the transition from saying simple sentences that express a single proposition to saying complex sentences.

As young children learn the special features of their own language, there are extensive regularities in how they acquire that specific language (Hoff, 2014). For example, all children learn the prepositions *on* and *in* before other prepositions.

However, some children encounter obstacles to language development, including speech and hearing problems. To read about an individual who works with children who have speech/language problems, see the *Connecting with Careers* profile.

Understanding Phonology and Morphology   During the preschool years, most children gradually become more sensitive to the sounds of spoken words and become increasingly capable of producing all the sounds of their language (Vihman, 2014). By the time children are 3 years of age, they can produce all the vowel sounds and most of the consonant sounds (Stoel-Gammon & Sosa, 2010).

By the time children move beyond two-word utterances, they demonstrate a knowledge of morphology rules (Park & others, 2012). Children begin using the plural and possessive forms of nouns (such as *dogs* and *dog's*). They put appropriate endings on verbs (such as *-s* when the subject is third-person singular and *-ed* for the past tense). They use prepositions (such as *in* and *on*), articles (such as *a* and *the*), and various forms of the verb *to be* (such as "I was going to the store"). Some of the best evidence for changes in children's use of morphological rules occurs in their overgeneralization of the rules, as when a preschool child says "foots" instead of "feet," or "goed" instead of "went."

Sharla Peltier, Speech Therapist

A speech therapist is a health professional who works with individuals who have a communication disorder. Sharla Peltier, a speech therapist in Manitoulin, Ontario, Canada, works with Native American children in the First Nations schools. She conducts screenings for speech/language and hearing problems and assesses infants as young as 6 months of age as well as school-aged children. She works closely with community health nurses to identify hearing problems.

Diagnosing problems is only about half of what Peltier does in her work. She especially enjoys treating speech/language and hearing problems. She conducts parent training sessions to help parents understand and help with their children's language problem. As part of this training, she guides parents in communicating more effectively with their children.

For more information about what speech therapists do, see the Careers in Life-Span Development appendix.

Speech therapist Sharla Peltier, helping a young child improve his language and communication skills.
Courtesy of Sharla Peltier

In a classic experiment that was designed to study children's knowledge of morphological rules, such as how to make a plural, Jean Berko (1958) presented preschool children and first-grade children with cards such as the one shown in Figure 5. Children were asked to look at the card while the experimenter read aloud the words on the card. Then the children were asked to supply the missing word. This might sound easy, but Berko was interested in the children's ability to apply the appropriate morphological rule—in this case to say "wugs" with the *z* sound that indicates the plural.

Although the children's answers were not perfect, they were much better than they could have attained by chance. What makes Berko's study impressive is that most of the words were made up for the experiment. Thus, the children could not base their responses on remembering past instances of hearing the words. That they could make the plurals or past tenses of words they had never heard before was proof that they knew the morphological rules.

Changes in Syntax and Semantics   Preschool children also learn and apply rules of syntax (de Villiers & de Villiers, 2013). They show a growing mastery of complex rules for how words should be ordered (O'Grady, 2013).

Consider *wh-* questions, such as "Where is Daddy going?" or "What is that boy doing?" To ask these questions properly, the child must know two important differences between *wh-* questions and affirmative statements (for instance, "Mommy is going to work" and "That boy is waiting on the school bus"). First, a *wh-* word must be added at the beginning of the sentence. Second, the auxiliary verb must be inverted—that is, exchanged with the subject of the sentence. Young children learn quite early where to put the *wh-* word, but they take much longer to learn the auxiliary-inversion rule. Thus, preschool children might ask, "Where Daddy is going?" and "What that girl is doing?"

Gains in semantics also characterize early childhood. Vocabulary development is dramatic (Crain & Zhou, 2013). Some experts have concluded that between 18 months and 6 years of age, young children learn words at the rate of about one new word every waking hour (Gelman & Kalish, 2006)! By the time they enter first grade, it is estimated that children know about 14,000 words (Clark, 1993). However, there are individual variations in children's vocabulary, and children who enter elementary school with a small vocabulary are at risk for developing reading problems (Berninger, 2006).

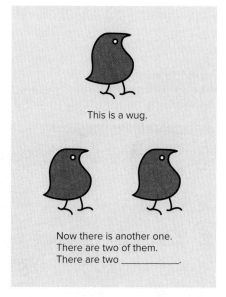

This is a wug.

Now there is another one.
There are two of them.
There are two _____.

FIGURE 5

STIMULI IN BERKO'S CLASSIC STUDY OF CHILDREN'S UNDERSTANDING OF MORPHOLOGICAL RULES. In Jean Berko's study, young children were presented cards such as this one with a "wug" on it. Then the children were asked to supply the missing word and say it correctly.

telegraphic speech The use of short, precise words without grammatical markers such as articles, auxiliary verbs, and other connectives.

Why can children learn so many new words so quickly? One possibility is **fast mapping,** which involves children's ability to make an initial connection between a word and its referent after only limited exposure to the word (Brady & Goodman, 2014; Kan, 2014; Woodward, Markman, & Fitzsimmons, 1994). Researchers have found that exposure to words on multiple occasions over several days results in more successful word learning than the same number of exposures in a single day (Childers & Tomasello, 2002).

What are some important aspects of how word learning optimally occurs? Kathy Hirsh-Pasek and Roberta Golinkoff (Harris, Golinkoff, & Hirsh-Pasek, 2011; Hirsh-Pasek & Golinkoff, 2014) emphasize six key principles in young children's vocabulary development:

1. *Children learn the words they hear most often.* They learn the words that they encounter when interacting with parents, teachers, siblings, peers, and also from books. They especially benefit from encountering words that they do not know.

2. *Children learn words for things and events that interest them.* Parents and teachers can direct young children to experience words in contexts that interest the children; playful peer interactions are especially helpful in this regard.

3. *Children learn words best in responsive and interactive contexts rather than passive contexts.* Children who experience turn-taking opportunities, joint focusing experiences, and positive, sensitive socializing contexts with adults encounter the scaffolding necessary for optimal word learning. They learn words less effectively when they are passive learners.

4. *Children learn words best in contexts that are meaningful.* Young children learn new words more effectively when new words are encountered in integrated contexts rather than as isolated facts.

5. *Children learn words best when they access clear information about word meaning.* Children whose parents and teachers are sensitive to words the children might not understand and provide support and elaboration with hints about word meaning learn words better than when parents and teachers quickly state a new word and don't monitor whether children understand its meaning.

6. *Children learn words best when grammar and vocabulary are considered.* Children who experience a large number of words and diversity in verbal stimulation develop a richer vocabulary and better understanding of grammar. In many cases, vocabulary and grammar development are connected.

How might a family's socioeconomic status influence parent-child communication and vocabulary growth in children? To read about this link, see the *Connecting with Research* interlude.

Advances in Pragmatics   Changes in pragmatics also characterize young children's language development (Waxman, 2013). A 6-year-old is simply a much better conversationalist than a 2-year-old is. What are some of the improvements in pragmatics during the preschool years?

Young children begin to engage in extended discourse (Aktar & Herold, 2008). For example, they learn culturally specific rules of conversation and politeness and become sensitive to the need to adapt their speech in different settings. Their developing linguistic skills and increasing ability to take the perspective of others contribute to their generation of more competent narratives.

As children get older, they become increasingly able to talk about things that are not here (Grandma's house, for example) and not now (what happened to them yesterday or might happen tomorrow, for example). A preschool child can tell you what she wants for lunch tomorrow, something that would not have been possible at the two-word stage of language development.

Around 4 to 5 years of age, children learn to change their speech style to suit the situation. For example, even 4-year-old children speak to a 2-year-old differently from the way they speak to a same-aged peer; they use shorter sentences with the 2-year-old. They also speak to an adult differently from the way they speak to a same-aged peer, using more polite and formal language with the adult (Shatz & Gelman, 1973).

What characterizes advances in pragmatics during early childhood?
© Hill Street Studios/Blend Images/age fotostock RF

fast mapping A process that helps to explain how young children learn the connection between a word and its referent so quickly.

What Characteristics of a Family Affect a Child's Language Development?

Socioeconomic status has been linked with how much parents talk to their children and with young children's vocabulary. Betty Hart and Todd Risley (1995) observed the language environments of children whose parents were professionals and children whose parents were on welfare. Compared with the professional parents, the parents on welfare talked much less to their young children, talked less about past events, and provided less elaboration. As indicated in Figure 6, the children of the professional parents had a much larger vocabulary at 36 months of age than the children whose parents were on welfare. A recent study also found that at 18 to 24 months of age, infants in low-SES families already had a smaller vocabulary and less efficient language processing than their infant counterparts in middle-SES families (Fernald, Marchman, & Weisleder, 2013).

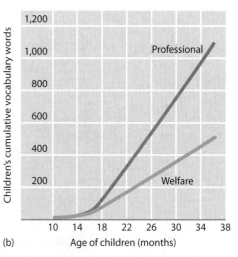

(a)   (b)

FIGURE 6

LANGUAGE INPUT IN PROFESSIONAL AND WELFARE FAMILIES AND YOUNG CHILDREN'S VOCABULARY DEVELOPMENT. (*a*) In this study (Hart & Risley, 1995), parents from professional families talked with their young children more than parents from welfare families. (*b*) All of the children learned to talk, but children from professional families developed vocabularies that were twice as large as the vocabularies of children from welfare families. Thus, by the time children go to preschool, they already have experienced considerable differences in language input in their families and developed different levels of vocabulary that are linked to their socioeconomic context. *Does this study indicate that poverty caused deficiencies in vocabulary development?*

Other research has linked how much mothers speak to their infants and the infants' vocabularies. For example, in one study by Janellen Huttenlocher and her colleagues (1991), infants whose mothers spoke more often to them had markedly higher vocabularies. By the second birthday, vocabulary differences were substantial.

However, a study of 1- to 3-year-old children living in low-income families found that the sheer amount of maternal talk was not the best predictor of a child's vocabulary growth (Pan & others, 2005). Rather, it was maternal language and literacy skills that were positively related to the children's vocabulary development. For example, when mothers used a more diverse vocabulary when talking with their children, their children's vocabulary benefited, but their children's vocabulary was not related to the total amount of time mothers spent talking to their children.

Children in low-income families are more likely to have less-educated parents, receive inadequate nutrition, live in low-income communities, and attend substandard schools than children in middle- and high-income families (Snow, Burns, & Griffin, 1998). However, living in a low-income family should not be used as the sole identifier in predicting whether children will have difficulties in language development, such as a low vocabulary and reading problems. If children growing up in low-income families experience effective instruction and support, they can develop effective language skills (Barbarin & Aikens, 2009)

These research studies and others (NICHD Early Child Care Research Network, 2005; Perkins, Finegood, & Swain, 2013) demonstrate the important effect that early speech input and poverty can have on the development of a child's language skills.

Early Literacy   Concern about the ability of U.S. children to read and write has led to a careful examination of preschool and kindergarten children's experiences, with the hope that a positive orientation toward reading and writing can be developed early in life (Beaty & Pratt, 2015; Lonigan, 2015). What should a literacy program for preschool children be like? Instruction should be built on what children already know about oral language, reading, and writing. Further, early precursors of literacy and academic success include language skills, phonological and syntactic knowledge, letter identification, and conceptual knowledge about print and its conventions and functions (Christie & others, 2014; Lonigan, 2015). Parents and

------------->
developmental connection

Conditions, Diseases, and Disorders

Dyslexia is a severe impairment in the ability to read and spell. Connect to "Schools, Achievement, and Work."

teachers need to provide a supportive environment to help children develop literacy skills (Heath & others, 2014; Tompkins, 2015).

So far, our discussion of early literacy has focused on U.S. children. Researchers have found that the extent to which phonological awareness is linked to learning to read effectively varies across language to some degree (McBride-Chang, 2004). For example, one study of second-grade students from Beijing, Hong Kong, Korea, and the United States revealed that phonological awareness may be more important for early reading development in English and Korean than for Chinese (McBride-Chang & others, 2005). Further, rates of dyslexia (severe reading disability) differ across countries and are linked with the spelling and phonetic rules that characterize the language (McCardle & others, 2011). English is one of the more difficult languages because of its irregular spellings and pronunciations. In countries where English is spoken, the rate of dyslexia is higher than in countries where the alphabet script is more phonetically pronounced.

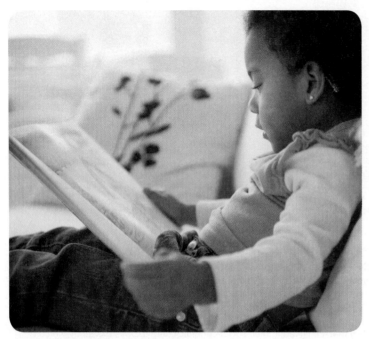

What are some strategies for increasing young children's literacy?
© JGI/Jamie Grill/Getty Images RF

Books can be valuable in enhancing children's communication skills (Vukelich, Christie, & Enz, 2012). What are some strategies for using books effectively with preschool children? Ellen Galinsky (2010) offered these recommendations:

· *Use books to initiate conversation with young children.* Ask them to put themselves in the places of the characters in the book and to imagine what the characters might be thinking or feeling.

· *Use* what *and* why *questions.* Ask young children to think about what is going to happen next in a story and then to see if it occurs.

· *Encourage children to ask questions about stories.*

· *Choose some books that play with language.* Creative books on the alphabet, including those with rhymes, often interest young children.

MIDDLE AND LATE CHILDHOOD

Upon entering school, children gain new skills that include increasing use of language to talk about things that are not physically present, knowledge of what a word is, and an ability to recognize and talk about sounds (Berko Gleason, 2003). They learn the *alphabetic principle*—the fact that the letters of the alphabet represent sounds of the language. As children develop during middle and late childhood, changes in their vocabulary and grammar continue to take place.

Vocabulary, Grammar, and Metalinguistic Awareness During middle and late childhood, children begin to organize their mental vocabulary in new ways. When asked to say the first word that comes to mind when they hear a word, young children typically provide a word that often follows the word in a sentence. For example, when asked to respond to "dog," the young child may say "barks." In response to the word "eat," they may say "lunch." At about 7 years of age, children begin to respond with a word that is the same part of speech as the stimulus word. For example, a child may now respond to the word "dog" with "cat" or "horse." To "eat," they now might say "drink." This type of reply is evidence that children have begun to categorize their vocabulary by parts of speech (Berko Gleason, 2003).

The process of categorizing becomes easier as children increase their vocabulary (Clark, 2012). Children's vocabulary increases from an average of about 14,000 words at 6 years of age to an average of about 40,000 words by 11 years of age.

Children make similar advances in grammar (Behrens, 2012). During the elementary school years, children's improvement in logical reasoning and analytical skills helps them understand such constructions as the appropriate use of comparatives (*shorter, deeper*) and subjunctives ("If you were president . . ."). During the elementary school years, children become increasingly able to understand and use complex grammar, such as the following sentence: *The boy who kissed his mother wore a hat.* They also learn to use language in a more connected way, producing connected discourse.

These advances in vocabulary and grammar during the elementary school years are accompanied by the development of **metalinguistic awareness,** which is knowledge about language, such as knowing what a preposition is or being able to discuss the sounds of a language (Tong, Deacon, & Cain, 2014). Metalinguistic awareness allows children "to think about their language, understand what words are, and even define them" (Berko Gleason, 2009, p. 4). It improves considerably during the elementary school years. Defining words becomes a regular part of classroom discourse, and children increase their knowledge of syntax as they study and talk about the components of sentences, such as subjects and verbs (Crain, 2012).

Children also make progress in understanding how to use language in culturally appropriate ways—pragmatics (Bryant, 2012). By the time they enter adolescence, most children know the rules for the use of language in everyday contexts—that is, what is appropriate to say and what is inappropriate to say.

Reading Before learning to read, children learn to use language to talk about things that are not present; they learn what a word is; and they learn how to recognize sounds and talk about them (Berko Gleason, 2003). If they develop a large vocabulary, their path to reading is eased. Children who begin elementary school with a small vocabulary are at risk when it comes to learning to read (Berko Gleason, 2003). Vocabulary development plays an important role in reading comprehension (Vacca & others, 2012).

How should children be taught to read? Currently, debate focuses on the whole-language approach versus the phonics approach (Lloyd & others, 2015; Reutzel & Cooter, 2015).

The **whole-language approach** stresses that reading instruction should parallel children's natural language learning. In some whole-language classes, beginning readers are taught to recognize whole words or even entire sentences, and to use the context of what they are reading to guess at the meaning of words. Reading materials that support the whole-language approach are whole and meaningful—that is, children are given material in its complete form, such as stories and poems, so that they learn to understand language's communicative function. Reading is connected with listening and writing skills. Although there are variations in whole-language programs, most share the premise that reading should be integrated with other skills and subjects, such as science and social studies, and that it should focus on real-world material. Thus, a class might read newspapers, magazines, or books, and then write about and discuss what they have read.

In contrast, the **phonics approach** emphasizes that reading instruction should teach basic rules for translating written symbols into sounds. Early phonics-centered reading instruction should involve simplified materials. Only after children have learned correspondence rules that relate spoken phonemes to the alphabet letters that are used to represent them should they be given complex reading materials such as books and poems (Fox, 2014). One study revealed that a computer-based phonics program improved first-grade students' reading skills (Savage & others, 2009).

Which approach is better? Research suggests that children can benefit from both approaches, but instruction in phonics needs to be emphasized (Del Campo & others, 2015; Tompkins, 2013). An increasing number of experts in the field of reading now conclude that direct instruction in phonics is a key aspect of learning to read (Dow & Baer, 2013).

Beyond the phonics/whole-language issue in learning to read, becoming a good reader includes learning to read fluently (Allington, 2015). Many beginning or poor readers do not recognize words automatically. Their processing capacity is consumed by the demands of word recognition, so they have less capacity to devote to comprehension of groupings of words as phrases or sentences. As their processing of words and passages becomes more automatic, it is said that their reading becomes more *fluent* (Fox, 2014). Metacognitive strategies, such as learning to monitor one's reading progress, getting the gist of what is being read, and summarizing, also are fundamental to becoming a good reader (McCormick, Dimmitt, & Sullivan, 2013).

Writing Children's writing emerges out of their early scribbles, which appear at around 2 to 3 years of age. In early childhood, children's motor skills usually develop to the point

developmental **connection**

Information Processing

Metacognition is cognition about cognition, or knowing about knowing. Connect to "Information Processing."

This teacher is helping a student sound out words. Researchers have found that phonics instruction is a key aspect of teaching students to read, especially beginning readers and students with weak reading skills.
© Gideon Mendel/Corbis

metalinguistic awareness Knowledge about language.

whole-language approach A teaching approach built on the idea that reading instruction should parallel children's natural language learning. Reading materials should be whole and meaningful.

phonics approach A teaching approach built on the idea that reading instruction should teach basic rules for translating written symbols into sounds.

that they can begin printing letters. Most 4-year-olds can print their first names. Five-year-olds can reproduce letters and copy several short words. They gradually learn to distinguish the distinctive characteristics of letters, such as whether the lines are curved or straight, open or closed. Through the early elementary grades, many children continue to reverse letters such as *b* and *d* and *p* and *q* (Temple & others, 1993). At this age, if other aspects of the child's development are normal, letter reversals do not predict literacy problems.

As they begin to write, children often invent spellings. Usually they base these spellings on the sounds of words they hear (Spandel, 2009).

Parents and teachers should encourage children's early writing but not be overly concerned about the formation of letters or spelling. Printing errors are a natural part of the child's growth. Corrections of spelling and printing should be selective and made in positive ways that do not discourage the child's writing and spontaneity.

Like becoming a good reader, becoming a good writer takes many years and lots of practice (Temple, Nathan, & Temple, 2013). Children should be given many writing opportunities (Tompkins, 2015). As their language and cognitive skills improve with good instruction, so will their writing skills. For example, developing a more sophisticated understanding of syntax and grammar serves as an underpinning for better writing. So do such cognitive skills as organization and logical reasoning. Through the course of the school years, students develop increasingly sophisticated methods of organizing their ideas. In early elementary school, they narrate and describe or write short poems. In late elementary and middle school, they can combine narration with reflection and analysis in projects such as book reports.

There are increasing concerns about students' writing competence (Soter, 2013). One study revealed that 70 to 75 percent of U.S. students in grades 4 through 12 are low-achieving writers (Persky, Dane, & Jin, 2003). Two studies—one of elementary school teachers, the other of high school teachers—raise concerns about the quality of writing instruction in U.S. schools (Gilbert & Graham, 2010; Kiuhara, Graham, & Hawken, 2009). The teachers in both studies reported that their college courses had inadequately prepared them to teach writing. The fourth- through sixth-grade teachers reported that they taught writing only 15 minutes a day. The high school teachers said that their writing assignments infrequently involved analysis and interpretation, and almost 50 percent of them had not assigned any multi-paragraph writing assignments in the span of one month's time.

The metacognitive strategies needed to be a competent writer are linked with those required to be a competent reader because the writing process involves competent reading and rereading during composition and revision (Dimmitt & McCormick, 2012; McCormick, Dimmitt, & Sullivan, 2013). Further, researchers have found that strategy instruction involving planning, drafting, revising, and editing improve older elementary school children's metacognitive awareness and writing competence (Harris & others, 2009).

As with reading, teachers play a critical role in students' development of writing skills. Effective writing instruction provides guidance about planning, drafting, and revising, not only in elementary school but through college (Mayer, 2008). A meta-analysis (use of statistical techniques to combine the results of studies) revealed that the following interventions were the most effective in improving fourth- through twelfth-grade students' writing quality: (1) strategy instruction, (2) summarization, (3) peer assistance, and (4) setting goals (Graham & Perin, 2007).

Second-Language Learning and Bilingualism   Are there sensitive periods in learning a second language? That is, if individuals want to learn a second language, how important is the age at which they begin to learn it? For many years, it was claimed that if individuals did not learn a second language prior to puberty they would never reach native-language speakers' proficiency in the second language (Johnson & Newport, 1991). However, recent research indicates a more complex conclusion: Sensitive periods likely vary across different language systems (Thomas & Johnson, 2008). Thus, for late language learners, such as adolescents and adults, new vocabulary is easier to learn than new sounds or new grammar (Neville, 2006). For example, children's ability to pronounce words with a native-like accent in a second language typically decreases with age, with an especially sharp drop occurring after the age of about 10 to 12. Also, adults tend to learn a second language faster than children, but their final level of second-language attainment is not as high as children's. And the way children and adults learn a second language differs somewhat. Compared with adults, children are less sensitive to feedback, less likely to use explicit strategies, and more likely to learn a second language from large amounts of input (Thomas & Johnson, 2008).

Students in the United States are far behind their counterparts in many developed countries in learning a second language. For example, in Russia, schools have 10 grades, called *forms*, which roughly correspond to the 12 grades in American schools. Russian children begin school at age 7 and begin learning English in the third form. Because of this emphasis on teaching English, most Russian citizens under the age of 40 today are able to speak at least some English. The United States is the only technologically advanced Western nation that does not have a national foreign-language requirement at the high school level, even for students in rigorous academic programs.

Some aspects of children's ability to learn a second language are transferred more easily to the second language than others (Pena & Bedore, 2009). Children who are fluent in two languages perform better than their single-language counterparts on tests of control of attention, concept formation, analytical reasoning, inhibition, cognitive flexibility, cognitive complexity, and cognitive monitoring (Bialystok, 2001, 2007, 2011, 2014, 2015; Bialystok & Craik, 2010; Sullivan & others, 2015). They also are more conscious of the structure of spoken and written language and better at noticing errors of grammar and meaning, skills that benefit their reading ability (Bialystok, 1997; Kuo & Anderson, 2012). However, recent research indicates that bilingual children have a smaller vocabulary in each language than monolingual children (Bialystok, 2011).

Children in many countries learn more than one language. Shown here is author John Santrock observing a preschool in Fes, Morocco, in 2015. The young children sang songs in three different languages—Arabic, French, and English. *Do you think children in the United States should learn more than one language?*
Courtesy of Dr. John Santrock

Thus, overall, bilingualism is linked to more positive outcomes for both children's language and cognitive development. An especially important developmental question that many parents of infants and young children have is whether to teach them two languages simultaneously or just teach one language at a time to avoid confusion. The answer is that teaching infants and young children two languages simultaneously (as when a mother's native language is English and her husband's is Spanish) has numerous benefits and few drawbacks (Bialystok, 2014, 2015).

However, a different type of bilingualism occurs when immigrant children have learned only their native language at home and then must learn the main language of their new country at school. For example, in the United States, many immigrant children go from being monolingual in their home language to bilingual in that language and in English, only to end up monolingual speakers of English. This is called *subtractive bilingualism*, and it can have negative effects on children, who often become ashamed of their home language.

A current controversy related to bilingualism involves the millions of U.S. children who come from homes in which English is not the primary language and then later at school must also learn English (Echevarria, Richards-Tutor, & Vogt, 2015). What is the best way to teach these English language learners (ELLs)?

ELLs have been taught in one of two main ways: (1) instruction in English only, or (2) a *dual-language* (used to be called *bilingual*) approach that involves instruction in their home language and English (Haley & Austin, 2014). In a dual-language approach, instruction is given in both the ELL child's home language and English for varying amounts of time at certain grade levels. One of the arguments for the dual-language approach is the research discussed earlier demonstrating that bilingual children have more advanced information processing skills than monolingual children (Genesee & Lindholm-Leary, 2012).

If a dual-language strategy is used, too often it has been thought that immigrant children need only one or two years of this type of instruction. However, in general it takes immigrant children approximately three to five years to develop speaking proficiency and seven years to develop reading proficiency in English (Hakuta, Butler, & Witt, 2001). Also, immigrant children vary in their ability to learn English (Horowitz, 2013). Children who come from lower

A first- and second-grade bilingual English-Cantonese teacher instructing students in Chinese in Oakland, California. *What have researchers found about the effectiveness of bilingual education?*
© Elizabeth Crews

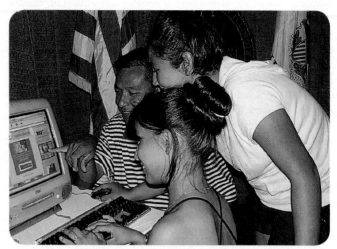
socioeconomic backgrounds have more difficulty than those from higher socioeconomic backgrounds (Hakuta, 2001; Hoff & Place, 2013). Thus, especially for immigrant children from low socioeconomic backgrounds, more years of dual-language instruction may be needed than they currently are receiving.

What have researchers found regarding outcomes of ELL programs? Drawing conclusions about the effectiveness of ELL programs is difficult because of variations across programs in the number of years they are in effect, type of instruction, quality of schooling other than ELL instruction, teachers, children, and other factors. Further, no effective experiments have been conducted that compare bilingual education with English-only education in the United States (Snow & Kang, 2006). Some experts have concluded that the quality of instruction is more important in determining outcomes than the language in which it is delivered (Lesaux & Siegel, 2003).

Nonetheless, other experts, such as Kenji Hakuta (2001, 2005), support the combined home language and English approach because (1) children have difficulty learning a subject when it is taught in a language they do not understand; and (2) when both languages are integrated in the classroom, children learn the second language more readily and participate more actively. In support of Hakuta's view, most large-scale studies have found that the academic achievement of ELLs is higher in dual-language programs than English-only programs. To read about the work of one ELL teacher, see the *Connecting with Careers* profile.

ADOLESCENCE

Language development during adolescence includes greater sophistication in the use of words. With an increase in abstract thinking, adolescents are much better than children at analyzing the role a word plays in a sentence.

Adolescents also develop more subtle abilities with words. They make strides in understanding **metaphor,** which is an implied comparison between unlike things. For example, individuals "draw a line in the sand" to indicate a nonnegotiable position; a political campaign is said to be a marathon, not a sprint; a person's faith is shattered. And adolescents become better able to understand and to use **satire,** which is the use of irony, derision, or wit to expose folly or wickedness. Caricatures are an example of satire. More advanced logical thinking also allows adolescents, from about 15 to 20 years of age, to understand complex literary works.

Most adolescents are also much better writers than children are. They are better at organizing ideas before they write, at distinguishing between general and specific points as they

developmental **connection**

Cognitive Theory

According to Piaget, at 11 to 15 years of age a new stage—formal operational thought—emerges that is characterized by thought that is more abstract, idealistic, and logical. Connect to "Cognitive Developmental Approaches."

metaphor An implied comparison between two unlike things.

satire The use of irony, derision, or wit to expose folly or wickedness.

write, at stringing together sentences that make sense, and at organizing their writing into an introduction, body, and concluding remarks.

Everyday speech changes during adolescence "and part of being a successful teenager is being able to talk like one" (Berko Gleason, 2005, p. 9). Young adolescents often speak a **dialect** with their peers that is characterized by jargon and slang (Cave, 2002). A dialect is a variety of language that is distinguished by its vocabulary, grammar, or pronunciation. For example, when meeting a friend, instead of saying hello, a young adolescent might say, "Sup?" ("What's up?"). Nicknames that are satirical and derisive ("Stilt," "Refrigerator," "Spaz") also characterize the dialect of young adolescents. Such labels might be used to show that one belongs to the group and to reduce the seriousness of a situation (Cave, 2002).

What are some changes in language development in adolescence?
© Digital Vision/PunchStock RF

ADULTHOOD AND AGING

Most research on language development has focused on infancy and childhood. It is generally thought that for most of adulthood individuals maintain their language skills.

In the adolescent and adult years, the development of an identity, a sense of who one is, is an important life task. A distinct personal linguistic style is part of one's special identity (Berko Gleason, 2009). Further psychological goals of early adulthood that call for expanded linguistic skills include entering the world of work and establishing intimate relations with others.

Language development during the adult years varies greatly among individuals, depending on such things as level of education and social and occupational roles. Actors, for instance, must learn not only to be heard by large audiences but also to speak the words of others using varying voices and regional dialects. Working people learn the special tones of voice and terminology associated with their own occupational language (Berko Gleason, 2005, p. 9).

What are some differences in the ways older and younger adults communicate?
© Corbis RF

The vocabulary of individuals often continues to increase throughout most of the adult years, at least until late adulthood (Schaie, 2012; Singh-Manoux & others, 2012). Many older adults "maintain or improve their knowledge of words and word meanings" (Burke & Shafto, 2004, p. 24).

In late adulthood, however, some decrements in language may appear. Among the most common language-related complaints reported by older adults is difficulty in retrieving words to use in conversation and in understanding spoken language in certain contexts (Clark-Cotton, Williams, & Goral, 2007). These often involve the *tip-of-the-tongue phenomenon*, in which individuals are confident that they can remember something but just can't quite seem to retrieve it from memory (Ossher, Flegal, & Lustig, 2013). Older adults also report that in less than ideal listening conditions they can have difficulty in understanding speech. This difficulty is most likely to occur when speech is rapid, when competing stimuli are present (a noisy room, for example), and when they can't see their conversation partner (in a telephone conversation, for example). The difficulty in understanding speech may be due to hearing loss (Benichov & others, 2012). In general, though, most language skills decline little among older adults who are healthy (Clark-Cotton & others, 2007; Thornton & Light, 2006).

Some aspects of the phonological skills of older adults differ from those of younger adults (Benichov & others, 2012). Older adults' speech is typically lower in volume, slower, less precisely articulated, and less fluent (more pauses, fillers, repetition, and corrections). Despite these age differences, the speech skills of most older adults are adequate for everyday communication. A recent study found that when retelling a story older adults were more likely than younger adults to compress discourse and less likely to improve the cohesiveness of their narratives (Saling, Laroo, & Saling, 2012).

Nonlanguage factors may be responsible for some of the declines in language skills that occur in older adults (Obler, 2009). Slower information-processing speed and a decline in working memory, especially in regard to keeping information in mind while processing, likely contribute to reduced language efficiency in older adults (Salthouse, 2013).

dialect A variety of language that is distinguished by its vocabulary, grammar, or pronunciation.

developmental connection

Conditions, Diseases, and Disorders

Alzheimer disease is a progressive brain disorder characterized by a gradual deterioration of memory, reasoning, language, and eventually physical function. Connect to "Health."

Language does change among individuals with Alzheimer disease (Obler, 2009). Word-finding/generating difficulties are one of the earliest symptoms of Alzheimer disease (Haugrud, Crossley, & Vrbancic, 2011). Individuals with Alzheimer disease especially have difficulty on tests of semantic verbal fluency, in which they have to say as many words as possible in a category (fruits or animals, for example) in a given time, typically one minute (Weakley & Schmitter-Edgecombe, 2014). Most individuals with the disease do retain much of their ability to produce well-formed sentences until the late stages of the disease. Nonetheless, they do make more grammatical errors than older adults without the disease (Huang, Meyer, & Federmeier, 2012).

Recently, interest has been generated in the possibility that bilingualism may delay the onset of Alzheimer disease (Fischer & Schweizer, 2014). A recent study found that the onset of Alzheimer disease occurred 4.5 years later in bilingual older adults (Alladi & others, 2013). Another recent study revealed that the onset of symptoms and first office visit for Alzheimer disease occurred several years later for bilingual than for monolingual older adults (Bialystok & others, 2014). It is not yet clear why this advantage occurs for bilingual older adults, but one explanation might be better executive function.

Review *Connect* Reflect

LG2 Describe how language develops through the life span

Review

- What are some key milestones of language development during infancy?
- How do language skills change during early childhood?
- How does language develop in middle and late childhood?
- How does language develop in adolescence?
- How do language skills change during adulthood and aging?

Connect

- What are some aspects of metacognition that might apply to the concept of metalinguistic awareness?

Reflect Your Own Personal Journey of Life

- How many languages can you speak and read? If and when you have children, do you want them to learn more than one language while they are young? Explain.

---

3 Biological and Environmental Influences

LG3 Discuss the biological and environmental contributions to language skills

Biological Influences

Environmental Influences

An Interactionist View of Language

We have described how language develops, but we have not explained what makes this amazing development possible. Everyone who uses language in some way "knows" its rules and has the ability to create an infinite number of words and sentences. Where does this knowledge come from? Is it the product of biology? Or is language learned and influenced by experiences?

BIOLOGICAL INFLUENCES

Some language scholars view the remarkable similarities in how children acquire language all over the world, despite the vast variation in language input they receive, as strong evidence that language has a biological basis. What role did evolution play in the biological foundations of language?

Evolution and the Brain's Role in Language The ability to speak and understand language requires a certain vocal apparatus as well as a nervous system with certain capabilities. The nervous system and vocal apparatus of humanity's predecessors changed over

Broca's area An area of the brain's left frontal lobe that is involved in producing words.

Wernicke's area An area of the brain's left hemisphere that is involved in language comprehension.

In the wild, chimps communicate through calls, gestures, and facial expressions, which evolutionary psychologists believe might be the roots of true language.
© Digital Vision/PunchStock RF

developmental **connection**

Brain Development

Much of our language processing takes place in the brain's left hemisphere. Connect to "Physical Development and Biological Aging."

hundreds of thousands or millions of years (Miyagawa & others, 2014; Pinker, 2015). With advances in the nervous system and vocal structures, *Homo sapiens* went beyond the grunting and shrieking of other animals to develop speech. Although estimates vary, many experts hold that humans acquired language about 100,000 years ago, which in evolutionary time represents a very recent acquisition. It gave humans an enormous edge over other animals and increased the chances of human survival (Arbib, 2012; Pinker, 2015).

As further support for the biological foundations of language, there is evidence that specific regions of the brain are predisposed to be used for language (Tando & others, 2014). Two regions involved in language were first discovered in studies of brain-damaged individuals: **Broca's area**, a region of the left frontal lobe of the brain that is involved in producing words, and **Wernicke's area**, a region of the brain's left hemisphere that is involved in language comprehension (see Figure 7). Damage to either of these areas produces types of **aphasia**, which is a loss or impairment of language processing. Individuals with damage to Broca's area have difficulty producing words correctly, while individuals with damage to Wernicke's area have poor comprehension and often produce fluent but incomprehensible speech.

Chomsky's Language Acquisition Device (LAD)
Linguist Noam Chomsky (1957) proposed that humans are biologically prewired to learn language at a certain time and in a certain way. He said that children are born into the world with a **language acquisition device (LAD)**, a biological endowment that enables the child to detect certain features and rules of language, including phonology, syntax, and semantics. Children are endowed by nature with the ability to detect the sounds of language, for example, and to follow rules such as how to form plurals and ask questions.

Chomsky's LAD is a theoretical construct, not a physical part of the brain. Is there evidence for the existence of a LAD? Supporters of the LAD concept cite the uniformity of language milestones across languages and cultures, evidence that children create language even in the absence of well-formed input, and biological foundations of language. But, as we will see, critics argue that even if infants have something like a LAD, it cannot fully explain the process of language acquisition.

ENVIRONMENTAL INFLUENCES

Decades ago, behaviorists opposed Chomsky's hypothesis and argued that language represents nothing more than chains of responses acquired through reinforcement (Skinner, 1957). A baby happens to babble "Ma-ma"; Mama rewards the baby with hugs and smiles; the baby says "Mama" more and more. Bit by bit, said the behaviorists, the baby's language is built

Broca's area   Wernicke's area

FIGURE 7
BROCA'S AREA AND WERNICKE'S AREA.
Broca's area is located in the frontal lobe of the brain's left hemisphere, and it is involved in the control of speech. Wernicke's area is a portion of the left hemisphere's temporal lobe that is involved in understanding language. *How does the role of these areas of the brain relate to lateralization, discussed in the chapter on "Physical Development and Biological Aging"?*

aphasia A loss or impairment of language processing resulting from damage to Broca's area or Wernicke's area.

language acquisition device (LAD) Chomsky's term that describes a biological endowment that enables the child to detect certain features and rules of language, including phonology, syntax, and semantics.

FIGURE **8**

SOCIAL INTERACTION AND BABBLING. One study focused on two groups of mothers and their 8-month-old infants (Goldstein, King, & West, 2003). One group of mothers was instructed to smile and touch their infants immediately after the babies cooed and babbled; the other group was also told to smile and touch their infants but in a random manner, unconnected to sounds the infants made. The infants whose mothers immediately responded in positive ways to their babbling subsequently made more complex, speech-like sounds, such as *da* and *gu*. The research setting for this study, which underscores how important caregivers are in the early development of language, is shown above.
Courtesy of Dr. Michael Goldstein

child-directed speech Language spoken in a higher pitch than normal, with simple words and sentences.

up. According to behaviorists, language is a complex learned skill, much like playing the piano or dancing.

There are several problems with the behavioral view of language learning. First, it does not explain how people create novel sentences—sentences that people have never heard or spoken before. Second, children learn the syntax of their native language even if they are not reinforced for doing so. Social psychologist Roger Brown (1973) spent long hours observing parents and their young children. He found that parents did not directly or explicitly reward or correct the syntax of most children's utterances. That is, parents did not say "good," "correct," "right," "wrong," and so on. Also, parents did not offer direct corrections such as "You should say two shoes, not two shoe." However, as we see shortly, many parents do expand on their young children's grammatically incorrect utterances and recast many of those that have grammatical errors (Bonvillian, 2005).

The behavioral view is no longer considered a viable explanation of how children acquire language. But a great deal of research describes ways in which children's environmental experiences influence their language skills (Hirsh-Pasek & Golinkoff, 2014). Many language experts argue that a child's experiences, the specific language to be learned, and the context in which learning takes place can strongly influence language acquisition (Goldfield & Snow, 2009).

Language is not learned in a social vacuum. Most children are bathed in language from a very early age (Kuhl, 2011). The Wild Boy of Aveyron, who never learned to communicate effectively, had lived in social isolation for years. If infants do not hear language or don't develop an emotional bond with an adult, the neural connections linked with language and emotion may be weakened (Berko Gleason, 2009).

Michael Tomasello (2003, 2006, 2011, 2014) stresses that young children are intensely interested in their social world and that early in their development they can understand the intentions of other people. His emphasizes that children learn language in specific contexts. For example, when a toddler and a father are jointly focused on a book, the father might say, "See the birdie." In this case, even a toddler understands that the father intends to name something and knows to look in the direction of the pointing. Through this kind of joint attention, early in their development children are able to use their social skills to acquire language (Tomasello, 2014). One study revealed that joint attention at 12 and 18 months predicted language skills at 24 months of age (Mundy & others, 2007).

The support and involvement of caregivers and teachers greatly facilitate a child's language learning (Hirsh-Pasek & Golinkoff, 2014). For optimal language development, experts increasingly recommend that parents and teachers provide young children with extensive opportunities to talk and be talked with (Hirsh-Pasek & Golinkoff, 2014). One study found that when mothers immediately smiled and touched their 8-month-old infants after they babbled, the infants subsequently made more complex speech-like sounds than when mothers responded to their infants in a random manner (Goldstein, King, & West, 2003) (see Figure 8).

Given that social interaction is a critical component for infants to learn language effectively, might they also be able to learn language effectively through television and videos? Researchers have found that infants and young children cannot effectively learn language (phonology or words) from television or videos (Kuhl, 2007; Roseberry & others, 2009). A recent study of toddlers found that frequent viewing of television increased the risk of delayed language development (Lin & others, 2015). Thus, just hearing language is not enough, even when infants seemingly are fully engaged in the experience. However, a recent study revealed that Skype provides some improvement in child language learning over videos and TV (Roseberry, Hirsh-Pasek, & Golinkoff, 2014), and older children can use information from television in their language development.

One intriguing component of the young child's linguistic environment is **child-directed speech,** language spoken in a higher pitch than normal with simple words and sentences. It is hard to use child-directed speech when not in the presence of a baby. As soon as you start talking to a baby, though, you shift into child-directed speech. Much of this is automatic and something most parents are not aware they are doing. As mentioned previously, even 4-year-olds speak in simpler ways to 2-year-olds than to their 4-year-old friends. Child-directed speech has the important function of capturing the infant's attention and maintaining communication. A recent study found that child-directed speech in a one-to-one social context at 11 to 14 months of age was linked to greater word production at two years of age than standard speech and speech in a group setting (Ramirez-Esparza, Garcia-Sierra, & Kuhl, 2014). Another recent study of low-SES Spanish-speaking families revealed that infants who experienced more child-directed speech were better at processing words in real time and had larger vocabularies at two years of age (Weisleder & Fernald, 2013).

Adults often use strategies other than child-directed speech to enhance the child's acquisition of language, including recasting, expanding, and labeling:

- **Recasting** is rephrasing something the child has said, perhaps turning it into a question or restating the child's immature utterance in the form of a fully grammatical sentence. For example, if the child says, "The dog was barking," the adult can respond by asking, "When was the dog barking?" Effective recasting lets the child indicate an interest and then elaborates on that interest.

What are some good strategies for parents and teachers to use to improve infants' and young children's language development?
© Roberto Westbrook/Getty Images

- **Expanding** is restating, in a linguistically sophisticated form, what a child has said. For example, a child says, "Doggie eat," and the parent replies, "Yes, the dog is eating."

- **Labeling** is identifying the names of objects. Young children are forever being asked to identify the names of objects. Roger Brown (1968) called this "the original word game" and claimed that much of a child's early vocabulary is motivated by this adult pressure to identify the words associated with objects.

Parents use these strategies naturally and in meaningful conversations. Parents do not (and should not) use any deliberate method to teach their children to talk, even for children who are slow in learning language. Children usually benefit when parents guide their children's discovery of language rather than overloading them with language; "following in order to lead" helps a child learn language. If children are not ready to take in some information, they are likely to tell you (perhaps by turning away). Thus, giving the child more information is not always better.

Infants, toddlers, and young children benefit when adults read books to and with them (shared reading) (Hirsh-Pasek & Golinkoff, 2014). In one study, reading daily to children at 14 to 24 months of age was positively related to the children's language and cognitive development at 36 months of age (Raikes & others, 2006). And in a recent study, Japanese mothers who used more elaborative information-seeking responses during joint picture-book reading at 20 months had children with a better productive vocabulary at 27 months (Murase, 2014).

Remember, the encouragement of language development, not drill and practice, is the key. Language development is not a simple matter of imitation and reinforcement. To read further about ways that parents can facilitate children's language development, see the *Connecting Development to Life* interlude.

Our discussion of environmental influences on language development has focused mainly on parents. However, children interact with many other people who can influence their language development, including teachers and peers. A study of more than 1,800 4-year-olds focused on ways in which peers might influence children's language development (Mashburn & others, 2009). In this study, peers' expressive language abilities were positively linked with young children's receptive and expressive language development.

AN INTERACTIONIST VIEW OF LANGUAGE

If language acquisition depended only on biology, then Genie and the Wild Boy of Aveyron (discussed at the beginning of the chapter) should have talked without difficulty. A child's experiences influence language acquisition. But we have seen that language does have strong biological foundations. No matter how much you converse with a dog, it won't learn to talk.

An interactionist view emphasizes that both biology and experience contribute to language development. This interaction of biology and experience can be seen in the variations in the acquisition of language. Children vary in their ability to acquire language, and this

recasting Rephrasing a statement that a child has said, perhaps turning it into a question, or restating a child's immature utterance in the form of a fully grammatical sentence.

expanding Restating, in a linguistically sophisticated form, what a child has said.

labeling Identifying the names of objects.

How Parents Can Facilitate Infants' and Toddlers' Language Development

Linguist Naomi Baron (1992) in *Growing Up with Language,* and more recently Ellen Galinsky (2010) in *Mind in the Making,* provided ideas to help parents facilitate their infants' and toddlers' language development. A summary of their ideas follows:

- *Be an active conversational partner.* Talk to your baby from the time it is born. Initiate conversation with the baby. If the baby is in a day-long child-care program, ensure that the baby receives adequate language stimulation from adults.
- *Talk in a slowed-down pace and don't worry about how you sound to other adults when you talk to your baby.* Talking in a slowed-down pace will help your baby detect words in the sea of sounds they experience. Babies enjoy and attend to the high-pitched sound of child-directed speech.
- *Use parent-look and parent-gesture, and name what you are looking at.* When you want your child to pay attention to something, look at it and point to it. Then name it—for example, by saying "Look, Alex, there's an airplane."
- *When you talk with infants and toddlers, be simple, concrete, and repetitive.* Don't try to talk to them in abstract, high-level ways and think you have to say something new or different all of the time. Using familiar words often will help them remember the words.
- *Play games.* Use word games like peek-a-boo and pat-a-cake to help infants learn words.
- *Remember to listen.* Since toddlers' speech is often slow and laborious, parents are often tempted to supply words and thoughts for them. Be patient and let toddlers express themselves, no matter how painstaking the process is or how great a hurry you are in.
- *Expand and elaborate language abilities and horizons with infants and toddlers.* Ask questions that encourage answers other than "Yes" and "No." Actively repeat, expand, and recast the utterances. Your toddler might say, "Dada." You could follow with "Where's Dada?" and then you might continue, "Let's go find him."

It is a good idea for parents to begin talking to their babies at the start. The best language teaching occurs when the talking is begun before the infant becomes capable of intelligible speech. *What are some other guidelines for parents to follow in helping their infants and toddlers develop their language skills?*
© John Carter/Science Source

- *Adjust to your child's idiosyncrasies instead of working against them.* Many toddlers have difficulty pronouncing words and making themselves understood. Whenever possible, make toddlers feel that they are being understood.
- *Resist making normative comparisons.* Be aware of the ages at which your child reaches specific milestones (such as the first word, first 50 words), but do not measure this development rigidly against that of other children. Such comparisons can bring about unnecessary anxiety.

The first suggestion for parents of infants is to "be an active conversational partner." What did you learn earlier in this chapter about the amount of conversation mothers have with their infants? Does the amount of conversation or the mother's literacy skills and vocabulary diversity have a stronger positive effect on infants' vocabulary?

variation cannot be readily explained by differences in environmental input alone. However, virtually every child benefits enormously from opportunities to talk and be talked with. Children whose parents and teachers provide them with a rich verbal environment show many positive outcomes (Beaty & Pratt, 2015). Parents and teachers who pay attention to what children are trying to say, expand their children's utterances, read to them, and label things in the environment, are providing valuable, if unintentional, benefits (Hirsh-Pasek & Golinkoff, 2014).

Review *Connect* Reflect

(LG3) Discuss the biological and environmental contributions to language skills

Review
- What are the biological foundations of language?
- What are the environmental aspects of language?
- How does an interactionist view describe language?

Connect
- Relate what you learned about the nature-nurture debate to understanding biological and environmental influences on the development of language skills.

Reflect *Your Own Personal Journey of Life*
- If and when you become a parent, how should you respond to your child's grammar when conversing with the child? Will you allow mistakes to continue and assume that your young child will grow out of them, or will you closely monitor your young child's grammar and correct mistakes whenever you hear them? Explain.

reach your **learning goals**

Language Development

1 What Is Language?

(LG1) Define language and describe its rule systems

Defining Language

Language's Rule Systems

- Language is a form of communication, whether spontaneous, written, or signed, that is based on a system of symbols. Language consists of all the words used by a community and the rules for varying and combining them. Infinite generativity is the ability to produce an endless number of meaningful sentences using a finite set of words and rules.

- The main rule systems of language are phonology, morphology, syntax, semantics, and pragmatics. Phonology is the sound system of a language, including the sounds used and the sound sequences that may occur in the language. Morphology refers to units of meaning in word formation. Syntax is the way words are combined to form acceptable phrases and sentences. Semantics involves the meaning of words and sentences. Pragmatics is the appropriate use of language in different contexts.

2 How Language Develops

(LG2) Describe how language develops through the life span

Infancy

Early Childhood

Middle and Late Childhood

- Among the milestones in infant language development are crying (birth), cooing (2 to 4 months), understanding first word (5 months), babbling (6 months), making the transition from universal linguist to language-specific listener (6 to 12 months), using gestures (8 to 12 months), detecting word boundaries (8 months), first word spoken (13 months), vocabulary spurt (18 months), rapid expansion of understanding words (18 to 24 months), and two-word utterances (18 to 24 months).

- Advances in phonology, morphology, syntax, semantics, and pragmatics continue in early childhood. The transition to complex sentences begins between 2 and 3 years and continues through the elementary school years. Fast mapping provides one explanation for how rapidly young children's vocabulary develops.

- In middle and late childhood, children become more analytical and logical in their approach to words and grammar. Current debate involving how to teach children to read focuses on the whole-language approach versus the phonics approach. Researchers have found strong evidence that the phonics approach should be used in teaching children to read but that children also benefit from the whole-language approach. Children's writing emerges out of scribbling. Advances in children's language and cognitive development provide the underpinnings for improved writing. Recent research indicates a complex conclusion about whether there are sensitive periods in learning a second language. Children who are fluent in two languages have more advanced information-processing skills. Instruction for English language learners (EELs) has taken one of two main forms: (1) instruction in English only, or (2) dual-language instruction in the child's home language and English. The majority of large-scale research studies have found a higher level of academic achievement when the dual-language approach is used.

Adolescence

· In adolescence, language changes include more effective use of words; improvements in the ability to understand metaphor, satire, and adult literary works; and improvements in writing.

Adulthood and Aging

· For many individuals, knowledge of words and word meanings continues unchanged or may even improve in later adulthood. However, some decline in language skills may occur in retrieving words for use in conversation, in understanding speech, in phonological skills, and in some aspects of discourse. These changes in language skills in older adults likely occur as a consequence of declines in memory or in speed of processing information, or as a result of disease.

3 Biological and Environmental Influences

 LG3 Discuss the biological and environmental contributions to language skills

Biological Influences

· In evolution, language clearly gave humans an enormous edge over other animals and increased their chances of survival. A substantial portion of language processing occurs in the brain's left hemisphere, with Broca's area and Wernicke's area being important left-hemisphere locations. Chomsky argues that children are born with the ability to detect basic features and rules of language. In other words, they are biologically prepared to learn language with a prewired language acquisition device (LAD).

Environmental Influences

· The behaviorists' view of language development—that children acquire language as a result of reinforcement—has not been supported. Adults help children acquire language through child-directed speech, recasting, expanding, and labeling. Environmental influences are demonstrated by differences in the language development of children as a consequence of being exposed to different language environments in the home. Parents should talk extensively with an infant, especially about what the baby is attending to.

An Interactionist View of Language

· An interactionist view emphasizes the contributions of both biology and experience in language.

key **terms**

aphasia	infinite generativity	metaphor	satire
Broca's area	labeling	morphology	semantics
child-directed speech	language	phonics approach	syntax
dialect	language acquisition device	phonology	telegraphic speech
expanding	(LAD)	pragmatics	Wernicke's area
fast mapping	metalinguistic awareness	recasting	whole-language approach

key **people**

Naomi Baron	Ellen Galinsky	Betty Hart	Patricia Kuhl
Jean Berko	Roberta Golinkoff	Kathy Hirsh-Pasek	Todd Risley
Roger Brown	Kenji Hakuta	Janellen Huttenlocher	Michael Tomasello
Noam Chomsky			

section four

Generations will depend on the ability of all procreating individuals to face their children.

—ERIK ERIKSON
Danish-born American psychoanalyst, 20th century

Socioemotional Processes and Development

As children develop, they need "the meeting eyes of love." They split the universe into two halves: "me and not me." They juggle the need to curb their will with becoming what they can freely. Children and youth want to fly but discover that first they have to learn to stand and walk and climb and dance. Adolescents try on one face after another, searching for a face of their own. As adults age, they seek satisfaction in their emotional lives and search for the meaning of life. This section contains four chapters: "Emotional Development and Attachment," "The Self, Identity, and Personality," "Gender and Sexuality," and "Moral Development, Values, and Religion."

chapter 10

EMOTIONAL DEVELOPMENT AND ATTACHMENT

chapter **outline**

preview

For many years, emotion was neglected in the study of life-span development. Today, emotion is increasingly important in conceptualizations of development. For example, even as infants, individuals show different emotional styles, display varying temperaments, and begin to form emotional bonds with their caregivers. In this chapter, we study how temperament and attachment change across the life span. But first, we examine emotion itself, exploring the functions of emotions in people's lives and the development of emotion from infancy through late adulthood.

1 Exploring Emotion   LG1   Discuss basic aspects of emotion

| What Are Emotions? | Emotion Regulation | Emotional Competence |

Imagine your life without emotion. Emotion is the color and music of life, as well as the tie that binds people together. How do psychologists define and classify emotions, and why are they important to development?

WHAT ARE EMOTIONS?

For our purposes, we will define **emotion** as feeling, or affect, that occurs when a person is in a state or an interaction that is important to him or her, especially to his or her well-being. In infancy, emotions have important roles in (1) communication with others and (2) behavioral organization. Through emotions, infants communicate important aspects of their lives such as joy, sadness, interest, and fear (Witherington & others, 2011). In terms of behavioral organization, emotions influence children's social responses and adaptive behavior as they interact with others in their world (Denham & Zinsser, 2015; Thompson, 2015).

When we think about emotions, a few dramatic feelings such as rage or glorious joy spring to mind. But emotions can be subtle as well, such as uneasiness in a new situation or the contentment a mother feels when she holds her baby. Psychologists classify the broad range of emotions in many ways, but almost all classifications designate an emotion as either positive or negative. Positive emotions include enthusiasm, joy, and love. Negative emotions include anxiety, anger, guilt, and sadness.

Emotions are influenced both by biological foundations and by a person's experience. Biology's importance to emotion also is apparent in the changes in a baby's emotional capacities (Frenkel & Fox, 2015). Certain regions of the brain that develop early in life (such as the brain stem, hippocampus, and amygdala) play a role in distress, excitement, and rage, and even infants display these emotions (Fox, Reeb-Sutherland, & Degnan, 2013; Kagan, 2013). But, as we discuss later in the chapter, infants only gradually develop the ability to regulate their emotions, and this ability is linked to the gradual maturation of frontal regions of the cerebral cortex that can exert control over other areas of the brain (Cuevas & others, 2012; Morasch & Bell, 2012).

Emotion regulation also can influence whether biological and experiential factors are linked to various developmental outcomes. For example, in G × E interaction, the short version of the serotonin transporter gene (5-HTTLPR) is linked to increased risk of depression when individuals often experience stressful environments. A recent study of 9- to 15-year-olds who were characterized by this gene-environment combination found that they were less likely to be depressed if they were effective at emotion regulation (Ford & others, 2014).

Social relationships provide the setting for the development of a rich variety of emotions (Lamb, 2015; Laible, Thompson, & Froimson, 2015; Thompson, 2014, 2015, 2016). When toddlers hear their parents quarreling, they often react with distress and inhibit their play. Well-functioning families make each other laugh and may develop a light mood to defuse conflicts. A recent study of 18- to 24-month-olds found that parents' elicitation of talk about emotions was associated with their toddlers' sharing and helping (Brownell & others, 2013). In another recent study of 10- to 12-year-olds, mothers of more anxious children were more likely to engage in psychologically controlling behavior intended to manipulate the children's emotional state, showed less warmth and interest in the children, and elaborated less during conversations about an emotionally negative event (Brumariu & Kerns, 2015).

Blossoms are scattered by the wind
And the wind cares nothing, but
The blossoms of the heart,
No wind can touch.

—Youshida Kenko
Buddhist monk, 14th century

developmental **connection**

Brain Development

The timing of maturation of the amygdala and prefrontal cortex is linked to adolescent risk taking. Connect to "Physical Development and Biological Aging."

emotion Feeling, or affect, that occurs when a person is engaged in an interaction that is important to him or her, especially to his or her well-being.

Biological evolution has endowed human beings with the capacity to be *emotional*, but cultural embeddedness and relationships with others provide diversity in emotional experiences (Chen, Fu, & Zhao, 2015; Chen & Schmidt, 2015; Cole & Tan, 2015; Ford & Mauss, 2015; Laible, Thompson, & Froimson, 2015). Emotional development and coping with stress are influenced by whether caregivers have maltreated or neglected children and whether children's caregivers are depressed or not (Hostinar & Gunnar, 2013). When infants become stressed, they show better biological recovery from the stressors when their caregivers engage in sensitive caregiving (Gunnar & Herrera, 2013).

A recent study documented how babies pick up on their mothers' stress (Waters, West, & Mendes, 2014). In this study, mothers were separated from their babies and asked to give a five-minute speech, with half of the mothers receiving a positive evaluation and the other half a negative evaluation. Mothers who received negative feedback reported an increase in negative emotion and cardiac stress, while those who were given positive feedback reported an increase in positive emotion. The babies quickly detected their mothers' stress, as reflected in an increased heart rate when reunited with them. And the greater the mother's stress response, the more her baby's heart rate increased.

Cultural variations characterize emotional development (Chen & others, 2015; Chen & Schmidt, 2015; Cole & Tan, 2015). For example, researchers have found that East Asian infants display less frequent and less positive and negative emotions than non-Latino White infants (Cole & Tan, 2007). Throughout childhood, East Asian parents encourage their children to show emotional reserve rather than to be emotionally expressive (Cole & Tan, 2007). Further, Japanese parents try to prevent children from experiencing negative emotions, whereas non-Latino White mothers more frequently respond after their children become distressed and then help them cope (Rothbaum & Trommsdorff, 2007).

How do Japanese mothers handle their infants' and children's emotional development differently from non-Latina White mothers?
© Jose Luis Pelaez Inc./Getty Images RF

EMOTION REGULATION

The ability to control one's emotions is a key dimension of development (Laible, Thompson, & Froimson, 2015). Emotion regulation consists of effectively managing arousal to adapt to circumstances and to reach a goal (Thompson, 2015). Arousal involves a state of alertness or activation, which can reach levels that are too high for effective functioning. Anger, for example, often requires regulation.

In infancy and early childhood, regulation of emotion gradually shifts from external sources to self-initiated, internal sources. Also, with increasing age, children are more likely to improve their use of cognitive strategies for regulating emotion, modulate their emotional arousal, become more adept at managing situations to minimize negative emotion, and choose effective ways to cope with stress.

Emotion regulation is involved in many aspects of children's and adolescents' development, and there are wide variations in children's and adolescents' ability to modulate their emotions (Thompson, 2015). Indeed, a prominent feature of children and adolescents with problems is that they often have difficulty managing their emotions. Ineffective emotion regulation is linked with a lower level of executive function, difficulty succeeding in school, a lower level of moral development (weak conscience and lack of internalization of rules, for example), failure to adequately cope with stress, and difficulty in peer relations (Raver & others, 2013; Rubin, Buknowski, & Bowker, 2015; Thompson, 2015).

Parents can play an important role in helping young children regulate their emotions (Kiel & Kalomiris, 2015; Wilson & others, 2014). Depending on how they talk with their children about emotion, parents can be described as taking an *emotion-coaching* or an *emotion-dismissing* approach (Gottman, 2014). The distinction between these approaches is most evident in the way the parent deals with the child's negative emotions (anger, frustration, sadness, and so on). *Emotion-coaching parents* monitor their children's emotions, view their children's negative emotions as opportunities for teaching, assist them in labeling emotions, and coach them in how to deal effectively with emotions. In contrast, *emotion-dismissing parents* view their role as to deny, ignore, or change negative emotions. Researchers have observed that emotion-coaching parents interact with their children in a less rejecting manner, use more scaffolding and praise, and are more nurturant than are emotion-dismissing parents (Gottman & DeClaire, 1997). Moreover, the children of emotion-coaching parents are better at soothing themselves when they got

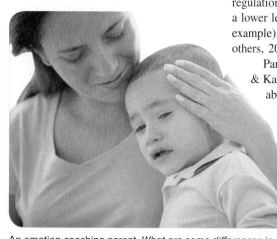

An emotion-coaching parent. What are some differences in emotion-coaching and emotion-dismissing parents?
© Jose Luis Pelaez Inc./Blend Images LLC RF

upset, are more effective in regulating their negative affect, focus their attention better, and have fewer behavior problems than the children of emotion-dismissing parents. One study found that fathers' emotion coaching was related to children's social competence (Baker, Fenning, & Crnic, 2011). Another study revealed that having emotion-dismissing parents was linked with children's poor emotion regulation (Lunkenheimer, Shields, & Cortina, 2007).

A challenge parents face is that young children typically don't want to talk about difficult emotional topics, such as being distressed or engaging in negative behaviors. Among the strategies young children use to avoid these conversations is to not talk at all, change the topic, push the parent away, or run away. Young children are more likely to openly discuss difficult emotional circumstances when they are securely attached to their mother.

EMOTIONAL COMPETENCE

In the "Intelligence" chapter, we briefly considered the concept of emotional intelligence. Here we examine a closely related concept, emotional competence, that focuses on the adaptive nature of emotional experience (Denham, Bassett, & Wyatt, 2015). Carolyn Saarni (1999; Saarni & others, 2006) notes that becoming emotionally competent involves developing a number of skills in social contexts, including the following:

developmental **connection**

Intelligence

Emotional intelligence involves perceiving and expressing emotions accurately, understanding emotion and emotional knowledge, using feelings to facilitate thought, and managing emotions effectively. Connect to "Intelligence."

Skill	Example
· Having awareness of one's emotional states	Being able to differentiate whether one feels sad or anxious
· Detecting others' emotions	Understanding when another person is sad rather than afraid
· Using the vocabulary of emotion terms in socially and culturally appropriate ways	Appropriately describing a social situation in one's culture when a person is feeling distressed
· Having empathetic and sympathetic sensitivity to others' emotional experiences	Being sensitive to other people when they are feeling distressed
· Recognizing that inner emotional states do not have to correspond to outer expressions	Recognizing that one can feel very angry yet manage one's emotional expression so that it appears more neutral
· Adaptively coping with negative emotions by using self-regulatory strategies that reduce the intensity or duration of such emotional states	Reducing anger by walking away from an aversive situation and engaging in an activity that takes one's mind off the aversive situation
· Having awareness that the expression of emotions plays a major role in relationships	Knowing that expressing anger toward a friend on a regular basis is likely to harm the friendship
· Viewing oneself overall as feeling the way one wants to feel	Striving to cope effectively with the stress in one's life and feeling that one is successfully doing this

As children acquire these emotional competence skills in a variety of contexts, they are more likely to effectively manage their emotions, become resilient in the face of stressful circumstances, and develop more positive relationships.

Review Connect Reflect

 Discuss basic aspects of emotion

Review

- How is *emotion* defined?
- What are some developmental changes in the regulation of emotion?
- What constitutes emotional competence, according to Saarni?

Connect

- How similar or different are the concepts of emotional intelligence and emotional competence?

Reflect *Your Own Personal Journey of Life*

- Think back to your childhood and adolescent years. How effective were you in regulating your emotions? Give some examples. Has your ability to regulate your emotions changed as you have grown older? Explain.

Joy

Sadness

Fear

Surprise

FIGURE 1

EXPRESSION OF DIFFERENT EMOTIONS IN INFANTS
(Joy): © BananaStock/PictureQuest RF; (Sadness): © The McGraw-Hill Companies, Inc./Jill Braaten, photographer; (Fear): © David Sacks/Getty Images; (Surprise): © EyeWire/Getty Images RF

primary emotions Emotions that are present in humans and other animals, emerge early in life, and are culturally universal; examples are joy, anger, sadness, fear, and disgust.

self-conscious emotions Emotions that require consciousness and a sense of "me"; they include empathy, jealousy, embarrassment, pride, shame, and guilt, most of which first appear at some point after 18 months of age when a sense of self becomes consolidated in toddlers.

basic cry A rhythmic pattern usually consisting of a cry, a briefer silence, a shorter inspiratory whistle that is higher pitched than the main cry, and then a brief rest before the next cry.

anger cry A cry similar to the basic cry but with more excess air forced through the vocal cords.

pain cry A sudden, initial loud cry followed by breath holding, without preliminary moaning.

Does an adult's emotional life differ from an adolescent's? Does a young child's emotional life differ from an infant's? Does an infant even have an emotional life? In this section, we trace the changes in emotion over the life span, looking not only at changes in emotional experience but also at the development of emotional competence.

INFANCY

What are some early developmental changes in emotions? What functions do infants' cries serve? When do infants begin to smile?

Early Emotions A leading expert on infant emotional development, Michael Lewis (2007, 2008, 2010, 2015) distinguishes between primary emotions and self-conscious emotions. **Primary emotions** are emotions that are present in humans and other animals; these emotions appear in the first six months of the human infant's development. Primary emotions include surprise, interest, joy, anger, sadness, fear, and disgust (see Figure 1 for infants' facial expressions of some of these early emotions). In Lewis' classification, **self-conscious emotions** require self-awareness that involves consciousness and a sense of "me." Self-conscious emotions include jealousy, empathy, embarrassment, pride, shame, and guilt—most of these occurring for the first time at some point after 18 months of age when a sense of self become consolidated in toddlers.

Researchers such as Joseph Campos (2005) and Michael Lewis (2007, 2010, 2015) debate about how early in the infant and toddler years these self-conscious emotions first appear and what their sequence is. As an indication of the controversy regarding when certain emotions first are displayed by infants, consider jealousy. Some researchers argue that jealousy does not emerge until approximately 18 months of age (Lewis, 2007), whereas others assert that it is displayed much earlier (Draghi-Lorenz, 2007; Hart & Behrens, 2013). Some research studies suggest that the appearance of jealousy might occur as early as 6 months of age (Hart & others, 2004). In one study, 6-month-old infants observed their mothers giving attention either to a lifelike baby doll (hugging or gently rocking it, for example) or to a book. When mothers directed their attention to the doll, the infants were more likely to display negative emotions, such as anger and sadness, which may have indicated their jealousy (Hart & Carrington, 2002) (see Figure 2). On the other hand, their expressions of anger and sadness simply may have reflected frustration about not being able to have the novel doll to play with. However, in a recent study, 9-month-old infants displayed jealousy-related behavior and EEG patterns characteristic of jealousy when their mothers gave attention to a social rival (Mize & others, 2014).

Debate about the onset of an emotion such as jealousy illustrates the complexity and difficulty of indexing early emotions. That said, some experts on infant socioemotional development, such as Jerome Kagan (2013), conclude that the structural immaturity of the infant brain makes it unlikely that emotions requiring thought—such as guilt, pride, despair, shame, empathy, and jealousy—can be experienced during the first year. Nonetheless, some leading researchers have argued that research now indicates that empathy can be expressed before the infant's first birthday (Davidov & others, 2013).

Emotional Expression and Social Relationships Emotional expression is involved in infants' first relationships. The ability of infants to communicate emotions permits coordinated interactions with their caregivers and the beginning of an emotional bond between them (Thompson, 2015). Not only do parents change their emotional expressions in response to infants' emotional expressions, but infants also modify their emotional expressions in response to their parents' emotional expressions. In other words, these interactions are mutually regulated (Bridgett

& others, 2009). Because of this coordination, the interactions are described as reciprocal, or synchronous, when all is going well. Sensitive, responsive parents help their infants grow emotionally, whether the infants respond in distressed or happy ways (Thompson, 2014). A recent study found that a higher level of maternal positive emotionality predicted more initial infant smiling and laughter, while a higher level of parental stress predicted a lower trajectory of infant smiling and laughter (Bridgett & others, 2013). Another recent study revealed that parents' elicitation of talk about emotion with toddlers was associated with the toddlers' sharing and helping behaviors (Brownell & others, 2013).

Cries and smiles are two emotional expressions that infants display when interacting with parents. These are babies' first forms of emotional communication.

Crying   Crying is the most important mechanism newborns have for communicating with their world. The first cry verifies that the baby's lungs have filled with air. Cries also may provide information about the health of the newborn's central nervous system. Newborns even tend to respond with cries and negative facial expressions when they hear other newborns cry (Dondi, Simion, & Caltran, 1999). However, a recent study revealed that newborns of depressed mothers showed less vocal distress when another infant cried, reflecting emotional and physiological dysregulation (Jones, 2012).

Babies have at least three types of cries:

· **Basic cry.** A rhythmic pattern that usually consists of a cry, followed by a briefer silence, then a shorter inspiratory whistle that is somewhat higher in pitch than the main cry, then another brief rest before the next cry. Some infancy experts stress that hunger is one of the conditions that incite the basic cry.
· **Anger cry.** A variation of the basic cry in which more excess air is forced through the vocal cords. The anger cry has a loud, harsh sound to it, almost like shouting.
· **Pain cry.** A sudden long, initial loud cry followed by breath holding; no preliminary moaning is present. The pain cry is stimulated by a high-intensity stimulus.

Most adults can determine whether an infant's cries signify anger or pain (Zeskind, 2007). Parents can distinguish between the various cries of their own baby better than those of another baby.

Smiling   Smiling is critical as a means of developing a new social skill and is a key social signal (Sauter & others, 2014; Witherington & others, 2011). Recent research found that smiling and laughter at 7 months of age were associated with self-regulation at 7 years of age (Posner & others, 2014).

Two types of smiling can be distinguished in infants:

· **Reflexive smile.** A smile that does not occur in response to external stimuli and appears during the first month after birth, usually during sleep.
· **Social smile.** A smile that occurs in response to an external stimulus, typically a face in the case of the young infant. Social smiling occurs as early as 4 to 6 weeks of age in response to a caregiver's voice (Messinger, 2008).

The infant's social smile can have a powerful impact on caregivers (Bates, 2008). Following weeks of endless demands, fatigue, and little reinforcement, an infant starts smiling at them and all of the caregivers' efforts are rewarded.

Fear   One of a baby's earliest emotions is fear, which typically first appears at about 6 months of age and peaks at about 18 months. However, abused and neglected infants can show fear as early as 3 months (Campos, 2005).

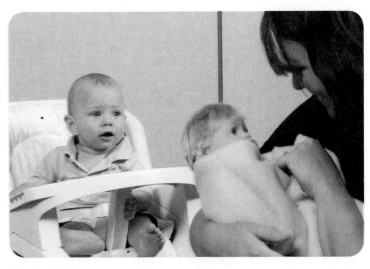

FIGURE **2**

IS THIS THE EARLY EXPRESSION OF JEALOUSY? In the study by Hart and Carrington (2002), the researchers concluded that the reactions of 6-month-old infants who observed their mothers giving attention to a baby doll may indicate the early appearance of jealousy because of the negative emotions—such as anger and sadness—they displayed. However, experts on emotional development, such as Joseph Campos (2009) and Jerome Kagan (2010), argue that emotions such as jealousy don't appear during the first year. *Why do they conclude that jealousy does not occur in the first year?*
© Kenny Braun/Braun Photography

What are some different types of cries?
© Andy Cox/The Image Bank/Getty Images

He who binds to himself a joy
Does the winged life destroy;
But he who kisses the joy as it flies
Lives in eternity's sun rise.

—WILLIAM BLAKE
English poet, 19th century

reflexive smile A smile that does not occur in response to external stimuli. It happens during the month after birth, usually during sleep.

social smile A smile in response to an external stimulus, which, early in development, typically is a face.

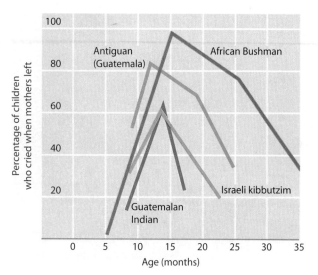

FIGURE **3**

SEPARATION PROTEST IN FOUR CULTURES. Note that separation protest peaked at about the same time in all four cultures in this study (13 to 15 months of age) (Kagan, Kearsley, & Zelazo, 1978). However, a higher percentage (100 percent) of infants in an African Bushman culture engaged in separation protest compared with only about 60 percent of infants in Guatemalan Indian and Israeli kibbutzim cultures. *What might explain the fact that separation protest peaks at about the same time in these cultures?*

Should a crying baby be given attention and soothed, or does this spoil the infant? Should the infant's age, the type of cry, and the circumstances be considered?
© Photodisc Collection/Getty Images RF

The most frequent expression of an infant's fear involves **stranger anxiety,** in which an infant shows a fear and wariness of strangers. Stranger anxiety usually emerges gradually. It first appears at about 6 months of age in the form of wary reactions. By age 9 months, the fear of strangers is often more intense, reaching a peak toward the end of the first year of life (Scher & Harel, 2008).

Not all infants show distress when they encounter a stranger. Besides individual variations, whether an infant shows stranger anxiety also depends on the social context and the characteristics of the stranger (Kagan, 2008).

Infants show less stranger anxiety when they are in familiar settings. It appears that when infants feel secure, they are less likely to show stranger anxiety.

In addition to stranger anxiety, infants experience fear of being separated from their caregivers. The result is **separation protest**—crying when the caregiver leaves. Separation protest is initially displayed by infants at approximately 7 to 8 months and peaks at about 15 months (Kagan, 2008). One study revealed that separation protest peaked at about 13 to 15 months in four different cultures (Kagan, Kearsley, & Zelazo, 1978). As indicated in Figure 3, the percentage of infants who engaged in separation protest varied across cultures, but the infants reached a peak of protest at about the same age—early in the second year of life.

Emotion Regulation and Coping   Earlier, we discussed some general developmental changes in emotion regulation across the childhood years. Here we examine in detail how infants develop emotion regulation and coping skills.

During the first year of life, the infant gradually develops an ability to inhibit, or minimize, the intensity and duration of emotional reactions. From early in infancy, babies put their thumbs in their mouths to soothe themselves. But at first, infants mainly depend on caregivers to help them soothe their emotions, as when a caregiver rocks an infant to sleep, sings lullabies to the infant, gently strokes the infant, and so on.

Later in infancy, when they become aroused, infants sometimes redirect their attention or distract themselves in order to reduce their arousal. By 2 years of age, toddlers can use language to define their feeling states and the context that is upsetting them (Kopp, 2008). A toddler might say, "Feel bad. Dog scare." This type of communication may allow caregivers to help the child in regulating emotion.

Contexts can influence emotion regulation (Thompson, 2015). Infants are often affected by fatigue, hunger, time of day, the people who are around them, and where they are. Infants must learn to adapt to different contexts that require emotion regulation. Further, new demands appear as the infant becomes older and parents modify their expectations. For example, a parent may take it in stride if a 6-month-old infant screams in a grocery store but may react very differently if a 2-year-old starts screaming.

To soothe or not to soothe—should a crying baby be given attention and soothed, or does this attention spoil the infant? Many years ago, the behaviorist John Watson (1928) argued that parents spend too much time responding to infant crying. As a consequence, he said, parents reward crying and increase its incidence. Some researchers have found that a caregiver's quick, soothing response to crying increased crying (Gewirtz, 1977). However, infancy experts Mary Ainsworth (1979) and John Bowlby (1989) stress that you can't respond too much to infant crying in the first year of life. They argue that a quick, comforting response to the infant's cries is an important ingredient in the development of a strong bond between the infant and caregiver. In one of Ainsworth's studies, infants whose mothers responded quickly when they cried at 3 months of age cried less later in the first year of life (Bell & Ainsworth, 1972).

Controversy continues to surround the question of whether or how parents should respond to an infant's cries. Some developmentalists argue that an infant cannot be spoiled in the first year of life, a view suggesting that parents should soothe a crying infant. This reaction should help infants develop a sense of trust and secure attachment to the caregiver. A recent study revealed that mothers' negative emotional reactions (anger and anxiety) to crying increased the risk of subsequent attachment insecurity (Leerkes, Parade, & Gudmundson, 2011). Another recent study found that problems in infant soothability at 6 months of age were linked to insecure attachment at 12 months of age (Mills-Koonce, Propper, & Barnette, 2012). And in yet another recent study, researchers discovered that emotionally reactive infants who also showed a high level of emotion regulation were more likely to have primary caregivers who engaged in positive parenting behavior during a parent-child interaction task (Ursache & others, 2013).

EARLY CHILDHOOD

The young child's growing awareness of self is linked to the ability to feel an expanding range of emotions. Young children, like adults, experience many emotions during the course of a day. At times, they also try to make sense of other people's emotional reactions and to control their own emotions.

Expressing Emotions   Recall from our earlier discussion that even young infants experience emotions such as joy and fear, but to experience self-conscious emotions, children must be able to refer to themselves and be aware of themselves as distinct from others (Lewis, 2008, 2010, 2015). Pride, shame, embarrassment, and guilt are examples of self-conscious emotions. Self-conscious emotions do not appear to develop until self-awareness appears in the second half of the second year of life.

During the early childhood years, emotions such as pride and guilt become more common (Lewis, 2015). They are especially influenced by parents' responses to children's behavior (Thompson, 2015). For example, a young child may experience shame when a parent says, "You should feel bad about biting your sister."

Understanding Emotions   Among the most important changes in emotional development in early childhood is an increased understanding of emotion (Denham, Bassett, & Wyatt, 2015; Denham & others, 2014). During early childhood, young children increasingly understand that certain situations are likely to evoke particular emotions, facial expressions indicate specific emotions, emotions affect behavior, and emotions can be used to influence others' emotions (Cole & others, 2009). In one study, young children's emotional understanding was linked to how extensively they engaged in prosocial behavior (Ensor, Spencer, & Hughes, 2010).

Between 2 and 4 years of age, children considerably increase the number of terms they use to describe emotions. During this time, they are also learning about the causes and consequences of feelings.

A young child expressing the emotion of shame, which occurs when a child evaluates his or her actions as not living up to standards. A child experiencing shame wishes to hide or disappear. *Why is shame called a self-conscious emotion?*
© James Woodson/Getty Images RF

When they are 4 to 5 years of age, children show an increased ability to reflect on emotions. They also begin to understand that the same event can elicit different feelings in different people. Moreover, they show a growing awareness that they need to manage their emotions to meet social standards (Denham & Zinsser, 2014). And, by 5 years of age, most children can accurately identify emotions that are produced by challenging circumstances and describe strategies they might call on to cope with everyday stress (Cole & others, 2009).

One program that is designed to improve young children's understanding of emotions is the Emotion-Based Prevention program (EBP) (Izard & others, 2008). This program consists of a teacher-conducted emotions course in the classroom, emotion tutoring and coaching teacher dialogues, and weekly parent messages that reinforce the lessons taught in the classroom. In the classroom component, teachers ask children to label or demonstrate emotional expressions, share ideas about what causes them to feel the emotions they described, compare expressions of different emotions and their intensities, and draw out or act out emotion expressions for their classmates. A recent study found that EBP was effective in improving Head Start children's emotion knowledge and the children who participated in the program showed a decrease in their expression of negative emotions and internalizing behaviors (Finion & others, 2015).

Regulating Emotions   Many researchers consider the growth of emotion regulation in children as fundamental to the development of social competence (Calkins & Dollar, 2014; Goodvin, Thompson, & Winer, 2015; Nelson & others, 2012). In a recent study of 5- to 7-year-olds, understanding others' emotions was linked to the children's emotion regulation (Hudson & Jacques, 2014).

Emotion regulation can be conceptualized as an important component of self-regulation or of executive function. Executive function is increasingly thought to be a key concept in describing the young child's higher-level cognitive functioning. Cybelle Raver and her colleagues (Blair & Raver, 2012; McCoy & Raver, 2011; Raver & others, 2011, 2012. 2013;

stranger anxiety An infant's fear of and wariness toward strangers; it tends to appear in the second half of the first year of life.

separation protest Reaction that occurs when infants experience a fear of being separated from a caregiver, which results in crying when the caregiver leaves.

Zhai, Raver, & Jones, 2012) are using various interventions, such as increasing caregiver emotional expressiveness, to improve young children's emotion regulation and reduce behavior problems in children growing up in poverty conditions.

MIDDLE AND LATE CHILDHOOD

During middle and late childhood, many children show marked improvement in understanding and managing their emotions. However, in some instances, as when they experience stressful circumstances, their coping abilities may be challenged.

Developmental Changes in Emotion   Here are some important developmental changes in emotions during the middle and late childhood years (Denham, Bassett, & Wyatt, 2007, 2015; Kuebli, 1994; Thompson, 2015; Wintre & Vallance, 1994):

· *Improved emotional understanding.* Children in elementary school develop an increased ability to understand such complex emotions as pride and shame. These emotions become less tied to the reactions of other people; they become more self-generated and integrated with a sense of personal responsibility. A child may feel a sense of pride about developing new reading skills or shame after hurting a friend's feelings. Also, during middle and late childhood as part of their understanding of emotions, children can engage in "mental time travel," in which they anticipate and recall the cognitive and emotional aspects of events (Lagattuta, 2014a, b).
· *Marked improvements in the ability to suppress or conceal negative emotional reactions.* Children now sometimes intentionally hide their emotions. Although a boy may feel sad that a friend does not want to play with him, he may decide not to share those feelings with his parents.
· *The use of self-initiated strategies for redirecting feelings.* In the elementary school years, children reflect more about emotional experiences and develop strategies to cope with their emotional lives. Children can more effectively manage their emotions by cognitive means, such as using distracting thoughts. A boy may be excited about his birthday party that will take place later in the afternoon, but still be able to concentrate on his schoolwork during the day.
· *An increased tendency to take into fuller account the events leading to emotional reactions.* A fourth-grader may become aware that her sadness today is influenced by her friend's moving to another town last week.
· *Development of a capacity for genuine empathy.* Two girls see another child in distress on the playground and run to the child and ask if they can help.

Coping with Stress   An important aspect of children's lives is learning how to cope with stress (Mash & Wolfe, 2013, 2016; Masten, 2014a, b; Morris, Thompson, & Morris, 2013). As children get older, they are able to more accurately appraise a stressful situation and determine how much control they have over it. Older children generate more coping alternatives to stressful conditions and make greater use of cognitive coping strategies (Saarni & others, 2006). For example, older children are better than younger children at intentionally shifting their thoughts to a topic that is less stressful. Older children are also better at reframing, or changing their perception of a stressful situation. For example, younger children may be very disappointed that their teacher did not say hello to them when they arrived at school. Older children may reframe this type of situation and think, "She may have been busy with other things and just forgot to say hello."

By 10 years of age, most children are able to use these cognitive strategies to cope with stress (Saarni & others, 2006). However, in families that have not been supportive and are characterized by turmoil or trauma, children may be so overwhelmed by stress that they do not use such strategies (Thabet & others, 2009).

Disasters can especially harm children's development and produce adjustment problems (Masten & others, 2015; Scheeringa, Cobham, & McDermott, 2014). Among the outcomes for children who experience disasters are acute stress reactions, depression, panic disorder, and post-traumatic stress disorder (Pfefferbaum, Newman, & Nelson, 2014). The likelihood that a child will face these problems following a disaster depends on factors such as the nature and severity of the disaster and the type of support available to the child.

Following are descriptions of recent studies of how various aspects of traumatic events and disasters affect children:

- In a study of mothers and their children aged 5 years and younger who were directly exposed to the 9/11 attacks in New York City, the mothers who developed post-traumatic stress disorder (PTSD) and depression were less likely to help their children regulate their emotions and behavior than mothers who were only depressed or only had PTSD (Chemtob & others, 2010). This outcome was linked to their children having anxiety, depression, aggression, and sleep problems.
- A study of the effects of the 2004 tsunami in Sri Lanka found that severe exposure to the tsunami combined with more exposure to other adversities, such as an ongoing war and family violence, was linked to poorer adjustment after the tsunami disaster (Catani & others, 2010).
- A research review revealed that children with disabilities are more likely than children without disabilities to live in poverty conditions, which increases their exposure to hazards and disasters (Peek & Stough, 2010). When a disaster occurs, children with disabilities have more difficulty escaping from the disaster.

What are some effective strategies to help children cope with traumatic events such as the mass shooting in December, 2012, at Sandy Hook Elementary School in Connecticut?
© Stephanie Keith/Polaris/Newscom

In research on disasters/trauma, the term *dose-response effects* is often used. A widely supported finding in this research area is that the more severe the disaster/trauma (dose), the worse the adaptation and adjustment (response) following the disaster/trauma (Masten, 2014a, b; Masten & Narayan, 2012; Masten & others, 2015).

Children who have developed a number of coping techniques have the best chance of adapting and functioning competently in the face of disasters and traumas (Ungar, 2015). Following are some recommendations for helping children cope with the stress of especially devastating events (Gurwitch & others, 2001, pp. 4–11):

- *Reassure children of their safety and security.* This step may need to be taken numerous times.
- *Allow children to retell events and be patient in listening to them.*
- *Encourage children to talk about any disturbing or confusing feelings.* Tell them that these are normal feelings after a stressful event.
- *Help children make sense of what happened.* Children may misunderstand what took place. For example, young children "may blame themselves, believe things happened that did not happen, believe that terrorists are in the school, etc. Gently help children develop a realistic understanding of the event" (p. 10).
- *Protect children from reexposure to frightening situations and reminders of the trauma.* This strategy includes limiting conversations about the event in front of the children and limiting exposure to media coverage of the event.

ADOLESCENCE

Adolescence has long been described as a time of emotional turmoil (Hall, 1904). Adolescents are not constantly in a state of "storm and stress," but emotional highs and lows do increase during early adolescence (Rosenblum & Lewis, 2003). Young adolescents can be on top of the world one moment and down in the dumps the next. In some instances, the intensity of their emotions seems out of proportion to the events that elicit them (Morris, Cui, & Steinberg, 2013). Young adolescents might sulk a lot, not knowing how to adequately express their feelings. With little or no provocation, they can blow up at their parents or siblings, a response that might reflect the defense mechanism of displacing their feelings onto another person. For some adolescents, such emotional swings can reflect serious problems. Girls are especially vulnerable to depression in adolescence (Nolen-Hoeksema, 2011). But it is important for adults to recognize that moodiness is a normal aspect of early adolescence and to understand that most adolescents make it through these moody times to become competent adults.

developmental **connection**

Brain Development

The amygdala, where much of emotion is processed in the brain, matures by early adolescence, and the prefrontal cortex continues developing through emerging adulthood. Connect to "Physical Development and Biological Aging."

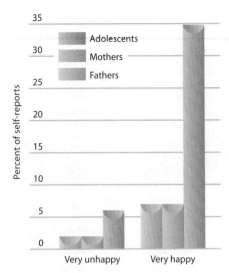

FIGURE 4

SELF-REPORTED EXTREMES OF EMOTION BY ADOLESCENTS, MOTHERS, AND FATHERS USING THE EXPERIENCE SAMPLING METHOD. In the study by Reed Larson and Maryse Richards (1994), adolescents and their mothers and fathers were beeped at random times by researchers using the experience sampling method. The researchers found that adolescents reported more emotional extremes than their parents did.

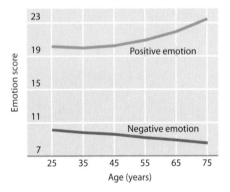

FIGURE 5

CHANGES IN POSITIVE AND NEGATIVE EMOTION ACROSS THE ADULT YEARS. Positive and negative scores had a possible range of 6 to 30, with higher scores reflecting positive emotion and lower scores negative emotion. Positive emotion increased in middle and late adulthood, while negative emotion declined.

fight or flight Taylor's view that when men experience stress, they are more likely to become aggressive, withdraw from social contact, or drink alcohol.

tend and befriend Taylor's view that when women experience stress, they are more likely to seek social alliances with others, especially female friends.

Reed Larson and Maryse Richards (1994) found that adolescents reported more extreme emotions and more fleeting emotions than their parents did. For example, adolescents were five times more likely to report being "very happy" and three times more likely to report being "very unhappy" than their parents (see Figure 4). These findings lend support to the perception of adolescents as moody and changeable (Rosenblum & Lewis, 2003).

ADULT DEVELOPMENT AND AGING

Like children, adults adapt more effectively when they are emotionally intelligent—when they are skilled at perceiving and expressing emotion, understanding emotion, using feelings to facilitate thought, and managing emotions effectively. (In the chapter on "Families, Lifestyles, and Parenting," we examine a number of aspects of relationships that involve emotions.)

Developmental changes in emotion continue through the adult years (English & Carstensen, 2014b). The changes often are characterized by an effort to create lifestyles that are emotionally satisfying, predictable, and manageable by making decisions about an occupation, a life partner, and other circumstances. Of course, not all individuals are successful in these efforts. A key theme of emotional development in adulthood is "the adaptive integration of emotional experience into satisfying daily life and successful relationships with others" (Thompson & Goodvin, 2007, p. 402).

Stress and Gender   Women and men differ in the way they experience and respond to stressors (Almeida & others, 2011). Women are more vulnerable to social stressors such as those involving romance, family, and work. For example, women experience higher levels of stress when things go wrong in romantic and marital relationships. Women also are more likely than men to become depressed when they encounter stressful life events such as a divorce or the death of a friend.

When men face stress, they are likely to respond in a **fight or flight** manner—become aggressive, withdraw from social contact, or drink alcohol. By contrast, according to Shelley Taylor and her colleagues (2011a, b, c, 2015, Taylor & others, 2000), when women experience stress, they are more likely to engage in a **tend and befriend** pattern, seeking social alliances with others, especially friends. Taylor argues that when women experience stress an influx of the hormone *oxytocin*, which is linked to nurturing in animals, is released.

Positive and Negative Emotions   Stereotypes suggest that older adults' emotional landscape is bleak and that most live sad, lonely lives. Researchers have found a different picture (Kunzmann, Kappes, & Wrosch, 2014). One study of a very large U.S. sample examined emotions at different ages (Mroczek & Kolarz, 1998). Older adults reported experiencing more positive emotion and less negative emotion than younger adults, and positive emotion increased with age in adults at an accelerating rate (see Figure 5). And a recent study of individuals from 22 to 93 years of age explored emotional experiences in the mornings and evenings (English & Carstensen, 2014b). Older adults reported experiencing more positive emotions than younger adults at both times of the day.

Overall, compared with younger adults, the feelings of older adults mellow. Emotional life is on a more even keel, with fewer highs and lows. It may be that although older adults have less extreme joy, they have more contentment, especially when they are connected in positive ways with friends and family. Compared with younger adults, older adults react less strongly to negative circumstances, are better at ignoring irrelevant negative information, and remember more positive than negative information (Shallcross & others, 2013; Windsor, Burns, & Byles, 2013). Recent research has also indicated that healthy older adults who age successfully show reduced responsiveness to regrets, not looking back with anger at missed opportunities in life (Brassen & others, 2012; Suri & Gross, 2012). Since opportunities to undo regrettable circumstances decrease with age, reduced connections with these situations may be a protective strategy to maintain well-being in old age.

One study revealed that positive emotion increased and negative emotion (except for sadness) decreased from 50 years of age through the mid-eighties (Stone & others, 2010). In this study, a pronounced decline in anger occurred from the early twenties onward and sadness was essentially unchanged from the early twenties through the mid-eighties. Another study found that aging was linked to more positive overall well-being and greater emotional stability (Carstensen

& others, 2011). In this study, adults who experienced more positive than negative emotions were more likely to remain alive over a 13-year period. Other research also indicates that happier people live longer (Frey, 2011). Thus, research consistently documents that the emotional life of older adults is more positive than stereotypes suggest (English & Carstensen, 2014b).

Changes in the Aging Brain   How might the brain be involved in the changes in older adults' emotion that take place?

Although links between the aging brain and emotion have only just begun to be studied, recent research suggests some possible connections (Dolcos, Katsumi, & Dixon, 2014; Samanez-Larkin & Carstensen, 2011). Reduced negative emotion in older adults may be associated with decreased physiological arousal of emotion due to aging in the amygdala and autonomic nervous system (Kaszniak & Menchola, 2012). More effective emotion regulation may be related to this reduction in subcortical activation and also to increased activation in the prefrontal cortex (Samanez-Larkin & Carstensen, 2011).

Socioemotional Selectivity Theory   One theory developed by Laura Carstensen (1991, 1998, 2006, 2009, 2011, 2014) stands out as important in thinking about developmental changes in adulthood, especially in older adults. **Socioemotional selectivity theory** states that older adults become more selective about their activities and social relationships in order to maintain social and emotional well-being. Because they place a high value on emotional satisfaction, older adults often spend more time with familiar individuals with whom they have had rewarding relationships. This theory argues that older adults deliberately withdraw from social contact with individuals peripheral to their lives while they maintain or increase contact with close friends and family members with whom they have had enjoyable relationships. This selective narrowing of social interaction maximizes positive emotional experiences and minimizes emotional risks as individuals become older. According to this theory, older adults systematically condense their social networks so that available social partners satisfy their emotional needs (Sims, Hogan, & Carstensen, 2015).

Is there research to support life-span differences in the composition of social networks? Researchers have found that the social networks of older adults are smaller than those of younger adults (Charles & Carstensen, 2010). In a recent study of individuals from 18 to 94 years of age, with increasing age in adulthood, they had fewer peripheral social contacts but retained close relationships with people who provided them with emotional support (English & Carstensen, 2014a).

Socioemotional selectivity theory also focuses on the types of goals that individuals are motivated to achieve (Carstensen & others, 2011; Sims & others, 2015). According to the theory, motivation for knowledge-related goals starts relatively high in the early years of life, peaks in adolescence and early adulthood, then declines in middle and late adulthood. The trajectory for emotion-related goals is high during infancy and early childhood, declines from middle childhood through early adulthood, and increases in middle and late adulthood.

Recent research paints a distinctly positive picture of aging in the emotional domain.

—LAURA CARSTENSEN
Contemporary psychologist, Stanford University

Laura Carstensen (*right*), in a caring relationship with an older woman. Her theory of socioemotional selectivity is gaining recognition as an important perspective on aging.
Courtesy of Dr. Laura Carstensen

socioemotional selectivity theory The theory that older adults become more selective about their activities and social relationships in order to maintain emotional well-being.

Review *Connect* **Reflect**

LG2 Describe the development of emotion through the life span

Review

- How does emotion develop in infancy?
- What characterizes emotional development in early childhood?
- What changes take place in emotion during middle and late childhood?
- How does emotion change in adolescence?
- What are some key aspects of emotional development in adulthood?

Connect

- How might cognitive development and language development be linked

to the development of emotion regulation and coping in young children?

Reflect *Your Own Personal Journey of Life*

- Imagine that you are the parent of an 8-month-old baby and you are having difficulty getting sufficient sleep because the baby wakes up crying in the middle of the night. How would you deal with this situation?

| Describing and Classifying Temperament | Biological Foundations and Experience | Goodness of Fit and Parenting |

Do you get upset a lot? Does it take much to get you angry or to make you laugh? Even at birth, babies seem to have different emotional styles. One infant is cheerful and happy much of the time; another baby seems to cry constantly. These tendencies reflect **temperament,** which involves individual differences in behavioral styles, emotions, and characteristic ways of responding. With regard to its link to emotion, temperament refers to individual differences in how quickly the emotion is shown, how strong it is, how long it lasts, and how soon it fades away (Campos, 2009).

Another way of describing temperament is in terms of predispositions toward emotional reactivity and self-regulation (Bates & Pettit, 2015). *Reactivity* involves variations in the speed and intensity with which an individual responds to situations with positive or negative emotions. *Self-regulation* involves variations in the extent or effectiveness of an individual's control of emotions.

DESCRIBING AND CLASSIFYING TEMPERAMENT

How would you describe your temperament or the temperament of a friend? Researchers have described and classified the temperaments of individuals in different ways (Bates & Pettit, 2015; Bould & others, 2014; Chen & Schmidt, 2015; Willoughby & others, 2015). Here we examine three of those ways.

Chess and Thomas' Classification Psychiatrists Alexander Chess and Stella Thomas (Chess & Thomas, 1977; Thomas & Chess, 1991) identified three basic types, or clusters, of temperament:

- An **easy child** is generally in a positive mood, quickly establishes regular routines in infancy, and adapts easily to new experiences.

"Oh, he's cute, all right, but he's got the temperament of a car alarm." © Barbara Smaller/The New Yorker Collection/www.cartoonbank.com.

What are some ways that developmentalists have classified infants' temperaments? Which classification makes the most sense to you, based on your observations of infants?
© Tom Merton/Getty Images RF

- A **difficult child** reacts negatively and cries frequently, engages in irregular daily routines, and is slow to accept change.
- A **slow-to-warm-up child** has a low activity level, is somewhat negative, and displays a low intensity of mood.

In their longitudinal investigation, Chess and Thomas found that 40 percent of the children they studied could be classified as easy, 10 percent as difficult, and 15 percent as slow to warm up. Notice that 35 percent did not fit any of the three patterns. Researchers have found that these three basic clusters of temperament are moderately stable across the childhood years. A recent study revealed that young children with a difficult temperament showed more problems when they experienced low-quality child care and fewer problems when they experienced high-quality child care than did young children with an easy temperament (Pluess & Belsky, 2009).

Kagan's Behavioral Inhibition   Another way of classifying temperament focuses on the differences between a shy, subdued, timid child and a sociable, extraverted, bold child (Asendorph, 2008). Jerome Kagan (2002, 2008, 2010, 2013) regards shyness with strangers (peers or adults) as one feature of a broad temperament category called *inhibition to the unfamiliar*. Beginning at about 7 to 9 months, inhibited children react to many aspects of unfamiliarity with initial avoidance, distress, or subdued affect. In Kagan's research, inhibition shows some continuity from infancy

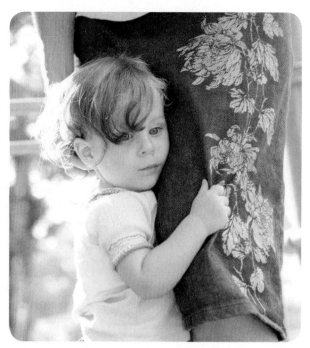

What characterizes an inhibited temperament?
© Girl Ray/Getty Images

through early childhood, although a substantial number of infants who are classified as inhibited become less so by 7 years of age. In recent research, having an inhibited temperament at 2 to 3 years of age was related to having social phobia symptoms at 7 years of age (Lahat & others, 2014). And recent findings also indicate that infants and young children who have an inhibited temperament are at risk for developing social anxiety disorder in adolescence and adulthood (Perez-Edgar & Guyer, 2014; Rapee, 2014).

Rothbart and Bates' Classification   New classifications of temperament continue to be forged. Mary Rothbart and John Bates (2006) argue that three broad dimensions best represent what researchers have found to characterize the structure of temperament: extraversion/surgency, negative affectivity, and effortful control (self-regulation):

- *Extraversion/surgency* includes approach, pleasure, activity, smiling, and laughter. Kagan's uninhibited children fit into this category.
- *Negative affectivity* includes "fear, frustration, sadness, and discomfort" (Rothbart, 2004, p. 495). These children are easily distressed; they may fret and cry often.

temperament An individual's behavioral style and characteristic way of responding.

easy child A temperament style in which the child is generally in a positive mood, quickly establishes regular routines, and adapts easily to new experiences.

difficult child A temperament style in which the child tends to react negatively and cry frequently, engages in irregular daily routines, and is slow to accept change.

slow-to-warm-up child A temperament style in which the child has a low activity level, is somewhat negative, and displays a low intensity of mood.

Kagan's inhibited children fit this category. A recent study revealed that preschool children with high levels of surgency and negative affectivity were more likely to engage in a number of obesity-related eating behaviors (Leung & others, 2014).

· *Effortful control* (self-regulation) includes "attentional focusing and shifting, inhibitory control, perceptual sensitivity, and low-intensity pleasure" (Rothbart, 2004, p. 495). Infants who are high on effortful control show an ability to keep their arousal from getting too high and have strategies for soothing themselves. By contrast, children low on effortful control are often unable to control their arousal; they become easily agitated and intensely emotional. A recent study found that young children higher in effortful control were more likely to wait longer to express anger and were more likely to use a self-regulatory strategy, distraction (Tan, Armstrong, & Cole, 2013). And another recent study revealed that effortful control was a strong predictor of academic success skills, including school readiness, math skills, and reading skills, in kindergarten children from low-income families (Morris & others, 2014)

The description of temperament categories so far reflects the development of normative capabilities of children, not individual differences in children. The development of these capabilities, such as effortful control, allows individual differences to emerge (Bates, 2008, 2012a, b; Bates & Pettit, 2015). For example, although maturation of the brain's prefrontal lobes must occur for any child's attention to improve and the child to achieve effortful control, some children develop effortful control while others do not. And it is these individual differences in children that are at the heart of temperament (Bates, 2008, 2012a, b; Bates & Pettit, 2015).

BIOLOGICAL FOUNDATIONS AND EXPERIENCE

How does a child acquire a certain temperament? Kagan (2002, 2008, 2010, 2013) argues that children inherit a physiology that biases them to have a particular type of temperament. However, through experience they may learn to modify their temperament to some degree (Bates & Pettit, 2015). For example, children may inherit a physiology that biases them to be fearful and inhibited, but they learn to reduce their fear and inhibition to some degree.

Biological Influences   Physiological characteristics have been linked with different temperaments (Mize & Jones, 2012). In particular, an inhibited temperament is associated with a unique physiological pattern that includes high and stable heart rate, high level of the hormone cortisol, and high activity in the right frontal lobe of the brain (Kagan, 2008). This pattern may be tied to the excitability of the amygdala, a structure of the brain that plays an important role in fear and inhibition. The temperament dimension of negative emotionality is linked to stress reactivity, which involves brain functioning (especially the hypothalamic-pituitary-adrenal (HPA) axis and its link to higher levels of cortisol) (Rothbart, 2011). And the development of effortful control is linked to advances in the brain's frontal lobes (Bates, 2008, 2012a, b).

What is heredity's role in the biological foundations of temperament? Twin and adoption studies suggest that heredity has a moderate influence on differences in temperament within a group of people (Buss & Goldsmith, 2007).

Too often the biological foundations of temperament are interpreted as meaning that temperament cannot develop or change. However, important self-regulatory dimensions of temperament such as adaptability, soothability, and persistence look very different in a 1-year-old and a 5-year-old (Easterbrooks & others, 2013). These temperament dimensions develop and change with the growth of the neurobiological foundations of self-regulation.

Gender and Temperament   Gender may be an important factor shaping the environmental context that influences temperament (Gaias & others, 2012). Parents might react differently to an infant's temperament depending on whether the baby is a boy or a girl. For example, in one study, mothers were more responsive to the crying of irritable girls than to the crying of irritable boys (Crockenberg, 1986).

Developmental Connections in Temperament   Is temperament in childhood linked with adjustment in adulthood? In one study, children who had an easy temperament at 3 to 5 years of age were likely to be well adjusted as young adults (Chess & Thomas, 1977). In contrast, many children who had a difficult temperament at 3 to 5 years of age were not well adjusted as

developmental **connection**

Nature and Nurture

Twin and adoption studies have been used in the effort to sort out hereditary and environmental influences on development. Connect to "Biological Beginnings."

308   CHAPTER 10   Emotional Development and Attachment

young adults. Also, other researchers have found that boys with a difficult temperament in child-hood are less likely as adults to continue their formal education, whereas girls with a difficult temperament in childhood are more likely to experience marital conflict as adults (Wachs, 2000).

Inhibition is another characteristic of temperament that has been studied extensively (Kagan, 2008, 2010, 2013). A recent study revealed that behavioral inhibition at 3 years of age was linked to shyness at age 7 (Volbrecht & Goldsmith, 2010). Also, research indicates that individuals with an inhibited temperament in childhood are less likely as adults to be assertive or to experience social support, and more likely to delay entering a stable job track (Asendorph, 2008).

In sum, these studies reveal some continuity between certain aspects of temperament in childhood and adjustment in early adulthood (Rothbart, 2011; Shiner & DeYoung, 2013; Wachs & Bates, 2011). However, keep in mind that these connections between childhood temperament and adult adjustment are based on only a small number of studies; more research is needed to verify these linkages.

Developmental Contexts   What accounts for the continuities and discontinuities between a child's temperament and an adult's personality? Physiological and hereditary factors likely are involved in continuity (Clauss, Avery, & Blackford, 2015). Links between temperament in child-hood and personality in adulthood also might vary, depending on the contexts that individuals experience (Bates & Pettit, 2015; Bates, Schermerhorn, & Goodnight, 2010; Wachs & Bates, 2011).

The reaction to an infant's temperament may depend, in part, on culture (Cole & Tan, 2007, 2015). For example, behavioral inhibition is more highly valued in China than in North America, and research-ers have found that Chinese children are more inhibited than Canadian infants are (Chen & others, 1998). The cultural differences in tem-perament were linked to parental attitudes and behavior. Canadian mothers of inhibited 2-year-olds were less accepting of their infants' inhibited temperament, while Chinese mothers were more accepting.

In short, many aspects of a child's environment can encourage or discourage the persistence of temperament characteristics (Bates & Pettit, 2015; Gartstein & others, 2010; Shiner & DeYoung, 2013). For example, a recent study found that fathers' internalizing problems (anxiety and depression, for example) were linked to a higher level of negative affectivity in 6-month-olds (Potapova, Gartstein, & Bridgett, 2014). And another recent study revealed that maternal

An infant's temperament can vary across cultures. *What do parents need to know about a child's temperament?*
© *MIXA/Getty Images RF*

Parenting and the Child's Temperament

What are the implications of temperamental variations for parenting? Although answers to this question necessarily are speculative, these conclusions regarding the best parenting strategies to use in relation to children's temperament were reached by temperament experts Ann Sanson and Mary Rothbart (1995):

- *Attention to and respect for individuality.* One implication is that it is difficult to generate general prescriptions for "good" parenting. A goal might be accomplished in one way with one child and in another way with another child, depending on the child's temperament. Parents need to be sensitive and remain flexible to the infant's signals and needs.

- *Structuring the child's environment.* Crowded, noisy environments can pose greater problems for some children (such as a "difficult child") than others (such as an "easygoing" child). We might also expect that a fearful, withdrawing child would benefit from slower entry into new contexts.

- *The "difficult child" and packaged parenting programs.* Programs for parents often focus on dealing with children who have "difficult" temperaments. In some cases, "difficult child" refers to Thomas and Chess' description of a child who reacts negatively, cries frequently, engages in irregular daily routines, and is slow to accept change. In others, the concept might be used to describe a child who is irritable, displays anger frequently, does not follow directions well, or shows some other negative characteristic. Acknowledging that some children are harder than others to parent is often helpful, and advice on how to handle specific difficult characteristics can be useful. However, whether a specific characteristic is difficult depends on its fit with the environment. To label a child "difficult" has the danger of becoming a self-fulfilling prophecy. If a child is identified as "difficult," people may treat the child in a way that actually elicits "difficult" behavior.

What are some good strategies for parents to adopt when responding to their infant's temperament?
© Corbis/age fotostock RF

Too often, we pigeonhole children into categories without examining the context (Bates, 2012a, b; Bates & Pettit, 2015; Rothbart, 2011). Nonetheless, caregivers need to take children's temperaments into account. Research does not yet allow for many highly specific recommendations, but in general, caregivers should (1) be sensitive to the individual characteristics of the child, (2) be flexible in responding to these characteristics, and (3) avoid applying negative labels to the child.

How does the advice to "structure the child's environment" relate to what you learned about the concept of "goodness of fit"?

---

developmental **connection**

Culture

Cross-cultural studies seek to determine culture-universal and culture-specific aspects of development. Connect to "Introduction."

goodness of fit The match between a child's temperament and the environmental demands the child must cope with.

negativity and child problem behavior were most strongly linked for children who were low in effortful control and living in chaotic homes (Chen, Deater-Deckard, and Bell, 2014). One useful way of thinking about temperament-environment connections involves the concept of goodness of fit, which we examine next.

GOODNESS OF FIT AND PARENTING

Goodness of fit refers to the match between a child's temperament and the environmental demands the child must cope with. Some temperament characteristics pose more parenting challenges than others, at least in modern Western societies (Bates & Pettit, 2015; Rothbart, 2011). When children are prone to distress, as exhibited by frequent crying and irritability, their parents may eventually respond by ignoring the child's distress or trying to force the child to "behave." In one research study, though, extra support and training for mothers of distress-prone infants improved the quality of mother-infant interaction (van den Boom, 1989). Researchers also have found that decreases in infants' negative emotionality are linked to higher levels of parental sensitivity, involvement, and responsiveness (Bates & Pettit, 2015; Penela & others, 2012).

To read further about some positive strategies for parenting that take into account the child's temperament, see the *Connecting Development to Life* interlude.

A final comment about temperament is that recently the *differential susceptibility model* and the *biological sensitivity to context model* have been proposed and studied (Belsky & Hartman, 2014; Belsky & others, 2015; Belsky & van Ijzendoorn, 2015; Ellis & others, 2011; Hartman & Belsky, 2015; Simpson & Belsky, 2016). According to these models, certain characteristics—such as a difficult temperament—that render children more vulnerable to difficulty in adverse contexts also make them more susceptible to optimal growth in very supportive conditions. These models offer a new perspective on "negative" temperament characteristics.

Review *Connect* Reflect

LG3 Characterize variations in temperament and their significance

Review
- How can temperament be described and classified?
- How is temperament influenced by biological foundations and experience?
- What is goodness of fit? What are some positive parenting strategies for dealing with a child's temperament?

Connect
- How is Chess and Thomas' classification of temperament similar to and different from Rothbart and Bates' classification?

Reflect *Your Own Personal Journey of Life*
- Consider your own temperament. We described a number of temperament categories. Which one best describes your temperament? Has your temperament changed as you have gotten older? If your temperament has changed, what factors contributed to the changes?

4 Attachment and Love   **LG4** Explain attachment and its development

| Infancy and Childhood | Adolescence | Adulthood |

So far, we have discussed how emotions and emotional competence change over the life span. We have also examined the role of emotional style—in effect, we have seen how emotions set the tone of our experiences in life. But emotions also write the lyrics because they are at the core of our relationships with others. Foremost among these relationships is **attachment,** a close emotional bond between two people. In this section, we focus on two types of attachment: the attachment between parents and children and the attachment between romantic partners.

INFANCY AND CHILDHOOD

Before we describe parent-child attachment in detail, we set the stage for its development by exploring the strength of social orientation among infants. We also examine infants' early development of social understanding.

Social Orientation/Understanding   In Ross Thompson's (2006, 2015, 2016) view, infants are socioemotional beings who show a strong interest in the social world and are motivated to orient to it and understand it. In previous chapters, we described many of the biological and cognitive foundations that contribute to the infant's development of social orientation and understanding. In this chapter we will call attention to relevant biological and cognitive factors as we explore social orientation; locomotion; intention, goal-directed behavior, and cooperation; and social referencing. Discussing biological, cognitive, and social processes together reminds us of an important aspect of development: these processes are intricately intertwined (Diamond, 2013).

Social Orientation   From early in their development, infants are captivated by their social world. Young infants will stare intently at faces and are attuned to the sounds of human voices, especially those of their caregivers (Lee & others, 2013). Later, they become adept at interpreting the meaning of facial expressions and voices (Otte & others, 2015).

attachment A close emotional bond between two people.

A mother and her baby engaging in face-to-face play. *At what age does face-to-face play usually begin, and when does it typically start decreasing in frequency?*
© Britt Erlanson/Getty Images

developmental **connection**

Developmental Theories

The dynamic systems view is increasingly used to explain how infants develop. Connect to "Motor, Sensory, and Perceptual Development."

FIGURE 6

THE COOPERATION TASK. The cooperation task consisted of two handles on a box, atop which was an animated musical toy, surreptitiously activated by remote control when both handles were pulled. The handles were placed far enough apart that one child could not pull both handles. The experimenter demonstrated the task, saying, "Watch! If you pull the handles, the doggie will sing" (Brownell, Ramani, & Zerwas, 2006).
Courtesy of Celia A. Brownell, University of Pittsburgh

Face-to-face play often begins to characterize caregiver-infant interactions when the infant is about 2 to 3 months of age. The focused social interaction of face-to-face play may include vocalizations, touch, and gestures (Leppänen & others, 2007). Such play results in part from many mothers' motivation to create a positive emotional state in their infants (Laible, Thompson, & Froimson, 2015).

In part because of such positive social interchanges between caregivers and infants, by 2 to 3 months of age infants respond differently to people and objects, showing more positive emotion to people than to inanimate objects such as puppets (Legerstee, 1997). At this age, most infants expect people to react positively when the infants initiate a behavior, such as a smile or a vocalization. This finding has been discovered by use of a method called the *still-face paradigm*, in which the caregiver alternates between engaging in face-to-face interaction with the infant and remaining still and unresponsive (MacLean & others, 2014; Montirosso & others, 2015; Planalp & Braungart-Rieker, 2015). As early as 2 to 3 months of age, infants show more withdrawal, negative emotions, and self-directed behavior when their caregivers are still and unresponsive (Adamson & Frick, 2003). The frequency of face-to-face play decreases after 7 months of age as infants become more mobile (Thompson, 2006). A recent study indicated that parental sensitivity during the still-face paradigm when infants were 3, 5, and 7 months old was linked to infants' emotional and behavioral trajectories in the paradigm, which in turn predicted secure and insecure attachment at 12 and 14 months of age (Braungart-Rieker & others, 2014).

Infants also learn about the social world through contexts other than face-to-face play with a caregiver (Bates & Pettit, 2015). Even though infants as young as 6 months of age show an interest in each other, their interaction with peers increases considerably in the second half of the second year. As increasing numbers of U.S. infants experience child care outside the home, they are spending more time in social play with peers (Lamb & Lewis, 2013). Later in the chapter, we further discuss child care.

Locomotion Recall from earlier in the chapter how important independence is for infants, especially in the second year of life. As infants develop the ability to crawl, walk, and run, they are able to explore and expand their social world. These newly developed self-produced locomotor skills allow the infant to independently initiate social interchanges on a more frequent basis (Laible, Thompson, & Froimson, 2015). The development of these gross motor skills is the result of a number of factors, including the development of the nervous system, the goal the infant is motivated to reach, and environmental support for the skill (Adolph & Robinson, 2015).

The infant's and toddler's push for independence also is likely paced by the development of locomotor skills (Campos, 2009). Locomotion is also important for its motivational implications. Once infants have the ability to move in goal-directed pursuits, the reward from these pursuits leads to further efforts to explore and develop skills.

Intention, Goal-Directed Behavior, and Cooperation Perceiving people as engaging in intentional and goal-directed behavior is an important social cognitive accomplishment that initially occurs toward the end of the first year (Thompson, 2015). Joint attention and gaze following help the infant to understand that other people have intentions (Tomasello, 2014). *Joint attention* occurs when the caregiver and infant focus on the same object or event. By their first birthday, infants have begun to direct the caregiver's attention to objects that capture their interest (Heimann & others, 2006).

One study involved presenting 1- and 2-year-olds with a simple cooperative task that consisted of pulling a lever to get an attractive toy (Brownell, Ramani, & Zerwas, 2006) (see Figure 6). Any coordinated actions of the 1-year-olds appeared to be more coincidental than cooperative, whereas the 2-year-olds' behavior was characterized as more actively cooperative efforts to reach a goal. In this study, the infants also were assessed with two social understanding tasks, observation of children's behavior in a joint attention task, and the parents' perceptions of the language the children use about the self and others (Brownell, Ramani, & Zerwas, 2006). Those with more advanced social understanding were more likely to cooperate. To cooperate, the children had to connect their own intentions with the peer's intentions and put this understanding to use in interacting with the peer to reach a goal.

Social Referencing   Another important social cognitive accomplishment in infancy is developing the ability to "read" the emotions of other people (Mireault & others, 2014). **Social referencing** is the term used to describe "reading" emotional cues in others to help determine how to act in a specific situation. The development of social referencing helps infants to interpret ambiguous situations more accurately, as when they encounter a stranger and need to know whether or not to fear the person (Pelaez, Virues-Ortega, & Gewirtz, 2012). By the end of the first year, a mother's facial expression—either smiling or fearful—influences whether an infant will explore an unfamiliar environment.

Infants become better at social referencing in the second year of life. At this age, they tend to "check" with their mother before they act; they look at her to see if she is happy, angry, or fearful.

Infants' Social Sophistication and Insight   In sum, researchers are discovering that infants are more socially sophisticated and insightful at younger ages than was previously envisioned (Thompson, 2006, 2015, 2016). Such sophistication and insight are reflected in infants' perceptions of others' actions as intentionally motivated and goal-directed, their motivation to share and participate in that intentionality, and their increase in emotion understanding and communication by their first birthday. The more advanced social cognitive skills of infants could be expected to influence their understanding and awareness of attachment to a caregiver.

What Is Attachment?   There is no shortage of theories about why infants become attached to a caregiver. Three theorists—Freud, Erikson, and Bowlby—proposed influential views.

Freud noted that infants become attached to the person or object that provides oral satisfaction. For most infants, this is the mother, since she is most likely to feed the infant. Is feeding as important as Freud thought? A classic study by Harry Harlow (1958) reveals that the answer is no (see Figure 7).

What is social referencing? What are some developmental changes in social referencing?
© Dan Lepp/Etsa/Corbis

social referencing "Reading" emotional cues in others to help determine how to act in a specific situation.

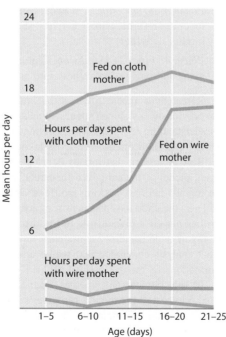

FIGURE 7

CONTACT TIME WITH WIRE AND CLOTH SURROGATE MOTHERS. Regardless of whether the infant monkeys were fed by a wire or a cloth mother, they overwhelmingly preferred to spend contact time with the cloth mother. *How do these results compare with what Freud's theory and Erikson's theory would predict about human infants?*
© Martin Rogers/The Image Bank/Getty Images

Harlow removed infant monkeys from their mothers at birth; for six months they were reared by surrogate (substitute) "mothers." One surrogate mother was made of wire, the other of cloth. Half of the infant monkeys were fed by the wire mother, half by the cloth mother. Periodically, the amount of time the infant monkeys spent with either the wire or the cloth mother was computed. Regardless of which mother fed them, the infant monkeys spent far more time with the cloth mother. Even if the wire mother but not the cloth mother provided nourishment, the infant monkeys spent more time with the cloth mother. And when Harlow frightened the monkeys, those "raised" by the cloth mother ran to the mother and clung to it; those raised by the wire mother did not. Whether the mother provided comfort seemed to determine whether the monkeys associated the mother with security. This study clearly demonstrated that feeding is not the crucial element in the attachment process and that contact comfort is important.

Physical comfort also plays a role in Erik Erikson's (1968) view of the infant's development. Recall Erikson's proposal that the first year of life represents the stage of trust versus mistrust. Physical comfort and sensitive care, according to Erikson (1968), are key to establishing a basic trust in infants. The infant's sense of trust, in turn, is the foundation for attachment and sets the stage for a lifelong expectation that the world will be a good and pleasant place to be.

The ethological perspective of British psychiatrist John Bowlby (1969, 1989) also stresses the importance of attachment in the first year of life and the responsiveness of the caregiver. Bowlby stresses that both infants and their primary caregivers are biologically predisposed to form attachments. He argues that the newborn is biologically equipped to elicit attachment behavior. The baby cries, clings, coos, and smiles. Later, the infant crawls, walks, and follows the mother. The immediate result is to keep the primary caregiver nearby; the long-term effect is to increase the infant's chances of survival.

Attachment does not emerge suddenly but rather develops in a series of phases, moving from a baby's general preference for human beings to a partnership with primary caregivers. Following are four such phases based on Bowlby's conceptualization of attachment (Schaffer, 1996):

In Bowlby's model, what are the four phases of attachment?
© Camille Tokerud/Getty Images RF

- *Phase 1: From birth to 2 months.* Infants instinctively direct their attachment to human figures. Strangers, siblings, and parents are equally likely to elicit smiling or crying from the infant.

- *Phase 2: From 2 to 7 months.* Attachment becomes focused on one figure, usually the primary caregiver, as the baby gradually learns to distinguish familiar from unfamiliar people.

- *Phase 3: From 7 to 24 months.* Specific attachments develop. With increased locomotor skills, babies actively seek contact with regular caregivers such as the mother or father.

- *Phase 4: From 24 months on.* Children become aware of others' feelings, goals, and plans and begin to take these into account in forming their own actions.

Researchers' recent findings that infants are more socially sophisticated and insightful than previously envisioned suggests that some of the characteristics of Bowlby's phase 4, such as understanding the goals and intentions of the attachment figure, appear to be developing in phase 3 as attachment security is taking shape.

Bowlby argued that infants develop an *internal working model* of attachment, a simple mental model of the caregiver, their relationship, and the self as deserving of nurturant care. The infant's internal working model of attachment with the caregiver influences the infant's and later, the child's, subsequent responses to other people. The internal model of attachment also has played a pivotal role in the discovery of links between attachment and subsequent emotional understanding, conscience development, and self-concept (Thompson, 2015). A recent analysis concluded that secure attachment enhances the positive processing of social information (Dykas & Cassidy, 2011).

In sum, attachment emerges from the social cognitive advances that allow infants to develop expectations for the caregiver's behavior and to determine the affective quality of their relationship (Thompson, 2015, 2016). These social cognitive advances include recognizing the caregiver's face, voice, and other features, as well as developing an internal

Strange Situation Ainsworth's observational measure of infant attachment to a caregiver that requires the infant to move through a series of introductions, separations, and reunions with the caregiver and an adult stranger in a prescribed order.

securely attached children Children who use the caregiver as a secure base from which to explore the environment.

insecure avoidant children Children who show insecurity by avoiding the mother.

insecure resistant children Children who might cling to the caregiver, then resist her by fighting against the closeness, perhaps by kicking or pushing away.

insecure disorganized children Children who show insecurity by being disorganized and disoriented.

working model of expecting the caregiver to provide pleasure in social interaction and relief from distress.

Individual Differences in Attachment   Although attachment to a caregiver intensifies midway through the first year, isn't it likely that the quality of babies' attachment experiences varies? Mary Ainsworth (1979) thought so. Ainsworth created the **Strange Situation,** an observational measure of infant attachment in which the infant experiences a series of introductions, separations, and reunions with the caregiver and an adult stranger in a prescribed order. In using the Strange Situation, researchers hope that their observations will provide information about the infant's motivation to be near the caregiver and the degree to which the caregiver's presence provides the infant with security and confidence.

Based on how babies respond in the Strange Situation, they are described as being securely attached or insecurely attached (in one of three ways) to the caregiver:

What is the nature of secure and insecure attachment? How are caregiving styles related to attachment classification?
© George Doyle/Stockbyte/Getty Images RF

· **Securely attached children** use the caregiver as a secure base from which to explore the environment. When in the presence of their caregiver, securely attached infants explore the room and examine toys that have been placed in it. When the caregiver departs, securely attached infants might protest mildly, and when the caregiver returns these infants reestablish positive interaction with her, perhaps by smiling or climbing onto her lap. Subsequently, they usually resume playing with the toys in the room.

· **Insecure avoidant children** show insecurity by avoiding the mother. In the Strange Situation, these babies engage in little interaction with the caregiver, are not distressed when she leaves the room, usually do not reestablish contact with her on her return, and may even turn their back on her. If contact is established, the infant usually leans away or looks away.

· **Insecure resistant children** often cling to the caregiver and then resist her by fighting against the closeness, perhaps by kicking or pushing away. In the Strange Situation, these babies often cling anxiously to the caregiver and don't explore the playroom. When the caregiver leaves, they often cry loudly and push away if she tries to comfort them on her return, then want to be held again.

· **Insecure disorganized children** are disorganized and disoriented. In the Strange Situation, these babies might appear dazed, confused, and fearful. To be classified as disorganized, babies must show strong patterns of avoidance and resistance or display certain specified behaviors, such as extreme fearfulness around the caregiver.

Evaluating the Strange Situation   Does the Strange Situation capture important differences among infants? As a measure of attachment, it may be culturally biased (Keller, 2013; Otto & Keller, 2013; Quinn & Mageo, 2013). For example, German and Japanese babies often show different patterns of attachment from those of American infants. As illustrated in Figure 8, German infants are more likely than U.S. infants to show an avoidant attachment pattern and Japanese infants are less likely than U.S. infants to display this pattern (van IJzendoorn & Kroonenberg, 1988). The avoidant pattern in German babies likely occurs because their caregivers encourage them to be independent (Grossmann & others, 1985). Also as shown in Figure 8, Japanese babies are more likely than American babies to be categorized as resistant. This may have more to do with the Strange Situation as a measure of attachment than with attachment insecurity itself. Japanese mothers rarely allow anyone unfamiliar with their babies to care for them. Thus, the Strange Situation might create considerably more stress for Japanese infants than for American infants, who are more accustomed to separation from their mothers (Miyake, Chen, & Campos, 1985). Even though there are cultural variations in attachment classification, the most frequent

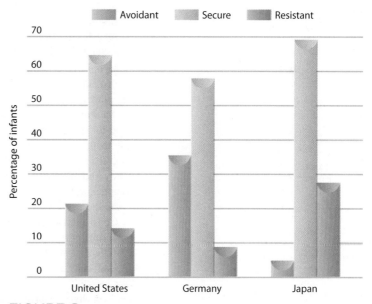

FIGURE 8

CROSS-CULTURAL COMPARISON OF ATTACHMENT. In one study, infant attachment in three countries—the United States, Germany, and Japan—was measured in the Ainsworth Strange Situation (van IJzendoorn & Kroonenberg, 1988). The dominant attachment pattern in all three countries was secure attachment. However, German infants were more avoidant and Japanese infants were less avoidant and more resistant than U.S. infants. *What are some explanations for differences in how German, Japanese, and American infants respond to the Strange Situation?*

classification in every culture studied so far is secure attachment (Jin & others, 2012; van IJzendoorn & Kroonenberg, 1988).

Some critics stress that behavior in the Strange Situation—like other laboratory assessments—might not indicate what infants would do in a natural environment. But researchers have found that infants' behaviors in the Strange Situation are closely related to how they behave at home in response to separation and reunion with their mothers (Pederson & Moran, 1996). Thus, many researchers stress that the Strange Situation continues to show merit as a measure of infant attachment.

Interpreting Differences in Attachment   Do individual differences in attachment matter? Ainsworth notes that secure attachment in the first year of life provides an important foundation for psychological development later in life. The securely attached infant moves freely away from the mother but keeps track of where she is through periodic glances. The securely attached infant responds positively to being picked up by others and, when put back down, freely moves away to play. An insecurely attached infant, by contrast, avoids the mother or is ambivalent toward her, fears strangers, and is upset by minor, everyday separations.

If early attachment to a caregiver is important, it should influence a child's social behavior later in development. For some children, early attachments seem to foreshadow later functioning (Ding & others, 2014; Frazier & Scharf, 2015; Gander & Buchheim, 2015; Umemura & Jacobvitz, 2014). In the extensive longitudinal study conducted by Alan Sroufe and his colleagues (2005; Sroufe, Coffino, & Carlson, 2010), early secure attachment (assessed by the Strange Situation at 12 and 18 months) was linked with positive emotional health, high self-esteem, self-confidence, and socially competent interaction with peers, teachers, camp counselors, and romantic partners through adolescence. Also, a recent meta-analysis concluded that secure attachment in infancy was related to social competence with peers in early childhood (Groh & others, 2014). Yet another study discovered that attachment security at 2 years of age was linked to lower rates of peer conflict at 3 years of age (Raikes & others, 2013). Further, a recent study revealed that infant attachment insecurity (especially insecure resistant attachment) and early childhood behavioral inhibition predicted adolescent social anxiety symptoms (Lewis-Morrarty & others, 2015). And a meta-analysis revealed that disorganized attachment was more strongly linked to externalizing problems (aggression and hostility, for example) than were avoidant and resistant attachment (Fearon & others, 2010).

Few studies have assessed infants' attachment security to the mother and the father separately. However, a recent study revealed that infants who were insecurely attached to their mother and father ("double-insecure") at 15 months of age had more externalizing problems (out-of-control behavior, for example) during the elementary school years than their counterparts who were securely attached to at least one parent (Kochanska & Kim, 2013).

An important issue regarding attachment is whether infancy is a critical or sensitive period for development. Many, but not all, research studies reveal the power of infant attachment to predict subsequent development (Fraley, Roisman, & Haltigan, 2012; Roisman & Groh, 2011; Thompson, 2015, 2016). In one longitudinal study, attachment classification in infancy did not predict attachment classification at 18 years of age (Lewis, Feiring, & Rosenthal, 2000). In this study, the best predictor of an insecure attachment classification at 18 was the occurrence of parental divorce in the intervening years.

Consistently positive caregiving over a number of years is likely an important factor in connecting early attachment with the child's functioning later in development. Indeed, researchers have found that early secure attachment and subsequent experiences, especially maternal care and life stresses, are linked with children's later behavior and adjustment (Thompson, 2015, 2016). For example, a longitudinal study revealed that changes in attachment security/insecurity from infancy to adulthood were linked to stresses and supports in socioemotional contexts (Van Ryzin, Carlson, & Sroufe, 2011). These results suggest that attachment continuity may be a reflection of stable social contexts as much as early working models. The study just described (Van Ryzin & others, 2011) reflects an increasingly accepted view of the development of attachment and its influence on development. That is, it is important to recognize that attachment security in infancy does not always by itself produce long-term positive outcomes, but rather is linked to later outcomes through connections with the way children and adolescents subsequently experience various social contexts as they develop (O'Conner & others, 2014).

developmental cascade model Involves connections across domains over time that influence developmental pathways and outcomes.

The Van Ryzin, Carlson, and Sroufe (2011) study reflects a **developmental cascade model,** which involves connections across domains over time that influence developmental pathways and outcomes (Cicchetti & Toth, 2015; Groh & others, 2014; Kim & Kochanska, 2015). Developmental cascades can include connections between a wide range of biological, cognitive, and socioemotional processes (attachment, for example), and also can involve social contexts such as families, peers, schools, and culture. Further, links can produce positive or negative outcomes at different points in development, such as infancy, early childhood, middle and late childhood, adolescence, and adulthood.

A recent meta-analysis supported these views just described (Pinquart, Feubner, & Ahnert, 2013). In this analysis of 127 research reports, the following conclusions were reached: (1) moderate stability of attachment security occurred from early infancy to adulthood, (2) no significant stability occurred for time intervals of more than 15 years, (3) attachment stability was greater when the time span was less than 2 years than when it was more than 5 years, and (4) securely attached children at risk were less likely to maintain attachment security, while insecurely attached children at risk were likely to continue to be insecurely attached.

Some developmentalists think that too much emphasis has been placed on the attachment bond in infancy. Jerome Kagan (2000), for example, emphasizes that infants are highly resilient and adaptive; he argues that they are evolutionarily equipped to stay on a positive developmental course, even in the face of wide variations in parenting. Kagan and others stress that genetic characteristics and temperament play more important roles in a child's social competence than the attachment theorists, such as Bowlby and Ainsworth, are willing to acknowledge (Bakermans-Kranenburg & others, 2007). For example, if some infants inherit a low tolerance for stress, this, rather than an insecure attachment bond, may be responsible for an inability to get along with peers. One study found links between disorganized attachment in infancy, a specific gene, and levels of maternal responsiveness. In this study, a disorganized attachment style developed in infancy only when infants had the short version of the serotonin transporter gene—5-HTTLPR (Spangler & others, 2009). Infants were not characterized by this attachment style when they had the long version of the gene (Spangler & others, 2009). Further, this gene-environment interaction occurred only when mothers showed a low level of responsiveness toward their infants. However, some researchers have not found support for gene-environment interactions related to infant attachment (Luijk & others, 2011; Roisman & Fraley, 2012).

Another criticism of attachment theory is that it ignores the diversity of socializing agents and contexts that exists in an infant's world. A culture's value system can influence the nature of attachment (van IJzendoorn & Sagi-Schwartz, 2008). Mothers' expectations for infants to be independent are high in northern Germany, whereas Japanese mothers are more strongly motivated to keep their infants close to them (Grossmann & others, 1985; Rothbaum & others, 2000). Not surprisingly, northern German infants tend to show less distress than Japanese infants when separated from their mothers. Also, in some cultures, infants show attachments to many people. Among the Hausa (who live in Nigeria), grandmothers and siblings provide a significant amount of care for infants (Harkness & Super, 1995). Infants in agricultural societies tend to form attachments to older siblings, who are assigned a major responsibility for younger siblings' care. Researchers recognize the importance of competent, nurturant caregivers in an infant's development (Grusec & Davidov, 2015). At issue, though, is whether or not secure attachment, especially to a single caregiver, is critical (Fraley, Roisman, & Haltigan, 2013; Thompson, 2015, 2016).

Despite such criticisms, there is ample evidence that security of attachment is important to development (Thompson, 2015, 2016). Secure attachment in infancy reflects a positive parent-infant relationship and provides a foundation that supports healthy socioemotional development in the years that follow.

Caregiving Styles and Attachment

Is the style of caregiving linked with the quality of the infant's attachment? Securely attached babies have caregivers who are sensitive to their signals and are consistently available to respond to their infants' needs (Jin & others, 2012). These caregivers often let their babies have an active part in determining the onset and pacing of interaction in the first year of life. One study revealed that maternal sensitivity in responding was linked to infant attachment security (Finger & others, 2009). Another study found that maternal sensitivity in parenting was linked with secure attachment in infants in two different cultures: the United States and Colombia (Posada & others, 2002).

developmental **connection**

Nature Versus Nurture

What is involved in gene-environment (G × E) interaction? Connect to "Biological Beginnings."

In the Hausa culture, siblings and grandmothers provide a significant amount of care for infants. *How might these variations in care affect attachment?*
© Penny Tweedie/Getty Images

How do the caregivers of insecurely attached babies interact with them? Caregivers of avoidant babies tend to be unavailable or rejecting (Posada & Kaloustian, 2011). They often don't respond to their babies' signals and have little physical contact with them. When they do interact with their babies, they may behave in an angry and irritable way. Caregivers of resistant babies tend to be inconsistent; sometimes they respond to their babies' needs, and sometimes they don't. In general, they tend not to be very affectionate with their babies and show little synchrony when interacting with them. Caregivers of disorganized babies often neglect or physically abuse them (Bernard & others, 2012). In some cases, these caregivers are depressed. In sum, caregivers' interactions with infants influence whether infants are securely or insecurely attached to the caregivers (Sroufe, Coffino, & Carlson, 2010).

Developmental Social Neuroscience and Attachment   The emerging field of *developmental social neuroscience* examines connections between socioemotional processes, development, and the brain (Vela, 2014; Steinberg, 2015a, b). Attachment is one of the main areas on which theory and research on developmental social neuroscience has focused. These connections of attachment and the brain involve the neuroanatomy of the brain, neurotransmitters, and hormones.

Theory and research on the role of the brain's regions in mother-infant attachment is just emerging (de Haan & Gunnar, 2009). One theoretical view proposed that the prefrontal cortex likely has an important role in maternal attachment behavior, as do the subcortical (areas of the brain lower than the cortex) regions of the mother's amygdala (which is strongly involved in emotion) and the hypothalamus (Gonzalez, Atkinson, & Fleming, 2009). An ongoing fMRI longitudinal study is exploring the possibility that different attachment patterns can be distinguished by different patterns of brain activity (Strathearn, 2007, 2011).

Research on the role of hormones and neurotransmitters in attachment has emphasized the importance of two neuropeptide hormones—oxytocin and vasopressin—in the formation of the maternal-infant bond (Carter, 2014). Oxytocin, a mammalian hormone that also acts as a neurotransmitter in the brain, is released in the mother during breast feeding and by contact and warmth (Ebstein & others, 2012). Oxytocin is especially thought to be a likely candidate in the formation of infant-mother attachment (Eapen & others, 2014; Feldman, 2012; Swain & others, 2014). A research review found strong links between levels or patterns of oxytocin and aspects of mother-infant attachment (Galbally & others, 2011).

Although oxytocin release is stimulated by birth and lactation in mothers, might it also be released in fathers? Oxytocin is secreted in males, and one research study found that at both 6 weeks and 6 months after birth, when fathers engage in more stimulation contact with babies, encouraged their exploration, and directed their attention to objects, the fathers' oxytocin levels increased (Gordon & others, 2010). In this study, mothers' behaviors that increased their oxytocin levels involved more affectionate parenting, such as gazing at their babies, expressing positive affect toward them, and touching them. A recent study also found that fathers with lower testosterone levels engaged in more optimal parenting with their infants (Weisman, Zagoory-Sharon, & Feldman, 2014). Also in this study, when fathers were administered oxytocin, their parenting behavior improved as evidenced in increased positive affect, social gaze, touch, and vocal synchrony when interacting with their infants.

The influence of these neuropeptides on the neurotransmitter dopamine in the mother's nucleus accumbens (a collection of neurons in the forebrain that are involved in pleasure) likely is important in motivating her approach to the baby (de Haan & Gunnar, 2009). Figure 9 shows the regions of the brain we have described that are likely to play important roles in infant-mother attachment.

In sum, it is likely that a number of brain regions, neurotransmitters, and hormones are involved in the development of infant-mother attachment (Swain & others, 2014). Key

developmental **connection**

Brain Development

Connections are increasingly being made between development, socioemotional processes, and the brain. Connect to "Introduction."

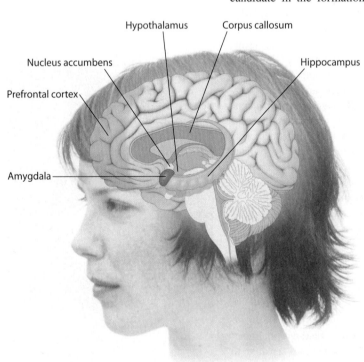

Hypothalamus   Corpus callosum

Nucleus accumbens

Hippocampus

Prefrontal cortex

Amygdala

FIGURE 9

REGIONS OF THE BRAIN PROPOSED AS LIKELY TO BE IMPORTANT IN INFANT-MOTHER ATTACHMENT. This illustration shows the brain's left hemisphere. The corpus callosum is the large bundle of axons that connect the brain's two hemispheres.

candidates for influencing this attachment are connections between the prefrontal cortex, amygdala, and hypothalamus; the neuropeptides oxytocin and vasopressin; and the activity of the neurotransmitter dopamine in the nucleus accumbens.

Mothers and Fathers as Caregivers An increasing number of U.S. fathers stay home full-time with their children (Lamb & Lewis, 2013). In a recent survey, the number of stay-at-home dads in the United States was estimated to be 2 million in 2012 (Livingston, 2014). The 2 million figure represents a significant increase from 1.6 million in 2004 and 1.1 million in 1989. A large portion of the full-time fathers have career-focused wives who provide most of the family's income. One study revealed that the stay-at-home fathers were as satisfied with their marriage as traditional parents, although they indicated that they missed their daily life in the workplace (Rochlen & others, 2008). In this study, the stay-at-home fathers reported that they tended to be ostracized when they took their children to playgrounds and often were excluded from parent groups.

An Aka pygmy father with his infant son. In the Aka culture, fathers were observed to be holding their infants or close to them 47 percent of the time (Hewlett, 1991).
Courtesy of Dr. Barry S. Hewlett

Can fathers take care of infants as competently as mothers can? Observations of fathers and their infants suggest that fathers have the ability to care for their infants as sensitively and responsively as mothers do (Clarke-Stewart & Parke, 2014; Shaw, 2013; Shwalb, Shwalb, & Lamb, 2013). A recent study found that infants who showed a higher level of externalizing, disruptive problems at one year of age had fathers who displayed a low level of engagement with them as early as the third month of life (Ramchandani & others, 2013). Another recent study revealed that fathers with a college-level education engaged in more stimulating physical activities with their infants than less-educated fathers did and that fathers in a conflicting couple relationship participated in less caregiving and physical play with their infants (Cabrera, Hofferth, & Chae, 2011).

Consider also the Aka pygmy culture in Africa, where fathers spend as much time interacting with their infants as mothers do (Hewlett, 2000; Hewlett & MacFarlan, 2010). A recent study also found that marital intimacy and partner support during prenatal development were linked to father-infant attachment following childbirth (Yu & others, 2012). Remember, however, that although fathers can be active, nurturing, involved caregivers with their infants, as Aka pygmy fathers are, in many cultures men have not chosen to follow this pattern (Parkinson, 2010). Also, if fathers have mental health problems, they may interact less effectively with their infants than fathers without such problems. A recent study revealed that depressed fathers focused more on their own needs than on their infants' needs and that they directed more negative and critical speech toward infants (Sethna, Murray, & Ramchandani, 2012).

Do fathers behave differently from mothers when interacting with their infants? Maternal interactions usually center on child-care activities—feeding, changing diapers, bathing (Lamb & Lewis, 2013). Paternal interactions are more likely to include play (Clarke-Stewart & Parke, 2014). Fathers engage in more rough-and-tumble play than mothers do. They bounce infants, throw them up in the air, tickle them, and so on (Lamb, 2013). Mothers do play with infants, but their play is less physical and arousing than that of fathers.

Child Care Many U.S. children today experience multiple caregivers. Most do not have a parent staying home to care for them; instead, the children have some type of care provided by others—"child care." Many parents worry that child care might reduce their infants' emotional attachment to them, retard the infants' cognitive development, fail to teach them how to control anger, and allow them to be unduly influenced by their peers. How extensive is child care? Are the worries of these parents justified?

Parental Leave Today far more young children are in child care than at any other time in history. About 2 million children in the United States currently receive formal, licensed child care, and uncounted millions of children are cared for by unlicensed baby-sitters.

Child-care policies around the world vary in eligibility criteria, duration of parental leaves, benefit level, and the extent to which parents take advantage of the policies (Burchinal & others, 2015; Tolani & Brooks-Gunn, 2008). Europe has led the way in creating new standards of parental leave: The European Union (EU) mandated a paid 14-week maternity leave in 1992. In most European countries today, working parents on

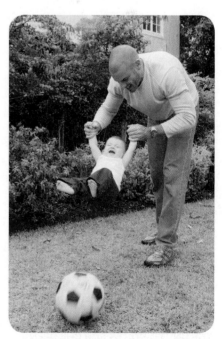

How do most fathers and mothers interact differently with infants?
© Polka Dot Images/Photolibrary RF

How are child-care policies in many European countries, such as Sweden, different from those in the United States?
© Matilda Lindeblad/Johner Images/Getty Images

We have all the knowledge necessary to provide absolutely first-rate child care in the United States. What is missing is the commitment and the will.

—Edward Zigler
Contemporary developmental psychologist, Yale University

FIGURE **10**

PRIMARY CARE ARRANGEMENTS IN THE UNITED STATES FOR CHILDREN UNDER 5 YEARS OF AGE WITH EMPLOYED MOTHERS

leave receive from 70 percent of the worker's prior wage to the full wage, and paid leave averages about 16 weeks (Tolani & Brooks-Gunn, 2008). The United States currently allows workers to take up to 12 weeks of unpaid leave to care for a newborn.

Most countries restrict eligibility for maternity benefits to women employed for a minimum time prior to childbirth (Tolani & Brooks-Gunn, 2008). In Denmark, even unemployed mothers are eligible for extended parental leave related to childbirth. In Sweden, parents can take an 18-month job-protected parental leave with benefits that can be shared by parents and applied to full-time or part-time work.

Variations in Child Care   Because the United States does not have a policy of paid leave for child care, child care in the United States has become a major national concern (Burchinal & others, 2015). Many factors influence the effects of child care, including the age of the child, the type of child care, and the quality of the program.

Child care settings in the United States vary extensively (Burchinal & others, 2015; Coley & others, 2013). Child care is provided in large centers with elaborate facilities and in private homes. Some child-care centers are commercial operations; others are nonprofit centers run by churches, civic groups, and employers. Some child-care providers are professionals; others are mothers who want to earn extra money. Infants and toddlers are more likely to be found in family child care and informal care settings, while older children are more likely to be in child care centers and preschool and early education programs. Figure 10 delineates primary care arrangements for children under 5 years of age with employed mothers (Clarke-Stewart & Miner, 2008).

In the United States, approximately 15 percent of children 5 years of age and younger attend more than one child-care arrangement. A study of 2- and 3-year-olds revealed that an increase in the number of child-care arrangements the children experienced was linked to an increase in behavioral problems and a decrease in prosocial behavior (Morrissey, 2009).

What constitutes a high-quality child-care program for infants? In high-quality child care (Clarke-Stewart & Miner, 2008, p. 273):

> . . . caregivers encourage the children to be actively engaged in a variety of activities, have frequent, positive interactions that include smiling, touching, holding, and speaking at the child's eye level, respond properly to the child's questions or requests, and encourage children to talk about their experiences, feelings, and ideas.

High-quality child care also involves providing children with a safe environment, access to age-appropriate toys and participation in age-appropriate activities, and a low caregiver-to-child ratio that allows caregivers to spend considerable time with children on an individual basis. A recent Australian study revealed that higher-quality child care that included positive child-caregiver relationships at 2 to 3 years of age was linked to children's better self-regulation of attention and emotion at 4 to 5 and 6 to 7 years of age (Gialamas & others, 2014). Quality of child care matters in children's development, and according to UNICEF, the United States meets or exceeds only 3 of 10 child care quality benchmarks. An analysis of U.S. child care studies found that a greater quantity of child care was a strong predictor of socioemotional problems (Jacob, 2009). However, a recent study in Norway (a country that meets or exceeds 8 of 10 UNICEF benchmarks) revealed that high quantity of child care there was not linked to children's externalizing problems (Zachrisson & others, 2013). To read about one individual who provides quality child care to individuals from impoverished backgrounds in the United States, see the *Connecting with Careers* profile.

A major, ongoing longitudinal study of U.S. child care was initiated by the National Institute of Child Health and Human Development (NICHD) in 1991. Data were collected on a diverse sample of almost 1,400 children and their families at ten locations across the United States over a period of seven years. Researchers used multiple methods (trained observers, interviews, questionnaires, and testing), and they measured many facets of children's development, including physical health, cognitive development, and socioemotional development. Following are some of the results of what is now referred to as the NICHD Study of Early Child Care and Youth Development, or NICHD SECCYD (NICHD Early Child Care Network, 2001, 2002, 2003, 2004, 2005, 2006, 2010).

·   *Patterns of use.* Many families placed their infants in child care very soon after the child's birth, and there was considerable instability in the child-care arrangements. By

Wanda Mitchell, Child-Care Director

Wanda Mitchell is the Center Director of the Hattie Daniels Day Care Center in Wilson, North Carolina. Her responsibilities include directing the operation of the center, which involves creating and maintaining an environment in which young children can learn effectively, and ensuring that the center meets state licensing requirements. Mitchell obtained her undergraduate degree from North Carolina A & T University, majoring in child development. Prior to her current position, she had been an education coordinator for Project Head Start and an instructor at Wilson Technical Community College. Describing her work, Mitchell says, "I really enjoy working in my field. This is my passion. After graduating from college, my goal was to advance in my field."

Wanda Mitchell, child-care director, working with some of the children at her center.
Courtesy of Wanda Mitchell

4 months of age, nearly three-fourths of the infants had entered some form of nonmaternal child care. Almost half of the infants were cared for by a relative when they first entered care; only 12 percent were enrolled in child-care centers. Low-income families were more likely than more affluent families to use child care, but infants from low-income families who were in child care averaged the same number of hours of child care as other income groups. In the preschool years, mothers who were single, those with more education, and families with higher incomes used more hours of center-based care than other families. Minority families and mothers with less education used more hours of care by relatives.

· *Quality of care.* Evaluations of quality of care were based on characteristics such as group size, child–adult ratio, physical environment, caregiver characteristics (such as formal education, specialized training, and child-care experience), and caregiver behavior (such as sensitivity to children). An alarming conclusion is that a majority of the child care in the first three years of life was of unacceptably low quality. Positive caregiving by nonparents in child-care settings was infrequent—only 12 percent of the children studied experienced positive nonparental child care (such as positive talk and language stimulation)! Further, infants from low-income families experienced a lower quality of child care than infants from higher-income families. When quality of caregivers' care was high, children performed better on cognitive and language tasks, were more cooperative with their mothers during play, showed more positive and skilled interaction with peers, and had fewer behavior problems. Caregiver training and good child-to-staff ratios were linked with higher cognitive and social competence when children were 54 months of age. In a recent study, high-quality infant-toddler child care was linked to better memory skills at the end of the preschool years (Li & others, 2013). In another recent study, higher-quality child care from birth to 4½ years of age was linked to higher cognitive-academic achievement at 15 years of age (Vandell & others, 2010). In this study, early high-quality care also was related to youth reports of less externalizing behavior (lower rates of delinquency, for example). Also, in a recent study, high-quality infant-toddler child care was linked to better memory skills at the end of the preschool years (Li & others, 2013).

What are some important findings from the national longitudinal study of child care conducted by the National Institute of Child Health and Human Development?
© Reena Rose Sibayan/The Jersey Journal/Landov Images

· *Amount of child care.* In general, when children spent 30 hours or more per week in child care, their development was less than optimal (Ramey, 2005). In a recent study, more hours of early non-relative child care was related to higher levels of risk taking and impulsivity at 15 years of age (Vandell & others, 2010).

·   *Family and parenting influences.* The influence of families and parenting was not weakened by extensive child care. Parents played a significant role in helping children to regulate their emotions. Especially important parenting influences were being sensitive to children's needs, being involved with children, and cognitively stimulating them. Indeed, parental sensitivity has been the most consistent predictor of a secure attachment, with child-care experiences being relevant in many cases only when mothers engage in insensitive parenting (Friedman, Melhuish, & Hill, 2011). An important point about the extensive NICHD research is that findings show that family factors are considerably stronger and more consistent predictors of a wide variety of child outcomes than are child-care aspects such as quality, quantity, and type.

·   *Home and child-care settings.* The worst outcomes for children occur when both home and child-care settings are of poor quality. For example, a recent study involving the NICHD SECCYD data revealed that worse socioemotional outcomes (higher levels of problem behavior, lower levels of prosocial behavior) for children occurred when they experienced both home and child-care environments that conferred risk (Watamura & others, 2011).

What are some strategies parents can follow in regard to child care? Child-care expert Kathleen McCartney (2003, p. 4) offered this advice:

·   *Recognize that the quality of your parenting is a key factor in your child's development.*
·   *Make decisions that will improve the likelihood you will be good parents.* "For some this will mean working full-time"—for personal fulfillment, income, or both. "For others, this will mean working part-time or not working outside the home."
·   *Monitor your child's development.* "Parents should observe for themselves whether their children seem to be having behavior problems." If problems arise, parents need to talk with their child-care providers and their pediatrician about their child's behavior.
·   *Take some time to find the best child care.* Observe different child-care facilities and be certain that you like what you see. "Quality child care costs money, and not all parents can afford the child care they want. However, state subsidies, and other programs like Head Start, are available for families in need."

Attachment in Middle and Late Childhood   Earlier you read about the importance of secure attachment in infancy and the role of sensitive parenting in attachment (Thompson, 2015). The attachment process continues to be an important aspect of children's development in the childhood years. In middle and late childhood, attachment becomes more sophisticated, and as children's social worlds expand to include peers, teachers, and others, they typically spend less time with parents.

Kathryn Kerns and her colleagues (Brumariu, Kerns, & Seibert, 2012; Kerns & Brumariu, 2016; Kerns & Seibert, 2012, 2016; Kerns, Siener, & Brumariu, 2011; Siener & Kerns, 2012) have studied links between attachment to parents and various child outcomes in middle and late childhood. They have found that during this period of development, secure attachment is associated with a lower level of internalized symptoms, anxiety, and depression in children (Brumariu & Kerns, 2011). For example, their research revealed that children who were less securely attached to their mothers reported having more anxiety (Brumariu, Kerns, & Seibert, 2012; Kerns & Brumariu, 2014). Also in this research, secure attachment was linked to a higher level of children's emotion regulation and less difficulty in identifying emotions. And their research indicates that insecure disorganized children (Type D) are most at risk for developing anxiety problems (Kerns & Brumariu, 2014).

ADOLESCENCE

Relationships between parents and children continue to be important into the adolescent years. But the adolescent's emotions may become more involved with people outside the family, especially with romantic partners. What do psychologists know about these relationships?

Attachment to Parents   The initial interest in attachment focused on infants and their caregivers. Developmentalists have recently begun to explore the role of secure attachment and related concepts, such as connectedness to parents, during adolescence (Dawson & others, 2014; Kobak & Kerig, 2015; Kobak & others, 2015; Zack & others, 2015). Secure attachment to parents in adolescence facilitates the adolescent's social competence and well-being, as reflected in such characteristics as self-esteem, emotional adjustment, and physical health (Hoeve & others, 2012). Recent research indicated that the most consistent outcomes of secure attachment in adolescence are positive peer relations and emotion regulation (Allen & Miga, 2010). In other recent research, Joseph Allen and his colleagues (2009) also found that adolescents who were securely attached at 14 years of age were more likely to report at age 21 that they were in an exclusive relationship, comfortable with intimacy in relationships, and attaining increased financial independence.

Dating and Romantic Relationships   Adolescents not only have attachments to their parents but also to romantic partners. Adolescents spend considerable time either dating or thinking about dating, which has gone far beyond its original courtship function to become a form of recreation, a source of status and achievement, and a setting for learning about close relationships (Furman & Rose, 2015; Suleiman & Deardorff, 2015; Young, Furman, & Laursen, 2014). One function of dating, though, continues to be mate selection.

Types of Dating and Developmental Changes   Three stages characterize the development of romantic relationships in adolescence (Connolly & McIsaac, 2009):

What are dating relationships like in adolescence?
© Digital Vision/Getty Images RF

- *Entry into romantic attractions and affiliations at about 11 to 13 years of age.* This initial stage is triggered by puberty. From 11 to 13, adolescents become intensely interested in romance, and it dominates many conversations with same-sex friends. Developing a crush on someone is common, and the crush often is shared with a same-sex friend. Young adolescents may or may not interact with the individual who is the object of their infatuation. When dating occurs, it usually takes place in a group setting.

- *Exploring romantic relationships at approximately 14 to 16 years of age.* At this point in adolescence, two types of romantic involvement occur: casual dating and group dating. Casual dating emerges between individuals who are mutually attracted. These dating experiences are often short-lived, last a few months at best, and usually endure for only a few weeks. *Dating in groups* is common and reflects embeddedness in the peer context. A friend often acts as a third-party facilitator of a potential dating relationship by communicating their friend's romantic interest and determining whether this attraction is reciprocated.

- *Consolidating dyadic romantic bonds at about 17 to 19 years of age.* At the end of the high school years, more serious romantic relationships develop. This is characterized by strong emotional bonds more closely resembling those in adult romantic relationships. These bonds often are more stable and enduring than earlier bonds, typically lasting one year or more.

Two variations on these stages in the development of romantic relationships in adolescence involve early and late bloomers (Connolly & McIsaac, 2009). Early bloomers include 15 to 20 percent of 11- to 13-year-olds who say that they currently are in a romantic relationship and 35 percent who indicate that they have had some prior experience in romantic relationships. A recent study found that early daters had more externalized problems throughout adolescents than on-time and late daters (Connolly & others, 2013). Late bloomers comprise approximately 10 percent of 17- to 19-year-olds who say that they have had no experience with romantic relationships and another 15 percent who report that they have not engaged in any romantic relationships that lasted more than four months.

In their early exploration of romantic relationships, today's adolescents often find comfort in numbers and begin hanging out together in heterosexual groups. Sometimes they just hang out at someone's house or get organized enough to get someone to drive them to a mall or a movie. Indeed, peers play an important role in adolescent romantic relationships. One study also found that young adolescents increase their participation in mixed-gender peer groups (Connolly & others, 2004). This participation was "not explicitly focused on dating but rather brought boys and girls together in settings in which heterosocial interaction might occur but is not obligatory" (p. 201).

Dating and Adjustment   Researchers have linked dating and romantic relationships with various measures of how well adjusted adolescents are (Furman & Rose, 2015; Soller, 2014). For example, a recent study of 200 tenth-graders revealed that those with more romantic experiences reported higher levels of social acceptance, friendship competence, and romantic competence—however, having more romantic experience also was linked with a higher level of substance use, delinquency, and sexual behavior (Furman, Low, & Ho, 2009). Also, among adolescent girls but not adolescent males, having an older romantic partner was linked with an increase in depressive symptoms, largely influenced by an increase in substance use (Haydon & Halpern, 2010). Dating and romantic relationships at an early age can be especially problematic (Connolly & McIsaac, 2009). A recent study found that romantic activity was linked to depression in early adolescent girls (Starr & others, 2012). Researchers also have found that early dating and "going with" someone are linked with adolescent pregnancy and problems at home and school (Florsheim, Moore, & Edgington, 2003).

Sociocultural Contexts and Dating   The sociocultural context is a strong influence on adolescents' dating patterns (Cheng & others, 2012). Values and religious beliefs of various cultures often dictate the age at which dating begins, how much freedom in dating is allowed, whether dates must be chaperoned by adults or parents, and the roles of males and females in dating. For example, Latino and Asian American cultures have more conservative standards regarding adolescent dating than does the Anglo-American culture.

Dating may be a source of cultural conflict for many adolescents whose families come from cultures in which dating begins at a later age with little freedom, especially for adolescent girls. One study found that Asian American adolescents were less likely to have been involved in a romantic relationship in the past 18 months than African American or Latino adolescents (Carver, Joyner, & Udry, 2003). In another study, Latina young adults in the midwestern United States reflected on their dating experiences during adolescence (Raffaelli & Ontai, 2001). They said that their parents had placed strict boundaries on their romantic involvement. As a result, the young women recalled that their adolescent dating experiences were filled with tension and conflict. Over half of the Latinas engaged in "sneak dating" without their parents' knowledge.

ADULTHOOD

Attachment and romantic relationships continue to be very important aspects of close relationships in adulthood. Let's explore attachment first, then examine different types of love.

Attachment   Earlier in this chapter, we discussed the importance of attachment in childhood and adolescence (Thompson, 2015). Are these earlier patterns of attachment related to adults' attachment styles?

Linking Infant Attachment to Adult Attachment   Although relationships with romantic partners differ from those with parents, romantic partners fulfill some of the same needs for adults as parents do for their children (Zayas & Hazan, 2014). Recall that *securely attached* infants are defined as those who use the caregiver as a secure base from which to explore the environment (Laible, Thompson, & Froimson, 2015). Similarly, adults may count on their romantic partners to be a secure base to which they can return and obtain comfort and security in stressful times (Zeifman & Hazan, 2008).

Do adult attachment patterns with partners reflect childhood attachment patterns with parents? In a retrospective study, Cindy Hazan and Phillip Shaver (1987) revealed that young adults who were securely attached in their romantic relationships were more likely to describe their early relationship with their parents as securely attached. In a longitudinal study, infants who were securely attached at 1 year of age were securely attached 20 years later in their adult romantic relationships (Steele & others, 1998). Also, a longitudinal study revealed that securely attached infants were in more stable romantic relationships in adulthood than their insecurely attached counterparts (Salvatore & others, 2011). However, in another longitudinal study links between early attachment styles and later attachment styles were lessened by

---

developmental **connection**

Sexuality

Early sexual intercourse is linked with a number of developmental outcomes. Connect to "Gender and Sexuality."

How are attachment patterns in childhood linked to relationships in emerging and early adulthood?
(left): © Runstudio/Taxi Japan/Getty Images; (right): © Jade/Getty Images RF

stressful and disruptive experiences such as the death of a parent or instability of caregiving (Lewis, Feiring, & Rosenthal, 2000).

A longitudinal study by Katherine Haydon and her colleagues (2012) provides insight into which aspects of early child development are linked to different aspects of attachment in emerging and early adulthood. In this study, adults who experienced higher-quality parenting in childhood were more likely to have secure attachment thoughts about early experiences with caregivers and about current romantic partners 20 years later. However, in this study, neither generalized attachment (adult thoughts about childhood relationships with caregivers) nor romantic attachment (thoughts about specific romantic partners) assessed in emerging and early adulthood were linked to infant attachment assessed at 12 months of age, which contradicts the view that infant attachment provides the basis for all subsequent attachment relationships. Also, in this study, ego resiliency (which involves flexibly regulating attention, affect, and behavior in response to changing environmental demands) assessed at 54 months of age was linked to more secure romantic representations in adulthood but not to adult representations of attachment to caregivers in childhood. This study reflects the *developmental cascade model* described earlier that emphasizes the importance of considering not only very early experiences but also later developmental changes and experiences in predicting relationship outcomes in adulthood.

Adult Attachment Styles   Hazan and Shaver (1987) measured attachment styles using the following brief assessment.

Read each paragraph and then place a check mark next to the one that best describes your interactions with others:

1. I find it relatively easy to get close to others and I am comfortable depending on them and having them depend on me. I don't worry about being abandoned or about someone getting too close to me.

2. I am somewhat uncomfortable being close to others. I find it difficult to trust them completely and to allow myself to depend on them. I get nervous when anyone gets too close to me and it bothers me when someone tries to be more intimate with me than I feel comfortable with.

3. I find that others are reluctant to get as close as I would like. I often worry that my partner doesn't really love me or won't want to stay with me. I want to get very close to my partner, and this sometimes scares people away.

secure attachment style An attachment style that describes adults who have positive views of relationships, find it easy to get close to others, and are not overly concerned or stressed out about their romantic relationships.

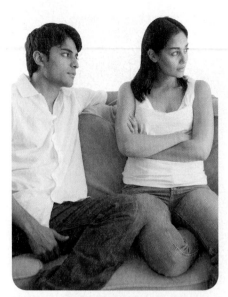

What are some key dimensions of attachment in adulthood, and how are they related to relationship patterns and well-being?
© Corbis RF

These items correspond to three attachment styles—secure attachment (option 1 in the list) and two insecure attachment styles (avoidant—option 2, and anxious—option 3):

- **Secure attachment style.** Securely attached adults have positive views of relationships, find it easy to get close to others, and are not overly concerned with, or stressed out about, their romantic relationships. These adults tend to enjoy sexuality in the context of a committed relationship and are less likely than others to have one-night stands.
- **Avoidant attachment style.** Avoidant individuals are hesitant about getting involved in romantic relationships and once in a relationship tend to distance themselves from their partner.
- **Anxious attachment style.** These individuals demand closeness, are less trusting, and are more emotional, jealous, and possessive.

The majority of adults (about 60 to 80 percent) describe themselves as securely attached, and not surprisingly adults prefer having a securely attached partner (Zeifman & Hazan, 2008).

Researchers are studying links between adults' current attachment styles and many aspects of their lives (Craparo & others, 2014; Hudson & others, 2014; Mikulincer & Shaver, 2014). For example, securely attached adults are more satisfied with their close relationships than insecurely attached adults, and the relationships of securely attached adults are more likely to be characterized by trust, commitment, and longevity. A recent meta-analysis of 94 samples of U.S. college students from 1988 to 2011 found the percentage of students with a secure attachment decreased in recent years while the percentage of students with insecure attachment styles increased (Konrath & others, 2014).

Benefits of Secure Attachment in Adulthood   The following recent studies confirmed the importance of adult attachment styles in people's lives:

- Attachment security predicted more positive romantic relationships (Holland & Roisman, 2010).
- In newlywed marriages, spouses were more likely to engage in infidelity when either they or their partner had an anxious attachment style (Russell, Baker, & McNulty, 2013).
- A national survey indicated that insecure attachment in adults was associated with the development of disease and chronic illness, especially cardiovascular system problems such as high blood pressure, heart attack, and stroke (McWilliams & Bailey, 2010).
- Adults with avoidant and anxious attachment patterns had a lower level of sexual satisfaction than their counterparts with a secure attachment pattern (Brassard & others, 2012).
- Secure attachment in adults was linked to fewer sleep disruptions than insecure avoidant and anxious attachment (Adams & McWilliams, 2015).

Leading experts Mario Mikulincer and Phillip Shaver (2014) have reached the following conclusions about the benefits of secure attachment:

1. Individuals who are securely attached have a well-integrated sense of self-acceptance, self-esteem, and self-efficacy.
2. They have the ability to control their emotions, are optimistic, and are resilient.
3. Facing stress and adversity, they activate cognitive representations of security, are mindful of what is happening around them, and mobilize effective coping strategies.

A recent meta-analysis concluded that securely attached individuals have better relationships with their partners than do individuals with avoidant or anxious attachment styles (Li & Chan, 2012).

If you have an insecure attachment style, are you stuck with it and does it doom you to have problematic relationships? Attachment categories are somewhat stable in adulthood, but adults do have the capacity to change their attachment thinking and behavior. Although attachment insecurities are linked to relationship problems, attachment style makes only a moderate-size contribution to relationship functioning because other factors contribute to relationship satisfaction and success. In the chapter on "Families, Lifestyles, and Parenting," we will discuss such factors in our coverage of marital relationships.

Attachment from Early to Late Adulthood   There has been far less research on how attachment influences the lives of aging adults than on effects of attachment in children,

avoidant attachment style An attachment style that describes adults who are hesitant about getting involved in romantic relationships and, once in a relationship, tend to distance themselves from their partner.

anxious attachment style An attachment style that describes adults who demand closeness, are less trusting, and are more emotional, jealous, and possessive.

adolescents, and young adults. A recent research review on attachment in older adults reached the following conclusions (Van Assche & others, 2013):

1. Older adults have fewer attachment relationships than younger adults (Cicirelli, 2010).
2. With increasing age, attachment anxiety decreases (Chopik, Edelstein, & Fraley, 2013).
3. In late adulthood, attachment security is associated with psychological and physical well-being (Bodner & Cohen-Fridel, 2010).
4. Insecure attachment is linked to more perceived negative caregiver burden in caring for patients with Alzheimer disease (Karantzas & others, 2010).

A recent large-scale study examined attachment anxiety and avoidance in individuals from 18 to 70 years of age (Chopik, Edelstein, & Fraley, 2013). In this study, attachment anxiety was highest among adults in their mid-twenties and lowest among middle-aged and older adults. Developmental changes in avoidant attachment were not as strong as in anxious attachment, although anxious attachment was highest for middle-aged adults and lowest for young adults and older adults. Also in this study, partnered adults showed lower levels of attachment anxiety and avoidance than single adults. Further, a recent study revealed that oxytocin was positively associated with diminished stress among securely attached older adults (Emeny & others, 2015).

Romantic Love   Think for a moment about songs and books that hit the top of the charts. Chances are, they're about love. Poets, playwrights, and musicians through the ages have lauded the fiery passion of romantic love—and lamented the searing pain when it fails. **Romantic love** is also called *passionate love* or *eros;* it has strong components of sexuality and infatuation, and it often predominates in the early part of a love relationship. A recent meta-analysis found that males show higher avoidance and lower anxiety about romantic love than females do (Del Giudice, 2011).

Well-known love researcher Ellen Berscheid (1988) says that romantic love is what we mean when we say that we are "in love" with someone. It is romantic love, she stresses, that we need to understand if we are to learn what love is all about. According to Berscheid, sexual desire is the most important ingredient of romantic love. We discuss sexuality in more detail in the chapter on "Gender and Sexuality."

Romantic love includes a complex intermingling of emotions—fear, anger, sexual desire, joy, and jealousy, for example. Obviously, some of these emotions are a source of anguish. One study found that romantic lovers were more likely than friends to be the cause of depression (Berscheid & Fei, 1977). And a recent study revealed that a heightened state of romantic love in young adults was linked to stronger depression and anxiety symptoms but better sleep quality (Bajoghli & others, 2014).

Recently, romantic attraction has not only taken place in person but also over the Internet. Forty million Americans use online dating services (about 40 percent of the U.S. singles pool) (Broussard, 2015). Is looking for love online likely to work out? It didn't work out so well in 2012 for Notre Dame linebacker Manti Te'o, whose online girlfriend turned out to be a "catfish," someone who fakes an identity online. However, online dating sites claim that their sites often have positive outcomes. A poll commissioned by match.com in 2009 reported that twice as many marriages occurred between individuals who met through an online dating site than between people who met in bars, clubs, and other social settings.

In 2010, Barbara Hassan, a 47-year-old divorcee from Texas, registered with match.com and within one day had three matches, all of whom appeared to be intelligent, attractive, and well off (Marinova, 2013). Barbara's first thoughts were that they were too good to be true, and those first thoughts were right. One of her matches said he was a construction engineer from Nigeria who had designed a building for orphans. She communicated with him for several months and then he asked her to send him $2,700 so he could come to the United States. That was enough to end the connection.

Connecting online for love turned out positively for two Columbia graduate students, Michelle Przybyksi and Andy Lalinde (Steinberg, 2011). They found out they lived only a few blocks away from each other, so soon after they communicated online through Date-myschool.com, a dating site exclusively for college students, they met in person, really hit it off, applied for a marriage license 10 days later, and eventually got married.

What are some changes in attachment in older adults?
© moodboard/Corbis RF

Love is a canvas furnished by nature and embroidered by imagination.

—VOLTAIRE
French essayist, 18th century

developmental **connection**

Sexuality

At the beginning of emerging adulthood, more than 60 percent of individuals have experienced sexual intercourse. Connect to "Gender and Sexuality."

romantic love Also called passionate love, or *eros*, this type of love has strong components of sexuality and infatuation, and it often predominates in the early part of a love relationship.

(*Left*) Manti Te'o; (*Right*) Michelle Przybyksi and Andy Lalinde.
Left: © John Biever/Sports Illustrated/Getty Images; Right: Courtesy of Michelle and Andres Lalinde
S. Nickalls, (2012, March 9). "Why college students shouldn't online date," The Tower, March 9, 2012. http://tower.arcadia.edu/?p=754. Copyright © 2012 by The Tower. All rights reserved. Used with permission.

However, in a recent editorial in *The Tower*, the student newspaper at Arcadia University in Philadelphia, Samantha Nickalls (2012) argued that online dating sites might be okay for people in their thirties and older but not for college students. She commented:

> The dating pool of our age is huge. Huge. After all, marriage is not on most people's minds when they're in college, but dating (or perhaps just hooking up) most certainly is. A college campus, in fact, is like living a dating service because the majority of people are looking for the same thing you are. As long as you put yourself out there, flirt a bit, and be friendly, chances are that people will notice.
>
> If this doesn't work for you right away, why should it really matter? As a college student, you have so many other huge things going on in your life—your career choice, your transition from kid to adult, your crazy social life. Unless you are looking to get married at age 20 (which is a whole other issue that I could debate for hours), dating shouldn't be the primary thing on your mind anyway. Besides, as the old saying goes, the best things come when you least expect them. Oftentimes, you find the best dates by accident—not by hunting them down.

Some critics argue that online romantic relationships lose the interpersonal connection, whereas others emphasize that the Internet may benefit shy or anxious individuals who find it difficult to meet potential partners in person (Holmes, Little, & Welsh, 2009). One problem with online matchmaking is that many individuals misrepresent their characteristics, such as how old they are, how attractive they are, and their occupation. Despite such dishonesty, researchers have found that romantic relationships initiated on the Internet are more likely than relationships established in person to last for more than two years (Bargh & McKenna, 2004). And in a recent large-scale study of more than 19,000 individuals, it was discovered that more than one-third of marriages now begin online and that these marriages are slightly less likely to break up and are characterized by slightly higher marital satisfaction than marriages than begin in offline contexts (Cacioppo & others, 2013).

affectionate love Also called companionate love, this type of love occurs when individuals desire to have another person near and have a deep, caring affection for the person.

triangular theory of love Sternberg's theory that love includes three components or dimensions—passion, intimacy, and commitment.

Affectionate Love Love is more than just passion. **Affectionate love,** also called companionate love, is the type of love that occurs when individuals desire to have the other person near and have a deep, caring affection for the person.

There is a growing belief that as love matures, passion tends to give way to affection (Sternberg, 2013). One investigation interviewed 102 happily married couples in early (average age 28), middle (average age 45), and late (average age 65) adulthood to explore the nature of age and sex differences in satisfying love relationships (Reedy, Birren, &

Schaie, 1981). As indicated in Figure 11, communication and sexual intimacy were more important in early adulthood, and feelings of emotional security and loyalty were more important in later-life love relationships. Young adult lovers also rated communication as more characteristic of their love than their older counterparts did. Aside from the age differences, however, there were some striking similarities in the nature of satisfying love relationships. At all ages, emotional security was ranked as the most important factor in love, followed by respect, communication, help and play behaviors, sexual intimacy, and loyalty. The findings in this research also suggested that women believe emotional security is more important in love than men do.

Sternberg's Triangular Theory of Love
Clearly, there is more to satisfying love relationships than sex (Berscheid, 2010). One theory of love that captures this idea has been proposed by Robert J. Sternberg (1988, 2013). His **triangular theory of love** states that love has three main components or dimensions—passion, intimacy, and commitment (see Figure 12):

· *Passion*, as described earlier, is physical and sexual attraction to another.
· *Intimacy* is the emotional feelings of warmth, closeness, and sharing in a relationship.
· *Commitment* is our cognitive appraisal of the relationship and our intent to maintain the relationship even in the face of problems.

According to Sternberg, if passion is the only ingredient (with intimacy and commitment low or absent), we are merely experiencing infatuation. This might happen in an affair or a one-night stand. But varying combinations of the dimensions of love create three qualitatively different types of love:

· A relationship marked by intimacy and commitment but low or lacking in passion is called *affectionate love,* a pattern often found among couples who have been married for many years.
· If passion and commitment are present but intimacy is not, Sternberg calls the relationship *fatuous* love, as when one person worships another from a distance.
· If passion, intimacy, and commitment are all strong, the result is *consummate love,* the fullest type of love.

Falling Out of Love
The collapse of a close relationship may feel tragic. In the long run, however, our happiness and personal development may benefit from getting over being in love and ending a close relationship.

In particular, falling out of love may be wise if you are obsessed with a person who repeatedly betrays your trust; if you are involved with someone who is draining you emotionally or financially; or if you are desperately in love with someone who does not return your feelings.

Being in love when love is not returned can lead to depression, obsessive thoughts, sexual dysfunction, inability to work effectively, difficulty in making new friends, and self-condemnation (Sbarra, 2012). Thinking clearly in such relationships is often difficult, because they are so colored by arousing emotions.

Some people get taken advantage of in relationships (Duck, 2011; Metts & Cupach, 2007). For example, without either person realizing it, a relationship can evolve in a way that creates dominant and submissive roles. Detecting this pattern is an important step toward learning either to reconstruct the relationship or to end it if the problems cannot be worked out. What other types of personal growth can follow romantic relationship breakups? To find out more about this aspect of relationships, see the *Connecting with Research* interlude.

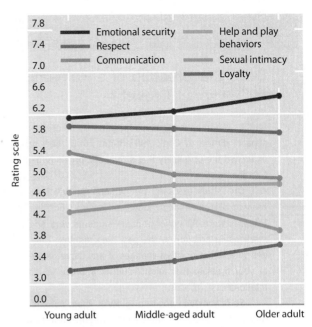

FIGURE 11
CHANGES IN SATISFYING LOVE RELATIONSHIPS ACROSS THE ADULT YEARS. In the investigation by Reedy, Birren, and Schaie (1981), emotional security was the most important factor in love at all ages. Sexual intimacy was more important in early adulthood, whereas emotional security and loyalty were more important in the love relationships of older adults. Young adult lovers also rated communication as more important in a love relationship than their older counterparts did.

FIGURE 12
STERNBERG'S TRIANGLE OF LOVE. Sternberg identified three dimensions that shape the experience we call love: passion, intimacy, and commitment. Various combinations of the three dimensions produce particular types of love.

connecting with research

Does the Breakup of a Romantic Relationship Present an Opportunity for Personal Growth?

Studies of romantic breakups have mainly focused on their negative aspects (Frazier & Cook, 1993; Kato, 2005). Few researchers have examined the possibility that a romantic breakup might lead to positive changes.

One study assessed the personal growth that can follow the breakup of a romantic relationship (Tashiro & Frazier, 2003). The participants were 92 undergraduate students who had experienced a relationship breakup in the past nine months. They were asked to describe "what positive changes, if any, have happened as a result of your breakup that might serve to improve your future romantic relationships" (p. 118).

Self-reported positive growth was common following a romantic breakup. Changes were categorized in terms of personal,

relational, and environmental positives. The most commonly reported types of growth were personal changes, which included feeling stronger and more self-confident, more independent, and better off emotionally. Relational positive changes included gaining relational wisdom, and environmental positive changes included having better friendships because of the breakup. Figure 13 provides examples of these positive changes. Women reported more positive growth than did men.

What other aspects of romantic dissolution might be interesting to study?

FIGURE 13
EXAMPLES OF POSITIVE CHANGES IN THE AFTERMATH OF A ROMANTIC BREAKUP

Change Category	Examples of Frequently Mentioned Responses
Personal positives	1. "I am more self-confident." 2. "Through breaking up I found I could handle more on my own." 3. "I didn't always have to be the strong one, it's okay to cry or be upset without having to take care of him."
Relational positives	1. "Better communication." 2. "I learned many relationship skills that I can apply in the future (for example, the importance of saying you're sorry)." 3. "I know not to jump into a relationship too quickly."
Environmental positives	1. "I rely on my friends more. I forgot how important friends are when I was with him." 2. "Concentrate on school more: I can put so much more time and effort toward school." 3. "I believe friends' and family's opinions count—will seek them out in future relationships."

Review Connect Reflect

 LG4 Explain attachment and its development

Review
- What is attachment? How does attachment develop in infancy and childhood? How are caregiving styles related to attachment? How does child care affect children's development?
- How does attachment develop in adolescence? What is the nature of dating and romantic relationships in adolescence?
- What are attachment and love like in different stages of adulthood?

Connect
- How is attachment similar or different in infancy and adolescence?

Reflect *Your Own Personal Journey of Life*
- How would you describe your attachment style? Why do you think you developed this attachment style?

reach your **learning goals**

Emotional Development and Attachment

1 Exploring Emotion — LG1 · Discuss basic aspects of emotion

What Are Emotions?

· Emotion is feeling, or affect, that expresses the pleasantness or unpleasantness of a person's state; it occurs when a person is engaged in an interaction that is important to him or her, especially to his or her well-being. Emotions can be classified as positive or negative and vary in intensity. Darwin described the evolutionary basis of emotions, and today psychologists note that emotions, especially facial expressions of emotions, have a biological foundation. Facial expressions of emotion are similar across cultures but display rules are not culturally universal. Biological evolution endowed humans to be emotional, but culture and relationships with others provide diversity in emotional experiences.

Emotion Regulation

· The ability to control one's emotions is a key dimension of development. Emotion regulation consists of effectively managing arousal to adapt and reach a goal. In infancy and early childhood, regulation of emotion gradually shifts from external sources to self-initiated, internal sources. Also with increasing age, children are more likely to increase their use of cognitive strategies for regulating emotion, modulate their emotional arousal, become more adept at managing situations to minimize negative emotion, and choose effective ways to cope with stress. Emotion-coaching parents have children who engage in more effective self-regulation of their emotions than do emotion-dismissing parents.

Emotional Competence

· Saarni argues that becoming emotionally competent involves developing a number of skills such as being aware of one's emotional states, discerning others' emotions, adaptively coping with negative emotions, and understanding the role of emotions in relationships.

2 Development of Emotion — LG2 · Describe the development of emotion through the life span

Infancy

· Infants display a number of emotions early in the first six months, including sadness, surprise, interest, joy, fear, and anger—although researchers debate the onset and sequence of these emotions. Lewis distinguishes between primary emotions and self-conscious emotions. Crying is the most important mechanism newborns have for communicating with their world. Babies have at least three types of cries—basic, anger, and pain cries. Controversy surrounds the question of whether babies should be soothed when they cry, although increasingly experts recommend immediately responding in a caring way during the first year. Social smiling in response to a caregiver's voice occurs as early as 4 weeks of age. Two fears that infants develop are stranger anxiety and separation from a caregiver (which is reflected in separation protest).

Early Childhood

· Young children's range of emotions expands during early childhood as they increasingly experience self-conscious emotions such as pride, shame, and guilt. Between 2 and 4 years of age, children use an increasing number of terms to describe emotion and learn more about the causes and consequences of feelings. At 4 to 5 years of age, children show an increased ability to reflect on emotions and understand that a single event can elicit different emotions in different people. Emotion regulation is a key aspect of competent socioemotional development in childhood.

Middle and Late Childhood

· In middle and late childhood, children show a growing awareness of the need to control and manage emotions to meet social standards. Also in this age period, they show enhanced emotional understanding, markedly improve their ability to suppress or conceal negative emotions, use self-initiated strategies for redirecting feelings, have an increased tendency to take into fuller account the events that lead to emotional reactions, and develop a genuine capacity for empathy.

Adolescence

· As individuals go through early adolescence, they are less likely to report being very happy. Moodiness is a normal aspect of early adolescence. Although pubertal change is associated with an increase in negative emotions, hormonal influences are often small, and environmental experiences may contribute more to the emotions of adolescents than hormonal changes do.

| Adult Development and Aging | | Older adults are better at controlling their emotions than younger adults are, and older adults experience more positive and less negative emotions than younger adults do. An important theory regarding developmental changes in emotion during adulthood, especially late adulthood, is Carstensen's socioemotional selectivity theory. Knowledge-related and emotion-related goals change across the life span; emotion-related goals become more important when individuals get older. |

3 Temperament

 Characterize variations in temperament and their significance

Describing and Classifying Temperament		Temperament is an individual's behavioral style and characteristic way of emotional responding. Developmentalists are especially interested in the temperament of infants. Chess and Thomas classified infants as (1) easy, (2) difficult, or (3) slow to warm up. Kagan argues that inhibition to the unfamiliar is an important temperament category. Rothbart and Bates' view of temperament identifies three aspects: (1) extraversion/surgency, (2) negative affectivity, and (3) effortful control (self-regulation).
Biological Foundations and Experience		Physiological characteristics are associated with different temperaments, and a moderate influence of heredity has been found in studies of the heritability of temperament. Children inherit a physiology that biases them to have a particular type of temperament, but through experience they learn to modify their temperament style to some degree. Very active young children are likely to become outgoing adults. In some cases, a difficult temperament is linked with adjustment problems in early adulthood. The link between childhood temperament and adult personality depends in part on context, which helps shape the reaction to a child and thus the child's experiences. For example, the reaction to a child's temperament depends in part on the child's culture.
Goodness of Fit and Parenting		Goodness of fit refers to the match between a child's temperament and the environmental demands the child must cope with. Goodness of fit can be an important aspect of a child's adjustment. Although research evidence is sketchy at this time, some general recommendations are that caregivers should (1) be sensitive to the individual characteristics of the child, (2) be flexible in responding to these characteristics, and (3) avoid negative labeling of the child.

4 Attachment and Love

 Explain attachment and its development

| Infancy and Childhood | | Infants show a strong interest in the social world and are motivated to understand it. Infants orient to the social world early in their development. Face-to-face play with a caregiver begins to occur at about 2 to 3 months of age. Newly developed self-produced locomotor skills significantly expand the infant's ability to initiate social interchanges and explore its social world more independently. Perceiving people as engaging in intentional and goal-directed behavior is an important social cognitive accomplishment that occurs toward the end of the first year. Social referencing increases in the second year of life. |

Attachment is a close emotional bond between two people. In infancy, contact comfort and trust are important in the development of attachment. Bowlby's ethological theory stresses that the caregiver and the infant are biologically predisposed to form an attachment. Attachment develops in four phases during infancy. Securely attached babies use the caregiver, usually the mother, as a secure base from which to explore the environment.

Three types of insecure attachment are avoidant, resistant, and disorganized. Ainsworth created the Strange Situation, an observational measure of attachment. Ainsworth notes that secure attachment in the first year of life provides an important foundation for psychological development later in life. The strength of the link between early attachment and later development has varied somewhat across studies. Some critics argue that attachment theorists have not given adequate attention to genetics and temperament. Other critics stress that attachment theorists have not adequately taken into account the diversity of social agents and contexts.

Cultural variations in attachment have been found, but in all cultures studied to date secure attachment is the most common classification. Caregivers of securely attached babies are sensitive to the babies' signals and are consistently available to meet their needs. Caregivers of avoidant babies tend to be unavailable or rejecting. Caregivers of resistant babies tend to be inconsistently available to their babies and usually are not very affectionate. Caregivers of disorganized babies often neglect or physically abuse their babies.

The mother's primary role when interacting with the infant is caregiving; the father's is playful interaction. More U.S. children are in child care now than at any earlier point in history. The quality of child care is uneven, and child care remains a controversial topic. Quality child care can be achieved and seems to have few adverse effects on children. In the NICHD child-care study, infants from low-income families were more likely to receive the lowest quality of care. Also, higher quality of child care was linked with fewer child problems.

Secure attachment continues to be important in the childhood years. Researchers have found that secure attachment to parents in middle and late childhood is linked lower levels of internalized symptoms, anxiety, and depression.

Adolescence

Securely attached adolescents show more competent behavior than their insecurely attached counterparts, with the most consistent outcomes involving positive peer relations and emotion regulation. Dating, or thinking about dating, becomes an important aspect of many adolescents' lives. Early dating is associated with developmental problems. Culture can exert a powerful influence on dating.

Adulthood

Three adult attachment styles are insecure attachment, avoidant attachment, and anxious attachment. Attachment styles in early adulthood are linked with a number of relationship patterns and developmental outcomes. For example, securely attached adults often show more positive relationship patterns than insecurely attached adults. Also, adults with avoidant and anxious attachment styles tend to be more depressed and have more relationship problems than securely attached adults. Older adults have fewer attachment relationships than younger adults, and attachment anxiety decreases in older adults. Romantic love and affectionate love are two important types of love. Romantic love tends to be more important in early adulthood; affectionate love is more likely to be important in later-life love relationships. Sternberg proposed a triangular theory of love that focuses on different combinations of (1) passion, (2) intimacy, and (3) commitment. The collapse of a close relationship can be traumatic, but for some individuals it results in increased self-confidence, relational wisdom, and being better off emotionally. For most individuals, falling out of love is painful and emotionally intense.

key **terms**

affectionate love	easy child	primary emotions	social referencing
anger cry	emotion	reflexive smile	social smile
anxious attachment style	fight or flight	romantic love	socioemotional selectivity theory
attachment	goodness of fit	secure attachment style	Strange Situation
avoidant attachment style	insecure avoidant children	securely attached children	stranger anxiety
basic cry	insecure disorganized children	self-conscious emotions	temperament
developmental cascade model	insecure resistant children	separation protest	tend and befriend
difficult child	pain cry	slow-to-warm-up child	triangular theory of love

key **people**

Mary Ainsworth	Erik Erikson	Kathleen McCartney	Robert J. Sternberg
John Bates	Harry Harlow	Cybelle Raver	Shelley Taylor
Ellen Berscheid	Cindy Hazan	Maryse Richards	Stella Thomas
John Bowlby	Jerome Kagan	Mary Rothbart	Ross Thompson
Joseph Campos	Kathryn Kerns	Carolyn Saarni	John Watson
Laura Carstensen	Reed Larson	Phillip Shaver	
Alexander Chess	Michael Lewis	Alan Sroufe	

chapter 11

THE SELF, IDENTITY, AND PERSONALITY

chapter outline

© Liz Von Hoene/Corbis

preview

Think about yourself for a few moments. Who are you? What are you like as a person? This chapter seeks to answer such questions by exploring the self, identity, and personality. We will examine these dimensions of people at different points in the life span, from infancy through late adulthood.

1 The Self — LG1 Discuss the main ways the self and understanding others are conceptualized and how they develop

Self-Understanding and Understanding Others

Self-Esteem and Self-Concept

Self-Regulation

What do we mean by the concepts of self, identity, and personality? Here are the definitions, and as you will see, there is considerable overlap among them:

· The **self** consists of all of the characteristics of a person.
· **Identity** is who a person is, representing a synthesis and integration of self-understanding.
· **Personality** refers to the enduring personal characteristics of individuals. Personality is usually viewed as the broadest of the three domains and as encompassing the other two (self and identity).

Theorists and researchers who focus on the self usually argue that the self is the central aspect of the individual's personality and that the self lends an integrative dimension to our understanding of different personality characteristics (Thompson, Winer, & Goodvin, 2011). Several aspects of the self have been studied more than others. These include self-understanding, self-esteem, and self-concept. Let's now turn our attention to how these aspects of the self develop across the life span.

When I say "I," I mean something absolutely unique and not to be confused with any other.

—Ugo Betti
Italian playwright, 20th century

SELF-UNDERSTANDING AND UNDERSTANDING OTHERS

What is self-understanding? **Self-understanding** is the cognitive representation of the self, the substance of self-conceptions. For example, an 11-year-old boy understands that he is a student, a boy, a football player, a family member, a video game lover, and a rock music fan. A 13-year-old girl understands that she is a middle school student, in the midst of puberty, a girl, a soccer player, a student council member, and a movie fan. Self-understanding is based, in part, on roles and membership categories (Harter, 2012, 2013). It provides the underpinnings for the development of identity. How does self-understanding develop across the life span?

Infancy Studying the self in infancy is difficult mainly because infants cannot tell us how they experience themselves. Infants cannot verbally express their views of the self. They also cannot understand complex instructions from researchers.

A rudimentary form of self-recognition—being attentive and positive toward one's image in a mirror—appears as early as 3 months of age (Mascolo & Fischer, 2007). However, a central, more complete index of self-recognition—the ability to recognize one's physical features—does not emerge until the second year (Thompson, 2006).

One ingenious strategy to test infants' visual self-recognition is the use of a mirror technique, in which first an infant's mother puts a dot of rouge on the infant's nose. Then an observer watches to see how often the infant touches its nose. Next, the infant is placed in front of a mirror, and observers detect whether nose touching increases. Why does this matter?

self All of the characteristics of a person.

identity Who a person is, representing a synthesis and integration of self-understanding.

personality The enduring personal characteristics of individuals.

self-understanding The individual's cognitive representation of the self, the substance of self-conceptions.

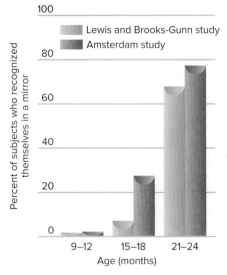

FIGURE 1

THE DEVELOPMENT OF SELF-RECOGNITION IN INFANCY. The graph shows the findings of two studies in which infants less than 1 year of age did not recognize themselves in the mirror. A slight increase in the percentage of infant self-recognition occurred around 15 to 18 months of age. By 2 years of age, a majority of children recognized themselves. *Why do researchers study whether infants recognize themselves in a mirror?*
© Digital Vision/Getty Images RF

The idea is that increased nose touching indicates that the infant recognizes the self in the mirror and is trying to touch or rub off the rouge because the rouge violates the infant's view of the self. Increased touching indicates that the infant realizes that it is the self in the mirror but that something is not right since the real self does not have a dot of rouge on it.

Figure 1 displays the results of two investigations that used the mirror technique. The researchers found that before they were 1 year old, infants did not recognize themselves in the mirror (Amsterdam, 1968; Lewis & Brooks-Gunn, 1979). Signs of self-recognition began to appear among some infants when they were 15 to 18 months old. By the time they were 2 years old, most children recognized themselves in the mirror. In sum, infants begin to develop a self-understanding called self-recognition at approximately 18 months of age (Hart & Karmel, 1996).

In one study, biweekly assessments from 15 to 23 months of age were conducted (Courage, Edison, & Howe, 2004). Self-recognition gradually emerged over this time, first appearing in the form of mirror recognition, followed by use of the personal pronoun "me" and then by recognizing a photo of themselves. These aspects of self-recognition are often referred to as the first indications of toddlers' understanding of the mental state of "me"—"that they are objects in their own mental representation of the world" (Lewis, 2005, p. 363).

Late in the second year and early in the third year, toddlers show other emerging forms of self-awareness that reflect a sense of "me" (Laible & Thompson, 2007). For example, they refer to themselves by saying "Me big"; they label internal experiences such as emotions; they monitor themselves, as when a toddler says, "Do it myself"; and they say that things are theirs (Bullock & Lutkenhaus, 1990; Fasig, 2000). One study revealed that it is not until the second year that infants develop a conscious awareness of their own bodies (Brownell & others, 2009). This developmental change in body awareness marks the beginning of children's representation of their own three-dimensional body shape and appearance, providing an early step in the development of their self-image and identity (Brownell, 2009).

The development of the self in infants and toddlers does not occur in a social vacuum (Thompson, 2015). Interactions with caregivers, older siblings, and others support the development of the self in infants and toddlers. Through labeling and describing physical aspects and internal states of infants and toddlers, these persons scaffold infants' and toddlers' self-development and understanding.

Early Childhood Recent research studies have revealed that young children are more psychologically aware—of themselves and others—than used to be thought (Thompson, 2015). This *self-awareness* reflects young children's expanding psychological sophistication.

Self-Understanding Because children can verbally communicate, research on self-understanding in childhood is not limited to visual self-recognition, as it is during infancy (Harter, 2012, 2013). Mainly through *interviews*, researchers have probed many aspects of children's self-understanding. Here are five main characteristics of self-understanding in young children:

· *Confusion of self, mind, and body.* Young children generally confuse self, mind, and body. Most young children conceive of the self as part of the body, which usually means the head. For them, the self can be described along many material dimensions, such as size, shape, and color.

· *Concrete descriptions.* Preschool children mainly think of themselves and define themselves in concrete terms. A young child might say, "I know my ABC's," "I can count," and "I live in a big house" (Harter, 2006). Although young children mainly describe themselves in terms of concrete, observable features and action tendencies, at about 4 to 5 years of age, as they hear others use psychological trait and emotion terms, they begin to include these in their own self-descriptions (Thompson, 2006). Thus, in a self-description, a 4-year-old might say, "I'm not scared. I'm always happy."

· *Physical descriptions.* Young children also distinguish themselves from others through many physical and material attributes. Says 4-year-old Sandra, "I'm different from Jennifer because I have brown hair and she has blond hair." Says 4-year-old Ralph, "I am different from Hank because I am taller, and I am different from my sister because I have a bicycle."

- *Active descriptions.* The active dimension is a central component of the self in early childhood. For example, preschool children often describe themselves in terms of activities such as play.

- *Unrealistic positive overestimations.* Self-evaluations during early childhood are often unrealistically positive and represent an overestimation of personal attributes (Harter, 2012, 2013). A young child might say, "I know all of my ABC's" but does not; or might comment, "I'm never scared," which is not the case. These unrealistic positive overestimations of the self occur because young children (1) have difficulty in differentiating their desired and actual competence, (2) cannot yet generate an ideal self that is distinguished from a real self, and (3) rarely engage in *social comparison*—exploring how they compare with others. Young children's self-evaluations also reflect an inability to recognize that they can possess opposite attributes, such as "good" and "bad" or "nice" and "mean" (Harter, 2006).

However, as in virtually all areas of human development, there are individual variations in young children's self-conceptions. In addition, there is increasing evidence that some children are vulnerable to negative self-attributions (Thompson, 2011). For example, one study revealed that insecurely attached preschool children whose mothers reported a high level of parenting stress and depressive symptoms had a lower self-concept than other young children in more positive family circumstances (Goodvin & others, 2008). This research indicates that young children's generally optimistic self-ascriptions do not buffer them from adverse, stressful family conditions.

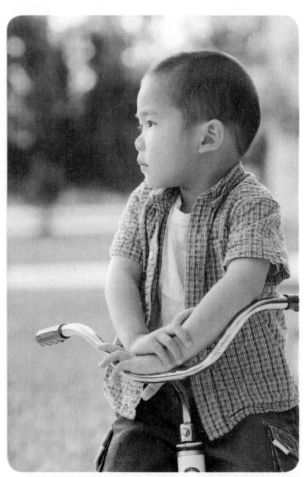

What characterizes young children's self-understanding?
© Kevin Dodge/Corbis

Understanding Others
Children also make advances in their understanding of others in infancy and early childhood (Carpendale & Lewis, 2015; Mills & Elashi, 2014; Rhodes & others, 2015; Thompson, 2014). As we saw in the chapter on "Information Processing," young children's theory of mind includes understanding that other people have emotions and desires. Recent research indicates that as early as 13 months of age, infants seem to consider another's perspective when predicting their actions (Choi & Luo, 2015).

At about 4 to 5 years, children not only start describing themselves in terms of psychological traits, but they also begin to perceive others in terms of psychological traits. Thus, a 4-year-old might say, "My teacher is nice."

An important part of children's socioemotional development is gaining an understanding that people don't always give accurate reports of their beliefs (Mills, 2013; Mills & Elashi, 2014). Researchers have found that even 4-year-olds understand that people may make statements that aren't true to obtain what they want or to avoid trouble (Lee & others, 2002). A recent study assessed preschool children's trust in the accuracy of an expert's comments (Landrum, Mills, & Johnston, 2013). In this study, in one condition, 5-year-olds trusted the expert's claim more than did 3-year-olds. However, in other conditions, preschoolers tended to trust a nice non-expert more than a mean expert, indicating that young children often are more likely to believe someone who is nice to them than someone who is an expert.

Both the extensive theory of mind research and the recent research on infants' and young children's social understanding underscore that they are not as egocentric as Piaget envisioned (Sokol, Snjezana, & Muller, 2010; Thompson, 2012). Piaget's concept of egocentrism has become so ingrained in people's thinking about young children that too often the current research on social awareness in infancy and early childhood has been overlooked. Research increasingly shows that young children are more socially sensitive and perceptive than previously envisioned, suggesting that parents and teachers can help them to better understand and interact in the social world by how they interact with them (Thompson, 2012, 2013). If young children are seeking to better understand various mental and emotional states

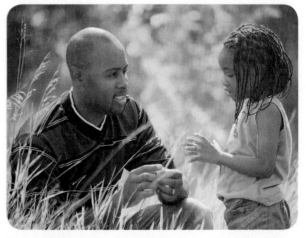

Young children are more psychologically aware of themselves and others than used to be thought. Some children are better than others at understanding people's feelings and desires, and to some degree, these individual differences are influenced by conversations caregivers have with young children about feelings and desires.
© Don Hammond/Design Pics/Corbis RF

(intentions, goals, feelings, desires) that they know underlie people's actions, then talking with them about these internal states can improve young children's understanding of them (Thompson, 2013).

However, there is ongoing debate about whether young children are socially sensitive or basically egocentric. Ross Thompson (2012, 2013) comes down on the side of viewing young children as socially sensitive, while Susan Harter (2012, 2013) argues that there is still evidence to support the conclusion that young children are essentially egocentric.

Whichever side is taken in this debate, it is important to underscore that social interactions and relationships with others contribute significantly to young children's development of the self and understanding of others. In Thompson's (2013) view, "When caregivers exuberantly applaud their child's accomplishments, focus their young child's attention on the consequences of misbehavior, acknowledge shared intentions, work to repair affective mismatches, or talk with their child about emotions, they act as *relational catalysts*, fostering the child's socioemotional growth and helping to refine the child's representations of who they are (and) what other people are like . . ." (p. 113).

Middle and Late Childhood   Children's self-understanding becomes more complex during middle and late childhood (Carpendale & Lewis, 2015). And their social understanding, especially in taking the perspective of others, also increases.

Self-Understanding   Five key changes characterize the increased complexity of children's self-understanding in middle and late childhood:

- *Psychological characteristics and traits.* In middle and late childhood, especially from 8 to 11 years of age, children increasingly describe themselves in terms of psychological characteristics and traits, in contrast with the more concrete self-descriptions of younger children. Older children are more likely to describe themselves as "*popular, nice, helpful, mean, smart,* and *dumb*" (Harter, 2006, p. 526).
- *Social descriptions.* In middle and late childhood, children begin to include social aspects such as references to social groups in their self-descriptions (Harter, 2006). For example, a child might describe herself as a Girl Scout, as a Catholic, or as someone who has two close friends.
- *Social comparison.* Children's self-understanding in middle and late childhood includes increasing reference to social comparison (Harter, 2006). That is, elementary-school-age children increasingly think about what they can do in comparison with others.
- *Real self and ideal self.* In middle and late childhood, children begin to distinguish between their real and ideal selves (Harter, 2006). This change involves differentiating their actual competencies from those they aspire to have and think are the most important.
  - *Realistic.* In middle and late childhood, children's self-evaluations become more realistic (Harter, 2006). This change may occur because of increased social comparison and perspective taking.

Understanding Others   **Perspective taking** is especially thought to be important in whether children develop prosocial or antisocial attitudes and behavior. In terms of prosocial behavior, taking another's perspective improves children's likelihood of understanding and sympathizing with others when they are distressed or in need. A recent study revealed that in children who were characterized as being emotionally reactive, good perspective-taking skills were linked to their ability to regain a neutral emotional state after being emotionally aroused (Bengtsson & Arvidsson, 2011). In this study, children who made gains in perspective-taking skills reduced their emotional reactivity over a two-year period.

Executive function is at work in perspective taking (Galinsky, 2010). Among the executive functions called on when young children engage in perspective taking are cognition inhibition (controlling one's own thoughts to consider the perspective of others) and cognitive flexibility (seeing situations in different ways).

developmental **connection**

Cognitive Processes

Executive function is an umbrella-like concept that encompasses a number of higher-level cognitive processes linked to the development of the brain's prefrontal cortex. Executive function involves managing one's thoughts to engage in goal-directed behavior and to exercise self-control. Connect to "Information Processing."

What are some changes in children's understanding of others in middle and late childhood?
© Paul Edmondson/Corbis

perspective taking The ability to assume another person's perspective and understand his or her thoughts and feelings.

In middle and late childhood, children become increasingly skeptical of some sources of information about psychological traits. A recent study of 6- to 9-year-olds revealed that older children were less trusting and more skeptical of others' distorted claims than were younger children (Mills & Elashi, 2014).

Adolescence   The development of self-understanding in adolescence is complex and involves a number of aspects of the self (Harter, 2012). The tendency to compare themselves with others continues to increase in the adolescent years. However, when asked whether they engage in social comparison, most adolescents deny it because they are aware that it is somewhat socially undesirable to do so.

Self-Understanding   Let's examine other ways in which the adolescent's self-understanding differs from the child's:

· *Abstract and idealistic thinking.* According to Piaget's theory of cognitive development, many adolescents begin thinking in more *abstract* and *idealistic* ways. When asked to describe themselves, adolescents are more likely than children to use abstract and idealistic labels. Consider 14-year-old Laurie's abstract description of herself: "I am a human being. I am indecisive. I don't know who I am." Also consider her idealistic description of herself: "I am a naturally sensitive person who really cares about people's feelings. I think I'm pretty good looking."

· *Self-consciousness.* Adolescents are more likely than children to be *self-conscious* about and preoccupied with their self-understanding. This self-consciousness and self-preoccupation reflect adolescent egocentrism.

· *Contradictions within the self.* As adolescents begin to differentiate their concept of the self into multiple roles in different relationship contexts, they sense potential contradictions between their differentiated selves (Harter, 2006, 2012). An adolescent might use this self-description: "I'm moody *and* understanding, ugly *and* attractive, bored *and* inquisitive, caring *and* uncaring, and introverted *and* fun-loving" (Harter, 1986). Young adolescents tend to view these opposing characteristics as contradictory, which can cause internal conflict. However, older adolescents and emerging adults begin to understand that an individual can possess opposing characteristics and to integrate these opposing self-labels into their emerging identity (Harter, 2006, 2012).

· *The fluctuating self.* The adolescent's self-understanding fluctuates across situations and across time (Harter, 2006). The adolescent's self continues to be characterized by instability until the adolescent constructs a more unified theory of self, usually not until late adolescence or even early adulthood.

· *Real and ideal selves.* The adolescent's emerging ability to construct ideal selves in addition to actual ones can be perplexing and agonizing to the adolescent. In one view, an important aspect of the ideal or imagined self is the possible self—what individuals might become, what they would like to become, and what they are afraid of becoming (Markus & Kitayama, 2010, 2012; Markus & Nurius, 1986). Thus, adolescents' **possible selves** include both what adolescents hope to be and what they dread they will become (Lee & others, 2015; Pierce, Schmidt, & Stoddard, 2015). The attributes of future positive selves (getting into a good college, being admired, having a successful career) can direct future positive states. The attributes of future negative selves (being unemployed, being lonely, not getting into a good college) can identify what is to be avoided. A recent study of adolescents in Hong Kong found that those reporting pragmatic support ("If I need to know something about the world, I can ask my parents," for example) had possible selves that were focused more on career and school, and they were more likely to think they could attain their hoped-for possible selves and avoid their feared possible selves (Zhu & others, 2015).

How does self-understanding change in adolescence?
© Image Source/Getty Images RF

developmental **connection**

Cognitive Theory

In Piaget's fourth stage of cognitive development, thought becomes more abstract, idealistic, and logical. Connect to "Cognitive Developmental Approaches."

What characterizes adolescents' possible selves?
© Stockbyte/PictureQuest RF

possible selves What adolescents hope to become as well as what they dread they will become.

What are some important aspects of social understanding in adolescence?
© SW Productions/Getty Images RF

Know thyself, for once we know ourselves, we may learn how to care for ourselves, but otherwise we never shall.

—SOCRATES
Greek philosopher, 5th century B.C.

What characterizes self-awareness and possible selves in young adults?
© Gareth Brown/Corbis

· *Self-integration.* In late adolescence and emerging adulthood, self-understanding becomes more integrative, with the disparate parts of the self more systematically pieced together (Harter, 2006, 2012, 2013). Older adolescents and emerging adults are more likely to detect inconsistencies in their earlier self-descriptions as they attempt to construct a general theory of self, an integrated sense of identity.

Understanding Others   Of course, becoming a competent adolescent involves not only understanding one's self but also understanding others. Among the aspects of understanding others that are important in adolescent development are perceiving others' traits, understanding multiple perspectives, and monitoring their social world.

As adolescence proceeds, teenagers develop a more sophisticated understanding of others. They come to understand that other people are complex and have public and private faces (Harter, 2006, 2012).

According to Robert Selman (1980), developmental changes in perspective taking begin with the egocentric viewpoint in early childhood and end with in-depth perspective taking in adolescence. Only recently has research on perspective taking in adolescence taken hold. Following are the results of two recent research investigations on this topic:

· In sixth through eighth grades, girls engaged in more social perspective taking than did boys (R. Smith, 2009; Smith & Rose, 2011) but they also experienced more empathic distress by taking on their friend's distress as their own than did boys.

· A lower level of perspective taking was linked to increased relational aggression (intentionally harming someone through strategies such as spreading vicious rumors) one year later in middle school students (Batanova & Loukas, 2011).

In the chapter titled "Intelligence," you read that an important cognitive activity in metacognition is cognitive monitoring, which can also be very helpful in social situations. As part of their increased awareness of themselves and others, adolescents monitor their social world more extensively than they did when they were children. Adolescents engage in a number of social cognitive monitoring activities on virtually a daily basis. For example, an adolescent might think, "I would like to get to know this guy better but he is not very open. Maybe I can talk to some other students about what he is like." Another adolescent might check incoming information about a club or a clique to determine if it is consistent with her impressions of the club or clique. Yet another adolescent might question someone or paraphrase what the person has just said about her feelings to make sure that he has accurately understood them. Adolescents' ability to monitor their social world may be an important aspect of their social maturity (Flavell, 1979).

Adulthood   As individuals move into the traditional college-age years and make the transition from adolescence to adulthood, they begin to engage in more self-reflection about what they want to do with their lives. The extended schooling that takes place in developed countries like the United States and Japan provides time for further self-reflection and understanding of one's self.

Self-Awareness   An aspect of self-understanding that becomes especially important in early adulthood is *self-awareness*—that is, the degree to which a young adult is aware of his or her psychological makeup, including strengths and weaknesses. Many individuals do not have very good awareness of their psychological makeup and skills, as well as the causes of their weaknesses (Hull, 2012). For example, how aware is the person that she or he is a good or bad listener, uses the best strategies to solve personal problems, and is assertive rather than aggressive or passive in resolving conflicts? Awareness of strengths and weaknesses in these and many other aspects of life is an important dimension of self-understanding throughout the adult years, and early adulthood is a time when individuals can benefit considerably from addressing some of their weaknesses.

Possible Selves   Another aspect of self-understanding that is important in the adult years involves possible selves (Markus & Kitayama, 2012). Recall that possible selves are what individuals might become, what they would like to become, and what they are afraid of becoming (Bolkan, Hooker, & Coehlo, 2015; Frazier & others, 2012; Hamman & others, 2013). Adults in their twenties mention many possible selves that they would like to become and might become. Some of these are unrealistic, such as being happy all of the time and being very rich. As individuals get older, they often describe fewer possible selves and portray them in more concrete and realistic ways. By middle age, individuals frequently describe their possible selves in terms of areas of their life in which they already have performed, such as "being good at my work" or "having a good marriage" (Cross & Markus, 1991). Also, when some individuals are middle-aged adults, their possible selves center on attaining hoped-for selves, such as acquiring material possessions, but when they become older adults, they are more concerned with maintaining what they have and preventing or avoiding health problems and dependency (J. Smith, 2009).

Many individuals continue to revise their possible selves as they go through the adult years (Bolkan & Hooker, 2012; Frazier & others, 2012). This ability to revise possible selves and adapt them to find a better match between desired and achieved goals may be an important aspect of maintaining positive self-esteem and psychological well-being as individuals get older (Bengtson, Reedy, & Gordon, 1985).

Life Review Another important aspect of self-understanding in adult-hood is the *life review*. Life review is prominent in Erikson's final stage of psychosocial development, which is integrity versus despair. Life review involves looking back at one's life experiences, evaluating them, interpreting them, and often reinterpreting them. As the past marches in review, the older adult surveys it, observes it, and reflects on it. Reconsideration of previous experiences and their meaning occurs, often with revision or expanded understanding taking place. This reorganization of the past may provide a more valid picture for the individual, bringing new and significant meaning to one's life. It may also help prepare the individual for death and in the process reduce fear.

What characterizes a life review in late adulthood?
© Corbis RF

One aspect of life review involves identifying and reflecting on not only the positive aspects of one's life but also on regrets as part of developing a mature wisdom and self-understanding (Korte & others, 2014; Randall, 2013). The hope is that by examining not only the positive aspects of one's life but also what an individual has regretted doing, a more accurate vision of the complexity of one's life and possibly increased life satisfaction will be attained (King & Hicks, 2007).

Although thinking about regrets can be helpful as part of a life review, recent research indicates that it is important for older adults to not dwell on regrets, especially since opportunities to undo regrettable actions decline with age (Suri & Gross, 2012). One study revealed that an important characteristic of older adults who showed a higher level of emotion regulation and successful aging was reduced responsiveness to regrets (Brassen & others, 2012).

Some clinicians use *reminiscence therapy* with their older clients, which involves discussing past activities and experiences with another individual or group (Blake, 2013; Fujiwara & others, 2012). The therapy may include the use of photographs, familiar items, and video/audio recordings. Researchers have found that reminiscence therapy improves the mood of older adults, including those with dementia (Subramaniam & Woods, 2012). A recent study with older adults who had dementia found that reminiscence therapy reduced their depressive symptoms and improved their self-acceptance and positive relations with others (Gonzalez & others, 2015). Also, a study with elderly institutionalized adults found that 8 weeks of group reminiscence therapy resulted in increased self-esteem, life satisfaction, and psychological well-being, and reduced depression (Melendez-Moral & others, 2013). And a recent meta-analysis of 128 studies found that reminiscence interventions made moderate improvements in integrity (as Erikson conceived it) and depression (Pinquart & Forstmeier, 2012). Smaller effects occurred for purpose in life, preparing for death, mastery, positive well-being, social integration, and cognitive performance. The largest improvements were made for depressive symptoms in depressed individuals and persons with chronic physical disease. Further, in a recent study, a variation of reminiscence therapy called *instrumental* reminiscence therapy (recalling the times one coped with stressful circumstances and analyzing what it took to adapt in those contexts) improved the adaptive ability and resilience of older adults in coping

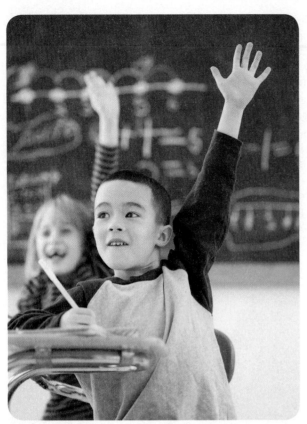

How is self-esteem related to school performance?
© Corbis RF

with adverse situations (Meléndez & others, 2015). In another version of reminiscence therapy, *attachment-focused* reminiscence therapy reduced depressive symptoms, perceived stress, and emergency room visits in older African Americans (Sabir & others, 2015).

Successful aging, though, doesn't mean thinking about the past all of the time. In one study, older adults who were obsessed about the past were not as well adjusted as older adults who integrated their past and present (Wong & Watt, 1991).

SELF-ESTEEM AND SELF-CONCEPT

High self-esteem and a positive self-concept are important characteristics of children's and adults' well-being (Baumeister, 2013; Hale & others, 2015; Kernis, 2013; Park & Park, 2015).

Self-esteem refers to global evaluations of the self. Self-esteem is also referred to as *self-worth*, or *self-image*. For example, a person may perceive that she or he is not merely a person but a *good* person. Of course, not all people have an overall positive image of themselves. **Self-concept** refers to domain-specific evaluations of the self. Individuals can make self-evaluations in many domains of their lives—academic, athletic, appearance, and so on. In sum, *self-esteem* refers to global self-evaluations, *self-concept* to domain-specific evaluations (Harter, 2006, 2012).

Investigators sometimes use the terms *self-esteem* and *self-concept* interchangeably and don't always precisely define them. However, the distinction between self-esteem as global self-evaluation and self-concept as domain-specific self-evaluation should help you keep the terms straight.

The foundations of self-esteem and self-concept emerge from the quality of parent-child interaction in infancy and early childhood. Children with high self-esteem are more likely to be securely attached to their parents and to have parents who engage in sensitive caregiving (Thompson, 2011, 2015).

Issues in Self-Esteem   What are the consequences of low self-esteem? Low self-esteem has been implicated in overweight and obesity, anxiety, depression, suicide, and delinquency (O'Brien, Bartoletti, & Leitzel, 2013; Zeigler-Hill, 2013). A recent study revealed that youth with low self-esteem had lower life satisfaction at 30 years of age (Birkeland & others, 2012).

Is self-esteem related to school and adult job performance? There are "only modest correlations between school performance and self-esteem, and these correlations do not indicate that high self-esteem causes good performance" (Baumeister & others, 2003, p. 1). Attempts to increase students' self-esteem have not produced improvements in academic performance (Davies & Brember, 1999).

In some studies, adult job performance is linked to self-esteem, but the correlations vary greatly and the direction of the causation is not clear (Baumeister & others, 2003). Occupational success might lead to higher self-esteem, but the opposite might occur.

Is self-esteem related to happiness? Self-esteem is strongly related to happiness, and it seems likely that high self-esteem increases happiness, whereas depression lowers it (Baumeister & others, 2003; Van Voorhees & others, 2008).

Is self-esteem related to physical appearance? Self-esteem is related to perceived physical appearance. For example, researchers have found that in adolescence, global self-esteem is correlated more strongly with physical appearance than with scholastic competence, social acceptance, behavioral conduct, and athletic competence (Harter, 1999) (see Figure 2). This association between perceived physical appearance and self-esteem is not confined to adolescence but holds across the life span from early childhood through middle age (Harter, 1999, 2006).

Is low self-esteem linked to depression? A large number of studies have found that individuals with low self-esteem report that they feel more depressed than individuals with high self-esteem (Baumeister & others, 2003). A recent study revealed that low and decreasing self-esteem in adolescence was linked to adult depression two decades later (Steiger &

self-esteem The global evaluative dimension of the self. Self-esteem is also referred to as self-worth or self-image.

self-concept Domain-specific evaluations of the self.

others, 2014). Low self-esteem has also been implicated in suicide attempts and anorexia nervosa (Brockmeyer & others, 2013; Fulginiti & Brekke, 2015; Kleiman & Riskind, 2013).

Does self-esteem in adolescence foreshadow adjustment and competence in adulthood? A New Zealand longitudinal study assessed self-esteem at 11, 13, and 15 years of age and adjustment and competence of the same individuals when they were 26 years old (Trzesniewski & others, 2006). The results revealed that adults characterized by poorer mental and physical health, worse economic prospects, and higher levels of criminal behavior were more likely to have had low self-esteem in adolescence than their better-adjusted, more competent adult counterparts.

An important point needs to be made about much of the research on self-esteem: It is correlational rather than experimental. Correlation does not equal causation. Thus, if a correlational study finds an association between self-esteem and depression, it could be equally likely that depression causes low self-esteem or that low self-esteem causes depression. A recent longitudinal study explored whether self-esteem is a cause or consequence of social support in youth (Marshall & others, 2014). In this study, self-esteem predicted subsequent changes in social support, but social support did not predict subsequent changes in self-esteem.

Developmental Changes Self-esteem fluctuates across the life span (Trzesniewski, Donnellan, & Robins, 2013). One cross-sectional study assessed the self-esteem of a very large, diverse sample of 326,641 individuals ranging from 9 to 90 years of age (Robins & others, 2002). About two-thirds of the participants were from the United States. The individuals were asked to respond to the statement "I have high self-esteem" on a scale from 1 to 5 with 1 meaning "strongly agree" and 5 meaning "strongly disagree." This research focused on both (a) developmental changes, and (b) gender differences. Self-esteem decreased in adolescence, increased in the twenties, leveled off in the thirties, rose in the fifties and sixties, and then dropped in the seventies and eighties (see Figure 3). In most age periods, the self-esteem of males was higher than the self-esteem of females. Let's now explore developmental changes in self-esteem in more detail.

Childhood and Adolescence Researchers have found that the accuracy of self-evaluations increases across the elementary school years (Harter, 2006, 2012). Young children tend to provide inflated views of themselves, but by about 8 years of age most children give more realistic appraisals of their skills (Harter, 2006). For example, older elementary school children who report a positive self-image of themselves in sports indeed are the ones who are reported by peers to be good at athletics.

Domain	Harter's U.S. Samples	Other Countries
Physical appearance	.65	.62
Scholastic competence	.48	.41
Social acceptance	.46	.40
Behavioral conduct	.45	.45
Athletic competence	.33	.30

FIGURE 2

CORRELATIONS BETWEEN GLOBAL SELF-ESTEEM AND DOMAINS OF COMPETENCE. *Note:* The correlations shown are the average correlations computed across a number of studies. The other countries in this evaluation were England, Ireland, Australia, Canada, Germany, Italy, Greece, the Netherlands, and Japan. Correlation coefficients can range from −1.00 to +1.00. The correlations between physical appearance and global self-esteem (.65 and .62) are moderately high.

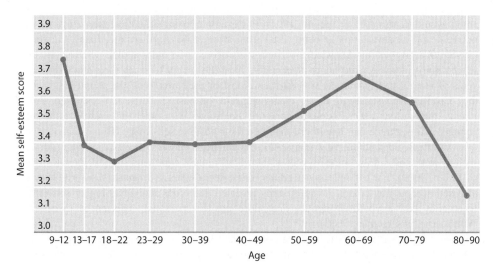

FIGURE 3

SELF-ESTEEM ACROSS THE LIFE SPAN. One cross-sectional study found that self-esteem was high in childhood, dropped in adolescence, increased through early and middle adulthood, then dropped in the seventies and eighties (Robins & others, 2002). More than 300,000 individuals were asked the extent to which they have high self-esteem on a 5-point scale, with 5 being "Strongly Agree" and 1 being "Strongly Disagree."

How does self-esteem change in adolescence?
© Ariel Skelley/Blend Images/Corbis RF

Adolescents in general have long been described as having low self-esteem (Robins & others, 2002). However, the majority of adolescents actually have a positive self-image. In an extensive cross-cultural study, Daniel Offer and his colleagues (1988) sampled the self-images of adolescents around the world—in the United States, Australia, Bangladesh, Hungary, Israel, Italy, Japan, Taiwan, Turkey, and West Germany. Almost three-fourths of the adolescents had a healthy self-image.

Some researchers note that gender differences in self-esteem emerge by early adolescence, and these were found in the study just described (Robins & others, 2002). Girls and boys enter first grade with roughly equivalent levels of self-esteem. Yet some research studies have shown that by the middle school years girls' self-esteem is significantly lower than boys' (American Association of University Women, 1992). For example, one study confirmed that male adolescents have higher self-esteem than do female adolescents (McLean & Breen, 2009). A recent study found that preexisting gender differences in self-esteem (higher in males) narrowed between the ninth and twelfth grades (Falci, 2012). In this study, adolescents from higher-SES backgrounds had higher self-esteem than did their lower-SES counterparts.

However, other researchers caution that the self-esteem of girls is only slightly lower than boys' and still in the positive range (Harter, 2006, 2012, 2013; Kling & others, 1999). Researchers also have found that after age 13, girls' self-esteem increases through the remainder of adolescence and in emerging adulthood (Baldwin & Hoffman, 2002).

A current concern is that too many of today's college students grew up receiving empty praise and as a consequence have inflated self-esteem (Graham, 2005; Stipek, 2005). Too often they were given praise for performance that was mediocre or even poor. When they are in college, they may have difficulty handling competition and criticism. The title of a book, *Dumbing Down Our Kids: Why American Children Feel Good About Themselves But Can't Read, Write, or Add* (Sykes, 1995), vividly captures the theme that many U.S. children's academic problems stem from receiving unmerited praise as part of an effort to prop up their self-esteem. In a series of studies, researchers found that inflated praise, although well intended, may cause children with low self-esteem to avoid important learning experiences such as tackling challenging tasks (Brummelman & others, 2014). And a recent study found that narcissistic parents especially overvalue their children's talents (Brummelman & others, 2015).

Adulthood   Are there differences in the self-esteem of young, middle-aged, and older adults? In the self-esteem study described earlier, self-esteem dropped in late adulthood (Robins & others, 2002). However, some researchers have not found any differences in self-esteem across the age periods of adulthood (McGue, Hirsch, & Lykken, 1993).

Given that older adults have more physical problems, why wouldn't they have lower self-esteem than young or middle-aged adults? One possible reason is that many older adults don't interpret their "losses" as negatively, and don't become as emotionally upset, as younger adults would (Carstensen & Freund, 1994). For example, being asked to retire at age 63 may not be nearly as devastating as being fired from a job at 40. Furthermore, Laura Carstensen (1998, 2008) argues that knowledge-related goals decrease in older adults, whereas emotion-related goals increase. And many older adults have the ability to reach their emotion-related goals of honing their social network to spend most of their time with the people with whom they have enjoyed satisfying close relationships in the past (Scheibe & Carstensen, 2010). Finally, many older adults choose to compare themselves with other older adults rather than younger adults, which can help them maintain their positive self-image (Brandstädter, 1999).

Although older adults may derive self-esteem from earlier successes in some domains such as work and family, some aspects of their lives require continued support for self-esteem (J. Smith, 2009). For example, older adults' self-esteem benefits when they are told they are nice and accepted by others. A recent study revealed that older adults had higher self-esteem when they had a youthful identity and more positive personal experiences (Westerhof, Whitbourne, & Freeman, 2012).

Why might self-esteem decline for some older adults? Explanations include deteriorating physical health and negative societal attitudes toward older adults, although these factors were

Even when older adults have physical problems, other aspects of their lives, such as spending time with people whose company they enjoy, can help to buffer any decline in their self-esteem.
© Norbert Schaefer/Corbis

not examined in the large-scale study just described. Researchers have found that in late adulthood, being widowed, institutionalized, or physically impaired, having a low religious commitment, and experiencing a decline in health are linked to low self-esteem (Giarrusso & Bengtson, 2007).

Strategies for Increasing Self-Esteem   What are some good strategies for increasing self-esteem? Five ways to improve self-esteem are (1) identify the causes of low self-esteem and the domains of competence important to the self, (2) provide emotional support and opportunities for social approval, (3) take responsibility for one's own self-esteem, (4) achieve goals, and (5) develop effective coping strategies.

Identifying sources of self-esteem—that is, competence in domains important to the self—is critical to improving self-esteem (Harter, 2012). Susan Harter (1990) points out that the self-esteem enhancement programs of the 1970s and 1980s, in which self-esteem itself was the target and individuals were encouraged to simply feel good about themselves, were ineffective. Rather, Harter notes that intervention must occur at the level of the *causes* of self-esteem if the individual's self-esteem is to improve significantly. Individuals have the highest self-esteem when they perform competently in domains that are important to them. Therefore, people should be encouraged to identify and value areas of competence.

Emotional support and social approval also powerfully influence self-esteem. Some children with low self-esteem come from conflicted families or conditions in which they experienced abuse or neglect—situations in which support was unavailable. In some cases, alternative sources of support can be implemented either informally through the encouragement of a teacher, a coach, or another significant adult or, more formally through programs such as Big Brothers and Big Sisters. As peer approval becomes increasingly important during adolescence, peer support is an important influence on the adolescent's self-esteem.

Developing self-confidence and believing that one has the ability to do what it takes to improve self-esteem are other good strategies. Although it is helpful to have the social support and emotional approval of others, it is also very important to take the initiative to increase one's own self-esteem.

Achievement can also improve an individual's self-esteem (Baumeister, 2013; Mruk & O'Brien, 2013). For example, self-esteem can be enhanced by the straightforward teaching of skills to individuals. People develop higher self-esteem when they know how to carry out the important tasks to accomplish goals and they realize that by carrying out these tasks they are more likely to reach their goals.

Self-esteem often increases when individuals face a problem and try to cope with it rather than avoid it (Frydenberg, 2008). When coping prevails, the individual often faces problems realistically, honestly, and nondefensively. This process leads to favorable self-evaluative thoughts, which then lead to self-generated approval and higher self-esteem. The converse is true of low self-esteem. Unfavorable self-evaluations trigger denial, deception, and avoidance in an attempt to disavow that which has already been glimpsed as true. This process leads to self-generated disapproval as a form of feedback to the self about personal inadequacy.

The living self has one purpose only: to come into its own fullness of being, as a tree comes into full blossom, or a bird into spring beauty, or a tiger into luster.

—**D. H. LAWRENCE**
English author, 20th century

How can parents help children develop higher self-esteem?
© Masterfile RF

SELF-REGULATION

Self-regulation involves the ability to control one's behavior without having to rely on others' help. Self-regulation includes the self-generation and cognitive monitoring of thoughts, feelings, and behaviors in order to reach a goal. An individual might develop better self-control in the physical, cognitive, or socioemotional domain than in other domains.

Throughout most of the life span, individuals who engage in self-regulation are better achievers and are more satisfied with their lives than their counterparts who let external factors dominate their lives (Eisenberg & others, 2014; McClelland & others, 2015). For example, researchers have found that, compared with low-achieving students, high-achieving students engage in greater self-regulation. They do this by setting more specific learning goals, using more strategies to learn and adapt, self-monitoring more, and more systematically evaluating their progress toward a goal (Schunk, Meece, & Pintrich, 2014; Wigfield & others, 2015).

self-regulation The ability to control one's behavior without having to rely on others for help.

Infancy and Early Childhood   In the chapter on "Emotional Development and Attachment" we discussed the importance of children learning to regulate their emotions as they develop. Emotion regulation is an important aspect of the overall development of self-regulation (Thompson, 2014, 2015). How do other aspects of self-regulation develop? Claire Kopp (1982, 1987, 2008) described a developmental process that begins early in life. Initially, beginning at about 12 to 18 months of age, infants depend completely on their caregivers for reminder signals about acceptable behaviors. At this age, infants begin to show compliance with caregivers' demands. For example, a parent might say, "No. Don't touch!" And the infant doesn't touch.

The next phase of developing self-regulation takes place at approximately 2 to 3 years of age. At this point, children begin to comply with the caregiver's expectations in the absence of external monitoring by the caregiver. Thus, most 2- to 3-year-old children are aware of where they may and may not play and which objects they may and may not touch if they are at home, on a playground, or in the homes of friends and relatives.

Nonetheless, at these young ages, there are clear limitations on self-regulation (Easterbrooks & others, 2013; Thompson, 2015). Given a strong stimulus, such as a ball rolling down the street or the motivation to explore an interesting place, toddlers often ignore safety and disregard exhortations. Also, only rudimentary aspects of delaying gratification are present at these early ages. For example, when 2-year-olds are confronted with an unexpected delay (such as not being able to go outside and play), they often whine and beg to engage in the activity. But there are clear signs of advances in self-initiated regulation, as when young children announce a toy cleanup without prompting from caregivers.

Preschoolers become better at self-control, learning how to resist temptation and giving themselves instructions that keep them focused (Thompson, 2006, 2015). Thus, toward the end of the preschool years, children might say to themselves, "No. I can't do that. I'm working," in response to a temptation to stop working and do something else, like play with an attractive toy.

Middle/Late Childhood and Adolescence   One of the most important aspects of the self in middle and late childhood is the increased capacity for self-regulation (Veenman, 2011). This increased capacity is characterized by deliberate efforts to manage one's behavior, emotions, and thoughts that lead to increased social competence and achievement (Winne & Nesbit, 2010). In a recent study, higher levels of self-control assessed at 4 years of age were linked to improvements in the math and reading achievement of early-elementary-school children living in predominantly rural and low-income contexts (Blair & others, 2015). Also, one study revealed that children from low-income families who had a higher level of self-regulation made better grades in school than their counterparts who had a lower level of self-regulation (Buckner, Mezzacappa, & Beardslee, 2009). Another study found that self-control increased from 4 to 10 years of age and that high self-control was linked to lower levels of deviant behavior (Vazsonyi & Huang, 2010). And a recent study of almost 17,000 3- to 7-year-old children revealed that self-regulation was a protective factor for children growing up in low socioeconomic (SES) conditions (Flouri, Midouhas, & Joshi, 2014). In this study, 7-year-old children with low self-regulation living in low-SES conditions had more emotional problems than their 3-year-old counterparts. Thus, low self-regulation was linked to an increase in low-SES children's emotional problems over time.

The increased capacity for self-regulation is linked to developmental advances in the brain's prefrontal cortex (Diamond, 2013). Increased focal activation in the prefrontal cortex is linked to improved cognitive control. Such cognitive control includes self-regulation.

Few studies of self-regulation have focused on adolescents. On the one hand, advances in cognitive skills (logical thinking, for example), increased introspection, and the greater independence of adolescence might lead to increased self-control. Also, advances in cognitive abilities provide adolescents with a better understanding of the importance of delaying gratification in exchange for something desirable (such as a good grade in a class) rather than seeking immediate gratification (listening to music rather than studying). On the other hand,

developmental connection

Information Processing

Cognitive control (inhibition and flexibility) increases from childhood through early adulthood. Connect to "Information Processing."

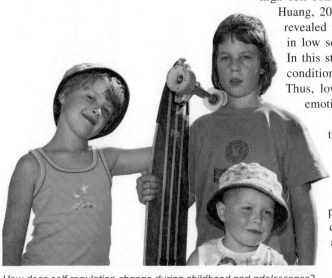

How does self-regulation change during childhood and adolescence?
© Roy Botterell/Corbis

an increased sense of invincibility (which can lead to risk taking), impulsiveness, and social comparison might produce less self-control.

A key component of self-regulation is engaging in *effortful control*, which involves inhibiting impulses and not engaging in destructive behavior, focusing and maintaining attention despite distractions, and initiating and completing tasks that have long-term value, even if they may seem unpleasant (Bates & Pettit, 2015). A recent study found that effortful control at 17 years of age predicted academic persistence and educational attainment at 23 to 25 years of age (Veronneau & others, 2014). In this study, effortful control was just as strong a predictor of educational attainment as were parents' education and past grade point average.

Some researchers emphasize the early development of self-regulation in childhood and adolescence as a key contributor to adult health and even longevity (Drake, Belsky, & Fearon, 2014; Reiss, Eccles, & Nielsen, 2014; Wigfield & others, 2015). For example, Nancy Eisenberg and her colleagues (2014) concluded that research indicates self-regulation fosters conscientiousness later in life, both directly and through its link to academic motivation/success and internalized compliance with norms.

Adulthood Self-control plays an important role in adult development (Bertrand, Graham, & Lachman, 2013). For example, higher levels of self-control are linked to better health and adjustment (Friedman & others, 2014; Reiss, Eccles, & Nielsen, 2014).

Self-control increases in early and middle adulthood (Gatz & Karel, 1993). Researchers have found a decline in perceived self-control of health and cognitive functioning in older adults (Bertrand, Graham, & Lachman, 2013; Bertrand & Lachman, 2003).

Although older adults are aware of age-related losses, most still effectively maintain a sense of self-control. Recent research indicates that self-control plays an important role in older adults' quality of life, including lower levels of depression and obesity (Levasseur & Couture, 2015; Privitera & others, 2015). The negative effects of age-typical problems, such as a decline in physical and cognitive skills and an increase in illness, may be buffered by a flexible, accommodating control style (Brandstädter & Renner, 1990).

Selective optimization with compensation theory states that successful aging is linked with three main factors: selection, optimization, and compensation (SOC). The theory states that individuals can produce new resources and allocate them effectively to tasks they want to master (Baltes & Smith, 2008; Freund, Nikitin, & Riediger, 2013; Hahn & Lachman, 2015; Martin & others, 2015).

Selection, optimization, and compensation involve the following:

· *Selection* is based on the concept that older adults have a reduced capacity and a loss of functioning, which require a reduction in performance in most life domains such as memory and physical skills.

· *Optimization* suggests that it is possible to maintain performance in some areas through continued practice and the use of new technologies. Examples might include doing crossword puzzles to maintain memory skills and exercising to optimize strength.

· *Compensation* becomes relevant when life tasks require a level of capacity beyond the current level of the older adult's performance potential. Older adults especially need to compensate in circumstances that impose high mental or physical demands, such as when thinking about and memorizing new material very rapidly, reacting quickly when driving a car, or running fast. When older adults develop an illness, the need for compensation increases.

According to selective optimization with compensation theory, what characterizes successful aging?
© Ariel Skelly/Blend Images/Getty Images RF

Selective optimization with compensation theory was proposed by Paul Baltes and his colleagues (Baltes, 2003; Baltes, Lindenberger, & Staudinger, 2006). They described the life of the pianist Arthur Rubinstein (1887–1982) to illustrate their theory. When he was interviewed at 80 years of age, Rubinstein said that three factors were responsible for his ability to maintain his status as an admired concert pianist into old age. First,

selective optimization with compensation theory The theory that successful aging is related to three factors: selection, optimization, and compensation.

Strategies for Effectively Engaging in Selective Optimization with Compensation

What are some good strategies that aging adults can use to attain selective optimization with compensation? According to Paul Baltes and his colleagues (Baltes, Lindenberger, & Staudinger, 2006; Freund & Baltes, 2002), the following strategies are likely to be effective:

Selection Strategies

- Focus on the most important goal at a particular time.
- Think about what you want in life, and commit yourself to one or two major goals.
- Realize that to reach a particular goal, you may need to abandon other goals.

Optimization Strategies

- Keep working on what you have planned until you are successful.
- Persevere until you reach your goal.

- When you want to achieve something, understand that you may need to wait until the right moment arrives.

Compensation

- When things don't go the way they used to, search for other ways to achieve what you want.
- If things don't go well for you, be willing to let others help you.
- When things don't go as well as in the past, keep trying other ways until you can achieve results that are similar to what you accomplished earlier in your life.

Which of the selection, optimization, and compensation strategies have you used? Which of the strategies would you benefit from using more?

---

he mastered the weakness of old age by reducing the scope of his performances and playing fewer pieces (which reflects selection). Second, he spent more time at practice than he had spent earlier in his life (which reflects optimization). Third, he used special strategies, such as slowing down before fast segments, thus creating the image of faster playing (which reflects compensation).

The process of selective optimization with compensation is likely to be effective whenever people pursue successful outcomes (Hutchinson & Nimrod, 2012; Freund, Nikitin, & Riediger, 2013). What makes SOC attractive to researchers in aging is that it makes explicit how individuals can manage and adapt to losses. By using SOC, they can continue to lead satisfying lives, although in a more restricted manner. Loss is a common dimension of old age, although there are wide variations in the nature of the losses involved. Because of these individual variations, the specific form of selection, optimization, and compensation will likely vary depending on the person's life history, pattern of interests, values, health, skills, and resources. To read about some strategies for effectively engaging in selective optimization with compensation, see the *Connecting Development to Life* interlude.

In Baltes' view (2003; Baltes & Smith, 2008), the selection of domains and life priorities is an important aspect of development. Life goals and priorities likely vary across the life course for most people. For many individuals, it is not just the sheer attainment of goals, but rather the attainment of *meaningful* goals, that makes life satisfying. In one study, younger adults were more likely to assess their well-being in terms of accomplishments and careers, whereas older adults were more likely to link well-being with good health and the ability to accept change. In addition, emotion-related goals become increasingly important for older adults (Carstensen, Smith, & Jaworksi, 2015; Carstensen & others, 2011).

In one cross-sectional study, the personal life investments of 25- to 105-year-olds were assessed (Staudinger, 1996) (see Figure 4). From 25 to 34 years of age, participants said that they personally invested more time in work, friends, family, and independence, in that order. From 35 to 54 and 55 to 65 years of age, family became more important to them than friends in terms of their personal investment. Little changed in the rank ordering of persons 70 to 84 years old, but for participants 85 to 105 years old, health became the most important personal investment. Thinking about life showed up for the first time on the most important list for those who were 85 to 105 years old.

25 to 34 Years	35 to 54 Years	55 to 65 Years	70 to 84 Years	85 to 105 Years
Work	Family	Family	Family	Health
Friends	Work	Health	Health	Family
Family	Friends	Friends	Cognitive fitness	Thinking about life
Independence	Cognitive fitness	Cognitive fitness	Friends	Cognitive fitness

FIGURE 4

DEGREE OF PERSONAL LIFE INVESTMENT AT DIFFERENT POINTS IN LIFE. Shown here are the top four domains of personal life investment at different points in life. The highest degree of investment is listed at the top (for example, work was the highest personal investment from 25 to 34 years of age, family from 35 to 84, and health from 85 to 105).

(left to right): © Ryan McVay/Getty Images RF; © image100/PunchStock RF; © Image Source/Getty Images RF; © Ned Frisk Photography/ Corbis RF; © Image Source/Getty Images RF

Review *Connect* Reflect

LG1 Discuss the main ways the self and understanding others are conceptualized and how they develop

Review

- How can the terms *self, identity,* and *personality* be defined? What is self-understanding, and how does it develop? How does understanding others develop?
- What are self-esteem and self-concept, and how do they develop? How is self-esteem related to performance, initiative, and happiness? Is there a dark side to high self-esteem? What are some ways to increase self-esteem?
- What is self-regulation, and how does it develop?

Connect

- How might the life reflection of older adults differ from the life reflection of individuals in middle adulthood?

Reflect *Your Own Personal Journey of Life*

- If a psychologist had interviewed you when you were 8 years old, 14 years old, and again today, would your self-understanding and self-esteem have been different at each of these ages?

2 Identity   **LG2**   Explain the key facets of identity development

What Is Identity?	Erikson's View	Some Contemporary Thoughts on Identity	Developmental Changes	Identity and Social Contexts

Who am I? What am I all about? What am I going to do with my life? What is different about me? How can I make it on my own? These questions reflect the search for an identity. By far the most comprehensive and provocative theory of identity development is Erik Erikson's. In this section, we examine his views on identity and some contemporary thoughts on identity. We also discuss research on how identity develops and how social contexts influence that development.

What are some important dimensions of identity?
© Digital Vision/Getty Images RF

WHAT IS IDENTITY?

Identity is a self-portrait composed of many pieces, including the following:

- The career and work path the person wants to follow (vocational/career identity)
- Whether the person is conservative, liberal, or middle-of-the-road (political identity)
- The person's spiritual beliefs (religious identity)
- Whether the person is single, married, divorced, and so on (relationship identity)
- The extent to which the person is motivated to achieve and is intellectually active (achievement, intellectual identity)
- Whether the person is heterosexual, homosexual, or bisexual (sexual identity)
- Which part of the world or country a person is from and how intensely the person identifies with his or her cultural heritage (cultural/ethnic identity)
- The kinds of things a person likes to do, which can include sports, music, hobbies, and so on (interests)
- The individual's personality characteristics, such as being introverted or extraverted, anxious or calm, friendly or hostile, and so on (personality)
- The individual's body image (physical identity)

ERIKSON'S VIEW

Questions about identity surface as common, virtually universal, concerns during adolescence. Some decisions made during adolescence might seem trivial, such as whom to date, whether or not to break up, which major to study, whether to study or play, whether or not to be politically active, and so on. Over the years of adolescence, however, such decisions begin to form the core of what the individual is all about as a human being—what is called his or her identity.

It was Erik Erikson (1950, 1968) who first understood the importance of identity questions to understanding adolescent development. Identity is now believed to be a key aspect of adolescent development because of Erikson's masterful thinking and analysis. His ideas reveal rich insights into adolescents' thoughts and feelings, and reading one or more of his books is worthwhile. A good starting point is *Identity: Youth and Crisis* (1968). Other works by Erikson that portray identity development are *Young Man Luther* (1962) and *Gandhi's Truth* (1969).

According to Erikson's theory, adolescents go through a developmental stage that he called **identity versus identity confusion.** Erikson states that in this fifth of his eight stages in the life span, adolescents are faced with deciding who they are, what they are all about, and where they are going in life. These questions about identity occur throughout life, but they become especially important for adolescents. Erikson maintains that adolescents face an overwhelming number of choices. As they gradually come to realize that they will be responsible for themselves and their own lives, adolescents search for what those lives are going to be.

The search for an identity during adolescence is aided by a **psychosocial moratorium,** which is Erikson's term for the gap between childhood security and adult autonomy. During this period, society leaves adolescents relatively free of responsibilities, which allows them to try out different identities. Adolescents in effect search their culture's identity files, experimenting with different roles and personalities. They may want to pursue one career one month (lawyer, for example) and another career the next month (doctor, actor, teacher, social worker, or astronaut, for example). They may dress neatly one day, sloppily the next. This experimentation is a deliberate effort on the part of adolescents to find out where they fit into the world. Most adolescents eventually discard undesirable roles.

Youth who successfully cope with conflicting identities emerge with a new sense of self that is both refreshing and acceptable. Adolescents who do not successfully resolve this identity crisis suffer what Erikson calls identity confusion. The confusion takes one of two courses: Individuals withdraw, isolating themselves from peers and family, or they immerse themselves in the world of peers and lose their identity in the crowd.

SOME CONTEMPORARY THOUGHTS ON IDENTITY

Contemporary views of identity development suggest that it is a lengthy process, in many instances more gradual and less cataclysmic than Erikson's use of the term *crisis* implies

Erik Erikson.
© Bettmann/Corbis

"Who are you?" said the caterpillar. Alice replied rather shyly, "I—I hardly know, sir, just at present—at least I know who I was when I got up this morning, but I must have changed several times since then."

—LEWIS CARROLL
English writer, 19th century

identity versus identity confusion Erikson's fifth stage of development, which occurs during the adolescent years; adolescents are faced with finding out who they are, what they are all about, and where they are going in life.

psychosocial moratorium Erikson's term for the gap between childhood security and adult autonomy that adolescents experience as part of their identity exploration.

(Azmitia, Syed, & Radmacher, 2013; Coté, 2015; Kroger, 2015). Resolution of the identity issue during adolescence and emerging adulthood does not mean that identity will be stable through the remainder of one's life. An individual who develops a healthy identity is flexible and adaptive, open to changes in society, in relationships, and in careers. This openness ensures numerous reorganizations of identity throughout the individual's life.

Identity formation neither happens neatly nor is it usually cataclysmic (McLean & Syed, 2015; Rivas-Drake & others, 2014; Schwartz & others, 2013, 2015a, b, c). At the bare minimum, it involves commitment to a vocational direction, an ideological stance, and a sexual orientation. Synthesizing the components of identity can be a long, drawn-out process, with many negations and affirmations of various roles. Identity development happens in bits and pieces. Decisions are not made once and for all, but must be made again and again (Schwartz & others, 2015a, b, c).

One way that researchers are examining identity changes in depth is to use a *narrative approach*. This involves asking individuals to tell their life stories and evaluate the extent to which their stories are meaningful and integrated (Habermas & Kober, 2015; McAdams, 2012; McAdams & McLean, 2013; McAdams & Zapata-Gietl, 2015; Pasupathi, 2015; Singer & Kasmark, 2015; Syed, 2013).

What are some contemporary thoughts about identity formation and development?
© Somos/Veer/Getty Images RF

The term *narrative identity* "refers to the stories people construct and tell about themselves to define who they are for themselves and others. Beginning in adolescence and young adulthood, our narrative identities are the stories we live by" (McAdams, Josselson, & Lieblich, 2006, p. 4). A recent study using the narrative identity approach revealed that from age 11 to 18, boys increasingly engaged in thinking about the meaningfulness of their lives, especially meaning related to the self as changing (McLean, Breen, & Fournier, 2010). In other research, relationship, autonomy, and mortality events were important contributors to searching for a meaningful identity in late adolescence and emerging adulthood (McLean & Pratt, 2006; McLean & Thorne, 2006). There also is increasing evidence that the effective management of difficult life events and circumstances contributes to the development of a meaningful identity in emerging adulthood (Pals, 2006).

A recent study used both identity status and narrative approaches to examine college students' identity domains. In both approaches, the interpersonal domain was most frequently described (McLean & others, 2015). In the interpersonal domain, dating and friendships were frequently mentioned, although there was no mention of gender roles. In the narrative domain, family stories were common.

DEVELOPMENTAL CHANGES

Although questions about identity may be especially important during adolescence and emerging adulthood, identity formation neither begins nor ends during these years (Kroger, 2015; Luyckx & Robitschek, 2014; McAdams & Zapata-Gietl, 2015). It begins with the appearance of attachment, the development of the sense of self, and the emergence of independence in infancy; the process reaches its final phase with a life review and integration in old age. But for Erikson, it is in adolescence that identity begins to be such a key dimension of individuals' lives. Why might that be so? What is important about identity development in adolescence, especially late adolescence, is that for the first time, physical development, cognitive development, and socioemotional development advance to the point at which the individual can sort through and synthesize childhood identities and identifications to construct a viable path toward adult maturity.

Identity Statuses How do individual adolescents go about the process of forming an identity? Eriksonian researcher James Marcia (1980, 1994) analyzed Erikson's theory of identity development and concluded that it involves four statuses of identity, or ways of resolving the identity crisis: identity diffusion, identity foreclosure, identity moratorium, and identity achievement. What determines an individual's identity status? Marcia classifies

		Has the person made a commitment?	
		Yes	No
Has the person explored meaningful alternatives regarding some identity question?	Yes	Identity Achievement	Identity Moratorium
	No	Identity Foreclosure	Identity Diffusion

FIGURE 5
MARCIA'S FOUR STATUSES OF IDENTITY

crisis A period of identity development during which the individual is exploring alternatives.

commitment A personal investment in identity.

identity diffusion Marcia's term for the status of individuals who have not yet experienced a crisis (explored meaningful alternatives) or made any commitments.

identity foreclosure Marcia's term for the status of individuals who have made a commitment but have not experienced a crisis.

identity moratorium Marcia's term for the status of individuals who are in the midst of a crisis but whose commitments are either absent or vaguely defined.

identity achievement Marcia's term for the status of individuals who have undergone a crisis and have made a commitment.

individuals based on the existence or extent of their crisis or commitment (see Figure 5). **Crisis** is defined as a period of identity development during which the individual explores alternatives. Most researchers use the term *exploration* rather than *crisis*. **Commitment** is a personal investment in identity.

The four statuses of identity are as follows:

- **Identity diffusion** is the status of individuals who have not yet experienced a crisis or made any commitments. Not only are they undecided about occupational and ideological choices, but they are also likely to show little interest in such matters.

- **Identity foreclosure** is the status of individuals who have made a commitment but have not experienced a crisis. This occurs most often when parents hand down commitments to their adolescents, usually in an authoritarian way, before adolescents have had a chance to explore different approaches, ideologies, and vocations on their own.

- **Identity moratorium** is the status of individuals who are in the midst of a crisis but whose commitments are either absent or only vaguely defined.

- **Identity achievement** is the status of individuals who have undergone a crisis and have made a commitment.

Let's explore some examples of Marcia's identity statuses. Thirteen-year-old Sarah has neither begun to explore her identity in any meaningful way nor made an identity commitment; she is *identity diffused*. Eighteen-year-old Tim's parents want him to be a medical doctor, so he is planning on majoring in premedicine in college and has not explored other options; he is *identity foreclosed*. Nineteen-year-old Sasha is not quite sure what life paths she wants to follow, but she recently went to the counseling center at her college to find out about different careers; she is in *identity moratorium* status. Twenty-one-year-old Marcelo extensively explored several career options in college, eventually getting his degree in science education, and is looking forward to his first year of teaching high school students; he is *identity achieved*. These examples focused on the career dimension of identity, but keep in mind that identity has a number of dimensions.

Marcia's approach has been sharply criticized by some researchers who conclude that it oversimplifies Erikson's concepts of crisis and commitment and doesn't examine them deeply enough (Coté, 2009, 2015; Luyckx & Robitschek, 2014).

Early Adolescence to Adulthood   During early adolescence, most youth are primarily in the identity statuses of *diffusion, foreclosure*, or *moratorium*. According to Marcia (1987, 1996), at least three aspects of the young adolescent's development are important to identity formation. Young adolescents must be confident that they have parental support, must have an established sense of industry, and must be able to take a self-reflective stance toward the future.

Researchers have developed a consensus that the key changes in identity are most likely to take place in emerging adulthood, the period from about 18 to 25 years of age, not adolescence (Schwartz & others, 2015a, b). One study found that as individuals aged from early adolescence to emerging adulthood, they increasingly engaged in in-depth exploration of their identity (Klimstra & others, 2010). Alan Waterman (1985, 1992) has found that from the years preceding high school through the last few years of college, the number of individuals who are identity achieved increases, whereas the number of individuals who are identity diffused decreases. Many young adolescents are identity diffused. College upperclassmen are more likely than high school students or college freshmen to be identity achieved.

Why might college produce some key changes in identity? Increased complexity in the reasoning skills of college students combined with a wide range of new experiences that highlight contrasts between home and college and between themselves and others stimulate them to reach a higher level of integrating various dimensions of their identity (Phinney, 2008). College contexts serve as a virtual "laboratory" for identity development through such experiences as diverse coursework and exposure to peers from diverse backgrounds. Also, one of emerging adulthood's key themes is not having many social commitments, which gives individuals considerable independence in developing a life path (Arnett, 2012; Arnett & Fischel, 2013).

How does identity change in emerging adulthood?
© BananaStock/JupiterImages RF

A meta-analysis of 124 studies revealed that during adolescence and emerging adulthood, identity moratorium status rose steadily to age 19 and then declined; identity achievement rose across late adolescence and emerging adulthood; and foreclosure and diffusion statuses declined across the high school years but fluctuated in the late teens and emerging adulthood (Kroger, Martinussen, & Marcia, 2010). The studies also found that a large portion of individuals were not identity achieved by the time they reached their twenties.

Resolution of the identity issue during adolescence and emerging adulthood does not mean that identity will be stable through the remainder of life (McAdams & Cox, 2011). Many individuals who develop positive identities follow what are called "MAMA" cycles; that is, their identity status changes from *m*oratorium to *a*chievement to *m*oratorium to *a*chievement (Marcia, 1994). These cycles may be repeated throughout life (Francis, Fraser, & Marcia, 1989). Marcia (2002) points out that the first identity is just that—it is not, and should not be expected to be, the final product.

Researchers have shown that identity consolidation—the process of refining and enhancing the identity choices that are made in emerging adulthood—continues well into early adulthood and possibly into the early part of middle adulthood (Kroger, 2012, 2015). Further, as individuals move from early to middle adulthood they become more certain about their identity. For example, a longitudinal study of college women found that identity certainty increased from the thirties through the fifties (Stewart, Ostrove, & Helson, 2001).

> As long as one keeps searching, the answers come.
>
> —**Joan Baez**
> *American folk singer, 20th century*

IDENTITY AND SOCIAL CONTEXTS

Social contexts influence an adolescent's identity development (Schwartz & others, 2012). Questions we will explore in this regard are: Do family and peer relationships influence identity development? How are culture and ethnicity linked to identity development?

Family Processes   Parents are important figures in the adolescent's development of identity (Cooper, 2011; Cooper, Gonzales, & Wilson, 2015). For example, one study found that poor communication between mothers and adolescents, as well as persistent conflicts with friends, was linked to less positive identity development (Reis & Youniss, 2004). Catherine Cooper and her colleagues (Cooper, 2011; Cooper, Behrens, & Trinh, 2009; Cooper & Grotevant, 1989) have found that a family atmosphere that promotes both individuality and connectedness is important to the adolescent's identity development:

· **Individuality** consists of two dimensions: self-assertion, which is the ability to have and communicate a point of view; and separateness, which is the use of communication patterns to express how one is different from others.
· **Connectedness** also consists of two dimensions: mutuality, which involves sensitivity to and respect for others' views; and permeability, which involves openness to others' views.

> developmental **connection**
> **Attachment**
> Even while adolescents seek autonomy, attachment to parents is important; secure attachment in adolescence is linked to a number of positive outcomes. Connect to "Emotional Development and Attachment."

individuality Characteristic consisting of two dimensions: self-assertion, the ability to have and communicate a point of view; and separateness, the use of communication patterns to express how one is different from others.

connectedness Characteristic consisting of two dimensions: mutuality, sensitivity to and respect for others' views; and permeability, openness to others' views.

Identity and Peer/Romantic Relationships   Researchers have recently found that the capacity to explore one's identity during adolescence and emerging adulthood is linked to the quality of friendships and romantic relationships (Galliher & Kerpelman, 2012). For example, a recent study found that an open, active exploration of identity when adolescents are comfortable with close friends contributes to the positive quality of the friendship (Doumen & others, 2012). In another study, friends were often a safe context for exploring identity-related experiences, providing sort of a testing ground for how self-disclosing comments are viewed by others (McLean & Jennings, 2012).

In terms of links between identity and romantic relationships in adolescence and emerging adulthood, two individuals in a romantic relationship are both in the process of constructing their own identities and each person provides the other with a context for identity exploration (Pittman & others, 2011). The extent of their secure attachment with each other can influence how each partner constructs his or her own identity.

Cultural and Ethnic Identity   Most research on identity development has historically been based on data obtained from adolescents and emerging adults in the United States and Canada, especially those who are non-Latino Whites (Cooper, Gonzalez, & Wilson, 2015; Schwartz & others, 2012). Many of these individuals have grown up in cultural contexts that value individual autonomy. However, in many countries around the world, adolescents and emerging adults have grown up influenced by a collectivist emphasis on fitting in with the group and connecting with others. The collectivist emphasis is especially prevalent in East Asian countries such as China. Researchers have found that self-oriented identity exploration may not be the main process through which identity achievement is attained in East Asian countries (Schwartz & others, 2012). Rather, East Asian adolescents and emerging adults may develop their identity through identification with and imitation of others in the cultural group (Bosma & Kunnen, 2001). This emphasis on interdependence in East Asian cultures includes an emphasis on adolescents and emerging adults accepting and embracing social and family roles (Berman & others, 2011). Thus, some patterns of identity development, such as the foreclosed status, may be more adaptive in East Asian countries than in North American countries (Cheng & Berman, 2012).

Identity development may take longer in some countries than in others (Azmitia, 2015; Schwartz & others, 2012). For example, research indicates that Italian youth may postpone significant identity exploration beyond adolescence and emerging adulthood, not settling on an identity until their mid- to late-twenties (Crocetti, Rabaglietti, & Sica, 2012). This delayed identity development is strongly influenced by many Italian youth living at home with their parents until 30 years of age and older.

Seth Schwartz and his colleagues (2012) recently pointed out that while everyone identifies with a particular "culture," many individuals in cultural majority groups take their cultural identity for granted. Thus, many adolescents and emerging adults in the cultural majority of non-Latino Whites in the United States likely don't spend much time thinking of themselves as "White American." However, for many adolescents and emerging adults who have grown up as a member of an ethnic minority group in the United States or emigrated from another country, cultural dimensions likely are an important aspect of their identity. Researchers recently have found that at both the high school and college level, Latino students were more likely than non-Latino White students to indicate that their cultural identity was an important dimension of their overall self-concept (Urdan, 2012).

Throughout the world, ethnic minority groups have struggled to maintain their ethnic identities while blending in with the dominant culture (Erikson, 1968; Liu & others, 2009).

Ethnic identity is an enduring aspect of the self that includes a sense of membership in an ethnic group, along with the attitudes and feelings related to that membership (Murry & others, 2015; Phinney, 2006; Spencer, Swanson, & Harpalani, 2015). Thus, for adolescents from ethnic minority groups, the process of identity formation has an added dimension: the choice between two or more sources of identification—their own ethnic group and the mainstream, or dominant, culture (Cooper, Gonzalez, & Wilson, 2015; Syed & Juang, 2014; Umana-Taylor & others, 2014). Many adolescents resolve this choice by developing a **bicultural identity.** That is, they identify in some ways with their ethnic

ethnic identity An enduring aspect of the self that includes a sense of membership in an ethnic group, along with the attitudes and feelings related to that membership.

bicultural identity Identifying both with one's own ethnic minority group and with the majority culture.

Armando Ronquillo, High School Counselor

Armando Ronquillo is a high school counselor and admissions advisor at Pueblo High School in a low-income area of Tucson, Arizona. More than 85 percent of the students have a Latino background. Ronquillo was named the top high school counselor in the state of Arizona in 2000.

Ronquillo especially works with Latino students to guide them in developing a positive identity. He talks with them about their Latino background and what it's like to have a bicultural identity—preserving important aspects of their Latino heritage but also pursuing what is important to be successful in the contemporary culture of the United States.

Ronquillo believes that helping students stay in school and getting them to think about the lifelong opportunities provided by a college education will benefit their identity development. He also works with parents to help them understand that sending their child to college can be doable and affordable.

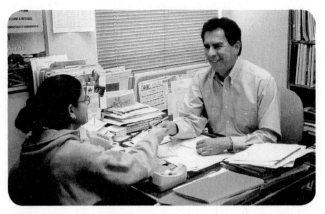

Armando Ronquillo counsels a Latina high school student about college.
Courtesy of Armando Ronquillo

For more information about what school counselors do, see the Careers in Life-Span Development appendix.

group and in other ways with the majority culture (Basilio & others, 2014; Knight & others, 2015). A study of Mexican American and Asian American college students found that they identified both with the American mainstream culture and with their culture of origin (Devos, 2006).

Time is another aspect that influences ethnic identity. The indicators of identity often differ for each succeeding generation of immigrants (Phinney, 2006; Phinney & Vedder, 2013). First-generation immigrants are likely to be secure in their identities and unlikely to change much; they may or may not develop a new identity. The degree to which they begin to feel "American" appears to be related to whether or not they learn English, develop social networks beyond their ethnic group, and become culturally competent in their new country. Second-generation immigrants are more likely to think of themselves as "American"—possibly because citizenship is granted at birth. For second-generation immigrants, ethnic identity is likely to be linked to retention of their ethnic language and social networks. In the third and later generations, the issues become more complex. Broad social factors may affect the extent to which members of this generation retain their ethnic identities. For example, media images may influence whether members of an ethnic group will continue to identify with their group and retain parts of its culture. Discrimination may force people to see themselves as cut off from the majority group and encourage them to seek the support of their own ethnic culture.

Researchers are also increasingly finding that a positive ethnic identity is related to positive outcomes for ethnic minority adolescents (Brittian & others, 2015). For example, a recent study found that Asian American adolescents' ethnic identity was associated with high self-esteem, positive relationships, academic motivation, and lower levels of depression over time (Kiang, Witkow, & Champagne, 2013). Another study indicated that Navajo adolescents' positive ethnic heritage was linked to higher self-esteem, school connectedness, and social functioning (Jones & Galliher, 2007). To read about one individual who guides Latino adolescents in developing a positive identity, see the *Connecting with Careers* profile.

One adolescent girl, 16-year-old Michelle Chin, made these comments about ethnic identity development: "My parents do not understand that teenagers need to find out who they are, which means a lot of experimenting, a lot of mood swings, a lot of emotions and awkwardness. Like any teenager, I am facing an identity crisis. I am still trying to figure out whether I am a Chinese American or an American with Asian eyes." *What are some other aspects of developing an ethnic identity in adolescence?*
© *Red Chopsticks/Getty Images RF*

Review Connect Reflect

LG2 Explain the key facets of identity development

Review

- What does an identity involve?
- What is Erikson's view of identity?
- What are some contemporary thoughts on identity?
- What are the four identity statuses, and how do they change developmentally?
- How do social contexts influence identity?

Connect

- Connect the concept of adolescents' "possible selves" to Erikson's view of adolescence as a time of identity versus identity confusion.

Reflect *Your Own Personal Journey of Life*

- Do you think your parents influenced your identity development? If so, how?

3 Personality

LG3 Describe personality and its development in adulthood

Trait Theories and the Big Five Factors of Personality

Views on Adult Personality Development

Generativity

Stability and Change

Earlier in the chapter, personality was defined as the enduring personal characteristics of individuals. Personality psychologists use many strategies to better understand the enduring characteristics of individuals. Some of them study the overall personality of individuals; some come up with a list of traits that best describe individuals; others zero in on specific traits or characteristics, such as being introverted or extraverted.

We've considered several major personality theories—psychoanalytic theories and the social cognitive theory of Albert Bandura. You might wish to review those theories at this time. Here our exploration of personality focuses on trait theory, several views of personality development in adulthood, and studies of stability and change in personality during adulthood.

TRAIT THEORIES AND THE BIG FIVE FACTORS OF PERSONALITY

Trait theories state that personality consists of broad dispositions, called traits, that tend to produce characteristic responses. In other words, people can be described in terms of the basic ways they behave, such as whether they are outgoing and friendly or whether they are dominant and assertive (De Bolle & others, 2015; Fairbairn & others, 2015). Although trait theorists disagree about which traits make up personality, they agree that traits are the foundation of personality (Costa & others, 2014; Hill, Nickel, & Roberts, 2014).

Big Five Factors of Personality One trait theory that has received considerable attention involves the **Big Five factors of personality**—the view that personality is made up of openness to experience, conscientiousness, extraversion, agreeableness, and neuroticism (see Figure 6). (Notice that if you create an acronym from these trait names, you will get the word *OCEAN*.) A number of research studies point toward these five factors as important dimensions of personality (Costa & McCrae, 1995, 2013; Costa & others, 2014; McCrae & Costa, 2006).

Evidence for the importance of the Big Five factors indicates that they are related to such important aspects of a person's life as health, intelligence and cognitive functioning, achievement and work, and relationships (Bertrand, Graham, & Lachman, 2013; English &

trait theories Theories emphasizing that personality consists of broad dispositions, called traits, which tend to produce characteristic responses.

Big Five factors of personality The view that personality is made up of openness to experience, conscientiousness, extraversion, agreeableness, and neuroticism.

Openness	**C**onscientiousness	**E**xtraversion	**A**greeableness	**N**euroticism (emotional stability)
• Imaginative or practical	• Organized or disorganized	• Sociable or retiring	• Softhearted or ruthless	• Calm or anxious
• Interested in variety or routine	• Careful or careless	• Fun-loving or somber	• Trusting or suspicious	• Secure or insecure
• Independent or conforming	• Disciplined or impulsive	• Affectionate or reserved	• Helpful or uncooperative	• Self-satisfied or self-pitying

FIGURE 6

THE BIG FIVE FACTORS OF PERSONALITY. Each of the broad super traits encompasses more narrow traits and characteristics. Use the acronym OCEAN to remember the Big Five personality factors (openness, conscientiousness, extraversion, agreeableness, neuroticism).

Carstensen, 2014; Hampson & others, 2015; Hill & others, 2014). The following research supports these links:

· *Openness to experience.* Individuals high on openness to experience are more likely to be tolerant (McCrae & Sutin, 2009), have superior cognitive functioning, achievement, and IQ across the life span (Briley, Domiteaux, & Tucker-Drob, 2014; Sharp & others, 2010), and experience success as entrepreneurs (Zhao, Seibert, & Lumpkin, 2010).

· *Conscientiousness.* Individuals high in conscientiousness often do well in a variety of life domains (Mike & others, 2015). For example, they have better health and less stress (Gartland & others, 2014), better-quality friendships (Jensen-Campbell & Malcolm, 2007), achieve better grade point averages in college (McAbee & Oswald, 2013), engage in less substance abuse (Walton & Roberts, 2004), and gamble less (Hwang & others, 2012). A recent study found that conscientiousness was linked to better cognitive status and less cognitive decline in older adults (Luchetti & others, 2015).

· *Extraversion.* Individuals high in *extraversion* are more likely than others to engage in social activities (Emmons & Diener, 1986), have fewer sleep problems (Hintsanen & others, 2014), and have a more positive sense of well-being in the future (Soto, 2015).

· *Agreeableness.* People who are high in agreeableness are more likely to be generous and altruistic (Caprara & others, 2010), have more satisfying romantic relationships (Donnellan, Larsen-Rife, & Conger, 2005), view other people positively (Wood, Harms, & Vazire, 2010), and lie less about themselves in online dating profiles, (Hall & others, 2010).

· *Neuroticism.* People high in neuroticism are more likely to feel negative emotion than positive emotion in daily life and to experiencing more lingering negative states (Widiger, 2009), have more health complaints (Carver & Connor-Smith, 2010), be more drug dependent (Valero & others, 2014), have a higher coronary heart disease risk (Lee & others, 2014), and have a lower sense of well-being 40 years later (Gale & others, 2013).

Researchers have found that several of the Big Five factors of personality continue to change in late adulthood (Roberts, Donnellan, & Hill, 2013). In one study, perceived social support predicted increased conscientiousness in older adults (Hill & others, 2014). And in another study, more severe depression in older adults was associated with higher neuroticism and lower extraversion and conscientiousness (Koorevaar & others, 2013).

An adolescent with a high level of conscientiousness organizes his daily schedule and plans how to use his time effectively. *What are some characteristics of conscientiousness? How is it linked to adolescents' competence?*
© Tim Pannell/Corbis

Optimism Another important personality characteristic is **optimism,** which involves having a positive outlook on the future and minimizing problems. Optimism is often referred to as a style of thinking.

Somewhat surprising is that little research has recently been conducted on children's optimism. One recent study did find that from 5 to 10 years of age children increasingly understood that thinking positively improves emotions and that thinking negatively makes them worse (Bamford & Lagattuta, 2012). In *The Optimistic Child*, Martin Seligman (2007) described how parents, teachers, and coaches can instill optimism in children, which he argues helps to make them more resilient and less likely to develop depression.

optimism A style of thinking that involves having a positive outlook on the future and minimizing problems.

In examining optimism in adolescents, one study found that having an optimistic style of thinking predicted a reduction in suicidal ideation for individuals who had experienced negative and potentially traumatic life events (Hirsch & others, 2009). Another study revealed that adolescents with an optimistic thinking style had a lower risk of developing depressive symptoms than their pessimistic counterparts (Patton & others, 2011).

Researchers increasingly are finding that optimism is linked to being healthier and living longer (Boelen, 2015). A recent study involving adults 50 years of age and older revealed that being optimistic and having an optimistic spouse were both associated with better health and physical functioning (Kim, Chopik, & Smith, 2014). Also, in a recent study of 40- to 85-year-olds, individuals who were prepared for physical losses but also had an optimistic outlook on the future had better physical functioning and a lower level of depressive symptoms (Wurm & Benyamini, 2014). And a 12-year longitudinal study of Danish older adults who were 92 to 93 years of age when the study began found optimistic men and women had a lower risk of dying during the 12 years of the study (Engberg & others, 2013).

Trait-Situation Interaction   The trait theories have identified a number of characteristics that are important to consider when attempting to understand an individual's personality (Ashcraft, 2015). The trait approach also has led to advances in the assessment of personality through the development of numerous personality tests. However, some psychologists note that the trait approach gives too little attention to environmental factors and puts too much emphasis on stability. These criticisms initially were leveled by social cognitive theorist Walter Mischel (1968). Mischel argued that personality often changes according to the situation. Thus, an individual may behave very differently at a party from the way he would in the library.

Today, most personality psychologists believe that personality is a product of *trait-situation interaction*. In other words, both traits and situational (context) factors must be considered to understand personality (Burger, 2015; Engler, 2014). Also, some people are more consistent on some traits and other people are consistent on other traits.

VIEWS ON ADULT PERSONALITY DEVELOPMENT

Two important perspectives on adult development are the stage-crisis view and the life-events approach. In examining these approaches, we discuss the extent to which adults experience a midlife crisis and consider how life events influence the individual's development.

The Stage-Crisis View   Erikson's theory, which we discussed earlier, is a stage-crisis view. Here we describe the view of Daniel Levinson and examine the concept of a midlife crisis.

Levinson's Seasons of a Man's Life   In *The Seasons of a Man's Life*, clinical psychologist Daniel Levinson (1978) reported the results of extensive interviews with 40 middle-aged men. The interviews were conducted with hourly workers, business executives, academic biologists, and novelists. Levinson bolstered his conclusions with information from the biographies of famous men and the development of memorable characters in literature. Although Levinson's major focus was midlife change, he described a number of stages and transitions in the life span, as shown in Figure 7.

Levinson emphasizes that developmental tasks must be mastered at each of these stages. In early adulthood, the two major tasks to be mastered are exploring the possibilities for adult living and developing a stable life structure. Levinson sees the twenties as a *novice phase* of adult development. At the end of one's teens, a transition from dependence to independence should occur. This transition is marked by the formation of a dream—an image of the kind

Era of late adulthood:
60 to 120

Late adult transition: Age 60 to 65

Culminating life structure for middle adulthood:
55 to 60

Age 50 transition:
50 to 55

Entry life structure for middle adulthood:
45 to 50

Middle adult transition: Age 40 to 45

Culminating life structure for early adulthood:
33 to 40

Age 30 transition:
28 to 33

Entry life structure for early adulthood:
22 to 28

Early adult transition: Age 17 to 22

FIGURE 7

LEVINSON'S PERIODS OF ADULT DEVELOPMENT.
According to Levinson, adulthood has three main stages, which are surrounded by transition periods. Specific tasks and challenges are associated with each stage.
(top to bottom): © Amos Morgan/Getty Images RF; © image100/Corbis RF;
© BananaStock/JupiterImages RF

of life the youth wants to have, especially in terms of a career and marriage. The novice phase is a time of reasonably free experimentation and of testing the dream in the real world.

From about age 28 to 33, a young man goes through a transition period in which he must face the more serious question of determining his goals. During the thirties, he usually focuses on family and career development. In the later years of this period, he enters a phase of Becoming One's Own Man (or BOOM, as Levinson calls it). By age 40, he has reached a stable location in his career, has outgrown his earlier, more tenuous attempts at learning to become an adult, and now must look forward to the kind of life he will lead as a middle-aged adult.

According to Levinson, the transition to middle adulthood lasts about five years (ages 40 to 45) and requires the adult male to come to grips with four major conflicts that have existed in his life since adolescence: (1) being young versus being old, (2) being destructive versus being constructive, (3) being masculine versus being feminine, and (4) being attached to others versus being separated from them. Seventy to eighty percent of the men Levinson interviewed found the midlife transition tumultuous and psychologically painful, as many aspects of their lives came into question. According to Levinson, the success of the midlife transition rests on how effectively the individual reduces the polarities and accepts each of them as an integral part of his being.

The original Levinson data included no females. However, Levinson (1987, 1996) subsequently reported that his stages, transitions, and the crisis of middle age hold for females as well as males.

> Mid-life crises are greatly exaggerated in America.
>
> —George Vaillant
> *Contemporary psychologist, Harvard University*

Midlife Crises   Levinson (1978) views midlife as a crisis, believing that the middle-aged adult is suspended between the past and the future, trying to cope with this gap that threatens life's continuity. George Vaillant (1977) concludes that just as adolescence is a time for detecting parental flaws and discovering the truth about childhood, the forties are a decade of reassessing and recording the truth about the adolescent and adulthood years. However, whereas Levinson sees midlife as a crisis, Vaillant notes that only a minority of adults experience a midlife crisis:

> Just as pop psychologists have reveled in the not-so-common high drama of adolescent turmoil, also the popular press, sensing good copy, had made all too much of the mid-life crisis. The term *mid-life crisis* brings to mind some variation of the renegade minister who leaves behind four children and the congregation that loved him in order to drive off in a magenta Porsche with a 25-year-old striptease artiste. As with adolescent turmoil, mid-life crises are much rarer in community samples. (Vaillant, 1977, pp. 222–223)

Vaillant's study—called the Grant Study—involved a follow-up of Harvard University men in their early thirties and in their late forties who initially had been interviewed as undergraduates. Other research has also found that midlife is not characterized by pervasive crises. For example, a longitudinal study of 2,247 individuals found few midlife crises (McCrae & Costa, 1990). The emotional well-being of these individuals did not significantly decrease during their middle-aged years (see Figure 8). In fact, some studies have documented psychological gains among middle-aged adults. For example, one study revealed that individuals from 40 to 60 years of age were less nervous and worried than those under 40. The middle-aged adults reported a growing sense of control in their work as well as increased financial security, greater environmental mastery (ability to handle daily responsibilities), and more autonomy than their younger counterparts.

Adult development experts have become virtually unanimous in their belief that midlife crises have been exaggerated (Lachman & Kranz, 2010; Pudrovska, 2009). In sum, there is a consensus that (1) the stage theories place too much emphasis on crises in development, especially midlife crises; and (2) there often is considerable individual variation in the way people experience the stages, a topic that we turn to next.

Individual Variations   Stage theories especially focus on the universals of adult personality development. They try to pin down stages that all individuals go through in their adult lives. These theories do not adequately address individual variations in adult development. In an extensive study of a random sample of 500 men at midlife, it was concluded that there is extensive individual variation among men (Farrell & Rosenberg, 1981). In the individual variations view, middle-aged adults interpret, shape, alter, and give meaning to their lives (Arpanantikul, 2004).

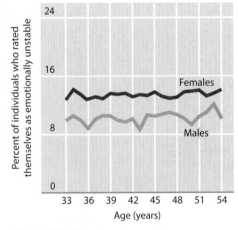

FIGURE 8

EMOTIONAL INSTABILITY AND AGE. In one longitudinal study, the emotional instability of individuals was assessed from age 33 to age 54 (McCrae & Costa, 1990). No significant increase in emotional instability occurred during the middle-aged years

FIGURE 9

A CONTEMPORARY LIFE-EVENTS FRAMEWORK FOR INTERPRETING ADULT DEVELOPMENTAL CHANGE. According to the contemporary life-events approach, the influence of a life event depends on the event itself, on mediating variables, on the life-stage and sociohistorical context, and on the individual's appraisal of the event and coping strategies.

contemporary life-events approach
Approach emphasizing that how a life event influences the individual's development depends not only on the event but also on mediating factors, the individual's adaptation to the life event, the life-stage context, and the sociohistorical context.

It also is important to recognize that some individuals may experience a midlife crisis in some contexts of their lives but not others (Lachman, 2004). Thus, turmoil and stress may characterize one area of a person's life (such as work) while things are going smoothly in another context (such as family).

Researchers have found that in one-third of the cases in which individuals have reported having a midlife crisis, the crisis is triggered by life events such as a job loss, financial problems, or illness (Wethington, Kessler, & Pixley, 2004). Let's further explore the role of life events in midlife development.

The Life-Events Approach   An alternative to the stage approach to adult development is the life-events approach (Luhmann & others, 2012; Schwarzer & Luszczynska, 2013). In the early version of the life-events approach, life events were viewed as taxing circumstances for individuals, forcing them to change their personality (Holmes & Rahe, 1967). Events such as the death of a spouse, divorce, marriage, and so on were believed to involve varying degrees of stress, and therefore likely to influence the individual's development. A recent study found that stressful life events were associated with cardiovascular disease in middle-aged women (Kershaw & others, 2014).

Today's life-events approach is more sophisticated (Cui & Vaillant, 1996; Hultsch & Plemons, 1979). The **contemporary life-events approach** emphasizes that how life events influence the individual's development depends not only on the event but also on *mediating factors* (physical health and family supports, for example), the individual's *adaptation to the life event* (appraisal of the threat and coping strategies, for example), the *life-stage context*, and the *sociohistorical context* (see Figure 9).

Consider how the life event of divorce might affect personality. A divorce is likely to be more stressful for individuals who are in poor health and have little family support. One individual may perceive it as highly stressful (less adaptive) rather than a challenge while another may develop coping strategies to effectively deal with it (more adaptive). And a divorce may be more stressful after many years of marriage when adults are in their fifties than when they have been married only a few years and are in their twenties (an example of life-stage context). Finally, adults may be able to cope more effectively with divorce today than several decades ago because divorce has become more commonplace and accepted in today's society (an example of sociohistorical context).

Though the life-events approach is a valuable addition to understanding adult development, it has some drawbacks. One drawback is that the life-events approach places too much emphasis on change. It does not adequately recognize the stability that, at least to some degree, characterizes adult development. Another drawback is that it may not be life's major events that are the primary sources of stress, but our daily experiences (Almeida & others, 2011; Aldwin & others, 2014; Totenhagen & others, 2012). Enduring a boring but tense job or living in poverty does not show up on scales of major life events. Yet the everyday pounding from these conditions can add up to a highly stressful life and eventually lead to illness. Greater insight into the source of life's stresses might come from focusing more on daily hassles and daily uplifts (Jacob & others, 2014). Researchers have found that young and middle-aged adults experience a greater daily frequency of stressors than older individuals do (Almeida & Horn, 2004). A recent study also found that stressful daily hassles were linked to increased anxiety and lower physical well-being (Falconier & others, 2015).

The manner in which different stressors affect health varies—life events often produce prolonged arousal, whereas daily stressors are linked to spikes in arousal (Piazza & others, 2010). Consider the effects of caring for a spouse who has Alzheimer disease. In this case, a life event (spouse diagnosed with an incurable disease) produces chronic stress for the caregiver, which also is linked to the daily stressors involved in caring for the individual.

GENERATIVITY

Erikson (1968) argues that middle-aged adults face the issue of **generativity versus stagnation,** which is the name Erikson gave to the seventh stage in his life-span theory. Generativity encompasses adults' desire to leave a legacy of themselves to the next generation (Busch & Hofer, 2012; Rubinstein & others, 2015). By contrast, stagnation (sometimes called "self-absorption") develops when individuals sense that they have done nothing for the next generation.

Does research support Erikson's theory that generativity is an important dimension of middle age? Yes, it does (McAdams & Cox, 2011; Newton & Stewart, 2012). In George Vaillant's (2002) longitudinal studies of aging, generativity (defined in this study as "taking care of the next generation") in middle age was more strongly related than intimacy to whether individuals would have an enduring and happy marriage at 75 to 80 years of age. One participant in Vaillant's studies said, "From twenty to thirty I learned how to get along with my wife. From thirty to forty I learned how to be a success at my job, and at forty to fifty I worried less about myself and more about the children" (p. 114). A recent analysis of Vaillant's data found that achieving generativity was associated with better later life health and adjustment to aging (Landes & others, 2014).

Other research also supports Erikson's (1968) view on the importance of generativity in middle age. In one study, Carol Ryff (1984) examined the views of women and men at different ages and found that middle-aged adults especially were concerned about generativity. In a longitudinal study of Smith College women, the desire for generativity increased as the participants aged from their thirties to their fifties (Stewart, Ostrove, & Helson, 2001) (see Figure 10). And in a recent study, generativity was strongly linked to middle-aged adults' positive social engagement in contexts such as family life and community activities (Cox & others, 2010).

Middle-aged adults can develop generativity in a number of ways (Kotre, 1984). Through biological generativity, adults conceive and give birth to an infant. Through parental generativity, adults provide nurturance and guidance to children. Through work generativity, adults develop skills that are passed down to others. And through cultural generativity, adults create, renovate, or conserve some aspect of culture that ultimately survives.

STABILITY AND CHANGE

An important issue in life-span development is the extent to which individuals show stability in their development versus the extent to which they change. A number of longitudinal studies have assessed stability and change in the personalities of individuals at different points in their lives (Hopwood & others, 2011; McAdams & Olson, 2010; Roberts, Donnellan, & Hill, 2013; Roberts & Mroczek, 2008). A common finding is that in most cases, the less time between measurements of personality characteristics, the more stability they show. Thus, if we measure a person's introversion/extraversion at the age of 20 and then again at age 30, we are likely to find more stability than if we assess the person at age 20 and then at age 40.

Costa and McCrae's Baltimore Study   Earlier we discussed the Big Five factors in personality as an important trait theory. Paul Costa and Robert McCrae (1998, 2013; McCrae & Costa, 2006) have studied the Big Five factors of approximately a thousand college-educated women and men from 20 to 96 years of age. Longitudinal data collection initially began in the 1950s to the mid-1960s on people of varying ages and is ongoing. Costa and McCrae found a great deal of stability across the adult years in the Big Five personality factors—openness to experience, conscientiousness, extraversion, agreeableness, and neuroticism.

However, more recent research indicates greater developmental changes in the Big Five personality factors in adulthood (Roberts, Donnellan, & Hill, 2013; Soto & others, 2011). For example, a recent study found that emotional stability, extraversion, openness, and agreeableness were lower in early adulthood, peaked between 40 and 60 years of age, and decreased in late adulthood, while conscientiousness showed a continuous increase from early adulthood to late adulthood (Specht, Egloff, & Schukle, 2011). Most research studies find that the greatest change occurs in early adulthood (Lucas & Donnellan, 2011; Roberts, Walton, & Viechtbauer, 2006).

Might some Big Five factors be related to how long older adults live? To find out, read the *Connecting with Research* interlude.

developmental **connection**

Life-Span Perspective

Erikson's early adulthood stage is intimacy versus isolation, and his late adulthood stage is integrity versus despair. Connect to "Introduction."

Generativity

Feeling needed by people

Effort to ensure that young people get their chance to develop

Influence in my community or area of interest

A new level of productivity or effectiveness

Appreciation and awareness of older people

Having a wider perspective

Interest in things beyond my family

Identity certainty

A sense of being my own person

Excitement, turmoil, confusion about my impulses and potential (reversed)

Coming near the end of one road and not yet finding another (reversed)

Feeling my life is moving well

Searching for a sense of who I am (reversed)

Wishing I had a wider scope to my life (reversed)

Anxiety that I won't live up to opportunities (reversed)

Feeling secure and committed

FIGURE **10**

ITEMS USED TO ASSESS GENERATIVITY AND IDENTITY CERTAINTY. These items were used to assess generativity and identity certainty in the longitudinal study of Smith College women (Stewart, Ostrove, & Helson, 2001). In the assessment of identity certainty, five of the items involved reversed scoring. For example, if an individual scored high on the item "Searching for a sense of who I am," it was an indication of identity uncertainty rather than identity certainty.

generativity versus stagnation The seventh stage in Erikson's life-span theory; it encompasses adults' desire to leave a legacy of themselves to the next generation.

Are Personality Traits Related to Longevity?

Researchers have found that some personality traits are associated with the mortality of older adults (Mroczek, Spiro, & Griffin, 2006; Noftle & Fleeson, 2010). A recent meta-analysis found that higher levels of openness to experience were linked to living longer (Ferguson & Bibby, 2012). In one study, 883 older Catholic clergy were given the NEO Five-Factor Inventory that assesses the Big Five factors of personality (Wilson & others, 2004). The clergy were followed for five years, during which 182 of the 883 clergy died. At the beginning of the study, the average age of the clergy was 75, and 69 percent of them were women. Risk of death nearly doubled in clergy who had a high score on neuroticism (90th percentile) compared with those who had a low score (10th percentile) and was halved in clergy who were very high in conscientiousness compared with those who were very low. Results for extraversion were mixed, whereas agreeableness and openness were not related to mortality. And in a recent study, a higher level of conscientiousness predicted greater longevity in older adults (Hill & others, 2012).

Why might a high score on neuroticism and a low score on conscientiousness lead to an earlier death? Researchers have found that older adults who are highly neurotic react more emotionally to stressful circumstances than their low-neuroticism counterparts (Mroczek, Spiro, & Griffin, 2006). Over many years, high neuroticism may elevate harmful stress hormones and produce physical damages to the cardiovascular system, thus contributing to mortality. By contrast, individuals who score high on conscientiousness engage in more healthy behaviors than those who score low. For example, low-conscientiousness individuals engage in more risky behaviors, such as excessive drinking and impulsive behaviors that lead to fatal accidents. It also has been proposed that they tend to have less healthy diets and are less likely to exercise regularly than highly conscientious individuals (Mroczek, Spiro, & Griffin, 2006).

An increasing number of studies are finding that conscientiousness is the Big Five factor that best predicts longevity (Wilson & others, 2015). A longitudinal study of more than 1,200 individuals across seven decades revealed that the Big Five personality factor of conscientiousness predicted lower mortality risk from childhood through late adulthood (Martin, Friedman, & Schwartz, 2007).

Another longitudinal study recently underscored the importance of the link between neuroticism and mortality in a sample of more than 1,600 aging men (Mroczek & Spiro, 2007). A high level of neuroticism and an increasing level of neuroticism were related to lower survival across an 18-year period (see Figure 11).

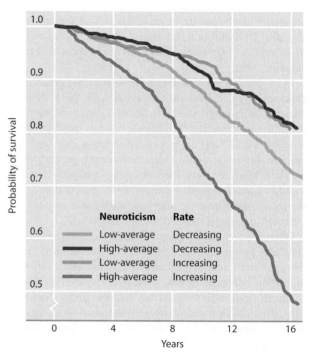

FIGURE 11

LINK BETWEEN NEUROTICISM AND SURVIVAL IN AGING MEN. *Note:* At the beginning of the study, the men were 43 to 91 years old. During the 18-year period of the study, 30 percent of the participants died, with more than 70 percent of the deaths due to cardiovascular disease and cancer.

An increasing number of researchers and theorists who study the Big Five are focusing on the role of conscientiousness and how it is linked to health and longevity (English & Carstensen, 2014; Friedman & others, 2014; Roberts & others, 2014). In a longitudinal study, children's conscientiousness predicted their physical health 40 years later (Hampson & others, 2013). And a recent study of 66- to 102-year-olds revealed that the self-discipline component of conscientiousness was a strong predictor of living longer, with individuals who had high self-discipline showing a 34 percent increase in survival time (Costa & others, 2014).

What type of studies might researchers conduct to identify early precursors of personality traits such as conscientiousness and neuroticism in an effort to increase longevity?

Berkeley Longitudinal Studies Most longitudinal studies indicate that neither extreme stability nor extreme change characterizes most people's personalities as they go through the adult years. One of the longest-running inquiries is the series of analyses called the Berkeley Longitudinal Studies. Initially, more than 500 children and their parents were studied in the late 1920s and early 1930s. The book *Present and Past in Middle Life* (Eichorn & others, 1981) profiles these individuals as they became middle-aged.

The results from early adolescence through a portion of midlife did not support either extreme in the debate over whether personality is characterized by stability or change. Some characteristics were more stable than others, however. The most stable characteristics were the degree to which individuals were intellectually oriented, self-confident, or open to new experiences. The characteristics that changed the most included the extent to which the individuals were nurturant or hostile and whether they had good self-control.

John Clausen (1993), one of the researchers in the Berkeley Longitudinal Studies, holds that too much attention has been given to discontinuities for all members of the human species, as exemplified in the adult stage theories. Rather, he stresses that some people experience recurrent crises and change a great deal over the life course, whereas others lead more stable, continuous lives and change far less.

What characterized the development of women in Ravenna Helson's Mills College Study?
© Sean Justice/Corbis RF

Helson's Mills College Studies   Another longitudinal investigation of adult personality development was conducted by Ravenna Helson and her colleagues (George, Helson, & John, 2011; Helson, 1997; Helson & Wink, 1992; Roberts, Helson, & Klohnen, 2002). They initially studied 132 women who were seniors at Mills College in California in the late 1950s. In 1981, when the women were 42 to 45 years old, they were studied again.

Helson and her colleagues distinguished three main groups among the Mills women: family-oriented (participants who had children), career-oriented (whether or not they also wanted families), and those who followed neither path (women without children who pursued only low-level work). Despite their different college profiles and their diverging life paths, the women in all three groups experienced some similar psychological changes over their adult years. However, the women in the third group changed less than those committed to career or family.

During their early forties, many of the women shared the concerns that stage theorists such as Levinson found in men: concern for young and old, introspectiveness, interest in roots, and awareness of limitations and death. However, the researchers in the Mills College Study concluded that rather than being in a midlife crisis, what the Mills women experienced was midlife *consciousness*. They also indicated that commitment to the tasks of early adulthood—whether to a career or family (or both)—helped women learn to control their impulses, develop interpersonal skills, become independent, and work hard to achieve goals. Women who did not commit themselves to one of these lifestyle patterns faced fewer challenges and did not develop as fully as the other women (Rosenfeld & Stark, 1987). In the Mills study, some women moved toward becoming "pillars of society" in their early forties to early fifties (Helson & Wink, 1992).

George Vaillant's Studies   George Vaillant (2002) has conducted three longitudinal studies of adult development and aging: (1) a sample of 268 socially advantaged Harvard graduates born about 1920 (called the "Grant Study"); (2) a sample of 456 socially disadvantaged inner-city men born about 1930; and (3) a sample of 90 middle-SES, intellectually gifted women born about 1910. These individuals have been assessed numerous times (in most cases every two years), beginning in the 1920s to 1940s and continuing today for those still living. The main assessments involve extensive interviews with the participants, their parents, and teachers.

Vaillant categorized 75- to 80-year-olds as "happy-well," "sad-sick," or "dead." He used data collected from these individuals when they were 50 years of age to predict which categories they were likely to end up in at 75 to 80 years of age. Alcohol abuse and smoking at age 50 were the best predictors of which individuals would be dead at 75 to 80 years of age. Other factors at age 50 were linked with being in the "happy-well" category at 75 to 80 years of age: getting regular exercise; avoiding being overweight; being well educated; having a stable marriage; being future-oriented; being thankful and forgiving; empathizing with others; being active with other people; and having good coping skills. Wealth and income at age 50 were not linked with being in the "happy-well" category at 75 to 80 years of age. The results for one of Vaillant's studies, the Grant Study of Harvard men, are shown in Figure 12.

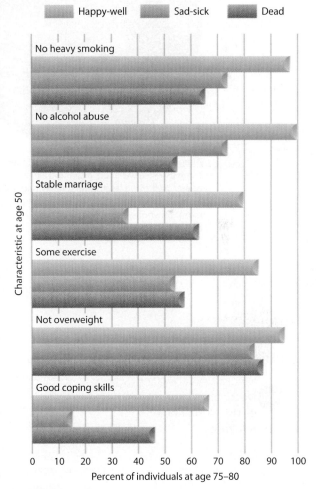

FIGURE 12

LINKS BETWEEN CHARACTERISTICS AT AGE 50 AND HEALTH AND HAPPINESS AT AGE 75 TO 80. In a longitudinal study, the characteristics shown above at age 50 were related to whether individuals were happy-well, sad-sick, or dead at age 75 to 80 (Vaillant, 2002).

developmental **connection**

Life-Span Perspective

The extent to which development is characterized by stability and/or change is one of life-span development's key issues. Connect to "Introduction."

Conclusions What can we conclude about stability and change in personality development during the adult years? According to a recent research review by leading researchers Brent Roberts and Daniel Mroczek (2008), there is increasing evidence that personality traits continue to change during the adult years, even into late adulthood. However, in the recent meta-analysis of 92 longitudinal studies described earlier, the greatest change in personality traits occurred in early adulthood—from about 20 to 40 years of age (Roberts, Walton, & Viechtbauer, 2006).

Thus, people show more stability in their personality when they reach midlife than when they were younger adults (Nye & others, 2015; Roberts, Donnellan, & Hill, 2013). These findings support what is called a *cumulative personality model of personality development*, which states that with time and age people become more adept at interacting with their environment in ways that promote increased stability in personality (Caspi & Roberts, 2001).

This does not mean that change is absent throughout middle and late adulthood. Ample evidence shows that social contexts, new experiences, and sociohistorical changes can affect personality development, but the changes in middle and late adulthood are usually not as great as in early adulthood (Mroczek, Spiro, & Griffin, 2006).

In general, changes in personality traits across adulthood also occur in a positive direction (George, 2010; Staudinger & Jacobs, 2010). Over time, "people become more confident, warm, responsible, and calm" (Roberts & Mroczek, 2008, p. 33). Such positive changes equate with becoming more socially mature.

In sum, recent research contradicts the old view that stability in personality begins to set in at about 30 years of age (Roberts, Donnellan, & Hill, 2013; Nye & others, 2015). Although there are some consistent developmental changes in the personality traits of large numbers of people, at the individual level people can show unique patterns of personality traits, and these patterns often reflect life experiences related to themes of their specific developmental period (Roberts & Mroczek, 2008). For example, researchers have found that individuals who are in a stable marriage and a solid career track become more socially dominant, conscientious, and emotionally stable as they go through early adulthood (Roberts & Wood, 2006). And, for some of these individuals, there is greater change in their personality traits than for other individuals (Roberts, Donnellan, & Hill, 2013).

At age 55, actor Jack Nicholson said, "I feel exactly the same as I've always felt: a slightly reined-in voracious beast." Nicholson felt his personality had not changed much. Some others might think they have changed more. *To what extent does personality change or stay the same through adulthood?*
© Noel Vasquez/Getty Images

Review Connect Reflect

 Describe personality and its development in adulthood

Review

- What are trait theories? What are the Big Five factors of personality?
- What are some views of adult development of personality?
- What is Erikson's view of middle-aged adults?
- What are some major longitudinal studies of adult personality development, and what implications do they have for the stability/change issue?

Connect

- This section discussed four different longitudinal studies. What are the pros and cons of using a longitudinal study to collect data?

Reflect *Your Own Personal Journey of Life*

- Think about the Big Five factors of personality for a few moments. Using the Big Five factors, describe your own personality.

The Self, Identity, and Personality

1 The Self

 LG1 Discuss the main ways the self and understanding others are conceptualized and how they develop

> Self-Understanding and
> Understanding Others

- There is considerable overlap in the concepts of self, identity, and personality. Self consists of all characteristics of a person, identity is who a person is, and personality comprises the enduring personal characteristics of individuals. Self-understanding is the cognitive representation of the self, the substance of self-conceptions. Developmental changes in self-understanding include the construction of the self in infancy in terms of self-recognition and transformations in self-understanding in childhood (including perspective taking). Self-understanding in early childhood is characterized by confusion of self, mind, and body; concrete, physical, and active descriptions; and unrealistic positive overestimations. Young children display more sophisticated self-understanding and understanding of others than was previously thought. Self-understanding in middle and late childhood involves an increase in the use of psychological characteristics and traits, social descriptions, and social comparison; distinction between the real and ideal self; and an increase in realistic self-evaluations. Social understanding also increases in middle and late childhood, especially in taking the perspective of others. Self-definition in adolescence is more abstract and idealistic, involves more contradictions within the self, is more fluctuating, includes concern about the real self versus the ideal self, is characterized by increased self-consciousness, and is more integrative. Increases in social understanding in adolescence involve greater skepticism of others' reports of their traits, more in-depth perspective taking, and social cognitive monitoring. Developments in adults' self-understanding include expanded self-awareness, revision of possible selves, and life reviews of older adults.

> Self-Esteem and
> Self-Concept

- Self-esteem refers to global evaluations of the self; it is also called self-worth and self-image. Self-concept consists of domain-specific evaluations of the self. Self-esteem can change over time, and low self-esteem is linked with depression. The accuracy of self-evaluations increases across the elementary school years. Some studies have found that self-esteem decreases in adolescence, but overall, most adolescents still have positive self-esteem. Important aspects of self-esteem include the degree to which it is linked to performance. This varies, as there are only moderate correlations with school performance and varying correlations with job performance; individuals with high self-esteem have greater initiative and this can produce positive or negative outcomes. Self-esteem is strongly correlated with happiness, but there is a dark side to high self-esteem in that some individuals who have high self-esteem are conceited and narcissistic. Five ways to increase self-esteem are through (1) identifying the causes of low self-esteem and the domains of competence important to the self, (2) providing emotional support and social approval, (3) taking responsibility for self-esteem, (4) achieving goals, and (5) developing effective coping strategies.

> Self-Regulation

- Self-regulation involves the ability to control one's behavior without having to rely on others' help. Two-year-olds may show rudimentary forms of self-regulation, but many preschoolers show increased self-regulation. Elementary-school-aged children increase their self-regulation. In adolescence, some changes may increase self-regulation, while others decrease it. Self-control increases in early and middle adulthood. Self-regulation may vary by domain. For example, older adults often show less self-regulation in the physical domain than younger adults. Baltes proposed the selective optimization with compensation theory of self-regulation. Many older adults show a remarkable ability to engage in self-regulation despite encountering losses.

2 Identity

 LG2 Explain the key facets of identity development

> What Is Identity?

- Identity is a self-portrait with many pieces, including vocational/career identity, political identity, religious identity, relationship identity, sexual identity, and cultural/ethnic identity.

Erikson's View	Identity versus identity confusion is Erikson's fifth developmental stage, which individuals experience during the adolescent years. At this time, adolescents examine who they are, what they are all about, and where they are going in life. Erikson describes the psychosocial moratorium between childhood dependence and adult independence that adolescents experience, which promotes identity exploration.
Some Contemporary Thoughts on Identity	In the contemporary view, identity development is more gradual than Erikson's term *crisis* implies, is extraordinarily complex, neither begins nor ends with adolescence, and emphasizes multiple identities.
Developmental Changes	According to Marcia, various combinations of crisis and commitment produce four identity statuses: identity diffused, identity foreclosed, identity moratorium, and identity achieved. A number of experts stress that the key developmental changes in identity occur in the late teens and early twenties. "MAMA" (moratorium-achievement-moratorium-achievement) cycles may continue throughout adulthood.
Identity and Social Contexts	Adolescents' identity development advances when their relationship with their parents includes both individuality and connectedness. Friendships and romantic relationships influence adolescents' identity development. Cross-cultural variations in identity occur. Ethnic identity may present special issues for members of ethnic minority groups, and they may confront these issues for the first time in adolescence. A positive ethnic identity is increasingly linked to positive outcomes for ethnic minority adolescents.

3 Personality

LG3 Describe personality and its development in adulthood

Trait Theories and the Big Five Factors of Personality	Trait theories state that personality consists of broad dispositions, called traits, that tend to produce characteristic responses. One trait theory that has received considerable attention is the Big Five factors of personality, which consist of openness to experience, conscientiousness, extraversion, agreeableness, and neuroticism. Also, optimism is linked with a number of positive developmental outcomes, including better health and living longer. Today most psychologists stress that personality is a product of trait-situation interaction.
Views on Adult Personality Development	Two of the important adult developmental views are the stage-crisis view and the life-events approach. Levinson's and Erikson's theories are stage-crisis views. Midlife crises do not occur nearly as much as the stereotype suggests. What does arise is a midlife consciousness that focuses on such matters as how to adapt to aging. The life-events approach argues that life events and how people adapt to them are important in understanding adult development. There is considerable variation in how people go through the adult stages of development and in how they experience and adapt to life events.
Generativity	Erikson argues that middle-aged adults face a significant issue in life—generativity versus stagnation—which is the name he gave to the seventh stage in his life-span theory. Generativity encompasses adults' desire to leave a legacy of themselves to the next generation.
Stability and Change	Four longitudinal studies that have addressed stability and change in adult development are Costa and McCrae's Baltimore Study, the Berkeley Longitudinal Studies, Helson's Mills College Study, and Vaillant's studies. The longitudinal studies have shown both stability and change in adult personality development. The cumulative personality model states that with time and age personality becomes more stable. Change in personality traits occurs more in early adulthood than middle and late adulthood, but a number of aspects of personality do continue to change after early adulthood. Change in personality traits across adulthood occurs in a positive direction, reflecting social maturity. At the individual level, changes in personality are often linked to life experiences related to a specific developmental period. Some people change more than others.

key **terms**

bicultural identity
Big Five factors of personality
commitment
connectedness
contemporary life-events
    approach
crisis
ethnic identity

generativity versus stagnation
identity
identity achievement
identity diffusion
identity foreclosure
identity moratorium
identity versus identity
    confusion

individuality
optimism
personality
perspective taking
possible selves
psychosocial moratorium
selective optimization with
    compensation theory

self
self-concept
self-esteem
self-regulation
self-understanding
trait theories

key **people**

Paul Baltes
John Clausen
Paul Costa
Erik Erikson

Susan Harter
Ravenna Helson
Claire Kopp
Daniel Levinson

James Marcia
Robert McCrae
Walter Mischel
Daniel Mroczek

Brent Roberts
Ross Thompson
George Vaillant
Alan Waterman

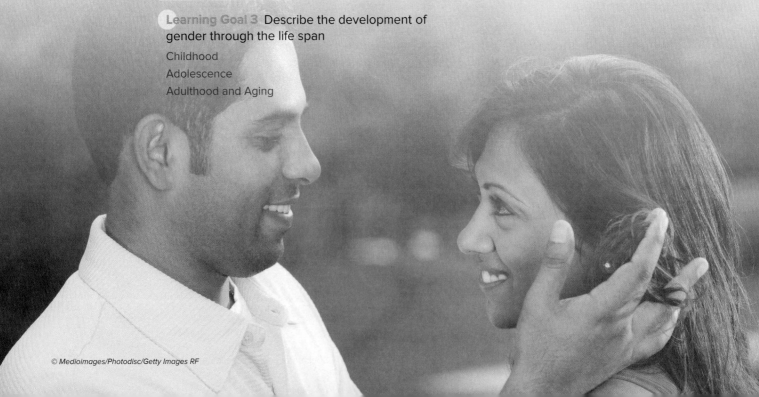

GENDER AND SEXUALITY

chapter **outline**

© Medioimages/Photodisc/Getty Images RF

preview

As females and males, human beings are involved in the existence and continuation of life. Gender and sexuality—our lives as females and males—are important aspects of human development and are the topics of this chapter.

1 Biological, Social, and Cognitive Influences on Gender

LG1 Explain biological, social, and cognitive influences on gender

- Biological Influences
- Social Influences
- Cognitive Influences

Gender refers to the characteristics of people as males and females. **Gender identity** involves a sense of one's own gender, including knowledge, understanding, and acceptance of being male or female (Perry, 2012). **Gender roles** are sets of expectations that prescribe how females or males should think, act, and feel. During the preschool years, most children increasingly act in ways that match their culture's gender roles. **Gender-typing** refers to acquisition of a traditional masculine or feminine role. For example, fighting is more characteristic of a traditional masculine role and crying is more characteristic of a traditional feminine role.

One aspect of gender identity involves knowing whether you are a boy or a girl. Until recently, it was thought that this aspect of gender identity emerged at about 2½ years of age. However, a longitudinal study that explored the acquisition of gender labels in infancy and their implications for gender-typed play revealed that gender identity likely emerges before children are 2 years old (Zosuls & others, 2009). In this study, infants began using gender labels on average at 19 months of age, with girls beginning to use gender labels earlier than boys. This gender difference became present at 17 months and increased at 21 months. Use of gender labels was linked to gender-typed play, indicating that knowledge of gender categories may affect gender-typing earlier than age 2. Another study revealed that sex-typed behavior (boys playing with cars and girls with jewelry, for example) increased during the preschool years, and children who engaged in the most sex-typed behavior during the preschool years were still doing so at 8 years of age (Golombok & others, 2008).

> We are born twice over; the first time for existence, the second time for life; once as human beings and later as men or as women.
>
> **—JEAN-JACQUES ROUSSEAU**
> *French-born Swiss philosopher, 18th century*

BIOLOGICAL INFLUENCES

It was not until the 1920s that researchers confirmed the existence of human sex chromosomes, the genetic material that determines our sex. Humans normally have 46 chromosomes, arranged in pairs. A 23rd pair with two X-shaped chromosomes produces a female. A 23rd pair with an X chromosome and a Y chromosome produces a male.

Hormones The two classes of hormones that have the most influence on gender are estrogens and androgens. Both estrogens and androgens occur in females and males, but in very different concentrations.

Estrogens primarily influence the development of female physical sex characteristics and help regulate the menstrual cycle. Estrogens are a general class of hormones. An example of an important estrogen is estradiol. In females, estrogens are produced mainly by the ovaries.

gender The characteristics of people as females or males.

gender identity Involves a sense of one's own gender, including knowledge, understanding, and acceptance of being male or female.

gender role A set of expectations that prescribe how females or males should think, act, or feel.

gender-typing Acquisition of a traditional masculine or feminine role.

estrogens A class of sex hormones—an important one of which is estradiol—that primarily influences the development of female sex characteristics and helps regulate the menstrual cycle.

developmental **connection**

Biological Processes

The genetic difference in males and females occurs in the 23rd pair of chromosomes: the male's Y chromosome is smaller than the female's X chromosome. Connect to "Biological Beginnings."

developmental **connection**

Biological Processes

Hormones are powerful chemical substances secreted by the endocrine glands and carried through the body by the bloodstream. Connect to "Physical Development and Biological Aging."

Androgens primarily promote the development of male genitals and secondary sex characteristics. One important androgen is testosterone. Androgens are produced by the adrenal glands in males and females, and by the testes in males.

During the first few weeks of gestation, female and male embryos look alike. Male sex organs start to differ from female sex organs when a gene on the Y chromosome directs a small piece of tissue in the embryo to turn into testes. Once the tissue has turned into testes, they begin to secrete testosterone. Because in females there is no Y chromosome, the tissue turns into ovaries. To explore biological influences on gender, researchers have studied individuals who are exposed to unusual levels of sex hormones early in development (Hines, 2013, 2015). Here are four examples of the problems that may occur as a result of such exposure (Lippa, 2005, pp. 122–124, 136–137):

· *Congenital adrenal hyperplasia (CAH).* Some girls have this condition, which is caused by a genetic defect. Their adrenal glands enlarge, resulting in abnormally high levels of androgens. Although CAH girls are XX females, they vary in how much their genitals look like male or female genitals. Their genitals may be surgically altered to look more like those of a typical female (Gonzalez & Ludwikowski, 2014). Although CAH girls usually grow up to think of themselves as girls and women, they are less content with being a female and show a stronger interest in being a male than non-CAH girls (Berenbaum & Bailey, 2003; Hall & others, 2004). They like sports and enjoy playing with boys and boys' toys. CAH girls usually don't like typical girl activities such as playing with dolls and wearing makeup.

· *Androgen-insensitive males.* Because of a genetic error, a small number of XY males don't have androgen cells in their bodies. Their bodies look female, they develop a female gender identity, and they usually are sexually attracted to males.

· *Pelvic field defect.* A small number of newborns have a disorder called pelvic field defect, which in boys involves a missing penis. These XY boys have normal amounts of testosterone prenatally but usually are castrated just after being born and raised as females. One study revealed that despite the efforts by parents to rear them as girls, most of the XY children insisted that they were boys (Reiner & Gearhart, 2004). Apparently, normal exposure to androgens prenatally had a stronger influence on their gender identity than being castrated and raised as girls.

· *Early loss of penis and sexual reassignment.* In an intriguing case, one of two identical twin boys lost his penis due to an errant circumcision. The twin who lost his penis was surgically reassigned to be a girl and reared as a girl. Bruce (the real name of the boy) became "Brenda." Early indications were that the sex reassignment had positive outcomes (Money, 1975), but later it was concluded that "Brenda" had not adjusted well to life as a girl (Diamond & Sigmundson, 1997). As a young adult, Brenda became David and lived as a man with a wife and adopted children (Colapinto, 2000). Tragically in 2004, when David was 38 years old, he committed suicide.

Although sex hormones alone do not dictate behavior, researchers have found links between sex hormone levels and certain behaviors (Hines, 2013, 2015). The most established effects of testosterone on humans involve aggressive behavior and sexual behavior (Hyde & DeLamater, 2014). Levels of testosterone are correlated with sexual behavior in boys during puberty (Udry & others, 1985). And one study revealed that a higher fetal testosterone level measured from amniotic fluid was linked to increased male-typical play, such as increased aggression, in 6- to 10-year-old boys and girls (Auyeung & others, 2009).

androgens A class of sex hormones—an important one of which is testosterone—that primarily promotes the development of male genitals and secondary sex characteristics.

social role theory Eagly's theory that psychological gender differences are caused by the contrasting social roles of women and men.

The Evolutionary Psychology View Evolutionary psychology emphasizes that adaptation during the evolution of humans produced psychological differences between males and females (Buss, 2012, 2015; Buss & Penke, 2014). Evolutionary psychologists argue that primarily because of their differing roles in reproduction, males and females faced different pressures in primeval environments when the human species was evolving. In particular, because having multiple sexual liaisons improves the likelihood that males will pass on their genes, natural selection favored males who adopted short-term mating strategies. These males competed with other males to acquire more resources in order to access females. Therefore, say evolutionary psychologists, males evolved dispositions that favor violence, competition, and risk taking (Schmitt & others, 2012).

In contrast, according to evolutionary psychologists, females' contributions to the gene pool were improved by securing resources for their offspring, which was promoted by obtaining long-term mates who could support a family. As a consequence, natural selection favored females who devoted effort to parenting and chose mates who could provide their offspring with resources and protection. Females developed preferences for successful, ambitious men who could provide these resources (Buss, 2012, 2015).

Critics of evolutionary psychology argue that its hypotheses are backed by speculations about prehistory, not evidence, and that in any event people are not locked into behavior that was adaptive in the evolutionary past. Critics also claim that the evolutionary view pays little attention to cultural and individual variations in gender differences (Hyde & Else-Quest, 2013).

SOCIAL INFLUENCES

Many social scientists do not locate the cause of psychological gender differences in biological dispositions. Rather, they argue that these differences are due to social experiences. Three theories that reflect this view have been influential.

Alice Eagly (2001, 2010, 2012, 2013) proposed **social role theory,** which states that psychological gender differences result from the contrasting roles of women and men. In most cultures around the world, women have less power and status than men do, and they control fewer resources (UNICEF, 2015). Compared with men, women perform more domestic work, spend fewer hours in paid employment, receive lower pay, and are more thinly represented in the highest levels of organizations. In Eagly's view, as women adapted to roles with less power and less status in society, they showed more cooperative, less dominant profiles than men. Thus, the social hierarchy and division of labor are important causes of gender differences in power, assertiveness, and nurture (Eagly & Antonakis, 2014; Eagly, Gartzia, & Carli, 2014).

The **psychoanalytic theory of gender** stems from Sigmund Freud's view that the preschool child develops a sexual attraction to the opposite-sex parent. At 5 or 6 years of age, the child renounces this attraction because of anxious feelings. Subsequently, the child identifies with the same-sex parent, unconsciously adopting the same-sex parent's characteristics. However, developmentalists do not hold that gender development proceeds as Freud proposed. Children become gender-typed much earlier than 5 or 6 years of age, and they become masculine or feminine even when the same-sex parent is not present in the family.

The social cognitive approach provides an alternative explanation of how children develop gender-typed behavior (see Figure 1). According to the **social cognitive theory of gender,**

developmental **connection**

Biological Processes

Evolutionary psychology emphasizes the importance of adaptation, reproduction, and "survival of the fittest" in shaping behavior. Connect to "Biological Beginnings."

Sex differences are adaptations to the differing restrictions and opportunities that a society provides for its men and women.

—ALICE EAGLY

Contemporary psychologist, Northwestern University

developmental **connection**

Theories

Freud proposed that individuals go through five stages of psychosocial development. Connect to "Introduction."

developmental **connection**

Social Cognitive Theory

Social cognitive theory holds that behavior, environment, and person (cognitive) factors are the key aspects of development. Connect to "Introduction."

Theory	Processes	Outcome
Psychoanalytic theory	Sexual attraction to opposite-sex parent at 3 to 5 years of age; anxiety about sexual attraction and subsequent identification with same-sex parent at 5 to 6 years of age	Gender behavior similar to that of same-sex parent
Social cognitive theory	Rewards and punishments of gender-appropriate and -inappropriate behavior by adults and peers; observation and imitation of models' masculine and feminine behavior	Gender behavior

FIGURE 1

PARENTS INFLUENCE THEIR CHILDREN'S GENDER DEVELOPMENT BY ACTION AND EXAMPLE

psychoanalytic theory of gender Theory that stems from Freud's view that preschool children develop a sexual attraction to the opposite-sex parent, then at 5 or 6 years of age renounce the attraction because of anxious feelings, subsequently identifying with the same-sex parent and unconsciously adopting the same-sex parent's characteristics.

social cognitive theory of gender The idea that children's gender development occurs through observation and imitation of gender behavior, as well as through the rewards and punishments children experience for behaviors believed to be appropriate or inappropriate for their gender.

"How is it gendered?"
© Edward Koren/The New Yorker Collection/
www.cartoonbank.com

children's gender development occurs through observation and imitation, and through the rewards and punishments children experience for gender-appropriate and gender-inappropriate behavior (Bussey & Bandura, 1999; Leaper, 2015).

Parents   Parents, by action and example, influence their children's and adolescents' gender development. Parents often use rewards and punishments to teach their daughters to be feminine ("Karen, you are being a good girl when you play gently with your doll") and their sons to be masculine ("Keith, a boy as big as you is not supposed to cry").

Mothers and fathers often interact differently with their children and adolescents (Leaper, 2015). Mothers are more involved with their children and adolescents than are fathers, although fathers increase the time they spend in parenting when they have sons, and they are less likely to become divorced when they have sons (Galambos, Berenbaum, & McHale, 2009). Mothers' interactions with their children and adolescents often center on caregiving and teaching activities, whereas fathers' interactions often involve leisure activities (Galambos & others, 2009).

Parents frequently interact differently with sons and daughters, and these gendered interactions that begin in infancy usually continue through childhood and adolescence (Leaper, 2015). In reviewing research on this topic, Phyllis Bronstein (2006) reached these conclusions:

· *Mothers' socialization strategies.* In many cultures, mothers socialize their daughters to be more obedient and responsible than their sons. They also place more restrictions on daughters' autonomy.

· *Fathers' socialization strategies.* Fathers pay more attention to sons than to daughters, engage in more activities with sons, and put forth more effort to promote sons' intellectual development.

Thus, according to Bronstein (2006, pp. 269–270), "Despite an increased awareness in the United States and other Western cultures of the detrimental effects of gender stereotyping, many parents continue to foster behaviors and perceptions that are consonant with traditional gender role norms."

Other Adults, Media, and Peers   Children also learn about gender from observing other adults in the neighborhood and in the media (Brannon, 2012). As children get older, peers become increasingly important. Peers extensively reward and punish gender behavior (Leaper, 2013, 2015; Rubin, Bukowski, & Bowker, 2015). For example, when children play in ways that the culture says are sex-appropriate, they tend to be rewarded by their peers. Those who engage in activities that are considered sex-inappropriate tend to be criticized or abandoned by their peers. It is generally more accepted for girls to act like boys than for boys to act like girls; thus, use of the term *tomboy* to describe masculine girls is often thought of as less derogatory than the term *sissy* to describe feminine boys (Pasterski, Golombok, & Hines, 2011).

From 4 to about 12 years of age, children spend a large majority of their free play time exclusively with others of their own sex (Maccoby, 2002). What kind of socialization takes place in these same-sex play groups? In one study, researchers observed preschoolers over a period of six months (Martin & Fabes, 2001). The more time boys spent interacting with other boys, the more their activity level, rough-and-tumble play, and sex-typed choice of toys and games increased, and the less time boys spent near adults. By contrast, the more time the preschool girls spent interacting with other girls, the more their activity level and aggression decreased, and the more their girl-type play activities and time spent near adults increased. A recent study of preschool children (average age: 4 years) found that children selected playmates of the same sex who engaged in similar levels of gender-typed activities (Martin & others, 2013). In selecting a playmate, comparisons of sex of child and activity revealed that sex of the playmate was more important than activity. After watching elementary school children repeatedly play in same-sex groups, two researchers characterized the playground as "gender school" (Luria & Herzog, 1985). Continuing in adolescence and the adulthood years through late adulthood, friendships also mainly consist of same-sex peers (Mehta & Strough, 2009, 2010).

What role does gender play in children's peer relations?
Left: © Tom Prettyman/PhotoEdit; Right: © Cindy Charles/PhotoEdit

Schools and Teachers   Some observers have expressed concern that schools and teachers have biases against both boys and girls (Mullola & others, 2012). What evidence exists that the classroom setting is biased against boys? Here are some factors to consider (DeZolt & Hull, 2001):

· Compliance, following rules, and being neat and orderly are valued and reinforced in many classrooms. These are behaviors that usually characterize girls more than boys.

· A large majority of teachers are females, especially at the elementary school level. This trend may make it more difficult for boys than for girls to identify with their teachers and model their teachers' behavior. A recent study revealed that male teachers perceived boys more positively and saw them as more educationally competent than did female teachers (Mullola & others, 2012).

· Boys are more likely than girls to have a learning disability, ADHD, and to drop out of school.

· Boys are more likely than girls to be criticized by their teachers.

· School personnel tend to stereotype boys' behavior as problematic.

What evidence is there that the classroom setting is biased against girls? Consider the views of Myra and David Sadker (2005):

· In a typical classroom, girls are more compliant and boys are more rambunctious. Boys demand more attention, and girls are more likely to quietly wait their turn. Teachers are more likely to scold and reprimand boys, as well as send boys to school authorities for disciplinary action. Educators worry that girls' tendency to be compliant and quiet comes at a cost: diminished assertiveness.

· In many classrooms, teachers spend more time watching and interacting with boys, whereas girls work and play quietly on their own. Most teachers don't intentionally favor boys by spending more time with them, yet somehow the classroom frequently ends up with this type of gendered profile.

· Boys get more instruction than girls and more help when they have trouble with a question. Teachers often give boys more time to answer a question, more hints at the correct answer, and further tries if they give the wrong answer.

· Girls and boys enter first grade with roughly equal levels of self-esteem. Yet by the middle school years, girls' self-esteem is lower than boys'.

Thus, there is evidence of gender bias against both males and females in schools. Many school personnel are not aware of their gender-biased attitudes. These attitudes are deeply

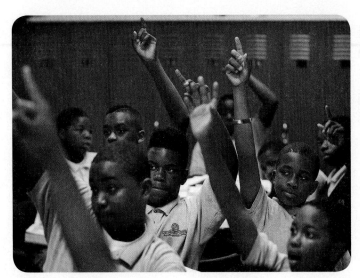

What are some recent changes in single-sex education in the United States? What does research say about whether single-sex education is beneficial?
© Jim Weber/The Commercial Appeal/Landov

entrenched in and supported by the general culture. Increasing awareness of gender bias in schools is clearly an important strategy in reducing such bias.

Might single-sex education be better for children than coed education? The argument for single-sex education is that it eliminates distraction from the other sex and reduces sexual harassment. Single-sex public education has increased dramatically in recent years. In 2002, only 12 public schools in the U.S. provided single-sex education; in the 2011–2012 school year, 116 public schools were single-sex and an additional 390 provided such experiences (NASSPE, 2012).

The increase in single-sex education has especially been fueled by its inclusion in the No Child Left Behind legislation as a means of improving the educational experiences and academic achievement of low-income students of color. It appears that many of the public schools offering single-sex education have a high percentage of such youth (Klein, 2012). However, recent research reviews concluded that there have been no documented benefits of single-sex education, especially in the highest-quality studies (Goodkind, 2013; Halpern & others, 2011; Pahlke, Hyde, & Allison, 2014). One review, titled "The Pseudoscience of Single-Sex Schooling," by Diane Halpern and her colleagues (2011) concluded that single-sex education is highly misguided, misconstrued, and unsupported by any valid scientific evidence. They emphasize that among the many arguments against single-sex education, the strongest is its reduction in the opportunities for boys and girls to work together in a supervised, purposeful environment.

There has been a special call for single-sex public education for one group of adolescents—African American boys—because of their historically poor academic achievement and high dropout rate from school (Mitchell & Stewart, 2013). In 2010, Urban Prep Academy for Young Men became the first all-male, all African American public charter school. One hundred percent of its first graduates enrolled in college, despite the school's location in a section of Chicago where poverty, gangs, and crime predominate. Because so few public schools focus solely on educating African American boys, it is too early to tell whether this type of single-sex education can be effective across a wide range of participants.

COGNITIVE INFLUENCES

Observation, imitation, rewards, and punishment—these are the mechanisms by which gender develops, according to social cognitive theory. Interactions between the child and the social environment are viewed as the main keys to gender development. Some critics who adopt a cognitive approach argue that social cognitive explanations pay too little attention to the child's own mind and understanding, portraying the child as passively acquiring gender roles (Martin, Ruble, & Szkrybalo, 2002).

One influential cognitive theory is **gender schema theory,** which states that gender-typing emerges as children gradually develop gender schemas of what is gender-appropriate and gender-inappropriate in their culture (Martin & Ruble, 2010). A *schema* is a cognitive structure, a network of associations that guide an individual's perceptions. A *gender schema* organizes the world in terms of female and male. Children are internally motivated to perceive the world and to act in accordance with their developing schemas. Bit by bit, children pick up what is gender-appropriate and gender-inappropriate in their culture, using this information to develop gender schemas that shape how they perceive the world and what they remember (Conry-Murray, Kim, & Turiel, 2012). Children are motivated to act in ways that conform to these gender schemas. Thus, gender schemas fuel gender-typing. How effectively do gender schemas extend to young children's judgments about occupations, for instance? For more information on this topic, see the *Connecting with Research* interlude.

In sum, cognitive factors contribute to the way children think and act as males and females. Through biological, social, and cognitive processes, children develop their gender attitudes and behaviors (Hines, 2013; Leaper, 2013).

gender schema theory The theory that gender-typing emerges as children gradually develop gender schemas of what is gender-appropriate and gender-inappropriate in their culture.

What Are Young Children's Gender Schemas About Occupations?

In one study, researchers interviewed children 3 to 7 years old about 10 traditionally masculine occupations (airplane pilot, car mechanic) and feminine occupations (clothes designer, secretary), using questions such as these (Levy, Sadovsky, & Troseth, 2000):

- *Example of a traditionally masculine occupation item.* An airplane pilot is a person who "flies airplanes for people." Who do you think would do the best job as an airplane pilot, a man or a woman?
- *Example of a traditionally feminine occupation item.* A clothing designer is a person "who draws up and makes clothes for people." Who do you think would do the best job as a clothes designer, a man or a woman?

As indicated in Figure 2, the children had well-developed gender schemas, in this case reflected in stereotypes, of occupations. They "viewed men as more competent than women in masculine occupations, and rated women as more competent than men in feminine occupations" (p. 993). Also, "girls' ratings of women's competence at feminine occupations were substantially higher than their ratings of men's competence at masculine occupations. Conversely, boys' ratings of men's competence at masculine occupations were considerably greater than their ratings of women's competence at

feminine occupations" (p. 1002). These findings demonstrate that children as young as 3 to 4 years of age have strong gender schemas regarding the perceived competencies of men and women in gender-typed occupations.

The researchers also asked the children to select from a list of emotions how they would feel if they grew up to have each of the 10 occupations. Girls said they would be happy with the feminine occupations and angry or disgusted with the masculine occupations. As expected, boys said they would be happy if they had the masculine occupations but angry and disgusted with the feminine occupations. However, the boys' emotions were more intense (more angry and disgusted) in desiring to avoid the feminine occupations than girls in wanting to avoid the masculine occupations. This finding supports other research that indicates gender roles often constrict boys more than girls (Matlin, 2012).

Children in this study were at the height of gender stereotyping. Most older children, adolescents, and adults become more flexible about occupational roles (Leaper, 2013). What does our understanding of this flexibility suggest about the role of education in reducing gender-based stereotypes?

	Boy	Girl
"Masculine Occupations"		
Percentage who judged men more competent	87	70
Percentage who judged women more competent	13	30
"Feminine Occupations"		
Percentage who judged men more competent	35	8
Percentage who judged women more competent	64	92

FIGURE 2

CHILDREN'S JUDGMENTS ABOUT THE COMPETENCE OF MEN AND WOMEN IN GENDER-STEREOTYPED OCCUPATIONS

Review Connect Reflect

 LG1 Explain biological, social, and cognitive influences on gender

Review

- What is gender? What are some components of gender?
- How does biology influence gender?
- How do cognitive factors influence gender development?

Connect

- Compare biological, social, and cognitive influences on gender.

Reflect *Your Own Personal Journey of Life*

- Which theory of gender development do you think best explains your gender development? Explain. What might an eclectic view of gender development be like? (You might want to review the discussion of an eclectic theoretical view in the "Introduction" chapter.)

2 Gender Stereotypes, Similarities, and Differences

LG2 Discuss gender stereotypes, similarities, and differences

Gender Stereotyping

Gender Similarities and Differences

First imagine that this is a photograph of a baby girl. *What expectations would you have for her?* Then imagine that this is a photograph of a baby boy. *What expectations would you have for him?*
© Getty Images RF

To what extent do real behavioral differences exist between males and females? Are many of the reported differences just stereotypes?

GENDER STEREOTYPING

Gender stereotypes are general impressions and beliefs about females and males. For example, men are powerful; women are weak. Men make good physicians; women make good nurses. Men are good with numbers; women are good with words. Women are emotional; men are not. All of these are stereotypes. They are generalizations about a group that reflect widely held beliefs. Recent research has found that gender stereotypes are, to a great extent, still present in today's world, in the lives of both children and adults (Leaper, 2013, 2015). Researchers also have found that boys' gender stereotypes are more rigid than girls' (Blakemore, Berenbaum, & Liben, 2009).

Traditional Masculinity and Femininity A classic study in the early 1970s assessed which traits and behaviors college students believed were characteristic of females and which they believed were characteristic of males (Broverman & others, 1972). The traits associated with males were labeled *instrumental:* they included characteristics such as being independent, aggressive, and power-oriented. The traits associated with females were labeled *expressive:* they included characteristics such as being warm and sensitive.

Thus, the instrumental traits associated with males suited them for the traditional masculine role of going out into the world as the breadwinner. The expressive traits associated with females paralleled the traditional feminine role of being the sensitive, nurturing caregiver in the home. These roles and traits, however, are not just different; they also are unequal in terms of social status and power. The traditional feminine characteristics are childlike, suitable for someone who is dependent and subordinate to others. The traditional masculine characteristics suit one to deal competently with the wider world and to wield authority.

Developmental Changes in Gender Stereotyping Earlier we described how young children stereotype occupations as being "masculine" or "feminine." When do children begin to engage in gender stereotyping? In one study, gender stereotyping by children was present even in 2-year-olds, but increased considerably by 4 years of age (Gelman, Taylor, & Nguyen, 2004).

Gender stereotyping continues to change during middle and late childhood and adolescence (Martin & Ruble, 2010). A study of 3- to 10-year-old U.S. children revealed that girls and older children used a higher percentage of gender stereotypes (Miller & others, 2009). In this study, appearance stereotypes were more prevalent on the part of girls, whereas activity (sports, for example) and trait (aggressive, for example) stereotyping was more commonly engaged in by boys. During middle and late childhood, children expanded the range and extent of their gender stereotyping in areas such as occupations, sports, and school tasks. In early adolescence, gender stereotyping might increase again, a topic we will address shortly. By late adolescence, gender attitudes become more flexible.

gender stereotypes General impressions and beliefs about females and males.

GENDER SIMILARITIES AND DIFFERENCES

What is the reality behind gender stereotypes? Let's examine some of the differences between the sexes, keeping the following information in mind:

· The differences are averages and do not apply to all females or all males.
· Even when gender differences occur, there often is considerable overlap between males and females.
· The differences may be due primarily to biological factors, sociocultural factors, or both.

First, we examine physical similarities and differences, and then we turn to cognitive and socioemotional similarities and differences.

Physical Similarities and Differences We could devote pages to describing physical differences between the average man and the average woman. For example, women have about twice the body fat of men, most of it concentrated around breasts and hips. In males, fat is more likely to go to the abdomen. On average, males grow to be 10 percent taller than females. Androgens (the "male" hormones) promote the growth of long bones; estrogens (the "female" hormones) stop such growth at puberty.

Many physical differences between men and women are tied to health. From conception onward, females have a longer life expectancy than males, and females are less likely than males to develop physical or mental disorders. Females are more resistant to infection, and their blood vessels are more elastic than males'. Males have higher levels of stress hormones, which cause faster clotting and higher blood pressure.

Just how much does gender matter when it comes to brain structure and activity? Among the differences that have been discovered are the following:

· One part of the hypothalamus involved in sexual behavior tends to be larger in men than in women (Swaab & others, 2001).
· An area of the parietal lobe that functions in visuospatial skills tends to be larger in males than in females (Frederikse & others, 2000).
· The areas of the brain involved in emotional expression tend to show more metabolic activity in females than in males (Gur & others, 1995).
· Female brains are approximately 10 percent smaller than male brains (Giedd & others, 2012). However, female brains have more folds; the larger folds (called convolutions) allow more surface brain tissue within the skulls of females than males (Luders & others, 2004).

Although some gender differences in brain structure and function have been found, many of these differences are small or research results are inconsistent regarding the differences. Also, when gender differences in the brain have been detected, in many cases they have not been directly linked to psychological differences (Blakemore & others, 2009). Although research on gender differences in the brain is still in its infancy, it is likely that there are far more similarities than differences in the brains of females and males (Hyde, 2007). Similarities and differences in the brains of males and females could be due to evolution and heredity as well as experiences.

What are some developmental changes in children's gender stereotyping? What are some cautions in interpreting gender differences?
(top): © Peter Dazeley/Getty Images; (bottom): © Turbo/Corbis Images

Cognitive Similarities and Differences No gender differences occur in overall intellectual ability, but in some cognitive areas gender differences do appear (Galambos & others, 2009; Ganley, Vasilyeva, & Dulaney, 2014; Halpern, 2012). Some gender experts, such as Janet Shibley Hyde (2007, 2014), stress that the cognitive differences between females and males have been exaggerated. For example, Hyde points out that there usually is considerable overlap in the distributions of female and male scores on visuospatial tasks (see Figure 3). However, some researchers have found that males have better visuospatial skills than females (Halpern, 2012). Despite equal participation in the National Geography Bee, in most years all 10 finalists have been boys (Liben, 1995). Also, a research review concluded that boys have better visuospatial skills than girls (Halpern

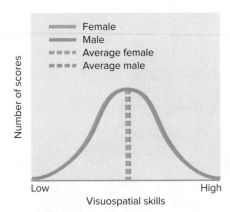

Legend:
— Female
— Male
- - - - Average female
- - - - Average male

Number of scores (y-axis)
Visuospatial skills (x-axis: Low → High)

FIGURE 3

VISUOSPATIAL SKILLS OF MALES AND FEMALES. Notice that, although an average male's visuospatial skills are higher than an average female's, scores for the two sexes almost entirely overlap. Not all males have better visuospatial skills than all females—the overlap indicates that, although the average male score is higher, many females outperform most males on such tasks.

"So according to the stereotype, you can put two and two together, but I can read the handwriting on the wall."
Copyright © 1994 Joel Pett. Reprinted by permission.

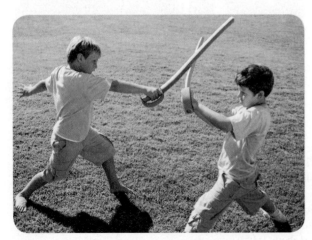

What gender differences characterize aggression?
© Corbis RF

& others, 2007). A recent research review found that having a stronger masculine gender role was linked to better spatial ability in males and females (Reilly & Neuman, 2013).

Are there gender differences in math ability? A very large-scale study of more than 7 million U.S. students in grades 2 through 11 revealed no differences in math scores for boys and girls (Hyde & others, 2008). And a recent meta-analysis found no gender differences in math scores for adolescents (Lindberg & others, 2010). Further, in the National Assessment of Educational Progress (2014) there were virtually no gender differences in math scores at the fourth- and eighth-grade levels.

Despite the similarities in math achievement scores for boys and girls, a recent research review concluded that girls have more negative math attitudes and that parents' and teachers' expectations for children's math competence are often gender-biased in favor of boys (Gunderson & others, 2012). And in a recent study, 6- to 12-year-olds reported that math is mainly for boys (Cvencek, Meltzoff, & Greenwald, 2011).

Are there gender differences in reading and writing skills? There is strong evidence that females outperform males in reading and writing. In the most recent National Assessment of Educational Progress (2014) report, girls had higher reading achievement than boys in both fourth- and eighth-grade assessments (National Assessment of Educational Progress, 2014). Girls also have consistently outperformed boys in writing skills in the National Assessment of Educational Progress in fourth-, eighth-, and twelfth-grade assessments.

With regard to school achievement, girls earn better grades and complete high school at a higher rate than boys (Halpern, 2012). Males are more likely than females to be assigned to special/remedial education classes. Girls are more likely than boys to be engaged with academic material, be attentive in class, put forth more academic effort, and participate more in class (DeZolt & Hull, 2001).

Keep in mind that measures of achievement in school or scores on standardized tests may reflect many factors besides cognitive ability. For example, performance in school may in part reflect attempts to conform to gender roles or differences in motivation, self-regulation, or other socioemotional characteristics (Eccles, 2014; Watt & Eccles, 2008; Wigfield & others, 2015).

Socioemotional Similarities and Differences Are "men from Mars" and "women from Venus"? Perhaps the gender differences that most fascinate people are those regarding how males and females relate to each other as people. For just about every imaginable socioemotional characteristic, researchers have examined whether there are differences between males and females. Here we examine just two that have been closely studied: (1) aggression and (2) emotion and its regulation.

One of the most consistent gender differences identified is that boys are more physically aggressive than girls (Coyne, Nelson, & Underwood, 2011). The difference occurs in all cultures and appears very early in children's development. The difference in physical aggression is especially pronounced when children are provoked.

Although boys are consistently more physically aggressive than girls, might girls show as much or more verbal aggression, such as yelling, than boys? When verbal aggression is examined, gender differences typically disappear or aggression is even more pronounced in girls (Eagly & Steffen, 1986).

Recently, increased interest has been directed toward *relational aggression*, which involves harming someone by manipulating a relationship. Relational aggression includes such behaviors as trying to make others dislike a certain individual by spreading malicious rumors about the person (Busching & Krahe, 2015; Kawabata, Tseng, & Crick, 2014; Orpinas, McNicholas, & Nahapetyan, 2015). Relational aggression increases in middle and late childhood (Dishion & Piehler, 2009). Mixed findings have characterized research on whether girls show more relational aggression than boys, but one consistent finding is that relational aggression comprises a greater percentage of overall aggression for girls than for boys (Putallaz & others, 2007). And a research review revealed that girls engage in more relational aggression than boys in adolescence but not in childhood (Smith, Rose, & Schwartz-Mette, 2010). Further, in a longitudinal study, preschool relational aggression predicted adolescent relational aggression for girls but not for boys (Nelson & others, 2014).

Gender differences occur in some aspects of emotion (Nolen-Hoeksema, 2012). Females express emotion more openly than males, are better than males at decoding emotion, smile more, cry more, and are happier (Brody & Hall, 2008; Gross, Frederickson, & Levenson, 1994; LaFrance, Hecht, & Paluck, 2003). Males report experiencing and expressing more anger than females (Kring, 2000). Girls also are better at reading others' emotions and more likely to show empathy than are boys (Blakemore & others, 2009). A recent meta-analysis found that females are better than males at recognizing nonverbal displays of emotion (Thompson & Voyer, 2014). A recent meta-analysis also revealed that overall gender differences in children's emotional expression were small, with girls showing more positive emotion (sympathy, for example) and more internalized emotions (sadness and anxiety, for example) (Chaplin & Aldao, 2013). In this analysis, the gender difference in positive emotions became more pronounced with age as girls more strongly expressed positive emotions than boys in middle and late childhood and in adolescence.

An important skill is to be able to regulate and control one's emotions and behavior (Thompson, 2015). Boys usually show less self-regulation than girls (Blakemore & others, 2009). This low self-control can translate into behavior problems.

Researchers have found that girls are more "people oriented" and boys are more "things oriented" (Galambos & others, 2009). In a recent research review, this conclusion was supported by findings that girls spend more time and energy building relationships, while boys spend more time alone, playing video games, and playing sports; that girls work at part-time jobs that are people-oriented such as waitressing and babysitting, while boys are more likely to take part-time jobs that involve manual labor and using tools; and girls are interested in careers that are more people-oriented, such as teaching and social work, while boys are more likely to be interested in object-oriented careers, such as mechanics and engineering (Perry & Pauletti, 2011). Researchers have found that adolescent girls engage in more self-disclosure (communication of intimate details about themselves) in close relationships, are better at actively listening in a conversation than are boys, and emphasize affiliation or collaboration (Hall, 2011; Leaper, 2013). Adolescent girls are especially likely to engage in self-disclosure and emotional support in friendship than are boys (Leaper, 2013). By contrast, boys are more likely to value self-assertion and dominance than are girls in their interactions with friends and peers (Rose & Rudolph, 2006; Leaper, 2013).

Gender Controversy   Controversy continues about the extent of gender differences and what might cause them (Leaper, 2013, 2015; Hyde, 2014). As we saw earlier, evolutionary psychologists such as David Buss (2012) argue that gender differences are extensive and caused by the adaptive problems people have faced across their evolutionary history. Alice Eagly (2012, 2013) also concludes that gender differences are substantial but reaches a very different conclusion about their cause. She traces gender differences to social conditions that have resulted in women having less power and controlling fewer resources than men do.

By contrast, Janet Shibley Hyde (2007, 2014) concludes that gender differences have been greatly exaggerated, with these comparisons being especially fueled by popular books such as John Gray's (1992) *Men Are from Mars, Women Are from Venus* and Deborah Tannen's (1990) *You Just Don't Understand*. She argues that the research indicates females and males are similar on most psychological factors. In a research review, Hyde (2005) summarized the results of 44 meta-analyses of gender differences and similarities. A *meta-analysis* is a statistical analysis that combines the results of many different studies. Gender differences in most areas—including math ability and communication—were either nonexistent or small. Gender differences in physical aggression were moderate. The largest difference occurred on motor skills (favoring males), followed by sexuality (males masturbate more and are more likely to endorse sex in a casual, uncommitted relationship) and physical aggression (males are more physically aggressive than are females).

Hyde's summary of meta-analyses is unlikely to quiet the controversy about gender differences and similarities, but further research should be conducted to provide a basis for more accurate judgments on this topic.

Gender in Context   In thinking about gender, it is important to consider the context of behavior (Leaper, 2013, 2015). Gender behavior often varies across contexts. Consider helping

developmental **connection**

Nature and Nurture
Bronfenbrenner's ecological theory emphasizes the importance of contexts; in his theory, the macrosystem includes cross-cultural comparisons. Connect to "Introduction."

In China, females and males are usually socialized to behave, feel, and think differently. The old patriarchal traditions of male supremacy have not been completely uprooted. Chinese women still make considerably less money than Chinese men do, and, in rural China (such as here in the Lixian Village of Sichuan), male supremacy still governs many women's lives.
© Richard Mayer/age fotostock

behavior. Males are more likely to help in contexts in which a perceived danger is present and they feel competent to help (Eagly & Crowley, 1986). For example, males are more likely than females to help a person who is stranded by the roadside with a flat tire; automobile problems are an area in which many males feel competent. In contrast, when the context involves volunteering time to help a child with a personal problem, females are more likely to help than males are, because there is little danger present and females feel more competent at nurturing. In many cultures, girls show more caregiving behavior than boys do.

Context is also relevant to gender differences in the display of emotions (Shields, 1998). Consider anger. Males are more likely to show anger toward strangers, especially other males, when they think they have been challenged. Males also are more likely than females to turn their anger into aggressive action, especially when their culture endorses such action (Tavris & Wade, 1984).

In many cultures around the world, traditional gender roles continue to guide the behavior of males and females (UNICEF, 2015). In China and Iran, for instance, it is still widely accepted for males to engage in dominant behavior and females to behave in subordinate ways. Many Western cultures, such as the United States, have become more flexible about gender behavior and allow for more diversity. For example, although a girl's father might promote traditional femininity, her friends might engage in many traditionally masculine activities and her teachers might encourage her to be assertive.

In the United States, the cultural backgrounds of children and adolescents influence how boys and girls will be socialized. In one study, Latino and Latina adolescents were socialized differently as they were growing up (Raffaelli & Ontai, 2004). Latinas experienced far greater restrictions than Latinos in having curfews, interacting with members of the other sex, getting a driver's license, getting a job, and being involved in after-school activities.

Review Connect Reflect

 LG2 Discuss gender stereotypes, similarities, and differences

Review
- What is gender stereotyping, and how extensive is it?
- What are some physical, cognitive, and socioemotional differences between men and women?

Connect
- Compare cognitive and socioemotional similarities and differences based on gender. What are your conclusions?

Reflect *Your Own Personal Journey of Life*
- How do your gender behavior and thoughts stack up against the similarities and differences in gender we discussed?

3 Gender Development Through the Life Span   **LG3** Describe the development of gender through the life span

Childhood   Adolescence   Adulthood and Aging

In this section we will focus further on gender-related developmental changes in the childhood years. In addition, we will look at some changes that take place in adolescence and adulthood, including the influence of gender roles in adolescence and some of the ways in which gender roles might shift as people age.

CHILDHOOD

The amount, timing, and intensity of gender socialization differs for girls and boys (Beal, 1994). Boys receive earlier and more intense gender socialization than girls do. The social cost of deviating from the expected male role is higher for boys than is the cost for girls of deviating from the expected female role, in terms of peer rejection and parental disapproval.

Imagine a girl who is wearing a toy holster, bandanna, and cowboy hat, running around in the backyard pretending to herd cattle. Now imagine a boy who is wearing a flowered hat, ropes of pearls, and lipstick, pretending to cook dinner on a toy stove. Which of these do you have a stronger reaction to—the girl's behavior or the boy's? Probably the boy's. Researchers have found that "effeminate" behavior in boys elicits more negative reactions than does "masculine" behavior in girls (Martin, 1990).

Boys might have a more difficult time learning the masculine gender role because male models are less accessible to young children and messages from adults about the male role are not always consistent. For example, most mothers and teachers would like boys to behave in masculine ways, but also to be neat, well mannered, and considerate. However, fathers and peers usually want boys to be independent and to engage in rough-and-tumble play. The mixed messages make it difficult for boys to figure out how to act.

Although gender roles have become more flexible in recent years, the flexibility applies more for girls than for boys (Beal, 1994). Girls can count on receiving approval if they are ambitious, competitive, and interested in sports, but relatively few adults are equally supportive of boys' being gentle, interested in fashion, and motivated to sign up for ballet classes. Instrumental traits and masculine gender roles may be evolving into a new norm for everyone.

Concern about the ways boys are being brought up has been called a "national crisis of boyhood" by William Pollack (1999) in his book *Real Boys*. Pollack says that little has been done to change what he calls the "boy code." The boy code tells boys they should not show their feelings and should act tough, says Pollack. Boys learn the boy code in many contexts—sandboxes, playgrounds, schoolrooms, camps, hangouts—and are taught the code by parents, peers, coaches, teachers, and other adults. Pollack, as well as many others, argues that boys would benefit from being socialized to express their anxieties and concerns and to better regulate their aggression.

ADOLESCENCE

Early adolescence is another transitional point that seems to be especially important in gender development. Young adolescents have to cope with the enormous changes of puberty. These changes are intensified by their expanding cognitive abilities, which make them acutely aware of how they appear to others. Relations with others change extensively as dating begins and sexuality is experienced.

As females and males experience the physical and social changes of early adolescence, they must come to terms with new definitions of their gender roles (Belansky & Clements, 1992; Priess & Lindberg, 2011a, b). During early adolescence, individuals develop the adult, physical aspects of their sex. Some theorists and researchers have proposed that, with the onset of puberty, girls and boys experience an intensification of gender-related expectations. Puberty might signal to socializing others—parents, peers, and teachers, for example—that the adolescent is beginning to approach adulthood and therefore should begin to behave in ways that more closely resemble the stereotypical female or male adult. The **gender-intensification hypothesis** states that psychological and behavioral differences between boys and girls become greater during early adolescence because of increased pressures to conform to traditional masculine and feminine gender roles (Galambos, 2004; Hill & Lynch, 1983).

Some researchers have reported evidence of gender intensification in early adolescence (Hill & Lynch, 1983). A recent study found no evidence for intensification in masculinity or femininity in young adolescents (Priess, Lindberg, & Hyde, 2009). The jury is still out on the validity of the gender-intensification hypothesis, but recent research has raised questions about its accuracy (Galambos & others, 2009; Priess & Lindberg, 2011a).

Gender intensification may create special problems for boys. Adopting a strong masculine role in adolescence is increasingly being found to be associated with problem behaviors. Joseph Pleck (1995) argues that what has defined traditional masculinity includes behaviors that do not have social approval but nonetheless validate the adolescent boy's masculinity. That is, in the male adolescent culture, male adolescents perceive that they will be thought of as more masculine if they engage in premarital sex, drink alcohol, take drugs, and participate in delinquent activities. A recent study revealed that both boys and girls who engaged in extreme gender-typed (hyper-gender) behaviors had lower levels of school engagement and school attachment (Ueno & McWilliams, 2010).

Are gender roles more flexible for boys or for girls?

(top): © Ariel Skelley/Corbis; (bottom): © image100/Corbis RF

developmental **connection**

Biological Processes

Girls enter puberty approximately two years earlier than boys, with pubertal change peaking on average at age 11½ in girls and 13½ in boys. Connect to "Physical Development and Biological Aging."

gender-intensification hypothesis The view that psychological and behavioral differences between boys and girls become greater during early adolescence because of increased socialization pressures to conform to traditional gender roles.

What are some gender differences in communication?
© Jetta Productions/David Atkinson/Getty Images RF

ADULTHOOD AND AGING

How might women's and men's development vary as they go through their adult years? How might gender be linked with aging?

Gender and Communication Stereotypes about differences in men's and women's attitudes toward communication and about differences in how they communicate with each other have spawned countless cartoons and jokes. Are the supposed differences real?

When Deborah Tannen (1990) analyzed the talk of women and men, she found that many wives complained about their husbands by saying that "He doesn't listen to me anymore" and "He doesn't talk to me anymore." Lack of communication, although high on women's lists of reasons for divorce, is mentioned much less often by men.

Communication problems between men and women may come in part from differences in their preferred ways of communicating. Tannen distinguishes *rapport talk* from *report talk*. **Rapport talk** is the language of conversation; it is a way of establishing connections and negotiating relationships. **Report talk** is talk that is designed to give information; this category of communication includes public speaking. According to Tannen, women enjoy rapport talk more than report talk, and men's lack of interest in rapport talk bothers many women. In contrast, men prefer to engage in report talk. Men hold center stage through verbal performances such as telling stories and jokes. They learn to use talk as a way to get and keep attention.

How extensive are gender differences in communication? Research has yielded somewhat mixed results. Recent studies do reveal some gender differences (Anderson, 2006). One study of a sampling of students' e-mails found that people could guess the writer's gender two-thirds of the time (Thompson & Murachver, 2001). Another study revealed that women make 63 percent of phone calls and when talking to another woman stay on the phone longer (7.2 minutes) than men do when talking with other men (4.6 minutes) (Smoreda & Licoppe, 2000). However, meta-analyses suggest that overall gender differences in communication are small in both children and adults (Hyde, 2005, 2014; Leaper & Smith, 2004).

Women's Development Tannen's analysis of women's preference for rapport talk suggests that women place a high value on relationships and focus on nurturing their connections with others. This view echoes some ideas of Jean Baker Miller (1986), who has been an important voice in stimulating the examination of psychological issues from a female perspective. Miller argues that when researchers examine what women have been doing in life, a large part of it is active participation in the development of others. In Miller's view, women often try to interact with others in ways that will foster the other person's development along many dimensions—emotional, intellectual, and social.

Most experts stress that it is important for women not only to maintain their competency in relationships but to be self-motivated, too (Brabek & Brabek, 2006). As Harriet Lerner (1989) concludes in her book *The Dance of Intimacy*, it is important for women to bring to their relationships nothing less than a strong, assertive, independent, and authentic self. She emphasizes that competent relationships are those in which the separate "I-ness" of both persons can be appreciated and enhanced while the partners remain emotionally connected with each other.

In sum, Miller, Tannen, and other gender experts such as Carol Gilligan note that women are more relationship-oriented than men are—and that this relationship orientation should be valued more highly in our culture than it currently is. Critics of this view of gender differences in relationships contend that it is too stereotypical (Hyde & Else-Quest, 2013; Matlin, 2012). They argue that there is greater individual variation in the relationship styles of men and women than this view acknowledges.

In the field of the psychology of women, there is increased interest in women of color. To read about the work and views of one individual in this field, see the *Connecting with Careers* profile.

Men's Development The male of the species—what is he really like? What are his concerns? According to Joseph Pleck's (1995) role-strain view, male roles are contradictory

------------->
developmental connection

Peers

How is adult friendship different among female friends, male friends, and cross-gender friends? Connect to "Peers and the Sociocultural World."

rapport talk The language of conversation; a way to establish connections and negotiate relationships; preferred by women.

report talk Language designed to give information; a communication style preferred by men.

382 CHAPTER 12 Gender and Sexuality

Cynthia de las Fuentes, College Professor and Counseling Psychologist

Cynthia de las Fuentes is a professor at Our Lady of the Lake University in San Antonio. She obtained her undergraduate degree in psychology and her doctoral degree in counseling psychology at the University of Texas in Austin. Among the courses she teaches are the psychology of women, Latino psychology, and counseling theories.

Dr. de las Fuentes is president of the Division of the Psychology of Women in the American Psychological Association. "'Many young women,'

Cynthia de las Fuentes.
Courtesy of Dr. Cynthia de las Fuentes

she says, 'take for granted that the women's movement has accomplished its goals—like equal pay for women, or reproductive rights—and don't realize that there is still work to be done.' . . . She's interested in learning about people's intersecting identities, like female and Latina, and how the two work together" (Winerman, 2005, pp. 66–67).

For more information about what college professors do, see the Careers in Life-Span Development appendix.

and inconsistent. Men not only experience stress when they violate men's roles, they also are harmed when they act in accord with men's roles. Here are some of the areas where men's roles can cause considerable strain (Levant, 2001):

· *Health.* Men die 8 to 10 years earlier than women do. They have higher rates of stress-related disorders, alcoholism, car accidents, and suicide. Men are more likely than women to be the victims of homicide. In sum, the male role is hazardous to men's health.

· *Male-female relationships.* Too often, the male role involves expectations that men should be dominant, powerful, and aggressive and should control women. "Real men," according to many traditional definitions of masculinity, look at women in terms of their bodies, not their minds and feelings, have little interest in rapport talk and relationships, and do not consider women equal to men in work or many other aspects of life. Thus, the traditional view of the male role encourages men to disparage women, be violent toward women, and refuse to have equal relationships with women.

· *Male-male relationships.* Too many men have had too little interaction with their fathers, especially fathers who are positive role models. Nurturing and being sensitive to others have been considered aspects of the female role, not the male role. And the male role emphasizes competition rather than cooperation. All of these aspects of the male role have left men with inadequate positive, emotional connections with other males.

To reconstruct their masculinity in more positive ways, Ron Levant (2001) suggests that every man should (1) reexamine his beliefs about manhood, (2) separate out the valuable aspects of the male role, and (3) get rid of those parts of the masculine role that are destructive. All of these involve becoming more "emotionally intelligent"—that is, becoming more emotionally self-aware, managing emotions more effectively, reading emotions better (one's own emotions and those of others), and being motivated to improve close relationships.

Gender and Aging Do our gender roles change when we become older adults? Some developmentalists maintain there is decreasing femininity in women and decreasing masculinity in men when they reach late adulthood (Gutmann, 1975). The evidence suggests that older men do become more *feminine*—nurturant, sensitive, and so on—but it appears that older women do not necessarily become more *masculine*—assertive, dominant, and so on (Turner, 1982). A longitudinal study revealed that as men entered their sixties, they endorsed more feminine items on a list of personal characteristics, which increased their classification as *androgynous* (combination of masculine and feminine traits) (Hyde, Krajnik, & Skuldt-Niederberger, 1991).

Tom Cruise (*left*) played Jerry Maguire in the movie *Jerry Maguire* with 6-year-old Ray, son of Jerry's love interest. Images of nurturing and nurtured males were woven throughout the movie. Jerry's relationship with Ray was a significant theme in the movie. It is through the caring relationship with Ray that Jerry makes his first genuine movement toward emotional maturity. The boy is guide to the man (Shields, 1998). Many experts on gender stress that men and boys would benefit from engaging in more nurturant behaviors.
© TriStar Pictures/Photofest

In a more recent cross-sectional study of individuals from 12 to 80 years and older, men in their seventies were more likely than adolescents and younger men to endorse androgynous traits (Strough & others, 2007). Also in this study, women in their eighties and older were less likely than younger and middle-aged women to endorse masculine and androgynous traits. Keep in mind that cohort effects are especially important to consider in areas such as gender roles. As sociohistorical changes take place and are assessed more frequently in life-span investigations, what were once perceived to be age effects may turn out to be cohort effects (Jackson, Govia, & Sellers, 2011; Schaie, 2012). For example, in the study described above (Strough & others, 2007), the early-adult and middle-aged women were "baby boomers," likely influenced by the women's movement as they were growing up and developing their identity. However, the oldest-old women likely had already established their gender identity when the women's movement began, which might explain why they were less likely than younger women to endorse masculine and androgynous traits.

A possible double jeopardy also faces many women—the burden of both ageism and sexism (Meyer & Parker, 2011; UNICEF, 2006). In developing countries, the poverty rate for older adult females is almost double that for older adult males.

Not only is it important to be concerned about older women's double jeopardy of ageism and sexism, but special attention also needs to be devoted to female ethnic minority older adults (Jackson & others, 2011). Many, but not all, immigrant ethnic groups traditionally have relegated the woman's role to family maintenance. Many important decisions may be made by a woman's husband or parents, and she is often not expected to seek an independent career or enter the workforce unless the family is in dire financial need.

Some ethnic minority groups may define an older woman's role as unimportant, especially if she is unable to contribute financially. However, in some ethnic minority groups, an older woman's social status improves. For example, older African American women can express their own needs and can be given status and power in the community. Despite their positive status in the African American family and the African American culture, African American women over the age of 70 are the poorest population group in the United States. Three of five older African American women live alone; most of them are widowed. The low incomes of older African American women translate into less than adequate access to health care. Substantially lower incomes for African American older women are related to the kinds of jobs they have held. Frequently these jobs are not covered by Social Security or, in the case of domestic service, the incomes of these women are not reported even when reporting is legally required.

A portrayal of older African American women in cities reveals some of their survival strategies. They highly value the family as a system of mutual support and aid, adhere to the American work ethic, and view religion as a source of strength.

In sum, older African American women have faced considerable stress in their lives. In dealing with this stress, they have shown remarkable adaptiveness, resilience, responsibility, and coping skills. However, many older African American women would benefit considerably from improved support.

developmental **connection**

Culture

Aging presents special challenges for ethnic minority individuals. Connect to "Peers and the Sociocultural World."

A special concern is the stress faced by African American elderly women. *What are some ways they cope with stress?*
© Bob Thomas/Corbis

Review Connect Reflect

LG3 Describe the development of gender through the life span

Review
- What are some developmental changes in gender during childhood?
- How does gender development change during adolescence?
- How does gender development change during adulthood?

Connect
- Relate this chapter's gender-intensification hypothesis to what you've learned about identity development in adolescence. What are your conclusions?

Reflect *Your Own Personal Journey of Life*
- How have your gender attitudes and behavior changed since childhood? Are the changes mainly age-related or do they reflect cohort effects?

4 Exploring Sexuality (LG4) Characterize influences on sexuality, the nature of sexual orientation, and some sexual problems

| Biological and Cultural Factors | Sexual Orientation | Sexually Transmitted Infections | Forcible Sexual Behavior and Sexual Harasssment |

Now that we have studied the gender aspects of being female and male, let's turn our attention to the sexual aspects. To explore sexuality, we examine biological and cultural factors, sexual orientation, sexually transmitted infections, and forcible sexual behavior and sexual harassment.

BIOLOGICAL AND CULTURAL FACTORS

We don't need sex for everyday survival the way we need food and water, but we do need it for the survival of the species. With this important role of sex in mind, let's examine some biological and cultural factors involved in sexuality.

Biological Factors   In our discussion of gender, we identified two main classes of sex hormones: estrogens (which primarily promote the development of female physical sex characteristics) and androgens (which mainly promote the development of male physical sex characteristics). The pituitary gland in the brain monitors hormone levels but is itself regulated by the hypothalamus. The pituitary gland sends out a signal to the testes or ovaries to manufacture a hormone; then the pituitary gland, through interaction with the hypothalamus, detects when the optimal level of the hormone is reached and maintains this level.

As we move from lower to higher animals, the role of hormones becomes less clear, especially in females. For human males, higher androgen levels are associated with sexual motivation and orgasm frequency (Knussmann, Christiansen, & Couwenbergs, 1986). Nonetheless, sexual behavior is so individualized in humans that it is difficult to distinguish the effects of hormones.

Cultural Factors   Sexual motivation also is influenced by cultural factors (Hock, 2013). The range of sexual values across cultures is substantial. Some cultures consider sexual pleasures "weird" or "abnormal." Consider the people who live on the small island of Ines Beag off the coast of Ireland. They are some of the most sexually repressed people in the world. They know nothing about tongue kissing or hand stimulation of the penis, and they detest nudity. For both females and males, premarital sex is out of the question (Messinger, 1971).

In contrast, consider the Mangaian culture in the South Pacific. In Mangaia, young boys are taught about masturbation and are encouraged to engage in it as much as they like. At age 13, the boys undergo a ritual that initiates them into sexual manhood. First, their elders instruct them about sexual strategies, including how to help their female partner have orgasms. Then, two weeks later, the boy has intercourse with an experienced woman who helps him hold back ejaculation until she can achieve orgasm with him. By the end of adolescence, Mangalans have sex virtually every day.

As reflected in the behavior of the people in these two different cultures, our sexual motivation is influenced by **sexual scripts.** These are stereotyped patterns of expectations for how people should behave sexually (Sakaluk & others, 2014). Two well-known sexual scripts are the traditional religious script and the romantic script. In the **traditional religious script,** sex is acceptable only within marriage. Extramarital sex is taboo, especially for women. Sex means reproduction and sometimes affection. In the **romantic script,** sex is synonymous with love. If we develop a relationship with someone and fall in love, it is acceptable to have sex with the person whether or not we are married.

You probably are familiar with some sex differences in sexual scripts (Masters & others, 2013). Females tend to link sexual intercourse with love more than males do, and males are more likely to emphasize sexual conquest. Some sexual scripts involve a double standard; for

sexual scripts Stereotyped patterns of expectancies for how people should behave sexually.

traditional religious script View that sex is acceptable only within marriage; extramarital sex is taboo, especially for women; and sex means reproduction and sometimes affection.

romantic script A perspective in which sex is synonymous with love; belief that if we develop a relationship with someone and fall in love, it is acceptable to have sex with the person whether we are married or not.

Noncohabiting

Men

23% / 25% / 26% / 19% / 7%

Women

32% / 23% / 24% / 15% / 5%

Cohabiting (married)

Men

1% / 13% / 43% / 36% / 7%

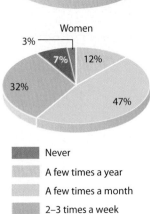

Women

3% / 12% / 47% / 32% / 7%

■ Never

▨ A few times a year

▨ A few times a month

▨ 2–3 times a week

■ 4 or more times a week

FIGURE 4

THE SEX IN AMERICA SURVEY. The percentages show noncohabiting and cohabiting (married) males' and females' responses to the question "How often have you had sex in the past year?" in a 1994 survey (Michael & others, 1994). *What was one feature of the Sex in America survey that made it superior to most surveys of sexual behavior?*

example, it is okay for male adolescents to have sex but not females, and if the female gets pregnant it's viewed as her fault for not using contraception. A recent study of young adult men found two main sexual scripts: (1) a traditional male "player" script, and (2) a script that emphasized mutual sexual pleasure (Morrison & others, 2014).

SEXUAL ORIENTATION

A national study of sexual behavior in the United States among adults 25 to 44 years of age found that 98 percent of the women and 97 percent of the men said that they had ever engaged in vaginal intercourse (Chandra & others, 2011). Also in this study, 89 percent of the women and 90 percent of the men reported that they had ever had oral sex with an opposite-sex partner, and 36 percent of the women and 44 percent of the men stated that they had ever had anal sex with an opposite-sex partner.

More extensive information about adult sexual patterns comes from the 1994 Sex in America survey. In this well-designed, comprehensive study of American adults' sexual patterns, Robert Michael and his colleagues (1994) interviewed more than 3,000 people from 18 to 59 years of age who were randomly selected, a sharp contrast from earlier samples that consisted of unrepresentative groups of volunteers.

Heterosexual Attitudes and Behavior Here are some of the key findings from the 1994 Sex in America survey:

· Americans tend to fall into three categories: One-third have sex twice a week or more, one third a few times a month, and one-third a few times a year or not at all.

· Married (and cohabiting) couples have sex more often than noncohabiting couples (see Figure 4).

· Most Americans do not engage in kinky sexual acts. When asked about their favorite sexual acts, the vast majority (96 percent) said that vaginal sex was "very" or "somewhat" appealing. Oral sex was in third place, after an activity that many have not labeled a sexual act—watching a partner undress.

· Adultery is clearly the exception rather than the rule. Nearly 75 percent of the married men and 85 percent of the married women in the survey indicated that they had never been unfaithful.

· Men think about sex far more often than women do—54 percent of the men said they thought about it every day or several times a day, whereas 67 percent of the women said they thought about it only a few times a week or a few times a month.

In sum, one of the most powerful messages in the 1994 survey was that Americans' sexual lives are more conservative than was previously believed. Although 17 percent of the men and 3 percent of the women said they had had sex with at least 21 partners, the overall impression from the survey was that sexual behavior is ruled by marriage and monogamy for most Americans.

How extensive are gender differences in sexuality? A meta-analysis revealed that men reported having slightly more sexual experiences and more permissive attitudes than women regarding most aspects of sexuality (Peterson & Hyde, 2010). For the following factors, stronger differences were found: Men said that they engaged more often in masturbation, pornography use, and casual sex, and they expressed more permissive attitudes about casual sex than their female counterparts.

Given all the media and public attention directed toward the negative aspects of sexuality—such as adolescent pregnancy, sexually transmitted infections, rape, and so on—it is important to underscore that research strongly supports the role of sexuality in well-being (Brody, 2010). For example, in a Swedish study frequency of sexual intercourse was strongly linked to life satisfaction for both women and men (Brody & Costa, 2009).

Sources of Sexual Orientation Until the end of the nineteenth century, it was generally believed that people were either heterosexual or homosexual. Today, sexual orientation is viewed less as an either/or proposition than as a continuum from exclusive male-female relations to exclusive same-sex relations (Crooks & Baur, 2014). Some individuals are also **bisexual,** being sexually attracted to people of both sexes.

People sometimes think that bisexuality is simply a steppingstone to homosexuality, while others view it as a sexual orientation itself or as an indicator of sexual fluidity (King, 2014). Evidence supports the notion that bisexuality is a stable orientation that involves attraction to both sexes (King, 2014; Mock & Eibach, 2012).

Compared with men, women are more likely to change their sexual patterns and desires (Knight & Morales Hope, 2012). Women are more likely than men to have sexual experiences with same- and opposite-sex partners, even if they identify themselves strongly as being heterosexual or lesbian (King, 2014). Also, women are more likely than men to identify themselves as bisexual (Gates, 2011).

In the Sex in America survey, 2.7 percent of the men and 1.3 percent of the women reported having had same-sex relations in the past year (Michael & others, 1994). Why are some individuals lesbian, gay, or bisexual (LGB) and others heterosexual? Speculation about this question has been extensive.

All people, regardless of their sexual orientation, have similar physiological responses during sexual arousal and seem to be aroused by the same types of tactile stimulation. Investigators typically find no differences between LGBs and heterosexuals in a wide range of attitudes, behaviors, and adjustments (Fingerhut & Peplau, 2013).

Recently, researchers have explored the possible biological basis of same-sex relations. The results of hormone studies have been inconsistent. If gay males are given male sex hormones (androgens), their sexual orientation doesn't change. Their sexual desire merely increases. A very early prenatal critical period might influence sexual orientation (Hines, 2013, 2015). In the second to fifth months after conception, exposure of the fetus to hormone levels characteristic of females might cause the individual (male or female) to become attracted to males (Ellis & Ames, 1987). If this critical-period hypothesis turns out to be correct, it would explain why clinicians have found that sexual orientation is difficult, if not impossible, to modify.

Researchers have also examined genetic influences on sexual orientation by studying twins. A Swedish study of almost 4,000 twins found that only about 35 percent of the variation in homosexual behavior in men and 19 percent in women could be explained by genetic differences (Langstrom & others, 2010). This result suggests that although genes likely play a role in sexual orientation, they are not the only factor (King, 2013).

An individual's sexual orientation—same-sex, heterosexual, or bisexual—is most likely determined by a combination of genetic, hormonal, cognitive, and environmental factors (Hyde & DeLamater, 2014; King, 2014). Most experts on same-sex relations believe that no one factor alone causes sexual orientation and that the relative weight of each factor can vary from one individual to the next.

What likely determines whether a male or female has a same-sex orientation?
(all): © 2009 JupiterImages Corporation RF

Attitudes and Behavior of Lesbians and Gays Many gender differences that appear in heterosexual relationships occur in same-sex relationships (Diamond & Savin-Williams, 2015; Savin-Williams & Cohen, 2015). For example, lesbians have fewer sexual partners than gays, and lesbians have less permissive attitudes about casual sex outside a primary relationship than gays (Fingerhut & Peplau, 2013).

According to psychologist Laura Brown (1989), lesbians and gays experience life as a minority in a dominant, majority culture. For lesbians and gays, developing a *bicultural identity* creates new ways of defining themselves. Brown believes that lesbians and gays adapt best when they don't define themselves in polarities, such as trying to live in an encapsulated lesbian or gay world completely divorced from the majority culture or completely accepting the dictates and biases of the majority culture. A special concern is discrimination and prejudice toward sexual minority individuals (Saewyc, 2011). A recent study of 15-year-olds found that sexual minority status was linked to depression mainly via peer harassment (Martin-Storey & Crosnoe, 2012).

SEXUALLY TRANSMITTED INFECTIONS

Sexually transmitted infections (STIs) are diseases that are primarily contracted through sex—penile-vaginal intercourse as well as oral-genital and anal-genital sex. STIs affect about

bisexuality Sexual attraction to people of both sexes.

sexually transmitted infections (STIs) Diseases that are contracted primarily through sexual contact, including oral-genital contact, anal-genital contact, and vaginal intercourse.

one of every six U.S. adults (National Center for Health Statistics, 2014). Among the most prevalent STIs are bacterial infections—such as gonorrhea, syphilis, and chlamydia—and STIs caused by viruses—such as AIDS (acquired immune deficiency syndrome), genital herpes, and genital warts. Figure 5 describes these sexually transmitted infections.

No single disease has had a greater impact on sexual behavior, or created more public fear in the last several decades, than infection with the human immunodeficiency virus (HIV) (Crooks & Baur, 2014). HIV is a virus that destroys the body's immune system. Once a person is infected with HIV, the virus breaks down and overpowers the immune system, which leads to AIDS. An individual sick with AIDS has such a weakened immune system that a common cold can be life-threatening.

In 2012, more than 1 million people in the United States were living with an HIV infection (National Center for Health Statistics, 2014). In 2012, male-male sexual contact continued to be the most frequent AIDS transmission category. Because of education and the development of more effective drug treatments, deaths due to HIV/AIDS have begun to decline in the United States (National Center for Health Statistics, 2014).

Globally, the total number of individuals living with HIV was 34 million at the end of 2010, with 22 million of these individuals with HIV living in sub-Saharan Africa (UNAIDS, 2011). Approximately half of all new HIV infections around the world occur in the 15- to 24-year-old age category. The good news is that global rates of HIV infection fell nearly 25 percent from 2001 to 2009 with substantial decreases in India and South Africa (UNAIDS, 2011). In a recent study, only 49 percent of 15- to 24-year-old females in low- and middle-income countries knew that using a condom helps to prevent HIV infection, compared with 74 percent of young males (UNAIDS, 2011).

STI	Description/cause	Incidence	Treatment
Gonorrhea	Commonly called the "drip" or "clap." Caused by the bacterium *Neisseria gonorrhoeae*. Spread by contact between infected moist membranes (genital, oral-genital, or anal-genital) of two individuals. Characterized by discharge from penis or vagina and painful urination. Can lead to infertility.	500,000 cases annually in U.S.	Penicillin, other antibiotics
Syphilis	Caused by the bacterium *Treponema pallidum*. Characterized by the appearance of a sore where syphilis entered the body. The sore can be on the external genitals, vagina, or anus. Later, a skin rash breaks out on palms of hands and bottom of feet. If not treated, can eventually lead to paralysis or even death.	100,000 cases annually in U.S.	Penicillin
Chlamydia	A common STI named for the bacterium *Chlamydia trachomatis*, an organism that spreads by sexual contact and infects the genital organs of both sexes. A special concern is that females with chlamydia may become infertile. It is recommended that adolescent and young adult females have an annual screening for this STI.	About 3 million people in U.S. annually.	Antibiotics
Genital herpes	Caused by a family of viruses with different strains. Involves an eruption of sores and blisters. Spread by sexual contact.	One of five U.S. adults	No known cure but antiviral medications can shorten outbreaks
AIDS	Caused by a virus, the human immunodeficiency virus (HIV), which destroys the body's immune system. Semen and blood are the main vehicles of transmission. Common symptoms include fevers, night sweats, weight loss, chronic fatigue, and swollen lymph nodes.	More than 300,000 cumulative cases of HIV virus in U.S. 25–34-year-olds; epidemic incidence in sub-Saharan countries	New treatments have slowed the progression from HIV to AIDS; no cure
Genital warts	Caused by the human papillomavirus, which does not always produce symptoms. Usually appear as small, hard, painless bumps in the vaginal area or around the anus. Very contagious. Certain high-risk types of this virus cause cervical cancer and other genital cancers. May recur despite treatment. A new HPV preventive vaccine, Gardasil, has been approved for girls and women 9–26 years of age.	About 5.5 million new cases annually; considered the most common STI in the U.S.	A topical drug, freezing, or surgery

FIGURE 5
SEXUALLY TRANSMITTED INFECTIONS

A youth group presents a play in the local marketplace in Morogoro, Tanzania. The play is designed to educate the community about HIV and AIDS.
© Wendy Stone/Corbis

A 13-year-old boy pushes his friends around in his barrow during his break from his work as a barrow boy in a sub-Saharan Africa community. He became the breadwinner in the family because both of his parents died of AIDS.
© Louise Gubb/Corbis Saba

What are some good strategies for protecting against HIV and other sexually transmitted infections? They include the following:

- *Knowing your own and your partner's risk status.* Anyone who has had previous sexual activity with another person might have contracted an STI without being aware of it. Spend time getting to know a prospective partner before you have sex. Use this time to inform the other person of your STI status and inquire about your partner's. Remember that many people lie about their STI status.

- *Obtaining medical examinations.* Many experts recommend that couples who want to begin a sexual relationship have a medical checkup to rule out STIs before they engage in sex. If cost is an issue, contact your campus health service or a public health clinic.

- *Having protected, not unprotected, sex.* When used correctly, latex condoms help to prevent many STIs from being transmitted. Condoms are most effective in preventing gonorrhea, syphilis, chlamydia, and HIV. They are less effective against the spread of herpes.

- *Not having sex with multiple partners.* One of the best predictors of getting an STI is having sex with multiple partners. Having more than one sex partner elevates the likelihood that you will encounter an infected partner.

FORCIBLE SEXUAL BEHAVIOR AND SEXUAL HARASSMENT

Too often, sex involves the exercise of power. Here we briefly look at three of the problems that may result: two types of rape and sexual harassment.

Rape   **Rape** is forcible sexual intercourse with a person who does not give consent. Legal definitions of rape differ from state to state. For example, in some states, husbands are not prohibited from forcing their wives to have intercourse, although this has been challenged in several of those states.

rape Forcible sexual intercourse, oral sex, or anal sex with a person who does not give consent. Legal definitions of rape differ from state to state.

What are some characteristics of date or acquaintance rape?
© Creasource/Corbis

Because victims may be reluctant to suffer the consequences of reporting rape, the actual number of incidents is not easily determined (Krebs, 2014; Walfield, 2015). A recent meta-analysis found that 60 percent of rape victims do not acknowledge that they have been raped, with the percentage of unacknowledged rape especially high in college students (Wilson & Miller, 2015).

Rape occurs most often in large cities, where it has been reported that 8 of every 10,000 women 12 years and older are raped each year. Nearly 200,000 rapes are reported each year in the United States. Although most victims of rape are women, rape of men does occur (McLean, Balding, & White, 2005). A recent study of college women who had been raped revealed that only 11.5 percent of them reported the rape to authorities and of those in which the rape involved drugs and/or alcohol, only 2.7 percent of the rapes were reported (Wolitzky-Taylor & others, 2011). Men in prisons are especially vulnerable to rape, usually by heterosexual males who use rape as a means of establishing their dominance and power (Barth, 2012).

A national study found that 7.4 percent of U.S. ninth- through twelfth-grade students reported that they had been physically forced to have intercourse against their will (Eaton & others, 2010). In this study, 10.5 percent of the female students and 4.5 percent of the male students reported having been forced to have sexual intercourse.

Why does rape of females occur so often in the United States? Among the causes given are that males are socialized to be sexually aggressive, to regard women as inferior beings, and to view their own pleasure as the most important objective in sexual relations (Beech, Ward, & Fisher, 2006; Davies, Gilston, & Rogers, 2012; Rudman, Fetterolf, & Sanchez, 2013). Researchers have found that male rapists share the following characteristics: aggression enhances their sense of power or masculinity; they are angry at women in general; and they want to hurt and humiliate their victims (Yarber, Sayad, & Strong, 2013). A recent study revealed that a higher level of men's sexual narcissism (assessed by these factors: sexual exploitation, sexual entitlement, low sexual empathy, and sexual skill) was linked to a greater likelihood that they would engage in sexual aggression (Widman & McNulty, 2010). Another recent study also revealed that regardless of whether or not the victim was using substances, sexual assault was more likely to occur when the offender was using substances (Brecklin & Ullman, 2010).

Rape is a traumatic experience for the victims and those close to them (Littleton, 2014; Padmanabhanunni & Edwards, 2015). As victims strive to get their lives back to normal, they may experience depression, fear, anxiety, increased substance use, and suicidal thoughts for months or years (Bryan & others, 2013; Iverson & others, 2015). Sexual dysfunctions, such as reduced sexual desire and an inability to reach orgasm, occur in 50 percent of female rape victims (Sprei & Courtois, 1988). Recovery depends on the victim's coping abilities, psychological adjustments prior to the assault, and social support (Kelly, 2011). Parents, partner, and others close to the victim can provide important support for recovery, as can mental health professionals (Ahrens & Aldana, 2012).

An increasing concern is **date or acquaintance rape,** which is coercive sexual activity directed at someone with whom the victim is at least casually acquainted (Angelone, Mitchell, & Grossi, 2015; Sabina & Ho, 2014; Turchik & Hassija, 2014). By some estimates, one in three adolescent girls will be involved in a controlling, abusive relationship before she graduates from high school, and two-thirds of college freshman women report having been date raped or having experienced an attempted date rape at least once (Watts & Zimmerman, 2002). About two-thirds of college men admit that they fondle women against their will, and half admit to forcing sexual activity.

A number of colleges and universities have identified a "red zone"— a period of time early in the first year of college when women are at especially high risk for unwanted sexual experiences. One study revealed that first-year women were more at risk for unwanted sexual experiences, especially early in the fall term, than second-year women (Kimble & others, 2008).

Sexual Harassment **Sexual harassment** is a manifestation of power by one person over another. It takes many forms—from inappropriate sexual remarks and physical contact

date or acquaintance rape Coercive sexual activity directed at someone with whom the victim is at least casually acquainted.

sexual harassment Sexual persecution that can take many forms—from sexist remarks and physical contact (patting, brushing against someone's body) to blatant propositions and sexual assaults.

(patting, brushing against one's body) to blatant propositions and sexual assaults. Millions of women experience sexual harassment each year in work and educational settings (Cantalupo, 2014). Sexual harassment of men by women also occurs but to a far lesser extent than sexual harassment of women by men.

In a survey of 2,000 college women, 62 percent reported having experienced sexual harassment while attending college (American Association of University Women, 2006). Most of the college women said that the sexual harassment involved noncontact forms such as crude jokes, remarks, and gestures. However, almost one-third said that the sexual harassment was physical in nature.

Sexual harassment can result in serious psychological consequences for the victim. A study of almost 1,500 college women revealed that when they had been sexually harassed they reported increases in psychological distress, physical illness, and disordered eating (Huerta & others, 2006).

The elimination of such exploitation requires the improvement of work and academic environments. These types of improvements help to provide equal opportunities for people to develop a career and obtain an education in a climate free of sexual harassment (Nielsen & Einarsen, 2012).

Review Connect Reflect

LG4 Characterize influences on sexuality, the nature of sexual orientation, and some sexual problems

Review

- How do biology and culture influence sexuality?
- What is the nature of heterosexual and homosexual attitudes and behavior?
- What are some common sexually transmitted infections? What are some good strategies for protecting against STIs?
- What is the nature of forcible sexual behavior and sexual harassment?

Connect

- How might our acceptance of sexual scripts be linked to ethnic identity?

Reflect *Your Own Personal Journey of Life*

- Have you ever experienced (or unwittingly committed) an act of sexual harassment?

5 Sexuality Through the Life Span   **LG5** Summarize how sexuality develops through the life span

Childhood

Adolescence and Emerging Adulthood

Adult Development and Aging

So far we have discussed a number of aspects of human sexuality. Now, let's explore sexuality at different points in development, beginning with childhood.

CHILDHOOD

Most psychologists doubt Freud's claim that preschool children have a strong sexual attraction to the parent of the other sex. But what are some aspects of child sexuality?

A majority of children engage in some sex play, usually with friends or siblings (Carroll, 2013). Child sex play includes exhibiting or inspecting the genitals. Much of this child sex play is likely motivated by curiosity. There does not appear to be any link between such sexual play and sexual adjustment in adolescence or adulthood.

As the elementary school years progress, sex play with others usually declines, although romantic interest in peers may be present. Curiosity about sex remains high throughout the elementary school years, and children may ask many questions about reproduction and sexuality (Gordon & Gordon, 1989). However, the main surge in sexual interest takes place not in childhood but in early adolescence.

ADOLESCENCE AND EMERGING ADULTHOOD

Adolescence is a critical juncture in the development of sexuality as pubertal changes unfold and individuals develop a sexual identity. And emerging adulthood provides further opportunities for individuals to explore the sexual aspects of their lives.

Adolescence   Adolescence is a time of sexual exploration and experimentation, of sexual fantasies and realities, of incorporating sexuality into one's identity. Adolescents have an almost insatiable curiosity about sexuality. They think about whether they are sexually attractive, how to do sex, and what the future holds for their sexual lives. The majority of adolescents eventually manage to develop a mature sexual identity, but most experience times of vulnerability and confusion (Tolman & McClelland, 2011).

Adolescence is a bridge between the asexual child and the sexual adult. Every society gives some attention to adolescent sexuality. In some societies, adults clamp down and protect adolescent females from males by chaperoning them. Other societies promote very early marriage. Yet others allow some sexual experimentation.

In the United States, children and adolescents learn a great deal about sex from television (Bersamin & others, 2010). The messages come from TV commercials, which use sex to sell just about everything, as well as from the content of TV shows. A research review concluded that adolescents who view more sexual content on TV are likely to initiate sexual intercourse earlier than their peers who view less sexual content on TV (Brown & Strasburger, 2007).

A special concern is *sexting,* which involves sending sexually explicit images, videos, or sexually explicit text messages via electronic communication. A recent national study of 13- to 18-year-olds found that 7 percent reported sending or showing someone sexual pictures of themselves (Ybarra & Mitchell, 2014). In this study, sharing sexual photos was linked to a wide range of sexual behaviors including oral sex and vaginal sex.

The American Academy of Pediatrics (2010) issued a policy statement on sexuality, contraception, and the media. It pointed out that television, film, music, and the Internet are all becoming increasingly explicit, yet information about abstinence, sexual responsibility, and birth control rarely is included in these media outlets. One study revealed that adolescents who reported ever visiting a sexually explicit Web site were more sexually permissive and were more likely to have had multiple lifetime sexual partners, to have had more than one sexual partner in the last three months, and to have used alcohol or other substances at their last sexual encounter than their counterparts who reported having never visited a sexually explicit Web site (Braun-Courville & Rojas, 2009). A recent study of Korean boys fund that high risk of Internet addiction was linked to having sexual intercourse experience (Sung & others, 2013).

Developing a Sexual Identity   Mastering emerging sexual feelings and forming a sense of sexual identity is a multifaceted and lengthy process (Diamond & Savin-Williams, 2015; Savin-Williams, 2015). It involves learning to manage sexual feelings (such as sexual arousal and attraction), developing new forms of intimacy, and learning the skills to regulate sexual behavior to avoid undesirable consequences. An adolescent's sexual identity is influenced by *social norms* related to sex—the extent to which adolescents perceive that their peers are having sex, using protection, and so on. These social norms have important influences on adolescents' sexual behavior. For example, one study revealed that when adolescents perceived that their peers were sexually permissive, the adolescents had a higher rate of initiating sexual intercourse and engaging in risky sexual practices (Potard, Courtois, & Rusch, 2008). An individual's sexual identity also can be linked to other developing identities, which are discussed in the chapter on "The Self, Identity, and Personality."

An adolescent's sexual identity involves activities, interests, styles of behavior, and an indication of sexual orientation (whether an individual has same-sex or other-sex attractions)

developmental **connection**

Technology

Media influences on adolescents and emerging adults include the digitally mediated social environment. Connect to "Peers and the Sociocultural World."

Sexual arousal emerges as a new phenomenon in adolescence, and it is important to view sexuality as a normal aspect of adolescent development.

—Shirley Feldman
Contemporary psychologist, Stanford University

developmental **connection**

Identity

Identity can be conceptualized in terms of identity statuses: diffused, foreclosed, moratorium, and achievement. Connect to "The Self, Identity, and Personality."

(Buzwell & Rosenthal, 1996; Savin-Williams & Cohen, 2015). For example, some adolescents have a high anxiety level about sex, others a low level. Some adolescents are strongly aroused sexually, others less so. Some adolescents are very active sexually, others not at all (Haydon & others, 2012). Some adolescents are sexually inactive in response to their strong religious upbringing, while others attend church regularly but their religious training does not inhibit their sexual activity (Thorton & Camburn, 1989).

It is commonly believed that most gay and lesbian individuals quietly struggle with same-sex attractions in childhood, do not engage in heterosexual dating, and gradually recognize that they are gay or lesbian in mid to late adolescence (Savin-Williams, 2015). Many youth do follow this developmental pathway, but others do not. For example, many youth have no recollection of same-sex attractions and experience a more abrupt sense of their same-sex attraction in late adolescence. Researchers also have found that the majority of adolescents with same-sex attractions also experience some degree of other-sex attractions (Garofalo & others, 1999). Even though some adolescents who are attracted to same-sex individuals fall in love with these individuals, others claim that their same-sex attractions are purely physical (Diamond & Savin-Williams, 2015).

In sum, gay and lesbian youth have diverse patterns of initial attraction, often have bisexual attractions, and may feel physical or emotional attraction to same-sex individuals but do not always fall in love with them (Savin-Williams, 2015).

The Timing and Frequency of Adolescent Sexual Behaviors   The timing of sexual initiation varies by country as well as by gender and other socioeconomic characteristics. In one cross-cultural study, among females, the proportion having first intercourse by age 17 ranged from 72 percent in Mali to 47 percent in the United States and 45 percent in Tanzania (Singh & others, 2000). The percentage of males who had their first intercourse by age 17 ranged from 76 percent in Jamaica to 64 percent in the United States and 63 percent in Brazil. Within the United States, male, African American, and inner-city adolescents report being the most sexually active, whereas Asian American adolescents have the most restrictive sexual timetable (Feldman, Turner, & Araujo, 1999).

What is the current profile of sexual activity of adolescents? In a U.S. national survey conducted in 2013, 64 percent of twelfth-graders reported having experienced sexual intercourse, compared with 30 percent of ninth-graders (Kann & others, 2014). By age 20, 77 percent of U.S. youth report having engaged in sexual intercourse (Dworkin & Santelli, 2007). Nationally, in 2013, 49 percent of twelfth-graders, 40 percent of eleventh-graders, 29 percent

What are some developmental pathways of same-sex attraction in adolescence?
© Marilyn Humphries/The Image Works

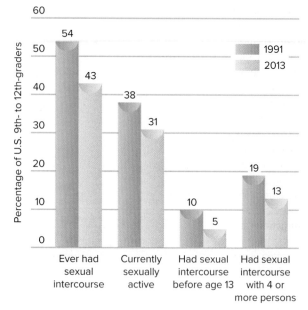

FIGURE 6

SEXUAL ACTIVITY OF U.S. ADOLESCENTS FROM 1991 TO 2013

of tenth-graders, and 20 percent of ninth-graders recently reported that they were currently sexually active (Kann & others, 2014).

What trends in adolescent sexual activity have occurred in recent decades? From 1991 to 2013, fewer adolescents reported any of the following: ever having had sexual intercourse, currently being sexually active, having had sexual intercourse before the age of 13, and having had sexual intercourse with four or more persons during their lifetime (Kann & others, 2014) (see Figure 6).

Sexual initiation varies by ethnic group in the United States (Kann & others, 2014). African Americans are likely to engage in sexual behaviors earlier than other ethnic groups, whereas Asian Americans are likely to engage in them later (Feldman, Turner, & Araujo, 1999). In a more recent national U.S. survey (2014) of ninth- to twelfth-graders, 61 percent of African Americans, 49 percent of Latinos, and 44 percent of non-Latino Whites said they had experienced sexual intercourse (Kann & others, 2014). In this study, 14 percent of African Americans (compared with 6 percent of Latinos and 3 percent of non-Latino Whites) said they had their first sexual experience before 13 years of age.

Recent research indicates that oral sex is now a common occurrence among U.S. adolescents (Fava & Bay-Cheng, 2012; Song & Halpern-Felsher, 2010). In a national survey, 55 percent of U.S. 15- to 19-year-old boys and 54 percent of girls in the same age group said they had engaged in oral sex (National Center for Health Statistics, 2002).

A recent study also found that among female adolescents who reported having vaginal sex first, 31 percent reported having a teen pregnancy, whereas among those who initiated oral-genital sex first, only 8 percent reported having a teen pregnancy (Reese & others, 2013). Thus, how adolescents initiate their sex lives may have positive or negative consequences for their sexual health.

Sexual Risk Factors in Adolescence   Many adolescents are not emotionally prepared to handle sexual experiences, especially in early adolescence. Early sexual activity is linked with risky behaviors such as drug use, delinquency, and school-related problems (Chan & others, 2015; Coley & others, 2013; Skinner & others, 2015). A recent study confirmed that early engagement in sexual intercourse (prior to 14 years of age) is associated with high-risk sexual factors (forced sex, using drugs/alcohol at last sex, not using a condom at last sex, having multiple partners in last month, and becoming pregnant or causing a pregnancy), as well as experiencing dating violence (Kaplan & others, 2013). Also, a recent study of more than 3,000 Swedish adolescents revealed that sexual intercourse before age 14 was linked to risky behaviors such as an increased number of sexual partners, experience of oral and anal sex, negative health behaviors (smoking, drug and alcohol use), and antisocial behavior (being violent, stealing, running away from home) at 18 years of age (Kastbom & others, 2015).

In a longitudinal study of 10- to 25-year-olds, early sexual intercourse and affiliation with deviant peers were linked to substance-use disorders in emerging adulthood (Cornelius & others, 2007). A recent study of adolescents in five countries, including the United States, found that substance use was related to early sexual intercourse (Madkour & others, 2010). Another recent study revealed that alcohol use, early menarche, and poor parent-child communication were linked to early sexually intimate behavior in girls (Hipwell & others, 2011).

In addition to having sex in early adolescence, other risk factors for sexual problems in adolescence include contextual factors such as socioeconomic status (SES) and poverty, family/parenting and peer factors, and school-related influences (Van Ryzin & others, 2011). The percentage of sexually active young adolescents is higher in low-income areas of inner cities (Silver & Bauman, 2006).

A number of family factors are associated with sexual risk-taking (de Looze & others, 2015; Widman & others, 2014). For example, a recent study found that difficulties and disagreements between Latino adolescents and their parents were linked to the adolescents' early sex initiation (Cordova & others, 2014). A research review indicated that the following aspects of connectedness predicted sexual and reproductive health outcomes for youth: family connectedness, parent-adolescent communication about sexuality, parental monitoring, and partner connectedness (Markham & others, 2010).

What are some risks for early initiation of sexual intercourse?
© Stockbyte/PunchStock RF

Also, having older sexually active siblings or pregnant/parenting teenage sisters places adolescent girls at increased risk for pregnancy (Miller, Benson, & Galbraith, 2001).

Peer relations, school experiences, and involvement in sports also are linked to sexual risk-taking in adolescence. Recent research indicated that associating with more deviant peers in early adolescence was related to having more sexual partners at age 16 (Lansford & others, 2010). And a recent research review found that school connectedness was linked to positive sexuality outcomes (Markham & others, 2010). Further, in a recent study adolescent females who skipped school or failed a test were more likely to frequently have sexual intercourse and less likely to use contraceptives (Hensel & Sorge, 2014). Also, a recent study found that adolescent males who play sports engage in a higher level of sexual risk taking while adolescent females who play sports engage in a lower level of sexual risk taking (Lipowski & others, 2015).

Cognitive and personality factors are increasingly implicated in sexual risk taking in adolescence. Two such cognitive factors are attention problems and self-regulation (the ability to control one's emotions and behavior). A longitudinal study revealed that attention problems and high rates of aggressive, disruptive behavior at school entry increased the risk of multiple problem behaviors (school maladjustment, antisocial behavior, and substance use) in middle school, which in turn was linked to early initiation of sexual activity (Schofield & others, 2008). Another longitudinal study found that weak self-regulation at 8 to 9 years of age and risk proneness (tendency to seek sensation and make poor decisions) at 12 to 13 years of age set the stage for sexual risk taking at 16 to 17 years of age (Crockett, Raffaelli, & Shen, 2006). And a recent study also found that a high level of impulsiveness was linked to early adolescent sexual risk taking (Khurana & others, 2012).

Contraceptive Use   Sexual intercourse is a normal activity necessary for procreation, but if appropriate safeguards are not taken it brings the risk of unintended pregnancy and sexually transmitted infections (Carroll, 2013). Both of these risks can be reduced significantly by using certain forms of contraception, particularly condoms (Breheny & Stephens, 2004).

Many sexually active adolescents still do not use contraceptives, or they use them inconsistently (Amialchuk & Gerhardinger, 2015; Finer & Philbin, 2013; Vasilenko, Kreager, & Lefkowitz, 2015). In 2013, 34 percent of sexually active adolescents had not used a condom the last time they had sexual intercourse (Kann & others, 2014). In the recent national U.S. survey (2014), among sexually active adolescents, ninth-graders (63 percent), tenth-graders (62 percent), and eleventh graders (62 percent) reported that they had used a condom during their last sexual intercourse more than did twelfth-graders (53 percent) (Kann & others, 2014). Researchers have found that U.S. adolescents are less likely to use condoms than their European counterparts (Jorgensen & others, 2015).

Younger adolescents are less likely than older adolescents to take contraceptive precautions. A recent study also found that 50 percent of U.S. 15- to 19-year-old girls with unintended pregnancies ending in live births were not using any birth control method when they got pregnant, and 34 percent believed they could not get pregnant at the time (Centers for Disease Control and Prevention, 2012). Also, a recent study found that a greater age difference between sexual partners in adolescence is associated with less consistent condom use (Volpe & others, 2013).

Sexually Transmitted Infections   Earlier, we described sexually transmitted infections. Here we focus on their incidence among adolescents. Every year more than 3 million American adolescents (about one-fourth of those who are sexually experienced) acquire an STI (Centers for Disease Control and Prevention, 2014b). In a single act of unprotected sex with an infected partner, a teenage girl has a 1 percent risk of getting infected with HIV, a 30 percent risk of acquiring genital herpes, and a 50 percent chance of contracting gonorrhea. In some areas of the United States, as many as 25 percent of sexually active adolescents have contracted chlamydia. Adolescents have a higher incidence of gonorrhea and of chlamydia than young adults.

As we discussed earlier, a special concern is the high incidence of AIDS in sub-Saharan Africa (Renju & others, 2011; UNICEF, 2013). Adolescent girls in many African countries are vulnerable to being infected with HIV by adult men. Approximately six times as many adolescent girls as boys have AIDS in these countries, whereas in the United States adolescent males are more likely to have AIDS than their female counterparts (Centers for Disease

developmental connection

Development of the Self

One of the most important aspects of the self in middle and late childhood is the increased capacity for self-regulation. Connect to "The Self, Identity, and Personality."

Sixteen-year-old Alberto's maternal grandmother was a heroin addict who died of cancer at 40. His father, just 17 when Alberto was born, has been in prison most of Alberto's life. His mother and stepfather are not married but have lived together for a dozen years and have four other children. Alberto's stepbrother dropped out of school when he was 17, fathered a child, and is unemployed. But Alberto, who lives in the Bronx in New York City, has different plans for his own future. He says he wants to be a dentist "like the kind of woman who fixed his teeth at Bronx-Lebanon Hospital Center clinic when he was a child" (Bernstein, 2004, p. A22). And Alberto, along with his girlfriend, Jasmine, wants to remain a virgin until he is married.
© Suzanne DeChillo/The New York Times/Redux Pictures

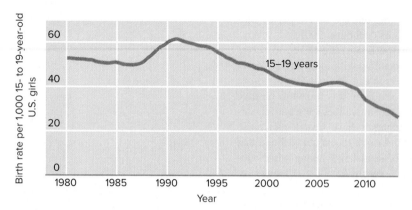

FIGURE 7

BIRTH RATES FOR U.S. 15- TO 19-YEAR-OLD GIRLS FROM 1980 TO 2013.
Source: Martin & others (2015).

- - - - - - - - ➤

developmental **connection**

Culture

The high school dropout rate for Latino adolescents is higher than any other ethnic group, except Native American adolescents. Connect to "Schools, Achievement, and Work."

Control and Prevention, 2014b). In Kenya, 25 percent of 15- to 19-year-old girls are HIV-positive compared with 4 percent of the boys.

Adolescent Pregnancy In cross-cultural comparisons, the United States continues to have one of the highest adolescent pregnancy and childbearing rates in the industrialized world, despite a considerable decline in the 1990s (Cooksey, 2009). The U.S. adolescent pregnancy rate is eight times as high as in the Netherlands. This dramatic difference exists in spite of the fact that U.S. adolescents are no more sexually active than their counterparts in the Netherlands. In the United States, 82 percent of pregnancies to mothers 15 to 19 years of age are unintended (Koh, 2014). A recent cross-cultural comparison found that among 21 countries, the United States had the highest adolescent pregnancy rate among 15- to 19-year-olds and Switzerland the lowest (Sedgh & others, 2015). Despite the negative comparisons of the United States with many other developed countries, there have been some encouraging trends in U.S. adolescent pregnancy rates. In 2013, the U.S. birth rate for 15- to 19-year-olds was 26.5 births per 1,000 females, the lowest rate ever recorded, which represents a dramatic decrease from the 61.8 births for the same age range in 1991 (Martin & others, 2015) (see Figure 7). There also has been a substantial decrease in adolescent pregnancies across ethnic groups in recent years. Reasons for the decline include school/community health classes, increased contraceptive use, and fear of sexually transmitted infections such as AIDS.

Ethnic variations characterize adolescent pregnancy (Bartlett & others, 2014; Centers for Disease Control and Prevention, 2014a; Kappeler & Farb, 2014). Latina adolescents are more likely than African American and non-Latina White adolescents to become pregnant (Martin & others, 2015). Also, daughters of teenage mothers are at risk for teenage childbearing, thus perpetuating an intergenerational cycle. A study using data from the National Longitudinal Survey of Youth revealed that daughters of teenage mothers were 66 percent more likely to become teenage mothers themselves (Meade, Kershaw, & Ickovics, 2008). In this study, conditions that increased the likelihood that daughters of the teenage mothers would become pregnant included low parental monitoring and poverty.

The consequences of America's high adolescent pregnancy rate are cause for great concern (Lau, Lin, & Flores, 2015; Siegel & Brandon, 2014). Adolescent pregnancy creates health and developmental outcome risks for both the baby and the mother (Bartlett & others, 2014; Kappeler & Farb, 2014). Infants born to adolescent mothers are more likely to have low birth weights—a prominent factor in infant mortality—as well as neurological problems and childhood illness (Malamitsi-Puchner & Boutsikou, 2006). A recent study assessed the reading and math achievement trajectories of children born to adolescent and non-adolescent mothers with different levels of education (Tang & others, 2015). In this study, higher levels of maternal education were linked to growth in achievement through the eighth grade. Nonetheless, the achievement of children born to adolescent mothers never reached the levels of children born to adult mothers.

Adolescent mothers also are more likely to be depressed and drop out of school than their peers (Siegel & Brandon, 2014). Although many adolescent mothers resume their education later in life, they generally do not catch up economically with women who bear children in their twenties. A longitudinal study revealed that these characteristics of adolescent mothers were related to their likelihood of having problems as emerging adults: a history of school problems, delinquency, hard substance use, and mental health problems (Oxford & others, 2006). Also, a recent study of African American urban youth found that at 32 years of age women who had been teenage mothers were more likely to be unemployed, live in poverty, depend on welfare, and not have completed college than women who became mothers during adulthood (Assini-Meytin & Green, 2015). In this study, at 32 years of age, men who had been teenage fathers were less likely to be employed than were men who had fathered children during adulthood.

Researchers have found that adolescent mothers interact less effectively with their infants than do adult mothers. A recent study revealed that adolescent mothers spent more time in

Lynn Blankinship, Family and Consumer Science Educator

Lynn Blankinship is a family and consumer science educator. She has an undergraduate degree in her specialty from the University of Arizona and has taught for more than 20 years, the last 14 at Tucson High Magnet School.

Blankinship received the Tucson Federation of Teachers Educator of the Year Award for 1999–2000 and was honored in 1999 as the Arizona Association of Family and Consumer Science Teacher of the Year.

Blankinship especially enjoys teaching life skills to adolescents. One of her favorite activities is having students care for an automated baby that imitates the needs of real babies. She says that this program has a profound impact on students because the baby must be cared for around the clock for the duration of the assignment. Blankinship also coordinates real-world work experiences and training for students in several child-care facilities in the Tucson area.

Lynn Blankinship (*center*) with students carrying their automated babies.
Courtesy of Lynn Blankinship

For more information about what family and consumer science educators do, see the Careers in Life-Span Development appendix.

negative interactions and less time in play and positive interactions with their infants than did adult mothers (Riva Crugnola & others, 2014). A recent intervention, "My Baby and Me," that involved frequent (55), intensive home visitation coaching sessions with adolescent mothers across three years resulted in improved maternal behavior and child outcomes (Guttentag & others, 2014).

Although the consequences of America's high adolescent pregnancy rate are cause for great concern, it often is not pregnancy alone that leads to negative consequences for an adolescent mother and her offspring (Cavazos-Rehg & others, 2010a, b). Adolescent mothers are more likely to come from low-SES backgrounds (Joyner, 2009). Many adolescent mothers also were not good students before they became pregnant (Malamitsi-Puchner & Boutsikou, 2006). However, not every adolescent female who bears a child lives a life of poverty and low achievement. Thus, although adolescent pregnancy is a high-risk circumstance and adolescents who do not become pregnant generally fare better than those who do, some adolescent mothers do well in school and have positive outcomes (Schaffer & others, 2012).

All adolescents can benefit from comprehensive sexuality education, beginning prior to adolescence and continuing through adolescence (Asheer & others, 2014). Family and consumer science educators teach life skills, such as effective decision making, to adolescents. To read about the work of one family and consumer science educator, see the *Connecting with Careers* profile. And to learn more about ways to reduce adolescent pregnancy, see the *Connecting Development to Life* interlude.

Emerging Adulthood At the beginning of emerging adulthood (age 18), surveys indicate that slightly more than 60 percent of individuals have experienced sexual intercourse, but by the end of emerging adulthood (age 25), most individuals have had sexual intercourse (Lefkowitz & Gillen, 2006). Also, the average age of marriage in the United States is currently 29 for males and 26.5 for females (U.S. Census Bureau, 2014). Thus, emerging adulthood is a time frame during which most individuals are both sexually active and unmarried.

Uncertainty characterizes many emerging adults' sexual relationships. Consider a recent study of emerging adult daters and cohabitors that found nearly half reported a reconciliation (a breakup followed by a reunion) (Halpern-Meekin & others, 2013). One study of 18- to

Reducing Adolescent Pregnancy

One strategy for reducing adolescent pregnancy, called the Teen Outreach Program (TOP), focuses on engaging adolescents in volunteer community service and stimulates discussions that help adolescents appreciate the lessons they learn through volunteerism (Dryfoos & Barkin, 2006). In one study, 695 adolescents in grades 9 to 12 were randomly assigned to either a Teen Outreach group or a control group (Allen & others, 1997). They were assessed at both program entry and program exit nine months later. The rate of pregnancy was substantially lower for the Teen Outreach adolescents. These adolescents also had a lower rate of school failure and academic suspension.

Currently, a major controversy in sex education is whether schools should have an abstinence-only program or a program that emphasizes contraceptive knowledge (Kraft & others, 2012). Two research reviews found that abstinence-only programs did not delay the initiation of sexual intercourse and did not reduce HIV-risk behaviors (Kirby, Laris, & Rolleri, 2007; Underhill, Montgomery, & Operario, 2007). Further, one study revealed that adolescents who experienced comprehensive sex education were less likely to report adolescent pregnancies than those who were given abstinence-only sex education or no education (Kohler, Manhart, & Lafferty, 2008). Some sex

education programs are starting to include abstinence-plus sexuality, an approach that promotes abstinence as well as contraceptive use (Nixon & others, 2011; Realini & others, 2010). A recent study found that sex education about abstinence and birth control was associated with healthier sexual behaviors, such as using some form of contraception at first sex, than no instruction at all (Lindberg & Maddow-Zimet, 2012). For girls whose behavior was tracked in this study, condom use at first sex was more likely among those who received instruction about both abstinence and birth control.

Also, in 2010, the U.S. government launched the Teen Pregnancy Prevention (TPP) Program under the direction of the newly created Office of Adolescent Health (Koh, 2014). Currently, a number of studies are being funded by the program in the effort to find ways to reduce the rate of adolescent pregnancy.

A number of leading experts on adolescent sexuality now conclude that sex education programs that emphasize contraceptive knowledge do not increase the incidence of sexual intercourse and are more likely to reduce the risk of adolescent pregnancy and sexually transmitted infections than abstinence-only programs (Constantine, 2008; Eisenberg & others, 2008; Hyde & DeLamater, 2014). What additional research might help expand the reach of such programs?

What are some characteristics of sexual patterns in emerging adulthood?
© 2/Sri Maiava Rusden/Ocean/Corbis RF

26-year-olds revealed that perceived relationship commitment, though not formal relationship commitment (usually indexed by marriage), was linked to sexual enjoyment (Galinsky & Sonenstein, 2013).

Casual sex is more common in emerging adulthood than it is during the late twenties (Fielder & others, 2013). A recent trend has involved "hooking up" to have non-relationship sex (from kissing to intercourse) (Olmstead & others, 2015; Roberson, Olmstead, & Fincham, 2015; Vrangalova, 2015a, b). A recent study indicated that 40 percent of 22-year-olds reported having had a recent casual sexual partner (Lyons & others, 2015). A recent study also revealed that 20 percent of first-year college women on one large university campus had engaged in at least one hookup over the course of the school year (Fielder & others, 2013). In this study, impulsivity, sensation seeking, and alcohol use were among the predictors of a higher likelihood of hooking up. And in another recent study of more than 3,900 18- to 25-year-olds, having casual sex was negatively linked to well-being and positively related to psychological distress (Bersamin & others, 2014).

In addition to hooking up, another type of casual sex that has recently increased among emerging adults is "friends with benefits," which involves a relationship formed by the integration of friendship and sexual intimacy without an explicit commitment characteristic of an exclusive romantic relationship (Owen, Fincham, & Manthos, 2013). In a study of almost 8,000 emerging adults, males had more permissive sexual attitudes, especially regarding sexual encounters, than did females (Sprecher, Treger, & Sakaluk, 2013).

ADULT DEVELOPMENT AND AGING

Earlier in our coverage of sexual orientation, we examined a number of basic ideas about heterosexual and gay/lesbian attitudes and behavior. Much of what we said there applied to young adults. Here we focus on changes in middle adulthood and late adulthood.

Middle Adulthood   What kinds of changes characterize the sexuality of women and men as they go through middle age? **Climacteric** is a term used to describe the midlife transition in which fertility declines.

Menopause   **Menopause** is the time in middle age, usually during the late forties or early fifties, when a woman's menstrual periods cease. The average age at which U.S. women have their last period is 51 (Wise, 2006). However, there is a large variation in the age at which menopause occurs—from 39 to 59 years of age. Later menopause is linked with increased risk of breast cancer (Mishra & others, 2009).

The average age at menarche, a girl's first menstruation, has significantly decreased since the mid-nineteenth century, occurring as much as four years earlier in some countries (Susman & Dorn, 2013). Has there been a similar earlier onset in the occurrence of menopause? No, there hasn't been a corresponding change in menopause, and there is little or no correlation between the onset of menarche and the onset of menopause (Gosden, 2007). However, researchers have found that early-onset menopause is linked to a higher risk of cardiovascular disease and stroke (Kaur, Singh, & Ahula, 2012).

Perimenopause is the transitional period from normal menstrual periods to no menstrual periods at all, which often takes up to 10 years (McNamara, Batur, & DeSapri, 2015). Perimenopause occurs most often in the forties but can occur in the thirties (Mendoza & others, 2013). One study of 30- to 50-year-old women found that depressed feelings, headaches, moodiness, and heart palpitations were the perimenopausal symptoms that these women most frequently discussed with health-care providers (Lyndaker & Hulton, 2004). Lifestyle factors such as whether women are overweight, smoke, drink heavily, or exercise regularly during perimenopause influence aspects of their future health status such as whether they develop cardiovascular disease or chronic illnesses (ESHRE Capri Workshop Group, 2011; Gallicchio & others, 2015).

In menopause, production of estrogen by the ovaries declines dramatically, and this decline produces uncomfortable symptoms in some women—"hot flashes," nausea, fatigue, and rapid heartbeat, for example (Brockie & others, 2014; Santen & others, 2014).

Cross-cultural studies also reveal wide variations in the menopause experience (Lerner-Geva & others, 2010; Perez-Alcala & others, 2013). For example, hot flashes are uncommon in Mayan women (Beyene, 1986). Asian women report fewer hot flashes than women in Western societies (Payer, 1991). It is difficult to determine the extent to which these cross-cultural variations are due to genetic, dietary, reproductive, or cultural factors.

Menopause overall is not the negative experience for most women it was once thought to be (Henderson, 2011). Most women do not have severe physical or psychological problems related to menopause. For example, a recent research review concluded that there is no clear evidence that depressive disorders occur more often during menopause than at other times in a woman's reproductive life (Judd, Hickey, & Bryant, 2012).

However, the loss of fertility is an important marker for women—it means that they have to make final decisions about having children. Women in their thirties who have never had children sometimes speak about being "up against the biological clock" because they cannot postpone choices about having children much longer.

Until recently, hormone replacement therapy was often prescribed as a treatment for unpleasant side effects of menopause. *Hormone replacement therapy (HRT)* augments the declining levels of reproductive hormone production by the ovaries (Gambacciani & Levancini, 2015; Pabon & others, 2014). HRT can consist of various forms of estrogen, usually in combination with a progestin.

The National Institutes of Health recommends that women who have not had a hysterectomy and who are currently taking hormones consult with their doctor to determine whether they should continue the treatment. If they are taking HRT for short-term relief of menopausal symptoms, the benefits may outweigh the risks. Recent research has indicated that when women start HRT in their fifties and continue its use for 5 to 30 years, there is an increase in 1.5 quality life years for the women (Hodis & Mack, 2014). And a recent meta-analysis concluded that HRT was linked to decreased lung cancer in females, especially nonsmoking females and females with BMI less than 25kg/m (Yao & others, 2013).

Many middle-aged women are seeking alternatives to HRT such as regular exercise, dietary supplements, herbal remedies, relaxation therapy, acupuncture, and nonsteroidal medications (Al-Safi & Santoro, 2014; Buhling & others, 2014). A recent study revealed

climacteric The midlife transition in which fertility declines.

menopause The complete cessation of a woman's menstrual cycles, which usually occurs during the late forties or early fifties.

perimenopause The transitional period from normal menstrual periods to no menstrual periods at all, which often takes up to 10 years.

© McGraw-Hill Companies, Inc./Suzie Ross, Photographer

that in sedentary women, aerobic training for 6 months decreased menopausal symptoms, especially night sweats, mood swings, and irritability (Moilanen & others, 2012). Another recent study found that yoga improved the quality of life of menopausal women (Reed & others, 2014).

Hormonal Changes in Middle-Aged Men   Do men go through anything like the menopause that women experience? That is, is there a male menopause? During middle adulthood, most men do not lose their capacity to father children, although there usually is a modest decline in their sexual hormone level and activity (Yassin & others, 2011). They experience hormonal changes in their fifties and sixties, but nothing like the dramatic drop in estrogen that women experience. Testosterone production begins to decline about 1 percent a year during middle adulthood, and sperm count usually shows a slow decline, but men do not lose their fertility in middle age. What has been referred to as "male menopause," then, probably has less to do with hormonal change than with the psychological adjustment men must make when they are faced with declining physical energy and with family and work pressures. Testosterone therapy has not been found to relieve such symptoms, suggesting that they are not induced by hormonal change.

The gradual decline in men's testosterone levels in middle age can reduce their sexual drive (Goel & others, 2009). Their erections are less full and less frequent, and men require more stimulation to achieve them. Researchers once attributed these changes to psychological factors, but increasingly they find that as many as 75 percent of the erectile dysfunctions in middle-aged men stem from physiological problems. Smoking, diabetes, hypertension, elevated cholesterol levels, and lack of exercise are responsible for many erectile problems in middle-aged men (Cao & others, 2013; Giagulli & others, 2013).

Recently, there has been a dramatic surge of interest in *testosterone replacement therapy (TRT)* (Hwang & Miner, 2015; Morgentaler, Feibus, & Baum, 2015; Rahnema & others, 2014; Ullah, Riche, & Koch, 2014). For many decades, it was thought that TRT increased the risk of prostate cancer, but recent research reviews indicate that is not the case, at least when TRT lasts one year or less (Cui & others, 2014; Khera & others, 2014). It is now accepted that TRT can improve sexual functioning, muscle strength, and bone health (Isidori & others, 2014; Mayo Clinic, 2014). Two recent studies found that TRT improved older men's sexual function as well as their moods (Miner & others, 2013; Okada & others, 2014). Further, a recent study found that a higher testosterone level was linked to better episodic memory in middle-aged males (Panizzon & others, 2014). However, a recent research review concluded that the benefit-risk ratio for older adult men is uncertain (Isidori & others, 2014). Men who have prostate cancer or breast cancer should not take TRT, and men who are at risk for blood clotting (those who have atrial fibrillation, for example) also should not use TRT (Osterberg, Bernie, & Ramasamy, 2014).

Erectile dysfunction (ED) is a common condition in aging men, being present in approximately 50 percent of men 40 to 70 years of age (Berookhim & Bar-Chama, 2011). Treatment for men with erectile dysfunction has focused on the drug Viagra and on similar drugs, such as Levitra and Cialis (Kim & others, 2015; McMahon, 2014). Viagra works by allowing increased blood flow into the penis, which produces an erection. Its success rate is in the 60 to 85 percent range (Claes & others, 2010).

Sexual Attitudes and Behavior   Although the ability of men and women to function sexually shows little biological decline in middle adulthood, sexual activity usually occurs on a less frequent basis than in early adulthood (Welch, 2011). Career interests, family matters, decreased energy levels, and routine may contribute to this decline (Avis & others, 2009).

In the Sex in America survey (described earlier in this chapter), the frequency of having sex was greatest for individuals aged 25 to 29 years old (47 percent had sex twice a week or more) and dropped off for individuals in their fifties (23 percent of 50- to 59-year-old males said they had sex twice a week or more, while only 14 percent of the females in this age group reported this frequency) (Michael & others, 1994). Note, though, that the

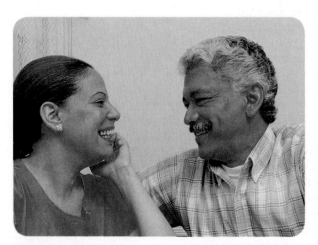

How frequently do middle-aged U.S. adults engage in sexual intercourse?
© Rhoda Sidney/PhotoEdit

Sex in America survey may underestimate the frequency of sexual activity of middle-aged adults because the data were collected prior to the widespread use of erectile dysfunction drugs such as Viagra.

Living with a spouse or partner makes all the difference in whether people engage in sexual activity, especially for women over 40 years of age. In one study conducted as part of the Midlife in the United States Study (MIDUS), 95 percent of women in their forties with partners said that they had been sexually active in the last six months, compared with only 53 percent of those without partners (Brim, 1999). By their fifties, 88 percent of women living with a partner had been sexually active in the last six months, but only 37 percent of those who were neither married nor living with someone reported having had sex in the last six months.

A large-scale study of U.S. adults 40 to 80 years of age found that premature ejaculation (26 percent) and erectile difficulties (22 percent) were the most common sexual problems of older men, whereas lack of sexual interest (33 percent) and lubrication difficulties (21 percent) were the most common sexual problems of older women (Laumann & others, 2009).

A person's health in middle age is a key factor in sexual activity during this period (Field & others, 2013). A recent study of adults 55 years and older revealed that their level of sexual activity was associated with their physical and mental health (Bach & others, 2013).

FIGURE **8**

SEXUAL ACTIVITY IN OLDER ADULTS WITH A PARTNER

Late Adulthood Too often it has been assumed that older adults do not have sexual desires (Inelmen & others, 2012). Aging does induce some changes in human sexual performance, more so in men than in women, but many older adults do have sexual desires (Mroczek & others, 2013). Orgasm becomes less frequent in males, occurring in every second to third act of intercourse rather than every time. More direct stimulation usually is needed to produce an erection. From 65 to 80 years of age, approximately one out of four men has serious problems getting or keeping erections; for those over 80 years of age, the percentage rises to one out of two men (Butler & Lewis, 2002). Even when intercourse is impaired by infirmity, other relationship needs persist, among them closeness, sensuality, and being valued as a man or a woman (Bouman, 2008).

An interview study of more than 3,000 adults 57 to 85 years of age revealed that many older adults are sexually active as long as they are healthy (Lindau & others, 2007) (see Figure 8). Sexual activity did decline through the later years of life: 73 percent of 57- to 64-year-olds, 53 percent of 65- to 74-year-olds, and 26 percent of 75- to 85-year-olds reported that they were sexually active. Even in the sexually active oldest group (75 to 85), more than 50 percent said they still had sex at least two to three times a month. Fifty-eight percent of sexually active 65- to 74-year-olds and 31 percent of 75- to 85-year-olds said they engaged in oral sex. As with middle-aged and younger adults, older adults who did not have a partner were far less likely to be sexually active than those who had a partner. For older adults with a partner who reported not having sex, the main reason was poor health, especially the male partner's physical health. However, with recent advances in erectile dysfunction medications such as Viagra, an increasing number of older men, especially the young old, are able to have an erection (Lochlainn & Kenny, 2013; Lowe & Costabile, 2012; Rubio-Aurioles & others, 2012). Also, as indicated earlier, there has been a dramatic increase in testosterone replacement therapy in middle-aged adults, but the benefit-risk ratio of testosterone replacement therapy is uncertain for older males (Isidori & others, 2014).

As indicated in Figure 8, older women had a lower rate of sexual activity than did men. Indeed, a challenge for a sexually interested older woman is not having a partner. At 70 years of age, only about 35 percent of women have a partner compared with approximately 70 percent of men of the same age. Many older women's husbands have died, and many older men are with younger women.

At this point, we have discussed many aspects of sexuality, but we have not examined three influential factors that are explored in the chapter on "Moral Development, Values, and Religion."

What are some characteristics of sexuality in older adults? How does sexual activity change as older adults go through the late adulthood period?
© Emma Rian/Corbis

Review Connect Reflect

LG5 Summarize how sexuality develops through the life span

Review

- What is the nature of child sexuality?
- How do adolescents develop a sexual identity? How does sexual behavior develop?
- What are some risk factors for sexual problems during adolescence?
- What are some patterns of behavior for emerging adults?
- How does sexuality change in middle adulthood? How does sexuality change in late adulthood?

Connect

- In this section you read that the production of estrogen by the ovaries declines dramatically in menopause. What have you learned about the role of estradiol, a type of estrogen, in puberty?

Reflect *Your Own Personal Journey of Life*

- How would you describe your sexual identity? What contributed to this identity?

reach your **learning goals**

Gender and Sexuality

1 Biological, Social, and Cognitive Influences on Gender

LG1 Explain biological, social, and cognitive influences on gender

Biological Influences

Gender refers to the characteristics of people as males and females. Key aspects of gender include gender roles and gender-typing (the process by which children acquire the thoughts, feelings, and behaviors that are considered appropriate for their gender). Biological influences on gender include heredity, hormones, and evolution. A 23rd pair of chromosomes with two X-shaped chromosomes produces a female; a 23rd pair with an X and a Y chromosome produces a male. Estrogens primarily influence the development of female physical sex characteristics and help regulate the menstrual cycle. Androgens primarily promote the development of male genitals and secondary sex characteristics. To explore biological influences on gender, researchers have studied individuals who are exposed to unusual levels of sex hormones early in prenatal development. Evolutionary psychology argues that adaptation during the evolution of humans produced psychological differences between males and females.

Social Influences

Three theories have been influential in arguing that psychological differences between the genders are due to social factors. Social role theory states that gender differences result from the contrasting roles of women and men. The psychoanalytic theory of gender stems from Freud's view that the preschool child develops a sexual attraction to the opposite-sex parent, then at 5 or 6 years of age renounces the attraction because of anxious feelings, subsequently identifies with the same-sex parent and unconsciously adopts the characteristics of the same-sex parent. The social cognitive theory of gender states that children learn about gender through observation and imitation and through reward and punishment for gender-appropriate and gender-inappropriate behavior. Parents, other adults, the media, peers, and schools and teachers influence children's gender development.

Cognitive Influences

Gender schema theory states that gender-typing emerges as children gradually develop gender schemas of what is gender-appropriate and gender-inappropriate in their culture.

2 Gender Stereotypes, Similarities, and Differences

 LG2 Discuss gender stereotypes, similarities, and differences

Gender Stereotyping

- Gender stereotypes are general impressions and beliefs about males and females. Gender stereotypes are widespread. Gender stereotyping changes developmentally; it is present even at 2 years of age but increases considerably in early childhood. In middle and late childhood, children become more flexible in their gender attitudes, but gender stereotyping may increase again in early adolescence. By late adolescence, gender attitudes are often more flexible.

Gender Similarities and Differences

- There are a number of physical differences in males and females, small or nonexistent cognitive differences, and some socioemotional differences (males are more physically aggressive and active, but engage in less emotional self-regulation; females show a stronger interest in relationships; and females are more people-oriented, boys more object-oriented). Controversy continues to occur regarding how extensive gender differences are and what causes the differences. Gender in context is an important concept—gender behavior often varies across contexts, not only within a particular culture but also across cultures.

3 Gender Development Through the Life Span

 LG3 Describe the development of gender through the life span

Childhood

- Children form many ideas about what the sexes are like from about 1½ to 3 years of age. The amount, timing, and intensity of gender socialization are different for girls and for boys. Boys receive earlier and more intense gender socialization than girls do.

Adolescence

- During early adolescence, females and males must come to terms with new definitions of their gender roles as they experience the extensive changes of puberty. There is continued controversy about whether all young adolescents experience gender intensification.

Adulthood and Aging

- Many experts argue that it is important for women to retain their relationship strengths but also to put more energy into self-development. Tannen stresses that many women prefer rapport talk and many men prefer report talk. Men have been successful at achieving career goals, but the male role involves considerable strain. There is diversity in men's experiences, just as there is in women's. Men seem to become more nurturant and sensitive when they get older, but there is mixed evidence about whether women tend to become more assertive and dominant as they get older.

4 Exploring Sexuality

 LG4 Characterize influences on sexuality, the nature of sexual orientation, and some sexual problems

Biological and Cultural Factors

- The role of hormones in human sexual behavior is difficult to specify. Sexual motivation is also influenced by cultural factors. Sexual scripts in cultures influence sexual behavior. In some sexual scripts, females link sexual intercourse with love more than do males, the female is blamed if she becomes pregnant, and males tend to emphasize sexual conquest.

Sexual Orientation

- An individual's sexual preference—heterosexual, homosexual, or bisexual—likely is the result of a combination of genetic, hormonal, cognitive, and environmental factors. In the 1994 Sex in America survey, Americans' sexual lives were reported to be more conservative than in earlier surveys. Sexual orientation is generally viewed as a continuum. Regardless of sexual orientation, most people emphasize the importance of trust, affection, and shared interests in a relationship.

Sexually Transmitted Infections

- Sexually transmitted infections (STIs) are contracted primarily through sexual contact. The STI that has received the most attention in recent years is AIDS. Gonorrhea, syphilis, chlamydia, genital herpes, and HPV are among the most common STIs. Some good strategies for protecting against STIs include knowing your own and your partner's risk status; obtaining screening for STIs; avoiding unprotected sex; and not having sex with multiple partners.

Forcible Sexual Behavior and Sexual Harassment

- Rape is forcible sexual intercourse, oral sex, or anal sex with a person who does not give consent. Rape usually produces traumatic reactions in its victims. Sexual harassment occurs when one person uses his or her power over another individual in a sexual manner.

Childhood

- A majority of children engage in some sex play, usually with siblings or friends. Their motivation is probably mainly curiosity, and there does not appear to be a link between childhood sex play and adolescent or adult sexual adjustment.

Adolescence and Emerging Adulthood

- Adolescence is a time of sexual exploration and sexual experimentation. Mastering emerging sexual feelings and forming a sense of sexual identity are two challenges of the period. Gay and lesbian youth have diverse patterns of initial attraction, often have bisexual attractions, and may experience same-sex emotional or physical attractions. National U.S. data indicate that by age 19, four out of five individuals have had sexual intercourse. A dramatic increase in oral sex has occurred in adolescence, although many adolescents are unaware of the health risks associated with oral sex. Risk factors for sexual problems include early sexual activity, engaging in delinquency and excessive drinking, living in a low-SES neighborhood, ineffective parenting, and having an older sibling who engages in sex. Contraceptive use by adolescents is increasing. About one in four sexually experienced adolescents acquires a sexually transmitted infection (STI). The adolescent pregnancy rate in the United States is high but has been decreasing in recent years. Emerging adults have sexual intercourse less frequently than young adults; males have more casual sexual partners and are less selective than females in their partner choice; and by the end of emerging adulthood, most people have had sexual intercourse.

Adult Development and Aging

- Menopause usually occurs during the late forties or early fifties. Perimenopause, the transition from normal menstrual periods to no menstrual periods at all, often takes up to 10 years. Hormone replacement therapy (HRT) augments the declining levels of reproductive hormone production by the ovaries. HRT consists of various forms of estrogen, and usually progestin. Although HRT reduces many short-term symptoms of menopause, its long-term use is no longer recommended by the National Institutes of Health because of its association with increased risks of coronary heart disease and stroke. Men do not experience an inability to father children in middle age, although their testosterone level drops. In late adulthood, sexual changes do occur, more so for men than for women.

key terms

androgens	gender-intensification	perimenopause	sexual scripts
bisexuality	hypothesis	psychoanalytic theory of gender	sexually transmitted
climacteric	gender role	rape	infections (STIs)
date or acquaintance rape	gender schema theory	rapport talk	social cognitive theory
estrogens	gender stereotypes	report talk	of gender
gender	gender-typing	romantic script	social role theory
gender identity	menopause	sexual harassment	traditional religious script

key people

Phyllis Bronstein	Sigmund Freud	Ron Levant	Joseph Pleck
Laura Brown	Janet Shibley Hyde	Robert Michael	Deborah Tannen
Alice Eagly	Harriet Lerner	Jean Baker Miller	

chapter 13

MORAL DEVELOPMENT, VALUES, AND RELIGION

chapter outline

preview

Just as a person's emotional life and sexual life change with age, a person's moral life and spiritual life also develop through the life span. In this chapter we examine how moral development proceeds. We also explore how people go beyond questions of right and wrong to search for values, religion, spirituality, and meaning at different points in their lives.

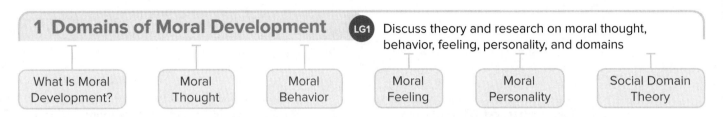

1 Domains of Moral Development

LG1 Discuss theory and research on moral thought, behavior, feeling, personality, and domains

What Is Moral Development? | Moral Thought | Moral Behavior | Moral Feeling | Moral Personality | Social Domain Theory

Moral development has been a topic of great concern to societies, communities, and families. It is also one of the oldest topics of interest to those who are curious about human nature. Philosophers and theologians have talked about it and written about it for many centuries. In the twentieth century, psychologists began theorizing about and studying moral development.

WHAT IS MORAL DEVELOPMENT?

Moral development involves changes in thoughts, feelings, and behaviors regarding standards of right and wrong. Moral development has an intrapersonal dimension, which regulates a person's activities when she or he is not engaged in social interaction, and an *interpersonal* dimension, which regulates social interactions and arbitrates conflict (Walker, 2004, 2006). To understand moral development, we need to consider five basic questions:

· First, how do individuals reason or think about moral decisions?
· Second, how do individuals actually behave in moral circumstances?
· Third, how do individuals feel about moral matters?
· Fourth, what characterizes an individual's moral personality?
· Fifth, how is the moral domain different from social conventional and personal domains?

As we consider various theories and domains in the following sections, keep in mind that thoughts, behaviors, feelings, and personality often are interrelated. For example, if the focus is on an individual's behavior, it is still important to evaluate the person's reasoning. Also, emotions can distort moral reasoning. And moral personality encompasses thoughts, behavior, and feeling.

MORAL THOUGHT

How do individuals think about what is right and wrong? Are children able to evaluate moral questions in the same way that adults can? Jean Piaget had some thoughts about these questions. So did Lawrence Kohlberg.

Piaget's Theory   Interest in how children think about moral issues was stimulated by Piaget (1932), who extensively observed and interviewed children from the ages of 4 through 12. Piaget watched children play marbles to learn how they used and thought about the game's rules. He also asked children about ethical issues—theft, lies, punishment, and justice, for example. Piaget concluded that children go through two distinct stages in how they think about morality:

· From 4 to 7 years of age, children display **heteronomous morality,** the first stage of moral development in Piaget's theory. Children think of justice and rules as unchangeable properties of the world, removed from the control of people.

moral development Changes in thoughts, feelings, and behaviors regarding standards of right and wrong.

heteronomous morality (Piaget) The first stage of moral development in Piaget's theory, occurring at 4 to 7 years of age. Justice and rules are conceived of as unchangeable properties of the world, removed from the control of people.

- From 7 to 10 years of age, children are in a transition showing some features of the first stage of moral reasoning and some features of the second stage, autonomous morality.

- From about 10 years of age and older, children show **autonomous morality.** They become aware that rules and laws are created by people, and in judging an action, they consider the actor's intentions as well as the consequences.

Because young children are heteronomous moralists, they judge the rightness or goodness of behavior by considering its consequences, not the intentions of the actor. For example, to the heteronomous moralist, breaking twelve cups accidentally is worse than breaking one cup intentionally. As children develop into moral autonomists, intentions assume paramount importance.

The heteronomous thinker also believes that rules are unchangeable and are handed down by all-powerful authorities. When Piaget suggested to young children that they use new rules in a game of marbles, they resisted. By contrast, older children—moral autonomists—accept change and recognize that rules are merely convenient conventions, subject to change.

The heteronomous thinker also believes in **immanent justice,** the concept that if a rule is broken, punishment will be meted out immediately. The young child believes that a violation is connected automatically to its punishment. Thus, young children often look around worriedly after doing something wrong, expecting inevitable punishment. Immanent justice also implies that if something unfortunate happens to someone, the person must have transgressed earlier. Older children, who are moral autonomists, recognize that punishment occurs only if someone witnesses the wrongdoing and that, even then, punishment is not inevitable.

How do these changes in moral reasoning occur? Piaget argued that, as children develop, they become more sophisticated in thinking about social matters, especially about the possibilities and conditions of cooperation. Piaget stressed that this social understanding comes about through the mutual give-and-take of peer relations. In the peer group, where others have power and status similar to the child's, plans are negotiated and coordinated, and disagreements are reasoned about and eventually settled. Parent-child relations, in which parents have the power and children do not, are less likely to advance moral reasoning, because rules are often handed down in an authoritarian way.

From Ross Thompson's perspective, young children are not as egocentric as Piaget envisioned. Thompson (2012) further elaborates on this view, arguing that recent research indicates that young children often show a non-egocentric awareness of others' goals, feelings, and desires and how such internal states are influenced by the actions of others. These ties between advances in moral understanding and theory of mind indicate that young children possess cognitive resources that allow them to be aware of others' intentions and know when someone violates a moral prohibition. One study of 3-year-olds found that they were less likely to offer assistance to an adult they had previously observed being harmful to another person (Vaish, Carpenter, & Tomasello, 2010).

However, because of limitations in their self-control skills, social understanding, and cognitive flexibility, young children's moral advancements often are inconsistent and vary across situations. They still have a long way to go before they have the capacity for developing a consistent moral character and making ethical judgments.

Kohlberg's Theory

A second major perspective on moral development was proposed by Lawrence Kohlberg (1958, 1986). Piaget's cognitive stages of development serve as the underpinnings for Kohlberg's theory, but Kohlberg suggested that there are six stages of moral development. These stages, he argued, are universal. Development from one stage to another, said Kohlberg, is fostered by opportunities to take the perspective of others and to experience conflict between one's current stage of moral thinking and the reasoning of someone at a higher stage.

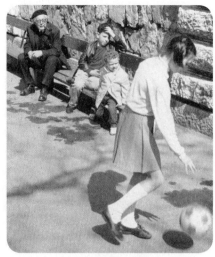

Piaget extensively observed and interviewed 4- to 12-year-old children as they played games to learn how they used and thought about the games' rules.
© Yves de Braine/Black Star/Stock Photo

developmental **connection**

Cognitive Theory

In which of Piaget's cognitive stages is a 5-year-old heteronomous thinker likely to be? Connect to "Cognitive Developmental Approaches."

How is this child's moral thinking likely to be different about stealing a cookie depending on whether he is in Piaget's heteronomous or autonomous stage?
© Tom Grill/Corbis RF

autonomous morality The second stage of moral development in Piaget's theory, displayed by children about 10 years of age and older. At this stage, children become aware that rules and laws are created by people and that in judging an action they should consider the actor's intentions as well as the consequences.

immanent justice Belief that if a rule is broken, punishment will be meted out immediately.

Lawrence Kohlberg.
Harvard University Archives, UAV 605.295.8, Box 7, Kohlberg

Kohlberg arrived at his view after 20 years of using a unique interview with children. In the interview, children are presented with a series of stories in which characters face moral dilemmas. The following is the most popular Kohlberg dilemma:

> In Europe a woman was near death from a special kind of cancer. There was one drug that the doctors thought might save her. It was a form of radium that a druggist in the same town had recently discovered. The drug was expensive to make, but the druggist was charging ten times what the drug cost him to make. He paid $200 for the radium and charged $2,000 for a small dose of the drug. The sick woman's husband, Heinz, went to everyone he knew to borrow the money, but he could only get together $1,000, which is half of what it cost. He told the druggist that his wife was dying and asked him to sell it cheaper or let him pay later. But the druggist said, "No, I discovered the drug, and I am going to make money from it." So Heinz got desperate and broke into the man's store to steal the drug for his wife. (Kohlberg, 1969, p. 379)

This story is one of 11 that Kohlberg devised to investigate the nature of moral thought. After reading the story, the interviewee answers a series of questions about the moral dilemma. Should Heinz have stolen the drug? Was stealing it right or wrong? Why? Is it a husband's duty to steal the drug for his wife if he can get it no other way? Would a good husband steal? Did the druggist have the right to charge that much when there was no law setting a limit on the price? Why or why not?

The Kohlberg Stages   Based on the answers interviewees gave for this and other moral dilemmas, Kohlberg identified three levels of moral thinking, each of which is characterized by two stages (see Figure 1). A key concept in understanding progression through the levels and stages is that people's morality becomes more internal or mature. That is, their reasons for their moral decisions or values begin to go beyond the external or superficial reasons they gave when they were younger to more complex coordinations of multiple perspectives. Each stage integrates previous stages into a qualitatively different type of thought. Let's further examine Kohlberg's stages.

Preconventional reasoning is the lowest level of moral reasoning, said Kohlberg. At this level, good and bad are interpreted in terms of external rewards and punishments.

- *Stage 1.* **Heteronomous morality** is the first stage in preconventional reasoning. At this stage, moral thinking is tied to punishment. For example, children think that they must obey because they fear punishment for disobedience.
- *Stage 2.* **Individualism, instrumental purpose, and exchange** is the second stage of preconventional reasoning. At this stage, individuals reason that pursuing their own interests is the right thing to do, but they let others do the same. Thus, they think that what is right involves an equal exchange. They reason that if they are nice to others, others will be nice to them in return.

preconventional reasoning The lowest level in Kohlberg's theory of moral development. The individual's moral reasoning is controlled primarily by external rewards and punishments.

heteronomous morality (Kohlberg) The first stage of preconventional reasoning in Kohlberg's theory, in which moral thinking is tied to punishment.

LEVEL 1	LEVEL 2	LEVEL 3
Preconventional Level	**Conventional Level**	**Postconventional Level**
Stage 1 Heteronomous Morality *Children obey because adults tell them to obey. People base their moral decisions on fear of punishment.*	**Stage 3** Mutual Interpersonal Expectations, Relationships, and Interpersonal Conformity *Individuals value trust, caring, and loyalty to others as a basis of moral judgments.*	**Stage 5** Social Contract or Utility and Individual Rights *Individuals reason that values, rights, and principles undergird or transcend the law.*
Stage 2 Individualism, Instrumental Purpose, and Exchange *Individuals pursue their own interests but let others do the same. What is right involves equal exchange.*	**Stage 4** Social Systems Morality *Moral judgments are based on understanding and the social order, law, justice, and duty.*	**Stage 6** Universal Ethical Principles *The person has developed moral judgments that are based on universal human rights. When faced with a dilemma between law and conscience, a personal, individualized conscience is followed.*

FIGURE 1

KOHLBERG'S THREE LEVELS AND SIX STAGES OF MORAL DEVELOPMENT

Psychoanalytic Theory According to Sigmund Freud, guilt and the desire to avoid feeling guilty are the foundation of moral behavior. In Freud's theory, the *superego* is the moral branch of personality. The superego consists of two main components: the ego ideal and the conscience. The **ego ideal** rewards the child by conveying a sense of pride and personal value when the child acts according to ideal standards approved by the parents. The **conscience** punishes the child for behaviors disapproved by the parents, making the child feel guilty and worthless.

How does the superego and hence guilt develop? According to Freud, children fear losing their parents' love and being punished for their unacceptable sexual attraction toward the opposite-sex parent. To reduce anxiety, avoid punishment, and maintain parental affection, children identify with the same-sex parent. Through this identification, children *internalize* the parent's standards of right and wrong, which reflect societal prohibitions, and hence develop their superego. Also, the child turns inward the hostility that was previously aimed externally at the same-sex parent. This inwardly directed hostility is then experienced self-punitively (and unconsciously) as guilt. In the psychoanalytic account of moral development, children conform to societal standards to avoid guilt. In this way, self-control replaces parental control.

Freud's claims regarding the formation of the ego ideal and conscience cannot be verified. However, researchers can examine the extent to which children feel guilty when they misbehave. Contemporary views of conscience emphasize that conscience is rooted in close relationships, constructed from advances in children's self-understanding and understanding of others, and linked to their emotions (Thompson, 2014).

Contemporary views also stress that the development of conscience goes well beyond discipline encounters with parents to include communication about emotion and conversations with parents about relationships (Thompson, 2014).

Grazyna Kochanska and her colleagues (Kochanska & Aksan, 2007; Kochanska & others, 2002, 2005, 2008; Kochanska, Koenig, & others, 2010) have conducted a number of studies that explore children's conscience development. In a research review of these studies involving children's conscience, she concluded that young children are aware of right and wrong, have the capacity to show empathy toward others, experience guilt, indicate discomfort following a transgression, and are sensitive to violating rules (Kochanska & Aksan, 2007). In one study, Kochanska and her colleagues (2002) observed 106 preschool children in laboratory situations in which they were led to believe that they had damaged valuable objects. In these mishaps, the behavioral indicators of guilt that were coded by observers included avoiding gaze (looking away or down), body tension (squirming, backing away, hanging head down, covering face with hands), and distress (looking uncomfortable, crying). Girls expressed more guilt than boys did. Children with a more fearful temperament expressed more guilt. Children of mothers who used power-oriented discipline (such as spanking, slapping, and yelling) displayed less guilt. In another study, young children with a history of stronger internalization of both parents' rules were more competent and better socialized (Kochanska, Woodard, & others, 2010).

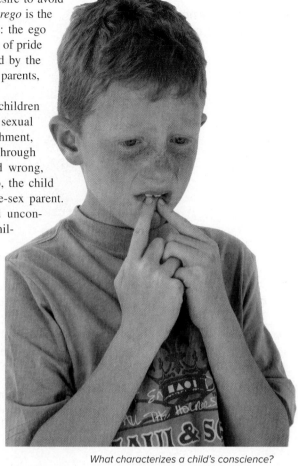

What characterizes a child's conscience?
© Martin Harvey/Corbis

Empathy Positive feelings, such as empathy, contribute to the child's moral development (Malti & Ongley, 2014; Yoo, Feng, & Day, 2013). Feeling **empathy** means reacting to another's feelings with an emotional response that is similar to the other's feelings (Damon, 1988). To empathize is not just to sympathize; it is to put oneself in another's place emotionally.

Although empathy is an emotional state, it has a cognitive component—the ability to discern another's inner psychological states, or what we have previously discussed as *perspective taking* (Eisenberg, Spinrad, & Morris, 2014). Infants have the capacity for some purely empathic responses, but for effective moral action, children must learn to identify a wide range of emotional states in others and to anticipate what kinds of actions will improve another person's emotional state.

What are the milestones in children's development of empathy? According to an analysis by child developmentalist William Damon (1988), changes in empathy take place in early infancy, at 1 to 2 years of age, in early childhood, and at 10 to 12 years of age.

ego ideal The component of the superego that rewards the child by conveying a sense of pride and personal value when the child acts according to ideal standards approved by the parents.

conscience The component of the superego that punishes the child for behaviors disapproved of by parents by making the child feel guilty and worthless.

empathy Reacting to another's feelings with an emotional response that is similar to the other's feelings.

FIGURE **2**

**DAMON'S DESCRIPTION OF
DEVELOPMENTAL CHANGES IN EMPATHY**

Age Period	Nature of Empathy
Early infancy	Characterized by global empathy, the young infant's empathic response does not distinguish between feelings and needs of self and others.
1 to 2 years of age	Undifferentiated feelings of discomfort at another's distress grow into more genuine feelings of concern, but infants cannot translate realization of others' unhappy feelings into effective action.
Early childhood	Children become aware that every person's perspective is unique and that someone else may have a different reaction to a situation. This awareness allows the child to respond more appropriately to another person's distress.
10 to 12 years of age	Children develop an emergent orientation of empathy for people who live in unfortunate circumstances—the poor, the handicapped, and the socially outcast. In adolescence, this newfound sensitivity may give a humanitarian flavor to the individual's ideological and political views.

Global empathy is the young infant's empathic response in which clear boundaries between the feelings and needs of the self and those of another have not yet been established. For example, one 11-month-old infant fought off her own tears, sucked her thumb, and buried her head in her mother's lap after she had seen another child fall and hurt himself. Not all infants cry every time someone else is hurt, though. Many times, an infant will stare at another's pain with curiosity. Although global empathy is observed in some infants, it does not consistently characterize all infants' behavior.

When they are 1 to 2 years of age, infants may feel genuine concern for the distress of other people, but only when they reach early childhood can they respond appropriately to another person's distress. This ability depends on children's new awareness that people have different reactions to situations. By late childhood, they may begin to feel empathy for the unfortunate. To read further about Damon's description of the developmental changes in empathy from infancy through adolescence, see Figure 2.

The Contemporary Perspective on the Role of Emotion in Moral Development We have seen that classical psychoanalytic theory emphasizes the power of unconscious guilt in moral development but that other theorists, such as Damon, emphasize the role of empathy. Today, many child developmentalists believe that both positive feelings—such as empathy, sympathy, admiration, and self-esteem—and negative feelings—such as anger, outrage, shame, and guilt—contribute to children's moral development (Eisenberg, Spinrad, Morris, 2013; Lapsley & Carlo, 2014; Malti & Ongley, 2014). When strongly experienced, these emotions influence children to act in accord with standards of right and wrong. *Sympathy*—an other-oriented emotional response in which the observer experiences emotions that are the same or similar to what the other person is feeling—often motivates prosocial behavior (Eisenberg, Spinrad, & Knafo, 2015; Eisenberg, Spinrad, & Morris, 2013, 2014). A recent study indeed found that young children's sympathy predicted whether they would share or not (Ongley & Malti, 2014).

Emotions such as empathy, shame, guilt, and anxiety over other people's violations of standards are present early in development and undergo developmental change throughout childhood and beyond (Damon, 1988). These emotions provide a natural base for children's acquisition of moral values, motivating them to pay close attention to moral events (Thompson, 2014). However, moral emotions do not operate in a vacuum to build a child's moral awareness, and they are not sufficient in themselves to generate moral responses. They do not give the "substance" of moral regulation—the rules, values, and standards of behavior that children need to understand and act on. Moral emotions are inextricably interwoven with the cognitive and social aspects of children's development (Narváez, 2010b).

Consider a recent study in which 18- to 30-month-olds interacted with a parent during book reading and play with toys, contexts that provide opportunities for parental talk about emotions and mental states (Drummond & others, 2014). In an empathic helping task, in which children had to read and understand the experimenter's internal state to understand his need and help to lessen his distress (bring him a blanket as he shivered and pretended he was

developmental **connection**

Emotional Development

Parents play an important role in the development of children's emotions. Connect to "The Self, Identity, and Personality."

cold, for example), those who helped more quickly had parents who labeled emotion and mental states more frequently during joint play and who were more likely to elicit this talk during book reading.

MORAL PERSONALITY

So far we have examined three key dimensions of moral development: thoughts, behavior, and feelings. Recently, there has been a surge of interest in a fourth dimension: personality (Walker, 2013, 2014; Walker, Frimer, & Dunlop, 2011). Thoughts, behavior, and feelings can all be involved in an individual's moral personality. For many years, skepticism surrounded the idea that a set of moral characteristics or traits could be discovered that would constitute a core of moral personality. Much of this skepticism stemmed from the results of Hartshorne and May's (1928–1930) classic study, and Walter Mischel's (1968) social learning theory and research, which argued that situations trump traits when attempts are made to predict moral behavior. Mischel's (2004) subsequent research and theory and Bandura's (2012) social cognitive theory have emphasized the importance of "person" factors while still recognizing situational variation. Until recently, though, there has been little interest in studying what might constitute a moral personality. Three aspects of moral personality that have recently been emphasized are (1) moral identity, (2) moral character, and (3) moral exemplars.

Moral Identity   A central aspect of the recent interest in the role of personality in moral development focuses on **moral identity.** Individuals have a moral identity when moral notions and commitments are central to their life (Walker, 2014). In this view, behaving in a manner that violates this moral commitment places the integrity of the self at risk (Lapsley & Stey, 2014).

Recently, Darcia Narváez (2010b) concluded that a mature moral individual cares about morality and being a moral person. For these individuals, moral responsibility is central to their identity. Mature moral individuals engage in moral metacognition, including moral self-monitoring and moral self-reflection. Moral self-monitoring involves monitoring one's thoughts and actions related to moral situations, and engaging in self-control when it is needed. Moral self-reflection encompasses critical evaluations of one's self-judgments and efforts to minimize bias and self-deception.

Sam Hardy and his colleagues (Hardy & others, 2013, 2014) also emphasize that identity is a way of caring about morality. Thus, when morality becomes an important aspect of your identity, you have a greater sense of obligation. If you do something immoral, you are not just violating an abstract principle (as in Kohlberg's moral reasoning theory), you are violating who you are.

What are some outcomes of having a moral identity? A recent study of 9,500 college students revealed that moral identity predicted all five health outcomes assessed (anxiety, depression, hazardous alcohol use, sexual risk taking, and self-esteem) (Hardy & others, 2013). A recent study of 15- to 18-year-olds found that a higher level of moral identity could possibly reduce the negative effects of moral disengagement and low self-regulation (Hardy, Bean, & Olsen, 2015).

Daniel Hart and his colleagues (Hart, 2005; Hart & Matsuba, 2010; Hart, Matsuba, & Atkins, 2008, 2014; Hart & others, 2011; Hart, Richardson, & Wilkenfeld, 2011; Matsuba, Murzyn, & Hart, 2014) argue that poor urban neighborhoods provide contexts that work against the formation of moral identity and commitment to moral projects. Living in high-poverty contexts often undermines moral attitudes and tolerance for divergent viewpoints. And high-poverty neighborhoods have fewer opportunities for effective engagement in the community because they lack an extensive network of organizations that support projects connected to moral goals. There are fewer opportunities for volunteering in such contexts. Hart and his colleagues advocate providing more service learning and community opportunities as a way of improving youths' moral attitudes and identity.

Moral Character   James Rest (1995) argued that moral character has not been adequately emphasized in moral development. In Rest's view, *moral character* involves having the strength of your convictions, persisting, and overcoming distractions and obstacles. If individuals don't have moral character, they may wilt under pressure or fatigue, fail to follow

developmental **connection**

Identity

According to James Marcia, what are the four statuses of identity development? Connect to "The Self, Identity, and Personality."

moral identity The aspect of personality that is present when individuals have moral notions and commitments that are central to their lives.

Rosa Parks (*left photo*, sitting in the front of a bus after the U.S. Supreme Court ruled that segregation was illegal on her city's bus system) and Andrei Sakharov (*right photo*) are moral exemplars. Parks (1913–2005), an African American seamstress in Montgomery, Alabama, became famous for her quiet, revolutionary act of not giving up her bus seat to a non-Latino White man in 1955. Her heroic act is cited by many historians as the beginning of the modern civil rights movement in the United States. Across the next four decades, Parks continued to work for progress in civil rights. Sakharov (1921–1989) was a Soviet physicist who spent several decades designing nuclear weapons for the Soviet Union and came to be known as the father of the Soviet hydrogen bomb. However, later in his life he became one of the Soviet Union's most outspoken critics and worked relentlessly to promote human rights and democracy.
(Left): © Bettmann/Corbis; (right): © Alain Nogues/Sygma/Corbis

through or become distracted and discouraged, and fail to behave morally. Moral character presupposes that the person has set moral goals and that achieving those goals involves the commitment to act in accord with those goals. Rest (1995) also concluded that motivation has not been adequately emphasized in moral development. In Rest's view, *moral motivation* involves prioritizing moral values over other personal values.

Lawrence Walker (2002) has studied moral character by examining people's conceptions of moral excellence. Among the moral virtues people emphasize are "honesty, truthfulness, and trustworthiness, as well as those of care, compassion, thoughtfulness, and considerateness. Other salient traits revolve around virtues of dependability, loyalty, and conscientiousness" (Walker, 2002, p. 74). In Walker's perspective, these aspects of moral character provide a foundation for positive social relationships and functioning.

Moral Exemplars   **Moral exemplars** are people who have lived exemplary lives. Moral exemplars have a moral personality, identity, character, and set of virtues that reflect moral excellence and commitment (Walker, 2013, 2014; Walker, Frimer, & Dunlop, 2011). The point of studying and conducting research on moral exemplars is to be able to characterize the ideal endpoint of moral development and understand how people got there.

One study examined the personality of exemplary young adults to determine what characterized their moral excellence (Matsuba & Walker, 2004). Forty young adults were nominated by executive directors of a variety of social organizations (such as Big Brothers, AIDS Society, and Ronald McDonald House) as moral exemplars based on their extraordinary moral commitment to these social organizations. They were compared with 40 young adults matched in age, education, and other variables who were attending a university. The moral exemplars were more advanced in moral reasoning, further along in developing an identity, and more likely to be in close relationships.

SOCIAL DOMAIN THEORY

Social domain theory states that there are different domains of social knowledge and reasoning, including moral, social conventional, and personal domains. In social domain theory, children's and adolescents' moral, social conventional, and personal knowledge and reasoning emerge from their attempts to understand and deal with different forms of social

moral exemplars People who have a moral personality, identity, character, and set of virtues that reflect moral excellence and commitment.

social domain theory Theory that identifies different domains of social knowledge and reasoning, including moral, social conventional, and personal domains. These domains arise from children's and adolescents' attempts to understand and deal with different forms of social experience.

experience (Killen & Smetana, 2015; Smetana, 2011a, b, 2013; Turiel, 2014, 2015). In the view of leading experts Judith Smetana (2013) and Eliot Turiel (2014, 2015), social domain theory emphasizes that the key aspects of morality involve judgments about welfare, justice, and rights as well as struggles that individuals have with moral issues in their social lives. Social domain theory stresses that children, even very young ones, are motivated to evaluate and make sense of their social world (Smetana, Jambon, & Ball, 2014).

Social conventional reasoning focuses on conventional rules that have been established by social consensus in order to control behavior and maintain the social system. The rules themselves are arbitrary, such as raising your hand in class before speaking, using one staircase at school to go up and the other to go down, not cutting in front of someone standing in line to buy movie tickets, and stopping at a stop sign when driving. There are sanctions if we violate these conventions, although the rules can be changed by consensus.

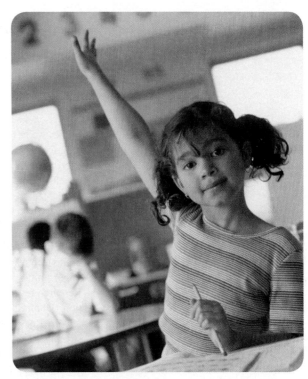

How does social conventional reasoning differ from moral reasoning? What are some examples of social conventional reasoning?
© Jim Craigmyle/Corbis

In contrast, moral reasoning focuses on ethical issues and rules of morality. Unlike conventional rules, moral rules are not arbitrary. They are obligatory, widely accepted, and somewhat impersonal (Turiel, 2015). Rules pertaining to lying, cheating, stealing, and physically harming another person are moral rules because violation of these rules affronts ethical standards that exist apart from social consensus and convention. Moral judgments involve concepts of justice, whereas social conventional judgments are concepts of social organization. Violating moral rules is usually more serious than violating conventional rules.

The social conventional approach is a serious challenge to Kohlberg's approach because Kohlberg argued that social conventions are a stop-over on the road to higher moral sophistication. For proponents of social conventional reasoning, social conventional reasoning is not lower than postconventional reasoning but rather something that needs to be disentangled from the moral thread (Killen & Smetana, 2015; Smetana, Jambon, & Ball, 2014; Turiel, 2014, 2015).

Recently, a distinction also has been made between moral and conventional issues, which are viewed as legitimately subject to adult social regulation, and personal issues, which are more likely subject to the child's or adolescent's independent decision making and personal discretion (Killen & Smetana, 2015). Personal issues include control over one's body, privacy, and choice of friends and activities. Thus, some actions belong to a *personal* domain not governed by moral strictures or social norms.

social conventional reasoning Focuses on conventional rules established by social consensus and convention, as opposed to moral reasoning, which stresses ethical issues.

Review Connect Reflect

 Discuss theory and research on moral thought, behavior, feeling, personality, and domains

Review

- What is moral development?
- What are Piaget's and Kohlberg's theories of moral development? What are some criticisms of Kohlberg's theory? What is social conventional reasoning?
- What processes are involved in moral behavior? What is the social cognitive theory of moral development?
- How are moral feelings related to moral development?
- What characterizes moral personality?
- What is the nature of social domain theory?

Connect

- How is joint attention similar to or different from the concept of perspective taking?

Reflect *Your Own Personal Journey of Life*

- Which of the five approaches—cognitive, psychoanalytic, behavioral/social cognitive, personality, and social domain—we have discussed do you think best describes the way you have developed morally? Explain.

So far, we have examined the four principal domains of moral development—thoughts, behaviors, feelings, and personality. We saw that both Piaget and Kohlberg noted that peer relations exert an important influence on moral development. What other contexts play a role in moral development? In particular, what are the roles of parents and schools?

PARENTING

Both Piaget and Kohlberg held that parents do not provide unique or essential inputs to children's moral development. Parents, in their view, are responsible for providing role-taking opportunities and cognitive conflict, but peers play the primary role in moral development. Research reveals siblings and peers, as well as parents, contribute to children's moral maturation (Dunn, 2014; Grusec & others, 2014; Yoo, Feng, & Day, 2013).

In Ross Thompson's (2006, 2009, 2014) view, young children are moral apprentices, striving to understand what is moral. They can be assisted in this quest by the "sensitive guidance of adult mentors in the home who provide lessons about morality in everyday experiences" (Thompson, 2009). Among the most important aspects of the relationship between parents and children that contribute to children's moral development are relational quality, proactive strategies, and conversational dialogue.

developmental connection

Attachment

Securely attached infants use the caregiver as a secure base from which to explore the environment. Connect to "Emotional Development and Attachment."

Relational Quality Parent-child relationships introduce children to the mutual obligations of close relationships that involve warmth and responsibility (Laible & Thompson, 2007; Thompson, 2009, 2014). Parents' obligations include engaging in positive caregiving and guiding children to become competent human beings. Children's obligations include responding appropriately to parents' initiatives and maintaining a positive relationship with parents.

In terms of relationship quality, secure attachment may play an important role in children's moral development. A secure attachment can place the child on a positive path for internalizing parents' socializing goals and family values. In one study, secure attachment in infancy was linked to early conscience development (Laible & Thompson, 2000). In another study, early secure attachment defused a maladaptive trajectory toward antisocial outcomes (Kochanska, Barry, & others, 2010). In yet another study, securely attached children's willing, cooperative stance was linked to positive future socialization outcomes (such as internalizing mothers' prohibitions) and a lower incidence of externalizing problems (high level of aggression, for example) (Kochanska, Woodard, & others, 2010).

Proactive Strategies An important parenting strategy is to proactively avert potential misbehavior by children before it takes place (Thompson, McGinley, & Meyer, 2006). With younger children, being proactive means using diversion, such as distracting their attention or moving them to alternative activities. With older children, being proactive may involve talking with them about values that the parents deem important. Transmitting these values can help older children and adolescents to resist temptations that inevitably emerge in contexts such as peer relations and the media that can be outside the scope of direct parental monitoring.

Conversational Dialogue Conversations related to moral development can benefit children, whether they occur as part of a discipline encounter or outside the encounter in the everyday stream of parent-child interaction (Thompson, 2009, 2014). The conversations can be planned or spontaneous and can focus on topics such as past events (for example, a child's prior misbehavior or positive moral conduct), shared future events (for example, going

What are some aspects of relationships between parents and children that contribute to children's moral development?
© Simon Jarratt/Corbis RF

somewhere that may involve a temptation and requires positive moral behavior), and immediate events (for example, talking with the child about a sibling's tantrums). Even when they are not intended to teach a moral lesson or explicitly encourage better moral judgment, such conversations can contribute to children's moral development.

Further, a recent study found parents' talk about emotions was associated with toddlers' sharing and helping (Brownell & others, 2013). In this study, children who helped and shared more quickly and frequently, especially in tasks that required complex emotional understanding, had parents who more often asked them to label and explain emotions displayed in books. Importantly, it was the parents' elicitation of emotion talk rather than parents' own production of emotion labels and explanations that was linked to toddlers' prosocial behavior.

Parenting Recommendations Nancy Eisenberg and her colleagues (Eisenberg, Spinrad, & Morris, 2013; Eisenberg & Valiente, 2002) suggest that parents who adopt the following strategies are more likely to have children who behave morally:

- Are warm and supportive, use inductive reasoning, and engage in authoritative parenting
- Are not punitive and do not use love withdrawal as disciplinary strategies
- Provide opportunities for the children to learn about others' perspectives and feelings
- Involve children in family decision making and in the process of thinking about moral decisions
- Model moral behaviors and thinking themselves, and provide opportunities for their children to do so
- Provide information about what behaviors are expected and why
- Foster an internal rather than an external sense of morality
- Help children to understand and regulate negative emotion rather than becoming overaroused

Parents who show this configuration of behaviors likely foster in their children concern and caring about others, and create a positive parent-child relationship. One study found that adolescents' moral motivation was positively linked to the quality of their relationship with their parents (Malti & Buchmann, 2010). In another study, mothers' authoritative parenting, but not fathers', contributed to adolescents' subsequent engagement in prosocial behavior one year later (Padilla-Walker & others, 2012). Other research also has found that mothers are more likely to influence adolescents' prosocial behavior than are fathers (Carlo & others, 2011).

In addition, parenting recommendations based on Ross Thompson's (2009, 2013; Laible & Thompson, 2007; Thompson, McGinley, & Meyer, 2006) analysis of parent-child relations suggest that children's moral development is likely to benefit when there are mutual parent-child obligations involving warmth and responsibility, when parents use proactive strategies, and when parents engage children in conversational dialogue. Further, young children's prosocial behavior increases when parents elicit children's talk about emotions.

> Both theory and empirical data support the conclusion that parents play an important role in children's moral development.
>
> **—NANCY EISENBERG**
> *Contemporary psychologist, Arizona State University*

SCHOOLS

No matter how parents treat their children at home, they may feel that they have little control over a great deal of their children's moral education. Children spend extensive time away from their parents at school, and the time spent can influence children's moral development (Narváez, 2014; Nucci, Krettenauer, & Narváez, 2014).

The Hidden Curriculum More than 80 years ago, educator John Dewey (1933) recognized that even when schools do not have specific programs in moral education, they provide moral education through a "hidden curriculum." The **hidden curriculum** is conveyed by the moral atmosphere that is a part of every school. The moral atmosphere is created by school and classroom rules, the moral orientation of teachers and school administrators, and text materials. Teachers serve as models of ethical or unethical behavior (Sanger, 2008). Classroom rules and peer relations at school transmit attitudes about cheating, lying, stealing, and consideration for others. And through its rules and regulations, the school administration infuses the school with a value system.

hidden curriculum The pervasive moral atmosphere that characterizes every school.

Recently, increased attention has been directed to the influence of classroom and school climate as part of the hidden curriculum. Darcia Narváez (2010a, 2014) argues that attention should be given to the concept of "sustaining climates." In her view, a sustaining classroom climate is more than a positive learning environment and more than a caring context. Sustaining climates involve focusing on students' sense of purpose, social engagement, community connections, and ethics. In sustaining classroom and school climates, students learn skills for flourishing and reaching their potential and help others to do so as well.

Character Education   Currently 40 of 50 states have mandates regarding **character education,** a direct education approach that involves teaching students a basic moral literacy to prevent them from engaging in immoral behavior and doing harm to themselves or others (Arthur, 2014; Narváez, 2014). The argument is that behaviors such as lying, stealing, and cheating are wrong, and students should be taught this throughout their education (Davidson, Lickona, & Khmelkov, 2008).

Every school should have an explicit moral code that is clearly communicated to students. According to traditional views of character education, any violations of the code should be met with sanctions. Newer approaches advocate a more democratic solution. Instruction in specified moral concepts, such as cheating, can take the form of example and definition, class discussions and role playing, or rewards for students exhibiting proper behavior. More recently, assisting students to develop a care perspective that involves considering others' feelings and helping others has been accepted as a relevant aspect of character education (Noddings, 2008, 2014).

Lawrence Walker (2002) argues that it is important for character education to involve more than a listing of moral virtues on a classroom wall. Instead, he emphasizes that children and adolescents need to participate in critical discussions of values; they need to discuss and reflect on how to incorporate virtues into their daily lives. Walker also advocates exposing children to moral exemplars worthy of emulating and getting them to participate in community service. The character education approach reflects the moral personality domain of moral development discussed earlier in the chapter.

Values Clarification   A second approach to providing moral education is **values clarification**—that is, helping people to clarify what their lives mean and what is worth working for. Unlike character education, which tells students what their values should be, values clarification encourages students to define their own values and understand the values of others (Williams & others, 2003).

Advocates of values clarification say it is value-free. However, critics argue that its content offends community standards and that the values-clarification exercises fail to stress the right behavior.

Cognitive Moral Education   A third approach to moral education, **cognitive moral education,** is based on the belief that students should learn to value such things as democracy and justice as their moral reasoning develops (Snarey, 2014). Kohlberg's theory has served as the foundation for a number of cognitive moral education programs. In a typical program, high school students meet in a semester-long course to discuss a number of moral issues. The instructor acts as a facilitator rather than as a director of the class. The goal is for students to develop more advanced notions of concepts such as cooperation, trust, responsibility, and community (Power & Higgins-D'Alessandro, 2008, 2014).

Service Learning   **Service learning** is a form of education that promotes social responsibility and service to the community. In service learning, adolescents engage in activities such as tutoring, helping older adults, working in a hospital, assisting at a child-care center, or cleaning up a vacant lot to make a play area. An important goal of service learning is for adolescents to become less self-centered and more strongly motivated to help others (Hart, Matsuba, & Atkins, 2008, 2014). Service learning is often more effective when two conditions are met (Nucci, 2006): (1) students are given some degree of choice in the service activities in which they participate, and (2) students are provided opportunities to reflect about their participation.

Service learning takes education out into the community (Hart, Matsuba, & Atkins, 2014; Zaff & others, 2010). Adolescent volunteers tend to be extraverted, committed to others, and have a high level of self-understanding (Eisenberg & Morris, 2004). Also, one study revealed

character education A direct moral education program in which students are taught moral literacy to prevent them from engaging in immoral behavior.

values clarification A moral education program in which students are helped to clarify their purpose in life and decide what is worth working for. Students are encouraged to define their own values and understand others' values.

cognitive moral education A moral education program based on the belief that students should learn to value things like democracy and justice as their moral reasoning develops; Kohlberg's theory has been the basis for many of the cognitive moral education programs.

service learning A form of education that promotes social responsibility and service to the community.

that adolescent girls participated in service learning more than adolescent boys (Webster & Worrell, 2008).

Researchers have found that service learning benefits adolescents in a number of ways (Zaff & others, 2010). These improvements include higher grades in school, increased goal setting, higher self-esteem, an enhanced sense of empowerment to make a difference for others, and an increased likelihood that they will serve as volunteers in the future. In one study, 74 percent of African American and 70 percent of Latino adolescents said that service-learning programs could have a "fairly or very big effect" on keeping students from dropping out of school (Bridgeland, DiIulio, & Wulsin, 2008).

Recently, interest has been shown in the role that civic engagement might play in adolescents' identity and moral development (Flanagan, Beyers, & Zukauskiene, 2012). A recent study found that compared with adolescents who had a diffused identity status, those who were identity achieved were more involved in volunteering in their community (Crocetti, Jahromi, & Meeus, 2012). In this study, adolescents' volunteer activity also was linked to their values, such as social responsibility, and the view that they, along with others, could make an impact on their community. Another recent study revealed that adolescents' volunteer activities provided opportunities to explore and reason about moral issues (van Goethem & others, 2012).

An analysis revealed that 26 percent of U.S. public high schools require students to participate in service learning (Metz & Youniss, 2005). The benefits of service learning, for both the volunteer and the recipient, suggest that more adolescents should be required to participate in such programs (Enfield & Collins, 2008; Zaff & others, 2010).

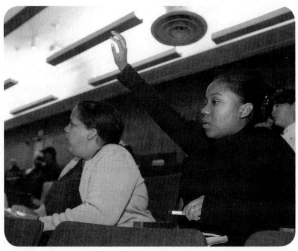

Jewel Cash, seated next to her mother, participating in a crime-watch meeting at a community center during high school. As an adolescent, she was an exemplar of teenage community involvement. The mayor of Boston said she was "everywhere." Jewel swayed a neighborhood group to support her proposal for a winter jobs program. She was raised in one of Boston's housing projects by her mother, a single parent. She has been a member of the Boston Student Advisory Council, mentored children, volunteered at a women's shelter, and was a member of a neighborhood crime-watch organization (Silva, 2005). As an emerging adult, Jewel works with a public consulting group and has continued to help others as a mentor and community organizer.
© Matthew J. Lee/The Boston Globe/Getty Images

Cheating   A moral education concern is whether students cheat and how to handle the cheating if it is discovered (Anderman & Anderman, 2010). Academic cheating can take many forms, including plagiarism, using "cheat sheets" during an exam, copying from a neighbor during a test, purchasing papers, and falsifying lab results. A 2006 survey revealed that 60 percent of secondary school students said they had cheated on a test in school during the past year, and one-third of the students reported that they had plagiarized information from the Internet in the past year (Josephson Institute of Ethics, 2006). A recent study with 8- to 12-year-olds found that a majority of them cheated in a game that required them to report the accuracy of their success in the game, and older children cheated less than the younger ones (Ding & others, 2014). Also in this study, children with better working memory and inhibitory control cheated less.

Why do students cheat? Among the reasons students give for cheating are pressure to get high grades, time constraints, poor teaching, and lack of interest (Stephens, 2008). In terms of poor teaching, "students are more likely to cheat when they perceive their teacher to be incompetent, unfair, and uncaring" (Stephens, 2008, p. 140).

A long history of research also implicates the power of the situation in determining whether students cheat (Hartshorne & May, 1928 1930; Vandehey, Diekhoff, & LaBeff, 2007). For example, students are more likely to cheat when they are not being closely monitored during a test; when they know their peers are cheating; when they know that another student has cheated without being caught; and when student scores are made public (Anderman & Murdock, 2007; Carrell, Malmstrom, & West, 2008; Harmon, Lambrinos, & Kennedy, 2008).

Certain personality traits also are linked to cheating. One study revealed that college students who engaged in academic cheating were characterized by the personality traits of low conscientiousness and low agreeableness (Williams, Nathanson, & Paulhus, 2010).

Why do students cheat? What are some strategies teachers can adopt to prevent cheating?
© Eric Audras/PhotoAlto/Getty Images RF

Among the strategies for decreasing academic cheating are preventive measures such as making sure students are aware of what constitutes cheating, explaining the consequences if they do cheat, closely monitoring students' behavior while they are taking tests, and emphasizing the importance of being a moral, responsible individual who practices academic integrity. In promoting academic integrity, many colleges have instituted an honor code that emphasizes self-responsibility, fairness, trust, and scholarship. However, few secondary schools have developed honor codes. The Center for Academic Integrity (www.academicintegrity.org/) has extensive materials available to help schools develop academic integrity policies.

An Integrative Approach   Darcia Narváez (2006, 2008, 2010a, b, 2014) emphasizes an *integrative approach* to moral education that encompasses both the reflective moral thinking and commitment to justice advocated in Kohlberg's approach, and developing virtues as advocated in the character education approach. She highlights the Child Development Project as an excellent example of an integrative moral education approach. In the Child Development Project, students are given multiple opportunities to discuss other students' experiences, which inspires empathy and perspective taking, and they participate in exercises that encourage them to reflect on their own behaviors in terms of values such as fairness and social responsibility (Battistich, 2008; Solomon, Watson, & Battistich, 2002). Adults coach students in ethical decision making and guide them in becoming more caring individuals. Students experience a caring community, not only in the classroom but also in after-school activities and through parental involvement in the program. Research evaluations of the Child Development Project indicate that it is related to an improved sense of community, an increase in prosocial behavior, better interpersonal understanding, and an increase in social problem solving (Battistich, 2008; Solomon & others, 1990).

Another integrative moral education program that is being implemented is called *integrative ethical education* (Narváez, 2006, 2008, 2010a, b, 2014; Narváez & others, 2004). This program builds on the concept of expertise development within a supportive community. The goal is to turn moral novices into moral experts by educating students about four ethical skills that moral experts possess: ethical sensitivity, ethical judgment, ethical focus, and ethical action (Narváez, 2010a, 2014).

Review Connect Reflect

 Explain how parents and schools influence moral development

Review
- What are some effective parenting strategies for advancing children's moral development?
- What is the hidden curriculum? What are some contemporary approaches to moral education?

Connect
- What parenting strategies might best prevent students from cheating?

Reflect *Your Own Personal Journey of Life*
- How do you think your parents influenced your moral development?

---

3 Prosocial and Antisocial Behavior   Describe the development of prosocial and antisocial behavior

Prosocial Behavior   Antisocial Behavior

Service learning encourages positive moral behavior. This behavior is not just moral behavior but behavior that is intended to benefit other people, and psychologists call it prosocial behavior (Carlo, 2014; Eisenberg & others, 2015). Of course, people have always engaged in antisocial behavior as well. In this section, we take a closer look at prosocial and antisocial behavior, focusing on how they develop.

PROSOCIAL BEHAVIOR

Caring about the welfare and rights of others, feeling concern and empathy for them, and acting in a way that benefits others are all components of prosocial behavior (Carlo, 2014; Eisenberg, Spinrad, & Morris, 2014). What motivates this behavior, and how does it develop in children?

Altruism and Reciprocity The purest forms of prosocial behavior are motivated by **altruism,** an unselfish interest and voluntary effort in helping another person. Human acts of altruism are plentiful. Think of the hardworking laborer who places $5 in a Salvation Army kettle, the volunteers at homeless shelters, the person who donates a kidney so someone else can live. Altruism is found throughout the human world. It is also taught by every widely practiced religion in the world—Christianity, Judaism, Islam, Hinduism, Buddhism. The circumstances most likely to evoke altruism are empathy for an individual in need or a close relationship between the benefactor and the recipient (Batson, 1989).

The notion of *reciprocity*, which is the obligation to return a favor with a favor, pervades human interactions all over the world. Fund-raisers try to exploit the norm of reciprocity when they send free calendars or other knickknacks in the mail, hoping that you'll feel obligated to reciprocate with a donation to their cause. People feel guilty when they do not reciprocate, and they may feel angry if someone else does not reciprocate. Reciprocity or altruism may motivate many important prosocial behaviors, including sharing.

Do Infants Have Moral Awareness and Engage in Prosocial Behavior?
Recently, researchers have explored whether infants and toddlers have a moral awareness and motivation for prosocial behavior. How can moral awareness and prosocial behavior be studied in preverbal infants? Just as adults do, babies tend to look at something they find interesting or surprising. And when they are given a choice between looking at two things, babies look longer at the more pleasing thing. Based on these assumptions, several studies using the violation of expectations technique described in Renee Baillargeon's research (described in the chapter on "Cognitive Developmental Approaches") have found that characters who hinder or harm others are viewed more negatively by infants as young as four months of age and that they will act to punish hinderers and to reward helpers (Hamlin, 2013, 2014; Hamlin & others, 2011, 2015). At this point, it is wise to interpret these conclusions with caution until they have been confirmed by more research and other measures. Other research indicates that during their second year, children will offer assistance to an unfamiliar experimenter, building on their capacities for shared intentionality and awareness of others' goals and intentions (Thompson & Newton, 2013; Warneken & Tomasello, 2006).

This research indicating that older infants and toddlers possess an intuitive sense of fairness that they use in evaluating observed behavior suggests the presence of an early foundation for moral awareness that is not anticipated in Piaget's and Kohlberg's theories of moral development. Next, we further explore sharing and fairness, focusing on the childhood and adolescent years.

Sharing and Fairness William Damon (1988) described a developmental sequence through which sharing develops in children. Unlike the recent research just described that indicates toddlers can engage in sharing and fairness and have a moral awareness, Damon proposed that sharing during the first three years of life is done for nonempathetic reasons such as the fun of social play or simply for imitation. Then, at about 4 years of age, a combination of empathetic awareness and adult encouragement produces a sense of obligation on the part of the child to share with others. Most 4-year-olds are not selfless saints, however. Children believe they have an obligation to share but do not necessarily think they should be as generous to others as they are to themselves. Neither do their actions always support their beliefs, especially when they covet an object. What is important developmentally is that the child has developed a belief that sharing is an obligatory part of a social relationship and involves a question of right and wrong. These early ideas about sharing set the stage for giant strides that children make in the years that follow.

developmental **connection**

Cognitive Development

Infants as young as four months of age were more likely to make visually guided reaches toward a puppet who acted as a helper rather than toward a puppet who acted as a hinderer to others' efforts to achieve their goals (Hamlin, 2013, 2014). Connect to the chapter on "Cognitive Developmental Approaches."

How does children's sharing change from the preschool to the elementary school years?
© Norbert Schaefer/Corbis

altruism An unselfish interest and voluntary effort in helping another person.

By the start of the elementary school years, children begin to express more complicated notions of what is fair. Throughout history, varied definitions of fairness have been used as the basis for distributing goods and resolving conflicts. These definitions involve the principles of equality, merit, and benevolence—*equality* means that everyone is treated the same; *merit* means giving extra rewards for hard work, a talented performance, or other laudatory behavior; *benevolence* means giving special consideration to individuals in a disadvantaged condition.

Equality is the first of these principles used regularly by elementary school children. It is common to hear 6-year-old children use the word *fair* as synonymous with *equal* or *same*. By the mid to late elementary school years, children also believe that equality means special treatment for those who deserve it—a belief that applies the principles of merit and benevolence.

Benevolence can be evident early in life. A recent study found that even 5-year-olds were inclined to give more to poor than to wealthy individuals, thus indicating that their motivation to help the poor overruled their otherwise dominant inclination to share resources equally (Paulus, 2014). However, in this study 3-year-olds did not share more resources with poor than wealthy individuals. Another recent study revealed that 8-year-olds were more likely to donate resources to needy peers than were 4-year-olds (Ongley, Nola, & Malti, 2014).

Parental advice and prodding certainly foster standards of sharing, but the give-and-take of peer requests and arguments provides the most immediate stimulation of sharing. Parents can set examples that children carry into their interactions and communication with peers, but parents are not present during all of their children's peer exchanges. The day-to-day construction of fairness standards is done by children in collaboration and negotiation with each other. Over the course of many years and thousands of encounters, children's understanding of concepts such as equality, merit, benevolence, and compromise deepens. With this understanding comes a greater consistency and generosity in children's sharing (Damon, 1988).

How does prosocial behavior change through childhood and adolescence? Prosocial behavior occurs more often in adolescence than in childhood, although examples of caring for others and comforting someone in distress occur even during the preschool years (Eisenberg, Spinrad, & Knafo, 2015).

Why might prosocial behavior increase in adolescence? Cognitive changes involving advances in abstract, idealistic, and logical reasoning as well as increased empathy and emotional understanding likely are involved. With such newfound cognitive abilities, young adolescents increasingly sympathize with members of abstract groups with whom they have little experience, such as people living in poverty in other countries (Eisenberg, Spinrad, & Knafo, 2015; Eisenberg, Spinrad, & Morris, 2013). The increase in volunteer opportunities in adolescence also contributes to more frequent prosocial behavior.

Are there different types of prosocial behavior? In a recent study, Gustavo Carlo and his colleagues (2010, pp. 340–341) investigated this question and confirmed the presence of six types of prosocial behavior in young adolescents:

- altruism ("One of the best things about doing charity work is that it looks good.")
- public ("Helping others while I'm being watched is when I work best.")
- emotional ("I usually help others when they are very upset.")
- dire ("I tend to help people who are hurt badly.")
- anonymous ("I prefer to donate money without anyone knowing.")
- compliant ("I never wait to help others when they ask for it.")

In this study, adolescent girls reported more emotional, dire, compliant, and altruistic behavior than did boys, while boys engaged in more public prosocial behavior. Parental monitoring was positively related to emotional, dire, and compliant behavior but not the other types of behavior. Compliant, anonymous, and altruistic prosocial behavior were positively related to religiosity.

Research on prosocial behavior is often conceptualized in a global and unidimensional manner. The study by Carlo and others (2010) illustrates the important point that in thinking about and studying prosocial behavior it is important to consider its dimensions.

Two other aspects of prosocial behavior are forgiveness and gratitude. **Forgiveness** is an aspect of prosocial behavior that occurs when the injured person releases the injurer from

forgiveness An aspect of prosocial behavior that occurs when the injured person releases the injurer from possible behavioral retaliation.

possible behavioral retaliation (Klatt & Enright, 2009). In one investigation, individuals from the fourth grade through college and adulthood were asked questions about forgiveness (Enright, Santos, & Al-Mabuk, 1989). The individuals were especially swayed by peer pressure in their willingness to forgive others. A recent study of older adults revealed that women were more likely to forgive than men, individuals were more likely to forgive family members than non-family members, and forgiveness was more likely to be extended to people who were still alive than those who were dead (Hantman & Cohen, 2010). Also, a recent study revealed that when adolescents encountered hurtful experiences in school settings if they disliked the transgressor they had more hostile thoughts, feelings of anger, and avoidance/revenge tendencies than when they liked the transgressing peer (Peets, Hodges, & Salmivalli, 2012).

Gratitude is a feeling of thankfulness and appreciation, especially in response to someone doing something kind or helpful (Grant & Gino, 2010). Interest in studying adolescents' gratitude or lack thereof is increasing. Consider the following recent studies:

- Gratitude was linked to a number of positive aspects of development in young adolescents, including satisfaction with one's family, optimism, and prosocial behavior (Froh, Yurkewicz, & Kashdan, 2009).
- Adolescents' expression of gratitude was linked to having fewer depressive symptoms (Lambert, Fincham, & Stillman, 2012).
- Chinese adolescents who had a higher level of gratitude were less likely to engage in suicide ideation and attempts (Li & others, 2012).
- A longitudinal study assessed the gratitude of adolescents at 10 to 14 years of age (Bono, 2012). Four years after the initial assessment, the most grateful adolescents (top 20 percent) had a stronger sense of the meaning of life, were more satisfied with their life, were happier and more hopeful, and had a lower level of negative emotions and were less depressed than the least grateful students (bottom 20 percent).

Gender and Prosocial Behavior   Are there gender differences in prosocial behavior during childhood and adolescence? Research concludes that differences exist (Eisenberg, Spinrad, & Morris, 2013). For example, across childhood and adolescence, females engage in more prosocial behavior than males. The largest gender difference occurs for kind and considerate behavior with a smaller difference for sharing.

Compared with antisocial behavior such as juvenile delinquency, less attention has been given to prosocial behavior in adolescence. We still do not have adequate research information about such topics as how youth perceive prosocial norms and how school policies and peers influence prosocial behavior (Siu, Shek, & Law, 2012).

Ninety-eight-year-old volunteer Iva Broadus plays cards with 10-year-old DeAngela Williams in Dallas, Texas. In 2008 Iva was recognized as the oldest volunteer in the Big Sister program in the United States. Iva said that the card-playing helped to keep her memory and thinking skills good and could help DeAngela's as well. *What are some other positive outcomes of volunteering as an older adult?*
© Dallas Morning News, photographer Jim Mahoney

Altruism and Volunteerism in Older Adults   A study of 21,000 individuals 50 to 79 years of age in 21 countries revealed that one-third give back to society, saying that they volunteer now or have volunteered in the past (HSBC Insurance, 2007). In this study, about 50 percent who volunteered reported that they did so for at least one-half day each week. And a large-scale U.S. study revealed that volunteering steadily increased from 57 years of age to 85 years of age (Cornwell, Laumann, & Schumm, 2008).

Are older adults more altruistic than younger adults? In a series of recent studies, older adults were more likely to behave in altruistic ways and to value contributions to the public good than younger adults were (Freund & Blanchard-Fields, 2014). For example, in two of the studies, older adults were more likely than younger adults to donate money for a good cause.

A common perception is that older adults need to receive help rather than to give help themselves. However, researchers recently have found that when older adults engage in altruistic behavior and volunteering they benefit from these activities (Anderson & others, 2014; Morrow-Howell, 2010; Tang, Choi, & Morrow-Howell, 2010). One study followed 423 older adult couples for five years (Brown & others, 2003). At the beginning of the study, the couples were asked about the extent to which they had given or received emotional or practical help in the past year. Five years later, those who

gratitude A feeling of thankfulness and appreciation, especially in response to someone's doing something kind or helpful.

said they had helped others were half as likely to have died. One possible reason for this finding is that helping others may reduce the output of stress hormones, which improves cardiovascular health and strengthens the immune system. And a study of adults 65 years of age and older who were institutionalized and had functional limitations revealed that an increased risk of dying over a six-year period occurred only for those who never or almost never volunteered (Okun & others, 2010).

Researchers have found that volunteering as an older adult is associated with a number of additional positive outcomes (Anderson & others, 2014). An early study of individuals 65 years and older found that volunteer workers were more satisfied with their lives than non-volunteers and were less depressed and anxious (Hunter & Linn, 1980). In another study, being a volunteer as an older adult was associated with more positive affect and less negative affect (Greenfield & Marks, 2004). Among the reasons for the positive outcomes of volunteering are its provision of constructive activities and productive roles, social integration, and enhanced meaningfulness.

ANTISOCIAL BEHAVIOR

Most children and adolescents at one time or another act out or do things that are destructive or troublesome for themselves or others. If these behaviors occur often, psychiatrists diagnose them as conduct disorders. If these behaviors result in illegal acts by juveniles, society labels them *delinquents*. Both problems are much more common in males than in females (Farrington, 2009; Thio, 2010).

Conduct Disorder   **Conduct disorder** refers to age-inappropriate actions and attitudes that violate family expectations, society's norms, and the personal or property rights of others. Children with conduct problems show a wide range of rule-violating behaviors, from swearing and temper tantrums to severe vandalism, theft, and assault (Mash & Wolfe, 2016). A recent study found that youth with conduct disorder characterized by its onset in childhood had more cognitive impairment (especially in executive function), psychiatric symptoms, and serious violent offenses than youth with conduct disorder characterized by the onset of antisocial behavior in adolescence (Johnson & others, 2015).

As part of growing up, most children and youth break the rules from time to time—they fight, skip school, break curfew, steal, and so on. As many as 50 percent of the parents of 4- to 6-year-old children report that their children steal, lie, disobey, or destroy property at least some of the time (Achenbach, 1997). Most of these children show a decrease in antisocial behavior from 4 to 18 years of age, but adolescents who are referred to psychological clinics for therapy continued to show high rates of antisocial behavior (Achenbach, 1997).

It has been estimated that about 5 percent of children show serious conduct problems. These children are often described as showing an *externalizing*, or *undercontrolled*, pattern of behavior. Children who show this pattern often are impulsive, overactive, and aggressive and engage in delinquent actions (Okado & Bierman, 2015).

Conduct problems in children are best explained by a confluence of causes, or risk factors, operating over time (Conduct Problems Prevention Research Group, 2011, 2015; Dodge & McCourt, 2010). These include possible genetic inheritance of a difficult temperament, ineffective parenting, and living in a neighborhood where violence is the norm. In a recent study in 10 urban schools serving primarily African American children from low-income backgrounds, the children were randomly assigned to either a "pre-kindergarten as usual" control condition or an intervention that consisted of a family program (13 weeks of behavioral parenting strategies) and a professional development training program for early childhood teachers (Dawson-McClure & others, 2015). For boys, but not girls, the intervention led to lower rates of conduct problems two years later.

Juvenile Delinquency   Closely linked with conduct disorder is **juvenile delinquency,** which refers to actions taken by an adolescent in breaking the law or engaging in behavior that is considered illegal. Like other categories of disorders, juvenile delinquency is a broad concept; legal infractions range from littering to murder. Because the adolescent technically becomes a juvenile delinquent only after being judged guilty of a crime by a court of law, official records do not accurately reflect the number of illegal acts juvenile delinquents commit.

What are some characteristics of conduct disorder?
© Stockdisc/PunchStock RF

conduct disorder Age-inappropriate actions and attitudes that violate family expectations, society's norms, and the personal or property rights of others.

juvenile delinquency Actions taken by an adolescent in breaking the law or engaging in illegal behavior.

One issue in juvenile justice is whether an adolescent who commits a crime should be tried as an adult (Cauffman & others, 2015; Steinberg, 2012). Some psychologists have proposed that individuals 12 and under should not be evaluated under adult criminal laws and that those 17 and older should be (Cauffman & others, 2015; Shulman & Steinberg, 2015). They also recommend that individuals 13 to 16 years of age be given some type of individualized assessment to determine whether they will be tried in a juvenile court or an adult criminal court.

Frequency   Estimates of the number of juvenile delinquents in the United States are sketchy, but FBI statistics indicate that at least 2 percent of all youth are involved in juvenile court cases. For both male and female delinquents, rates for property offenses are higher than rates for other offenses (such as offenses against persons, drug offenses, and public order offenses). Arrests for delinquency are much higher for adolescent males than for adolescent females (Puzzanchera & Robson, 2014).

© Comstock Images/Alamy RF

Developmental Changes and Pathways   As adolescents become emerging adults, do their rates of delinquency and crime change? Research indicates that theft, property damage, and physical aggression decrease from 18 to 26 years of age (Schulenberg & Zarrett, 2006). The peak ages for property damage are 16 to 18 years for males and 15 to 17 years for females. However, the peak ages for violence are 18 to 19 years for males and 19 to 21 years for females (Farrington, 2004).

A distinction is made between early-onset (before age 11) and late-onset (after age 11) antisocial behavior. Early-onset antisocial behavior is associated with more negative developmental outcomes than late-onset antisocial behavior (Schulenberg & Zarrett, 2006). Early-onset antisocial behavior is more likely to persist into emerging adulthood and is associated with more mental health and relationship problems (Roisman, Aguilar, & Egeland, 2004; Stouthamer-Loeber & others, 2004).

In the Pittsburgh Youth Study, a longitudinal study involving more than 1,500 inner-city boys, three developmental pathways to delinquency were identified (Loeber, Burke, & Pardini, 2009; Loeber & Farrington, 2001; Stouthamer-Loeber & others, 2002):

· *Authority conflict.* Youth on this pathway showed stubbornness prior to age 12, then moved on to defiance and avoidance of authority.
· *Covert.* This pathway included minor covert acts, such as lying, followed by property damage and moderately serious delinquency, then serious delinquency.
· *Overt.* This pathway included minor aggression followed by fighting and violence.

One individual whose goal is to reduce juvenile delinquency and help at-risk adolescents cope more effectively with their lives is Rodney Hammond. To read about his work, see the *Connecting with Careers* profile.

Causes of Delinquency   What causes delinquency? Many causes have been proposed, including heredity, identity problems, community influences, and family experiences. Erik Erikson (1968), for example, noted that adolescents whose development has restricted them from acceptable social roles or made them feel that they cannot measure up to the demands placed on them may choose a negative identity. Adolescents with a negative identity may find support for their delinquent image among peers, reinforcing the negative identity. For Erikson, delinquency is an attempt to establish an identity, although a negative one.

Although delinquency is less exclusively a phenomenon of lower socioeconomic status today than it was in the past, some characteristics of lower-class culture might promote delinquency (Dawson-McClure & others, 2015). The norms of many lower-SES peer groups and gangs are antisocial, or counterproductive, to the goals and norms of society at large. Getting into and staying out of trouble are prominent features of life for some adolescents in low-income neighborhoods. Adolescents from low-income backgrounds may sense that they can gain attention and status by performing antisocial actions. Furthermore, adolescents in communities with high crime rates observe many models who engage in criminal activities. Quality schooling, educational funding, and organized neighborhood activities may be lacking in these communities (Leventhal & Brooks-Gunn, 2011). One study found that youth whose

connecting with careers

Rodney Hammond, Health Psychologist

Rodney Hammond described how his college experiences influenced his choice of career: "When I started as an undergraduate at the University of Illinois Champaign-Urbana, I hadn't decided on my major. But to help finance my education, I took a part-time job in a child development research program sponsored by the psychology department. There, I observed inner-city children in settings designed to enhance their learning. I saw first-hand the contribution psychology can make, and I knew I wanted to be a psychologist" (American Psychological Association, 2003, p. 26).

Rodney Hammond went on to obtain a doctorate in school and community psychology with a focus on children's development. For a number of years, he trained clinical psychologists at Wright State University in Ohio and directed a program to reduce violence in ethnic minority youth. There, he and his associates taught at-risk youth how to use social skills to effectively manage conflict and to recognize situations that could lead to violence. Today, Hammond is director of Violence Prevention at the Centers for Disease Control and Prevention in Atlanta. Hammond says that if you are interested in people and problem solving, psychology is a wonderful way to put the two together.

(*Source:* American Psychological Association, 2003, pp. 26–27)

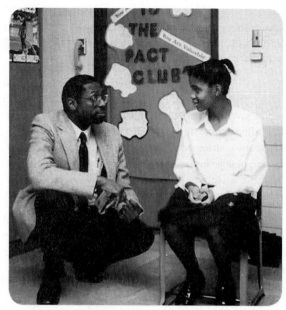

Rodney Hammond counsels an adolescent girl about the risks of adolescence and how to cope effectively with them.
Courtesy of Dr. Rodney Hammond

What are some factors that influence whether adolescents will become delinquents?
© Chuck Savage/Corbis

families had experienced repeated poverty were more than twice as likely to be delinquent at 14 and 21 years of age (Najman & others, 2010).

Certain characteristics of families are also associated with delinquency (Burke & Loeber, 2015; Van Ryzin & Dishion, 2012). Parents of delinquents are less skilled in discouraging antisocial behavior and in encouraging prosocial behavior than are parents of nondelinquents. Parental monitoring of adolescents is especially important in determining whether an adolescent becomes a delinquent (Henneberger & others, 2013). One study found that early parental monitoring in adolescence and ongoing parental support were linked to a lower incidence of criminal behavior in emerging adulthood (Johnson & others, 2011). Also, one study found that low rates of delinquency from 14 to 23 years of age were associated with an authoritative parenting style (Murphy & others, 2012). Family discord and inconsistent and inappropriate discipline are also associated with delinquency (Capaldi & Shortt, 2003).

Rare are the studies that actually demonstrate in an experimental design that changing parenting practices in childhood is related to a lower incidence of juvenile delinquency in adolescence. However, one study by Marion Forgatch and her colleagues (2009) randomly assigned divorced mothers with sons to an experimental group (mothers received extensive parenting training) and a control group (mothers received no parenting training) when their sons were in the first to third grades. The parenting training consisted of 14 parent group meetings that especially focused on improving parenting practices with their sons (skill encouragement, limit setting, monitoring, problem solving, and positive involvement). Best practices for emotion regulation, managing interparental conflict, and talking with children about divorce also were included in the sessions. Improved parenting practices and reduced contact with deviant peers were linked with lower rates of delinquency in the experimental group than in the control group at a nine-year follow-up assessment.

Family therapy is often effective in reducing delinquency (Baldwin & others, 2012). A recent meta-analysis found that of five program types (case management, individual treatment, youth court, restorative justice, and family treatment), family treatment was the only one that was linked to a reduction in recidivism for juvenile

Does Intervention Reduce Juvenile Delinquency?

Fast Track is an intervention that attempts to lower the risk of juvenile delinquency and other problems (Conduct Problems Prevention Research Group, 2007, 2010a, b, 2011, 2015; Dodge & McCourt, 2010; Jones & others, 2010; Miller & others, 2011). Schools in four areas (Durham, North Carolina; Nashville, Tennessee; Seattle, Washington; and rural central Pennsylvania) were identified as high-risk based on neighborhood crime and poverty data. Researchers screened more than 9,000 kindergarten children in the four schools and randomly assigned 891 of the highest-risk and moderate-risk children to intervention or control conditions. The average age of the children when the intervention began was 6.5 years.

The 10-year intervention consisted of behavior management training of parents, social cognitive skills training of children, reading tutoring, home visitations, mentoring, and a revised classroom curriculum that was designed to increase socioemotional competence and decrease aggression. Outcomes were assessed in the third, sixth, and ninth grades for the following behavioral problems:

- *Conduct disorder* (multiple instances of behaviors such as truancy, running away, fire setting, cruelty to animals, breaking and entering, and excessive fighting across a six-month period)
- *Oppositional defiant disorder* (an ongoing pattern of disobedient, hostile, and defiant behavior toward authority figures)
- *Attention deficit hyperactivity disorder* (having one or more of these characteristics over a period of time: inattention, hyperactivity, and impulsivity)
- *Any externalizing disorder* (presence of any of the three disorders previously described)

- *Self-reported antisocial behavior* (a list of 34 behaviors, such as skipping school, stealing, and attacking someone with an intent to hurt the person)

The extensive intervention was successful only for children and adolescents who were identified as the highest risk in kindergarten, and it resulted in lowering their incidence of conduct disorder, attention deficit hyperactivity disorder, any externalized disorder, and antisocial behavior. Positive outcomes for the intervention occurred as early as the third grade and continued through the ninth grade. For example, in the ninth grade the intervention reduced the likelihood that the highest-risk kindergarten children would develop conduct disorder by 75 percent, attention deficit hyperactivity disorder by 53 percent, and any externalized disorder by 43 percent.

Recently, data have been reported through age 19 (Miller & others, 2011). Findings indicate that the comprehensive Fast Track intervention was successful in reducing youth arrest rates (Conduct Problems Prevention Research Group, 2011). Also, a recent study found that the intervention's impact on adolescents' antisocial behavior was linked to three social cognitive processes: reducing hostile-attribution biases, improving responses to social problems, and devaluing aggression (Dodge, Godwin, & Conduct Problems Prevention Research Group, 2013).

What might be some other strategies for intervening in the lives of high-risk children to reduce their likelihood of become juvenile delinquents?

offenders (Schwalbe & others, 2012). Another recent research review revealed that prevention programs focused on improving the family context were more effective in reducing persistent delinquency than were individual and group-based programs (de Vries & others, 2015).

An increasing number of studies have found that siblings can have a strong influence on delinquency (Bank, Burraston, & Snyder, 2004). In one study, high levels of hostile sibling relationships and older sibling delinquency were linked with younger sibling delinquency in both brother pairs and sister pairs (Slomkowski & others, 2001).

Having delinquent peers increases the risk of becoming delinquent (Yu & others, 2013). For example, one study found that peer rejection and having deviant friends at 7 to 13 years of age were linked with increased delinquency at 14 to 15 years of age (Vitaro, Pedersen, & Brendgen, 2007).

Lack of success in school also is associated with delinquency. A recent study found that poor academic performance and reduced attachment to school at age 15 predicted a higher level of criminal activity at 17 to 19 years of age (Savolainen & others, 2012).

Cognitive factors, such as low self-control, low intelligence, and lack of sustained attention, are also implicated in delinquency. For example, one study revealed that low-IQ serious delinquents were characterized by low self-control (Koolhof & others, 2007). And in one study, mothers' reports of their son's impulsiveness at 15 years of age predicted their arrest record up to 6 years in the future (Bechtold & others, 2014).

Does intervening in the lives of children who show early conduct problems help reduce their delinquency risk in adolescence? See the *Connecting with Research* interlude to find out how researchers have tried to answer this question.

developmental connection

Parenting

A neglectful parenting style is linked with lower levels of self-control in children. Connect to "Families, Lifestyles, and Parenting."

4 Values, Religion, Spirituality, and Meaning in Life

LG4 Characterize the development of values, religion, spirituality, and meaning in life

Values   Religion and Spirituality   Meaning in Life

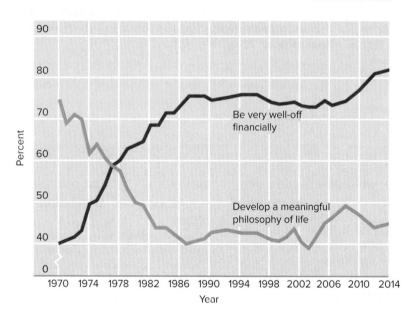

FIGURE 3

CHANGING FRESHMAN LIFE GOALS, 1970 TO 2014. In the last four decades, a significant change has occurred in the life goals of college freshmen. A far greater percentage of today's college freshmen state that an "essential" or "very important" life goal is to be well-off financially, and far fewer state that developing a meaningful philosophy of life is an "essential" or "very important" life goal.

values Beliefs and attitudes about the way things should be.

James Garbarino (1999) has interviewed a number of young killers. He concludes that nobody really knows precisely why a tiny minority of youth kill, but that the cause might be a lack of a spiritual center. In many of the youth killers he interviewed, Garbarino found a spiritual or emotional emptiness in which the youth sought meaning in the dark side of life. Are spirituality and religion important in your life? How much time have you spent thinking about the meaning of life? What are your values?

VALUES

Values are beliefs and attitudes about the way things should be. They involve what is important to us. We attach value to all sorts of things: politics, religion, money, sex, education, helping others, family, friends, career, recognition, self-respect, and so on. We carry with us values that influence our thoughts, feelings, and actions. One way to measure what people value is to ask them what their goals are. Over the past four decades, traditional-aged college students have shown an increased concern for personal well-being and a decreased concern for the well-being of others, especially for the disadvantaged (Eagan & others, 2014). As shown in Figure 3, today's college freshmen are more strongly motivated to be well-off financially and less motivated to develop a meaningful philosophy of life than were their counterparts of 40 or even 20 years ago. In 2014, 82 percent of students (the highest percentage ever in this survey) viewed becoming well-off financially as an "essential" or a "very important" objective compared with only 42 percent in 1971.

There are, however, some signs that U.S. college students are shifting toward a stronger interest in the welfare of society. In the survey just described, interest in developing a meaningful philosophy of life increased from 39 percent to 45 percent of U.S. freshmen from 2001 through 2014 (Eagan & others, 2014) (see Figure 3). Also in this survey, the percentage of college freshmen who said the chances are very good that they will participate in volunteer or community service programs increased from 18 percent in 1990 to 34 percent in 2014 (Eagan & others, 2014).

Our discussion of values corresponds to William Damon's (2008) view proposed in *The Path to Purpose: Helping Children Find Their Calling in Life*. Damon concluded that a major difficulty confronting today's youth is their lack of a clear sense of what they want to do with their lives—that too many youth are essentially "rudderless." Damon (2008, p. 8) found that only about 20 percent of 12- to 22-year-olds in the United States expressed "a clear vision of where they want to go, what they want to accomplish in life, and why." He argues that their goals and values too often focus on the short term, such as getting a good grade on a test this week and finding a date for a dance, rather than developing a plan for the future based on positive values. The types of questions that adults can pose to youth to guide them in the direction of developing more purposeful values include "What's most important in your life? Why do you care about those things? . . . What does it mean to be a good person?" (Damon, 2008, p. 135).

RELIGION AND SPIRITUALITY

In Damon's (2008) view, one long-standing source for discovering purpose in life is religion. Religion and spirituality play important roles in the lives of many people around the world (King & Boyatzis, 2015; Koenig, 2014, 2015; Koenig & others, 2015a, b; Olson & others, 2012; Park, 2013).

Is religion different from spirituality? Recent analysis by Pamela King and her colleagues (King, Carr, & Boiter, 2011; King & Boyatzis, 2015) provides the following distinctions:

· **Religion** is an organized set of beliefs, practices, rituals, and symbols that increases an individual's connection to a sacred or transcendent other (God, higher power, or ultimate truth).

· **Religiousness** refers to the degree of affiliation with an organized religion, participation in its prescribed rituals and practices, connection with its beliefs, and involvement in a community of believers.

· **Spirituality** involves experiencing something beyond oneself in a transcendent manner and living in a way that benefits others and society.

What developmental changes characterize the influence of religion, religiousness, and spirituality in people's lives?

Childhood, Adolescence, and Emerging Adulthood
Societies use many methods—such as Sunday schools, parochial education, and parental teaching—to ensure that people will carry on a religious tradition. In a recent national study, 63 percent of parents with children at home said they pray or read Scripture with their children and 60 percent reported that they send their children to religious education programs (Pew Research Center, 2008). Does this religious socialization work? In many cases it does (Paloutzian, 2000).

In general, individuals tend to adopt the religious teachings of their upbringing. For instance, individuals who are Catholics by the time they are 25 years of age, and who were raised as Catholics, likely will continue to be Catholics throughout their adult years. If a religious change or reawakening occurs, it is most likely to take place during adolescence. However, it is important to consider the quality of the parent-adolescent relationship (Ream & Savin-Williams, 2003). Adolescents who have a positive relationship with their parents or are securely attached to them are likely to adopt the religious orientation of their parents (Dudley, 1999). Adolescents who have a negative relationship with their parents or are insecurely attached to them may disaffiliate from religion or seek religion-based attachments that are missing in their family system (Streib, 1999).

Religious issues are important to many adolescents, but during the twenty-first century religious interest among adolescents has declined. In a 2010 national study of American college freshmen, 73 percent said they had attended religious services frequently or occasionally during their senior year in high school, down from a high of 85 percent in 1997 (Pryor, DeAngelo, & Blake, 2011).

As an adolescent, Nina Vasan founded ACS Teens, a nationwide group of teen volunteers who support the efforts of the American Cancer Society. Nina's organization has raised hundreds of thousands of dollars for cancer research, helped change state tobacco laws, and conducted a number of cancer control programs. In Nina's words, "I realized that teenagers like myself could make a big difference in the fight against cancer. I knew that the best way to help was to start a teen organization. . . . To be a beneficial part of the human race, it is essential and fundamental to give back to the community and others" (Vasan, 2002, p. 1). Nina completed her MD degree at Harvard University Medical School and currently is Resident Physician in Psychiatry at Stanford University Hospital. In 2013, she published her first book (with co-author Jennifer Przybylo), *Do Good Well*. The book reflects Nina's motivation to get others involved in leadership and to encourage them to take action in improving people's lives, especially those who are less fortunate. *Do Good Well* became a #1 Amazon Best Seller.
© Newscom

Religion enlightens, terrifies, subdues; it gives faith, inflicts remorse, inspires resolutions, and inflames devotion.

—HENRY NEWMAN
English churchman and writer, 19th century

religion An organized set of beliefs, practices, rituals, and symbols that increases an individual's connection to a sacred or transcendent other (God, higher power, or higher truth).

religiousness The degree of affiliation with an organized religion, participation in prescribed rituals and practices, connection with its beliefs, and involvement in a community of believers.

spirituality Experiencing something beyond oneself in a transcendent manner and living in a way that benefits others and society.

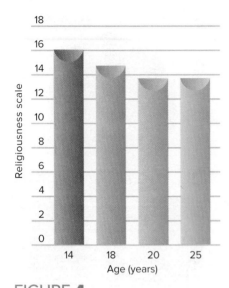

FIGURE 4

DEVELOPMENTAL CHANGES IN RELIGIOUSNESS FROM 14 TO 25 YEARS OF AGE. *Note:* The religiousness scale ranged from 0 to 32, with higher scores indicating stronger religiousness.

developmental **connection**

Identity

In addition to religious/spiritual identity, what are some other identity components? Connect to "The Self, Identity, and Personality."

A developmental study revealed that religiousness declined from 14 to 20 years of age in the United States (Koenig, McGue, & Iacono, 2008) (see Figure 4). In this study, religiousness was assessed with items such as frequency of prayer, frequency of discussing religious teachings, frequency of deciding moral actions for religious reasons, and the overall importance of religion in everyday life. As indicated in Figure 4, more change in religiousness occurred from 14 to 18 years of age than from 20 to 25 years of age. Also, attending religious services was highest at 14 years of age, declined from 14 to 18 years of age, and increased at 20 years of age. More change occurred in attending religious services than in religiousness. Another study found that across the first three semesters of college, students were less likely to attend religious services or engage in religious activities (Stoppa & Lefkowitz, 2010).

Analysis of the World Values Survey of 18- to 24-year-olds revealed that emerging adults in less developed countries were more likely to be religious than their counterparts in more developed countries (Lippman & Keith, 2006). For example, emerging adults' reports of religion being very important in their lives ranged from a low of 0 in Japan to 93 percent in Nigeria, and belief in God ranged from a low of 40 percent in Sweden to a high of 100 percent in Pakistan.

Religion and Cognitive Development   Adolescence and emerging adulthood can be especially important junctures in religious development (King & Boyatzis, 2015). Even if children have been indoctrinated into a religion by their parents, because of advances in their cognitive development adolescents and emerging adults may question what their own religious beliefs truly are.

Many of the cognitive changes thought to influence religious development involve Piaget's cognitive developmental stages. More so than in childhood, adolescents think abstractly, idealistically, and logically. The increase in abstract thinking lets adolescents consider various ideas of religious and spiritual concepts. For example, an adolescent might ask how a loving God can possibly exist given the extensive suffering of many people in the world (Good & Willoughby, 2008). Adolescents' increased idealistic thinking provides a foundation for thinking about whether religion provides the best route to a better, more ideal world than the present. And adolescents' increased logical reasoning gives them the ability to develop hypotheses and systematically sort through different answers to spiritual questions (Good & Willoughby, 2008).

Religion and Identity Development   During adolescence and emerging adulthood, especially emerging adulthood, identity development becomes a central focus (Erikson, 1968; Kroger, 2015). Adolescents and emerging adults look for answers to questions like these: "Who am I? What am I all about as a person? What kind of life do I want to lead?" As part of their search for identity, adolescents and emerging adults begin to grapple in more sophisticated, logical ways with such questions as "Why am I on this planet? Is there really a God or higher spiritual being, or have I just been believing what my parents and the church imprinted in my mind? What really are my religious views?" An analysis of the link between identity and spirituality concluded that adolescence and adulthood can serve as gateways to a spiritual identity that "transcends, but not necessarily excludes, the assigned religious identity in childhood" (Templeton & Eccles, 2006, p. 261).

A recent study of Latino, African American, Asian, and non-Latino White adolescents revealed that their religious identity remained stable across high school grades but that religious participation declined (Lopez, Huynh, & Fuligni, 2011). In this study, Latino and Asian adolescents had the highest levels of religious identity, while Latino adolescents had the highest level of religious participation.

The Positive Role of Religion in Adolescents' Lives   Researchers have found that various aspects of religion are linked with positive outcomes for adolescents (King & Boyatzis, 2015). A recent study revealed that parents' religiousness during youths' adolescence was positively related to youths' own religiousness during adolescence (Spilman & others, 2013). Another recent study found that when youth attend religious services with parents, this activity increases the positive influence of parenting on their psychological well-being (Petts, 2014). Religion plays a role in adolescents' health and has an influence on whether they engage in problem behaviors (King & Boyatzis, 2015; King, Ramos, & Clardy, 2013). A recent meta-analysis found that spirituality/religiosity was positively related to well-being, self-esteem, and three of the big five factors of personality (conscientiousness, agreeableness, openness) (Yonker, Schnabelrauch, & DeHaan, 2012). In this meta-analysis, spirituality/religion was negatively associated with risk behavior and depression. Also in a national random sample of more than 2,000 11- to 18-year-olds, those who had a stronger interest in religion were less likely to smoke, drink alcohol, use marijuana, be truant from school, engage in delinquent activities, and be depressed than their low-religiosity counterparts (Sinha, Cnaan, & Gelles, 2007).

Many religious adolescents also adopt their religion's message about caring and concern for people (Lerner & others, 2013; Saroglou, 2013). For example, in one survey religious youth were almost three times as likely to engage in community service as nonreligious youth (Youniss, McLellan, & Yates, 1999).

How does religious thinking change in adolescence? How is religion linked to adolescents' health?
© Christopher Futcher/Getty Images RF

Adulthood and Aging   What roles do religion and spirituality play in the lives of adults? Is religion related to adults' health? Is there a point in adult development at which understanding of the meaning of life increases? How do religious beliefs affect the lives of older adults?

Many children and adolescents show an interest in religion, and many religious institutions created by adults (such as this Muslim school in Malaysia) are designed to introduce them to religious benefits and ensure that they will carry on a religious tradition.
© Paul Chesley/Getty Images

What roles do religion and spirituality play in adults' lives?
© Erik S. Lesser/epa/Corbis

Religion and Spirituality in Adulthood   How religious are Americans? A national poll of more than 35,000 U.S. adults found that 92 percent said they believe in God, 75 percent reported that they pray at least weekly and 58 percent said they pray every day, 56 percent said that religion is very important, and 39 percent indicated that they attend religious services at least weekly (Pew Research Center, 2008). In the MacArthur Study of Midlife Development, more than 70 percent of U.S. individuals surveyed said they are religious and consider spirituality a major part of their lives (Brim, 1999).

Gender and ethnic differences characterize religious interest and participation. Females have consistently shown a stronger interest in religion than males have (Idler, 2006). Compared with men, women participate more in both organized and personal forms of religion, are more likely to believe in a higher power or presence, and are more likely to feel that religion is an important dimension of their lives. Regarding ethnicity, African Americans and Latinos show higher rates of religious participation than do non-Latino White Americans (Idler, 2006).

In thinking about religion and adult development, it is important to consider individual differences. Religion is a powerful influence in some adults' lives, whereas it plays little or no role in others' lives (Myers, 2000). Further, the influence of religion in people's lives may change as they develop. In John Clausen's (1993) longitudinal investigation, some individuals who had been strongly religious in their early-adult years became less so in middle age; others became more religious in middle age.

Religion and Health   How might religion be linked to physical health? Some cults and religious sects encourage behaviors that are damaging to health, such as ignoring sound medical advice (Williams & Sternthal, 2007). For individuals in the religious mainstream, researchers increasingly are finding that religion is positively linked to health (McCullough & Willoughby, 2009). Researchers have found that religious commitment helps to moderate blood pressure and that religious attendance is linked to a reduction in hypertension (Gillum & Ingram, 2007). And a recent study found that older adults who had a higher level of religious identification were less likely to be depressed (Ysseldyk, Haslam, & Haslam, 2013).

Why might religion be linked to physical health?
© Hill Street Studios/Blend Images/age fotostock RF

Gabriel Dy-Liacco, Professor and Pastoral Counselor

Gabriel Dy-Liacco currently is a professor in religious and pastoral counseling at Regent University in the Virginia Beach, Virginia, area. He obtained his Ph.D. in pastoral counseling from Loyola College in Maryland and also has experience as a psychotherapist in mental health settings such as a substance-abuse program, military family center, psychiatric clinic, and community mental health center. Earlier in his career he was a pastoral counselor at the Pastoral Counseling and Consultation Centers of Greater Washington, DC, and taught at Loyola University in Maryland. As a pastoral counselor, he works with adolescents and adults in the aspects of their lives that they show the most concern about—psychological, spiritual, or the interface of both. Having lived in Peru, Japan, and the Philippines, he brings considerable multicultural experience to teaching and counseling settings.

Also, a number of studies have confirmed a positive association between religious participation and longevity (Oman & Thoresen, 2006). For example, a recent study revealed that religious attendance was linked to increased longevity (Kim, Smith, & Kang, 2014).

Why might religion promote physical health? There are several possible answers (Hill & Butter, 1995):

- *Lifestyle issues.* For example, religious individuals have lower rates of drug use than their nonreligious counterparts (Gartner, Larson, & Allen, 1991).
- *Social networks.* Well-connected individuals have fewer health problems (Benjamins & Finlayson, 2007). Religious groups, meetings, and activities provide social connectedness for individuals.
- *Coping with stress.* Religion offers a source of comfort and support when individuals are confronted with stressful events (Weber & Pargament, 2014). A recent study revealed that highly religious individuals were less likely than their moderately religious, somewhat religious, and nonreligious counterparts to be psychologically distressed (Park, 2013).

Religious counselors often advise people about mental health and coping (Fayard & Koenig, 2015; Koenig, 2015a, b). To read about the work of one religious counselor, see the *Connecting with Careers* profile. In the *Connecting Development to Life* interlude we further explore links between religion and coping.

Religion in Older Adults

In many societies around the world, older adults are the spiritual leaders in their churches and communities. For example, in the Catholic Church, more popes have been elected in their eighties than in any other 10-year period of the human life span.

The religious patterns of older adults have increasingly been studied (Krause, 2012; Krause & Hayward, 2014; Sun & others, 2012). A longitudinal study found that religious service attendance was stable in middle adulthood, increased in late adulthood, then declined later in the older adult years (Hayward & Krause, 2013a). Also, a research review concluded that individuals with a stronger spiritual/religious orientation were more likely to live longer (Lucchetti, Lucchetti, & Koenig, 2011). Another study revealed that religious attendance at least weekly was linked to a lower risk of mortality than for people who never attended religious services (Gillum & others, 2008).

In one study of individuals from their early thirties through their late sixties and early seventies, a significant increase in spirituality occurred between late middle adulthood (mid-fifties/early sixties) and late adulthood (late sixties/mid-seventies) (Wink & Dillon, 2002) (see Figure 5). The spirituality of women increased more than that of men. In this study, spirituality in late adulthood was linked with religiosity in early adulthood (thirties). This finding supports the idea that early religious involvement predisposes individuals to further spiritual development. And a recent survey found that 77 percent of 30- to 49-year-olds and 84 percent of 50- to 64-year-olds reported having a religious affiliation (compared with 67 percent of 18- to 29-year-olds and 90 percent of adults 90 years of age and older) (Pew Research, 2012).

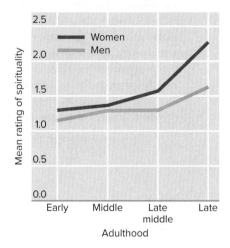

FIGURE 5

LEVEL OF SPIRITUALITY IN FOUR ADULT AGE PERIODS. In a longitudinal study, the spirituality of individuals in four different adult age periods—early (thirties), middle (forties), late middle (mid-fifties/early sixties), and late (late sixties/early seventies) adulthood—was assessed (Wink & Dillon, 2002). Based on responses to open-ended questions in interviews, the spirituality of the individuals was coded on a 5-point scale with 5 being the highest level of spirituality and 1 the lowest.

Religion and Coping

Is religion linked to individuals' ability to cope with stress? Some psychologists have categorized prayer and religious commitment as defensive coping strategies, arguing that they are less effective in helping individuals cope than are life-skill, problem-solving strategies. However, religious coping often benefits individuals during times of high stress (Koenig, 2015a, b; Park & Iacocca, 2014; Weber & Pargament, 2014). For example, a recent study found that coping styles that relied on collaboration with others and turning to religious groups were more strongly related to improved psychological adjustment than a self-directed coping style (Ross & others, 2009).

A recent interest in linking religion and coping focuses on **meaning-making coping**, which involves drawing on beliefs, values, and goals to change the meaning of a stressful situation, especially in times of high levels of stress such as when a loved one dies. In Crystal Park's (2005, 2007, 2010, 2012a, b, 2013) view, individuals who are religious experience more disruption

How is religion linked to the ability to cope with stress?
© Image Source/Getty Images RF

personal growth. A recent study revealed that personal religiosity decreased the negative effects of a spouse's death on the psychological well-being of widowed individuals (Momtaz & others, 2010).

In sum, various dimensions of religiousness can help some individuals cope more effectively with challenges that arise (Koenig, 2014, 2015; Koenig & others, 2015a, b; Olson & others, 2012; Park, 2012a, b; Weber & Pargament, 2014). Religious beliefs can shape a person's psychological perception of pain or disability. Religious cognitions can play an important role in maintaining hope and stimulating motivation toward recovery. Because of its effectiveness in reducing distress, religious coping can help prevent denial of the problem and thus facilitate early recognition and more appropriate health-seeking behavior. Religion also can forestall the development of anxiety and depression disorders by promoting communal or social interaction (Weber & Pargament, 2014). Houses of religious worship are a readily available, acceptable, and inexpensive source of support for many individuals,

of their beliefs, values, and goals immediately after the death of a loved one than do individuals who are not religious. Initially, religion is linked with more depressed feelings about a loved one's death. Over time, however, as religious individuals search for meaning in their loss, they often become less depressed and show better adjustment. Thus, religion can serve as a meaning system through which bereaved individuals are able to reframe their loss and even find avenues of especially the elderly. The socialization provided by religious organizations can help prevent isolation and loneliness (Koenig & Larson, 1998).

How would you explain successful coping strategies in those who are not religious? How is religion linked to the ability to cope with stress? What characterizes the search for meaning in life?

Individuals over 65 years of age are more likely than younger people to say that religious faith is the most significant influence in their lives, that they try to put religious faith into practice, and that they attend religious services (Gallup & Bezilla, 1992). A recent study of more than 500 African Americans 55 to 105 years of age revealed that they had a strong identification with religious institutions and high levels of attendance and participation in religious activities (Williams, Keigher, & Williams, 2012).

Is religion related to a sense of well-being and life satisfaction in old age? In one study, older adults' self-esteem was highest when they had a strong religious commitment and lowest when they had little religious commitment (Krause, 1995). In another study, older adults who derived a sense of meaning in life from religion had higher levels of life satisfaction, self-esteem, and optimism (Krause, 2003). And in a recent study, older adults who reported having a higher level of spirituality had more resilience in the face of stressful and difficult circumstances (Vahia & others, 2011).

Religion can meet some important psychological needs in older adults, helping them to face impending death, to find and maintain a sense of meaningfulness in life, and to accept

meaning-making coping Drawing on beliefs, values, and goals to change the meaning of a stressful situation, especially in times of high levels of stress such as when a loved one dies.

the inevitable losses of old age (Koenig, 2012; Park, 2012a, b). Socially, the religious community can serve many functions for older adults, such as providing social activities, social support, and the opportunity to assume teaching and leadership roles. A recent study revealed that over a period of seven years, older adults who attended church regularly increased the amount of emotional support they gave and received but decreased the amount of tangible support they gave and received (Hayward & Krause, 2013b).

MEANING IN LIFE

Austrian psychiatrist Viktor Frankl's mother, father, brother, and wife died in the concentration camps and gas chambers in Auschwitz, Poland. Frankl survived the concentration camp and went on to write about meaning in life. In his book, *Man's Search for Meaning*, Frankl (1984) emphasized each person's uniqueness and the finiteness of life. He believed that examining the finiteness of our existence and the certainty of death adds meaning to life. If life were not finite, said Frankl, we could spend our life doing just about whatever we pleased because time would continue forever.

Frankl said that the three most distinct human qualities are spirituality, freedom, and responsibility. Spirituality, in his view, does not have a religious underpinning. Rather, it refers to a human being's uniqueness—of spirit, philosophy, and mind. Frankl proposed that people need to ask themselves such questions as why they exist, what they want from life, and what their life means.

It is in middle adulthood that individuals begin to be faced with death more often, especially the deaths of parents and other older relatives. Also faced with fewer years ahead of them than behind them, many individuals in middle age begin to ask and evaluate the questions that Frankl proposed. And, as we indicated in the discussion of religion and coping, meaning-making coping is especially helpful in times of chronic stress and loss.

Researchers are increasingly studying the factors involved in a person's exploration of meaning in life and whether developing a sense of meaning in life is linked to positive developmental outcomes. Many individuals state that religion played an important role in increasing their exploration of meaning in life (Krause, 2008, 2009). Studies also suggest that individuals who have found a sense of meaning in life are more physically healthy and happier, and experience less depression, than their counterparts who report that they have not discovered meaning in life (Debats, 1990; Krause, 2009).

Having a sense of meaning in life can lead to clearer guidelines for living one's life and enhanced motivation to take care of oneself and reach goals. A higher level of meaning in life also is linked to a higher level of psychological well-being and physical health (Park, 2012a, b).

Roy Baumeister and Kathleen Vohs (2002, pp. 610–611) argue that the quest for a meaningful life can be understood in terms of four main needs for meaning that guide how people try to make sense of their lives:

·   *Need for purpose*. "Present events draw meaning from their connection with future events." Purposes can be divided into (1) goals and (2) fulfillments. Life can be oriented toward a future anticipated state, such as living happily ever after or being in love.

·   *Need for values*. This "can lend a sense of goodness or positive characterization of life and justify certain courses of action. Values enable people to decide whether certain acts are right or wrong." Frankl's (1984) view of meaning in life emphasized value as the main form of meaning that people need.

·   *Need for a sense of efficacy*. This involves the "belief that one can make a difference. A life that had purposes and values but no efficacy would be tragic. The person might know what is desirable but could not do anything with that knowledge." With a sense of efficacy, people believe that they can control their environment, which has positive physical and mental health benefits (Bandura, 2012).

·   *Need for self-worth*. Most individuals want to be good, worthy persons. Self-worth can be pursued individually, such as finding out that one is very good at doing something, or collectively, as when people gain self-esteem from belonging to a group or category of people.

What characterizes the search for meaning in life?
© Michael Prince/Corbis

Review *Connect* **Reflect**

LG4 Characterize the development of values, religion, spirituality, and meaning in life

Review
- What are values? How are the values of U.S. college students changing?
- How do individuals experience religion and spirituality at different points in the life span?
- How do people seek meaning in life?

Connect
- How might the search for meaning in life connect with what you have

learned about developmental personality changes in adults, especially in middle age?

Reflect *Your Own Personal Journey of Life*
- What characterizes your quest for a meaningful life?

reach your **learning goals**

Moral Development, Values, and Religion

1 Domains of Moral Development

LG1 Discuss theory and research on moral thought, behavior, feeling, personality, and domains

What Is Moral Development?

Moral Thought

- Moral development involves changes in thoughts, feelings, and behaviors regarding right and wrong. Moral development has intrapersonal and interpersonal dimensions.

- Piaget distinguished between the heteronomous morality of younger children and the autonomous morality of older children. Kohlberg developed a provocative theory of moral reasoning. He argued that development of moral reasoning consists of three levels—preconventional, conventional, and postconventional—and six stages (two at each level). Kohlberg argued that these stages were age related. Influences on the Kohlberg stages include cognitive development, imitation and cognitive conflict, peer relations, and perspective taking. Criticisms of Kohlberg's theory have been made, especially by Gilligan, who advocates a stronger care perspective. Other criticisms focus on the inadequacy of moral reasoning to predict moral behavior, the intuitiveness of moral thought, the role of emotion, and cultural and family influences.

Moral Behavior

- The processes of reinforcement, punishment, and imitation have been used to explain the acquisition of moral behavior, but they provide only a partial explanation. Situational variability is stressed by behaviorists. Cognitions can play a role in resistance to temptation and self-control. Social cognitive theory of morality emphasizes a distinction between moral competence and moral performance.

Moral Feeling

- In Freud's theory, the superego is the moral branch of personality. The superego consists of the ego ideal and the conscience. According to Freud, guilt is the foundation of children's moral behavior. Empathy is an important aspect of moral feelings, and it changes developmentally. In the contemporary perspective, both positive and negative feelings contribute to moral development.

Moral Personality

- Recently, there has been a surge of interest in studying moral personality. This interest has focused on moral identity, moral character, and moral exemplars. People who have a moral identity value moral notions and commitments to such an extent that behaving in a manner that violates this moral commitment would place the integrity of the self at risk. Moral character involves having the strength of your convictions, and persisting and overcoming distractions and obstacles. Moral character also means having certain virtues, such as honesty, truthfulness, loyalty, and compassion. Moral exemplars' identity, character, and virtues reflect moral commitment and excellence.

Social Domain Theory

- Social domain theory states that there are different domains of social knowledge and reasoning, including moral, social conventional, and personal domains.

2 Contexts of Moral Development

 Explain how parents and schools influence moral development

Parenting

· Warmth and responsibility in mutual obligations of parent-child relationships provide important foundations for the child's positive moral growth. Moral development can be advanced by these parenting strategies: being warm and supportive rather than punitive; providing opportunities to learn about others' perspectives and feelings; involving children in family decision making; modeling moral behaviors; averting misbehavior before it takes place; and engaging in conversational dialogue related to moral development.

Schools

· The hidden curriculum, initially described by Dewey, is the distinctive moral atmosphere that is present in each school. Contemporary approaches to moral education include character education, values clarification, cognitive moral education, service learning, and integrative ethical education. Cheating is a moral education concern and can take many forms. Various situational aspects influence whether students will cheat or not.

3 Prosocial and Antisocial Behavior

 Describe the development of prosocial and antisocial behavior

Prosocial Behavior

· Altruism, which is an unselfish interest and voluntary effort in helping another person, and reciprocity often motivate prosocial behaviors (behaviors intended to help others) such as sharing. Recent research has focused on whether infants and toddlers have moral awareness and can engage in prosocial behavior. Damon described a sequence by which children develop their understanding of fairness and come to share more consistently. Peers play a key role in this development. Altruism is linked to having a longer life. Volunteering is associated with higher life satisfaction, less depression and anxiety, better physical health, and more positive affect and less negative affect.

Antisocial Behavior

· Conduct disorder involves age-inappropriate actions and attitudes that violate family expectations, society's norms, and the personal or property rights of others. The disorder is more common in boys than in girls. Juvenile delinquency refers to actions taken by an adolescent in breaking the law or engaging in illegal behavior. In the Pittsburgh Youth Study, pathways to delinquency included conflict with authority, minor covert acts followed by property damage and more serious acts, and overt acts of minor aggression followed by fighting and violence. Associating with peers and friends who are delinquents, low parental monitoring, ineffective discipline, having an older sibling who is a delinquent, living in an urban, high-crime area, having low self-control, and having low intelligence are also linked with delinquency,

4 Values, Religion, Spirituality, and Meaning in Life

 Characterize the development of values, religion, spirituality, and meaning in life

Values

· Values are beliefs and attitudes about the way people think things should be. Over the last four decades, traditional-age college students have shown an increased interest in personal well-being and a decreased interest in the welfare of others.

Religion and Spirituality

· Distinctions have been made between the concepts of religion, religiousness, and spirituality. Many children, adolescents, and emerging adults show an interest in religion, and religious institutions strive to introduce them to religious beliefs. Cognitive changes in adolescence—such as increases in abstract, idealistic, and logical thinking—increase the likelihood that adolescents will seek a better understanding of religion and spirituality. As part of their search for identity, many adolescents and emerging adults begin to grapple with more complex aspects of religion. A downturn in religious interest among college students has occurred. When adolescents have a positive relationship with parents or are securely attached to them, they often adopt their parents' religious beliefs. Various aspects of religion are linked with positive outcomes in adolescent development. Religion is an important dimension of many American adults' lives as well as the lives of people around the world. Females tend to have a stronger interest in religion than males do. Although some people in certain religious sects try to avoid using medical treatment, individuals in the religious mainstream generally enjoy a positive or neutral link between religion and physical health. Religious interest often increases in late adulthood.

Meaning in Life

Frankl argued that people need to face the finiteness of their life in order to understand life's meaning. Faced with the death of older relatives and less time to live themselves, middle-aged adults increasingly examine life's meaning. Baumeister described four main needs that guide how people try to make sense of their lives: (1) need for purpose, (2) need for values, (3) need for a sense of efficacy, and (4) need for self-worth.

key terms

altruism
autonomous morality
care perspective
character education
cognitive moral education
conduct disorder
conscience
conventional reasoning
ego ideal
empathy
forgiveness

gratitude
heteronomous morality
    (Kohlberg)
heteronomous morality (Piaget)
hidden curriculum
immanent justice
individualism, instrumental
    purpose, and exchange
justice perspective
juvenile delinquency
meaning-making coping

moral development
moral exemplars
moral identity
mutual interpersonal
    expectations, relationships,
    and interpersonal conformity
postconventional reasoning
preconventional reasoning
religion
religiousness
service learning

social cognitive theory
    of morality
social contract or utility and
    individual rights
social conventional reasoning
social domain theory
social systems morality
spirituality
universal ethical principles
values
values clarification

key people

Albert Bandura
Roy Baumeister
Gustavo Carlo
William Damon
John Dewey
Nancy Eisenberg
Marion Forgatch

Viktor Frankl
Sigmund Freud
James Garbarino
Carol Gilligan
Jonathan Haidt
Sam Hardy
Hugh Hartshorne

Grazyna Kochanska
Lawrence Kohlberg
Mark May
Walter Mischel
Darcia Narváez
Crystal Park
Jean Piaget

James Rest
Judith Smetana
Ross Thompson
Eliot Turiel
Lawrence Walker

It is not enough for parents to understand children. They must also accord children the privilege of understanding them.

—**Milton Saperstein,**
American psychiatrist and writer, 20th century

© Ariel Skelly/Corbis

Social Contexts of Development

As children develop, their small world widens and they discover new contexts and people. As they grow through childhood, their parents still cradle their lives, but their lives also are shaped by successive choirs of peers and friends. Parents can give adolescents both roots and wings. When some adults become parents, they recognize for the first time how much effort their parents put into rearing them. In recent decades, increasing numbers of adults have chosen to get married later or not at all. As people age, they come to sense that the generations of living things pass in a short while, and, like runners, they pass on the torch of life. This section contains three chapters: "Families, Lifestyles, and Parenting," "Peers and the Sociocultural World," and "Schools, Achievement, and Work."

chapter 14

FAMILIES, LIFESTYLES, AND PARENTING

chapter **outline**

preview

Love and attachment are two important aspects of family life. Beyond these emotional ties, what else goes on in families that influences development? And how do the choices that adults make about family life affect their development and the development of their children? These are some of the questions that we will consider in this chapter.

1 Family Processes **LG1** Describe some important family processes

| Reciprocal Socialization | Family as a System | Sociocultural and Historical Influences | Multiple Developmental Trajectories |

As we examine the family and other social contexts of development, consider Urie Bronfenbrenner's (1986, 2004; Bronfenbrenner & Morris, 2006) ecological theory, which we discussed in the "Introduction" chapter. Bronfenbrenner analyzes the social contexts of development in terms of five environmental systems:

· The *microsystem*, or the setting in which the individual lives, such as a family, the world of peers, schools, work, and so on

· The *mesosystem*, which consists of links between microsystems, such as the connection between family processes and peer relations

· The *exosystem*, which consists of influences from another setting (such as parents' work) that the individual does not experience directly

· The *macrosystem*, or the culture in which the individual lives, such as an ethnic group or a nation

· The *chronosystem*, or sociohistorical circumstances, such as the increased numbers of working mothers, divorced parents, stepparent families, gay and lesbian parents, and multiethnic families in the United States in the last 30 to 40 years

developmental **connection**

Environment

An important contribution of Bronfenbrenner's ecological theory is its focus on a range of social contexts that influence the child's development. Connect to "Introduction."

RECIPROCAL SOCIALIZATION

Socialization between parents and children is not a one-way process. Parents do socialize children, but socialization in families is reciprocal (Maccoby, 2015; Qin & Pomerantz, 2013; Ram & others, 2014). **Reciprocal socialization** is socialization that is bidirectional; children socialize parents just as parents socialize children. These reciprocal interchanges and mutual influence processes are sometimes referred to as *transactional* (Kuczynski, Parkin, & Pitman, 2015; Sameroff, 2009).

For example, the interaction of mothers and their infants is sometimes symbolized as a dance in which successive actions of the partners are closely coordinated. This coordinated dance can assume the form of synchrony—that is, each person's behavior depends on the partner's previous behavior. Or the interaction can be reciprocal in a precise sense, in which the actions of the partners can be matched, as when one partner imitates the other or when there is mutual smiling. An important example of early synchronized interaction is mutual gaze or eye contact. In one study, the mother and infant engaged in a variety of behaviors while they looked at each other; by contrast, when they looked away from each other, the rate of such

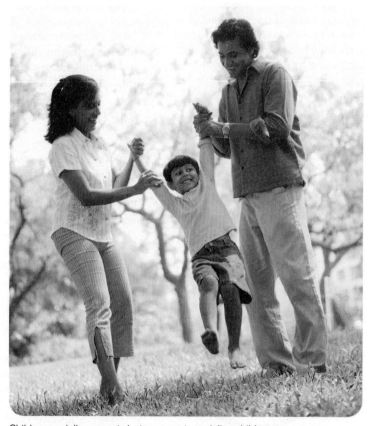

Children socialize parents just as parents socialize children.
© Floresco Productions/Corbis RF

reciprocal socialization Socialization that is bidirectional in that children socialize parents just as parents socialize children.

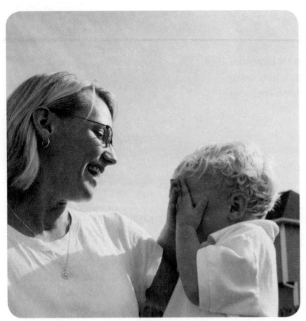

How does the game of peek-a-boo reflect the concept of scaffolding?
© Tracy Powell/Getty Images

developmental **connection**

Genetic Influences

Genotype-environment correlations. shared and non-shared environments, and gene × environment interactions (G × E) reflect ways that the genetic heritage of children can be conceptualized and possibly influence parent-child relationships. Connect to "Biological Beginnings."

behaviors dropped considerably (Stern & others, 1977). In another study, synchrony in parent-child relationships was positively related to children's social competence (Harrist, 1993).

Another example of synchronization occurs in *scaffolding*, which means adjusting the level of guidance to fit the child's performance (Guttentag & others, 2014). The parent responds to the child's behavior with scaffolding, which in turn affects the child's behavior. For example, in the game peek-a-boo, parents initially cover their babies, then remove the covering, and finally register "surprise" at the babies' reappearance. As infants become more skilled at peek-a-boo, they gradually do some of the covering and uncovering. Parents try to time their actions in such a way that the infant takes turns with the parent. In addition to peek-a-boo, other caregiver games such as pat-a-cake and "so-big" exemplify scaffolding and turn-taking sequences.

Scaffolding can be used to support children's efforts at any age. A study of Hmong families living in the United States revealed that maternal scaffolding of young children's problem solving the summer before kindergarten, especially in the form of cognitive support, predicted the children's reasoning skills in kindergarten (Stright, Herr, & Neitzel, 2009). Also, a recent study found that maternal scaffolding was associated with a higher verbal IQ level of preschool children born with a very low birth weight (Lowe & others, 2014).

Increasingly, genetic and epigenetic factors are being studied to discover not only parental influences on children but also children's influence on parents (Avinun & Knafo-Noam, 2015; Belsky & others, 2015; Bornstein & Leventhal, 2015; Harold & others, 2013; Hartman & Belsky, 2015; Plomin, 2013). Recall that the *epigenetic view* emphasizes that development is the result of an ongoing, bidirectional interchange between heredity and the environment (Lickliter & Honeycutt, 2015; Moore, 2013). For example, harsh, hostile parenting is associated with negative outcomes for children, such as being defiant and oppositional (Deater-Deckard, 2013). This likely reflects bidirectional influences rather than a unidirectional parenting effect. That is, the parents' harsh, hostile parenting and the children's defiant, oppositional behavior may mutually influence each other. In this bidirectional influence, the parents' and children's behavior may have genetic linkages as well as experiential connections.

FAMILY AS A SYSTEM

As a social system, the family can be thought of as a constellation of subsystems defined in terms of generation, gender, and role. Divisions of labor among family members define particular sub-units, and attachments define others. Each family member participates in several subsystems—some dyadic (involving two people) and some polyadic (involving more than two people) (Gavazzi, 2013). The father and child represent one dyadic subsystem, the mother and father another; the mother-father-child represent one polyadic subsystem, the mother and two siblings another.

These subsystems interact with and influence each other. Thus, as Figure 1 illustrates, the marital relationship, parenting, and infant/child behavior can have both direct and indirect effects on each other (Belsky, 1981). The link between marital relationships and parenting has recently received increased attention (Ulbricht & others, 2013). The most consistent findings are that compared with unhappily married parents, happily married parents are more sensitive, responsive, warm, and affectionate toward their children (Grych, 2002).

Researchers have found that promoting marital satisfaction often leads to good parenting. The marital relationship is an important support for parenting (Cox & others, 2008). When parents report more intimacy and better communication in their marriage, they are more affectionate with their children (Grych, 2002). Thus, marriage-enhancement programs may end up improving parenting and helping children. Programs that focus on parenting skills might also benefit from including attention to the participants' marriages.

Thus, a positive family climate for children and adolescents involves not only effective parenting but also a positive relationship between parents, whether they are married or divorced. A longitudinal study found that a positive family climate (based on positive interaction between spouses and between parents and a seventh-grader) was linked to the degree of positive engagement the adolescents later showed toward their own spouses almost 20 years later in early adulthood (Ackerman & others, 2013).

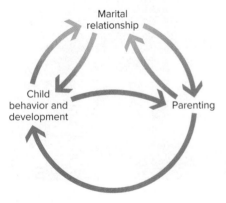

Marital
relationship

Child
behavior and
development

Parenting

FIGURE 1

INTERACTION BETWEEN CHILDREN AND THEIR PARENTS: DIRECT AND INDIRECT EFFECTS

SOCIOCULTURAL AND HISTORICAL INFLUENCES

Family development does not occur in a social vacuum. Important sociocultural and historical influences affect family processes, which reflect Bronfenbrenner's concepts of the macrosystem and chronosystem (Bronfenbrenner & Morris, 2006). Both great upheavals such as war, famine, or mass immigration and subtle transitions in ways of life may stimulate changes in families (Elder & Shanahan, 2006; Masten & others, 2015). One example is the effect on U.S. families of the Great Depression of the 1930s. During its height, the Depression produced economic deprivation, adult discontent, and depression about living conditions. It also increased marital conflict, inconsistent child rearing, and unhealthy lifestyles—heavy drinking, demoralized attitudes, and health problems—especially in fathers (Elder, 1980).

A major change in families during the last several decades has been the dramatic increase in the immigration of Latino and Asian families into the United States (Leventhal, Dupere, & Shuey, 2015; Murry & others, 2015). These families often experience stressors uncommon to or less prominent among longtime residents, such as language barriers, dislocations and separations from support networks, the dual struggle to preserve identity and to acculturate, and changes in socioeconomic status (Fuligni & Tsai, 2015; McLoyd, Purtell, & Hardaway, 2015; Nieto & Yoshikawa, 2014; Schwartz & others, 2015a, b, c). We discuss ethnic variations in families more extensively in the chapter on "Peers and the Sociocultural World."

Subtle changes in a culture have significant influences on the family (Duncan, Magnuson, & Votruba-Drzal, 2015; Mistry & Dutta, 2015). Such changes include the longevity of older adults; movement to urban and suburban areas; widespread use of television, computers, and the Internet; and a general dissatisfaction and restlessness.

Early in the twentieth century, middle-aged and older adults were often closely linked to the family (Mead, 1978). Today, older parents may have lost some of their socializing role in the family as many of their children moved considerable distances away. However, as we see later in the chapter, in the twenty-first century an increasing number of grandparents are raising their grandchildren.

In the twentieth century, many families moved from farms and small towns to urban and suburban settings (Mead, 1978). In the small towns and farms, individuals were surrounded by lifelong neighbors, relatives, and friends. Today, neighborhood and extended-family support systems are not nearly as prevalent. Families now move all over the country, often uprooting children from a school and peer group they have known for a considerable length of time. And it is not unusual for this type of move to occur every several years, as one or both parents are transferred from job to job.

Further, an increasing number of children are growing up in transnational families, who move back and forth between the United States and Mexico or between the United States and China (Alcantara, Molina, & Kawachi, 2015; Asgary & others, 2015; Parke, 2013). In some cases, these children are left behind in their home country or in other cases they are sent back to be raised by grandparents during their early childhood years. Such children

- - - - - - - - - ➤
developmental **connection**

Family

Many families who have immigrated into the United States in recent decades, such as Mexican Americans and Asian Americans, come from collectivist cultures in which family obligation is strong. Connect to "Peers and the Sociocultural World."

Two important changes in families are the increased mobility of families and the increase in media use. *What are some other changes?*
(left): © Tom & Dee Ann McCarthy/Corbis; (right): © Franco Vogt/Corbis

developmental **connection**

Family

Recent research indicates that children's and adolescents' media use/screen time have increased dramatically in the last decade. Connect to "Peers and the Sociocultural World."

might benefit from economic remittances but suffer emotionally from prolonged separation from parents.

Media use and screen time also play a major role in the changing family (Boniel-Nissim & others, 2015; Calvert, 2015; Prot & others, 2015). Many children who watch television or use computers find that parents are too busy working to share this experience with them. Children increasingly experience a world in which their parents are not participants. Instead of interacting in neighborhood peer groups, children come home after school and watch television or log on to a computer. Among the historical changes related to computers, consider the dramatic increase in young people's participation on Internet social networking sites (Shin & Ismail, 2014).

Another change in families has been an increase in general dissatisfaction and restlessness (Mead, 1978). The result of such restlessness and the tendency to divorce and remarry has been a hodgepodge of family structures, with far greater numbers of divorced and remarried families than ever before. Later in the chapter, we will discuss in greater detail these aspects of the changing social world of the child and the family.

MULTIPLE DEVELOPMENTAL TRAJECTORIES

multiple developmental trajectories Refers to the fact that adults follow one trajectory or pattern of development and children another one.

The concept of **multiple developmental trajectories** refers to the fact that adults follow one trajectory or pattern of development and children another one (Clarke-Stewart & Parke, 2014; Parke & Buriel, 2006). Observing how adult and child developmental trajectories mesh is important for understanding the timing of entry into various family tasks. Adult developmental trajectories include timing of entry into cohabitation, marriage, or parenthood; child developmental trajectories include timing of child care and entry into middle school. The timing of some family tasks and changes is planned, such as reentry into the workforce or delaying parenthood, whereas the timing of others is not, such as job loss or divorce (Parke & Buriel, 2006).

Review *Connect* Reflect

LG1 Describe some important family processes

Review

- What characterizes reciprocal socialization?
- How does the family function as a system?
- How do sociocultural and historical circumstances influence families?
- What is meant by the concept of multiple developmental trajectories?

Connect

- Compare mothers' and fathers' socialization strategies with this section's description of reciprocal socialization.

Reflect *Your Own Personal Journey of Life*

- Reflect for several moments on your own family as you were growing up, and give some examples of the family processes discussed in this section as you experienced them in your own family.

2 The Diversity of Adult Lifestyles

LG2 Discuss the diversity of adult lifestyles and how they influence people's lives

| Single Adults | Cohabiting Adults | Married Adults | Divorced Adults | Remarried Adults | Gay and Lesbian Adults |

A striking social change in recent decades has been the decreased stigma attached to individuals who do not maintain what were long considered conventional families. Adults today choose many lifestyles and form many types of families (Benokraitis, 2012; Klinenberg, 2012). They live alone, cohabit, marry, divorce, or live with someone of the same sex.

In his book *The Marriage-Go-Round*, sociologist Andrew Cherlin (2009) concluded that the United States has more marriages and remarriages, more divorces, and more short-term cohabiting (living together) relationships than most countries. Combined, these lifestyles create more turnover and movement in and out of relationships in the United States than in virtually any other country. Let's explore these varying relationship lifestyles.

SINGLE ADULTS

Recent decades have seen a dramatic rise in the percentage of single adults (Klinenberg, 2012, 2013). In 2009 for the first time in history the proportion of U.S. individuals 25 to 34 years of age who had never been married (46 percent) exceeded those who were married (45 percent) (U.S. Census Bureau, 2013). The increasing number of single adults is the result of rising rates of cohabitation and a trend toward postponing marriage. There actually are a lower percentage of single adults in the United States than in many other countries such as Great Britain, Germany, and Japan. Also the fastest growth in individuals adopting a single adult lifestyle is occurring in rapidly developing countries such as China, India, and Brazil (Klinenberg, 2012, 2013).

Even when singles enjoy their lifestyles and are highly competent individuals, they often are stereotyped (Schwartz & Scott, 2012). Stereotypes associated with being single range from the "swinging single" to the "desperately lonely, suicidal" single. Of course, most single adults are somewhere between these extremes.

Common challenges faced by single adults may include forming intimate relationships with other adults, confronting loneliness, and finding a niche in a society that is marriage-oriented. Bella DePaulo (2006, 2011) argues that society has a widespread bias against unmarried adults that is seen in everything from missed perks in jobs to deep social and financial prejudices.

Advantages of being single include having time to make decisions about one's life course, time to develop personal resources to meet goals, freedom to make autonomous decisions and pursue one's own schedule and interests, opportunities to explore new places and try out new things, and privacy. Compared with married adults, single adults are more likely to spend time with friends and neighbors, go out to restaurants, and attend art classes and lectures (Klinenberg, 2012, 2013). Once adults reach the age of 30, they may face increasing pressure to settle down and get married. This is when many single adults make a conscious decision to marry or to remain single.

A nationally representative U.S. survey of more than 5,000 single adults 21 years of age and older who were not in a committed relationship revealed that men are more interested in love, marriage, and children than their counterparts were in earlier generations (Match.com, 2011). In this study, today's women desire more independence in their relationships than their mothers did. Across every age group, more women than men reported wanting to pursue their own interests, have personal space, have their own bank account, have regular nights out with girlfriends, and take vacations on their own. In a second nationally representative survey, many single adults reported that they were looking for love but not marriage (Match.com, 2012). In this survey, 39 percent of the single adults were uncertain about whether they wanted to get married, 34 percent said they did want to marry, and 27 percent said they didn't want to get married.

Approximately 8 percent of all individuals in the United States who reach the age of 65 have never been married. Contrary to the popular stereotype, older adults who have never been married seem to have the least difficulty coping with loneliness in old age. Many of them discovered long ago how to live autonomously and how to become self-reliant.

COHABITING ADULTS

Cohabitation refers to living together in a sexual relationship without being married. Cohabitation has undergone considerable changes in recent years (Copen, Daniels, & Mosher, 2013; Manning & others, 2014; Smock & Gupta, 2013; Tach & Eads, 2015). There has been a dramatic increase in the number of cohabiting U.S. couples since 1970, with more than 75 percent cohabiting prior to getting married (The National Marriage Project, 2011). And the upward trend shows no sign of letting up—from 3.8 million cohabiting couples in 2000 to 7.5 million cohabiting couples in 2010, as shown in Figure 2 (U.S. Census Bureau, 2011). Cohabiting rates are even higher in some countries—in Sweden, for example, cohabitation before marriage is virtually universal (Stokes & Raley, 2009).

Some couples view their cohabitation not as a precursor to marriage but as an ongoing lifestyle (Klinenberg, 2012; Rose-Greenland & Smock, 2013). These couples do not want the official aspects of marriage. In the United States, cohabiting arrangements tend to be short-lived,

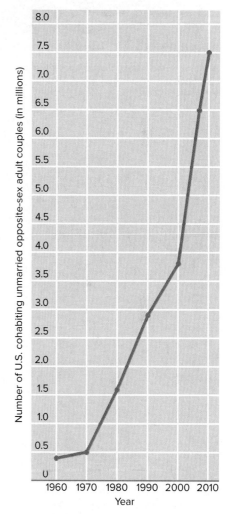

FIGURE **2**

THE INCREASE IN COHABITATION IN THE UNITED STATES. Since 1970, there has been a dramatic increase in the number of unmarried adults living together in the United States.

cohabitation Living together in a sexual relationship without being married.

What are some potential advantages and disadvantages of cohabitation?
© Image Source/Corbis RF

with one-third lasting less than a year (Hyde & DeLamater, 2014). Fewer than 1 out of 10 last five years. Of course, it is easier to dissolve a cohabitation relationship than to divorce.

A recent study revealed that young adults' main reasons for cohabiting are to spend time together, share expenses, and evaluate compatibility (Huang & others, 2011). In this study, gender differences emerged regarding drawbacks in cohabiting: men were more concerned about their loss of freedom while women were more concerned about delays in getting married.

Couples who cohabit face certain problems (James, 2014; Rhoades, Stanley, & Markman, 2009). Disapproval by parents and other family members can place emotional strain on the cohabiting couple. Some cohabiting couples have difficulty owning property jointly. Legal rights regarding the dissolution of the relationship are less certain than in a divorce. A recent study also found that following the transition from dating to cohabitation, relationships were characterized by more commitment, lower satisfaction, more negative communication, and more physical aggression than when dating (noncohabiting) (Rhoades, Stanley, & Markham, 2012).

Cohabitation and Marital Stability/Happiness   If a couple lives together before they marry, does cohabiting help or harm their chances of later having a stable and happy marriage? The majority of studies have found lower rates of marital satisfaction and higher rates of divorce in couples who lived together before getting married (Blumberg, Vahratian, & Blumberg, 2014; Rose-Greenland & Smock, 2013). However, recent research indicates that the link between marital cohabitation and marital instability in first marriages has weakened in recent cohorts (Copen, Daniels, & Mosher, 2013; Smock & Gupta, 2013).

What might explain the finding that cohabiting is linked with divorce more than not cohabiting? The most frequently given explanation is that the less traditional lifestyle of cohabitation may attract less conventional individuals who are not great believers in marriage in the first place. An alternative explanation is that the experience of cohabiting changes people's attitudes and habits in ways that increase their likelihood of divorce.

Recent research has provided clarification of cohabitation outcomes. One meta-analysis found that the link between cohabitation and marital instability did not hold up when only cohabitation with the eventual marital partner was examined, indicating that these cohabitors may attach more long-term positive meaning to living together (Jose, O'Leary, & Moyer, 2010). Another study also revealed that for first marriages, cohabiting with the spouse without first being engaged was linked to more negative interaction and a higher probability of divorce than cohabiting after engagement (Stanley & others, 2010). In contrast, premarital cohabitation prior to a second marriage placed couples at risk for divorce regardless of whether they were engaged. A recent study also found that the marriages of couples who were cohabiting but not engaged were less likely to survive to the 10- to 15-year mark than the marriages of their counterparts who were engaged when they cohabited (Copen, Daniels, & Mosher, 2013). Also, one analysis indicated that cohabiting does not have a negative effect on marriage if the couple did not have any previous live-in lovers and did not have children prior to the marriage (Cherlin, 2009). And a recent study concluded that the risk of marital dissolution between cohabitors and those who married without previously cohabiting was much smaller when they cohabited in their mid-twenties and later (Kuperberg, 2014).

Cohabiting Older Adults   An increasing number of older adults cohabit (Vespa, 2012; Wu, Schimmele, & Quellet, 2015). In the middle of the twentieth century, hardly any older adults cohabited. In 2010, 3 percent of older adults were cohabiting (U.S. Census Bureau, 2011). It is expected that the number of cohabiting older adults will increase even further as the large cohort of baby boomers become 65 years of age and older and bring their historically more nontraditional values about love, sex, and relationships to late adulthood. In many cases, cohabiting among older couples is more for companionship than for love. In other cases—for example, when one partner faces the potential for expensive care—a couple may decide to maintain their assets separately and thus not marry. One study found that older adults who cohabited had a more positive, stable relationship than younger adults who cohabited, although older adults who cohabited were less likely to make plans to marry their partner (King & Scott, 2005). In one recent study, cohabiting older adults were less likely to receive partner care than married older adults (Noel-Miller, 2011).

MARRIED ADULTS

Until about 1930, stable marriage was widely accepted as the endpoint of adult development. In the last 70 to 80 years, however, personal fulfillment both inside and outside marriage has emerged as a goal that competes with marital stability. The changing norm of male-female equality in marriage and increasingly high expectations for what a marital relationship should be have produced marital relationships that are more fragile and intense than they were earlier in the twentieth century (Lavner & Bradbury, 2012). A recent study found that newlyweds who had a high level of general dispositional optimism were more satisfied with their marriages over the first year of the marriage while newlyweds who had a high level of relationship-specific optimism had more marital problems during this time frame (Neff & Geers, 2013).

© Steve Cole/Getty Images RF

Marital Trends   In recent years, marriage rates in the United States have declined. In a recent year (2011), the marriage rate was 6.2 per 1,000 individuals, down from 8.2 in 2000 (National Center for Vital Statistics, 2013). In 2012, 48.6 percent of Americans were married, down from 72 percent in 1960 (U.S. Census Bureau, 2013).

More adults are remaining single longer, with 27 percent of U.S. adults currently having never married (Pew Research Center, 2010). In 2011, the U.S. average age for a first marriage climbed to 28.7 years for men and 26.5 years for women, higher than at any other point in history (Pew Research Center, 2011). In 1980, the average age for a first marriage in the United States was 24 years for men and 21 years for women. In addition, the increase in cohabitation and a slight decline in the percentage of divorced individuals who remarry contribute to the decline in marriage rates in the United States (Copen & others, 2012).

Despite declining marriage rates, the United States is still a marrying society (Popenoe, 2009; Welch, 2015). In 2010, by 40 years of age 77 percent of individuals had ever been married, although this figure is substantially below the figure of 93 percent in the 1960s (Pew Research Center, 2011). In a recent national poll, more than 40 percent of Americans under 30 believed that marriage was headed for extinction, yet only 5 percent of those young adults said they didn't want to get married (Pew Research Center, 2010). These findings may reflect marriage's role as a way to show friends and family that you have a successful social life (Cherlin, 2009).

An increasing number of children are growing up in families where the parents have cohabited but never married, a circumstance that is far more likely to occur when the mother has a low level of education (Pew Research Center, 2015). In a recent study, women with lower levels of education were more likely to give birth in a cohabiting relationship established prior to conception (Gibson-Davis & Rackin, 2014). In the same study, the probability that a less-educated mother would have a conventional married birth was only 11.5 percent compared with 78.4 percent for highly educated mothers.

How happy are people who do marry? As indicated in Figure 3, the percentage of married individuals in the U.S. who said their marriages were "very happy" declined from the

> When two people are under the influence of the most violent, most insane, most delusive, and most transient of passions, they are required to swear that they will remain in that excited, abnormal, and exhausting condition continuously until death do them part.
>
> —GEORGE BERNARD SHAW
> *Irish playwright, 20th century*

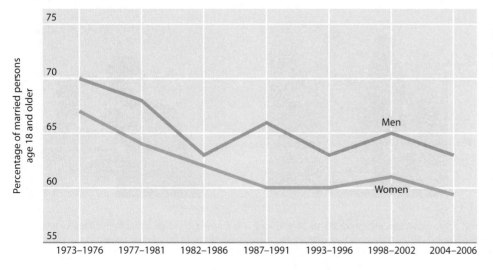

FIGURE 3

PERCENTAGE OF MARRIED PERSONS AGE 18 AND OLDER WITH "VERY HAPPY" MARRIAGES

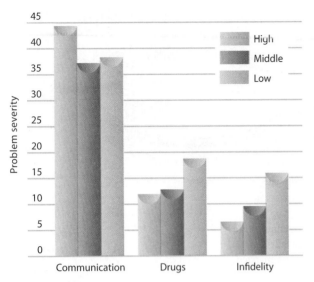

FIGURE **4**

SEVERITY OF SPECIFIC RELATIONSHIP PROBLEMS IN LOW-, MIDDLE-, AND HIGH-INCOME HOUSEHOLDS

1970s through the early 1990s, increased around the turn of the century, but recently has begun to decline again (Popenoe, 2009). Notice in Figure 3 that married men consistently report being happier than married women.

Social Contexts   Contexts within a culture and across cultures are powerful influences on marriage. A U.S. study found that although poor communication was rated as a relatively severe problem regardless of household income, it was rated as most severe in high-income households (Karney, Garvin, & Thomas, 2003) (see Figure 4). By contrast, drugs and infidelity were rated as more severe problems in low-income households.

Many aspects of marriage vary across cultures. For example, as part of China's efforts to control population growth, a 1981 law set the minimum age for marriage at 22 years for males and 20 for females. Further, in many parts of the world, such as India, arranged marriages are common.

The traits that people look for in a marriage partner vary around the world. In one large-scale study of 9,474 adults from 37 cultures on six continents and five islands, people varied most regarding how much they valued chastity—desiring a marital partner with no previous experience in sexual intercourse (Buss & others, 1990). Chastity was the most important characteristic in selecting a marital partner in China, India, Indonesia, Iran, Taiwan, and the Palestinian Arab culture. Adults from Ireland and Japan placed moderate importance on chastity. In contrast, adults in Sweden, Finland, Norway, the Netherlands, and Germany generally said that chastity was not important in selecting a marital partner.

Domesticity is also valued in some cultures and not in others. In the same study, adults from the Zulu culture in South Africa, Estonia, and Colombia placed a high value on housekeeping skills in their marital preference. By contrast, adults in the United States, Canada, and all Western European countries except Spain said that housekeeping skill was not an important trait in selecting their partner.

Religion plays an important role in marital preferences in many cultures. For example, Islam stresses the honor of the male and the purity of the female. It also emphasizes the woman's role in childbearing, child rearing, educating children, and instilling the Islamic faith in children.

International comparisons of marriage also reveal that individuals in Scandinavian countries marry later than Americans, whereas their counterparts in many African, Asian, Latin American, and Eastern European countries marry younger (Waite, 2009). In Denmark, for example, almost 80 percent of the women and 90 percent of the men aged 20 to 24 have never been married. In Hungary, less than 40 percent of the women and 70 percent of the men aged 20 to 24 have never been married. In Scandinavian countries, cohabitation is popular among young adults; however, most Scandinavians eventually marry (Popenoe, 2008). In Sweden, on average, women delay marriage until they are 31, men until they are 33. Some countries, such as Hungary, encourage early marriage and childbearing to offset declines in

(a)

(b)

(c)

(a) In Scandinavian countries, cohabitation is popular; only a small percentage of 20- to 24-year-olds are married. *(b)* Islam stresses male honor and female purity. *(c)* Japanese young adults live at home longer with their parents before marrying than young adults in most other countries.
(a): © Johner Images/Getty Images RF; (b): © Image Source/age fotostock RF; (c): © BloomImage/Getty Images RF.

the population. Like Scandinavian countries, Japan has a high proportion of unmarried young people. However, rather than cohabiting as the Scandinavians do, unmarried Japanese young adults tend to live with their parents before marrying.

What Makes Marriages Work   John Gottman (1994; Gottman & Gottman, 2009; Gottman & Silver, 1999; Gottman & others, 1998) has been studying married couples' lives since the early 1970s. He uses many methods to analyze what makes marriages work. Gottman interviews couples about the history of their marriage, their philosophy about marriage, and how they view their parents' marriages. He videotapes spouses talking with each other about how their day went and evaluates what they say about the good and bad times of their marriages. Gottman also uses physiological measures to measure their heart rate, blood flow, blood pressure, and immune functioning moment by moment. He checks back with the couples every year to see how their marriage is faring. Gottman's research represents the most extensive assessment of marital relationships available. Currently he and his colleagues are following 700 couples in seven studies.

John Gottman has conducted extensive research on what makes marriages work.
Courtesy of The Gottman Institute, www.gottman.com

In his research, Gottman has identified the following factors as important predictors of success in marriage:

- *Establishing love maps.* Individuals in successful marriages have personal insights and detailed maps of each other's life and world. They aren't psychological strangers. In good marriages, partners are willing to share their feelings with each other. They use these "love maps" to express not only their understanding of each other but also their fondness and admiration.

- *Nurturing fondness and admiration.* In successful marriages, partners sing each other's praises. More than 90 percent of the time, when couples put a positive spin on their marriage's history, their marriage is likely to have a positive future.

- *Turning toward each other instead of away.* In good marriages, spouses are adept at turning toward each other regularly. They see each other as friends. This friendship doesn't keep arguments from occurring, but it can prevent differences from overwhelming the relationship. In these good marriages, spouses respect each other and appreciate each other's points of view despite disagreements.

- *Letting your partner influence you.* Bad marriages often involve one spouse who is unwilling to share power with the other. Although power-mongering is more common in husbands, some wives also show this trait. A willingness to share power and to respect the other person's point of view is a prerequisite to compromising. A study revealed that equality in decision making was one of the main factors that predicted positive marriage quality (Amato & others, 2007).

- *Overcoming gridlock.* One partner wants the other to attend church, but the other is an atheist. One partner is a homebody, but the other wants to go out and socialize a lot. Such problems often produce gridlock. Gottman stresses that the key to ending gridlock is not to solve the problem but to move from gridlock to dialogue and to be patient.

- *Creating shared meaning.* The easier it is for partners to speak candidly and respectfully with each other, the more likely it is that they will create shared meaning in their marriage. This also includes sharing goals with one's spouse and working together to achieve each other's goals.

Unlike most approaches to helping couples, mine is based on knowing what makes marriages succeed rather than fail.

—JOHN GOTTMAN
Contemporary psychologist, University of Washington

In a provocative book titled *Marriage: A History*, Stephanie Coontz (2005) concluded that marriages in America today are fragile not because Americans have become self-centered and career-minded but because expectations for marriage have become unrealistically high compared with those of previous generations. However, she states that many marriages today are better than in the past, citing the increase in marriages that are equitable, loving, intimate, and protective of children. To make a marriage work, she emphasizes (as does Gottman) that partners need to develop a deep friendship, show respect for each other, and embrace commitment.

Premarital Education   Premarital education occurs in a group and focuses on relationship advice. Might premarital education improve the quality of a marriage and possibly reduce the chances that the marriage will end in divorce? Researchers have found that it can

What makes marriages work? What are the benefits of having a good marriage?
© Image Source Pink/Alamy RF

(Markman & others, 2013; Owen & others, 2011; Williamson & others, 2015). For example, a survey of more than 3,000 adults revealed that premarital education was linked to a higher level of marital satisfaction and commitment to a spouse, a lower level of destructive marital conflict, and a 31 percent lower likelihood of divorce (Stanley & others, 2006). The premarital education programs in the study ranged from several hours to 20 hours, with a median of 8 hours. It is recommended that premarital education begin approximately six months to a year before the wedding. Also, a recent study revealed that participating in premarital education predicted a higher quality of marriage (Rhoades & Stanley, 2014).

The Benefits of a Good Marriage   Are there any benefits to having a good marriage? There are several (Benokraitis, 2015; Seccombe, 2015). Individuals who are happily married live longer, healthier lives than either divorced individuals or those who are unhappily married (Shor & others, 2012; Prouix & Snyder-Rivas, 2013; Robles, 2014). A survey of U.S. adults 50 years and older also revealed that a lower portion of adult life spent in marriage was linked to an increased likelihood of dying at an earlier age (Henretta, 2010). And a recent large-scale analysis of data from a number of studies indicated a positive effect of marriage on life span, with being married benefitting the longevity of men more than women (Rendall & others, 2011). Further, an unhappy marriage can shorten a person's life by an average of four years (Gove, Style, & Hughes, 1990).

Marriage in Middle and Late Adulthood   What is marriage like for middle-aged adults? How does marriage change in late adulthood?

Middle Adulthood   Even some marriages that were difficult and rocky during early adulthood improve during middle adulthood (Wickrama & others, 2004). Although the partners may have lived through a great deal of turmoil, they eventually discover a deep and solid foundation on which to anchor their relationship. In middle adulthood, the partners may have fewer financial worries, less housework and chores, and more time to spend with each other. Partners who engage in mutual activities usually view their marriage more positively.

What are some adaptations that many married middle-aged and older adults need to make?
© Ronnie Kaufman/Corbis

In midlife, most individuals who are married voice considerable satisfaction with being married. In one large-scale study of individuals in middle adulthood, 72 percent of those who were married said their marriage was either "excellent" or "very good" (Brim, 1999). Possibly by middle age, many of the worst marriages already have dissolved.

Might relationship skills in emerging adulthood predict marital adjustment in middle age? A longitudinal study revealed that individuals with higher levels of emotional intimacy skills in their early twenties were more likely to have well-adjusted marriages in middle age than their counterparts with lower levels of intimacy skills in their twenties (Boden, Fischer, & Niehuis, 2010).

Late Adulthood   In 2012, 58 percent of U.S. adults over 65 years of age were married (U.S. Census Bureau, 2013). Older men (72 percent) were far more likely to be married than older women (45 percent). In 2012, 27 percent of U.S. adults over 65 years of age were widowed (U.S. Census Bureau, 2013). There were more than four times as many widows (8.5 million) as widowers (2.1 million).

Individuals who are in a marriage or a partnership in late adulthood are usually happier, are less distressed, and live longer than those who are single (Piazza & Charles, 2012; Strout & Howard, 2012). One study found that older adults were more satisfied with their marriages than were young and middle-aged adults (Bookwala & Jacobs, 2004). Indeed, the majority of older adults evaluate their marriages as happy or very happy (Huyck, 1995). In a study of octogenarians, marital satisfaction helped to protect their happiness from being affected by daily fluctuations in perceived health (Waldinger & Schulz, 2010). Also, a longitudinal study of adults 75 years of age and older revealed that individuals who were married were less likely to die during a seven-year time span (Rasulo, Christensen, & Tomassini, 2005). And

Grow old along with me!

The best is yet to be,

The last of life,

For which the first was made.

—ROBERT BROWNING

English poet, 19th century

a recent study found that older adult men reported higher marital satisfaction than did older adult women (Boerner & others, 2014).

In late adulthood, married individuals are more likely to find themselves having to care for a sick partner with a limiting health condition (Blieszner & Roberto, 2012). The stress of caring for a spouse who has a chronic disease can place demands on intimacy.

DIVORCED ADULTS

During the mid-twentieth century divorce reached epidemic proportions in the United States (Braver & Lamb, 2013). However, the divorce rate declined in recent decades after peaking at 5.1 divorces per 1,000 people in 1981 and had declined to 4.0 divorces per 1,000 people in 2000 and 3.6 divorces per 1,000 people in 2011 (National Center for Vital Statistics, 2013). The 2011 figure (3.6) compares with a marriage rate of 6.8 per 1,000 people.

Although the divorce rate has dropped, the United States still has one of the highest divorce rates in the world. Russia has the highest divorce rate (4.7 divorces per 1,000 people) (UNSTAT, 2011). In the United States, nearly half of first marriages will break up within 20 years (Copen, Daniels, & Mosher, 2013).

Individuals in some groups have a higher incidence of divorce than others do (Amato, 2010). Youthful marriage, low educational level, low income, not having a religious affiliation, having parents who are divorced, and having a baby before marriage are factors that are associated with increased rates of divorce (Hoelter, 2009). And characteristics of one's partner that increase the likelihood of divorce include alcoholism, psychological problems, domestic violence, infidelity, and inadequate division of household labor (Hoelter, 2009).

Certain personality traits also have been found to predict divorce. In a recent study focused on the Big Five personality factors, low levels of agreeableness and conscientiousness, and high levels of neuroticism and openness to experience, were linked to daily experiences that over time negatively impacted relationship quality and eventually led to a marital breakup (Solomon & Jackson, 2014).

Earlier, we indicated that researchers have not been able to pin down a specific age that is the best time to marry in order to reduce the likelihood of divorce. However, if a divorce is going to occur, it usually takes place early in a marriage; most occur in the fifth to tenth years of marriage (National Center for Health Statistics, 2000) (see Figure 5). For example, a recent study found that divorce peaked in Finland at approximately 5 to 7 years after a marriage, and then the rate of divorce gradually declined (Kulu, 2014). This timing may reflect an effort by partners in troubled marriages to stay in the marriage and try to work things out. If after several years these efforts have not improved the relationship, they may then seek a divorce.

Even those adults who initiated their divorce go through challenges after a marriage dissolves (Tamers & others, 2014). Both divorced women and divorced men complain of loneliness, diminished self-esteem, anxiety about the unknowns in their lives, and difficulty forming satisfactory new intimate relationships.

The stress of separation and divorce places both men and women at risk for psychological and physical difficulties (Kulik & Heine-Cohen, 2011). Separated and divorced women and men have higher rates of psychiatric disorders, admission to psychiatric hospitals, clinical depression, alcoholism, and psychosomatic problems such as sleep disorders than do married adults (Braver & Lamb, 2013; Breslau & others, 2011; Keyes, Hatzenbuehler, & Hasin, 2011).

There are gender differences in the process and outcomes of divorce (Braver & Lamb, 2013). Women are more likely to sense that something is wrong with the marriage and are more likely to seek a divorce than are men. Women also show better emotional adjustment and are more likely to perceive divorce as offering a "second chance" to increase their happiness, improve their social lives, and seek better work opportunities. However, divorce typically has a more negative economic impact on women that it does on men.

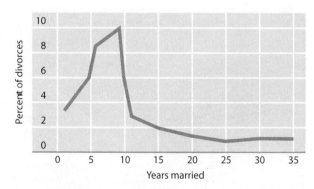

FIGURE 5

THE DIVORCE RATE IN RELATION TO NUMBER OF YEARS MARRIED. Shown here is the percentage of divorces as a function of how long couples have been married. Notice that most divorces occur in the early years of marriage, peaking in the fifth to tenth years of marriage.

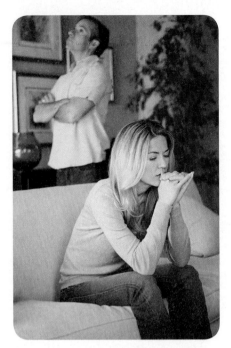

What are some strategies for coping with divorce?
© Image Source/Getty Images RF

Coping with Divorce Psychologically, one of the most common characteristics of divorced adults is difficulty trusting someone else in a romantic relationship. Following a divorce, though, people's lives can take diverse turns (Tashiro, Frazier, & Berman, 2006). Strategies to produce positive outcomes for divorced adults include the following (Hetherington & Kelly, 2002):

· Think of divorce as a chance to grow personally and to develop more positive relationships.
· Make decisions carefully. The consequences of your decisions regarding work, lovers, and children may last a lifetime.
· Focus more on the future than the past. Think about what is most important to help you go forward in your life, and then set some challenging goals and plan how to reach them.
· Use your strengths and resources to cope with difficulties.
· Don't expect to be successful and happy in everything you do. "The road to a more satisfying life is bumpy and will have many detours" (p. 109).
· Remember that "you are never trapped by one pathway. Most of those who were categorized as defeated immediately after divorce gradually moved on to a better life, but moving onward usually requires some effort" (p. 109).

Divorced Middle-Aged and Older Adults A survey by AARP (2004) of more than 1 million 40- to 79-year-olds who were divorced at least once in their forties, fifties, or sixties found that staying married because of their children was by far the main reason many people took so long to become divorced. Despite the worry and stress involved in going through the divorce process, three out of four of the divorcees said they had made the right decision to dissolve their marriage and reported a positive outlook on life. Sixty-six percent of the divorced women said they had initiated the divorce, compared with only 41 percent of the divorced men. The divorced women were much more afraid of having financial problems (44 percent) than the divorced men were (11 percent). Following are the main reasons these middle-aged and older adults cited for their divorce:

Main Causes of Divorce for Women

· Verbal, physical, or emotional abuse (23 percent)
· Alcohol or drug abuse (18 percent)
· Cheating (17 percent)

Main Causes of Divorce for Men

· No obvious problems, just fell out of love (17 percent)
· Cheating (14 percent)
· Different values, lifestyles (14 percent)

In 2012, 1 percent of women and 12 percent of men 65 years and older in the United States were divorced or separated (U.S. Census Bureau, 2013). Many of these individuals were divorced or separated before they entered late adulthood (Carr & Pudrovska, 2011). The majority of divorced older adults are women, due to their greater longevity. Men are more likely to remarry, thus removing themselves from the pool of divorced older adults (Peek, 2009). Divorce is far less common among older adults than younger adults, likely reflecting cohort effects rather than age effects since divorce was somewhat rare when current cohorts of older adults were young (Peek, 2009).

There are social, financial, and physical consequences of divorce for older adults (Butrica & Smith, 2012). Divorce can weaken kinship ties when it occurs in later life, especially in the case of older men. Divorced older women are less likely to have adequate financial resources than married older women, and older adults who are divorced have more health problems than those who are not (Bennett, 2006).

What are some characteristics of divorce in middle-aged adults?
© Denkou Images/Alamy RF

In sum, divorce in midlife may have positive outcomes for some individuals and negative outcomes for others (Bourassa, Sbarrra, & Whisman, 2015; Pudrovska, 2009). A recent study found that women who became divorced at 40 to 59 years of age reported being more lonely following the divorce than men who became divorced in this age period (Nicolaisen & Thorsen, 2014). Another recent study of middle-aged women found that those in very low-quality marriages gained life satisfaction following a divorce (Bourassa & others, 2015).

REMARRIED ADULTS

Data indicate that the remarriage rate in the United States has recently declined, going from 50 of every 1,000 divorced or widowed Americans in 1990 to 29 of every 1,000 in 2011 (U.S. Census Bureau, 2013). One reason for the decline is the dramatic increase in cohabitation in recent years.

Adults who remarry usually do so rather quickly, with approximately 50 percent remarrying within three years after they initially divorce (Sweeney, 2009, 2010). Men remarry sooner than women. Men with higher incomes are more likely to remarry than their counterparts with lower incomes. Remarriage occurs sooner for partners who initiate a divorce (especially in the first several years after divorce and for older women) than for those who do not initiate it (Sweeney, 2009, 2010). And some remarried individuals are more adult-focused, responding more to the concerns of their partner, while others are more child-focused, responding more to the concerns of their children (Anderson & Greene, 2011).

Adjustment Evidence on the benefits of remarriage is mixed. Remarried families are more likely to be unstable than first marriages, with divorce more likely to occur—especially in the first several years of the remarried family—than in first marriages (Waite, 2009). While approximately 50 percent of first marriages end in divorce within 20 years, that figure rises to 67 percent for second marriages and 73 percent for third marriages (Banschick & Tabatsky, 2011).

Adults who remarry have lower levels of mental health (higher rates of depression, for example) than adults in first marriages, but remarriage often improves the financial status of remarried adults, especially women (Waite, 2009). Researchers have found that remarried adults' marital relationships tend to be more egalitarian and more likely to be characterized by shared decision making than first marriages (Waite, 2009). Remarried wives also report that they have more influence on financial matters in their new family than do wives in first marriages (Waite, 2009). The complex histories and multiple relationships make adjustment difficult in a stepfamily (Pann & Crosbie-Burnett, 2005). Only one-third of stepfamily couples stay married.

Why do remarried adults find it so difficult to stay married? For one thing, many remarry not for love but for financial reasons, for help in rearing children, and to ease loneliness. They also might carry into the stepfamily negative patterns that produced failure in an earlier marriage. Remarried couples also experience more stress in rearing children than do parents in never-divorced families (Ganong, Coleman, & Hans, 2006). A recent study revealed that positive attitudes about divorce, low marital quality, and divorce proneness were more common among remarried persons than among their counterparts in first marriages (Whitton & others, 2013).

Among the strategies that can help remarried couples cope with the stress of living in a stepfamily are these (Visher & Visher, 1989):

· *Have realistic expectations*. Allow time for loving relationships to develop, and look at the complexity of the stepfamily as a challenge to overcome.
· *Develop new positive relationships within the family*. Create new traditions and ways of dealing with difficult circumstances. Allocation of time is especially important because so many people are involved. The remarried couple needs to allot some time for each person to spend alone.

Remarriage and Aging Rising divorce rates, increased longevity, and better health have led to an increase in remarriage by older adults. What happens when an older adult wants to remarry or does remarry? Researchers have found that some older adults perceive negative social pressure about their decision to remarry (McKain, 1972). These negative sanctions range from raised eyebrows to rejection by adult children. However, the majority of adult children support the decision of their older adult parents to remarry. Researchers have found that remarried parents and stepparents provide less financial and emotional support to adult stepchildren than do parents in first marriages (White, 1994).

GAY AND LESBIAN ADULTS

The legal and social context of marriage creates barriers to breaking up that do not usually exist for same-sex partners (Brown & Henriquez, 2011). But in other ways, researchers have found that gay and lesbian relationships are similar—in their satisfactions, loves, joys, and conflicts—to heterosexual relationships (Crooks & Baur, 2014). For example, like heterosexual couples, gay and lesbian couples need to find a balance of romantic love, affection, autonomy, and equality that is acceptable to both partners (Fingerhut & Peplau, 2013; Hope, 2009). And like heterosexual couples, many gay and lesbian couples are creating families that include children.

Lesbian couples especially place a high priority on equality in their relationships. Indeed, some researchers have found that gay and lesbian couples are more flexible in their gender roles than heterosexual individuals are (Marecek, Finn, & Cardell, 1988). And a recent study of couples revealed that over the course of ten years of cohabitation, partners in gay and lesbian relationships showed a higher average level of relationship quality than heterosexual couples did (Kurdek, 2008).

There are a number of misconceptions about gay and lesbian couples (Cohler & Michaels, 2013; Diamond, 2013). Contrary to stereotypes, one partner is masculine and the other feminine in only a small percentage of gay and lesbian couples. Only a small segment of the gay population has a large number of sexual partners, and this is uncommon among lesbians. Furthermore, researchers have found that gay and lesbian couples prefer long-term, committed relationships (Fingerhut & Peplau, 2013). About half of committed gay couples do have an open relationship that allows the possibility of sex (but not affectionate love) outside of the relationship. Lesbian couples usually do not have this type of relationship.

A special concern is the stigma, prejudice, and discrimination that lesbian, gay, and bisexual individuals experience because of widespread social devaluation of same-sex relationships (Cochran & others, 2013). However, a recent study indicated that many individuals in these relationships saw stigma as bringing them closer together and strengthening their relationship (Frost, 2011).

What are some characteristics of lesbian and gay relationships?
(left): © 2009 JupiterImages Corporation RF;
(right): © Jack Star/PhotoLink/Getty Images RF

Review *Connect* Reflect

LG2 Discuss the diversity of adult lifestyles and how they influence people's lives

Review
- What characterizes single adults?
- What are the lives of cohabiting adults like?
- What are some key aspects of the lives of married adults?
- How does divorce affect adults?
- What are the lives of remarried adults like?
- What characterizes the lifestyles of gay and lesbian adults?

Connect
- What have you learned about the sexual attitudes and behaviors of lesbians and gays?

Reflect *Your Own Personal Journey of Life*
- Which type of lifestyle are you living today? What do you think are its advantages and disadvantages? If you could have a different lifestyle, which one would it be? Why?

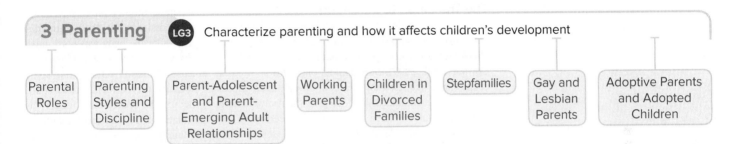

3 Parenting

LG3 Characterize parenting and how it affects children's development

Parental Roles • Parenting Styles and Discipline • Parent-Adolescent and Parent-Emerging Adult Relationships • Working Parents • Children in Divorced Families • Stepfamilies • Gay and Lesbian Parents • Adoptive Parents and Adopted Children

Just as there are diverse lifestyles that adults can adopt, so are there diverse styles of parenting and diverse types of parents. Before we examine these diverse styles and types, let's explore the roles of parents.

PARENTAL ROLES

Many adults plan when to be parents and consider how parenting will fit with their economic situation. For others, the discovery that they are about to become parents is a startling surprise. In either event, the prospective parents may have mixed emotions and romantic illusions about having a child (Carl, 2012). The needs and expectations of parents have stimulated many myths about parenting.

Some recent media accounts portray many parents as unhappy, feeling little joy in caring for their children. However, recent research found that parents were more satisfied with their lives than were nonparents, felt relatively better on a daily basis than did nonparents, and had more positive feelings related to caring for their children than from other daily activities (Nelson & others, 2013). Also, a recent research review concluded that parents are unhappy when they experience more negative emotions, financial problems, sleep problems, and troubled marriages (Nelson, Kushlev, & Lyubomirsky, 2014). In this review, it was concluded that parents are happy when they experience meaning in life, satisfaction of basic needs, more positive emotions, and positive social roles.

Currently, there is a tendency for couples to have fewer children. The number of one-child families is increasing. Is there a best time to have children? What are some of the restrictions individuals face when they become parents? These are some of the questions we now consider.

Timing of Parenthood Like the age when individuals first marry, the age at which individuals have children has been increasing (Lauer & Lauer, 2012). In 2012, the average age at which women gave birth for the first time was 26, up from 21 years of age in 2001 (U.S. Census Bureau, 2013). A recent national poll of 40- to 50-year-old U.S. women found that those with a master's degree or higher first became mothers at 30; in comparison, the average age for women with a high school diploma was just 24 (Pew Research Center, 2015).

As birth control has become common practice, many individuals consciously choose when they will have children and how many children they will rear. The number of one-child

I looked on child rearing not only as a work of love and duty but as a profession that was fully as interesting and challenging as any honorable profession in the world and one that demanded the best that I could bring to it.

—ROSE KENNEDY
U.S. public figure and philanthropist, 20th century

We never know the love of our parents until we have become parents.

—HENRY WARD BEECHER
American clergyman, 19th century

families is increasing, for example, and U.S. women overall are having fewer children or not having children at all. The percentage of 40- to 44-year-old U.S. women who remain childless increased from 10 percent in 1976 to 20 percent in 2006 (U.S. Census Bureau, 2008).

What are some of the advantages of having children early or late? Some of the advantages of having children early (in the twenties) are these: (1) the parents are likely to have more physical energy—for example, they can cope better with such matters as getting up in the middle of the night with infants and waiting up until adolescents come home at night; (2) the mother is likely to have fewer medical problems with pregnancy and childbirth; and (3) the parents may be less likely to build up expectations for their children, as do many couples who have waited many years to have children.

There are also advantages to having children later (in the thirties): (1) the parents have had more time to consider their goals in life, such as what they want from their family and career roles; (2) the parents are more mature and are able to benefit from their experiences to engage in more competent parenting; and (3) the parents are better established in their careers and have more income for child-rearing expenses.

The Transition to Parenting   Whether people become parents through pregnancy, adoption, or stepparenting, they face disequilibrium and must adapt (Florsheim, 2014). In a longitudinal investigation of couples from late pregnancy until 3½ years after the baby was born, most couples enjoyed more positive marital relations before the baby was born than after (Cowan & Cowan, 2000, 2009). Still, almost one-third showed an increase in marital satisfaction. Some couples said that the baby had both brought them closer together and moved them farther apart; being parents enhanced their sense of themselves and gave them a new, more stable identity as a couple. Babies opened men up to a concern with intimate relationships, and the demands of juggling work and family roles stimulated women to manage family tasks more efficiently and pay attention to their own personal growth. A recent study revealed that when new mothers had low marital satisfaction it often was linked to reductions in quality time spent with husbands and perceptions of unequal sharing of housework (Dew & Wilcox, 2011).

The Bringing Baby Home project is a workshop for new parents that helps couples strengthen their relationship, understand and become acquainted with their baby, resolve conflict, and develop parenting skills (Gottman, Gottman, & Shapiro, 2009). Evaluations of the project revealed that participants were better able to work together as parents, fathers were more involved with their baby and sensitive to the baby's behavior, mothers had a lower incidence of postpartum depression symptoms, and their babies showed better overall development than the babies of participants in a control group (Gottman, 2012; Shapiro & Gottman, 2005).

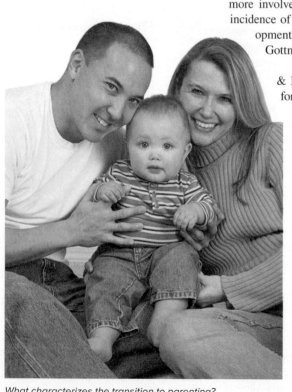

Other recent studies have explored the transition to parenthood (Brown, Feinberg, & Kan, 2012). One study found similar negative change in relationship satisfaction for married and cohabiting women during the transition to parenthood (Mortensen & others, 2012). Another study revealed that mothers experienced unmet expectations in the transition to parenting, with fathers doing less than the mothers had anticipated (Biehle & Mickelson, 2012).

Parents as Managers of Children's Lives   Parents can play important roles as managers of children's opportunities, as monitors of their lives, and as social initiators and arrangers (Caruthers, Van Ryzin, & Dishion, 2014; Lowe & Dotterer, 2013; Parke & Buriel, 1998, 2006). An important developmental task of childhood and adolescence is to learn how to make competent decisions in an increasingly independent manner. To help children and adolescents reach their full potential, an important parental role is to be an effective manager—one who finds information, makes contacts, helps structure choices, and provides guidance. Parents who fulfill this important managerial role help children and adolescents to avoid pitfalls and to work their way through the myriad choices and decisions they face.

Managing and Guiding Infants' Behavior   In addition to sensitive parenting involving warmth and caring that can result in infants being securely attached to their parents, other important aspects of parenting infants involve managing and guiding their behavior in an attempt to reduce or eliminate

What characterizes the transition to parenting?
© Frare/Davis Photography/Brand X/Corbis RF

undesirable behaviors (Holden, Vittrup, & Rosen, 2011). This management process includes (1) being proactive and childproofing the environment so infants won't encounter potentially dangerous objects or situations, and (2) engaging in corrective methods when infants engage in undesirable behaviors, such as excessive fussing and crying, throwing objects, and so on.

One study assessed discipline and corrective methods that parents had used by the time their infants were 12 and 24 months old (Vittrup, Holden, & Buck, 2006) (see Figure 6). Notice in Figure 6 that the main method parents used by the time infants were 12 months old was diverting the infants' attention, followed by reasoning, ignoring, and negotiating. Also note in Figure 6 that more than one-third of parents had yelled at their infant, about one-fifth had slapped the infant's hands or threatened the infant, and approximately one-sixth had spanked the infant by their first birthday.

As infants move into the second year of life and become more mobile and capable of exploring a wider range of environments, parental management of the toddler's behavior often includes increased corrective feedback and discipline (Holden & others, 2011). As indicated in Figure 6, in the study just described, yelling increased from 36 percent at 1 year of age to 81 percent by 2 years of age, slapping the infant's hands increased from 21 percent at 1 year to 31 percent by age 2, and spanking increased from 14 percent at 1 to 45 percent by 2 (Vittrup & others, 2006).

A special concern is that such corrective discipline tactics not become abusive. Too often what starts out as mild to moderately intense discipline on the part of parents can move into highly intense anger. Later in this chapter, you will read more extensively about the use of punishment with children and child maltreatment.

Parents as Regulators of Children's Activities   Parents can serve as regulators of opportunities for their children's activities (Tilton-Weaver & others, 2013). From infancy through adolescence, mothers are more likely than fathers to have a managerial role in guiding and managing the activities in which children participate. In infancy, this might involve taking a child to a doctor and arranging for child care; in early childhood, it might involve a decision about which preschool the child should attend and contacting other parents who have young children whom their child can play with; in middle and late childhood, it might include directing the child to take a bath, to match their clothes and wear clean clothes, and to put away toys; in adolescence, it could involve participating in a parent-teacher conference and subsequently managing the adolescent's homework activity. Researchers have found that family-management practices are related to students' grades and self-responsibility (Lowe & Dotterer, 2013).

Parental Monitoring and Adolescents' Information Management
A key aspect of the managerial role of parenting is effective monitoring, which is especially important as children move into the adolescent years (Lowe & Dotterer, 2013; Smetana, 2011a, b). Monitoring includes supervising adolescents' choice of social settings, activities, and friends as well as their academic efforts. A recent study found that a higher level of parental monitoring in the last year of high school was linked to a lower probability of alcohol dependence in the first year of college (Kaynak & others, 2013). And a recent study found that a high level of parental monitoring within the context of parental warmth was linked to positive academic outcomes for ethnic minority youth (Lowe & Dotterer, 2013). A recent meta-analysis also concluded that low parental monitoring was associated with adolescent depression (Yap & others, 2014). And in another recent study, low parental monitoring was a key factor in predicting a developmental trajectory of delinquency and substance use in adolescence (Wang & others, 2014).

A current interest involving parental monitoring focuses on adolescents' management of their parents' access to information, especially disclosing or concealing details about their activities (Keijsers & Laird, 2014; Smetana,

Method	12 Months	24 Months
Spank with hand	14	45
Slap infant's hand	21	31
Yell in anger	36	81
Threaten	19	63
Withdraw privileges	18	52
Time-out	12	60
Reason	85	100
Divert attention	100	100
Negotiate	50	90
Ignore	64	90

FIGURE 6

PARENTS' METHODS FOR MANAGING AND CORRECTING INFANTS' UNDESIRABLE BEHAVIOR.
Shown here are the percentages of parents who had used various corrective methods by the time the infants were 12 and 24 months old.
Source: Based on data presented in Table 1 in Vittrup, Holden, & Buck (2006).

What characterizes adolescents' management of their parents' access to information?
© Ryan McVay/Getty Images RF

developmental **connection**

Moral Development

Lack of adequate parental monitoring is linked to juvenile delinquency. Connect to "Moral Development, Values, and Religion."

Parenting is a very important profession, but no test of fitness for it is ever imposed in the interest of children.

—GEORGE BERNARD SHAW
Irish playwright, 20th century

Robinson, & Rote, 2015). When parents engage in positive parenting practices, adolescents are more likely to disclose information (Rote & others, 2012). For example, disclosure increases when parents ask adolescents questions and when adolescents' relationship with parents is characterized by a high level of trust, acceptance, and quality (Smetana & others, 2015). Researchers have found that adolescents' disclosure to parents about their whereabouts, activities, and friends is linked to positive adolescent adjustment (Laird & Marrero, 2010). A recent study of U.S. and Chinese young adolescents found that adolescents' disclosure to parents was linked with a higher level of academic competence (better learning strategies, autonomous motivation, and better grades) over time (Cheung, Pomerantz, & Dong, 2012).

To read about one individual who helps parents become more effective in managing their children's lives, see the *Connecting with Careers* profile.

PARENTING STYLES AND DISCIPLINE

A few years ago, there was considerable interest in Mozart CDs that were marketed with the promise that playing them would enrich infants' and young children's brains. Some of the parents who bought them probably thought, "I don't have enough time to spend with my children so I'll just play these CDs and then they won't need me as much." Similarly, one-minute bedtime stories have been marketed for parents to read to their children (Walsh, 2000). There are one-minute bedtime bear books, puppy books, and so on. Parents who buy them know it is a good idea to read to their children, but they don't want to spend a lot of time doing it. Behind the popularity of these products is an unfortunate theme that suggests that parenting can be done quickly, with little or no inconvenience (Sroufe, 2000).

What is wrong with these quick-fix parenting strategies? Good parenting takes time and effort (Grusec & others, 2013). You can't do it in a minute here and a minute there. You can't do it with CDs or DVDs.

A recent survey of American parents found that approximately half of fathers and one-fourth of mothers reported feeling that they were not spending enough time with their children (Pew Research Center, 2013). Nonetheless, in this survey, both mothers and fathers are spending more time with their children than the previous generation of parents did.

Of course, it's not just the quantity of time parents spend with children that is important for children's development—the quality of the parenting is clearly important (Clarke-Stewart & Parke, 2014). For example, a recent study found that maternal scaffolding, sensitivity, and support for autonomy were linked to better executive function in preschool children (Blair, Raver, & Berry, 2014). To further understand variations in parenting, let's consider the styles parents use when they interact with their children, how they discipline their children, and coparenting.

Baumrind's Parenting Styles   Diana Baumrind (1971, 2012) argues parents should be neither punitive nor aloof. Rather, they should develop rules for their children and be affectionate with them. She has described four types of parenting styles:

- **Authoritarian parenting** is a restrictive, punitive style in which parents exhort the child to follow their directions and respect their work and effort. The authoritarian parent places firm limits and controls on the child and allows little verbal exchange. For example, an authoritarian parent might say, "You will do it my way or else." Authoritarian parents also might spank the child frequently, enforce rules rigidly but not explain them, and show rage toward the child. Children of authoritarian parents are often unhappy, fearful, and anxious about comparing themselves with others, fail to initiate activity, and have weak communication skills. Sons of authoritarian parents may behave aggressively (Hart & others, 2003).

- **Authoritative parenting** encourages children to be independent but still places limits and controls on their actions. Extensive verbal give-and-take is allowed, and parents are warm and nurturant toward the child. An authoritative parent might put his arm around the child in a comforting way and say, "You know you should not have done that. Let's talk about how you can handle the situation better next time." Authoritative parents show pleasure and support in response to children's constructive behavior. They also expect mature, independent, and age-appropriate behavior by children. Children whose parents are authoritative are often cheerful, self-controlled, self-reliant, and achievement-oriented; they tend to maintain friendly relations with peers, cooperate with adults, and cope well with stress. A recent study of Chinese adolescents revealed that authoritative parenting positively predicted parent-adolescent attachment, which in turn was associated with a higher level of adolescent self-esteem and positive attachment to peers (Cai & others, 2013).

- **Neglectful parenting** is a style in which the parent is very uninvolved in the child's life. Children whose parents are neglectful develop the sense that other aspects of the parents' lives are more important than they are. These children tend to be socially incompetent. Many have poor self-control and don't handle independence well. They frequently have low self-esteem, are immature, and may be alienated from their family. In adolescence, they may show patterns of truancy and delinquency.

- **Indulgent parenting** is a style in which parents are highly involved with their children but place few demands or controls on them. Such parents let their children do what they want. The result is that the children never learn to control their own behavior and always expect to get their way. Some parents deliberately rear their children in this way because they believe the combination of warm involvement and few restraints will produce a creative, confident child. However, children whose parents are indulgent rarely learn respect for others and tend to have difficulty controlling their behavior. They might be domineering, egocentric, and noncompliant, and have difficulties in peer relations.

These four classifications of parenting involve combinations of acceptance and responsiveness on the one hand and demand and control on the other (Maccoby & Martin, 1983). How these dimensions combine to produce authoritarian, authoritative, neglectful, and indulgent parenting is shown in Figure 7.

Parenting Styles in Context   Do the benefits of authoritative parenting transcend the boundaries of ethnicity, socioeconomic status, and household composition? Although some exceptions have been found, evidence linking authoritative parenting with competence on the part of the child occurs in research across a wide range of ethnic groups, social strata, cultures, and family structures (Morris, Cui, & Steinberg, 2012).

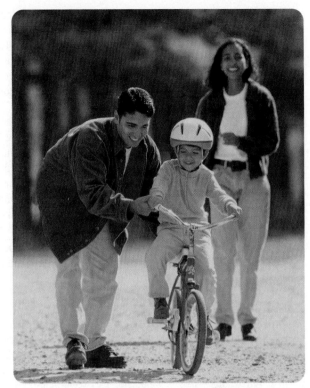

	Accepting, responsive	Rejecting, unresponsive
Demanding, controlling	Authoritative	Authoritarian
Undemanding, uncontrolling	Indulgent	Neglectful

FIGURE 7

CLASSIFICATION OF PARENTING STYLES. The four types of parenting styles (authoritative, authoritarian, indulgent, and neglectful) involve the dimensions of acceptance and responsiveness, on the one hand, and demand and control on the other. For example, authoritative parenting involves being both accepting/responsive and demanding/controlling.
© Ariel Skelley/Corbis

authoritarian parenting A restrictive, punitive style in which parents exhort the child to follow their directions and to respect their work and effort. Firm limits are placed on the child, and little verbal exchange is allowed.

authoritative parenting A style that encourages children to be independent but still places limits and controls on children's actions; extensive verbal give-and-take is allowed, and parents are warm and nurturant toward the child.

neglectful parenting A style in which the parent is very uninvolved in the child's life.

indulgent parenting A style in which parents are very involved with their children but place few demands or controls on them.

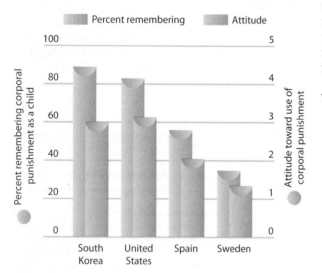

According to Ruth Chao, what type of parenting style do many Asian American parents use?
© Blend Images/SuperStock RF

developmental **connection**

Family

The effects of parenting tactics used by Chinese and Chinese American parents have been described in two recent books—*Battle Hymn of the Tiger Mom* and *Tiger Babies Strike Back*—and researchers have studied parenting in Chinese and Chinese American families. Connect to "Schools, Achievement, and Work."

Other research with ethnic groups suggests that some aspects of the authoritarian style may be associated with positive child outcomes (Parke & Buriel, 2006). Elements of the authoritarian style may take on different meanings and have different effects depending on the context. For example, Asian American parents often continue aspects of traditional Asian child-rearing practices that have sometimes been described as authoritarian. The parents exert considerable control over their children's lives. However, Ruth Chao (2005, 2007; Chao & Otsuki-Clutter, 2011; Chao & Tseng, 2002) argues that the style of parenting used by many Asian American parents is distinct from the domineering control of the authoritarian style. Instead, Chao argues that the control reflects concern and involvement in their children's lives and is best conceptualized as a type of training. The high academic achievement of Asian American children may be a consequence of their "training" parents (Stevenson & Zusho, 2002). In recent research involving Chinese American adolescents and their parents, parental control was endorsed as were the Confucian parental goals of perseverance, hard work in school, obedience, and sensitiveness to parents' wishes (Russell, Crockett, & Chao, 2010).

Further Thoughts on Parenting Styles Several caveats about parenting styles are in order. First, the parenting styles do not capture the important themes of reciprocal socialization and synchrony. Keep in mind that children socialize parents, just as parents socialize children (Bush & Peterson, 2013; Kuczynski & others, 2015). Second, many parents use a combination of techniques rather than a single technique, although one technique may be dominant. Although consistent parenting is usually recommended, the wise parent may sense the importance of being more permissive in certain situations, more authoritarian in some circumstances, and more authoritative in others. Moreover, parenting styles often are talked about as if both parents have the same style, but this is not always the case. Also, some critics argue that the concept of parenting style is too broad and that more research needs to be conducted to "unpack" parenting styles by studying the influence of various components of the styles (Maccoby, 2007). For example, is parental monitoring more important than warmth in predicting child and adolescent outcomes?

Punishment Use of corporal (physical) punishment is legal in every state in the United States. A national survey of U.S. parents with 3- and 4-year-old children found that 26 percent of parents reported spanking their children frequently, and 67 percent reported yelling at their children frequently (Regalado & others, 2004). A recent study of more than 11,000 U.S. parents indicated that 80 percent of the parents reported spanking their children by the time they reached kindergarten (Gershoff & others, 2012). A cross-cultural comparison found that individuals in the United States were among those with the most favorable attitudes toward corporal punishment and were most likely to remember it being used by their parents (see Figure 8) (Curran & others, 2001). Physical punishment is illegal in 41 countries, mainly to provide children with protection from abuse and exploitation (Committee on the Rights of the Child, 2014).

What are some reasons for avoiding spanking or similar punishments? They include the following:

· When adults punish a child by yelling, screaming, or spanking, they are presenting children with out-of-control models for handling stressful situations. Children may imitate this behavior.

· Punishment can instill fear, rage, or avoidance. For example, spanking the child may cause the child to avoid being near the parent and to fear the parent.

· Punishment tells children what not to do rather than what to do. Children should be given constructive feedback, such as "Why don't you try this?"

· Parents might unintentionally become so angry when they are punishing the child that they become abusive (Knox, 2010).

Most child psychologists recommend handling misbehavior by reasoning with the child, especially explaining the consequences of the child's actions for others. *Time out*, in which the child is removed from a setting that offers positive reinforcement, can also be effective. For example, when the child has misbehaved, a parent might forbid TV viewing for a specified time.

FIGURE 8

CORPORAL PUNISHMENT IN DIFFERENT COUNTRIES. A 5-point scale was used to assess attitudes toward corporal punishment, with scores closer to 1 indicating an attitude against its use and scores closer to 5 suggesting an attitude favoring its use. *Why are studies of corporal punishment correlational studies, and how does that affect their usefulness?*

Are Marital Conflict, Individual Hostility, and the Use of Physical Punishment Linked?

A longitudinal study assessed couples across the transition to parenting to investigate possible links between marital conflict, individual adult hostility, and the use of physical punishment with young children (Kanoy & others, 2003). Before the birth of the first child, the level of marital conflict was observed in a marital problem-solving discussion; answers to questionnaires regarding individual characteristics were also obtained. Thus, these characteristics of the couples were not influenced by characteristics of the child. When the children were 2 and 5 years old, the couples were interviewed about the frequency and intensity of their physical punishment of the children. At both ages, the parents' level of marital conflict was again observed in a marital problem-solving discussion.

The researchers found that both hostility and marital conflict were linked with the use of physical punishment. Individuals with high rates of hostility on the prenatal measures used more frequent and more severe physical punishment with their children. The same was evident for marital conflict—when marital conflict was high, both mothers and fathers were more likely to use physical punishment in disciplining their young children.

If parents who have a greater likelihood of using physical punishment can be identified in prenatal classes, these families could be encouraged to use other forms of discipline before they develop a pattern of physically punishing their children. How might counselors help prevent this pattern from developing? How do most child psychologists recommend handling a child's misbehavior?

Debate about the effects of punishment on children's development continues (Deater-Deckard, 2013; Ferguson, 2013; Gershoff, 2013; Grusec & others, 2013; Knox, 2010; Laible, Thompson, & Froimson, 2015; Lansford & Deater-Deckard, 2012; Theunissen, Vogels, & Reijneveld, 2015). Several recent longitudinal studies also have found that physical punishment of young children is associated with higher levels of aggression later in childhood and adolescence (Berlin & others, 2009; Gershoff & others, 2012; Lansford & others, 2014; Taylor & others, 2010). However, a recent meta-analysis that focused on longitudinal studies revealed that the negative outcomes of punishment on children's internalizing and externalizing problems were minimal (Ferguson, 2013). A research review of 26 studies concluded that only severe or predominant use of spanking, not mild spanking, compared unfavorably with alternative discipline practices (Larzelere & Kuhn, 2005). In addition to considering whether physical punishment is mild or out-of-control, another factor in evaluating effects on children's development involves cultural contexts. Recently researchers have found that physical punishment has less harmful effects in countries where corporal punishment is considered normal, but in all countries studied, corporal punishment was linked to increased child aggression and anxiety (Lansford & others, 2005, 2012).

Thus, in the view of some experts, it is still difficult to determine whether the effects of physical punishment are harmful to children's development, although such a view might be distasteful to some individuals (Grusec & others, 2013; Ferguson, 2013). Also, as with other research on parenting, research on punishment is correlational in nature, making it difficult to discover causal factors. Also, consider the concept of reciprocal socialization discussed at the beginning of this chapter, which emphasizes bidirectional child and parent influences. Researchers have found links between children's early behavioral problems and parents' greater use of physical punishment over time (Laible & others, 2015; Sheehan & Watson, 2008). Nonetheless, a large majority of leading experts on parenting conclude that physical punishment has harmful effects on children and should not be used.

In a recent research review, Elizabeth Gershoff (2013) concluded that the defenders of spanking have not produced any evidence that spanking produces positive outcomes for children and that negative outcomes of spanking have been replicated in many studies. Also, one thing that is clear is that when physical punishment involves abuse, it can be very harmful to children's development, as discussed later in this chapter (Cicchetti & Toth, 2015).

Considering the family as a system (as discussed earlier in this chapter), what connections might be found between marital relationships and parenting practices? To read about a family systems study involving marital conflict and the use of physical punishment, see the *Connecting with Research* interlude.

How do most child psychologists recommend handling a child's misbehavior?
© Image Source/PunchStock/Getty Images RF

Darla Botkin, Marriage and Family Therapist

Darla Botkin is a marriage and family therapist who teaches, conducts research, and engages in marriage and family therapy. She is on the faculty of the University of Kentucky. Botkin obtained a bachelor's degree in elementary education with a concentration in special education and then went on to receive a master's degree in early childhood education. She spent the next six years working with children and their families in a variety of settings, including child care, elementary school, and Head Start. These experiences led Darla to recognize the interdependence of the developmental settings that children and their parents experience (such as home, school, and work). She returned to graduate school and obtained a Ph.D. in family studies from the University of Tennessee. She then became a faculty member in the Family Studies program at the University of Kentucky. Completing further coursework and clinical training in marriage and family therapy, she became certified as a marriage and family therapist.

Botkin's current interests include working with young children in family therapy, understanding gender and ethnic issues in family therapy, and exploring the role of spirituality in family wellness.

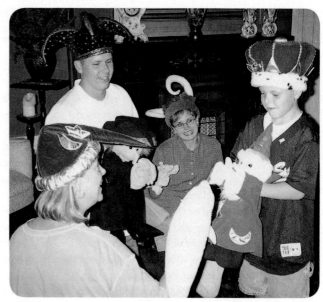

Darla Botkin (left) conducts a family therapy session.
Courtesy of Dr. Darla Botkin

For more information about what marriage and family therapists do, see the Careers in Life-Span Development appendix.

What characterizes coparenting?
© Jim Craigmyle/Corbis

coparenting The support that parents provide one another in jointly raising a child.

Coparenting   The relationship between marital conflict and the use of punishment highlights the importance of **coparenting,** which is the support that parents provide one another in jointly raising a child. Poor coordination between parents, undermining of the other parent, lack of cooperation and warmth, and disconnection by one parent are conditions that place children at risk for problems (Fagan & Lee, 2014; Garneu & Adler-Baeder, 2015; Goldberg & Carlson, 2015; Gonzales, Jones, & Parent, 2014; Lewin & others, 2015). For example, one study revealed that coparenting influenced young children's effortful control above and beyond maternal and paternal parenting by themselves (Karreman & others, 2008). Another study found that greater father involvement in young children's play was linked to an increase in supportive coparenting (Jia & Schoppe-Sullivan, 2011). And a recent study found that parents' joint involvement predicted that adolescents would engage in fewer risky behaviors (Riina & McHale, 2014). In this study, there was a bidirectional influence: adolescents' engagement in a lower level of risk behaviors predicted higher levels of joint parental involvement. Also, in a recent study, unmarried African American parents who were instructed in coparenting techinques during the prenatal period and also one month after the baby was born showed improvements in rapport, communication, and problem-solving skills when the baby was three months old (McHale, Salman-Engin, & Coovert, 2015).

Parents who do not spend enough time with their children or who have problems in child rearing can benefit from counseling and therapy. To read about the work of marriage and family therapist Darla Botkin, see the *Connecting with Careers* profile.

Child Maltreatment   Unfortunately, punishment sometimes leads to the abuse of infants and children (Cicchetti, 2013; Cicchetti & Toth, 2015). In 2009, approximately 702,000 U.S. children were found to be victims of child abuse at least once during that year (U.S. Department of Health and Human Services, 2010). Eighty-one percent of these children were abused by a parent or parents. Laws in many states now require physicians and teachers to report suspected cases of child abuse, yet many cases go unreported, especially those involving battered infants.

Whereas the public and many professionals use the term **child abuse** to refer to both abuse and neglect, developmentalists increasingly use the term **child maltreatment** (Cicchetti, 2013; Cicchetti & Toth, 2015; Jackson & Deye, 2015). This term does not have quite the emotional impact of the term *abuse* and acknowledges that maltreatment includes diverse conditions.

Types of Child Maltreatment The four main types of child maltreatment are physical abuse, child neglect, sexual abuse, and emotional abuse (Jackson, Kissoon, & Greene, 2015; National Clearinghouse on Child Abuse and Neglect, 2013):

· **Physical abuse** is characterized by the infliction of physical injury as a result of punching, beating, kicking, biting, burning, shaking, or otherwise harming a child. The parent or other person may not have intended to hurt the child; the injury may have resulted from excessive physical punishment (Flaherty & others, 2014; Villodas & others, 2015).

· **Child neglect** is characterized by failure to provide for the child's basic needs (O'Hara & others, 2015; Ross & Juarez, 2014). Neglect can be physical (abandonment, for example), educational (allowing chronic truancy, for example), or emotional (marked inattention to the child's needs, for example) (Horner, 2014). Child neglect is by far the most common form of child maltreatment. In every country where relevant data have been collected, neglect occurs up to three times as often as abuse (Potthast, Neuner, & Catani, 2014).

· **Sexual abuse** includes fondling a child's genitals, intercourse, incest, rape, sodomy, exhibitionism, and commercial exploitation through prostitution or the production of pornographic materials (Collin-Vezina & others, 2015; Williams & others, 2014). Unlike physical abuse, many cases of sexual abuse produce no outward physical signs that abuse has taken place.

· **Emotional abuse** (psychological/verbal abuse/mental injury) includes acts or omissions by parents or other caregivers that have caused, or could cause, serious behavioral, cognitive, or emotional problems (Shin & others, 2015; Sorbo & others, 2013).

Eight-year-old Donnique Hein lovingly holds her younger sister, 6-month-old Maria Paschel, after a meal at Laura's Home, a crisis shelter run by the City Mission of Cleveland.
© Joshua Gunter/The Plain Dealer/Landov Images

Although any of these forms of child maltreatment may be found separately, they often occur in combination. Emotional abuse is almost always present when other forms are identified.

The Context of Abuse No single factor causes child maltreatment (Cicchetti, 2013). A combination of factors, including the culture, neighborhood, family, and development, likely contribute to child maltreatment.

The extensive violence that takes place in American culture is reflected in the occurrence of violence in the family (Leppakoski, Flinck, & Paavilainen, 2015). A regular diet of violence appears on television screens, and parents often resort to power assertion as a disciplinary technique. In China, where physical punishment is rarely used to discipline children, the incidence of child abuse is reportedly very low.

The family itself is obviously a key part of the context of abuse (Diderich & others, 2014). Among the family and family-associated characteristics that may contribute to child maltreatment are parenting stress, substance abuse, social isolation, single parenting, and socioeconomic difficulties (especially poverty) (Cicchetti & Toth, 2015). The interactions of all family members should be considered, regardless of who performs the violent acts against the child (Kim & Cicchetti, 2004). For example, even though the father may be the one who physically abuses the child, contributions by the mother, the child, and siblings also should be evaluated.

Were parents who abuse children abused by their own parents? A 30-year longitudinal study found that offspring of parents who had engaged in child maltreatment and neglect are at risk for engaging in child neglect and sexual maltreatment themselves (Widom, Cazja, & Dumont, 2015). It is estimated that about one-third of parents who were abused when they were young abuse their own children (Cicchetti & Toth, 2015). Thus, some, but not a majority, of parents are locked into an intergenerational transmission of abuse (Dixon, Browne, & Hamilton-Giachritsis, 2005).

Child maltreatment involves grossly inadequate and destructive aspects of parenting.

—DANTE CICCHETTI
Contemporary developmental psychologist, University of Minnesota

child abuse The term used most often by the public and many professionals to refer to both abuse and neglect.

child maltreatment The term increasingly used by developmentalists in referring not only to abuse and neglect but also to diverse conditions.

physical abuse Infliction of physical injury by punching, beating, kicking, biting, burning, shaking, or otherwise harming a child.

child neglect Failure to provide for a child's basic needs, including physical, educational, or emotional needs.

sexual abuse Fondling a child's genitals, intercourse, incest, rape, sodomy, exhibitionism, and commercial exploitation through prostitution or the production of pornographic materials.

emotional abuse Acts or omissions by parents or other caregivers that have caused, or could cause, serious behavioral, cognitive, or emotional problems.

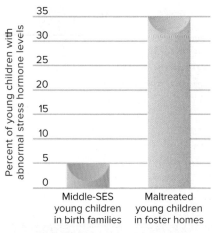

FIGURE 9

ABNORMAL STRESS HORMONE LEVELS IN YOUNG CHILDREN IN DIFFERENT TYPES OF REARING CONDITIONS

Developmental Consequences of Abuse Among the consequences of child maltreatment are poor emotion regulation, attachment problems, problems in peer relations, difficulty in adapting to school, and other psychological problems such as depression and delinquency during childhood and adolescence (Cicchetti & Banny, 2014; Cicchetti & Toth, 2015). As shown in Figure 9, maltreated young children in foster care were more likely to show abnormal stress hormone levels than middle-SES young children living with their birth family (Gunnar & Fisher, 2006). In this study, the abnormal stress hormone levels were mainly present in the foster children who experienced neglect, best described as "institutional neglect" (Fisher, 2005). Adolescents who experienced abuse or neglect as children are more likely than adolescents who were not maltreated as children to engage in violent romantic relationships, suicide attempts, delinquency, sexual risk taking, and substance abuse (Miller & others, 2013). Further, a recent study revealed that young adults who experienced child maltreatment, especially physical abuse, at any age were more likely to be depressed and engage in suicide ideation as adults (Dunn & others, 2013). In this study, child maltreatment at 3 to 5 years of age was associated more strongly with depression in early adulthood than other childhood age periods. And a recent study revealed that a significant increase in suicide attempts before age 18 occurred with repeated child maltreatment (Jonson-Reid, Kohl, & Drake, 2012).

Later, during the adult years, individuals who were maltreated as children are more likely to experience physical, emotional, and sexual problems (Lacelle & others, 2012). A 30-year longitudinal study found that middle-aged adults who had experienced child maltreatment had increased risk for diabetes, lung disease, malnutrition, and vision problems (Widom & others, 2012). Another study revealed that young adults who had experienced child maltreatment, especially physical abuse, at any age were more likely to be depressed and to engage in suicidal ideation as adults (Dunn & others, 2013). Further, adults who were maltreated as children often have difficulty establishing and maintaining healthy intimate relationships (Dozier, Stovall-McClough, & Albus, 2009). As adults, maltreated children are also at higher risk for violent behavior toward other adults—especially dating partners and marital partners—as well as for substance abuse, anxiety, and depression (Miller-Perrin, Perrin, & Kocur, 2009). One study also revealed that adults who had experienced child maltreatment were at increased risk for financial and employment-related difficulties (Zielinski, 2009).

An important research agenda is to discover how to prevent child maltreatment or intervene in children's lives when they have been maltreated (Petersen, Joseph, & Feit, 2014). In one study of maltreating mothers and their 1-year-olds, two treatments were effective in reducing child maltreatment: (1) home visitation that emphasized improved parenting, coping with stress, and increasing support for the mother; and (2) parent-infant psychotherapy that focused on improving maternal-infant attachment (Cicchetti, Toth, & Rogosch, 2005).

PARENT–ADOLESCENT AND PARENT–EMERGING ADULT RELATIONSHIPS

Even the best parents may find their relationship with their child strained during adolescence, yet attachment to parents is an important aspect of adolescent development. As individuals become emerging adults, their relationship with their parents changes.

Parent-Adolescent Relationships Important aspects of parent-adolescent relationships include autonomy/attachment and conflict. First, we explore the young adolescent's push for autonomy.

Autonomy and Attachment The young adolescent's push for autonomy and responsibility puzzles and angers many parents. Parents see their teenager slipping from their grasp. They may have an urge to assert stronger control as the adolescent seeks autonomy and responsibility. Heated emotional exchanges may ensue, with either side calling names, making threats, and doing whatever seems necessary to gain control. Most parents anticipate that their

> When I was a boy of 14, my father was so ignorant I could hardly stand to have the man around. But when I got to be 21, I was astonished at how much he had learnt in 7 years.

> —MARK TWAIN
> *American writer and humorist, 19th century*

teenager will have some difficulty adjusting to the changes that adolescence brings, but few parents can imagine and predict just how strong will be an adolescent's desire to spend time with peers or how much adolescents will want to show that it is they—not their parents—who are responsible for their successes and failures.

The ability to attain autonomy and gain control over one's behavior in adolescence is acquired through appropriate adult reactions to the adolescent's desire for control (McElhaney & Allen, 2012). At the onset of adolescence, the average individual does not have the knowledge to make mature decisions in all areas of life. As the adolescent pushes for autonomy, the wise adult relinquishes control in those areas in which the adolescent can make reasonable decisions but continues to guide the adolescent to make reasonable decisions in areas where the adolescent's knowledge is more limited. Gradually, adolescents acquire the ability to make mature decisions on their own (Laursen & Collins, 2009). In a recent study, young adolescents' perception that their parents promoted more psychological autonomy and less psychological control predicted fewer depressive symptoms two years later (Sher-Censor, Parke, & Coltrane, 2010).

Expectations about the appropriate timing of adolescent autonomy often vary across cultures, parents, and adolescents (McElhaney & Allen, 2012). For example, expectations for early autonomy on the part of adolescents are more prevalent in non-Latino Whites, single parents, and adolescents themselves than they are in Asian Americans or Latinos, married parents, and parents themselves (Feldman & Rosenthal, 1999). Nonetheless, although Latino cultures may place a stronger emphasis on parental authority and restrict adolescent autonomy, a recent study revealed that regardless of where they were born, Mexican-origin adolescent girls living in the United States expected autonomy at an earlier age than their mothers preferred (Bamaca-Colbert & others, 2012). Another recent study of Mexican immigrant mothers and their U.S.-raised 13- to 14-year-old daughters explored future autonomy expectations when the daughters reach 15 years of age (Romo, Mireles-Rios, & Lopez-Tello, 2014). In this study, the daughters hoped for less strict rules regarding social activities while mothers reported that they still expected to exert control, although they were willing to allow more autonomy in personal matters such as physical appearance and to allow the daughter to group date.

Gender differences characterize autonomy-granting in adolescence, with boys being given more independence than girls are allowed to have. In one study, this was especially true in those U.S. families with a traditional gender-role orientation (Bumpus, Crouter, & McHale, 2001). Even while adolescents seek autonomy, parent-child attachment remains important (Gorrese & Ruggieri, 2012). Mothers maintain closer emotional ties with adolescents, especially daughters, than fathers do (Collins & Steinberg, 2006).

One of the most widely discussed aspects of socioemotional development in infancy is secure attachment to caregivers (Thompson, 2015). In the past several decades, researchers have explored whether secure attachment also might be an important element in adolescents' relationships with their parents (de Vries & others, 2015; Glazebrook, Townsend, & Sayal, 2015; Kobak & Kerig, 2015; Zack & others, 2015). For example, Joseph Allen and his colleagues (2009) found that adolescents who were securely attached at age 14 were more likely to report at age 21 that they were in an exclusive relationship, comfortable with intimacy in relationships, and moving toward financial independence. In a recent analysis, it was concluded that the most consistent outcomes of secure attachment in adolescence involve positive peer relations and development of the adolescent's emotion regulation capacities (Allen & Miga, 2010). Recent research studies have found that adolescents who had attempted suicide were less securely attached to their mothers and fathers (Sheftall & others, 2013), and avoidant attachment predicted suicidal behavior in adolescents (Sheftall, Schoppe-Sullivan, & Bridge, 2014). Further, a recent study revealed that insecure attachment with mothers and fathers was linked to a lower level of parents' knowledge about adolescents' whereabouts (Jones & others, 2015).

Parent-Adolescent Conflict   Although attachment to parents may remain strong during adolescence, the connectedness is not always smooth. Early adolescence is a time when conflict with parents escalates (Laursen & Collins, 2009; Moed & others, 2015). Much of the conflict involves the everyday issues of family life, such as keeping a bedroom clean,

What strategies can parents use to guide adolescents in effectively handling their increased motivation for autonomy?
© Myrleen Pearson/PhotoEdit

developmental **connection**

Attachment

Securely attached infants use the caregiver as a secure base from which to explore the environment. Connect to "Emotional Development and Attachment."

Conflict with parents increases in early adolescence. *What is the nature of this conflict in a majority of American families?*
© BananaStock/PunchStock RF

dressing neatly, getting home by a certain time, and not talking incessantly on the phone. The conflicts rarely involve major dilemmas such as drugs and delinquency.

The increased conflict in early adolescence may be due to a number of factors: the biological changes of puberty, cognitive changes involving increased idealism and logical reasoning, social changes focused on independence and identity, maturational changes in parents, and expectations that are violated by parents and adolescents (Collins & Steinberg, 2006). Adolescents compare their parents with an ideal standard and then criticize their flaws. Many parents see their adolescent changing from a compliant child to someone who is noncompliant, oppositional, and resistant to parental standards. Also, early-maturing adolescents experience more conflict with their parents than do adolescents who mature late or on time (Collins & Steinberg, 2006).

It is not unusual to hear parents of young adolescents ask, "Is it ever going to get better?" Things usually do get better as adolescents move from early to late adolescence. Conflict with parents often escalates during early adolescence, remains somewhat stable during the high school years, and then lessens as the adolescent reaches 17 to 20 years of age. Parent-adolescent relationships become more positive if adolescents go away to college than if they live at home while attending college (Sullivan & Sullivan, 1980).

The everyday conflicts that characterize parent-adolescent relationships may serve a positive function. These minor disputes and negotiations facilitate the adolescent's transition from being dependent on parents to becoming an autonomous individual. For example, in one study, adolescents who expressed disagreement with their parents explored identity development more actively than did adolescents who did not express disagreement with their parents (Cooper & others, 1982). One way for parents to cope with the adolescent's push for independence and identity is to recognize that adolescence is a decade-long transitional period in the journey to adulthood, rather than an overnight accomplishment. Recognizing that conflict and negotiation can serve a positive developmental function can further tone down parental hostility. Understanding parent-adolescent conflict, though, is not simple (Riesch & others, 2003). A high degree of intense conflict characterizes some parent-adolescent relationships and if prolonged is associated with a number of adolescent problems, such as running away from home, juvenile delinquency, dropping out of school, adolescent pregnancy, and substance abuse (Fuligni, 2012; Rengasamy & others, 2013). For example, a recent study found that a higher level of parent-adolescent conflict was associated with higher levels of adolescent anxiety, depression, and aggression, and lower levels of self-esteem (Smokowski & others, 2015).

In sum, the old model of parent-adolescent relationships suggested that parent-adolescent conflict is intense and stressful throughout adolescence. The new model emphasizes that most parent-adolescent conflict is moderate rather than intense and that the moderate conflict can serve a positive function. Figure 10 summarizes the old and new models of parent-adolescent relationships, which include changes in thinking about attachment and autonomy.

Old Model

Autonomy, detachment from parents; parent and peer worlds are isolated

Intense, stressful conflict throughout adolescence; parent-adolescent relationships are filled with storm and stress on virtually a daily basis

New Model

Attachment and autonomy; parents are important support systems and attachment figures; adolescent-parent and adolescent-peer worlds have some important connections

Moderate parent-adolescent conflict is common and can serve a positive developmental function; conflict greater in early adolescence

FIGURE **10**

OLD AND NEW MODELS OF PARENT-ADOLESCENT RELATIONSHIPS
© BananaStock/PunchStock RF

Still, a high degree of conflict characterizes some parent-adolescent relationships. According to one estimate, parents and adolescents engage in prolonged, intense, repeated, unhealthy conflict in about one in five families (Montemayor, 1982). In other words, 4 to 5 million American families encounter serious, highly stressful parent-adolescent conflict. And this prolonged, intense conflict is associated with a number of adolescent problems—movement out of the home, juvenile delinquency, school dropout, pregnancy and early marriage, membership in religious cults, and drug abuse (Brook & others, 1990).

When families emigrate to another country, adolescents typically acculturate more quickly to the norms and values of their new country than do their parents (Fuligni, 2012). This likely occurs because of immigrant adolescents' exposure in school to the language and culture of the host country. The norms and values immigrant adolescents experience are especially likely to diverge from those of their parents in areas such as autonomy and romantic relationships. Such divergences are likely to increase parent-adolescent conflict in immigrant families. Andrew Fuligni (2012) argues that these conflicts aren't always expressed in open conflict but are often present in underlying, internal feelings. For example, immigrant adolescents may feel that their parents want them to give up their personal interests for the sake of the family, but the adolescents don't think this is fair. Such acculturation-based conflict focuses on issues related to core cultural values and is likely to occur in immigrant families, such as Latino and Asian American families, who come to the United States to live (Juang & Umana-Taylor, 2012).

Conclusions   We have seen that parents play very important roles in adolescent development. Although adolescents are moving toward independence, they still need to stay connected with families. Competent adolescent development is most likely when adolescents have parents who show them warmth and mutual respect, demonstrate sustained interest in their lives, recognize and adapt to their cognitive and socioemotional development, communicate expectations for high standards of conduct and achievement, and display constructive ways of dealing with problems and conflict (Small, 1990). These ideas coincide with Diana Baumrind's (1971, 1991, 2012) authoritative parenting style.

Emerging Adults' Relationships with Their Parents   For the most part, emerging adults' relationships with their parents improve when they leave home. They often grow closer psychologically to their parents and share more with them than they did before they left home (Arnett, 2007, 2015). However, challenges in the parent–emerging adult relationship involve the emerging adult's possessing adult status in many areas while still depending on parents in some manner (Fingerman, Cheng, & others, 2012; Swartz & others, 2011). Many emerging adults can make their own decisions about where to live, whether to stay in college, which lifestyle to adopt, whether to get married, and so on. At the same time, parents often provide support for their emerging adult children even after they leave home. This might be accomplished through loans and monetary gifts for education or purchase of a car, financial contributions to living arrangements, and emotional support.

In successful emerging adulthood, individuals separate from their parents without cutting off ties completely or fleeing to some substitute emotional refuge. Complete cutoff from parents rarely solves emotional problems. Emerging adulthood is a time for young people to sort out emotionally what they will take along from the family of origin, what they will leave behind, and what they will create.

The vast majority of studies of parenting have focused on outcomes for children and adolescents and have involved mothers rather than fathers. A recent study revealed that parents act as "scaffolding" and "safety nets" to support their children's successful transition through emerging adulthood (Swartz & others, 2011).

WORKING PARENTS

More than one of every two U.S. mothers with a child under the age of 5 is in the labor force; more than two of every three with a child from 6 to 17 years of age work outside the home. Maternal employment is a part of modern life, but its effects continue to be debated.

According to one adolescent girl, Stacey Christensen, age 16: "I am lucky enough to have open communication with my parents. Whenever I am in need or just need to talk, my parents are there for me. My advice to parents is to let your teens grow at their own pace, be open with them so that you can be there for them. We need guidance; our parents need to help but not be too overwhelming."
© Stockbyte/Getty Images RF

What are some strategies that can benefit the relationship between emerging adults and their parents?
© Comstock Images/Getty Images RF

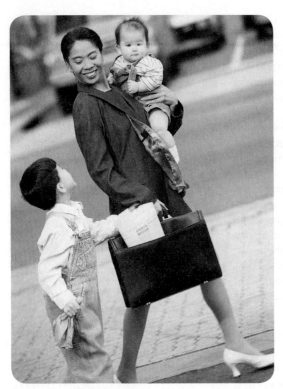

How does work affect parenting?
© Photodisc Collection/Getty Images RF

developmental **connection**

Social Contexts

Research consistently shows that family factors are considerably better at predicting children's developmental outcomes than are child-care experiences. Connect to "Emotional Development and Attachment."

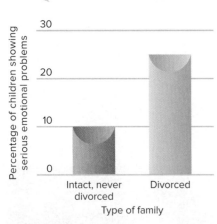

FIGURE 11

DIVORCE AND CHILDREN'S EMOTIONAL PROBLEMS. In Hetherington's research, 25 percent of children from divorced families showed serious emotional problems compared with only 10 percent of children from intact, never-divorced families. However, keep in mind that a substantial majority (75 percent) of the children from divorced families did not show serious emotional problems.

Most research on parental work has focused on young children and the mother's employment (Brooks-Gunn, Han, & Waldfogel, 2010). However, the effects of parental work involve the father as well as the mother when matters such as work schedules, work-family stress, and unemployment are considered (Clarke-Stewart & Parke, 2014; O'Brien & others, 2014). Recent research indicates that the nature of parents' work matters more to children than whether one parent works outside the home (Clarke-Stewart & Parke, 2014; Goodman & others, 2011). And a recent study of almost 3,000 adolescents found a negative association between the father's, but not the mother's, unemployment and the adolescents' health (Bacikova-Sleskova, Benka, & Orosova, 2014).

Work can have positive and negative effects on parenting (Crouter & McHale, 2005). Ann Crouter (2006) described how parents bring their experiences at work into their homes. She concluded that parents who have poor working conditions, such as long hours, overtime work, stressful work, and lack of autonomy on the job, are likely to be more irritable at home and to engage in less effective parenting than their counterparts who have better working conditions at their jobs. A consistent finding is that children (especially girls) of working mothers engage in less gender stereotyping and have more egalitarian views of gender (Goldberg & Lucas-Thompson, 2008). Also, a recent study revealed that mothers' positive mood after work was linked with adolescents' reports of more positive affect, better sleep quality, and longer sleep duration (Lawson & others, 2014). Further, this study indicated that mothers with more positive work experiences had adolescents who reported less negative affect and fewer physical health problems.

CHILDREN IN DIVORCED FAMILIES

It is estimated that 40 percent of children born to married parents in the United States will experience their parents' divorce (Hetherington & Stanley-Hagan, 2002). Let's examine some important questions about children in divorced families:

Are children better adjusted in intact, never-divorced families than in divorced families? Most researchers agree that children from divorced families show poorer adjustment than their counterparts in nondivorced families (Amato & Anthony, 2014; Arkes, 2015; Braver & Lamb, 2013; Hetherington, 2006; Lansford, 2012, 2013; Robbers & others, 2012; Wallerstein, 2008; Weaver & Schofield, 2015) (see Figure 11). Those who have experienced multiple divorces are at greater risk. Children in divorced families are more likely than children in nondivorced families to have academic problems, to show externalized problems (such as acting out and delinquency) and internalized problems (such as anxiety and depression), to be less socially responsible, to have less competent intimate relationships, to drop out of school, to become sexually active at an earlier age, to take drugs, to associate with antisocial peers, to have low self-esteem, and to be less securely attached as young adults (Lansford, 2009, 2013). In a recent study, individuals who had experienced their parents' divorce were at higher lifetime risk for engaging in a suicide attempt (Alonzo & others, 2014). One study revealed that adolescent girls with divorced parents were especially vulnerable to developing symptoms of depression (Oldehinkel & others, 2008). Nonetheless, keep in mind that a majority of children in divorced families do not have significant adjustment problems (Ahrons, 2007). One study found that 20 years after their parents had divorced when they were children, approximately 80 percent of adults concluded that their parents' decision to divorce had been a wise one (Ahrons, 2004).

However, a recent study concluded that childhood divorce was linked to an increased number of cohabiting/marital partnerships and negative partner relationships the children had from 16 to 30 years of age (Fergusson, McLeod, & Horwood, 2014). An important point is that the outcomes just described for the life event of childhood divorce was explained by a variety of other factors and social contexts—parental history of illicit drug use, experience of childhood sexual abuse, lower-SES status at the child's birth, and parental history of criminality.

Note that marital conflict may have negative consequences for children in the context of marriage or divorce (Cummings & Davies, 2010). A longitudinal study revealed that conflict

in nondivorced families was associated with emotional problems in children (Amato, 2006). Indeed, many of the problems that children from divorced homes experience begin during the predivorce period, a time when parents are often in active conflict with each other. Thus, when children from divorced homes show problems, the problems may be due not only to the divorce but also to the marital conflict that led to it (Thompson, 2008).

E. Mark Cummings and his colleagues (Cummings, El-Sheikh, & Kouros, 2009; Cummings & Miller, 2015; Cummings & others, 2012; Cummings & Valentino, 2015; Koss & others, 2013, 2014; Yan, Cheung, & Cummings, 2015) have proposed *emotional security theory*, which has its roots in attachment theory and states that children appraise marital conflict in terms of their sense of security and safety in the family. These researchers make a distinction between marital conflict that is negative for children (such as hostile emotional displays and destructive conflict tactics) and marital conflict that can be positive for children (such as marital disagreement that involves a calm discussion of each person's perspective and working together to reach a solution). In a recent study, Cummings and his colleagues (2012) found that parental conflict in their children's kindergarten year was linked to children's emotional insecurity later in childhood, which in turn was associated with adolescent adjustment, including higher levels of depression and anxiety.

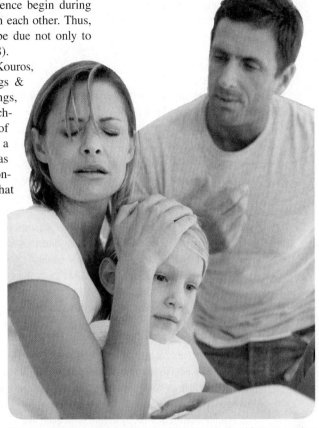

What concerns are involved in whether parents should stay together for the sake of the children or become divorced?
© Image Source/PunchStock/Getty Images RF

Should parents stay together for the sake of the children?

Whether parents should stay in an unhappy or conflicted marriage for the sake of their children is one of the most commonly asked questions about divorce (Deutsch & Pruett, 2009; Hetherington, 2006; Ziol-Guest, 2009). If the stresses and disruptions in family relationships associated with an unhappy, conflictual marriage that erode the well-being of children are reduced by the move to a divorced, single-parent family, divorce can be advantageous. However, if the diminished resources and increased risks associated with divorce also are accompanied by inept parenting and sustained or increased conflict, not only between the divorced couple but also among the parents, children, and siblings, the best choice for the children would be that an unhappy marriage be retained (Hetherington & Stanley-Hagan, 2002). It is difficult to determine how these "ifs" will play out when parents either remain together in an acrimonious marriage or become divorced.

How much do family processes matter in divorced families?

In divorced families, family processes matter a great deal (Braver & Lamb, 2013; Hetherington, 2006; Lansford, 2012, 2013; Narayan & others, 2015; Warshak, 2014). When the divorced parents have a harmonious relationship and use authoritative parenting, the adjustment of adolescents is improved (Hetherington, 2006). When the divorced parents can agree on child-rearing strategies and can maintain a cordial relationship with each other, frequent visits by the non-custodial parent usually benefit the child (Fabricius & others, 2010). Following a divorce, father involvement with children drops off more than mother involvement, especially for fathers of girls. In a recent study, children were more likely to have behavior problems if their post-divorce home environment was less supportive and stimulating, their mother was less sensitive and more depressed, and if their household income was lower (Weaver & Schofield, 2015). Also, a recent study in divorced families revealed that an intervention focused on improving the mother-child relationship was linked to improvements in relationship quality that increased children's coping skills over the short term (6 months) and long term (6 years) (Velez & others, 2011).

What factors influence an individual child's vulnerability to suffering negative consequences as a result of living in a divorced family?

Among the factors involved in the child's risk and vulnerability are the child's adjustment prior to the divorce, as well as the child's personality and temperament, and the custody situation (Hetherington, 2006). Children whose parents later divorce show poorer adjustment before the breakup (Amato & Booth, 1996). Children who are socially mature and responsible, who show few behavioral problems, and who have an easy temperament are better able to cope

As marriage has become a more optional, less permanent institution in contemporary America, children and adolescents are encountering stresses and adaptive challenges associated with their parents' marital transitions.

—E. MAVIS HETHERINGTON
Contemporary psychologist, University of Virginia

Communicating with Children About Divorce

Ellen Galinsky and Judy David (1988) developed a number of guidelines for communicating with children about divorce:

- *Explain the separation.* As soon as daily activities in the home make it obvious that one parent is leaving, tell the children. If possible, both parents should be present when children are told about the separation to come. The reasons for the separation are very difficult for young children to understand. No matter what parents tell children, children can find reasons to argue against the separation. It is extremely important for parents to let the children know who will take care of them and to describe the specific arrangements for seeing the other parent.

- *Explain that the separation is not the child's fault.* Young children often believe their parents' separation or divorce is their own fault. Therefore, it is important to tell children that they are not the cause of the separation. Parents need to repeat this point a number of times.

- *Explain that it may take time to feel better.* Tell young children that it's normal not to feel good about what is happening and that many other children feel this way when their parents become separated. It is also okay for divorced parents to share some of their emotions with children, by saying something like "I'm having

a hard time since the separation just like you, but I know it's going to get better after a while." Such statements are best kept brief and should not criticize the other parent.

- *Keep the door open for further discussion.* Tell your children to come to you any time they want to talk about the separation. It is healthy for children to express their pent-up emotions in discussions with their parents and to learn that the parents are willing to listen to their feelings and fears.

- *Provide as much continuity as possible.* The less children's worlds are disrupted by the separation, the easier their transition to a single-parent family will be. This guideline means maintaining the rules already in place as much as possible. Children need parents who care enough not only to give them warmth and nurturance but also to set reasonable limits.

- *Provide support for your children and yourself.* After a divorce or separation, parents are as important to children as they were before the divorce or separation. Divorced parents need to provide children with as much support as possible. Parents function best when other people are available to give them support as adults and as parents. Divorced parents can find people who provide practical help and with whom they can talk about their problems.

How well do these strategies complement E. Mavis Hetherington's six strategies for divorced adults, discussed earlier in this chapter?

---

with their parents' divorce. Children with a difficult temperament often have problems coping with their parents' divorce (Hetherington, 2006). In a recent study, higher levels of predivorce maternal sensitivity and child IQ served as protective factors in reducing child problems after the divorce (Weaver & Schofield, 2015). Joint custody works best for children when the parents can get along with each other (Clarke-Stewart & Parke, 2014).

What role does socioeconomic status play in the lives of children in divorced families? Custodial mothers experience the loss of about one-fourth to one-half of their predivorce income, in comparison with a loss of only one-tenth by custodial fathers (Emery, 1999). This income loss for divorced mothers is accompanied by increased workloads, high rates of job instability, and residential moves to less desirable neighborhoods with inferior schools (Braver & Lamb, 2013). A recent study found that children from families with higher incomes before the separation/divorce had fewer internalizing problems (Weaver & Schofield, 2015).

In sum, many factors affect how divorce influences a child's development (Hetherington, 2006; Warshak, 2014). To read about some strategies for helping children cope with the divorce of their parents, see the *Connecting Development to Life* interlude.

STEPFAMILIES

Not only are parents divorcing more, they are also getting remarried more (Ganong, Coleman, & Russell, 2015; van Eeden-Moorefield & Pasley, 2013). The number of remarriages involving children has grown steadily in recent years. About half of all children whose parents divorce will have a stepparent within four years of parental separation. However, divorces occur at a 10 percent higher rate in remarriages than in first marriages (Cherlin & Furstenberg, 1994).

In some cases, the stepfamily may have been preceded by the death of the spouse. However, by far the largest number of stepfamilies are preceded by divorce rather than death.

Three common types of stepfamily structure are (1) stepfather, (2) stepmother, and (3) blended or complex. In stepfather families, the mother typically had custody of the children and remarried, introducing a stepfather into her children's lives. In stepmother families, the father usually had custody and remarried, introducing a stepmother into his children's lives. In a blended or complex stepfamily, both parents bring children from previous marriages to live in the newly formed stepfamily.

In E. Mavis Hetherington's (2006) most recent longitudinal analyses, children and adolescents who had been in a simple stepfamily (stepfather or stepmother) for a number of years were adjusting better than in the early years of the remarried family and were functioning well in comparison with children and adolescents in conflictual nondivorced families and children and adolescents in complex (blended) stepfamilies. More than 75 percent of the adolescents in long-established simple stepfamilies described their relationships with their stepparents as "close" or "very close." Hetherington (2006) concluded that in long-established simple stepfamilies, adolescents seem eventually to benefit from the presence of a stepparent and the resources provided by the stepparent.

How does living in a stepfamily influence a child's development?
© Todd Wright/Blend Images/Getty Images RF

Children often have better relationships with their custodial parents (mothers in stepfather families, fathers in stepmother families) than with stepparents (Santrock, Sitterle, & Warshak, 1988). Also, children in simple stepfamilies (stepmother, stepfather) often show better adjustment than their counterparts in complex (blended) stepfamilies (Anderson & others, 1999; Hetherington & Kelly, 2002).

As in divorced families, children in stepfamilies show more adjustment problems than children in nondivorced families (Hetherington & Kelly, 2002). The adjustment problems are similar to those found among children of divorced parents—academic problems and lower self-esteem, for example (Anderson & others, 1999). However, it is important to recognize that a majority of children in stepfamilies do not have problems. In one analysis, 25 percent of children from stepfamilies showed adjustment problems compared with 10 percent in intact, never-divorced families (Hetherington & Kelly, 2002). Adolescence is an especially difficult time in stepfamilies (Anderson & others, 1999). This difficulty may occur because becoming part of a stepfamily exacerbates normal adolescent concerns about identity, sexuality, and autonomy.

GAY AND LESBIAN PARENTS

Increasingly, gay and lesbian couples are creating families that include children (Patterson, 2013, 2014; Patterson & D'Augelli, 2013; Patterson & Farr, 2014; Patterson, Farr, & Hastings, 2015) (see Figure 12). Approximately 33 percent of lesbian couples and 23 percent of gay couples are parents (Patterson, 2004). There may be more than 1 million gay and lesbian parents in the United States today.

An important aspect of gay and lesbian families with children is the sexual identity of parents at the time of a child's birth or adoption (Patterson, 2013, 2014). The largest group of children with gay and lesbian parents are likely those who were born in the context of heterosexual relationships, with one or both parents only later identifying themselves as gay or lesbian. Gay and lesbian parents may be single or they may have same-gender partners. In addition, gays and lesbians are increasingly choosing parenthood through donor insemination or adoption. Researchers have found that the children created through new reproductive technologies—such as in vitro fertilization—are as well adjusted as their counterparts conceived by natural means (Golombok, 2011a, b; Golombok & Tasker, 2010).

Earlier in the chapter, we describe the positive outcomes of coparenting for children. A recent study compared the incidence of coparenting in adoptive heterosexual, lesbian, and gay couples with preschool-aged children (Farr & Patterson, 2013). Both self-reports and observations found that lesbian and gay couples shared child care more than heterosexual couples, with lesbian couples being the most supportive and gay couples the least supportive. Further, a recent study revealed more positive parenting in adoptive gay father families

FIGURE 12

PERCENTAGE OF GAY AND LESBIAN COUPLES WITH CHILDREN: 1990 AND 2000. *Why do you think more lesbian couples have children than gay couples?*

developmental **connection**

Sexuality

Regardless of sexual orientation, most males and females emphasize the importance of affection, trust, and shared interests in a relationship. Connect to "Gender and Sexuality."

and fewer child externalizing problems in these families than in heterosexual families (Golombok & others, 2014).

Another issue focuses on custody arrangements for adolescents. Many gays and lesbians have lost custody of their adolescents to heterosexual spouses following divorce. For this reason, many gay fathers and lesbian mothers are noncustodial parents.

Researchers have found few differences between children growing up with gay fathers and lesbian mothers and children growing up with heterosexual parents (Patterson, 2013, 2014; Patterson & others, 2015). For example, children growing up in gay or lesbian families are just as popular with their peers, and there are no differences between the adjustment and mental health of children living in these families and children living in heterosexual families (Hyde & DeLamater, 2014). Also, the overwhelming majority of children growing up in a gay or lesbian family have a heterosexual orientation (Golombok & Tasker, 2010).

ADOPTIVE PARENTS AND ADOPTED CHILDREN

Another variation in the type of family in which children live involves adoption, the social and legal process by which a parent-child relationship is established between persons unrelated at birth (Fisher, 2015). As we see next, an increase in diversity has characterized the adoption of children in the United States in recent years.

The Increased Diversity of Adopted Children and Adoptive Parents A number of changes have characterized adoptive children and adoptive parents in the last three to four decades (Brodzinsky & Pinderhughes, 2002; Kim, Reichwald, & Lee, 2013). In the first half of the twentieth century, most U.S. adopted children were healthy, non-Latino White infants who were adopted at birth or soon after; however, in recent decades as abortion became legal and contraception increased, fewer of these infants became available for adoption. Increasingly, U.S. couples have adopted a much wider diversity of children—from other countries, from other ethnic groups, children with physical and/or mental problems, and children who had been neglected or abused (Kim, Reichwald, & Lee, 2013).

Changes also have characterized adoptive parents in the last three to four decades (Brodzinsky & Pinderhughes, 2002). In the first half of the twentieth century, most adoptive parents were people from non-Latino White middle or upper socioeconomic status backgrounds who were married and did not have any type of disability. However, in recent decades, increased diversity has characterized adoptive parents. Many adoption agencies today have no income requirements for adoptive parents and now allow adults from a wide range of backgrounds to adopt children, including single adults, gay and lesbian adults, and older adults. Further, many adoptions involve other family members (such as aunts, uncles, or grandparents); currently, 30 percent of U.S. adoptive placements are with relatives (Ledesma, 2012). And slightly more than 50 percent of U.S. adoptions occur through the foster care system; recently, more than 100,000 children in the U.S. foster care system were waiting for someone to adopt them (Ledesma, 2012).

Three pathways to adoption are (1) domestic adoption from the public welfare system, (2) domestic infant adoption through private agencies and intermediaries, and (3) international adoption (Grotevant & McDermott, 2014). In the next decade, the mix of U.S. adoptions is likely to include fewer domestic infant and international adoptions and more adoptions via the child welfare system (Grotevant & McDermott, 2014).

The changes in adoption practice over the last several decades make it difficult to generalize about the average adopted child or average adoptive parent (Woolgar & Scott, 2013). As we see next, though, some researchers have provided useful comparisons between adopted children and nonadopted children and their families.

An increasing number of Hollywood celebrities are adopting children from developing countries. Actress Angelina Jolie (*above*) carrying adopted daughter Zahara with adopted sons Maddox and Pax alongside them.
© Jackson Lee/Tom Meinelt/Newscom

Developmental Outcomes for Adopted and Nonadopted Children How do adopted children fare after they are adopted? A recent research review concluded that adopted children are at higher risk for externalizing (aggression and conduct problems, for example), internalizing (anxiety and depression, for example), and attention problems (ADHD, for example) (Grotevant & McDermott, 2014). However, a majority of adopted children and adolescents (including those adopted at older ages, transracially, and across national borders) adjust effectively, and their parents report considerable satisfaction with their decision to adopt (Brodzinsky & Pinderhughes, 2002; Castle & others, 2010).

An ongoing issue in adopting children is whether there should be any connection with children's biological parents (Farr & others, 2014). Open adoption involves sharing identifying information and having contact with the biological parents, versus closed adoption, which consists of not having such sharing and contact. Most adoption agencies today offer adoptive parents the opportunity to have either an open or a closed adoption. A longitudinal study found that when their adopted children reached adulthood, adoptive parents described open adoption positively and saw it as serving the child's best interests (Siegel, 2013). Another longitudinal study found that birth mothers, adoptive parents, and birth children who had contact were more satisfied with their arrangements than those who did not have contact (Grotevant & others, 2013). Also, in this study, contact was linked to more optimal adjustment for adolescents and emerging adults (Grotevant & others, 2013). Further, birth mothers who were more satisfied with their contact arrangements had less unresolved grief 12 to 20 years after placement.

What are some strategies for parenting adopted children at different points in their development?
© Photodisc/Getty Images RF

Parenting Adopted Children   Many of the keys to effectively parenting adopted children are no different from those for effectively parenting biological children: be supportive and caring; be involved and monitor the child's behavior and whereabouts; be a good communicator; and help the child learn to develop self-control. However, parents of adopted children face some unique circumstances. They need to recognize the differences involved in adoptive family life, communicate about these differences, show respect for the birth family, and support the child's search for self and identity.

Because many children begin to ask where they came from when they are about 4 to 6 years old, this is a natural time for parents to begin talking in simple ways to children about their adoption status (Warshak, 2008). Some parents (although not as many as in the past) decide not to tell their children about the adoption. This secrecy may create psychological risks for the child if he or she later finds out about the adoption.

Review Connect Reflect

LG3 Characterize parenting and how it affects children's development

Review
- What are some parental roles?
- What are four main parenting styles? Which parenting style is most often linked with children's social competence? Is physical punishment a wise choice by parents? Does coparenting have positive effects on children? What is the nature of child maltreatment?
- How can parent–adolescent relationships and parent–emerging adult relationships be described?
- What are the effects of working parents on children's development?
- How does divorce affect children's development?
- What influence does growing up in a stepfamily have on children's development?
- What characterizes gay and lesbian parenting?

- How do the lives of adoptive parents and adopted children differ from the lives of nonadoptive parents and nonadopted children?

Connect
- How does what you learned about working parents in this chapter connect with the discussion of child care in the chapter on "Emotional Development"?

Reflect *Your Own Personal Journey of Life*
- What characterized your relationship with your parents during middle school and high school? Has your relationship with your parents changed since then? Does it involve less conflict? What do you think are the most important aspects of parenting adolescents competently?

As important as child-parent relationships are to children's development, other family relationships are also important. Here we briefly examine sibling relationships, grandparenting and great-grandparenting, and intergenerational relationships.

SIBLING RELATIONSHIPS AND BIRTH ORDER

What are sibling relationships like? How extensively does birth order influence behavior?

Sibling Relationships Approximately 80 percent of American children have one or more siblings—that is, sisters and brothers (Dunn, 2007, 2015). If you grew up with siblings, you probably have a rich memory of aggressive, hostile interchanges. Siblings in the presence of each other when they are 2 to 4 years of age, on average, have a conflict once every 10 minutes, and then the conflicts decrease somewhat from 5 to 7 years of age (Kramer, 2006). What do parents do when they encounter siblings having a verbal or physical confrontation? One study revealed that they do one of three things: (1) intervene and try to help them resolve the conflict, (2) admonish or threaten them, or (3) do nothing at all (Kramer & Perozynski, 1999). Of interest is that in families with two siblings 2 to 5 years of age, the most frequent parental reaction is to do nothing at all. A recent review concluded that sibling relationships in adolescence are more egalitarian and not as close or as intense as sibling relationships during childhood (East, 2009). Indeed, beginning in adolescence, sibling companionship begins to decline in many cultures as boys and girls become increasingly involved in the world beyond their family (McHale, Updegraff, & Whiteman, 2013).

Negative aspects of sibling relationships, such as high conflict, are linked to negative outcomes for children and adolescents (Dunn, 2015). The negative outcomes can develop not only through conflict but also through direct modeling of a sibling's behavior, as when a younger sibling has an older sibling who has poor study habits and engages in delinquent behavior. By contrast, close and supportive sibling relationships can buffer the negative effects of stressful circumstances in children's and adolescents' lives.

Laurie Kramer (2006), who conducted a number of research studies on siblings, says that not intervening and letting sibling conflict escalate is not a good strategy. She developed a program titled "More Fun with Sisters and Brothers," which teaches 4- to 8-year-old siblings social skills for carrying out positive interactions (Kramer & Radey, 1997). Among the social skills taught in the program are how to appropriately initiate play, how to accept and refuse invitations to play, how to take another's perspective, how to deal with angry feelings, and how to manage conflict.

However, conflict is only one of the many dimensions of sibling relations (Buist, Dekovic, & Prinzie, 2013; Dunn, 2015; Feinberg & others, 2013; Howe, Ross, & Recchia, 2011; McHale, Updegraff, & Whiteman, 2013). Sibling relationships include helping, sharing, teaching, fighting, and playing, and siblings can act as emotional supports, rivals, and communication partners. One study found that adolescent siblings spent an average of 10 hours a week together, with an average of 12 percent of that time spent in constructive pursuits (creative activities such as art, music, and hobbies; sports; religious activities; and games) and 25 percent in nonconstructive activities (watching TV and hanging out) (Tucker, McHale, & Crouter, 2003).

Judy Dunn (2007, 2015), a leading expert on sibling relationships, described three important characteristics of sibling relationships:

· *Emotional quality of the relationship.* Intense positive and negative emotions are often expressed by siblings toward each other. Many children and adolescents have mixed feelings toward their siblings.

What characterizes children's sibling relationships?
(all): © RubberBall Productions/Getty Images RF

- *Familiarity and intimacy of the relationship.* Siblings typically know each other very well, and this intimacy suggests that they can either provide support or tease and undermine each other, depending on the situation.
- *Variation of the relationship.* Some siblings describe their relationships more positively than others. Thus, there is considerable variation in sibling relationships. We've indicated that many siblings have mixed feelings about each other, but some children and adolescents mainly describe their sibling in warm, affectionate ways, whereas others primarily talk about how irritating and mean a sibling is.

Do parents usually favor one sibling over others—and if so, does it make a difference in an adolescent's development? One study of 384 adolescent sibling pairs revealed that 65 percent of their mothers and 70 percent of their fathers showed favoritism toward one sibling (Shebloski, Conger, & Widaman, 2005). When favoritism of one sibling occurred, it was linked to lower self-esteem and sadness in the less-favored sibling. Indeed, equality and fairness are major concerns of siblings' relationships with each other and how they are treated by their parents (Campione-Barr, 2011; Campione-Barr, Greer, & Kruse, 2013; Campione-Barr & Smetana, 2010).

What role might sibling conflict play in adolescent development? High levels of sibling conflict and low levels of sibling warmth can be detrimental to adolescent development. A recent meta-analysis found that less sibling conflict and higher sibling warmth were associated with fewer internalizing and externalizing problems (Buist, Dekovic, & Prinzie, 2013).

In some instances, siblings may be stronger socializing influences on the child than parents are (Cicirelli, 1994). Someone close in age to the child—such as a sibling—may be able to understand the child's problems and communicate more effectively than parents can. In dealing with peers, coping with difficult teachers, and discussing taboo subjects such as sex, siblings may have more influence than parents.

Is sibling interaction the same around the world? In industrialized societies such as the United States, parents tend to delegate responsibility for younger siblings to older siblings primarily to give the parents freedom to pursue other activities. However, in nonindustrialized countries such as Kenya, the older sibling's role as a caregiver to younger siblings has much more importance. In industrialized countries, the older sibling's caregiving role is often discretionary; in nonindustrialized countries, it is more obligatory (Cicirelli, 1994).

Birth Order   Whether a child has older or younger siblings has been linked to development of certain personality characteristics. For example, one review concluded that "firstborns are the most intelligent, achieving, and conscientious, while later-borns are the most rebellious, liberal, and agreeable" (Paulhus, 2008, p. 210). Compared with later-born children, firstborn children have also been described as more adult-oriented, helpful, conforming, and self-controlled. However, when such birth-order differences are reported, they often are small.

What might account for even small differences related to birth order? Proposed explanations usually point to variations in interactions with parents and siblings associated with being in a specific position in the family. This is especially true in the case of the firstborn child (Teti, 2001). The oldest child is the only one who does not have to share parental love and affection with other siblings—until another sibling comes along. An infant requires more attention than an older child; thus the firstborn sibling receives less attention after the newborn arrives. Does this result in conflict between parents and the firstborn? In one research study, mothers became more negative, coercive, and restraining and played less with the firstborn following the birth of a second child (Dunn & Kendrick, 1982).

What is the only child like? The popular conception is that the only child is a "spoiled brat" with undesirable characteristics such as dependency, lack of self-control, and self-centered behavior. But researchers present a more positive portrayal of the only child. Only children often are achievement-oriented and display a desirable personality, especially in comparison with later-borns and children from large families (Falbo & Poston, 1993).

So far, our discussion suggests that birth order might be a strong predictor of behavior. However, an increasing number of family researchers stress that when all of the factors that influence behavior are considered, birth order by itself shows limited ability to predict behavior.

Think about some of the other important factors in children's lives beyond birth order that influence their behavior. They include heredity, models of competency or incompetency that parents present to children on a daily basis, peer influences, school influences, socioeconomic

The one-child family is becoming much more common in China because of the strong motivation to limit the population growth in the People's Republic of China. The policy is still relatively new, and its effects on children have not been fully examined. *In general, though, what have researchers found the only child to be like?*
© Image Source/Getty Images RF

factors, sociohistorical factors, and cultural variations. When someone says firstborns are always like this but last-borns are always like that, the person is making overly simplistic statements that do not adequately take into account the complexity of influences on a child's development.

Sibling Relationships in Adulthood   Sibling relationships persist over the entire life span for most adults (Bedford, 2009). Eighty-five percent of today's adults have at least one living sibling. Sibling relationships in adulthood may be extremely close, apathetic, or highly rivalrous, but the majority of sibling relationships in adulthood have been found to be close (Cicirelli, 2009). Those siblings who are psychologically close to each other in adulthood tended to be that way in childhood. It is rare for sibling closeness to develop for the first time in adulthood (Dunn, 1984). A recent study revealed that adult siblings often provide practical and emotional support to each other (Voorpostel & Blieszner, 2008).

GRANDPARENTING AND GREAT-GRANDPARENTING

The increase in longevity is influencing the nature of grandparenting (Dunifon, 2013). In 1900 only 4 percent of 10-year-old children had four living grandparents. but in 2000 that figure had risen to more than 40 percent. And in 1990 only about 20 percent of adults 30 years of age had living grandparents, a figure that is projected to increase to 80 percent in 2020 (Hagestad & Uhlenberg, 2007). Further increases in longevity are likely to support this trend in the future, although the current trend of delaying childbearing is likely to undermine it (Szinovacz, 2009).

Grandparent Roles   Grandparents play important roles in the lives of many grandchildren (de Toledo & Brown, 2013; Dunifon, 2013; Newton & Stewart, 2012; Patterson & others, 2015). Many adults become grandparents for the first time during middle age. Researchers have consistently found that grandmothers have more contact with grandchildren than do grandfathers (Watson, Randolph, & Lyons, 2005). Perhaps women tend to define their role as grandmothers as part of their responsibility for maintaining ties between family members across generations. Men may have fewer expectations about the grandfather role and see it as more voluntary.

Three prominent meanings are attached to being a grandparent (Neugarten & Weinstein, 1964). For some older adults, being a grandparent is a source of biological reward and continuity. For others, being a grandparent is a source of emotional self-fulfillment, generating feelings of companionship and satisfaction that may have been missing in earlier adult-child relationships. And for yet others, being a grandparent is a remote role.

The grandparent role may have different functions in different families, in different ethnic groups and cultures, and in different situations (Szinovacz, 2009). For example, in one study of White, African American, and Mexican American grandparents and grandchildren, the Mexican American grandparents saw their grandchildren more frequently, provided more support for the grandchildren and their parents, and had more satisfying relationships with their grandchildren (Bengtson, 1985). And in a study of three generations of families in Chicago, grandmothers had closer relationships with their children and grandchildren and gave more personal advice than grandfathers did (Hagestad, 1985).

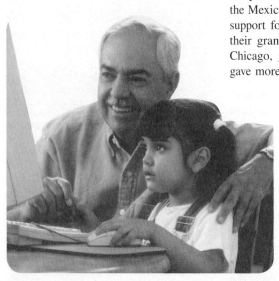

What is the changing profile of grandparents in the United States?
© Jose Luis Pelaez, Inc./Corbis

The Changing Profile of Grandparents   In 2009, 7.8 million children lived with at least one grandparent, a 64 percent increase since 1981 when 4.7 million children were living with at least one grandparent (U.S. Census Bureau, 2011). Divorce, adolescent pregnancies, and drug use by parents are the main reasons that grandparents are thrust back into the "parenting" role they thought they had shed (de Toledo & Brown, 2013). One study revealed that grandparent involvement was linked with better adjustment when it occurred in single-parent and stepparent families than in two-parent biological families (Attar-Schwartz & others, 2009).

Grandparents who are full-time caregivers for grandchildren are at elevated risk for health problems, depression, and stress (Silverstein, 2009). A recent review concluded that grandparents raising grandchildren are especially at risk for developing depression (Hadfield, 2014).

Caring for grandchildren is linked with these problems in part because full-time grandparent caregivers are often characterized by low-income minority status, and by not being married (Minkler & Fuller-Thompson, 2005). Grandparents who are part-time caregivers are less likely to have the negative health profiles that full-time grandparent caregivers have. In a recent study of part-time grandparent caregivers, few negative effects on grandparents were found (Hughes & others, 2007).

As divorce and remarriage have become more common, a special concern of grandparents is visitation privileges with their grandchildren. In the last 10 to 15 years, more states have passed laws giving grandparents the right to petition a court for visitation privileges with their grandchildren, even if a parent objects. Whether such forced visitation rights for grandparents are in the child's best interest is still being debated.

Great-Grandparenting   Because of increased longevity, more grandparents today than in the past are also great-grandparents. At the turn of the previous century, the three-generation family was common, but now the four-generation family is common. One contribution of great-grandparents is to transmit family history by telling their children, grandchildren, and great-grandchildren where the family came from, what their members achieved, what they endured, and how their lives changed over the years (Harris, 2002).

There has been little research on great-grandparenting. One study examined the relationship between young adults and their grandparents and great-grandparents (Roberto & Skoglund, 1996). The young adults interacted with and participated in more activities with their grandparents than with their great-grandparents. They also perceived their grandparents to have a more defined role and to be more influential in their lives than great-grandparents.

At the beginning of the twentieth century, the three-generation family was common, but now the four-generation family is common as well. Thus, an increasing number of grandparents are also great-grandparents. The four-generation family shown here is the Jordans—author John Santrock's mother-in-law, daughter, granddaughter, and wife.
Courtesy of Dr. John Santrock

INTERGENERATIONAL RELATIONSHIPS

Family is important to most people. When 21,000 adults aged 40 to 79 in 21 countries were asked, "When you think of who you are, you think mainly of _____," 63 percent said "family," 9 percent said "religion," and 8 percent said "work" (HSBC Insurance, 2007). In this study, in all 21 countries, middle-aged and older adults expressed a strong feeling of responsibility between generations in their family, with the strongest intergenerational ties indicated in Saudi Arabia, India, and Turkey. More than 80 percent of the middle-aged and older adults reported that adults have a duty to care for their parents (and parents-in-law) in time of need later in life.

The generations of living things pass in a short time, and like runners hand on the torch of life.

—LUCRETIUS
Roman poet, 1st century B.C.

The Empty Nest and Its Refilling   An important event in a family is the launching of a child into adult life. Parents face new adjustments as a result of the child's absence. Students usually think that their parents suffer from their absence. In fact, parents who live vicariously through their children might experience the **empty nest syndrome,** which includes a decline in marital satisfaction after children leave the home. For most parents, however, marital satisfaction does not decline after children have left home. Rather, for most parents marital satisfaction increases during the years after child rearing (Fingerman & Baker, 2006). With their children gone, marital partners have time to pursue careers and other interests and more time for each other. A recent study revealed that the transition to an empty nest increased marital satisfaction and this increase was linked to an increase in the quality of time—but not the quantity of time—spent with partners (Gorchoff, John, & Helson, 2008).

In today's uncertain economic climate, the refilling of the empty nest is becoming a common occurrence as adult children return to live at home after several years of college, after graduating from college, or to save money after taking a full-time job (Fingerman, Cheng, & others, 2012; Fingerman, Pillemer, & others, 2012). Young adults also may move back in with their parents after an unsuccessful career or a divorce. And some individuals don't leave home at all until their middle to late twenties because they cannot financially support themselves. Numerous labels have been applied to these young adults who return to their parents' homes to live, including "boomerang kids" and "B2B" (or Back-to-Bedroom) (Furman, 2005).

The middle generation has always provided support for the younger generation, even after the nest is bare. Through loans and monetary gifts for education, and through emotional support, the middle generation has helped the younger generation. Adult children appreciate the

Middle-aged and older adults around the world show a strong sense of family responsibility. A recent study of middle-aged and older adults in 21 countries revealed that the strongest intergenerational ties were in Saudi Arabia.
© Reza/National Geographic/Getty Images

empty nest syndrome View that a decline in marital satisfaction occurs when children leave home; however, research indicates that for most parents there is an upswing in marital satisfaction when children are launched into an adult life.

What are some strategies that can help parents and their young adult children get along better?
© Tom Grill/Corbis RF

financial and emotional support their parents provide them at a time when they often feel considerable stress about their career, work, and lifestyle. And parents feel good that they can provide this support.

However, as with most family living arrangements, there are both pluses and minuses when adult children live with their parents. One of the most common complaints voiced by both adult children and their parents is a loss of privacy. The adult children complain that their parents restrict their independence, cramp their sex lives, reduce their music listening, and treat them as children rather than adults. Parents often complain that their quiet home has become noisy, that they stay up late worrying about when their adult children will come home, that meals are difficult to plan because of conflicting schedules, that their relationship as a married or partnered couple has been invaded, and that they have to shoulder too much responsibility for their adult children. In sum, when adult children return home to live, the changes in family life require considerable adaptation on the part of parents and their adult children.

When adult children ask to return home to live, parents and their adult children should agree on the conditions and expectations beforehand. For example, they might discuss and agree on whether young adults will pay rent, wash their own clothes, cook their own meals, do any household chores, pay their phone bills, come and go as they please, be sexually active or drink alcohol at home, and so on. If these conditions aren't negotiated at the beginning, conflict often results because the expectations of parents and young adult children will likely be violated.

Recent research indicates that today's parents and their emerging adult/young adult children have more contact with each other than did earlier generations, with the connection especially accelerating in the first decade of the twenty-first century (Fingerman, Chan, & others, 2012; Fingerman, Pillemer, & others, 2012). Keeping in touch has become easier with advances in technology, and today's emerging and young adults frequently text their parents and become friends with their parents on Facebook. Recent research indicates that today's emerging adults and young adults appreciate their parents' emotional and financial support. Nonetheless, there is concern when this parental support becomes too intense, in which case it can restrict emerging and young adults' development of autonomy (Fingerman, Chan, & others, 2012; Fingerman, Pillemer, & others, 2012). The term "helicopter parents" has been applied to this type of support. A recent study of emerging adults found that helicopter parenting was positively linked to parental involvement and other aspects of positive parenting, such as guidance, disclosure, and emotional support, but negatively related to parental granting of autonomy and school engagement (Padilla-Walker & Nelson, 2012).

As discussed in the next section, a considerable degree of ambivalence characterizes intergenerational relationships in many families, with middle-aged adults playing a key role in connecting generations.

The Midlife Generation   Adults in midlife play important roles in the lives of the young and the old (Antonucci, Birditt, & Ajrouch, 2013; Fingerman & others, 2014; Luong, Rauers, & Fingerman, 2015). Middle-aged adults share their experience and transmit values to the younger generation. They may be launching children and experiencing the empty nest, adjusting to having grown children return home, or becoming grandparents. They also may be giving or receiving financial assistance, caring for a widowed or sick parent, or adapting to being the oldest generation after both parents have died.

Middle-aged adults have been described as the "sandwich," "squeezed," or "overload" generation because of the responsibilities they have for their adolescent and young adult children on the one hand and their aging parents on the other (Etaugh & Bridges, 2010; Pudrovska, 2009). However, Karen Fingerman and her colleagues (Fingerman & Birditt, 2011; Fingerman, Sechrest, & Birditt, 2013) offer an alternative view, concluding that in the United States, a "sandwich" generation, in which the middle generation cares for both grown children and aging parents simultaneously, occurs less often than a "pivot" generation, in which the middle generation alternates attention between the demands of grown children and aging parents.

Many middle-aged adults experience considerable stress when their parents become very ill and die. One survey found that when adults enter midlife, 41 percent have both parents alive, but that 77 percent leave midlife with no parents alive (Bumpass & Aquilino, 1994). By middle age, more than 40 percent of adult children (most of them daughters) provide care for aging parents or parents-in-law (Bliezner & Roberto, 2012). However, researchers recently have found that middle-aged parents are more likely to provide support to their grown children than to their parents (Fingerman & others, 2011). In this research, when middle-aged adults have a parent with a disability, their support for that parent increases. The support might involve locating a nursing home and monitoring its quality, procuring medical services, arranging public service assistance, and handling finances. In some cases, adult children provide direct assistance with daily living, including such activities as eating, bathing, and dressing. Even less severely impaired older adults may need help with shopping, housework, transportation, home maintenance, and bill paying.

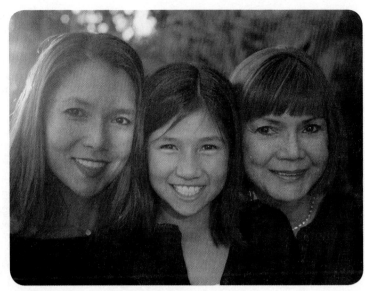

What is the nature of intergenerational relationships?
© Steve Casimiro/The Image Bank/Getty Images

In most cases researchers have found that relationships between aging parents and their children are characterized by ambivalence (Fingerman & others, 2014; Luong & others, 2015). Perceptions include love, reciprocal help, and shared values on the positive side and isolation, family conflicts and problems, abuse, neglect, and caregiver stress on the negative side. A recent study found that middle-aged adults positively supported family responsibility to emerging adult children but were more ambivalent about providing care for aging parents, viewing it as both a joy and a burden (Igarashi & others, 2013). A recent study, though, revealed that affection and support, reflecting solidarity, were more prevalent than ambivalence in intergenerational relationships (Hogerbrugge & Komter, 2012).

With each new generation, personality characteristics, attitudes, and values are replicated or changed (Antonucci, Birditt, & Ajrouch, 2013). As older family members die, their biological, intellectual, emotional, and personal legacies are carried on in the next generation. Their children become the oldest generation and their grandchildren the second generation. As adult children become middle-aged, they often develop more positive perceptions of their parents (Field, 1999). Both similarity and dissimilarity across generations are found. For example, similarity between parents and an adult child is most noticeable in religion and politics, least in gender roles, lifestyle, and work orientation.

The following studies provide further evidence of the importance of intergenerational relationships in development:

· The motivation of adult children to provide social support to their older parents was linked with earlier family experiences (Silverstein & others, 2002). Children who spent more time in shared activities with their parents and were given more financial support by them earlier in their lives provided more support to their parents when they became older.

· Children of divorce were disproportionately more likely to end their own marriage than were children from intact, never-divorced families, although the transmission of divorce across generations has declined in recent years (Wolfinger, 2011).

· Adult children of divorce who were classified as securely attached were less likely to divorce in the early years of their marriage than their insecurely attached counterparts (Crowell, Treboux, & Brockmeyer, 2009).

· Parents who smoked early and often, and persisted in becoming regular smokers, were more likely to have adolescents who became smokers (Chassin & others, 2008).

Gender   Gender differences also characterize intergenerational relationships (Etaugh & Bridges, 2010; Luong & others, 2015). Women have an especially important role in maintaining family relationships across generations. Women's relationships across generations are typically closer than other family bonds (Merrill, 2009). In one study, mothers and their daughters had much closer relationships during their adult years than mothers and sons, fathers and daughters, and fathers and sons (Rossi, 1989). Also in this study, married men were more involved with their wives' kin than with their own. And maternal grandmothers and maternal aunts were cited twice as often as their counterparts on the paternal side of the family as the most important or loved relative. Also, a recent study revealed that mothers' intergenerational ties were more influential for grandparent-grandchild relationships than fathers' were (Monserud, 2008).

Review Connect Reflect

 LG4 Explain other aspects of family relationships

Review
- How do siblings interact with each other? How is birth order linked with developmental outcomes?
- What is the nature of grandparenting and great-grandparenting?
- How do intergenerational relationships influence development?

Connect
- Connect what you have learned about longevity to this chapter's discussion

of grandparenting and great-grandparenting.

Reflect *Your Own Personal Journey of Life*
- Do you have a sibling? If so, what is your relationship like? Has it changed over the years? If you don't have a sibling, how do you think your life would have been different with one or more siblings?

reach your **learning goals**

Families, Lifestyles, and Parenting

1 Family Processes

 LG1 Describe some important family processes

Reciprocal Socialization

Family as a System

Sociocultural and Historical Influences

Multiple Developmental Trajectories

- Reciprocal socialization is socialization that is bidirectional; children socialize parents just as parents socialize children. Synchrony and scaffolding are two important types of reciprocal socialization.
- The family system consists of subsystems defined by generation, gender, and role. These subsystems interact with each other and can have direct and indirect effects on each other.
- Sociocultural and historical contexts influence families, reflecting Bronfenbrenner's concepts of macrosystem and chronosystem. Both great upheavals such as war and subtle transitions in ways of life may influence families. A major change in families in the last several decades has been the extensive immigration of Latino and Asian families into the United States.
- Adults follow one developmental trajectory and children another one. Observing how these trajectories mesh is important for understanding timing of entry into various family tasks.

2 The Diversity of Adult Lifestyles

LG2 Discuss the diversity of adult lifestyles and how they influence people's lives

Single Adults

- Being single has become an increasingly prominent lifestyle. There are advantages and disadvantages to being single, autonomy being one of the advantages. Intimacy, loneliness, and finding a positive identity in a marriage-oriented society are concerns of single adults. Approximately 8 percent of 65-year-old adults have never been married. Many of them cope effectively with loneliness in old age.

Cohabiting Adults

· Cohabitation is an increasingly prevalent lifestyle for many adults that offers some advantages as well as problems. Cohabitation does not lead to greater marital happiness but rather to no differences or to differences suggesting that it is not good for a marriage. An increasing number of older adults cohabit, in many cases more for companionship than for love.

Married Adults

· Even though adults are remaining single longer and the divorce rate is high, Americans still show a strong predilection for marriage. The age at which individuals marry, expectations about what the marriage will be like, and the developmental course of marriage vary not only over time within a culture but also across cultures. John Gottman has conducted extensive research on what makes marriages work. In his research, the following factors are among the most important for having a good marriage: establishing love maps, nurturing fondness and admiration, turning toward each other instead of away, letting your partner influence you, overcoming gridlock, and creating shared meaning. Premarital education is associated with positive relationship outcomes. The benefits of marriage include better physical and mental health and a longer life. A majority of middle-aged adults who are married say their marriage is very good or excellent. The time from retirement until death is sometimes called the final stage in the marital process. Married older adults are often happier than single older adults.

Divorced Adults

· The U.S. divorce rate increased dramatically in the twentieth century but began to decline in the 1980s. Divorce is complex and emotional. In the first year following divorce, a disequilibrium in the divorced adult's behavior occurs, but by several years after the divorce, more stability has been achieved. The divorced displaced homemaker may encounter excessive stress; however, men do not go through a divorce unscathed. There are social, financial, and physical consequences of divorce for older adults.

Remarried Adults

· Divorced adults remarry on average within four years of their divorce. Stepfamilies are complex and adjustment is difficult. Only about one-third of stepfamily couples stay remarried. Rising divorce rates, increased longevity, and better health have led to an increase in remarriage by older adults.

Gay and Lesbian Adults

· One of the most striking findings about gay and lesbian couples is how similar they are to heterosexual couples—for example, gay and lesbian couples prefer committed, long-term relationships and work to find a balance of romantic love, affection, and autonomy. There are many misconceptions about gay and lesbian adults.

3 Parenting

LG3 Characterize parenting and how it affects children's development

Parental Roles

· Currently, there is a trend toward having fewer children and choosing when to have children. The transition to parenting involves a great deal of adaptation for many people. A key aspect of being a competent parent is effectively managing children's lives and understanding adolescents' information management.

Parenting Styles and Discipline

· Authoritarian, authoritative, neglectful, and indulgent are four main parenting styles. Authoritative parenting is the style most often associated with children's social competence. Physical punishment is widely used by U.S. parents, but there are a number of reasons why it is not a good choice. Coparenting can have positive effects on children's development if it is accompanied by parental warmth and cooperation. The four main types of child maltreatment are physical abuse, child neglect, sexual abuse, and emotional abuse. An understanding of child abuse requires information about cultural, familial, and community influences. Child maltreatment places the child at risk for a number of developmental problems.

Parent–Adolescent and Parent–Emerging Adult Relationships

· Adolescents seek to be independent, but secure attachment to parents is a positive influence on development. Conflict with parents often increases in adolescence but usually is moderate rather than severe. An increasing number of emerging adults are returning home to live with their parents, often for economic reasons. Both emerging adults and their parents need to adapt when emerging adults return home to live.

Working Parents

· In general, having both parents employed full-time outside the home has not been shown to have negative effects on children. However, the nature of parents' work can affect the quality of their parenting.

Children in Divorced Families	· Overall, divorce is linked with adjustment problems in children, but not for all children. Whether parents should stay together for the sake of the children is a difficult question to answer. Family processes, such as harmony between parents, quality of parenting, and support systems, matter in the development of children of divorced parents. So does socioeconomic status.
Stepfamilies	· Children in stepparent families have more problems than their counterparts in nondivorced families. Adolescence is an especially difficult time for remarriage of parents to occur. Restabilization takes longer in stepfamilies than in divorced families.
Gay and Lesbian Parents	· Researchers have found few differences between children growing up with gay or lesbian parents and children growing up with heterosexual parents.
Adoptive Parents and Adopted Children	· Although adopted children and adolescents have more problems than their nonadopted counterparts, the vast majority of adopted children adapt effectively. When adoption occurs very early in development, the outcomes for the child are improved. Because of the dramatic changes that have occurred in adoption in recent decades, it is difficult to generalize about characteristics of the average adopted child or average adoptive family.

4 Other Family Relationships

 LG4 Explain other aspects of family relationships

Sibling Relationships and Birth Order	· Siblings interact with each other in positive and negative ways. Birth order is related in certain ways to child characteristics, but some critics argue that birth order is not a good predictor of behavior. Sibling relationships persist over the entire life span for most adults.
Grandparenting and Great-Grandparenting	· There are different grandparent roles and styles. Grandmothers spend more time with grandchildren than grandfathers do, and the grandmother role involves greater expectations for maintaining ties across generations than the grandfather role. The profile of grandparents is changing because of factors such as divorce and remarriage. An increasing number of U.S. grandchildren live with their grandparents. Because of increased longevity, more grandparents today are also great-grandparents. One contribution of great-grandparents is their knowledge of family history.
Intergenerational Relationships	· For most families, there is an upswing in marital satisfaction when children are launched into adulthood. Family members usually maintain contact across generations. Mothers and daughters have the closest relationships. The middle-aged generation plays an important role in linking generations. In many families, ambivalence characterizes intergenerational relationships.

key terms

authoritarian parenting	child neglect	empty nest syndrome	neglectful parenting
authoritative parenting	cohabitation	indulgent parenting	physical abuse
child abuse	coparenting	multiple developmental	reciprocal socialization
child maltreatment	emotional abuse	trajectories	sexual abuse

key people

Joseph Allen	Ann Crouter	Karen Fingerman	E. Mavis Hetherington
Diana Baumrind	E. Mark Cummings	John Gottman	Laurie Kramer

chapter **15**

PEERS AND THE SOCIOCULTURAL WORLD

chapter **outline**

1 Peer Relations in Childhood and Adolescence

Learning Goal 1 Discuss peer relations in childhood and adolescence

Exploring Peer Relations
Peer Statuses
Bullying
Gender and Peer Relations
Adolescent Peer Relations

2 Friendship

Learning Goal 2 Explain the role of friendship through the life span

Functions of Friendship
Friendship During Childhood
Friendship During Adolescence and Emerging Adulthood
Adult Friendship

3 Play and Leisure

Learning Goal 3 Describe the developmental aspects of play and leisure

Childhood
Adolescence
Adulthood

4 Aging and the Social World

Learning Goal 4 Summarize the social aspects of aging

Social Theories of Aging
Stereotyping of Older Adults
Social Support and Social Integration
Successful Aging

5 Sociocultural Influences

Learning Goal 5 Evaluate sociocultural influences on development

Culture
Socioeconomic Status and Poverty
Ethnicity

© Kevin Dodge/Corbis

preview

The social worlds outside the family play important roles in life-span development. As we go through life, we interact with a convoy of people through peer relations, friendships, cliques, and support systems in many different cultural worlds.

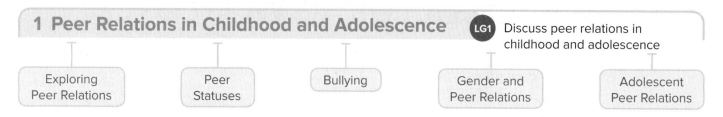

1 Peer Relations in Childhood and Adolescence

LG1 Discuss peer relations in childhood and adolescence

- Exploring Peer Relations
- Peer Statuses
- Bullying
- Gender and Peer Relations
- Adolescent Peer Relations

As children grow older, peer relations consume increasing amounts of their time. In some cases these relations are positive influences, in others negative.

EXPLORING PEER RELATIONS

Some important questions involving peer relations are the following: What are the functions of a child's peer group? How are peer relations and adult-child relations linked? What are some developmental changes in peer relations during childhood? What role does social cognition play in peer relations? How is emotion regulation involved in peer relations?

Functions of Peer Groups **Peers** are individuals of about the same age or maturity level. Peer groups provide a source of information and comparison about the world outside the family. Children receive feedback about their abilities from their peer group. They evaluate what they can do in terms of whether it is better than, as good as, or worse than what other children do. It is hard to make such comparisons at home because siblings are usually older or younger.

Researchers have found that children's peer relations can have long-term consequences. For example, a recent study indicated that low peer status in childhood (low acceptance/likeability) was linked to increased probability of being unemployed and having mental health problems in adulthood (Almquist & Brannstrom, 2014).

Both Jean Piaget (1932) and Harry Stack Sullivan (1953) stressed that children learn reciprocity through interaction with their peers. Children explore the meanings of fairness and justice by working through disagreements with peers. They also learn to be keen observers of peers' interests and perspectives in order to smoothly integrate themselves into ongoing peer activities. A recent study found that children who associated with peers who engaged in prosocial behavior at age 9 had a higher level of self-control at age 10, while those who associated with peers who engaged in deviant behavior at age 9 had a lower level of self-control at age 10 (Meldrum & Hay, 2012).

Susceptibility to peer influences can have both negative and positive consequences (Rubin, Bukowski, & Bowker, 2015; Rulison, Kreager, & Osgood, 2014). For example, a longitudinal study of adolescents and emerging adults from 13 to 23 years of age revealed that adolescents' autonomy from peer influences predicted long-term success in avoiding problematic behavior but also more difficulty in establishing strong friendships in emerging adulthood (Allen, Chango, & Swedo, 2014). Further, peer relations are linked to adolescents' patterns of drug use, delinquency, depression, sexual activity, and self-injury (Barrocas & others, 2015; Choukas-Bradley & others, 2014; Evans, Simons, & Simons, 2015). One study found that having friends who engage in delinquent behavior is associated with early onset and more persistent delinquency (Evans

What are some functions of a peer group?
© Ariel Skelley/Corbis

peers Individuals who share the same age or maturity level.

& others, 2015). A recent study revealed that among negative interactions with parents (being yelled at by a parent, for example), teachers (getting into trouble with a teacher, for example), and peers, negative peer events (such as getting into a fight or argument with another kid, for example) were most likely to account for maintaining depressive symptoms across a two-year period in early adolescence (Herres & Kobak, 2014). Another recent study found that college students with risky social networks (friends who drink, for example) were ten times more likely to engage in heavy drinking (Mason, Zaharakis, & Benotsch, 2014).

Being rejected or overlooked by peers leads some children to feel lonely or hostile. Further, rejection and neglect by peers are related to an individual's subsequent mental health difficulties and criminal problems. Withdrawn children who are rejected by peers or victimized and lonely are at risk for depression. Children who are aggressive with their peers are at risk for developing a number of problems, including conduct problems, delinquency, and dropping out of school (Chen, Drabick, & Burgers, 2015; Prinstein, Brechwald, & Cohen, 2011). Peers can also undermine parental values and control (Masten, 2005).

Keep in mind that the influences of peer experiences vary according to the type of peer experience, developmental status, and outcome (such as achievement, delinquency, depression, and so on) (Choukas-Bradley & Prinstein, 2013; Foshee & others, 2013; Prinstein & Giletta, 2015). "Peers" and "peer group" are global concepts. For example, "peer group" might refer to acquaintances, members of a clique, neighborhood associates, a friendship network, or an activity group (Brown, 1999).

Adult-Child and Peer Relations   Parents may influence their children's peer relations in many ways, both direct and indirect (Caruthers & others, 2014; Chan, Brown, and Von Bank, 2015; Ninio, 2015; Pallini & others, 2014). Parents affect their children's peer relations through their interactions with their children, how they manage their children's lives, and the opportunities they provide to their children (Brown & Bakken, 2011). One study revealed that warmth, advice giving, and provision of opportunities by mothers and fathers were linked to children's social competence (high prosocial behavior, low aggression), and subsequently to social acceptance (being well liked by peers and teachers) one year later (McDowell & Parke, 2009).

Basic lifestyle decisions by parents—their choices of neighborhoods, churches, schools, and their own friends—largely determine the pool from which their children select possible friends. These choices in turn affect which children their children meet, their purpose in interacting, and eventually which children become their friends.

Children and adolescents live in a connected world with parents and peers, not one in which parents and peers are disconnected from each other (Caruthers, Van Ryzin, & Dishion, 2014). A recent study found that parent-adolescent attachment was positively related to peer attachment (Cai & others, 2013). Another recent study found that when mothers coached their preschool daughters about the negative aspects of peer conflicts involving relational aggression (harming someone by manipulating a relationship), the daughters engaged in lower rates of relational aggression (Werner & others, 2014).

Do these findings indicate that children's peer relations always are wedded to parent-child relationships? Although parent-child relationships influence children's subsequent peer relations, children also learn other modes of relating through their relationships with peers. For example, rough-and-tumble play occurs mainly with other children, not in parent-child interaction. In times of stress, children more often turn to parents than to peers for support. Parent-child relationships teach children how to relate to authority figures. With their peers, children are likely to interact on a much more equal basis and to learn a mode of relating based on mutual influence.

Some researchers have found that parents and adolescents perceive that parents have little authority over adolescents' choices in some areas but more authority over choices in other areas (Killen & Smetana, 2015). For example, Judith Smetana's (2008, 2011a, b) research has revealed that both parents and adolescents view peer relations as an arena in which parents have little authority to dictate adolescents' choices, in contrast with moral, religious, and educational arenas in which parents are perceived to have more authority.

Peer Contexts   Peer interaction is influenced by contexts that can include the type of peer the individual interacts with—such as an acquaintance, a crowd, a clique, a friend, or a romantic partner—and the situation or location where they interact—such as a school, neighborhood, community center, dance, religious setting, sporting event, and so on, as well as the culture in which the individual lives (Brown & Larson, 2009). As they interact with peers in these various

How are parent-child and peer relationships connected?
(top): © iStockphoto.com/monkeybusinessimages RF;
(bottom): © Aramanda/Fotolia RF

developmental **connection**

Attachment

Securely attached infants use the caregiver as a secure base from which to explore their environment. Connect to "Emotional Development and Attachment."

contexts, individuals are likely to encounter different messages and different opportunities to engage in adaptive or maladaptive behavior that can influence their development (Brechwald & Prinstein, 2011; Prinstein & Giletta, 2015).

Individual Difference Factors   Individual differences among peers also are important considerations in understanding peer relations (Brechwald & Prinstein, 2011; Prinstein & Giletta, 2015). Among the wide range of individual differences that can affect peer relations are personality traits such as how shy or outgoing an individual is. For example, a very shy individual is more likely than a gregarious individual to be neglected by peers and to feel anxious about introducing himself or herself to new peers. One individual difference factor that has been found to impair peer relations is the trait of negative emotionality, which involves a relatively low threshold for experiencing anger, fear, anxiety, and irritation. For example, one recent study revealed that adolescents characterized by negative emotionality tended to engage in negative interpersonal behavior when interacting with a friend or a romantic partner (Hatton & others, 2008). Other individual differences include the individual's openness to peer influence and the status/power of the individual compared with the status/power of the other peer or peer group (Brown & others, 2008). Being in a subordinate social position decreases the likelihood that the individual will influence other peers but increases the probability that the individual will be open to peer influence.

Developmental Changes in Childhood   Around the age of 3, children already prefer to spend time with same-sex rather than opposite-sex playmates, and this preference increases in early childhood. During these same years, the frequency of peer interaction, both positive and negative, picks up considerably (Hartup, 1983). Although aggressive interaction and rough-and-tumble play increase, the proportion of aggressive exchanges, compared with friendly exchanges, decreases. Many preschool children spend considerable time in peer interaction just playing, conversing with peers, trying out roles, and negotiating rules (Rubin, Bukowski, & Bowker, 2015). In early childhood, children distinguish between friends and nonfriends (Howes, 2009). For most young children, a friend is someone to play with. Young preschool children are more likely than older children to have friends of different gender and ethnicity (Howes, 2009).

As children enter the elementary school years, reciprocity becomes especially important in peer interchanges. Children play games, interact in groups, and cultivate friendships. Until about 12 years of age, their preference for same-sex groups increases. The amount of time children spend in peer interaction also rises during middle and late childhood and adolescence. Researchers estimate that the percentage of time spent in social

What are some developmental changes in peer relations during childhood?
© Rachel Epstein/PhotoEdit

interaction with peers increases from approximately 10 percent at 2 years of age to more than 30 percent in middle and late childhood (Rubin, Bukowski, & Parker, 2006). Other changes in peer relations as children move through middle and late childhood involve an increase in the size of their peer group and peer interaction that is less closely supervised by adults (Rubin & others, 2006).

Social Cognition   A boy accidentally trips and knocks another boy's soft drink out of his hand. That boy misinterprets the encounter as hostile, which leads him to retaliate aggressively against the boy who tripped. Through repeated encounters of this kind, the aggressive boy's classmates come to perceive him as habitually acting in inappropriate ways.

This example demonstrates the importance of *social cognition*—thoughts about social matters, such as the aggressive boy's interpretation of an encounter as hostile and his classmates' perception of his behavior as inappropriate (Carpendale & Lewis, 2015; Vetter & others, 2013). Children's social cognition about their peers becomes increasingly important for understanding peer relationships in middle and late childhood. Of special interest are the ways in which children process information about peer relations and their social knowledge (Dodge, 2011a, b; Lansford & others, 2010).

Kenneth Dodge (1983, 2011a, b) argues that children go through six steps in processing information about their social world. They selectively attend to social cues, attribute intent, generate goals, access behavioral scripts from memory, make decisions, and enact behavior.

Dodge has found that aggressive boys are more likely to perceive another child's actions as hostile when the child's intention is ambiguous. And, when aggressive boys search for cues to determine a peer's intention, they respond more rapidly, less efficiently, and less reflectively than do nonaggressive boys. These are among the social cognitive factors believed to be involved in children's and adolescents' conflicts.

Social knowledge also is involved in children's ability to get along with peers (Carpendale & Lewis, 2015). They need to know what goals to pursue in poorly defined or ambiguous situations, how to initiate and maintain a social bond, and what scripts to follow to get other children to be their friends. For example, as part of the script for getting friends, it helps to know that making positive comments to the peer will make the peer like the child more.

Regulation of Emotion and Peer Relations   Emotions play a strong role in determining whether a child's peer relationships are successful (Rowsell & others, 2014; Vetter & others, 2013). Moody and emotionally negative children are often rejected by their peers, whereas emotionally positive children are often popular (Stocker & Dunn, 1990; Martinez & others, 2015). The ability to modulate one's emotions is an important skill that benefits children in their relationships with peers.

PEER STATUSES

Which children are likely to be popular with their peers and which ones tend to be disliked? Developmentalists address these and similar questions by examining sociometric status, a term that describes the extent to which children are liked or disliked by their peer group (Cillessen

developmental **connection**

Social Cognition

Social cognition refers to the processes involved in understanding the world around us, especially how we think and reason about others. Connect to "The Self, Identity, and Personality."

& van den Berg, 2012; Rubin & others, 2015). Sociometric status is typically assessed by asking children to rate how much they like or dislike each of their classmates. Or it may be assessed by asking children to nominate the children they like the most and those they like the least.

Developmentalists have distinguished five peer statuses (Wentzel & Asher, 1995):

· **Popular children** are frequently nominated as a best friend and are rarely disliked by their peers.

· **Average children** receive an average number of both positive and negative nominations from their peers.

· **Neglected children** are infrequently nominated as a best friend but are not disliked by their peers.

· **Rejected children** are infrequently nominated as someone's best friend and are actively disliked by their peers.

· **Controversial children** are frequently nominated both as someone's best friend and as being disliked.

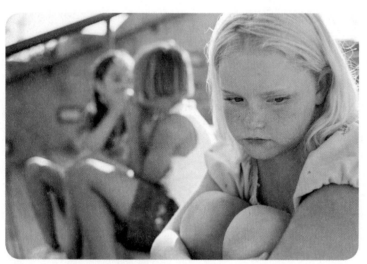

What are some statuses that children have with their peers?
© BananaStock RF

Peer rejection contributes to subsequent problems of adaptation, including antisocial behavior.

—JOHN COIE
Contemporary developmental psychologist, Duke University

popular children Children who are frequently nominated as a best friend and are rarely disliked by their peers.

average children Children who receive an average number of both positive and negative nominations from their peers.

neglected children Children who are infrequently nominated as a best friend but are not disliked by their peers.

rejected children Children who are infrequently nominated as a best friend and are actively disliked by their peers.

controversial children Children who are frequently nominated both as someone's best friend and as being disliked.

Popular children have a number of social skills that contribute to their being well liked (Asher & McDonald, 2009). Researchers have found that popular children give out reinforcements, listen carefully, maintain open lines of communication with peers, are happy, control their negative emotions, show enthusiasm and concern for others, and are self-confident without being conceited (Hartup, 1983; Rubin, Bukowski, & Parker, 2006). In a recent study, the popularity of adolescents with their peers was associated with their dating popularity (Houser, Mayeux, & Cross, 2014). Also, a recent study of 13- to 23-year-olds revealed that early adolescent pseudomature behavior (trying to appear mature or be "cool" among peers, such as engaging in minor delinquency or precocious romantic involvement) was associated with a desire to be popular with peers (Allen & others, 2014). In this study, early adolescent pseudomature behavior was linked to long-term problems in close relationships, substance abuse, and a higher level of criminal behavior.

Neglected children engage in low rates of interaction with their peers and are often described as shy by peers. The goal of many training programs for neglected children is to help them attract attention from their peers in positive ways and to hold that attention by asking questions, by listening in a warm and friendly way, and by saying things about themselves that relate to the peers' interests. They also are taught to enter groups more effectively.

Rejected children often have more serious adjustment problems than those who are neglected. One study found that in kindergarten, children who were rejected by their peers were less likely to engage in classroom participation, more likely to express a desire to avoid school, and more likely to report being lonely than children who were accepted by their peers (Buhs & Ladd, 2002). A recent study revealed a link between peer rejection and depression in adolescence (Platt, Kadosh, & Lau, 2013). The combination of being rejected by peers and being aggressive especially forecasts problems (Hymel & others, 2011). Peer rejection is consistently linked to the development and maintenance of conduct problems (Chen & others, 2015).

John Coie (2004, pp. 252–253) gave three reasons why aggressive peer-rejected boys have problems in social relationships:

· "First, the rejected, aggressive boys are more impulsive and have problems sustaining attention. As a result, they are more likely to be disruptive of ongoing activities in the classroom and in focused group play.

· Second, rejected, aggressive boys are more emotionally reactive. They are aroused to anger more easily and probably have more difficulty calming down once aroused. Because of this they are more prone to become angry at peers and attack them verbally and physically. . . .

· Third, rejected children have fewer social skills in making friends and maintaining positive relationships with peers."

Not all rejected children are aggressive (Rubin & others, 2015). Although aggression and its related characteristics of impulsiveness and disruptiveness underlie rejection about half the time, approximately 10 to 20 percent of rejected children are shy.

How can rejected children be trained to interact more effectively with their peers? Rejected children may be taught to more accurately assess whether the intentions of their peers are negative (Fontaine & others, 2010). They may be asked to engage in role playing or to discuss hypothetical situations involving negative encounters with peers, such as when a peer cuts into a line ahead of them. In some programs, children are shown videotapes of appropriate peer interaction and asked to draw lessons from what they have seen (Ladd, Buhs, & Troop, 2004).

BULLYING

Significant numbers of students are victimized by bullies (Connell, Morris, & Piquero, 2015; Thornberg & Jungert, 2014; Tsitsika & others, 2014; Waasdorp & Bradshaw, 2015). In a national survey of more than 15,000 students in grades 6 through 10, nearly one of every three students said that they had experienced occasional or frequent involvement as a victim or perpetrator in bullying (Nansel & others, 2001). In this study, bullying was defined as verbal or physical behavior intended to disturb someone less powerful (see Figure 1). Boys are more likely to be bullies than girls, but gender differences regarding victims of bullying are less clear (Salmivalli & Peets, 2009).

Who is likely to be bullied? In the study just described, boys and younger middle school students were most likely to be affected (Nansel & others, 2001). Children who said they were bullied reported more loneliness and difficulty in making friends, while those who did the bullying were more likely to have low grades and to smoke and drink alcohol.

Researchers have found that anxious, socially withdrawn, and aggressive children are often the victims of bullying (Hanish & Guerra, 2004). Anxious and socially withdrawn children may be victimized because they are nonthreatening and unlikely to retaliate if bullied, whereas aggressive children may be the targets of bullying because their behavior is irritating to bullies (Rubin & others, 2015). A recent study revealed that having supportive friends was linked to a lower level of bullying and victimization (Kendrick, Jutengren, & Stattin, 2012). Further, a recent meta-analysis indicated that positive parenting behavior (including having good communication, a warm relationship, being involved, and engaging in supervision of their children) was related to a lesser likelihood that a child would become either a bully/ victim or a victim at school (Lereya, Samara, & Wolke, 2013).

The social context of the peer group also plays an important role in bullying (Hilliard & others, 2014; Troop-Gordon & Ladd, 2014). Recent research indicates that 70 to 80 percent of victims and their bullies are in the same school classroom (Salmivalli & Peets, 2009). Classmates are often aware of bullying incidents and in many cases witness bullying. In many cases, bullies torment victims to gain higher status in the peer group and bullies need others to witness their power displays. Many bullies are not rejected by the peer group. A recent longitudinal study explored the costs and benefits of bullying in the context of the peer group (Reijntjes & others, 2013). In this study children were initially assessed at 10 years of age and then followed into early adolescence. The results indicated that although young bullies may be on a developmental trajectory that over the long run is problematic, in the shorter term personal benefits of bullying often outweigh disadvantages. Frequent bullying was linked to high social status as indexed by perceived popularity in the peer group, and bullies also were characterized by self-perceived personal competence.

What are the outcomes of bullying? A recent study revealed that peer victimization in the fifth grade was associated with worse physical and mental health in the tenth grade (Bogart & others, 2014). Researchers have found that children who are bullied are more likely to experience depression, engage in suicidal ideation, and attempt suicide than their counterparts who have not been the victims of bullying (Hensley, 2013; Undheim, 2013; Yen & others, 2014). A recent study revealed that peer victimization during the elementary school years was linked to stress and suicidal ideation (Kowalski & others, 2014). Another study indicated that peer victimization during the elementary school years was a leading indicator of internalizing problems (depression, for example) in adolescence (Schwartz & others, 2015). Also, a longitudinal study of more than 6,000 children found that children who were the victims of peer bullying from 4 to 10 years of age were more likely to engage in suicidal ideation at 11½ years of age (Winsper & others, 2012). And three meta-analyses concluded that engaging in bullying during middle

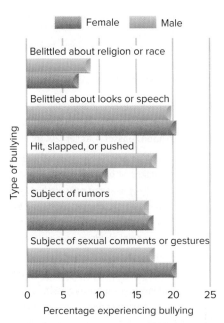

FIGURE 1

BULLYING BEHAVIORS AMONG U.S. YOUTH. This graph shows the type of bullying most often experienced by U.S. youth. The percentages reflect the extent to which bullied students said that they had experienced a particular type of bullying. In terms of gender, note that when they were bullied, boys were more likely to be hit, slapped, or pushed than girls were.

Who is likely to be bullied? What are some outcomes of bullying?
© Design Pics Inc./Alamy RF

How Are Perspective Taking and Moral Motivation Linked to Bullying?

One study explored the roles that perspective taking and moral motivation play in the lives of bullies, bully-victims, victims, and prosocial children (Gasser & Keller, 2009):

- *Bullies* are highly aggressive toward other children but are not victims of bullying.
- *Bully-victims* not only are highly aggressive toward other children but also are the recipients of other children's bullying.
- *Victims* are passive, non-aggressive respondents to bullying.
- *Prosocial children* engage in positive behaviors such as sharing, helping, comforting, and empathizing.

Teacher and peer ratings in 34 classrooms of 7- and 8-year-old students were used to classify 212 boys and girls into the aforementioned four categories. On a five-point scale (from never to several times a week), teachers rated (1) how often the child bullied others and (2) how often the child was bullied. The ratings focused on three types of bullying and being victimized: physical, verbal, and excluding others. On a four-point scale (from not applicable to very clearly applicable), teachers also rated children's prosocial behavior on three items: "willingly shares with others," "comforts others if necessary," and "empathizes with others." Peer ratings assessed children's nominations of which children in the classroom acted as bullies, were victimized by bullies, and engaged in prosocial behavior. Combining the teacher and peer ratings after eliminating those that did not agree on which children were bullies, victims, or prosocial children, the final sample consisted of 49 bullies, 80 bully-victims, 33 victims, and 50 prosocial children.

Children's perspective-taking skills were assessed using theory of mind tasks, and moral motivation was examined by interviewing children about aspects of right and wrong in stories about children's transgressions. In one theory of mind task, children were tested to see whether they understood that people may have false beliefs about another individual. In another theory of mind task, children were assessed to determine whether they understood that people sometimes hide their emotions by showing emotions that differ from what they really feel. A moral interview also was conducted in which children were told four moral transgression stories (with content about being unwilling to share with a classmate, stealing candy from a classmate, hiding a victim's shoes, and verbally bullying a victim) and then asked to judge whether the acts were right or wrong and how the participants in the stories likely felt.

The results of the study indicated that only bully-victims—but not bullies—were deficient in perspective taking. Further analysis revealed that both aggressive groups of children—bullies and bully-victims—had a deficiency in moral motivation. The analyses were consistent with a portrait of bullies as socially competent and knowledgeable in terms of perspective-taking skills and ability to interact effectively with peers. However, bullies use this social knowledge for their own manipulative purposes. The analysis also confirmed the picture of the bully as being morally insensitive. Another recent study also found that bullying was linked to moral disengagement (Obermann, 2011).

How can researchers ensure that results that might help prevent bullying are properly applied in school settings (and not, for instance, used to label potential bullies or segregate potential victims)?

---

school is linked to an increased likelihood of antisocial and criminal behavior later in adolescence and adulthood (Kim & others, 2011; Losel & Bender, 2011; Ttofi & others, 2011). Further, a recent analysis concluded that bullying can have long-term effects, including difficulty in forming lasting relationships and problems in the workplace (Wolke & Lereya, 2015).

An increasing concern is peer bullying and harassment on the Internet (called *cyber bullying*) (Barlett, 2015; Bonanno & Hymel, 2013). A recent study involving third- to sixth-graders revealed that engaging in cyber aggression was related to loneliness, lower self-esteem, fewer mutual friendships, and lower peer popularity (Schoffstall & Cohen, 2011). Further, recent research found that cyber bullying was more strongly associated with suicidal ideation that traditional bullying (van Geel, Vedeer, & Tanilon, 2014). Also, a recent meta-analysis concluded that being the victim of cyber bullying was linked to stress and suicidal ideation (Kowalski & others, 2014). And another recent meta-analysis revealed that cyber bullying occurred twice as much as traditional bullying and that those who engaged in cyber bullying were likely to also have engaged in traditional bullying (Modecki & others, 2014). Further, a longitudinal study found that adolescents experiencing social and emotional difficulties were more likely to be both cyber bullied and traditionally bullied than traditionally bullied only (Cross, Lester, & Brown, 2015). In this study, adolescents targeted in both ways stayed away from school more than their counterparts who were traditionally bullied only. Information about preventing cyber bullying can be found at www.stopcyberbullying.org/.

What leads some children to become bullies and others to fall victim to bullying? To read further about bullying, see the *Connecting with Research* interlude.

Extensive interest is being directed to preventing and treating bullying and victimization (Cantone & others, 2015; Low & others, 2014; Olweus, 2013). A research review revealed mixed results for school-based intervention (Vreeman & Carroll, 2007). School-based interventions vary greatly, ranging from involving the whole school in an anti-bullying campaign to providing individualized social skills training (Strohmeier & Noam, 2012). One of the most promising bullying intervention programs has been created by Dan Olweus (2003, 2013). This program focuses on 6- to 15-year-olds with the goal of decreasing opportunities and rewards for bullying. School staff are instructed in ways to improve peer relations and make schools safer. When properly implemented, the program reduces bullying by 30 to 70 percent (Olweus, 2003). A recent research review concluded that interventions focused on the whole school, such as Olweus', are more effective than interventions involving classroom curricula or social skills training (Cantone & others, 2015).

GENDER AND PEER RELATIONS

We know that boys are far more likely to be involved in bullying than girls are. Indeed, there is increasing evidence that gender plays an important role in peer relations, as we saw in the chapter on "Gender and Sexuality" (Furman & Rose, 2015). Gender influences the composition of children's groups, their size, and the interaction within groups (Maccoby, 2002):

· *Gender composition.* Around the age of 3, children already prefer to spend time with same-sex playmates. From 4 to 12 years of age, this preference for playing in same-sex groups increases (see Figure 2).

· *Group size.* From about 5 years of age onward, boys tend to associate in larger clusters than girls do. Girls are more likely than boys to play in groups of two or three.

· *Interaction in same-sex groups.* Boys are more likely to participate in organized group games than girls are. They also are more likely to engage in rough-and-tumble play, competition, conflict, ego displays, risk taking, and dominance seeking. And, more than girls' groups, boys' groups seek to attain a group goal (Benenson, Apostolaris, & Parnass, 1997). By contrast, girls are more likely to engage in "collaborative discourse."

ADOLESCENT PEER RELATIONS

Peers play powerful roles in the lives of adolescents (Furman & Rose, 2015; Rancourt & others, 2014; Wentzel, 2013). And just as there are gender differences in peer relations in childhood as you just read, a recent meta-analysis concluded that adolescent girls show stronger peer attachment, especially related to trust and communication, than do adolescent boys (Gorrese & Ruggieri, 2012).

Unlike children, whose groups are usually informal collections of friends or neighborhood acquaintances, adolescents are often members of formal and heterogeneous groups, including adolescents who may not be friends or neighborhood acquaintances. Adolescent groups are also more likely than childhood groups to include boys and girls.

Do these and other peer groups matter? Yes, they do. Researchers have found that the standards of peer groups and the influence of crowds and cliques become increasingly important during adolescence (Brown & others, 2008).

Peer Pressure   Young adolescents conform more to peer standards than children do (Badaly, 2013; Teunissen & others, 2014). Around the eighth and ninth grades, conformity to peers—especially to their antisocial standards—peaks (Brechwald & Prinstein, 2011; Brown & Larson, 2009). At this point, adolescents are most likely to go along with a peer to steal hubcaps off a car, draw graffiti on a wall, or steal cosmetics from a store counter. One study found that U.S. adolescents are more likely than Japanese adolescents to put pressure on their peers to resist parental influence (Rothbaum & others, 2000). Adolescents are more likely to conform to their peers when they are uncertain about their social identity and when they are in the presence of someone they perceive to have higher status than they do (Prinstein & Dodge, 2008; Prinstein & Giletta, 2015; Prinstein & others, 2009). A recent study of young adolescent

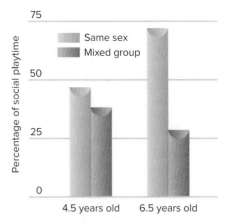

FIGURE 2

DEVELOPMENTAL CHANGES IN PERCENTAGE OF TIME SPENT IN SAME-SEX AND MIXED-GROUP SETTINGS. Observations of children show that they are more likely to play in same-sex than mixed-sex groups. This tendency increases between 4 and 6 years of age.

What characterizes peer pressure in adolescence? What characterizes adolescent cliques? How are they different from crowds?
© Jose Luis Pelaez, Inc./Blend Images/Getty Images RF

Latinas revealed that a peer resistance skill-building game involving avatar-based reality technology was effective in strengthening the girls' peer-resistance skills and tendencies to be pressured into risky behavior (Norris & others, 2013).

Cliques and Crowds   Cliques and crowds assume more important roles in the lives of adolescents than in the lives of children (Brown & Dietz, 2009; Doornwaard & others, 2012; Rubin & others, 2013). **Cliques** are small groups that range from 2 to about 12 individuals and average about 5 or 6 individuals. The clique members are usually of the same sex and about the same age.

Cliques can form because adolescents engage in similar activities, such as being in a club or on a sports team. Some cliques also form because of friendship. Several adolescents may form a clique because they have spent time with each other, share mutual interests, and enjoy each other's company. Not necessarily friends, they often develop a friendship if they stay in the clique. What do adolescents do in cliques? They share ideas and hang out together. Often they develop an in-group identity in which they believe that their clique is better than other cliques.

Crowds are larger than cliques and less personal. Adolescents are usually members of a crowd based on reputation, and they may or may not spend much time together. Many crowds are defined by the activities adolescents engage in (such as "jocks" who are good at sports or "druggies" who take drugs). A recent study indicated that adolescents who identify with some crowds ("populars," for example) have fewer externalizing problem behaviors than their counterparts who identify with other crowds ("metal heads," for example) (Doornwaard & others, 2012). In this study, some crowds had a higher level of internalizing problems ("nonconformists," for example) than others ("jocks," for example).

cliques Small groups that range from 2 to 12 individuals and average about 5 or 6 individuals. Clique members usually are of the same age and same sex and often engage in similar activities, such as belonging to a club or participating in a sport.

crowds The crowd is a larger group than a clique. Adolescents usually are members of a crowd based on reputation and may not spend much time together. Many crowds are defined by the activities in which adolescents engage.

Review Connect Reflect

LG1 Discuss peer relations in childhood and adolescence

Review

- What are peers, and what are the functions of peer groups? What are Piaget's and Sullivan's views on peers? How are the worlds of parents and peers distinct but coordinated? What is the developmental course of peer relations in childhood? How is social cognition involved in peer relations? What role does emotion regulation play in peer relations?
- Describe five types of peer statuses.
- What is the nature of bullying?
- How is gender involved in children's peer relations?
- How do adolescent peer groups differ from childhood peer groups? What are peer pressure and conformity like in adolescence? How are cliques and crowds involved in adolescent

development? What are some cultural variations in adolescent peer relations?

Connect

- Most developmentalists agree that peers play an important role in the development of moral reasoning. Of the five peer status groups you learned about in this section of the chapter, in which one(s) do you think children would have the least opportunity to fully develop their moral reasoning capacities and why?

Reflect *Your Own Personal Journey of Life*

- Think back to your childhood and adolescent years. Which peer status would you use to describe yourself? How influential do you think your peer status was on your development?

2 Friendship   Explain the role of friendship through the life span

| Functions of Friendship | Friendship During Childhood | Friendship During Adolescence and Emerging Adulthood | Adult Friendship |

The world of peers is one of varying acquaintances; we interact with some people we barely know, and with others we know well, every day. It is to the latter type—friends—that we now turn.

FUNCTIONS OF FRIENDSHIP

Why are friendships important? They serve the following functions (Gottman & Parker, 1987):

· *Companionship.* Friendship provides a familiar partner and playmate, someone who is willing to spend time with us and join in collaborative activities.
· *Stimulation.* Friendship provides interesting information, excitement, and amusement.
· *Ego support.* Friendship provides the expectation of support, encouragement, and feedback, which helps us maintain an impression of ourselves as competent, attractive, and worthwhile individuals.
· *Social comparison.* Friendship provides information about where we stand vis-à-vis others and how we are doing.
· *Affection and intimacy.* Friendship provides a warm, close, trusting relationship with another individual. **Intimacy in friendships** is characterized by self-disclosure and the sharing of private thoughts. Research reveals that intimate friendships may not appear until early adolescence (Berndt & Perry, 1990).

FRIENDSHIP DURING CHILDHOOD

Children's friendships are typically characterized by similarity (referred to as homophily, the tendency to associate with similar others) (Neal, Neal, & Cappella, 2014). Similarity is a central aspect of friendship that may or may not be beneficial (Prinstein & Dodge, 2008; Prinstein & Giletta, 2015). Throughout childhood, friends are more similar than dissimilar in terms of age, sex, ethnicity, and many other factors. Friends often have similar attitudes toward school, similar educational aspirations, and closely aligned achievement orientations.

Although having friends can be a developmental advantage, not all friendships are alike (Deutsch & others, 2015; Furman & Rose, 2015; Mason & others, 2014). People differ in the company they keep—that is, who their friends are. Developmental advantages occur when children have friends who are socially skilled, supportive, and oriented toward academic achievement (Chow, Tan, & Buhrmester, 2015; Jones & Magee, 2014; Wentzel, 2013). However, it is not developmentally advantageous to have coercive, conflict-ridden, and poor-quality friendships (Hartup, 2009). A recent study found that students who engaged in classroom aggressive-disruptive behavior were more likely to have aggressive friends (Powers & Bierman, 2013). To read about strategies for helping children develop friendships, see the *Connecting Development to Life* interlude.

FRIENDSHIP DURING ADOLESCENCE AND EMERGING ADULTHOOD

How are adolescent friendships different from childhood friendships? What characterizes friendship in emerging adulthood?

Adolescence   For most children, being popular with their peers is a strong motivator. The focus of their peer relations is on being liked by classmates and being included in games or lunchroom conversations. Beginning in early adolescence, however, teenagers typically prefer to have a smaller number of friendships that are more intense and intimate than those of young children.

Harry Stack Sullivan (1953) has been the most influential theorist in the study of adolescent friendships. Sullivan argued that friends are also important in shaping the development of children and adolescents. Everyone, said Sullivan, has basic social needs, such as the need for secure attachment, playful companionship, social acceptance, intimacy, and sexual relations. Whether or not these needs are fulfilled largely determines our emotional well-being. For example, if the need for playful companionship goes unmet, then we become bored and depressed; if the need for social acceptance is not met, we suffer a lowered sense of self-worth.

What characterizes children's friendships?
© Rolf Bruderer/Corbis

intimacy in friendship Self-disclosure and the sharing of private thoughts.

connecting development to life

Effective and Ineffective Strategies for Making Friends

Here are some strategies that adults can recommend to children and adolescents for making friends (Wentzel, 1997):

- *Initiate interaction.* Learn about a friend: Ask for his or her name, age, favorite activities. Use these prosocial overtures: Introduce yourself, start a conversation, and invite him or her to do things.
- *Be nice.* Show kindness, be considerate, and compliment the other person.
- *Engage in prosocial behavior.* Be honest and trustworthy: Tell the truth, keep promises. Be generous, share, and be cooperative.
- *Show respect for yourself and others.* Have good manners, be polite and courteous, and listen to what others have to say. Have a positive attitude and personality.
- *Provide social support.* Show you care.

And here are some ineffective strategies for making friends that adults can recommend that children and adolescents avoid using (Wentzel, 1997):

- *Be psychologically aggressive.* Show disrespect and have bad manners. Use others, be uncooperative, don't share, ignore others, gossip, and spread rumors.
- *Present yourself negatively.* Be self-centered, snobby, conceited, and jealous; show off, care only about yourself. Be mean, have a bad attitude, be angry, throw temper tantrums, and start trouble.
- *Behave antisocially.* Be physically aggressive, yell at others, pick on them, make fun of them, be dishonest, tell secrets, and break promises.

These suggestions were developed for adults to recommend to children. Do you think there is any period of the life span in which they would not be appropriate? Are some more effective in some periods of the life span than in others? If so, which ones and why?

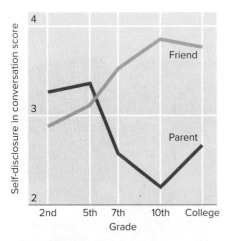

FIGURE 3

DEVELOPMENTAL CHANGES IN SELF-DISCLOSING CONVERSATIONS. Self-disclosing conversations with friends increased dramatically in adolescence while self-disclosure with parents declined in an equally dramatic fashion. However, self-disclosing conversations with parents began to pick up somewhat during the college years. The measure of self-disclosure involved a five-point rating scale completed by the children and youth, with a higher score representing greater self-disclosure. The data shown represent the means for each age group.

During adolescence, said Sullivan, friends become increasingly important in meeting social needs. In particular, Sullivan argued that the need for intimacy intensifies during early adolescence, motivating teenagers to seek out close friends. If adolescents fail to forge such close friendships, they often experience loneliness and a reduced sense of self-worth.

Many of Sullivan's ideas have withstood the test of time. For example, adolescents report disclosing intimate and personal information to their friends more often than do younger children (Buhrmester, 1998) (see Figure 3). Adolescents also say they depend more on friends than on parents to satisfy their needs for companionship, reassurance of worth, and intimacy. The ups and downs of experiences with friends shape adolescents' well-being (Rubin & others, 2013).

Are the friendships of adolescent girls more intimate than the friendships of adolescent boys? Girls' friendships in adolescence are more likely to focus on intimacy; boys' friendships tend to emphasize power and excitement (Furman & Rose, 2015; Rose & others, 2012). Boys may discourage one another from openly disclosing their problems because self-disclosure is not considered masculine (Maccoby, 1998).

A study of third- through ninth-graders, though, revealed that one aspect of girls' social support in friendship may have costs as well as benefits (Rose, Carlson, & Waller, 2007). In the study, girls' co-rumination (as reflected in excessively discussing problems) predicted not only an increase in positive friendship quality but also an increase in further co-rumination as well as an increase in depressive and anxiety symptoms. One implication of the research is that some girls who are vulnerable to developing internalized problems may go undetected because they have supportive friendships.

The study just described indicates that the characteristics of an adolescent's friends can influence whether the friends have a positive or negative influence on the adolescent. Positive friendship relationships in adolescence are associated with a host of positive outcomes, including lower rates of delinquency, substance abuse, risky sexual behavior, and bullying victimization, and a higher level of academic achievement and exercise (Lopes, Gabbard, & Rodriques, 2013; Furman & Rose, 2015; Wentzel, 2013). Not having a close relationship with a best friend, having less contact with friends, having friends who are depressed, and experiencing peer rejection all increase depressive tendencies in adolescents (Harris, Qualter,

& Robinson, 2013; Platt, Kadosh, & Lau, 2013; Waller & Rose, 2013). Researchers have found that interacting with delinquent peers and friends greatly increases the risk of becoming delinquent (Deutsch & others, 2012).

Although most adolescents develop friendships with individuals who are close to their own age, some adolescents become best friends with younger or older individuals. Do older friends encourage adolescents to engage in delinquent behavior or early sexual behavior? Adolescents who interact with older youth do engage in these behaviors more frequently, but it is not known whether the older youth guide younger adolescents toward deviant behavior or whether the younger adolescents were already prone to deviant behavior before they developed the friendship with the older youth (Billy, Rodgers, & Udry, 1984). A study also revealed that over time from the sixth through tenth grades girls were more likely to have older male friends, which places some girls on a developmental trajectory for engaging in problem behavior (Poulin & Pedersen, 2007).

Emerging Adulthood   Many aspects of friendship are the same in emerging adulthood as they were in adolescence. One difference was found, however, in a longitudinal study (Collins & van Dulmen, 2006). Close relationships—between friends, family members, and romantic partners—were more integrated and similar in emerging adulthood than they were in adolescence. Also in this study, the number of friendships declined from the end of adolescence through emerging adulthood.

Another research study indicated that best friendships often decline in satisfaction and commitment in the first year of college (Oswald & Clark, 2003). In this study, maintaining communication with high school friends and keeping the same best friends across the transition to college lessened the decline.

ADULT FRIENDSHIP

As in childhood and adolescence, adult friends tend to be similar in a number of ways. Among the similarities in friendship during the adult years are occupational status, ethnicity, age, marital status, income, education, gender, and religion (Rawlins, 2009).

Gender Differences   As in the childhood and adolescent years, there are gender differences in adult friendships. Women have more close friends than men do, and their friendships are more intimate (Wood, 2011, 2012). When adult female friends get together, they often talk, whereas adult male friends are more likely to engage in activities, especially outdoors. Thus, the adult male pattern of friendship often involves keeping one's distance while sharing useful information. When women talk with their friends, they expect to be able to express their feelings, reveal their weaknesses, and discuss their problems. They anticipate that their friends will listen at length and be sympathetic. In contrast, men are less likely to

A man's growth is seen in the successive choirs of his friends.

—RALPH WALDO EMERSON
American author and poet, 19th century

developmental **connection**

Gender

Deborah Tannen emphasizes gender differences in report talk and rapport talk. Connect to "Gender and Sexuality."

How is adult friendship different among female friends, male friends, and cross-gender friends?
(left to right): © Stockbyte/PunchStock RF; © BananaStock RF; © Ingram Publishing/age fotostock RF

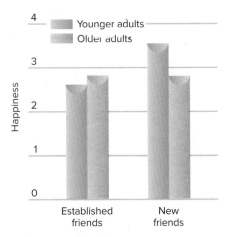

FIGURE **4**

HAPPINESS OF YOUNGER ADULTS AND OLDER ADULTS WITH NEW AND ESTABLISHED FRIENDS. *Note:* The happiness scale ranged from 0 to 6, with participants rating how intensely they experienced happiness (0 = not at all, 6 = extremely intense). Older adults' mean age 71; younger adults' mean age 23.

What are some characteristics of older adults' friendships?
© George Shelley/Corbis

talk about their weaknesses with their friends, and they want practical solutions to their problems rather than sympathy (Tannen, 1990). Also, adult male friendships are more competitive than those of women (Sharkey, 1993). For example, male friends disagree with each other more. Keep in mind, however, that these differences in same-sex adult friendship tend to be small (Sabini, 1995).

What about female-male friendship? Cross-gender friendships are more common among adults than among elementary school children, but not as common as same-gender friendships (Wood, 2011, 2012). Cross-gender friendships can provide both opportunities and problems. The opportunities involve learning more about common feelings and interests and shared characteristics, as well as acquiring knowledge and understanding of beliefs and activities that historically have been typical of the other gender.

Problems can arise in cross-gender friendships because of different expectations. For example, a woman might expect sympathy from a male friend but might receive a directive solution rather than a shoulder to cry on (Tannen, 1990). Another problem that can plague adult cross-gender friendship is unclear sexual boundaries, which can produce tension and confusion (Swain, 1992).

Friendship in Late Adulthood   In early adulthood, friendship networks expand as new social connections are made away from home. In late adulthood, new friendships are less likely to be forged, although some adults do seek out new friendships, especially following the death of a spouse (Zettel-Watson & Rook, 2009).

Aging expert Laura Carstensen and her colleagues (1998, 2009; Carstensen, Mikels, & Mather, 2006; Charles & Carstensen, 2010; Sims, Hogan, & Carstensen, 2015) concluded that people choose close friends over new friends as they grow older. And as long as they have several close people in their network, they seem content, says Carstensen. Supporting Carstensen's view, researchers found that in comparison with younger adults, older adults said they tended to experience less intense positive emotions with new friends and equal levels of positive emotions with established friends (Charles & Piazza, 2007) (see Figure 4).

The following four studies document the importance of friendship in older adults:

· A recent study found that activities with friends increased positive affect and life satisfaction in older adults (Huxhold, Miche, & Schuz, 2014).

· Friendships were more important than family relationships in predicting mental health in adults 60 years and older (Fiori, Antonucci, & Cortina, 2006).

· Older adults 75 years of age and older who maintained close ties with friends were less likely to die across a seven-year age span (Rasulo, Christensen, & Tomassini, 2005). The findings were stronger for women than for men.

· Unmarried older adults embedded in a friend-focused network fared better physically and psychologically than unmarried older adults in a restricted network with little friend contact (Fiori, Smith, & Antonucci, 2007).

Review Connect Reflect

Explain the role of friendship through the life span

Review
• What are five functions of friendship?
• What is the developmental significance of friendship during childhood?
• How can adolescents' friendships be characterized? What is Sullivan's view on friendship? What are friendships in emerging adulthood like?
• How do friendships vary in adulthood based on gender and age?

Connect
• Connect this section's discussion of friendship in late adulthood with what you've learned about health and aging.

Reflect *Your Own Personal Journey of Life*
• What characterizes your relationships with friends at this point in your life? How are your friendships different from what they were like when you were younger?

Peers and friends often engage in play and enjoy leisure activities together. Let's explore the developmental aspects of play and leisure.

CHILDHOOD

An extensive amount of peer interaction during childhood involves play; however, social play is but one type of play. **Play** is a pleasurable activity that is engaged in for its own sake.

Play's Functions   Play is an important aspect of children's development (Bergen, 2015; Hirsh-Pasek & Golinkoff, 2014; Johnson & others, 2015; Lillard, 2015). Theorists have focused on different aspects of play and highlighted a long list of functions (Henricks, 2015a, b).

According to Freud and Erikson, play helps the child master anxieties and reduce conflicts (Demanachick, 2015). Because tensions are relieved in play, the child can cope more effectively with life's problems. Play permits the child to work off excess physical energy and release pent-up tensions. Therapists use **play therapy** both to allow the child to work off frustrations and to analyze the child's conflicts and ways of coping with them. Children may feel less threatened and be more likely to express their true feelings in the context of play (Clark, 2015; Demanachick, 2015; Yanof, 2013).

Piaget (1962) maintained that play advances children's cognitive development. At the same time, he said that children's cognitive development constrains the way they play. Play permits children to practice their competencies and skills in a relaxed, pleasurable way (Hirsh-Pasek & Golinkoff, 2014). Piaget thought that cognitive structures need to be exercised, and play provides the perfect setting for this exercise (DeLisi, 2015). For example, children who have just learned to add or multiply begin to play with numbers in different ways as they perfect these operations, laughing as they do so.

Vygotsky (1962) also considered play to be an excellent setting for cognitive development. He was especially interested in the symbolic and make-believe aspects of play, as when a child substitutes a stick for a horse and rides the stick as if it were a horse (Bodrova & Leong, 2015). For young children, the imaginary situation is real. Parents should encourage such imaginary play, because it advances the child's cognitive development, especially creative thought. Both Piaget and Vygotsky described play as the work of the child.

Daniel Berlyne (1960) described play as exciting and pleasurable in itself because it satisfies our exploratory drive. This drive involves curiosity and a desire for information about something new or unusual. Play is a means whereby children can safely explore and seek out new information. Play encourages exploratory behavior by offering children the possibilities of novelty, complexity, uncertainty, surprise, and incongruity.

More recently, play has been described as an important context for the development of language and communication skills (Christie & Roskos, 2015; Hirsh-Pasek & Golinkoff, 2014). Language and communication skills may be enhanced through discussions and negotiations regarding roles and rules in play as young children practice various words and phrases. These types of social interactions during play can benefit young children's literacy skills (Gunning, 2013). Play is a central focus of the child-centered kindergarten and is thought to be an essential aspect of early childhood education (Kostelnik & others, 2015; Morrison, 2014, 2015).

An increasing concern is that the large number of hours children spend with electronic media, such as television and computers, takes time away from play (Linn, 2008). An important agenda for parents is to include ample time for play in their children's lives.

Types of Play   The contemporary perspective on types of play emphasizes both cognitive and social aspects of play (Bergen, 2015; Hirsh-Pasek

> You are troubled at seeing him spend his early years in doing nothing. What! Is it nothing to be happy? Is it nothing to skip, to play, to run about all day long? Never in his life will he be so busy as now.
>
> —JEAN-JACQUES ROUSSEAU
> *Swiss-born French philosopher, 18th century*

developmental **connection**

Cognitive Development

Vygotsky emphasized that children mainly develop their ways of thinking and understanding through social interaction. Connect to "Cognitive Developmental Approaches."

play A pleasurable activity that is engaged in for its own sake.

play therapy Therapy that lets children work off frustrations while therapists analyze their conflicts and coping methods.

© iStockphoto.com/cujo19 RF

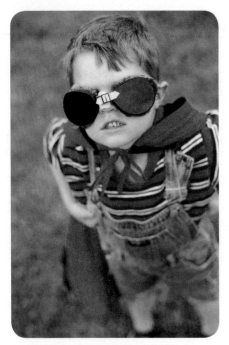

A preschool "superhero" at play.
© Dann Tardif/LWA/Corbis

- - - - - - - - - - ➤

developmental **connection**

Education

The child-centered kindergarten emphasizes the education of the whole child and
the importance of play in young children's
development. Connect to "Schools, Achievement, and Work."

sensorimotor play Behavior by infants to
derive pleasure from exercising their
sensorimotor schemes.

practice play Play that involves repetition of
behavior when new skills are being learned
or when mastery and coordination of skills are
required for games or sports.

pretense/symbolic play Play that occurs
when a child transforms aspects of the
physical environment into symbols.

social play Play that involves interaction with
peers.

constructive play Combination of
sensorimotor/practice play with symbolic
representation.

games Activities that are engaged in for
pleasure and include rules.

leisure The pleasant times when individuals
are free to pursue activities and interests of
their own choosing.

& Golinkoff, 2014; Lillard, 2015). Among the most widely studied types of children's play today are sensorimotor and practice play, pretense/symbolic play, social play, constructive play, and games.

Sensorimotor and Practice Play   **Sensorimotor play** is behavior by infants to derive pleasure from exercising their sensorimotor schemes. The development of sensorimotor play follows Piaget's description of sensorimotor thought. Infants initially engage in exploratory and playful visual and motor transactions in the second quarter of the first year of life. By the end of the third quarter, infants begin to select novel objects for exploration and play, especially responsive objects such as toys that make noise or bounce. At 12 months of age, infants enjoy making things work and exploring cause and effect.

Practice play involves repetition of behavior when new skills are being learned or when physical or mental mastery and coordination of skills are required for games or sports. Sensorimotor play, which often involves practice play, is primarily confined to infancy, whereas practice play can be engaged in throughout life. During the preschool years, children frequently engage in practice play. Although practice play declines in the elementary school years, practice play activities such as running, jumping, sliding, twirling, and throwing balls or other objects are frequently observed on the playgrounds at elementary schools.

Pretense/Symbolic Play   **Pretense/symbolic play** occurs when the child transforms aspects of the physical environment into symbols. Between 9 and 30 months of age, children increase their use of objects in symbolic play. They learn to transform objects—substituting them for other objects and acting toward them as if they were those other objects (Smith, 2007). For example, a preschool child treats a table as if it were a car and says, "I'm fixing the car," as he grabs a leg of the table.

Many experts on play consider the preschool years the "golden age" of symbolic/ pretense play that is dramatic or sociodramatic in nature. This type of make-believe play often appears at about 18 months of age and reaches a peak at 4 to 5 years of age, then gradually declines.

Some child psychologists conclude that pretense/symbolic play is an important aspect of young children's development and often reflects advances in their cognitive development, especially as an indication of symbolic understanding (Lillard, 2015; Lillard, Pinkham, & Smith, 2011). For example, Catherine Garvey (2000) and Angeline Lillard (2006, 2015) emphasize that hidden in young children's pretend play narratives are capacities for role-taking, balancing of social roles, metacognition (thinking about thinking), testing of the reality-pretense distinction, and numerous nonegocentric capacities that reveal the remarkable cognitive skills of young children.

Social Play   **Social play** is play that involves interaction with peers. Social play increases dramatically during the preschool years (Power, 2011). Social play includes varied interchanges such as turn taking, conversations about numerous topics, social games and routines, and physical play (Sumaroka & Bornstein, 2008). Social play often involves a high degree of pleasure on the part of the participants (Sumaroka & Bornstein, 2008).

Constructive Play   **Constructive play** combines sensorimotor/practice play with symbolic representation. Constructive play occurs when children engage in the self-regulated creation of a product or a solution (Sawyer & DeZutter, 2007). Constructive play increases in the preschool years as symbolic play increases and sensorimotor play decreases. In the preschool years, some practice play is replaced by constructive play. For example, instead of moving their fingers around and around in finger paint (practice play), children are more likely to draw the outline of a house or a person in the paint (constructive play). Constructive play is also a frequent form of play in the elementary school years, both within and outside the classroom.

Games   **Games** are activities that are engaged in for pleasure and have rules. Often they involve competition. Preschool children may begin to participate in social games that involve simple rules of reciprocity and turn taking. However, games take on a much stronger role in the lives of elementary school children.

In sum, play ranges from an infant's simple exercise of a new sensorimotor skill to a preschool child's riding a tricycle to an older child's participation in organized games.

Note that children's play can involve a combination of the play categories we have discussed. For example, social play can be sensorimotor (rough-and-tumble), symbolic, or constructive.

Trends in Play   Kathy Hirsh-Pasek, Roberta Golinkoff, and Dorothy Singer (Hirsh-Pasek & others, 2009; Singer, Golinkoff, & Hirsh-Pasek, 2006) are concerned about the limited amount of time for free play that young children have, reporting that it has declined considerably in recent decades. They especially are worried about young children's playtime being restricted at home and school so they can spend more time on academic subjects. They also point out that many schools have eliminated recess. And it is not just the decline in free play time that bothers them. They underscore that learning in playful contexts captivates children's minds in ways that enhance their cognitive and socioemotional development. In fact, Singer, Golinkoff, and Hirsh-Pasek's (2006) first book on play was titled: *Play = Learning*. Among the cognitive benefits of play they described are these skills: creative, abstract thinking; imagination; attention, concentration, and persistence; problem-solving; social cognition, empathy, and perspective taking; language; and mastering new concepts. Among the socioemotional experiences and development they believe play promotes are enjoyment, relaxation, and self-expression; cooperation, sharing, and turn-taking; anxiety reduction; and self-confidence. With so many positive cognitive and socioemotional outcomes of play, clearly it is important that we find more time for play in young children's lives (Dyson, 2015; Lillard, 2015).

Kathy Hirsh-Pasek interacts with a young child in a play context. *What are some of the benefits of play for children, according to Hirsh-Pasek and her colleagues?*
© Temple University, photo by Joseph V. Labolito

ADOLESCENCE

Leisure refers to the pleasant times when individuals are free to pursue activities and interests of their own choosing—hobbies, sports, or reading, for example. How much leisure time do U.S. adolescents have compared with adolescents in other countries? How do U.S. adolescents use their leisure time?

Figure 5 indicates that U.S. adolescents spend more time in leisure activities than do adolescents in other industrialized countries (Larson & Verma, 1999). About 40 to 50 percent of U.S. adolescents' waking hours (not counting summer vacation) is spent in leisure activities, compared with 25 to 35 percent in East Asia and 35 to 45 percent in Europe. Whether this additional leisure time is a liability or an asset for U.S. adolescents, of course, depends on how they use it.

developmental **connection**

Culture

In the research of Harold Stevenson and his colleagues, the longer students were in school, the wider the gap was between Asian and U.S. students in math achievement. Connect to "Schools, Achievement, and Work."

Activity	Nonindustrial, Unschooled Populations	Postindustrial, Schooled Populations		
		United States	Europe	East Asia
TV viewing	Insufficient data	1.5 to 2.5 hours	1.5 to 2.5 hours	1.5 to 2.5 hours
Talking	Insufficient data	2 to 3 hours	Insufficient data	45 to 60 minutes
Sports	Insufficient data	30 to 60 minutes	20 to 80 minutes	0 to 20 minutes
Structured voluntary activities	Insufficient data	10 to 20 minutes	10 to 20 minutes	0 to 10 minutes
Total free time	4 to 7 hours	6.5 to 8.0 hours	5.5 to 7.5 hours	4.0 to 5.5 hours

Note: The estimates in the table are averaged across a 7-day week, including weekdays and weekends. The data for nonindustrial, unschooled populations come primarily from rural peasant populations in developing countries.

FIGURE 5

AVERAGE DAILY LEISURE TIME OF ADOLESCENTS IN DIFFERENT REGIONS OF THE WORLD

The largest amounts of U.S. adolescents' free time are spent engaging in screen-based activities, hanging out, and engaging in unstructured leisure activities, often with friends. U.S. and European adolescents spend more time in voluntary structured activities—such as sports, hobbies, and organizations—than East Asian adolescents do.

According to Reed Larson (2001; Larson & Dawes, 2013), in terms of optimal development U.S. adolescents may have too much unstructured time because when they are allowed to choose what to do with their time, they typically engage in unchallenging leisure activities such as hanging out and watching TV. Although relaxation and social interaction are important aspects of adolescence, it seems unlikely that spending large numbers of hours per week in unchallenging activities fosters development. Structured voluntary activities may hold more promise for adolescent development than unstructured time, especially if adults give

How do U.S. adolescents spend their time differently from European and East Asian adolescents?
© *Allan Shoemake/Getty Images RF*

responsibility to adolescents, challenge them, and provide competent guidance in these activities (Mahoney, Larson, & Eccles, 2004).

ADULTHOOD

As adults, not only must we learn how to work well, but we also need to learn how to relax and enjoy leisure (Iwasaki, 2008). In an analysis of what U.S. adults regret the most, not engaging in more leisure was one of the top six regrets (Roese & Summerville, 2005).

Leisure can be an especially important aspect of middle adulthood (Mannell, 2000). By middle adulthood, more money is available to many individuals, and there may be more free time and paid vacations. In short, midlife changes may produce expanded opportunities for leisure. For many individuals, middle adulthood is the first time in their lives when they have the opportunity to diversify their interests.

In one study, 12,338 men 35 to 57 years of age were assessed each year for five years regarding whether they took vacations or not (Gump & Matthews, 2000). Then the researchers examined the medical and death records over nine years for men who lived for at least a year after the last vacation survey. Compared with those who never took vacations, men who went on annual vacations were 21 percent less likely to die over the nine years and 32 percent less likely to die of coronary heart disease. The qualities that lead men to avoid taking a vacation tend to promote heart disease, such as not trusting anyone to fill in while they are gone or fearing that they will get behind in their work and someone will replace them. These are behaviors that sometimes have been described as part of the Type A behavioral pattern.

Adults at midlife need to begin preparing psychologically for retirement. Participating in constructive and fulfilling leisure activities in middle adulthood is an important part of this preparation (Kelly, 1996). If adults develop leisure activities that they can continue into retirement, the transition from work to retirement can be less stressful.

How much leisure activity do older adults get? A national study revealed that more than half of U.S. adults 60 years and older spend no time in leisure activities (Hughes, McDowell, & Brody, 2008). In this study, 27 percent of the older adults participated in 2½ hours or more of leisure time activities per week. Older adults who were male, younger, non-Latino White, had a higher income status and education, were married, and reported being in better health were more likely to engage in leisure activities.

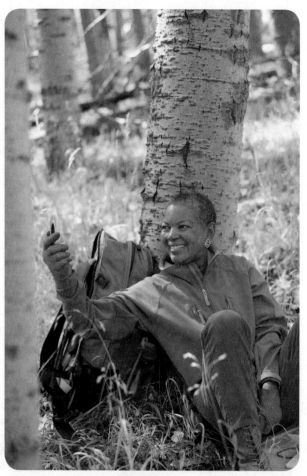

Sigmund Freud once commented that the two things adults need to do well to adapt to society's demands are to work and to love. To his list we add "to play." In our fast-paced society, it is all too easy to get caught up in the frenzied, hectic pace of our achievement-oriented work world and ignore leisure and play. *Imagine your life as a middle-aged adult. What would be the ideal mix of work and leisure? What leisure activities do you want to enjoy as a middle-aged adult?*
© Marc Romanelli/Getty Images

Review Connect Reflect

 Describe the developmental aspects of play and leisure

Review

- What are the functions of play? What are the different types of play?
- What is leisure? How do adolescents use their discretionary time?
- What are some key aspects of leisure in adulthood?

Connect

- How might friendship and moral development interact during adolescence?

Reflect *Your Own Personal Journey of Life*

- Do you think your life as a child and now as an adult is too structured and leaves too little time for play? Did you have too much unstructured time as an adolescent? Explain.

Social Theories of Aging   Stereotyping of Older Adults   Social Support and Social Integration   Successful Aging

What happens to our social world when we get older? Does it shrink? Do we become more selective and spend more time with our closest friends? How do social experiences influence the aging process? In this section we'll explore some theories of aging that give social experiences an important role.

SOCIAL THEORIES OF AGING

Socioemotional selectivity theory states that older adults become more selective about their social networks and often seek greater emotional quality in relationships with friends and family. Researchers have found extensive support for socioemotional selectivity theory (Charles & Carstensen, 2010; English & Carstensen, 2014; Sims, Hogan, & Carstensen, 2015). Let's consider two other social theories of aging.

Disengagement theory states that to cope effectively, older adults should gradually withdraw from society. This theory was proposed half a century ago (Cumming & Henry, 1961). In this view, older adults develop increasing self-preoccupation, lessen emotional ties with others, and show decreasing interest in society's affairs. By following these strategies of disengagement, it was thought that older adults would enjoy enhanced life satisfaction. This theory generated a storm of protest and met with a quick death. We present it because of its historical relevance. Although not formally proposed until 1961, it summarized the prevailing beliefs about older adults in the first half of the twentieth century.

Activity theory states that the more active and involved older adults are, the more satisfied they will be with their lives. Thus, activity theory is the exact opposite of disengagement theory. Researchers have found strong support for activity theory, beginning in the 1960s and continuing into the twenty-first century (Neugarten, Havighurst, & Tobin, 1968). One longitudinal study found that a greater overall activity level (which included social activities such as visiting relatives or friends, solitary activities such as hobbies, and productive activities such as volunteer work and gardening) at the beginning of the study was related to greater happiness, better physical and cognitive functioning, and reduced mortality six years later (Menec, 2003). Also, a recent study of Canadian older adults revealed that those who were more physically active had higher life satisfaction and greater social interaction than their physically inactive counterparts (Azagba & Sharaf, 2014). In sum, when older adults are active, energetic, and productive, they age more successfully and are happier than if they disengage from society.

developmental **connection**

Social Contexts

Socioemotional selectivity theory also focuses on the types of goals individuals are motivated to achieve as they go through the adult years. Connect to "Emotional Development and Attachment."

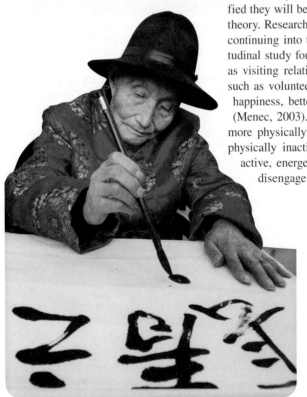

One-hundred-year-old He Jingming demonstrates his calligraphy skills in China. *How does his behavior contradict stereotyping of older adults?*
© Claro Cortes IV/Reuters/Corbis

STEREOTYPING OF OLDER ADULTS

Social participation by older adults is often discouraged by **ageism,** which is prejudice against others because of their age, especially prejudice against older adults (Bodner & Cohen-Fridel, 2014). Older adults are often perceived as incapable of thinking clearly, learning new things, enjoying sex, contributing to the community, or holding responsible jobs. Because of their age, older adults might not be hired for new jobs or might be eased out of old ones; they might be shunned socially; and they might be edged out of their family life.

Ageism is widespread (Anderson & others, 2013; North & Fiske, 2013a, b). One study found that men were more likely to negatively stereotype older adults than were women (Rupp, Vodanovich, & Crede, 2005). Research indicates that the most frequent form of ageism is disrespect for older adults, followed by assumptions about ailments or frailty caused by age (Palmore, 2004). However, the increased number of adults living to older ages has led to active efforts to improve society's image of older adults, obtain better living conditions for older adults, and gain political clout to address issues involving this group.

SOCIAL SUPPORT AND SOCIAL INTEGRATION

Social support and social integration play important roles in the physical and mental health of older adults (Cramm & Nieboer, 2015; Lee, Kahana, & Kahana, 2015; Li, Ji, & Chen, 2014; Utz & others, 2014). In the *social convoy* model of social relations, individuals go through life embedded in a personal network of individuals to whom they give, and from whom they receive, social support (Antonucci Birditt, & Ajrouch, 2013). Social support can help individuals of all ages cope more effectively with life's challenges (Ikeda & others, 2013). For older adults, social support is related to their physical and mental health (Lee & others, 2015; Lieverse & others, 2013). It is linked with a reduction in symptoms of disease, with the ability to meet one's own health-care needs, and increased longevity (Rook & others, 2007). A higher level of social support also is related to a lower probability of an older adult being institutionalized and depressed (Heard & others, 2011). Further, a recent study revealed that older adults who experienced a higher level of social support showed later cognitive decline than their counterparts with a lower level of social support (Dickinson & others, 2011).

Social integration also plays an important role in the lives of many older adults (Hawkley & Cacioppo, 2013; Li & Zhang, 2015; Stephens, Breheny, & Mansvelt, 2015). A recent study found that older adults with higher levels of social integration were less depressed (Ivan Santini & others, 2015).

Researchers have found that older adults tend to report being less lonely than younger adults and less lonely than would be expected based on their circumstances (Schnittker, 2007). Their reports of feeling less lonely than younger adults likely reflect their more selective social networks and greater acceptance of loneliness in their lives (Koropeckyj-Cox, 2009). In one study, the most consistent factor that predicted loneliness in older adults at 70, 78, and 85 years of age was not being married (Stessman & others, 2014). In other research with 60- to 80-year-olds, the partner's death was a stronger indicator of loneliness for men than for women (Nicolaisen & Thorsen, 2014).

Recently, researchers also have explored the extent to which loneliness and social isolation are linked to various outcomes in elderly adults (Boss, Kang, & Branson, 2015; Skingley, 2013). Both loneliness and social isolation are associated with increased health problems and mortality (Luo & others, 2012). Also, a recent study of elderly adults revealed that both loneliness and social isolation were associated with decreases in cognitive functioning 4 years later (Shankar & others, 2013). However, another recent study found that social isolation was a better predictor of mortality than loneliness (Steptoe & others, 2013).

What role does social support play in the health of older adults?
© Frank Conaway/age fotostock

What characterizes social integration in the lives of older adults?
© Yellow Dog Productions/Getty Images RF

SUCCESSFUL AGING

Throughout this book, we have called attention to the positive aspects of aging. In fact, examining the positive aspects of aging is an important trend in life-span development and is likely to benefit future generations of older adults (Cheng, 2014; Cosco & others, 2014; Johnson & Mutchler, 2014; Rowe & Kahn, 2015).

There are many robust, healthy older adults. With a proper diet, an active lifestyle, mental stimulation and flexibility, positive coping skills, good social relationships and support, and the absence of disease, many abilities can be maintained or in some cases even improved as we get older (Antonucci, Birditt, & Ajrouch, 2013). Even when individuals develop a disease, improvements in medical technology mean that increasing numbers of older adults can continue to lead active, constructive lives (Siegler, Bosworth, & others, 2013; Siegler, Elias, & others, 2013). A recent Canadian study found that the predicted self-rated probability of aging successfully was 41 percent for those 65 to 74, 33 percent for those 75 to 84, and 22 percent for those 85+ years of age (Meng & D'Arcy, 2014). In this study, being younger, married, a

disengagement theory The theory that, to cope effectively, older adults should gradually withdraw from society; this theory is no longer supported.

activity theory The theory that the more active and involved older adults are, the more likely they are to be satisfied with their lives.

ageism Prejudice against people because of their age, especially prejudice against older adults.

Eighty-two-year-old Warren Buffett, one of the world's richest individuals, continues to have a very active, successful life. He recently donated more than $30 billion to several foundations, with the bulk of the money given to the Bill and Melinda Gates Foundation, which plans to use it to reduce poverty, improve education, and solve health problems.
© Nati Harnik/AP Images

regular drinker, healthy, and satisfied with life were associated with successful aging. Presence of disease was linked to a significant decline in successful aging. A recent study found that having multiple chronic diseases was linked to a lower level of successful aging (Hsu, 2015). Having selective positive family and friendship relationships is associated with successful aging (English & Carstensen, 2014; Huxhold, Miche, & Schüz, 2014). A recent study of 90- to 91-year-olds found that living circumstances, especially owning one's own home and living there as long as possible; independence in various aspects of life; good health; and a good death were described as important themes of successful aging (Nosraty & others, 2015). In this study, social and cognitive aspects were thought to be more important than physical health.

Being active is especially important to successful aging (Parisi & others, 2014; Solberg & others, 2014). Older adults who exercise regularly, attend meetings, participate in religious activities, and go on trips are more satisfied with their lives than their counterparts who disengage from society (Berchicci & others, 2014). Older adults who engage in challenging cognitive activities are more likely to retain their cognitive skills for a longer period of time (Park & others, 2014; Rebok & others, 2014). Older adults who are emotionally selective, optimize their choices, and compensate effectively for losses increase their chances of aging successfully (Freund, Nikitin, & Riediger, 2013). And a very important agenda is to continue improving our understanding of how people can live longer, healthier, more productive and satisfying lives (Nagamatsu & others, 2014; Park, Han, & Kang, 2014).

Review Connect Reflect

 LG4 Summarize the social aspects of aging

Review
- What are three social theories of aging?
- How extensively are older adults stereotyped?
- What roles do social support and social integration play in the development of older adults?
- What are some important aspects of successful aging?

Connect
- Connect the research on intergenerational relationships with this section's discussion of successful aging.

Reflect *Your Own Personal Journey of Life*
- Consider your parents, grandparents, and possibly even great-grandparents who are still alive. How have their social lives changed as they have aged?

5 Sociocultural Influences   **LG5** Evaluate sociocultural influences on development

| Culture | Socioeconomic Status and Poverty | Ethnicity |

developmental **connection**

Theories

In Bronfenbrenner's ecological theory, the macrosystem is the environmental system that involves the influence of culture on children's development. Connect to "Introduction."

Personal relations with friends and other peers form only part of the social world outside the family that influences development. As we have seen throughout this book, development is also influenced by the sociocultural context. Here we take a closer look at three aspects of that context: culture, socioeconomic status, and ethnicity.

CULTURE

Culture refers to the behavior, patterns, beliefs, and all other products of a group of people that are passed on from generation to generation. It results from the interaction between people and their environment over many years. **Cross-cultural studies** compare aspects of two or more cultures, providing information about the degree to which development is similar, or universal, across cultures, or is instead culture-specific.

One study revealed that from the beginning of the seventh grade through the end of the eighth grade, U.S. adolescents valued academics less and their motivational behavior also decreased (Wang & Pomerantz, 2009). By contrast, the value placed on academics by Chinese adolescents did not change across this time frame and their motivational behavior was sustained. In the chapter on "Schools, Achievement, and Work," we discuss in greater detail the higher math and science achievement of Asian children in comparison with U.S. children.

The concept of culture is broad; it includes many components and can be analyzed in many ways (Goodnow & Lawrence, 2015; Mistry & Dutta, 2015). Cross-cultural expert Richard Brislin (1993) described a number of characteristics of culture:

· Culture is made up of ideals, values, and assumptions about life that guide people's behavior.

· Culture consists of those aspects of the environment that people make.

· Culture is transmitted from generation to generation, with responsibility for the transmission resting on the shoulders of parents, teachers, and community leaders.

· When their cultural values are violated or their cultural expectations are ignored, people react emotionally.

· It is not unusual for people to accept a cultural value at one point in their lives and reject it at another point. For example, rebellious adolescents and young adults might accept a culture's values and expectations after having children of their own.

© Cartesia/Getty Images RF

Classical research by American psychologist Donald Campbell and his colleagues (Brewer & Campbell, 1976; Campbell & LeVine, 1968) revealed that people in all cultures tend to do the following things:

· think that what happens in their culture is "natural" and "correct" and that what happens in other cultures is "unnatural" and "incorrect";

· perceive their cultural customs as universally valid—that is, conclude that "what is good for us is good for everyone";

· behave in ways that favor their cultural group; and

· feel hostile toward other cultural groups.

In other words, people in all cultures tend to display **ethnocentrism**, the tendency to consider one's own group superior to others.

The Relevance of Culture for the Study of Life-Span Development
Global interdependence is an inescapable reality (Matsumoto & Juang, 2013). Children, adolescents, and adults are not just citizens of one country; they are citizens of the world—a world that, through advances in transportation and technology, has become increasingly connected. By better understanding cultures around the world, we may be able to interact more effectively with each other and make this planet a more hospitable, peaceful place (Mistry & Dutta, 2015).

Individualism and Collectivism
What cultural differences are significant in life-span development? One finding in cross-cultural research is that cultures around the world tend to take two very different orientations to life and social relations. That is, cultures tend to emphasize either individualism or collectivism:

· **Individualism** involves giving priority to personal goals rather than to group goals; it emphasizes values that serve the self, such as feeling good, obtaining personal distinction through achievement, and preserving independence.

· **Collectivism** emphasizes values that serve the group by subordinating personal goals to preserve group integrity, supporting interdependence of the members, and promoting harmonious relationships.

Figure 6 summarizes some of the main characteristics of individualistic and collectivistic cultures. Many Western cultures, such as those of the United States, Canada, Great Britain, and the Netherlands, are described as individualistic; many Eastern cultures, such as those of China, Japan, India, and Thailand, are described as collectivistic. A recent study from 1970

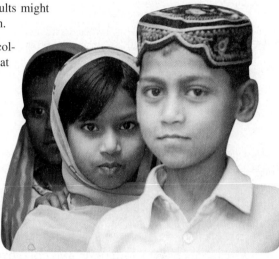
What is culture? How does it influence people's lives?
© Annabelle Breakey/The Image Bank/Getty Images

culture The behavior, patterns, beliefs, and all other products of a group of people that are passed on from generation to generation.

cross-cultural studies Studies that compare aspects of two or more cultures to provide information about the degree to which development is similar or universal across the cultures, or is instead culture-specific.

ethnocentrism The tendency to consider one's own group superior to other groups.

individualism Giving priority to personal goals rather than to group goals; emphasizing values that serve the self, such as feeling good, obtaining personal distinction through achievement, and preserving independence.

collectivism Emphasizing values that serve the group by subordinating personal goals to preserve group integrity, supporting interdependence of members, and promoting harmonious relationships.

Individualistic	Collectivistic
Focuses on individual.	Focuses on groups.
Self is determined by personal traits independent of groups; self is stable across contexts.	Self is defined by in-group terms; self can change with context.
Private self is more important.	Public self is most important.
Personal achievement, competition, power are important.	Achievement is for the benefit of the in-group; cooperation is stressed.
Cognitive dissonance is frequent.	Cognitive dissonance is infrequent.
Emotions (such as anger) are self-focused.	Emotions (such as anger) are often relationship based.
People who are the most liked are self-assured.	People who are the most liked are modest, self-effacing.
Values: pleasure, achievement, competition, freedom.	Values: security, obedience, in-group harmony, personalized relationships.
Many casual relationships.	Few, close relationships.
Save own face.	Save own and other's face.
Independent behaviors: swimming, sleeping alone in room, privacy.	Interdependent behaviors: co-bathing, co-sleeping.
Relatively rare mother-child physical contact.	Frequent mother-child physical contact (such as hugging, holding).

FIGURE 6

CHARACTERISTICS OF INDIVIDUALISTIC AND COLLECTIVISTIC CULTURES

to 2008 found that although China still is characterized by collectivistic values, the frequency of words used in China to index individualistic values increased (Zeng & Greenfield, 2015).

Many of the assumptions about contemporary ideas in fields like life-span development were developed in individualistic cultures (Triandis, 1994, 2001, 2007). Consider the flurry of self-terms in psychology that have an individualistic focus: *self-actualization, self-awareness, self-efficacy, self-reinforcement, self-criticism, self-serving, selfishness,* and *self-doubt* (Lonner, 1988).

Self-conceptions are related to culture. In one study, American and Chinese college students completed 20 sentences beginning with "I am _____" (Trafimow, Triandis, & Goto, 1991). As indicated in Figure 7, the American college students were much more likely than the Chinese students to describe themselves with personal traits ("I am assertive," for example), than to identify themselves by their group affiliations ("I am a member of the math club," for example). However, a recent study found that from 1990 to 2007, Chinese 18- to 65-year-olds increasingly included more individualistic characteristics in their descriptions of what constitutes happiness and well-being (Steele & Lynch, 2013).

Some social scientists note that many problems in Western cultures are intensified by the Western cultural emphasis on individualism. The rates of suicide, drug abuse, crime, teenage pregnancy, divorce, child abuse, and mental disorders are higher in individualistic cultures than in collectivistic ones. A recent study across 62 countries found that reported student aggressive behavior for fourth- and eighth-graders was higher in individualistic countries than in collectivistic cultures (Bergmuller, 2013).

Critics of the concept of individualistic and collectivistic cultures argue that these terms are too broad and simplistic, especially with globalization increasing (Greenfield, 2009; Sugimura & Mizokami, 2013). Regardless of their cultural background, people need both a positive sense of self and connectedness to others to develop fully as human beings. Carolyn Tamis-LeMonda and her colleagues (2008) emphasize that in many families, children are not reared in environments that uniformly endorse either individualistic or collectivistic values, thoughts, and actions. Rather, in many families, children are "expected to be quiet, assertive, respectful, curious, humble, self-assured, independent, dependent, affectionate, or reserved depending on the situation, people present, children's age, and social-political and economic circles." Nonetheless, a number of studies continue to find differences between individualistic and collectivistic cultures in a number of areas (Boer & Fischer, 2013; Eichbaum, 2015; Grossman & Varnum, 2015; Papadopoulos, Foster, & Caldwell, 2013; Willis, 2012).

Media/Screen Time If the amount of time spent in an activity is any indication of its importance, there is no doubt that media viewing and screen time play important roles in children's and adolescents' lives (Busschaert & others, 2015; Calvert, 2015; Calvert & Wartella, 2014; Sterin, 2014). Few developments in society in the second half of the twentieth century had a greater impact on children than television. Television continues to have a strong influence on children's development, but children's use of other media and information/communication devices has led to the use of the term *screen time*, which encompasses the total amount of time individuals spend watching television or DVDs, playing video games, and using computers or mobile media such as iPhones (Lloyd & others, 2014). Television is still the elephant in young children's media life, with 2- to 4-year-old children watching TV approximately 2 to 4 hours per day (Roberts & Foehr, 2008).

To better understand various aspects of U.S. children's and adolescents' media use/screen time, the Kaiser Family Foundation funded national surveys in 1999, 2004, and 2009. The 2009 survey included more than 2,000 8- to 18-year-olds and documented that children's and adolescents' media use had increased dramatically in recent years (Rideout, Foehr, & Roberts, 2010). Today's youth live in a world in which they are encapsulated by media. In this survey, in 2009, 8- to 11-year-olds used media 5 hours and 29 minutes a day, but 11- to 14-year-olds used media an average of 8 hours and 40 minutes a day and 15- to 18-year-olds an average of 7 hours and 58 minutes a day (see Figure 8). Thus, daily media use jumps by more than 3 hours in early adolescence. The largest increases in media use in early adolescence are for TV viewing and video gaming. TV use by youth increasingly has involved watching TV on the Internet, an iPod/MP3 player, or on a cell phone. As indicated in Figure 8, time spent listening to music and using computers also increases considerably among 11- to 14-year-old adolescents. Based on the 2009 survey, adding up the daily media use figures to obtain weekly media use leads to the staggering levels of more than 60 hours a week of media use by 11- to 14-year-olds and almost 56 hours a week by 15- to 18-year-olds.

A major trend in the use of technology is the dramatic increase in media multitasking (Sanbonmatsu & others, 2013). In the 2009 survey, when the amount of time spent multitasking was included in computing media use, 11- to 14-year-olds spent nearly 12 hours a day (as compared with almost 9 hours a day when multitasking was not included) exposed to media (Rideout & others, 2010). In this survey, 39 percent of seventh- to twelfth-graders said "most of the time" they use two or more media concurrently, such as surfing the Web while listening to music. In some cases, media multitasking—such as text messaging, listening to an iPod, and updating a YouTube site—is engaged in at the same time as doing homework. It is hard to imagine that this allows a student to do homework efficiently. Consider the following recent studies:

- A comparison of heavy and light media multitaskers revealed that heavy media multitaskers were more susceptible to interference from irrelevant information (Ophir, Nass, & Wagner, 2009).
- For 8- to 12-year-old girls, a higher level of media multitasking was linked to negative social well-being, while a higher level of face-to-face communication was associated with positive social-well-being indicators such as greater social success, feeling more normal, and having fewer friends whom parents thought were a bad influence (Pea & others, 2012).
- Heavy media multitaskers were more likely to be depressed and have social anxiety than their counterparts who engaged in a lower incidence of media multitasking (Becker, Alzahabi, & Hopwood, 2013).
- Individuals often engaged in media multitasking because they were less capable of blocking out distractions and focusing on a single task (Sanbonmatsu & others, 2013).

Mobile media, such as cell phones and iPods, are mainly driving the increased media use by adolescents. For example, in the 2004 survey, only 18 percent of youth owned an iPod or MP3 player, but in 2009, 76 percent owned them; in 2004, 39 percent owned a cell phone, a figure that had jumped to 66 percent by 2009 (Rideout & others, 2010).

Television   Many children spend more time in front of the television set than they spend interacting with their parents. Although it is only one of the many mass media that affect children's behavior, television may be the

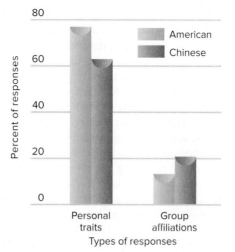

FIGURE 7

AMERICAN AND CHINESE SELF-CONCEPTIONS. College students from the United States and China completed 20 "I am" sentences. Both groups filled in personal traits more than group affiliations. However, the Chinese students filled in the blanks with group affiliations more often than the U.S. students did.

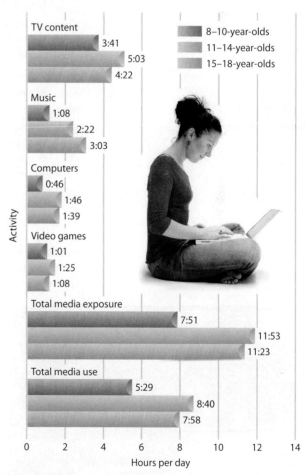

FIGURE 8

DEVELOPMENTAL CHANGES IN THE AMOUNT OF TIME U.S. 8- TO 18-YEAR-OLDS SPEND WITH DIFFERENT TYPES OF MEDIA
© istockphoto.com/Dan Wilton RF

"Mrs. Horton, could you stop by school today?" Copyright © 1981 Martha F. Campbell. Reprinted by permission.

most influential. The persuasive capabilities of television are staggering (Sterin, 2014). The 20,000 hours of television watched by the time the average American adolescent graduates from high school are greater than the number of hours spent in the classroom.

Television can have positive or negative effects on children's and adolescents' development. Television can have a positive influence by presenting motivating educational programs, increasing children's and adolescents' information about the world beyond their immediate environment, and providing models of prosocial behavior (Wilson, 2008).

Some types of TV shows are linked to positive outcomes for children (Calvert, 2015). For example, a recent meta-analysis of studies in 14 countries found positive outcomes for watching the TV show *Sesame Street* in three areas: cognitive, learning about the world, and social reasoning and attitudes toward outgroups (Mares & Pan, 2013).

However, television can have a negative influence on children and adolescents by making them passive learners, distracting them from doing homework, teaching them stereotypes, providing them with violent models of aggression, and presenting them with unrealistic views of the world (Matos, Ferreira, & Haase, 2012). Further, researchers have found that a high level of TV viewing is linked to a greater incidence of obesity in children and adolescents (Escobar-Chaves & Anderson, 2008).

The extent to which children and adolescents are exposed to violence and aggression on television raises special concerns (DeWall, Anderson, & Bushman, 2013). A research review concluded that children and adolescents who experience a heavy media diet of violence are more likely to perceive the world as a dangerous place and to view aggression as more acceptable than their counterparts who see media violence less frequently (Wilson, 2008). Also, another research review concluded that there is strong evidence that media violence is a risk factor for aggressive behavior but less evidence linking it to juvenile delinquency and crime (Escobar-Chaves & Anderson, 2008). Much of the media violence described in these two recent research reviews comes from television, but as we see next, it also includes violent video games.

Video Games Violent video games, especially those that are highly realistic, also raise concerns about their effects on children and adolescents (DeWall & others, 2013). Correlational studies indicate that children and adolescents who extensively play violent electronic games are more aggressive and more likely to engage in delinquent acts than their counterparts who spend less time playing the games or do not play them at all (DeWall & others, 2013; Gentile, 2011). Further, a recent study revealed that video game consumption was linked to rape myth acceptance (shifting blame for sexual assault from the perpetrator to the victim) through connections with interpersonal aggression and hostile sexism (Fox & Potocki, 2015). Many recently developed video games have increased their sexualized portrayal of females to appeal to a male audience.

Some critics (Ferguson, 2013) argue that conclusions about the negative effects of video game violence have been overstated and others think that too much attention has been given to the negative outcomes of video games and too little research has been conducted on possible positive outcomes for some types of video games (Adachi & Willoughby, 2013).

How might playing violent video games be related to adolescent aggression?
© Bernhard Classen/imageBroker/age fotostock

Are there any positive outcomes when adolescents play video games? Researchers found that middle-school students who played prosocial video games subsequently behaved in more prosocial ways (Gentile & others, 2009). Research also indicates that playing video games can improve adolescents' visuospatial skills (Schmidt & Vandewater, 2008). A recent study found that playing action video games improved attentional control (Chisholm & Kingstone, 2015). Further, researchers have revealed that video games requiring exercise are linked to weight loss in overweight adolescents (Bond, Richards, & Calvert, 2013; Calvert, 2015; Calvert, Bond, & Staiano, 2013). For example, a recent experimental study found that overweight adolescents lost more weight when they participated in a 10-week competitive exergame video condition (video games that require gross motor activity—in this study the Nintendo Wii EA Sports Active video game was used) than their overweight counterparts who were involved in a cooperative exergame condition or a no-video-game-play control condition (Staiano, Abraham, & Calvert, 2012). The weight loss in the competitive condition also was linked to improved executive function in this study.

Media/Screen Time, Learning, and Children's Development The effects of media/screen time on children depend on how old children are and the type of media involved (Calvert, 2015; Lauricella, Gola, & Calvert, 2011). A research review reached the following conclusions about media/screen viewing by infants and young children (Kirkorian, Wartella, & Anderson, 2008):

· *Infancy.* Learning from media is difficult for infants and toddlers, and they learn much more easily from direct experiences with people.

· *Early childhood.* At about 3 years of age, children can learn from media with educational material if the media use effective strategies such as repeating concepts a number of times, use images and sounds that get young children's attention, and use children's rather than adults' voices. However, the vast majority of media young children experience is geared toward entertainment rather than education.

The American Academy of Pediatrics (2001) recommends that children under 2 years of age not watch television because doing so is likely to reduce direct interactions with parents. One study found that the more hours of TV viewed per day by 1- and 3-year-olds, the more likely they were to have attention problems at 7 years of age (Christakis & others, 2004), and a recent study also revealed that daily TV exposure at 18 months was linked to increased inattention/hyperactivity at 30 months of age (Cheng & others, 2010). A study of 2- to 48-month-olds indicated that each hour of audible TV was linked to a reduction in child vocalizations (Christakis & others, 2009), and another study revealed that 8- to 16-month-olds who viewed baby DVDs/videos had poor language development (Zimmerman, Christakis, & Meltzoff, 2007).

A recent study revealed that 12 percent of 2- to 4-year-old U.S. children use computers every day and 22 percent of 5- to 8-year-olds use computers daily (Common Sense Media, 2011). A recent recommendation stated that for children 2 to 4 years of age, screen time should be limited to no more than 1 hour per day (Tremblay & others, 2012). Many children spend more time with various screen media than they do interacting with their parents and peers.

Screen time can have a negative influence on children by making them passive learners, distracting them from doing homework, teaching them stereotypes, providing them with violent models of aggression, and presenting them with unrealistic views of the world. A higher degree of parental monitoring of children's media use was linked to a number of positive outcomes (more sleep, better school performance, less aggressive behavior, and more prosocial behavior for third- through fifth-graders) (Gentile & others, 2014). And a recent study found that parents' reduction of their own screen time is associated with decreased child screen time (Xu, Wen, & Rissel, 2015).

Among other concerns about children having so much screen time are decreasing time spent in play, less time interacting with peers, decreased physical activity, an increase in being overweight or obese, poor sleep habits, and higher rates of aggression (Falbe & others, 2015; Herman & others, 2015). A recent research review found that when their screen time exceeded

What have researchers found about infants who watch TV and videos?
© Davo Blair/Alamy

two hours a day, children and adolescents were more likely to be overweight or obese (Atkin & others, 2014). Another research review concluded that a higher level of screen time at 4 to 6 years of age was linked to increased obesity and lower physical activity from preschool through adolescence (te Velde & others, 2012). Further, a recent study of 9- to 11-year-olds revealed that a higher number of screens in a child's bedroom was associated with higher obesity and lower sleep efficiency (Chaput & others, 2014). Also, a recent study found that greater screen time was associated with adolescent obesity (Mitchell & others, 2013). And a recent research review concluded that more extensive screen time was linked to more adverse sleep outcomes in children and adolescents, with the most negative associations involving computer use, video games, and mobile devices (Hale & Guan, 2015). Further, a recent study of Canadian youth found that duration of screen time was linked to depression and anxiety (Maras & others, 2015). The more children and adolescents watch TV, the lower their school

How much screen time is recommended for young children?
© Jekaterina Nikitina/Getty Images

achievement (Comstock & Scharrer, 2006). A recent study revealed that the greater the amount of screen time among young adolescents, the lower their academic achievement (Syvaoja & others, 2013). Why might TV watching be negatively linked to children's achievement? Three possibilities involve interference, displacement, and self-defeating tastes/preferences (Comstock & Scharrer, 2006). In terms of interference, having a television on while doing homework can distract children while they are doing cognitive tasks. In terms of displacement, television can take time and attention that could otherwise be spent engaging in achievement-related tasks such as homework, reading, writing, and mathematics.

Are media use/screen time linked to children's creativity? A recent research review concludes that there is a negative association between children's TV viewing and their creativity. An exception, though, is when children watch educational TV content that is designed to teach creativity through the use of imaginative characters (Calvert & Valkenburg, 2011).

Technology and Digitally Mediated Communication Culture involves change, and nowhere is that change greater than in the technological revolution individuals are experiencing with increased use of computers and the Internet (Lever-Duffy & McDonald, 2015; Smaldino & others, 2015). Society still relies on some basic nontechnological competencies—for example, good communication skills, positive attitudes, and the ability to solve problems and to think deeply and creatively. But how people pursue these competencies is changing in ways and at a speed that few people had to cope with in previous eras. For youth to be adequately prepared for tomorrow's jobs, technology needs to become an integral part of their lives (Roblyer & Doering, 2013).

The digitally mediated social environment of youth includes e-mail, instant messaging, social networking sites such as Facebook, chat rooms, videosharing and photosharing, multiplayer online computer games, and virtual worlds. The remarkable increase in the popularity of Facebook was reflected in its supplanting of Google in 2010 as the most frequently visited Internet site. Most of these digitally mediated social interactions began on computers but more recently have also shifted to cell phones, especially smartphones (Underwood & others, 2012).

A national survey revealed dramatic increases in adolescents' use of social media and text messaging (Lenhart & others, 2010). In 2009, nearly three-fourths of U.S. 12- to 17-year-olds reported that they used social networking sites. Eighty-one percent of 18- to 24-year-olds had created a profile on a social networking site, and 31 percent of them visited a social networking site several times a day. More emerging adult women visited a social networking site several times a day (33 percent) than did their male counterparts (24 percent).

Text messaging has now become the main way that adolescents connect with their friends, surpassing face-to-face contact, e-mail, instant messaging, and voice calling (Lenhart & others, 2010). A recent survey of 12- to 17-year-olds found that they send an average of 60 text messages per day (Lenhart, 2012). A special concern is *sexting,* which involves sending sexually explicit images, videos, or sexually explicit text messages via electronic communication. However, voice mail is the primary way that most adolescents prefer to connect with parents.

Special concerns have emerged about children's and adolescents' access to information on the Internet, which has been largely unregulated (Straubhaar, LaRose, & Davenport, 2014).

What characterizes the online social environment of adolescents?
© Digital Vision/Alamy RF

Youth can access adult sexual material, instructions for making bombs, and other information that is inappropriate for them.

A recent study of college students—mean age 20 years old—found that when the Internet was used for shopping, entertainment, and pornography, negative outcomes included higher levels of drinking and drug use, greater numbers of sexual partners, worse relationships with friends and parents, and lower self-worth. By contrast, when college students used the Internet for schoolwork, positive outcomes included a lower level of drug use and higher self-worth (Padilla-Walker & others, 2010).

Clearly, parents need to monitor and regulate adolescents' use of the Internet. Consider Bonita Williams, who began to worry about how obsessed her 15-year-old daughter, Jade, had become with MySpace (Kornblum, 2006). She became even more concerned when she discovered that Jade was posting suggestive photos of herself and giving her cell phone number to people in different parts of the United States. She grounded her daughter, blocked MySpace at home, and moved Jade's computer from her bedroom into the family room.

The following studies explored the role of parents in guiding adolescents' use of the Internet and media:

- Parents' high estimates of online dangers were not matched by their low rates of setting limits and monitoring their adolescents' online activities (Rosen, Cheever, & Carrier, 2008). Also in this study, adolescents who perceived that their parents had an indulgent parenting style (high warmth and involvement but low levels of strictness and supervision) reported engaging in the most risky online behavior, such as meeting someone in person whom they had initially contacted on the Internet.
- Both maternal and paternal authoritative parenting predicted proactive monitoring of adolescent media use, including restriction of certain media from adolescent use and parent-adolescent discussion of exposure to questionable media content (Padilla-Walker & Coyne, 2011).
- Problematic mother-adolescent (age 13) relationships (such as insecure attachment and autonomy conflicts) predicted emerging adults' preference for online communication and greater probability of forming a relationship of poor quality with someone they had met online (Szwedo, Mikami, & Allen, 2011).

The Internet and Aging Adults   The Internet plays an increasingly important role in providing access to information and communication for adults as well as youth (Berner & others, 2015; Cook & others, 2015; Schmidt, Wahl, & Plischke, 2014; Shahrokni & others, 2015). How well are older adults keeping up with changes in technology? A 2013 national survey conducted by the Pew Research Center found that 59 percent of U.S. older adults reported that they use the Internet (in 2000, only 13 percent of older adults said they use the Internet) (Smith, 2014). This survey identified two distinct groups of older adult Internet users: (1) those who are younger, more highly educated, and more affluent; and (2) those who are older, less affluent, and who have significant health or disability challenges. Also in this recent survey, once older adults begin using the Internet, it becomes an integral part of their daily lives. Among those 65 years and older who use the Internet, 71 percent report going online every day or almost every day (compared with 88 percent of 18- to 29-year-olds, 84 percent of 30- to 49-year-olds, and 79 percent of 50- to 64-year-olds). Among adults 75 years of age and older, Internet use drops off considerably.

Links between older adults' use of technology and their cognitive development also are being studied. One study found that frequent computer use was linked to higher performance on cognitive tasks in older adults (Tun & Lachman, 2010). And researchers are examining the role that video games could play in maintaining or improving older adults' cognitive skills (McDougall & House, 2012). For example, researchers found that a lengthy 40-hour video game training program improved older adults' attention and memory (Smith & others, 2009). And a recent study revealed that a brain training game that elderly adults played about 15 minutes a day for 4 weeks improved their executive function and speed of processing information (Nouchi & others, 2012).

Researchers also have found connections between Internet use and social relationships. One study revealed that older adults' increased use of the Internet was associated with greater ease in meeting new people, feeling less isolated, and feeling more connected with friends and family (Cotten, Anderson, & McCullough, 2014). A longitudinal study also revealed that Internet use by older adults reduced their likelihood of being depressed by one-third (Cotten & others, 2014). As with children and younger adults, cautions about the accuracy of information on the Internet—especially regarding topics such as health care—should always be kept in mind (Miller & Bell, 2012).

Aging and Culture   Culture plays an important role in aging (Gold & Amthor, 2011). What promotes a good old age in most cultures? What factors are associated with whether older adults are accorded a position of high status in a culture? Seven factors are most likely to predict high status for the elderly in a culture (Sangree, 1989):

- Older persons have valuable knowledge.
- Older persons control key family/community resources.

Are older adults keeping up with changes in technology?
© Sami Sarkis/Getty Images RF

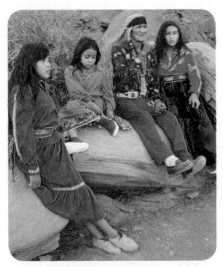

Cultures differ in the amount of prestige they give to older adults. In Navajo culture, older adults are especially treated with respect because of their wisdom and extensive life experiences. *What are some other factors that are linked with respect for older adults in a culture?*
© Suzi Moore-McGregor/Woodfin Camp & Associates

· Older persons are permitted to engage in useful and valued functions as long as possible.

· There is role continuity throughout the life span.

· Age-related role changes involve greater responsibility, authority, and advisory capacity.

· The extended family is a common family arrangement in the culture, and the older person is integrated into the extended family.

In general, respect for older adults is greater in collectivistic cultures (such as China and Japan) than in individualistic cultures (such as the United States). However, some researchers are finding that this collectivistic/individualistic difference in respect accorded to older adults is not as strong as it used to be and that in some cases older adults in individualistic cultures receive considerable respect (Antonucci, Vandewater, & Lansford, 2000).

SOCIOECONOMIC STATUS AND POVERTY

Analyzing cultures represents just one way to understand the social context of life-span development. Another approach focuses on inequalities present in every society (McLoyd, Mistry, & Hardaway, 2014; Weisner & Duncan, 2014). That is, how do people in a particular society differ in their access to economic, social, and psychological resources, and how do these differences affect their development through life?

What Is Socioeconomic Status?   **Socioeconomic status (SES)** refers to a grouping of people with similar occupational, educational, and economic characteristics. Generally, members of a society (1) hold occupations that vary in prestige, with some individuals having more access than others to higher-status occupations; (2) attain different levels of education, with some individuals having more access than others to better education; (3) possess different economic resources; and (4) have different degrees of power to influence a community. These differences go together. That is, people with prestigious occupations tend also to have higher levels of educational attainment, more economic resources, and greater power. These differences in the ability to control resources and to participate in society's rewards produce unequal opportunities for people (Duncan, Magnuson, & Votruba-Drzal, 2015; Yoshikawa, Aber, & Beardslee, 2012). Socioeconomic differences have been described as a "proxy for material, human, and social capital within and beyond the family" (Huston & Ripke, 2006, p. 425).

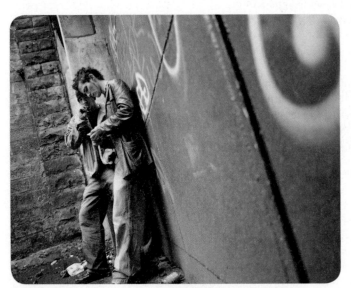

What characterizes socioeconomic variations in neighborhoods?
© BananaStock/PunchStock RF

The number of different socioeconomic statuses depends on the community's size and complexity. In most investigators' descriptions of socioeconomic status, two broad categories—low SES and middle SES—are used, although as many as five categories are delineated. Sometimes low SES is described as low-income, working class, or blue collar; sometimes middle SES is described as middle-income, managerial, or white collar. Examples of low-SES occupations are factory worker and maintenance worker. Examples of middle-SES occupations include managerial and professional careers (doctor, lawyer, teacher, accountant, and so on).

Socioeconomic Variations in Neighborhoods and Families   A parent's SES is likely linked to the neighborhoods in which children live and the schools they attend (Chen, Howard, & Brooks-Gunn, 2011). Such variations in neighborhood settings can influence children's adjustment (Duncan & others, 2015).

Neighborhood crime and isolation have been linked with low self-esteem and psychological distress in children (Leventhal, Dupere, & Shuey, 2015). Further, schools in low-income neighborhoods have fewer resources than schools in higher-income neighborhoods, and they are more likely to have more students with lower achievement test scores, low rates of graduation, and smaller percentages of graduates going on to college (Garbarino & Asp, 1981).

socioeconomic status (SES) A grouping of people with similar occupational, educational, and economic characteristics.

In the United States and most other Western cultures, differences have been found in child rearing among different SES groups (Hoff, Laursen, & Tardif, 2002, p. 246):

- Lower-SES parents (1) "are more concerned that their children conform to society's expectations," (2) "create a home atmosphere in which it is clear that parents have authority over children," (3) use physical punishment more in disciplining their children, and (4) are more directive and less conversational with their children.

- Higher-SES parents (1) "are more concerned with developing children's initiative and ability to delay gratification," (2) "create a home atmosphere in which children are more nearly equal participants and in which rules are discussed as opposed to being laid down" in an authoritarian manner, (3) are less likely to use physical punishment, and (4) are less directive and more conversational with their children.

Nevertheless, a sizable portion of children from low-SES backgrounds are very competent and perform well in school; some perform better than many middle-SES students. When children from low-SES backgrounds achieve well in school, it is not unusual to find a parent or parents making special sacrifices to provide the conditions that contribute to academic success.

So far we have focused on the challenges that many adolescents from low-income families face. However, research by Suniya Luthar and her colleagues (Ansary & Luthar, 2009; Luthar, 2006; Luthar, Barkin, & Crossman, 2013; Luthar & Goldstein, 2008) found that adolescents from affluent families also face challenges. In her research, adolescents from affluent families are vulnerable to high rates of substance abuse. Also, in the affluent families she has studied, males tend to have more adjustment difficulties than females, with affluent female adolescents being more likely to attain superior levels of academic success.

Poverty

When sixth-graders in a poverty-stricken area of St. Louis were asked to describe a perfect day, one boy said he would erase the world, then he would sit and think. Asked if he wouldn't rather go outside and play, the boy responded, "Are you kidding, out there?" (Children's Defense Fund, 1992). The world is a dangerous and unwelcoming place for too many of America's children, especially those who live in poverty (Children's Defense Fund, 2011). Some children are resilient and cope with the challenges of poverty without any major setbacks, but too many struggle unsuccessfully (Duncan & others, 2015; Evans & Kim, 2013; Murry & others, 2015). Each child of poverty who reaches adulthood unhealthy, unskilled, or alienated keeps our nation from being as competent and productive as it could be.

Poverty Rates   Children who grow up in poverty represent a special concern (Duncan, 2012; Duncan & others, 2015; Heberle & Carter, 2015). In 2013, 19.9 percent of U.S. children and adolescents lived in families with incomes below the poverty line (De Navas-Walt & Proctor, 2014). The U.S. poverty rate for children and adolescents was higher than it had been in 2001 (16.2 percent) but down from a peak of 22.7 percent in 1993 and also down from 21.8 percent in 2012. The U.S. figure of 19.9 percent of children and adolescents living in poverty is much higher than figures from other industrialized nations. For example, Canada has a child poverty rate of 9 percent and Sweden has a rate of 2 percent.

Poverty in the United States is demarcated along ethnic and family structure lines (De Navas-Walt & Proctor, 2014). In 2013, African American (27.2 percent) and Latino (23.5 percent) families with children and adolescents had especially high rates of poverty (compared with 12.3 percent of their non-Latino White counterparts). And compared with non-Latino White children and adolescents, ethnic minority children and adolescents are more likely to experience persistent poverty over many years and to live in isolated, poor neighborhoods where social supports are minimal and threats to positive development abundant (Jarrett, 1995) (see Figure 9).

In 2013, 39.6 percent of single-mother families lived in poverty, nearly five times the poverty rate for married-couple families (7.6 percent). More than half (51.9 percent) of the single-mother families who lived in poverty lived in extreme poverty, with incomes below half of the federal poverty level (about $9,900 for a family of three), which means a family budget of about $200 a week.

developmental **connection**

Environment

Reducing the poverty level and improving the lives of children living in poverty are important goals of U.S. social policy. Connect to "Introduction."

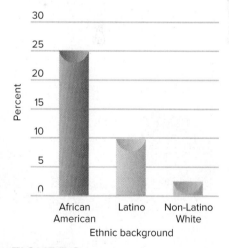

FIGURE **9**

PERCENTAGES OF YOUTH UNDER 18 WHO ARE LIVING IN DISTRESSED NEIGHBORHOODS. *Note:* A distressed neighborhood is defined by high levels (at least one standard deviation above the norm) of (1) poverty; (2) female-headed families: (3) high school dropout rate; (4) unemployment; and (5) reliance on public assistance programs.

(*Top*) Children playing in Nueva Era, a low-income area on the outskirts of Nuevo Laredo, Mexico. (*Bottom*) Children living in the poverty section of the South Bronx in New York City. *How does poverty affect the development of children like these?*

(*Top*) © Janet Jarman/Corbis; (*Bottom*) © Andy Levin/Science Source

Psychological Ramifications of Poverty Poor children are often exposed to poor health conditions, inadequate housing and homelessness, less effective schools, environmental toxins, and violence (Bradley, 2015). What are the psychological ramifications of living in poverty? First, the poor are often powerless. At work, they rarely are the decision makers; rules are handed down to them. Second, the poor are often vulnerable to disaster. They are not likely to be given notice before they are laid off from work, and they usually do not have financial resources to fall back on when problems arise. Third, their alternatives are restricted. Only a limited number of jobs are open to them. Even when alternatives are available, the poor might not know about them or be prepared to make a wise decision because of inadequate education and inability to read well. Fourth, being poor means having less prestige.

One research review concluded that compared with their economically more advantaged counterparts, poor children experience widespread environmental inequities (Evans, 2004). For example, one study found that a higher percentage of children in poor families than in middle-income families were exposed to family turmoil, separation from a parent, violence, crowding, excessive noise, and poor housing (Evans & English, 2002).

Persistent and long-standing poverty can have especially damaging effects on children (Duncan & others, 2015; Evans, Li, & Sepanski Whipple, 2013). One study revealed that the more years children spent in poverty, the higher were their physiological indices of stress (Evans & Kim, 2007). And a recent study found that persistent economic hardship as well as very early poverty was linked to lower cognitive functioning in children at 5 years of age (Schoon & others, 2012). Another recent study revealed that poverty-related adversity in family and school contexts in early childhood was linked to less effective executive function in second and third grades (Cybele Raver & others, 2013). Also, a recent study found that youth living in neighborhoods where poverty increased from the time they were 11 to 19 years of age experienced high levels of *allostatic load*, which involves a wearing down of the body's physiological systems due to stressors (Brody & others, 2014). However, for youth who experienced high levels of emotional support, allostatic load did not increase across this time frame when poverty increased.

Feminization of Poverty The term **feminization of poverty** refers to the fact that far more women than men live in poverty. A special concern is the high percentage of children and adolescents growing up in mother-headed households in poverty (Ward & Edelstein, 2014). In 2008, 36.5 percent of female-headed families lived in poverty compared with only 6.4 percent of married-couple families (Federal Interagency Forum on Child and Family Statistics, 2010).

Vonnie McLoyd (1998) concluded that because poor, single mothers are more distressed than their middle-SES counterparts are, they tend to show lower levels of support, nurturance, and involvement with their children. Among the reasons for the high poverty rate of single mothers are women's low pay, infrequent awarding of alimony payments, and poorly enforced child support by fathers (Graham & Beller, 2002).

Families and Poverty One study documented the important links among economic well-being, parenting behavior, and social adjustment (Mistry & others, 2002). Lower levels of economic well-being and elevated perceptions of economic pressure were linked with parenting behavior. Distressed parents reported feeling less effective and capable in disciplining their children and were observed to be less affectionate in parent-child interactions. In turn, less optimal parenting predicted lower teacher ratings of children's social behavior and higher ratings of behavior problems.

Benefits provided to low-income parents may have positive outcomes for children (Widom & Nikulina, 2012). For example, the Minnesota Family Investment Program (MFIP) was primarily designed to improve the lives of adults—specifically, to move adults off the welfare rolls and into paid employment. A key element of the program was its guarantee that adults who participated in the program would receive more money if they worked

Vonnie McLoyd (*right*) has conducted a number of important investigations of the roles of poverty, ethnicity, and unemployment in children's and adolescents' development. She has found that economic stressors often diminish children's and adolescents' belief in the utility of education and their achievement strivings.

Courtesy of Vonnie McLoyd

than if they did not. When the adults' income rose, how did it affect their children? A study of the effects of MFIP found that increases in the incomes of working poor parents were linked with benefits for their children (Gennetian & Miller, 2002). The children's achievement in school improved and their behavior problems decreased.

Might intervention with families of children living in poverty improve children's school performance? In an experimental study, Aletha Huston and her colleagues (2006) evaluated the effects on adolescent development of a program called New Hope, which is designed to increase parental employment and reduce family poverty. They randomly assigned families with 6- to 10-year-old children living in poverty to the New Hope program or to a control group. To adults living in poverty who were employed 30 or more hours a week, New Hope provided benefits that included a wage supplement ensuring that net income increased as parents earned more, subsidized child care for any child under age 13, and health insurance. Management services were provided to New Hope participants to assist them with job searches and other needs. The New Hope program was available to the experimental group families for three years (until the children were 9 to 13 years old). Two years after the program ended, the program's effects on the children were examined when they were 11 to 16 years old. Compared with adolescents in the control group, New Hope adolescents were more competent at reading, earned higher grades in school, were less likely to be in special education classes, had more positive social skills, and were more likely to participate in formal after-school arrangements. New Hope parents reported better psychological well-being and a greater sense of self-efficacy in managing their adolescents than parents in the control group did. In a further assessment, the influence of the New Hope program on adolescents and emerging adults 9 to 19 years old after they left the program was evaluated (McLoyd & others, 2011). Positive outcomes were especially apparent among African American males, who were more optimistic about their future employment and career prospects.

Schools and school programs are the focus of some poverty interventions. A recent study assessed the effects of the Positive Action program in 14 urban, low-income Chicago schools across 6 years from grades 3 to 8 (Lewis & others, 2013). The Positive Action program is a K–12 curriculum that focuses on self-concept, self-control and responsibility, physical and mental health, honesty, getting along with others, and continually striving for self-improvement. The program includes teacher, counselor, family, and community training and activities to improve school-wide atmosphere. In comparison with control group schools that did not include the Positive Action program, students in the program engaged in a lower rate of violence-related behavior and received fewer disciplinary referrals and suspensions from school.

In another recent study, more than 500 ninth- to twelfth-grade students living in low-income settings in Los Angeles were chosen through a random admissions lottery to attend high-performing public charter schools (Wong & others, 2014). Compared with a control group of students who did not attend the high-performing charter schools, the students attending the charter schools had higher scores on math and English standardized tests and were less likely to drop out of school.

SES, Poverty, and Aging Another group of special concern consists of older adults who are poor (Kohon & Carder, 2014). Researchers have found that poverty in late adulthood is linked to an increase in physical and mental health problems (Cagney & others, 2014; Sztramko & others, 2013). Poverty also is linked to lower levels of physical and cognitive fitness in older adults (Basta & others, 2008). A recent study found that processing speed was slower in older adults living in poverty (Zhang & others, 2015). And one study revealed that low SES increases the risk of earlier death in older adults (Krueger & Chang, 2008).

Census data suggest that the overall number of older people living in poverty has declined since the 1960s, but in 2012, 9.1 percent of older adults in the United States still were living in poverty (U.S. Census Bureau, 2013). In 2010, U.S. women 65 years and older (10.7 percent) were much more likely to live in poverty than their male counterparts (6.2 percent) (U.S. Census Bureau, 2012). Nineteen percent of single, divorced, or widowed women 65 years and older lived in poverty. There is a special concern about poverty among older women and considerable discussion about the role of Social Security in providing a broad economic safety net for them (Jokinen-Gordon, 2012).

What are some characteristics of older U.S. adults living in poverty conditions?
© Syracuse Newspapers/The Image Works

feminization of poverty The fact that far more women than men live in poverty. Women's lower income, divorce, infrequent awarding of alimony, and poorly enforced child support by fathers—which usually leave women with less money than they and their children need to adequately function—are the likely causes.

Poverty rates among ethnic minorities are two to three times higher than the rate for non-Latino Whites. Combining the effects of age, gender, and ethnicity, 41 percent of older Latinas and 31 percent of older African American women lived in poverty in 2010 (U.S. Census Bureau, 2011). Also, the oldest-old are the age subgroup of older adults most likely to be living in poverty.

ETHNICITY

As our discussion of poverty and aging indicated, differences in SES often overlap with ethnic differences. The United States is a showcase for these differences because it has been a great magnet for people from many ethnic groups. Cultural heritages from every continent have connected and mixed here (Phinney & others, 2013a, b). Native Americans, European Americans, African Americans, Latinos, Chinese Americans, and other groups have retained parts of their culture of origin, lost other parts, and seen some elements transformed as they became part of the mainstream culture.

Immigration   Relatively high rates of minority immigration have contributed to growth in the proportion of ethnic minorities in the U.S. population. And this growth of ethnic minorities is expected to continue throughout the twenty-first century. Today the United States is more ethnically diverse than ever before (Banks, 2014). Ninety-three languages are spoken in Los Angeles alone.

Asian Americans are expected to be the fastest-growing ethnic group of adolescents in coming decades, with a growth rate of almost 600 percent by 2100. Latino adolescents are projected to increase almost 400 percent by 2100. Figure 10 shows the actual numbers of adolescents in different ethnic groups in the year 2000, as well as the numbers projected through 2100. Notice that by 2100, Latino adolescents are expected to outnumber non-Latino White adolescents.

Immigrants often experience special stressors (Renzetti & Kennedy-Bergen, 2015; Yu & Singh, 2012). These include language barriers, separation from support networks, changes in SES, and the challenges of preserving ethnic identity while adapting to the majority culture (Lessow-Hurley, 2013).

Parents and children in immigrant families may be at different stages of acculturation, the process of adapting to the majority culture. The result may be conflict over cultural values (Phinney & others, 2013a, b). One study examined values in immigrant (Vietnamese, Armenian, and Mexican) and nonimmigrant families (African American and European American) (Phinney, 1996). In all groups, parents endorsed family obligations more than adolescents did, and the differences between generations generally increased with time spent in the United States.

Ethnicity and Families   Families within different ethnic groups in the United States differ in their size, structure, composition, reliance on kinship networks, and levels of income and education (McLoyd, Purtell, & Hardaway, 2015; Murry & others, 2015; Parke, 2013). Large and extended families are more common among minority groups than among the non-Latino White majority. For example, 19 percent of Latino families have three or more children, compared with 14 percent of African American and 10 percent of non-Latino White families. African American and Latino children interact more with their grandparents, aunts, uncles, cousins, and more distant relatives than do non-Latino White children.

Single-parent families are more common among African Americans and Latinos than among non-Latino White Americans (Hattery & Smith, 2007). In comparison with two-parent households, single parents often have more limited resources of

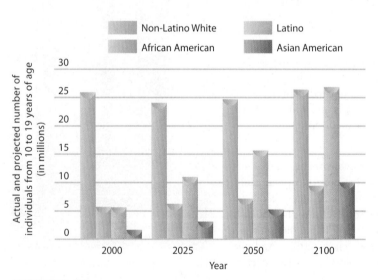

FIGURE 10

ACTUAL AND PROJECTED NUMBERS OF U.S. ADOLESCENTS AGED 10 TO 19, 2000 TO 2100. In 2000, there were more than 25 million non-Latino White adolescents 10 to 19 years of age in the United States, whereas the numbers for ethnic minority groups were substantially lower. However, projections for 2025 through 2100 reveal dramatic increases in the numbers of Latino and Asian American adolescents to the point at which in 2100 it is projected that there will be more Latino than non-Latino White adolescents in the United States and more Asian American than African American adolescents.

time, money, and energy (Wright & others, 2012). Ethnic minority parents also tend to be less educated and are more likely to live in low-income circumstances than are their non-Latino White counterparts. Still, many impoverished ethnic minority families manage to find ways to raise competent children (Gamble & Modry-Mandell, 2008).

Recently immigrated families may face special problems. Many individuals in immigrant families are dealing with the problem of being undocumented. Living in an undocumented family can affect children's developmental outcomes through parents being unwilling to sign up for services for which they eligible, conditions linked to low-wage work and lack of benefits, increased stress, discrimination, and a lack of cognitive stimulation in the home (Marks & others, 2015; Yoshikawa & others, 2013).

Poverty contributes to the stressful life experiences of many ethnic minority children (McLoyd, Purtell, & Hardaway, 2015). But even when they are not poor, economic advantage does not enable ethnic minority children to escape entirely the prejudice and discrimination directed at them (Marks & others, 2015). Although middle-SES ethnic minority children have more resources available to counter the destructive influences of prejudice and discrimination, they still cannot completely avoid the pervasive influence of negative stereotypes about ethnic minority groups.

Vonnie McLoyd (1990) concluded that ethnic minority children experience a disproportionate share of the adverse effects of poverty and unemployment in the United States today. Thus, many ethnic minority children experience a double disadvantage: (1) prejudice and discrimination because of their ethnic minority status, and (2) the stressful effects of poverty. Some aspects of home life can help protect ethnic minority children from injustice. The community and the family can filter out destructive racist messages, and parents can present alternative frames of reference to offset those presented by the majority. The extended family also can serve as an important buffer to stress (Harris & Graham, 2007; Hayashino & Chopra, 2009).

Latino immigrants in the Rio Grande Valley, Texas. *What are some characteristics of the families who have recently immigrated to the United States?*
© Allison Wright/Corbis

Research indicates that many members of families that have recently immigrated to the United States adopt a bicultural orientation, selecting characteristics of the U.S. culture that help them to survive and advance, while still retaining aspects of their culture of origin (Cooper, 2011; Kao & Huang, 2015; Schwartz & others, 2015). Immigration also involves cultural brokering, which has increasingly occurred in the United States as children and adolescents serve as mediators (cultural and linguistic) for their immigrant parents (Villanueva & Buriel, 2010).

However, while many ethnic/immigrant families adopt a bicultural orientation, parenting in many ethnic minority families also focuses on issues associated with promoting children's ethnic pride, knowledge of their ethnic group, and awareness of discrimination (Simpkins & others, 2013).

In adopting characteristics of the U.S. culture, Latino families are increasingly embracing the importance of education (Cooper, 2011). Although their school dropout rates have remained higher than those of other ethnic groups, toward the end of the first decade of the twenty-first century they declined considerably (National Center for Education Statistics, 2010). Ross Parke and his colleagues (2011) have found that Latino families are retaining a strong commitment to family when they immigrate to the United States despite facing challenges advancing economically. For example, divorce rates for Latino families are lower than for non-Latino White families of similar socioeconomic status.

However, there are variations in immigrant Latino families' experiences and how much their children and adolescents change as they are exposed to American culture. A recent study found that following their immigration, Mexican American adolescents spent less time with their family and identified less with family values (Updegraff & others, 2012). However, in this study, teens with stronger family values in early adolescence were less likely to engage in risky behavior in late adolescence.

Of course, individual families vary, and how successfully ethnic minority families deal with stress depends on many factors (Marks & others, 2015;

What characterizes families in different ethnic groups in the United States?
© Ocean/Corbis RF

Norma Thomas, Social Work Professor and Administrator

Norma Thomas.
Courtesy of Dr. Norma Thomas

Dr. Norma Thomas has worked for more than three decades in the field of aging. She obtained her undergraduate degree in social work from Pennsylvania State University and her doctoral degree in social work from the University of Pennsylvania. Thomas' activities are varied. Earlier in her career, as a social work practitioner, she provided services to older adults of color in an effort to improve their lives. She currently is a professor and academic administrator at Widener University in Chester, Pennsylvania, a fellow of the Institute of Aging at the University of Pennsylvania, and the chief executive officer and cofounder of the Center on Ethnic and Minority Aging (CEMA). CEMA was formed to provide research, consultation, training, and services to benefit aging individuals of color, their families, and their communities. Thomas has created numerous community service events that benefit older adults of color, especially African Americans and Latinos. She has also been a consultant to various national, regional, and state agencies in her effort to improve the lives of aging adults of color.

Murry & others, 2015; Parke, 2013). Whether the parents are native-born or immigrants, how long the family has been in the United States, its socioeconomic status, and its national origin all make a difference. The characteristics of the family's social context also influence its adaptability. What are the attitudes toward the family's ethnic group within its neighborhood or city? Can the family's children attend good schools? Are there community groups that welcome people from the family's ethnic group? Do members of the family's ethnic group form community groups of their own?

Ethnicity and Aging   Of special concern are ethnic minority older adults, especially African Americans and Latinos, who are overrepresented in poverty statistics (U.S. Census Bureau, 2013). Comparative information about African Americans, Latinos, and non-Latino Whites indicates a possible double jeopardy for elderly ethnic minority individuals. They face problems related to both ageism and racism (Allen, 2015; Hatzfeld, Laveist, & Gaston-Johansson, 2012; Nadimpalli & others, 2015). One study of more than 4,000 older adults found that African Americans perceived more discrimination than did non-Latino Whites (Barnes & others, 2004). Both the wealth and the health of ethnic minority older adults decrease more rapidly than for elderly non-Latino Whites (Thorpe & others, 2013). Older ethnic minority individuals are more likely to become ill but less likely to receive treatment (Hinrichsen, 2006). They also are more likely to have a history of less education, longer periods of unemployment, worse housing conditions, higher levels of stress, and shorter life expectancies than their older non-Latino White counterparts (Gee, Walsemann, & Brondolo, 2012; Santiago & others, 2012). And many ethnic minority workers never enjoy the Social Security and Medicare benefits to which their earnings contribute, because they die before reaching the age of eligibility for benefits (Ciol & others, 2008).

Despite the stress and discrimination older ethnic minority individuals face, many of these older adults have developed coping mechanisms that have allowed them to survive in the dominant non-Latino White world (Kingston & Bartholomew, 2009). Extension of family networks helps older minority group individuals cope with having only the bare essentials of living and gives them a sense of being loved (Antonucci & others, 2000). Churches in African American and Latino communities provide avenues for meaningful social participation, feelings of power, and a sense of internal satisfaction (Hill & others, 2006). And residential concentrations of ethnic minority groups give their older members a sense of belonging. Thus, it is important to consider individual variations in the lives of aging minorities. To read about one individual who is providing help for aging minorities, see the *Connecting with Careers* profile.

Review Connect Reflect

LG5 Evaluate sociocultural influences on development

Review

- How can culture, cross-cultural comparisons, and individualism/collectivism be defined? What are some outcomes of the increase in media use? How is culture related to development?
- What is socioeconomic status? How are socioeconomic status and poverty linked to development?
- What is ethnicity? How is ethnicity involved in development? What aspects of ethnicity are important to recognize?

Connect

- Compare what you learned in this section about the digitally mediated world of children and adolescents with the chapter's earlier discussion of the importance of play. What are your conclusions?

Reflect *Your Own Personal Journey of Life*

- No matter how well intentioned people are, their life circumstances likely have given them some prejudices. If they don't have prejudices toward people with different cultural and ethnic backgrounds, other kinds of people may bring out prejudices in them. For example, prejudices can be developed about people who have certain religious or political convictions, people who are unattractive or too attractive, people with a disability, and people who live in a nearby town. As a parent or teacher, how would you attempt to reduce children's prejudices?

reach your **learning goals**

Peers and the Sociocultural World

1 Peer Relations in Childhood and Adolescence

LG1 Discuss peer relations in childhood and adolescence

Exploring Peer Relations

· Peers are individuals who are at about the same age or maturity level. Peers provide a means of social comparison and a source of information about the world outside the family. Good peer relations may be necessary for normal social development. The inability to "plug in" to a social network is associated with a number of problems. Peer relations can be both positive and negative. Piaget and Sullivan stressed that peer relations provide the context for learning the reciprocal aspects of relationships. Healthy family relations usually promote healthy peer relations. Parents can model or coach their children in ways of relating to peers. Parents' choices of neighborhoods, churches, schools, and their own friends influence the pool from which their children might select possible friends. Rough-and-tumble play occurs mainly in peer relations rather than in parent-child relations. In times of stress, children usually turn to parents rather than peers. Peer relations have a more equal basis than parent-child relations. Contexts and individual difference factors influence peer relations. The frequency of peer interaction, both positive and negative, increases in the preschool years. Children spend even more time with peers in the elementary and secondary school years. Social information-processing skills and social knowledge are important dimensions of social cognition in peer relations. Emotion regulation plays an important role in determining whether a child's peer relationships are successful.

Peer Statuses

· Popular children are frequently nominated as a best friend and are rarely disliked by their peers. Average children receive an average number of both positive and negative nominations from their peers. Neglected children are infrequently nominated as a best friend but are not disliked by their peers. Rejected children are infrequently nominated as a best friend and are actively disliked by their peers. Controversial children are frequently nominated both as a best friend and as being disliked by peers.

Bullying	· Significant numbers of students are bullied, and bullying can result in short-term and long-term negative effects for the victim. Anxious, withdrawn children and aggressive children often are victims of bullying, and boys are far more likely to be involved in bullying than girls are.
Gender and Peer Relations	· Gender is linked to peer relations in several ways. From 4 to 12 years of age, preference for playing in same-sex groups increases. Boys' groups are larger than girls', and they participate in more organized games than girls do. Boys are more likely to engage in rough-and-tumble play, competition, ego displays, risk taking, and dominance, whereas girls are more likely to engage in collaborative discourse. Peers play more important roles in adolescents' lives in some cultures than in others, with some countries restricting adolescents' access to peers, especially for girls.
Adolescent Peer Relations	· Childhood groups are less formal and less heterogeneous than adolescent groups; childhood groups are also more likely to have same-sex participants. The pressure to conform to peers is strong during adolescence, especially during the eighth and ninth grades. Cliques and crowds assume more importance in the lives of adolescents than in the lives of children. Membership in certain crowds—especially jocks and populars—is associated with increased self-esteem. Independents also show high self-esteem.

2 Friendship

 LG2 Explain the role of friendship through the life span

Functions of Friendship	· The functions of friendship include companionship, stimulation, ego support, social comparison, and intimacy/affection.
Friendship During Childhood	· Throughout childhood and adolescence, friends are generally similar—in terms of age, sex, ethnicity, and many other factors. Although having friends is usually a developmental advantage, the quality of friendships varies and having a coercive, conflict-ridden friendship can be harmful.
Friendship During Adolescence and Emerging Adulthood	· Sullivan argued that there is a dramatic increase in the psychological importance of intimacy among close friends in adolescence. He believed friendships were important sources of support for adolescents, and research findings generally support his view. The friendships of adolescent girls are more intimate than those of adolescent boys. Adolescents who become friends with older individuals engage in more deviant behaviors than their counterparts with same-age friends. Many aspects of friendship are the same in emerging adulthood as in adolescence, although the transition to college can bring changes in friendship.
Adult Friendship	· Friendships play an important role in adult development, especially in providing emotional support. Female, male, and female-male friendships often have different characteristics. Regardless of age, friendship is an important aspect of relationships. In old age, there often is more change in male than in female friendships.

3 Play and Leisure

LG3 Describe the developmental aspects of play and leisure

Childhood	· The functions of play include affiliation with peers, tension release, advances in cognitive development, and exploration. The contemporary perspective emphasizes both social and cognitive aspects of play. The most widely studied types of play include sensorimotor and practice play, pretense/symbolic play, social play, constructive play, and games.
Adolescence	· Leisure refers to the pleasant times when individuals are free to pursue activities and interests of their own choosing—hobbies, sports, or reading, for example. U.S. adolescents have more discretionary time than do adolescents in other industrialized countries, but they often fill this time with unchallenging activities such as hanging out and watching television. U.S. adolescents spend more time in voluntary structured activities—such as hobbies, sports, and organizations—than do East Asian adolescents. Some scholars argue that U.S. adolescents have too much unstructured discretionary time that should be replaced with more challenging activities.

| Adulthood | | As adults, we not only need to learn to work well, but we also need to learn to enjoy leisure. Midlife may be an especially important time for leisure because of expanded free time, because of the availability of more money to many individuals, and because of the need for psychological preparation for an active retirement. |

4 Aging and the Social World

 Summarize the social aspects of aging

| Social Theories of Aging | | Disengagement theory, in which older adults gradually withdraw from society, has not held up, but socioemotional selectivity theory and activity theory are viable theories of aging. |

| Stereotyping of Older Adults | | There is extensive stereotyping of older adults, and ageism is a common occurrence. |

| Social Support and Social Integration | | Social support is an important aspect of helping people cope with stress. Older adults usually have less integrated social networks and engage in less social activity than their younger counterparts, although these findings may be influenced by cohort effects. |

| Successful Aging | | Increasingly, the positive aspects of aging are being studied. Factors that are linked with successful aging include an active lifestyle, positive coping skills, good social relationships and support, and self-efficacy. |

5 Sociocultural Influences

 Evaluate sociocultural influences on development

| Culture | | Culture refers to the behavior, patterns, beliefs, and all other products of a group of people that are passed on from generation to generation. Cross-cultural comparisons involve the comparison of one culture with one or more other cultures to gain information about the degree to which aspects are universal or culture-specific. One way that the influence of culture has been studied is to characterize cultures as individualistic (giving priority to personal rather than group goals) or collectivistic (emphasizing values that serve the group). There is substantial concern about the extensive increase in media/screen time by U.S. children and adolescents. Many experts argue that exposure to television violence is linked to increased aggression. Heavy TV watching is linked to lower school achievement. Children and youth also spend substantial amounts of time on the Internet. Large numbers of adolescents and college students engage in social networking on Facebook. Although older adults are less likely to have a computer and to use the Internet than younger adults, they are the fastest-growing age segment of Internet users. Respect for the aged may vary across cultures. Factors that predict high status for older adults across cultures range from the perception that they have valuable knowledge to the belief that they serve useful functions. |

| Socioeconomic Status and Poverty | | Socioeconomic status (SES) is the grouping of people with similar occupational, educational, and economic characteristics. The neighborhoods and families of children have SES characteristics that are related to children's development. Parents from low-SES families are more concerned that their children conform to society's expectations, have an authoritarian parenting style, use physical punishment more in disciplining their children, and are more directive and less conversational with their children than higher-SES parents. Poverty is defined by economic hardship. The subculture of the poor is often characterized not only by economic hardship but also by social and psychological difficulties. Persistent, long-lasting poverty especially has adverse effects on children's development. Older adults who live in poverty are a special concern. |

| Ethnicity | | Ethnicity is based on cultural heritage, nationality characteristics, race, religion, and language. Immigration brings a number of challenges as people adapt to their new culture. Although not all ethnic minority families are poor, poverty contributes to the stress of many ethnic minority families and between ethnic minority groups and the non-Latino White majority. African American and Latino children are more likely than non-Latino White American children to live in single-parent families, to have larger families, and to maintain extended family connections. A special concern involves ethnicity and aging. |

key terms

activity theory	cross-cultural studies	individualism	popular children
ageism	crowds	intimacy in friendship	practice play
average children	culture	leisure	pretense/symbolic play
cliques	disengagement theory	neglected children	rejected children
collectivism	ethnocentrism	peers	sensorimotor play
constructive play	feminization of poverty	play	social play
controversial children	games	play therapy	socioeconomic status (SES)

key people

Daniel Berlyne	Kenneth Dodge	Angeline Lillard	Ross Parke
Richard Brislin	Catherine Garvey	Suniya Luthar	Harry Stack Sullivan
Donald Campbell	Aletha Huston	Vonnie McLoyd	
John Coie	Reed Larson		

chapter 16

SCHOOLS, ACHIEVEMENT, AND WORK

chapter outline

1 Schools

Learning Goal 1 Describe the role of schools in development

Contemporary Approaches to Student Learning and Assessment
Schools and Developmental Status
Educating Children with Disabilities
Socioeconomic Status and Ethnicity in Schools

2 Achievement

Learning Goal 2 Explain the key aspects of achievement

Extrinsic and Intrinsic Motivation
Mastery Motivation and Mindset
Self-Efficacy
Goal Setting, Planning, and Self-Monitoring
Expectations
Ethnicity and Culture

3 Careers, Work, and Retirement

Learning Goal 3 Discuss career development, work, and retirement

Career Development
Work
Retirement

© KidStock/Blend Images/Getty Images RF

preview

This chapter is about becoming educated, achieving, and working. We will begin the chapter by exploring the importance of schools in development and then examine many aspects of a topic that is closely linked to success in school and life—achievement. The final section of the chapter focuses on key aspects of career development, the role of work across the life span, and retirement as a help or a hindrance to our development.

1 Schools LG1 Describe the role of schools in development

| Contemporary Approaches to Student Learning and Assessment | Schools and Developmental Status | Educating Children with Disabilities | Socioeconomic Status and Ethnicity in Schools |

developmental connection

Cognitive Theory

Piaget's and Vygotsky's theories can be applied to children's education. Connect to "Cognitive Developmental Approaches."

We discuss many aspects of schools throughout this book, but especially in the chapters on cognitive processes and development. These chapters cover topics such as the applications of Piaget's and Vygotsky's theories to education, strategies for encouraging children's critical thinking in schools, applications of Gardner's and Sternberg's theories of intelligence to education, and bilingual education. Among the topics related to schools that we explore here are contemporary approaches to student learning, education for individuals at different developmental levels, educating children with disabilities, and the impact of socioeconomic status and ethnicity in schools.

Is this classroom more likely constructivist or direct instruction? Explain.
© Elizabeth Crews

The whole art of teaching is the art of awakening the natural curiosity of young minds.

—ANATOLE FRANCE
French novelist, 20th century

constructivist approach A learner-centered approach that emphasizes the individual's active, cognitive construction of knowledge and understanding with guidance from the teacher.

direct instruction approach A teacher-centered approach characterized by teacher direction and control, high expectations for students' progress, and maximum time spent on academic tasks.

CONTEMPORARY APPROACHES TO STUDENT LEARNING AND ASSESSMENT

Because there are so many approaches to education, controversy swirls about the best way to teach children (Burden & Byrd, 2013; McCombs, 2013). There also is considerable interest in finding the best way to hold schools and teachers accountable for whether children are learning (McMillan, 2014; Popham, 2014).

Constructivist and Direct Instruction Approaches The **constructivist approach** is learner centered, and it emphasizes the importance of individuals actively constructing their knowledge and understanding with guidance from the teacher. In the constructivist view, teachers should not attempt to simply pour information into children's minds. Rather, children should be encouraged to explore their world, discover knowledge, reflect, and think critically, with careful monitoring and meaningful guidance from the teacher (Borich, 2014). Constructivists believe that for too long in American education children have been required to sit still, be passive learners, and rotely memorize irrelevant as well as relevant information (Webb, Metha, & Jordan, 2013). Today, constructivism may include an emphasis on collaboration—children working with each other in their efforts to know and understand (Mahn & John-Steiner, 2013).

By contrast, the **direct instruction approach** is structured and teacher centered. It is characterized by teacher direction and control, high teacher expectations for students' progress, maximum time spent by students on academic tasks, and efforts by the teacher to keep negative affect to a minimum. An important goal in the direct instruction approach is maximizing student learning time (Kilbane & Milman, 2014; Parkay, 2016).

Advocates of the constructivist approach argue that the direct instruction approach turns children into passive learners and does not adequately challenge them to think in critical and creative ways (Estes & Mintz, 2015; Joyce, Weil, & Calhoun, 2015). The direct instruction

enthusiasts say that the constructivist approaches do not give enough attention to the content of a discipline, such as history or science. They also believe that the constructivist approaches are too relativistic and vague.

Some experts in educational psychology believe that many effective teachers use both a constructivist and a direct instruction approach rather than using either approach exclusively (Bransford & others, 2006; Parkay, 2016). Further, some circumstances may require a constructivist approach, others a direction instruction approach. For example, experts increasingly recommend an explicit, intellectually engaging direct instruction approach when teaching students with a reading or a writing disability (Berninger, 2006).

Accountability   Since the 1990s, the U.S. public and governments at every level have demanded increased accountability from schools. One result has been the spread of state-mandated tests to measure just what students have or have not learned (Russell & Airasian, 2012; Powell, 2015; Waugh & Gronlund, 2013). Many states have identified objectives for students in their state and created tests to measure whether students are meeting those objectives. This approach became national policy in 2002 when the No Child Left Behind (NCLB) legislation was signed into law.

Advocates argue that statewide standardized testing will have a number of positive effects. These include improved student performance; more time teaching the subjects that are tested; high expectations for all students; identification of poorly performing schools, teachers, and administrators; and improved confidence in schools as test scores rise.

Critics argue that the NCLB legislation is doing more harm than good (Sadker & Zittleman, 2012). One criticism stresses that using a single test as the sole indicator of students' progress and competence presents a very narrow view of students' skills (Lewis, 2007). This criticism is similar to the one leveled at IQ tests. To assess student progress and achievement, many psychologists and educators emphasize that a number of measures should be used, including tests, quizzes, projects, portfolios, classroom observations, and so on. Also, the tests used as part of NCLB don't measure creativity, motivation, persistence, flexible thinking, or social skills (Stiggins, 2008). Critics point out that teachers end up spending far too much class time "teaching to the test" by drilling students and having them memorize isolated facts at the expense of teaching that focuses on thinking skills, which students need for success in life (Brookhart & Nitko, 2015; Pressley, 2007). Also, some individuals are concerned that No Child Left Behind educational policy overlooks the needs of students who are gifted because of its primary focus on raising the achievement level of students who are not doing well (Clark, 2008).

Consider also the following: Each state is allowed to establish different criteria for what constitutes passing or failing grades on tests designated for NCLB inclusion. An analysis of NCLB data indicated that almost every fourth-grade student in Mississippi knows how to read but only half of Massachusetts' students do (Birman & others, 2007). Clearly, Mississippi's standards for passing the reading test are far below those of Massachusetts. In the recent analysis of state-by-state comparisons, many states have taken the safe route by choosing a low passing score. Thus, while one of NCLB's goals was to raise standards for achievement in U.S. schools, apparently allowing states to set their own standards has instead lowered achievement standards in many schools.

Despite such criticisms, the U.S. Department of Education is committed to implementing No Child Left Behind, and schools are making accommodations to meet the requirements of this law. Indeed, most educators support high expectations and high standards of excellence for students and teachers. At issue, however, is whether the tests and procedures mandated by NCLB are the best means of achieving these high standards (Darling-Hammond, 2011; McMillan, 2014; Popham, 2014; Witte, 2012).

In 2009, the Common Core State Standards Initiative was endorsed by the National Governors Association in an effort to implement more rigorous state guidelines for educating students. The Common Core Standards specify what students should know and the skills they should develop at each grade level in various content areas (Common Core State Standards Initiative, 2014). A large majority of states have agreed to implement the Standards, but they have generated considerable controversy. Some critics argue that they are simply a further effort by the federal government to control education and that

What are some of the most important purposes of standardized tests?
© Image Source/Alamy RF

they emphasize a "one size fits all" approach that pays little attention to individual variations in students. Supporters say that the Standards provide much-needed detailed guidelines and important milestones for students to achieve.

SCHOOLS AND DEVELOPMENTAL STATUS

Let's now explore how schools work for students at different developmental levels. We will begin with early childhood education.

Early Childhood Education   How do early education programs treat children, and how do the children fare? Our exploration of early childhood education focuses on variations in programs, education for children who are disadvantaged, and some controversies in early childhood education.

What are some characteristics of the child-centered kindergarten?
© image100/PunchStock RF

Variations in Early Childhood Education   There are many variations in the way young children are educated (Burchinal & others, 2015; Feeney, Moravcik, & Nolte, 2016; Morrison, 2014, 2015). The foundation of early childhood education is the child-centered kindergarten.

Nurturing is a key aspect of the **child-centered kindergarten,** which emphasizes the education of the whole child and concern for his or her physical, cognitive, and socioemotional development (Morrison, 2014, 2015). Instruction is organized around children's needs, interests, and learning styles. Emphasis is on the process of learning, rather than what is learned (Kostelnik & others, 2015; Weissman & Hendrick, 2014). The child-centered kindergarten honors three principles: (1) each child follows a unique developmental pattern; (2) young children learn best through firsthand experiences with people and materials; and (3) play is extremely important in the child's total development. *Experimenting, exploring, discovering, trying out, restructuring, speaking,* and *listening* are frequent activities in excellent kindergarten programs. Such programs are closely attuned to the developmental status of 4- and 5-year-old children.

Larry Page and Sergey Brin, founders of the highly successful Internet search engine, Google, said that their early years at Montessori schools were a major factor in their success (International Montessori Council, 2006). During an interview with Barbara Walters, they said they learned how to be self-directed and self-starters at Montessori (ABC News, 2005). They commented that Montessori experiences encouraged them to think for themselves and allowed them the freedom to develop their own interests.
© James Leynse/Corbis

Montessori schools are patterned on the educational philosophy of Maria Montessori (1870–1952), an Italian physician-turned-educator who at the beginning of the twentieth century crafted a revolutionary approach to young children's education. The **Montessori approach** is a philosophy of education in which children are given considerable freedom and spontaneity in choosing activities. They are allowed to move from one activity to another as they desire. The teacher acts as a facilitator rather than a director. The teacher shows the child how to perform intellectual activities, demonstrates interesting ways to explore curriculum materials, and offers help when the child requests it (Isaacs, 2012). "By encouraging children to make decisions from an early age, Montessori programs seek to develop self-regulated problem solvers who can make choices and manage their time effectively" (Hyson, Copple, & Jones, 2006, p. 14). The number of Montessori schools in the United States has expanded dramatically in recent years, from one school in 1959 to 355 schools in 1970 to more than 4,000 today.

Some developmental psychologists favor the Montessori approach, but others believe that it neglects children's socioemotional development. For example, although the Montessori approach fosters independence and the development of cognitive skills, it deemphasizes verbal interaction between the teacher and child and between peers. Montessori's critics also argue that it restricts imaginative play and that its heavy reliance on self-corrective materials may not adequately allow for creativity and for a variety of learning styles.

Many educators and psychologists conclude that preschoolers and young elementary school children learn best through active, hands-on teaching methods such as games and dramatic play. They know that children develop at varying rates and that schools need to allow for these individual differences (Feeney, Moravcik, & Nolte, 2016). They also argue

child-centered kindergarten Education that involves the whole child by considering both the child's physical, cognitive, and socioemotional development and the child's needs, interests, and learning styles.

Montessori approach An educational philosophy in which children are given considerable freedom and spontaneity in choosing activities and are allowed to move from one activity to another as they desire.

that schools should focus on supporting children's socioemotional development as well as their cognitive development. Educators refer to this type of schooling as **developmentally appropriate practice (DAP),** which is based on knowledge of the typical development of children within a particular age span (age appropriateness), as well as on the uniqueness of the individual child (individual appropriateness). DAP emphasizes the importance of creating settings that reflect children's interests and capabilities while encouraging them to be active learners (Bredekamp, 2014; Follari, 2015). Desired outcomes for DAP include thinking critically, working cooperatively, solving problems, developing self-regulatory skills, and enjoying learning. The emphasis in DAP is on the process of learning rather than on its content.

Do developmentally appropriate educational practices improve young children's development? Some researchers have found that young children in developmentally appropriate classrooms are likely to feel less stress, be more motivated, be more socially skilled, have better work habits, be more creative, have better language skills, and demonstrate better math skills than children in developmentally inappropriate classrooms (Hart & others, 2003). However, not all studies find DAP to have significant positive effects (Hyson, Copple, & Jones, 2006). Among the reasons that it is difficult to generalize about research on developmentally appropriate education is that individual programs often vary, and developmentally appropriate education is an evolving concept. Recent changes in the concept have given more attention to how strongly academic skills should be emphasized and how they should be taught.

What are some important aspects of developmentally appropriate practice?
© BananaStock/PunchStock RF

Education for Young Children Who Are Disadvantaged   For many years, U.S. children from low-income families did not receive any education before they entered the first grade. Often when they began first grade they were already several steps behind their classmates in readiness to learn. In the summer of 1965, the federal government began an effort to break the cycle of poverty and poor education for young children through **Project Head Start.** Head Start is a compensatory program designed to give children from low-income families the opportunity to acquire skills and experiences that are important for success in school (Hustedt, Friedman, & Barnett, 2012; Zigler & Styfco, 2010). After almost half a century, Head Start continues to be the largest federally funded program for U.S. children, with almost 1 million children enrolled in it annually. In 2007, 3 percent of Head Start children were 5 years old, 51 percent were 4 years old, 36 percent were 3 years old, and 10 percent were under age 3 (Administration for Children & Families, 2008).

Early Head Start was established in 1995 to serve children from birth to age 3. In 2007, half of all new funds appropriated for Head Start programs were used for the expansion of Early Head Start. Researchers have found these programs to have positive effects. For example, a recent study revealed that Early Head Start had a protective effect on risks that young children might experience in relation to parenting stress, language development, and self-control (Ayoub, Vallotton, & Mastergeorge, 2011). Another recent study revealed language benefits for Early Head Start children (Love & others, 2013).

Head Start programs are not all created equal. One estimate is that 40 percent of the 1,400 Head Start programs are of questionable quality (Zigler & Styfco, 1994). More attention needs to be given to developing consistently high-quality Head Start programs (Hillemeier & others, 2013). One person who is strongly motivated to make Head Start a valuable learning experience for young children from disadvantaged backgrounds is Yolanda Garcia. To read about her work, see the *Connecting with Careers* profile.

Evaluations support the positive influence of quality early childhood programs on both the cognitive and social worlds of disadvantaged young children (Bierman & others, 2014; Lamy, 2012). A recent study found that one year of Head Start was linked to higher performance in early math, early reading, and receptive vocabulary (Miller & others, 2014). Also, a national evaluation of Head Start revealed that the program had a positive influence on the language and cognitive development of 3- and 4-year-olds (Puma & others, 2010). However, by the end of the first grade, there were few lasting outcomes. One exception was a larger vocabulary for those who went to Head Start as 4-year-olds and better oral comprehension for those who went to Head Start as 3-year-olds. Another recent study found that when young children initially began Head Start, they were well below their more academically advantaged

developmentally appropriate practice (DAP) Education that focuses on the typical developmental patterns of children (age appropriateness) and the uniqueness of each child (individual appropriateness). Such practice contrasts with developmentally inappropriate practice, which has an academic, direct instruction emphasis focused largely on abstract paper-and-pencil activities, seatwork, and rote/drill practice activities.

Project Head Start Compensatory prekindergarten education designed to provide children from low-income families the opportunity to acquire skills and experiences important for school success.

Yolanda Garcia, Director of Children's Services, Head Start

Yolanda Garcia has been the director of the Children's Services Department of the Santa Clara, California, County Office of Education since 1980. As director, she is responsible for managing child development programs for 2,500 3- to 5-year-old children in 127 classrooms. Her training includes two master's degrees, one in public policy and child welfare from the University of Chicago and another in educational administration from San Jose State University.

Garcia has served on many national advisory committees that have resulted in improvements in the staffing of Head Start programs. Most notably, she served on the Head Start Quality Committee that recommended the development of Early Head Start and revised performance standards for Head Start programs. Garcia currently is a member of the American Academy of Sciences Committee on the Integration of Science and Early Childhood Education.

Yolanda Garcia, Director of Children's Services/Head Start, works with a Head Start child in Santa Clara, California.
Courtesy of Yolanda Garcia

peers in literacy and math (Hindman & others, 2010). However, by the end of the first grade, the Head Start children were on par with national averages in literacy and math.

One high-quality early childhood education program (although not a Head Start program) is the Perry Preschool program in Ypsilanti, Michigan, a two-year preschool program that includes weekly home visits from program personnel. In analyses of the long-term effects of the program, adults who had been in the Perry Preschool program were compared with a control group of adults from the same background who had not received the enriched early childhood education (Schweinhart & others, 2005; Weikert, 1993). Those who had been in the Perry Preschool program had fewer teen pregnancies and better high school graduation rates, and at age 40 they were more likely to be in the workforce, own a home, and have a savings account, and they'd also had fewer arrests.

Controversy Over Curriculum   A current controversy in early childhood education involves what the curriculum for early childhood education should be (Follari, 2015; Morrison, 2014, 2015). On one side are those who advocate a child-centered, constructivist approach much like that emphasized by the National Association for the Education of Young Children (NAEYC), along the lines of developmentally appropriate practice. On the other side are those who advocate an academic, direct-instruction approach.

In practice, many high-quality early childhood education programs encompass both academic and constructivist approaches. Many education experts such as Lilian Katz (1999), however, worry about academic approaches that place too much pressure on young children to achieve and don't provide opportunities to actively construct knowledge. Competent early childhood programs should focus on both cognitive development and socioemotional development, not exclusively on cognitive development (Bredekamp, 2014; NAEYC, 2009).

Elementary School   For many children, entering the first grade signals a change from being a "home-child" to being a "school-child"—a situation in which they experience new roles and obligations. Children take up the new role of being a student, interact, develop new relationships, adopt new reference groups, and develop new standards by which to judge themselves. School provides children with a rich source of new ideas to shape their sense of self.

What is the curriculum controversy in early childhood education?
© Ronnie Kaufman/The Stock Market/Corbis

Too often, however, early schooling proceeds mainly on the basis of negative feedback. For example, children's self-esteem in the later years of elementary school is lower than it is in the earlier years, and older children rate themselves as less smart, less good, and less hardworking than do younger ones (Eccles, 2003).

Educating Adolescents   How do students experience the transition from elementary to middle or junior high school? What are the characteristics of effective schools for adolescents?

The Transition to Middle or Junior High School   The transition to middle school or junior high school can be stressful. Why? The transition takes place at a time when many changes—in the individual, in the family, and in school—are occurring simultaneously (Eccles & Roeser, 2013; Wigfield & others, 2015). These changes include puberty and related concerns about body image; the emergence of at least some aspects of formal operational thought, including accompanying changes in social cognition; increased responsibility and decreased dependency on parents; change to a larger, more impersonal school structure; change from one teacher to many teachers and from a small, homogeneous set of peers to a larger, more heterogeneous set of peers; and an increased focus on achievement and performance and their assessment. Also, when students make the transition to middle or junior high school, they experience the **top-dog phenomenon,** moving from being the oldest, biggest, and most powerful students in the elementary school to being the youngest, smallest, and least powerful students in the middle or junior high school. A recent study in North Carolina schools revealed that sixth-grade students attending middle schools were far more likely to be cited for discipline problems than their counterparts who were attending elementary schools (Cook & others, 2008).

There can also be positive aspects to the transition to middle or junior high school. Students are more likely to feel grown up, have more subjects from which to select, have more opportunities to spend time with peers and locate compatible friends, and enjoy increased independence from direct parental monitoring. They also may be more challenged intellectually by academic work.

Effective Schools for Young Adolescents   Educators and psychologists worry that junior high and middle schools have become watered-down versions of high schools, mimicking their curricular and extracurricular schedules. Critics argue that these schools should offer activities that reflect a wide range of individual differences in biological and psychological development among young adolescents (Casas, 2011). The Carnegie Foundation (1989) issued an extremely negative evaluation of U.S. middle schools. It concluded that most young adolescents attended massive, impersonal schools, learned from irrelevant curricula, trusted few adults in school, and lacked access to health care and counseling. It recommended that the nation develop smaller "communities" or "houses" to lessen the impersonal nature of large middle schools; have lower student-to-counselor ratios (10 to 1 instead of several hundred to 1); involve parents and community leaders in schools; develop new curricula; have teachers team teach in more flexibly designed curriculum blocks that integrate several disciplines; boost students' health and fitness with more in-school physical education programs; and help students who need public health care to get it. More than two decades later, many of the Carnegie Foundation's recommendations have not been implemented, and middle schools throughout the nation continue to need a major redesign if they are to be effective in educating adolescents (Wigfield & others, 2015).

High School   Just as there are concerns about U.S. middle school education, so are there concerns about U.S. high school education (Bill and Melinda Gates Foundation, 2011). Critics stress that many high schools foster passivity and that schools should create a variety of

As children make the transition to elementary school, they interact and develop relationships with new and significant others. School provides them with a rich source of new ideas to shape their sense of self.
© Ariel Skelley/Blend Images/Getty Images RF

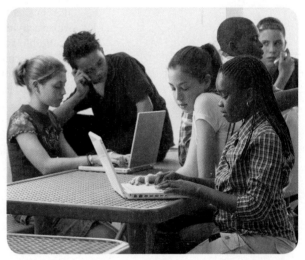

The transition from elementary to middle or junior high school occurs at the same time as a number of other developmental changes. *What are some of these other developmental changes?*
© Creatas/PunchStock RF

top-dog phenomenon The circumstance of moving from the top position in elementary school to the youngest, smallest, and least powerful position in middle or junior high school.

pathways for students to achieve an identity. Many students graduate from high school with inadequate reading, writing, and mathematical skills; of these, many go on to college and must enroll in remediation classes there. Other students drop out of high school and do not have skills that would allow them to obtain decent jobs, much less to be informed citizens.

Robert Crosnoe's (2011) recent book, *Fitting In, Standing Out*, highlighted another major problem with U.S. high schools: How the negative social aspects of adolescents' lives undermine their academic achievement. In his view, adolescents become immersed in complex peer group cultures that demand conformity. High school is supposed to be about getting an education but in reality for many youth it is as much about navigating the social worlds of peer relations that may or may not value education and academic achievement. The adolescents who fail to fit in, especially those who are obese or gay, become stigmatized. Crosnoe recommends increased school counseling services, expanded extracurricular activities, and improved parental monitoring to reduce such problems (Crosnoe & Benner, 2015).

Adolescents in U.S. schools usually have a wide array of extracurricular activities they can participate in beyond their academic courses. These activities include such diverse activities as sports, academic clubs, band, drama, and math clubs. Researchers have found that participation in extracurricular activities is linked to higher grades, greater school engagement, less likelihood of dropping out of school, improved probability of going to college, higher self-esteem, and lower rates of depression, delinquency, and substance abuse (Vandell & others, 2015). A recent study also revealed that the more adolescents participated in organized out-of-school activities, the more likely they were to be characterized by positive outcomes—educational attainment, civic engagement, and psychological flourishing—in emerging adulthood (Mahoney & Vest, 2012). Adolescents benefit from a breadth of extracurricular activities more than focusing on a single extracurricular activity.

In the last half of the twentieth century and the first decade of the twenty-first century, U.S. high school dropout rates declined (National Center for Education Statistics, 2014). In the 1940s, more than half of U.S. 16- to 24-year-olds had dropped out of school; by 2012, this figure had decreased to 6.6 percent. The dropout rate of Latino adolescents remains high, although it has been decreasing considerably in the twenty-first century (from 28 percent in 2000 to 12.7 percent in 2012). The lowest dropout rate in 2013 occurred for Asian American adolescents (3.4 percent), followed by non-Latino White adolescents (5.1 percent), African American adolescents (7.9 percent), and Latino adolescents (11.7 percent) (Child Trends, 2014).

Gender differences characterize U.S. dropout rates, with males more likely to drop out than females in 2012 (7.3 versus 5.9 percent) (National Center for Education Statistics, 2014). The gender gap in dropout rates for Latino adolescents still favors females—11.3 percent for females, 12.7 percent for males—but that gender gap has come down considerably in recent years.

Students in the technology training center at Wellpinit Elementary/High School located on the Spokane Indian reservation in Washington. An important educational goal is to increase the high school graduation rate of Native American adolescents.
© Ed Kashi/Corbis

The average U.S. high school dropout rates just described mask some very high dropout rates in low-income areas of inner cities. For example, in cities such as Detroit, Cleveland, and Chicago, dropout rates are above 50 percent. Also, the percentages cited earlier are for 16- to 24-year-olds. When dropout rates are calculated in terms of students who do not graduate from high school within four years, the percentage of students is also much higher than in Figure 1. Thus, in considering high school dropout rates, it is important to examine age, the number of years it takes to complete high school, and various contexts including ethnicity, gender, and school location.

Students drop out of school for many reasons. In one study, almost 50 percent of the dropouts cited school-related reasons for leaving school, such as not liking school or being expelled or suspended (Rumberger, 1995). Twenty percent of the dropouts (but 40 percent of the Latino students) cited economic reasons for leaving school. One-third of the female students dropped out for personal reasons, such as pregnancy or marriage. A recent study revealed that when children's parents were involved in their school in middle and late childhood and when parents and adolescents had good relationships in early adolescence, a positive trajectory toward academic success was the likely outcome (Englund, Egeland, & Collins, 2008). By contrast, those who had poor relationships with their parents were more likely to drop out of high school even if they were doing well academically and behaviorally.

"I Have a Dream" (IHAD) is an innovative, comprehensive, long-term dropout prevention program administered by the National "I Have a Dream" Foundation in New York. Since the National IHAD Foundation was created in 1986, it has grown to comprise more than 180 projects in 64 cities and 27 states serving more than 15,000 children ("I Have a Dream" Foundation, 2015). Local IHAD projects around the country "adopt" entire grades (usually the third or fourth) from public elementary schools, or corresponding age cohorts from public housing developments. These children—"Dreamers"—are then provided with a program of academic, social, cultural, and recreational activities throughout their elementary, middle school, and high school years. When participants complete high school, IHAD provides the tuition assistance necessary for them to attend a state or local college or vocational school.

The IHAD program was created in 1981, when philanthropist Eugene Lang made an impromptu offer of college tuition to a class of graduating sixth-graders at P.S. 121 in East Harlem. Evaluations of IHAD programs have found dramatic improvements in grades, test scores, and school attendance, as well as a reduction in behavioral problems of Dreamers. In a recent analysis of the I Have a Dream program in Houston, 91 percent of the participants received passing grades in reading/English, 83 percent said they liked school, 98 percent said getting good grades is important to them, 100 percent said they plan to graduate from high school, and 94 percent reported they plan to go to college ("I Have a Dream" Foundation, 2015).

These adolescents are participating in the "I Have a Dream" (IHAD) Program, a comprehensive, long-term dropout prevention program that has been very successful. *What are some other strategies for reducing high school dropout rates?*
Courtesy of "I Have a Dream" Foundation of Boulder County (www.ihadboulder.org)

College and Adult Education   Having a college degree is a strong asset. College graduates can enter careers that will earn them considerably more money in their lifetimes than those who do not go to college, and income differences between college graduates and high school graduates continue to grow (*Occupational Outlook Handbook,* 2014–2015). Recent media accounts have highlighted the dramatically rising costs of a college education and somewhat bleak job prospects for recent college graduates, raising questions about whether a college education is worth it. However, recent data show that individuals with a bachelor's degree make over $20,000 a year more on the average than those with only a high school degree (Daly & Bengali, 2014). Recent data also indicate that in the United States a college graduate will make approximately $830,000 more on average than a high school graduate will earn (Daly & Bengali, 2014).

Individuals with a college education live two years longer on the average than their counterparts who only graduate from high school. What is the transition to college like? Are adults seeking more education than in the past?

Transition to College   Just as the transition from elementary school to middle or junior high school involves change and possible stress, so does the transition from high school to college. The two transitions have many parallels. Going from being a senior in high school to being a freshman in college replays the top-dog phenomenon of transferring from the oldest and most powerful group of students to the youngest and least powerful group of students that occurred earlier as adolescence began. For many students, the transition from high school to college involves movement to a larger, more impersonal school structure; interaction with peers from more diverse geographical and sometimes more diverse ethnic backgrounds; and increased focus on achievement and its assessment. And like the transition from elementary to middle or junior high school, the transition from high school to college can involve positive features. Students are more likely to feel grown up, have more subjects from which to select, have more time to spend with

The transition from high school to college often involves positive as well as negative features. In college, students are likely to feel grown up, be able to spend more time with peers, have more opportunities to explore different lifestyles and values, and enjoy greater freedom from parental monitoring. However, college involves a larger, more impersonal school structure and an increased focus on achievement and its assessment. *What was your transition to college like?*
© Stockbyte/PunchStock RF

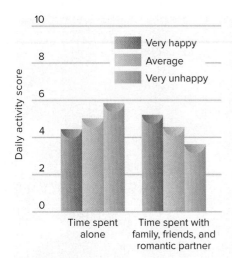

FIGURE 1

DAILY ACTIVITY SELF-RATINGS AND COLLEGE STUDENTS' HAPPINESS. In this study of undergraduates, the daily activity scores reflect mean times with 0 representing no time and 8 reflecting 8 hours per day (Diener & Seligman, 2002). Students were classified as very happy, average, or very unhappy based on their self-ratings.

learning disabilities Disabilities in which children experience difficulty in learning that involves understanding or using spoken or written language; the difficulty can appear in listening, thinking, reading, writing, and spelling. A learning disability also may involve difficulty in doing mathematics. To be classified as a learning disability, the learning problem is not primarily the result of visual, hearing, or motor disabilities; intellectual disability; emotional disorders; or environmental, cultural, or economic disadvantage.

dyslexia A learning disability that involves a severe impairment in the ability to read and spell.

dysgraphia A learning disability that involves difficulty in handwriting.

dyscalculia Also known as developmental arithmetic disorder, this term refers to a learning disability that involves difficulty in math computation.

attention deficit hyperactivity disorder (ADHD) A disability in which children consistently show one or more of the following characteristics: (1) inattention, (2) hyperactivity, and (3) impulsivity.

peers, have more opportunities to explore different lifestyles and values, enjoy greater independence from parental monitoring, and be challenged intellectually by academic work (Santrock & Halonen, 2013).

Today's college students experience more stress and are more depressed than in the past, according to a national study of more than 300,000 freshmen at more than 500 colleges and universities (Eagan & others, 2014). In 2014, 35 percent (up from 16 percent in 1985 and 27 percent in 2009) said they frequently "felt overwhelmed with what I have to do." In 2014, college females were more than twice as likely as their male counterparts to say that they felt overwhelmed with all they had to do. And college freshmen in 2014 indicated that they felt more depressed than their counterparts from the 1980s had indicated. The pressure to succeed in college, get a great job, and make lots of money were pervasive concerns of these students.

What makes college students happy? One study of 222 undergraduates compared the upper 10 percent of college students who were very happy with average and very unhappy college students (Diener & Seligman, 2002). The very happy college students were highly social, more extraverted, and had stronger romantic and social relationships than the less happy college students, who spent more time alone (see Figure 1).

Adult Education   An increasing number of adults older than the traditional college age go to school (Smith & Reio, 2007). Adult education refers to all forms of schooling and learning in which adults participate. Adult education includes literacy training, community development, university credit programs, on-the-job training, and continuing professional education (Comings, 2007). Institutions that offer education to adults include colleges, libraries, museums, government agencies, businesses, and churches.

In 1985, individuals over the age of 25 represented 45 percent of the enrollment in credit courses in the United States. In the second decade of the twenty-first century, that figure is now over 50 percent. A large and expanding number of college students are adults who pursue education and advanced degrees on a part-time basis (Smith & Reio, 2007). The increase in adult education is a result of increased leisure time for some individuals and the need to update information and skills for others. Some older adults simply take educational courses because they enjoy learning and want to keep their minds active.

Women represent the majority of adult learners—almost 60 percent. In the 35-and-over age group, women constitute an even greater percentage of the enrollment in adult education—almost 70 percent. Some of these women devoted their early adult lives to parenting and decided to go back to school to enter a new career.

Going back to a classroom after being away from school for a long time can be stressful. However, returning students should realize that they bring a wealth of experience to college and should feel good about the contributions they can make.

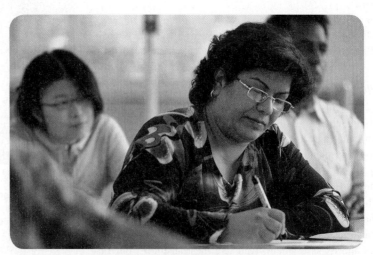

Many immigrants to the United States, such as this Spanish-speaking woman enrolled in an English class, take adult education classes. *What are some trends in adult education?*
© Newscom

EDUCATING CHILDREN WITH DISABILITIES

So far we have discussed schools that are experienced by the majority of U.S. students. Of all children in the United States, 13 percent from 3 to 21 years of age in the United States received special education or related services in 2011–2012, an increase of 3 percent since 1980–1981 (Condition of Education, 2014). Figure 2 shows the five largest groups of students with a disability who were served by federal programs during the 2011–2012 school year (Condition of Education, 2014).

As indicated in Figure 2, students with a learning disability were by far the largest group of students with a disability to be given special education, followed by children with speech or language impairments, intellectual disability, and emotional disturbance. Note that the U.S. Department of Education includes both students with a learning disability and students with ADHD in the category of learning disability.

Learning Disabilities The U.S. government defines whether a child should be classified as having a learning disability in the following way: A child with a **learning disability** has difficulty in learning that involves understanding or using spoken or written language, and the difficulty can appear in listening, thinking, reading, writing, and spelling. A learning disability also may involve difficulty in doing mathematics (Kucian & von Aster, 2015). To be classified as a learning disability, the learning problem is not primarily the result of visual, hearing, or motor disabilities; intellectual disability; emotional disorders; or due to environmental, cultural, or economic disadvantage (Swanson, 2014).

About three times as many boys as girls are classified as having a learning disability. Among the explanations for this gender difference are a greater biological vulnerability among boys and *referral bias*. That is, boys are more likely to be referred by teachers for treatment because of troublesome behavior.

Approximately 80 percent of children with a learning disability have a reading problem (Shaywitz, Gruen, & Shaywitz, 2007). Three types of learning disabilities are dyslexia, dysgraphia, and dyscalculia:

- **Dyslexia** is a category reserved for individuals with a severe impairment in their ability to read and spell (Ramus, 2014; Thompson & others, 2015).
- **Dysgraphia** is a learning disability that involves difficulty in handwriting (Berninger & others, 2015; Fischer-Baum & Rapp, 2014). Children with dysgraphia may write very slowly, their writing products may be virtually illegible, and they may make numerous spelling errors because of their inability to match up sounds and letters.
- **Dyscalculia,** also known as developmental arithmetic disorder, is a learning disability that involves difficulty in math computation (Cowan & Powell, 2014; Kucian & von Aster, 2015).

The precise causes of learning disabilities have not yet been determined (Vaughn & Bos, 2015). To reveal any regions of the brain that might be involved in learning disabilities, researchers use brain-imaging techniques such as magnetic resonance imaging (Shaywitz, Lyon, & Shaywitz, 2006) (see Figure 3). This research indicates that it is unlikely that learning disabilities reside in a single, specific brain location. More likely, learning disabilities are due to problems with integrating information from multiple brain regions or subtle difficulties in brain structures and functions.

Interventions with children who have a learning disability often focus on improving reading ability (Templeton & Gehsmann, 2014). Intensive instruction in reading over a period of time by a competent teacher can help many children (Berninger & Dunn, 2012; Del Campo & others, 2015).

Attention Deficit Hyperactivity Disorder (ADHD) **Attention deficit hyperactivity disorder (ADHD)** is a disability in which children consistently show one or more of the following characteristics over a period of time: (1) inattention, (2) hyperactivity, and (3) impulsivity. Children who are inattentive have such difficulty focusing on any one thing that they may

Disability	Percentage of All Children in Public Schools
Learning disabilities	4.7
Speech and language impairments	2.8
Intellectual disability	0.9
Autism	0.9
Emotional disturbance	0.8

FIGURE 2

U.S. CHILDREN WITH A DISABILITY WHO RECEIVE SPECIAL EDUCATION SERVICES. Figures are for the 2011–2012 school year and represent the five categories with the highest numbers and percentage of children. Both learning disability and attention deficit hyperactivity disorder are combined in the learning disabilities category (Condition of Education, 2014).

FIGURE 3

BRAIN SCANS AND LEARNING DISABILITIES. An increasing number of studies are using MRI brain scans to examine the brain pathways involved in learning disabilities. Shown here is 9-year-old Patrick Price, who has dyslexia. Patrick is going through an MRI scanner disguised by drapes to look like a child-friendly castle. Inside the scanner, children must lie virtually motionless as words and symbols flash on a screen, and they are asked to identify them by clicking different buttons.
© Manuel Balce Ceneta/AP Images

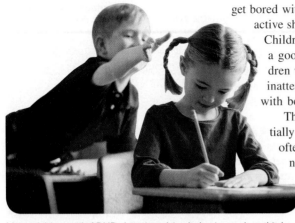

Many children with ADHD show impulsive behavior, such as this boy reaching to pull a girl's hair. *How would you handle this situation if you were a teacher and this were to happen in your classroom?*
© Nicole Hill/Rubberball/Getty Images RF

get bored with a task after only a few minutes—or even seconds. Children who are hyperactive show high levels of physical activity, seeming to be almost constantly in motion. Children who are impulsive have difficulty curbing their reactions; they do not do a good job of thinking before they act. Depending on the characteristics that children with ADHD display, they can be diagnosed as (1) ADHD with predominantly inattention, (2) ADHD with predominantly hyperactivity/impulsivity, or (3) ADHD with both inattention and hyperactivity/impulsivity.

The number of children diagnosed and treated for ADHD has increased substantially in recent decades. The disorder is diagnosed as much as four to nine times as often in boys as in girls. There is controversy, however, about the increased diagnosis of ADHD (Friend, 2014; Watson & others, 2014). Some experts attribute the increase mainly to heightened awareness of the disorder; others are concerned that many children are being incorrectly diagnosed.

A recent study examined the possible misdiagnosis of ADHD (Bruchmiller, Margraf, & Schneider, 2012). In this study, child psychologists, psychiatrists, and social workers were given vignettes of children with ADHD (some vignettes matched the diagnostic criteria for the disorder, while others did not). Whether each child was male or female varied. The researchers assessed whether the mental health professionals gave a diagnosis of ADHD to the child described in the vignette. The professionals overdiagnosed ADHD almost 20 percent of the time, and regardless of the symptoms described, boys were twice as likely as girls to be given a diagnosis of ADHD.

Definitive causes of ADHD have not been found. However, a number of causes have been proposed. Some children likely inherit a tendency to develop ADHD from their parents (Lee & Song, 2014). Other children likely develop ADHD because of damage to their brain during prenatal or postnatal development (Strickland, 2014). Among early possible contributors to ADHD are cigarette and alcohol exposure, as well as a high level of maternal stress during prenatal development and low birth weight (Glover, 2014; Yochum & others, 2014). For example, a recent study revealed that cigarette smoking during pregnancy was linked to ADHD in 6- to 7-year-old children (Sciberras, Ukoumunne, & Efron, 2011).

As with learning disabilities, the development of brain-imaging techniques is leading to a better understanding of ADHD (Berger & others, 2015; Chiang & others, 2015; Li & others, 2014). One study revealed that peak thickness of the cerebral cortex occurred three years later (10.5 years) in children with ADHD than in children without ADHD (peak at 7.5 years) (Shaw & others, 2007). The delay was more prominent in the prefrontal regions of the brain that are especially important in attention and planning (see Figure 4). Another study also found delayed development in the brain's frontal lobes among children with ADHD, which likely was due to delayed or decreased myelination (Nagel & others, 2011). Researchers also are exploring the roles that various neurotransmitters, such as serotonin and dopamine, might play in ADHD (Gold & others, 2014; Kollins & Adcock, 2014).

The delays in brain development just described are in areas linked to executive function. An increasing interest in the study of children with ADHD is their difficulty on tasks involving executive function, such as behavioral inhibition when necessary, use of working memory, and effective planning (Dovis & others, 2015; Dunn & Kroenenberger, 2013; Saarinen & others, 2015). Researchers also have found deficits in theory of mind in children with ADHD (Buhler & others, 2011; Mary & others, 2015).

Adjustment and optimal development also are difficult for children who have ADHD, so it is important that the diagnosis be accurate (Bolea-Alamanac & others, 2014; Feldman & Reiff, 2014). Children diagnosed with ADHD have an increased risk of school dropout, adolescent pregnancy, substance use problems, and antisocial behavior (Molina & Pelham, 2014).

Experts previously thought that most children "grow out" of ADHD. However, recent evidence suggests that as many as 70 percent of adolescents (Sibley & others, 2012) and 66 percent of adults (Buitelaar, Karr, & Asherton, 2010) who were diagnosed as children continue to experience ADHD symptoms.

Stimulant medication such as Ritalin or Adderall (which has fewer side effects than Ritalin) is effective in improving the attention of many children with ADHD, but it usually does not improve their attention to the same level as children who do not have ADHD (Sclar & others, 2012). A meta-analysis concluded that behavior management treatments are effective in reducing the effects of ADHD (Fabiano & others, 2009). Researchers have often found

Prefrontal cortex   Prefrontal cortex

▮ Greater than 2 years delay
▮ 0 to 2 years delay

FIGURE 4

REGIONS OF THE BRAIN IN WHICH CHILDREN WITH ADHD HAD A DELAYED PEAK IN THE THICKNESS OF THE CEREBRAL CORTEX. *Note:* The greatest delays occurred in the prefrontal cortex.

that a combination of medication (such as Ritalin) and behavior management improves the behavior of children with ADHD better than medication alone or behavior management alone, although not in all cases (Parens & Johnston, 2009).

The sheer number of ADHD diagnoses has prompted speculation that psychiatrists, parents, and teachers are in fact labeling normal childhood behavior as psychopathology (Mash & Wolfe, 2013; Molina & Pelham, 2014). One reason for concern about overdiagnosing ADHD is that the form of treatment in well over 80 percent of cases is psychoactive drugs, including stimulants such as Ritalin and Adderall (Garfield & others, 2012). Further, there is increasing concern that children who are given stimulant drugs such as Ritalin or Adderall are at risk for developing substance abuse problems, although results on this concern so far have been mixed (Nogueira & others, 2014; Zulauf & others, 2014).

Recently, researchers have been exploring the possibility that neurofeedback might improve the attention of children with ADHD (Gevensleben & others, 2014; Marx & others, 2015; Steiner & others, 2014a, b; Zuberer, Brandeis, & Drechsler, 2015). Neurofeedback trains individuals to become more aware of their physiological responses so that they can attain better control over their brain's prefrontal cortex, where executive control primarily occurs. Individuals with ADHD have higher levels of electroencephalogram (EEG) abnormalities, such as lower beta waves that involve attention and memory, and lower sensorimotor rhythms (which involve control of movements). Neurofeedback produces audiovisual profiles of brain waves so that individuals can learn how to achieve normal EEG functioning. In a recent study, 7- to 14-year-olds with ADHD were randomly assigned either to take Ritalin or to undergo 40 sessions of a neurofeedback treatment (Meisel & others, 2013). Both groups showed a lower level of ADHD symptoms six months after the treatment, but only the neurofeedback group performed better academically.

Mindfulness training also recently has been given to children and adolescents with ADHD (Anderson & Guthery, 2015; Cassone, 2015; Converse & others, 2014). In a recent study, 11- to 15-year-old adolescents with ADHD received eight weeks of mindfulness training (van de Weijer-Bergsma & others, 2012). Immediately after and eight weeks following the training, the adolescents' attention improved and they engaged in fewer behavioral problems, although at 16 weeks post-training the effects had waned.

Exercise also is being investigated as a possible treatment for children with ADHD (Berwid & Halperin, 2012; Cassone, 2015; Huang & others, 2015; Pan & others, 2015). A recent study found that a single 20-minute bout of moderately intense aerobic exercise improved the neurocognitive function and inhibitory control of children with ADHD (Pontifex & others, 2013). Among the reasons given as to why exercise might reduce ADHD symptoms in children are (1) better allocation of attention resources, (2) positive influence on prefrontal cortex functioning, and (3) exercise-induced dopamine release (Chang & others, 2012).

Autism Spectrum Disorders

Autism spectrum disorders (ASDs), also called pervasive developmental disorders, range from the more severe disorder called *autistic disorder* to the milder disorder called *Asperger syndrome.* Autism spectrum disorders are characterized by problems in social interaction, problems in verbal and nonverbal communication, and repetitive behaviors (Wheeler, Mayton, & Carter, 2015; Wilczynski & others, 2014). Children with these disorders may also show atypical responses to sensory experiences (National Institute of Mental Health, 2015). Intellectual disability is present in some children with autism; others show average or above-average intelligence (Volkmar & others, 2014). Autism spectrum disorders can often be detected in children as young as 1 to 3 years of age.

In 2013, the American Psychiatric Association proposed that in the new DSM-5 psychiatric classification of disorders, autistic disorder, Asperger syndrome, and several other autistic variations ought to be consolidated in the overarching category of autism spectrum disorder (Autism Research Institute, 2015). Distinctions will be made in terms of the severity of problems based on amount of support needed due to challenges involving social communication, restricted interests, and repetitive behaviors. Critics of this proposal argue that the umbrella category proposed for autism spectrum disorder masks the heterogeneity that characterizes the subgroups of autism (Lai & others, 2013).

Recent estimates of autism spectrum disorders indicate that they are increasing in occurrence or are increasingly being detected and labeled (Neal, 2009). These disorders were once thought to affect only 1 in 2,500 individuals, However, the most recent estimate

developmental **connection**

Cognitive Processes

Mindfulness training is being used to improve students' executive function. Connect to "Information Processing."

developmental **connection**

Conditions, Diseases, and Disorders

Autistic children have difficulty in developing a theory of mind, especially in understanding others' beliefs and emotions. Connect to "Information Processing."

What characterizes autism spectrum disorders?
© Pixland/PunchStock RF

autism spectrum disorders (ASDs) Also called pervasive developmental disorders, these range from the severe disorder labeled autistic disorder to the milder disorder called Asperger syndrome. Children with these disorders are characterized by problems in social interaction, verbal and nonverbal communication, and repetitive behaviors.

FIGURE **5**

A SCENE FROM THE DVD ANIMATIONS USED IN A STUDY BY BARON-COHEN AND OTHERS (2007). *What did they do to improve autistic children's ability to read facial expressions?*
The Autism Research Trust

is that 1 in 88 children had an autism spectrum disorder in 2008 (Centers for Disease Control & Prevention, 2012). In the most recent survey, autism spectrum disorders were identified five times more often in boys than in girls.

Autistic disorder is a severe developmental autism spectrum disorder that has its onset in the first three years of life and includes deficiencies in social relationships; abnormalities in communication; and restricted, repetitive, and stereotyped patterns of behavior.

Asperger syndrome is a relatively mild autism spectrum disorder in which the child has relatively good verbal language skills, milder nonverbal language problems, and a restricted range of interests and relationships (Helles & others, 2015; Soares & Patel, 2012). Children with Asperger syndrome often engage in obsessive, repetitive routines and preoccupations with a particular subject. For example, a child may be obsessed with baseball scores or specific videos on YouTube.

What causes the autism spectrum disorders? The current consensus is that autism is a brain dysfunction characterized by abnormalities in brain structure and neurotransmitters (Conti & others, 2015; Doll & Broadie, 2014; Lisiecka & others, 2015; Nomi & Uddin, 2015). Recent interest has focused on a lack of connectivity between brain regions as a key factor in autism (Fakhoury, 2015; Verly & others, 2014).

Genetic factors also are likely to play a role in the development of the autism spectrum disorders (Ch'ng & others, 2015; Ning & others, 2015; Rutter & Thapar, 2014; Sandin & others, 2014). One study revealed that mutations—missing or duplicated pieces of DNA on chromosome 16—can raise a child's risk of developing autism 100-fold (Weiss & others, 2008). There is no evidence that family socialization causes autism.

Boys are estimated to be five times more likely to have autism spectrum disorders than girls are (Centers for Disease Control and Prevention, 2015). Expanding on autism's male linkage, Simon Baron-Cohen (2008, 2009, 2011) recently argued that autism reflects an extreme male brain, especially indicative of males' less effective ability to show empathy and read facial expressions and gestures. In an attempt to improve these skills in 4- to 8-year-old autistic boys, Baron-Cohen and his colleagues (2007) produced a number of animations on a DVD that put faces with different emotions on toy trains and tractor characters in a boy's bedroom (see Figure 5) (see www.thetransporters.com for a look at a number of the facial expression animations in addition to the one shown in Figure 5). After the autistic children watched the animations 15 minutes every weekday for one month, their ability to recognize emotions on real faces in a different context equaled that of children without autism.

Children with autism benefit from a well-structured classroom, individualized instruction, and small-group instruction (Simmons, Lanter, & Lyons, 2014; Wheeler, Mayton, & Carter, 2015). Behavior modification techniques are sometimes effective in helping autistic children learn (Odom & others, 2014; Zirpoli, 2016).

Educational Issues   Until the 1970s most U.S. public schools either refused enrollment to children with disabilities or inadequately served them. This changed in 1975 when Public Law 94-142, the Education for All Handicapped Children Act, required that all students with disabilities be given a free, appropriate public education. In 1990, Public Law 94-142 was recast as the Individuals with Disabilities Education Act (IDEA). IDEA was amended in 1997 and then reauthorized in 2004 and renamed the Individuals with Disabilities Education Improvement Act.

IDEA spells out broad mandates for services to children with disabilities of all kinds (Kirk, Gallagher, & Coleman, 2015). These services include evaluation and eligibility determination, appropriate education and an individualized education plan (IEP), and education in the least restrictive environment (LRE) (Hallahan, Kauffman, & Pullen, 2015).

autistic disorder A severe autism spectrum disorder that has its onset in the first three years of life and includes deficiencies in social relationships; abnormalities in communication; and restricted, repetitive, and stereotyped patterns of behavior.

Asperger syndrome A relatively mild autism spectrum disorder in which the child has relatively good verbal language skills, milder nonverbal language problems, and a restricted range of interests and relationships.

An **individualized education plan (IEP)** is a written statement that spells out a program that is specifically tailored for a student with a disability. The **least restrictive environment (LRE)** is a setting that is as similar as possible to the one in which children who do not have a disability are educated. This provision of the IDEA has given a legal basis to efforts to educate children with a disability in the regular classroom (Smith & Tyler, 2014; Turnbull & others, 2016). The term **inclusion** describes educating a child with special educational needs full-time in the regular classroom (Friend, 2014; Salend, 2016). Recent analysis indicated that the percentage of time students with disabilities spend in the regular classroom reached its highest level (61 percent) since it had been assessed (Condition of Education, 2014).

IDEA mandates free, appropriate education for all children. *What services does IDEA mandate for children with disabilities?*
© Richard Hutchings/Science Source

Many legal changes regarding children with disabilities have been extremely positive (Smith & others, 2016; Vaughn, Bos, & Schumm, 2014). Compared with several decades ago, far more children today are receiving competent, specialized services. For many children, inclusion in the regular classroom, with modifications or supplemental services, is appropriate. However, some leading experts on special education argue that some children with disabilities may not benefit from inclusion in the regular classroom (Hallahan, Kauffman, & Pullen, 2015). James Kauffman and his colleagues, for example, advocate a more individualized approach that does not necessarily involve full inclusion but allows options such as special education outside the regular classroom with trained professionals and adapted curricula (Kauffman, McGee, & Brigham, 2004). They go on to say, "We sell students with disabilities short when we pretend that they are not different from typical students. We make the same error when we pretend that they must not be expected to put forth extra effort if they are to learn to do some things—or learn to do something in a different way" (p. 620). Like general education, special education should challenge students with disabilities to become all they can be.

SOCIOECONOMIC STATUS AND ETHNICITY IN SCHOOLS

Children from low-income, ethnic minority backgrounds have more difficulties in school than do their middle-socioeconomic-status, non-Latino White counterparts. Why? Critics argue that schools have not done a good job of educating low-income, ethnic minority students to overcome the barriers to their achievement (Banks, 2015; Bennett, 2015). And recent comparisons of student achievement indicate that U.S. students have lower achievement in math and science than students in a number of countries, especially those in East Asia (TIMMS, 2008).

The Education of Students from Low-Income Backgrounds Many children in poverty face problems that present barriers to their learning (Crosnoe & Leventhal, 2014; Duncan, Magnuson, & Votruba-Drzal, 2015). They might have parents who don't set high educational standards for them, who are incapable of reading to them, or who don't have enough money to pay for educational materials and experiences, such as books and trips to zoos and museums. They might be malnourished or live in areas where crime and violence are a way of life. One study revealed that neighborhood disadvantage (involving characteristics such as low neighborhood income and high unemployment) was linked to less consistent, less stimulating, and more punitive parenting, and ultimately to negative child outcomes such as behavioral problems and low verbal ability (Kohen & others, 2008). Another study revealed that the longer children experienced poverty, the more detrimental the poverty was to their cognitive development (Najman & others, 2009).

Compared with schools in higher-income areas, schools in low-income areas are more likely to have higher percentages of students with low achievement test scores, lower graduation rates, and smaller percentages of students going to college; they are more likely to have young teachers with less experience, larger proportions of noncredentialed or nonqualified teachers, and substitute teachers regularly filling in to teach; they are more likely to encourage rote learning; and they are less likely to provide adequate support for English-language learners (Crosnoe & Benner, 2015). Too few schools in low-income neighborhoods provide students with environments that are conducive to learning (Koppelman, 2014; Leventhal, Dupere, & Shuey, 2015).

developmental **connection**

Environment

Socioeconomic differences are a proxy for material, human, and social capital within and beyond the family (Huston & Ripke, 2006). Connect to "Peers and the Sociocultural World."

individualized education plan (IEP) A written statement that spells out a program tailored to a child with a disability. The plan should be (1) related to the child's learning capacity, (2) specially constructed to meet the child's individual needs and not merely a copy of what is offered to other children, and (3) designed to provide educational benefits.

least restrictive environment (LRE) A setting that is as similar as possible to the one in which children without a disability are educated.

inclusion Education of a child with special educational needs full-time in the regular classroom.

In *The Shame of the Nation*, Jonathan Kozol (2005) criticized the inadequate quality and lack of resources in many U.S. schools, especially those in the poverty areas of inner cities that have high concentrations of ethnic minority children. Kozol praises teachers like Angela Lively (*above*), who keeps a box of shoes in her Indianapolis classroom for students in need.
© Michael Conroy/AP Images

Many of the schools' buildings and classrooms are old and crumbling. In sum, far too many schools in low-income neighborhoods provide students with environments that are not conducive to effective learning (Bradley, 2015).

Ethnicity in Schools More than one-third of all African American and almost one-third of all Latino students attend schools in the 47 largest city school districts in the United States, compared with only 5 percent of all White and 22 percent of all Asian American students. Many of these inner-city schools are still segregated, are grossly underfunded, and do not provide adequate opportunities for children to learn effectively. Thus, the effects of socioeconomic status (SES) and the effects of ethnicity are often intertwined (Murry & others, 2015).

Even outside inner-city schools, school segregation remains a factor in U.S. education (Banks, 2014; Cushner, McClelland, & Safford, 2015). Almost one-third of all African American and Latino students attend schools in which 90 percent or more of the students are from minority groups (Banks, 2010, 2014, 2015).

The school experiences of students from different ethnic groups vary considerably. African American and Latino students are much less likely than non-Latino White or Asian American students to be enrolled in academic, college preparatory programs and are much more likely to be enrolled in remedial and special education programs. Asian American students are far more likely than other ethnic minority groups to take advanced math and science courses in high school. African American students are twice as likely as Latinos, Native Americans, or Whites to be suspended from school.

However, it is very important to note that diversity characterizes every ethnic group (Bennett, 2015). For example, the higher percentage of Asian American students in advanced classes is mainly true for students with Chinese, Taiwanese, Japanese, Korean, and East Indian cultural backgrounds, but students with Hmong and Vietnamese cultural backgrounds have had less academic success.

Following are some strategies for improving relationships among ethnically diverse students:

· *Turn the class into a jigsaw classroom.* When Elliot Aronson was a professor at the University of Texas at Austin, the school system contacted him for ideas on how to reduce the increasing racial tension in classrooms. Aronson (1986) developed the concept of a "jigsaw classroom," in which students from different cultural backgrounds are placed in a cooperative group in which they have to construct different parts of a project to reach a common goal. Aronson used the term *jigsaw* because he saw that the technique resembled a group of students cooperating to put different pieces together to complete a jigsaw puzzle. How might this process work? Team sports, drama productions, and musical performances are examples of contexts in which students cooperatively participate to reach a common goal.

· *Encourage students to have positive personal contact with diverse other students.* Contact alone does not do the job of improving relationships with diverse others. For example, busing ethnic minority students to predominantly non-Latino White schools, or vice versa, has not reduced prejudice or improved interethnic relations (Minuchin & Shapiro, 1983). What matters is what happens after children get to school. Especially beneficial in improving interethnic relations is sharing one's worries, successes, failures, coping strategies, interests, and other personal information with people of other ethnicities. When this sharing happens, people tend to look at others as individuals rather than as members of a homogeneous group.

· *Encourage students to engage in perspective taking.* Exercises and activities that help students see others' perspectives can improve interethnic relations. These help students "step into the shoes" of peers who are culturally different and to discover what it feels like to be treated in fair or unfair ways.

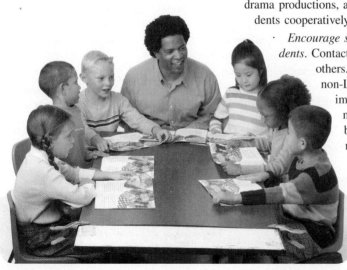

What are some features of a jigsaw classroom?
© McGraw-Hill Companies, Inc./Ken Karp, Photographer

James Comer, Child Psychiatrist

James Comer grew up in a low-income neighborhood in East Chicago, Indiana, and credits his parents with leaving no doubt about the importance of education. He obtained a B.A. degree from Indiana University. He went on to obtain a medical degree from Howard University College of Medicine, a Master of Public Health degree from the University of Michigan School of Public Health, and psychiatric training at the Yale University School of Medicine's Child Study Center. He currently is the Maurice Falk Professor of Child Psychiatry at the Yale University Child Study Center and an associate dean at the Yale University Medical School. During his years at Yale, Comer has concentrated his career on promoting a focus on child development as a way of improving schools. His efforts in support of healthy development of young people are known internationally.

Dr. Comer perhaps is best known for the founding of the School Development program in 1968, which promotes the collaboration of parents, educators, and community to improve social, emotional, and academic outcomes for children. His concept of teamwork is currently improving the educational environment in more than 600 schools throughout the United States.

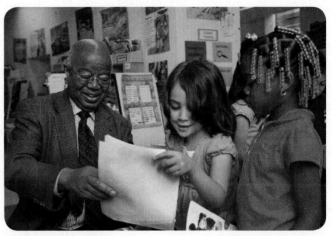

James Comer is shown with some of the inner-city children who attend a school that became a better learning environment because of Comer's intervention.
© Chris Volpe

- *Reduce bias.* Teachers can reduce bias by displaying images of children from diverse ethnic and cultural groups, selecting play materials and classroom activities that encourage cultural understanding, helping students resist stereotyping, and working with parents.
- *View the school and community as a team.* James Comer (2004, 2006, 2010) emphasizes that a community, team approach is the best way to educate children. Three important aspects of the Comer Project for Change are (1) a governance and management team that develops a comprehensive school plan, assessment strategy, and staff development plan; (2) a mental health or school support team; and (3) a parents' program. Comer holds that the entire school community should have a cooperative rather than an adversarial attitude. The Comer program is currently operating in more than 600 schools in 26 states. To read further about James Comer's work, see the *Connecting with Careers* profile.

Review *Connect* Reflect

 Describe the role of schools in development

Review
- What are some contemporary approaches to student learning?
- How do schools change as children develop?
- What are learning disabilities, ADHD, and autism spectrum disorders? What is involved in educating children with disabilities?
- What roles do socioeconomic status and ethnicity play in schools?

Connect
- What did you learn in this section about educating children that might connect with what you've learned about socioeconomic status and ethnicity?

Reflect *Your Own Personal Journey of Life*
- What was your middle or junior high school like? How did it measure up to the Carnegie Foundation's recommendations?

2 Achievement   LG2 Explain the key aspects of achievement

- Extrinsic and Intrinsic Motivation
- Mastery Motivation and Mindset
- Self-Efficacy
- Goal-Setting, Planning, and Self-Monitoring
- Expectations
- Ethnicity and Culture

Life is a gift . . . Accept it.

Life is a puzzle . . . Solve it.

Life is an adventure . . . Dare it.

Life is an opportunity . . . Take it.

Life is a mystery . . . Unfold it.

Life is a mission . . . Fulfill it.

Life is a struggle . . . Face it.

Life is a goal . . . Achieve it.

—AUTHOR UNKNOWN

In any classroom, whoever the teacher is and whatever approach is used, some children achieve more than others. Why? Among the reasons for variations in achievement are characteristics of the child and sociocultural contexts related to motivation.

EXTRINSIC AND INTRINSIC MOTIVATION

The behavioral perspective emphasizes the importance of extrinsic motivation. **Extrinsic motivation** involves doing something to obtain something else (the activity is a means to an end). Extrinsic motivation is often influenced by external incentives such as rewards and punishments. For example, a student may study for a test in order to obtain a good grade.

Whereas the behavioral perspective emphasizes extrinsic motivation in achievement, the cognitive perspective stresses the importance of intrinsic motivation. **Intrinsic motivation** involves the internal motivation to do something for its own sake (the activity is an end in itself). For example, a student may study hard for a test because he or she enjoys the content of the course.

Parental intrinsic/extrinsic motivational practices are linked to children's motivation. In one study, children had higher intrinsic motivation in math and science from 9 to 17 years of age when their parents engaged in task-intrinsic practices (encouraging children's pleasure and engagement in learning) than when their parents engaged in task-extrinsic practices (providing external rewards and consequences contingent on children's performance) (Gottfried & others, 2009).

Let's first consider the intrinsic motivation of self-determination and personal choice. Next, we'll identify some developmental changes in intrinsic and extrinsic motivation as students move up the educational ladder. Finally, we will draw some conclusions about intrinsic and extrinsic motivation.

Self-Determination and Choice   One view of intrinsic motivation emphasizes that students want to believe that they are doing something because of their own will, not because of external success or rewards (Deci, Koestner, & Ryan, 2001). Students' internal motivation and intrinsic interest in school tasks increase when they have opportunities to make choices and take responsibility for their learning (Stipek, 2002). In one study, students who were given some choice of activities and when to do them, and were encouraged to take personal responsibility for their behavior, had higher achievement gains and were more likely to graduate from high school than a control group (deCharms, 1984). The architects of self-determination theory, Richard Ryan and Edward Deci (2009), refer to teachers who create circumstances for students to engage in self-determination as autonomy-supportive teachers.

Developmental Shifts in Intrinsic and Extrinsic Motivation   Many psychologists and educators stress that it is important for children to develop intrinsic motivation as they grow older. However, as students move from the early elementary school years to the high school years, intrinsic motivation tends to decline (Harter, 1996). In one study, the biggest drop in intrinsic motivation and largest increase in extrinsic motivation occurred between the sixth and seventh grades (Harter, 1981).

Jacquelynne Eccles and her colleagues (Eccles, 2004; Eccles & Roeser, 2013; Wigfield & others, 2006, 2015) identified some specific changes in the school context that help to explain the decline in intrinsic motivation. Middle and junior high schools are more impersonal, more formal, more evaluative, and more competitive than elementary schools. Students compare themselves more with other students because they are increasingly graded in terms of their relative performance on assignments and standardized tests.

extrinsic motivation Doing something to obtain something else (the activity is a means to an end).

intrinsic motivation Doing something for its own sake; involves factors such as self-determination and opportunities to make choices.

Conclusions About Intrinsic and Extrinsic Motivation   An overwhelming conclusion of motivation research is that teachers should encourage students to become intrinsically motivated (Eccles & Roeser, 2010; Sosic-Vasic & others, 2015). Similarly, teachers should create learning environments that promote students' cognitive engagement and self-responsibility for learning (Anderman, Gray, & Chang, 2013). That said, the real world includes both intrinsic and extrinsic motivation, and too often intrinsic and extrinsic motivation have been pitted against each other as polar opposites. In many aspects of students' lives, both intrinsic and extrinsic motivation are at work (Cameron & Pierce, 2008; Wigfield & others, 2015). Further, intrinsic and extrinsic motivation can operate simultaneously. Thus, a student may work hard in a course because she enjoys the content and likes learning about it (intrinsic) and because she wants to earn a good grade (extrinsic) (Schunk, 2012). Keep in mind, though, that many educational psychologists suggest that extrinsic motivation by itself is not a good strategy.

MASTERY MOTIVATION AND MINDSET

The increasingly competitive, impersonal atmosphere of middle schools obviously does not discourage all students. To some, these characteristics represent a challenge. How students typically respond to challenges has a lot to do with how much they achieve (Wigfield & others, 2015). Becoming cognitively engaged and self-motivated to improve are reflected in individuals with mastery motivation. These individuals also have a growth mindset—a belief that they can produce positive outcomes if they put forth sufficient effort.

Mastery Motivation   Carol Dweck and her colleagues (Dweck, 2012, 2013; Dweck & Elliott, 1983; Dweck, Mangels, & Good, 2004; Murphy & Dweck, 2010) have found that individuals respond in two distinct ways to difficult or challenging circumstances. People who display a **mastery orientation** are task-oriented—they concentrate on learning strategies and implementing the process of achievement rather than focusing on their ability or the outcome. By contrast, those with a **helpless orientation** seem trapped by the experience of difficulty, and they attribute their difficulty to lack of ability. They frequently say such things as "I'm not very good at this," even though they might earlier have demonstrated their ability through many successes. And, once they view their behavior as failure, they often feel anxious, and their performance worsens even further. Figure 6 describes some behaviors that might reflect helplessness (Stipek, 2002).

In contrast, mastery-oriented individuals often instruct themselves to pay attention, to think carefully, and to remember strategies that have worked for them in previous situations. They frequently report feeling challenged and excited by difficult tasks, rather than being threatened by them (Dweck, 2012). A study revealed that seventh- to eleventh-grade students' mastery goals were linked to how much effort they put forth in mathematics (Chouinard, Karsenti, & Roy, 2007).

Another issue in motivation involves whether to adopt a mastery or a performance orientation. Individuals with a **performance orientation** are focused on winning, rather than on an achievement outcome, and believe that happiness results from winning. Does this focus mean that mastery-oriented individuals do not like to win and that performance-oriented individuals are not motivated to experience the self-efficacy that comes from being able to take credit for one's accomplishments? No. A matter of emphasis or degree is involved, though. For mastery-oriented individuals, winning isn't everything; for performance-oriented individuals, skill development and self-efficacy take a backseat to winning.

The U.S. government's No Child Left Behind Act (NCLB) emphasizes testing and accountability. Although NCLB may motivate some teachers and students to work harder, motivation experts worry that it encourages a performance rather than a mastery motivation orientation on the part of students (Schunk, 2012).

A final point needs to be made about mastery and performance goals: They are not always mutually exclusive. Students can be both mastery- and performance-oriented, and researchers have found that mastery goals combined with performance goals often benefit students' success (Schunk, 2012).

Mindset   Carol Dweck's (2006, 2007, 2012) most recent analysis of motivation for achievement stresses the importance of developing a **mindset,** which she defines as the cognitive view individuals develop for themselves. She concludes that individuals have one of

The student:
- Says "I can't"
- Doesn't pay attention to teacher's instructions
- Doesn't ask for help, even when it is needed
- Does nothing (for example, stares out the window)
- Guesses or answers randomly without really trying
- Doesn't show pride in successes
- Appears bored, uninterested
- Is unresponsive to teacher's exhortations to try
- Is easily discouraged
- Doesn't volunteer answers to teacher's questions
- Maneuvers to get out of or to avoid work (for example, has to go to the nurse's office)

FIGURE 6
BEHAVIORS THAT SUGGEST A HELPLESS ORIENTATION

mastery orientation A perspective in which one is task-oriented—concerned with learning strategies and the process of achievement rather than the outcome.

helpless orientation An orientation in which one seems trapped by the experience of difficulty and attributes one's difficulty to a lack of ability.

performance orientation An orientation in which one focuses on winning, rather than on achievement outcome; happiness is thought to result from winning.

mindset The cognitive view individuals develop for themselves that views their potential either as fixed or as capable of growth.

A screen from Carol Dweck's Brainology program, which is designed to cultivate children's growth mindset.
Courtesy of Dr. Carol S. Dweck

two mindsets: (1) a *fixed mindset*, in which they believe that their qualities are carved in stone and cannot change; or (2) a *growth mindset*, in which they believe their qualities can change and improve through their effort. A fixed mindset is similar to a helpless orientation; a growth mindset is much like having mastery motivation.

In *Mindset*, Dweck (2006) argued that individuals' mindsets influence whether they will be optimistic or pessimistic, shape their goals and how hard they will strive to reach those goals, and affect many aspects of their lives, including achievement and success in school and sports. Dweck says that mindsets begin to be shaped as children and adolescents interact with parents, teachers, and coaches, who themselves have either a fixed mindset or a growth mindset.

Dweck and her colleagues (Blackwell & Dweck, 2008; Blackwell, Trzesniewski, & Dweck, 2007; Dweck & Master, 2009) recently incorporated information about the brain's plasticity into their effort to improve students' motivation to achieve and succeed. In one study, they assigned two groups of students to eight sessions of either (1) study skills instruction or (2) study skills instruction plus information about the importance of developing a growth mindset (called *incremental theory* in the research) (Blackwell & others, 2007). One of the exercises in the growth mindset group was titled "You Can Grow Your Brain," and it emphasized that the brain is like a muscle that can change and grow as it gets exercise and develops new connections. Students were informed that the more you challenge your brain to learn, the more your brain cells grow. Both groups had a pattern of declining math scores prior to the intervention. Following the intervention, math scores of the group who had received only the study skills instruction continued to decline, but the group that received the combination of study skills instruction plus the growth mindset emphasis reversed the downward trend and improved their math achievement. In a recent study conducted by Dweck and her colleagues (Paunesku & others, 2015), underachieving high school students read online modules about how the brain changes when people learn and study hard. Following the online exposure about the brain and learning, the underachieving students improved their grade point averages.

In other work, Dweck has been creating a computer-based workshop, "Brainology," to teach students that their intelligence can change (Blackwell & Dweck, 2008). Students experience six modules about how the brain works and how the students can make their brain improve. After the program was tested in 20 New York City schools, students strongly endorsed the value of the computer-based brain modules. Said one student, "I will try harder because I know that the more you try the more your brain knows" (Dweck & Master, 2009, p. 137).

Dweck and her colleagues also recently have found that a growth mindset can prevent negative stereotypes from undermining achievement. For example, women who believe that math ability can be learned are protected from negative gender stereotyping about math (Good, Rattan, & Dweck, 2012). And other research recently indicated that willpower is a virtually nonlimited mindset that predicts how long people will work and resist temptations during stressful circumstances (Dweck, 2012; Job, Dweck, & Walton, 2010; Job & others, 2015; Miller & others, 2012). Also in a longitudinal study of university students, a nonlimited theory predicted better self-regulation (improvements in time management and less procrastination, unhealthy eating, and impulsive spending) (Job & others, 2015). In this study, among students taking a heavy course load, those who with a nonlimited theory got higher grades.

SELF-EFFICACY

self-efficacy The belief that one can master a situation and produce favorable outcomes.

Albert Bandura's (1997, 2001, 2009, 2010, 2012) social cognitive theory stresses that a critical factor in whether or not students achieve is **self-efficacy,** the belief that one can master a situation and produce favorable outcomes. Self-efficacy is the belief that "I can";

helplessness is the belief that "I cannot." Students with high self-efficacy endorse statements such as "I know that I will be able to learn the material in this class" and "I expect to be able to do well at this activity."

Dale Schunk (2012, 2016) has applied the concept of self-efficacy to many aspects of students' achievement. In his view, self-efficacy influences a student's choice of activities. Students with low self-efficacy for learning may avoid many learning tasks, especially those that are challenging. By contrast, those with high self-efficacy eagerly work at learning tasks (Schunk & Zimmerman, 2013). High-self-efficacy students are more likely than low-self-efficacy students to expend effort and persist longer at a learning task.

Children's and adolescents' development is influenced by their parents' self-efficacy. A recent study revealed a number of positive developmental outcomes, including more daily opportunities for optimal functioning, better peer relations, and fewer problems, for children and adolescents whose parents had high self-efficacy (Steca & others, 2011).

GOAL SETTING, PLANNING, AND SELF-MONITORING

Self-efficacy and achievement improve when individuals set goals that are specific, proximal, and challenging (Schunk, 2012, 2016). A nonspecific, fuzzy goal is "I want to be successful." A more concrete, specific goal is "I want to make the honor roll by the end of the semester."

Students can set both long-term (distal) and short-term (proximal) goals. It is okay for individuals to set some long-term goals, such as "I want to graduate from high school" or "I want to go to college," but they also need to create short-term goals, which are steps along the way. "Getting an A on the next math test" is an example of a short-term, proximal goal. So is "Doing all of my homework by 4 p.m. Sunday."

Another good strategy is to set challenging goals. A challenging goal is a commitment to self-improvement. Strong interest and involvement in activities are sparked by challenges. Goals that are easy to reach generate little interest or effort. However, goals should be optimally matched to the individual's skill level. If goals are unrealistically high, the result will be repeated failures that lower the individual's self-efficacy.

It is not enough just to set goals. In order to achieve, it also is important to plan how to reach those goals. Being a good planner means managing time effectively, setting priorities, and being organized.

Individuals should not only plan their next week's activities but also monitor how well they are sticking to their plan. Once engaged in a task, they need to monitor their progress, judge how well they are doing on the task, and evaluate the outcomes to regulate what they do in the future (Wigfield & others, 2006, 2015). High-achieving children are often self-regulatory learners (Schunk, 2016; Schunk & Zimmerman, 2013). For example, high-achieving children monitor their learning and systematically evaluate their progress toward a goal more than low-achieving students do. Encouraging children to monitor their learning conveys the message that they are responsible for their own behavior and that learning requires their active, dedicated participation (Wigfield, Klauda, & Cambria, 2011).

Barry Zimmerman and his colleagues (Zimmerman, 2012; Zimmerman & Kitsantas, 1997; Zimmerman & Labuhn, 2012) have developed a model of self-regulation in achievement contexts that has three phrases:

· *Forethought.* Adolescents assess task demands, set goals, and estimate their ability to reach the goals.
· *Performance.* Adolescents create self-regulating strategies such as managing time, attentional focusing, help seeking, and metacognition.
· *Self-Reflection.* Adolescents evaluate their performance, including attributions about factors that affected the outcome and how satisfied they are with their behavior.

In addition to planning and self-regulation/monitoring, delaying gratification is an important aspect of reaching goals—especially long-term goals (Cheng, Shein, & Chiou, 2012; Schlam & others, 2013). Delay of gratification involves postponing immediate rewards in order to attain larger, more valuable rewards at a later point in time. While adolescents may

They can because they think they can.

—Virgil
Roman poet, 1st century B.C.

developmental **connection**

Cognitive Theory

Social cognitive theory holds that behavior, environment, and person/cognitive factors are the key influences on development. Connect to "Introduction."

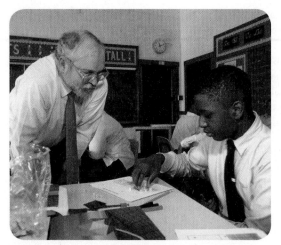

A student and a teacher at Langston Hughes Elementary School in Chicago, a school whose teachers have high expectations for students. *How do teachers' expectations influence students' achievement?*
© Ralf-Finn Hestoft/Corbis

developmental **connection**

Culture

Ethnicity refers to characteristics rooted in cultural heritage, including nationality, race, religion, and language. Connect to "Introduction" and "Peers and the Sociocultural World."

UCLA educational psychologist Sandra Graham talks with adolescent boys about motivation. She has conducted a number of studies which reveal that middle-socioeconomic-status African American students—like their White counterparts—have high achievement expectations and attribute success to internal factors such as effort rather than external factors such as luck.
Courtesy of Dr. Sandra Graham

prefer to hang out with friends today rather than working on a project that is due for a class assignment later in the week, their decision not to delay gratification can have negative consequences for their academic achievement.

EXPECTATIONS

Expectations play important roles in children's and adolescents' achievement (Wigfield & others, 2015). These expectations involve not only the expectations of children and adolescents themselves but also the expectations of parents, teachers, and other adults.

How hard students will work can depend on how much they expect to accomplish. If they expect to succeed, they are more likely to work hard to reach a goal than if they expect to fail. Jacquelynne Eccles (2007) defined expectations for students' success as beliefs about how well they will do on upcoming tasks, in either the immediate or long-term future. Three aspects of ability beliefs, according to Eccles, are students' beliefs about how good they are at a particular activity, how good they are in comparison with other individuals, and how good they are in relation to their performance in other activities.

How hard students work also depends on the value they place on the goal (Wigfield & Cambria, 2010). Indeed, the combination of expectancy and value has been the focus of a number of efforts to better understand students' achievement motivation. In Eccles' (2007) model, students' expectancies and values are assumed to directly influence their performance, persistence, and task choice.

Researchers have found that parents' expectations are linked with children's and adolescents' academic achievement (Burchinal & others, 2002). One longitudinal study revealed that children whose mothers had higher academic expectations for them in the first grade were more likely to reach a higher level of educational attainment in emerging adulthood (age 23) than children whose mothers had lower expectations for them in the first grade (Englund & others, 2004).

Too often parents attempt to protect children's and adolescents' self-esteem by setting low standards (Graham, 2005; Stipek, 2005). In reality, it is more beneficial to set standards that challenge them and to expect the highest level of performance that they are capable of achieving.

Teachers' expectations also are important influences on children's achievement (Rubie-Davies, 2011). In an observational study of twelve classrooms, teachers with high expectations spent more time providing a framework for students' learning, asked higher-level questions, and were more effective in managing students' behavior than teachers with average or low expectations (Rubie-Davies, 2007).

ETHNICITY AND CULTURE

How do ethnicity and culture influence children's achievement? Of course, diversity exists within every group in terms of achievement. But Americans have been especially concerned about two questions related to ethnicity and culture. First, does their ethnicity deter ethnic minority children from high achievement in school? And second, is there something about American culture that accounts for the poor performance of U.S. children in math and science?

Ethnicity   Analyzing the effects of ethnicity in the United States is complicated by the fact that a disproportionate number of ethnic minorities have low socioeconomic status. Disentangling the effects of SES and ethnicity can be difficult, and many investigations overlook the socioeconomic status of ethnic minority students. In many instances, when ethnicity and socioeconomic status are investigated, socioeconomic status predicts achievement better than ethnicity does. Students from middle- and upper-income families fare better than their counterparts from low-income backgrounds in a host of achievement situations—for example, expectations for success, achievement aspirations, and recognition of the importance of effort (Wigfield & others, 2015). A longitudinal study revealed that African American children or children from low-income families benefited more than children from higher-income families when they did homework more frequently, had Internet access at home, and had a community library card (Xia, 2010).

Sandra Graham (1986, 1990) has conducted a number of studies that reveal stronger differences in achievement connected with socioeconomic status than with ethnicity. She is struck by how consistently middle-income African American students, like their non-Latino White middle-income counterparts, have high achievement expectations and understand that failure is usually due to a lack of effort. An especially important factor in the lower achievement of students from low-income families regardless of their ethnic background is lack of adequate resources to support students' learning, such as an up-to-date computer in the home or even any computer at all (Schunk, Pintrich, & Meece, 2008).

Cross-Cultural Comparisons   Since the early 1990s, the poor performance of American children and adolescents in math and science has been well publicized. In a recent large-scale international comparison of 15-year-olds in 65 countries, the top five scores in reading, math, and science were held by Asian countries (Shanghai-China, South Korea, Singapore, Hong Kong-China, and Taipei-China), with the exception of 15-year-olds from Finland being third in reading and second in science (OECD, 2010). Shanghai-China 15-year-olds held first place among the 65 countries in all three academic areas. In this study, U.S. 15-year-olds placed seventeenth in reading, thirty-second in math, and twenty-third in science. The international rankings for reading and math are shown in Figure 7.

Harold Stevenson's (1995, 2000; Stevenson, Hofer, & Randel, 1999; Stevenson & others, 1990) research has explored the reasons for the poor performance of American students. Stevenson and his colleagues have completed five cross-cultural comparisons of students in the United States, China, Taiwan, and Japan. In these studies, Asian students consistently outperform American students. And, the longer the students are in school, the wider the gap becomes between Asian and American students—the lowest difference is in the first grade, the highest in the eleventh grade (the highest grade studied).

To learn more about the reasons for these large cross-cultural differences, Stevenson and his colleagues spent thousands of hours observing in classrooms as well as interviewing and surveying teachers, students, and parents. They found that the Asian teachers spent more of their time teaching math than did the American teachers. For example, more than one-fourth of total classroom time in the first grade was spent on math instruction in Japan, compared with only one-tenth of the time in the U.S. first-grade classrooms. Also, the Asian students were in school an average of 240 days a year, compared with 178 days in the United States.

In addition to the substantially greater time spent on math instruction in the Asian schools than the American schools, differences were found between the Asian and American parents. The American parents had much lower expectations for their children's education and

Reading		Mathematics	
1. China: Shanghai	556	1. China: Shanghai	600
2. Korea	539	2. Singapore	562
3. Finland	536	3. China: Hong Kong	555
4. China: Hong Kong	533	4. Korea	546
5. Singapore	526	5. Chinese Taipei	543
6. Canada	524	6. Finland	541
7. New Zealand	521	7. Liechtenstein	536
8. Japan	520	8. Switzerland	534
9. Australia	515	9. Japan	529
10. Netherlands	508	10. Canada	527
11. Belgium	506	11. Netherlands	526
12. Norway	503	12. China: Macao	525
13. Estonia	501	13. New Zealand	519
14. Switzerland	501	14. Belgium	515
15. Iceland	500	15. Australia	514
16. Poland	500	16. Germany	513
17. United States	500	17. Estonia	512
18. Liechtenstein	499	18. Iceland	507
19. Germany	497	19. Denmark	503
20. Sweden	497	20. Slovenia	501
21. France	496	21. Norway	498
22. Ireland	496	22. France	497
23. Chinese Taipei	495	23. Slovak Republic	497
24. Denmark	495	24. Austria	496
25. Hungary	494	25. OECD average	496
26. United Kingdom	494	26. Poland	495
27. OECD average	493	27. Sweden	494
28. Portugal	489	28. Czech Republic	493
29. China: Macao	487	29. United Kingdom	492
30. Italy	486	30. Hungary	490
31. Latvia	484	31. Luxembourg	489
32. Greece	483	32. United States	487

FIGURE 7

INTERNATIONAL COMPARISONS OF 15-YEAR-OLDS' READING AND MATH SCORES

Source: OECD (2010). *Strong performers and successful reformers in education: Lessons from PISA for the United States.* Paris, France: OECD.

Asian grade schools intersperse studying with frequent periods of activities. This approach helps children maintain their attention and likely makes learning more enjoyable. Shown here are Japanese fourth-graders making wearable masks. *What are some differences in the way children in many Asian countries are taught compared with children in the United States?*
© Eiji Miyazawa/Stock Photo/Black Star

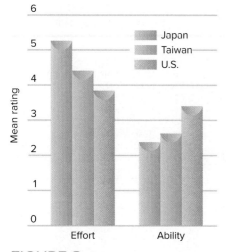

FIGURE 8

MOTHERS' BELIEFS ABOUT THE FACTORS RESPONSIBLE FOR CHILDREN'S MATH ACHIEVEMENT IN THREE COUNTRIES. In one study, mothers in Japan and Taiwan were more likely to believe that their children's math achievement was due to effort rather than innate ability, whereas U.S. mothers were more likely to believe their children's math achievement was due to innate ability (Stevenson, Lee, & Stigler, 1986). If parents believe that their children's math achievement is due to innate ability and their children are not doing well in math, the implication is that they are less likely to think their children will benefit from putting forth more effort. (From Stevenson et al., 1986, Figure 6, "Mathematics Achievement of Chinese, Japanese, and American Children," *Science*, vol. 231, pp. 693–699. Reprinted with permission from AAAS.)

achievement than did the Asian parents. Also, the American parents were more likely to believe that their children's math achievement was due to innate ability; the Asian parents were more likely to say that their children's math achievement was the consequence of effort and training (see Figure 8). The Asian students were more likely to do math homework than were the American students, and the Asian parents were far more likely to help their children with their math homework than were the American parents (Chen & Stevenson, 1989).

A recent study examined factors that might account for the superior academic performance of Asian American children (Hsin & Xie, 2014). In this study, the Asian American advantage was mainly due to children exerting greater academic effort and not to advantages in tested cognitive abilities or sociodemographic factors.

Eva Pomerantz (2014) recently offered the following recommendations for parents of children and adolescents regarding motivation to do well in school:

· *Keep in mind that ability is not fixed and can change.* Although it is difficult and takes a lot of patience, understand that children's and adolescents' abilities can improve.

· *Be involved.* One of the most important things parents can do is to become involved in their children's and adolescents' academic life and talk often with them about what they are learning.

· *Support autonomy and self-initiative.* An important aspect of children's and adolescents' motivation to do well in school is whether they are made to feel that they are responsible for their learning and must be self-motivated.

· *Be positive.* Too often schoolwork and homework can be frustrating for children and adolescents. Interact with them in positive ways and let them know that life is often tough but that you are confident that they can do well and overcome difficulties.

· *Understand that each child and adolescent is different.* Get to know your child or adolescent—don't let them be a psychological stranger to you. Be sensitive to their unique characteristics and know that sometimes you need to adapt to such idiosyncrasies.

In the *Connecting with Research* interlude, you can read further about efforts to discover why parenting practices are likely to be an important aspect of the lower achievement of U.S. children compared with East Asian children, as well as potential implications for other aspects of children's development.

Review *Connect* Reflect

 Explain the key aspects of achievement

Review

• What are intrinsic motivation and extrinsic motivation? How are they related to achievement?

• How are mastery, helpless, and performance orientations linked with achievement?

• What is self-efficacy, and how is it related to achievement?

• Why are goal setting, planning, and self-monitoring important in achievement?

• How are expectations involved in an individual's achievement motivation?

• How do cultural, ethnic, and socioeconomic variations influence achievement?

Connect

• One of Carol Dweck's exercises in the growth-mindset group was titled "You Can Grow Your Brain." Can you actually grow your brain? What physical changes, if any, are still occurring in the brain in middle and late childhood and in adolescence?

Reflect *Your Own Personal Journey of Life*

• Think about several of your own past schoolmates who showed low motivation in school. Why do you think they behaved that way? What teaching strategies might have helped them?

Parenting and Children's Achievement: My Child Is My Report Card, Tiger Moms, and Tiger Babies Strike Back

There is rising concern that U.S. children are not reaching their full potential, which ultimately will reduce the success of the United States in competing with other countries (Pomerantz, 2013; Qu & Pomerantz, 2015; Qu, Pomerantz, & Deng, 2015). Eva Pomerantz is interested in determining how parents can maximize their children's motivation and achievement in school while also maintaining positive emotional adjustment. To this end, Pomerantz and her colleagues are conducting research with children and their parents not only in the United States but also in China, where children often attain higher levels of achievement than their U.S. counterparts (Pomerantz, Cheung, & Qin, 2012; Pomerantz & Kempner, 2013; Pomerantz, Kim, & Cheung, 2012; Qu & Pomerantz, 2015; Qu, Pomerantz, & Deng, 2015).

As indicated earlier regarding Harold Stevenson's research, East Asian parents spend considerably more time helping their children with homework than do U.S. parents (Chen & Stevenson, 1989). Pomerantz's research indicates that East Asian parental involvement in children's learning is present as early as the preschool years and continues during the elementary school years (Cheung & Pomerantz, 2012; Ng, Pomerantz, & Deng, 2014; Ng, Pomerantz, & Lam, 2013; Siegler & Mu, 2008). In East Asia, children's learning is considered to be a far greater responsibility of parents than in the United States (Ng, Pomerantz, & Lam, 2013; Pomerantz, Kim, & Cheung, 2012). In a recent study, a decline in U.S. young adolescents' but not Chinese young adolescents' sense of responsibility to parents occurred (Qu & Pomerantz, 2015). The U.S. adolescents' decline in sense of responsibility to parents was linked to the lower value they placed on school and their lower engagement in school as they went from the beginning of the seventh grade to the end of eighth grade (Qu & Pomerantz, 2015).

However, a recent study revealed that when U.S. parents are more involved in their children's learning, the children's achievement benefits (Cheung & Pomerantz, 2012). In this study, more than 800 U.S. and Chinese young adolescents reported on their parents' involvement in their learning and their motivation in school every six months from the fall of seventh grade to the end of eighth grade. The researchers also collected data on children's self-regulated learning strategies and grades. Over time, the more involved parents were in children's learning, the more strongly motivated children were to do well academically for parent-oriented reasons, which improved children's self-regulated learning and grades.

In addition to studying parental involvement in children's learning, Pomerantz and her colleagues also are conducting research on the role of parental control in children's achievement. In a recent study in which the title of the resulting article included the phrase "My Child Is My Report Card," Chinese mothers exerted more control (especially psychological control) over their children than did U.S. mothers (Ng, Pomerantz, & Deng, 2014). Also in this study, Chinese mothers' self-worth was more contingent on their children's achievement than was the case for U.S. mothers.

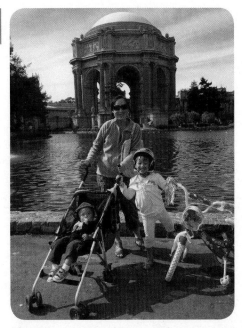

Qing Zhou, who has recently conducted research on authoritarian parenting of immigrant children, with her children. *What are the results of her research?*
Courtesy of Qing Zhou

Pomerantz's research reflects the term "training parents," a variation of authoritarian parenting in which many Asian parents train their children to achieve high levels of academic success. In 2011, Amy Chua's book, *Battle Hymn of the Tiger Mom*, sparked considerable interest in the role of parenting in children's achievement. Chua uses the term *Tiger Mom* to mean a mother who engages in strict disciplinary practices. In another recent book, *Tiger Babies Strike Back*, Kim Wong Keltner (2013) argues that the Tiger Mom parenting style can be so demanding and confining that being an Asian American child is like being in an "emotional jail." She says that the Tiger Mom authoritarian style does provide some advantages for children, such as emphasizing the value of going for what you want and not taking no for an answer, but that too often the outcome is not worth the emotional costs that accompany it.

Recent research on Chinese-American immigrant families with first- and second-grade children has found that the children with authoritarian (highly controlling) parents are more aggressive, are more depressed, have a higher anxiety level, and show poorer social skills than children whose parents engage in non-authoritarian styles (Zhou & others, 2012). Qing Zhou (2013), lead author on the study just described and the director of the University of California's Culture and Family Laboratory, is conducting workshops to teach Chinese mothers positive parenting strategies such as using listening skills, praising their children for good behavior, and spending more time with their children in fun activities.

In sum, while an authoritarian, psychologically controlling style of parenting may be associated with higher levels of achievement, especially in Asian children, there are concerns that this parenting style also may produce more emotional difficulties in children.

What do you think are the best parenting strategies overall for rearing children to reach high levels of achievement and to be emotionally healthy?

The quality of schooling children experience and the achievement orientation they develop provide the foundation for career success and the type of work they pursue when they become adults. Choosing a career, developing in a career, working, and coping with retirement—these are important themes in adulthood.

CAREER DEVELOPMENT

When you were a child, what were your thoughts about a career? How did your thinking about careers change as you became an adolescent? What are your thoughts now?

"Your son has made a career choice, Mildred. He's going to win the lottery and travel a lot."
Copyright © 2011; reprinted courtesy of Bunny Hoest.

Developmental Changes Many children have idealistic fantasies about what they want to be when they grow up. For example, many young children want to be superheroes, sports stars, or movie stars. In the high school years, they often have begun to think about careers in a somewhat less idealistic way. In their late teens and early twenties, their career decision making has usually turned more serious as they explore different career possibilities and zero in on the career they want to enter. In college, this focus often means choosing a major or specialization that is designed to lead to work in a specific field. By their early and mid-twenties, many individuals have completed their education or training and entered a full-time occupation. From the mid-twenties through the remainder of early adulthood, individuals often seek to establish their emerging career in a particular field. They may work hard to move up the career ladder and improve their financial standing.

Phyllis Moen (2009a) described the *career mystique*—ingrained cultural beliefs that engaging in hard work for long hours through adulthood will automatically lead to status, security, and happiness. That is, many individuals have an idealized concept of a career path toward achieving the American dream by upward mobility through occupational ladders. However, the lockstep career mystique has never been a reality for many individuals, especially ethnic minority individuals, women, and poorly educated adults. Further, the career mystique has increasingly become a myth for many individuals in middle-income occupations as global outsourcing of jobs and changes in the U.S. economy during the 2007–2009 recession have meant reduced job security for millions of Americans.

Monitoring the Occupational Outlook As you explore the type of work you are likely to enjoy and in which you can succeed, it is important to become knowledgeable about different fields and companies. Occupations may have many job openings one year but few in another year as economic conditions change. Thus, it is critical to keep up with the occupational outlook in various fields. An excellent resource for doing this is the U.S. government's *Occupational Outlook Handbook*, which is revised every two years.

According to the 2014–2015 handbook, industrial/organizational psychologists, personal care aides, interpreters and translators, genetic counselors, physicians' assistants, information security analysts, and physical therapists are among the job categories that are projected to be the fastest-growing through 2022. Projected job growth varies widely by educational requirements. Jobs that require a college degree are expected to grow the fastest. Most of the highest-paying occupations require a college degree. To read about the work of one individual who advises college students about careers, see the *Connecting with Careers* profile.

"Did you think the ladder of success would be straight up?"
© Joseph Farris/The Yorker Collection/www.cartoonbank.com.

WORK

Work is one of the most important activities in people's lives. Our developmental coverage of work begins with adolescence and concludes with late adulthood.

Grace Leaf, College/Career Counselor and College Administrator

For many years, Grace Leaf was a counselor at Spokane Community College in Washington. In 2014, she became Vice President of Instruction at Lower Columbia College in Spokane. She has a master's degree in educational leadership and is working toward a doctoral degree in educational leadership at Gonzaga University in Washington. Her job as a college counselor involved teaching orientation sessions for international students, conducting individual and group advising, and doing individual and group career planning. Grace tries to connect students with goals and values and helps them design an educational program that fits their needs and visions.

College counselors help students to cope with adjustment problems, identify their abilities and interests, develop academic plans, and explore career options. Some have an undergraduate degree, others a master's degree like Grace Leaf. Some college counselors have a graduate degree in counseling; others may have an undergraduate degree in psychology or another discipline.

For more information about what career counselors do, see the Careers in Life-Span Development appendix.

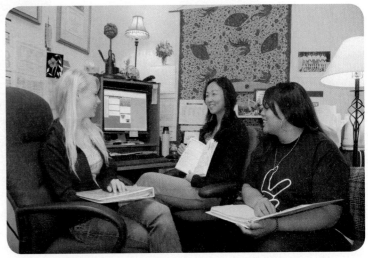

Grace Leaf counsels college students at Spokane Community College about careers.
Courtesy of Grace Leaf

Work in Adolescence One of the greatest changes in adolescents' lives in recent years has been the increased number of adolescents who work part-time and still attend school on a regular basis. Our discussion of adolescents and work focuses on the sociohistorical context of adolescent work and the advantages and disadvantages of part-time work at this stage of life.

Even though education keeps many of today's youth from holding full-time jobs, it has not prevented them from working part-time while going to school (Staff, Messersmith, & Schulenberg, 2009). In 1940, only 1 of 25 tenth-grade males attended school and simultaneously worked part-time. In the 1970s, the number had increased to 1 in 4. Today, it is estimated that 80 to 90 percent of adolescents are employed at some point during high school (Staff & others, 2009). As adolescents go from the eighth to the twelfth grade, their likelihood of working and the average number of hours they work during the school year increase (Staff & others, 2009). In the eighth through tenth grades, the majority of students don't work in paid employment during the school year, but in the twelfth grade only one-fourth don't engage in paid employment during the school year. Almost 10 percent of employed twelfth-graders work more than 30 hours per week during the school year.

What are some advantages and disadvantages of part-time work during adolescence?
© *Corey Lowenstein/MCT/Landov Images*

Overall, the weight of the evidence suggests that spending large amounts of time in paid labor produces limited developmental benefits for youth, and for some it is associated with risky behavior and costs to physical health (Larson, Wilson, & Rickman, 2009). For example, one research study found that it was not just working that affected adolescents' grades—more important was how many hours they worked per week (Greenberger & Steinberg, 1986). Tenth-graders who worked more than 14 hours a week suffered a drop in grades. Eleventh-graders worked up to 20 hours a week before their grades dropped. When adolescents spend more than 20 hours per week working, there is little time to study for tests and to complete homework assignments. In addition, working adolescents felt less involved in school, were absent more, and said that they did not enjoy school as much as their nonworking counterparts did. Adolescents who worked long hours also were more frequent users of alcohol and marijuana. Also, a recent study found that high school students with paid part-time jobs were more likely to drink alcohol, binge drink, and use marijuana (Leeman & others, 2014).

Some youth, though, are engaged in challenging work activities, are provided constructive supervision by adults, and experience favorable work conditions (Staff & others, 2009). For example, work may benefit adolescents in low-income, urban contexts by providing them with economic benefits and adult monitoring. These factors may increase school engagement and decrease delinquency.

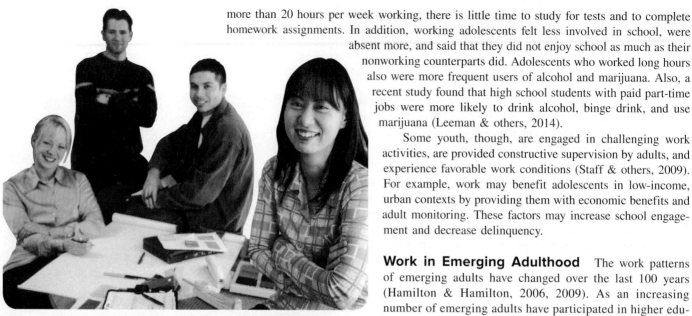

These emerging adults are college graduates who have started their own business. Emerging adults follow a diversity of work and educational pathways. *What are some of these variations in education and work that characterize emerging adults?*
© Jose Luis Pelaez, Inc./Corbis

Work in Emerging Adulthood The work patterns of emerging adults have changed over the last 100 years (Hamilton & Hamilton, 2006, 2009). As an increasing number of emerging adults have participated in higher education, many leave home and begin their careers at later ages. Changing economic conditions have made the job market more competitive for emerging adults and increased the demand for more highly skilled workers (Gauthier & Furstenberg, 2005).

A diversity of school and work patterns characterizes emerging adults (Borges & others, 2008; Hamilton & Hamilton, 2009). Some emerging adults are attending college full-time; others are working full-time. Some emerging adults work full-time immediately after high school, others after they graduate from college. Many emerging adults who attend college drop out and enter the workforce before they complete their degree; some of these individuals return to college later. Some emerging adults are attending two-year colleges, others four-year colleges; and some are working part-time while going to college but others are not.

The nature of the transition from school to work in emerging adulthood is strongly influenced by the individual's level of education (Hamilton & Hamilton, 2009; Swanson, 2013). In the last two decades, the job market for emerging adults with only a high school education has worsened. The MacArthur Foundation Research Network on Emerging Adults recently concluded that for emerging adults who don't go to college, the problem is not being unable to find any job at all but being unable to get a good job (Settersten, Furstenberg, & Rumbaut, 2005). The Research Network also stated that community colleges are an underutilized resource for connecting high schools and employers. A special concern is the large number of students who begin their college education in a community college but drop out before getting a degree (Horn & Nevill, 2006).

What about work during college? To read about the pluses and minuses of working during college, see the *Connecting Development to Life* interlude.

Work in Adulthood Both Sigmund Freud and the Russian Count Leo Tolstoy described love and work as the two most important things that adults need to do well. We discussed love in the chapter on "Emotional Development." Let's now explore work in the adult years.

The Work Landscape Do you work to live or live to work? Most individuals spend about one-third of their lives at work. In one survey, 35 percent of Americans worked 40 hours a week, but 18 percent worked 51 hours or more per week (Center for Survey Research at the University of Connecticut, 2000). Only 10 percent worked less than 30 hours a week.

Work defines people in fundamental ways (Blustein, 2013; Parker, 2014). It is an important influence on their financial standing, housing, the way they spend their time, where they live, their friendships, and their health (Allen, 2013). Some people define their identity through their work. Work also creates a structure and rhythm to life that is often missed when individuals do not work for an extended period. When they are unable to work, many individuals experience emotional distress and low self-esteem.

Working During College

The percentage of full-time U.S. college students who also held jobs increased from 34 percent in 1970 to 47 percent in 2008, then declined to 41 percent in 2011 (down from a peak of 52 percent in 2000) (National Center for Education Statistics, 2013). In this recent survey, 74 percent of part-time U.S. college students were employed, down from 81 percent in 2008.

Working can pay for schooling or help offset some of the costs, but working also can restrict students' opportunities to learn. For those who identified themselves primarily as students, one national study found that as the number of hours worked per week increased, their grades suffered (National Center for Education Statistics, 2002) (see Figure 9). Thus, college students need to carefully examine whether the number of hours they work is having a negative impact on their college success.

Of course, jobs also can contribute to a student's education. More than 1,000 colleges in the United States offer *cooperative (co-op) programs*, which are paid apprenticeships in specific fields. (You may not be permitted to participate in a co-op program until your junior year.) Other useful opportunities for working while going to college include internships and part-time or summer jobs relevant to your field of study. In a national survey of employers, almost 60 percent said their entry-level college hires had co-op or internship experience (Collins, 1996). Participating in these work experiences can be a key factor in landing the job you want when you graduate.

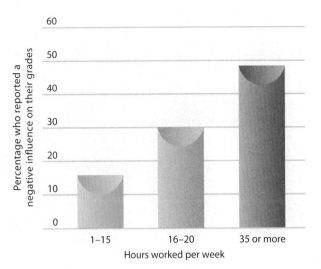

FIGURE 9

THE RELATION BETWEEN HOURS WORKED PER WEEK IN COLLEGE AND GRADES. Among students working to pay for school expenses, 16 percent of those working 1 to 15 hours per week reported that working negatively influenced their grades (National Center for Education Statistics, 2002). Thirty percent of college students who worked 16 to 20 hours a week said the same, as did 48 percent who worked 35 hours or more per week.

As unpaid internships become more common, some students complain that they are merely a way for organizations to obtain free labor. How can student interns ensure that they have a rewarding experience in spite of not being paid?

Special concerns about work in emerging adults are the unemployment rate of college graduates as well as the high percentage of recent college graduates who have had to take jobs that do not require a college degree. In 2013, the unemployment rate for recent college graduates dropped to 5.6 percent, down from 6.4 percent at the peak of the 2009 recession (Gabor, 2014). Among 22-year-olds with a college degree who found jobs in 2013, more than 50 percent were in jobs that did not require a college degree (Center for Economic and Policy Research, 2014).

A trend in the U.S. workforce is the disappearing long-term career for an increasing number of adults, especially men in private-sector jobs (Greenhaus & Callanan, 2013). Among the reasons for the disappearance of many long-term jobs is the dramatic increase in technology and companies' use of cheaper labor in other countries.

An important consideration regarding work is how stressful it is (Demsky, Ellis, & Fritz, 2014). A national survey of U.S. adults revealed that 55 percent indicated they were less productive because of stress (American Psychological Association, 2007). In this study, 52 percent reported that they had considered or made a career decision, such as looking for a new job, declining a promotion, or quitting a job, because of stress in the workplace (American Psychological Association, 2007). In this survey, main sources of stress included low salaries (44 percent), lack of advancement opportunities (42 percent), uncertain job expectations (40 percent), and long hours (39 percent). A recent study

What are some characteristics of work settings linked with employees' stress?
© Dann Tardif/LWA/Corbis

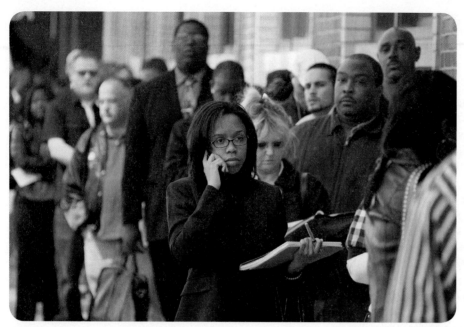

The economic recession that hit in 2007 resulted in millions of Americans losing their jobs, such as the individuals in line here waiting to apply for unemployment benefits in Chicago. *What are some of the potential negative outcomes of the stress caused by job loss?*
© Scott Olson/Getty Images

revealed that stressors at work were linked to arterial hypertension in employees (Lamy & others, 2015).

Many adults hold changing expectations about work, yet employers often aren't meeting their expectations (Grzywacz, 2009; Hall & Mirvis, 2013; Richardson & Schaeffer, 2013). For example, current policies and practices often were designed for a single-breadwinner (male) workforce and an industrial economy, making these policies and practices out of step with a workforce of women and men, and of single parents and dual earners. Many workers today want flexibility and greater control over the duration and timing of their work, and yet most employers offer little flexibility, even though policies like flex-time may be "on the books."

Unemployment Unemployment produces stress regardless of whether the job loss is temporary, cyclical, or permanent (Jalles & Andresen, 2014; Kalousova & Burgard, 2014). Problems with banks and the economic recession toward the end of the first decade of the twenty-first century have produced very high unemployment rates, especially in the United States. Researchers have found that unemployment is related to increased rates of physical problems (such as hypertension, heart attack, and stroke), mental problems (such as depression and anxiety), substance abuse, and marital difficulties (Garrido & Lopez-Valcárcel, 2015; Rizvi & others, 2015; Zagozdzon & others, 2014). In a recent study, unemployment was associated with higher rates of tobacco and illicit drug use, as well as heavy alcohol use (Compton & others, 2014).

Another recent study revealed that 90 or more days of unemployment was associated with subsequent cardiovascular disease across an 8-year follow-up period (Lundin & others, 2014). Further, a recent study found that involuntary job loss was linked to an increase in attempted suicide and suicide (Milner & others, 2014) and another study indicated that unemployment was linked to a higher suicide rate during the recession of 2007–2009 in the United States (Phillips & Nugent, 2014). And in a recent study, unemployment was associated with higher mortality but the connection was stronger for those who were unmarried (Van Hedel & others, 2015).

Stress related to unemployment comes not only from a loss of income and the resulting financial hardships but also from decreased self-esteem (Howe & others, 2012). Individuals who cope best with unemployment have financial resources to rely on, often savings or the earnings of other family members. The support of understanding, adaptable family members also helps individuals to cope with unemployment. Job counseling and self-help groups can provide practical advice on job searching, résumé writing, and interviewing skills, and also can lend emotional support (van Hooft, 2014).

Might unemployment be linked to certain characteristics in childhood? Longitudinal data revealed that low self-control in childhood was linked to the emergence and persistence of unemployment from 21 to 50 years of age (Daly & others, 2015).

Dual-Career Couples Dual-career couples may have special problems finding a balance between work and family life (Allen, 2013; Aazami, Shamsuddin, & Akmal, 2015; Shimazu & others, 2014). If both partners are working, who cleans up the house or calls the repairman or takes care of the other endless details involved in maintaining a home? If the couple has children, who is responsible for making sure that the children get to school or to piano practice; who writes the notes to approve field trips or attends parent-teacher conferences or schedules dental appointments?

Although single-earner married families still make up a sizable minority of families, the number of two-earner couples has increased considerably in recent decades. A recent projection indicates that women's share of the U.S. labor force will increase through 2022 (*Occupational Outlook Handbook*, 2014). As more U.S. women work outside the home, the division of responsibility for work and family has changed in three ways: (1) U.S. husbands are taking increased responsibility for maintaining the home; (2) U.S. women are taking increased responsibility for breadwinning; and (3) U.S. men are showing greater interest in their families and parenting.

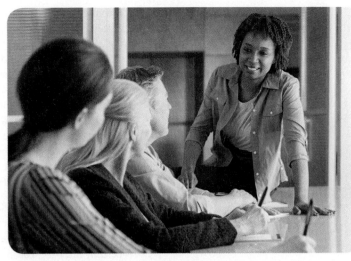

As more women have worked outside the home, how has the division of responsibility for work and family changed?
© Image Source/Getty Images RF

Many jobs have been designed for single earners, usually male breadwinners, without taking account of family responsibilities and the realities of people's lives (Richardson & Schaeffer, 2013). Consequently, many dual-earner couples engage in a range of adaptive strategies to coordinate their work and manage the family side of the work-family equation (Moen, 2009b; Wang & Repetti, 2014). Researchers have found that even though couples may strive for gender equality in dual-earner families, gender inequalities persist (Cunningham, 2009). For example, women still do not earn as much as men in the same jobs, and this inequity perpetuates gender divisions in how much time each partner spends in paid work, homemaking, and caring for children. Thus, dual-earner career decisions often are made in favor of men's greater earning power, and women end up spending more time than men in homemaking and caring for children (Moen, 2009b). A recent study indicated that women reported more family interference from work than did men (Allen & Finkelstein, 2014). Another recent study found that partner coping, having a positive attitude toward multiple roles, using planning and management skills, and not having to cut back on professional responsibilities were linked to better relationships between dual earners (Matias & Fontaine, 2015).

Careers and Work in Middle Adulthood   The role of work—whether a person works in a full-time career, in a part-time job, as a volunteer, or as a homemaker—is central during middle age. Middle-aged adults may reach their peak in position and earnings but also be saddled with financial burdens from rent or mortgage, child care, medical bills, home repairs, college tuition, or bills from nursing homes for care of an elderly parent.

In the United States, approximately 80 percent of individuals 40 to 59 years of age are employed. In the 51-to-59 age group, slightly less than 25 percent do not work. More than half of this age group say that a health condition or an impairment limits the type of paid work that they do (Sterns & Huyck, 2001). Also, a recent study found that difficulty managing different job demands was associated with poor health in middle-aged adults (Nabe-Nielsen & others, 2014).

However, leading Finnish researcher Clas-Hakan Nygard (2013) concludes from his longitudinal research that the ability to work effectively peaks during middle age because of increased motivation, work experience, employer loyalty, and better strategic thinking. Nygard also has found that the quality of work done by employees in middle age is linked to how much their work is appreciated and how well they get along with their immediate supervisors. And Nygard and his colleagues discovered that work ability in middle age was linked to mortality and disability 28 years later (von Bonsdorff & others, 2011, 2012).

Do middle-aged workers perform their work as competently as younger adults? Age-related declines occur in some occupations, such as air traffic controllers and professional athletes, but for most jobs, no differences have been found in the work performance of young adults and middle-aged adults (Salthouse, 2012).

The progression of career trajectories in middle age is diverse, with some individuals having stable careers, whereas others move in and out of the labor force, experiencing layoffs and unemployment (Lachman, 2004). Middle-aged adults also may experience age-related discrimination in some job situations. Finding a job in midlife may be difficult because technological advances may render the midlife worker's skills outdated.

Some midlife career changes are the consequence of losing one's job; others are self-motivated (Moen, 1998; Moen & Spencer, 2006). Among the work issues that some people face in midlife are recognizing limitations in career progress, deciding whether to change jobs or careers, considering whether to rebalance family and work, and planning for retirement (Brand, 2014; Sterns & Huyck, 2001).

The recent economic downturn and recession in the United States has forced some middle-aged individuals into premature retirement because of job loss and fear of not being able to reenter the work force (Cahill, Giandrea, & Quinn, 2015). Such premature retirement also may result in accumulating insufficient financial resources to cover an increasingly long retirement period (de Wind & others, 2014).

A final point to make about career development in middle adulthood is that cognitive factors earlier in development are linked to occupational attainment in middle age. In one study, task persistence at 13 years of age was related to occupational success in middle age (Andersson & Bergman, 2011).

Work in Late Adulthood   In 2000, 23 percent of U.S. 65- to 69-year-olds were in the workforce; in 2015, this percentage had jumped to 32 percent (Short, 2015). Among 70- to 74-year-olds, 13 percent were in the workforce in 2000, but this percentage had increased to 19 percent in 2015. The increase in the percentage of older U.S. workers has occurred more for women than men. For example, the labor force participation of women aged 75 and over has risen 78 percent since 2000, while participation in the workforce by men aged 75 and over has increased 37 percent (Short, 2015). As mentioned earlier, these increases likely are driven mainly by the need to have adequate money to meet living expenses in old age. The U.S. Labor Department projects that by 2020 35 percent of 65- to 74-year-old men and 28 percent of 65- to 74-year-old women will be in the workforce (Hayutin, Beals, & Borges, 2013).

Cognitive ability is one of the best predictors of job performance in older adults. And older workers have lower rates of absenteeism, fewer accidents, and increased job satisfaction compared with their younger counterparts (Warr, 1994). Thus the older worker can be of considerable value to a company, above and beyond the older worker's cognitive competence. Changes in federal law now allow individuals over the age of 65 to continue working (Shore & Goldberg, 2005). Also, remember that substantively complex work is linked with a higher level of intellectual functioning (Schooler, 2007). Further, a recent study found that working in an occupation with a high level of mental demands was linked to higher levels of cognitive functioning before retirement and a slower rate of cognitive decline after retirement (Fisher & others, 2014). In sum, a cognitively stimulating work context promotes successful aging (Bowen, Noack, & Staudinger, 2011).

Several recent studies also have found that older adults who work have better physical profiles than those who retire. For example, a recent study found that physical functioning declined faster in retirement than in full-time work for employees 65 years of age and older with the difference not explained by absence of chronic diseases and lifestyle risks (Stenholm & others, 2014). Another study revealed that retirement increased the risk of having a heart attack in older adults (Olesen & others, 2014).

In sum, age affects many aspects of work (Sterns & Sterns, 2013). Nonetheless, many studies of work and aging—such as evaluation of hiring and performance—have yielded inconsistent results. Important contextual factors—such as age composition of departments or applicant pools, occupations, and jobs—all affect decisions about older workers. It also is important to recognize that ageist stereotypes of workers and of tasks can limit older workers' career opportunities and can encourage early retirement or other forms of downsizing that adversely affect older workers (Finkelstein & Farrell, 2007).

RETIREMENT

How is retirement in the United States similar to and different from retirement in other countries? What factors predict whether individuals will adapt well to retirement?

Retirement in the United States and Other Countries   What are some life paths that retired individuals follow? Do many people return to the workforce at some point after they have retired? What is retirement like in other countries?

The option to retire is a twentieth-century phenomenon in the United States (Coe & others, 2012). It exists largely thanks to the implementation in 1935 of the Social Security system, which gives benefits to older workers when they retire. On average, today's workers will spend 10 to 15 percent of their lives in retirement. One survey revealed that as baby boomers move into their sixties, they expect to delay retirement longer than their parents or grandparents did (Frey, 2007). In 2011, in the United States, the average age of retirement for men was 64 and for women 62 (Munnell, 2011).

In the past, when most people reached an accepted retirement age—usually at some point during their sixties—retirement meant a one-way exit from full-time work to full-time leisure (Williamson, 2011). Leading expert Phyllis Moen (2007) described how today, when people reach their sixties, the life path they follow is less clear:

· Some don't retire—they continue in their career jobs.
· Some retire from their career work and then take up a new and different job.
· Some retire from career jobs but do volunteer work.
· Some retire from a postretirement job and go on to yet another job.
· Some move in and out of the workforce, so they never really have a "career" job from which they retire.
· Some who are in poor health move to a disability status and eventually into retirement.
· Some who are laid off define it as "retirement."

Increasingly both spouses are in the workforce and both expect to retire. Historically retirement has been a male transition, but today more and more couples have to plan two retirements—his and hers (Moen, Kelly, & Magennis, 2008).

Approximately 7 million retired Americans return to work after they have retired (Putnam Investments, 2006). On average, retired adults return to the labor force four years after retirement (Hardy, 2006). In many instances, these postretirement jobs pay much less than the preretirement jobs did. In one study of older adults who returned to work, approximately two-thirds said they were happy they had done so, whereas about one-third indicated they were forced to go back to work to meet financial needs (Putnam Investments, 2006).

The recent economic downturn, high unemployment rate, and potential changes in Social Security and health insurance coverage for retired individuals in the United States has made having enough money for retirement an even greater concern (Bosworth, 2012). A 2012 survey indicated that confidence in having enough money to live comfortably in retirement had dropped to 14 percent (Helman, Copeland, & VanDerhei, 2012). In this survey, the percent of workers who reported that they expect to retire after the age of 65 grew to 37 percent (compared to 11 percent in 1991). In regard to retirement income, the two main worries of individuals as they approach retirement are: (1) drawing retirement income from savings, and (2) paying for health care expenses (Yakoboski, 2011).

Just as the life path after individuals reach retirement age may be varied, so are their reasons for working. For example, some older adults who reach retirement age work for financial reasons, others to stay busy, and yet others "to give back" (Moen, 2007).

Work and Retirement Around the World A large-scale study of 21,000 individuals aged 40 to 79 in 21 countries examined patterns of work and retirement (HSBC Insurance, 2007). On average, 33 percent of individuals in their sixties and 11 percent in their seventies were still in some kind of paid employment. In this study, 19 percent of those in their seventies in the United States were still working. A substantial percentage of individuals expect to continue working as long as possible before retiring (HSBC Insurance, 2007).

In the study of work and retirement in 21 countries, Japanese retirees missed the work slightly more than they expected and the money considerably less than they expected (HSBC Insurance, 2007). U.S. retirees missed both the work and the money slightly less than they expected. German retirees were the least likely to miss the work, Turkish and Chinese retirees the most likely to miss it. Regarding the money, Japanese and Chinese retirees were the least likely to miss it, Turkish retirees the most likely to miss it.

Ninety-two-year-old Russell "Bob" Harrell (*right*) puts in 12-hour days at Sieco Consulting Engineers in Columbus, Indiana. A highway and bridge engineer, he designs and plans roads. James Rice (age 48), a vice president of client services at Sieco, says that Bob wants to learn something new every day and that he has learned many life lessons from being around him. Harrell says he is not planning on retiring. *What are some variations in work and retirement in older adults?*
© Greg Sailor

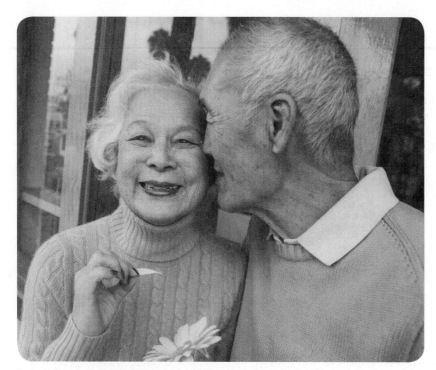

In the recent cross-national study, to what extent did Japanese retirees miss the work and the money in comparison with U.S. retirees?
© Ronnie Kaufman/Blend Images LLC RF

Early retirement policies were introduced by many companies in the 1970s and 1980s with an intent to make room for younger workers (Coe & others, 2012). However, in the 21-country study, there was some indication that an increasing number of adults are beginning to reject the early retirement option as they hear about people who retired and then regretted it. In the 21-country study, on average only 12 percent of individuals in their forties and fifties expected to take early retirement, whereas 16 percent in their sixties and seventies had taken early retirement. Only in Germany, South Korea, and Hong Kong did a higher percentage of individuals expect earlier retirement than in the past.

Adjustment to Retirement   Retirement is a process, not an event (Wang, 2012; Wang & Shi, 2014). Much of the research on retirement has been cross-sectional rather than longitudinal and has focused on men rather than women. One study found that men had higher morale when they had retired within the last two years compared with men who had been retired for longer periods of time (Kim & Moen, 2002). Another study revealed that retired married and remarried women reported being more satisfied with their lives and in better health than retired women who were widowed, separated, divorced, or had never been married (Price & Joo, 2005). One study indicated that women spend less time planning for retirement than men do (Jacobs-Lawson, Hershey, & Neukam, 2005). And a recent study revealed that a higher level of financial assets and job satisfaction were more strongly linked to men's higher psychological well-being in retirement, while preretirement social contacts were more strongly related to women's psychological well-being in retirement (Kubicek & others, 2010).

Older adults who adjust best to retirement are healthy, have adequate incomes, are active, are better educated, have an extended social network including both friends and family, and usually were satisfied with their lives before they retired (Damman, Henkens, & Kalmijn, 2015). Older adults with inadequate incomes and poor health, and those who must adjust to other stress that occurs at the same time as retirement, such as the death of a spouse, have the most difficult time adjusting to retirement (Reichstadt & others, 2007). A study also found that individuals who had difficulty adjusting to retirement had a strong attachment to work, including full-time jobs and a long work history, lack of control over the transition to retirement, and low self-efficacy (van Solinge & Henkens, 2005).

The U.S. retirement system is in transition (Butrica, Smith, & Iams, 2012). Following are the results of a 2007 survey on retirement (Helman, VanDerhei, & Copeland, 2007):

· Half of the workers were not confident about their pension benefits.
· Many workers count on benefits that won't be there when they retire.
· Workers often don't heed advice about retirement even when they are provided the advice.
· Workers overestimate long-term care coverage.
· Most workers' savings are modest.
· Many workers know little about the Social Security income they will receive when they retire.

Flexibility is also a key factor in whether individuals adjust well to retirement (Wang, 2012; Wang & Shi, 2014). When people retire, they no longer have the structured environment they had when they were working,

What are some keys to adjusting effectively in retirement?
© Bronwyn Kidd/Getty Images RF

so they need to be flexible and discover and pursue their own interests (Eisdorfer, 1996). Cultivating interests and friends unrelated to work improves adaptation to retirement (Zarit & Knight, 1996).

Planning and then successfully carrying out the plan is an important aspect of adjusting well in retirement (Williamson, 2011). A special concern in retirement planning involves the fact that women are likely to live longer than men and more likely to live alone (less likely to remarry and more likely to be widowed) (Moen, 2007).

Individuals who view retirement planning only in terms of finances don't adapt as well to retirement as those who have a more balanced retirement plan (Birren, 1996). It is important not only to plan financially for retirement but to consider other areas of life as well (Sener, Terzioglu, & Karabulut, 2007). In addition to financial planning, questions individuals need to ask about retirement include: What am I going to do with my leisure time? What am I going to do to stay active? What am I going to do socially? What am I going to do to keep my mind alert?

Review Connect Reflect

 LG3 Discuss career development, work, and retirement

Review
- What is involved in developing a career?
- What are some key aspects of work?
- What characterizes retirement?

Connect
- U.S. adolescents spend more time in unstructured leisure activities than East Asian adolescents do. How might establishing challenging lifelong leisure activities in

adolescence benefit an individual at retirement age?

Reflect *Your Own Personal Journey of Life*
- At what age would you like to retire? Or would you prefer to continue working as long as you are healthy? At what age did your father and/or mother retire, if they are no longer working? How well did they adjust to retirement?

---

reach your **learning goals**

Schools, Achievement, and Work

1 Schools

LG1 Describe the role of schools in development

Contemporary Approaches to Student Learning and Assessment

· Contemporary approaches to student learning include the direct instruction approach and the constructivist approach. Today, many effective teachers use both a constructivist approach and a direct instruction approach. Increased concern by the public and government in the United States has produced extensive state-mandated testing, which has both strengths and weaknesses and is controversial. The most visible example of the increased state-mandated testing is the No Child Left Behind federal legislation.

Schools and Developmental Status

· The child-centered kindergarten emphasizes the education of the whole child, with special attention to individual variation, the process of learning, and the importance of play in development. The Montessori approach allows children to choose from a range of activities while teachers serve as facilitators. Developmentally appropriate practice focuses on the typical patterns of children (age appropriateness) and the uniqueness of each child (individual appropriateness). Such practice contrasts with developmentally inappropriate practice, which ignores the concrete, hands-on approach to learning. The U.S. government has tried to break the poverty cycle with programs such as Head Start. Model programs have been shown to have positive effects on children who live in poverty. Controversy surrounds early childhood education curricula. On the one side are the child-centered, constructivist advocates; on the other are those who advocate a direct instruction, academic approach. A special concern is that early elementary school education proceeds too much on the basis of providing negative feedback to children. The transition from elementary school to middle or junior high school can be stressful. Successful schools for young adolescents focus on individual differences, show a deep concern for what is known about early adolescence, and emphasize social as well as cognitive development. There are concerns about dropping out of high school and improving the high school experience. The transition to college can involve a number of positive and negative experiences.

Educating Children with Disabilities

An estimated 14 percent of U.S. children receive special education or related services. Slightly less than 45 percent of students with disabilities are classified as having a learning disability. In the federal government classification, this category includes attention deficit hyperactivity disorder, or ADHD. Children with learning disabilities have difficulty in learning that involves understanding or using spoken or written language, and the difficulty can appear in listening, thinking, reading, writing, and spelling. A learning disability also may involve difficulty in doing mathematics. To be classified as a learning disability, the learning problem is not primarily the result of visual, hearing, or motor disabilities; intellectual disability; emotional disorders; or environmental, cultural, or economic disadvantage. Dyslexia is a category of learning disabilities that involves a severe impairment in the ability to read and spell. Attention deficit hyperactivity disorder (ADHD) is a disability in which individuals consistently show problems in one or more of these areas: (1) inattention, (2) hyperactivity, and (3) impulsivity. ADHD has been increasingly diagnosed. Autism is a severe disorder with an onset in the first three years of life, and it involves abnormalities in social relationships and communication. It also is characterized by repetitive behaviors. The current consensus is that autism involves an organic brain dysfunction. Autism spectrum disorders (ASD) range from the classical, severe form of autism to a milder condition known as Asperger syndrome. In 1975, Public Law 94-142, the Education for All Handicapped Children Act, required that all children with disabilities be given a free, appropriate public education. This law was renamed the Individuals with Disabilities Education Act (IDEA) in 1990 and updated in 2004. IDEA includes requirements that children with disabilities receive an individualized education plan (IEP), which is a written plan that spells out a program tailored to the child, and that they be educated in the least restrictive environment (LRE), which is a setting that is as similar as possible to the one in which children without disabilities are educated. Today's trend is toward inclusion, although some aspects of inclusion have recently been criticized.

Socioeconomic Status and Ethnicity in Schools

Children living in poverty face problems at home and at school that present barriers to learning. The school experiences of children from different ethnic groups vary considerably. A number of strategies can be adopted to improve relationships with diverse others.

2 Achievement Explain the key aspects of achievement

Extrinsic and Intrinsic Motivation

Extrinsic motivation involves doing something to obtain something else (a means to an end). Intrinsic motivation involves the internal motivation to do something for its own sake (an end in itself). Overall, most experts recommend that teachers create a classroom climate in which students are intrinsically motivated to learn. One view of intrinsic motivation emphasizes its self-determining characteristics. Giving students some choice and providing opportunities for personal responsibility increase intrinsic motivation. When rewards are used, they should convey information about task mastery rather than external control. Researchers have found that as students move from the early elementary school years to high school, their intrinsic motivation declines, especially during the middle school years. Intrinsic motivation is typically favored by educational psychologists, although in many aspects of achievement, both intrinsic and extrinsic factors are at work.

Mastery Motivation and Mindset	· A mastery orientation is preferred over helpless or performance orientations in achievement situations. Mindset is the cognitive view, either fixed or growth, that individuals develop for themselves. Dweck argues that a key aspect of optimal development is guiding children and adolescents to develop a growth mindset.
Self-Efficacy	· Self-efficacy is the belief that one can master a situation and produce positive outcomes. Bandura stresses that self-efficacy is a critical factor that determines whether students will achieve. Schunk argues that self-efficacy influences a student's choice of tasks, with low-efficacy students avoiding many learning tasks.
Goal Setting, Planning, and Self-Monitoring	· Setting specific, proximal (short-term), and challenging goals benefits students' self-efficacy and achievement. Being a good planner means managing time effectively, setting priorities, and being organized. Self-monitoring is a key aspect of self-regulation that benefits student learning.
Expectations	· Students' expectations for success and the value they place on what they want to achieve influence their motivation. The combination of expectancy and value has been the focus of a number of efforts to understand students' achievement motivation. Individuals benefit when their parents, teachers, and other adults have high expectations for their achievement.
Ethnicity and Culture	· In most investigations, socioeconomic status predicts achievement better than ethnicity. U.S. children do more poorly on math and science achievement tests than children in Asian countries such as China, Taiwan, and Japan.

3 Careers, Work, and Retirement   LG3 Discuss career development, work, and retirement

Career Development	· Many young children have idealistic fantasies about a career. In the late teens and early twenties, their career thinking has usually become more serious. By their early to mid-twenties, many individuals have started in a career. In the remainder of early adulthood, they seek to establish their career and start moving up the career ladder. Service-producing industries will account for the most jobs in America in the next decade. Jobs that require a college education will be the fastest-growing and highest-paying.
Work	· Work defines people in fundamental ways and is a key aspect of their identity. Most individuals spend about one-third of their adult lives at work. People often become stressed if they are unable to work, but work also can produce stress, as when there is a heavy workload and time pressure. Working part-time during adolescence can have advantages or disadvantages, although working too many hours harms students' grades. Working during college can have negative outcomes when students work long hours, or positive outcomes when students participate in co-op programs, internships, or part-time or summer work relevant to their field of study. The work patterns of emerging adults have changed over the last 100 years, and diverse school and work patterns now characterize emerging adults. The nature of the transition from school to work is strongly influenced by the individual's educational level. Many emerging adults change jobs, which can involve searching or floundering. Unemployment produces stress regardless of whether the job loss is temporary, cyclical, or permanent. The increasing number of women who work in careers outside the home has led to new work-related issues. There has been a considerable increase in the time men spend in household work and child care. For many people, midlife is a time of reflection, assessment, and evaluation of their current work and what they plan to do in the future. Midlife job or career changes can be self-motivated or forced on individuals. Some individuals continue a life of strong work productivity throughout late adulthood. An increasing number of older U.S. men and women are working, and since the mid-1990s there has been a substantial rise in the percentage of older adults who work full-time and a considerable decrease in the percentage of older adults who work part-time.
Retirement	· A retirement option for older workers is a late-twentieth-century phenomenon in the United States. The United States has extended the mandatory retirement age upward, and efforts have been made to reduce age discrimination in work-related circumstances. The pathways individuals follow when they reach retirement age today are less clear than in the past. Individuals who are healthy, have adequate incomes, are active, are better educated, have an extended social network of friends and family, and are satisfied with their lives before they retire adjust best to retirement.

key terms

Asperger syndrome
attention deficit hyperactivity
 disorder (ADHD)
autism spectrum disorders
 (ASDs)
autistic disorder
child-centered kindergarten
constructivist approach

developmentally appropriate
 practice (DAP)
direct instruction approach
dyscalculia
dysgraphia
dyslexia
extrinsic motivation
helpless orientation

inclusion
individualized education plan
 (IEP)
intrinsic motivation
learning disabilities
least restrictive environment
 (LRE)

mastery orientation
mindset
Montessori approach
performance orientation
Project Head Start
self-efficacy
top-dog phenomenon

key people

Elliot Aronson
Albert Bandura
James Comer
Robert Crosnoe

Carol Dweck
Jacquelynne Eccles
Sandra Graham
James Kauffman

Phyllis Moen
Maria Montessori
Clas-Hakan Nygard
Eva Pomerantz

Dale Schunk
Harold Stevenson
Barry Zimmerman

section **six**

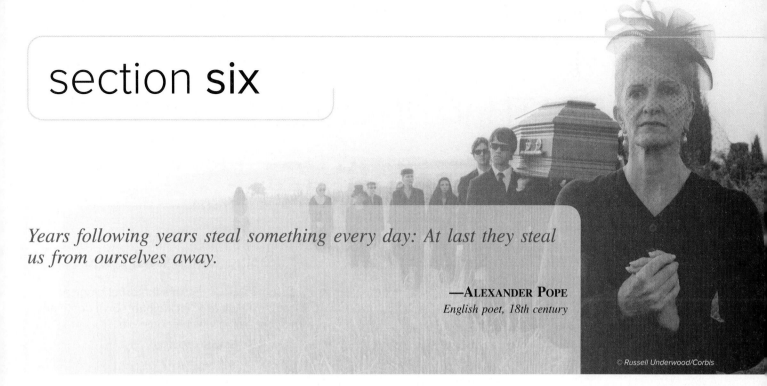

Years following years steal something every day: At last they steal us from ourselves away.

—**ALEXANDER POPE**
English poet, 18th century

© Russell Underwood/Corbis

Endings

Our life ultimately ends—when we approach life's grave sustained and soothed with unfaltering trust or rave at the close of day; when at last years steal us from ourselves, and when we are linked to our children's children's children by an invisible cable that runs from age to age. This final section contains one chapter: "Death, Dying, and Grieving."

chapter **17**

DEATH, DYING, AND GRIEVING

chapter outline

1 The Death System and Cultural Contexts

Learning Goal 1 Describe the death system and its cultural and historical contexts

The Death System and Its Cultural Variations

Changing Historical Circumstances

2 Defining Death and Life/Death Issues

Learning Goal 2 Evaluate issues in determining death and decisions regarding death

Issues in Determining Death

Decisions Regarding Life, Death, and Health Care

3 A Developmental Perspective on Death

Learning Goal 3 Discuss death and attitudes about it at different points in development

Causes of Death

Attitudes Toward Death at Different Points in the Life Span

Suicide

4 Facing One's Own Death

Learning Goal 4 Explain the psychological aspects involved in facing one's own death and the contexts in which people die

Kübler-Ross' Stages of Dying

Perceived Control and Denial

The Contexts in Which People Die

5 Coping with the Death of Someone Else

Learning Goal 5 Identify ways to cope with the death of another person

Communicating with a Dying Person

Grieving

Making Sense of the World

Losing a Life Partner

Forms of Mourning

© Fuse/Getty Images RF

preview

In this final chapter, we will explore many aspects of death and dying. Among the questions that we will ask are these: What characterizes the death system and its cultural and historical contexts? How can death be defined? What are some links between development and death? How do people face their own death? How do individuals cope with the death of someone they love?

1 The Death System and Cultural Contexts

 LG1 Describe the death system and its cultural and historical contexts

- The Death System and Its Cultural Variations
- Changing Historical Circumstances

Every culture has a death system, and variations in this death system occur across cultures. Also, when, where, and how people die have changed historically in the United States.

THE DEATH SYSTEM AND ITS CULTURAL VARIATIONS

Robert Kastenbaum (2004, 2009, 2012) emphasizes that a number of components compose the *death system* in any culture. These components include the following:

- *People.* Because death is inevitable, everyone is involved with death at some point, both their own death and the deaths of others. Some individuals have a more systematic role with death, such as those who work in the funeral industry or belong to the clergy, as well as people who work in life-threatening contexts, such as firefighters and the police.
- *Places or contexts.* These include hospitals, funeral homes, cemeteries, hospices, battlefields, and memorials (such as the Vietnam Veterans Memorial Wall in Washington, D.C.).
- *Times.* Death involves times or occasions—such as Memorial Day in the United States and the Day of the Dead in Mexico—which are set aside to honor those who have died. Also, anniversaries of disasters such as D-Day in World War II, 9/11/2001, and Hurricane Sandy in 2012, as well as the 2004 tsunami in Southeast Asia that took approximately 100,000 lives, are times when those who died are remembered in special ways such as ceremonies.
- *Objects.* Many objects in a culture are associated with death, including caskets and various colored objects such as clothes, armbands, and hearses. In the United States, black is associated with death but in China white is linked to death.
- *Symbols.* Symbols such as a skull and crossbones, as well as last rites in the Catholic religion and various religious ceremonies, are connected to death.

Kastenbaum (2004, 2007, 2009, 2012) also argues that the death system serves certain functions in a culture. These functions include *issuing warnings and predictions* (by such providers as weather-forecasting services and the media, laboratories that analyze test results, and doctors that communicate with patients and their families); *preventing death* (by people such as firefighters, the police, physicians, and researchers who work to improve safety and find cures for diseases); *caring for the dying* (by various health professionals such as physicians and nurses, as well as places where dying individuals are cared for, such as hospitals or hospices); *disposing of the dead* (removal of the body, embalming or cremation, and so on); *social consolidation after death* (coping and adapting by family members and friends of the deceased, who often need support and counseling); *making sense of the death* (how people in the society try to understand death); and

> Sustained and soothed by an unfaltering trust, approach thy grave, Like one who wraps the drapery of his couch About him, and lies down to pleasant dreams.
>
> **—WILLIAM CULLEN BRYANT**
> *American poet, 19th century*

In October, 2012, Hurricane Sandy resulted in the deaths of more than 200 people in eight countries. Damage was especially severe in the coastal areas of New Jersey and New York.
© Kristin Callahan/Ace Pictures/Newscom

Death System Function	Hurricane Katrina
Warnings and predictions	Long-standing recognition of vulnerability; clear advance warning of impending disaster.
Preventing death	The hurricane itself could not be prevented; loss of life, social disorganization, and massive property destruction could have been sharply reduced by better advance planning and emergency response.
Caring for the dying	Medical care was interrupted and undermined by damage to hospitals and communications.
Disposing of the dead	Recovering bodies was delayed, and there were major problems in identifying bodies.
Social consolidation after death	Community cohesiveness and support were negatively impacted by evacuation, scattering of family members, and limited response by overwhelmed human service agencies.
Making sense of death	There was intense criticism of government agencies, whose alleged failures contributed to death and destruction.
Killing	The media reported spikes in lethal violence after the hurricane, but those reports were later found to be inaccurate.

FIGURE 1

HURRICANE KATRINA AND DEATH SYSTEM FUNCTIONS

FIGURE 2

A RITUAL ASSOCIATED WITH DEATH. Family memorial day at the national cemetery in Seoul, South Korea.
© Ahn Young-joon/AP Images

killing (when, how, and for what reasons people in the culture can be killed, such as criminals, and whether the death penalty should be given to some individuals). Figure 1 describes the functions of the death system in the context of Hurricane Katrina in 2005 (Kastenbaum, 2007, 2009).

What are some cultural variations in the death system? To live a full life and to die with glory were the prevailing goals of the ancient Greeks. Individuals are more conscious of death in times of war, famine, and plague. Whereas Americans are conditioned from early in life to live as though they were immortal, in much of the world this fiction cannot be maintained. Death crowds the streets of Calcutta in daily overdisplay, as it does the scrubby villages of Africa's Sahel. Children live with the ultimate toll of malnutrition and disease, mothers lose as many babies as survive into adulthood, and it is rare that a family remains intact for many years. Even in peasant areas where life is better, and health and maturity may be reasonable expectations, the presence of dying people in the house, the large attendance at funerals, and the daily contact with aging adults prepare the young for death and provide them with guidelines on how to die. By contrast, in the United States it is not uncommon to reach adulthood without having talked about death or experienced the death of someone close.

Most societies throughout history have had philosophical or religious beliefs about death, and most societies have a ritual that deals with death (Gordon, 2015; Masaki & Asai, 2013; Morita & others, 2015). Death may be seen as a punishment for one's sins, an act of atonement, or a judgment of a just God. For some, death means loneliness; for others, death is a quest for happiness. For still others, death represents redemption, a relief from the trials and tribulations of the earthly world. Some embrace death and welcome it; others abhor and fear it. For those who welcome it, death may be seen as the fitting end to a fulfilled life. From this perspective, how we depart from life is influenced by how we have lived.

In most societies, death is not viewed as the end of existence—although the biological body has died, the spiritual body is believed to live on (Qazi & others, 2013). This religious perspective is favored by most Americans as well (Gowan, 2003). Cultural variations in attitudes toward death include belief in reincarnation, which is an important aspect of the Hindu and Buddhist religions (Dillon, 2003; Setta & Shemie, 2015). In the Gond culture of India, death is believed to be caused by magic and demons. The members of the Gond culture react angrily to death. In the Tanala culture of Madagascar, death is believed to be caused by natural forces. The members of the Tanala culture show a much more peaceful reaction to death than their counterparts in the Gond culture. Figure 2 shows a ritual associated with death in South Korea.

In many ways, we in the United States are death avoiders and death deniers (Gold, 2011). This denial can take many forms:

- The tendency of the funeral industry to gloss over death and fashion lifelike qualities in the dead
- The adoption of euphemistic language for death—for example, exiting, passing on, never say die, and good for life, which implies forever
- The persistent search for a fountain of youth
- The rejection and isolation of the aged, who may remind us of death
- The adoption of the concept of a pleasant and rewarding afterlife, suggesting that we are immortal
- The medical community's emphasis on prolonging biological life rather than on diminishing human suffering

CHANGING HISTORICAL CIRCUMSTANCES

One historical change involves the age group that death most often strikes. Two hundred years ago, almost one of every two children died before the age of 10, and one parent died before children grew up. Today, death occurs most often among older adults (Carr, 2009). Life expectancy has increased from 47 years for a person born in 1900 to 79 years for someone born today (U.S. Census Bureau, 2015). In 1900, most people died at home, cared for by their family. As our population has aged and become more mobile, a larger number of older adults die apart from their families (Carr, 2009). In the United States today, more than 80 percent of all deaths occur in institutions or hospitals. The care of a dying older person has shifted away from the family and minimized our exposure to death and its painful surroundings.

developmental **connection**

Life Expectancy

The upper boundary of the human life span is 122 years of age (based on the oldest age documented). Connect to "Introduction."

Review *Connect* Reflect

LG1 Describe the death system and its cultural and historical contexts

Review
- What characterizes the death system in a culture? What are some cultural variations in the death system?
- What are some changing sociohistorical circumstances regarding death?

Connect
- You just read about how changes in life expectancy over time have affected the experience of death. What did you learn about life expectancy and life span from other chapters?

Reflect *Your Own Personal Journey of Life*
- How extensively have death and dying been discussed in your family? Explain.

2 Defining Death and Life/Death Issues

LG2 Evaluate issues in determining death and decisions regarding death

Issues in Determining Death

Decisions Regarding Life, Death, and Health Care

Is there one point in the process of dying that is the point at which death takes place, or is death a more gradual process? What are some decisions individuals can make about life, death, and health care?

ISSUES IN DETERMINING DEATH

Twenty-five years ago, determining whether someone was dead was simpler than it is today. The end of certain biological functions—such as breathing and blood pressure, and the rigidity of the body (rigor mortis)—were considered to be clear signs of death. In the past several decades, defining death has become more complex (Barron, 2015; Burkle & Pope, 2015; Nair-Collins, Northrup, & Olcese, 2015; Taylor & others, 2014; Veatch, 2015).

Brain death is a neurological definition of death, which states that a person is brain dead when all electrical activity of the brain has ceased for a specified period of time. A flat EEG (electroencephalogram) recording for a specified period of time is one criterion of brain death. The higher portions of the brain often die sooner than the lower portions. Because the brain's lower portions monitor heartbeat and respiration, individuals whose higher brain areas have died may continue breathing and have a heartbeat (Macdougall & others, 2014). The definition of brain death currently followed by most physicians includes the death of both the higher cortical functions and the lower brain stem functions.

Some medical experts argue that the criteria for death should include only higher cortical functioning. If the cortical death definition were adopted, then physicians could claim a

brain death A neurological definition of death—an individual is dead when all electrical activity of the brain has ceased for a specified period of time.

person is dead who has no cortical functioning, even though the lower brain stem is functioning. Supporters of the cortical death policy argue that the functions we associate with being human, such as intelligence and personality, are located in the higher cortical part of the brain. They believe that when these functions are lost, the "human being" is no longer alive.

DECISIONS REGARDING LIFE, DEATH, AND HEALTH CARE

In cases of catastrophic illness or accidents, patients might not be able to respond adequately to participate in decisions about their medical care. To prepare for this situation, some individuals make choices earlier.

Advance Care Planning   *Advance care planning* refers to the process of patients thinking about and communicating their preferences about end-of-life care (Anderson, 2015; Chiarchiaro, Arnold, & White, 2015; Harrison & McGee, 2014; Silveira, Witala, & Piette, 2014). For many patients in a coma, it is not clear what their wishes regarding termination of treatment might be if they still were conscious. A recent study found that advance care planning decreased life-sustaining treatment, increased hospice use, and decreased hospital use (Brinkman-Stoppelenburg, Rietjens, & van der Heide, 2014). Recognizing that some terminally ill patients might prefer to die rather than linger in a painful or vegetative state, the organization "Choice in Dying" created the *living will,* a legal document that reflects the patient's advance care planning. A recent study of older adults found that advance care planning was associated with improved quality of care at the end of life, including less in-hospital death and greater use of hospice care (Bischoff & others, 2013).

Physicians' concerns over malpractice suits and the efforts of people who support the living will concept have produced natural death legislation. Laws in all 50 states now accept an *advance directive,* such as a living will An advance directive states such preferences as whether life-sustaining procedures should or should not be used to prolong the life of an individual when death is imminent (Mitchell & Dale, 2015). An advance directive must be signed while the individual still is able to think clearly (Lum, Sudore, & Bekelman, 2015). A study of end-of-life planning revealed that only 15 percent of patients 18 years of age and older had a living will (Clements, 2009). Almost 90 percent of the patients reported that it was important to discuss health care wishes with their family, but only 60 percent of them had done so. A recent research review concluded that physicians have a positive attitude toward advance directives (Coleman, 2013).

Recently, Physician Orders for Life-Sustaining Treatment (POLST), a document that is more specific than previous advance directives, was created (Ibrahim & others, 2015; Buck & Fahlberg, 2014). POLST translates treatment preferences into medical orders such as those involving cardiopulmonary resuscitation, extent of treatment, and artificial nutrition via a tube (Hickman, Keevern, & Hammes, 2015; Mirarchi & others, 2015). POLST requires the health care professional and the patient or surrogate to confer and to state what the wishes of the patient are. POLST is currently available or being considered in 34 states.

Terri Schiavo (*right*) with her mother in an undated photo. *What issues does the Terri Schiavo case raise?*

© Handout Courtesy of the Schiavo Family/Corbis

Euthanasia   **Euthanasia** ("easy death") is the act of painlessly ending the lives of individuals who are suffering from an incurable disease or severe disability (Gormley-Fleming & Campbell, 2014; Macleod, 2015; Tomlinson & others, 2015). Sometimes euthanasia is called "mercy killing." Distinctions are made between two types of euthanasia: passive and active. **Passive euthanasia** occurs when a person is allowed to die by withholding available treatment, such as withdrawing a life-sustaining device. For example, this might involve turning off a respirator or a heart-lung machine. **Active euthanasia** occurs when death is deliberately induced, as when a lethal dose of a drug is injected.

Technological advances in life-support devices raise the issue of quality of life (Bloodworth, Bloodworth, & Ely, 2015). Nowhere was this more apparent than in the highly publicized case of Terri Schiavo, who suffered severe brain damage related to cardiac arrest and a lack of oxygen to the brain. She went into a coma and spent 15 years in a vegetative state. Across the 15 years, whether passive euthanasia should be implemented, or whether she should be kept in the vegetative state with the hope that her condition might change for the better, was debated between family members and eventually at a number of levels in the judicial system. At one point toward the end of her life in early spring 2005, a judge ordered her feeding tube be removed. However, subsequent appeals led to its reinsertion twice. The feeding tube was removed a third and final time on March 18, 2005, and she died 13 days later. Withholding the life-support system allowed Terri Schiavo to die from passive euthanasia.

Should individuals like Terri Schiavo be kept alive in a vegetative state? The trend is toward acceptance of passive euthanasia in the case of terminally ill patients (Seay, 2011). However, one study revealed that family members were reluctant to have their relatives disconnected from a ventilator but rather wanted an escalation of treatment for them (Sviri & others, 2009). In this study, most of the individuals said that in similar circumstances they would not want to be chronically ventilated or resuscitated.

The most widely publicized cases of active euthanasia involve "assisted suicide." Jack Kevorkian, a Michigan physician, assisted a number of terminally ill patients in ending their lives. After a series of trials, Kevorkian was convicted in the state of Michigan of second-degree murder and served eight years in prison.

Assisted suicide is now legal in these countries: Netherlands, Belgium, Luxembourg, Switzerland, Germany, Albania, Columbia, and Japan. The United States government has no official policy on assisted suicide and leaves the decision up to each of the states. Currently, five states allow assisted suicide—Oregon, Washington, Montana, New Mexico, and Vermont. The manner in which assisted suicide is performed involves the physician giving the patient an overdose of muscle relaxants or sedatives, which causes a coma and then death. In states where assisted suicide is illegal, the crime is typically considered manslaughter or a felony. Canada has yet to approve assisted suicide, but a recent study indicated that a majority of Canadians favored a change to Canada's Criminal Code that would make assisted suicide legal (Schafer, 2013).

A Dutch study of almost 7,000 dying persons revealed that only 7 percent requested passive or active euthanasia, and of those who requested it, approximately one-third of the requests were granted (Onwuteaka-Philipsen & others, 2010). Also, a recent study found that approximately 50 percent of the requests for euthanasia were granted in Belgium (Van Wesemael & others, 2011). And another study found that in the Netherlands approximately 75 percent of the requests for euthanasia came from cancer patients and the main reason for the requests was pain (van Alphen, Donker, & Marquet, 2010).

A recent research review also revealed that the percentage of physician-assisted deaths ranged from 0.1 to 0.2 percent in the United States and Luxembourg to 1.8 to 2.9 percent in the Netherlands (Steck & others, 2013). In this review, the percentage of assisted suicide cases reported to authorities has increased in recent years and the individuals who die through assisted suicide are most likely to be males from 60 to 75 years of age.

Why is euthanasia so controversial? Those in favor of euthanasia argue that death should be calm and dignified, not full of agony, pain, and prolonged suffering. Those against euthanasia stress that it is a criminal act of murder in most states in the United States and in most countries. Many religious individuals, especially Christians, say that taking a life for any reason is against God's will and is an act of murder.

Dr. Jack Kevorkian assisted a number of people in Michigan to end their lives through active euthanasia. *Where do you stand on the use of active euthanasia?*
© Jeff Kowalsky/ZumaPress/Newscom

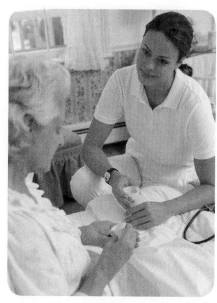

What characterizes hospice care?
© Comstock Images/PictureQuest RF

Needed: Better Care for Dying Individuals Too often, death in America is lonely, prolonged, and painful. Scientific advances sometimes have made dying harder by delaying the inevitable. Also, even though painkillers are available, too many people experience severe pain during the last days and months of life. Many health-care professionals have not been trained to provide adequate end-of-life care or to understand its importance.

Care providers are increasingly interested in helping individuals experience a "good death" (McIlfatrick & Hasson, 2014; Meffert & others, 2015). One view is that a good death involves physical comfort, support from loved ones, acceptance, and appropriate medical care. For some individuals, a good death involves accepting one's impending death and not feeling like a burden to others (Carr, 2012).

Hospice is a program committed to making the end of life as free from pain, anxiety, and depression as possible (Carlisle, 2015; Guo & Jacelon, 2014; Holden & others, 2015).

euthanasia The act of painlessly ending the lives of persons who are suffering from incurable diseases or severe disabilities; sometimes called "mercy killing."

passive euthanasia The withholding of available treatments, such as life-sustaining devices, allowing the person to die.

active euthanasia Death induced deliberately, as by injecting a lethal dose of a drug.

hospice A program committed to making the end of life as free from pain, anxiety, and depression as possible. The goals of hospice contrast with those of a hospital, which are to cure disease and prolong life.

Kathy McLaughlin, Home Hospice Nurse

Kathy McLaughlin is a home hospice nurse in Alexandria, Virginia. She provides care for individuals with terminal cancer, Alzheimer disease, and other diseases. There currently is a shortage of home hospice nurses in the United States.

Kathy says that she has seen too many people dying in pain, away from home, hooked up to needless machines. In her work as a home hospice nurse, she comments, "I know I'm making a difference. I just feel privileged to get the chance to meet this person who is not going to be around much longer. I want to enjoy the moment with this person. And I want them to enjoy the moment. They have great stories. They are better than novels" (McLaughlin, 2003, p. 1).

Hospice nurses like Kathy McLaughlin care for terminally ill patients and seek to make their remaining days of life as pain-free and comfortable as possible. They typically spend several hours a day in the terminally ill patient's home, serving not just as a medical caregiver but also as an emotional caregiver. Hospice nurses usually coordinate the patient's care through an advising physician.

A hospice nurse must be a registered nurse (RN) who is also certified as a hospice worker. The educational requirement is an

Kathy McLaughlin with her hospice patient Mary Monteiro.
Courtesy of the Family of Mary Monteiro

undergraduate degree in nursing; some hospice nurses also have graduate degrees in nursing. To be a certified hospice nurse requires a current license as an RN, a minimum of two years of experience as an RN in hospice-nursing settings, and passing an exam administered by the National Board for the Certification of Hospice Nurses.

Traditionally, a hospital's goals have been to cure illness and prolong life; by contrast, hospice care emphasizes **palliative care,** which involves reducing pain and suffering and helping individuals die with dignity (Guevara-Lopez, Altamirano-Bustamante, & Viesca-Trevino, 2015; Holloway & others, 2014; Kelley & others, 2014; Moore, 2015). However, U.S. hospitals recently have rapidly expanded their provision of palliative care. A recent study found that more than 85 percent of mid- to large-size U.S. hospitals have a palliative care team (Morrison, 2013). Hospice-care professionals work together to treat the dying person's symptoms, make the individual as comfortable as possible, show interest in the person and the person's family, and help everyone involved cope with death (Hugel & others, 2014; Melia, 2014; Reville & Foxwell, 2014; Webb, Horton, & Johnson, 2015).

Today many hospice programs are home-based, a blend of institutional and home care designed to humanize the end-of-life experience for the dying person (Sokol, 2013). Too often people don't get hospice care until very late and as a result don't experience its full benefits. To read about the work of a home hospice nurse, see the *Connecting with Careers* profile.

palliative care Emphasized in hospice care; involves reducing pain and suffering and helping individuals die with dignity.

Review Connect Reflect

 Evaluate issues in determining death and decisions regarding death

Review
- What are some issues regarding the determination of death?
- What are some decisions to be made regarding life, death, and health care?

Connect
- In this section you learned that hospices try to provide adequate pain management for dying patients. What

did you learn about older adults in the chapter on "Motor, Sensory, and Perceptual Development" that might help them deal with pain better than younger adults?

Reflect *Your Own Personal Journey of Life*
- Have you signed an advance directive (living will)? Why or why not?

3 A Developmental Perspective on Death

LG3 Discuss death and attitudes about it at different points in development

```
Causes
of Death

Attitudes Toward Death at
Different Points in the Life Span

Suicide
```

Today in the United States, the deaths of older adults account for approximately two-thirds of the 2 million deaths that occur each year. Thus, what we know about death, dying, and grieving mainly is based on information about older adults. Youthful death is far less common. When, where, and how people die have changed historically in the United States (Leming & Dickinson, 2011).

CAUSES OF DEATH

Death can occur at any point in the human life span. Death can occur during prenatal development through miscarriages or stillborn births. Death can also occur during the birth process or in the first few days after birth, which usually happens because of a birth defect or because infants have not developed adequately to sustain life outside the uterus. *Sudden infant death syndrome* (SIDS), in which infants stop breathing (usually during the night) and die without apparent cause (Moon & Fu, 2012), is the leading cause of infant death in the United States, with the risk highest at 2 to 4 months of age (NICHD, 2015).

In childhood, death occurs most often because of accidents or illness. Accidental death in childhood can be the consequence of an event such as an automobile accident, drowning, poisoning, fire, or a fall from a high place. Major illnesses that cause death in children are heart disease, cancer, and birth defects.

Compared with childhood, death in adolescence is more likely to occur because of motor vehicle accidents, suicide, and homicide. Many motor vehicle accidents that cause death in adolescence are alcohol-related. We will examine suicide in greater depth shortly.

Older adults are more likely to die from chronic diseases, such as heart disease and cancer, whereas younger adults are more likely to die from accidents. Older adults' diseases often incapacitate before they kill, which produces a course of dying that slowly leads to death. Of course, many young and middle-aged adults die of illnesses such as heart disease and cancer.

> **developmental connection**
>
> **Conditions, Diseases, and Disorders**
>
> Nearly 3,000 deaths of infants each year in the United States are attributed to SIDS. Connect to "Physical Development and Biological Aging."

ATTITUDES TOWARD DEATH AT DIFFERENT POINTS IN THE LIFE SPAN

The ages of children and adults influence the way they experience and think about death (Sarwar, Mangewala, & Baron, 2013). A mature, adult-like conception of death includes an understanding that death is final and irreversible, that death represents the end of life, and that all living things die. Most researchers have found that as children grow, they gradually develop a more mature approach to death (Hayslip & Hansson, 2003).

Childhood   Most researchers note that infants do not have even a rudimentary concept of death. However, as infants develop an attachment to a caregiver, they can experience loss or separation and an accompanying anxiety. But young children do not perceive time the way adults do. Even brief separations may be experienced as total losses. For most infants, the reappearance of the caregiver provides a continuity of existence and a reduction of anxiety. We know very little about the infant's actual experiences with bereavement, although the loss of a parent, especially if the caregiver is not replaced, can negatively affect the infant's health.

Even children 3 to 5 years of age have little or no idea of what death means. They may confuse death with sleep or ask in a puzzled way, "Why doesn't it move?" Preschool-aged children rarely get upset by the sight of a dead animal or by being told that a person has died. They believe that the dead can be brought back to life spontaneously by magic or by giving them food or medical treatment. Young children often believe that only people who

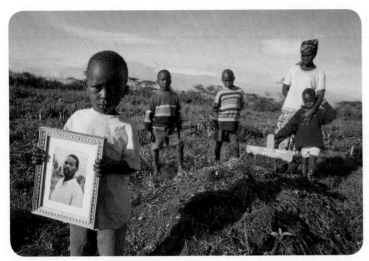

Three- to nine-year-old children with their mother visiting their father's grave in Kenya. *What are some developmental changes in children's conceptions of death?*
© Per-Anders Pettersson/Getty Images

want to die, or who are bad or careless, actually die. They also may blame themselves for the death of someone they know well, illogically reasoning that the event may have happened because they disobeyed the person who died.

Sometime in the middle and late childhood years more realistic perceptions of death develop. In one early investigation of children's perception of death, children 3 to 5 years of age denied that death exists, children 6 to 9 years of age believed that death exists but happens to only some people, and children 9 years of age and older recognized death's finality and universality (Nagy, 1948). In a review of research on children's conception of death, it was concluded that children probably do not view death as universal and irreversible until about 9 years of age (Cuddy-Casey & Orvaschel, 1997). Most children under 7 do not see death as likely. Those who do see it as likely perceive it as reversible.

An expert on death and dying, Robert Kastenbaum (2009, 2012) has a different perspective on developmental dimensions of death and dying. He notes that even very young children are acutely aware of and concerned about separation and loss, just as attachment theorist John Bowlby (1980) pointed out. Kastenbaum also says that many children work hard at trying to understand death. Thus, instead of viewing young children as having illogical perceptions of death, Kastenbaum thinks a more accurate stance is to view them as having concerns about death and striving to understand it.

The death of a parent is especially difficult for children. When a child's parent dies, the child's school performance and peer relationships often worsen. For some children, as well as adults, a parent's death can be devastating and result in a hypersensitivity about death, including a fear of losing others close to the individual. In some cases, loss of a sibling can result in similar negative outcomes. However, a number of factors, such as the quality of the relationship and type of the death (whether due to an accident, long-standing illness, suicide, or murder, for example), can influence a child's response following the death of a person close to him or her.

Most psychologists stress that honesty is the best strategy in discussing death with children. Treating the concept as unmentionable is thought to be an inappropriate strategy, yet most of us have grown up in a society in which death is rarely discussed.

In addition to honesty, what other strategies can be adopted in discussing death with children? The best response to the child's query about death might depend on the child's maturity level. For example, a preschool child requires a less elaborate explanation than an older child. Death can be explained to preschool children in simple physical and biological terms. Actually, what young children need more than elaborate explanations of death is reassurance that they are loved and will not be abandoned. Regardless of children's ages, adults should be sensitive and sympathetic, encouraging them to express their own feelings and ideas.

developmental **connection**

Cognitive Development

In Piaget's theory, adolescents think more abstractly, idealistically, and logically than do children. Connect to "Cognitive Developmental Approaches."

What are children's and adolescents' attitudes about death? What are some good strategies for helping children and adolescents understand death?
Photo by Molly Hayden, U.S. Army Garrison-Hawaii Public Affairs

Adolescence Adolescents develop more abstract conceptions of death than children do. For example, adolescents describe death in terms of darkness, light, transition, or nothingness (Wenestam & Wass, 1987). They also develop religious and philosophical views about the nature of death and whether there is life after death.

Recall the concepts of adolescent egocentrism and personal fable—adolescents' preoccupation with themselves and their beliefs that they are invincible and unique. If that is the case, it would not be unusual for some adolescents to think that they are somehow immune to death and that death is something that happens to other people but not to them. However, some recent research studies suggest that rather than perceiving themselves to be invulnerable, adolescents are more likely to portray themselves as vulnerable to experiencing a premature death (Fischhoff & others, 2010).

Adulthood There is no evidence that a special orientation toward death develops in early adulthood. An increase in consciousness about death accompanies individuals' awareness that they are aging, which usually intensifies in middle adulthood. In our discussion of middle adulthood, we considered that midlife is a time when adults begin to think more about how much time is left in their lives. Researchers have found that middle-aged adults actually fear death more than do young adults or older adults (Kalish & Reynolds, 1976). Older adults, though, think about death more and talk about it more in conversation with others than do middle-aged and young adults. They also have more direct experience with death as their friends and relatives become ill and die (Hayslip & Hansson, 2003). Older adults are forced to examine the meanings of life and death more frequently than are younger adults.

Younger adults who are dying often feel cheated more than do older adults who are dying (Kalish, 1987). Younger adults are more likely to think they have not had the opportunity to do what they want to do with their lives. Younger adults perceive they are losing what they might achieve; older adults perceive they are losing what they have attained.

In older adults, one's own death may take on an appropriateness it lacked in earlier years. Some of the increased thinking and conversing about death, and an increased sense of integrity developed through a positive life review, may help older adults accept death. Older adults are less likely to have unfinished business than are younger adults. They usually do not have children who need to be guided to maturity, their spouses are more likely to be dead, and they are less likely to have work-related projects that require completion. Lacking such anticipations, death may be less emotionally painful to them. Even among older adults, however, attitudes toward death vary (Whitbourne & Meeks, 2011).

How might older adults' attitudes about death differ from those of younger adults?
© Ned Frisk Photography/Corbis RF

SUICIDE

What are some of the factors that place people at risk for suicide? They include serious physical illnesses, mental disorders, feelings of hopelessness, social isolation, failure in school and work, loss of loved ones, serious financial difficulties, drug use, and a prior suicide attempt.

There are cultural differences in suicide (Hjelmeland, 2011). The highest rate of suicide reported since 2010 for males is in Greenland (117 per 100,000 population); the lowest for males occurs in Middle Eastern countries, for example, Pakistan (1.45 per 100,000 population). The highest rate of suicide reported since 2010 for females is South Korea (17.3 per 100,000 population) and the lowest rate is in Slovakia (2.8 per 100,000 population). In 2012, in the United States the suicide rate per 100,000 population for males was 20.3 and for females was 5.4 (Centers for Disease Control and Prevention, 2013). Suicide rates have been rising in the United States in the last decade, more for male than females.

Adolescence Suicide behavior is rare in childhood but escalates in adolescence and then increases further in emerging adulthood (Park & others, 2006). Suicide is the third leading cause of death among 10- to 19-year-olds today in the United States (U.S. Census Bureau, 2015). After increasing to high levels in the 1990s, suicide rates in adolescents have declined in recent years. Emerging adults have triple the suicide rate of adolescents (Park & others, 2006).

Although a suicide threat should always be taken seriously, far more adolescents contemplate or attempt it unsuccessfully than actually commit it. As indicated in Figure 3, in the last two decades there has been a considerable decline in the percentage of adolescents who think about committing suicide, although from 2009 to 2013 this percentage increased from 14 to 17 percent (Kann & others, 2014). In this national study, in 2013, 8 percent attempted suicide and 2 percent engaged in suicide attempts that required medical attention. Approximately 4,600 adolescents commit suicide each year (Centers for Disease Control and Prevention, 2015).

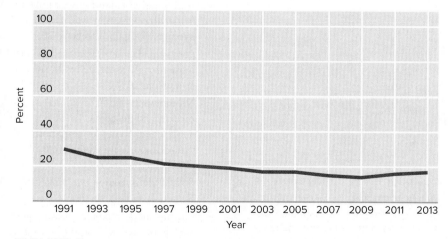

FIGURE 3

PERCENTAGE OF U.S. NINTH- TO TWELFTH-GRADE STUDENTS WHO SERIOUSLY CONSIDERED ATTEMPTING SUICIDE IN THE PREVIOUS MONTH FROM 1991 TO 2013

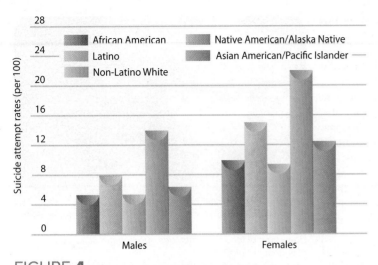

FIGURE 4

SUICIDE ATTEMPTS BY U.S. ADOLESCENTS FROM DIFFERENT ETHNIC GROUPS. *Note:* Data shown are for one-year rates of self-reported suicide attempts.

The suicidal behavior of adolescents varies not only by gender but also by ethnicity (Schrijvers, Bollen, & Sabbe, 2012; Wong & others, 2012). As shown in Figure 4, Native American/Alaska Native adolescent females are the most likely and African American males the least likely to attempt suicide (Goldston & others, 2008). However, Native American/Alaska Native adolescents are the most likely and non-Latino White females the least likely to actually commit suicide (Goldston & others, 2008). A major risk factor in the high rate of suicide attempts by NA/AN adolescents is their elevated rate of alcohol abuse.

Distal, or earlier, experiences often are involved in suicide attempts as well (Hardt & others, 2015; Lopez-Castroman & others, 2015; Shah & Bhandarkar, 2011). The adolescent may have a long-standing history of family instability and unhappiness. Just as a lack of affection and emotional support, high control, and pressure for achievement by parents during childhood are related to adolescent depression, such combinations of family experiences also are likely to show up as distal factors in adolescents' suicide attempts.

What is the psychological profile of the suicidal adolescent? Suicidal adolescents often have depressive symptoms. Although not all depressed adolescents are suicidal, depression is the most frequently cited factor associated with adolescent suicide (Mirkovic & others, 2015; Thapar & others, 2012). A sense of hopelessness, low self-esteem, and high self-blame also are associated with adolescent suicide (O'Donnell & others, 2004). A recent study found that college students with greater severity of depression and a higher level of hopelessness were at risk for engaging in suicidal ideation (Farabaugh & others, 2012). In another recent study, both depression and hopelessness were predictors of adolescents who repeated a suicide attempt across a six-month period (Consoli & others, 2015). The following studies document a number of factors linked with adolescent suicide attempts:

- The most common link between self-reported adolescent suicide attempts and drug use was any lifetime use of tranquilizers or sedatives (Kokkevi & others, 2012).
- Perception of being overweight increased the risk of suicidal ideation and attempts by adolescent girls but not boys (Dave & Rashad, 2009).
- Data from the National Longitudinal Study of Adolescent Health indicated that the following factors indicated suicide risk: depressive symptoms, a sense of hopelessness, engaging in suicidal ideation, having a family background of suicidal behavior, and having friends with a history of suicidal behavior (Thompson, Kuruwita, & Foster, 2009).
- Authoritative parenting was linked to fewer adolescent suicide attempts; rejecting/neglecting parenting was associated with a greater likelihood of adolescent suicide attempts (Donath & others, 2014).
- Peer victimization was related to suicidal ideation and suicide attempts, with cyberbullying more strongly associated with suicidal ideation than traditional bullying (van Geel, Vedder, & Tanilon, 2014).
- No national studies have been conducted of suicide rates in gay, lesbian, and bisexual adolescents. However, a recent study in Boston found that sexual minority adolescents living in neighborhoods with higher rates of lesbian, gay, and bisexual crimes reported a higher rate of suicidal ideation and attempts (Duncan & Hatzenbuehler, 2014).
- Sexual victimization was linked to a risk for suicide attempts in adolescence (Plener, Singer, & Goldbeck, 2011).
- Playing sports predicted lower suicidal ideation in boys and venting by talking to others was associated with lower suicidal ideation in girls (Kim & others, 2014).
- Overweight middle school students were more likely to think about, plan, and attempt suicide than their counterparts who were not overweight (Whetstone, Morrissey, & Cummings, 2007).

developmental **connection**

Peer Relationships

Bullying victimization is associated with suicide-related thoughts and behavior. Connect to "Peers and the Sociocultural World."

In some instances, suicides in adolescence occur in clusters. That is, when one adolescent commits suicide, other adolescents who find out about it also commit suicide. Such "copycat" suicides raise the issue of whether or not suicides should be reported in the media; a news report might plant the idea of committing suicide in other adolescents' minds.

Adulthood and Aging Suicide is increasing among U.S. adults. In 2009, the number of deaths from suicide surpassed the number of deaths from automobile crashes (Centers for Disease Control and Prevention, 2013). A recent analysis found that for U.S. adults 35 to 64 years of age, the suicide rate increased 28.4 percent from 13.7 per 100,000 population in 1999 to 17.6 in 2010 (Centers for Disease Control and Prevention, 2013).

In 2012, in the United States the highest suicide rate per 100,000 population was 19.8 for 45- to 59-year-olds, with the second highest rate (17) occurring for those 75 years of age and older. In 2012, younger age groups had lower suicide rates than middle-aged and older adults. In 2012, adolescents and young adults had a suicide rate of 10.9 per 100,000 population (Centers for Disease Control and Prevention, 2013).

Older non-Latino White men are more likely to commit suicide than any other group (Garand & others, 2006). One study found that African Americans are less likely to commit suicide than non-Latino Whites, but African Americans commit suicide at a younger age (median age of 34 years compared with 44 years for non-Latino Whites) (Garlow, Purselle, & Heninger, 2005). For all adult age groups (as for adolescents), males are more likely to commit suicide than are females (Fung & Chan, 2011; Schrijvers & others, 2012). The older adult most likely to commit suicide is a male who lives alone, has lost his spouse, and is experiencing failing health (Heisel, 2006). A recent study revealed that perceiving oneself as burdensome also may be a contributing factor in suicide attempts by older adults (Corna & others, 2010).

Are there factors that differentiate individuals who just think about suicide from those who actually attempt it? A study of more than 7,000 adults revealed that suicide attempters were more likely than suicide ideators to be unemployed, have poor health, and have relationship problems (Fairweather & others, 2006).

Older adults are more likely to plan their suicide than adolescents, while impulsivity is more likely to be involved in adolescent suicide behavior (Demircin & others, 2011). Older adults also are more likely to actually commit suicide than are adolescents, with one in four attempts by older adults resulting in death (Demircin & others, 2011). A surviving spouse is especially at risk for depression or suicide (De Leo, 2002).

It is important to know what to do and what not to do when someone is likely to attempt suicide. Figure 5 provides some valuable guidance.

What to do	**What not to do**
1. Ask direct, straightforward questions in a calm manner: "Are you thinking about hurting yourself?"	1. Do not ignore the warning signs.
2. Assess the seriousness of the suicidal intent by asking questions about feelings, important relationships, who else the person has talked with, and the amount of thought given to the means to be used. If a gun, pills, a rope, or other means have been obtained and a precise plan has been developed, clearly the situation is dangerous. Stay with the person until help arrives.	2. Do not refuse to talk about suicide if a person approaches you about it.
3. Be a good listener and be very supportive without being falsely reassuring.	3. Do not react with humor, disapproval, or repulsion.
4. Try to persuade the person to obtain professional help and assist him or her in getting this help.	4. Do not give false reassurances by saying such things as "Everything is going to be OK." Also do not give out simple answers or platitudes, such as "You have everything to be thankful for."
	5. Do not abandon the individual after the crisis has passed or after professional help has commenced.

FIGURE 5

WHAT TO DO AND WHAT NOT TO DO WHEN SOMEONE IS LIKELY TO ATTEMPT SUICIDE

Review

- What are some developmental changes in the cause of death?
- What are some attitudes about death at different points in development?
- Why do people commit suicide? What are some links of suicide to development?

Connect

- In this section you learned that children 3 to 5 years of age often believe the dead can be brought back to life spontaneously, by magic or by giving them food or medical treatment. During which of Piaget's stages of development is a child's cognitive world dominated by egocentrism and magical beliefs?

Reflect *Your Own Personal Journey of Life*

- What is your current attitude about death? Has it changed since you were an adolescent? If so, how?

---

4 Facing One's Own Death

LG4 Explain the psychological aspects involved in facing one's own death and the contexts in which people die

Kübler-Ross' Stages of Dying	Perceived Control and Denial	The Contexts in Which People Die

Man is the only animal that finds his own existence a problem he has to solve and from which he cannot escape. In the same sense man is the only animal who knows he must die.

—ERICH FROMM
American psychotherapist, 20th century

Knowledge of death's inevitability permits us to establish priorities and structure our time accordingly. As we age, these priorities and structurings change in recognition of diminishing future time. Values concerning the most important uses of time also change. For example, when asked how they would spend six remaining months of life, younger adults described such activities as traveling and accomplishing things they previously had not done; older adults described more inner-focused activities—contemplation and meditation, for example (Kalish & Reynolds, 1976).

Most dying individuals want an opportunity to make some decisions regarding their own life and death (Kastenbaum, 2012). Some individuals want to complete unfinished business; they want time to resolve problems and conflicts and to put their affairs in order.

KÜBLER-ROSS' STAGES OF DYING

We are all born to die, and our lives are in a way preparation for that finality. Dealing with one's own death usually only takes front and center in a person's life when they are nearing death, but we live with that awareness throughout our lives. However, as indicated earlier in this chapter, people (especially in the United States) often tend to deny death by trying to avoid the topic altogether.

Might there be a sequence of stages we go through as we face death? Elisabeth Kübler-Ross (1969) divided the behavior and thinking of dying persons into five stages: denial and isolation, anger, bargaining, depression, and acceptance.

Denial and isolation is Kübler-Ross' first stage of dying, in which the person denies that death is really going to take place. The person may say, "No, it can't be me. It's not possible." This is a common reaction to terminal illness. However, denial is usually only a temporary defense. It is eventually replaced with increased awareness when the person is confronted with such matters as financial considerations, unfinished business, and worry about the welfare of surviving family members.

Anger is Kübler-Ross' second stage of dying, in which the dying person recognizes that denial can no longer be maintained. Denial often gives way to anger, resentment, rage, and envy. The dying person's question is "Why me?" At this point, the person becomes increasingly difficult to care for as anger may become displaced and projected onto physicians, nurses, family members, and even God. The realization of loss is great, and those who symbolize life, energy, and competent functioning are especially salient targets of the dying person's resentment and jealousy.

denial and isolation Kübler-Ross' first stage of dying, in which the dying person denies that she or he is really going to die.

anger Kübler-Ross' second stage of dying, in which the dying person's denial gives way to anger, resentment, rage, and envy.

Bargaining is Kübler-Ross' third stage of dying, in which the person develops the hope that death can somehow be postponed or delayed. Some persons enter into bargaining or negotiation—often with God—as they try to delay their death. Psychologically, the person is saying, "Yes, me, but . . ." In exchange for a few more days, weeks, or months of life, the person promises to lead a reformed life dedicated to God or to the service of others.

Depression is Kübler-Ross' fourth stage of dying, in which the dying person perceives the certainty of his or her death. At this point, a period of depression or preparatory grief may appear. The dying person may become silent, refuse visitors, and spend much of the time crying or grieving. This behavior is normal and is an effort to disconnect the self from love objects. Attempts to cheer up the dying person at this stage should be discouraged, says Kübler-Ross, because the dying person has a need to contemplate impending death.

Acceptance is Kübler-Ross' fifth stage of dying, in which the person develops a sense of peace, an acceptance of one's fate, and—in many cases—a desire to be left alone. In this stage, feelings and physical pain may be virtually absent. Kübler-Ross describes this fifth stage as the end of the dying struggle, the final resting stage before death. A summary of Kübler-Ross' dying stages is presented in Figure 6.

What is the current evaluation of Kübler-Ross' theory about the stages of dying? According to Robert Kastenbaum (2009, 2012), there are some problems with Kübler-Ross' approach:

· The existence of the five-stage sequence has not been demonstrated by either Kübler-Ross or independent research.

· The stage interpretation neglected the patients' situations, including relationship support, specific effects of illness, family obligations, and institutional climate in which they were interviewed.

Despite these limitations, Kübler-Ross' pioneering efforts were important in calling attention to those who are attempting to cope with life-threatening illnesses. She did much to encourage attention to the quality of life for dying persons and their families.

Because of the criticisms of Kübler-Ross' stages, some psychologists prefer to describe them not as stages but as potential reactions to dying. At any one moment, a number of emotions may wax and wane. Hope, disbelief, bewilderment, anger, and acceptance may come and go as individuals try to make sense of what is happening to them.

In facing their own death, some individuals struggle until the end, desperately trying to hang on to their lives. Acceptance of death never comes for them. Some psychologists note that the harder individuals fight to avoid the inevitable death they face and the more they deny it, the more difficulty they will have in dying peacefully and in a dignified way; other psychologists argue that not confronting death until the end may be adaptive for some individuals (Lifton, 1977).

The extent to which people have found meaning and purpose in their lives is linked with how they approach death (Carr, 2012; Ozanne, Graneheim, & Strang, 2013; Park, 2012). One study revealed that individuals with a chronic, life-threatening illness—congestive heart failure—were trying to understand meaning in life (Park & others, 2008). Another study of 160 individuals with less than three months to live revealed that those who had found purpose and meaning in their lives felt the least despair in the final weeks, whereas dying individuals who saw no reason for living were the most distressed and wanted to hasten death (McClain, Rosenfeld, & Breitbart, 2003). In this and other studies, spirituality helped to buffer dying individuals from severe depression (Smith, McCullough, & Poll, 2003).

Do individuals become more spiritual as they get closer to death? A recent study of more than 100 patients with advanced congestive heart failure who were studied at two times six months apart found that as the patients perceived they were closer to death, they became more spiritual (Park, 2008).

PERCEIVED CONTROL AND DENIAL

Perceived control may work as an adaptive strategy for some older adults who face death. When individuals are led to believe they can influence and control events—such as prolonging

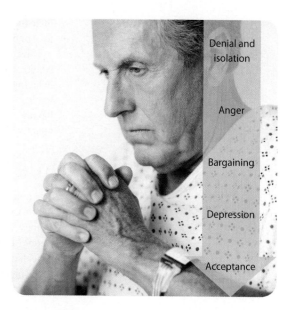

FIGURE 6

KÜBLER-ROSS' STAGES OF DYING. According to Elisabeth Kübler-Ross, we go through five stages of dying: denial and isolation, anger, bargaining, depression, and acceptance. *Does everyone go through these stages, or go through them in the same order? Explain.*
© Sean Justice/Corbis RF

developmental connection

Religion

Religion can fulfill some important psychological needs in older adults, helping them face impending death and accept the inevitable losses of old age. Connect to "Moral Development, Values, and Religion."

bargaining Kübler-Ross' third stage of dying, in which the dying person develops the hope that death can somehow be postponed.

depression Kübler-Ross' fourth stage of dying, in which the dying person perceives the certainty of her or his death. A period of depression or preparatory grief may appear.

acceptance Kübler-Ross' fifth stage of dying, in which the dying person develops a sense of peace, an acceptance of her or his fate, and, in many cases, a desire to be left alone.

their lives—they may become more alert and cheerful. Giving nursing home residents options for control can improve their attitudes and increase their longevity (Rodin & Langer, 1977).

Denial also may be a fruitful way for some individuals to approach death. It can be adaptive or maladaptive. Denial can be used to avoid the destructive impact of shock by delaying the necessity of dealing with one's death. Denial can insulate the individual from having to cope with intense feelings of anger and hurt—however, if denial keeps us from having a life-saving operation, it clearly is maladaptive. Denial is neither good nor bad; its adaptive qualities need to be evaluated on an individual basis.

THE CONTEXTS IN WHICH PEOPLE DIE

For dying individuals, the context in which they die is important (Hooyman & Kiyak, 2011). More than 50 percent of Americans die in hospitals, and nearly 20 percent die in nursing homes. Some people spend their final days in isolation and fear. An increasing number of people choose to die in the humane atmosphere of hospice care. A recent Canadian study revealed that 71 percent preferred to be at home if they were near death, 15 percent preferred a hospice/palliative care facility, 7 percent a hospital, and only 2 percent a nursing home (Wilson & others, 2013).

Hospitals offer several important advantages to the dying individual—for example, professional staff members are readily available, and the medical technology present may prolong life. But a hospital may not be the best place for many people to die. Although most individuals say they would rather die at home as indicated in the survey described above, many feel that they will be a burden at home, that there is limited space there, and that dying at home may alter relationships. Individuals who are facing death also worry about the competency and availability of emergency medical treatment if they remain at home.

Review Connect Reflect

 LG4 Explain the psychological aspects involved in facing one's own death and the contexts in which people die

Review
- What are Kübler-Ross' five stages of dying? What conclusions can be reached about them?
- What roles do perceived control and denial play in facing one's own death?
- What are the contexts in which people die?

Connect
- In this section you learned that the extent to which people have found meaning and purpose in their lives is linked with the way they approach death. In the chapter on "Moral Development, Values, and Religion," what did Roy Baumeister and Kathleen Vohs say are the four main needs for meaning that guide how people try to make sense of their lives?

Reflect Your Own Personal Journey of Life
- How do you think you will psychologically handle facing your own death?

5 Coping with the Death of Someone Else   **LG5** Identify ways to cope with the death of another person

| Communicating with a Dying Person | Grieving | Making Sense of the World | Losing a Life Partner | Forms of Mourning |

Loss can come in many forms in our lives—divorce, a pet's death, loss of a job—but no loss is greater than that which comes through the death of someone we love and care for: a parent, child, sibling, spouse, relative, or friend. In the ratings of life's stresses that require the most adjustment, death of a spouse is given the highest number. How should we communicate with a dying individual? How do we cope with the death of someone we love?

Communicating with a Dying Person

Effective strategies for communicating with a dying person include these:

1. Establish your presence, be at the same eye level; don't be afraid to touch the dying person—dying individuals are often starved for human touch.

2. Eliminate distraction—for example, ask whether it is okay to turn off the TV. Realize that excessive small talk can be a distraction.

3. Dying individuals who are very frail often have little energy. If the dying person you are visiting is very frail, you may not want to visit for very long.

4. Don't insist that the dying person feel acceptance about death if he or she wants to deny the reality of the situation; on the other hand, don't insist on denial if the dying individual indicates acceptance.

5. Allow the dying person to express guilt or anger; encourage the expression of feelings.

6. Don't be afraid to ask the person what the expected outcome for the illness is. Discuss alternatives and unfinished business.

7. Sometimes dying individuals don't have access to other people. Ask the dying person whether there is anyone he or she would like to see whom you can contact.

8. Encourage the dying individual to reminisce, especially if you have memories in common.

What are some good strategies for communicating with a dying person?
© Stockbroker/Photolibrary RF

9. Talk with the individual when she or he wishes to talk. If this is impossible, make a later appointment and keep it.

10. Express your regard for the dying individual. Don't be afraid to express love, and don't be afraid to say good-bye.

How would you adjust these strategies if the dying person were very young or very old?

COMMUNICATING WITH A DYING PERSON

Most psychologists stress that it is best for dying individuals to know that they are dying and that significant others know they are dying so they can interact and communicate with each other on the basis of this mutual knowledge. What are some of the advantages of this open awareness for the dying individual? First, dying individuals can close their lives in accord with their own ideas about proper dying. Second, they may be able to complete some plans and projects, can make arrangements for survivors, and can participate in decisions about a funeral and burial. Third, dying individuals have the opportunity to reminisce, to converse with others who have been important in their life, and to end life conscious of what life has been like. And fourth, dying individuals have more understanding of what is happening within their bodies and what the medical staff is doing to them (Kalish, 1981). In the *Connecting Development to Life* interlude, you can read further about effective communication strategies with a dying person.

GRIEVING

Grief is a complex emotional state that is an evolving process with multiple dimensions. Our exploration of grief focuses on dimensions of grieving and how coping may vary with the type of death.

Dimensions of Grieving **Grief** is the emotional numbness, disbelief, separation anxiety, despair, sadness, and loneliness that accompany the loss of someone we love. Grief is not a simple emotional state but rather a complex, evolving process with multiple dimensions (Barbosa, Sa, & Carlos-Rocha, 2014; Maccallum & others 2015; Romero, Ott, & Kelber, 2014). An important dimension of grief is pining for the lost person. Pining or yearning

Everyone can master grief but he who has it.

—**WILLIAM SHAKESPEARE**
English playwright, 17th century

grief The emotional numbness, disbelief, separation anxiety, despair, sadness, and loneliness that accompany the loss of someone we love.

reflects an intermittent, recurrent wish or need to recover the lost person. Another important dimension of grief is separation anxiety, which not only includes pining and preoccupation with thoughts of the deceased person but also focuses on places and things associated with the deceased, as well as crying or sighing (Root & Exline, 2014). Grief may also involve despair and sadness, which include a sense of hopelessness and defeat, depressive symptoms, apathy, loss of meaning for activities that used to involve the person who is gone, and growing desolation (Boer & others, 2014). A recent study found that older adults who were bereaved had more dysregulated cortisol patterns, indicative of the intensity of their stress (Holland & others, 2014). And a recent study found that college students who lost someone close to them in campus shootings had severe posttraumatic stress symptoms four months after the shootings and were more likely to experience severe grief one year after the shootings (Smith & others, 2015).

These feelings occur repeatedly shortly after a loss (Shear, 2012a, b). As time passes, pining and protest over the loss tend to diminish, although episodes of depression and apathy may remain or increase. The sense of separation anxiety and loss may continue to the end of one's life, but most of us emerge from grief's tears, turning our attention once again to productive tasks and regaining a more positive view of life (Lund & others, 2009; Mendes, 2015).

The grieving process is more like a roller-coaster ride than an orderly progression of stages with clear-cut time frames. The ups and downs of grief often involve rapidly changing emotions, meeting the challenges of learning new skills, detecting personal weaknesses and limitations, creating new patterns of behavior, and forming new friendships and relationships. For most individuals, grief becomes more manageable over time, with fewer abrupt highs and lows (Maciejewski & others, 2007). But many grieving spouses report that even though time has brought some healing, they have never gotten over their loss. They have just learned to live with it. A recent study found that individuals in the early stages of spousal bereavement are at increased risk for distress in situations with special significance for the couple, such as the late spouse's birthday or a wedding anniversary (Carr & others, 2014).

An estimated 80 to 90 percent of survivors experience normal or uncomplicated grief reactions that include sadness and even disbelief or considerable anguish. By six months after their loss, they accept it as a reality, are more optimistic about the future, and function competently in their everyday lives. However, six months after their loss, approximately 7 to 10 percent of bereaved individuals have difficulty moving on with their life, feel numb or detached, believe their life is empty without the deceased, and feel that the future has no meaning (Maccalum & Bryant, 2013; Shear, Ghesquiere, & Glickman, 2013). This type of grief, which involves enduring despair that remains unresolved over an extended period of time, has been labeled **complicated grief or prolonged grief disorder** (Prigerson & Maciejewski, 2014). Complicated grief usually has negative consequences for physical and mental health (Arizmendi & O'Connor, 2015; Marques & others, 2013; Shear, 2015). A person who loses someone on whom he or she was emotionally dependent is often at greatest risk for developing prolonged grief (Rodriquez Villar & others, 2012).

Complicated grief or prolonged grief disorder was recently considered for possible inclusion in DSM-V, the psychiatric classification system for mental health disorders (Bryant, 2012, 2013). Although it ended up not being included as a psychiatric disorder, it was described in an Appendix (American Psychiatric Association, 2013). The argument for not including complicated grief or prolonged grief as a psychiatric disorder was based on concerns that normal grieving would be turned into a medical condition.

Recently, there has been a substantial increase in research on complicated grief (Boelen, 2013; Supiano & Luptak, 2014). The following studies provide further information about the nature of complicated grief:

· Prolonged grief was more likely to occur when individuals had lost their spouse, lost a loved one unexpectedly, or had spent time with the deceased every day in the last week of the person's life (Fujisawa & others, 2010).

· Adults with depression were more likely to also have complicated grief (Sung & others, 2011).

· Complicated grief was more likely to be present in older adults when the grief occurred in response to the death of a child or a spouse (Newsom & others, 2011).

· Of individuals diagnosed with complicated grief, 40 percent reported at least one full or limited symptom grief-related panic attack in the past week (Bui & others, 2015).

What are some different types of grief?
© Digital Vision RF

Another type of grief is **disenfranchised grief,** which describes an individual's grief over a deceased person that is a socially ambiguous loss and can't be openly mourned or supported (Cavuoti, 2015; Gill & Lowes, 2014; Mortell, 2015). Examples of disenfranchised grief include a relationship that isn't socially recognized such as an ex-spouse, a hidden loss such as an abortion, and circumstances of the death that are stigmatized such as death because of AIDS. Disenfranchised grief may intensify an individual's grief because it cannot be publicly acknowledged. This type of grief may be hidden or repressed for many years, only to be reawakened by later deaths.

Dual-Process Model of Coping with Bereavement   The **dual-process model** of coping with bereavement consists of two main dimensions: (1) loss-oriented stressors and (2) restoration-oriented stressors (Stroebe, Schut, & Stroebe, 2005). Loss-oriented stressors focus on the deceased individual and can include grief work and both positive and negative reappraisal of the loss. A positive reappraisal of the loss might include acknowledging that death brought relief at the end of suffering, whereas a negative reappraisal might involve yearning for the loved one and rumination about the death. Restoration-oriented stressors involve the secondary stressors that emerge as indirect outcomes of bereavement (Caserta & others, 2014). They can include a changing identity (such as from "wife" to "widow") and mastering skills (such as dealing with finances). Restoration rebuilds "shattered assumptions about the world and one's own place in it" (Stroebe & others, 2005).

In the dual-process model, effective coping with bereavement often involves an oscillation between coping with loss and coping with restoration. Earlier models often emphasized a sequence of coping with loss through such strategies as grief work as an initial phase, followed by restoration efforts. However, in the dual-process model, coping with loss and engaging in restoration can be carried out concurrently (Richardson, 2007). According to this model, the person coping with death might be involved in grief group therapy while settling the affairs of the loved one. Oscillation might occur in the short term during a specific day as well as across weeks, months, and even years. Although loss and restoration coping can occur concurrently, over time there often is an initial emphasis on coping with loss followed by greater emphasis on restoration.

Coping and Type of Death   The impact of death on surviving individuals is strongly influenced by the circumstances under which the death occurs (Kristensen, Weisaeth, & Heir, 2012). Deaths that are sudden, untimely, violent, or traumatic are likely to have more intense and prolonged effects on surviving individuals and make the coping process more difficult for them (Maercker & Lalor, 2012). Such deaths often are accompanied by post-traumatic stress disorder (PTSD) symptoms, such as intrusive thoughts, flashbacks, nightmares, sleep disturbance, problems in concentrating, and others (Nakajima & others, 2012). The death of a child can be especially devastating and extremely difficult for parents (Caeymaex & others, 2013).

In sum, people grieve in a variety of ways (Carr, 2012). Thus, there is no one right, ideal way to grieve. There are many different ways to feel about a deceased person and no set series of stages that the bereaved must pass through to become well adjusted. What is needed is an understanding that healthy coping with the death of a loved one involves growth, flexibility, and appropriateness within a cultural context.

MAKING SENSE OF THE WORLD

One beneficial aspect of grieving is that it stimulates many individuals to try to make sense of their world (Carr, 2009, 2012; Park, 2010, 2012; Meert & others, 2015). A common occurrence is to go over again and again all of the events that led up to the death. In the days and weeks after the death, the closest family members share experiences with each other, sometimes reminiscing about family experiences. One study revealed that finding meaning in the death of a spouse was linked to a lower level of anger during bereavement (Kim, 2009). In a recent study, meaning-making following a child's death was examined (Meert & others, 2015). From 8 to 20 weeks following the child's death, the child's intensive care physician conducted a bereavement meeting with the parents. These meetings were conducted with 53 parents of 35 children who had died. Four meaning-

developmental **connection**

Stress and Coping

Meaning-making coping includes drawing on beliefs, values, and goals to change the meaning of a stressful situation, especially in times of chronic stress such as when a loved one dies. Connect to "Moral Development, Values, and Religion."

complicated grief or prolonged grief disorder Grief that involves enduring despair and remains unresolved over an extended period of time.

disenfranchised grief Grief involving a deceased person that is a socially ambiguous loss that can't be openly mourned or supported.

dual-process model A model of coping with bereavement that emphasizes oscillation between loss-oriented stressors and restoration-oriented stressors.

These restaurant workers, who lost their jobs on 9/11/01, have made a bittersweet return by establishing a New York restaurant they call their own. Colors, named for the many nationalities and ethnic groups among its owners, is believed to be the city's first cooperative restaurant. World-famous restaurant Windows on the World was destroyed and 73 workers killed when the Twin Towers were destroyed by terrorists. The former Windows survivors at the new venture planned to split 60 percent of the profits between themselves and to donate the rest to a fund to open other cooperative restaurants.
© Thomas Hinton/Splash News/Newscom

making processes were identified in the meetings: (1) sense making (seeking biomedical explanations for the death, revisiting parents' prior decisions and roles, and assigning blame); (2) benefit finding (exploration of possible positive consequences of the death, such as ways to help others, providing feedback to the hospital, and making donations); (3) continuing bonds (reminiscing about the child, sharing photographs, and participating in community events to honor the child); and (4) identity reconstruction (changes in the parents' sense of self, including changes in relationships, work, and home).

In trying to make sense of a person's death, each individual may offer a piece of death's puzzle. "When I saw him last Saturday, he looked as though he were rallying," says one family member. "Do you think it might have had something to do with his sister's illness?" remarks another. "I doubt it, but I heard from an aide that he fell going to the bathroom that morning," comments yet another. "That explains the bruise on his elbow," says the first individual. "No wonder he told me that he was angry because he could not seem to do anything right," chimes in a fourth family member. So it goes in the attempt to understand why someone who was rallying on Saturday was dead on Wednesday.

When a death is caused by an accident or a disaster, the effort to make sense of it is pursued more vigorously. As added pieces of news come trickling in, they are integrated into the puzzle. The bereaved want to put the death into a perspective that they can understand—divine intervention, a curse from a neighboring tribe, a logical sequence of cause and effect, or whatever it may be.

LOSING A LIFE PARTNER

In 2010 in the United States, 13 percent of men and 40 percent of women age 65 and older were widowed (U.S. Census Bureau, 2012). Those left behind after the death of an intimate partner often suffer profound grief and often endure financial loss, loneliness, increased physical illness, and psychological disorders, including depression (Das, 2013; Lee, 2014). A study of widowed individuals 75 years and older found that loss of a spouse increases the likelihood of psychiatric visits and an earlier death (Moller & others, 2011). In another study, becoming widowed was associated with a 48 percent increase in risk of mortality (Sullivan & Fenelon, 2014). In this study, mortality risk increased for men if their wives' deaths were not expected but for women unexpected death of a husband mattered less in terms of their mortality risk. A recent study also revealed that widowed individuals who reported higher marital quality subsequently had more symptoms of depression after their spouse died (Schaan, 2013). In another recent study, widowed individuals, especially those in age-heterogamous unions (where the partners were of significantly different ages), had worse mental health than married persons but not worse physical health (Choi & Vasunilashorn, 2014). Another recent study found that widowed individuals in 2011, especially women, reported fewer social and financial difficulties than their counterparts in 1979 had reported (Perrig-Chiello & others, 2015). Nonetheless, there were no differences in the depressive symptoms and psychological difficulties of the widowed individuals in the two different time periods.

Becoming widowed is likely to be especially difficult for individuals who have been happily married for a number of decades. In such circumstances, losing their spouse, who may also have been their best friend and the person with whom they lived a deeply connected life, can be an extremely emotional event that is difficult to cope with.

Surviving spouses seek to cope with the loss of their spouse in various ways (McKiernan & others, 2013; Park, 2012). In one study, widowed individuals were more likely to intensify their religious and spiritual beliefs following the death of a spouse, and this increase was linked with a lower level of grief (Brown & others, 2004). Another study revealed that finding meaning in the death of a spouse was linked to a lower level of anger during bereavement (Kim, 2009). And a recent study revealed that widowed persons who did not expect to be reunited with their loved ones in the afterlife reported more depression, anger, and intrusive thoughts at 6 and 18 months after their loss (Carr & Sharp, 2014).

How Is Widowhood Related to Women's Physical and Mental Health?

A three-year longitudinal study of more than 130,000 women 50 to 79 years of age in the United States, as part of the Women's Health Initiative, examined the relation of widowhood to physical and mental health, health behaviors, and health outcomes (Wilcox & others, 2003). Women were categorized as (1) remaining married, (2) transitioning from married to widowed, (3) remaining widowed, and (4) transitioning from widowed to married. Widows were further subdivided into the recently widowed (widowed for less than one year) and longer-term widowed (widowed for more than one year).

The measures used to assess the older women's health were:

- *Physical health.* Blood pressure was assessed after five minutes of quiet rest using the average of two readings with 30 seconds between the readings. Hypertension was defined as more than 140/90. Body mass index (BMI) was calculated and used to determine whether a woman was obese. A health survey assessed physical function and health status.
- *Mental health.* Depressive symptoms were assessed by a six-item depression scale, with participants rating the frequency of their depressed thoughts during the past week. The participant's self-report of antidepressant medicine use was also obtained. Information about social functioning and mental health was based on participants' responses on the Social Functioning Scale (Ware, Kosinski, & Dewey, 2000).
- *Health behaviors.* Dietary behaviors were assessed with a modified version of the National Cancer Institute Health Habits and

History Questionnaire. Participants also were asked if they smoked tobacco and, if so, how much. To assess physical activity, participants were asked how often they walked outside the home each week and the extent to which they engaged in strenuous or moderate exercise. To assess health-care use, they were asked whether they had visited their doctor in the past year.

- *Health outcomes.* Cardiovascular disease and cancer occurrences were assessed annually and any overnight hospitalizations were noted.

At the beginning of the three-year study, married women reported better physical and mental health, and better health in general, than widowed women. Women who remained married over the three-year period of the study showed stability in mental health, recent widows experienced marked impairments in mental health, and longer-term widows showed stability or slight improvements in mental health. Both groups of widows (recent and longer term) reported more unintentional weight loss across the three years.

These findings underscore the resilience of older women and their capacity to reestablish connections but point to the need for services that strengthen social support for those who have difficulty during the transition from marriage to widowhood. How might the study's specific findings be applied to new or improved social services for widowed women?

Many widows are lonely and benefit considerably from social support (Ben-Zur, 2012). The poorer and less educated they are, the lonelier they tend to be. The bereaved are also at increased risk for many health problems (Mechakra-Tahiri & others, 2010). How might you expect widowhood to affect a woman's physical and mental health, for instance? In the *Connecting with Research* interlude, researchers explore this link.

Optimal adjustment after a death depends on various factors. Women do better than men largely because, in our society, women are responsible for the emotional life of a couple, whereas men usually manage the finances and material goods (Fry, 2001). Thus, women have better networks of friends, closer relationships with relatives, and experience in taking care of themselves psychologically (Antonucci, Birditt, & Ajrouch, 2013). Older widows do better than younger widows, perhaps because the death of a partner is more expected for older women. For their part, widowers usually have more money than widows do, and they are far more likely to remarry.

One study found that psychological and religious factors—such as personal meaning, optimism, the importance of religion, and access to religious support—were related to the psychological well-being of older adults following the loss of a spouse (Fry, 2001). Other studies have indicated that religiosity and coping skills are related to well-being following the loss of a spouse in late adulthood (Whitbourne & Meeks, 2011; Wortmann & Park, 2008).

Two recent studies revealed that volunteering and helping behavior improved the well-being of widowed individuals. In one study, volunteering following spousal loss helped to protect against depressive symptoms and increased self-efficacy (Li, 2007). In another study,

developmental **connection**

Community

For older adults, social support is linked with a reduction in the symptoms of disease and mortality. Connect to "Peers and the Sociocultural World."

A widow with a photo of her husband who was recently killed in Afghanistan. *What are some factors that are related to the adjustment of a widow after the death of her husband?*
© Peter Power/Toronto Star/Getty Images

following spousal loss, engaging in helping behavior (providing instrumental support to others) was linked to an accelerated decline in the helper's depressive symptoms 6 to 18 months following spousal loss (Brown & others, 2008).

For either widows or widowers, social support helps them adjust to the death of a spouse (Antonucci & others, 2013; Powers, Bisconti, & Bergeman, 2014). The Widow-to-Widow program, begun in the 1960s, provides support for newly widowed women. Volunteer widows reach out to other widows, introducing them to others who may have similar problems, leading group discussions, and organizing social activities. The program has been adopted by the AARP and disseminated throughout the United States as the Widowed Persons Service. The model has since been adopted by numerous community organizations to provide support for those going through a difficult transition.

FORMS OF MOURNING

One decision facing the bereaved is what to do with the body. In the United States, in 2013, 45 percent of deaths were followed by cremation—a significant increase from a cremation rate of 14 percent in 1985 and 27 percent in 2000 (Cremation Association of North America, 2015). Cremation is more popular in the Pacific region of the United States, less popular in the South. Cremation also is more popular in Canada than in the United States and most popular of all in Japan and many other Asian countries. In the United States, the trend is away from public funerals and displaying the dead body in an open casket and toward private funerals followed by a memorial ceremony (Callahan, 2009).

The funeral industry has been the source of controversy in recent years. Funeral directors and their supporters argue that the funeral provides a form of closure to the relationship with the deceased, especially when there is an open casket. Their critics claim that funeral directors are just trying to make money and that embalming is grotesque. One way to avoid being exploited during bereavement is to purchase funeral arrangements in advance.

In some cultures, a ceremonial meal is held after death; in others, a black armband is worn for one year following a death. The family and the community have important roles in mourning in some cultures. Two of those cultures are the Amish and traditional Judaism (Worthington, 1989).

The Amish are a conservative group with approximately 80,000 members in the United States, Ontario, and several small settlements in South and Central America. The Amish live in a family-oriented society in which family and community support is essential for survival. Today, they live at the same unhurried pace as did their ancestors, using horses instead of cars and facing death with the same steadfast faith as their forebears. At the time of death, close neighbors assume the responsibility of notifying others of the death. The Amish community handles virtually all aspects of the funeral.

A funeral in the United States.
© Mike Kemp/Rubberball/Getty Images RF

A crowd gathered at a cremation ceremony in Bali, Indonesia, balancing decorative containers on their heads.
© Agung Parameswara/ZumaPress/Newscom

The funeral service is held in a barn in warmer months and in a house during colder months. Calm acceptance of death, influenced by a deep religious faith, is an integral part of the Amish culture. Following the funeral, a high level of support is given to the bereaved family for at least a year. Visits to the family, special scrapbooks and handmade items for the family, new work projects started for the widow, and quilting days that combine fellowship and productivity are among the supports given to the bereaved family. A profound example of the Amish culture's religious faith and acceptance of death occurred after Charles Roberts shot and killed five Amish schoolgirls and then apparently took his own life in October 2006 in the small town of Nickel Mines in Bart Township, Pennsylvania. Soon after the murders and suicide, members of the Amish community visited the widow of the murderer and offered their support and forgiveness.

A funeral procession of horse-drawn buggies on their way to the burial of five young Amish girls who were murdered in October 2006. A remarkable aspect of their mourning involved the outpouring of support and forgiveness they gave to the widow of the murderer.
© Glenn Fawcett/Baltimore Sun/MCT/Getty Images

The family and community also have specific and important roles in mourning in traditional Judaism. The program of mourning is divided into graduated time periods, each with its appropriate practices. The observance of these practices is required of the spouse and the immediate blood relatives of the deceased. The first period is aninut, the period between death and burial—which must take place within one day. The next two periods make up avelut, or mourning proper. The first of these is shivah, a period of seven days, which commences with the burial. It is followed by sheloshim, the 30-day period following the burial, including shivah. At the end of sheloshim, the mourning process is considered over for all but one's parents. For parents, mourning continues for 11 months, although observances are minimal.

The seven-day period of the shivah is especially important in traditional Judaism. The mourners, sitting together as a group through an extended period, have an opportunity to project their feelings to the group as a whole. Visits from others during shivah may help the mourner deal with feelings of guilt. After shivah, the mourner is encouraged to resume normal social interaction. In fact, it is customary for the mourners to walk together a short distance as a symbol of their return to society. In its entirety, the elaborate mourning system of traditional Judaism is designed to promote personal growth and to reintegrate the individual into the community.

Meeting in a Jewish graveyard.
© Gil Cohen Magen/Reuters/Landov Images

Some Final Comments   We have arrived at the end of *A Topical Approach to Life-Span Development*. I hope this edition and course have been a window to the life span of the human species and a window to your own personal journey in life.

Our study of the human life span has been long and complex. You have read about many physical, cognitive, and socioemotional changes that take place from conception through death. This is a good time to reflect on what you have learned. Which theories, studies, and ideas were especially interesting to you? What did you learn about your own development?

I wish you all the best in the remaining years of your journey though the human life span.

John W. Santrock

Review

- What are some strategies for communicating with a dying person?
- What is the nature of grieving?
- How is making sense of the world a beneficial outcome of grieving?
- What are some characteristics and outcomes of losing a life partner?
- What are some forms of mourning? What is the nature of the funeral?

Connect

- In this section you learned that one advantage of knowing you are dying is that you have the opportunity to reminisce. Which of Erikson's stages of development involves reflecting on the past and either piecing together a positive life review or concluding that one's life has not been well spent?

Reflect *Your Own Personal Journey of Life*

- What are considered appropriate forms of mourning in the culture in which you live?

reach your **learning goals**

Death, Dying, and Grieving

1 The Death System and Cultural Contexts

LG1 Describe the death system and its cultural and historical contexts

The Death System and Its Cultural Variations

· In Kastenbaum's view, every culture has a death system that involves people, places, times, objects, and symbols. He also argues that the death system serves certain functions in a culture that include issuing warnings and predictions, preventing death, caring for the dying, disposing of the dead, attaining social consolation after the death, making sense of the death, and killing. Most societies throughout history have had philosophical or religious beliefs about death, and most societies have rituals that deal with death. Most cultures do not view death as the end of existence—spiritual life is thought to continue. The United States has been described as more of a death-denying and death-avoiding culture than most cultures.

Changing Historical Circumstances

· When, where, and why people die have changed historically. Today, death occurs most often among older adults. More than 80 percent of all deaths in the United States now occur in a hospital or other institution; our exposure to death in the family has been minimized.

2 Defining Death and Life/Death Issues

LG2 Evaluate issues in determining death and decisions regarding death

Issues in Determining Death

· Twenty-five years ago, determining whether someone was dead was simpler than it is today. Brain death is a neurological definition of death which states that a person is brain dead when all electrical activity of the brain has ceased for a specified period of time. Medical experts debate whether this definition should include both the higher and lower brain functions or just the higher cortical functions. Most physicians use the cessation of brain function (both higher and lower) as a standard for determining death.

| Decisions Regarding Life, Death, and Health Care | · Decisions regarding life, death, and health care can involve advance care planning, euthanasia, and hospice care. Advance care planning can involve living wills and advance directives; recently, Physician Orders for Life-Sustaining Treatment, which is more specific than previous advance directives, was created. Euthanasia is the act of painlessly ending the life of a person who is suffering from an incurable disease or disability. Distinctions are made between active and passive euthanasia. Hospice care emphasizes reducing pain and suffering rather than prolonging life. |

3 A Developmental Perspective on Death

 LG3 Discuss death and attitudes about it at different points in development

| Causes of Death | · Although death is more likely to occur in late adulthood, it can come at any point in development. In children and younger adults, death is more likely to occur because of accidents; in older adults, death is more likely to occur because of chronic diseases. |

| Attitudes Toward Death at Different Points in the Life Span | · Infants do not have a concept of death. Preschool children also have little or no concept of death. Preschool children sometimes blame themselves for a person's death. During the elementary school years, children develop a more realistic orientation toward death. Most psychologists stress that honesty is the best strategy for helping children cope with death. Death may be glossed over in adolescence. Adolescents have more abstract, philosophical views of death than children do. There is no evidence that a special orientation toward death emerges in early adulthood. Middle adulthood is a time when adults show a heightened consciousness about death and death anxiety. The deaths of some persons, especially children and younger adults, are often perceived to be more tragic than those of others, such as very old adults, who have had an opportunity to live a long life. Older adults often show less death anxiety than middle-aged adults, but older adults experience and converse about death more. Attitudes about death may vary considerably among adults of any age. |

| Suicide | · Among the factors that place people at risk for suicide are serious physical illnesses, feelings of hopelessness, social isolation, failure in school and work, loss of loved ones, serious financial difficulties, and depression. Suicide behavior is rare in childhood but escalates in adolescence. Both earlier and later experiences can influence suicide. U.S. suicide rates remain rather stable in early and middle adulthood, then increase in late adulthood. |

4 Facing One's Own Death

 LG4 Explain the psychological aspects involved in facing one's own death and the contexts in which people die

| Kubler-Ross' Stages of Dying | · Kübler-Ross proposed five stages of dying: denial and isolation, anger, bargaining, depression, and acceptance. Not all individuals go through the same sequence. Critics emphasize that many individuals don't go through the stages in the order she proposed. |

| Perceived Control and Denial | · Perceived control and denial may work together as an adaptive orientation for the dying individual. Denial can be adaptive or maladaptive, depending on the circumstances. |

| The Contexts in Which People Die | · Most deaths in the United States occur in hospitals; this has advantages and disadvantages. Most individuals say they would rather die at home, but they worry that they will be a burden and they are concerned about the availability of medical care. |

5 Coping with the Death of Someone Else

 LG5 Identify ways to cope with the death of another person

| Communicating with a Dying Person | · Most psychologists recommend an open communication system with the dying. Communication should not dwell on pathology or preparation for death but should emphasize the dying person's strengths. |

Grieving	· Grief is the emotional numbness, disbelief, separation anxiety, despair, sadness, and loneliness that accompany the loss of someone we love. Grief is multidimensional and in some cases may last for years. Complicated grief or prolonged grief disorder involves enduring despair that remains unresolved over an extended period of time. In the dual-process model of coping with bereavement, oscillation occurs between two dimensions: loss-oriented stressors and restoration-oriented stressors. Grief and coping vary with the type of death. There are cultural variations in grieving.
Making Sense of the World	· The grieving process may stimulate individuals to strive to make sense out of their world; each individual may contribute a piece to death's puzzle.
Losing a Life Partner	· Usually the most difficult loss is the death of a spouse. The bereaved are at risk for many health problems, although there are variations in the distress experienced by a surviving spouse. Social support benefits widows and widowers.
Forms of Mourning	· Forms of mourning vary across cultures. Approximately 58 percent of corpses are disposed of by burial, 42 percent by cremation. An important aspect of mourning in many cultures is the funeral. In recent years, the funeral industry has been the focus of controversy. In some cultures, a ceremonial meal is held after death.

key **terms**

acceptance	brain death	depression	grief
active euthanasia	complicated grief or prolonged	disenfranchised grief	hospice
anger	grief disorder	dual-process model	palliative care
bargaining	denial and isolation	euthanasia	passive euthanasia

key **people**

Robert Kastenbaum   Elisabeth Kübler-Ross

glossary

A

A-not-B error   This error occurs when infants make the mistake of selecting the familiar hiding place (A) of an object rather than its new hiding place (B) as they progress into substage 4 in Piaget's sensorimotor stage.

acceptance   Kübler-Ross' fifth stage of dying, in which the dying person develops a sense of peace, an acceptance of her or his fate, and, in many cases, a desire to be left alone.

accommodation   Piagetian concept of adjusting schemes to fit new information and experiences.

accommodation of the eye   The eye's ability to focus and maintain an image on the retina.

active (niche-picking) genotype-environment correlations   Correlations that exist when children seek out environments they find compatible and stimulating.

active euthanasia   Death induced deliberately, as by injecting a lethal dose of a drug.

activity theory   The theory that the more active and involved older adults are, the more likely they are to be satisfied with their lives.

adolescent egocentrism   The heightened self-consciousness of adolescents, which is reflected in adolescents' beliefs that others are as interested in them as they are themselves, and in adolescents' sense of personal uniqueness and invincibility.

adoption study   A study in which investigators seek to discover whether, in behavior and psychological characteristics, adopted children are more like their adoptive parents, who provided a home environment, or more like their biological parents, who contributed their heredity. Another form of the adoption study compares adoptive and biological siblings.

aerobic exercise   Sustained activity that stimulates heart and lung functioning.

affectionate love   Also called companionate love, this type of love occurs when individuals desire to have another person near and have a deep, caring affection for the person.

affordances   Opportunities for interaction offered by objects that fit within our capabilities to perform activities.

ageism   Prejudice against people because of their age, especially prejudice against older adults.

altruism   An unselfish interest and voluntary effort in helping another person.

Alzheimer disease   A progressive, irreversible brain disorder characterized by a gradual deterioration of memory, reasoning, language, and eventually, physical function.

amygdala   A part of the brain's limbic system that is the seat of emotions such as anger.

androgens   A class of sex hormones—an important one of which is testosterone—that primarily promotes the development of male genitals and secondary sex characteristics.

anger   Kübler-Ross' second stage of dying, in which the dying person's denial gives way to anger, resentment, rage, and envy.

anger cry   A cry similar to the basic cry but with more excess air forced through the vocal cords.

animism   A facet of preoperational thought—the belief that inanimate objects have lifelike qualities and are capable of action.

anorexia nervosa   An eating disorder that involves the relentless pursuit of thinness through starvation.

anxious attachment style   An attachment style that describes adults who demand closeness, are less trusting, and are more emotional, jealous, and possessive.

Apgar Scale   A widely used method to assess the health of newborns at one and five minutes after birth; it evaluates an infant's heart rate, respiratory effort, muscle tone, body color, and reflex irritability.

aphasia   A loss or impairment of language processing resulting from damage to Broca's area or Wernicke's area.

Asperger syndrome   A relatively mild autism spectrum disorder in which the child has relatively good verbal language skills, milder nonverbal language problems, and a restricted range of interests and relationships.

assimilation   Piagetian concept in which children use existing schemes to incorporate new information.

attachment   A close emotional bond between two people.

attention   Focusing of mental resources.

attention deficit hyperactivity disorder (ADHD)   A disability in which children consistently show one or more of the following characteristics: (1) inattention, (2) hyperactivity, and (3) impulsivity.

authoritarian parenting   A restrictive, punitive style in which parents exhort the child to follow their directions and to respect their work and effort. Firm limits are placed on the child, and little verbal exchange is allowed.

authoritative parenting   A style that encourages children to be independent but still places limits and controls on children's actions; extensive verbal give-and-take is allowed, and parents are warm and nurturant toward the child.

autism spectrum disorders (ASDs)   Also called pervasive developmental disorders, these range from the severe disorder labeled autistic disorder to the milder disorder called Asperger syndrome. Children with these disorders are characterized by problems in social interaction, verbal and nonverbal communication, and repetitive behaviors.

autistic disorder   A severe autism spectrum disorder that has its onset in the first three years of life and includes deficiencies in social relationships; abnormalities in communication; and restricted, repetitive, and stereotyped patterns of behavior.

automaticity   The ability to process information with little or no effort.

autonomous morality   The second stage of moral development in Piaget's theory, displayed by children about 10 years of age and older. At this stage, children become aware that rules and laws are created by people and that in judging an action they should consider the actor's intentions as well as the consequences.

average children   Children who receive an average number of both positive and negative nominations from their peers.

avoidant attachment style   An attachment style that describes adults who are hesitant about getting involved in romantic relationships and, once in a relationship, tend to distance themselves from their partner.

B

bargaining   Kübler-Ross' third stage of dying, in which the dying person develops the hope that death can somehow be postponed.

basic cry   A rhythmic pattern usually consisting of a cry, a briefer silence, a shorter inspiratory whistle that is higher pitched than the main cry, and then a brief rest before the next cry.

Bayley Scales of Infant Development   Widely used scales, developed by Nancy Bayley, for assessing infant development. The current version, the Bayley-III, has five scales: cognitive, language, motor, socio-emotional, and adaptive; the first three are administered to the infant, the latter two to the caregiver.

behavior genetics   The field that seeks to discover the influence of heredity and environment on individual differences in human traits and development.

bicultural identity   Identifying both with one's own ethnic minority group and with the majority culture.

Big Five factors of personality   The view that these five key traits are the best way to characterize personality: openness to experience, conscientiousness, extraversion, agreeableness, and neuroticism.

biological processes   Processes that produce changes in an individual's physical nature.

bisexuality   Sexual attraction to people of both sexes.

bonding   The formation of a close connection, especially a physical bond between parents and their newborn in the period shortly after birth.

brain death   A neurological definition of death—an individual is dead when all electrical activity of the brain has ceased for a specified period of time.

brainstorming Technique in which individuals are encouraged to come up with creative ideas in a group, play off each other's ideas, and say practically whatever comes to mind that is relevant to a particular issue.

Broca's area An area of the brain's left frontal lobe that is involved in producing words.

Bronfenbrenner's ecological theory Bronfenbrenner's environmental systems theory that focuses on five environmental systems: microsystem, mesosystem, exosystem, macrosystem, and chronosystem.

bulimia nervosa An eating disorder in which the individual consistently follows a binge-and-purge eating pattern.

C

care perspective The moral perspective of Carol Gilligan; views people in terms of their connectedness with others and emphasizes interpersonal communication, relationships with others, and concern for others.

case study An in-depth look at a single individual.

cataracts A thickening of the lens of the eye that causes vision to become cloudy, opaque, and distorted.

cellular clock theory Leonard Hayflick's theory that the number of times human cells can divide is about 75 to 80. As we age, our cells become less able to divide.

centration Focusing attention on one characteristic to the exclusion of all others.

cephalocaudal pattern The sequence in which the fastest growth occurs at the top of the body—the head—with physical growth in size, weight, and feature differentiation gradually working from top to bottom.

character education A direct moral education program in which students are taught moral literacy to prevent them from engaging in immoral behavior.

child abuse The term used most often by the public and many professionals to refer to both abuse and neglect.

child-centered kindergarten Education that involves the whole child by considering both the child's physical, cognitive, and socioemotional development and the child's needs, interests, and learning styles.

child-directed speech Language spoken in a higher pitch than normal, with simple words and sentences.

child maltreatment The term increasingly used by developmentalists in referring not only to abuse and neglect but also to diverse conditions.

child neglect Failure to provide for a child's basic needs, including physical, educational, or emotional needs.

chromosomes Threadlike structures made up of deoxyribonucleic acid, or DNA.

chronic disorders Disorders characterized by slow onset and long duration.

climacteric The midlife transition during which fertility declines.

cliques Small groups that range from 2 to 12 individuals and average about 5 or 6 individuals. Clique members usually are of the same age and same sex and often engage in similar activities, such as belonging to a club or participating in a sport.

cognitive mechanics The "hardware" of the mind, reflecting the neurophysiological architecture of the brain as developed through evolution. Cognitive mechanics involves the speed and accuracy of the processes involving sensory input, visual and motor memory, discrimination, comparison, and categorization.

cognitive moral education A moral education program based on the belief that students should learn to value things like democracy and justice as their moral reasoning develops; Kohlberg's theory has been the basis for many of the cognitive moral education programs.

cognitive pragmatics The culture-based "software" of the mind. Cognitive pragmatics include reading and writing skills, language comprehension, educational qualifications, professional skills, and also the type of self-knowledge and life skills that helps us to master or cope with life.

cognitive processes Processes that involve changes in an individual's thought, intelligence, and language.

cohabitation Living together in a sexual relationship without being married.

cohort effects Characteristics attributable to a person's time of birth, era, or generation but not to actual age.

collectivism Emphasizing values that serve the group by subordinating personal goals to preserve group integrity, supporting interdependence of members, and promoting harmonious relationships.

commitment A personal investment in identity.

complicated grief or prolonged grief disorder Grief that involves enduring despair and remains unresolved over an extended period of time.

concepts Cognitive groupings of similar objects, events, people, or ideas.

concrete operational stage The third Piagetian stage, which lasts from approximately 7 to 11 years of age; children can perform concrete operations, and logical reasoning replaces intuitive reasoning as long as the reasoning can be applied to specific or concrete examples.

conduct disorder Age-inappropriate actions and attitudes that violate family expectations, society's norms, and the personal or property rights of others.

connectedness Characteristic consisting of two dimensions: mutuality, sensitivity to and respect for others' views; and permeability, openness to others' views.

conscience The component of the superego that punishes the child for behaviors disapproved of by parents by making the child feel guilty and worthless.

conservation The awareness that altering the appearance of an object or a substance does not change its basic properties.

constructive play Combination of sensorimotor/practice play with symbolic representation.

constructivist approach A learner-centered approach that emphasizes the individual's active, cognitive construction of knowledge and understanding with guidance from the teacher.

contemporary life-events approach Approach emphasizing that how a life event influences the individual's development depends not only on the event but also on mediating factors, the individual's adaptation to the life event, the life-stage context, and the sociohistorical context.

continuity-discontinuity issue Debate that focuses on the extent to which development involves gradual, cumulative change (continuity) or distinct stages (discontinuity).

controversial children Children who are frequently nominated both as someone's best friend and as being disliked.

conventional reasoning The second, or intermediate, level in Kohlberg's theory of moral development. At this level, individuals abide by the standards of others such as parents or the laws of society.

convergent thinking Thinking that produces one correct answer; characteristic of the kind of thinking required on conventional intelligence tests.

coparenting The support that parents provide one another in jointly raising a child.

core knowledge approach States that infants are born with domain-specific innate knowledge systems. Among these domain-specific knowledge systems are those involving space, number sense, object permanence, and language.

corpus callosum A large bundle of axon fibers that connects the brain's left and right hemispheres.

correlation coefficient A number based on a statistical analysis that is used to describe the degree of association between two variables.

correlational research A type of research that strives to describe the strength of the relationship between two or more events or characteristics.

creativity The ability to think in novel and unusual ways and to come up with unique solutions to problems.

crisis A period of identity development during which the individual is exploring alternatives.

critical thinking Thinking reflectively and productively, and evaluating the evidence.

cross-cultural studies Comparisons of one culture with one or more other cultures. These provide information about the degree to which development is similar, or universal, across cultures, and the degree to which it is culture-specific.

cross-sectional approach A research strategy in which individuals of different ages are compared at one time.

crowds The crowd is a larger group than a clique. Adolescents usually are members of a crowd based on reputation and may not spend much time together. Many crowds are defined by the activities in which adolescents engage.

crystallized intelligence An individual's accumulated information and verbal skills, which continues to increase with age.

culture The behavior, patterns, beliefs, and all other products of a group of people that are passed on from generation to generation.

culture-fair tests Intelligence tests that are designed to avoid cultural bias.

D

date or acquaintance rape Coercive sexual activity directed at someone with whom the victim is at least casually acquainted.

dementia A global term for any neurological disorder in which the primary symptom is deterioration of mental functioning.

denial and isolation Kübler-Ross' first stage of dying, in which the dying person denies that she or he is really going to die.

depression Kübler-Ross' fourth stage of dying, in which the dying person perceives the certainty of her or his death. A period of depression or preparatory grief may appear.

descriptive research A type of research that aims to observe and record behavior.

development The pattern of movement or change that begins at conception and continues through the human life span.

developmental cascade model Involves connections across domains over time that influence developmental pathways and outcomes.

developmentally appropriate practice (DAP) Education that focuses on the typical developmental patterns of children (age appropriateness) and the uniqueness of each child (individual appropriateness). Such practice contrasts with developmentally inappropriate practice, which has an academic, direct instruction emphasis focused largely on abstract paper-and-pencil activities, seatwork, and rote/drill practice activities.

dialect A variety of language that is distinguished by its vocabulary, grammar, or pronunciation.

difficult child A temperament style in which the child tends to react negatively and cry frequently, engages in irregular daily routines, and is slow to accept change.

direct instruction approach A teacher-centered approach characterized by teacher direction and control, high expectations for students' progress, and maximum time spent on academic tasks.

disenfranchised grief Grief involving a deceased person that is a socially ambiguous loss that can't be openly mourned or supported.

disengagement theory The theory that, to cope effectively, older adults should gradually withdraw from society; this theory is no longer supported.

dishabituation The recovery of a habituated response after a change in stimulation.

divergent thinking Thinking that produces many answers to the same question; characteristic of creativity.

divided attention Concentrating on more than one activity at the same time.

DNA A complex molecule that has a double helix shape and contains genetic information.

doula A caregiver who provides continuous physical, emotional, and educational support for the mother before, during, and after childbirth.

Down syndrome A chromosomally transmitted form of intellectual disability caused by the presence of an extra copy of chromosome 21.

dual-process model Theory stating that decision making is influenced by two cognitive systems—one analytical and one experiential—that compete with each other.

dynamic systems theory A theory proposed by Esther Thelen that seeks to explain how infants assemble motor skills for perceiving and acting.

dyscalculia Also known as developmental arithmetic disorder, this term refers to a learning disability that involves difficulty in math computation.

dysgraphia A learning disability that involves difficulty in handwriting.

dyslexia A learning disability that involves a severe impairment in the ability to read and spell.

E

easy child A temperament style in which the child is generally in a positive mood, quickly establishes regular routines, and adapts easily to new experiences.

eclectic theoretical orientation An orientation that does not follow any one theoretical approach but rather selects from each theory whatever is considered best in it.

ecological view The view proposed by the Gibsons that people directly perceive information in the world around them. Perception brings people in contact with the environment in order to interact with it and adapt to it.

ego ideal The component of the superego that rewards the child by conveying a sense of pride and personal value when the child acts according to ideal standards approved by the parents.

egocentrism The inability to distinguish between one's own and someone else's perspective; an important feature of preoperational thought.

elaboration Engagement in more extensive processing of information, benefiting memory.

embryonic period The period of prenatal development that occurs from two to eight weeks after conception. During the embryonic period, the rate of cell differentiation intensifies, support systems for the cells form, and organs appear.

emerging adulthood The developmental time frame occurring from approximately 18 to 25 years of age; this transitional period between adolescence and adulthood is characterized by experimentation and exploration.

emotion Feeling, or affect, that occurs when a person is engaged in an interaction that is important to him or her, especially to his or her well-being.

emotional abuse Acts or omissions by parents or other caregivers that have caused, or could cause, serious behavioral, cognitive, or emotional problems.

emotional intelligence The ability to perceive and express emotions accurately and adaptively, to understand emotion and emotional knowledge, to use feelings to facilitate thought, and to manage emotions in oneself and others.

empathy Reacting to another's feelings with an emotional response that is similar to the other's feelings.

empty nest syndrome View that a decline in marital satisfaction occurs when children leave home; however, research indicates that for most parents there is an upswing in marital satisfaction when children are launched into an adult life.

encoding The process by which information gets into memory.

epigenetic view Perspective that emphasizes that development is the result of an ongoing, bidirectional interchange between heredity and environment.

episodic memory Retention of information about the where and when of life's happenings.

equilibration A mechanism that Piaget proposed to explain how children shift from one stage of thought to the next.

Erikson's theory Theory that proposes eight stages of human development. Each stage consists of a unique developmental task that confronts individuals with a crisis that must be resolved.

estradiol A hormone associated in girls with breast, uterine, and skeletal development.

estrogens A class of sex hormones—an important one of which is estradiol—that primarily influences the development of female sex characteristics and helps regulate the menstrual cycle.

ethnic gloss Use of an ethnic label such as African American or Latino in a superficial way that portrays an ethnic group as being more homogeneous than it really is.

ethnic identity An enduring aspect of the self that includes a sense of membership in an ethnic group, along with the attitudes and feelings related to that membership.

ethnicity A characteristic based on cultural heritage, nationality characteristics, race, religion, and language.

ethnocentrism The tendency to consider one's own group superior to other groups.

ethology Theory stressing that behavior is strongly influenced by biology, is tied to evolution, and is characterized by critical or sensitive periods.

euthanasia The act of painlessly ending the lives of persons who are suffering from incurable diseases or severe disabilities; sometimes called "mercy killing."

evocative genotype-environment correlations Correlations that exist when the child's characteristics elicit certain types of environments.

evolutionary psychology A branch of psychology that emphasizes the importance of adaptation, reproduction, and "survival of the fittest" in shaping behavior.

executive attention Cognitive process involving planning actions, allocating attention to goals, detecting and compensating for errors, monitoring progress on tasks, and dealing with novel or difficult circumstances.

executive function   An umbrella-like concept that encompasses a number of higher-level cognitive processes linked to the development of the brain's prefrontal cortex. Executive function involves managing one's thoughts to engage in goal-directed behavior and to exercise self-control.

expanding   Restating, in a linguistically sophisticated form, what a child has said.

experiment   Carefully regulated procedure in which one or more factors believed to influence the behavior being studied are manipulated while all other factors are held constant.

expertise   Having extensive, highly organized knowledge and understanding of a particular domain.

explicit memory   Conscious memory of facts and experiences.

extrinsic motivation   Doing something to obtain something else (the activity is a means to an end).

F

fast mapping   A process that helps to explain how young children learn the connection between a word and its referent so quickly.

feminization of poverty   The fact that far more women than men live in poverty. Women's lower income, divorce, infrequent awarding of alimony, and poorly enforced child support by fathers—which usually leave women with less money than they and their children need to adequately function—are the likely causes.

fertilization   A stage in reproduction when an egg and a sperm fuse to create a single cell, called a zygote.

fetal alcohol spectrum disorders (FASD)   A cluster of abnormalities that may appear in the offspring of mothers who drink alcohol heavily during pregnancy.

fetal period   The prenatal period of development that begins two months after conception and lasts for seven months, on average.

fight or flight   Taylor's view that when men experience stress, they are more likely to become aggressive, withdraw from social contact, or drink alcohol.

fine motor skills   Motor skills that involve finely tuned movements, such as any activity that requires finger dexterity.

fluid intelligence   The ability to reason abstractly, which begins to decline in middle adulthood.

forgiveness   An aspect of prosocial behavior that occurs when the injured person releases the injurer from possible behavioral retaliation.

formal operational stage   The fourth and final Piagetian stage, which appears between the ages of 11 and 15; individuals move beyond concrete experiences and think in more abstract and logical ways.

fragile X syndrome   A chromosomal disorder involving an abnormality in the X chromosome, which becomes constricted and often breaks.

free-radical theory   A microbiological theory of aging stating that people age because when their cells metabolize energy, they generate waste that includes unstable oxygen molecules, known as free radicals, that damage DNA and other structures.

fuzzy trace theory   Theory stating that memory is best understood by considering two types of memory representations: verbatim memory trace and gist. In this theory, older children's better memory is attributed to the fuzzy traces created by extracting the gist of information.

G

games   Activities that are engaged in for pleasure and include rules.

gender   The characteristics of people as females or males.

gender identity   Involves a sense of one's own gender, including knowledge, understanding, and acceptance of being male or female.

gender-intensification hypothesis   The view that psychological and behavioral differences between boys and girls become greater during early adolescence because of increased socialization pressures to conform to traditional gender roles.

gender role   A set of expectations that prescribe how females or males should think, act, or feel.

gender schema theory   The theory that gender-typing emerges as children gradually develop gender schemas of what is gender-appropriate and gender-inappropriate in their culture.

gender stereotypes   General impressions and beliefs about females and males.

gender-typing   Acquisition of a traditional masculine or feminine role.

gene × environment (G × E) interaction   The interaction of a specific measured variation in DNA and a specific measured aspect of the environment.

generativity versus stagnation   The seventh stage in Erikson's life-span theory; it encompasses adults' desire to leave a legacy of themselves to the next generation.

genes   Units of hereditary information composed of DNA. Genes help cells to reproduce themselves and assemble proteins that direct body processes.

genotype   All of a person's actual genetic material.

germinal period   The period of prenatal development that takes place during the first two weeks after conception; it includes the creation of the zygote, continued cell division, and the attachment of the zygote to the wall of the uterus.

giftedness   Having above-average intelligence (an IQ of 130 or higher) and/or superior talent for something.

glaucoma   Damage to the optic nerve because of pressure created by a buildup of fluid in the eye.

gonadotropins   Hormones that stimulate the testes or ovaries.

gonads   The sex glands, which are the testes in males and the ovaries in females.

goodness of fit   The match between a child's temperament and the environmental demands the child must cope with.

grasping reflex   A reflex that occurs when something touches an infant's palms. The infant responds by grasping tightly.

gratitude   A feeling of thankfulness and appreciation, especially in response to someone's doing something kind or helpful.

grief   The emotional numbness, disbelief, separation anxiety, despair, sadness, and loneliness that accompany the loss of someone we love.

gross motor skills   Motor skills that involve large-muscle activities, such as walking.

H

habituation   Decreased responsiveness to a stimulus after repeated presentations of the stimulus.

helpless orientation   An orientation in which one seems trapped by the experience of difficulty and attributes one's difficulty to a lack of ability.

heritability   The portion of the variance in a population that is attributed to genes.

heteronomous morality (Kohlberg)   The first stage of preconventional reasoning in Kohlberg's theory, in which moral thinking is tied to punishment.

heteronomous morality (Piaget)   The first stage of moral development in Piaget's theory, occurring at 4 to 7 years of age. Justice and rules are conceived of as unchangeable properties of the world, removed from the control of people.

hidden curriculum   The pervasive moral atmosphere that characterizes every school.

hormonal stress theory   The theory that aging in the body's hormonal system can lower resistance to stress and increase the likelihood of disease.

hormones   Powerful chemical substances secreted by the endocrine glands and carried through the body by the bloodstream.

hospice   A program committed to making the end of life as free from pain, anxiety, and depression as possible. The goals of hospice contrast with those of a hospital, which are to cure disease and prolong life.

hypothalamus   A structure in the brain that is involved with eating and sexual behavior.

hypotheses   Specific assumptions and predictions that can be tested to determine their accuracy.

hypothetical-deductive reasoning   Piaget's formal operational concept that adolescents have the cognitive ability to develop hypotheses about ways to solve problems and can systematically deduce which is the best path to follow in solving the problem.

I

identity   Who a person is, representing a synthesis and integration of self-understanding.

identity achievement   Marcia's term for the status of individuals who have undergone a crisis and have made a commitment.

identity diffusion   Marcia's term for the status of individuals who have not yet experienced a crisis (explored meaningful alternatives) or made any commitments.

identity foreclosure   Marcia's term for the status of individuals who have made a commitment but have not experienced a crisis.

identity moratorium   Marcia's term for the status of individuals who are in the midst of a crisis but whose commitments are either absent or vaguely defined.

identity versus identity confusion   Erikson's fifth stage of development, which occurs during the adolescent years; adolescents are faced with finding out who they are, what they are all about, and where they are going in life.

imaginary audience   That aspect of adolescent egocentrism that involves feeling that one is the center of attention and sensing that one is on stage.

immanent justice   Belief that if a rule is broken, punishment will be meted out immediately.

implicit memory   Memory without conscious recollection—memory of skills and routine procedures that are performed automatically.

inclusion   Education of a child with special educational needs full-time in the regular classroom.

individualism   Giving priority to personal goals rather than to group goals; emphasizing values that serve the self, such as feeling good, obtaining personal distinction through achievement, and preserving independence.

individualism, instrumental purpose, and exchange   The second Kohlberg stage of preconventional reasoning. At this stage, individuals pursue their own interests but also let others do the same.

individuality   Characteristic consisting of two dimensions: self-assertion, the ability to have and communicate a point of view; and separateness, the use of communication patterns to express how one is different from others.

individualized education plan (IEP)   A written statement that spells out a program tailored to a child with a disability. The plan should be (1) related to the child's learning capacity, (2) specially constructed to meet the child's individual needs and not merely a copy of what is offered to other children, and (3) designed to provide educational benefits.

indulgent parenting   A style in which parents are very involved with their children but place few demands or controls on them.

infinite generativity   The ability to produce an endless number of meaningful sentences using a finite set of words and rules.

information-processing theory   Theory emphasizing that individuals manipulate information, monitor it, and strategize about it. Central to this theory are the processes of memory and thinking.

insecure avoidant children   Children who show insecurity by avoiding the mother.

insecure disorganized children   Children who show insecurity by being disorganized and disoriented.

insecure resistant children   Children who might cling to the caregiver, then resist her by fighting against the closeness, perhaps by kicking or pushing away.

intellectual disability   A condition of limited mental ability in which an individual has a low IQ, usually below 70 on a traditional test of intelligence, and has difficulty adapting to the demands of everyday life.

intelligence   The ability to solve problems and to adapt to and learn from experiences.

intelligence quotient (IQ)   An individual's mental age divided by chronological age, multiplied by 100; devised in 1912 by William Stern.

intermodal perception   The ability to integrate information about two or more sensory modalities, such as vision and hearing.

intimacy in friendship   Self-disclosure and the sharing of private thoughts.

intrinsic motivation   Doing something for its own sake; involves factors such as self-determination and opportunities to make choices.

intuitive thought substage   The second substage of preoperational thought, occurring between approximately 4 and 7 years of age. Children begin to use primitive reasoning and want to know the answers to all sorts of questions.

J

joint attention   Focus by individuals on the same object or event; requires an ability to track another's behavior, one individual to direct another's attention, and reciprocal interaction.

justice perspective   A moral perspective that focuses on the rights of the individual; individuals independently make moral decisions.

juvenile delinquency   Actions taken by an adolescent in breaking the law or engaging in illegal behavior.

K

kangaroo care   A way of holding a preterm infant so that there is skin-to-skin contact.

Klinefelter syndrome   A chromosomal disorder in which males have an extra X chromosome, making them XXY instead of XY.

L

labeling   Identifying the names of objects.

laboratory   A controlled setting from which many of the complex factors of the "real world" have been removed.

language   A form of communication, whether spoken, written, or signed, that is based on a system of symbols.

language acquisition device (LAD)   Chomsky's term that describes a biological endowment that enables the child to detect certain features and rules of language, including phonology, syntax, and semantics.

lateralization   Specialization of function in one hemisphere or the other of the cerebral cortex.

learning disabilities   Disabilities in which children experience difficulty in learning that involves understanding or using spoken or written language; the difficulty can appear in listening, thinking, reading, writing, and spelling. A learning disability also may involve difficulty in doing mathematics. To be classified as a learning disability, the learning problem is not primarily the result of visual, hearing, or motor disabilities; intellectual disability; emotional disorders; or environmental, cultural, or economic disadvantage.

least restrictive environment (LRE)   A setting that is as similar as possible to the one in which children without a disability are educated.

leisure   The pleasant times when individuals are free to pursue activities and interests of their own choosing.

life span   The upper boundary of life, which is the maximum number of years an individual can live. The maximum life span of humans is about 120 years of age.

life-span perspective   View of development as being lifelong, multidimensional, multidirectional, plastic, multidisciplinary, and contextual; involving growth, maintenance, and regulation of loss; and constructed through biological, sociocultural, and individual factors working together.

limbic system   The region of the brain where emotions and rewards are experienced.

long-term memory   A relatively permanent and unlimited type of memory.

longitudinal approach   A research strategy in which the same individuals are studied over a period of time, usually several years or more.

low birth weight infants   Infants who weigh less than 5½ pounds at birth.

M

macular degeneration   A vision problem in the elderly that involves deterioration of the macula of the retina.

mastery orientation   A perspective in which one is task-oriented—concerned with learning strategies and the process of achievement rather than the outcome.

meaning-making coping   Drawing on beliefs, values, and goals to change the meaning of a stressful situation, especially in times of high levels of stress such as when a loved one dies.

meiosis   A specialized form of cell division that occurs to form eggs and sperm (or gametes).

memory   Retention of information over time.

menarche   A girl's first menstrual period.

menopause   The complete cessation of a woman's menstrual cycles, which usually occurs during the late forties or early fifties.

menopause   The time in middle age, usually in the late forties or early fifties, when a woman's menstrual periods have ceased for one year.

mental age (MA)   An individual's level of mental development relative to that of others.

metacognition   Cognition about cognition, or "knowing about knowing."

metalinguistic awareness   Knowledge about language.

metamemory   Knowledge about memory.

metaphor   An implied comparison between two unlike things.

mindset   The cognitive view individuals develop for themselves that views their potential either as fixed or as capable of growth.

mitochondrial theory   The theory that aging is caused by the decay of the mitochondria, which are tiny cellular bodies that supply energy for cell function, growth, and repair.

mitosis   Cellular reproduction in which the cell's nucleus duplicates itself; two new cells are formed, each containing the same DNA as the original cell, arranged in the same 23 pairs of chromosomes.

Montessori approach   An educational philosophy in which children are given considerable freedom and spontaneity in choosing activities and are allowed to move from one activity to another as they desire.

moral development   Changes in thoughts, feelings, and behaviors regarding standards of right and wrong.

moral exemplars   People who have a moral personality, identity, character, and set of virtues that reflect moral excellence and commitment.

moral identity   The aspect of personality that is present when individuals have moral notions and commitments that are central to their lives.

Moro reflex   A startle response that occurs in reaction to a sudden, intense noise or movement. When startled, the newborn arches its back, throws its head back, and flings out its arms and legs. Then the newborn rapidly closes its arms and legs to the center of the body.

morphology   Units of meaning involved in word formation.

multiple developmental trajectories   Refers to the fact that adults follow one trajectory or pattern of development and children another one.

mutual interpersonal expectations, relationships, and interpersonal conformity   Kohlberg's third stage of moral development. At this stage, individuals value trust, caring, and loyalty to others as a basis of moral judgments.

myelination   The process of encasing axons with a myelin sheath, which helps increase the speed and efficiency of information processing.

N

natural childbirth   A childbirth method that attempts to reduce the mother's pain by decreasing her fear through education about childbirth stages and relaxation techniques during delivery.

naturalistic observation   Observing behavior in real-world settings.

nature-nurture issue   Debate about whether development is primarily influenced by nature or nurture. Nature refers to an organism's biological inheritance, nurture to its environmental experiences. The "nature proponents" claim biological inheritance is the more important influence on development; the "nurture proponents" claim that environmental experiences are more important.

neglected children   Children who are infrequently nominated as a best friend but are not disliked by their peers.

neglectful parenting   A style in which the parent is very uninvolved in the child's life.

neo-Piagetians   Developmentalists who have elaborated on Piaget's theory, emphasizing attention to children's strategies; information-processing speed; the task involved; and division of the problem into more precise, smaller steps.

neuroconstructivist view   Developmental perspective in which biological processes and environmental conditions influence the brain's development; the brain has plasticity and is context dependent; and cognitive development is closely linked with brain development.

neurogenesis   The generation of new neurons.

neurons   Nerve cells that handle information processing at the cellular level.

nonnormative life events   Unusual occurrences that have a major impact on an individual's life.

nonshared environmental experiences   The child's own unique experiences, both within the family and outside the family, that are not shared by another sibling; thus, experiences occurring within the family can be part of the "nonshared environment."

normal distribution   A symmetrical, bell-shaped curve with a majority of the cases falling in the middle of the possible range of scores and few scores appearing toward the extremes of the range.

normative age-graded influences   Influences that are similar for individuals in a particular age group.

normative history-graded influences Influences that are common to people of a particular generation because of historical circumstances.

O

object permanence   The Piagetian term for one of an infant's most important accomplishments: understanding that objects continue to exist even when they cannot directly be seen, heard, or touched.

operations   Reversible mental actions that allow children to do mentally what before they had done only physically.

optimism   A style of thinking that involves having a positive outlook on the future and minimizing problems.

organization   Piagetian concept of grouping isolated behaviors and thoughts into a higher-order, more smoothly functioning cognitive system.

organogenesis   Process of organ formation that takes place during the first two months of prenatal development.

osteoporosis   A disorder that involves an extensive loss of bone tissue and is the main reason many older adults walk with a marked stoop. Women are especially vulnerable to osteoporosis.

P

pain cry   A sudden, initial loud cry followed by breath holding, without preliminary moaning.

palliative care   Emphasized in hospice care; involves reducing pain and suffering and helping individuals die with dignity.

Parkinson disease   A chronic, progressive disease characterized by muscle tremors, slowing of movement, and partial facial paralysis.

passive euthanasia   The withholding of available treatments, such as life-sustaining devices, allowing the person to die.

passive genotype-environment correlations   Correlations that exist when the biological parents, who are genetically related to the child, provide a rearing environment for the child.

peers   Individuals who share the same age or maturity level.

perception   The interpretation of sensation.

performance orientation   An orientation in which one focuses on winning, rather than on achievement outcome; happiness is thought to result from winning.

perimenopause   The transitional period from normal menstrual periods to no menstrual periods at all, which often takes up to 10 years.

personal fable   The part of adolescent egocentrism that involves an adolescent's sense of personal uniqueness and invincibility.

personality   The enduring personal characteristics of individuals.

perspective taking   The ability to assume another person's perspective and understand his or her thoughts and feelings.

phenotype   Observable and measurable characteristics of an individual, such as height, hair color, and intelligence.

phenylketonuria (PKU)   A genetic disorder in which an individual cannot properly metabolize phenylalanine, an amino acid; PKU is now easily detected—but, if left untreated, results in intellectual disability and hyperactivity.

phonics approach   A teaching approach built on the idea that reading instruction should teach basic rules for translating written symbols into sounds.

phonology   The sound system of a language—includes the sounds used and how they may be combined.

physical abuse   Infliction of physical injury by punching, beating, kicking, biting, burning, shaking, or otherwise harming a child.

Piaget's theory   Theory stating that children actively construct their understanding of the world and go through four stages of cognitive development.

pituitary gland   An important endocrine gland that controls growth and regulates the activity of other glands.

play   A pleasurable activity that is engaged in for its own sake.

play therapy   Therapy that lets children work off frustrations while therapists analyze their conflicts and coping methods.

popular children   Children who are frequently nominated as a best friend and are rarely disliked by their peers.

possible selves What adolescents hope to become as well as what they dread they will become.

postconventional reasoning The highest level in Kohlberg's theory of moral development. At this level, the individual recognizes alternative moral courses, explores the options, and then decides on a personal moral code.

postformal thought Thinking that is reflective, relativistic, and contextual; provisional; realistic; and influenced by emotions.

postpartum depression A major depressive episode that typically occurs about four weeks after delivery; women with this condition have such strong feelings of sadness, anxiety, or despair that they have trouble coping with daily tasks during the postpartum period.

postpartum period The period after childbirth when the mother adjusts, both physically and psychologically, to the process of childbirth. This period lasts for about six weeks or until her body has completed its adjustment and returned to a near prepregnant state.

practice play Play that involves repetition of behavior when new skills are being learned or when mastery and coordination of skills are required for games or sports.

pragmatics The appropriate use of language in different contexts.

preconventional reasoning The lowest level in Kohlberg's theory of moral development. The individual's moral reasoning is controlled primarily by external rewards and punishments.

prefrontal cortex The highest level of the frontal lobes that is involved in reasoning, decision making, and self-control.

preoperational stage The second Piagetian developmental stage, which lasts from about 2 to 7 years of age; children begin to represent the world with words, images, and drawings.

prepared childbirth Developed by French obstetrician Ferdinand Lamaze, a childbirth strategy similar to natural childbirth but one that teaches a special breathing technique to control pushing in the final stages of labor and provides details about anatomy and physiology.

pretense/symbolic play Play that occurs when a child transforms aspects of the physical environment into symbols.

preterm infants Infants born three weeks or more before the pregnancy has reached its full term.

primary emotions Emotions that are present in humans and other animals, emerge early in life, and are culturally universal; examples are joy, anger, sadness, fear, and disgust.

Project Head Start Compensatory prekindergarten education designed to provide children from low-income families the opportunity to acquire skills and experiences important for school success.

prospective memory Remembering to do something in the future.

proximodistal pattern The sequence in which growth starts at the center of the body and moves toward the extremities.

psychoanalytic theories Theories that describe development as primarily unconscious and heavily colored by emotion. Behavior is merely a surface characteristic, and the symbolic workings of the mind must be analyzed to understand behavior. Early experiences with parents are emphasized.

psychoanalytic theory of gender Theory that stems from Freud's view that preschool children develop a sexual attraction to the opposite-sex parent, then at 5 or 6 years of age renounce the attraction because of anxious feelings, subsequently identifying with the same-sex parent and unconsciously adopting the same-sex parent's characteristics.

psychosocial moratorium Erikson's term for the gap between childhood security and adult autonomy that adolescents experience as part of their identity exploration.

puberty A brain-neuroendocrine process occurring primarily in early adolescence that provides stimulation for the rapid physical changes that occur in this period of development.

R

rape Forcible sexual intercourse, oral sex, or anal sex with a person who does not give consent. Legal definitions of rape differ from state to state.

rapport talk The language of conversation; a way to establish connections and negotiate relationships; preferred by women.

recasting Rephrasing a statement that a child has said, perhaps turning it into a question, or restating a child's immature utterance in the form of a fully grammatical sentence.

reciprocal socialization Socialization that is bidirectional in that children socialize parents just as parents socialize children.

reflexive smile A smile that does not occur in response to external stimuli. It happens during the month after birth, usually during sleep.

rejected children Children who are infrequently nominated as a best friend and are actively disliked by their peers.

religion An organized set of beliefs, practices, rituals, and symbols that increases an individual's connection to a sacred or transcendent other (God, higher power, or higher truth).

religiousness The degree of affiliation with an organized religion, participation in prescribed rituals and practices, connection with its beliefs, and involvement in a community of believers.

report talk Language designed to give information; a communication style preferred by men.

romantic love Also called passionate love, or *eros*, this type of love has strong components of sexuality and infatuation, and it often predominates in the early part of a love relationship.

romantic script A perspective in which sex is synonymous with love; belief that if we develop a relationship with someone and fall in love, it is acceptable to have sex with the person whether we are married or not.

rooting reflex A newborn's built-in reaction that occurs when the infant's cheek is stroked or the side of the mouth is touched. In response, the infant turns its head toward the side that was touched, in an apparent effort to find something to suck.

S

satire The use of irony, derision, or wit to expose folly or wickedness.

scaffolding In cognitive development, a term Vygotsky used to describe the changing level of support over the course of a teaching session, with the more-skilled person adjusting guidance to fit the child's current performance level.

schemas Mental frameworks that organize concepts and information.

schema theory Theory stating that people mold memories to fit information that already exists in their minds.

schemes In Piaget's theory, actions or mental representations that organize knowledge.

secure attachment style An attachment style that describes adults who have positive views of relationships, find it easy to get close to others, and are not overly concerned or stressed out about their romantic relationships.

securely attached children Children who use the caregiver as a secure base from which to explore the environment.

selective attention Focusing on a specific aspect of experience that is relevant while ignoring others that are irrelevant.

selective optimization with compensation theory The theory that successful aging is related to three factors: selection, optimization, and compensation.

self All of the characteristics of a person.

self-concept Domain-specific evaluations of the self.

self-conscious emotions Emotions that require consciousness and a sense of "me"; they include empathy, jealousy, embarrassment, pride, shame, and guilt, most of which first appear at some point after 18 months of age when a sense of self becomes consolidated in toddlers.

self-efficacy The belief that one can master a situation and produce favorable outcomes.

self-esteem The global evaluative dimension of the self. Self-esteem is also referred to as self-worth or self-image.

self-regulation The ability to control one's behavior without having to rely on others for help.

self-understanding The individual's cognitive representation of the self, the substance of self-conceptions.

semantic memory A person's knowledge about the world, including fields of expertise, general academic knowledge, and "everyday knowledge" about meanings of words, names of famous individuals, important places, and common things.

semantics The meanings of words and sentences.

sensation Reaction that occurs when information interacts with sensory receptors—the eyes, ears, tongue, nostrils, and skin.

sensorimotor play   Behavior by infants to derive pleasure from exercising their sensorimotor schemes.

sensorimotor stage   The first of Piaget's stages, which lasts from birth to about 2 years of age, during which infants construct an understanding of the world by coordinating sensory experiences (such as seeing and hearing) with physical, motoric actions.

separation protest   Reaction that occurs when infants experience a fear of being separated from a caregiver, which results in crying when the caregiver leaves.

seriation   The concrete operation that involves ordering stimuli along a quantitative dimension (such as length).

service learning   A form of education that promotes social responsibility and service to the community.

sexual abuse   Fondling a child's genitals, intercourse, incest, rape, sodomy, exhibitionism, and commercial exploitation through prostitution or the production of pornographic materials.

sexual harassment   Sexual persecution that can take many forms—from sexist remarks and physical contact (patting, brushing against someone's body) to blatant propositions and sexual assaults.

sexual scripts   Stereotyped patterns of expectancies for how people should behave sexually.

sexually transmitted infections (STIs)   Diseases that are contracted primarily through sexual contact, including oral-genital contact, anal-genital contact, and vaginal intercourse.

shape constancy   Recognition that an object remains the same even though its orientation to the viewer changes.

shared environmental experiences   Siblings' common experiences, such as their parents' personalities or intellectual orientation, the family's socioeconomic status, and the neighborhood in which they live.

short-term memory   Retention of information for up to 15 to 30 seconds, without rehearsal of the information. Using rehearsal, individuals can keep the information in short-term memory longer.

sickle-cell anemia   A genetic disorder that affects the red blood cells and occurs most often in African Americans.

size constancy   Recognition that an object remains the same even though the retinal image of the object changes as the viewer moves toward or away from the object.

slow-to-warm-up child   A temperament style in which the child has a low activity level, is somewhat negative, and displays a low intensity of mood.

small for date infants   Infants whose birth weights are below normal when the length of pregnancy is considered; also called small for gestational age infants. Small for date infants may be preterm or full-term.

social cognitive theory   Theoretical view that behavior, environment, and cognition are the key factors in development.

social cognitive theory of gender   The idea that children's gender development occurs through observation and imitation of gender behavior, as well as through the rewards and punishments children experience for behaviors believed to be appropriate or inappropriate for their gender.

social cognitive theory of morality   The theory that distinguishes between moral competence—the ability to produce moral behaviors—and moral performance—performing those behaviors in specific situations.

social constructivist approach   An emphasis on the social contexts of learning and construction of knowledge through social interaction. Vygotsky's theory reflects this approach.

social contract or utility and individual rights   The fifth Kohlberg stage of moral development. At this stage, individuals reason that values, rights, and principles undergird or transcend the law.

social conventional reasoning   Focuses on conventional rules established by social consensus and convention, as opposed to moral reasoning, which stresses ethical issues.

social domain theory   Theory that identifies different domains of social knowledge and reasoning, including moral, social conventional, and personal domains. These domains arise from children's and adolescents' attempts to understand and deal with different forms of social experience.

social play   Play that involves interaction with peers.

social policy   A government's course of action designed to promote the welfare of its citizens.

social referencing   "Reading" emotional cues in others to help determine how to act in a specific situation.

social role theory   Eagly's theory that psychological gender differences are caused by the contrasting social roles of women and men.

social smile   A smile in response to an external stimulus, which, early in development, typically is a face.

social systems morality   The fourth stage in Kohlberg's theory of moral development. Moral judgments are based on understanding the social order, law, justice, and duty.

socioeconomic status (SES)   A grouping of people with similar occupational, educational, and economic characteristics.

socioemotional processes   Processes that involve changes in an individual's relationships with other people, emotions, and personality.

socioemotional selectivity theory   The theory that older adults become more selective about their activities and social relationships in order to maintain emotional well-being.

source memory   The ability to remember where something was learned.

spirituality   Experiencing something beyond oneself in a transcendent manner and living in a way that benefits others and society.

stability-change issue   Debate as to whether and to what degree we become older renditions of our earlier selves (stability) or whether we develop into someone different from who we were at an earlier point in development (change).

standardized test   A test with uniform procedures for administration and scoring. Many standardized tests allow a person's performance to be compared with the performance of other individuals.

Strange Situation   Ainsworth's observational measure of infant attachment to a caregiver that requires the infant to move through a series of introductions, separations, and reunions with the caregiver and an adult stranger in a prescribed order.

stranger anxiety   An infant's fear of and wariness toward strangers; it tends to appear in the second half of the first year of life.

strategy construction   Creation of new procedures for processing information.

sucking reflex   A newborn's reaction of sucking an object placed in its mouth. The sucking reflex enables the infant to get nourishment before it has begun to associate a nipple with food.

sudden infant death syndrome (SIDS)   Condition that occurs when an infant stops breathing, usually during the night, and suddenly dies without an apparent cause.

sustained attention   The ability to maintain attention to a selected stimulus for a prolonged period of time.

symbolic function substage   The first substage of preoperational thought, occurring roughly between the ages of 2 and 4. In this substage, the young child gains the ability to represent mentally an object that is not present.

syntax   The ways words are combined to form acceptable phrases and sentences.

T

telegraphic speech   The use of short, precise words without grammatical markers such as articles, auxiliary verbs, and other connectives.

temperament   An individual's behavioral style and characteristic way of responding.

tend and befriend   Taylor's view that when women experience stress, they are more likely to seek social alliances with others, especially female friends.

teratogen   Any agent that can potentially cause a birth defect or negatively alter cognitive and behavioral outcomes.

testosterone   A hormone associated in boys with the development of the genitals, increased height, and voice changes.

theory   An interrelated, coherent set of ideas that helps to explain phenomena and make predictions.

theory of mind   Thoughts about how one's own mental processes work and the mental processes of others.

thinking   Manipulating and transforming information in memory, in order to reason, reflect, think critically, evaluate ideas and solve problems, and make decisions.

top-dog phenomenon   The circumstance of moving from the top position in elementary school to the youngest, smallest, and least powerful position in middle or junior high school.

traditional religious script View that sex is acceptable only within marriage; extramarital sex is taboo, especially for women; and sex means reproduction and sometimes affection.

trait theories Theories emphasizing that personality consists of broad dispositions, called traits, which tend to produce characteristic responses.

transitivity The ability to logically combine relations to understand certain conclusions. Piaget argued that an understanding of transitivity is characteristic of concrete operational thought.

triangular theory of love Sternberg's theory that love includes three components or dimensions—passion, intimacy, and commitment.

triarchic theory of intelligence Sternberg's theory that intelligence consists of analytical intelligence, creative intelligence, and practical intelligence.

Turner syndrome A chromosomal disorder in females in which either an X chromosome is missing, making the person XO instead of XX, or part of one X chromosome is deleted.

twin study A study in which the behavioral similarity of identical twins is compared with the behavioral similarity of fraternal twins.

U

universal ethical principles The sixth and highest stage in Kohlberg's theory of moral development. Individuals develop a moral standard based on universal human rights.

V

values Beliefs and attitudes about the way things should be.

values clarification A moral education program in which students are helped to clarify their purpose in life and decide what is worth working for. Students are encouraged to define their own values and understand others' values.

visual preference method A method developed by Fantz to determine whether infants can distinguish one stimulus from another by measuring the length of time they attend to different stimuli.

Vygotsky's theory Sociocultural cognitive theory that emphasizes how culture and social interaction guide cognitive development.

W

Wernicke's area An area of the brain's left hemisphere that is involved in language comprehension.

whole-language approach A teaching approach built on the idea that reading instruction should parallel children's natural language learning. Reading materials should be whole and meaningful.

wisdom Expert knowledge about the practical aspects of life that permits excellent judgment about important matters.

working memory A mental "workbench" where individuals manipulate and assemble information when making decisions, solving problems, and comprehending written and spoken language.

X

XYY syndrome A chromosomal disorder in which males have an extra Y chromosome.

Z

zone of proximal development (ZPD) Vygotsky's term for tasks that are too difficult for children to master alone but can be mastered with guidance and assistance from adults or more-skilled children.

zygote A single cell formed through fertilization.

references

A

Aalsma, M., Lapsley, D.K., & Flannery, D. (2006). Narcissism, personal fables, and adolescent adjustment. *Psychology in the Schools, 43,* 481–491.

AARP (2004). *The divorce experience: A study of divorce at midlife and beyond.* Washington, DC: Author.

Aatashak, S., Stannard, S.R., & Azizbeigi, K. (2015, in press). Cardiovascular risk factors adaptation to concurrent training in overweight sedentary middle-aged men. *Journal of Sports Medicine and Physical Fitness.*

Aazami, S., Shamsuddin, K., & Akmal, S. (2015). Examining behavioral coping strategies as mediators between work-family conflict and psychological distress. *Scientific World Journal, 2015,* 343075.

Abar, C.C., Jackson, K.M., Colby, S.M., & Barnett, N.P. (2015, in press). Parent-child discrepancies in reports of parental monitoring and their relationship to adolescent alcohol-related incidents. *Journal of Youth and Adolescence.*

Abbott, A. (2003). Restless nights, listless days. *Nature, 425,* 896–898.

ABC News (2005, December 12). Larry Page and Sergey Brin. Retrieved June 24, 2006, from www.Montessori.org/enews/barbaraWalters.html

Abyzov, A., & others (2013). Analysis of variable retroduplications in human populations suggests coupling of retrotransposition to cell division. *Genome Research, 23,* 2042–2052.

Accornero, V.H., & others (2007). Impact of prenatal cocaine exposure on attention and response inhibition as assessed by continuous performance tests. *Journal of Developmental and Behavioral Pediatrics, 28,* 195–205.

Achenbach, T.M. (1997). What is normal? What is abnormal? Developmental perspectives on behavioral and emotional problems. In S.S. Luthar, J.A. Burack, D. Cicchetti, & J.R. Weisz (Eds.), *Developmental psychopathology: Perspectives on adjustment, risk, and disorder.* New York: Cambridge University Press.

Ackerman, J.P., Riggins, T., & Black, M.M. (2010). A review of the effects of prenatal cocaine exposure among school-aged children. *Pediatrics, 125,* 554–565.

Ackerman, R.A., & others (2013). The interpersonal legacy of a positive family climate in adolescence. *Psychological Science, 24,* 243–250.

Adachi, P.J.C., & Willoughby, T. (2013). Do video games promote positive youth development? *Journal of Adolescent Research, 28,* 55–66.

Adams, G.C., & McWilliams, L.A. (2015, in press). Relationships between adult attachment style ratings and sleep disturbances in a nationally representative sample. *Journal of Psychosomatic Research.*

Adams, J.C. (2009). Immunocytochemical traits of type IV fibrocytes and their possible relation to cochlear function and pathology. *Journal of the Association for Research in Otolaryngology, 10,* 369–382.

Adamson, L., & Frick, J. (2003). The still face: A history of a shared experimental paradigm. *Infancy, 4,* 451–473.

Adler, N., Nadler, B., Eviater, Z., & Shamay-Tsoory, S.G. (2010). The relationship between theory of mind and autobiographical memory in high-functioning autism and Asperger syndrome. *Psychiatry, 178,* 214–216.

Administration for Children and Families (2008). *Statistical fact sheet, fiscal year 2008.* Washington, DC: Author.

Adolescent Sleep Working Group, AAP (2014). School start times for adolescents. *Pediatrics, 134,* 642–649.

Adolph, K.E. (1997). Learning in the development of infant locomotion. *Monographs of the Society for Research in Child Development, 62*(3, Serial No. 251).

Adolph, K.E., & Berger, S.E. (2005). Physical and motor development. In M.H. Bornstein & M.E. Lamb (Eds.), *Developmental psychology* (5th ed.). Mahwah, NJ: Erlbaum.

Adolph, K.E., & Berger, S.E. (2016, in press). Physical and motor development. In M.H. Bornstein & M.E. Lamb (Eds.), *Developmental Science* (7th ed.). New York: Psychology Press.

Adolph, K.E., Cole, W.G., & Vereijken, B. (2015, in press). Intra-individual variability in the development of motor skills in childhood. In M. Diehl, K. Hooker, & M.J. Sliwinski (Eds.), *Handbook of intraindividual variability across the life span.* New York: Routledge.

Adolph, K.E., & Joh, A.S. (2009). Multiple learning mechanisms in the development of action. In A. Needham & A. Woodward (Eds.), *Learning and the infant mind.* New York: Oxford University Press.

Adolph, K.E., Karasik, L.B., & Tamis-LeMonda, C.S. (2010). Moving between cultures: Cross-cultural research on motor development. In M. Bornstein & L.R. Cote (Eds.), *Handbook of cross-cultural developmental science, Vol. 1: Domains of development across cultures.* Clifton, NJ: Psychology Press.

Adolph, K.E., & Kretch, K.S. (2012). Infants on the edge: Beyond the visual cliff. In A. Slater & P. Quinn (Eds.), *Developmental psychology: Revisiting the classic studies.* New York: Oxford University Press.

Adolph, K.E., & Kretch, K.S. (2015, in press). Gibson's theory of perceptual learning. In J.D. Wright (Ed.), *International encyclopedia of the social and behavioral sciences* (2nd ed.). New York: Elsevier.

Adolph, K.E., & Robinson, S.R. (2013). The road to walking: What learning to walk tells us about development. In P. Zelazo (Ed.), *Oxford handbook of developmental psychology.* New York: Oxford University Press.

Adolph, K.E., & Robinson, S.R. (2015). Motor development. In R.M. Lerner (Ed.), *Handbook of child psychology and developmental science* (7th ed.). New York: Wiley.

Adolph, K.E., & Tamis-LeMonda, C.S. (2014). The costs and benefits of development: The transition from crawling to walking. *Child Development Perspectives, 8,* 187–192.

Adolph, K.E., & others (2012). How do you learn to walk? Thousands of steps and dozens of falls per day. *Psychological Science, 23*(11), 1387–1394.

Adriaanase, S.M., & others (2014). Widespread disruption of functional brain organization in early-onset Alzheimer's disease. *PLoS One, 9*(7), e102995.

Agency for Healthcare Research and Quality (2007). *Evidence report / Technology assessment number 153: Breastfeeding and maternal and infant health outcomes in developed countries.* Rockville, MD: U.S. Department of Health and Human Services.

Ahern, E.C., & Lamb, M.E. (2015, in press). Research-based child investigative interviewing. *Community Care Inform Children.*

Ahmed, R., Hustad, J.T., Lasalle, L., & Bosari, B. (2014). Hospitalizations for students with an alcohol-related sanction: Gender and pregaming as risk factors. *Journal of American College Health, 62,* 293–300.

Ahmed, S., & others (2011). Community kangaroo mother care: Implementation and potential for neonatal survival and health in very low-income settings. *Journal of Perinatology, 31,* 361–367.

Ahrens, C.E., & Aldana, E. (2012). The ties that bind: Understanding the impact of sexual assault disclosure on survivors' relationships with friends, family, and partners. *Journal of Trauma & Dissociation, 13,* 226–243.

Ahrons, C. (2004). *We're still family.* New York: Harper Collins.

Ahrons, C.R. (2007). Family ties after divorce: Long-term implications for children. *Family Process, 46,* 53–65.

Aiken Morgan, A., Sims, R.C., & Whitfield, K.E. (2010). Cardiovascular health and education as sources of individual variability in cognitive aging among African Americans. *Journal of Aging and Health, 22*(4), 477–503.

Ainsworth, M.D.S. (1979). Infant-mother attachment. *American Psychologist, 34,* 932–937.

Akbari, A., & others (2011). Parity and breastfeeding are preventive measures against breast cancer in Iranian women. *Breast Cancer, 18*(1), 51–55.

Aksglaede, L., & others (2013). 47, XXY Klinefelter syndrome: Clinical characteristics and age-specific recommendations for medical management. *American Journal of Medical Genetics C: Seminars in Medical Genetics, 163,* 55–63.

Aktar, N., & Herold, K. (2008). Pragmatic development. In M.M. Haith & J.B. Benson (Eds.), *Encyclopedia of infant and early childhood development.* New York: Elsevier.

Alberga, A.S., & others (2012). Healthy eating, aerobic and resistance training in youth (HEARTY): Study rationale, design, and methods. *Contemporary Clinical Trials, 33,* 839–847.

Albert, D., & Steinberg, L. (2011a). Judgment and decision making in adolescence. *Journal of Research on Adolescence, 21,* 211–224.

Albert, D., & Steinberg, L. (2011b). Peer influences on adolescent risk behavior. In M. Bardo, D. Fishbein, & R. Milich (Eds.), *Inhibitory control and drug abuse prevention: From research to translation.* New York: Springer.

Alcantara, C., Molina, K.M., & Kawachi, I. (2015). Transnational, social, and neighborhood ties and smoking among Latino immigrants: Does gender matter? *American Journal of Public Health, 105,* 741–749.

Alcauter, S., & others (2014). Development of thalamocortical connectivity during infancy and its cognitive correlations. *Journal of Neuroscience, 34,* 9067–9075.

Alderson-Day, B., & Fernyhough, C. (2014). More than one voice: Investigating the phenomenological properties of inner speech requires a variety of methods. *Consciousness and Cognition, 24,* 113–124.

Aldwin, C.M., Jeong, Y.J., Igarashi, H., & Spiro, A. (2014). Do hassles and uplifts change with age? Longitudinal findings from the VA Normative Aging Study. *Psychology and Aging, 29,* 57–71.

Alegret, M., & others (2014). Cognitive, genetic, and brain perfusion factors associated with four-year incidence of Alzheimer's disease from mild cognitive impairment. *Journal of Alzheimer's Disease, 41,* 739–748.

Alladi, S., & others (2013). Bilingualism delays age of onset of dementia, independent of education and immigration status. *Neurology, 81,* 1938–1944.

Allen, J.O. (2015, in press). Ageism as a risk factor for chronic disease. *Gerontologist.*

Allen, J.P., & Miga, E.M. (2010). Attachment in adolescence: A move to the next level of emotion regulation. *Journal of Social and Personal Relationships, 27,* 181–190.

Allen, J.P., Chango, J., & Szwedo, D. (2014). The adolescent relational dialectic and the peer roots of adult social functioning. *Child Development, 85,* 192–204.

Allen, J.P., Philliber, S., Herring, S., & Kuperminc, G.P. (1997). Preventing teen pregnancy and academic failure: Experimental evaluation of a developmentally-based approach. *Child Development, 68,* 729–742.

Allen, J.P., & others (2009, April). *Portrait of the secure teen as an adult.* Paper presented at the meeting of the Society for Research in Child Development, Denver.

Allen, T.D. (2013). The work-family role interface: A synthesis of the research from industrial and organizational psychology. In I.B. Weiner & others (Eds.), *Handbook of psychology* (2nd ed., Vol. 12). New York: Wiley.

Allen, T.D., & Finkelstein, L.M. (2014). Work-family conflict among members of full-time dual-earner couples: An examination of family life stage, gender, and age. *Journal of Occupational Health Psychology, 19,* 376–384.

Allington, R.L. (2015). *What really matters for middle school readers.* Upper Saddle River, NJ: Pearson.

Allstate Foundation (2005). *Chronic: A report on the state of teen driving.* Northbrook, IL: Author.

Almeida, D.M., & Horn, M.C. (2004). Is daily life more stressful during middle adulthood? In C.D. Ryff & R.C. Kessler (Eds.), *A portrait of midlife in the United States.* Chicago: University of Chicago Press.

Almeida, D.M., Piazza, J.R., Stawski, R.S., & Klein, L.C. (2011). The speedometer of life: Stress, health, and aging. In K.W. Schaie & S.L. Willis (Eds.), *Handbook of the psychology of aging* (7th ed.). New York: Elsevier.

Almquist, Y.B, & Brannstrom, L. (2014). Childhood peer status and the clustering of social, economic, and health-related circumstances in adulthood. *Social Science & Medicine, 105,* 67–75.

Alonge, O., & Hyder, A.A. (2014). Reducing the global burden of unintentional injuries. *Archives of Disease in Childhood, 99,* 62–69.

Alonzo, D., Thompson, R.G., Stohl, M., & Hasin, D. (2014). The influence of parental divorce and alcohol abuse on adult offspring risk of lifetime suicide attempt in the United States. *American Journal of Orthopsychiatry, 84,* 316–320.

Al-Safi, Z.A., & Santoro, N. (2014). Menopausal hormone therapy and menopausal symptoms. *Fertility and Sterility, 101,* 905–915.

Alzheimer's Association (2010). *Alzheimer's disease facts and figures.* Chicago: Author.

Alzheimer's Association (2014). *Alzheimer's disease facts and figures.* Chicago: Author.

Amabile, T.M. (1993). (Commentary). In D. Goleman, P. Kaufman, & M. Ray (Eds.), *The creative spirit.* New York: Plume.

Amabile, T.M., & Hennessey, B.A. (1992). The motivation for creativity in children. In A.K. Boggiano & T.S. Pittman (Eds.), *Achievement and motivation.* New York: Cambridge University Press.

Amato, P.R. (2006). Marital discord, divorce, and children's well-being: Results from a 20-year longitudinal study of two generations. In A. Clarke-Stewart & J. Dunn (Eds.), *Families count.* New York: Cambridge University Press.

Amato, P.R. (2010). Research on divorce: Continuing trends and new developments. *Journal of Marriage and the Family, 72*(3), 650–666.

Amato, P.R., & Anthony, C.J. (2014). Estimating the effects of parental divorce and death with fixed effects models. *Journal of Marriage and the Family, 76,* 370–386.

Amato, P.R., & Booth, A. (1996). A prospective study of divorce and parent-child relationships. *Journal of Marriage and the Family, 58,* 356–365.

Amato, P.R., Booth, A., Johnson, D.R., & Rogers, S.J. (2007). *Alone together: How marriage in America is changing.* Cambridge, MA: Harvard University Press.

American Academy of Pediatrics (2001). Committee on Public Education: Children, adolescents, and television. *Pediatrics, 107,* 423–426.

American Academy of Pediatrics (2010). Policy statement—sexuality, contraception, and the media. *Pediatrics, 126,* 576–582.

American Academy of Pediatrics Section on Breastfeeding (2012). Breastfeeding and the use of human milk. *Pediatrics, 129,* e827–e841.

American Academy of Pediatrics Task Force on Infant Positioning and SIDS (2000). Changing concepts of sudden infant death syndrome. *Pediatrics, 105,* 650–656.

American Association of University Women (1992). *How schools shortchange girls: A study of major findings on girls and education.* Washington, DC: Author.

American Association of University Women (2006). *Drawing the line: Sexual harassment on campus.* Washington, DC: Author.

American Psychiatric Association (2013). *Diagnostic and Statistical Manual of Mental Disorders, Fifth Edition (DSM-V).* Washington, DC: Author.

American Psychological Association (2003). *Psychology: Scientific problem solvers.* Washington, DC: Author.

American Psychological Association (2007). *Stress in America.* Washington, DC: Author.

Amialchuk, A., & Gerhardinger, L. (2015). Contraceptive use and pregnancies in adolescents' romantic relationships: Role of relationship activities and parental attitudes and communication. *Journal of Developmental and Behavioral Pediatrics, 36,* 86–97.

Amsterdam, B.K. (1968). *Mirror behavior in children under two years of age.* Unpublished doctoral dissertation, University of North Carolina, Chapel Hill.

Anastasi, A., & Urbina, S. (1996). *Psychological testing* (7th ed.). Upper Saddle River, NJ: Prentice-Hall.

Anderman, E.M., & Anderman, E.M. (2010). *Classroom motivation.* Upper Saddle River, NJ: Pearson.

Anderman, E.M., & Murdock, T.B. (Eds.). (2007). *Psychology of academic cheating.* San Diego: Academic Press.

Anderman, E.M., Gray, D.L., & Chang, Y. (2013). Motivation and classroom learning. In I.B. Weiner & others (Eds.), *Handbook of psychology* (2nd ed., Vol. 7). New York: Wiley.

Andersen, S.L., Sebastiani, P., Dworkis, D.A., Feldman, L., & Perls, T.T. (2012). Health span approximates life span among many supercentenarians: Compression of morbidity at the approximate limit of life span. *Journals of Gerontology A: Biological Sciences and Medical Sciences, 67,* 395–405.

Anderson, E.R., & Greene, S.M. (2011). "My child and I are a package deal": Balancing adult and child concerns in repartnering after divorce. *Journal of Family Psychology, 25,* 741–750.

Anderson, E., Greene, S.M., Hetherington, E.M., & Clingempeel, W.G. (1999). The dynamics of parental remarriage. In E.M. Hetherington (Ed.), *Coping with divorce, single parenting, and remarriage.* Mahwah, NJ: Erlbaum.

Anderson, K.A., Richardson, V.E., Fields, N.L., & Harootyan, R.A. (2013). Inclusion or exclusion? Exploring barriers to employment for low-income workers. *Journal of Gerontological Social Work, 56,* 318–334.

Anderson, M.L., & Finlay, B.L. (2014). Allocating structure to function: The strong links between neuroplasticity and natural selection. *Frontiers in Human Neuroscience, 7,* 918.

Anderson, N.D., & others (2014). The benefits of volunteering among seniors: A critical review and recommendations for future research. *Psychological Bulletin, 140,* 1505–1533.

Anderson, P.A. (2006). The evolution of biological sex differences in communication. In K. Dindia & D.J. Canary (Eds.), *Sex differences and similarities in communication.* Mahwah, NJ: Erlbaum.

Anderson, P.J., & others (2011). Attention problems in a representative sample of extremely preterm/extremely low birth weight children. *Developmental Neuropsychology, 36,* 57–73.

Anderson, S.B., & Guthery, A.M. (2015). Mindfulness-based psychoeducation for parents of children with attention-deficit/hyperactivity disorder: An applied clinical project. *Journal of Child and Adolescent Psychiatric Nursing, 28,* 43–49.

Anderson, S.E., Gooze, R.A., Lemeshow, S., & Whitaker, R.C. (2012). Quality of early maternal-child relationship and risk of adolescent obesity. *Pediatrics, 129,* 132–140.

Anderson, W.G. (2015). Quantifying the value of palliative care and advance care planning. *Critical Care Medicine, 43,* 1147–1149.

Andersson, H., & Bergman, L.R. (2011). The role of task persistence in young adolescence for successful educational and occupational attainment in middle adulthood. *Developmental Psychology, 47,* 950–960.

Andersson, U. (2010). The contribution of working memory capacity to foreign language comprehension in children. *Memory, 18*(4), 458–472.

Ang, M., Evans, J.R., & Mehta, J.S. (2012). Manual small incision cataract surgery (MSICS) with posterior chamber intraocular lens versus extracapsular cataract extraction (ECCE) with posterior chamber intraocular lens for age-related cataract. *Cochrane Database of Systematic Reviews.* doi:10.1002/14651858.CD008811 .pub2

Angel, L., Fay, S., Bouazzaoui, B., & Isingrini, M. (2011). Two hemispheres for better memory in old age: Role of executive functioning. *Journal of Cognitive Neuroscience, 23,* 3767–3777.

Angelone, D.J., Mitchell, D., & Grossi, L. (2015, in press). Men's perceptions of an acquaintance rape: The role of relationship length, victim resistance, and gender role attitudes. *Journal of Interpersonal Violence.*

Anguera, J.A., & others (2013). Video game training enhances cognitive control in older adults. *Nature, 501,* 97–101.

Ansado, J., & others (2013). Coping with task demand in aging using neural compensation and neural reserve triggers primarily intra-hemispheric-based neurofunctional reorganization. *Neuroscience Research, 75,* 295–304.

Ansary, N.S., & Luthar, S.S. (2009). Distress and academic achievement among adolescents of affluence: A study of externalizing and internalizing problem behaviors and school performance. *Development and Psychopathology, 21,* 319–341.

Anthony, D., George, P., & Eaton, C.B. (2014). Cardiac risk factors: New cholesterol and blood pressure management guidelines. *Family Physician Essentials, 421,* 28–43.

Antonenko, D., & Floel, A. (2014). Healthy aging by staying selectively connected: A mini-review. *Gerontology, 60*(1), 3–9.

Antonucci, T.C., Ajrouch, K., & Birditt, K. (2014). The convoy model: Explaining social relations from a multidisciplinary perspective. *Gerontologist, 54,* 82–92.

Antonucci, T.C., Birditt, K.S., & Ajrouch, K.J. (2013). Social relationships and aging. In I.B. Weiner & others (Eds.), *Handbook of psychology* (2nd ed., Vol. 6). New York: Wiley.

Antonucci, T.C., Vandewater, E.A., & Lansford, J.E. (2000). Adulthood and aging: Social processes and development. In A. Kazdin (Ed.), *Encyclopedia of psychology.* New York: American Psychological Association and Oxford University Press.

Anyaegbu, E., & Dharnidharka, V.R. (2014). Hypertension in the teenager. *Pediatric Clinics of North America, 61,* 131–151.

Apalasamy, Y.D., & Mohamed, Z. (2015, in press). Obesity and genomics: Role of technology in unraveling the complex genetic architecture of obesity. *Human Genetics.*

Apostolopoulos, V., Borkoles, E., Polman, R., & Stojanovska, L. (2014). Physical and immunological aspects of exercise in chronic diseases. *Immunotherapy, 6,* 1145–1157.

Arbib, M.A. (2012). *How the brain got language.* New York: Oxford University Press.

Ardelt, M. (2010). Are older adults wiser than college students? A comparison of two age cohorts. *Journal of Adult Development, 17,* 193–207.

Argyri, L., & others (2014). Molecular basis for increased risk for late-onset Alzheimer's disease due to the naturally occurring Leu28Pro mutation in apolipoprotein E4. *Journal of Biological Chemistry, 289,* 12931–12945.

Ariceli, G., Castro, J., Cesena, J., & Toro, J. (2005). Anorexia nervosa in male adolescents: Body image, eating attitudes, and psychological traits. *Journal of Adolescent Health, 36,* 221–226.

Arizmendi, B.J., & O'Connor, M.F. (2015, in press). What is "normal" in grief? *Australian Critical Care.*

Arkes, J. (2015). The temporal effects of divorces and separations on children's academic achievement and problem behavior. *Journal of Divorce and Remarriage, 56,* 25–42.

Arnett, J.J. (2006). Emerging adulthood: Understanding the new way of coming of age. In J.J. Arnett & J.L. Tanner (Eds.), *Emerging adults in America.* Washington, DC: American Psychological Association.

Arnett, J.J. (2007). Socialization in emerging adulthood. In J.E. Grusec & P.D. Hastings (Eds.), *Handbook of socialization.* New York: Guilford.

Arnett, J.J. (2014a). *Emerging adulthood* (2nd ed.). New York: Oxford University Press.

Arnett, J.J. (2014b). *Getting to 30: A parent's guide to the 20-something years.* New York: Workman.

Arnett, J.J. (2015). Socialization in emerging adulthood. In J.E. Grusec & P.D. Hastings (Eds.), *Handbook of socialization* (2nd ed.). New York: Guilford.

Arnett, J.J. (Ed.) (2012). *Adolescent psychology around the world.* New York: Psychology Press.

Arnett, J.J., & Fischel, E. (2013). *When will my grown-up kid grow up?* New York: Workman.

Aronow, W.S. (2007). Cardiovascular system. In J.E. Birren (Ed.), *Encyclopedia of gerontology* (2nd ed.). San Diego: Academic Press.

Aronson, E. (1986, August). *Teaching students things they think they already know about: The case of prejudice and desegregation.* Paper presented at the meeting of the American Psychological Association, Washington, DC.

Arpanantikul, M. (2004). Midlife experiences of Thai women. *Journal of Advanced Nursing, 47,* 49–56.

Arterberry, M.E. (2008). Perceptual development. In M.M. Haith & J.B. Benson (Eds.), *Encyclopedia of infant and early childhood development.* Oxford, UK: Elsevier.

Artero, A., Artero, A., Tarin, J.J., & Cano, A. (2015). The impact of moderate wine consumption on health. *Maturitas, 80,* 3–13.

Arthur, J. (2014). Traditional approaches to character education in Britain and America. In L. Nucci, T. Krettenauer, & D. Narváez (Eds.), *Handbook of moral and character education* (2nd ed.). New York: Routledge.

Asendorph, J.B. (2008). Shyness. In M.M. Haith & J.B. Benson (Eds.), *Encyclopedia of infant and early childhood development.* Oxford, UK: Elsevier.

Asgary, R., & others (2015, in press). Malnutrition prevalence and nutrition barriers in children under 5 years: A mixed methods study in Madagascar. *International Health.*

Ashcraft, D. (2015). *Personality theories workbook* (6th ed.). Boston: Cengage.

Asheer, S., Berger, A., Meckstroth, A., Kisker, E., & Keating, B. (2014). Engaging pregnant and parenting teens: Early challenges and lessons learned from the Evaluation of Adolescent Pregnancy Prevention Approaches. *Journal of Adolescent Health, 54*(Suppl. 3), S84–S91.

Asher, S.R., & McDonald, K.L. (2009). The behavior basis of acceptance, rejection, and perceived popularity. In K.H. Rubin, W.M. Bukowski, & B. Laursen (Eds.), *Handbook of peer interactions, relationships, and groups.* New York: Guilford.

Aslin, R.N. (2012). Infant eyes: A window on cognitive development. *Infancy, 17,* 126–140.

Aslin, R.N., Jusczyk, P.W., & Pisoni, D.B. (1998). Speech and auditory processing during infancy: Constraints on and precursors to language. In W. Damon (Ed.), *Handbook of child psychology* (5th ed., Vol. 2). New York: Wiley.

Aslin, R.N., & Lathrop, A.L. (2008). Visual perception. In M.M. Haith & J.B. Benson (Eds.), *Encyclopedia of infant and early childhood development.* Oxford, UK: Elsevier.

Aspen Institute (2013). *Two generations, one future.* Washington, DC: Aspen Institute.

Assini-Meytin, L.C., & Green, K.M. (2015, in press). Long-term consequences of adolescent parenthood among African-American youth: A propensity score matching approach. *Journal of Adolescent Health.*

Atkin, A.J., & others (2014). Prevalence and correlates of screen time in youth: An international perspective. *American Journal of Preventive Medicine, 47,* 803–807.

Atkinson, J., & Braddick, O. (2013). Visual development. In P.D. Zelazo (Ed.), *Oxford handbook of developmental psychology.* New York: Oxford University Press.

Attar-Schwartz, S., Tan, J.P., Buchanan, A., Flouri, E., & Griggs, J. (2009). Grandparenting and adolescent adjustment in two-parent biological, lone-parent, and step-families. *Journal of Family Psychology, 23*(1), 67–75.

Austad, S.N. (2011). Sex differences in aging. In E.J. Masoro & S.N. Austad (Eds.), *Handbook of the biology of aging* (7th ed.). New York: Elsevier.

Autism Research Institute (2015). *DSM-V and autism.* New York: Autism Research Institute.

Auyeung, B., & others (2009). Fetal testosterone predicts sexually differentiated childhood behavior in girls and boys. *Psychological Science, 20,* 144–148.

Avila, J., & others (2014). Sources of extracellular tau and its signaling. *Journal of Alzheimer's Disease, 40*(Suppl. 1), S7–S15.

Avinun, R., & Knafo-Noam, A. (2015). Socialization, genetics, and their interplay in development. In J.E. Grusec & P.D. Hastings (Eds.), *Handbook of socialization* (2nd ed.). New York: Guilford.

Avis, N.E., & others (2009). Longitudinal changes in sexual functioning as women transition through menopause: Results from the Study of Women's Health Across the Nation. *Menopause, 16,* 425–426.

Avis, N.E., & others (2015, in press). Duration of menopausal symptoms over the menopausal transition. *JAMA Internal Medicine.*

Ayoub, C., Vallotton, C.D., & Mastergeorge, A.M. (2011). Developmental pathways to integrated social skills: The role of parenting and early intervention. *Child Development, 82,* 583–600.

Azagba, S., & Sharaf, M.F. (2014). Physical inactivity among older Canadian adults. *Journal of Physical Activity and Health, 11*(1), 99–108.

Azmitia, M. (2015). Reflections on the cultural lenses of identity development. In K.C. McLean & M. Syed (Eds.), *Oxford handbook of identity development.* New York: Oxford University Press.

Azmitia, M., Syed, M., & Radmacher, K.A. (2013). Finding your niche: Identity and emotional support in emerging adults' adjustment to the transition to college. *Journal of Research in Adolescence, 23,* 744–761.

B

Bach, L.E., Mortimer, J.A., Vandeweerd, C., & Corvin, J. (2013). The association of physical and mental health with sexual activity in older adults in a retirement community. *Journal of Sexual Medicine, 10*(11), 2671–2678.

Bachman, J.G., & others (2002). *The decline in substance use in young adulthood.* Mahwah, NJ: Erlbaum.

Bachman, J.G., & others (2008). *The education-drug use connection.* Clifton, NJ: Psychology Press.

Bacikova-Sleskova, M., Benka, J., & Orosova, O. (2014). Parental employment status and adolescents' health: The role of financial situation, parent-adolescent relationship, and adolescents' resilience. *Psychology and Health, 30,* 400–422.

Badaly, D. (2013). Peer similarity and influence for weight-related outcomes in adolescence: A meta-analytic review. *Clinical Psychology Review, 33,* 1218–1236.

Baddeley, A.D. (1990). *Human memory: Theory and practice.* Boston: Allyn & Bacon.

Baddeley, A.D. (2001). *Is working memory still working?* Paper presented at the meeting of the American Psychological Association, San Francisco.

Baddeley, A.D. (2007). *Working memory, thought and action.* New York: Oxford University Press.

Baddeley, A.D. (2010a). Long-term and working memory: How do they interact? In L. Backman & L. Nyberg (Eds.), *Memory, aging, and the brain.* New York: Psychology Press.

Baddeley, A.D. (2010b). Working memory. *Current Biology, 20,* 136–140.

Baddeley, A.D. (2012). Prefatory. *Annual Review of Psychology* (Vol. 63). Palo Alto, CA: Annual Reviews.

Baddeley, A.D. (2013). On applying cognitive psychology. *British Journal of Psychology, 104,* 443–456.

Badger, J.L., & others (2014). Parkinson's disease in a dish—using stem cells as a molecular tool. *Neuropharmacology, 76* Pt. A, 88–96.

Badowski, M., & others (2014). The influence of intrinsic and extrinsic factors on immune system aging. *Immunobiology, 219,* 482–485.

Baer, J., & Kaufman, J.C. (2013). *Being creative inside and outside the classroom.* The Netherlands: Sense Publishers.

Bagshaw, A.T., & others (2013). No effect of genome-wide copy number variation on measures of intelligence in a New Zealand birth cohort. *PLoS One, 8*(1), e55208.

Bahrick, H.P. (1984). Semantic memory content in permastore: Fifty years of memory for Spanish learned in school. *Journal of Experimental Psychology: General, 113,* 1–35.

Bahrick, H.P., Bahrick, P.O., & Wittlinger, R.P. (1975). Fifty years of memory for names and faces: A cross-sectional approach. *Journal of Experimental Psychology: General, 104,* 54–75.

Bahrick, L.E. (2010). Intermodal perception and selective attention to intersensory redundancy: Implications for social development and autism. In J.G. Bremner & T.D. Wachs (Eds.), *Wiley-Blackwell handbook of infant development* (2nd ed.). New York: Wiley.

Bahrick, L.E., & Hollich, G. (2008). Intermodal perception. In M.M. Haith & J.B. Benson (Eds.), *Encyclopedia of infant and early childhood development.* Oxford, UK: Elsevier.

Bailey, H.R., Dunlosky, J., & Hertzog, C. (2014). Does strategy training reduce age-related deficits in working memory? *Gerontology, 60,* 346–356.

Baillargeon, R. (1995). The object concept revisited: New directions in the investigation of infants' physical knowledge. In C. E. Granrud (Ed.), *Visual perception and cognition in infancy.* Hillsdale, NJ: Erlbaum.

Baillargeon, R. (2004). The acquisition of physical knowledge in infancy: A summary in eight lessons. In U. Goswami (Ed.), *Blackwell handbook of childhood cognitive development.* Malden, MA: Blackwell.

Baillargeon, R. (2008). Innate ideas revisited: For a principle of persistence in infants' physical reasoning. *Perspectives on Psychological Science, 3,* 2–13.

Baillargeon, R. (2016, in press). Cognitive development in infancy. *Annual Review of Psychology* (Vol. 67). Palo Alto, CA: Annual Reviews.

Baillargeon, R., & Carey, S. (2012). Core cognition and beyond: The acquisition of physical and numerical knowledge. In S. Pauen & M. Bornstein (Eds.), *Early childhood development and later achievement.* New York: Cambridge University Press.

Baillargeon, R., & DeVos, J. (1991). Object permanence in young children: Further evidence. *Child Development, 62*(1991), 1227–1246.

Baillargeon, R., Li, J., Gertner, Y., & Wu, D. (2011). How do infants reason about physical events? In U. Goswami (Ed.), *Wiley-Blackwell handbook of childhood cognitive development* (2nd ed.). New York: Wiley.

Baillargeon, R., & others (2012). Object individuation and physical reasoning in infancy: An integrative account. *Language, Learning, and Development, 8,* 4–46.

Bajoghli, H., & others (2014). "I love you more than I can stand!"—romantic love, symptoms of depression and anxiety, and sleep complaints are related among young adults. *International Journal of Psychiatry and Clinical Practice, 18,* 169–174.

Bakeman, R., & Brown, J.V. (1980). Early interaction: Consequences for social and mental development at three years. *Child Development, 51,* 437–447.

Baker, J.K., Fenning, R.M., & Crnic, K.A. (2011). Emotion socialization by mothers and fathers: Coherence among behaviors and associations with parent attitudes and children's competence. *Social Development, 20,* 412–430.

Bakermans-Kranenburg, M.J., Breddels-Van Bardewijk, F., Juffer, M.K., Velderman, M.H., & van IJzendoorn, M.H. (2007). Insecure mothers with temperamentally reactive infants. In F. Juffer, M.J. Bakermans-Kranenburg, & M.H. van IJzendoorn (Eds.), *Promoting positive parenting.* Mahwah, NJ: Erlbaum.

Baldwin, S.A., Christian, S., Berkeljon, A., & Shadish, W.R. (2012). The effects of family therapies for adolescent delinquency and substance abuse: A meta-analysis. *Journal of Marital and Family Therapy, 38,* 281–304.

Baldwin, S.A., & Hoffman, J.P. (2002). The dynamics of self-esteem: A growth-curve analysis. *Journal of Youth and Adolescence, 31,* 101–113.

Ball, K., Edwards, J.D., Ross, L.A., & McGwin, G. (2010). Effects of cognitive training interventions with older adults: A randomized controlled trial. *Journal of the American Geriatrics Society, 55,* 1–10.

Baltes, P.B. (1987). Theoretical propositions of life-span developmental psychology: On the dynamics between growth and decline. *Developmental Psychology, 23,* 611–626.

Baltes, P.B. (1993). The aging mind: Potentials and limits. *Gerontologist, 33,* 580–594.

Baltes, P.B. (2000). Life-span developmental theory. In A. Kazdin (Ed.), *Encyclopedia of psychology.* New York: Oxford University Press.

Baltes, P.B. (2003). On the incomplete architecture of human ontogeny: Selection, optimization, and compensation as foundation of developmental theory. In U.M. Staudinger & U. Lindenberger (Eds.), *Understanding human development.* Boston: Kluwer.

Baltes, P.B., & Kunzmann, U. (2004). The two faces of wisdom: Wisdom as a general theory of knowledge and judgment about excellence in mind and virtue vs. wisdom as everyday realization in people and products. *Human Development, 47,* 290–299.

Baltes, P.B., & Lindenberger, U. (1997). Emergence of a powerful connection between sensory and cognitive functions across the adult life span: A new window to the study of cognitive aging? *Psychology and Aging, 12,* 12–21.

Baltes, P.B., Lindenberger, U., & Staudinger, U. (2006). Life span theory in developmental psychology. In W. Damon & R. Lerner (Eds.), *Handbook of child psychology* (6th ed.). New York: Wiley.

Baltes, P.B., Reuter Lorenz, P., & Rosler, F. (Eds.) (2012). *Life development and the brain: The perspective of biocultural co-constructivism.* New York: Cambridge University Press.

Baltes, P.B., & Smith, J. (2003). New frontiers in the future of aging: From successful aging of the young to the dilemmas of the fourth age. *Gerontology, 49,* 123–135.

Baltes, P.B., & Smith, J. (2008). The fascination of wisdom: Its nature, ontogeny, and function. *Perspectives on Psychological Science, 3,* 56–64.

Bamaca Colbert, M.Y., Umana Taylor, A.J., Espinosa-Hernandez, G., & Brown, A.M. (2012). Behavioral autonomy and expectations among Mexican-origin mother-daughter dyads: An examination of within-group variability. *Journal of Adolescence, 35,* 691–176.

Bamford, C., & Lagattuta, K.H. (2012). Looking on the bright side: Children's knowledge about the benefits of positive versus negative thinking. *Child Development, 83,* 667–682.

Bandura, A. (1997). *Self-efficacy.* New York: W.H. Freeman.

Bandura, A. (1998, August). *Swimming against the mainstream: Accentuating the positive aspects of humanity.* Paper presented at the meeting of the American Psychological Association, San Francisco.

Bandura, A. (2001). Social cognitive theory. *Annual Review of Psychology* (Vol. 52). Palo Alto, CA: Annual Reviews.

Bandura, A. (2002). Selective moral disengagement in the exercise of moral agency. *Journal of Moral Education, 31,* 101–119.

Bandura, A. (2009). Social and policy impact of social cognitive theory. In M. Mark, S. Donaldson, & B. Campbell (Eds.), *Social psychology and program/policy evaluation.* New York: Guilford.

Bandura, A. (2010a). Self-efficacy. In D. Matsumoto (Ed.), *Cambridge dictionary of psychology.* New York: Cambridge University Press.

Bandura, A. (2010b). Self-reinforcement. In D. Matsumoto (Ed.), *Cambridge dictionary of psychology.* New York: Cambridge University Press.

Bandura, A. (2012). Social cognitive theory. *Annual Review of Clinical Psychology* (Vol. 8). Palo Alto, CA: Annual Reviews.

Bank, L., Burraston, B., & Snyder, J. (2004). Sibling conflict and ineffective parenting as predictors of adolescent boys' antisocial behavior and peer difficulties: Additive and interactive effects. *Journal of Research on Adolescence, 14,* 99–125.

Banks, J.A. (2014). *Introduction to multicultural education* (5th ed.). Upper Saddle River, NJ: Pearson.

Banks, J.A. (2015). *Cultural diversity and eduction* (6th ed.). Upper Saddle River, NJ: Pearson.

Banks, J.A. (Ed.). (2010). *Routledge international handbook of multicultural education.* New York: Routledge.

Banks, S., & Dinges, D.F. (2008). Behavioral and physiological consequences of sleep restriction. *Journal of Clinical Sleep Medicine, 15,* 519–528.

Banschick, M.R., & Tabatsky, D. (2011). *The intelligent divorce: Taking care of yourself.* New York: Intelligent Book Press.

Banuelos, C., & others (2014). Prefrontal cortical GABAergic dysfunction contributes to age-related working memory impairment. *Journal of Neuroscience, 34,* 3457–3466.

Bao, J.M., & others (2014). Association between FOXO3A gene polymorphisms and human longevity: A meta-analysis. *Asian Journal of Andrology, 16,* 446–452.

Barbarin, O., & Aikens, N. (2009). Supporting parental practices in the language and literacy development of young children. In O. Barbarin & H. Wasik (Eds.), *Handbook of child development and education.* New York: Guilford.

Barbosa, V., Sa, M., & Carlos Rocha, J. (2014). Randomized controlled trial of cognitive narrative intervention for complicated grief in widowhood. *Aging and Mental Health, 18,* 354–326.

Barbot, B., & Tinio, P.P. (2015). Where is the "g" in creativity? A specialization-differentiation hypothesis. *Frontiers in Human Neuroscience, 8,* 1041.

Bardach, S.H., & Rowles, G.D. (2012). Geriatric education in the health professions: Are we making progress? *The Gerontologist, 52*(5), 607–618.

Barger, J.L. (2013). An adipocentric perspective of resveratrol as a calorie restriction mimetic. *Annals of the New York Academy of Sciences, 1290,* 122–129.

Bargh, J.A., & McKenna, K.Y.A. (2004). The Internet and social life. *Annual Review of Psychology* (Vol. 55). Palo Alto, CA: Annual Reviews.

Barlett, C.P. (2015). Predicting adolescents' cyberbullying behavior: A longitudinal risk analysis. *Journal of Adolescence, 41,* 86–95.

Barnes, D.C., & Wilson, D.A. (2014). Sleep and olfactory cortical plasticity. *Frontiers in Behavioral Neuroscience, 22*(8), 134.

Barnes, L.L., & others (2004). Racial difference in perceived discrimination in a community population of older blacks and whites. *Journal of Aging and Health, 16,* 315–317.

Barnett, J.E., & Francis, A.L. (2012). Using higher-order thinking questions to foster critical thinking: A classroom study. *Educational Psychology, 32,* 201–211.

Baron, C. (2012). Using the gradient of human cortical bone properties to determine age-related bone changes via ultrasonic guided waves. *Ultrasound in Medicine and Biology, 38,* 972–981.

Baron, N.S. (1992). *Growing up with language.* Reading, MA: Addison-Wesley.

Baron-Cohen, S. (2008). Autism, hypersystematizing, and truth. *Quarterly Journal of Experimental Psychology, 61,* 64–75.

Baron-Cohen, S. (2009). Autism: The empathizing-systematizing (E-S) theory. *Annals of the New York Academy of Sciences, 1156,* 68–80.

Baron-Cohen, S. (2011). The empathizing-systematizing (E-S) theory of autism: A cognitive developmental account. In U. Goswami (Ed.), *Wiley-Blackwell handbook of childhood cognitive development* (2nd ed.). New York: Wiley-Blackwell.

Baron-Cohen, S., Golan, O., Chapman, E., & Granader, Y. (2007). Transported to a world of emotions. *The Psychologist, 20,* 76–77.

Barrocas, A.L., & others (2015). Nonsuicidal self-injury in adolescence: Longitudinal course, trajectories, and interpersonal predictors. *Journal of Abnormal Child Psychology, 43,* 369–380.

Barron, R.S. (2015). Death: Past, present, and future. *Journal of Critical Care, 30,* 214–215.

Bartel, M.A., Weinstein, J.R., & Schaffer, D.V. (2012). Directed evolution of novel adeno-associated viruses for therapeutic gene delivery. *Gene Therapy, 19*(6), 694–700.

Barth, T. (2012). Relationships and sexuality of imprisoned men in the German penal system—A survey of inmates in a Berlin prison. *International Journal of Law and Psychiatry, 35,* 153–158.

Bartlett, J.D., & others (2014). An ecological analysis of infant neglect by adolescent mothers. *Child Abuse and Neglect, 38,* 723–734.

Bartsch, K., & Wellman, H.M. (1995). *Children talk about the mind.* New York: Oxford University Press.

Bascandziev, I., & Harris, P.L. (2011). The role of testimony in young children's solution of a gravity-driven invisible displacement task. *Cognitive Development, 25,* 233–246.

Basilio, C.D., & others (2014). The Mexican-American Biculturalism Scale: Bicultural comfort, ease, and advantage for adolescents and adults. *Psychological Assessment, 26,* 539–555.

Bassil, K.L., & others (2014). Impact of late preterm and early term infants on Canadian Neonatal Intensive Care Units. *American Journal of Perinatology, 31*(4), 269–278.

Basta, N.E., Matthews, F.E., Chatfield, M.D., Byrnes, C., & MRC-FFAS (2008). Community-level socio-economic status and cognitive and functional impairment in the older population. *European Journal of Public Health, 18,* 48–54.

Basterfield, L., & others (2015). Longitudinal associations between sports participation, body composition, and physical activity from childhood to adolescence. *Journal of Science and Medicine in Sport, 18*(2), 178–182.

Bastos, F.N., & others (2013). Investigation of characteristics and risk factors of sports injuries in young soccer players: A retrospective study. *International Archives of Medicine, 6,* 14.

Batanova, M.D., & Loukas, A. (2011). Social anxiety and aggression in early adolescents: Examining the moderating roles of empathic concern and perspective taking. *Journal of Youth and Adolescence, 40,* 1534–1543.

Bates, J.E. (2008). Unpublished review of J.W. Santrock's *Children,* 11th ed. (New York: McGraw-Hill).

Bates, J.E. (2012a). Behavioral regulation as a product of temperament and environment. In S.L. Olson & A.J. Sameroff (Eds.), *Biopsychosocial regulatory processes in the development of childhood behavioral problems.* New York: Cambridge University Press.

Bates, J.E. (2012b). Temperament as a tool in promoting early childhood development. In S.L. Odom, E.P. Pungello, & N. Gardner-Neblett (Eds.), *Infants, toddlers, and families in poverty.* New York: Guilford.

Bates, J.E., & Pettit, G.S. (2015). Temperament, parenting, and social development. In J.E. Grusec & P.D. Hastings (Eds.), *Handbook of socialization* (2nd ed.). New York: Guilford.

Bates, J.E., Schermerhorn, A.C., & Goodnight, J.A. (2010). Temperament and personality through the life span. In A. Freund, M. Lamb, & R.M. Lerner (Eds.), *Handbook of life-span development.* New York: Wiley.

Bateson, P. (2015). Human evolution and development: An ethological perspective. In R.M. Lerner (Ed.), *Handbook of child psychology and developmental science* (7th ed.). New York; Wiley.

Batson, C.D. (1989). Personal values, moral principles, and the three-path model of prosocial motivation. In N. Eisenberg & J. Reykowski (Eds.), *Social and moral values.* Hillsdale, NJ: Erlbaum.

Battistich, V.A. (2008). The Child Development Project: Creating caring school communities. In L. Nucci & D. Narváez (Eds.), *Handbook of moral and character education.* Clifton, NJ: Psychology Press.

Bauer, M.E., & others (2013). Psychoneuroendocrine interventions aimed at attenuating immunosenescence. *Biogerontology, 14,* 9–20.

Bauer, P.J. (2006). Event memory. In W. Damon & R. Lerner (Eds.), *Handbook of child psychology* (6th ed.). New York: Wiley.

Bauer, P.J. (2009). Neurodevelopmental changes in infancy and beyond: Implications for learning and memory. In O.A. Barbarin & B.H. Wasik (Eds.), *Handbook of child development and early education.* New York: Oxford University Press.

Bauer, P.J. (2013). Memory. In P.D. Zelazo (Ed.), *Oxford handbook of developmental psychology.* New York: Oxford University Press.

Bauer, P.J., & Fivush, R. (Eds.) (2014). *Wiley-Blackwell handbook of children's memory.* New York: Wiley.

Bauer, P.J., & Larkina, M. (2014). The onset of childhood amnesia in childhood: A prospective investigation of the course and determinants of forgetting of early-life events. *Memory, 22,* 907–924.

Bauer, P.J., & Larkina, M. (2015, in press). Childhood amnesia in the making: Different distributions of autobiographical memories in children and adolescents. *Journal of Experimental Psychology: General.*

Bauer, P.J., Wenner, J.A., Dropik, P.L., & Wewerka, S.S. (2000). Parameters of remembering and forgetting in the transition from infancy to early childhood. *Monographs of the Society for Research in Child Development, 65*(4, Serial No. 263).

Bauerlein, M. (2008). *The dumbest generation: How the digital age stupefies young Americans and jeopardizes our future (Or, don't trust anyone under 30).* New York: Tarcher.

Bauman, R.W. (2015, in press). *Microbiology with diseases by body system* (4th ed.). Upper Saddle River, NJ: Pearson.

Baumeister, R.F. (2013). Self-esteem. In E. Anderson (Ed.), *Psychology of classroom learning: An encyclopedia.* Detroit: Macmillan.

Baumeister, R.F., Campbell, J.D., Krueger, J.I., & Vohs, K.D. (2003). Does high self-esteem cause better performance, interpersonal success, happiness, or healthier lifestyles? *Psychological Science in the Public Interest, 4*(1), 1–44.

Baumeister, R.F., & Vohs, K.D. (2002). The pursuit of meaningfulness in life. In C.R. Snyder & S.J. Lopez (Eds.), *Handbook of positive psychology.* New York: Oxford University Press.

Baumrind, D. (1971). Current patterns of parental authority. *Developmental Psychology Monographs, 4*(I, Pt. 2).

Baumrind, D. (1991). Effective parenting during the early adolescent transition. In P.A. Cowan & E.M. Hetherington (Eds.), *Advances in family research* (Vol. 2). Hillsdale, NJ: Erlbaum.

Baumrind, D. (2012). Authoritative parenting revisited: History and current status. In R. Larzelere, A.S. Morris, & A.W. Harrist (Eds.), *Authoritative parenting.* Washington, DC: American Psychological Association.

Bayley, N. (1969). *Manual for the Bayley Scales of Infant Development.* New York: Psychological Corporation.

Bayley, N. (2006). *Bayley Scales of Infant and Toddler Development* (3rd ed.). San Antonio: Harcourt Assessment.

Baysinger, C.L. (2010). Imaging during pregnancy. *Anesthesia and Analgesia, 110,* 863–867.

Beal, C.R. (1994). *Boys and girls: The development of gender roles.* New York: McGraw-Hill.

Beaty, J.J., & Pratt, L. (2015). *Early literacy in preschool and kindergarten* (4th ed.). Upper Saddle River, NJ: Pearson.

Beauchamp, G., & Mennella, J.A. (2009). Early flavor learning and its impact on later feeding behavior. *Journal of Pediatric Gastroenterology and Nutrition, 48*(Suppl. 1), S25–S30.

Bechtold, A.G., Bushnell, E.W., & Salapatek, P. (1979, April). *Infants' visual localization of visual and auditory targets.* Paper presented at the meeting of the Society for Research in Child Development, San Francisco.

Bechtold, J., Cavanagh, C., Shulman, E.P., & Caufmann, E. (2014). Does mother know best? Adolescent and mother reports of impulsivity and subsequent delinquency. *Journal of Youth and Adolescence, 43,* 1903–1913.

Becker, M.W., Alzahabi, R., & Hopwood, C.J. (2013). Media multitasking is associated with symptoms of depression and social anxiety. *Cyberpsychology, Behavior, and Social Networking, 16,* 132–135.

Beckmann, M.M., & Stock, O.M. (2013). Antenatal massage for reducing perineal trauma. *Cochrane Database of Systematic Reviews, 4:* CD005123.

Bedford, V.H. (2009). Sibling relationships: Adulthood. In D. Carr (Eds.), *Encyclopedia of the life course and human development.* Boston: Gale Cengage.

Beduer. A., & others (2015, in press). Detection of Alzheimer's disease amyloid-beta plaque deposition by deep brain impedance profiling. *Journal of Neural Engineering.*

Beebe, D.W., Rose, D., & Amin, R. (2010). Attention, learning, and arousal of experimentally sleep-restricted adolescents in a simulated classroom. *Journal of Adolescent Health, 47,* 523–525.

Beech, A.R., Ward, T., & Fisher, D. (2006). The identification of sexual or violent motivations in men who assault women: Implications for treatment. *Journal of Interpersonal Violence, 21,* 1635–1653.

Beeghly, M., & others (2006). Prenatal cocaine exposure and children's language functioning at 6 and 9.5 years: Moderating effects of child age, birthweight, and gender. *Journal of Pediatric Psychology, 31,* 98–115.

Begus, K., & Southgate, V. (2012). Infant pointing serves an interrogative function. *Developmental Science, 15*(5), 611–617.

Behrens, H. (2012). Grammatical categories. In E.L. Bavin (Ed.), *Cambridge handbook of child language.* New York: Cambridge University Press.

Belansky, E.S., & Clements, P. (1992, March). *Adolescence: A crossroads for gender-role transcendence or gender-role intensification.* Paper presented at the meeting of the Society for Research on Adolescence, Washington, DC.

Belk, C., & Borden Maier, V. (2016, in press). *Biology* (5th ed.). Upper Saddle River, NJ: Pearson.

Bell, M.A. (2015, in press). Bringing the field of infant cognition and perception toward a biopsychosocial perspective. In S.D. Calkins (Ed.), *Handbook of infant development.* New York: Guilford.

Bell, M.A., & Cuevas, K. (2012). Using EEG to study cognitive development: Issues and practices. *Journal of Cognition and Development, 13,* 281–294.

Bell, M.A., & Cuevas, K. (2014). Psychobiology of executive function in early development. In J.A. Griffin, L.S. Freund, & P. McCardle (Eds.), *Executive function in preschool children.* Washington, DC: American Psychological Association.

Bell, M.A., & Cuevas, K. (2015). Psychobiology of executive function in early development. In J.A. Griffin & others (Eds.), *Executive function in preschool age children.* Washington, DC: American Psychological Association.

Bell, M.A., & Fox, N.A. (1992). The relations between frontal brain electrical activity and cognitive development during infancy. *Child Development, 63,* 1142–1163.

Bell, M.A., Kraybill, J.H., & Diaz, A. (2014). Reactivity, regulation, and remembering: Associations between temperament and memory. In P.J. Bauer & R. Fivush (Eds.), *Handbook on the development of children's memory.* New York: Wiley.

Bell, R.D., & others (2012). Apolipoprotein E controls cerebrovascular integrity via cyclophilin A. *Nature, 485,* 512–516.

Bell, S.M., & Ainsworth, M.D.S. (1972). Infant crying and maternal responsiveness. *Child Development, 43,* 1171–1190.

Belsky, J. (1981). Early human experience: A family perspective. *Developmental Psychology, 17,* 3–23.

Belsky, J., & Hartman, S. (2014). Gene-environment interaction in evolutionary perspective: Differential susceptibility to environmental influences. *World Psychiatry, 13,* 87–89.

Belsky, J., & van Ijzendoorn, M.H. (2015, in press). What works for whom? Genetic moderation of intervention efficacy. *Development and Psychopathology.*

Belsky, J., & others (2015, in press). Differential susceptibility to effects of maternal sensitivity? A study of candidate plasticity genes. *Development and Psychopathology.*

Bendersky, M., & Sullivan, M.W. (2007). Basic methods in infant research. In A. Slater & M. Lewis (Eds.), *Introduction to infant development* (2nd ed.). New York: Oxford University Press.

Benenson, J.F., Apostolaris, N.H., & Parnass, J. (1997). Age and sex differences in dyadic and group interaction. *Developmental Psychology, 33,* 538–543.

Bengtson, V.L. (1985). Diversity and symbolism in grandparental roles. In V.L. Bengtson & J. Robertson (Eds.), *Grandparenthood.* Newbury Park, CA: Sage.

Bengtson, V.L., Reedy, M.N., & Gordon, C. (1985). Aging and self-conceptions: Personality processes and social contexts. In J.E. Birren & K.W. Schaie (Eds.), *Handbook of the psychology of aging.* New York: Van Nostrand Reinhold.

Bengtsson, H., & Arvidsson, A. (2011). The impact of developing social perspective-taking skills on emotionality in middle and late childhood. *Social Development, 20,* 353–375.

Benichov, J., Cox, L.C., Tun, P.A., & Wingfield, A. (2012). Word recognition within a linguistic context: Effects of age, hearing acuity, verbal ability, and cognitive function. *Ear and Hearing, 33,* 250–256.

Benjamins, M.R., & Finlayson, M. (2007). Using religious services to improve health: Findings from a sample of middle-aged and older adults with multiple sclerosis. *Journal of Aging and Health, 19,* 537–553.

Bennett, C.I. (2015). *Comprehensive multicultural education* (8th ed.). Upper Saddle River, NJ: Pearson.

Bennett, K.M. (2006). Does marital status and marital status change predict physical health in older adults? *Psychological Medicine, 36,* 1313–1320.

Bennett, S.A., Bagot, C.N., & Arya, R. (2012). Pregnancy loss and thrombophilia: The elusive link. *British Journal of Hematology, 157*(5), 529–542.

Benokraitis, N. (2015). *Marriage and families* (8th ed.). Upper Saddle River, NJ: Pearson.

Benowitz-Fredericks, C.A., Garcia, K., Massey, M., Vassagar, B., & Borzekowski, D.L. (2012). Body image, eating disorders, and the relationship to adolescent media use. *Pediatric Clinics of North America, 59,* 693–704.

Ben-Zur, H. (2012). Loneliness, optimism, and well-being among married, divorced, and widowed individuals. *Journal of Psychology, 146,* 23–36.

Bera, A., & others (2014). Effects of kangaroo care on growth and development of low birthweight babies up to 12 months of age: A controlled clinical trial. *Acta Pediatrica, 103,* 643–650.

Berardi, N., Sale, A., & Maffei, L. (2015). Brain structural and functional development: Genetics and experience. *Developmental Medicine and Child Neurology, 57*(Suppl. 2), S4–S9.

Berchicci, M., & others (2014). Benefits of physical exercise on basic visuo-motor functions across age. *Frontiers in Aging Neuroscience, 6,* 48.

Berenbaum, S.A., & Bailey, J.M. (2003). Effects on gender identity of prenatal androgens and genital appearance: Evidence from girls with congenital adrenal hyperplasia. *Journal of Clinical Endocrinology and Metabolism, 88,* 1102–1106.

Berens, A.E., & Nelson, C.A. (2015, in press). The science of early adversity: Is there a role for large institutions in the care of vulnerable children? *Lancet.*

Berge, J.M., & others (2015, in press). The protective role of family meals for youth obesity: 10-year longitudinal associations. *Journal of Pediatrics.*

Bergen, D. (2015). Psychological approaches to the study of play. In J.E. Johnson & others (Eds.), *Handbook of the study of play.* Blue Ridge Summit, PA: Rowman & Littlefield.

Berger, I., Remington, A., Leitner, Y., & Leviton, A. (2015). Brain development and the attention spectrum. *Frontiers in Human Neuroscience, 9,* 23.

Berger, S.E., Chan, G., & Adolph, K.E. (2014). What cruising infants understand about support for locomotion. *Infancy, 19,* 117–137.

Bergmuller, S. (2013). The relationship between cultural individualism-collectivism and student aggression across 62 countries. *Aggressive Behavior, 39,* 182–200.

Berk, L.E. (1994). Why children talk to themselves. *Scientific American, 271*(5), 78–83.

Berk, L.E., & Spuhl, S.T. (1995). Maternal interaction, private speech, and task performance in preschool children. *Early Childhood Research Quarterly, 10,* 145–169.

Berko Gleason, J. (2003). Unpublished review of J.W. Santrock's *Life-span development,* 9th ed. (New York: McGraw-Hill).

Berko Gleason, J. (2005). The development of language: An overview. In J. Berko Gleason & N.B. Ratner (Eds.), *The development of language* (6th ed.). Boston: Allyn & Bacon.

Berko Gleason, J. (2009). The development of language: An overview. In J. Berko Gleason & N.B. Ratner (Eds.), *The development of language* (7th ed.). Boston: Allyn & Bacon.

Berko, J. (1958). The child's learning of English morphology. *Word, 14,* 150–177.

Berlin, L.J., & others (2009). Correlates and consequences of spanking and verbal punishment for low-income White, African-American, and Mexican American toddlers. *Child Development, 80,* 1403–1420.

Berlyne, D.E. (1960). *Conflict, arousal, and curiosity.* New York: McGraw-Hill.

Berman, M.G., & others (2013). Dimensionality of brain networks linked to life-long individual differences in self-control. *Nature Communications, 4,* 1373.

Berman, S.L., You, Y., Schwartz, S., Teo, G., & Mochizuki, K. (2011). Identity exploration, commitment, and distress: A cross-national investigation in China, Taiwan, Japan, and the United States. *Child Youth Care Forum, 40,* 65–75.

Bernard, J.P., & others (2013). Combined screening for open spina bifida at 11–13 weeks using fetal biparietal diameter and maternal serum markers. *American Journal of Obstetrics and Gynecology, 209,* e1–e5.

Bernard, K., & others (2012). Enhancing attachment organization among maltreated children: Results from a randomized clinical trial. *Child Development, 83,* 623–636.

Berndt, T.J., & Perry, T.B. (1990). Distinctive features and effects of early adolescent friendships. In R. Montemayor (Ed.), *Advances in adolescent research.* Greenwich, CT: JAI Press.

Berner, J., & others (2015, in press). Factors influencing Internet usage in older adults (65 years and above) living in rural and urban Sweden. *Health Informatics.*

Bernier, A., & others (2013). Sleep and cognition in preschool years: Specific links to executive functioning. *Child Development., 84*(5), 1542–1553.

Berninger, V.W. (2006). Learning disabilities. In W. Damon & R. Lerner (Eds.), *Handbook of child psychology* (6th ed.). New York: Wiley.

Berninger, V., & Dunn, M. (2012). Brain and behavioral response to intervention for specific reading, writing, and math disabilities: What works for whom? In B. Wong & D. Butler (Eds.), *Learning about LD* (4th ed.). New York: Elsevier.

Berninger, V., & others (2015). Computer instruction in handwriting, spelling, and composing for students with specific learning disabilities in grades 4 to 9. *Computers & Education, 81,* 154–168.

Bernstein, N. (2004, March 7). Young love, new caution. *The New York Times,* p. A22.

Berntsen, D., & Rubin, D.C. (2002). Emotionally charged autobiographical memories across the life span: The role of happy, sad, traumatic, and involuntary memories. *Psychology and Aging, 17,* 636–652.

Berookhim, B.M., & Bar-Chama, N. (2011). Medical implications of erectile dysfunction. *Medical Clinics of North America, 95,* 213–221.

Berry, A., & others (2012). Sustained hippocampal neurogenesis in females is amplified in P66 (Shc-/-) mice: An animal model of healthy aging. *Hippocampus, 22*(12), 2249–2259.

Berry, J.W. (2015). Acculturation. In J.E. Grusec & P.D. Hastings (Eds.), *Handbook of socialization* (2nd ed.). New York: Guilford.

Berryman, N., & others (2013). Executive functions, physical fitness, and mobility in well-functioning older adults. *Experimental Gerontology, 48,* 1402–1409.

Bersamin, M.M., Bourdeau, B., Fisher, D.A., & Grube, J.W. (2010). Television use, sexual behavior, and relationship status at last oral sex and vaginal intercourse. *Sexuality and Culture, 14,* 157–168.

Bersamin, M.M., & others (2014). Risky business: Is there an association between casual sex and mental health among emerging adults? *Journal of Sex Research, 51,* 43–51.

Berscheid, E. (1988). Some comments on love's anatomy: Or, whatever happened to old-fashioned lust? In R.J. Sternberg (Ed.), *Anatomy of love.* New Haven, CT: Yale University Press.

Berscheid, E. (2010). Love in the fourth dimension. *Annual Review of Psychology* (Vol. 61). Palo Alto, CA: Annual Reviews.

Berscheid, E., & Fei, J. (1977). Sexual jealousy and romantic love. In G. Clinton & G. Smith (Eds.), *Sexual jealousy.* Englewood Cliffs, NJ: Prentice-Hill.

Bertenthal, B.I. (2008). Perception and action. In M.M. Haith & J.B. Benson (Eds.), *Encyclopedia of infant and early childhood development.* Oxford, UK: Elsevier.

Bertenthal, B.I., Longo, M.R., & Kenny, S. (2007). Phenomenal permanence and the development of predictive tracking in infancy. *Child Development, 78,* 350–363.

Bertoglio, K., & Hendren, R.L. (2009). New developments in autism. *Psychiatric Clinics of North America, 32,* 1–14.

Bertorelle, R., & others (2014). Telomeres, telomerase, and colorectal cancer. *World Journal of Gastroenterology, 20,* 1940–1950.

Bertrand, R., Graham, E.K., & Lachman, M.E. (2013). Personality development in adulthood and old age. In I.B. Weiner & others (Eds.), *Handbook of psychology* (2nd ed., Vol. 6). New York: Wiley.

Bertrand, R.M., & Lachman, M.E. (2003). Personality development in adulthood and old age. In I.B. Weiner (Ed.), *Handbook of psychology* (Vol. 6). New York: Wiley.

Berwid, O.G., & Halperin, J.M. (2012). Emerging support for a role of exercise in attention-deficit/hyperactivity disorder intervention planning. *Current Psychiatry Reports, 14,* 543–551.

Best, J.R. (2010). Effects of physical activity on children's executive function: Contributions of experimental research on aerobic exercise. *Developmental Review, 30*(4), 331–351.

Betts, D., Smith, C.A., & Hannah, D.G. (2012). Acupuncture as a therapeutic treatment option for threatened miscarriage. *BMC Complementary and Alternative Medicine, 12,* 20.

Betts, K.S., Williams, G.M., Najman, J.M., & Alati, R. (2014). Maternal depressive, anxious, and stress symptoms during pregnancy predict internalizing problems in adolescence. *Depression and Anxiety, 31,* 9–18.

Beuker, K.T., Rommelse, N.N, Donders, R., & Buitelaar, J.K. (2013). Development of early communication skills in the first two years of life. *Infant Behavior and Development, 36,* 71–83.

Bevan, D., Wittkowski, A., & Wells, A. (2013). A multiple-baseline study of the effects associated with metacognitive therapy in postpartum depression. *Journal of Midwifery and Women's Health, 58,* 69–75.

Beyene, Y. (1986). Cultural significance and physiological manifestations of menopause: A biocultural analysis. *Culture, Medicine and Psychiatry, 10,* 47–71.

Bhullar, N., Schutte, N.S., & Malouff, J.M. (2013). The nature of well-being: The roles of hedonic and eudaimonic processes and trait emotional intelligence. *Journal of Psychology, 147,* 1–16.

Bialystok, E. (1997). Effects of bilingualism and biliteracy on children's emerging concepts of print. *Developmental Psychology, 33,* 429–440.

Bialystok, E. (2001). *Bilingualism in development: Language, literacy, and cognition.* New York: Cambridge University Press.

Bialystok, E. (2007). Acquisition of literacy in preschool children: A framework for research. *Language Learning, 57,* 45–77.

Bialystok, E. (2011). *Becoming bilingual: Emergence of cognitive outcomes of bilingualism in immersion education.* Paper presented at the meeting of the Society for Research in Child Development, Montreal.

Bialystok, E. (2014). Language experience changes language and cognitive ability: Implications for social policy. In B. Spolsky, O. Inbar-Lourie, & M. Tannenbaum (Eds.), *Challenges for language education and policy.* New York: Routledge.

Bialystok, E. (2015, in press). The impact of bilingualism on cognition. In R. Scott & S. Kosslyn (Eds.), *Emerging trends in the social and behavioral sciences.* New York: Wiley.

Bialystok, E., & Craik, F.I.M. (2010). Cognitive and linguistic progressing in the bilingual mind. *Current Directions in Psychological Science, 19,* 19–23.

Bialystok, E., Craik, F.I., Binns, M.A., Ossher, L., & Freedman, M. (2014). Effects of bilingualism on the age of onset and progression of MCI and AD: Evidence from executive function tests. *Neuropsychology, 28,* 290–304.

Bian, Z., & Andersen, G.J. (2008). Aging and the perceptual organization of 3-D scenes. *Psychology and Aging, 23,* 342–352.

Bick, J., & others (2015, in press). Effect of early institutionalization and foster care on long-term white matter development: A randomized clinical trial. *JAMA Pediatrics.*

Biehle, S.N., & Mickelson, K.D. (2012). First-time parents' expectations about the division of childcare and play. *Journal of Family Psychology, 26,* 36–45.

Bielak, A.A., Cherbuin, N., Bunce, D., & Anstey, K.J. (2014). Preserved differentiation between physical activity and cognitive performance across young, middle, and older adulthood across eight years. *Journals of Gerontology B: Psychological Sciences and Social Sciences, 69,* 523–532.

Bierman, K.L., & others (2014). Effects of Head Start REDI on children's outcomes 1 year later in different kindergarten contexts. *Child Development, 85*(1), 140–159.

Bigler, R. (2015). Cognition in developing social identities and beliefs. In R.M. Lerner (Ed.), *Handbook of child psychology and developmental science* (7th ed.). New York: Wiley.

Bihlmeyer, N.A., & others (2015, in press). Genetic diversity is a predictor of mortality in humans. *BMC Genetics.*

Bill and Melinda Gates Foundation (2011). *College-ready education.* Retrieved August 21, 2011, from www.gatesfoundation.org/college-ready-education/Pages/default.aspx

Billy, J.O.G., Rodgers, J.L., & Udry, J.R. (1984). Adolescent sexual behavior and friendship choice. *Social Forces, 62,* 653–678.

Birch, L.L., & Doub, A.E. (2014). Learning to eat: Birth to 2 years. *American Journal of Clinical Nutrition, 99,* 723S–728S.

Birch, S., & Bloom, P. (2003). Children are cursed: An asymmetric bias in mental state attribution. *Psychological Science, 14,* 283–286.

Birkeland, M.S., Melkevick, O., Holsen, I., & Wold, B. (2012). Trajectories of global self-esteem development during adolescence. *Journal of Adolescence, 35,* 43–54.

Birman, B.F., & others (2007). *State and local implementation of the "No Child Left Behind Act." Volume II—Teacher quality under "NCLB": Interim report.* Jessup, MD: U.S. Department of Education.

Birren, J.E. (Ed.). (1996). *Encyclopedia of gerontology.* San Diego: Academic Press.

Birren, J.E. (2002). Unpublished review of J.W. Santrock's *Life-span development,* 9th ed. (New York: McGraw-Hill).

Bischoff, K.E., Sudore, R., Miao, Y., Boscardin, W.J., & Smith, A.K. (2013). Advance care planning and the quality of end-of-life care in older adults. *Journal of the American Geriatrics Society, 61,* 209–214.

Bjorklund, D.F. (2012). *Children's thinking* (5th ed.). Boston: Cengage.

Bjorklund, D.F., & Pellegrini, A.D. (2002). The origins of human nature. New York: Oxford University Press.

Bjorklund, D.F., & Rosenbaum, K. (2000). Middle childhood: Cognitive development. In A. Kazdin (Ed.), *Encyclopedia of psychology.* New York: Oxford University Press.

Black, M.M., & Dewey, K.G. (2014). Promoting equity through integrated early child development nutrition interventions. *Annals of the New York Academy of Sciences, 1308,* 1–10.

Blackwell, L.S., & Dweck, C.S. (2008). *The motivational impact of a computer-based program that teaches how the brain changes with learning.* Unpublished manuscript, Department of Psychology, Stanford University, Palo Alto, CA.

Blackwell, L.S., Trzesniewski, K.H., & Dweck, C.S. (2007). Implicit theories of intelligence predict achievement across an adolescent transition: A longitudinal study and an intervention. *Child Development, 78,* 246–263.

Blaga, O.M., & others (2009). Structure and continuity of intellectual development in early childhood. *Intelligence, 37,* 106–113.

Blair, C., & Raver, C.C. (2012). Child development in the context of poverty: Experiential canalization of brain and behavior. *American Psychologist, 67,* 309–318.

Blair, C., Raver, C.C., & Berry, D.J. (2014). Two approaches estimating the effect of parenting on the development of executive function in early childhood. *Developmental Psychology, 50,* 554–565.

Blair, C., & Razza, R.P. (2007). Relating effortful control, executive functioning, and false belief understanding to emerging math and literacy ability in kindergarten. *Child Development, 78,* 647–663.

Blair, C., & others (2015). Multiple aspects of self-regulation uniquely predict mathematics but not letter-word knowledge in the early elementary grades. *Developmental Psychology, 5,* 459–472.

Blair, S.N. (1990, January). Personal communication. Aerobics Institute, Dallas.

Blair, S.N., & others (1989). Physical fitness and all-cause mortality: A prospective study of healthy men and women. *Journal of the American Medical Association, 262,* 2395–2401.

Blake, J.S. (2015). *Nutrition and you* (3rd ed.). Upper Saddle River, NJ: Pearson.

Blake, M. (2013). Group reminiscence therapy for adults with dementia: A review. *British Journal of Community Nursing, 18,* 228–233.

Blakemore, J.E.O., Berenbaum, S.A., & Liben, L.S. (2009). *Gender development.* Clifton, NJ: Psychology Press.

Blakemore, S-J., & Mills, K. (2014). The social brain in adolescence. *Annual Review of Psychology* (Vol. 65). Palo Alto, CA: Annual Reviews.

Blanchard-Fields, F. (2007). Everyday problem solving and emotion. *Current Directions in Psychological Science, 16,* 26–31.

Blass, E. (2008). Suckling. In M.M. Haith & J.B. Benson (Eds.), *Encyclopedia of infant and early childhood development.* Oxford, UK: Elsevier.

Blieszner, R., & Roberto, K.A. (2012). Partner and friend relationships in adulthood. In S.K. Whitbourne & M. Sliwinski (Eds.), *Wiley-Blackwell handbook of adult development and aging.* New York: Wiley.

Bloodworth, M., Bloodworth, N., & Ely, E.W. (2015). A template for non-religious-based discussions about euthanasia. *Lincare Quarterly, 82,* 49–54.

Bloom, B. (1985). *Developing talent in young people.* New York: Ballantine.

Bloom, L. (1998). Language acquisition in its developmental context. In W. Damon (Ed.), *Handbook of child psychology* (5th ed., Vol. 2). New York: Wiley.

Bloom, L., Lifter, K., & Broughton, J. (1985). The convergence of early cognition and language in the second year of life: Problems in conceptualization and measurement. In M. Barrett (Ed.), *Single word speech.* London: Wiley.

Bloom, P., & German, T.P. (2000). Two reasons to abandon the false belief task as a test of theory of mind. *Cognition, 77,* B25–B31.

Bloomer, R.J., & others (2011). A 21-day Daniel Fast improves selected biomarkers of antioxidant status and oxidative stress in men and women. *Nutrition and Metabolism, 8,* 17.

Bloor, C., & White, F. (1983). Unpublished manuscript. La Jolla, CA: University of California at San Diego.

Blumberg, S.J., Vahratian, A., & Blumberg, J.H. (2014). Marriage, cohabitation, and men's use of preventive health services. *NCHS Data Brief, 154,* 1–8.

Blumel, J.E., Lavin, P., Vellejo, M.S., & Sarra, S. (2014). Menopause or climacteric, just a semantic discussion or has it clinical implications? *Climacteric, 17,* 235–241.

Blustein, D.L. (2013). The psychology of working: A new perspective in a new era. In D.L. Blustein (Ed.), *Oxford handbook of the psychology of working.* New York: Oxford University Press.

Boccardi, V., & others (2015, in press). Stn1 is critical for telomere maintenance and long-term viability of somatic human cells. *Aging Cell.*

Boccia, M., Silveri, M.C., & Guariglia, C. (2014). Visuo-perceptive priming in Alzheimer's disease: Evidence for a multi-componential implicit memory system. *Journal of Alzheimer's Disease, 40,* 455–463.

Boden, J.S., Fischer, J.L., & Niehuis, S. (2010). Predicting marital adjustment from young adults' initial levels of and changes in emotional intimacy over time: A 25-year longitudinal study. *Journal of Adult Development, 17,* 121–134.

Bodner, E., & Cohen-Fridel, S. (2010). Relations between attachment styles, ageism, and quality of life in late life. *International Psychogeriatrics, 22,* 1353–1361.

Bodner, E., & Cohen-Fridel, S. (2014). The paths leading from attachment to ageism: A structural equation model approach. *Death Studies, 38,* 423–429.

Bodrova, E., & Leong, D.J. (2007). *Tools of the mind* (2nd ed.). Geneva, Switzerland: International Bureau of Education, UNESCO.

Bodrova, E., & Leong, D.J. (2015). Standing 'A head taller than himself': Vygotskian and post-Vygotskian views on children's play. In J.E. Johnson & others (Eds.), *Handbook of the study of play.* Blue Ridge Summit, PA: Rowan & Littlefield.

Bodrova, E., Leong, D.J., & Akhutina, T.V. (2011). When everything new is well-forgotten old: Vygotsky/ Luria insights in the development of executive functions. In *New Directions for Child and Adolescent Development, 133,* 11–28.

Boelen, P.A. (2013). Symptoms of prolonged grief, depression, and adult separation anxiety: Distinctiveness and correlates. *Psychiatry Research, 207,* 68–72.

Boelen, P.A. (2015, in press). Optimism in prolonged grief and depression following loss: A three-wave longitudinal study. *Psychiatry Research.*

Boer, D., & Fischer, R. (2013). How and when do personal values guide our attitudes and sociality? Explaining cross-cultural variability in attitude-value linkages. *Psychological Bulletin, 139,* 1113–1147.

Boer, L.M., & others (2014). Assessing the stages of the grieving process in chronic obstructive pulmonary disease (COPD): Validation of the Acceptance of Disease and Impairments Questionnaire (ADIQ). *International Journal of Behavioral Medicine, 21,* 561–570.

Boerner, K., Jopp, J.S., Carr, D., Sosinsky, L., & Kim, S.K. (2014). "His" and "her" marriage? The role of positive and negative characteristics in global marital satisfaction among older adults. *Journals of Gerontology B: Psychological Sciences and Social Sciences, 69,* 579–589.

Bogart, L.M., & others (2014). Peer victimization in fifth grade and health in tenth grade. *Pediatrics, 133,* 440–447.

Bolea-Alamanac, B., & others (2014). Evidence-based guidelines for the pharmacological management of attention deficit hyperactivity disorder: Update on recommendations from the British Association of Psychopharmacology. *Journal of Psychopharmacology, 28,* 179–203.

Bolkan, C., & Hooker, K. (2012). Self-regulation and social cognition in adulthood: The gyroscope of personality. In S.K. Whitbourne & M.J. Sliwinski (Eds.), *Wiley-Blackwell handbook of aging.* New York: Wiley.

Bolkan, C., Hooker, K., & Coehlo, D. (2015). Possible selves and depressive symptoms in later life. *Research on Aging, 37,* 41–62.

Bonaccorso, C.M., & others (2015). Fragile X mental retardation protein (FMRP) interacting proteins exhibit different expression patterns during development. *International Journal of Developmental Neuroscience, 42,* 15–23.

Bonanno, R.A., & Hymel, S. (2013). Cyber bullying and internalizing difficulties: Above and beyond the impact of traditional forms of bullying. *Journal of Youth and Adolescence, 42,* 685–697.

Bond, B.J., Richards, M.N., & Calvert, S.L. (2013). Media and pediatric obesity. In D. Lemish (Ed.), *The handbook of children and the media.* New York: Routledge.

Boniel-Nissim, M., & others (2015). International trends in electronic media communication among 11- to 15-year-olds in 30 countries from 2002 to 2010: Association with ease of communication with friends of the opposite sex. *European Journal of Public Health, 25*(Suppl. 2), S41–S45.

Bono, G. (2012, August 5). *Searching for the developmental role of gratitude: A 4-year longitudinal analysis.* Paper presented at the American Psychological Association, Orlando.

Bonvillian, J. (2005). Unpublished review of J.W. Santrock's *Topical approach to life-span development,* 3rd ed. (New York: McGraw-Hill).

Booij, G.E. (2013). Morphological analysis. In B. Eeine & H. Narrog (Eds.), *Oxford handbook of linguistics.* New York: Oxford University Press.

Bookwala, J., & Jacobs, J. (2004). Age, marital processes, and depressed affect. *The Gerontologist, 44,* 328–338.

Boraska, V., & others (2014). A genome-wide study of anorexia nervosa. *Molecular Psychiatry, 19,* 1085–1094.

Borella, E., Caretti, B., Zanoni, G., Zavagnin, M., & De Beni, R. (2013). Working memory training in old age: An examination of transfer and maintenance effects. *Archives of Clinical Neuropsychology, 28,* 331–347.

Borges, N.J., McNally, C.J., Maguire, C.P., Werth, J.L., & Britton, P.J. (2008). Work, health, diversity, and social justice: Expanding and extending the discussion. *The Counseling Psychologist, 36,* 127–131.

Borges, S.M., Radanovic, M., & Forienza, O.V. (2015, in press). Functional mobility in a divided attention task in older adults with cognitive impairment. *Journal of Motor Behavior.*

Borich, G.D. (2014). *Effective teaching methods* (8th ed.). Upper Saddle River, NJ: Pearson.

Bornstein, M.H. (1975). Qualities of color vision in infancy. *Journal of Experimental Child Psychology, 19,* 401–409.

Bornstein, M.H., & Leventhal, T. (2015). Children in bioecological landscapes of development. In R.M. Lerner (Ed.), *Handbook of child psychology and developmental science* (7th ed.). New York: Wiley.

Boron, J.B., Willis, S.L., & Schaie, K.W. (2007). Cognitive training gain as a predictor of mental status. *Journals of Gerontology B: Psychological Sciences and Social Sciences, 62B,* P45–P52.

Borrell, L.N., & Samuel, L. (2014). Body mass index categories and mortality risk in U.S. adults: The effect of overweight and obesity on advancing death. *American Journal of Public Health, 104,* 512–519.

Borst, G., & others (2013). Inhibitory control efficiency in a Piaget-like class-inclusion task in school-age children and adults: A developmental negative priming study. *Developmental Psychology, 49,* 1366–1374.

Bosma, H.A., & Kunnen, E.S. (2001). Determinants and mechanisms in ego identity development: A review and synthesis. *Developmental Review, 21,* 39–66.

Boss, L., Kang, D.H., & Branson, S. (2015). Loneliness and cognitive function in the older adult: A systematic review. *International Psychogeriatrics, 27,* 541–553.

Bosworth, B. (2012, February). *Economic consequences of the great recession: Evidence from the Panel Study of Income Dynamics.* Chestnut Hill, MA: Center for Retirement Research at Boston College.

Boucher, J., Mayes, A., & Bigham, S. (2012). Memory in autism spectrum disorder. *Psychological Bulletin, 138,* 458–496.

Bould, H., & others (2014). Association between early temperament and depression at 18 years. *Depression and Anxiety, 31,* 729–736.

Bouman, W.P. (2008). Sexuality in later life. In R. Jacoby, C. Oppenheimer, T. Dening, & A. Thomas (Eds.), *Oxford textbook of old age psychiatry.* New York: Oxford University Press.

Bourassa, K.J., Sharra, D.A., & Whisman, M.A. (2015, in press). Women in very low quality marriages gain life satisfaction following divorce. *Journal of Family Psychology.*

Bowen, C.E., Noack, M.G., & Staudinger, U.M. (2011). Aging in the work context. In K.W. Schaie & S.L. Willis (Eds.), *Handbook of the psychology of aging* (7th ed.). New York: Elsevier.

Bower, T.G.R. (1966). Slant perception and shape constancy in infants, *Science, 151,* 832–834.

Bowlby, J. (1969). *Attachment and loss* (Vol. 1). London: Hogarth Press.

Bowlby, J. (1980). *Attachment and loss* (Vol. 3). New York: Basic Books.

Bowlby, J. (1989). *Secure and insecure attachment.* New York: Basic Books.

Buckner, J.C., Mezzacappa, E., & Beardslee, W.R. (2009). Self-regulation and its relations to adaptive functioning in low-income youths. *American Journal of Orthopsychiatry, 79,* 19–30.

Bucur, B., & Madden, D.J. (2007). Information processing/cognition. In J.E. Birren (Ed.), *Encyclopedia of gerontology* (2nd ed.). San Diego: Academic Press.

Bucur, B., & Madden, D.J. (2010). Effects of adult age and blood pressure on executive function and speed of processing. *Experimental Aging Research, 36,* 153–168.

Bugenthal, D.B., Corpuz, R., & Beaulieu, D.A. (2015). An evolutionary approach to socialization. In J.E. Grusec & P.D. Hastings (Eds.), *Handbook of socialization* (2nd ed.). New York: Guilford.

Buhler, E., & others (2011). Differential diagnosis of autism spectrum disorder and attention deficit hyperactivity disorder by means of inhibitory control and 'theory of mind.' *Journal of Autism and Developmental Disorders, 41,* 718–726.

Buhling, K.J., & others (2014). The use of complementary and alternative medicine by women transitioning through menopause in Germany: Results of a survey of women aged 45–60 years. *Complementary Therapies in Medicine, 22,* 94–98.

Buhrmester, D. (1998). Need fulfillment, interpersonal competence, and the developmental contexts of early adolescent friendship. In W.M. Bukowski & A.F. Newcomb (Eds.), *The company they keep: Friendship in childhood and adolescence.* New York: Cambridge University Press.

Buhs, E.S., & Ladd, G.W. (2002). Peer rejection as antecedent of young children's school adjustment: An examination of mediating processes. *Developmental Psychology, 37,* 550–560.

Bui, E., & others (2015). Grief-related panic symptoms in complicated grief. *Journal of Affective Disorders, 170,* 213–216.

Buist, K.L., Dekovic, M., & Prinzie, P. (2013). Sibling relationship quality and psychopathology of children and adolescents: A meta-analysis. *Clinical Psychology Review, 33,* 97–106.

Buitelaar, J., Karr, C., & Asherton, P. (2010). *ADHD in adulthood.* New York: Cambridge University Press.

Bulf, H., & Valenza, E. (2014). Object-based visual attention in 8-month-old infants: Evidence from an eye-tracking study. *Developmental Psychology, 57,* 238–248.

Bullock, M., & Lutkenhaus, P. (1990). Who am I? Self-understanding in toddlers. *Merrill-Palmer Quarterly, 36,* 217–238.

Bumpass, L., & Aquilino, W. (1994). *A social map of midlife: Family and work over the middle life course.* Center for Demography and Ecology, University of Wisconsin, Madison, WI.

Bumpus, M.F., Crouter, A.C., & McHale, S.M. (2001). Parental autonomy granting during adolescence: Exploring gender differences in context. *Developmental Psychology, 37,* 163–173.

Burchinal, M., Magnuson, K., Powell, D., & Hong, S.S. (2015). Early child care and education. In R.M. Lerner (Ed.), *Handbook of child psychology and developmental science* (7th ed.). New York: Wiley.

Burchinal, M.R., Peisner-Feinberg, E., Pianta, R., & Howes, C. (2002). Development of academic skills from preschool through second grade: Family and classroom predictors of developmental trajectories. *Journal of School Psychology, 40*(5), 415–436.

Burchinal, M.R., & others (2015). Early child care and education. In R.M. Lerner (Ed.), *Handbook of child psychology and developmental science* (7th ed.). New York: Wiley.

Burden, P.R., & Byrd, D.M. (2013). *Methods for effective teaching* (6th ed.). Upper Saddle River, NJ: Pearson.

Burger, J.M. (2015). *Personality* (9th ed.). Boston: Cengage.

Burke, D.M., & Shafto, M.A. (2004). Aging and language production. *Current Directions in Psychological Science, 13,* 21–24.

Burke, J.D., & Loeber, R. (2015). The effectiveness of the Stop Now and Plan (SNAP) program for boys at risk for violence and delinquency. *Prevention Science, 16,* 242–253.

Burke-Adams, A. (2007). The benefits of equalizing standards and creativity: Discovering a balance in instruction. *Gifted Child Quarterly, 30,* 58–63.

Burkle, C.M., & Pope, T.M. (2015). Brain death: Legal obligations and the courts. *Seminars in Neurology, 35,* 174–179.

Burns, C., Dunn, A., Brady, M., Starr, N., & Blosser, C. (2013). *Pediatric primary care* (5th ed.). New York: Elsevier.

Burt, S.A. (2014). Research review: The shared environment as a key source of variability in child and adolescent psychopathology. *Journal of Child Psychology and Psychiatry, 55,* 304–312.

Burton, E., & others (2015). Effectiveness of exercise programs to reduce falls in older people with dementia living in the community: A systematic review and meta-analysis. *Clinical Interventions in Aging, 9,* 421–434.

Burton, R.V. (1984). A paradox in theories and research in moral development. In W.M. Kurtines & J.L. Gewirtz (Eds.), *Morality, moral behavior, and moral development.* New York: Wiley.

Busch, H., & Hofer, J. (2012). Self-regulation and milestones of adult development: Intimacy and generativity. *Developmental Psychology, 48,* 282–293.

Busching, R., & Krahe, B. (2015, in press). The girls set the tone: Gendered classroom norms and the development of aggression in adolescence. *Personality and Social Psychology Bulletin.*

Bush, K.R., & Peterson, G.W. (2013). Parent-child relationships in diverse contexts. In G.W. Peterson & K.R. Bush (Eds.), *Handbook of marriage and the family* (3rd ed.). New York: Springer.

Bushnell, I.W.R. (2003). Newborn face recognition. In O. Pascalis & A. Slater (Eds.), *The development of face processing in infancy and early childhood.* New York: NOVA Science.

Buss, D.M. (2008). *Evolutionary psychology* (3rd ed.). Boston: Allyn & Bacon.

Buss, D.M. (2012). *Evolutionary psychology* (4th ed.). Boston: Allyn & Bacon.

Buss, D.M. (2015). *Evolutionary psychology* (5th ed.). Upper Saddle River, NJ: Pearson.

Buss, D.M., & Penke, L. (2014). Evolutionary personality psychology. In M. Mikulincer & P.R. Shaver (Eds.), *APA handbook personality and social psychology.* Washington, DC: APA Books.

Buss, D.M., & others (1990). International preferences in selecting mates: A study of 37 cultures. *Journal of Cross-Cultural Psychology, 21,* 5–47.

Buss, K.A., & Goldsmith, H.H. (2007). Biobehavioral approaches to early socioemotional development. In C.A. Brownell & C.B. Kopp (Eds.), *Socioemotional development in the toddler years.* New York: Guilford.

Busschaert, C., & others (2015). Tracking and predictors of screen time from early adolescence to early adulthood: A 10-year follow-up study. *Journal of Adolescent Health, 56,* 440–448.

Bussey, K., & Bandura, A. (1999). Social cognitive theory of gender development and differentiation. *Psychological Review, 106,* 676–713.

Butler, R.N., & Lewis, M. (2002). *The new love and sex after 60.* New York: Ballantine.

Butrica, B.A., & Smith, K.E. (2012). The retirement prospects of divorced women. *Social Security Bulletin, 72*(1), 11–22.

Butrica, B.A., Smith, K.E., & Iams, H.M. (2012). This is not your parents' retirement: Comparing retirement income across generations. *Social Security Bulletin, 72,* 37–58.

Buttelmann, D., Over, H., Carpenter, M., & Tomasello, M. (2014). Eighteen-month-olds understand false beliefs in an unexpected-contents task. *Journal of Experimental Child Psychology, 119,* 120–126.

Buttermore, E.D., Thaxton, C.L., & Bhat, M.A. (2013). Organization and maintenance of molecular domains in myelinated axons. *Journal of Neuroscience Research, 91*(5), 603–622.

Buttitta, M., Iliescu, C., Rousseau, A., & Guerrien, A. (2014). Quality of life in overweight and obese children and adolescents: A literature review. *Quality of Life Research, 23,* 1117–1139.

Buzwell, S., & Rosenthal, D. (1996). Constructing a sexual self: Adolescents' sexual self-perceptions and sexual risk-taking. *Journal of Research on Adolescence, 6,* 489–513.

Byard, R.W. (2013). Breastfeeding and sudden infant death syndrome. *Journal of Pediatric Child Health, 49,* E353.

Byrnes, J.P. (2012). How neuroscience contributes to our understanding of learning and development in typically developing and special needs students. In K.R. Harris, S. Graham, & T. Urdan (Eds.), *APA educational psychology handbook.* Washington, DC: American Psychological Association.

C

Cabeza, R. (2002). Hemispheric asymmetry reduction in older adults: The HAROLD model. *Psychology and Aging, 17,* 85–100.

Cabeza, R., & Dennis, N.A. (2013). Frontal lobes and aging: Deterioration and compensation. In D.T. Stuss & R.T. Knight (Eds.), *Principles of frontal lobe function* (2nd ed.). New York: Oxford University Press.

Cabrera, N.J., Hofferth, S.L., & Chae, S. (2011). Patterns and predictors of father-infant engagement across race/ethnic groups. *Early Childhood Research Quarterly, 26,* 365–375.

Cacioppo, J.T., Cacioppo, S., Gonzaga, G.C., Ogburn, E.L., & VanderWheele, T.J. (2013). Marital satisfaction and break-ups differ across on-line and off-line meeting venues. *Proceedings of the National Academy of Sciences, 110*(25), 10135–10140.

Caetano, J., & Delgado Alves, J. (2015, in press). Heart rate and cardiovascular protection. *European Journal of Internal Medicine.*

Caeymaex, L., & others (2013). Perceived role in end-of-life decision making in the NICU affects long-term parental grief response. *Archives of Disease in Childhood: Fetal and Neonatal Edition, 98*(1), F26–F31.

Cagney, K.A., Browning, C.R., Iveniuk, J., & English, N. (2014). The onset of depression during the great recession: Foreclosure and older adult mental health. *American Journal of Public Health, 104,* 498–505.

Cahill, K.E., Giandrea, M.D., & Quinn, J.F. (2015, in press). Retirement patterns and the macroeconomy, 1992–2010: The prevalence and determinants of bridge jobs, retirement, and reentry among three recent cohorts of older Americans. *Gerontologist.*

Cai, L., Chan, J.S., Yan, J.H., & Peng, K. (2014). Brain plasticity and motor practice in cognitive aging. *Frontiers in Aging Neuroscience, 6,* 31.

Cai, M., Hardy, S.A., Olsen, J.A., Nelson, D.A., & Yamawaki, N. (2013). Adolescent-parent attachment as a mediator of relationships between parenting and adolescent social behavior and well-being in China. *International Journal of Psychology, 48,* 1185–1190.

Cain, M.A., Bornick, P., & Whiteman, V. (2013). The maternal, fetal, and neonatal effects of cocaine exposure in pregnancy. *Clinical Obstetrics and Gynecology, 56,*124–132.

Cain, N., & Gradisar, M. (2010). Electronic media use and sleep in school-aged children and adolescents. *Sleep Medicine, 11,* 735–742.

Calamaro, C.J., Mason, T.B., & Ratcliffe, S.J. (2009). Adolescents living the 24/7 lifestyle: Effects of caffeine and technology on sleep duration and daytime functioning. *Pediatrics, 123,* e1005–e1010.

Caldwell, B.A., & Redeker, N.S. (2015, in press). Maternal stress and psychological status and sleep in minority preschool children. *Public Health Nursing.*

Calkins, S.D., & Dollar, J. (2014). Caregiving influences on emotional regulation: Educational implications of a behavioral perspective. In R. Pekrun & L. Linnebrink-Garcia (Eds.), *International handbook of emotions in education.* New York: Routledge.

Callaghan, B.L., Li, S., & Richardson, R. (2014). The elusive engram: What can infantile amnesia tell us about memory? *Trends in Neuroscience, 37,* 47–53.

Callaghan, M.F., & others (2014). Widespread age-related differences in the human brain microstructure revealed by quantitative magnetic resonance imaging. *Neurobiology of Aging, 35,* 1862–1872.

Callaghan, T., & Corbit, J. (2015). The development of symbolic representation. In R.M. Lerner (Ed.), *Handbook of child psychology and developmental science* (7th ed.). New York: Wiley.

Callahan, D. (2009). Death, mourning, and medical practice. *Perspectives in Biological Medicine, 52,* 103–115.

Calvert, S.L. (2015). Children and digital media. In R.M. Lerner (Ed.), *Handbook of child psychology and developmental science* (7th ed.). New York: Wiley.

Calvert, S.L., Bond, B.J., & Staiano, A.E. (2013). Electronic game changers for the obesity crisis. In F. Blumberg (Ed.), *Learning by playing: Frontiers of video gaming in education.* New York: Oxford University Press.

Calvert, S.L., & Valkenburg, P.M. (2011). The influence of television, video games, and the Internet on children's creativity. In M. Taylor (Ed.), *Handbook of the development of imagination.* New York: Oxford University Press.

Calvert, S.L., & Wartella, E.A. (2014). Children and electronic media. In E.T. Gershoff, R.S. Mistry, & D.A. Crosby (Eds.), *Societal contexts of child development.* New York: Oxford University Press.

Calzo, J.P., Sonneville, K.R., Haines, E.A., Field, E.A., & Austin, S.B. (2012). The development of associations of body mass index, body dissatisfaction, and shape concern in adolescent boys and girls. *Journal of Adolescent Health, 51,* 517–523.

Cameron, J., & Pierce, D. (2008). Intrinsic versus extrinsic motivation. In N.J. Salkind (Ed.), *Encyclopedia of educational psychology.* Thousand Oaks, CA: Sage.

Campbell, D.T., & LeVine, K.A. (1968). Ethnocentrism and intergroup relations. In R. Abelson & others (Eds.), *Theories and cognitive consistency: A sourcebook.* Chicago: Rand-McNally.

Campbell, F.A. (2007). The malleability of the cognitive development of children of low-income African-American families: Intellectual test performance over twenty-one years. In P.C. Kyllonen, R.D. Roberts, & L. Stankov (Eds.), *Extending intelligence.* Mahwah, NJ: Erlbaum.

Campbell, F.A., Pungello, E.P., Miller-Johnson, S., Burchinal, M., & Ramey, C.T. (2001). The

development of cognitive and academic abilities: Growth curves from an early childhood educational experiment. *Developmental Psychology, 37,* 231–243.

Campbell, F.A., & others (2012). Adult outcomes as a function of an early childhood educational program: An Abecedarian Project follow-up. *Developmental Psychology, 48,* 1033–1043.

Campbell, I.G., Grimm, K.J., de Bie, E., & Feinberg, I. (2012). Sex, puberty, and the timing of sleep EEG measured in adolescent brain maturation. *Proceedings of the National Academy of Sciences U.S.A., 109,* 5740–5743.

Campbell, L., Campbell, B., & Dickinson, D. (2004). *Teaching and learning through multiple intelligences* (3rd ed.). Boston: Allyn & Bacon.

Campione-Barr, N. (2011). Sibling conflict. *Encyclopedia of family health.* Thousand Oaks, CA: Sage.

Campione-Barr, N., Greer, K.B., & Kruse, A. (2013). Differential associations between domains of sibling conflict and adolescent emotional adjustment. *Child Development, 84*(3), 938–954.

Campione-Barr, N., & Smetana, J.G. (2010). "Who said you could wear my sweater?" Adolescent siblings' conflicts and associations with relationship quality. *Child Development, 81,* 464–471.

Campos, J.J. (2005). Unpublished review of J.W. Santrock's *Life-span development,* 11th ed. (New York: McGraw-Hill).

Campos, J.J. (2009). Unpublished review of J.W. Santrock's *Life-span development,* 13th ed. (New York: McGraw-Hill).

Campos, J.J., Langer, A., & Krowitz, A. (1970). Cardiac responses on the visual cliff in prelocomotor human infants. *Science, 170,* 196–197.

Candow, D.G., & Chilibeck, P.D. (2005). Differences in size, strength, and power of upper and lower body muscle groups in young and older men. *Journals of Gerontology A: Biological Sciences and Medical Sciences, 60,* 148A–156A.

Cantalupo. N.C. (2014). Institution-specific victimization surveys: Addressing legal and practical disincentives to gender-based violence reporting on college campuses. *Trauma, Violence, and Abuse, 15,* 227–241.

Cantone, E., & others (2015). Interventions on bullying and cyberbullying in schools: A systematic review. *Clinical Practice and Epidemiology in Mental Health, 11*(Suppl. 1), S58–S76.

Cao, S., & others (2013). Smoking and risk of erectile dysfunction: Systematic review of observational studies with meta-analysis. *PLoS One, 8*(4), e60443.

Capaldi, D.M., & Shortt, J.W. (2003). Understanding conduct problems in adolescence from a lifespan perspective. In G.R. Adams & M.D. Berzonsky (Eds.), *Blackwell handbook of adolescence.* Malden, MA: Blackwell.

Caprara, G.V., & others (2010). The contributions of agreeableness and self-efficacy beliefs to prosociality. *European Journal of Personality, 24,* 36–55.

Capurro, A., & others (2015). Computational deconvolution of genome wide expression data from Parkinson's and Huntington's disease brain tissues using population-specific expression analysis. *Frontiers of Neuroscience, 8,* 441.

Carey, D.P. (2007). Is bigger really better? The search for brain size and intelligence in the twenty-first century. In S. Della Sala (Ed.), *Tall tales about the mind and brain: Separating fact from fiction.* Oxford, UK: Oxford University Press.

Carl, J.D. (2012). *Short introduction to the U.S. Census.* Upper Saddle River, NJ: Pearson.

Carlisle, D. (2015). Best of both worlds at hospital hospice. *Nursing Standard, 29,* 22–23.

Carlo, G. (2014). The development and correlates of prosocial moral behaviors. In M. Killen & J.G. Smetana (Eds.), *Handbook of moral development* (2nd ed.). New York: Psychology Press.

Carlo, G., Knight, G.P., McGinley, M., Zamboanga, B.L., & Jarvis, L.H. (2010). The multidimensionality of prosocial behaviors and evidence of measurement equivalence in Mexican American and European American early adolescents. *Journal of Research on Adolescence, 20,* 334–358.

Carlo, G., Mestre, M.V., Samper, P., Tur, A., & Armenta, B.E. (2011). The longitudinal relations among dimensions of parenting styles, sympathy, prosocial moral reasoning, and prosocial behaviors. *International Journal of Behavioral Development, 35,* 116–124.

Carlozzi, N.E., Kirsch, N.L., Kisala, P.A., & Tulsky, D.S. (2015). An examination of the Wechsler Adult Intelligence Scales, Fourth Edition (WAIS-V), in individuals with complicated mild, moderate, and severe traumatic brain injury (TBI). *Clinical Neuropsychology.*

Carlson, S.M., Claxton, L.J., & Moses, L.J. (2015, in press). The relation between executive function and theory of mind is more than skin deep. *Journal of Cognition and Development.*

Carlson, S.M., & White, R. (2011). Unpublished research. Institute of Child Development, University of Minnesota, Minneapolis.

Carlson, S.M., & White, R. (2013). Executive function and imagination. In M. Taylor (Ed.), *Handbook of imagination.* New York: Oxford University Press.

Carlson, S.M., White, R., & Davis-Unger, A.C. (2014). Evidence for a relation between executive function and pretense representation in preschool children. *Cognitive Development, 29,* 1–16.

Carlson, S.M., Zelazo, P.D., & Faja, S. (2013). Executive function. In P.D. Zelazo (Ed.), *Oxford handbook of developmental psychology.* New York: Oxford University Press.

Carnegie Foundation (1989). *Turning points: Preparing youth for the 21st century.* New York: Author.

Carnes, B.A., Olshansky, S.J., & Hayflick, L. (2013). Can human biology allow most of us to become centenarians? *Journals of Gerontology A: Biological Sciences and Medical Sciences, 68,* 136–142.

Carpendale, J.I., & Chandler, M.J. (1996). On the distinction between false belief understanding and subscribing to an interpretive theory of mind. *Child Development, 67,* 1686–1706.

Carpendale, J.I.M., & Lewis, C. (2015). The development of social understanding. In R.M. Lerner (Ed.), *Handbook of child psychology and developmental science* (7th ed.). New York: Wiley.

Carr, D. (2009). Death and dying. In D. Carr (Eds.), *Encyclopedia of the life course and human development.* Boston: Gale Cengage.

Carr, D. (2012). "I don't want to die like that. . .": The impact of significant others' death quality on advance care planning. *Gerontologist, 52*(6), 770–781.

Carr, D., & Pudrovska, T. (2011). Divorce and widowhood in later life. In R. Blieszner & V.H. Bedford (Eds.), *Handbook of aging and the family.* Santa Barbara, CA: Praeger.

Carr, D., & Sharp, S. (2014). Do afterlife beliefs affect psychological adjustment to late-life spousal loss? *Journals of Gerontology B: Psychological Sciences and Social Sciences, 69,* 103–112.

Carr, D., Sonnega, J., Nesse, R.M., & House, J.S. (2014). Do special occasions trigger psychological distress among older bereaved spouses? An empirical assessment of clinical wisdom? *Journals of*

Gerontology B: Psychological Sciences and Social Sciences. 69, 113–122.

Carr, R., & Peebles, R. (2012). Developmental considerations of media exposure risk for eating disorders. In J. Lock (Ed.), *Oxford handbook of child and adolescent eating disorders: Developmental perspectives.* New York: Oxford University Press.

Carrell, S.E., Malmstrom, F.V., & West, J.E. (2008). Peer effects in academic cheating. *Journal of Human Resources, 43*, 173–207.

Carretti, B., Caldarola, N., Tencati, C., & Cornoldi, C. (2014). Improving reading comprehension in reading and listening settings: The effect of two training programs focusing on metacognition and working memory. *British Journal of Educational Psychology, 84*(Pt. 2), 194–210.

Carriere, J.S., Cheyne, J.A., Solman, G.J., & Smilek, D. (2010). Age trends for failures in sustained attention. *Psychology and Aging, 25*(3), 569–574.

Carrizzo, A., & others (2013). Antioxidant effects of resveratrol in cardiovascular, cerebral, and metabolic diseases. *Food and Chemical Toxicology, 61*, 215–226.

Carroll, J.L. (2013). *Sexuality now* (4th ed.). Boston: Cengage.

Carskadon, M.A. (Ed.). (2002). *Adolescent sleep patterns.* New York: Cambridge University Press.

Carskadon, M.A. (2004). Sleep difficulties in young people. *Archives of Pediatric and Adolescent Health, 158*, 597–598.

Carskadon, M.A. (2005). Sleep and circadian rhythms in children and adolescents: Relevance for athletic performance of young people. *Clinical Sports Medicine, 24*, 319–328.

Carskadon, M.A. (2006, April). *Adolescent sleep: The perfect storm.* Paper presented at the meeting of the Society for Research on Adolescence, San Francisco.

Carskadon, M.A. (2011a). Sleep in adolescents: The perfect storm. *Pediatric Clinics of North America, 58*, 637–647.

Carskadon, M.A. (2011b). Sleep's effects on cognition and learning in adolescence. *Progress in Brain Research, 190*, 137–143.

Carskadon, M.A., & Tarokh, L. (2014). Developmental changes in sleep biology and potential effects on adolescent behavior and caffeine use. *Nutrition Review, 72*(Suppl. 1), S60–S64.

Carstensen, L.L. (1991). Selectivity theory: Social activity in life-span context. *Annual Review of Gerontology and Geriatrics, 11*, 195–217.

Carstensen, L.L. (1998). A life-span approach to social motivation. In J. Heckhausen & C. Dweck (Eds.), *Motivation and self-regulation across the life span.* New York: Cambridge University Press.

Carstensen, L.L. (2006). The influence of a sense of time on human development. *Science, 312*, 1913–1915.

Carstensen, L.L. (2008, May). *Long life in the 21st century.* Paper presented at the meeting of the Association for Psychological Science, Chicago.

Carstensen, L.L. (2009). *A long bright future.* New York: Random House.

Carstensen, L.L. (2011). *A long bright future: Happiness, health, and financial health in an age of increased longevity.* New York: Public Affairs.

Carstensen, L.L. (2014). Our aging population may just save us all. In P. Irving (Ed.), *The upside of aging.* New York: Wiley.

Carstensen, L.L., & Freund, A.M. (1994). Commentary: The resilience of the aging self. *Developmental Review, 14*, 81–92.

Carstensen, L.L., Mikels, J.A., & Mather, M. (2006). Aging and the intersection of cognition, motivation and emotion. In J. Birren & K.W. Schaie (Eds.), *Handbook of the psychology of aging* (6th ed.). San Diego: Academic Press.

Carstensen, L.L., Smith, K., & Jaworski, D. (2015, in press). Selectivity as an emotion regulation strategy: Lessons from older adults. *Current Opinion in Psychology.*

Carstensen, L.L., & others (2011). Emotional experience improves with age: Evidence based on over 10 years of sampling. *Psychology and Aging, 26*, 21–33.

Carter, C.S. (2014). Oxytocin pathways and the evolution of human behavior. *Annual Review of Psychology* (Vol. 65). Palo Alto, CA: Annual Reviews.

Cartwright, K.B., Galupo, M.P., Tyree, S.D., & Jennings, J.G. (2009). Reliability and validity of the Complex Postformal Thought Questionnaire: Assessing adults' cognitive development. *Journal of Adult Development, 16*, 183–189.

Cartwright, R., Agargun, M.Y., Kirkby, J., & Friedman, J.K. (2006). Relation of dreams to waking concerns. *Psychiatry Research, 141*, 261–270.

Caruthers, A.S., Van Ryzin, M.J., & Dishion, T.J. (2014). Preventing high-risk sexual behavior in early adulthood with family interventions in adolescence: Outcomes and developmental processes. *Prevention Science, 15*(Suppl. 1), S59–S69.

Carver, C.S., & Connor-Smith, J. (2010). Personality and coping. *Annual Review of Psychology* (Vol. 61). Palo Alto, CA: Annual Reviews.

Carver, K., Joyner, K., & Udry, J.R. (2003). National estimates of adolescent romantic relationships. In P. Florsheim (Eds.), *Adolescent romantic relationships and sexual behavior.* Mahwah, NJ: Erlbaum.

Casas, M. (2011). *Enhancing student learning in middle school.* New York: Routledge.

Case, R. (1987). Neo-Piagetian theory: Retrospect and prospect. *International Journal of Psychology, 22*, 773–791.

Case, R. (1999). Conceptual development in the child and the field: A personal view of the Piagetian legacy. In E.K. Skolnick, K. Nelson, S.A. Gelman, & P.H. Miller (Eds.), *Conceptual development.* Mahwah, NJ: Erlbaum.

Case, R., Kurland, D.M., & Goldberg, J. (1982). Operational efficiency and the growth of short-term memory span. *Journal of Experimental Child Psychology, 33*, 386–404.

Caserta, M., Utz, R., Lund, D., Swenson, K.L., & de Vries, B. (2014). Coping processes among bereaved spouses. *Death Studies, 38*, 145–155.

Casey, B.J. (2015). The adolescent brain and self-control. *Annual Review of Psychology* (Vol. 66). Palo Alto, CA: Annual Reviews.

Casey, B.J., Jones, R.M., & Somerville, L.H. (2011). Braking and accelerating of the adolescent brain. *Journal of Research on Adolescence, 21*, 21–33.

Caspi, A., & Roberts, B.W. (2001). Personality development across the life course: The argument for change and continuity. *Psychological Inquiry, 12*, 49–66.

Caspi, A., & others (2003). Influence of life stress on depression: Moderation by a polymorphism in the 5-HTT gene. *Science, 301*, 386–389.

Cassidy, J., & others (2011). Enhancing infant attachment security: An examination of treatment efficacy and differential susceptibility. *Development and Psychopathology, 23*, 131–148.

Cassoff, J., Knauper, B., Michaelsen, S., & Gruber, R. (2013). School-based sleep promotion programs: Effectiveness, feasibility, and insights for future research. *Sleep Medicine Reviews, 17*(3), 207–214.

Cassone, A.R. (2015). Mindfulness training as an adjunct to evidence-based treatment for ADHD within families. *Journal of Attention Disorders, 19*, 147–157.

Castle, J., & others (2010). Parents' evaluation of adoption success: A follow-up study of intercountry and domestic adoptions. *American Journal of Orthopsychiatry, 79*, 522–531.

Castrodale, V., & Rinehart, S. (2014). The golden hour: Improving the stabilization of the very low birth-weight infant. *Advances in Neonatal Care, 14*, 914.

Catani, C., & others (2010). Tsunami, war, and cumulative risk in the lives of Sri Lankan school children. *Child Development, 81*, 1176–1191.

Cauffman, E., Shulman, E., Bechtold, J., & Steinberg, L. (2015). Children and the law. In R.M. Lerner (Ed.), *Handbook of child psychology and developmental science* (7th Ed.). New York: Wiley.

Cavanagh, S.E. (2009). Puberty. In D. Carr (Ed.), *Encyclopedia of the life course and human development.* Boston: Gale Cengage.

Cavazos-Rehg, P.A., & others (2010a). Number of sexual partners and associations with initiation and intensity of substance abuse. *AIDS Behavior, 15*(4), 869–874.

Cavazos-Rehg, P.A., & others (2010b). Understanding adolescent parenthood from a multisystemic perspective. *Journal of Adolescent Health, 46*, 525–531.

Cave, R.K. (2002, August). *Early adolescent language: A content analysis of child development and educational psychology textbooks.* Unpublished doctoral dissertation, University of Nevada, Reno.

Cavuoti, C. (2015, in press). Giving a voice to the disenfranchised. Book review. *Death Studies.*

Ceci, S.J. (2000). Bronfenbrenner, Urie. In A. Kazdin (Ed.), *Encyclopedia of psychology.* Washington, DC, & New York: American Psychological Association and Oxford University Press.

Ceci, S.J., & Gilstrap, L.L. (2000). Determinants of intelligence: Schooling and intelligence. In A. Kazdin (Ed.), *Encyclopedia of psychology.* New York: Oxford University Press.

Ceci, S.J., Papierno, P.B., & Kulkofsky, S. (2007). Representational constraints on children's suggestibility. *Psychological Science, 18*, 503–509.

Center for Economic and Policy Research (2014, May). *A college degree is no guarantee.* Washington, DC: Author.

Center for Survey Research at the University of Connecticut (2000). *Hours on the job.* Storrs: University of Connecticut, Center for Survey Research.

Centers for Disease Control and Prevention (2008). *National Health Interview Study.* Atlanta: Author.

Centers for Disease Control and Prevention (2012). *Breastfeeding.* Atlanta: Author.

Centers for Disease Control and Prevention (2012). *By the numbers full year 2011: Health measures from the National Health Interview Study, January–December 2011.* Atlanta: Author.

Centers for Disease Control and Prevention (2012). CDC estimates 1 in 88 children in the United States has been identified as having an autism spectrum disorder. CDC Division of News & Electronic Media, http://www.cdc.gov/media/releases/2012/p0329_autism_disorder.html

Centers for Disease Control and Prevention (2012). Prepregnancy contraceptive use among teens with unintended pregnancies resulting in live births—Pregnancy Risk Assessment Monitoring System (PRAMS), 2004-2008. *MMWR Morbidity and Mortality Weekly Report, 61*(2), 25–29.

Centers for Disease Control and Prevention (2012, January 13). Vital signs: Binge drinking prevalence, frequency, and intensity among adults—United States, 2010. *Morbidity and Mortality Weekly Report (MMWR), 61*(1), 14–19.

Centers for Disease Control and Prevention (2013). Suicide among adults aged 35–64—United States, 1999–2010. *MMWR Morbidity and Mortality Weekly Report, 62,* 321–325.

Centers for Disease Control and Prevention (2014). *Adolescent pregnancy.* Atlanta, GA: U.S. Department of Health and Human Services.

Centers for Disease Control and Prevention (2014). *Body mass index for children and teens.* Atlanta: Centers for Disease Control and Prevention.

Centers for Disease Control and Prevention (2014). *How much physical activity do older adults need?* Atlanta: Author.

Centers for Disease Control and Prevention (2014). *Sexually transmitted disease surveillance.* Atlanta, GA: U.S. Department of Health and Human Services.

Centers for Disease Control and Prevention (2015). *Autism.* Atlanta: Author.

Centers for Disease Control and Prevention (2015). *Injury prevention and control: Division of Violence Prevention.* Retrieved April 21, 2015, from www.cdcgov/violenceprevention/pub/youth_suicide.html

Central Intelligence Agency (2012). *The world factbook: Life expectancy at birth.* Washington, DC: CIA.

Cerpa, V.J., & others (2015, in press). Prenatal-perinatal nicotine alters neonatal raphe neurons: Meaning for sudden infant death syndrome. *American Journal of Respiratory Cell and Molecular Biology.*

Cerqueira, F.M., Cunha, F.M., Laurindo, F.R., & Kowaltowski, A.J. (2012). Calorie restriction increases cerebral mitochondrial respiratory capacity in a NO mediated mechanism: Impact on neuronal survival. *Free Radical and Biological Medicine, 52,* 1236–1241.

Ch'ng, C., Kwok, W., Rogic, S., & Pavlidis, P. (2015, in press). Meta-analysis of gene expression in autism spectrum disorder. *Autism Research.*

Chan, C.H., & others (2015). Sexual initiation and emotional/behavioral problems in Taiwanese adolescents: A multivariate response profile analysis. *Archives of Sexual Behavior, 44,* 717–727.

Chan, H.Y., Brown, B.B., & Von Bank, H. (2015). Adolescent disclosure of information about peers: The mediating role of perceptions of parents' right to know. *Journal of Youth and Adolescence, 44,* 1048–1065.

Chan, M.Y., Haber, S., Drew, L.M., & Park, D.C. (2015, in press). Training older adults to use tablet computers: Does it enhance cognitive function? *Gerontologist.*

Chance, P. (2014). *Learning and behavior* (7th ed.). Boston: Cengage.

Chandra, A., Mosher, W.D., Copen, C., & Sionean, C. (2011, March 3). Sexual behavior, sexual attraction, and sexual identity in the United States: Data from the 2006–2008 National Survey of Family Growth. *National Health Statistics Reports, 36,* 1–28.

Chang, H.Y., & others (2014). Prenatal maternal depression is associated with low birth weight through shorter gestational age in term infants in Korea. *Early Human Development, 90,* 15–20.

Chang, Y.K., Liu, S., Yu, H.H., & Lee, Y.H. (2012). Effect of acute exercise on executive function in children with attention deficit hyperactivity disorder. *Archives of Clinical Neuropsychology, 27,* 225–237.

Chao, R., & Tseng, V. (2002). Parenting of Asians. In M.H. Bornstein (Ed.), *Handbook of parenting* (2nd ed., Vol. 4). Mahwah, NJ: Erlbaum.

Chao, R.K. (2005, April). *The importance of Guan in describing control of immigrant Chinese.* Paper presented at the meeting of the Society for Research in Child Development, Atlanta.

Chao, R.K. (2007, March). *Research with Asian Americans: Looking back and moving forward.* Paper presented at the meeting of the Society for Research in Child Development, Boston.

Chao, R.K., & Otsuki-Clutter, M. (2011). Racial and ethnic differences: Sociocultural and contextual explanations. *Journal of Research on Adolescence, 21,* 47–60.

Chaplin, J.E., & others (2012). Improvements in behavior and self-esteem following growth hormone treatment in short prepubertal children. *Hormone Research in Pediatrics, 75*(4), 291–303.

Chaplin, T.M., & Aldao, A. (2013). Gender differences in emotion expression in children: a meta-analytic review. *Psychological Bulletin, 139,* 735–765.

Chaput, J.P., & others (2014). Electronic screens in children's bedroooms and adiposity, physical activity, and sleep: Do the number and types of electronic devices matter? *Canadian Journal of Public Health, 105,* e273–e279.

Charles, S.T., & Carstensen, L.L. (2010). *Social and emotional aging.* In S. Fiske & S. Taylor (Eds.), *Annual Review of Psychology* (Vol. 61). Palo Alto, CA: Annual Reviews.

Charles, S.T., & Piazza, J.R. (2007). Memories of social interactions: Age differences in emotional intensity. *Psychology and Aging, 22,* 300–309.

Charness, N., & Bosman, E.A. (1992). Human factors and aging. In F.I.M. Craik & T.A. Salthouse (Eds.), *The handbook of aging and cognition.* Hillsdale, NJ: Erlbaum.

Chassin, L., & others (2008). Multiple trajectories of cigarette smoking and the intergenerational transmission of smoking: A multigenerational, longitudinal study of a midwestern community sample. *Health Psychology, 27,* 819–828.

Chauhan, G., & others (2015, in press). Association of Alzheimer's disease GWAS loci with MRI markers of brain aging. *Neurobiology of Aging.*

Chavarria, M.C., & others (2014). Puberty in the corpus callosum. *Neuroscience, 265,* 1–8.

Chemtob, C.M., & others (2010). Impact of maternal posttraumatic stress disorder and depression following exposure to the September 11 attacks on preschool children's behavior. *Child Development, 81,* 1129–1141.

Chen, C., & Stevenson, H.W. (1989). Homework: A cross-cultural examination. *Child Development, 60*(3), 551–561.

Chen, C.P., & others (2014). Prenatal diagnosis and molecular cytogenetic characterization of de novo pure partial trisomy 6p associated with microcephaly, craniosynostosis, and abnormal maternal serum biochemistry. *Gene, 536,* 425–429.

Chen, D., Drabick, D.A., & Burgers, D.E. (2015, in press). A developmental perspective on peer rejection, deviant peer affiliation, and conduct problems among youth. *Child Psychiatry and Human Development.*

Chen, D., & Guarente, L. (2007). SIR2: A potential target for calorie restriction mimetics. *Trends in Molecular Medicine, 13,* 64–71.

Chen, J., & others (2014). Genetic and environmental influences on depressive symptoms in Chinese children. *Behavior Genetics, 44,* 36–44.

Chen, J.A., & others (2015, in press). A multiancestral genome-wide exome array study of Alzheimer disease, frontotemporal dementia, and progressive supranuclear palsy. *JAMA Neurology.*

Chen, J.J., Howard, K.S., & Brooks-Gunn, J. (2011). How do neighborhoods matter across the life span? In K.L. Fingerman, C.A. Berg, J. Smith, & T.C. Antonucci (Eds.), *Handbook of life-span development.* New York: Springer.

Chen, N., Deater-Deckard, K., & Bell, M.A. (2014). The role of temperament by family interactions in child maladjustment. *Journal of Abnormal Child Psychology, 42,* 1251–1262.

Chen, S.H., Zhou, Q., Main, A., & Lee, E.H. (2015, in press). Chinese American immigrant parents' emotional expression in the family: Relations with parents' cultural orientations and children's emotion-related regulation. *Cultural Diversity and Ethnic Minority Psychology.*

Chen, X., Fu, R., & Zhao, S. (2015). Culture and socialization. In J.E. Grusec & P.D. Hastings (Eds.), *Handbook of socialization* (2nd ed.). New York: Guilford.

Chen, X., & Schmidt, L.A. (2015). Temperament and personality. In R.M. Lerner (Ed.), *Handbook of child psychology and developmental science* (7th ed.). New York: Wiley.

Chen, X., & others (1998). Childrearing attitudes and behavioral inhibition in Chinese and Canadian toddlers: A cross-cultural study. *Developmental Psychology, 34,* 677–686.

Cheng, E.R., Cohen, A., & Goodman, E. (2015). The role of perceived discrimination during childhood and adolescence in understanding racial and socioeconomic influences on depression in young adulthood. *Journal of Pediatrics, 166,* 370–377.

Cheng, M., & Berman, S.L. (2012). Globalization and identity development: A Chinese perspective. *New Directions in Child and Adolescent Development, 138,* 103–121.

Cheng, M.H., Lee, S.J., Wang, P.H., & Fuh, J.L. (2007). Does menopausal transition affect the quality of life? A longitudinal study of middle-aged women in Kinmen. *Menopause, 14,* 885–890.

Cheng, S., & others (2010). Early television exposure and children's behavioral and social outcomes at age 30 months. *Journal of Epidemiology, 20*(Suppl. 2), S482–S489.

Cheng, S.T. (2014). Defining successful aging: The need to distinguish pathways from outcomes. *International Psychogeriatrics, 26,* 527–531.

Cheng, Y., Lou, C., Gao, E., Emerson, M.R., & Zabin, L.S. (2012). The relationship between contact and unmarried adolescents' and young adults' traditional beliefs in three East Asian cities: A cross-cultural analysis. *Journal of Adolescent Health, 50*(Suppl. 3), S4–S11.

Cheng, Y.Y., Shein, P.P., & Chiou, W.B. (2012). Escaping the impulse to immediate gratification: The prospect concept promotes a future-oriented mindset, prompting an inclination towards delayed gratification. *British Journal of Psychology, 103,* 129–141.

Cherlin, A.J. (2009). *The marriage-go-round.* New York: Random House.

Cherlin, A.J., & Furstenberg, F.F. (1994). Stepfamilies in the United States: A reconsideration. In J. Blake & J. Hagen (Eds.), *Annual Review of Sociology* (Vol. 20). Palo Alto, CA: Annual Reviews.

Chess, S., & Thomas, A. (1977). Temperamental individuality from childhood to adolescence. *Journal of Child Psychiatry, 16,* 218–226.

Cheung, C., & Pomerantz, E.M. (2012). Why does parents' involvement in children's learning enhance children's achievement? The role of parent-oriented motivation. *Journal of Educational Psychology, 104*(3), 820–832.

Cheung, C.S., Pomerantz, E.M., & Dong, W. (2012). Does adolescents' disclosure to their parents matter for their academic adjustment? *Child Development, 84*(2), 693–710.

Chi, M.T. (1978). Knowledge structures and memory development. In R.S. Siegler (Ed.), *Children's thinking: What develops?* Hillsdale, NJ: Erlbaum.

Chiang, H.L., & others (2015). Altered white matter tract property related to impaired focused attention, sustained attention, cognitive impulsivity, and vigilance in attention-deficit/hyperactivity disorder. *Journal of Psychiatry and Neuroscience, 40,* 140106.

Chiarchiaro, J., Arnold, R.M., & White, D.B. (2015). Reengineering advance care planning to create scalable, patient-, and family-centered interventions. *JAMA, 313,* 1103–1104.

Chick, C.F., & Reyna, V.F. (2012). A fuzzy trace theory of adolescent risk taking: Beyond self-control and sensation seeking. In V.F. Reyna & others (Eds.), *The adolescent brain.* Washington, DC: American Psychological Association.

Child Trends (2014, October). *High school dropout rates.* Bethesda, MD: Child Trends.

Childers, J.B., & Tomasello, M. (2002). Two-year-olds learn novel nouns, verbs, and conventional actions from massed or distributed exposures. *Developmental Psychology, 38,* 967–978.

Children's Defense Fund (1992). *The state of America's children, 1992.* Washington, DC: Author.

Children's Defense Fund (2011). *The state of America's children, 2011.* Washington, DC: Author.

Chiou, W.B., Chen, S.W., & Liao, D.C. (2014). Does Facebook promote self-interest? Enactment of indiscriminate one-to-many communication on online social networking sites decreases prosocial behavior. *Cyberpsychology, Behavior, and Social Networking, 17,* 68–73.

Chisholm, D.J., Manganello, J.A., Kelleher, K.J., & Marshal, M.P. (2014). Health literacy, alcohol expectancies, and alcohol use in teens. *Patient Education and Counseling, 97,* 291–296.

Chisholm, J.D., & Kingstone, A. (2015, in press). Action video games and improved attentional control: Disentangling selection- and response-based processes. *Psychonomic Bulletin and Review.*

Chiu, M., Wesson, V., & Sadavoy, J. (2014). Improving caregiver competence, stress coping, and well-being in informal dementia caregivers. *World Journal of Psychiatry, 3*(3), 65–73.

Choi, K.H., & Vasunilashorn, S. (2014). Widowhood, age heterogamy, and health: The role of selection, marital quality, and health behaviors. *Journals of Gerontology B: Psychological Sciences and Social Sciences, 69,* 123–134.

Choi, S., & Gopnik, A. (1995). Early acquisition of verbs in Korean: A cross-linguistic study. *Journal of Child Language, 22,* 497–529.

Choi, Y.J., & Luo, Y. (2015). 13-month-olds' understanding of social interaction. *Psychological Science, 26,* 274–283.

Chomsky, N. (1957). *Syntactic structures.* The Hague: Mouton.

Chopik, W.J., Edelstein, R.S., & Fraley, R.C. (2013). From the cradle to the grave: Age differences in attachment from early adulthood to old age. *Journal of Personality, 81*(2), 171–183.

Chouinard, R., Karsenti, T., & Roy, N. (2007). Relations among competence beliefs, utility value, achievement goals, and effort in mathematics. *British Journal of Educational Psychology, 77,* 501–517.

Choukas-Bradley, S., Giletta, M., Widman, L., Cohen, G.L., & Prinstein, M.J. (2014). Experimentally measured susceptibility to peer influence and adolescent sexual behavior trajectories: A preliminary study. *Developmental Psychology, 50,* 2221–2227.

Choukas-Bradley, S., & Prinstein, M.J. (2013). Peer relationships and the development of psychopathology. In M. Lewis & K.D. Rudolph (Eds.), *Handbook of developmental psychopathology* (3rd ed.). New York: Springer.

Chow, C.M., Tan, C.C., & Buhrmester, D. (2015, in press). Interdependence of depressive symptoms, school involvement, and academic performance between adolescent friends: A dyadic analysis. *British Journal of Educational Psychology.*

Christakis, D.A., & others (2009). Audible television and decreased adult words, infant vocalizations, and conversational turns. *Archives of Pediatric & Adolescent Medicine, 163,* 554–558.

Christakis, D.A., Zimmerman, F.J., DiGiuseppe, D.L., & McCarty, C.A. (2004). Early television exposure and subsequent attentional problems in children. *Pediatrics, 113,* 708–713.

Christensen, L.B., Johnson, R.B., & Turner, L.A. (2015). *Research methods* (12th ed.). Upper Saddle River, NJ: Pearson.

Christie, J., Enz, B.J., Vukelilch, C., & Roskos, K.A. (2014). *Teaching language and literacy* (5th ed.). Upper Saddle River, NJ: Pearson.

Christie, J.F., & Roskos, K.A. (2015). How does play contributed to literacy? In J.E. Johnson & others (Eds.), *Handbook of the study of play.* Blue Ridge Summit, PA: Rowan & Littlefield.

Christodoulidou, A., & others (2013). The roles of telomerase in the generation of polyploidy during neoplastic cell growth. *Neoplasia, 15,* 156–168.

Chua, A. (2011). *Battle hymn of the tiger mom.* New York: Penguin.

Chuang, Y.F., & others (2014). Cardiovascular risks and brain function: A functional magnetic resonance imaging study of executive function in older adults. *Neurobiology of Aging, 35,* 1396–1403.

Chui, H., Hoppmann, C.A., Gerstorf, D., Walker, R., & Luszcz, M.A. (2014). Social partners and momentary affect in the oldest-old: The presence of others benefits affect depending on who we are and who we are with. *Developmental Psychology, 50,* 1728–1740.

Chung, J.K., Park, S.H., Lee, W.J., & Lee, S.J. (2009). Bilateral cataract surgery: A controlled clinical trial. *Japan Journal of Ophthalmology, 53,* 107–113.

Cicchetti, D. (2013). Developmental psychopathology. In P. Zelazo (Ed.), *Oxford handbook of developmental psychology.* New York: Oxford University Press.

Cicchetti, D., & Banny, A. (2014). A developmental psychopathology perspective on child maltreatment. In M. Lewis & K. Rudolph (Eds.), *Handbook of developmental psychopathology.* New York: Springer.

Cicchetti, D., & Toth, S.L. (2015). A multilevel perspective on child maltreatment. In R.M. Lerner (Ed.), *Handbook of child psychology and developmental science* (7th ed.). New York: Wiley.

Cicchetti, D., Toth, S.L., & Rogosch, F.A. (2005). *A prevention program for child maltreatment.* Unpublished manuscript, University of Rochester, Rochester, NY.

Cicirelli, V.G. (1994). Sibling relationships in cross-cultural perspective. *Journal of Marriage and Family, 56,* 7–20.

Cicirelli, V.G. (2009). Sibling relationships, later life. In D. Carr (Eds.), *Encyclopedia of the life course and human development.* Boston: Gale Cengage.

Cicirelli, V.G. (2010). Attachment relationships in old age. *Journal of Social and Personal Relationships, 27,* 191–199.

Cillessen, A.H.N., & van den Berg, Y.H.M. (2012). Popularity and school adjustment. In A.M. Ryan & G.W. Ladd (Eds.), *Peer relationships and adjustment at school.* Charlotte, NC: Information Age Publishing.

Ciol, M.A., & others (2008). Minority disparities in disability between Medicare beneficiaries. *Journal of the American Geriatrics Society, 56,* 444–453.

Citkovitz, C., Schnyer, R.N., & Hoskins, I.A. (2011). Acupuncture during labour: Data are more promising than a recent review suggests. *British Journal of Obstetrics and Gynecology, 118,* 101.

Claes, H.I., & others (2010). Understanding the effects of sildenafil treatment on erection maintenance and erection hardness. *Journal of Sexual Medicine, 7,* 2184–2191.

Clancy, S.M., & Hoyer, W.J. (1994). Age and skill in visual search. *Developmental Psychology, 30,* 545–552.

Clark, B. (2008). *Growing up gifted* (7th ed.). Upper Saddle River, NJ: Prentice Hall.

Clark, C.D. (2015). Play interventions and therapy. In J.E. Johnson & others (Eds.), *Handbook of the study of play.* Blue Ridge Summit, PA: Rowan & Littlefield.

Clark, E.V. (1993). *The lexicon in acquisition.* New York: Cambridge University Press.

Clark, E.V. (2012). Lexical meaning. In E.L. Bavin (Ed.), *Cambridge handbook of child language.* New York: Cambridge University Press.

Clark, E.V. (2014). Pragmatics in acquisition. *Journal of Child Language, 41*(Suppl. 1), S105–S116.

Clark-Cotton, M.R., Williams, R.K., & Goral, M. (2007). Language and communication in aging. In J.E. Birren (Ed.), *Encyclopedia of gerontology* (2nd ed.). San Diego: Academic Press.

Clarke-Stewart, A.K., & Miner, J.L. (2008). Child and day care, effects of. In M.M. Haith & J.B. Benson (Eds.), *Encyclopedia of infant and early childhood development.* Oxford, UK: Elsevier.

Clarke-Stewart, A.K., & Parke, R.D. (2014). *Social development* (2nd ed.). New York: Wiley.

Clausen, J.A. (1993). *American lives.* New York: Free Press.

Clauss, J.A., Avery, S.N., & Blackford, J.U. (2015, in press). The nature of individual differences in inhibited temperament and risk for psychiatric disease: A review and meta-analysis. *Progress in Neurobiology.*

Clay, O.J., & others (2009). Visual function and cognitive speed of processing mediate age-related decline in memory span and fluid intelligence. *Journal of Aging and Health, 21,* 547–566.

Clearfield, M.W., Diedrich, F.J., Smith, L.B., & Thelen, E. (2006). Young infants reach correctly in A-not-B tasks: On the development of stability and perseveration. *Infant Behavior and Development, 29,* 435–444.

Clements, J.M. (2009). Patient perceptions on the use of advance directives and life-prolonging technology. *American Journal of Hospice and Palliative Care, 26,* 270–276.

Cleveland, M.J., Feinberg, M.E., Osgood, D.W., & Moody, J. (2012). Do peers' parents matter? A new link between positive parenting and adolescent substance use. *Journal of Studies on Alcohol and Drugs, 73,* 423–433.

Cliffordson, C., & Gustafsson, J-E. (2008). Effects of age and schooling on intellectual performance: Estimates obtained from analysis of continuous variation in age and length of schooling. *Intelligence, 36,* 143–152.

Clifton, R.K., Morrongiello, B.A., Kulig, J.W., & Dowd, J.M. (1981). Developmental changes in auditory localization in infancy. In R.N. Aslin, J.R. Alberts, & M.R. Petersen (Eds.), *Development of perception* (Vol. 1). Orlando, FL: Academic Press.

Clifton, R.K., Muir, D.W., Ashmead, D.H., & Clarkson, M.G. (1993). Is visually guided reaching in early infancy a myth? *Child Development, 64,* 1099–1110.

Clinkinbeard, S.S., Simi, P., Evans, M.K., & Anderson, A.L. (2011). Sleep and delinquency: Does amount of sleep matter? *Journal of Youth and Adolescence, 40*(7), 916–930.

Cluett, E.R., & Burns, E. (2009). Immersion in water in labour and birth. *Cochrane Database of Systematic Reviews,* CD000111.

Cochran, B.N., & others (2013). Mental health characteristics of sexual minority veterans. *Journal of Homosexuality, 60,* 419–435.

Coe, N.B., von Gaudecker, H.M., Lindeboom, M., & Maurer, J. (2012). The effect of retirement on cognitive functioning. *Health Economics, 21,* 913–927.

CogMed (2013). *CogMed: Working memory is the engine of learning.* Upper Saddle River, NJ: Pearson.

Cohen-Woods, S., Craig, I.W., & McGuffin, P. (2013). The current state of play on the molecular genetics of depression. *Psychological Medicine, 43*(4), 673–687.

Cohler, B., & Michaels, S. (2013). Emergent adulthood in lesbian and gay lives. In G.W. Peterson & K.R. Bush (Eds.), *Handbook of marriage and the family* (3rd ed.). New York: Springer.

Coie, J.D. (2004). The impact of negative social experiences on the development of antisocial behavior. In J.B. Kupersmidt & K.A. Dodge (Eds.), *Children's peer relations: From development to intervention.* Washington, DC: American Psychological Association.

Colangelo, N.C., Assouline, S.G., & Gross, M.U.M. (2004). *A nation deceived: How schools hold back America's brightest students.* The Templeton National Report on Acceleration. Retrieved March 6, 2005, from http://nationdeceived.org/

Colapinto, J. (2000). *As nature made him.* New York: Simon & Schuster.

Colbert, B.J., & Gonzalez, L. (2016, in press). *Microbiology.* Boston: Cengage.

Colby, A., Kohlberg, L., Gibbs, J., & Lieberman, M. (1983). A longitudinal study of moral judgment. *Monographs of the Society for Research in Child Development, 48* (21, Serial No. 201).

Colcombe, S.J., & Kramer, A.F. (2003). Fitness effects on the cognitive function of older adults: A meta-analytic study. *Psychological Science, 14,* 125–130.

Colcombe, S.J., & others (2006). Aerobic exercise training increases brain volume in aging humans. *Journals of Gerontology: Medical Sciences, 61A,* 1166–1170.

Cole, M.W., Yarkoni, T., Repovs, G., Anticevic, A., & Braver, T.S. (2012). Global connectivity of prefrontal cortex predicts cognitive control and intelligence. *Journal of Neuroscience, 32,* 8988–8999.

Cole, P.M., Dennis, T.A., Smith-Simon, K.E., & Cohen, L.H. (2009). Preschoolers' emotion regulation strategy understanding: Relations with emotion socialization and child self-regulation. *Social Development, 18*(2), 324–352.

Cole, P.M., & Tan, P.Z. (2007). Emotion socialization from a cultural perspective. In J.E. Grusec & P.D. Hastings (Eds.), *Handbook of socialization.* New York: Guilford.

Cole, P.M., & Tan, P.Z. (2015). Emotion socialization from a cultural perspective. In J.E. Grusec & P.D. Hastings (Eds.), *Handbook of socialization* (2nd ed.). New York: Guilford.

Coleman, A.M. (2013). Physicians' attitudes toward advance directives: A literature review of variables impacting on physicians' attitude toward advance directives. *American Journal of Hospice and Palliative Care, 30,* 696–706.

Coleman, P.D. (1986, August). *Regulation of dendritic extent: Human aging brain and Alzheimer's disease.* Paper presented at the meeting of the American Psychological Association, Washington, DC.

Coleman-Phox, K., Odouli, R., & Li, D-K. (2008). Use of a fan during sleep and the risk of sudden infant death syndrome. *Archives of Pediatric and Adolescent Medicine, 162,* 963–968.

Coley, R.L., Votruba-Drzal, E., Miller, P.L., & Koury, A. (2013). Timing, extent, and type of child care and children's functioning in kindergarten. *Developmental Psychology, 49,* 1859–1873.

Coley, R.L., & others (2013). Sexual partner accumulation from adolescence through early adulthood: The role of family, peer, and school norms. *Journal of Adolescent Health, 53,* 91–97.

Collins, C.E., & others (2011). Parent diet modification, child activity, or both in obese children: An RCT. *Pediatrics, 127,* 619–627.

Collins, M. (1996, Winter). The job outlook for 96 grads. *Journal of Career Planning,* 51–54.

Collins, W.A., & Steinberg, L. (2006). Adolescent development in interpersonal context. In W. Damon & R. Lerner (Eds.), *Handbook of child psychology* (6th ed.). New York: Wiley.

Collins, W.A., & van Dulmen, M. (2006). The significance of middle childhood peer competence for work and relationships in early adulthood. In A.C. Huston & M.N. Ripke (Eds.), *Developmental contexts in middle childhood.* New York: Cambridge University Press.

Collin-Vezina, D., & others (2015, in press). A preliminary mapping of individual, relational, and social factors that impede disclosure of childhood sexual abuse. *Child Abuse and Neglect.*

Colman, R.J., & others (2009). Caloric restriction delays disease onset and mortality in rhesus monkeys. *Science, 325,* 201–204.

Colom, R., & others (2009). Gray matter correlates of fluid, crystallized, and spatial intelligence. *Intelligence, 37,* 124–135.

Colom, R., Karama, S., Jung, R.E., & Haier, R.J. (2010). Human intelligence and brain networks. *Dialogues in Clinical Neuroscience, 12,* 489–501.

Columbo, J., Brez, C.C., & Curtindale, L.M. (2013). Infant perception and cognition. In I.B. Weiner & others (Eds.), *Handbook of psychology* (2nd ed., Vol. 6). New York: Wiley.

Comer, J. (2004). *Leave no child behind.* New Haven, CT: Yale University Press.

Comer, J. (2006). Child development: The under-weighted aspect of intelligence. In P.C. Kyllonen, R.D. Roberts, & L. Stankov (Eds.), *Extending intelligence.* Mahwah, NJ: Erlbaum.

Comer, J. (2010). Comer School Development Program. In J. Meece & J. Eccles (Eds.), *Handbook of research on schools, schooling, and human development.* New York: Routledge.

Comings, J. (2007). Persistence: Helping adult students reach their goals. In J. Comings, B. Garner, & C. Smith (Eds.), *Review of adult learning and literacy* (Vol. 7). Mahwah, NJ: Erlbaum.

Committee on the Rights of the Child (2014). *The Convention on the Rights of the Child and its treaty body—the Committee on the Rights of the Child.* Retrieved April 14, 2015, from http://endcorporalpunishment.org/pages/hrlaw/crc_session.html

Common Core State Standards Initiative (2014). *Common Core.* Retrieved on June 1, 2014, from www.core standards.org/

Common Sense Media (2011). *Zero to eight: Children's media use in America.* Retrieved June 21, 2012, from www.commonsensemedia.org/research

Commoner, B. (2002). Unraveling the DNA myth: The spurious foundation of genetic engineering. *Harper's Magazine, 304,* 39–47.

Commons, M.L., & Richards, F.A. (2003). Four postformal stages. In J. Demick & C. Andreoletti (Eds.), *Handbook of adult development.* New York: Kluwer.

Commons, M.L., Sinnott, J.D., Richards, F.A., & Armon, C. (1989). *Adult development, Vol. 1: Comparisons and applications of developmental models.* New York: Praeger.

Compton, W.M., Gfoerer, J., Conway, I.P., & Finger, M.S. (2014). Unemployment and substance outcomes in the United States 2002–2010. *Drug and Alcohol Dependence, 142,* 350–353.

Comstock, G., & Scharrer, E. (2006). Media and popular culture. In W. Damon & R. Lerner (Eds.), *Handbook of child psychology* (6th ed.). New York: Wiley.

Conde-Agudelo, A., & Diaz-Rossello, J.L. (2014). Kangaroo mother care to reduce morbidity and mortality in low birthweight infants. *Cochrane Database of Systematic Reviews, 4,* CD002771.

Condition of Education (2014). *Participation in education.* Washington, DC: U.S. Office of Education.

Conduct Problems Prevention Research Group (2007). The Fast Track randomized controlled trial to prevent externalizing psychiatric disorders: Findings from grades 3 to 9. *Journal of the American Academy of Child and Adolescent Psychiatry, 46,* 1250–1262.

Conduct Problems Prevention Research Group (2010a). The difficulty of maintaining positive intervention effects: A look at disruptive behavior, deviant peer relations, and social skills during the middle school years. *Journal of Early Adolescence, 30,* 593–624.

Conduct Problems Prevention Research Group (2010b). Fast Track intervention effects on youth arrests and delinquency. *Journal of Experimental Criminology, 6,* 131–157.

Conduct Problems Prevention Research Group (2011). The effects of Fast Track preventive intervention on the development of conduct disorder across childhood. *Child Development, 82,* 331–345.

Conduct Problems Prevention Research Group (2015). Impact of early intervention on psychopathology, crime, and well-being at age 25. *American Journal of Psychiatry, 71,* 59–70.

Cong, X., Ludington-Hoe, S.M., & Walsh, S. (2011). Randomized crossover trial of kangaroo care to reduce biobehavioral pain responses in preterm infants: A pilot study. *Biological Research for Nursing, 13,* 204–216.

Connell, N.M., Morris, R.G., & Piquero, A.R. (2015, in press). Predicting bullying: Exploring the contribution of negative life experiences in predicting adolescent bullying behavior. *International Journal of Offender Therapy and Comparative Criminology.*

Connolly, J., Craig, W., Goldberg, A., & Pepler, D. (2004). Mixed-gender groups, dating, and romantic relationships in early adolescence. *Journal of Research on Adolescence, 14,* 185–207.

Connolly, J.A., & Mcisaac, C. (2009). Romantic relationships in adolescence. In R.M. Lerner & L. Steinberg (Eds.), *Handbook of adolescent psychology* (3rd ed.). New York: Wiley.

Connolly, J.A., Nguyen, H.N., Pepler, D., Craig, W., & Jiang, D. (2013). Developmental trajectories of romantic stages and associations with problem behaviors during adolescence. *Journal of Adolescence, 36*(6), 1013–1024.

Conry-Murray, C., Kim, J.M., & Turiel, E. (2012, April). *U.S. and Korean children's judgments of gender norm violations.* Paper presented at the Gender Development Research conference, San Francisco.

Consoli, A., & others (2015). Risk and protective factors for suicidality at 6-month follow-up in adolescent inpatients who attempted suicide: An exploratory model. *Canadian Journal of Psychology, 60*(Suppl. 2), S27–S36.

Constantine, N.A. (2008). Editorial: Converging evidence leaves policy behind: Sex education in the United States. *Journal of Adolescent Health, 42,* 324–326.

Contant, T.L., Bass, J.E., & Carin, A.A. (2015). *Teaching science through inquiry and investigation* (12th ed.). Upper Saddle River, NJ: Pearson.

Conti, E., & others (2015). The first 1000 days of the autistic brain: A systematic review of diffusion imaging studies. *Frontiers in Human Neuroscience, 9,* 159.

Converse, A.K., Ahlers, E.O., Travers, B.G., & Davidson, R.J. (2014). Tai chi training reduces self-report of inattention in healthy young adults. *Frontiers in Human Neuroscience, 8,* 13.

Cook, M., & Birch, R. (1984). Infant perception of the shapes of tilted plane forms. *Infant Behavior and Development, 7,* 389–402.

Cook, P.J., MacCoun, R., Muschkin, C., & Vigdor, J. (2008). The negative impacts of starting middle school in the sixth grade. *Journal of Policy Analysis and Management, 27,* 104–121.

Cook, R.F., Hersch R.K., Schlossberg, D., & Leaf, S.L. (2015). A Web-based health promotion program for older workers: Randomized controlled trial. *Journal of Medical Internet Research, 17,* e82.

Cooksey, E.C. (2009). Sexual activity, adolescent. In D. Carr (Ed.), *Encyclopedia of the life course and human development.* Boston: Gale Cengage.

Coombs, N., Stamatakis, E., & Lee, I.M. (2015, in press). Physical inactivity in older adults: Implications for life expectancy among non-overweight and overweight or obese individuals. *Obesity Research and Clinical Practice.*

Coontz, S. (2005). *Marriage: A history.* New York: Penguin.

Cooper, C.R. (2011). *Bridging multiple worlds.* New York: Oxford University Press.

Cooper, C.R., Behrens, R., & Trinh, N. (2009). Identity development. In R.A. Shweder & others (Eds.), *The Chicago companion to the child.* Chicago: University of Chicago Press.

Cooper, C.R., Gonzalez, E., & Wilson, A.R. (2015). Identities, cultures, and schooling: How students navigate racial-ethnic, indigenous, immigrant, social class, and gender identities on their pathways through school. In K.C. McLean & M. Syed (Eds.), *Oxford handbook of identity development.* New York: Oxford University Press.

Cooper, C.R., & Grotevant, H.D. (1989, April). *Individuality and connectedness in the family and adolescent's self and relational competence.* Paper presented at the meeting of the Society for Research in Child Development, Kansas City.

Cooper, C.R., Grotevant, H.D., Moore, M.S., & Condon, S.M. (1982, August). *Family support and conflict: Both foster adolescent identity and role taking.* Paper presented at the meeting of the American Psychological Association, Washington, DC.

Copen, C.E., Daniels, C.E., & Mosher, W.D. (2013, April 4). First premarital cohabitation in the United States: 2006–2010 National Survey of Family Growth. *National Health Statistics Reports, 64,* 1–16.

Copen, C.E., Daniels, K., Vespa, J., & Mosher, W.D. (2012, March 22). First marriages in the United States: Data from the 2006–2010 National Survey of Family Growth. *National Health Statistics Reports, 49,* 1–22.

Cordier, S. (2008). Evidence for a role of paternal exposure in developmental toxicity. *Basic and Clinical Pharmacology and Toxicology, 102,* 176–181.

Cordova, D., Huang, S., Lally, M., Estrada, Y., & Prado, G. (2014). Do parent-adolescent discrepancies in family functioning increase the risk of Hispanic adolescent HIV risk behaviors? *Family Process, 53,* 348–363.

Corna, D.R., Cukrowicz, K.C., Linton, K., & Prabhu, F. (2010). The mediating effect of perceived burdensomeness on the relation between depressive symptoms and suicide ideation in a community sample of older adults. *Aging and Mental Health, 50,* 785–797.

Cornelissen, K.K., & others (2015). The influence of personal BMI on body size estimations and sensitivity to body size change in anorexia spectrum disorders. *Body Image, 13C,* 75–85.

Cornelius, J.R., Clark, D.B., Reynolds, M., Kirisci, L., & Tarter, R. (2007). Early age of first sexual intercourse and affiliation with deviant peers predict development of SUD: A prospective longitudinal study. *Addictive Behavior, 32,* 850–854.

Cornwell, B., Laumann, E.O., & Schumm, L.P. (2008). The social connectedness of older adults. *American Sociological Review, 73,* 185–203.

Corso, J.F. (1977). Auditory perception and communication. In J.E. Birren & K.W. Schaie (Eds.), *Handbook of the psychology of aging* (2nd ed.). New York: Van Nostrand Reinhold.

Cortes, E., Basra, R., & Kelleher, C.J. (2011). Waterbirth and pelvic floor injury: A retrospective study and postal survey using ICIQ modular long form questionnaires. *European Journal of Obstetrics, Gynecology, and Reproductive Biology, 155,* 27–30.

Cosco, T.D., & others (2014). Operational definitions of successful aging: A systematic review. *International Psychogeriatrics, 26,* 373–381.

Cosmides, L. (2013). Evolutionary psychology. *Annual Review of Psychology* (Vol. 64). Palo Alto, CA: Annual Reviews.

Costa, P.T., & McCrae, R.R. (1995). Solid ground on the wetlands of personality: A reply to Black. *Psychological Bulletin, 117,* 216–220.

Costa, P.T., & McCrae, R.R. (1998). Personality assessment. In H.S. Friedman (Ed.), *Encyclopedia of mental health* (Vol. 3). San Diego: Academic Press.

Costa, P.T., & McCrae, R.R. (2013). A theoretical context for adult temperament. In T.D. Wachs & others (Eds.), *Temperament in context.* New York: Psychology Press.

Costa, P.T., & others (2014). Personality facets and all-causes mortality among Medicare patients aged 66 to 102 years: A follow-up study of Weiss and Costa (2005). *Psychosomatic Medicine, 76,* 370–378.

Costley, K.C. (2012). An overview of the life, central concepts, including classroom applications for Lev Vygotsky. *ERIC,* ED529565.

Coté, J.E. (2009). Identify formation and self development in adolescence. In R.M. Lerner & L. Steinberg (Eds.), *Handbook of adolescent psychology* (3rd ed.). New York: Wiley.

Coté, J.E. (2015). Identity-formation research from a critical perspective: Is a social science developing? In K.C. McLean & M. Syed (Eds.), *Oxford handbook of identity development.* New York: Oxford University Press.

Cotten, S.R., Anderson, W.A., & McCullough, B.M. (2013). Impact of Internet use on loneliness and contact with others among older adults: Cross-sectional analysis. *Journal of Medical Internet Research, 152),* e39.

Cotten, S.R., Ford, G., Ford, S., & Hale, T.M. (2014). Internet use and depression among retired older adults in the United States: A longitudinal analysis. *Journals of Gerontology B: Psychological Sciences and Social Sciences, 69,* 763–771.

Coubart, A., & others (2014). Dissociation between small and larger numerosities in newborn infants. *Developmental Science, 17,* 11–22.

Council of Economic Advisors (2000). *Teens and their parents in the 21st century: An examination of trends in teen behavior and the role of parent involvement.* Washington, DC: Author.

Courage, M.L., Edison, S.C., & Howe, M.L. (2004). Variability in the early development of visual self-recognition. *Infant Behavior and Development, 27,* 509–532.

Court, F., & others (2014). Genome-wide parent-of-origin DNA methylation analysis reveals the intricacies of the human imprintome and suggests a germline methylation independent establishment of imprinting. *Genome Research, 24,* 554–569.

Cowan, M.K. (2015). *Microbiology* (4th ed.). New York: McGraw-Hill.

Cowan, N, (2014). Short-term and working memory in childhood. In P. Bauer & R. Fivush (Eds.), *Wiley-Blackwell handbook of children's memory.* New York: Wiley.

Cowan, P., & Cowan, C. (2000). *When partners become parents: The big life change for couples.* Mahwah, NJ: Erlbaum.

Cowan, P.A., & Cowan, C.P. (2009). How working with couples fosters children's development: From prevention science to public policy. In M.S. Schultz, M.K. Pruett, P.K. Kerig, & R.D. Parke (Eds.), *Feathering the nest: Couple relationships, couples interventions, and children's development.* Washington, DC: American Psychological Association.

Cowan, R., & Powell, D. (2014). The contributions of domain-general and numerical factors to third-grade arithmetic skills and mathematical learning disability. *Journal of Educational Psychology, 106,* 214–229.

Cox, K.S., Wilt, J., Olson, B., & McAdams, D.P. (2010). Generativity, the Big Five, and psychosocial adaptation in midlife adults. *Journal of Personality, 78,* 1185–1208.

Cox, M.J., & others (2008). Marital relationship. In M.M. Haith & J.B. Benson (Eds.), *Encyclopedia of infant and early childhood development.* Oxford, UK: Elsevier.

Coxon, J.P., Van Impe, A., Wenderoth, N., & Swinnen, S.P. (2012). Aging and inhibitory control of action: Cortio-subthalamic connection strength predicts stopping performance. *Journal of Neuroscience, 32,* 8401–8412.

Coyne, S.M., Nelson, D.A., & Underwood, M. (2011). Aggression in children. In P.K. Smith & C.H. Hart (Eds.), *Wiley-Blackwell handbook of childhood social development* (2nd ed.). New York: Wiley.

Craft, C.S., & others (2014). The extracellular matrix protein MAGP1 supports thermogenesis and protects against obesity and diabetes through regulation of TGFB. *Diabetes, 63,* 920–932.

Crain, S. (2012). Sentence scope. In E.L. Bavin (Ed.), *Cambridge handbook of child language.* New York: Cambridge University Press.

Crain, S., & Zhou, P. (2013). Semantics and pragmatics: Acquisition of logical connectives and focus. In C.T.J. Huang & R. Sybesma (Eds.), *Encyclopedia of Chinese language and linguistics.* The Netherlands: Brill.

Cramm, J.M., & Nieboer, A.P. (2015). Social cohesion and belonging predict the well-being of community-dwelling older people. *BMC Geriatrics, 15*(1), 30.

Crane, J.D., Macneil, L.G., & Tarnopolsky, M.A. (2013). Long-term aerobic exercise is associated with greater muscle strength throughout the life span. *Journals of Gerontology A: Biological Sciences and Medical Sciences, 68*(6), 631–638.

Craparo, G., Gori, A., Petruccelli, I., Cannella, V., & Simonelli, C. (2014). Intimate partner violence: Relationships between alexithymia, depression, attachment styles, and coping strategies of battered women. *Journal of Sexual Medicine, 11,* 1484–1494.

Cremation Association of North America (2015). *Statistics about cremation trends.* Retrieved April 21, 2015, from www.cremationassociation.org/Media/Cremation Statistics/tabid/95/Default.aspx

Crocco, P., & others (2015, in press). Population-specific association of genes for telomere-associated proteins with longevity in an Italian population. *Biogerontology.*

Crocetti, E., Jahromi, P., & Meeus, W. (2012). Identity and civic engagement in adolescence. *Journal of Adolescence, 35,* 521–532.

Crocetti, E., Rabaglietti, E., & Sica, L.S. (2012). Personal identity in Italy. *New Directions in Child and Adolescent Development, 138,* 87–102.

Crockenberg, S.B. (1986). Are temperamental differences in babies associated with predictable differences in caregiving? In J.V. Lerner & R.M. Lerner (Eds.), *Temperament and social interaction during infancy and childhood*. San Francisco: Jossey-Bass.

Crockett, L.J., Raffaelli, M., & Shen, Y-L. (2006). Linking self-regulation and risk proneness to risky sexual behavior: Pathways through peer pressure and early substance use. *Journal of Research on Adolescence, 16*, 503–525.

Crooks, R.L., & Baur, K. (2014). *Our sexuality* (12th ed.). Boston: Cengage.

Crosnoe, R. (2011). *Fitting in, standing out*. New York: Cambridge University Press.

Crosnoe, R., & Benner, A.D. (2015). Children at school. In R.M. Lerner (Ed.), *Handbook of child psychology and developmental science* (7th ed.). New York: Wiley.

Crosnoe, R., & Leventhal, T. (2014). School- and neighborhood-based interventions to improve the lives of disadvantaged children. In E.T. Gershoff, R.S. Mistry, & D.A. Crosby (Eds.), *Societal contexts of child development*. New York: Oxford University Press.

Cross, D., Lester, L., & Barnes, A. (2015). A longitudinal study of the social and emotional predictors and consequences of cyber and traditional bullying victimization. *International Journal of Public Health, 60*, 207–217.

Cross, S., & Markus, H. (1991). Possible selves across the lifespan. *Human Development, 34*, 230–255.

Crouter, A.C. (2006). Mothers and fathers at work. In A. Clarke-Stewart & J. Dunn (Eds.), *Families count*. New York: Cambridge University Press.

Crouter, A.C., & McHale, S. (2005). The long arm of the job revisited: Parenting in dual-earner families. In T. Luster & L. Okagaki (Eds.), *Parenting*. Mahwah, NJ: Erlbaum.

Crowell, J.A., Treboux, D., & Brockmeyer, S. (2009). Parental divorce and adult children's attachment representations and marital status. *Attachment and Human Development, 11*, 87–101.

Crowley, K., Callahan, M.A., Tenenbaum, H.R., & Allen, E. (2001). Parents explain more to boys than to girls during shared scientific thinking. *Psychological Science, 12*, 258–261.

Cruchaga, C., & others (2014). Rare encoding variants in the phospholipase D3 gene confer risk for Alzheimer's disease. *Nature, 505*, 550–554.

Csikszentmihalyi, M. (1996). *Creativity*. New York: HarperCollins.

Cuddy-Casey, M., & Orvaschel, H. (1997). Children's understanding of death in relation to child suicidality and homicidality. *Death Studies, 17*, 33–45.

Cuenca-Garcia, M., & others (2014). Dietary indices, cardiovascular risk factors, and mortality in middle-aged adults: Findings from the Aerobics Center Longitudinal Study. *Annals of Epidemiology, 24*, 297–303.

Cuevas, K., & Bell, K.A. (2014). Infant attention and early childhood executive function. *Child Development, 85*(2), 397–404.

Cuevas, K., Swingler, M.M., Bell, M.A., Marcovitch, S., & Calkins, S.D. (2012). Measures of frontal functioning and the emergence of inhibitory control processes at 10 months of age. *Developmental Cognitive Neuroscience, 2*, 235–243.

Cuevas, K., & others (2014). What's mom got to do with it? Contributions of maternal executive function and caregiving to the development of executive function acorss early childhood. *Developmental Science, 17*, 224–238.

Cui, X., & Vaillant, G.E. (1996). Antecedents and consequents of negative life events in adulthood: A longitudinal study. *American Journal of Psychiatry, 153*, 123–126.

Cui, Y., Zong, H., Yan, H., & Zhang, Y. (2014). The effect of testosterone replacement therapy on prostate cancer: A systematic review and meta-analysis. *Prostate Cancer and Prostatic Diseases, 17*, 132–143.

Culicover, P.W. (2013). Simpler syntax. In B. Heine & H. Narrog (Eds.), *Oxford handbook of linguistic analysis*. New York: Oxford University Press.

Cumming, E., & Henry, W. (1961). *Growing old*. New York: Basic Books.

Cummings, E.M., & Davies, P.T. (2010). *Marital conflict and children: An emotional security perspective*. New York: Guilford.

Cummings, E.M., El-Sheikh, M., & Kouros, C.D. (2009). Children and violence: The role of children's regulation in the marital aggression–child adjustment link. *Clinical Child and Family Psychology Review, 12*(1), 3–15.

Cummings, E.M., George, M.R.W., McCoy, K.P., & Davies, P.T. (2012). Interparental conflict in kindergarten and adolescent adjustment: Prospective investigation of emotional security as an explanatory mechanism. *Child Development, 83*, 1703–1715.

Cummings, E.M., & Miller, L.M. (2015, in press). Emotional security theory: An emerging theoretical model for youths' psychological and physiological responses across multiple developmental contexts. *Current Directions in Psychological Science*.

Cummings, E.M., & Valentino, K.V. (2015). Developmental psychopathology. In R.M. Lerner (Ed.), *Handbook of child psychology and developmental science* (7th ed.). New York: Wiley.

Cummings, M. (2014). *Human heredity* (10th ed.). Boston: Cengage.

Cunningham, M. (2009). Housework. In D. Carr (Ed.), *Encyclopedia of the life course and human development*. Boston: Gale Cengage.

Cunningham, S.A., Kramer, M.R., & Narayan, K.M. (2014). Incidence of childhood obesity in the United States. *New England Journal of Medicine, 370*, 403–411.

Curran, K., DuCette, J., Eisenstein, J., & Hyman, I. A. (2001, August). *Statistical analysis of the cross-cultural data: The third year*. Paper presented at the meeting of the American Psychological Association, San Francisco.

Currie, C., & others (2012). Is obesity at individual and national level associated with lower age at menarche? Evidence from 34 countries in the Health Behavior in School-aged Children study. *Journal of Adolescent Health, 50*, 621–626.

Cushner, K., McClelland, A., & Safford, P. (2015). *Human diversity in education* (8th ed.). New York: McGraw-Hill.

Cuzzolaro, M. (2014). Eating and weight disorders: Studies on anorexia, bulimia, and obesity turns 19. *Eating and Weight Disorders, 19*, 1–2.

Cvencek, D., Meltzoff, A.N., & Greenwald, A.G. (2011). Math-gender stereotypes in elementary school children. *Child Development, 82*, 766–779.

Cvijetic, S., & others (2014). Influence of nutrition and lifestyle on bone mineral density of children from adoptive and biological families. *Journal of Epidemiology, 24*, 209–215.

Cybele Raver, C., McCoy, D.C., Lowenstein, A.E., & Pess, R. (2013). Predicting individual differences in low-income children's executive control from early to middle childhood. *Developmental Science, 16*, 394–408.

D

D'Aoust, L.N., & others (2015). Examination of candidate exonic variants for association to Alzheimer disease in the Amish. *PLoS One, 10*(21), e0118043.

D'Apolito, K. (2013). Breastfeeding and substance abuse. *Clinical Obstetrics and Gynecology, 56*, 202–211.

da Costa Souza, A., & Ribeiro, S. (2015, in press). Sleep deprivation and gene expression. *Current Topics in Behavioral Neurosciences*.

da Cruz, A.C., & others (2014). Oxidative stress and aging: Correlation with clinical parameters. *Aging: Clinical and Experimental Research, 26*, 7–12.

da Luz, M.H., & others (2015). Dopamine induces the accumulation of insoluble prion protein and affects autophagic flux. *Frontiers in Cellular Neuroscience, 9*, 12.

da Rocha, A.F., Rocha, F.T., & Massad, E. (2011). The brain as a distributed intelligent processing system: An EEG study. *PLoS One, 6*, e17355.

da Rosa, G., & others (2014). Examination of important life experiences of the oldest-old: Cross-cultural comparisons of U.S. and Japanese centenarians. *Journal of Cross-Cultural Gernontology, 29*, 109–130.

Dahl, R.E. (2004). Adolescent brain development: A period of vulnerabilities and opportunities. *Annals of the New York Academy of Sciences, 1021*, 1–22.

Dahlberg, L., & McKee, K.J. (2014). Correlates of social and emotional loneliness in older people: Evidence from an English community study. *Aging and Mental Health, 18*, 504–514.

Dahlen, H.G., Dowling, H., Schmied, V., & Tracy, S. (2013). Maternal and perinatal outcomes amongst low risk women giving birth in water compared to six birth positions on land: A descriptive cross sectional study in a birth center over 12 years. *Midwifery, 29*, 759–764.

Dale, B., & others (2014). Utility of the Stanford-Binet Intelligence Scales, 5th ed., with ethnically diverse preschoolers. *Psychology in the Schools, 51*, 581–590.

Daly, M., Delaney, L., Egan, M., & Baumeister, R.F. (2015, in press). Childhood self-control and unemployment through the life span: Evidence from two British cohort studies. *Psychological Science*.

Daly, M.C., & Bengali, L. (2014, May 5). Is it still worth it to go to college? *FRBSF Economic Letter*, 1–6.

Damasio, A.R. (1994). Descartes' error and the future of human life. *Scientific American, 271*, 144.

Damman, M., Henkens, K., & Kalmijn, M. (2015, in press). Missing work after retirement: The role of life histories in the retirement adjustment process. *Gerontologist*.

Damon, W. (1988). *The moral child*. New York: Free Press.

Damon, W. (2008). *The path to purpose*. New York: Free Press.

Dan, B., Pelc, K., de Meireir, L., & Cheron, G. (2015). Phenotypic plasticity and the perception-action-cognition-environment paradigm in neurodevelopmental genetic disorders. *Developmental Medicine and Child Neurology, 57*(Suppl. 2), S52–S54.

Daniels, H. (2011). Vygotsky and psychology. In U. Goswami (Ed.), *Wiley-Blackwell handbook of childhood cognitive development* (2nd ed.). New York: Wiley-Blackwell.

Danielson, Y.S., & others (2012). Factors associated with low self-esteem in children with overweight. *Obesity Facts, 5*, 722–733.

Danner, D., Snowdon, D., & Friesen, W. (2001). Positive emotions in early life and longevity: Findings from the Nun Study. *Journal of Personality and Social Psychology, 80*(5), 804–813.

Darcy, E. (2012). Gender issues in child and adolescent eating disorders. In J. Lock (Ed.), *Oxford handbook of child and adolescent eating disorders: Developmental perspectives*. New York: Oxford University Press.

Darling-Hammond, N. (2011). Testing, No Child Left Behind, and educational equity. In L.M. Stulberg & S.L. Weinberg (Eds.), *Diversity in higher education*. New York: Routledge.

Darwin, C. (1859). *On the origin of species.* London: John Murray.

Das, A. (2013). Spousal loss and health in late life: Moving beyond emotional trauma. *Journal of Aging Health, 25,* 221–242.

Davanzo, R., & others (2013). Intermittent kangaroo mother care: A NICU protocol. *Journal of Human Lactation, 29*(3), 332–338.

Dave, D., & Rashad, I. (2009). Overweight status, self-perception, and suicide behaviors among adolescents. *Social Science & Medicine, 68,* 1685–1691.

Davidov, M., Zhan-Waxler, C., Roth-Hanania, C., & Knafo, A. (2013). Concern for others in the first year of life: Theory, evidence, and avenues of research. *Child Development Perspectives, 7,* 126–131.

Davidson, D. (1996). The effects of decision characteristics on children's selective search of predecisional information. *Acta Psychologica, 92,* 263–281.

Davidson, J., & Davidson, B. (2004). *Genius denied: How to stop wasting our brightest young minds.* New York: Simon & Schuster.

Davidson, M., Lickona, T., & Khmelkov, V. (2008). A new paradigm for high school character education. In L. Nucci & D. Narváez (Eds.), *Handbook of moral and character education.* Clifton, NJ: Psychology Press.

Davies, G., & others (2011). Genome-wide association studies establish that human intelligence is highly heritable and polygenic. *Molecular Psychiatry, 16,* 996–1005.

Davies, J., & Brember, I. (1999). Reading and mathematics attainments and self-esteem in years 2 and 6: An eight-year cross-sectional study. *Educational Studies, 25,* 145–157.

Davies, M., Gilston, J., & Rogers, P. (2012). Examining the relationship between male rape myth acceptance, female rape myth acceptance, victim blame, homophobia, gender roles, and ambivalent sexism. *Journal of Interpersonal Violence, 27*(14), 2807–2823.

Davies, P.T., & Cicchetti, D. (2014). How and why does the 5-HTTLPR gene moderate associations between maternal unresponsiveness and children's problems? *Child Development, 85,* 484–500.

Davis, B.E., Moon, R.Y., Sachs, M.C., & Ottolini, M.C. (1998). Effects of sleep position on infant motor development: *Pediatrics, 102,* 1135–1140.

Davis, C.L., & Cooper, S. (2011). Fitness, fatness, cognition, behavior, and academic achievement among overweight children: Do cross-sectional associations correspond to exercise trial outcomes? *Preventive Medicine, 52*(Suppl. 1), S65–S69.

Davis, C.L., & others (2011). Exercise improves executive function and alters neural activation in overweight children. *Health Psychology, 30,* 91–98.

Davis, C.L., & others (2012). Exercise dose and diabetes risk in overweight and obese children: A randomized controlled trial. *Journal of the American Medical Association, 308,* 1103–1112.

Davis, L., & Keyser, J. (1997). *Becoming the parent you want to be: A sourcebook of strategies for the first five years.* New York: Broadway Books.

Davis, M.C., Burke, H.M., Zautra, A.J., & Stark, S. (2013). Arthritis and musculoskeletal conditions. In I.B. Weiner & others (Eds.), *Handbook of psychology* (2nd ed., Vol. 9). New York: Wiley.

Davis, S.W., Kragel, J.E., Madden, D.J., & Cabeza, R. (2012). The architecture of cross-hemispheric communication in the aging brain: Linking behavior to functional structural connectivity. *Cerebral Cortex, 22,* 232–242.

Dawson, A.E., & others (2014). Adolescent insecure attachment as a predictor of maladaptive coping and externalizing behaviors in emerging adulthood. *Attachment and Human Development, 116,* 462–478.

Dawson-McClure, S., & others (2015). A population-level approach to promoting healthy child development and school success in low-income, urban neighborhoods: Impact of parenting and child conduct problems. *Prevention Science, 16,* 279–290.

Day, N.L., Goldschmidt, L., & Thomas, C.A. (2006). Prenatal marijuana exposure contributes to the prediction of marijuana use at age 14. *Addiction, 101,* 1313–1322.

Day, R.H., & McKenzie, B.E. (1973). Perceptual shape constancy in early infancy. *Perception, 2,* 315–320.

De Bolle, M., & others (2015). The emergence of sex differences in personality traits in early adolescence: A cross-sectional, cross-cultural study. *Journal of Personality and Social Psychology, 108,* 171–185.

de Frias, C.M., & Dixon, R.A. (2014). Lifestyle engagement affects cognitive status differences and trajectories on executive functions in older adults. *Archives of Clinical Neuropsychology, 29,* 16–25.

de Frias, C.M., Schaie, K.W., & Willis, S. (2014). Hypertension moderates the effect of APOE on 21-year cognitive trajectories. *Psychology and Aging, 29,* 431–439.

De Giovanni, N., & Marchetti, D. (2012). Cocaine and its metabolites in the placenta: A systematic review of the literature. *Reproductive Toxicology, 33*(1), 1–14.

de Guzman, N.S., & Nishina, A. (2014). A longitudinal study of body dissatisfaction and pubertal timing in an ethnically diverse adolescent sample. *Body Image, 11,* 68–71.

de Haan, M. (2015). Neuroscientific methods with children. In R.M. Lerner (Ed.), *Handbook of child psychology and developmental science* (7th ed.). New York: Wiley.

de Haan, M., & Gunnar, M.R. (Eds.). (2009). *Handbook of developmental social neuroscience.* New York: Guilford.

de Jongh, B.E., Mackley, A., Jain, N., Locke, R., & Paul, D.A. (2015, in press). Effects of advanced maternal age and race/ethnicity on placental weight and placental weight/birthweight ratio in very low birthweight infants. *Maternal and Child Health Journal.*

de la Cuesta-Benjumea, C. (2011). Strategies for the relief of burden in advanced dementia care-giving. *Journal of Advanced Nursing, 67*(8), 1790–1799.

De Leo, D. (2002). Struggling against suicide: The need for an integrative approach. *Crisis, 23,* 23–31.

de Looze, M., & others (2015). Parent-adolescent sexual communication and its association with adolescent sexual behaviors: A nationally representative analysis in the Netherlands. *Journal of Sexual Research, 52,* 257–268.

De Navas-Walt, C., & Proctor, B.D. (2014). *Income and poverty in the United States, 2013.* Washington, DC: U.S. Census Bureau.

de Planell-Saguer, M., Lovinsky-Desir, S., & Miller, R.L. (2014). Epigenetic regulation: The interface between prenatal and early life exposure and asthma susceptibility. *Environmental and Molecular Mutagenesis, 55,* 231–243.

de Toledo, S., & Brown, D.E. (2013). *Grandparents as parents* (2nd ed.). New York: Guilford.

de Villiers, J., & de Villiers, P. (2013). Syntax acquisition. In P.D. Zelazo (Ed.), *Oxford handbook of developmental psychology.* New York: Oxford University Press.

de Vries, S.L., Hoeve, M., Assink, M., Stams, G.J., & Asscher, J.J. (2015). Practitioner review: Effective ingredients of prevention programs for youth at risk of persistent juvenile delinquency—recommendations for clinical practice. *Journal of Child Psychology and Psychiatry, 56,* 108–121.

de Vries, S.L., Hoeve, M., Stams, G.J., & Asscher, J.J. (2015, in press). Adolescent-parent attachment and externalizing behavior: The mediating role of individual and social factors. *Journal of Abnormal Child Psychology.*

de Wind, A.W., & others (2014). Health, job characteristics, skills, and social and financial factors in relation to early retirement—results from a longitudinal study in the Netherlands. *Scandinavian Journal of Work, Environment, and Health, 40,* 186–194.

de Wit, L., & others (2010). Depression and obesity: A meta-analysis of community-based studies. *Psychiatry Research, 178,* 230–235.

Deary, I. (2012). Intelligence. *Annual Review of Psychology* (Vol. 63). Palo Alto, CA: Annual Reviews.

Deater-Deckard, K. (2013). The social environment and the development of psychopathology. In P.D. Zelazo (Ed.), *Oxford handbook of developmental psychology.* New York: Oxford University Press.

Debats, D.L. (1990). The Life Regard Index: Reliability and validity. *Psychological Reports, 67,* 27–34.

DeCasper, A.J., & Spence, M.J. (1986). Prenatal maternal speech influences newborns' perception of speech sounds. *Infant Behavior and Development, 9,* 133–150.

deCharms, R. (1984). Motivation enhancement in educational setting. In R. Arnes & C. Arnes (Eds.), *Research on motivation in education* (Vol. 1). Orlando, FL: Academic Press.

Deci, E.L., Koestner, R., & Ryan, R.M. (2001). Extrinsic rewards and intrinsic motivation in education: Reconsidered once again. *Review of Educational Research, 71,* 1–28.

Dedon, P.C., & Begley, T.H. (2014). A system of RNA modifications and biased codon use control cellular stress response at the level of transition. *Chemical Research in Toxicology, 27,* 330–337.

DeJong, W., DeRicco, B., & Schneider, S.K. (2010). Pregaming: An exploratory study of strategic drinking by college students in Pennsylvania. *Journal of American College Health, 58,* 307–316.

Del Campo, L., Buchanan, W.R., Abbott, R.D., & Berninger, V.W. (2015). Levels of phonology related to reading and writing in middle and late childhood. *Reading and Writing, 28,* 183–198.

Del Giudice, M. (2011). Sex differences in romantic attachment: A meta-analysis. *Personality and Social Psychology Bulletin, 37,* 193–214.

DeLisi, R. (2015). Piaget's sympathetic but unromantic account of children's play. In J.E. Johnson & others (Eds.), *Handbook of the study of play.* Blue Ridge Summit, PA: Rowan & Littlefield.

DeLoache, J.S., Simcock, G., & Macari, S. (2007). Planes, trains, automobiles—and tea-sets: Extremely intense interests in very young children. *Developmental Psychology, 43,* 1579–1586.

Demanachick, S.P. (2015). The interpretation of play: Psychoanalysis and beyond. In J.E. Johnson & others (Eds.), *Handbook of the study of play.* Blue Ridge Summit, PA: Rowan & Littlefield.

Demiray, B., Gulgoz, S., & Bluck, S. (2009). Examining the life story account of the reminiscence bump: Why we remember more from early adulthood. *Memory, 17,* 708–723.

Demircin, S., Akkoyun, M., Yilmaz, R., & Gokdogan, M.R. (2011). Suicide of elderly persons: Towards a framework for prevention. *Geriatrics & Gerontology International, 11,* 107–113.

Dempster, F.N. (1981). Memory span: Sources of individual and developmental differences. *Psychological Bulletin, 80,* 63–100.

Demsky, C.A., Ellis, M.A., & Fritz, C. (2014). Shrugging it off: Does psychological detachment from work mediate the relationship between workplace aggression and work-family conflict? *Journal of Occupational Health and Psychology, 19,* 195–205.

Denard, P.J., & others (2010). Back pain, neurogenic symptoms, and physical function in relation to spondylolisthesis among elderly men. *Spine Journal, 10,* 865–887.

Denham, S.A., Bassett, H.H., & Wyatt, T. (2007). The socialization of emotional competence. In J.E. Grusec & P.D. Hastings (Eds.), *Handbook of socialization.* New York: Guilford.

Denham, S.A., Bassett, H.H., & Wyatt, T. (2015). The socialization of emotional competence. In J.E. Grusec & P.D. Hastings (Eds.), *Handbook of socialization* (2nd ed.). New York: Guilford.

Denham, S.A., & Zinsser, K.M. (2015). Promoting social and emotional learning in early childhood. In T.P. Gullotta & M. Bloom (Eds.), *Encyclopedia of primary prevention and health promotion* (2nd ed.). New York: Academic/Plenum Publishers.

Denham, S.A., & others (2014). "I know how you feel": Preschoolers' emotion knowledge contributes to early school success. *Journal of Early Childhood Research, 28,* 182–202.

Denmark, F.L., Russo, N.F., Frieze, I.H., & Eschuzur, J. (1988). Guidelines for avoiding sexism in psychological research: A report of the ad hoc committee on nonsexist research. *American Psychologist, 43,* 582–585.

Denney, N.W. (1986, August). *Practical problem solving.* Paper presented at the meeting of the American Psychological Association, Washington, DC.

Denney, N.W. (1990). Adult age differences in traditional and practical problem solving. *Advances in Psychology, 72,* 329–349.

Dennis, M., & others (2014). Functional plasticity in childhood brain disorders: When, what, how, and whom to assess. *Neuropsychology Review, 24*(4), 389–408.

Dennis, N.A., & Cabeza, R. (2008). Neuroimaging of healthy cognitive aging. In F.I.M. Craik & T.A. Salthouse (Eds.), *Handbook of aging and cognition* (3rd ed.). Mahwah, NJ: Erlbaum.

DePaulo, B. (2006). *Singled out.* New York: St. Martin's Press.

DePaulo, B. (2011). Living single: Lightening up those dark, dopey myths. In W.R. Cupach & B.H. Spitzberg (Eds.), *The dark side of close relationships.* New York: Routledge.

Der Ananian, C., & Prohaska, T.R. (2007). Exercise and physical activity. In J.E. Birren (Ed.), *Encyclopedia of gerontology* (2nd ed.). San Diego: Academic Press.

Derebail, V.K., & others (2014). Sickle trait in African-American hemodialysis patients and higher erythropoiesis-stimulating agent dose. *Journal of the American Society of Nephrology, 25*(4), 819–826.

DeRosa, D.A., & Abruscato, J. (2015). *Teaching children science* (8th ed.). Upper Saddle River, NJ: Pearson.

Destan, N., Hembacher, E., Ghetti, S., & Roebers, C.M. (2014). Early metacognitive abilities: The interplay of monitoring and control processes in 5- to 7-year-old children. *Journal of Experimental Child Psychology, 126,* 213–228.

Deustch, A.R., Chernyavskiy, P., Steinley, D., & Slutske, W.S. (2015). Measuring peer socialization for adolescent substance use: A comparison of perceived and actual friends' substance use effects. *Journal of Studies on Alcohol and Drugs, 76,* 267–277.

Deutsch, A.R., Crockett, L.J., Wolf, J.M., & Russell, S.T. (2012). Parent and peer pathways to adolescent delinquency: Variations by ethnicity and neighborhood context. *Journal of Youth and Adolescence, 41,* 1078–1094.

Deutsch, R., & Pruett, M.K. (2009). Child adjustment and high-conflict divorce. In R.M. Galatzer-Levy,

L. Kraus, & J. Galatzer-Levy (Eds.), *The scientific basis of custody decisions* (2nd ed.). New York: Wiley.

Devaney, S.A., Palomaki, G.E., Scott, J.A., & Bianchi, D.W. (2011). Noninvasive fetal sex determination using cell-free fetal DNA: A systematic review and meta-analysis. *Journal of the American Medical Association, 306,* 627–636.

Devos, T. (2006). Implicit bicultural identity among Mexican American and Asian American college students. *Cultural Diversity and Ethnic Minority Psychology, 12,* 381–402.

Dew, J., & Wilcox, W.B. (2011). "If momma ain't happy": Explaining declines in marital satisfaction among new mothers. *Journal of Marriage and the Family, 73,* 1–12.

DeWall, C.N., Anderson, C.A., & Bushman, B.J. (2013). Aggression. In I.B. Weiner & others (Eds.), *Handbook of psychology* (2nd ed., Vol. 5). New York: Wiley.

Dewey, J. (1933). *How we think.* Lexington, MA: D.C. Heath.

DeZolt, D.M., & Hull, S.H. (2001). Classroom and school climate. In J. Worell (Ed.), *Encyclopedia of women and gender.* San Diego: Academic Press.

Di Florio, A., & others (2014). Mood disorders and parity—a clue to the etiology of the postpartum trigger. *Journal of Affective Disorders, 152,* 334–349.

Di Nardo, W., & others (2014). The effects of cochlear implantation on quality of life in the elderly. *European Archives of Otorhinolaryngology, 271,* 65–73.

Diamond, A. (2013). Executive functions. *Annual Review of Psychology* (Vol. 64). Palo Alto, CA: Annual Reviews.

Diamond, A., Barnett, W.S., Thomas, J., & Munro, S. (2007). Preschool program improves cognitive control. *Science, 318,* 1387–1388.

Diamond, A., & Lee, K. (2011). Interventions shown to aid executive function development in children 4 to 12 years old. *Science, 333,* 959–964.

Diamond, A.D. (1985). Development of the ability to use recall to guide action as indicated by infants' performance on A-not-B. *Child Development, 56,* 868–883.

Diamond, L.M. (2013). Concepts of female sexual orientation. In C. Patterson & A.R. D'Augelli (Eds.), *The psychology of sexual orientation.* New York: Cambridge University Press.

Diamond, L.M., & Savin-Williams, R.C. (2015). Same-sex activity in adolescence: Multiple meanings and implications. In R.F. Fassinger & S.L. Morrow (Eds.), *Sex in the margins.* Washington, DC: American Psychological Association.

Diamond, M., & Sigmundson, H.K. (1997). Sex reassignment at birth: Long-term review and clinical implications. *Archives of Pediatric and Adolescent Medicine, 151,* 295–304.

Dickens, B.M. (2014). Ethical and legal aspects of noninvasive prenatal genetic diagnosis. *International Journal of Gynecology and Obstetrics, 124,* 181–184.

Dickinson, W.J., & others (2011). Change in stress and social support as predictors of cognitive decline in older adults with and without depression. *International Journal of Geriatric Psychiatry, 26,* 1267–1274.

Diderich, H.M., & others (2014). Facilitators and barriers to the successful implementation of a protocol to detect child abuse based on parental characteristics. *Child Abuse and Neglect, 38,* 1822–1831.

Diego, M.A., Field, T., & Hernandez-Reif, M. (2008). Temperature increases in preterm infants during massage therapy. *Infant Behavior and Development, 31,* 149–152.

Diego, M.A., Field, T., & Hernandez-Reif, M. (2014). Preterm infant weight gain is increased by massage therapy and exercise via different underlying mechanisms. *Early Human Development, 90,* 137–140.

Diekelmann, S. (2014). Sleep for cognitive enhancement. *Frontiers in Systems Neuroscience, 8,* 46.

Diener, E. (2015). *Subjective well-being.* Retrieved February 17, 2015, from http://internal.psychology.illinois.edu/~ediener/SWLS.html

Diener, E., Emmons, R.A., Larson, R.J., & Griffin, S. (1985). The Satisfaction with Life Scale. *Journal of Personality Assessment, 49,* 71–75.

Diener, E., & Seligman, M.E.P. (2002). Very happy people. *Psychological Science, 13,* 81–84.

DiLeonardo, M.J. (2015). *Talking about weight with your child.* Retrieved February 25, 2015, from www.webmd.com/parenting/raising-fit-kids/weight/talk-child-...

Dillon, J. (2003). Reincarnation: The technology of death. In C.D. Bryant (Ed.), *Handbook of death and dying.* Thousand Oaks, CA: Sage.

Dimitropoulos, G., & others (2015, in press). Family-based treatment with transition age youth with anorexia nervosa: A qualitative summary of application in clinical practice. *Journal of Eating Disorders.*

Dimmitt, C., & McCormick, C.B. (2012). Metacognition in education. In K.R. Harris, S. Graham, & T. Urdan (Eds.), *Handbook of educational psychology.* Washington, DC: American Psychological Association.

Ding, X.P., & others (2014). Elementary school children's cheating behavior and its cognitive correlates. *Journal of Experimental Child Psychology, 121,* 85–95.

Ding, Y.H., & others (2014). The relation of infant attachment to attachment and cognitive and behavioral outcomes in early childhood. *Early Human Development, 90,* 459–464.

Ding, Z., & others (2014). Estimating telomere length from whole genome sequence data. *Nucleic Acids Research, 42*(9), e75.

Dionne, G., & others (2011). Associations between sleep-wake consolidation and language development: A developmental twin study. *Sleep, 34,* 987–995.

Dishion, T.J., & Piehler, T.F. (2009). Deviant by design: Peer contagion in development, interventions, and schools. In K.H. Rubin, W.M. Bukowski, & B. Laursen (Eds.), *Handbook of peer interactions, relationships, and groups.* New York: Guilford.

Dixon, L., Browne, K., & Hamilton-Giachritsis, C. (2005). Risk factors of parents abused as children: A mediational analysis of the intergenerational continuity of child maltreatment (Part I). *Journal of Child Psychology and Psychiatry and Allied Disciplines, 46,* 47–54.

Dixon, R.A., McFall, G.P., Whitehead, B.P., & Dolcos, S. (2013). Cognitive development and aging. In I.B. Weiner & others (Eds.), *Handbook of psychology* (2nd ed., Vol. 6). New York: Wiley.

Doane, L.D., & Thurston, E.C. (2014). Associations among sleep, daily experiences, and loneliness in adolescence: Evidence of moderating and bidirectional pathways. *Journal of Adolescence, 37,* 145–154.

Dodge, K.A. (1983). Behavioral antecedents of peer social status. *Child Development, 54,* 1386–1399.

Dodge, K.A. (2011a). Context matters in child and family policy. *Child Development, 82,* 433–442.

Dodge, K.A. (2011b). Social information processing models of aggressive behavior. In M. Mikulincer & P.R. Shaver (Eds.), *Understanding and reducing aggression, violence, and their consequences.* Washington, DC: American Psychological Association.

Dodge, K.A., Godwin, J., & The Conduct Problems Prevention Research Group (2013). Social-information-processing patterns mediate the impact of preventive intervention on adolescent antisocial behavior. *Psychological Science, 24,* 456–465.

Dodge, K.A., & McCourt, S.N. (2010). Translating models of antisocial behavioral development into efficacious intervention policy to prevent adolescent violence. *Developmental Psychobiology, 52*(3), 277–285.

Dolcos, S., Katsumi, Y., & Dixon, R.A. (2014). The role of arousal in the spontaneous regulation of emotions in healthy aging: A fMRI investigation. *Frontiers in Psychology, 5,* 681.

Doll, C.A., & Broadie, K. (2014). Impaired activity-dependent neural circuit assembly and refinement in autism spectrum disorder genetic models. *Frontiers in Cellular Neuoroscience, 8,* 30.

Domsch, H., Lohaus, A., & Thomas, H. (2009). Influence of information processing and disengagement on infants' looking behavior. *Infant and Child Development, 19,* 161–174.

Donatelle, R.J. (2015). *Health: The basics* (11th ed.). Upper Saddle River, NJ: Pearson.

Donath, C., Graessel, E., Baier, D., Bleich, S., & Hillemacher, T. (2014). Is parenting style a predictor of suicide attempts in a representative sample of adolescents? *BMC Pediatrics, 14*(1), 113.

Dondi, M., Simion, F., & Caltran, G. (1999). Can newborns discriminate between their own cry and the cry of another newborn infant? *Developmental Psychology, 35*(2), 418–426.

Donegan, S., & others (2010). Two food-assisted maternal and child health nutrition programs helped mitigate the impact of economic hardship on child stunting in Haiti. *Journal of Nutrition, 140,* 1139–1145.

Dong, M., & others (2015, in press). Multiple genetic variants associated with primary biliary cirrhosis in a Han Chinese population. *Clinical Reviews in Allergy and Immunology.*

Donnellan, M.B., Larsen-Rife, D., & Conger, R.D. (2005). Personality, family history, and competence in early adult romantic relationships. *Journal of Personality and Social Psychology, 88,* 562–576.

Donnelly, N., & Storchova, Z. (2015, in press). Causes and consequence of protein folding stress in aneuploidy cells. *Cell Cycle.*

Doornwaard, S.M., Branje, S., Meeus, W.H.J., & ter Bogt, T.F.M. (2012). Development of adolescents' peer crowd identification in relation to changes in problem behaviors. *Developmental Psychology, 48,* 1366–1380.

Dorey, E., Chang, N., Liu, Q.Y., Yang, Z., & Zhang, W. (2014). Apolipoprotein E., amyloid-beta, and neuroinflammation in Alzheimer's disease. *Neuoroscience Bulletin, 30*(2), 317–330.

Dorffner, G., Vitr, M., & Anderer, P. (2015). The effects of aging on sleep architecture in healthy subjects. *Advances in Experimental Medicine and Biology, 821,* 93–100.

Dorheim, S.K., Bjorvatn, B., & Eberhard-Gran, M. (2014). Can insomnia in pregnancy predict postpartum depression? A longitudinal, population-based study. *PLoS One, 9*(4), e94674.

Doty, R.L., & Shah, M. (2008). Taste and smell. In M.M. Haith & J.B. Benson (Eds.), *Encyclopedia of infant and early childhood development.* Oxford, UK: Elsevier.

Doumen, S., & others (2012). Identity and perceived peer relationship quality in emerging adulthood: The mediating role of attachment-related emotions. *Journal of Adolescence, 35,* 1417–1425.

Dovis, S., Van der Oord, S., Wiers, R.W., & Prins, P.J. (2015). Improving executive functioning in children with ADHD: Training multiple executive functions within the context of a computer game. A randomized double-blind placebo controlled trial. *PLoS One, 10*(4), e0121651.

Dow, R.S., & Baer, G.T. (2013). *Self-paced phonics* (5th ed.). Boston: Allyn & Bacon.

Dowda, M., & others (2009). Policies and characteristics of the preschool environment and physical activity of young children. *Pediatrics, 123,* e261–e266.

Dozier, M., Stovall-McClough, K.C., & Albus, K.E. (2009). Attachment and psychopathology in adulthood. In J. Cassidy & P.R. Shaver (Eds.), *Handbook of attachment* (2nd ed.). New York: Guilford.

Draghi-Lorenz, R. (2007, July). *Self-conscious emotions in young infants and the direct perception of self and others in interaction.* Paper presented at the meeting of the International Society for Research on Emotions, Sunshine Coast, Australia.

Drake, K., Belsky, J., Fearon, R.M.P. (2014). From early attachment to engagement with learning in school: The role of self-regulation and persistence. *Developmental Psychology, 50,* 1350–1361.

Drake, K.M., & others (2012). Influence of sports, physical education, and active commuting to school on adolescent weight status. *Pediatrics, 130,* e296–e304.

Dregan, A., & Armstrong, D. (2010). Adolescent sleep disturbances as predictors of adult sleep disturbances—A cohort study. *Journal of Adolescent Health, 46,* 482–487.

Drollette, E.S., & others (2014). Acute exercise facilitates brain function and cognition in children who need it most: An ERP study of individual differences in inhibitory control capacity. *Developmental Cognitive Neuroscience, 7,* 53–64.

Drummond, J., Paul, E.F., Waugh, W.E., Hammong, S.I., & Brownell, C.A. (2014). Here, there, and everywhere: Emotion and mental state talk in different social contexts predicts empathic helping in toddlers. *Frontiers in Psychology, 5,* 361.

Dryfoos, J.G., & Barkin, C. (2006). *Adolescence: Growing up in America today.* New York: Oxford University Press.

Du, M., & others (2012). Physical activity, sedentary behavior, and leukocyte telomere length in women. *American Journal of Epidemiology, 175,* 414–422.

Duan, X., Dan, Z., & Shi, J. (2014). The speed of information processing of 9- to 13-year-old intellectually gifted children. *Psychology Reports, 112,* 20–32.

Dublin, S., & others (2014). Neuropathologic changes associated with atrial fibrillation in a population-based autopsy cohort. *Journals of Gerontology A: Biological Sciences and Medical Sciences, 69,* 609–615.

Dubois, J., & others (2014). The early development of brain white matter: A review of imaging studies in fetuses, newborns, and infants. *Neuroscience, 276,* 48–71.

Duck, S. (2011). *Rethinking relationships.* Thousand Oaks, CA: Sage.

Dudley, R.L. (1999). Youth religious commitment over time: Longitudinal study of retention. *Review of Religious Research, 41,* 110–121.

Dudova, I., & others (2014). Screening for autism in preterm children with extremely low and very low birth weight. *Neuropsychiatric Disease and Treatment, 10,* 277–282.

Duff, D., Tomblin, J.B., & Catts, H. (2015, in press). The influence of reading on vocabulary growth: A case for a Matthew effect. *Journal of Speech, Language, and Hearing Research.*

Duggan, K.A., & Friedman, H.S. (2014). Lifetime biopsychosocial trajectories of the Terman gifted children: Health, well-being, and longevity. In D.K. Simonton (Ed.), *Wiley-Blackwell handbook of genius.* New York: Oxford University Press.

Duggan, P.M., Lapsley, D.K., & Norman, K. (2000, April). *Adolescent invulnerability and personal uniqueness: Scale development and initial contact validation.* Paper presented at the biennial meeting of the Society for Research in Child Development, Chicago.

Duke, J., & others (2011). A study of burn hospitalizations for children younger than 5 years of age: 1983–2008. *Pediatrics, 127*(4), e971–e977.

Duke, S.A., Balzer, B.W., & Steinbeck, K.S. (2014). Testosterone and its effects on human male adolescent mood and behavior: A systematic review. *Journal of Adolescent Health, 55,* 315–322.

Dulas, M.R., & Duarte, A. (2014). Aging affects the interaction between attentional control and source memory: An fMRI study. *Journal of Cognitive Neuroscience. 26,* 2653–2669,

Duncan, D.T., & Hatzenbuehler, M.L. (2014). Lesbian, gay, bisexual, and transgender hate crimes and suicidality among a population-based sample of sexual-minority adolescents in Boston. *American Journal of Public Health, 104,* 272–278.

Duncan, G.J. (2012). Give us this day our daily breadth. *Child Development, 83,* 6–15.

Duncan, G.J., & Magnuson, K. (2013). The long reach of early childhood poverty. In W-J. Yeung & Y. Mui-Teng (Eds.), *Economic stress, human capital, and families in Asia: Research and policy challenges.* New York: Springer.

Duncan, G.J., Magnuson, K., & Votruba-Drzal, E. (2015). Children and socioeconomic status. In R.M. Lerner (Ed.), *Handbook of child psychology and developmental science* (7th ed.). New York: Wiley.

Dunifon, R. (2013). The influence of grandparents on the lives of children and adolescents. *Child Development Perspectives, 7*(1), 55–60.

Dunn, D.W., & Kronenberger, W.G. (2013). Attention deficit. *Handbook of clinical psychology, 111,* 257–261.

Dunn, E.C., McLaughlin, K.A., Slopen, N., Rosand, J., & Smoller, J.W. (2013). Developmental timing of child maltreatment and symptoms of depression and suicidal ideation in young adulthood: Results from the National Longitudinal Study of Adolescent Health. *Depression and Anxiety, 30,* 955–964.

Dunn, J. (1984). Sibling studies and the developmental impact of critical incidents. In P.B. Baltes & O.G. Brim (Eds.), *Life-span development and behavior* (Vol. 6). Orlando, FL: Academic Press.

Dunn, J. (2007). Siblings and socialization. In J.E. Grusec & P.D. Hastings (Eds.), *Handbook of socialization.* New York: Guilford.

Dunn, J. (2014). Moral development in early childhood and social interaction in the family. In M. Killen & J.G. Smetana (Eds.), *Handbook of moral development* (2nd ed.). New York: Psychology Press.

Dunn, J. (2015). Siblings. In J.E. Grusec & P.D. Hastings (Eds.), *Handbook of socialization* (2nd ed.). New York: Guilford.

Dunn, J., & Kendrick, C. (1982). *Siblings.* Cambridge, MA: Harvard University Press.

Dunphy-Lelii, S., Labounty, J., Lane, J.D., & Wellman, H.M. (2014). The social context of infant intention understanding. *Journal of Cognitive Development, 15,* 60–77.

Durham, R., & Chapman, L. (2014). *Maternal-newborn nursing* (2nd ed.). Philadelphia: F.A. Davis.

Durrant, R., & Ellis, B.J. (2013). Evolutionary psychology. In I.B. Weiner & others (Eds.), *Handbook of psychology* (2nd ed.,Vol. 3). New York: Wiley.

Durston, S., & others (2006). A shift from diffuse to focal cortical activity with development. *Developmental Science, 9,* 1–8.

Dvornyk, V., & Waqar-ul-Haq, H. (2012). Genetics of age at menarche: A systematic review. *Human Reproduction Update, 18,* 198–210.

Dweck, C.S. (2006). *Mindset.* New York: Random House.

Dweck, C.S. (2007). Boosting achievement with messages that motivate. *Education Canada, 47,* 6–10.

Dweck, C.S. (2012). Mindsets and human nature: Promoting change in the Middle East, the school yard, the racial divide, and willpower. *American Psychologist, 67,* 614–622.

Dweck, C.S. (2013). Social development. In P. Zelazo (Ed.), *Oxford handbook of developmental psychology.* New York: Oxford University Press.

Dweck, C.S., & Elliott, E. (1983). Achievement motivation. In P. Mussen (Ed.), *Handbook of child psychology* (4th ed., Vol. 4). New York: Wiley.

Dweck, C.S., & Master, A. (2009). Self-theories and motivation: Students' beliefs about intelligence. In K.R. Wentzel & A. Wigfield (Eds.), *Handbook of motivation at school.* New York: Routledge.

Dweck, C.S., Mangels, J.A., & Good, C. (2004). Motivational effects on attention, cognition, and performance. In D.Y. Dai & R.J. Sternberg (Eds.), *Motivation, emotion and cognition.* Mahwah, NJ: Erlbaum.

Dworkin, S.L., & Santelli, J. (2007). Do abstinence-plus interventions reduce sexual risk behavior among youth? *PloS Medicine, 4,* 1437–1439.

Dykas, M.J., & Cassidy, J. (2011). Attachment and the processing of information across the life span: Theory and evidence. *Psychological Bulletin, 137,* 19–46.

Dyson, J.C. (2015). Play in America: An historical overview. In J.E. Johnson & others (Eds.), *Handbook of the study of play.* Blue Ridge Summit, PA: Rowan & Littlefield.

E

Eagan, K., & others (2014). *The American college freshman: National norms for fall 2014.* Los Angeles: Higher Education Research Institute, UCLA.

Eagly, A.H. (2001). Social role theory of sex differences and similarities. In J. Worrell (Ed.), *Encyclopedia of women and gender.* San Diego: Academic Press.

Eagly, A.H. (2010). Gender roles. In J. Levine & M. Hogg (Eds.), *Encyclopedia of group process and intergroup relations.* Thousand Oaks, CA: Sage.

Eagly, A.H. (2012). Women as leaders: Paths through the labyrinth. In M.C. Bligh & R. Riggio (Eds.), *When near is far and far is near: Exploring distance in leader-follower relationships.* New York: Wiley Blackwell.

Eagly, A.H. (2013). Science and politics: A reconsideration. In M.K. Ryan & N.R. Branscombe (Eds.), *Sage handbook of gender and psychology.* Thousand Oaks, CA: Sage.

Eagly, A.H., & Antonakis, J. (2014). Leadership. In G. Borgida & J. Bargh (Eds.), *APA handbook of personality and social psychology.* Washington, DC: APA Books.

Eagly, A.H., & Crowley, M. (1986). Gender and helping behavior: A meta-analytic review of the social psychological literature. *Psychological Bulletin, 100,* 283–308.

Eagly, A.H., Gartzia, L., & Carli, L.L. (2014). Female advantage: Revisited. In S. Kumra, R. Simpson, & R. Burke (Eds.), *Oxford handbook of gender in organizations.* New York: Oxford University Press.

Eagly, A.H., & Steffen, V.J. (1986). Gender and aggressive behavior: A meta-analytic review of the social psychological literature. *Psychological Bulletin, 100,* 309–330.

Eapen, V., & others (2014). Separation anxiety, attachment, and inter-personal representations: Disentangling the role of oxytocin in the perinatal period. *PloS One, 9,* e107745.

East, P. (2009). Adolescent relationships with siblings. In R.M. Lerner & L. Steinberg (Eds.), *Handbook of adolescent psychology* (3rd ed.). New York: Wiley.

Easterbrooks, M.A., Bartlett, J.D., Beeghly, M., & Thompson, R.A. (2013). Social and emotional development in infancy. In I.B. Weiner & others (Eds.), *Handbook of psychology* (2nd ed., Vol. 6). New York: Wiley.

Eaton, D.K., & others (2008). Youth risk behavior surveillance—United States, 2007. *MMWR, 57,* 1–131.

Eaton, D.K., & others (2010, June 4). Youth risk behavior surveillance—United States, 2009. *MMWR, 59,* 1–141.

Eaton, D.K., & others (2012). Youth risk behavior surveillance—United States 2011. *MMWR, 61,* 1–162.

Eaton, W.O. (2008). Milestones: Physical. In M. M. Haith & J.B. Benson (Eds.), *Encyclopedia of infant and early childhood development.* Oxford, UK: Elsevier.

Ebstein, R.P., Knafo, A., Mankuta, D., Chew, S.H., & Lai, P.S. (2012). The contributions of oxytocin and vasopressin pathway genes to human behavior. *Hormones and Behavior, 61,* 359–379.

Eccles, J. (2003). Education: Junior and high school. In G. Adams & M. Berzonsky (Eds.), *Blackwell handbook of adolescence.* Malden, MA: Blackwell.

Eccles, J.S. (2004). Schools, academic motivation, and stage-environment fit. In R. Lerner & L. Steinberg (Eds.), *Handbook of adolescent psychology.* New York: Wiley.

Eccles, J.S. (2007). Families, schools, and developing achievement-related motivations and engagement. In J.E. Grusec & P.D. Hastings (Eds.), *Handbook of socialization.* New York: Guilford.

Eccles, J.S. (2014). Gender and achievement choices. In E.T. Gershoff, R.S. Mistry, & D.A. Crosby (Eds.), *Societal contexts of child development.* New York: Oxford University Press.

Eccles, J.S., & Roeser, R.W. (2010). Schools, academic motivation, and stage-environment fit. In J. Meece & J. Eccles (Eds.), *Handbook of research on schools, schooling, and human development.* New York: Routledge.

Eccles, J.S., & Roeser, R.W. (2013). Schools as developmental contexts during adolescence. In I.B. Weiner & others (Eds.), *Handbook of psychology* (2nd ed., Vol. 6). New York: Wiley.

Echevarria, J.J., Richards-Tutor, C., & Vogt, M. J. (2015). *Response to intervention (RTI) and English learners: Using the SIOP model* (2nd ed.). Upper Saddle River, NJ: Pearson.

Eckert, G.P., Lipka, U., & Muller, W.E. (2012). Omega-3 fatty acids in neurodegenerative diseases: Focus on mitochondria. *Prostaglandins, Leukotrienes, and Essential Fatty Acids, 88*(1), 105–114.

Ednick, M., & others (2010). Sleep-related respiratory abnormalities and arousal pattern in achondroplasia during early infancy. *Journal of Pediatrics, 155,* 510–515.

Edwards, J.D., Bart, E., O'Connor, M.L., & Cissell, G. (2010). Ten years down the road: Predictors of driving cessation. *Gerontologist, 50,* 393–399.

Edwards, J.D., Delahunt, P.B., & Mahncke, H.W. (2009). Cognitive speed of processing training delays driving cessation. *Journal of Gerontology B. Psychological Sciences and Social Sciences, 64B,* 1262–1267.

Eichbaum, Q. (2015). The problem with competencies in global health education. *Academic Medicine, 90,* 414–417.

Eichorn, D.H., Clausen, J.A., Haan, N., Honzik, M.P., & Mussen, P.H. (Eds.). (1981). *Present and past in middle life.* New York: Academic Press.

Eisdorfer, C. (1996, December). Interview. *APA Monitor,* p. 35.

Eisenberg, M.E., Bernat, D.H., Bearinger, L.H., & Resnick, M.D. (2008). Support for comprehensive sexuality education: Perspectives from parents of school-aged youth. *Journal of Adolescent Research, 42,* 352–359.

Eisenberg, N., Duckworth, A., Spinrad, L., & Valiente, C. (2014). Conscientiousness and healthy aging. *Developmental Psychology, 50,* 1331–1349.

Eisenberg, N., & Morris, A.S. (2004). Moral cognitions and prosocial responding in adolescence. In R. Lerner & L. Steinberg (Eds.), *Handbook of adolescent psychology* (2nd ed.). New York: Wiley.

Eisenberg, N., Spinrad, T.L., & Knafo, A. (2015). Prosocial development. In R.M. Lerner (Ed.), *Handbook of child psychology and developmental science* (7th ed.). New York: Wiley.

Eisenberg, N., Spinrad, T.L., & Morris, A.S. (2013). Prosocial development. In P.D. Zelazo (Ed.), *Oxford handbook of developmental psychology.* New York: Oxford University Press.

Eisenberg, N., Spinrad, T.L., & Morris, A.S. (2014). Empathy-related responding in children. In M. Killen & J.G. Smetana (Eds.), *Handbook of moral development* (2nd ed.). New York: Psychology Press.

Eisenberg, N., & Valiente, C. (2002). Parenting and children's prosocial and moral development. In M.H. Bornstein (Ed.), *Handbook of parenting* (2nd ed.). Mahwah, NJ: Erlbaum.

Ekblad, A., & others (2015, in press). Amniotic fluid—a source for clinical therapeutics in the newborn. *Stem Cells and Development.*

Ekin, A., & others (2014). Chromosomal and structural anomalies in fetuses with open neural tube defects. *Journal of Obstetrics and Gynecology, 34,* 156–159.

Eklund, K., Tanner, N., Stoll, K., & Anway, L. (2015, in press). Identifying emotional and behavioral risk among gifted and nongifted children: A multi-gate, multi-informant approach. *School Psychology Quarterly.*

El Haj, M., & Allain, P. (2012). Relationship between source monitoring in episodic memory and executive function in normal aging. *Geriatrie et Psychologie Neuropsychiatrie du Viellissement, 10,* 19–205.

Elbourne, P. (2012). *Meaning.* New York: Oxford University Press.

Elder, D. (2015). Reducing the risk of sudden infant death syndrome—a steady gain but still room for improvement. *New Zealand Medical Journal, 128,* 13–14.

Elder, G.H. (1980). Adolescence in historical perspective. In J. Adelson (Ed.), *Handbook of adolescent psychology.* New York: Wiley.

Elder, G.H., & Shanahan, M.J. (2006). The life course and human development. In W. Damon & R. Lerner (Eds.), *Handbook of child psychology* (6th ed.). New York: Wiley.

Elder, G.H., Shanahan, M.J., Jennings, J.A. (2015). Human development in time and place. In R.M. Lerner (Ed.), *Handbook of child psychology and developmental science* (7th ed.). New York: Wiley.

Eliasieh, K., Liets, L.C., & Chalupa, L.M. (2007). Cellular reorganization in the human retina during normal aging. *Investigative Ophthalmology and Visual Science, 48,* 2824–2830.

Elisa, C., & others (2014). How to classify the oldest old according to their health status: A study on 1,160 subjects belonging to 552 90+ Italian sib-ships characterized by familial longevity recruited within the GEHA EU Project. *Mechanisms of Aging and Development, 134,* 560–569.

Elkind, D. (1976). *Child development and education: A Piagetian perspective.* New York: Oxford University Press.

Elkind, D. (1978). Understanding the young adolescent. *Adolescence, 13,* 127–134.

Elliott, E.M., & others (2011). Working memory in the oldest-old: Evidence from output serial position curves. *Memory and Cognition, 10,* 20–27.

Ellis, B.J., Boyce, W.T., Belsky, J., Bakersman-Kranenburg, M.J., & van Ijzendoorn, M.H. (2011). Differential susceptibility to the environment: An evolutionary-neurodevelopmental theory. *Development and Psychopathology, 23,* 7–28.

Ellis, L., & Ames, M.A. (1987). Neurohormonal functioning and sexual orientation. *Psychological Bulletin, 101,* 233–258.

Ellison, A., & others (2014). Functional interaction between right parietal and bilateral frontal cortices during visual search tasks revealed using functional magnetic imaging and transcranial direct current stimulation. *PLoS One, 9*(4), e93767.

El-Sheikh, M. (2013). *Auburn University Child Sleep, Health, and Development Center.* Auburn, AL: Auburn University.

El-Sheikh, M., & Buckhalt, J.A. (2015, in press). Moving sleep and child development research forward: Priorities and recommendations from the SRCD-sponsored forum on sleep and child development. In M. El-Sheikh & A. Sadeh (Eds.), *Sleep and development: Advancing theory and research.* Monographs of the Society for Research in Child Development.

El-Sheikh, M., & others (2013). Economic adversity and children's sleep problems: Multiple indicators and moderation of health. *Health Psychology, 32,* 849–859.

Emeny, R.T., & others (2015). Oxytocin-induced coping with stressful events in old age depends on attachment: Findings from the cross-sectional KORA Age study. *Psychoneuroimmunology, 56,* 132–142.

Emery, R.E. (1999). *Renegotiating family relationships* (2nd ed.). New York: Guilford.

Emes, R.D., & Grant, S.G.N. (2013). Evolution of synapse complexity and diversity. *Annual Review of Neuroscience* (Vol. 35). Palo Alto, CA: Annual Reviews.

Emmons, R.A., & Diener, E. (1986). Situation selection as a moderator of response consistency and stability. *Journal of Personality and Social Psychology, 51,* 1013–1019.

Enfield, A., & Collins, D. (2008). The relationships of service-learning, social justice, multicultural competence, and civic engagement. *Journal of College Student Development, 49,* 95–109.

Engberg, H., & others (2013). Optimism and survival: Does an optimistic outlook predict better survival at advanced ages? A twelve-year follow-up of Danish nonagenarians. *Aging: Clinical and Experimental Research, 25,* 517–525.

Engler, B. (2014). *Personality theories* (9th ed.). Boston: Cengage.

English, T., & Carstensen, L.L. (2014a). Emotional experience in the mornings and the evenings: Consideration of age differences in specific emotions by time of day. *Frontiers in Psychology, 5,* 185.

English, T., & Carstensen, L.L. (2014b). Selective narrowing of social networks across adulthood is associated with improved emotional experience in life. *International Journal of Behavioral Development, 38,* 195–202.

English, T., & Carstensen, L.L. (2014c). Will interventions targeting conscientiousness improve aging outcomes? *Developmental Psychology, 50,* 1478–1481.

Englund, M.M., Egeland, B., & Collins, W.A. (2008). Exceptions to high school dropout predictions in a low-income sample: Do adults make a difference? *Journal of Social Issues, 64,* 77–93.

Englund, M.M., Luckner, A.E., Whaley, G.J.L., & Egeland, B. (2004). Children's achievement in early elementary school: Longitudinal effects of parental involvement, expectations, and quality of assistance. *Journal of Educational Psychology, 96,* 723–730.

Enomoto, H., & others (2015, in press). Effects of L-Dopa and pramipexole on plasticity induced

by QPS in human motor cortex. *Journal of Neural Transmission.*

Enright, R.D., Santos, M.J., & Al-Mabuk, R. (1989). The adolescent as forgiver. *Journal of Adolescence, 12,* 95–110.

Ensembl Human (2008). *Explore the Homo sapiens genome.* Retrieved April 14, 2008, from www.ensembl .org/Homo_sapiens/index.html

Ensor, R., Spencer, D., & Hughes, C. (2010). "You feel sad?" Emotion understanding mediates effects of verbal ability and mother-child mutuality on prosocial behaviors: Findings from 2 to 4 years. *Social Development, 20*(1), 93–110.

Erickson, K.I., & others (2011). Exercise training increases the size of the hippocampus and improves memory. *Proceedings of the National Academy of Sciences U.S.A., 108,* 3017–3022.

Erickson, K.I., Gildengers, A.G., & Butters, M.A. (2013). Physical activity and brain plasticity in late adulthood. *Dialogues in Clinical Neuroscience, 15*(1), 99–108.

Ericsson, K.A., Krampe, R., & Tesch-Romer, C. (1993). The role of deliberate practice in the acquisition of expert performance. *Psychological Review, 100,* 363–406.

Erikson, E.H. (1950). *Childhood and society.* New York: Norton.

Erikson, E.H. (1962). *Young man Luther.* New York: Norton.

Erikson, E.H. (1968). *Identity: Youth and crisis.* New York: Norton.

Erikson, E.H. (1969). *Gandhi's truth.* New York: Norton.

Ernst, M., & Spear, L.P. (2009). Reward systems. In M. de Haan & M.R. Gunnar (Eds.), *Handbook of developmental social neuroscience.* New York: Guilford.

Escobar-Chaves, S.L., & Anderson, C.A. (2008). Media and risky behavior. *The Future of Children, 18*(1), 147–180.

ESHRE Capri Workshop Group (2011). Perimenopausal risk factors and future health. *Human Reproduction Update, 17,* 706–717.

Espie, J., & Eisler, I. (2015). Focus on anorexia nervosa: Modern psychological treatment and guidelines for the adolescent patient. *Adoleslcent Health, Medicine, and Therapeutics, 6,* 9–16.

Estes, T.H., & Mintz, S.L. (2016, in press). *Instruction: A models approach* (7th ed.). Upper Saddle River, NJ: Pearson.

Etaugh, C., & Bridges, J.S. (2010). *Women's lives* (2nd ed.). Boston: Allyn & Bacon.

Evans, G.W. (2004). The environment of childhood poverty. *American Psychologist, 59,* 77–92.

Evans, G.W., & English, G.W. (2002). The environment of poverty. *Child Development, 73,* 1238–1248.

Evans, G.W., & Kim, P. (2007). Childhood poverty and health: Cumulative risk exposure and stress dysregulation. *Psychological Science, 18,* 953–957.

Evans, G.W., & Kim, P. (2013). Childhood poverty, chronic stress, self-regulation, and coping. *Child Development Perspectives, 7*(1), 43–48.

Evans, G.W., Li, D., & Sepanski Whipple, S. (2013). Cumulative risk and child development. *Psychological Bulletin, 139,* 1342–1396.

Evans, S.Z., Simons, L.G., & Simons, R.L. (2015, in press). Factors that influence trajectories of delinquency throughout adolescence. *Journal of Youth and Adolescence.*

Evers, A.W., & others (2014). Does stress affect the joints? Daily stressors, stress vulnerability, immune and HPA axis activity, and short-term disease and symptom

fluctuations in rheumatoid arthritis. *Annals of the Rheumatic Diseases, 73,* 1683–1688.

Ezkurdia, I., & others (2014). The shrinking human protein coding complement: Are there fewer than 20,000 genes? *bioRxiv,* doi:10.1101/001909.

F

Fabiano, G.A., & others (2009). A meta-analysis of behavioral treatments for attention deficit/hyperactivity disorder. *Clinical Psychology Review, 29*(2), 129–140.

Fabricius, W.V., Braver, S.L., Diaz, P., & Schenck, C. (2010). Custody and parenting time: Links to family relationships and well-being after divorce. In M.E. Lamb (Ed.), *The role of the father in child development* (5th ed.). New York: Wiley.

Fagan, J., & Lee, Y. (2014). Longitudinal associations among fathers' perception of coparenting, partner relationship quality, and paternal stress during early childhood. *Family Process, 53,* 80–96.

Fagan, J.F. (1992). Intelligence: A theoretical viewpoint. *Current Directions in Psychological Science, 1,* 82–86.

Fagan, J.F. (2011). Intelligence in infancy. In R.J. Sternberg & S.B. Kaufman (Eds.), *Cambridge handbook of intelligence.* New York: Cambridge University Press.

Fagan, J.F., Holland, C.R., & Wheeler, K. (2007). The prediction, from infancy, of adult IQ and achievement. *Intelligence, 35,* 225–231.

Fagundes, C.P., Glaser, R., & Kiecolt-Glaser, J.K. (2013). Stressful early life experiences and immune dysregulation across the lifespan. *Brain, Behavior, and Immunity, 27,* 8–12.

Fagundes, C.P., & others (2013). Depressive symptoms enhance stress-induced inflammatory responses. *Brain, Behavior, and Immunity, 31,* 172–176.

Fairbairn, C.E., & others (2015, in press). Extraversion and the rewarding effects of alcohol in a social context. *Journal of Abnormal Psychology.*

Fairweather, A.K., Anstey, K.J., Rodgers, B., & Butterworth, P. (2006). Factors distinguishing suicide attempters from suicide ideators in a community sample: Social issues and physical health problems. *Psychological Medicine, 31,* 1–11.

Fakhoury, M. (2015, in press). Autistic spectrum disorders: A review of clinical features, theories, and diagnosis. *International Journal of Neuroscience.*

Falbe, J., & others (2015). Sleep duration, restfulness, and screens in the sleep environment. *Pediatrics, 135,* e367–e375.

Falbo, T., & Poston, D.L. (1993). The academic personality and physical outcomes of only children in China. *Child Development, 64,* 18–35.

Falci, C.D. (2012). Self-esteem and mastery trajectories in high school by social class and gender. *Social Science Research, 40,* 586–601.

Falconier, M.K., & others (2015, in press). Stress from daily hassles in couples: Its effects on intradyadic relationship satisfaction, and physical and psychological well-being. *Journal of Marital and Family Therapy.*

Fandakova, Y., Lindenberger, U., & Shing, Y.L. (2013). Deficits in process-specific prefrontal and hippocampal activations contribute to adult age differences in episodic memory interference. *Cerebral Cortex, 24,* 1832–1844.

Fantz, R.L. (1963). Pattern vision in newborn infants. *Science, 140,* 286–297.

Farabaugh, A., & others (2012). Depression and suicide ideation in college students. *Psychopathology, 45,* 228–234.

Farioli-Vecchioli, S., & others (2014). Running rescues defective adult neurogenesis by shortening the length of the cell cycle of neural stem and progenitor cells. *Stem Cells, 32,* 1968–1982.

Farr, R.H., & Patterson, C.J. (2013). Coparenting among lesbian, gay, and heterosexual couples: Associations with adopted children's outcomes. *Child Development, 84,* 226–240.

Farr, R.H., & others (2014). Adoptees' contact with birth relatives in emerging adulthood. *Journal of Adolescent Behavior, 29,* 45–66.

Farrell, M.J. (2012). Age-related changes in the structure and function of brain regions involved in pain processing. *Pain Medicine, 13*(Suppl. 2), S37–S43.

Farrell, M.P., & Rosenberg, S.D. (1981). *Men at mid-life.* Boston: Auburn House.

Farrell, S.W., Fitzgerald, S.J., McAuley, P., & Barlow, C.E. (2010). Cardiorespiratory fitness, adiposity, and all-cause mortality in women. *Medicine and Science in Sports Exercise, 42*(11), 2006–2012.

Farrington, D. (2004). Conduct disorder, aggression, and delinquency. In R. Lerner & L. Steinberg (Eds.), *Handbook of adolescent psychology.* New York: Wiley.

Farrington, D.P. (2009). Conduct disorder, aggression, and delinquency. In R.M. Lerner & L. Steinberg (Eds.), *Handbook of adolescent psychology* (3rd ed.). New York: Wiley.

Fasig, L. (2000). Toddlers' understanding of ownership: Implications for self-concept development. *Social Development, 9,* 370–382.

Fatusi, A.O., & Hindin, M.J. (2010). Adolescents and youths in developing countries: Health and development issues in context. *Journal of Adolescence, 33,* 499–508.

Fava, N.M., & Bay-Cheng, L.Y. (2012). Young women's adolescent experiences of oral sex: Relation of age of initiation to sexual motivation, sexual coercion, and psychological functioning. *Journal of Adolescence, 35*(5), 1191–1201.

Fearon, R.P., & others (2010). The significance of insecure attachment and disorganization in the development of children's externalizing behavior: A meta-analytic study. *Child Development, 81,* 435–456.

Federal Interagency Forum on Child and Family Statistics (2010). *America's children: Key indicators of well-being.* Washington, DC: U.S. Government Printing Office.

Fedor, A., Garcia, S., & Gunstad, J. (2015). The effects of a brief, water-based exercise intervention on cognitive function in older adults. *Archives of Clinical Neuropsychology, 30,* 139–147.

Feeney, M.P., & Sanford, C.A. (2004). Age effects in the middle ear: Wideband acoustical measures. *Journal of the Acoustical Society of America, 116,* 3546–3558.

Feeney, S., Moravcik, E., & Nolte, S. (2016, in press). *Who am I in the lives of children?* (10th ed.). Upper Saddle River, NJ: Pearson.

Feinberg, M.E., Sakuma, K-L., Hostetler, M., & McHale, S.M. (2013). Enhancing sibling relationships to prevent adolescent problem behaviors: Theory, design, and feasibility. *Siblings Are Special: Evaluation and Program Planning, 36*(1), 97–106.

Feldhusen, J. (1999). Giftedness and creativity. In M.A. Runco & S.R. Pritzker (Eds.), *Encyclopedia of creativity.* San Diego: Academic Press.

Feldman, H.M., & Reiff, M.I. (2014). Clinical practice: Attention deficit-hyperactivity disorder in children and adolescents. *New England Journal of Medicine, 370,* 838–846.

Feldman, R. (2012). Oxytocin and social affiliation in humans. *Hormones and Behavior, 61,* 380–391.

Feldman, R., Rosenthal, Z., & Eidelman, A.I. (2014). Maternal-preterm skin-to-skin contact enhances child physiologic organization and cognitive control across the first 10 years of life. *Biological Psychiatry, 75,* 56–64.

Feldman, S.S., & Rosenthal, D.A. (1999). *Factors influencing parents' and adolescents' evaluations of parents as sex communicators.* Unpublished manuscript, Stanford Center on Adolescence, Stanford University.

Feldman, S.S., Turner, R., & Araujo, K. (1999). Interpersonal context as an influence on sexual timetables of youths: Gender and ethnic effects. *Journal of Research on Adolescence, 9,* 25–52.

Feng, L., & others (2012). Tea drinking and cognitive function in oldest-old Chinese. *Journal of Nutrition, Health, and Aging, 16,* 754–758.

Feng, Z., Wang, W.W., Jones, K., & Li, Y. (2012). An exploratory multilevel analysis of income, income inequality, and self-rated health of the elderly in China. *Social Science and Medicine, 75,* 2481–2492.

Ferencz, B., & Gerritsen, L. (2015, in press). Genetics and underlying pathology of dementia. *Neuropsychology Review.*

Ferguson, C.J. (2013). Spanking, corporal punishment, and negative long-term outcomes: A meta-analytic review of longitudinal studies. *Clinical Psychology Review, 33,* 196–208.

Ferguson, C.J. (2013). Violent video games and the Supreme Court. *American Psychologist, 69,* 57–74.

Ferguson, E., & Bibby, P.A. (2012). Openness to experience and all-cause mortality: A meta-analysis and r (equivalent) from risk ratios and odd ratios. *British Journal of Health Psychology, 17,* 85–102.

Fergusson, D.M., Horwood, L.J., & Shannon, F.T. (1987). Breastfeeding and subsequent social adjustment in 6- to 8-year-old children. *Journal of Child Psychology and Psychiatry, 28,* 378–386.

Fergusson, D.M., McLeod, G.F., & Horwood, L.J. (2014). Parental separation/divorce in childhood and partnership outcomes at age 30. *Journal of Child Psychology and Psychiatry, 55,* 352–360.

Fernald, A., Marchman, V.A., & Weisleder, A. (2013). SES differences in language processing skill and vocabulary are evident at 18 months. *Developmental Science, 16,* 234–248.

Ferrer, E., & others (2013). White matter maturation supports the development of reasoning ability through its influence on processing speed. *Developmental Science, 16,* 941–951.

Fetterman, A.K., Kruger, N.N., & Robinson, M.D. (2015, in press). Sex-linked mating strategies diverge with a manipulation of genital salience. *Motivation and Emotion.*

Field, D. (1999). A cross-cultural perspective on continuity and change in social relations in old age: Introduction to a special issue. *International Journal of Aging and Human Development, 48,* 257–262.

Field, N., & others (2013). Associations between health and sexual lifestyles in Britain: Findings from the third National Survey of Sexual Attitudes and Lifestyles (Natsal-3). *Lancet, 382,* 1830–1844.

Field, T., & others (1986). Tactile/kinesthetic stimulation effects on preterm neonates. *Pediatrics, 77,* 654–658.

Field, T.M. (2001). Massage therapy facilitates weight gain in preterm infants. *Current Directions in Psychological Science, 10,* 51–55.

Field, T.M. (2007). *The amazing infant.* Malden, MA: Blackwell.

Field, T.M. (2010). Postpartum depression effects on early interactions, parenting, and safety practices: A review. *Infant Behavior and Development, 33,* 1–6.

Field, T.M., Diego, M., & Hernandez-Reif, M. (2008). Prematurity and potential predictors. *International Journal of Neuroscience, 118,* 277–289.

Field, T.M., Diego, M., & Hernandez-Reif, M. (2010). Preterm infant massage therapy research: A review. *Infant Behavior and Development, 33,* 115–124.

Field, T.M., Diego, M., & Hernandez-Reif, M. (2011). Preterm infant massage therapy research: A review. *Infant Behavior and Development, 34,* 383–389.

Fielder, R.L., Walsh, J.L., Carey, K.B., & Carey, M.P. (2013). Predictors of sexual hookups: A theory-based, prospective study of first-year college women. *Archives of Sexual Behavior, 42,* 1425–1441.

Fields, R. (2013). *Drugs in perspective* (8th ed.). New York: McGraw-Hill.

Finch, C.E. (2009). The neurobiology of middle-age has arrived. *Neurobiology of Aging, 30.*

Finch, C.E. (2011). Inflammation and aging. In E. Masoro & S. Austad (Eds.), *Handbook of the biology of aging* (7th ed.). New York: Elsevier.

Finer, L.B., & Philbin, J.M. (2013). Sexual initiation, contraceptive use, and pregnancy among young adolescents. *Pediatrics, 131,* 886–891.

Finer, S., & others (2015, in press). Maternal gestational diabetes is associated with genome-wide DNA methylation variation in placenta and cord blood of exposed offspring. *Human Molecular Genetics.*

Finger, B., Hans, S.L., Bernstein, V.J., & Cox, S.M. (2009). Parent relationship quality and infant-mother attachment. *Attachment and Human Development, 11,* 285–306.

Fingerhut, A.W., & Peplau, L.A. (2013). Same-sex romantic relationships. In C.J. Patterson & A.R. D'Augelli (Eds.), *Handbook of psychology and sexual orientation.* New York: Oxford University Press.

Fingerman, K.L., & Baker, B. (2006). Socioemotional aspects of aging. In J. Wilmouth & K. Ferraro (Eds.), *Perspectives in gerontology* (3rd ed.). New York: Springer.

Fingerman, K.L., & Birditt, K.S. (2011). Adult children and aging parents. In K.W. Schaie (Ed.), *Handbook of the psychology of aging* (7th ed.). New York: Elsevier.

Fingerman, K.L., Birditt, K.S., Nussbaum, J., & Schroeder, D. (2014). Generational juggling: midlife. In A.L. Vangelisti (Ed.), *Handbook of family communication* (2nd ed.). New York: Elsevier.

Fingerman, K.L., Pillemer, K.A., Silverstein, M., & Suitor, J.J. (2012). The Baby Boomers' intergenerational relationships. *Gerontologist, 52,* 199–209.

Fingerman, K.L., Sechrest, J., & Birditt, K.S. (2013). Intergenerational relationships in a changing world. *Gerontology, 59,* 64–70.

Fingerman, K.L., & Tennant, P. (2015, in press). Friends and acquaintances in late life. In S. Whitbourne (Ed.), *Encyclopedia of adulthood and aging.* New York: Wiley.

Fingerman, K.L., & others (2011). Who gets what and why: Help middle-aged adults provide to parents and grown children. *Journal of Gerontology B: Psychological Sciences and Social Sciences, 66,* 87–98.

Fingerman, K.L., & others (2012). Helicopter parents and landing pad kids: Intense parental support of grown children. *Journal of Marriage and the Family, 74*(4), 880–896.

Finlon, K.J., & others (2015, in press). Emotion-based preventive intervention: Effectively promoting emotion knowledge and adaptive behavior among at-risk preschoolers. *Development and Psychopathology.*

Finkelstein, E.A., & others (2012). Obesity and severe obesity forecasts through 2030. *American Journal of Preventive Medicine, 42,* 563–570.

Finkelstein, L.M., & Farrell, S.K. (2007). An expanded view of age bias in the workplace. In K.S. Shultz & G.A. Adams (Eds.), *Aging and work in the 21st century.* Mahwah, NJ: Erlbaum.

Fiori, K.L., Antonucci, T.C., & Cortina, K.S. (2006). Social network typologies and mental health among older adults. *Journals of Gerontology B: Psychological Sciences and Social Sciences, 61,* P25–P32.

Fiori, K.L., Smith, J., & Antonucci, T.C. (2007). Social network types among older adults: A multidimensional approach. *Journals of Gerontology B: Psychological Sciences and Social Sciences, 62,* P322–P330.

Fiori, M., & others (2014). What is the Ability Emotional Intelligence Test (MSCEIT) good for? An evaluation using item response theory. *PLoS One, 9*(6), e08827.

Fischer, C.E., & Schweizer, T.A. (2014). How does speaking another language reduce the risk of dementia? *Expert Reviews of Neuroptherapeutics, 14,* 469–471.

Fischer-Baum, S., & Rapp, B. (2014). The analysis of perseverations in acquired dysgraphia reveals the internal structure of orthographic representations. *Cognitive Neuropsychology. 31,* 237–265.

Fischhoff, B., Bruine de Bruin, W., Parker, A.M., Millstein, S.G., & Halpern-Felsher, B.L. (2010). Adolescents' perceived risk of dying. *Journal of Adolescent Health, 46,* 265–269.

Fisher, G.G., & others (2014). Mental work demands, retirement, and longitudinal trajectories of cognitive functioning. *Journal of Occupational Health Psychology, 19,* 231–242.

Fisher, K.R., Hirsh-Pasek, K., Newcombe, N., & Golinkoff, R.M. (2013). Taking shape: Supporting preschoolers' acquisition of geometric knowledge through guided play. *Child Development, 84,* 1872–1878.

Fisher, P.A. (2005, April). *Translational research on underlying mechanisms of risk among foster children: Implications for prevention science.* Paper presented at the meeting of the Society for Research in Child Development, Washington, DC.

Fisher, P.A. (2015). Review: Adoption, fostering, and the needs of looked-after and adopted children. *Child and Adolescent Mental Health, 20,* 5–12.

Fitzgerald, A., Fitzgerald, N., & Aherne, C. (2012). Do peers matter? A review of peer and/or friends' influence on physical activity among American adolescents. *Journal of Adolescence, 35,* 941–958.

Fitzpatrick, K.K. (2012). Developmental considerations when treating anorexia nervosa in adolescents and young adults. In J. Lock (Ed.), *Oxford handbook of child and adolescent eating disorders: Developmental perspectives.* New York: Oxford University Press.

Fivush, R. (2010). The development of autobiographical memory. *Annual Review of Psychology* (Vol. 62). Palo Alto, CA: Annual Reviews.

Fivush, R., & Haden, C.A. (1997). Narrating and representing experience: Preschoolers' developing autobiographical accounts. In P. van den Broek, P.J. Bauer, & T. Bourg (Eds.), *Developmental spans in event representations and comprehension: Bridging fictional and actual events.* Mahwah, NJ: Erlbaum.

Fizke, E., Barthel, D., Peters, T., & Rakoczy, H. (2014). Executive function plays a role in coordinating different perspectives, particularly when one's own perspective is involved. *Cognition, 130,* 315–334.

Fjell, A.M., & Walhovd, K.B. (2010). Structural brain changes in aging: Courses, causes, and consequences. *Reviews in the Neurosciences, 21,* 187–122.

Flaherty, E.G., & others (2014). Evaluating children with fractures for child physical abuse. *Pediatrics, 133,* e477–e489.

Flanagan, C., Beyers, W., & Zukauskiene, R. (2012). Editorial: Political and civic engagement development in adolescence. *Journal of Adolescence, 35,* 471–473.

Flanagan, J.C., Gordon, K.C., Moore, T.M., & Stuart, G.L. (2015). Women's stress, depression, and relationship adjustment profiles as they relate to intimate partner violence and mental health during pregnancy and postpartum. *Psychology of Violence, 5,* 66–71.

Flavell, J.H. (1971). First discussant's comments: What is memory development the development of? *Human Development, 14,* 272–278.

Flavell, J.H. (1976). Metacognitive aspects of problem solving. In L.B. Resnick (Ed.), *The nature of intelligence.* Englewood Cliffs, NJ: Prentice Hall.

Flavell, J.H. (1979). Metacognition and cognitive monitoring. A new area of psychological inquiry. *American Psychologist, 34,* 906–911.

Flavell, J.H. (2004). Theory-of-mind development. *Merrill-Palmer Quarterly, 50,* 274–290.

Flavell, J.H., Friedrichs, A., & Hoyt, J. (1970). Developmental changes in memorization processes. *Cognitive Psychology, 1,* 324–340.

Flavell, J.H., Green, F.L., & Flavell, E.R. (1993). Children's understanding of the stream of consciousness. *Child Development, 64,* 95–120.

Flavell, J.H., Green, F.L., & Flavell, E.R. (1995). The development of children's knowledge about intentional focus. *Developmental Psychology, 31,* 706–712.

Flavell, J.H., Green, F.L., & Flavell, E.R. (1998). The mind has a mind of its own: Developing knowledge about mental uncontrollability. *Cognitive Development, 13,* 127–138.

Flavell, J.H., Green, F.L., & Flavell, E.R. (2000). Development of children's awareness of their own thoughts. *Journal of Cognition and Development, 1,* 97–112.

Flavell, J.H., Miller, P.H., & Miller, S. (2002). *Cognitive development* (4th ed.). Upper Saddle River, NJ: Prentice Hall.

Flavell, J.H., Mumme, D., Green, F., and Flavell, E. (1992). Young children's understanding of different types of beliefs. *Child Development, 63,* 960–977.

Fletcher, B.R., & Rapp, P.R. (2013). Normal neurocognitive aging. In I.B. Weiner & others (Eds.), *Handbook of psychology* (2nd ed.). New York: Wiley.

Fletcher-Watson, S., McConnell, F., Manola, E., & McConachie, H. (2014). Interventions based on the theory of mind cognitive model for autism spectrum disorder. *Cochrane Database of Systematic Reviews, 3,* CD008785.

Flicek, P., & others (2013). Ensembl 2013. *Nucleic Acids Research, 41,* D48–D55.

Flint, M.S., Baum, A., Chambers, W.H., & Jenkins, F.J. (2007). Induction of DNA damage, alteration of DNA repair, and transcriptional activation by stress hormones. *Psychoneuroendocrinology, 32,* 470–479.

Flom, R., & Pick, A.D. (2003). Verbal encouragement and joint attention in 18-month-old infants. *Infant Behavior and Development, 26,* 121–134.

Florsheim, P. (2014). *The young parenthood program.* New York: Oxford University Press.

Florsheim, P., Moore, D., & Edgington, C. (2003). Romantic relationships among pregnant and parenting adolescents. In P. Florsheim (Ed.), *Adolescent romantic relations and sexual behavior.* Mahwah, NJ: Erlbaum.

Flouri, E., Midouhas, E., & Joshi, H. (2014). Family poverty and trajectories of children's emotional and behavioral problems: The moderating role of self-regulation and verbal cognitive ability. *Journal of Abnormal Child Psychology, 42,* 1043–1056.

Flynn, J.R. (1999). Searching for justice: The discovery of IQ gains over time. *American Psychologist, 54,* 5–20.

Flynn, J.R. (2007). The history of the American mind in the 20th century: A scenario to explain gains over time and a case for the irrelevance of *g.* In P.C. Kyllonen, R.D. Roberts, & L. Stankov (Eds.), *Extending intelligence.* Mahwah, NJ: Erlbaum.

Flynn, J.R. (2011). Secular changes in intelligence. In R.J. Sternberg & S.B. Kaufman (Eds.), *Cambridge handbook of intelligence.* New York: Cambridge University Press.

Flynn, J.R. (2013). *Are we getting smarter?* New York: Cambridge University Press.

Flynn, J.R., & Rossi-Case, L. (2012). IQ gains in Argentina between 1964 and 1998. *Intelligence, 40,* 145–150.

Follari, L. (2015). *Foundations and best practices in early childhood education* (4th ed.). Upper Saddle River, NJ: Merrill.

Foltynie, T. (2015, in press). Can Parkinson's disease be cured by stimulating neurogenesis? *Journal of Clinical Investigation.*

Fontaine, R.G., & others (2010). Does response evaluation and decision (RED) mediate the relation between hostile attributional style and antisocial behavior in adolescence? *Journal of Abnormal Child Psychology, 38,* 615–626.

Fontana, L., & Hu, F.B. (2014, in press). Optimal body weight for health and longevity: Bridging basic, clinical, and population research. *Aging Cell.*

Ford, B.Q., & Mauss, I.B. (2015, in press). *Current Opinion in Psychology.*

Ford, B.Q., & others (2014). Emotion regulation moderates the risk associated with the 5-HTT gene and stress in children. *Emotion, 14,* 930–939.

Ford, D.Y. (2012). Gifted and talented education: History, issues, and recommendations. In K.R. Harris, S. Graham, & T. Urdan (Eds.), *APA handbook of educational psychology.* Washington, DC: American Psychological Association.

Forgatch, M.S., Patterson, G.R., Degarmo, D.S., & Beldavs, Z.G. (2009). Testing the Oregon delinquency model with 9-year follow-up of the Oregon Divorce Study. *Development and Psychopathology, 21,* 637–660.

Foshee, V.A., & others (2013). The peer context and the development of the perpetration of adolescent dating violence. *Journal of Youth and Adolescence, 42,* 471–486.

Foster, G.A., Alviar, A., Neumeir, R., & Wootten, A. (2012). A tri-service perspective on the implementation of a centering pregnancy model in the military. *Journal of Obstetric, Gynecological, and Neonatal Nursing, 41,* 315–321.

Fowler-Brown, A., & Kahwati, L.C. (2004). Prevention and treatment of overweight in children and adolescents. *American Family Physician, 69,* 2591–2598.

Fox, B.J. (2014). *Phonics and word study for the teacher of reading* (11th ed.). Upper Saddle River, NJ: Pearson.

Fox, J., & Potocki, B. (2015, in press). Lifetime videogame consumption, interpersonal aggression, hostile sexism, and rape myth acceptance: A cultivation perspective. *Journal of Interpersonal Violence.*

Fox, M.K., & others (2010). Food consumption patterns of young preschoolers: Are they starting off on the right path? *Journal of the American Dietetic Association, 110*(Suppl. 12), S52–S59.

Fox, N.A., Reeb-Sutherland, C., & Degnan, K.A. (2013). Personality and emotional development. In P.D. Zelazo (Ed.), *Oxford handbook of developmental psychology.* New York: Oxford University Press.

Fragala, M.S., Kenny, A.M., & Kuchel, G.A. (2015). Muscle quality in aging: A multi-dimensional approach to muscle functioning with applications for treatment. *Sports Medicine.*

Fragala, M.S. & others (2014). Muscle quality index improves with resistance exercise training in older adults. *Experimental Gerontology, 53,* 1–6.

Fraley, C., & Roisman, G.I. (2015). Early attachment experiences and romantic functioning: Developmental pathways, emerging issues, and future directions. In J.A. Simpson & W.S. Rholes (Eds.), *Attachment theory and research.* New York: Guilford.

Fraley, R.C., Roisman, G.I., & Haltigan, J.D. (2013). The legacy of early experiences in development: Formalizing alternative models of how early experiences are carried forward over time. *Developmental Psychology, 49*(1), 109–126.

Francis, J., Fraser, G., & Marcia, J.E. (1989). *Cognitive and experimental factors in moratorium-achievement (MAMA) cycles.* Unpublished manuscript. Department of Psychology, Simon Fraser University, Burnaby, British Columbia.

Frankl, V. (1984). *Man's search for meaning.* New York: Basic Books.

Franklin, A., Vevis, L., Ling, Y., & Hurlbert, A. (2010). Biological components of color preference in infancy. *Developmental Science, 13,* 346–354.

Franklin, N.C., Lavie, C.J., & Arena, R.A. (2015, in press). Personal health technology: A new era in cardiovascular disease prevention. *Postgraduate Medicine.*

Fraser, S. (Ed.). (1995). *The bell curve wars: Race, intelligence, and the future of America.* New York: Basic Books.

Frazier, L.D., Barreto, M.L., & Newman, F.L. (2012). Self-regulation and eudaimonic well-being across adulthood. *Experimental Aging Research, 38,* 394–410.

Frazier, P.A., & Cook, S.W. (1993). Correlates of distress following heterosexual relationship dissolution. *Journal of Social and Personal Relationships, 10,* 55–67.

Frazier, P.A., & Scharf, R.J. (2015). Parent-infant attachment. *Pediatrics in Review, 36,* 36–41.

Frederikse, M., & others (2000). Sex differences in inferior lobule volume in schizophrenia. *American Journal of Psychiatry, 157,* 422–427.

Frenkel, T.I., & Fox, N.A. (2015). Caregiver socialization factors influencing socioemotional development in infancy and childhood: A neuroscience perspective. In J.E. Grusec & P.D. Hastings (Eds.), *Handbook of socialization* (2nd ed.). New York: Guilford.

Freud, S. (1917). *A general introduction to psychoanalysis.* New York: Washington Square Press.

Freund, A.M., & Baltes, P.B. (2002). Life-management strategies of selection, optimization, and compensation: Measurement by self-report and construct validity. *Journal of Personality and Social Psychology, 82,* 642–662.

Freund, A.M., & Blanchard-Fields, F. (2014). Age-related differences in altruism across adulthood: Making personal financial gain versus contributing to the public good. *Developmental Psychology, 50,* 1125–1136.

Freund, A.M., Nikitin, J., & Riediger, M. (2013). Successful aging. In I.D. Weiner & others (Eds.), *Handbook of psychology* (2nd ed., Vol. 6). New York: Wiley.

Frey, B.S. (2011). Happy people live longer. *Science, 331,* 542–543.

Frey, W.H. (2007). *Mapping the growth of older America: Seniors and boomers in the early 21st century.* Washington, DC: The Brookings Institution.

Friedman, D. (2013). The cognitive aging of episodic memory: A view based on the event-related brain potential. *Frontiers in Behavioral Neuroscience, 7,* 1–15.

Friedman, H.S., & others (2014). A new life-span approach to conscientiousness and health: Combining the pieces of the causal puzzle. *Developmental Psychology, 50,* 1377–1389.

Friedman, J. (2013). Twin separation. Retrieved February 14, 2013, from http://christinabaglivitinglof.com/twin-pregnancy/six-twin-experts-tell-all/

Friedman, S.L., Melhuish, E., & Hill, C. (2011). Childcare research at the dawn of a new millennium: Update. In J.G. Bremner & T.D. Wachs (Eds.), *Wiley-Blackwell handbook of infant development* (2nd ed.). New York: Wiley.

Friedman, W.J. (2014). Development of memory for the times of past events. In P. Bauer & R. Fivush (Eds.), *Wiley handbook of children's memory.* New York: Wiley.

Friend, M. (2014). *Special education* (4th ed.). Upper Saddle River, NJ: Pearson.

Froh, J.J., Yurkewicz, C., & Kashdan, T.B. (2009). Gratitude and subjective well-being in early adolescence: Examining gender differences. *Journal of Adolescence, 32,* 633–650.

Frost, D.M. (2011). Stigma and intimacy in same-sex relationships: A narrative approach. *Journal of Family Psychology, 25,* 1–10.

Fry, P.S. (2001). The unique contribution of key existential factors to the prediction of psychological well-being of older adults following spousal loss. *The Gerontologist, 41,* 69–81.

Frydenberg, E. (2008). *Adolescent coping.* Clifton, NJ: Psychology Press.

Fuglset, T.S., Endestad, T., Landro, N.I., & Ro, O. (2014). Brain structure alterations associated with weight changes in young females with anorexia nervosa: A case series. *Neurocase, 21,* 169–177.

Fuhs, M.W., Nesbitt, K.T., Farran, D.C., & Dong, N. (2014). Longitudinal associations between executive functioning and academic skills across content areas. *Developmental Psychology, 50,* 1698–1709.

Fujisawa, D., & others (2010). Prevalence and determinants of complicated grief in general population. *Journal of Affective Disorders, 127*(1–3), 352–358.

Fujiwara, E., & others (2012). Usefulness of reminiscence therapy for community mental health. *Psychiatry and Clinical Neuroscience, 66,* 74–79.

Fukunaga, A., Uematsu, H., & Sugimoto, K. (2005). Influences of age on taste perception and oral somatic sensation. *Journals of Gerontology A: Biological Sciences and Medical Sciences, 60,* 109A–113A.

Fulginiti, A., & Brekke, J.S. (2015, in press). Escape from discrepancy: Self-esteem and quality of life as predictors of current suicide ideation among individuals with schizophrenia. *Community Mental Health.*

Fuligni, A.J. (2012). Gaps, conflicts, and arguments between adolescents and their parents. *New Directions for Child and Adolescent Development, 135,* 105–110.

Fuligni, A.J., & Tsai, K.M. (2015). Developmental flexibility in the age of globalization: Autonomy and identity development among immigrant adolescents. *Annual Review of Psychology* (Vol. 66). Palo Alto, CA: Annual Reviews.

Fuligni, A.J., Tsai, K.M., Krull, J.L., & Gonzalez, N.A. (2015). Daily concordance between parent and adolescent sleep habits. *Journal of Adolescent Health, 56,* 244–250.

Fung, Y.L., & Chan, Z.C. (2011). A systematic review of suicidal behavior in old age: A gender perspective. *Journal of Clinical Nursing, 20,* 2109–2124.

Furman, E. (2005). *Boomerang nation.* New York: Fireside.

Furman, W., & Rose, A.J. (2015). Friendships, romantic relationships, and other dyadic peer relationships in childhood and adolescence: A unified relational perspective. In R.M. Lerner (Ed.), *Handbook of child psychology and developmental science* (7th ed.). New York: Wiley.

Furman, W., Low, S., & Ho, M. (2009). Romantic experience and psychosocial adjustment in middle adolescence. *Journal of Clinical Child and Adolescent Psychology, 38,* 1–16.

Furstenberg, F.F. (2006). Growing up healthy: Are adolescents the right target group? *Journal of Adolescent Health, 39,* 303–304.

Furth, H.G., & Wachs, H. (1975). *Thinking goes to school.* New York: Oxford University Press.

Furukawa, S., Sameshima, H., & Ikenoue, T. (2014). The impact of cesarean section on neonatal outcome of infants born at 23 weeks gestation. *Early Human Development, 90,* 113–118.

G

Gabor, M. (2014, March). New college degree in hand: Now what? *Monthly Labor Review.* Washington, DC: U.S. Department of Labor.

Gaias, L.M., & others (2012). Cross-cultural temperamental differences in infants, children, and adults in the United States of America and Finland, *53,* 119–128.

Gaillard, A., & others (2014). Predictors of postpartum depression: Prospective study of 264 women followed during pregnancy and postpartum. *Psychiatry Research, 215,* 341–346.

Gaither, S.E., Pauker, K., & Johnson, S.P. (2012). Biracial and monoracial infant own-race face perception: An eye tracking study. *Developmental Science, 15*(6), 775–782.

Galambos, N.L. (2004). Gender and gender role development in adolescence. In R. Lerner & L. Steinberg (Eds.), *Handbook of adolescence.* New York: Wiley.

Galambos, N.L., Berenbaum, S.A., & McHale, S.M. (2009). Gender development in adolescence. In R.M. Lerner & L. Steinberg (Eds.), *Handbook of adolescent psychology.* New York: Wiley.

Galambos, N.L., Howard, A.L., & Maggs, J.L. (2011). Rise and fall of sleep quality with student experiences across the first year of the university. *Journal of Research on Adolescence, 21,* 342–349.

Galbally, M., Lewis, A.J., IJzendoorn, M., & Permezel, M. (2011). The role of oxytocin in mother-infant relations: A systematic review of human studies. *Harvard Review of Psychiatry, 19,* 1–14.

Gale, C.R., Booth, T., Mottus, R., Kuh, D., & Deary, J.J. (2013). Neuroticism and extraversion in youth predict mental wellbeing and life satisfaction 40 years later. *Journal of Research in Personality, 47,* 687–697.

Galinsky, A.M., & Sonenstein, F.L. (2013). Relationship commitment, perceived equity, and sexual enjoyment among young adults in the United States. *Archives of Sexual Behavior, 42,* 93–104.

Galinsky, E. (2010). *Mind in the making.* New York: HarperCollins.

Galinsky, E., & David, J. (1988). *The preschool years: Family strategies that work—from experts and parents.* New York: Times Books.

Galland, B.C., Taylor, B.J., Edler, D.E., & Herbison, P. (2012). Normal sleep patterns in infants and children: A systematic review of observational studies. *Sleep Medicine Review, 16,* 213–222.

Gallicchio, L., & others (2015, in press). Risk factors for hot flashes among women undergoing the menopausal transition: Baseline results from the Midlife Women's Health Study. *Menopause.*

Galliher, R.V., & Kerpelman, J.L. (2012). The intersection of identity development and peer relationship processes in adolescence and young adulthood: Contributions of the special issue. *Journal of Adolescence, 35,* 1409–1415.

Galloway, J.C., & Thelen, E. (2004). Feet first: Object exploration in young infants. *Infant Behavior & Development, 27,* 107–112.

Gallup (2013a). *U.S. obesity rate climbing in 2013.* Washington, DC: Gallup.

Gallup (2013b). *No major change in Americans' exercise habits in 2011.* Washington, DC: Gallup.

Gallup, G.W., & Bezilla, R. (1992). *The religious life of young Americans.* Princeton, NJ: Gallup Institute.

Galupo, M.P., Cartwright, K.B., & Savage, L.S. (2010). Cross-category friendships and postformal thought among college students. *Journal of Adult Development, 17,* 208–214.

Gambacciani, M., & Levancini, M. (2015). Hormone replacement therapy: Who should be treated? *Minerva Ginecologica, 67*(3), 249–255.

Gamble, W.C., & Modry-Mandell, K. (2008). Family relations and the adjustment of young children of Mexican descent: Do family cultural values moderate these associations? *Social Development, 17,* 358–379.

Gander, M., & Buchheim, A. (2015). Attachment classification, psychophysiology, and frontal EEG asymmetry across the lifespan: A review. *Frontiers in Human Neuroscience, 19*(9), 79.

Gandhi, S., & Abramov, A.Y. (2012). Mechanism of oxidative stress in neurodegeneration. *Oxidative Medicine and Cellular Longevity, 2012,* 428010.

Ganguli, M., & others (2014). Vascular risk factors and cognitive decline in a population sample. *Alzheimer Disease and Associated Disorders, 28,* 9–15.

Ganley, C.M., Vasilyeva, M., & Dulaney, A. (2014). Spatial ability mediates the gender difference in middle school students' science performance. *Child Development, 85,* 1419–1432.

Ganong, L., Coleman, M., & Hans, J. (2006). Divorce as a prelude to stepfamily living and the consequences of re-divorce. In M. Fine & J.H. Harvey (Eds.), *Handbook of divorce and relationship dissolution.* Mahwah, NJ: Erlbaum.

Ganong, L., Coleman, M., & Russell, L. (2015). Children in diverse families. In R.M. Lerner (Ed.), *Handbook of child psychology and developmental science* (7th ed.). New York: Wiley.

Ganzach, Y., & Fried, I. (2012). The role of intelligence in the formation of well-being: From job rewards to job satisfaction. *Intelligence, 40,* 333–342.

Gao, W., & others (2015, in press). Development of human brain cortical network architecture during infancy. *Brain Structure and Function.*

Garand, L., Mitchell, A.M., Dietrick, A., Hijjawi, S.P., & Pan, D. (2006). Suicide in older adults: Nursing assessment of suicide risk. *Issues in Mental Health Nursing, 27,* 355–370.

Garbarino, J. (1999). *Lost boys: Why our sons turn violent and how we can save them.* New York: Free Press.

Garbarino, J., & Asp, C.E. (1981). *Successful schools and competent students.* Lexington, MA: Lexington Books.

Garcia-Hermoso, A., Saavedra, J.M., & Escalante, Y. (2013). Effects of exercise on resting blood pressure in obese children: A meta-analysis of randomized controlled trials. *Obesity Reviews, 14,* 919–928.

Gardner, H. (1983). *Frames of mind.* New York: Basic Books.

Gardner, H. (1993). *Multiple intelligences.* New York: Basic Books.

Gardner, H. (2002). The pursuit of excellence through education. In M. Ferrari (Ed.), *Learning from extraordinary minds.* Mahwah, NJ: Erlbaum.

Gardner, M., & Steinberg, L. (2005). Peer influence on risk taking, risk preference, and risky decision making in adolescence and adulthood. *Developmental Psychology, 41,* 625–635.

Gardner, M.K. (2014). Theories of intelligence. In M.A. Bray & T.J., Kehle (Eds.), *Oxford handbook of school psychology.* New York: Oxford University Press.

Gardosi, J., & others (2013). Maternal and fetal risk factors for stillbirth: Population-based study. *British Medical Journal, 346,* f108.

Garfield, C.F., & others (2012). Trends in attention deficit hyperactivity disorder ambulatory diagnosis and medical treatment in the United States, 2000–2010. *Academic Pediatrics, 12,* 110–116.

Garlow, S.J., Purselle, D., & Heninger, M. (2005). Ethnic differences in patterns of suicide across the life cycle. *American Journal of Psychiatry, 162,* 319–323.

Garneau, C.L., & Adler-Baeder, F. (2015, in press). Changes in stepparents' coparenting and parenting following participation in a community-based relationship education program. *Family Process.*

Garofalo, R. (2010). Cytokines in human milk. *Journal of Pediatrics, 156*(Suppl. 2), S36–S40.

Garofalo, R., Wolf, R.C., Wissow, L.S., Woods, E.R., & Goodman, E. (1999). Sexual orientation and risk of suicide attempts among a representative sample of youth. *Archives of Pediatrics and Adolescent Medicine, 153,* 487–493.

Gartland, N., O'Connor, D.B., Lawton, R., & Ferguson, R. (2014). Investigating the effects of conscientiousness on daily stress, affect, and physical symptom processes: A daily diary study. *British Journal of Health Psychology, 19,* 311–328.

Gartner, J., Larson, D.B., & Allen, G.D. (1991). Religious commitment and mental health: A review of the empirical literature. *Journal of Psychology and Theology, 19,* 6–25.

Gartstein, M.A., Slobodskaya, H.R., Putnam, S.P., & Kirchhoff, C. (2010). Cross-cultural evaluation of temperament development: Japan, United States of American, Poland, and Russia. *International Journal of Psychology and Psychological Therapy, 10,* 55–75.

Garvey, C. (2000). *Play* (Enlarged Ed.). Cambridge, MA: Harvard University Press.

Gaspar, A., & others (2015). Oxidative stress and neurodegenerative diseases: Looking for a therapeutic solution inspired on benzopyran chemistry. *Current Topics in Medicinal Chemistry.*

Gasser, L., & Keller, M. (2009). Are the competent morally good? Perspective taking and moral motivation of children involved in bullying. *Social Development, 18*(4), 798–816.

Gates, G.J. (2011). *How many people are lesbian, gay, bisexual, and transgender?* Los Angeles: Williams Institute, School of Law.

Gates, W. (1998, July 20). Charity begins when I'm ready (interview). *Fortune Magazine.*

Gatz, M., & Karel, M.J. (1993). Individual change in perceived control over 20 years. Special issue: Planning and control processes across the life span. *International Journal of Behavioral Development, 16*(2), 305–322.

Gauthier, A.H., & Furstenberg, F.F. (2005). Historical trends in the patterns of time use among young adults in developed countries. In R.A. Setterson, F.F. Furstenberg, & R.G. Rumbaut (Eds.), *On the frontier of adulthood: Theories, research, and social policy.* Chicago: University of Chicago Press.

Gauvain, M. (2013). Sociocultural contexts of development. In P.D. Zelazo (Ed.), *Oxford handbook of developmental psychology.* New York: Oxford University Press.

Gauvain, M., & Perez, S. (2015). Cognitive development in the context of culture. In R.M. Lerner (Ed.), *Handbook of child psychology and developmental science* (7th ed.). New York: Wiley.

Gavazzi, S. (2013). Theory and research pertaining to families with adolescents. In G.W. Peterson & K.R. Bush (Eds.), *Handbook of marriage and the family* (3rd ed.). New York: Springer.

Gawlik, S., & others (2014). Prevalence of paternal perinatal depressiveness and its link to partnership satisfaction and birth concerns. *Archives of Women's Mental Health, 17,* 49–56.

Gee, C.C., Walsemann, K.M., & Brondolo, E. (2012). A life course perspective on how racism may be related to health inequities. *American Journal of Public Health, 102,* 967–974.

Gelman, R. (1969). Conservation acquisition: A problem of learning to attend to relevant attributes. *Journal of Experimental Child Psychology, 7,* 67–87.

Gelman, R., & Williams, E.M. (1998). Enabling constraints for cognitive development and learning. In W. Damon (Ed.), *Handbook of child psychology* (5th ed., Vol. 4). New York: Wiley.

Gelman, S.A., & Kalish, C.W. (2006). Conceptual development. In W. Damon & R. Lerner (Eds.), *Handbook of child psychology* (6th ed.). New York: Wiley.

Gelman, S.A., & Opfer, J.E. (2004). Development of the animate-inanimate distinction. In U. Goswami (Ed.), *Blackwell handbook of childhood cognitive development.* Malden, MA: Blackwell.

Gelman, S.A., Taylor, M.G., & Nguyen, S.P. (2004). Mother-child conversations about gender. *Monographs of the Society for Research in Child Development, 69*(1, Serial No. 275).

Gems, D. (2014). Evolution of sexually dimorphic longevity in humans. *Aging, 6,* 84–91.

Gems, D., & Partridge, L. (2013). Genetics of longevity in model organisms: Debates and paradigm shifts. *Annual Review of Physiology* (Vol. 75). Palo Alto, CA: Annual Reviews.

Genesee, F., & Lindholm-Leary, K. (2012). The education of English language learners. In K. Harris, S. Graham, & T. Urdan (Eds.), *APA educational psychology handbook.* Washington, DC: American Psychological Association.

Gennetian, L.A., & Miller, C. (2002). Children and welfare reform: A view from an experimental welfare reform program in Minnesota. *Child Development, 73,* 601–620.

Gentile, D.A. (2011). The multiple dimensions of video game effects. *Child Development Perspectives, 5,* 75–81.

Gentile, D.A., & others (2009). The effects of prosocial video games on prosocial behaviors: International evidence from correlational, longitudinal, and experimental studies. *Personality and Social Psychology Bulletin, 35,* 752–763.

Gentile, D.A., & others (2014). Protective effects of parental monitoring of children's media use: A prospective study. *JAMA Pediatrics, 168,* 479–484.

George, L.G., Helson, R., & John, O.P. (2011). The "CEO" of women's work lives: How Big Five conscientiousness, extraversion, and openness predict 50 years of work experiences in a changing sociocultural context. *Journal of Personality and Social Psychology, 101,* 812–830.

George, L.K. (2010). Still happy after all these years: Research frontiers on subjective well-being in later life. *Journals of Gerontology B: Psychological Sciences and Social Sciences, 65B,* 331–339.

Gershoff, E.T. (2013). Spanking and development: We know enough now to stop hitting our children. *Child Development Perspectives, 7,* 133–137.

Gershoff, E.T., Lansford, J.E., Sexton, H.R., Davis-Kean, P., & Sameroff, A. (2012). Longitudinal links between spanking and children's externalizing behaviors in a national sample of White, Black, Hispanic, and Asian American families. *Child Development, 83,* 838–843.

Gerson, S.A., & Woodward, A.L. (2014). The joint role of trained, untrained, and observed actions at the origins of goal recognition. *Infant Behavior and Development, 37*(1), 94–104.

Gesell, A. (1934). *An atlas of infant behavior.* New Haven, CT: Yale University Press.

Gevensleben, H., & others (2014). Neurofeedback in ADHD: Further pieces of the puzzle. *Brain Topography, 27,* 20–32.

Gewirtz, J. (1977). Maternal responding and the conditioning of infant crying: Directions of influence within the attachment-acquisition process. In B.C. Etzel, J.M. LeBlanc, & D.M. Baer (Eds.), *New developments in behavioral research.* Hillsdale, NJ: Erlbaum.

Ghetti, S., & Alexander, K.W. (2004). "If it happened, I would remember it": Strategic use of event memorability in the rejection of false autobiographical events. *Child Development, 75,* 542–561.

Ghosh, S., Feingold, E., Chakaborty, S., & Dey, S.K. (2010). Telomere length is associated with types of chromosome 21 nondisjunction: A new insight into the maternal age effect on Down syndrome birth. *Human Genetics, 127*(4), 403–409.

Giaguilli, V.A., & others (2013). Managing erectile dysfunction in heart failure. *Endocrine, Metabolic, and Immune Disorders Drug Targets, 13,* 125–134.

Gialamas, A., & others (2014). Quality of childcare influences children's attentiveness and emotional regulation at school entry. *Journal of Pediatrics, 165,* 813–819.

Giallo, R., & others (2015, in press). The emotional-behavioral functioning of children exposed to maternal depressive symptoms across pregnancy and early childhood: A prospective Australian pregnancy cohort study. *European Child and Adolescent Psychiatry.*

Giangregorio, L.M., & others (2015). Too fit to fracture: Outcomes of a Delphi consensus process on physical activity and exercise recommendations for adults with osteoporosis with or without vertebral fractures. *Osteoporosis International, 26,* 891–910.

Giarrusso, R., & Bengtson, V.L. (2007). Self-esteem. In J.E. Birren (Ed.), *Encyclopedia of gerontology* (2nd ed.). San Diego: Academic Press.

Gibbs, J.C., Basinger, K.S., Grime, R.L., & Snarey, J.R. (2007). Moral judgment across cultures: Revisiting Kohlberg's universality claims. *Developmental Review, 27,* 443–500.

Gibson, E.J. (1969). *Principles of perceptual learning and development.* New York: Appleton-Century-Crofts.

Gibson, E.J. (1989). Exploratory behavior in the development of perceiving, acting, and the acquiring of knowledge. *Annual Review of Psychology* (Vol. 39). Palo Alto, CA: Annual Reviews.

Gibson, E.J. (2001). *Perceiving the affordances.* Mahwah, NJ: Erlbaum.

Gibson, E.J., & Walk, R.D. (1960). The "visual cliff." *Scientific American, 202,* 64–71.

Gibson, E.J., & others (1987). Detection of the traversability of surfaces by crawling and walking infants. *Journal of Experimental Psychology: Human Perception and Performance, 13,* 533–544.

Gibson, J.J. (1966). *The senses considered as perceptual systems.* Boston: Houghton Mifflin.

Gibson, J.J. (1979). *The ecological approach to visual perception.* Boston: Houghton Mifflin.

Gibson-Davis, C., & Rackin, H. (2014). Marriage or carriage? Trends in union context and birth type by education. *Journal of Marriage and the Family, 76,* 506–519.

Giedd, J.N. (2007, September 27). Commentary in S. Jayson, "Teens driven to distraction." *USA Today,* pp. D1–2.

Giedd, J.N., & others (2012). Automatic magnetic resonance imaging of the developing child and adolescent brain. In V.F. Reyna & others (Eds.), *The adolescent brain.* Washington, DC: American Psychological Association.

Gielen, S., Sandri, M., Erbs, S., & Adams, V. (2011). Exercise-induced modulation of endothelial nitric oxide production. *Current Pharmaceutical Biotechnology, 12*(9), 1375–1384.

Gilbert, G., & Graham, S. (2010). Teaching writing to students in grades 4–6: A national survey. *Elementary School Journal, 110,* 494–518.

Gilbertson, S.L., & Graves, B.A. (2014). Motivating parents to promote cardiovascular health in children. *Journal of Cardiovascular Nursing, 30,* E8–E18.

Gill, P., & Lowes, L. (2014). Renal transplant failure and disenfranchised grief: Participants' experiences in first year post-graft failure. *International Journal of Nursing Studies, 51,* 1271–1280.

Gillen-O'Neel, C., Huynh, V.W., & Fuligni, A.J. (2013). To study or to sleep? The academic costs of extra studying at the expense of sleep. *Child Development, 84*(1), 133–142.

Gilligan, C. (1982). *In a different voice.* Cambridge, MA: Harvard University Press.

Gilligan, C. (1992, May). *Joining the resistance: Girls' development in adolescence.* Paper presented at the symposium on development and vulnerability in close relationships, Montreal.

Gilligan, C. (1996). The centrality of relationships in psychological development: A puzzle, some evidence, and a theory. In G.G. Noam & K.W. Fischer (Eds.), *Development and vulnerability in close relationships.* Hillsdale, NJ: Erlbaum.

Gilligan, C., Spencer, R., Weinberg, M.K., & Bertsch, T. (2003). On the listening guide: A voice-centered relational model. In P.M. Carnic & J.E. Rhodes (Eds.), *Qualitative research in psychology.* Washington, DC: American Psychological Association.

Gillum, R.F., & Ingram, D.D. (2007). Frequency of attendance at religious services, hypertension, and blood pressure: The third National Health and Nutrition Examination Survey. *Psychosomatic Medicine, 68,* 382–385.

Gillum, R.F., King, D.E., Obisesan, T.O., & Koenig, H.G. (2008). Frequency of attendance at religious services and mortality in a U.S. national cohort. *Annals of Epidemiology, 18,* 124–129.

Gimovsky, A., Khodak-Gelman, S., & Larsen, J. (2014). Making chorionic villus sampling painless for both the patient and the physician. *Journal of Ultrasound Medicine, 33,* 355–357.

Glaser, R., & Kiecolt-Glaser, J.K. (2005). Stress-induced immune dysfunction: Implications for health. *Nature Review: Immunology, 5,* 243–251.

Glass, L., Ware, A.L., & Mattson, S.N. (2014). Neurobehavioral, neurologic, and neuroimaging characteristics of fetal alcohol spectrum disorders. *Handbook of Clinical Neurology, 125,* 435–462.

Glavind, J., & Uldhjerg, N. (2015, in press). Elective Cesarean delivery at 38 and 39 weeks: Neonatal and maternal risks. *Current Opinion in Obstetrics and Gynecology.*

Glazebrook, K., Townsend, E., & Sayal, K. (2015, in press). The role of attachment style in predicting repetition of adolescent self-harm: A longitudinal study. *Suicide and Life-Threatening Behavior.*

Glover, V. (2014). Maternal depression, anxiety, and stress during pregnancy and child outcome: What needs to be done. *Best Practice and Research: Clinical Obstetrics and Gynecology, 28,* 25–35.

Goel, A., Sinha, R.J., Delela, D., Sankhwar, S., & Singh, V. (2009). Andropause in Indian men: A preliminary cross-sectional study. *Urology Journal, 6,* 40–46.

Goga, A.E., & others (2012). Infant feeding practices at routine PMTCT site, South Africa: Results of a prospective observational study amongst HIV exposed and unexposed infants—birth to 9 months. *International Breastfeeding Journal, 7,* 4.

Gogtay, N., & Thompson, P.M. (2010). Mapping gray matter development: Implications for typical development and vulnerability to psychopathology. *Brain and Cognition, 72,* 6–15.

Gold, D. (2011). Death and dying. In R.H. Binstock & L.K. George (Eds.), *Handbook of aging and the social sciences* (7th ed.). New York: Elsevier.

Gold, M.S., Blum K., Oscar-Berman, M., & Braverman, E.R. (2014). Low dopamine function in attention deficit/hyperactivity disorder: Should genotyping signify early diagnosis in children? *Postgraduate Medicine, 126,* 153–177.

Gold, S.J., & Amthor, R.F. (2011). Life-span development and international migration. In K.L. Fingerman, C.A. Berg, J. Smith, & T.C. Antonucci (Eds.), *Handbook of life-span development.* New York: Springer.

Goldberg, J.S., & Carlson, M.J. (2015, in press). Patterns and predictors of coparenting after unmarried parents part. *Journal of Family Psychology.*

Goldberg, W.A., & Lucas-Thompson, R. (2008). Effects of maternal and paternal employment. In M.M. Haith & J.B. Benson (Eds.), *Encyclopedia of infant and early childhood development.* Oxford, UK: Elsevier.

Goldfield, B.A., & Snow, C.E. (2009). Individual differences: Implications for the study of language acquisition. In J. Berko Gleason & N.B. Ratner (Eds.), *The development of language.* Boston: Allyn & Bacon.

Goldin-Meadow, S. (2014a). Widening the lens: What the manual modality reveals about language, learning, and cognition. *Philosophical Transactions of the Royal Society, Series B, 369*(1651), 20130295.

Goldin-Meadow, S. (2014b). Language and the manual modality: How our hands help us talk and think. In N.J. Enfield & others (Eds.), *Cambridge handbook of linguistic anthropology.* New York: Cambridge University Press.

Goldin-Meadow, S. (2015). Nonverbal communication: The hand's role in talking and thinking. In R.M. Lerner (Ed.), *Handbook of child psychology and developmental science* (7th ed.). New York: Wiley.

Goldschmidt, L., Richardson, G.A., Willford, J., & Day, N.L. (2008). Prenatal marijuana exposure and intelligence test performance at age 6. *Journal of the American Academy of Child and Adolescent Psychiatry, 47*(3), 254–263.

Goldstein, M.H., King, A.P., & West, M.J. (2003). Social interaction shapes babbling: Testing parallels between birdsong and speech. *Proceedings of the National Academy of Sciences, 100,* 8030–8035.

Goldston, D.B., & others (2008). Cultural considerations in adolescent suicide prevention and psychosocial treatment. *American Psychologist, 63,* 14–31.

Goldstone, E., & Reynolds, A. (2014). Child development and behavior. In W. Hay, M. Levin, & M. Abzug (Eds.), *Pediatrics* (22nd ed.). New York: McGraw-Hill.

Goleman, D. (1995). *Emotional intelligence.* New York: Basic Books.

Goleman, D., Kaufman, P., & Ray, M. (1993). *The creative spirit.* New York: Plume.

Golombok, S. (2011a). Children in new family forms. In R. Gross (Ed.), *Psychology* (6th ed.). London: Hodder.

Golombok, S. (2011b). Why I study lesbian families. In S. Ellis, V. Clarke, E. Peel, & D. Riggs (Eds.), *LGBTQ psychologies.* New York: Cambridge University Press.

Golombok, S., & Tasker, F. (2010). Gay fathers. In M.E. Lamb (Ed.), *The role of the father in child development* (5th ed.). New York: Wiley.

Golombok, S., & others (2008). Development trajectories of sex-typed behavior in boys and girls: A longitudinal general population study of children aged 2.5–8 years. *Child Development, 79,* 1583–1593.

Golombok, S., & others (2014). Adoptive gay father families: Parent-child relationships and children's psychological adjustment. *Child Development, 85,* 456–468.

Gomes, R.S., & others (2011). Primary versus secondary hypertension in children followed up at an outpatient tertiary unit. *Pediatric Nephrology, 26,* 441–447.

Gomez-Pinilla, F., & Hillman, C. (2013). The influence of exercise on cognitive abilities. *Comprehensive Physiology, 3,* 403–428.

Goncu, A., & Gauvain, M. (2012). Sociocultural approaches in educational psychology. In K.H. Harris, S. Graham, & T. Urdan (Eds.), *APA educational psychology handbook.* Washington, DC: American Psychological Association.

Gonzales, M., Jones, D., & Parent, J. (2014). Coparenting experiences in African American families: An examination of single mothers and their nonmarital coparents. *Family Process, 53,* 33–54.

Gonzalez Rey, F.L. (2014). Advancing further the history of Soviet psychology: Moving forward from dominant representations in Western and Soviet psychology. *History of Psychology, 17,* 60–78.

Gonzalez, A., Atkinson, L., & Fleming, A.S. (2009). Attachment and the comparative psychobiology of mothering. In M. de Haan & M.R. Gunnar (Eds.), *Handbook of developmental social neuroscience.* New York: Guilford.

Gonzalez, J., & others (2015, in press). Reminiscence and dementia: A therapeutic intervention. *International Psychogeriatrics.*

Gonzalez, R., & Ludwikowski, B.M. (2014). Should the genitoplasty of girls with CAH be done in one or two stages? *Frontiers in Pediatrics, 1,* 54.

Gonzalez-Echavarri, C., & others (2015). Prevalence and significance of persistently positive antiphospholipid antibodies in women with preeclampsia. *Journal of Rheumatology, 42,* 2010–2013.

Good, C., Rattan, A., & Dweck, C.S. (2012). Why do women opt out? Sense of belonging and women's representation in mathematics. *Journal of Personality and Social Psychology, 102,* 700–717.

Good, M., & Willoughby, T. (2008). Adolescence as a sensitive period for spiritual development. *Child Development Perspectives, 2,* 32–37.

Goodkind, S. (2013). Single-sex public education for low-income youth of color: A critical theoretical review. *Sex Roles, 69,* 393–402.

Goodman, G.S. (2014). *Children's eyewitness testimony.* Cambridge, MA: Harvard University Press.

Goodman, G.S., Batterman-Faunce, J.M., & Kenney, R. (1992). Optimizing children's testimony: Research and social policy issues concerning allegations of child sexual abuse. In D. Cicchetti & S. Toth (Eds.), *Child abuse, child development and social policy.* Norwood, NJ: Ablex.

Goodman, W.B., & others (2011). Parental work stress and latent profiles of father-infant parenting quality. *Journal of Marriage and the Family, 73,* 588–604.

Goodnow, J.J., & Lawrence, J.A. (2015). Children and cultural context. In R.M. Lerner (Ed.), *Handbook of child psychology and developmental science* (7th ed.). New York: Wiley.

Goodvin, R., Meyer, S., Thompson, R.A., & Hayes, R. (2008). Self-understanding in early childhood: Associations with child attachment security and maternal negative affect. *Attachment and Human Development, 10,* 433–450.

Goodvin, R., Thompson, R.A., & Winer, A.C. (2015, in press). The individual child: Temperament, emotion, self, and personality. In M. Bornstein & M.E. Lamb (Eds.), *Developmental science* (7th ed.). New York: Psychology Press.

Gopinath, B., & others (2012). Severity of age-related hearing loss is associated with impaired activities of daily living. *Age and Aging, 41,* 195–200.

Gopnik, A. (2010). Commentary in E. Galinsky (2010), *Mind in the making.* New York: Harper Collins.

Gorby, H.E., Brownell, A.M., & Falk, M.C. (2010). Do specific dietary constituents and supplements affect mental energy? Review of the evidence. *Nutrition Reviews, 68,* 697–718.

Gorchoff, S.M., John, O.P., & Helson, R. (2008). Contextualizing change in marital satisfaction during middle age: An 18-year longitudinal study. *Psychological Science, 19,* 1194–1200.

Gordon, B.A., & others (2015, in press). Task-evolved fMRI changes in attention networks are associated with preclinical Alzheimer's disease biomarkers. *Neurobiology of Aging.*

Gordon, I., Zagoory-Sharon, O., Leckman, J.F., & Feldman, R. (2010). Oxytocin and the development of parenting in humans. *Biological Psychiatry, 68,* 377–382.

Gordon, M. (2015). Rituals in death and dying: Modern medical technologies enter the fray. *Rambam Maimonides Medical Journal, 6*(1), e0007.

Gordon, S., & Gordon, J. (1989). *Raising a child conservatively in a sexually permissive world.* New York: Simon & Schuster.

Gormley-Fleming, L., & Campbell, A. (2014). Rights of the child: To die? *British Journal of Nursing, 23,* 302–308.

Gorrese, A., & Ruggieri, R. (2012). Peer attachment: A meta-analytic review of gender and age differences and associations with parent attachment. *Journal of Youth and Adolescence, 41,* 650–672.

Gosden, R.G. (2007). Menopause. In J.E. Birren (Ed.), *Encyclopedia of gerontology* (2nd ed.). San Diego: Academic Press.

Gothe, N.P., & others (2014). Executive function processes predict mobility outcomes in older adults. *Journal of the American Geriatrics Society, 62,* 285–290.

Gottfried, A.E., Marcoulides, G.A., Gottfried, A.W., & Oliver, P.H. (2009). A latent curve model of motivational practices and developmental decline in math and science academic intrinsic motivation. *Journal of Educational Psychology, 101,* 729–739.

Gottlieb, G. (2007). Probabilistic epigenesis. *Developmental Science, 10,* 1–11.

Gottman, J.M. (1994). *Why marriages succeed or fail.* New York: Simon & Schuster.

Gottman, J.M. (2012). *Research on parenting.* Retrieved September 15, 2012, from www.gottman.com/parenting/research

Gottman, J.M. (2014). *Research on parenting.* Retrieved September 20, 2014, from www.gottman.com/parenting/research

Gottman, J.M., Coan, J., Carrere, S., & Swanson, C. (1998). Predicting marital happiness and stability from newlywed interactions. *Journal of Marriage and the Family, 60,* 5–22.

Gottman, J.M., & DeClaire, J. (1997). *The heart of parenting: Raising an emotionally intelligent child.* New York: Simon & Schuster.

Gottman, J.M., & Gottman, J.S. (2009). Gottman method of couple therapy. In A.S. Gurman (Ed.), *Clinical handbook of couple therapy* (4th ed.). New York: Guilford.

Gottman, J.M., Gottman, J.S., & Shapiro, A. (2009). A new couples approach to interventions for the transition to parenthood. In M.S. Schultz, M.K. Pruett, P.K. Kerig, & R.D. Parke (Eds.), *Feathering the nest: Couple relationships, couples interventions, and children's development.* Washington, DC: American Psychological Association.

Gottman, J.M., & Parker, J.G. (Eds.). (1987). *Conversations of friends.* New York: Cambridge University Press.

Gottman, J.M., & Silver, N. (1999). *The seven principles for making marriages work.* New York: Crown.

Gouin, K., & others (2011). Effects of cocaine use during pregnancy on low birthweight and preterm birth: Systematic and metanalyses. *American Journal of Obstetrics and Gynecology, 201,* e1–e12.

Gove, W.R., Style, C.B., & Hughes, M. (1990). The effect of marriage on the well-being of adults: A theoretical analysis. *Journal of Health and Social Behavior, 24,* 122–131.

Gowan, D.E. (2003). Christian beliefs concerning death and life after death. In C.D. Bryant (Ed.), *Handbook of death and dying.* Thousand Oaks, CA: Sage.

Grabenhenrich, L.B., & others (2014). Early-life determinants of asthma from birth to age 20 years: A German birth cohort study. *Journal of Allergy and Clinical Immunology, 133,* 979–988.

Graber, J.A. (2008). Pubertal and neuroendocrine development and risk for depressive disorders. In N.B. Allen & L. Sheeber (Eds.), *Adolescent emotional development and the emergence of depressive disorders.* New York: Cambridge University Press.

Graber, J.A. (2013). Pubertal timing and the development of psychopathology in adolescence and beyond. *Hormones and Behavior, 64,* 262–269.

Grace, F.M., & others (2015, in press). Age-related vascular endothelial function following lifelong sedentariness: Positive impact of cardiovascular conditioning without further improvement following low-frequency, high-intensity interval training. *Physiological Reports.*

Gradisar, M., Gardner, G., & Dohnt, H. (2011). Recent worldwide sleep patterns and problems during adolescence: A review and meta-analysis of age, region, and sleep. *Sleep Medicine, 12,* 110–118.

Graham, G.M., Holt-Hale, S., & Parker, M.A. (2013). *Children moving* (9th ed.). New York: McGraw-Hill.

Graham, J.H., & Beller, A.H. (2002). Non-resident fathers and their children: Child support and visitation from an economic perspective. In C.S. Tamis-LeMonda & N. Cabrera (Eds.), *The handbook of father involvement.* Mahwah, NJ: Erlbaum.

Graham, S. (1986, August). *Can attribution theory tell us something about motivation in Blacks?* Paper presented at the meeting of the American Psychological Association, Washington, DC.

Graham, S. (1990). Motivation in Afro-Americans. In G.L. Berry & J.K. Asamen (Eds.), *Black students: Psychosocial issues and academic achievement.* Newbury Park, CA: Sage.

Graham, S. (2005, February 16). Commentary in *USA Today,* p. 2D.

Graham, S., & Perin, D. (2007). A meta-analysis of writing instruction for adolescent students. *Journal of Educational Psychology, 99,* 445–476.

Grammas, P., & others (2014). A new paradigm for the treatment of Alzheimer's disease: Targeting vascular activation. *Journal of Alzheimer's Disease, 40,* 619–630.

Grant, A.M., & Gino, F. (2010). A little thanks goes a long way: Explaining why gratitude expressions motivate prosocial behavior. *Journal of Personality and Social Psychology, 98,* 946–955.

Graven, S. (2006). Sleep and brain development. *Clinical Perinatology, 33,* 693–706.

Gravetter, F.J., & Forzano, L.B. (2016, in press). *Research methods for the behavioral sciences* (5th ed.). Boston: Cengage.

Gray, J. (1992), *Men are from Mars, women are from Venus.* New York: Harper Collins.

Green, M.J., Espie, C.A., Hunt, K., & Benzeval, M. (2012). The longitudinal course of insomnia symptoms: Inequalities by sex and occupational class among two different age cohorts followed for 20 years in the west of Scotland. *Sleep, 35,* 815–823.

Greenberger, E., & Steinberg, L. (1986). *When teenagers work: The psychological and social costs of adolescent employment.* New York: Basic Books.

Greenfield, L.A., & Marks, N.F. (2004). Formal volunteering as a protective factor for older adults' psychological well-being. *Journals of Gerontology B: Psychological Sciences and Social Sciences, 59,* S258–S264.

Greenfield, P.M. (2009). Linking social change and developmental change: Shifting pathways of human development. *Developmental Psychology, 43,* 401–418.

Greenhaus, J., & Callanan, G.A. (2013). Career dynamics. In I.B. Weiner & others (Eds.), *Handbook of psychology* (2nd ed.). New York: Wiley.

Greer, F.R., Sicherer, S.H., Burks, A.W., & The Committee on Nutrition and Section on Allergy and Immunology (2008). Effect of early nutritional interventions on the development of atopic disease in infants and children: The role of maternal dietary restriction, breast feeding, timing of introduction of complementary foods, and hydrolyzed formulas. *Pediatrics, 121,* 183–191.

Gregoire, C.A., & others (2014). Untangling the influence of voluntary running, environmental complexity, social housing, and stress on adult hippocampal neurogenesis. *PLoS One, 9*(1), e86237.

Gregorson, M., Kaufman, J.C., & Snyder, H. (Eds.) (2013). *Teaching creatively and teaching creativity.* New York: Springer.

Gregory, R.J. (2014). *Psychological testing* (7th ed.). Boston: Cengage.

Greif, M.L., & Needham, A. (2012). The development of tool use early in life. In T. McCormack, C. Hoerl, & S. Butterfill (Eds.), *Tool use and causal cognition.* New York: Oxford University Press.

Griffin, I.J., Lee, H.C., Profit, J., & Tancedi, D.J. (2015, in press). The smallest of the small: Short-term outcomes of profoundly growth restricted and profoundly low birth weight preterm infants. *Journal of Perinatology.*

Griffiths, J.D., Marslen-Wilson, W.D., Stamatakis, E.A., & Tyler, L.K. (2013). Functional organization of the neural language system: Dorsal and ventral pathways are critical for syntax. *Cerebral Cortex, 23,* 139–147.

Grigorenko, E. (2000). Heritability and intelligence. In R.J. Sternberg (Ed.), *Handbook of intelligence.* New York: Cambridge University Press.

Grivell, R.M., Andersen, C., & Dodd, J.M. (2014). Prenatal versus postnatal repair procedures for spina bifida for improving infant and maternal outcomes. *Cochrane Database of Systematic Reviews, 10:* CD0008825.

Groh, A.M., & others (2014). The significance of attachment security for children's social competence with peers: A meta-analytic study. *Attachment and Human Development, 16,* 103–136.

Gronli, J., Soule, J., & Bramham, C.R. (2014). Sleep and protein-synthesis-dependent synaptic plasticity: Impacts of sleep loss and stress. *Frontiers in Behavioral Neuroscience, 7,* 224.

Gross, J.J., Frederickson, B.L., & Levenson, R.W. (1994). The psychology of crying. *Psychophysiology, 31,* 460–468.

Grossman, I., & Varnum, M.E. (2015). Social structure, infectious diseases, disasters, secularism, and cultural change in America. *Psychological Science, 26,* 311–324.

Grossmann, K., Grossmann, K.E., Spangler, G., Suess, G., & Unzner, L. (1985). Maternal sensitivity and newborns' orientation responses as related to quality of attachment in northern Germany. In I. Bretherton & E. Waters (Eds.), Growing points of attachment theory and research. *Monographs of the Society for Research in Child Development, 50*(1–2, Serial No. 209).

Grotevant, H., & McDermott, J.M. (2014). Adoption: Biological and social processes related to adoption. *Annual Review of Psychology* (Vol. 65). Palo Alto, CA: Annual Reviews.

Grotevant, H.D., McRoy, R.G., Wrobel, G.M., & Ayers-Lopez, S. (2013). Contact between adoptive and birth families: Perspectives from the Minnesota/Texas Adoption Research Project. *Child Development Perspectives, 7,* 193–198.

Gruber, K.J., Cupito, S.H., & Dobson, C.F. (2013). Impact of doulas on healthy birth outcomes. *Journal of Perinatal Education, 22,* 49–58.

Grusec, J.E. (2006). Development of moral behavior and a conscience from a socialization perspective. In M. Killen & J.G. Smetana (Eds.), *Handbook of moral development.* Mahwah, NJ: Erlbaum.

Grusec, J.E., Chaparro, M.P., Johnston, M., & Sherman, A. (2013). Social development and social relationships in middle childhood. In I.B. Weiner & others, *Handbook of psychology* (2nd ed., Vol. 6). New York: Wiley.

Grusec, J.E., Chaparro, M.P., Johnston, M., & Sherman, A. (2014). The development of moral behavior from a socialization perspective. In M. Killen & J.G. Smetana (Eds.), *Handbook of moral development* (2nd ed.). New York: Psychology Press.

Grusec, J.E., & Davidov, M. (2015). Analyzing socialization from a domain-specific perspective. In J.E. Grusec & P.D. Hastings (Eds.), *Handbook of socialization* (2nd ed.). New York: Guilford.

Grych, J.H. (2002). Marital relationships and parenting. In M.H. Bornstein (Ed.), *Handbook of parenting.* Mahwah, NJ: Erlbaum.

Grzywacz, J.G. (2009). Work-family conflict. In D. Carr (Ed.), *Encyclopedia of the life course and human development.* Boston: Gale Cengage.

Gu, X., Chen, H., & Gao, X. (2015). Nanotherapeutic strategies for treating Alzheimer's disease. *Therapeutic Delivery, 6,* 177–195.

Guevara-Lopez, U., Altamirano-Bustamante, M.M., & Viesca-Trevino, C. (2015). New frontiers in the future of palliative care: Real-world bioethical dilemmas and axiology of clinical practice. *BMC Medical Ethics, 16*(1), 11.

Guilford, J.P. (1967). *The structure of intellect.* New York: McGraw-Hill.

Guimard-Brunault, M., & others (2013). Back to basic: Do children with autism spontaneously look at screen displaying a face or an object? *Autism Research and Treatment.* doi:10.1155/2013/835247

Guiney, H., & Machado, L. (2013). Benefits of regular aerobic exercise for executive functioning in healthy populations. *Psychonomic Bulletin and Review, 20,* 73–86.

Guirado, G.N., & others (2012). Combined exercise training in asymptomatic elderly with controlled hypertension: Effects of functional capacity and cardiac diastolic function. *Medical Science Monitor, 28,* CR461–CR465.

Gump, B., & Matthews, K. (2000, March). *Annual vacations, health, and death.* Paper presented at the meeting of the American Psychosomatic Society, Savannah, GA.

Gunderson, E.A., Ramirez, G., Beilock, S.L., & Levine, S.C. (2012). The role of parents and teachers in the development of gender-related attitudes. *Sex Roles, 66,* 153–166.

Gunnar, M.R., & Fisher, P.A. (2006). Bringing basic research on early experience and stress neurobiology to bear on preventive interventions for neglected and maltreated children. *Development and Psychopathology, 18,* 651–677.

Gunnar, M.R., & Herrera, A.M. (2013). The development of stress reactivity: A neurobiological perspective. In P.D. Zelazo (Ed.), *Oxford handbook of developmental psychology.* New York: Oxford University Press.

Gunnar, M.R., Malone, S., & Fisch, R.O. (1987). The psychobiology of stress and coping in the human neonate: Studies of the adrenocortical activity in response to stress in the first week of life. In T. Field, P. McCasbe, & N. Scheiderman (Eds.), *Stress and coping.* Hillsdale, NJ: Erlbaum.

Gunning, T.G. (2013). *Creating literacy instruction for all children in grades pre-K to 4* (2nd ed.). Boston: Allyn & Bacon.

Guo, Q., & Jacelon, C.S. (2014). An integrative review of dignity in end-of-life care. *Palliative Medicine, 28,* 931–940.

Gur, R.C., & others (1995). Sex differences in regional cerebral glucose metabolism during a resting state. *Science, 267,* 528–531.

Gururaj, G. (2013). Injury prevention and care: An important public health agenda for health, survival, and safety of children. *Indian Journal of Pediatrics, 80*(Suppl. 1), S100–S108.

Gurwitch, R.H., Silovksy, J.F., Schultz, S., Kees, M., & Burlingame, S. (2001). *Reactions and guidelines for children following trauma/disaster.* Norman, OK: Department of Pediatrics, University of Oklahoma Health Sciences Center.

Gutchess, A.H., & others (2005). Aging and the neural correlates of successful picture encoding: Frontal activations compensate for decreased medial-temporal activity. *Journal of Cognitive Neuroscience, 17,* 84–96.

Gutmann, D.L. (1975). Parenthood: A key to the comparative study of the life cycle. In N. Datan & L. Ginsberg (Eds.), *Life-span developmental psychology: Normative life crises.* New York: Academic Press.

Guttentag, C.L., & others (2014). "My Baby & Me": Effects of an early, comprehensive parenting intervention on at-risk mothers and their children. *Developmental Psychology, 50,* 1482–1496.

Guttmannova, K., & others (2012). Examining explanatory mechanisms of the effects of early alcohol use on young adult alcohol competence. *Journal of Studies on Alcohol and Drugs, 73,* 379–390.

H

Habermas, T., & Kober, C. (2015). Autobiographical reasoning is constitutive for narrative identity: The role of the life story for personal continuity. In K.C. McLean & M. Syed (Eds.), *Oxford handbook of identity development.* New York: Oxford University Press.

Hadfield, J.C. (2014). The health of grandparents raising grandchildren: A literature review. *Journal of Gerontological Nursing, 40,* 32–42.

Hagestad, G.O. (1985). Continuity and connectedness. In V.L. Bengtson (Ed.), *Grandparent-hood*. Beverly Hills, CA: Sage.

Hagestad, G.O., & Uhlenberg, P. (2007). The impact of demographic changes on relations between the age groups and generations: A comparative perspective. In K.W. Schaie & P. Uhlenberg (Eds.), *Demographic changes and the well-being of older persons*. New York: Springer.

Hagman, J.O., & Frank, G.K.W. (2012). Developmental concerns in psychopharmacological treatment of children and adolescents with eating disorders. In J. Lock (Ed.), *Oxford handbook of child and adolescent eating disorders: Developmental perspectives*. New York: Oxford University Press.

Hahn, E.A., & Lachman, M.E. (2015). Everyday experiences of memory problems and control: The adaptive role of selective optimization with compensation in the context of memory. *Neuropsychology, Development, Cognition B: Aging, Neuropsychology, and Cognition, 22*, 25–41.

Haidt, J. (2006). *The happiness hypothesis*. New York: Basic Books.

Haidt, J. (2013). *The righteous mind*. New York: Random House.

Haier, R.J., Karama, S., Colom, R., Jung, R., & Johnson, W. (2014). A comment on "fractionating intelligence" and the peer review process. *Intelligence, 46*, 323–332.

Hakuta, K. (2001, April 5). *Key policy milestones and directions in the education of English language learners*. Paper prepared for the Rockefeller Foundation Symposium, Leveraging change: An emerging framework for educational equity. Washington, DC.

Hakuta, K. (2005, April). *Bilingualism at the intersection of research and public policy*. Paper presented at the meeting of the Society for Research in Child Development, Atlanta.

Hakuta, K., Butler, Y.G., & Witt, D. (2001). *How long does it take English learners to attain proficiency?* Berkeley, CA: The University of California Linguistic Minority Research Institute Policy Report 2000–1.

Hale, L., & Guan, S. (2015). Screen time and sleep among school-aged children and adolescents: A systematic review of the literature. *Sleep Medicine Reviews, 21*, 50–58.

Hale, N., Picklesimer, A.H., Billings, D.L., & Covington-Kolb, S. (2014). The impact of Centering Pregnancy group prenatal care on postpartum family planning. *American Journal of Obstetrics and Gynecology, 210*(50), e1–e7.

Hale, S. (1990). A global developmental trend in cognitive processing speed. *Child Development, 61*, 653–663.

Hale, W.J., & others (2015). Low self-esteem and positive beliefs about smoking: A destructive combination for male college students. *Addictive Behaviors, 46*, 94–99.

Haley, M.H., & Austin, T.Y. (2014). *Content-based second language teaching and learning* (2nd ed.). Upper Saddle River, NJ: Pearson.

Hall, C.B., & others (2009). Cognitive activities delay onset of memory decline in persons who develop dementia. *Neurology, 73*, 356–361.

Hall, C.M., & others (2004). Behavioral and physical masculinization are related to genotype in girls with congenital adrenal hyperplasia. *Journal of Clinical Endocrinology and Metabolism, 89*, 419–424.

Hall, D.T., & Mirvis, P.H. (2013). Redefining work, work identity, and career success. In D.L. Blustein (Ed.), *Oxford handbook of the psychology of working*. New York: Oxford University Press.

Hall, G.S. (1904). *Adolescence* (Vols. 1 & 2). Englewood Cliffs, NJ: Prentice Hall.

Hall, J.A. (2011). Sex differences in friendship expectations: A meta-analysis. *Journal of Social and Personal Relationships, 28*, 723–747.

Hall, J.A., Park, N., Song, H., & Cody, M.J. (2010). Strategic misrepresentation in online dating: The effects of gender, self-monitoring, and personality traits. *Journal of Social and Personal Relationships, 27*, 117–135.

Hall, J.R., & others (2013). Biomarkers of vascular risk, systematic inflammation, and microvascular pathology and neuropsychiatric symptoms in Alzheimer's disease. *Journal of Alzheimer's Disease, 35*(2), 363–371.

Hall, S.S., & others (2014). Using discrete trial training to identify specific learning impairments in boys with fragile X syndrome. *Journal of Autism and Developmental Disorders, 44*, 1659–1670.

Hall, W.J. (2008). Centenarians: Metaphor becomes reality. *Archives of Internal Medicine, 168*, 262–263.

Hallahan, D.P., Kauffman, J.M., & Pullen, P.C. (2015). *Exceptional learners* (13th ed.). Upper Saddle River, NJ: Pearson.

Halpern, D.F. (2012). *Sex differences in cognitive abilities* (2nd ed.). New York: Psychology Press.

Halpern, D.F., & others (2007). The science of sex differences in science and mathematics. *Psychological Science in the Public Interest, 8*, 1–51.

Halpern, D.F., & others (2011). The pseudoscience of single-sex schooling. *Science, 333*, 1706–1717.

Halpern-Meekin, S., Manning, W., Giordano, P.C., & Longmore, M.A. (2013). Relationship churning in emerging adulthood: On/off relationships and sex with an ex. *Journal of Adolescent Research, 28*, 166–188.

Halpin, K.S., Smith, K.Y., Widen, J.E., & Chertoff, M.E. (2010). Effects of universal newborn hearing screening on an early intervention program for children with hearing loss, birth to 3 yr of age. *Journal of the American Academy of Audiology, 21*, 169–175.

Halt, K., & Vainio, S. (2014). Coordination of kidney organogenesis by Wnt signaling. *Pediatric Nephrology, 29*, 737–744.

Hambrick, D.Z. (2014, December 2). Brain training doesn't necessarily make you smarter: Scientists doubt claims from brain training companies. *Scientific American*, pp. 1–8.

Hamilton, B.E., & Ventura, S.J. (2012, April). Birth rates for U.S. teenagers reach historic lows for all age and ethnic groups. *NCHS Data Brief, No. 89*, 1–8.

Hamilton, J.L., & others (2014). Pubertal timing and vulnerabilities to depression in early adolescence: Differential pathways to depressive symptoms by sex. *Journal of Adolescence, 37*, 165–174.

Hamilton, S.F., & Hamilton, M.A. (2006). School, work, and emerging adulthood. In J.J. Arnett & J.L. Tanner (Eds.), *Emerging adults in America*. Washington, DC: American Psychological Association.

Hamilton, S.F., & Hamilton, M.A. (2009). The transition to adulthood: Challenges of poverty and structural lag. In R.M. Lerner & L. Steinberg (Eds.), *Handbook of adolescent psychology* (3rd ed.). New York: Wiley.

Hamlin, J.K. (2013). Failed attempts to help and harm: Intention versus outcome in preverbal infants' social evaluations. *Cognition, 128*, 451–474.

Hamlin, J.K. (2013). Moral judgment and action in preverbal infants and toddlers: Evidence for an innate moral core. *Current Directions in Psychological Science, 22*, 186–193.

Hamlin, J.K. (2014). The origins of human morality: Complex socio-moral evaluations by preverbal infants. *Research and Perspectives in Social Neuroscience, 21*, 165–188.

Hamlin, J.K., Wynn, K., Bloom, P., & Mahajan, N. (2011). How infants and toddlers react to antisocial others. *Proceedings of the National Academy of Sciences, 108*, 19931–19936.

Hamlin, J.K., & others (2015, in press). The mentalistic basis of core social cognition: Experiments in preverbal infants and a computational model. *Developmental Science*.

Hamman, D., & others (2013). Teacher possible selves: How thinking about the future contributes to the formation of professional identity. *Self and Identity, 12*(3), 307–336.

Hampl, S., & Campbell, A. (2015). Recognizing obesity and its complications: The story of Score 1 for Health. *NASN School Nurse, 30*, 46–52.

Hampson, S.E., & others (2013). Childhood conscientiousness relates to objectively measured adult physical health four decades later. *Health Psychology, 32*, 925–938.

Hampson, S.E., & others (2015, in press). A life-span mechanism relating childhood conscientiousness to adult clinical health. *Health Psychology*.

Han, J.J., Leichtman, M.D., & Wang, Q. (1998). Autobiographical memory in Korean, Chinese, and American children. *Developmental Psychology, 34*, 701–713.

Hanish, L.D., & Guerra, N.G. (2004). Aggressive victims, passive victims, and bullies: Developmental continuity or developmental change? *Merrill-Palmer Quarterly, 50*, 17–38.

Hantman, S., & Cohen, O. (2010). Forgiveness in late life. *Journal of Gerontological Social Work, 53*, 613–630.

Haran, C., van Driel, M., Mitchell, B.L., & Brodribb, W.E. (2014). Clinical guidelines for postpartum women and infants in primary care—a systematic review. *BMC Pregnancy and Childbirth, 14*, 51.

Hardt, J., & others (2015). Suicidality and its relationship with depression, alcohol disorders, and childhood experiences of violence: Results from the ESEMeD study. *Journal of Affective Disorders, 175*, 168–174.

Hardy, M. (2006). Older workers. In R.H. Binstock & L.K. George (Eds.), *Handbook of aging and the social sciences* (6th ed.). San Diego: Academic Press.

Hardy, S.A., Bean, D.S., & Olsen, J.A. (2015, in press). Moral identity and adolescent prosocial and antisocial behaviors: Interactions with moral disengagement and self-regulation. *Journal of Youth and Adolescence*.

Hardy, S.A., & others (2013). The roles of identity formation and moral identity in college student mental health, health-risk behaviors, and psychological well-being. *Journal of Clinical Psychology, 69*, 364–382.

Hardy, S.A., & others (2014). Moral identity as moral ideal self: Links to adolescent outcomes. *Developmental Psychology, 50*, 45–57.

Harkins, S.W., Price, D.D., & Martinelli, M. (1986). Effects of age on pain perception. *Journal of Gerontology, 41*, 58–63.

Harkness, S., & Super, E.M. (1995). Culture and parenting. In M.M. Bornstein (Ed.), *Handbook of parenting* (Vol. 3). Hillsdale, NJ: Erlbaum.

Harlow, H.F. (1958). The nature of love. *American Psychologist, 13*, 673–685.

Harmon, O.R., Lambrinos, J., & Kennedy, P. (2008). Are online exams an invitation to cheat? *Journal of Economic Education, 39*, 116–125.

Harold, G.T., & others (2013). The nature of nurture: Disentangling passive genotype-environment correlation from family relationship influences on children's externalizing problems. *Journal of Family Psychology, 27*, 12–21.

Harper, K.M., Tunc-Ozcan, E., Graf, E.N., & Redel, E.E. (2014). Intergenerational effects of prenatal ethanol on glucose tolerance and insulin responses. *Physiological Genomics, 46*(5), 159–168.

Harrington, B.C., Jimerson, M., Haxton, C., & Jimerson, D.C. (2015). Initial evaluation, diagnosis, and treatment of anorexia nervosa and bulimia nervosa. *American Family Physician, 9,* 46–52.

Harris, G. (2002). *Grandparenting: How to meet its responsibilities.* Los Angeles: The Americas Group.

Harris, J., Golinkoff, R.M., & Hirsh-Pasek, K. (2011). Lessons from the crib for the classroom: How children really learn vocabulary. In S.B. Neuman & D.K. Dickinson (Eds.), *Handbook of early literacy research* (Vol. 3). New York: Guilford.

Harris, K.R., Graham, S., Brindle, M., & Sandmel, K. (2009). Metacognition and children's writing. In D.J. Hacker, J. Dunlosky, & A. Graesser (Eds.), *Handbook of metacognition in education.* New York: Elsevier.

Harris, P.L. (2000). *The work of the imagination.* New York: Oxford University Press.

Harris, P.L. (2006). Social cognition. In W. Damon & R. Lerner (Eds.), *Handbook of child psychology* (6th ed.). New York: Wiley.

Harris, R.A., Qualter, P., & Robinson, S.J. (2013). Loneliness trajectories from middle childhood to pre-adolescence: Impact on perceived health and sleep disturbance. *Journal of Adolescence, 36,* 1295–1304.

Harris, Y.R., & Graham, J.A. (2007). *The African American child.* New York: Springer.

Harrison, C. (2012). Aging: Telomerase gene therapy increases longevity. *Nature Reviews: Drug Discovery, 11,* 518.

Harrison, K., & McGee, H. (2014). Advance care planning in practice. *BMJ Supportive and Palliative Care, 4*(Suppl. 1), A87.

Harrist, A.W. (1993, March). *Family interaction styles as predictors of children's competence: The role of synchrony and nonsynchrony.* Paper presented at the biennial meeting of the Society for Research in Child Development, New Orleans.

Hart, B., & Risley, T.R. (1995). *Meaningful differences in the everyday experience of young Americans.* Baltimore: Paul H. Brookes.

Hart, C.H., Yang, C., Charlesworth, R., & Burts, D.C. (2003, April). *Early childhood teachers' curriculum beliefs, classroom practices, and children's outcomes: What are the connections?* Paper presented at the biennial meeting of the Society for Research in Child Development, Tampa, FL.

Hart, D. (2005). The development of moral identity. In G. Carlo & C.P. Edwards (Eds.), *Nebraska Symposium on Motivation* (Vol. 51). Lincoln, NE: University of Nebraska Press.

Hart, D., & Karmel, M.P. (1996). Self-awareness and self-knowledge in humans, great apes, and monkeys. In A. Russon, K. Bard, & S. Parker (Eds.), *Reaching into thought.* New York: Cambridge University Press.

Hart, D., & Matsuba, M.K. (2010). Urban neighborhoods as contexts for moral identity development. In D. Narváez & D.K. Lapsley (Eds.), *Moral personality, identity, and character.* New York: Cambridge University Press.

Hart, D., Matsuba, M.K., & Atkins, R. (2008). The moral and civic effects of learning to serve. In L. Nucci & D. Narváez (Eds.), *Handbook of moral and character education.* Clifton, NJ: Psychology Press.

Hart, D., Matsuba, M.K., & Atkins, R. (2014). The moral and civic effects of learning to serve. In L. Nucci, T. Krettenauer, & D. Narváez (Eds.), *Handbook of moral and character education* (2nd ed.). New York: Routledge.

Hart, D., Richardson, C., & Wilkenfeld, B. (2011). Citizenship and civic identity. In S. Schwartz, K. Luyckx, & V. Fignoles (Eds.), *Handbook of identity theory and research.* New York: Springer.

Hart, D., Watson, N.C., Dar, A., & Atkins, R. (2011). Prosocial tendencies, antisocial behavior, and moral development in childhood. In A. Slater & G. Bremner (Eds.), *Introduction to developmental psychology* (2nd ed.). Oxford, UK: Blackwell.

Hart, S., & Behrens, K.Y. (2013). Regulation of jealousy protest in the context of reunion following differential treatment. *Infancy, 18,* 1076–1110.

Hart, S., & Carrington, H. (2002). Jealousy in 6-month-old infants. *Infancy, 3,* 395–402.

Hart, S., Carrington, H., Tronick, E.Z., & Carroll, S.R. (2004). When infants lose exclusive maternal attention: Is it jealousy? *Infancy, 6,* 57–78.

Harter, S. (1981). A new self-report scale of intrinsic versus extrinsic orientation in the classroom: Motivational and informational components. *Development Psychology, 17,* 300–312.

Harter, S. (1986). Processes underlying the construction, maintenance, and enhancement of the self-concept of children. In J. Suls & A. Greenwald (Eds.), *Psychological perspectives on the self* (Vol. 3). Hillsdale, NJ: Erlbaum.

Harter, S. (1990). Processes underlying adolescent self-concept formation. In R. Montemayor, G.R. Adams, & T.P. Gullotta (Eds.), *From childhood to adolescence: A transitional period?* Newbury Park, CA: Sage.

Harter, S. (1996). Teacher and classmate influences on scholastic motivation, self-esteem, and level of voice in adolescents. In J. Juvonen & K.R. Wentzel (Eds.), *Social motivation.* New York: Cambridge University Press.

Harter, S. (1999). *The construction of the self.* New York: Guilford.

Harter, S. (2006). The self. In W. Damon & R. Lerner (Eds.), *Handbook of child psychology* (6th ed.). New York: Wiley.

Harter, S. (2012). *The construction of the self* (2nd ed.). New York: Wiley.

Harter, S. (2013). The development of self-esteem. In M.H. Kernis (Ed.), *Self-esteem issues and answers.* New York: Psychology Press.

Hartman, S., & Belsky, J. (2015). An evolutionary perspective on developmental plasticity: Differential susceptibility to environmental influences. In R. Scott & S. Kosslyn (Eds.), *Emerging trends in the social and behavioral sciences.* New York: Wiley.

Hartshorne, H., & May, M.S. (1928–1930). *Moral studies in the nature of character. Studies in deceit* (Vol. 1); *Studies in self-control* (Vol. 2); *Studies in the organization of character* (Vol. 3). New York: Macmillan.

Hartup, W.W. (1983). The peer system. In P.H. Mussen (Ed.), *Handbook of child psychology* (4th ed., Vol. 4). New York: Wiley.

Hartup, W.W. (2009). Critical issues and theoretical viewpoints. In K.H. Rubin, W.M. Bukowski, & B. Laursen (Eds.), *Handbook of peer interactions, relationships, and groups.* New York: Guilford.

Hasher, L. (2003, February 28). Commentary in "The wisdom of the wizened," *Science, 299,* 1300–1302.

Hasher, L., Chung, C., May, C.P., & Foong, N. (2001). Age, time of testing, and proactive interference. *Canadian Journal of Experimental Psychology, 56,* 200–207.

Hashim, H.A., Freddy, G., & Rosmatunisah, A. (2012). Relationships between negative affect and academic achievement among secondary school students: The mediating effects of habituated exercise. *Journal of Physical Activity and Health, 9,* 1012–1019.

Hastie, A.R., & others (2013). Rapid genome mapping in nanochannel arrays for highly complete and accurate de novo sequence assembly of the complex aegilops tauschii genome. *PLoS One 8*(2), e55864.

Hattery, A.J., & Smith, E. (2007). *African American families.* Thousand Oaks, CA: Sage.

Hatton, H., & others (2008). Family and individual difference predictors of trait aspects of negative interpersonal behaviors during emerging adulthood. *Journal of Family Psychology, 22,* 448–455.

Hatzfeld, J.J., Laveist, T.A., & Gaston-Johansson, F.G. (2012). Racial/ethnic disparities in the prevalence of selected chronic diseases among U.S. Air Force members, 2008. *Preventing Chronic Disease.* doi:10.5888/pcd9.110136.

Haugrud, N., Crossley, M., & Vrbancic, M. (2011). Clustering and switching strategies during verbal fluency performance differentiate Alzheimer's disease and healthy aging. *Journal of the International Alzheimer's Society, 17,* 1153–1157.

Hawi, Z., & others (2015, in press). The molecular genetic architecture of attention deficit hyperactivity disorder. *Molecular Psychiatry.*

Hawkes, C. (2006). Olfaction in neurodegenerative disorder. *Advances in Otorhinolaryngology, 63,* 133–151.

Hawkley, L.C., & Cacioppo, J.T. (2013). Social connection and relationships in successful aging. In J.M. Rippe (Ed.), *Encyclopedia of lifestyle medicine and health.* Thousand Oaks, CA: Sage.

Hayashino, D., & Chopra, S.B. (2009). Parenting and raising families. In N. Tewari & A. Alvarez (Eds.), *Asian American psychology.* Clifton, NJ: Psychology Press.

Haydon, A., & Halpern, G.T. (2010). Older romantic partners and depressive symptoms during adolescence. *Journal of Youth and Adolescence, 39,* 1240–1251.

Haydon, A.A., Herring, A.H., Prinstein, M.J., & Halpern, C.T. (2012). Beyond age at first sex: Patterns of emerging sexual behavior in adolescence and young adulthood. *Journal of Adolescent Health, 50,* 456–463.

Haydon, K.C., Collins, W.A., Salvatore, J.E., Simpson, J.A., & Roisman, G.I. (2012). Shared and distinctive origins and correlates of adult attachment representations: The developmental organization of romantic functioning. *Child Development, 83,* 1689–1702.

Hayflick, L. (1977). The cellular basis for biological aging. In C.E. Finch & L. Hayflick (Eds.), *Handbook of the biology of aging.* New York: Van Nostrand.

Hayslip, B., & Hansson, R. (2003). Death awareness and adjustment across the life span. In C.D. Bryant (Ed.), *Handbook of death and dying.* Thousand Oaks, CA: Sage.

Hayutin, A., Beals, M., & Borges, E. (2013). *The aging laborforce.* Palo Alto, CA: Stanford Center on Longevity.

Hayward, R.D., & Krause, N. (2013a). Changes in church-based social support relationships during older adulthood. *Journals of Gerontology B: Psychological Sciences and Social Sciences, 68,* 85–96.

Hayward, R.D., & Krause, N. (2013b). Patterns of change in religious service attendance across the life course: Evidence from a 34-year longitudinal study. *Social Science Research, 42,* 1480–1489.

Hazan, C., & Shaver, P.R. (1987). Romantic love conceptualized as an attachment process. *Journal of Personality and Social Psychology, 52,* 522–524.

He, K., & others (2014). ITIH family genes confer risk to schizophrenia and major depressive disorder in the Han Chinese population. *Progress in Neuro-psychopharmacology and biological psychiatry, 51,* 34–38.

Healey, M.K., Campbell, K.L., Hasher, L., & Ossher, L. (2010). Direct evidence for the role of inhibition in resolving interference. *Psychological Science, 21*(10), 1464–1470.

Healey, M.K., & Hasher, L. (2009). Limitations to the deficit attenuation hypothesis: Aging and decision making. *Journal of Consumer Psychology, 19,* 17–22.

Heard, E., & others (2011). Mediating effects of social support on the relationship among perceived stress, depression, and hypertension in African Americans. *Journal of the National Medical Association, 103,* 116 122.

Heath, S.M., & others (2014). A spotlight on preschool: The influence of family factors on children's early literacy skills. *PLoS One, 9,* e95255.

Heberle, A.E., & Carter, A.S. (2015, in press). Cognitive aspects of young children's experience of economic disadvantage. *Psychological Bulletin.*

Hegele, R.A., & others (2015, in press). Targeted next-generation sequencing in monogenic dyslipidemias. *Current Opinion in Lipidology.*

Heiman, G.W. (2014). *Basic statistics for the behavioral sciences* (7th ed.). Boston: Cengage.

Heiman, G.W. (2015). *Behavioral sciences STAT* (2nd ed.). Boston: Cengage.

Heimann, M., & others (2006). Exploring the relation between memory, gestural communication, and the emergence of language in infancy: A longitudinal study. *Infant and Child Development, 75,* 233–249.

Heisel, M.J. (2006). Suicide and its prevention in older adults. *Canadian Journal of Psychiatry, 51,* 143–154.

Helles, A., Gillberg, C.L., Gillberg, C., & Bilistedt, E. (2015, in press). Asperger syndrome in males over two decades: Stability and predictors of diagnosis. *Journal of Child Psychology and Psychiatry.*

Helman, R., Copeland, C., & VanDerhei, J. (2012). The 2012 Retirement Confidence Survey: Job insecurity, debt weigh on retirement confidence, savings. *EBRI Issue Brief, 369,* 5–32.

Helman, R., VanDerhei, J., & Copeland, C. (2007). The retirement system in transition: The 2007 Retirement Confidence Survey. *Employment Benefit Research Institute Issue Brief, 304*(1), 4–24.

Helmuth, L. (2003). The wisdom of the wizened. *Science, 299,* 1300–1302.

Helson, R. (1997, August). *Personality change: When is it adult development?* Paper presented at the meeting of the American Psychological Association, Chicago.

Helson, R., & Wink, P. (1992). Personality change in women from the early 40s to early 50s. *Psychology and Aging, 7,* 46–55.

Henderson, J., & others (2014). Laboring women who used a birthing pool in obstetric units in Italy: Prospective observational study. *BMC Pregnancy and Childbirth, 14*(1), 17.

Henderson, V.W. (2011). Gonadal hormones and cognitive aging: A midlife perspective. *Women's Health, 7,* 81–93.

Hendricks-Munoz, K.D., & others (2013). Maternal and neonatal nurse perceived value of kangaroo mother care and maternal care partnership in the Neonatal Intensive Care Unit. *American Journal of Perinatology 30*(10), 875–880.

Henneberger, A.K., Durkee, M.I., Truong, N., Atkins, A., & Tolan, P.H. (2013). The longitudinal relationship between peer violence and popularity and delinquency in adolescent boys: Examining effects by family functioning. *Journal of Youth and Adolescence, 42,* 1651–1660.

Hennessey, B. (2011). Intrinsic motivation and creativity: Have we come full circle? In R.A. Beghetto & J.C. Kaufman (Eds.), *Nurturing creativity in the classroom.* New York: Cambridge University Press.

Henninger, D.E., Madden, D.J., & Huettel, S.A. (2010). Processing speed and memory mediate age-related differences in decision making. *Psychology and Aging, 25,* 262–270.

Henretta, J.C. (2010). Lifetime marital history and mortality after age 50. *Journal of Aging and Health, 22*(8), 1198–1212.

Henricks, T.S. (2015a). Classical theories of play. In J.E. Johnson & others (Eds.), *Handbook of the study of play.* Blue Ridge Summit, PA: Rowan & Littlefield.

Henricks, T.S. (2015b). Modern theories of play. In J.E. Johnson & others (Eds.), *Handbook of the study of play.* Blue Ridge Summit, PA: Rowan & Littlefield.

Hensel, D.J., & Sorge, B.H. (2014). Adolescent women's daily academic behaviors, sexual behaviors, and sexually related emotions. *Journal of Adolescent Health, 55,* 845–847.

Hensley, V. (2013). Childhood bullying: A review and implications for health care professionals. *Nursing Clinics of North America, 48,* 203–213.

Herbers, J.E., & others (2011). Direct and indirect effects of parenting on academic functioning of young homeless children. *Early Education and Development, 22,* 77–104.

Herman, K.M., & others (2015). Correlates of sedentary behavior in 8- to 10-year-old children at elevated risk for obesity. *Applied Physiology, Nutrition, and Metabolism, 40,* 10–19.

Herman-Giddens, M.E., & others (2012). Secondary sex characteristics in boys: Data from the pediatric research in office settings network. *Pediatrics, 130,* e1058–e1068.

Hernandez, S.S., & others (2015, in press). What are the benefits of exercise for Alzheimer's disease? A systematic review of past 10 years. *Journal of Aging and Physical Activity.*

Hernandez-Reif, M., Diego, M., & Field, T. (2007). Preterm infants show reduced stress behaviors and activity after 5 days of massage therapy. *Infant Behavior and Development, 30,* 557–561.

Heron, M. (2013, December 20). Deaths: Leading causes for 2010. *National Vital Statistics Reports, 62*(6), 1–96.

Herres, J., & Kobak, R. (2015). The role of parent, teacher, and peer events in maintaining depressive symptoms during early adolescence. *Journal of Abnormal Child Psychology, 43,* 325–337.

Herting, M.M., Colby, J.B., Sowell, E.R., & Nagel, B.J. (2014). White matter connectivity and aerobic fitness in male adolescents. *Developmental Cognitive Neuroscience, 7,* 65–75.

Hertzog, C., & Dixon, R.A. (2005). Metacognition in midlife. In S.L. Willis & M. Martin (Eds.), *Middle adulthood: A lifespan perspective.* Thousand Oaks, CA: Sage.

Hertzog, C., Kramer, A.F., Wilson, R.S., & Lindenberger, U. (2009). Enrichment effects on adult cognitive development. *Psychological Perspectives in the Public Interest, 9,* 1–65.

Hess, T.M., Auman, C., Colcombe, S.J., & Rahhal, T.A. (2003). The impact of stereotype threat on age differences in memory performance. *Journals of Gerontology: Psychological and Social Sciences, 58B,* P3–P11.

Hetherington, E.M. (1993). An overview of the Virginia Longitudinal Study of Divorce and Remarriage with a focus on early adolescence. *Journal of Family Psychology, 7,* 39–56.

Hetherington, E.M. (2006). The influence of conflict, marital problem solving, and parenting on children's adjustment in nondivorced, divorced, and remarried families. In A. Clarke-Stewart & J. Dunn (Eds.), *Families count.* New York: Cambridge University Press.

Hetherington, E.M., & Kelly, J. (2002). *For better or for worse: Divorce reconsidered.* New York: Norton.

Hetherington, E.M., & Stanley-Hagan, M. (2002). Parenting in divorced and remarried families. In M. Bornstein (Ed.), *Handbook of parenting* (2nd ed.). Mahwah, NJ: Erlbaum.

Heuwinkel, M.K. (1996). New ways of learning: Five new ways of teaching. *Childhood Education, 72,* 27–31.

Hewlett, B.S. (1991). *Intimate fathers.* Ann Arbor, MI: University of Michigan Press.

Hewlett, B.S. (2000). Culture, history and sex: Anthropological perspectives on father involvement. *Marriage and Family Review, 29,* 324–340.

Hewlett, B.S., & MacFarlan, S.J. (2010). Fathers' roles in hunter-gatherer and other small-scale cultures. In M.E. Lamb (Ed.), *The role of the father in child development* (5th ed.). New York: Wiley.

Heyes, C. (2014). Rich interpretations of infant behavior are popular, but are they valid? A reply to Scott and Baillargeon. *Developmental Science, 17,* 665–666.

Heyman, G.D., Fu, G., & Lee, K. (2013). Selective skepticism: American and Chinese children's reasoning about evaluative feedback. *Developmental Psychology, 49,* 543–553.

Hibell, B., Andersson, B., Bjarnasson, T., & others (2004). *The ESPAD report 2003: Alcohol and other drug use among students in 35 European countries.* The Swedish Council for Information on Alcohol and Other Drugs (CAN) and Council of Europe Pompidou Group.

Hickman, S.E., Keevern, E., & Hammes, B.J. (2015). Use of the physician orders for life-sustaining treatment program in the clinical setting: A systematic review of the literature. *Journal of the American Geriatrics Society, 63,* 341–350.

Highfield, R. (2008, April 30). *Harvard's baby brain research lab.* Retrieved on January 24, 2009, from www.telegraph.co.uk/scienceandtechnology/science/sciencenews/3341166/Harvard

Hill, J.P., & Lynch, M.E. (1983). The intensification of gender-related role expectations during early adolescence. In J. Brooks-Gunn & A.C. Petersen (Eds.), *Girls at puberty: Biological and psychosocial perspectives.* New York: Plenum Press.

Hill, P.C., & Butter, E.M. (1995). The role of religion in promoting physical health. *Journal of Psychology and Christianity, 14,* 141–155.

Hill, P.L., Nickel, L.B., & Roberts, B.W. (2014). Are you in a healthy relationship? Linking conscientiousness to health via implementing and immunizing behaviors. *Journal of Personality, 82,* 485–492.

Hill, P.L., Turiano, N.A., Mroczek, D.K., & Roberts, B.W. (2012). Examining concurrent and longitudinal relations between personality traits and social well-being in adulthood. *Social Psychological and Personality Science, 3*(6), 698–705.

Hill, P.L., & others (2014). Perceived social support predicts increased conscientiousness during older adulthood. *Journals of Gerontology B: Psychological Sciences and Social Sciences.*

Hill, T.D., Burdette, A.M., Angel, J.L., & Angel, R.J. (2006). Religious attendance and cognitive functioning among older Mexican Americans. *Journals of Gerontology B: Psychological Sciences and Social Sciences, 61,* P31–P39.

Hillemeier, M.M., Morgan, P.L., Farkas, G., & Maczuga, S.A. (2013). Quality disparities in child care for at-risk children: Comparing Head Start and non-Head Start settings. *Journal of Maternal and Child Health, 17*(1), 180–188.

Hilliard, L.J., & others (2014). Beyond the deficit model: Bullying and trajectories of character virtues in adolescence. *Journal of Youth and Adolescence, 43,* 991–1003.

Hillman, C.H., Erickson, K.I., & Kramer, A.F. (2008). Be smart, exercise your heart: Exercise effects on the brain and cognition. *Nature Reviews: Neuroscience, 9,* 58–65.

Hillman, C.H., & others (2014). Effects of the FITKids randomized controlled trial on executive control and brain function. *Pediatrics, 134,* e1063–e1071.

Hindman, A.H., Skibbek, L.E., Miller, A., & Zimmerman, M. (2010). Ecological contexts and early learning: Contributions of child, family, and classroom factors during Head Start to literacy and mathematics growth through first grade. *Early Childhood Research Quarterly, 25,* 235–250.

Hines, M. (2013). Sex and sex differences. In P.D. Zelazo (Ed.), *Oxford handbook of developmental psychology.* New York: Oxford University Press.

Hines, M. (2015). Gendered development. In R.M. Lerner (Ed.), *Handbook of child psychology and developmental science* (7th ed.). New York: Wiley.

Hinrichsen, G.A. (2006). Why multicultural issues matter for practitioners working with older adults. *Psychology and Aging, 37,* 29–35.

Hintsanen, M., & others (2014). Five-factor personality traits and sleep: Evidence from two population-based cohort studies. *Health Psychology, 33,* 214–233.

Hipwell, A.E., Stepp, S.D., Keenan, K., Chung, T., & Loeber, R. (2011). Brief report: Parsing the heterogeneity of adolescent girls' sexual behavior: Relationships to individual and interpersonal factors. *Journal of Adolescence, 34,* 589–592.

Hirsch, J.K., Wolford, K., Lalonde, S.M., Brunk, L., & Parker-Morris, A. (2009). Optimistic explanatory style as a moderator of the association between negative life events and suicide ideation. *Crisis, 30,* 48–53.

Hirsh-Pasek, K., & Golinkoff, R.M. (2014). Early language and literacy: Six principles. In S. Gilford (Ed.), *Head Start teacher's guide.* New York: Teacher's College Press.

Hirsh-Pasek, K., Golinkoff, R.M., Singer, D., & Berk, L. (2009). *A mandate for playful learning in preschool: Presenting the evidence.* New York: Oxford University Press.

Hjelmeland, H. (2011). Cultural context is crucial in suicide research and prevention. *Crisis, 32,* 61–64.

Hochberg, C., & others (2012). Association of vision loss in glaucoma and age-related macular degeneration with IADL disability. *Investigative Ophthalmology and Visual Science, 53,* 3201–3206.

Hock, R.R. (2013). *Human sexuality* (3rd ed.). Upper Saddle River, NJ: Prentice Hall.

Hodapp, R.M., Griffin, M.M., Burke, M., & Fisher, M.H. (2011). Intellectual disabilities. In R.J. Sternberg & S.B. Kaufman (Eds.), *Cambridge handbook of intelligence.* New York: Cambridge University Press.

Hodis, H.N., & Mack, W.J. (2014). Hormone replacement therapy and the association with coronary heart disease and overall mortality: Clinical application of the timing hypothesis. *Journal of Steroid Biochemistry and Molecular Biology, 142,* 68–75.

Hoefnagels, M. (2015). *Biology* (3rd ed.). New York: McGraw-Hill.

Hoeljmakers, L., Lucassen, P.J., & Korosi, A. (2015). The interplay of early-life stress, nutrition, and immune activation programs adults hippocampal structure and function. *Frontiers in Molecular Neuroscience, 7,* 103.

Hoelter, L. (2009). Divorce and separation. In D. Carr (Ed.), *Encyclopedia of the life course and human development.* Boston: Gale Cengage.

Hoeve, M., & others (2012). A meta-analysis of attachment to parents and delinquency. *Journal of Abnormal Child and Adolescent Psychology, 40,* 771–785.

Hofer, S.M., Rast, P., & Piccinin, A.M. (2012). Methodological issues in research on adult development and aging. In S.K. Whitbourne & M.J. Sliwinski (Eds.), *Wiley-Blackwell handbook of adult development and aging.* New York: Wiley.

Hoff, E. (2014). *Language development* (5th ed.). Boston: Cengage.

Hoff, E., Laursen, B., & Tardif, T. (2002). Socioeconomic status and parenting. In M.H. Bornstein (Ed.), *Handbook of parenting* (2nd ed.). Mahwah, NJ: Erlbaum.

Hoff, E., & Place, S. (2013). Bilingual language learners. In S.L. Odom, E. Pungello, & N. Gardner-Neblett (Eds.), *Re-visioning the beginning: Developmental and health science contributions to infant/toddler programs for children and families living in poverty.* New York: Guilford.

Hoffmeyer, K., & others (2012). Wnt/B-catenin signaling regulates telomerase in stem cells and cancer cells. *Science, 336,* 1549–1554.

Hogan, C. (2014). Socioeconomic factors affecting infant sleep-related deaths in St. Louis. *Public Health Nursing, 31,* 10–18.

Hogan, C.L., Mata, J., & Carstensen, L.L. (2013). Exercise holds immediate benefits for affect and cognition in younger and older adults. *Psychology and Aging, 28,* 587–594.

Hogerbrugge, M.J., & Komter, A.E. (2012). Solidarity and ambivalence: Comparing two perspectives on intergenerational relations using longitudinal panel data. *Journals of Gerontology B: Psychological Sciences and Social Sciences, 67,* 372–383.

Hoglund, K., & others (2015, in press). Alzheimer's disease—recent biomarker developments in relation to updated diagnostic criteria. *Clinical Chimca Acta.*

Holahan, C.J., & others (2012). Wine consumption and 20-year mortality among late-life moderate drinkers. *Journal of Studies in Alcohol and Drugs, 73,* 80–88.

Holden, G.W., Vittrup, B., & Rosen, L.H. (2011). Families, parenting, and discipline. In M.K. Underwood & L.H. Rosen (Eds.), *Social development.* New York: Guilford.

Holden, T.R., & others (2015, in press). Hospice enrollment, local hospice utilization patterns, and rehospitalization in Medicare patients. *Journal of Palliative Medicine.*

Hollams, E.M., de Klerk, N.H., Holt, P.G., & Sly, P.D. (2014). Persistent effects of maternal smoking during pregnancy on lung function and asthma in adolescents. *American Journal of Respiratory and Critical Care Medicine, 189,* 401–407.

Hollan, M. (2012). Compulsory vaccination, the constitution, and the hepatitis B mandate for infants and young children. *Yale Journal of Health Policy, Law, and Ethics, 12,* 39–86.

Holland, A.S., & Roisman, G.I. (2010). Adult attachment security and young adults' dating relationships over time: Self-reported, observational, and physiological evidence. *Developmental Psychology, 46,* 552–557.

Holland, J.M., & others (2014). The unique impact of late-life bereavement and prolonged grief on diurnal cortisol. *Journals of Gerontology B: Psychological Sciences and Social Sciences, 69,* 4–11.

Holland, M.G., & Cawthon, D. (2015). Personal protective equipment and decontamination of adults and children. *Emergency Medicine Clinics of North Americam, 33,* 51–68.

Hollis, J.F., & others (2008). Weight loss during the intensive intervention phase of the weight-loss maintenance trial. *American Journal of Preventive Medicine, 35,* 118–126.

Holloway, R.G., & others (2014). Palliative and end-of-life care in stroke: A statement for healthcare professionals from the American Heart Association/American Stroke Association. *Stroke, 45,* 1887–1916.

Holman, C., & de Villers-Sidani, E. (2014). Indestructible plastic: The neuroscience of the aging brain. *Frontiers in Human Neuroscience, 8,* 219.

Holme, A.M., & others (2015). Placental glucose transfer: A human in vivo study. *PLoS One, 10*(2), e117084.

Holmes, R.M., Little, K.C., & Welsh, D. (2009). Dating and romantic relationships, adulthood. In D. Carr (Ed.), *Encyclopedia of the life course and human development.* Boston: Gale Cengage.

Holmes, T.H., & Rahe, R.H. (1967). The social readjustment rating scale. *Journal of Psychosomatic Research, 11,* 213–218.

Holsen, I., Carlson Jones, D., & Skogbrott Birkeland, M. (2012). Body image satisfaction among Norwegian adolescents and young adults: A longitudinal study of interpersonal relationships and BMI. *Body Image, 9,* 201–208.

Hong, X., & others (2015). Normal aging selectivity diminishes alpha lateralization in visual spatial attention. *Neuroimage, 106,* 353–363.

Honzik, M.P., MacFarlane, I.W., & Allen, L. (1948). The stability of mental test performance between two and eighteen years. *Journal of Experimental Education, 17,* 309–324.

Hood, B.M. (1995). Gravity rules for 2- to 4-year-olds? *Cognitive Development, 10,* 577–598.

Hoogendam, Y.Y., & others (2014). Older age relates to worsening of fine motor skills: A population-based study of middle-aged and elderly persons. *Frontiers in Aging Neuroscience, 6,* 259.

Hoogendam, Y.Y., & others (2014). Patterns of cognitive functioning in aging: The Rotterdam Study. *European Journal of Epidemiology, 29,* 133–140.

Hooper, P.L., Gurven, M., Winking, J., & Kaplan, H.S. (2015, in press). Inclusive fitness and differential productivity across the life course determine intergenerational transfers in a small-scale human society. *Proceedings B: Biological Sciences.*

Hooyman, N.R., & Kiyak, H.A. (2011). *Social gerontology* (9th ed.). Upper Saddle River, NJ: Pearson.

Hooyman, N., Kiyak, H.A., & Kawamoto, K. (2015). *Aging matters.* Upper Saddle River, NJ: Pearson.

Hope, D.A. (2009). Contemporary perspectives on lesbian, gay, and bisexual identities: Introduction. *Nebraska Symposium on Motivation, 54,* 1–4.

Hopkins, B. (1991). Facilitating early motor development: An intercultural study of West Indian mothers and their infants living in Britain. In J.K. Nugent, B.M. Lester, & T.B. Brazelton (Eds.), *The cultural context of infancy, Vol. 2: Multicultural and interdisciplinary approaches to parent-infant relations.* New York: Ablex.

Hopkins, B., & Westra, T. (1990). Motor development, maternal expectations, and the role of handling. *Infant Behavior and Development, 13,* 117–122.

Hopwood, C.J., & others (2011). Genetic and environmental influences on personality trait stability and growth during the transition to adulthood: A three-wave longitudinal study. *Journal of Personality and Social Psychology, 100,* 545–556.

Horn, J. (2007). Spearman, *g,* expertise, and the nature of human cognitive capacity. In P.C. Kyllonen, R.D. Robberts, & L. Stankov (Eds.), *Extending intelligence.* Mahwah, NJ: Erlbaum.

Horn, J.L., & Donaldson, G. (1980). Cognitive development II: Adulthood development of human abilities. In O.G. Brim & J. Kagan (Eds.), *Constancy and change in human development.* Cambridge, MA: Harvard University Press.

Horn, L., & Nevill, S. (2006). *Profile of undergraduates in U.S. postsecondary education institutions: 2003–2004, with a special analysis of community college students* (NCES 2006-184). Washington, DC: National Center for Education Statistics.

Horne, R.S., Franco, P., Adamson, T.M., Groswasser, J., & Kahn, A. (2002). Effects of body position on sleep and arousal characteristics in infants. *Early Human Development, 69,* 25–33.

Horner, G. (2014). Child neglect: Assessment and intervention. *Journal of Pediatric Health Care, 28,* 186–192.

Horowitz, E.K. (2013). *Becoming a second language teacher* (2nd ed.). Boston: Allyn & Bacon.

Hospital for Sick Children & others (2010). *Infant sleep.* Toronto: Author.

Hostinar, C.E., & Gunnar, M.R. (2013). The developmental psychobiology of stress and emotion in childhood. In I.B. Weiner & others (Eds.), *Handbook of psychology* (2nd ed., Vol. 6). New York: Wiley.

Houde, O., & others (2011). Functional magnetic resonance imaging study of Piaget's conservation-of-number task in preschool and school-age children:A neo-Piagetian approach. *Journal of Experimental Child Psychology, 110*(3), 332–346.

Houser, J.J., Mayeux, L., & Cross, C. (2014). Peer status and aggression as predictors of dating popularity in adolescence. *Journal of Youth and Adolescence, 44,* 683–695.

Howard, A., & Rogers, A.N. (2014). Role of translation factor 4G in lifespan regulation and age-related health. *Aging Research Reviews, 13,* 115–124.

Howe, G.W., Homberger, A.P., Weihs, K., Moreno, F., & Neiderhiser, J.M. (2012). Higher-order structure in the trajectories of depression and anxiety following sudden involuntary unemployment. *Journal of Abnormal Psychology, 121,* 325–338.

Howe, M.J.A., Davidson, J.W., Moore, D.G., & Sloboda, J.A. (1995). Are there early childhood signs of musical ability? *Psychology of Music, 23,* 162–176.

Howe, M.L. (2015). An adaptive view of memory development. In R.M. Lerner (Ed.), *Handbook of child psychology and developmental science* (7th ed.). New York: Wiley.

Howe, N., Ross, H.S., & Recchia, H. (2011). Sibling relationships in early and middle childhood. In P.K. Smith & C.H. Hart (Eds.), *Wiley-Blackwell handbook of social development.* New York: Wiley.

Howell, D.C. (2014). *Fundamental statistics for the behavioral sciences* (8th ed.). Boston: Cengage.

Howerton, C.L., & Bale, T.L. (2012). Prenatal programming: At the intersection of maternal stress and immune activation. *Hormones and Behavior, 62*(3), 237–242.

Howes, C. (2009). Friendship in early childhood. In K.H. Rubin, W.M. Bukowski, & B. Laursen (Eds.), *Handbook of peer interactions, relationships, and groups.* New York: Guilford.

Hoyer, W.J. (2015, in press). Brain aging: Behavioral, cognitive, and personality consequences. In J.D. Wright (Ed.), *International encyclopedia of the social and behavioral sciences* (2nd ed.). New York; Elsevier.

Hoyer, W.J., & Roodin, P.A. (2009). *Adult development and aging* (6th ed.). New York: McGraw-Hill.

Hoyert, D.L., & Xu, J.X. (2012). Deaths: Preliminary data for 2011. *National Vital Statistics Reports, 61*(6), 1–52.

Hritcu, L., Stefan, M., Brandsch, R., & Mihasan, M. (2015). Enhanced behavioral response by decreasing brain oxidative stress to 6-hydroxy-1-nicotine in Alzheimer's disease rat model. *Neuroscience Letters, 591C,* 41–47.

HSBC Insurance (2007). *The future of retirement: The new age—global report.* London: HSBC.

Hsin, A., & Xie, Y. (2014). Explaining Asian Americans' academic advantage over whites. *Proceedings of the National Academy of Sciences U.S.A., 111*(23), 8416–8421.

Hsu, H.C. (2015, in press). Trajectories of multimorbidity and impacts on successful aging. *Experimental Gerontology.*

Hsu, H.C., Chang, W.C., Chong, Y.S., & An, J.S. (2015, in press). Happiness and social determinants across age cohorts in Taiwan. *Journal of Health Psychology.*

Hsuan, C., & Rodriguez, H.P. (2014). The adoption and discontinuation of clinical services by local health departments. *American Journal of Public Health, 104,* 124–133.

Hu, J.K., Wang, X., & Wang, P. (2014). Testing gene-gene interactions in genome-wide association studies. *Genetic Epidemiology, 38,* 123–134.

Huang, C.J., & others (2015, in press). A preliminary examination of aerobic exercise effects on resting EEG in children with ADHD. *Journal of Attention Disorders.*

Huang, H.W., Meyer, A.M., & Federmeier, K.D. (2012). A "concrete view" of aging: Event-related potentials reveal age-related changes in basic integrated processes in language. *Neuropsychologia, 50,* 26–35.

Huang, J.H., DeJong, W., Towvim, L.G., & Schneider, S.K. (2009). Sociodemographic and psychobehavioral characteristics of U.S. college students who abstain from alcohol. *Journal of American College Health, 57,* 395–410.

Huang, K., & others (2014). MetaRef: A pan-genomic database for comparative and community microbial genomics. *Nucleic Acids Research, 42,* D618–D624.

Huang, O.S., & others (2013). Lack of awareness of common eye conditions in the community. *Ophthalmic Epidemiology, 20,* 52–60.

Huang, P.M., Smock, P.J., Manning, W.D., & Bergstrom-Lynch, C.A. (2011). He says, she says: Gender and cohabitation. *Journal of Family Issues, 32,* 876–905.

Huang, Y., & Spelke, E. (2015). Core knowledge and the emergence of symbols: The case of maps. *Journal of Cognition and Development, 16,* 81–96.

Hudson, A., & Jacques, S. (2014). Put on a happy face! Inhibitory control and socioemotional knowledge predict emotion regulation in 5- to 7-year-olds. *Journal of Experimental Child Psychology, 123,* 36–52.

Hudson, N.W., Fraley, R.C., Brumbaugh, C.C., & Vicary, A.M. (2014). Coregulation in romantic partners' attachment styles: A longitudinal investigation. *Personality and Social Psychology Bulletin, 40,* 845–857.

Huerta, M., Cortina, L.M., Pang, J.S., Torges, C.M., & Magley, V.J. (2006). Sex and power in the academy: Modeling sexual harassment in the lives of college women. *Personality and Social Psychology Bulletin, 32,* 616–628.

Hugel, H., Gavin, C., Mitchell, C., & Edwards, D. (2014). Hospice at home services—the importance of integration and medical support. *BMJ Supportive and Palliative Care* (Suppl. 1), A90–A91.

Hughes, C., & Devine, R.T. (2015). Individual differences in theory of mind: A social perspective. In R.M. Lerner (Ed.), *Handbook of child psychology and developmental science* (7th ed.). New York: Wiley.

Hughes, J.P., McDowell, M.A., & Brody, D.J. (2008). Leisure-time physical activity among U.S. adults 60 or more years of age: Result from NHANES 1999–2004. *Journal of Physical Activity and Health, 5,* 347–358.

Hughes, M.E., Waite, L.J., LaPierre, T.A., & Luo, Y. (2007). All in the family: The impact of caring for grandchildren on grandparents' health. *Journals of Gerontology B: Psychological Sciences and Social Sciences, 62*(2), S108–S119.

Hughes, P.C. (1978). In J.L. Fozard & S.J. Popkin, Optimizing adult development: Ends and means of an applied psychology of aging. *American Psychologist, 33,* 975–989.

Hull, J. (2012). A self-awareness model of the causes and effects of alcohol consumption. In K. Vohs & R.F. Baumeister (Eds.), *Self and identity.* Thousand Oaks, CA: Sage.

Hultsch, D.F., Hertzog, C., Small, B.J., & Dixon, R.A. (1999). Use it or lose it: Engaged lifestyle as a buffer of cognitive decline in aging? *Psychology and Aging, 14,* 245–263.

Hultsch, D.F., & Plemons, J.K. (1979). Life events and life-span development. In P.B. Baltes & O.G. Brim (Eds.), *Life-span development and behavior.* New York: Academic Press.

Hunt, E. (1995). *Will we be smart enough? A cognitive analysis of the coming work force.* New York: Russell Sage.

Hunt, S.R., Corazzini, K., & Anderson, R.A. (2014). Top nurse-management staffing and care quality in nursing homes. *Journal of Applied Gerontology, 33,* 51–74.

Hunter, K.I., & Linn, M.W. (1980). Psychosocial differences between elderly volunteers and non-volunteers. *International Journal of Aging and Human Development, 12,* 205–213.

Hur, K., Liang, J., & Lin, S.Y. (2014). The role of secondhand smoke in allergic rhinitis: A systematic review. *International Forum of Allergy and Rhinology, 4,* 110–116.

Hurt, H., Brodsky, N.L., Roth, H., Malmud, F., & Giannetta, J.M. (2005). School performance of children with gestational cocaine exposure. *Neurotoxicology and Teratology, 27,* 203–211.

Hustedt, J.T., Friedman, A.H., & Barnett, W.S. (2012). Investments in early education: Resources at the federal and state levels. In R.C. Pianta (Ed.), *Handbook of early childhood education.* New York: Guilford.

Huston, A.C., & Ripke, M.N. (2006). Experiences in middle childhood and children's development: A summary and integration of research. In A.C. Huston & M.N. Ripke (Eds.), *Developmental contexts in middle childhood.* New York: Cambridge University Press.

Huston, A.C., & others (2006). Effects of a poverty intervention program last from middle childhood to adolescence. In A.C. Huston & M.N. Ripke (Eds.), *Developmental contexts of middle childhood: Bridge to adolescence and adulthood.* New York: Cambridge University Press.

Hutchinson, S.L., & Nimrod, G. (2012). Leisure as a resource for successful aging by older adults with chronic health conditions. *International Journal of Aging and Human Development, 74,* 41–65.

Hutson, J.R., & others (2013). Adverse placental effect of formic acid on hCG secretion is mitigated by folic acid. *Alcohol and Alcoholism, 48,* 283–287.

Huttenlocher, J., Haight, W., Bruk, A., Seltzer, M., & Lyons, T. (1991). Early vocabulary growth: Relation to language input and gender. *Developmental Psychology, 27,* 236–248.

Huttenlocher, P.R., & Dabholkar, A.S. (1997). Regional differences in synaptogenesis in human cerebral cortex. *Journal of Comparative Neurology, 37*(2), 167–178.

Huxhold, O., Miche, M., & Schüz, B. (2014). Benefits of having friends in older ages: Differential effects of informal social activities on well-being in middle-aged and older adults. *Journals of Gerontology B: Psychological Sciences and Social Sciences, 69,* 366–375.

Huyck, M.H. (1995). Marriage and close relationships of the marital kind. In R. Blieszner & V.H. Bedford (Eds.), *Handbook of aging and the family.* Westport, CT: Greenwood Press.

Hwang, A.C., & others (2014). Predicting all-cause and cause-specific mortality by static and dynamic measurements of allostatic load: A 10-year population-based cohort study in Taiwan. *Journal of the American Medical Directors Association, 15,* 490–496.

Hwang, I.C., & others (2015). Statin therapy is associated with lower all-cause mortality in patients with non-obstructive coronary artery disease. *Atherosclerosis, 239,* 335–342.

Hwang, J.Y., & others (2012). Multidimensional comparison of personality characteristics of the Big Five model, impulsiveness, and affect in pathological gambling and obsessive-compulsive disorder. *Journal of Gambling Studies, 28,* 351–362.

Hwang, K., & Miner, M. (2015). Controversies in testosterone replacement therapy: Testosterone and cardiovascular disease. *Asian Journal of Andrology, 17,* 187–191.

Hyde, J.S. (2005). The gender similarities hypothesis. *American Psychologist, 60,* 581–592.

Hyde, J.S. (2007). *Half the human experience* (7th ed.). Boston: Houghton Mifflin.

Hyde, J.S. (2014). Gender similarities and differences. *Annual Review of Psychology* (Vol. 65). Palo Alto, CA: Annual Reviews.

Hyde, J.S., & DeLamater, J.D. (2014). *Understanding human sexuality* (12th ed.). New York: McGraw-Hill.

Hyde, J.S., & Else-Quest, N. (2013). *Half the human experience* (8th ed.). Boston: Cengage.

Hyde, J.S., Krajnik, M., & Skuldt-Niederberger, K. (1991). Androgyny across the life span: A replication and longitudinal follow-up. *Developmental Psychology, 27,* 516–519.

Hyde, J.S., Lindberg, S.M., Linn, M.C., Ellis, A.B., & Williams, C.C. (2008). Gender similarities characterize math performance. *Science, 321,* 494–495.

Hyde, Z., & others (2012). Prevalence and predictors of sexual problems in men aged 75–95 years: A population-based study. *Journal of Sexual Medicine, 9,* 442–453.

Hymel, S., Closson, L.M., Caravita, C.S., & Vaillancourt, T. (2011). Social status among peers: From sociometric attraction to peer acceptance to perceived popularity. In P.K. Smith & C.H. Hart (Eds.), *Wiley-Blackwell handbook of childhood social development* (2nd ed.). New York: Wiley.

Hysing, M., & others (2015). Sleep and school attendance in adolescence: Results from a large population-based study. *Scandinavian Journal of Public Health, 43,* 2–9.

Hyson, M.C., Copple, C., & Jones, J. (2006). Early childhood development and education. In W. Damon & R. Lerner (Eds.), *Handbook of child psychology* (6th ed.). New York: Wiley.

I

Ibrahim, J.E., MacPhail, A., Winbolt, M., & Grano, P. (2015, in press). Limitation of care orders in patients with a diagnosis of dementia. *Resuscitation.*

Ibrahim, R., & Eviatar, Z. (2012). The contribution of two hemispheres to lexical decision in different languages. *Behavioral and Brain Functions, 8,* 3.

"I Have a Dream" Foundation (2015). *About us.* Retrieved October 10, 2015, from http://www.ihad.org

Ickovics, J.R., & others (2011). Effects of group prenatal care on psychosocial risk in pregnancy: Results from a randomized controlled trial. *Psychology and Health, 26,* 235–250.

Idler, E. (2006). Religion and aging. In R.H. Binstock & L.K. George (Eds.), *Handbook of aging and the social sciences* (6th ed.). San Diego: Academic Press.

Igarashi, H., Hooker, K., Coehlo, D.P., & Maoogian, M.M. (2013). "My nest is full":

Intergenerational relationships at midlife. *Journal of Aging Studies, 27,* 102–112.

Ige, F., & Shelton, D. (2004). Reducing the risk of sudden infant death syndrome (SIDS) in African-American communities. *Journal of Pediatric Nursing, 19,* 290–292.

Ikeda, A., & others (2013). Social support and cancer incidence and mortality: The JPHC study cohort II. *Cancer Causes and Control, 24,* 847–860.

Inelmen, E.M., & others (2012). The importance of sexual health in the elderly: Breaking down barriers and taboos. *Aging: Clinical and Experimental Research, 24*(Suppl. 3), S31–S34.

International Montessori Council (2006). Larry Page and Sergey Brin, founders of Google.com, credit their Montessori education for much of their success on prime-time television. Retrieved June 24, 2006, from http://www.Montessori.org/enews/Barbara_walters.html

Ip, S., Chung, M., Raman, G., Trikalinos, T.A., & Lau, J. (2009). A summary of the Agency for Healthcare Research and Quality's evidence report on breastfeeding in developed countries. *Breastfeeding Medicine, 4*(Suppl. 1), S17–S30.

Irwin, C.E. (2010). Young adults are worse off than adolescents. *Journal of Adolescent Health, 46,* 405–406.

Isella, V., & others (2008). Age-related quantitative and qualitative changes in decision-making ability. *Behavioral Neurology, 19,* 59–63.

Ishak, S., Franchak, J.M., & Adolph, K.E. (2014). Fear of height in infants. *Current Directions in Psychological Science, 23,* 60–66.

Isidori, A.M., & others (2014). A critical analysis of the role of testosterone in erectile function: From pathophysiology to treatment—a systematic analysis. *European Urology, 65*(1), 99–112.

Isingrini, M., Perrotin, A., & Souchay, C. (2008). Aging, metamemory regulation, and executive functioning. *Progress in Brain Research, 169,* 377–392.

Ivan Santini, Z., Koyanagi, A., Tyrovolas, S., & Haro, J.M. (2015). The association of relationship quality and social networks with depression, anxiety, and suicidal ideation among older married adults: Findings from a cross-sectional analysis of the Irish Longitudinal Study on Aging (TILDA). *Journal of Affective Disorders, 179,* 134–141.

Iverson, K.M., King, M.W., Cunningham, K.C., & Resick, P.A. (2015). Rape survivors' trauma-related beliefs before and after cognitive processing therapy: Associations with PTSD and depression symptoms. *Behavior Research and Therapy.*

Iwasaki, Y. (2008). Pathways to meaning-making through leisure-like pursuits in global contexts. *Journal of Leisure Research, 40,* 231–249.

Iwata, S., & others (2012). Qualitative brain MRI at term and cognitive outcomes at 9 years after very preterm birth. *Pediatrics, 129,* e1138–1147.

Izard, C.E., & others (2008). Accelerating the development of emotional competence in Head Start children: Effects on adaptive and maladaptive behavior. *Development and Psychopathology, 20,* 369–397.

J

Jackson, A.M., & Deve, K. (2015, in press). Aspects of abuse: Consequences of childhood victimization. *Current Problems in Pediatric and Adolescent Health Care.*

Jackson, A.M., Kissoon, N., & Greene, C. (2015, in press). Aspects of abuse: Recognizing and responding to child maltreatment. *Current Problems in Pediatric and Adolescent Health Care.*

Jackson, J.S., Govia, I.O., & Sellers, S.L. (2011). Racial and ethnic influences over the life course. In

R.H. Binstock & L.K. George (Eds.), *Handbook of aging and the social sciences* (7th ed.). New York: Elsevier.

Jackson, M.I. (2015). Early childhood WIC participation, cognitive development and academic achievement. *Social Science and Medicine, 126,* 145–153.

Jackson, S.L. (2016, in press). *Research methods* (5th ed.). Boston: Cengage.

Jacob, J.I. (2009). The socioemotional effects of non maternal childcare on children in the USA: Critical review of recent studies. *Early Child Development and Care, 179,* 559–570.

Jacob, R., & others (2014). Daily hassles' role in health seeking behavior among low-income populations. *American Journal of Health Behavior, 38,* 297–306.

Jacobs, J.M., Hammerman-Rozenberg, R., Cohen, A., & Stressman, J. (2008). Reading daily predicts reduced mortality among men from a cohort of community-dwelling 70-year-olds. *Journals of Gerontology B: Psychological Sciences and Social Sciences, 63,* S73–S80.

Jacobs-Lawson, J.M., Hershey, D.A., & Neukam, K.A. (2005). Gender differences in factors that influence time spent planning for retirement. *Journal of Women and Aging, 16,* 55–69.

Jacobson, L.A., & others (2011). Working memory influences processing speed and reading fluency in ADHD. *Child Neuropsychology, 17*(3), 209–224.

Jaffee, S., & Hyde, J.S. (2000). Gender differences in moral orientation: A meta-analysis. *Psychological Bulletin, 126,* 703–726.

Jak, A.J. (2012). The impact of physical and mental activity on cognitive aging. *Current Topics in Behavioral Neurosciences, 10,* 273–291.

Jalles, J.T., & Andresen, M.A. (2014). Suicide and unemployment: A panel analysis of Canadian provinces. *Archives of Suicide Research, 18,* 14–27.

James, J.E., Kristijansson, A.L., & Sigfusdottir, I.D. (2011). Adolescence substance use, sleep, and academic achievement: Evidence of harm due to caffeine. *Journal of Adolescence, 34,* 665–673.

James, S. (2014). Longitudinal patterns of women's marital quality: The case of divorce, cohabitation, and race-ethnicity. *Marriage and Family Review, 50,* 738–763.

James, W. (1890/1950). *The principles of psychology.* New York: Dover.

Jan, J.E., & others (2010). Long-term sleep disturbances in children: A cause of neuronal loss. *European Journal of Pediatric Neurology, 14,* 380–390.

Jankowski, T., & Holas, P. (2014). Metacognitive model of mindfulness. *Consciousness and Cognition, 28C,* 64–80.

Jansen, A.G., & others (2015, in press). What twin studies tell us about the heritability of brain development, morphology, and function: A review. *Neuropsychology Review.*

Janssen, I. (2014). Active play: An important physical activity strategy in the fight against childhood obesity. *Canadian Journal of Public Health, 105,* e22–e27.

Janssen, I., & others (2005). Comparison of overweight and obesity prevalence in school-aged youth from 34 countries and their relationships with physical activity and dietary patterns. *Obesity Reviews, 6,* 123–132.

Janz, K.F., & others (2015). Top 10 research questions related to physical activity and bone health in children and adolescents. *Research Quarterly for Exercise and Sport, 86,* 5–12.

Jardri, R., & others (2012). Assessing fetal response to maternal speech using a noninvasive functional brain imaging technique. *International Journal of Developmental Neuroscience, 30,* 159–161.

Jaremka, L.M., & others (2014). Pain, depression, and fatigue: Loneliness as a longitudinal risk factor. *Health Psychology, 33,* 948–957.

Jarosinska, D., Polanska, K., Wityniak, B., & Hanke, W. (2014). Towards estimating the burden of disease attributable to second-hand smoke exposure in Polish children. *International Journal of Occupational Medicine and Environmental Health, 27,* 38–49.

Jarrett, R.L. (1995). Growing up poor: The family experiences of socially mobile youth in low-income African-American neighborhoods. *Journal of Adolescent Research, 10,* 111–135.

Jencks, C. (1979). *Who gets ahead? The determinants of economic success in America.* New York: Basic Books.

Jenkins, J.M., & Astington, J.W. (1996). Cognitive factors and family structure associated with theory of mind development in young children. *Developmental Psychology, 32,* 70–78.

Jensen, M.M., & others (2015). Prostate stem cell antigen interacts with nicotinic acetylcholine receptors and is affected in Alzheimer's disease. *Neurobiology of Aging, 36*(4), 1629–1638.

Jensen-Campbell, L.A., & Malcolm, K.T. (2007). The importance of conscientiousness in adolescent interpersonal relationships. *Personality and Social Psychology Bulletin, 33,* 368–383.

Ji, B.T., & others (1997). Parental cigarette smoking and the risk of childhood cancer among the offspring of nonsmoking mothers. *Journal of the National Cancer Institute, 89,* 238–244.

Jia, R., & Schoppe-Sullivan, S.J. (2011). Relations between coparenting and father involvement in families with preschool-age children. *Developmental Psychology, 47,* 106–118.

Jiang, H.Y., & others (2014). Diffusion of two botulinum toxins type A on the forehead: Double-blinded, randomized, controlled study. *Dermatologic Surgery, 40,* 184–192.

Jin, D., & Lee, H. (2015). A computational approach to identifying gene-microRNA modules in cancer. *PLoS Computational Biology, 11*(1), e1004042.

Jin, M.K., Jacobvitz, D., Hagen, N., & Jung, S.H. (2012). Maternal sensitivity and infant attachment security in Korea: Cross-cultural validation of the Strange Situation. *Attachment and Human Development, 14,* 33–44.

Jinesh, S. (2015, in press). Pharmaceutical aspects of anti-inflammatory TNF-blocking drugs. *Inflammopharmacology.*

Job, V., Dweck, C.S., & Walton, G.M. (2010). Ego-depletion—Is it all in your head? Implicit theories about willpower affect self-regulation. *Psychological Science, 21,* 1686–1693.

Job, V., Walton, G.M., Bernecker, K., & Dweck, C.S. (2015, in press). Implicit theories about willpower predict self-regulation and grades in everyday life. *Journal of Personality and Social Psychology.*

Joh, A.S., Jaswal, V.K., & Keen, R. (2011). Imaging a way out of the gravity bias: Preschoolers can visualize the solution to a spatial problem. *Child Development, 82,* 744–750.

Johansson, M., Forssman, L., & Bohlin, G. (2014). Individual differences in 10-month-olds' performance on the A-not-B task. *Scandinavian Journal of Psychology, 55,* 130–135.

Johnson, G.B. (2015). *The living world* (8th ed.). New York: McGraw-Hill.

Johnson, J.E., Eberle, S.G., Henricks, T.S., & Kuschner, D. (Eds.) (2015). *Handbook of the study of play.* Blue Ridge Summit, PA: Rowan & Littlefield.

Johnson, J.S., & Newport, E.L. (1991). Critical period effects on universal properties of language: The status of subjacency in the acquisition of a second language. *Cognition, 39,* 215–258.

Johnson, K.J., & Mutchler, J.E. (2014). The emergence of positive gerontology: From disengagement to social involvement. *Gerontologist, 54,* 93–100.

Johnson, L., Giordano, P.C., Manning, W.D., & Longmore, M.A. (2011). Parent-child elations and offending during young adulthood. *Journal of Youth and Adolescence, 40*(7), 786–799.

Johnson, M. (2008, April 30). Commentary in R. Highfield, *Harvard's baby brain research lab.* Retrieved January 24, 2008, from http://www.telegraph.co.uk/scienceandtechnology/science/sciencenews/3341166/Harvards-baby-brain-research-labl.html

Johnson, M.H., Grossmann, T., & Cohen-Kadosh, K. (2009). Mapping functional brain development: Building a social brain through interactive specialization. *Developmental Psychology, 45,* 151–159.

Johnson, M.H., Jones, E., & Gliga, T. (2015, in press). Brain adaptation and alternative developmental trajectories. *Development and Psychopathology.*

Johnson, S.P. (2004). Development of perceptual completion in infancy. *Psychological Science, 15,* 769–775.

Johnson, S.P. (2011). A constructivist view of object perception in infancy. In L.M. Oakes & others (Eds.), *Infant perception and cognition.* New York: Oxford University Press.

Johnson, S.P. (2013). Object perception. In P.D. Zelazo (Ed.), *Oxford handbook of developmental psychology.* New York: Oxford University Press.

Johnson, S.P., & Hannon, E.E. (2015). Perceptual development. In R.M. Lerner (Ed.), *Handbook of child psychology and developmental science* (7th ed.). New York: Wiley.

Johnson, V.A., & others (2015). Childhood- versus adolescent-onset antisocial youth with conduct disorder: Psychiatric illness, neuropsychological and psychosocial function. *PLoS One, 10*(4), e0121627.

Johnson, W., & Bouchard, T.J. (2014). Genetics of intellectual and personality traits associated with creative genius: Could geniuses be cosmobian dragon kings? In D.K. Simonton (Ed.), *Wiley-Blackwell handbook of genius.* New York: Wiley.

Johnston, L.D., O'Malley, P.M., Bachman, J.G., & Schulenberg, J.E. (2011). *Monitoring the Future national survey results on drug use, 1975–2010, Volume II: College students and adults ages 19–50.* Bethesda, MD: National Institute on Drug Abuse.

Johnston, L.D., O'Malley, P.M., Bachman, J.G., & Schulenberg, J.E. (2013). *Monitoring the Future national survey results on drug use, 1975–2012, Volume II: College students and adults ages 19–50.* Bethesda, MD: National Institute on Drug Abuse.

Johnston, L.D., O'Malley, P.M., Bachman, J.G., & Schulenberg, J.E. (2015). *Monitoring the Future national results on drug use: 2014 overview, key findings on adolescent drug use.* Ann Arbor: Institute of Social Research, University of Michigan.

Jokinen-Gordon, H. (2012). Still penalized? Parity, age at first birth, and women's income in later life. *Journal of Women and Aging, 24,* 227–241.

Jones, B.F., Reedy, E.J., & Weinberg, B.A. (2014). Age and scientific genius. In D.K. Simonton (Ed.), *Wiley-Blackwell handbook of genius.* New York: Wiley.

Jones, D., & others (2010). The impact of the Fast Track prevention trial on health services utilization by youth at risk for conduct problems. *Pediatrics, 125,* 130–136.

Jones, J.D., Ehrlich, K.B., Lejuez, C.W., & Cassidy, J. (2015). Parental knowledge of adolescent activities: Links with parental attachment style and adolescent substance use. *Journal of Family Psychology, 29,* 191–200.

Jones, L., & others (2012). Pain management for women in labor: An overview of systematic reviews. *Cochrane Database of Systematic Reviews, 14*(3), CD009234.

Jones, M.C. (1965). Psychological correlates of somatic development. *Child Development, 36,* 899–911.

Jones, M.D., & Galliher, R.V. (2007). Navajo ethnic identity: Predictors of psychosocial outcomes in Navajo adolescents, *Journal of Research on Adolescence, 17,* 683–696.

Jones, N.A. (2012). Delayed reactive cries demonstrate emotional and physiological dysregulation in newborns of depressed mothers. *Biological Psychiatry, 89,* 374–381.

Jones, S.C., & Magee, C.A. (2014). The role of family, friends, and peers in Australian adolescents' alcohol consumption. *Drug and Alcohol Review, 33,* 304–313.

Jonson-Reid, M., Kohl, P.L., & Drake, B. (2012). Child and adolescent outcomes of chronic child maltreatment. *Pediatrics, 129,* 839–845.

Jose, A., O'Leary, K.D., & Moyer, A. (2010). Does premarital cohabitation predict subsequent marital stability and marital quality? A meta-analysis. *Journal of Marriage and the Family, 72,* 105–116.

Josephson Institute of Ethics (2006). *2006 Josephson Institute report card on the ethics of American youth. Part one—integrity.* Los Angeles: Josephson Institute.

Josselyn, S.A., & Frankland, P.W. (2012). Infantile amnesia: A neurogenic hypothesis. *Learning and Memory, 19,* 423–433.

Joyce, B.R., Weil, M., & Calhoun, E. (2015). *Models of teaching* (9th ed.). Upper Saddle River, NJ: Pearson.

Joyner, K. (2009). Transition to parenthood. In D. Carr (Ed.), *Encyclopedia of the life course and human development.* Boston: Gale Cengage.

Juang, L.P., & Umana-Taylor, A.J. (2012). Family conflict among Chinese- and Mexican-origin adolescents and their parents in the U.S.: An introduction. *New Directions in Child and Adolescent Development, 135,* 1–12.

Judd, F.K., Hickey, M., & Bryant, C. (2012). Depression and midlife: Are we overpathologising the menopause? *Journal of Affective Disorders, 136,* 199–211.

Jurkowski, J.M., & others (2014). The empowerment of low-income parents engaged in a childhood obesity intervention. *Family and Community Health, 37,* 104–118.

K

Kadlecova, P., & others (2015, in press). Alcohol consumption at midlife and risk of stroke during 43 years of follow-up: Cohort and twin analysis. *Stroke.*

Kaffashi, F., Scher, M.S., Ludington-Hoe, S.M., & Loparo, K.A. (2013). An analysis of kangaroo care intervention using neonatal EEG complexity: A preliminary study. *Clinical Neurophysiology, 124,* 238–246.

Kagan, J. (2000). Temperament. In A. Kazdin (Ed.), *Encyclopedia of psychology.* New York: Oxford University Press.

Kagan, J. (2002). Behavioral inhibition as a temperamental category. In R.J. Davidson, K.R. Scherer, & H.H. Goldsmith (Eds.), *Handbook of affective sciences.* New York: Oxford University Press.

Kagan, J. (2008). Fear and wariness. In M.M. Haith & J.B. Benson (Eds.), *Encyclopedia of infant and early childhood development.* Oxford, UK: Elsevier.

Kagan, J. (2010). Emotions and temperament. In M.H. Bornstein (Ed.), *Handbook of cultural developmental science.* New York: Psychology Press.

Kagan, J. (2013). Temperamental contributions to inhibited and uninhibited profiles. In P.D. Zelazo (Ed.), *Oxford handbook of developmental psychology*. New York: Oxford University Press.

Kagan, J., Kearsley, R.B., & Zelazo, P.R. (1978). *Infancy: Its place in human development*. Cambridge, MA: Harvard University Press.

Kahrs, B.A., Jung, W.P., & Lockman, J.J. (2013). Motor origins of tool use. *Child Development, 84*(3), 810–816.

Kail, R.V. (2007). Longitudinal evidence that increases in processing speed and working memory enhance children's reasoning. *Psychological Science, 18*, 312–313.

Kaiser, L.L., & others (2015, in press). Correlates of food patterns in young Latino children at high risk for obesity. *Public Health Nutrition*.

Kalak, N., & others (2012). Daily morning running for 3 weeks improved sleep and psychological functioning in healthy adolescents compared to controls. *Journal of Adolescent Health, 51*(6), 615–622.

Kalish, R.A. (1981). *Death, grief, and caring relationships*. Monterey, CA: Brooks/Cole.

Kalish, R.A. (1987). Death. In G.L. Maddox (Ed.), *Encyclopedia of aging*. New York: Springer.

Kalish, R.A., & Reynolds, D.K. (1976). *An overview of death and ethnicity*. Farmingdale, NY: Baywood.

Kalousova, L., & Burgard, S.A. (2014). Unemployment, measured and perceived decline of economic resources: Contrasting three measures of recessionary hardships and their implications for adopting negative health behaviors. *Social Science and Medicine, 106*, 28–34.

Kamii, C. (1985). *Young children reinvent arithmetic: Implications of Piaget's theory*. New York: Teachers College Press.

Kamii, C. (1989). *Young children continue to reinvent arithmetic*. New York: Teachers College Press.

Kamiya, M., Sakurai, T., Ogama, N., Maki, Y., & Toba, K. (2014). Factors associated with increased caregivers' burden in several cognitive stages of Alzheimer's disease. *Geriatrics and Gerontology International, 14*(Suppl. 2), S45–S55.

Kan, P.F. (2014). Novel word retention in sequential bilingual children. *Journal of Child Language, 41*, 416–438.

Kancherla, V., Oakley, G.P., & Brent, R.L. (2014). Urgent global opportunities to prevent birth defects. *Seminars in Fetal and Neonatal Medicine, 19*, 153–160.

Kandler, C., Kornadt, A.E., Hagemeyer, B., & Neyer, F.J. (2015, in press). Patterns and sources of personality development in old age. *Journal of Personality and Social Psychology*.

Kang, H.K. (2014). Influence of culture and community perceptions on birth and perinatal care of immigrant women: Doulas' perspective. *Journal of Perinatal Education, 23*, 25–32.

Kann, L., & others (2014). Youth Risk Behavior Surveillance—United States, 2013. *MMWR Surveillance Summaries, 63*(4), 1–169.

Kanoy, K., Ulku-Steiner, B., Cox, M., & Burchinal, M. (2003). Marital relationship and individual psychological characteristics that predict physical punishment of children. *Journal of Family Psychology, 17*, 20–28.

Kantowitz, B.H., Roediger, H.L., & Elmes, D.G. (2015). *Experimental psychology* (10th ed.). Boston: Cengage.

Kao, T.A., & Huang, B. (2015, in press). Bicultural standing among immigrant adolescents: A concept analysis. *Journal of Holistic Nursing*.

Kaplan, D.L., Jones, E.J., Olson, E.C., & Yunzal-Butler, C.B. (2013). Early age of first sex and health risk in an urban adolescent population. *Journal of School Health, 83*, 350–356.

Kappeler, E.M., & Farb, A.F. (2014). Historical context for the creation of the Office of Adolescent Health and the Teen Pregnancy Prevention Program. *Journal of Adolescent Health, 54*(3, Suppl.), S3–S9.

Karantzas, G.C., Evans, L., & Foddy, M. (2010). The role of attachment in current and future parent caregiving. *Journals of Gerontology B: Psychological Sciences and Social Sciences, 65*, 573–580.

Karelitz, T.M., Jarvin, L., & Sternberg, R.J. (2010). The meaning of wisdom and its development throughout life. In W. Overton (Ed.), *Handbook of lifespan human development*. New York: Wiley.

Karlamangia, A.S., & others (2013). Biological correlates of adult cognition: Midlife in the United States (MIDUS). *Neurobiology of Aging, 35*(2), 387–394.

Karlsson, P., & others (2015, in press). Birth cohort differences in fluid cognition in old age: Comparisons of trends in levels and change trajectories over 30 years in three population-based samples. *Psychology and Aging*.

Karnes, F.A., & Stephens, K.R. (2008). *Achieving excellence: Educating the gifted and talented*. Upper Saddle River, NJ: Prentice Hall.

Karney, B.R., Garvin, C.W., & Thomas, M.S. (2003). *Family formation in Florida 2003 baseline survey of attitudes, beliefs, and demographics relating to marriage and family formation*. Gainesville, FL: The University of Florida. Retrieved from http://www.phhp.ufl.edu/~uspringe/FMP/Publications/REPORT.pdf

Karreman, A., van Tuiji, C., van Aken, M.A.G., & Dekovic, M. (2008). Parenting, coparenting, and effortful control in preschoolers. *Journal of Family Psychology, 22*, 30–40.

Kask, K., & others (2015, in press). Deletion of RIC8A in neural precursor cells leads to altered neurogenesis and neonatal lethality of mouse. *Developmental Neurobiology*.

Kassahn, K.S., Scott, H.S., & Fletcher, J.M. (2014). Ensuring clinical validity—modernizing genetic testing services. *Pathology, 46*(Suppl. 1), S27–S28.

Kastbom, A.A., Sydsjo, G., Bladh, M., Priee, G., & Svedin, C.G. (2015). Sexual debut before the age of 14 leads to poorer psychosocial health and risky behavior later in life. *Acta Pediatrica, 104*, 91–100.

Kastenbaum, R.J. (2004). *Death, society, and human experience* (8th ed.). Boston: Allyn & Bacon.

Kastenbaum, R.J. (2007). *Death, society, and human experience* (9th ed.). Boston: Allyn & Bacon.

Kastenbaum, R.J. (2009). *Death, society, and human experience* (10th ed.). Boston: Allyn & Bacon.

Kastenbaum, R.J. (2012). *Death, society, and human experience* (11th ed.). Upper Saddle River, NJ: Pearson.

Kaszniak, A.W., & Menchola, M. (2012). Behavioral neuroscience of emotion in aging. *Current Topics in Behavioral Neuroscience, 10*, 51–56.

Kato, T. (2005). The relationship between coping with stress due to romantic break-ups and mental health. *Japanese Journal of Social Psychology, 20*, 171–180.

Katz, L. (1999). Curriculum disputes in early childhood education. *ERIC Clearinghouse on Elementary and Early Childhood Education*, Document EDO-PS-99-13.

Katz, P.R., Karuza, J., Intrator, O., & Mor, V. (2009). Nursing home physician specialists: A response to the workforce crisis in long-term care. *Annals of Internal Medicine, 150*, 411–413.

Katzel, L.I., & Steinbrenner, G.M. (2012). Physical exercise and health. In S.K. Whitbourne & M.J. Sliwinski (Eds.), *Wiley-Blackwell handbook of adult development and aging*. New York: Wiley.

Kauffman, J.M., McGee, K., & Brigham, M. (2004). Enabling or disabling? Observations on changes in special education. *Phi Delta Kappan, 85*, 613–620.

Kaufman, J.C., & Sternberg, R.J. (2013). The creative mind. In C. Jones, M. Lorenzen, & R.F. Proctor (Eds.), *Handbook of psychology: Experimental psychology* (Vol. 4). New York: Wiley.

Kaur, A., & Phadke, S.R. (2012). Analysis of short stature cases referred for genetic evaluation. *Indian Journal of Pediatrics, 79*(12), 1597–1600.

Kaur, M., Singh, H., & Ahula, G.K. (2012). Cardiac performance in relation to age of onset of menopause. *Journal of the Indian Medical Association, 109*, 234–237.

Kavsek, M. (2013). The comparator model of infant visual habituation and dishabituation: Recent insights. *Developmental Psychobiology, 55*, 793–808.

Kawabata, Y., Tseng, W.L., & Crick, N.R. (2014). Adaptive, maladaptive, mediational, and bidirectional processes of relational and physical aggression, relational and physical victimization, and peer liking. *Aggressive Behavior, 40*, 273–287.

Kawagoe, T., & Sekiyama, K. (2014). Visually encoded working memory is closely associated with mobility in older adults. *Experimental Brain Research, 232*, 2035–2043.

Kawai, M., & others (2010). Developmental trends in mother-infant interaction from 4 months to 42 months: Using an observation technique. *Journal of Epidemiology, 20*(Suppl. 2), S427–S434.

Kaynak, O., & others (2013). Relationships among parental monitoring and sensation seeking on the development of substance use disorder among college students. *Addictive Behaviors, 38*, 1457–1463.

Kazanis, I. (2013). Neurogenesis in the adult mammalian brain: How much do we need, how much do we have? *Current Topics in Behavioral Neuroscience, 15*, 3–29.

Keage, H.A., & others (2012). What sleep characteristics predict cognitive decline in the elderly? *Sleep Medicine, 13*, 886–892.

Keating, D.P. (1990). Adolescent thinking. In S.S. Feldman & G.R. Elliott (Eds.), *At the threshold: The developing adolescent*. Cambridge, MA: Harvard University Press.

Keating, D.P. (2004). Cognitive and brain development. In R. Lerner & L. Steinberg (Eds.), *Handbook of adolescent psychology* (2nd ed.). New York: Wiley.

Keating, D.P. (2004). Cognitive and brain development. In R. Lerner & L. Steinberg (Ed.), *Handbook of adolescent psychology*. New York: Wiley.

Keen, R. (2005). Unpublished review of J.W. Santrock, *A topical approach to life-span development*, 3rd ed. (New York: McGraw-Hill).

Keen, R. (2011). The development of problem solving in young children: A critical cognitive skill. *Annual Review of Psychology* (Vol. 63). Palo Alto, CA: Annual Reviews.

Keen, R., Lee, M-H., & Adolph, K.E. (2014). Planning and action: A developmental progression for tool use. *Ecological Psychology, 26*, 98–108.

Kehle, T.J., & Bray, M.A. (2014). Individual differences. In M.A. Bray & T.J. Kehle (Eds.), *Oxford handbook of school psychology*. New York: Oxford University Press.

Keijsers, L., & Laird, R.D. (2014). Mother-adolescent monitoring dynamics and the legitimacy of parental authority. *Journal of Adolescence, 37*, 515–524.

Kell, H.J., & Lubinski, D. (2014). The study of mathematically precocious youth at maturity: Insights into elements of genius. In D.K. Simonton (Ed.), *Wiley-Blackwell handbook of genius*. New York: Wiley.

Kell, H.J., Lubinski, D., & Benbow, C.P. (2013). Who rises to the top? Early indicators. *Psychological Science, 24*, 648–659.

Keller, H. (2013). Attachment and culture. *Journal of Cross-Cultural Psychology, 44,* 175–194.

Kelley, A.S., & others (2014). Leveraging the Health and Retirement Study to advance palliative care research. *Journal of Palliative Medicine, 17,* 506–111.

Kellman, P.J., & Banks, M.S. (1998). Infant visual perception. In W. Damon (Ed.), *Handbook of child psychology* (5th ed., Vol. 2). New York: Wiley.

Kelly, A.J., Hertzog, C., Hayes, M.G., & Smith, A.D. (2012). The effects of age and focality on delay-execute prospective memory. *Neuropsychology, Development, and Cognition B. Aging, Neuropsychology, and Cognition, 20,* 101–124.

Kelly, D.J., & others (2007). Cross-race preferences for same-race face extend beyond the African versus Caucasian contrast in 3-month-old infants. *Infancy, 11,* 87–95.

Kelly, D.J., & others (2009). Development of the other-race effect in infancy: Evidence towards universality? *Journal of Experimental Child Psychology, 104,* 105–114.

Kelly, G.F. (2011). *Sexuality today* (10th ed.). New York: McGraw-Hill.

Kelly, J.P., Borchert, J., & Teller, D.Y. (1997). The development of chromatic and achromatic sensitivity in infancy as tested with the sweep VEP. *Vision Research, 37,* 2057–2072.

Kelly, J.R. (1996). Leisure. In J.E. Birren (Ed.), *Encyclopedia of gerontology* (Vol. 2). San Diego: Academic Press.

Kelly, Y., & others (2013). Light drinking versus abstinence in pregnancy—behavioral and cognitive outcomes in 7-year-old children: A longitudinal cohort study. *BJOG, 120,* 1340–1347.

Keltner, K.W. (2013). *Tiger babies strike back.* New York: William Morrow.

Kempe, A., & others (2015, in press). Collaborative centralized reminder/recall notification to increase immunization rates among young children: A comparative effectiveness trial. *JAMA Pediatrics.*

Kempermann, G., van Praag, H., & Gage, F.H. (2000). Activity-dependent regulation of neuronal plasticity and self repair. *Progress in Brain Research 127,* 35–48.

Kendler, K.S., & others (2012). Genetic and familial environmental influences on the risk for drug abuse: A national Swedish adoption study. *Archives of General Psychiatry, 69*(7), 690–697.

Kendrick, K., Jutengren, G., & Stattin, H. (2012). The protective role of supportive friends against bullying perpetration and victimization. *Journal of Adolescence, 35*(4), 1069–1080.

Kennedy, K.M., & others (2015). Lifespan age trajectory differences in functional brain activation under conditions of low and high processing demands. *Neuroimage, 104,* 31–34.

Kennedy, K.M., & others (2015, in press). BDNF val66met polymorphism affects aging of multiple types of memory. *Brain Research.*

Kennedy, K.M., & Raz, N. (2015, in press). Normal aging of the brain. In A.W. Toga (Ed.), *Brain mapping.* New York: Elsevier.

Kennell, J.H. (2006). Randomized controlled trial of skin-to-skin contact from birth versus conventional incubator for physiological stabilization in 1200 g to 2199 g newborns. *Acta Paediatrica (Sweden), 95,* 15–16.

Kennell, J.H., & McGrath, S.K. (1999). Commentary: Practical and humanistic lessons from the third world for perinatal caregivers everywhere. *Birth, 26,* 9–10.

Kennis, E., & others (2013). Long-term impact of strength training on muscle strength characteristics in older adults. *Archives of Physical Medicine and Rehabilitation, 94,* 2054–2060.

Kenyon, C. (2010). A pathway that links reproductive status to lifespan in *Caenorhabditis elegans. Annals of the New York Academy of Sciences, 1204,* 156–162.

Kernis, M.H. (Ed.) (2013). *Self-esteem issues and answers.* New York: Psychology Press.

Kerns, K.A., & Brumariu, L.E. (2014). Is insecure attachment a risk factor for the development of anxiety in childhood or adolescence? *Child Development Perspectives, 8,* 12–17.

Kerns, K.A., & Brumariu, L.E. (2016, in press). Attachment in middle childhood. In J. Cassidy & P. Shaver (Eds.), *Handbook of attachment* (3rd ed.). New York; Guilford.

Kerns, K.A., & Seibert, A.C. (2012). Finding your way through the thicket: Promising approaches to assessing attachment in middle childhood. In E. Waters, B. Vaughn, & H. Waters (Eds.), *Measuring attachment.* New York: Guilford.

Kerns, K.A., & Seibert, A.C. (2016, in press). Finding your way through the thicket: Promising approaches to assessing attachment in middle childhood. In E. Waters, B. Vaughn, & H. Waters (Eds.), *Measuring attachment.* New York: Guilford.

Kerns, K.A., Siener, S., & Brumariu, L.E. (2011). Mother-child relationships, family context, and child characteristics as predictors of anxiety symptoms in middle childhood. *Development and Psychopathology, 23,* 593–604.

Kershaw, K.N., & others (2014). Associations of stressful life events and social strain with incident cardiovascular disease in the Women's Health Initiative. *Journal of the American Heart Association, 3*(3), e000687.

Ketcham, C.J., & Stelmach, G.E. (2001). Age-related declines in motor control. In J.E. Birren & K.W. Schaie (Eds.), *Handbook of the psychology of aging* (5th ed.). San Diego: Academic Press.

Keyes, C.L., & Ryff, C.D. (1998). Generativity in adult lives: Social structural contours and quality of life consequences. In D.P. McAdams & E. de St. Aubin (Eds.), *Generativity and adult development.* Washington, DC: American Psychological Association.

Keyes, K.M., Hatzenbuehler, M.L., & Hasin, D.S. (2011). Stressful life experiences, alcohol consumption, and alcohol use disorders: The epidemiological evidence for four main types of stressors. *Psychopharmacology, 218*(1), 1–17.

Keyes, K.M., Maslowsky, J., Hamilton, A., & Schulenberg, J. (2015, in press). The great sleep recession: Changes in sleep duration among U.S. adolescents, 1991–2012. *Pediatrics.*

Khairullah, A., & others (2014). Testosterone trajectories and reference ranges in a large longitudinal sample of adolescent males. *PLoS One, 9*(9), e108838.

Khan, M.R., Berger, A.T., Wells, B.E., & Cleland, C.M. (2012). Longitudinal associations between adolescent alcohol use and adult sexual risk behavior and sexually transmitted infection in the United States: Assessment of differences by race. *American Journal of Public Health, 102,* 867–876.

Khera, M., Crawford, D., Morales, A., Salonia, A., & Morgentaler, A. (2014). A new era of testosterone and prostate cancer: From physiology to clinical implications. *European Urology, 65*(1), 115–123.

Khuc, K., & others (2012). Adolescent metabolic syndrome risk is increased with higher infancy weight gain and decreased with longer breast feeding. *International Journal of Pediatrics, 2012,* #478610.

Khurana, A., & others (2012). Early adolescent sexual debut: The mediating role of working memory ability, sensation seeking, and impulsivity. *Developmental Psychology, 48*(5), 1416–1428.

Khurana, S., & others (2013). Polyphenols: Benefits to the cardiovascular system in health and in aging. *Nutrients, 5,* 3779–3827.

Kiang, L., Witkow, M.R., & Champagne, M.C. (2013). Normative changes in ethnic and American identities and links with adjustment among Asian American adolescents. *Developmental Psychology, 49,* 1713–1722.

Kidd, C., Piantadosi, S.T., & Aslin, R.N. (2012). The Goldilocks effect: Human infants allocate attention to visual sequences that are neither too simple nor too complex. *PLoS One, 7*(5), e36399.

Kiecolt-Glaser, J.K., & others (2003). Chronic stress and age-related increases in the proinflammatory cytokine IL-6. *Proceedings of the National Academy of Science USA, 100,* 9090–9095.

Kiel, E.J., & Kalomiris, A.E. (2015). Current themes in understanding children's emotion regulation as development from within the parent-child relationship. *Current Opinion in Psychology, 3,* 11–16.

Kilbane, C.R., & Milman, N.B. (2014). *Teaching models.* Upper Saddle River, NJ: Pearson.

Kilic, S., & others (2012). Environmental tobacco smoke exposure during intrauterine period promotes granulosa cell apoptosis: A prospective, randomized study. *Journal of Maternal-Fetal and Neonatal Medicine, 25,* 1904–1908.

Killen, M., & Smetana, J.G. (2015). Morality: Origins and development. In R.M. Lerner (Ed.), *Handbook of child psychology and developmental science* (7th ed.). New York: Wiley.

Kim, E., & others (2015). Comparative efficacy of tadalafil once daily in men with erectile dysfunction who demonstrated previous partial responses to as-needed sildenafil, tadalafil, or vardenafil. *Current Medical Research and Opinion, 31,* 379–389.

Kim, E.S., Chopik, W.J., & Smith, J. (2014). Are people healthier if their partners are more optimistic? The dyadic effect of optimism on health among older adults. *Journal of Psychosomatic Research, 76,* 447–453.

Kim, H., & Pedersen, S. (2010). Young adolescents' metacognition and domain knowledge as predictors of hypothesis-development performance in a computer-supported context. *Educational Psychology, 30,* 565–582.

Kim, H.J., & others (2014). Long-term cognitive outcome of bilateral subthalamic deep brain stimulation in Parkinson's disease. *Journal of Neurology, 261,* 1090–1096.

Kim, J., & Cicchetti, D. (2004). A longitudinal study of child maltreatment, mother-child relationship quality and maladjustment: The role of self-esteem and social competence. *Journal of Abnormal Child Psychology, 32,* 341–354.

Kim, J., Smith, T.W., & Kang, J.H. (2015, in press). Religious affiliation, religious service attendance, and morality. *Journal of Religion and Health.*

Kim, J.E., & Moen, P. (2002). Retirement transitions, gender, and psychological well-being: A life-course, ecological model. *Journals of Gerontology B: Psychological Sciences and Social Sciences, 57,* P212–P222.

Kim, K., Cheng, Y.P., Zarit, S.H., & Fingerman, K.L. (2015). Relationships between adults and parents in Asia. In S.T. Cheng & others (Eds.), *Successful aging: Asian perspectives.* New York: Springer.

Kim, K.H. (2010, July 10). Interview. *Newsweek,* 42–48.

Kim, M.J., Catalano, R.F., Haggerty, K.P., & Abbott, R.D. (2011). Bullying at elementary school and problem behavior in young adulthood: A study of bullying, violence, and substance use from age 11 to age 21. *Criminal Behavior and Mental Health, 21,* 136–144.

Kim, O.M., Reichwald, R., & Lee, R. (2013). Cultural socialization in families with adopted Korean adolescents: A mixed-method, multi-informant study. *Journal of Adolescent Research, 28,* 69–95.

Kim, S., & Hasher, L. (2005). The attraction effect in decision making: Superior performance by older adults. *Quarterly Journal of Experimental Psychology, 58A,* 120–133.

Kim, S., & Kochanska, G. (2015, in press). Mothers' power assertion, children's negative, adversarial orientation; and future behavior problems in low-income families: Early maternal responsiveness as a moderator of the developmental cascade. *Journal of Family Psychology.*

Kim, S.H. (2009). The influence of finding meaning and worldview of accepting death on anger among bereaved older spouses. *Aging and Mental Health, 13,* 38–45.

Kim, S.M., Han, D.H., Trksak, G.H., & Lee, Y.S. (2014). Gender differences in adolescent coping behaviors and suicidal ideation. *Anxiety, Stress, and Coping, 27,* 439–454.

Kimble, M., Neacsiu, A.D., Flack, W.F., & Horner, J. (2008). Risk of unwanted sex for college women: Evidence for a red zone. *Journal of American College Health, 57,* 331–338.

Kim-Fuchs, C., & others (2014). Chronic stress accelerates pancreatic cancer growth and invasion: A critical role for beta-adrenergic signaling in the pancreatic microenvironment. *Brain, Behavior, and Immunity, 40,* 40–47.

King, L.A. (2014). *Psychology: An appreciative experience* (3rd ed.). New York: McGraw-Hill.

King, L.A., & Hicks, J.A. (2007). Whatever happened to "What might have been?" Regrets, happiness, and maturity. *American Psychologist, 62,* 625–636.

King, P.E., & Boyatzis, C.J. (2015). The nature and functions of religious and spiritual development in childhood and adolescence. In R.M. Lerner (Ed.), *Handbook of child psychology and developmental science* (7th ed.). New York: Oxford University Press.

King, P.E., Carr, A., & Boiter, C. (2011). Spirituality, religiosity, and youth thriving. In R.M. Lerner, J.V. Lerner, & J.B. Benson (Eds.), *Advances in child development and behavior: Positive youth development.* New York: Elsevier.

King, P.E., Ramos, J.S., & Clardy, C.E. (2013). Searching for the sacred: Religious and spiritual development among adolescents. In K.I. Pargament, J. Exline, & J. Jones (Eds.), *APA handbook of psychology, religion, and spirituality.* Washington, DC: American Psychological Association.

King, V., & Scott, M.E. (2005). A comparison of cohabiting relationships among older and younger adults. *Journal of Marriage and the Family, 67,* 271–285.

Kingston, E.R., & Bartholomew, J. (2009). Social Security. In D. Carr (Ed.), *Encyclopedia of the life course and human development.* Boston: Gale Cengage.

Kins, E., & Beyers, W. (2010). Failure to launch, failure to achieve criteria for adulthood. *Journal of Adolescent Research, 25,* 206–217.

Kirby, D.B., Laris, B.A., & Rolleri, L.A. (2007). Sex and HIV education programs: Their impact on sexual behavior of young people throughout the world. *Journal of Adolescent Health, 40,* 206–217.

Kirk, S.A., Gallagher, J.J., & Coleman, M.R. (2015). *Educating exceptional children* (14th ed.). Boston: Cengage.

Kirkham, N.Z., Wagner, J.B., Swan, K.A., & Johnson, S.P. (2012). Sound support: Intermodal information facilitates infants' perception of an occluded trajectory. *Infant Behavior and Development, 35,* 174–178.

Kirkorian, H.L., Anderson, D.R., & Keen, R. (2012). Age differences in online processing of video: An eye movement study. *Child Development, 83,* 497–507.

Kirkorian, H.L., Wartella, E.A., & Anderson, D.A. (2008). Media and young children's learning. *Future of Children, 18*(1), 39–61.

Kirk-Sanchez, N.J., & McGough, E.L. (2014). Physical exercise and cognitive performance in the elderly: Current perspectives. *Clinical Interventions in Aging, 9,* 51–62.

Kisilevsky, B.S., & others (2009). Fetal sensitivity to properties of maternal speech and language. *Infant Behavior and Development, 32,* 59–71.

Kitsantas, P., & Gaffney, K.F. (2010). Racial/ethnic disparities in infant mortality. *Journal of Perinatal Medicine, 38,* 87–94.

Kiuhara, S.A., Graham, S., & Hawken, L.S. (2009). Teaching writing to high school students: A national survey. *Journal of Educational Psychology, 101,* 136–160.

Klahr, A.M., & Burt, S.A. (2014). Elucidating the etiology of individual differences in parenting: A meta-analysis of behavioral genetic research. *Psychological Bulletin, 140,* 544–586.

Klatt, J., & Enright, R. (2009). Investigating the place of forgiveness within the positive youth development paradigm. *Journal of Moral Education, 38,* 35–52.

Klaus, M., & Kennell, H.H. (1976). *Maternal-infant bonding.* St. Louis: Mosby.

Kleiman, E.M., & Riskind, J.H. (2013). Utilized social support and self-esteem mediate the relationship between perceived social support and suicide ideation: A test of a multiple mediator model. *Crisis, 34*(1), 42–49.

Klein, S. (2012). *State of public school segregation in the United States 2007–2010.* Washington, DC: Feminist Majority Foundation.

Klima, C., Norr, K., Conderheld, S., & Handler, A. (2009). Introduction of Centering Pregnancy in a public health clinic. *Journal of Midwifery and Women's Health, 54,* 27–34.

Klimstra, T.A., Hale, W.W., Raaijmakers, Q.A., Branje, S.J.T., & Meeus, W.H. (2010). Identity formation in adolescence: Change or stability? *Journal of Youth and Adolescence, 39,* 150–162.

Klinenberg, E. (2012, February 4). Sunday Review: One's a crowd. *The New York Times,* Retrieved from http://www.nytimes.com/2012/02/05/opinion/sunday/living-alone-means-being-social.html?pagewanted=all&_r=0

Klinenberg, E. (2013). *Going solo: The extraordinary rise and surprising appeal of living alone.* New York: Penguin.

Kling, K.C., Hyde, J.S., Showers, C.J., & Buswell, B.N. (1999). Gender differences in self-esteem: A meta-analysis. *Psychological Bulletin, 125,* 470–500.

Knight, C.P., & others (2015, in press). Trajectories of Mexican American and mainstream cultural values among Mexican American adolescents. *Journal of Youth and Adolescence.*

Knight, L.F., & Morales Hope, D.A. (2012). Correlates of same-sex attractions and behaviors among self-identified heterosexual university students. *Archives of Sexual Behavior, 41,* 1199–1208.

Knox, M. (2010). On hitting children: A review of corporal punishment in the United States. *Journal of Pediatric Health Care, 24,* 103–107.

Knussmann, R., Christiansen, K., & Couwenbergs, C. (1986). Relations between sex hormone levels and sexual behavior in men. *Archives of Sexual Behavior, 15,* 429–445.

Ko, S.H., Chen, C.H., Wang, H.H., & Su, Y.T. (2014). Postpartum women's sleep quality and its predictors in Taiwan. *Journal of Nursing Scholarship, 46,* 74–81.

Ko, Y.L., Yang, C.L., Fang, C.L., Lee, M.Y., & Lin, P.C. (2013). Community-based postpartum exercise program. *Journal of Clinical Nursing, 22,* 2122–2131.

Kobak, R.R., & Kerig, P.K. (2015). Introduction to the special issue: Attachment-based treatments for adolescents. *Attachment and Human Development, 17,* 111–118.

Kobak, R.R., & others (2015). Attachment-based treatments for adolescents: The secure cycle as a framework for assessment, treatment, and evaluation. *Attachment and Human Development, 17,* 220–239.

Kochanska, G., & Aksan, N. (2007). Conscience in childhood: Past, present, and future. *Merrill-Palmer Quarterly, 50,* 299–310.

Kochanska, G., Aksan N., Prisco, T.R., & Adams, E.E. (2008). Mother-child and father-child mutually responsive orientation in the first two years and children's outcomes at preschool age: Mechanisms of influence. *Child Development, 79,* 30–44.

Kochanska, G., Barry, R.A., Stellern, S.A., & O'Bleness, J.J. (2010). Early attachment organization moderates the parent-child mutually coercive pathway to children's antisocial conduct. *Child Development, 80,* 1288–1300.

Kochanska, G., Forman, D.R., Aksan, N., & Dunbar, S.B. (2005). Pathways to conscience: Early mother-child mutually responsive orientation and children's moral emotion, conduct, and cognition. *Journal of Child Psychology and Psychiatry, 46,* 19–34.

Kochanska, G., Gross, J.N., Lin, M., & Nichols, K.E. (2002). Guilt in young children: Development, determinants, and relations with a broader set of standards. *Child Development, 73,* 461–482.

Kochanska, G., & Kim, S. (2013). Early attachment organization with both parents and future behavior problems: From infancy to middle childhood. *Child Development, 84*(1), 283–296.

Kochanska, G., Koenig, J.L., Barry, R.A., Kim, S., & Yoon, J.E. (2010). Children's conscience during toddler and preschool years, moral self, and a competent, adaptive development trajectory. *Development Psychology, 46,* 1320–1332.

Kochanska, G., & others (2010). Positive socialization mechanisms in secure and insecure parent-child dyads: Two longitudinal studies. *Journal of Child Psychology and Psychiatry, 51,* 998–1009.

Koeblinger, C., & others (2013). Fetal magnetic resonance imaging of lymphangiomas. *Journal of Perinatal Medicine, 41,* 437–443.

Koenig, H.G. (Ed.) (2012). Medicine meets modern spirituality. In J. van Hussteen & K. Chamcham (Eds.), *Templeton science and religion reader.* Philadelphia: Templeton Press.

Koenig, H.G. (2014). The spiritual care team: Enabling the practice of whole person medicine. *Religions, 5,* 1161–1174.

Koenig, H.G. (2015, in press). Religion, spirituality, and health: Review and update. *Advances in Mind-Body Medicine.*

Koenig, H.G., & Larson, D.B. (1998). Religion and mental health. In H.S. Friedman (Ed.), *Encyclopedia of mental health* (Vol. 3). San Diego: Academic Press.

Koenig, H.G., & others (2015a). Religious versus conventional cognitive-behavioral therapy for major depression in persons with chronic medical illness. *Journal of Nervous and Mental Disease, 203,* 243–251.

Koenig, H.G., & others (2015b, in press). Effects of religious vs. conventional cognitive-behavioral therapy on therapeutic alliance: A randomized clinical trial. *Psychotherapy Research.*

Koenig, L.B., McGue, M., & Iacono, W.G. (2008). Stability and change in religiousness during emerging adulthood. *Developmental Psychology, 44,* 523–543.

Koh, H. (2014). The Teen Pregnancy Prevention Program: An evidence-based public health program model. *Journal of Adolescent Health, 54*(Suppl. 1), S1–S2.

Kohen, D.E., Leventhal, T., Dahinten, V.S., & McIntosh, C.N. (2008). Neighborhood disadvantage: Pathways of effects for young children. *Child Development, 79,* 156–169.

Kohlberg, L. (1958). *The development of modes of moral thinking and choice in the years 10 to 16.* Unpublished doctoral dissertation, University of Chicago.

Kohlberg, L. (1969). Stage and sequence: The cognitive-developmental approach to socialization. In D.A. Goslin (Ed.), *Handbook of socialization theory and research.* Chicago: Rand McNally.

Kohlberg, L. (1986). A current statement on some theoretical issues. In S. Modgil & C. Modgil (Eds.), *Lawrence Kohlberg.* Philadelphia: Falmer.

Kohler, P.K., Manhart, L.E., & Lafferty, W.E. (2008). Abstinence-only and comprehensive sex education and the initiation of sexual activity and teen pregnancy. *Journal of Adolescent Health, 42,* 344–351.

Kohon, J., & Carder, P. (2014). Exploring identity and aging: Auto-photography and narratives of low-income older adults. *Journal of Aging Studies, 30,* 47–55.

Kok, R., & others (2014). Parenting, corpus callosum, and executive function in preschool children. *Child Neuropsychology, 20,* 583–606.

Kokkevi, A., & others (2012). Multiple substance use and self-reported suicide attempts by adolescents in 16 countries. *European Child and Adolescent Psychiatry, 21*(8), 443–450.

Kokotas, H., & others (2012). Biomarkers in primary open angle glaucoma. *Clinical Chemistry and Laboratory Medicine, 29,* 1–13.

Kolialexi, A. (2012). Early non-invasive detection of fetal Y chromosome sequences in maternal plasma using multiplex PCR. *European Journal of Obstetrics, Gynecology, and Reproductive Medicine, 161,* 34–37.

Kollins, S.H., & Adcock, R.A. (2014). ADHD, altered dopamine neurotransmission, and disrupted reinforcement processes: Implications for smoking and nicotine dependence. *Progress in Neuro-Psychopharmacology and Biological Psychiatry, 52,* 70–78.

Kolovou, G., & others (2014). Aging mechanisms and associated lipid changes. *Current Vascular Pharmacology, 12,* 682–689.

Kong, A., & others (2012). Rate of *de novo* mutations and the importance of father's age to disease risk. *Nature, 488,* 471–475.

Kong, A., & others (2013). Racial/ethnic differences in dietary intake among WIC families prior to food package revisions. *Journal of Nutrition Education and Behavior, 45,* 39–46.

Konrath, S.H., Chopik, W.J., Hsing, C.K., & O'Brien, E. (2014). Changes in adult attachment styles in American college students over time: A meta-analysis. *Personality and Social Psychology Bulletin, 18,* 326–348.

Koo, Y.J., & others (2012). Pregnancy outcomes according to increasing maternal age. *Taiwan Journal of Obstetrics and Gynecology, 51,* 60–65.

Koolhof, R., Loeber, R., Wei, E.H., Pardini, D., & D'Escury, A.C. (2007). Inhibition deficits of serious delinquent boys of low intelligence. *Criminal Behavior and Mental Health, 17,* 274–292.

Koolschijn, P.C., Peper, J.S., & Crone, E.A. (2014). The influence of sex steroids on structural brain maturation in adolescence. *PLoS One, 9*(1), e83929.

Koorevaar, A.M., & others (2013). Big Five personality factors and depression diagnosis, severity, and age of onset in older adults. *Journal of Affective Disorders, 151,* 178–185.

Kopp, C.B. (1982). The antecedents of self-regulation. *Developmental Psychology, 18,* 199–214.

Kopp, C.B. (1987). The growth of self-regulation: Caregivers and children. In N. Eisenberg (Ed.),

Contemporary topics in developmental psychology. New York: Wiley.

Kopp, C.B. (2008). Self-regulatory processes. In M.M. Haith & J.B. Benson (Eds.), *Encyclopedia of infant and early childhood development.* Oxford, UK: Elsevier.

Kopp, F., & Lindenberger, U. (2012). Effects of joint attention on long-term memory in 9-month-old infants: An event-related potentials study. *Developmental Science, 15,* 540–556.

Koppel, J., & Bernstsen, D. (2014). Does everything happen when you are young? Introducing the youth bias. *Journal of Experimental Psychology, 67,* 417–423.

Koppelman, K. (2014). *Understanding human differences* (4th ed.). Upper Saddle River, NJ: Pearson.

Koren, G., & Nordeng, H. (2012). Antidepressant use during pregnancy: The benefit-risk ratio. *American Journal of Obstetrics and Gynecology, 207*(3), 157–163.

Kornblum, J. (2006, March 9). How to monitor the kids? *USA Today, 1D,* p. 1.

Koropeckyj-Cox, T. (2009). Singlehood. In D. Carr (Ed.), *Encyclopedia of the life course and human development.* Boston: Gale Cengage.

Korte, J., Dorssaert, C.H., Westerhof, G.J., & Bohlmeijer, E.T. (2014). Life review in groups? An explorative analysis of social processes that facilitate or hinder the effectiveness of life review. *Aging and Mental Health, 18,* 376–384.

Korten, N.C., & others (2014). Heterogeneity of late-life depression: Relationship with cognitive functioning. *International Psychogeriatrics, 26,* 953–963.

Koss, K.J., & others (2013). Patterns of children's adrenocortical reactivity to interparental conflict and associations with child adjustment: A growth mixture modeling approach. *Developmental Psychology, 49*(2), 317–326.

Koss, K.J., & others (2014). Asymmetry in children's salivary cortisol and alpha-amylase in the context of marital conflict: Links to children's emotional security and adjustment. *Developmental Psychobiology, 56,* 836–849.

Kostelnik, M.J., Soderman, A.K., Whiren, A.P., & Rupiper, M. (2015). *Developmentally appropriate curriculum* (6th ed.). Upper Saddle River, NJ: Pearson.

Kostovic, I., Judas, M., & Sedmak, G. (2011). Developmental history of the subplate zone, subplate neurons, and interstitial white matter neurons: Relevance for schizophrenia. *International Journal of Developmental Neuroscience, 29*(3), 193–205.

Kotovsky, L., & Baillargeon, R. (1994). Calibration-based reasoning about collision events in 11-month-old infants. *Cognition, 51,* 107–129.

Kotre, J. (1984). *Outliving the self: Generativity and the interpretation of lives.* Baltimore: Johns Hopkins University Press.

Koulougliotti, C., & others (2014). The longitudinal association of young children's everyday routines to sleep duration. *Journal of Pediatric Health Care, 28*(1), 80–87.

Kouros, C.D., & El-Sheikh, M. (2015, in press). Daily mood and sleep: Reciprocal relations and links with adjustment problems. *Journal of Sleep Research.*

Kowalski, R.M., Giumetti, G.W., Schroeder, A.N., & Lattanner, M.R. (2014). Bullying in the digital age: A critical review and meta-analysis of cyberbullying research on youth. *Psychological Bulletin, 140,* 1073–1137.

Koziel, J.E., & Herbert, B.S. (2015). The telomerase inhibitor imetelstat alone, and in combination with trastuzumab, decreases the cancer cell population and self-renewal of HER2 (+) breast cancer cells. *Breast Cancer Research and Treatment.*

Kozol, J. (2005). *The shame of the nation.* New York: Crown.

Kraft, J.M., & others (2012). Sex education and adolescent sexual behavior: Do community characteristics matter? *Contraception, 86*(3), 276–280.

Kraftt, C.E., & others (2014). An eight-month randomized controlled exercise trial alters brain activation during cognitive tasks in overweight children. *Obesity, 22,* 232–242.

Krakoff, L.R., & others (2014). 2014 hypertension recommendations from the Eighth Joint National Committee Panel members raise concerns for elderly Black and female populations. *Journal of the American College of Cardiology, 64,* 394–402.

Kramer, A.F., & Madden, D.J. (2008). Attention. In F.I.M. Craik & T.A. Salthouse (Eds.), *Handbook of aging and cognition* (3rd ed.). Mahwah, NJ: Erlbaum.

Kramer, C.K. (2015). Weight loss is a useful therapeutic objective. *Canadian Journal of Cardiology, 31,* 211–215.

Kramer, L. (2006, July 10). Commentary in "How your siblings make you who you are" by J. Kluger. *Time,* 46–55.

Kramer, L., & Perozynski, L. (1999). Parental beliefs about managing sibling conflict. *Developmental Psychology, 35,* 489–499.

Kramer, L., & Radey, C. (1997). Improving sibling relationships among young children: A social skills training model. *Family Relations, 46,* 237–246.

Krause, N. (1995). Religiosity and self-esteem among older adults. *Journals of Gerontology B: Psychological Science, 50,* P236–P246.

Krause, N. (2003). Religious meaning and subjective well-being in late life. *Journals of Gerontology B: Psychological Science and Social Science, 58,* S160–S170.

Krause, N. (2008). The social foundations of religious meaning in life. *Research on Aging, 30*(4), 395–427.

Krause, N. (2009). Deriving a sense of meaning in late life. In V.L. Bengtson, D. Gans, N.M. Putney, & M. Silverstein (Eds.), *Handbook of theories of aging.* New York: Springer.

Krause, N. (2012). Valuing the life experience of old adults and change in depressive symptoms: Exploring an overlooked benefit of involvement in religion. *Journal of Aging Health, 24,* 227–249.

Krause, N., & Hayward, R.D. (2014). Religious involvement, practical wisdom, and self-rated health. *Journal of Aging and Health, 26,* 540–558.

Krebs, C. (2014). Measuring sexual victimization: On what fronts is the jury still out and do we need it to come in? *Trauma, Violence, and Abuse, 15,* 170–180.

Kremen, W.S., & others (2014). Genetic complexity of episodic memory: A twin approach to studies of aging. *Psychology and Aging, 29,* 404–417.

Kretch, K.S., Franchak, J.M., Adolph, K.E. (2014). Crawling and walking infants see the world differently. *Child Development, 85,* 1503–1518.

Kreutzer, M.A., Leonard, C., & Flavell, J.H. (1975). An interview study of children's knowledge about memory. *Monographs of the Society for Research in Child Development, 40*(1, Serial No. 159).

Kriemler, S., & others (2011). Effect of school-based interventions on activity and fitness in children and adolescents: A review of reviews and systematic update. *British Journal of Sports Medicine, 45,* 923–930.

Kring, A.M. (2000). Gender and anger. In A.H. Fischer (Ed.), *Gender and emotion.* New York: Cambridge University Press.

Kristensen, P., Weisaeth, L., & Heir, T. (2012). Bereavement and mental health after sudden and violent losses: A review. *Psychiatry, 75,* 76–97.

Kristjuhan, U., & Taidre, E. (2010). Postponed aging in university teachers. *Rejuvenation Research, 13*(2–3), 353–355.

Kroesbergen, E.H., van 't Noordende, J.E., & Kolkman, M.E. (2014). Training working memory in kindergarten children: Effects on working memory and early numeracy. *Child Neuropsychology, 20,* 23–37.

Kroger, J. (2012). The status of identity development in identity research. In P.K. Kerig, M.S. Schulz, & S.T. Hauser (Eds.), *Adolescence and beyond.* New York: Oxford University Press.

Kroger, J. (2015). Identity development through adulthood: The move toward "wholeness." In K.C. McLean & M. Syed (Eds.), *Oxford handbook of identity development.* New York: Oxford University Press.

Kroger, J., Martinussen, M., & Marcia, J.E. (2010). Identity change during adolescence and young adulthood: A meta-analysis. *Journal of Adolescence, 33,* 683–698.

Krstic, D., & Knuesel, I. (2013). Deciphering the mechanism underlying late-onset Alzheimer disease. *Nature Reviews: Neurology, 9,* 24–34.

Krueger, P.M., & Chang, V.W. (2008). Being poor and coping with stress: Health behaviors and the risk of death. *American Journal of Public Health, 98,* 889–896.

Kruger, J., Blanck, H.M., & Gillespie, C. (2006). Dietary and physical activity behaviors among adults successful at weight loss management. *International Journal of Behavioral Nutrition and Physical Activity, 3,* 17.

Krushkal, J., & others (2014). Epigenetic analysis of neurocognitive development at 1 year of age in a community-based pregnancy cohort. *Behavior Genetics, 44,* 113–125.

Kubicek, B., Korunka, C., Hoonakker, P., & Raymo, J.M. (2010). Work and family characteristics as predictors of early retirement in men and women. *Research on Aging, 32,* 467–498.

Kübler-Ross, E. (1969). *On death and dying.* New York: Macmillan.

Kucian, K., & von Aster, M. (2015). Developmental dyscalculia. *European Journal of Pediatrics, 174,* 1–13.

Kuczynski, L., Parkin, C.M., & Pitman, R. (2015). Socialization as dynamic process: A dialectical, transactional process. In J. Grusec & P.D. Hastings (Eds.), *Handbook of socialization* (2nd ed.). New York: Guilford.

Kudo, M.F., Lussier, C.M., & Swanson, H.L. (2015). Reading disabilities in chidren: A selective meta-analysis of the cognitive literature. *Research in Developmental Disabilities, 40C,* 51–62.

Kuebli, J. (1994, March). Young children's understanding of everyday emotions. *Young Children,* pp. 36–48.

Kuhl, P.K. (1993). Infant speech perception: A window on psycholinguistic development. *International Journal of Psycholinguistics, 9,* 33–56.

Kuhl, P.K. (2000). A new view of language acquisition. *Proceedings of the National Academy of Sciences, 97*(22), 11850–11857.

Kuhl, P.K. (2007). Is speech learning "gated" by the social brain? *Developmental Science, 10,* 110–120.

Kuhl, P.K. (2009). Linking infant speech perception to language acquisition: Phonetic learning predicts language growth. In J. Colombo, P. McCardle, & L. Freund (Eds.), *Infant pathways to language.* New York: Psychology Press.

Kuhl, P.K. (2011). Social mechanisms in early language acquisition: Understanding integrated brain systems and supporting language. In J. Decety & J. Cacioppo (Eds.), *Handbook of social neuroscience.* New York: Oxford University Press.

Kuhn, D. (1998). Afterword to Volume 2: Cognition, perception, and language. In W. Damon (Ed.), *Handbook of child psychology* (5th ed., Vol. 2). New York: Wiley.

Kuhn, D. (2008). Formal operations from a twenty-first-century perspective. *Human Development, 51,* 48–55.

Kuhn, D. (2009). Adolescent thinking. In R.M. Lerner & L. Steinberg (Eds.), *Handbook of adolescent psychology* (3rd ed.). New York: Wiley.

Kuhn, D. (2011). What is scientific thinking and how does it develop? In U. Goswami (Ed.), *Wiley-Blackwell handbook of childhood cognitive development* (2nd ed.). New York: Wiley-Blackwell.

Kuhn, D. (2013). Reasoning. In P.D. Zelazo (Ed.), *Oxford handbook of developmental psychology.* New York: Oxford University Press.

Kuhn, D., Cheney, R., & Weinstock, M. (2000). The development of epistemological understanding. *Cognitive Development, 15,* 309–328.

Kuhn, D., & Franklin, S. (2006). The second decade: What develops (and how)? In W. Damon & R. Lerner (Eds.), *Handbook of child psychology* (6th ed.). New York: Wiley.

Kuhn, D., Schauble, L., & Garcia-Mila, M. (1992). Cross-domain development of scientific reasoning. *Cognition and Instruction, 9,* 285–327.

Kulik, L., & Heine-Cohen, E. (2011). Coping resources, perceived stress, and adjustment among Israeli women: Assessing effects. *Journal of Social Psychology, 151,* 5–30.

Kulmala, J., & others (2013). Perceived stress symptoms in midlife predict disability in old age: A 28-year prospective study. *Journals of Gerontology A: Biological Sciences and Medical Sciences, 68,* 984–991.

Kulu, H. (2014). Marriage duration and divorce: The seven year itch or a lifelong itch? *Demography, 51,* 881–893.

Kumar, R., & others (2014). Interactions between the FTO and GNB3 genes contribute to varied phenotypes in hypertension. *PLoS One, 8*(5), e63934.

Kuncel, N.R., Rose, M., Ejogu, K., & Yang, Z. (2014). Cognitive ability and socio-economic status relations with job performance. *Intelligence, 46,* 203–208.

Kunzmann, U., Kappes, C., & Wrosch, C. (2014). Emotional aging: A discrete emotions perspective. *Frontiers in Psychology, 5,* 380.

Kunzweiler, C. (2007). Twin individuality. *Fresh Ink: Essays from Boston College's First-Year Writing Seminar, 9*(1), 2–3.

Kuo, L.J., & Anderson, R.C. (2012). Effects of early bilingualism on learning phonological regularities in a new language. *Journal of Experimental Child Psychology, 111,* 455–467.

Kuo, M.C., Kiu, I.P., Ting, K.H., & Chan, C.C. (2014). Age-related effects on perceptual and semantic encoding in memory. *Neuroscience, 261,* 95–106.

Kuperberg, A. (2014). Age at coresidence, premarital cohabitation, and marriage dissolution: 1985–2009. *Journal of Marriage and Family, 76,* 352–369.

Kurdek, L.A. (2008). Change in relationship quality for partners from lesbian, gay male, and heterosexual couples. *Journal of Family Psychology, 22,* 701–711.

Kwan, M.Y., Cairney, J., Faulkner, G.E., & Pullenayegum, E.E. (2012). Physical activity and other health-risk behaviors during the transition into early adulthood: A longitudinal cohort study. *American Journal of Preventive Medicine, 42,* 14–20.

Kymre, I.G. (2014). NICU nurses' ambivalent attitudes in skin-to-skin care practice. *International Journal of Qualitative Studies on Health and Well-Being, 9,* 23297.

L

Labouvie-Vief, G. (1986, August). *Modes of knowing and life-span cognition.* Paper presented at the meeting of the American Psychological Association, Washington, DC.

Labouvie-Vief, G. (2009). Cognition and equilibrium regulation in development and aging. In V. Bengtson & others (Eds.), *Handbook of theories of aging.* New York: Springer.

Labouvie-Vief, G., Gruhn, D., & Studer, J. (2010). Dynamic integration of emotion and cognition: Equilibrium regulation in development and aging. In M.E. Lamb, A. Freund, & R.M. Lerner (Eds.), *Handbook of life-span development* (Vol. 2). New York: Wiley.

LaBrie, J.W., Hummer, J., Kenney, S., Lac, A., & Pedersen, E. (2011). Identifying factors that increase the likelihood for alcohol-induced blackouts in the prepartying context. *Substance Use and Misuse, 46,* 992–1002.

Lacelle, C., Hebert, M., Lavoie, F., Vitaro, F., & Tremblay, R.E. (2012). Sexual health in women reporting a history of child sexual abuse. *Child Abuse and Neglect, 36,* 247–259.

Lachman, M., & Kranz, E. (2010). The midlife crisis. In I. Wiener & E. Craighead (Eds.), *The Corsini encyclopedia of psychology* (4th ed.). New York: Wiley.

Lachman, M.E. (2004). Development in midlife. *Annual Review of Psychology* (Vol. 55). Palo Alto, CA: Annual Reviews.

Lachman, M.E., Agrigoroaei, S., Murphy, C., & Tun, P.A. (2010). Frequent cognitive activity compensates for education difference in episodic memory. *American Journal of Geriatric Psychiatry, 18,* 4–10.

Lachman, M.E., Neupert, S., & Agrigoraei, S. (2011). The relevance of control beliefs for health and aging. In K.W. Schaie & S.L. Willis (Eds.), *Handbook of the psychology of aging* (7th ed.). New York: Elsevier.

Ladd, G., Buhs, E., & Troop, W. (2004). School adjustment and social skills training. In P.K. Smith & C.H. Hart (Eds.), *Wiley-Blackwell handbook of childhood social development.* Malden, MA: Blackwell.

LaFrance, M., Hecht, M.A., & Paluck, E.L. (2003). The contingent smile: A meta-analysis of sex differences in smiling. *Psychological Bulletin, 129,* 305–334.

Lafreniere, D., & Mann, N. (2009). Anosmia: Loss of smell in the elderly. *Otolaryngologic Clinics of North America, 42,* 123–131.

Lagattuta, K.H. (2014a). *Children and emotion. New insights into developmental affective science.* Basel, Switzerland: Karger.

Lagattuta, K.H. (2014b). Linking past, present, and future: Children's ability to connect mental states and emotions across time. *Child Development Perspectives, 8,* 90–95.

Lahat, A., & others (2014). Early behavioral inhibition and increased error monitoring predict later social phobia symptoms in childhood. *Journal of the American Academy of Child and Adolescent Psychiatry, 53,* 447–455.

Lai, M-C., Lombardo, M.V., Chakrabarti, B., & Baron-Cohen, S. (2013). Subgrouping the autism "spectrum": Reflections on DSM-5. *PLoS Biology, 11*(4), e1001544.

Laible, D.J., & Thompson, R.A. (2000). Mother-child discourse, attachment security, shared positive affect, and early conscience development. *Child Development, 71,* 1424–1440.

Laible, D.J., & Thompson, R.A. (2007). Early socialization: A relationship perspective. In J.E. Grusec & P.D. Hastings (Eds.), *Handbook of socialization.* New York: Guilford.

Laible, D.J., Thompson, R.A., & Froimson, J. (2015). Early socialization: The influence of close relationships. In J.E. Grusec & P.D. Hastings (Eds.), *Handbook of socialization* (2nd ed.). New York: Guilford.

Laird, R.D., & Marrero, M.D. (2010). Information management and behavior problems: Is concealing misbehavior necessarily a sign of trouble? *Journal of Adolescence, 33,* 297–308.

Lakoski, S., & others (2013, June 2). *Exercise lowers cancer risk in middle-aged men.* Paper presented at the American Society of Clinical Oncology meeting, Chicago, IL.

Lamb, M.E. (1994). Infant care practices and the application of knowledge. In C.B. Fisher & R.M. Lerner (Eds.), *Applied developmental psychology.* New York: McGraw-Hill.

Lamb, M.E. (2013). Commentary: Early experience, neurobiology, plasticity, vulnerability, and resilience. In D. Narváez & others (Eds.), *Evolution, early experience, and human development.* New York: Oxford University Press.

Lamb, M.E. (2015). Unraveling the processes that underlie social, emotional, and personality development: A preliminary survey of the terrain. In R.M. Lerner (Ed.), *Handbook of child psychology and developmental science* (7th ed.). New York: Wiley.

Lamb, M.E., Bornstein, M.H., & Teti, D.M. (2002). *Development in infancy* (4th ed.). Mahwah, NJ: Erlbaum.

Lamb, M.E., & Lewis, C. (2013). Father-child relationships. In C.S. Tamis-LeMonda & N. Cabrera (Eds.), *Handbook of father involvement* (2nd ed.). New York: Psychology Press.

Lamb, M.E., Malloy, L.C., Hershkowitz, I., & La Rooy, D. (2015). Children and the law. In R.E. Lerner (Ed.), *Handbook of child psychology and developmental science* (7th ed.). New York: Wiley.

Lambert, N.M., Fincham, F.D., & Stillman, T.F. (2012). Gratitude and depressive symptoms: The role of positive reframing and positive emotion. *Cognition and Emotion, 26,* 615–633.

Lampard, A.M., Byrne, S.M., McLean, N., & Fursland, A. (2012). The Eating Disorder Inventory-2 perfectionism scale: Factor structure and associations with dietary restraint and weight and shape concern in eating disorders. *Eating Behaviors, 13,* 49–53.

Lamy, C. (2012). Poverty is a knot, preschool is an untangler. In R.C. Pianta (Ed.), *Handbook of early childhood education.* New York: Guilford.

Lamy, S., & others (2015, in press). Psychological and organizational work factors and incidence of arterial hypertension among female healthcare workers: Results of the Organisation des Soins et Sante des Soignants cohort. *Journal of Hypertension.*

Lanciano, T., & Curci, A. (2014). Incremental validity of emotional intelligence ability in predicting academic achievement. *American Journal of Psychology, 127,* 447–461.

Landes, S.D., Ardelt, M., Vaillant, G.E., & Waldinger, R.J. (2014). Childhood diversity, midlife generativity, and later life well-being. *Journals of Gerontology B: Psychological Sciences and Social Sciences, 69,* 942–952.

Landrum, A.R., Mills, C.M., & Johnston, A.M. (2013). When do children trust the expert? Benevolence information influences children's trust more than expertise. *Developmental Science, 16,* 622–638.

Lane, H. (1976). *The wild boy of Aveyron.* Cambridge, MA: Harvard University Press.

Lange, B.S., & others (2010). The potential of virtual reality and gaming to assist successful aging with disability. *Physical Medicine and Rehabilitation Clinics of North America, 21,* 339–356.

Langer, E.J. (2005). *On becoming an artist.* New York: Ballantine.

Lango Allen, H., & others (2014). Next generation sequencing of chromosomal arrangements in patients with split-hand/split-foot malformation provides evidence for DYNC111 exonic enhancers of DLX5/6 expression in humans. *Journal of Medical Genetics.*

Langstrom, N., Rahman, Q., Carlstrom, E., & Lichtenstein, P. (2010). Genetic and environmental effects on same-sex behavior: A population study of twins in Sweden. *Archives of Sexual Behavior, 39,* 75–80.

Lankford, L., & others (2015). Early gestation chorionic villi-derived stromal cells for fetal tissue engineering. *World Journal of Stem Cells, 7,* 195–207.

Lansford, J.E. (2009). Parental divorce and children's adjustment. *Perspectives on Psychological Science, 4,* 140–152.

Lansford, J.E. (2012). Divorce. In R.J.R. Levesque (Ed.), *Encyclopedia of adolescence.* New York: Springer.

Lansford, J.E. (2013). Single- and two-parent families. In J. Hattie & E. Anderman (Eds.), *International handbook of student achievement.* New York: Routledge.

Lansford, J.E., & Deater-Deckard, K. (2012). Childrearing discipline and violence in developing countries. *Child Development, 83*(1), 62–75.

Lansford, J.E., Malone, P.S., Dodge, K.A., Petti, G.S., & Bates, J.E. (2010). Developmental cascades of peer rejection, social information processing biases, and aggression during middle school. *Development and Psychopathology, 22,* 593–602.

Lansford, J.E., Wager, L.B., Bates, J.E., Pettit, G.S., & Dodge, K.A. (2012). Forms of spanking and children's externalizing problems. *Family Relations, 61*(2), 224–236.

Lansford, J.E., Yu, T., Erath, S., Pettit, G.S., Bates, J.E., & Dodge, K.A. (2010). Developmental precursors of number of sexual partners from age 16 to 22. *Journal of Research on Adolescence, 20,* 651–677.

Lansford, J.E., & others (2005). Cultural normativeness as a moderator of the link between physical discipline and children's adjustment: A comparison of China, India, Italy, Kenya, Philippines, and Thailand. *Child Development, 76,* 1234–1246.

Lansford, J.E., & others (2014). Corporal punishment, maternal warmth, and child adjustment: A longitudinal study in eight countries. *Journal of Clinical Child and Adolescent Psychology, 43,* 670–685.

Lapsley, D., & Carlo, G. (2014). Moral development at the crossroads: New trends and possible futures. *Developmental Psychology, 50,* 1–7.

Lapsley, D., & Stey, P.C. (2014). Moral self-identity as the aim of education. In L. Nucci, T. Krettenauer, & D. Narváez (Eds.), *Handbook of moral and character education* (2nd ed.). New York: Routledge.

Lapsley, D.K., & Hill, P.L. (2010). Subjective invulnerability, optimism bias, and adjustment in emerging adulthood. *Journal of Youth and Adolescence, 39,* 847–857.

Larsen, J.K., & others (2015). How parental dietary behavior and food parenting practices affect children's dietary behavior. Interacting sources of influence? *Appetite, 89,* 246–257.

Larson, R., & Richards, M.H. (1994). *Divergent realities.* New York: Basic Books.

Larson, R., & Verma, S. (1999). How children and adolescents spend time around the world: Work, play, and developmental opportunities. *Psychological Bulletin, 125,* 701–736.

Larson, R.W. (2001). How U.S. children spend time: What it does (and doesn't) tell us about their development. *Current Directions in Psychological Science, 10,* 160–164.

Larson, R.W., & Dawes, N.P. (2013). Cultivating intrinsic motivation in American youth programs. In M. Csikszentmihalyi (Ed.), *Education and youth development in cross-cultural psychology: Contributions from positive psychology.* New York: Springer.

Larson, R.W., Wilson, S., & Rickman, A. (2009). Globalization, societal change, and adolescence across the world. In R.M. Lerner & L. Steinberg (Eds.), *Handbook of adolescent psychology* (3rd ed.). New York: Wiley.

Larzelere, R.E., & Kuhn, B.R. (2005). Comparing child outcomes of physical punishment and alternative disciplinary tactics: A meta-analysis. *Clinical Child and Family Psychology Review, 8,* 1–37.

Lau, M., Lin, H., & Flores, G. (2015, in press). Clusters of factors identify a high prevalence of pregnancy involvement among U.S. adolescent males. *Maternal and Child Health Journal.*

Lauer, R.H., & Lauer, J.C. (2012). *Marriage and the family* (8th ed.). New York: McGraw-Hill.

Laumann, E.O., Glasser, D.B., Never, R.C., & Moreira, E.D. (2009). A population-based survey of sexual activity, sexual problems, and associated help-seeking behavior patterns in mature adults in the United States of America. *International Journal of Impotence Research, 21,* 171–178.

Launay, F. (2015). Sports-related overuse injuries in children. *Orthopedics and Traumatology: Surgery, and Research, 101*(S1), S139–S147.

Lauricella, A.R., Gola, A.H., & Calvert, S.L. (2011). Toddlers' learning from socially meaningful video characters. *Media Psychology, 14,* 216–232.

Laursen, B., & Collins, W.A. (2009). Parent-child relationships during adolescence. In R.M. Lerner & L. Steinberg (Eds.), *Handbook of adolescent psychology* (3rd ed.). New York: Wiley.

Lavalliere, M., & others (2011). Changing lanes in a simulator: Effects of aging on the control of the vehicle and visual inspection of mirrors and the blind spot. *Traffic Injury Prevention, 12,* 191–200.

Lavender, J.M., & others (2014). Dimensions of emotion dysregulation in bulimia nervosa. *European Eating Disorders Review, 22,* 212–216.

Lavner, J.A., & Bradbury, T.N. (2012). Why do even satisfied newlyweds eventually go on to divorce? *Journal of Family Psychology, 26,* 1–10.

Lawson, K.M., & others (2014). Daily positive spillover and crossover from mothers' work to youth health. *Journal of Family Psychology, 28,* 897–907.

Leach, P. (1990). *Your baby and child: From birth to age five.* New York: Knopf.

Leaper, C. (2013). Gender development during childhood. In P.D. Zelazo (Ed.), *Oxford handbook of developmental psychology.* New York: Oxford University Press.

Leaper, C. (2015). Gender development from a social-cognitive perspective. In R.M. Lerner (Ed.), *Handbook of child psychology and developmental science* (7th ed.). New York: Wiley.

Leaper, C., & Smith, T.E. (2004). A meta-analytic review of gender variations in children's language use: Talkativeness, affiliative speech, and assertive speech. *Developmental Psychology, 40,* 993–1027.

Ledesma, K. (2012). A place to call home. *Adoptive Families.* Retrieved August 8, 2012, from www.adoptivefamilies.com/articles.php?aid=2129

Lee, C.K., & others (2015). Prospective effects of possible selves on alcohol consumption in adolescents. *Research in Nursing & Health, 38,* 71–81.

Lee, G.R. (2014). Current research on widowhood: Devastation and human resilience. *Journals of Gerontology B: Psychological Sciences and Social Sciences, 69,* 2–3.

Lee, H.B., & others (2014). Five-factor model personality traits as predictors of incident coronary heart disease in the community: A 10.5-year cohort study based on the Baltimore epidemiological catchment area follow-up study. *Psychosomatics, 55,* 352–361.

Lee, I.M., & Skerrett, P.J. (2001). Physical activity and all-cause mortality: What is the dose-response relation? *Medical Science and Sports Exercise, 33*(Suppl. 6), S459–S471.

Lee, J.E., Kahana, B., & Kahana, E. (2015, in press). Social support and cognitive functioning as resources for elderly persons with chronic arthritis pain. *Aging and Mental Health.*

Lee, J.H., Jang, A.S., Park, S.W., Kim, D.J., & Park, C.S. (2014). Gene-gene interaction between CCR3 and Eotaxin genes: The relationship with blood eosinophilia in asthma. *Allergy, Asthma, and Immunology Research, 6,* 55–60.

Lee, J.H., & Park, C.S. (2014). Gene-gene interactions among MCP genes polymorphisms in asthma. *Allergy, Asthma, and Immunology Research, 6,* 333–340.

Lee, K., Cameron, C.A., Doucette, J., & Talwar, V. (2002). Phantoms and fabrications: Young children's detection of implausible lies. *Child Development, 73,* 1688–1702.

Lee, K., Quinn, P.C., Pascalis, O., & Slater, A. (2013). Development of face processing ability in childhood. In P.D. Zelazo (Ed.), *Oxford handbook of developmental psychology.* Oxford, UK: Oxford University Press.

Lee, K.Y., & others (2011). Effects of combined radiofrequency radiation exposure on the cell cycle and its regulatory proteins. *Bioelectromagnetics, 32,* 169–178.

Lee, T-W., Wu, Y-T., Yu, Y., Wu, H-C., & Chen, T-J. (2012). A smarter brain is associated with stronger neural interaction in healthy young females: A resting EEG coherence study. *Intelligence, 40,* 38-48.

Lee, Y.H., & Song, G.G. (2014). Genome-wide pathway analysis in attention-deficit/hyperactivity disorder. *Neurological Sciences, 35,* 1189–1196.

Leedy, P.D., & Ormrod, J.E. (2016, in press). *Practical research* (11th ed.). Upper Saddle River, NJ: Pearson.

Leeman, R.F., & others (2014). Impulsivity, sensation-seeking, and part-time job status in relation to substance use and gambling in adolescents. *Journal of Adolescent Health, 54,* 460–466.

Leerkes, E.M., Parade, S.H., & Gudmundson, J.A. (2011). Mothers' emotional reactions to crying pose risk for subsequent attachment insecurity. *Journal of Family Psychology, 25,* 635–643.

Lefkowitz, E.S., & Gillen, M.M. (2006). "Sex is just a normal part of life": Sexuality in emerging adulthood. In J.J. Arnett & J.L. Tanner (Eds.), *Emerging adults in America.* Washington, DC: American Psychological Association.

Leger, D., Beck, F., Richard, J.B., & Godeau, E. (2012). Total sleep time severely drops in adolescence. *PLoS One, 7*(10), e45204.

Legerstee, M. (1997). Contingency effects of people and objects on subsequent cognitive functioning in 3-month-old infants. *Social Development, 6,* 307–321.

Lehman, H.C. (1960). The age decrement in outstanding scientific creativity. *American Psychologist, 15,* 128–134.

Lehrer, R., & Schauble, L. (2006). Scientific thinking and scientific literacy. In W. Damon & R. Lerner (Eds.), *Handbook of child psychology* (6th ed.). New York: Wiley.

Leming, M.R., & Dickinson, G.E. (2011). *Understanding death, dying, and bereavement* (7th ed.). Boston: Cengage.

Lempers, J.D., Flavell, E.R., & Flavell, J.H. (1977). The development in very young children of tacit knowledge concerning visual perception. *Genetic Psychology Monographs, 95,* 3–53.

Lenhart, A. (2012). Teens, smartphones, and texting: Texting volume is up while the frequency of voice calling is down. Retrieved May 2, 2013, from http://pewinternet.org/~/medai/Files/Reorts/2012/PIP_Teens_Smartphones_and-Texting.pdf

Lenhart, A., Purcel, K., Smith, A., & Zickuhr, K. (2010). *Social media and mobile Internet use among teens and young adults.* Washington, DC: Pew Research Center.

Lennon, E.M., Gardner, J.M., Karmel, B.Z., & Flory, M.J. (2008). Bayley Scales of Infant Development. In M.M. Haith & J.B. Benson (Eds.), *Encyclopedia of infant and early childhood development.* Oxford, UK: Elsevier.

Lenoir, C.P., Mallet, E., & Calenda, E. (2000). Siblings of sudden infant death syndrome and near miss in about 30 families: Is there a genetic link? *Medical Hypotheses, 54,* 408–411.

Lenz, M., & others (2012). Increased excitability of somatosensory cortex in aged humans is associated with impaired tactile acuity. *Journal of Neuroscience, 32,* i1811–i1816.

Leon, J., & others (2015). A combination of physical and cognitive exercise improves reaction time in 61-84-years-old persons. *Journal of Aging and Physical Activity, 23,* 72–77.

Leone, J.E., Mullin, E.M., Maurer-Starks, S.S., & Rovito, M.J. (2014). The Adolescent Body Image Satisfaction Scale (ABISS) for males: Exploratory factor analysis and implications for strength and conditioning professionals. *Journal of Strength and Conditioning Research, 28,* 2657–2668.

Lepage, J.F., & others (2014). Brain morphology in children with 47, XYY syndrome: A voxel- and surface-based morphometric study. *Genes, Brain, and Behavior, 113,* 127–134.

Leppakoski, T.H., Flinck, A., & Paavilainen, E. (2015). Greater commitment to the domestic violence training is required. *Journal of Interprofessional Care, 29*(3), 281–283.

Leppanen, J.M., Moulson, M., Vogel-Farley, V.K., & Nelson, C.A. (2007). An ERP study of emotional face processing in the adult and infant brain. *Child Development, 78,* 232–245.

Lereya, S.T., Samara, M., & Wolke, D. (2013). Parenting behavior and the risk of becoming victim and a bully/victim: A meta-analysis study. *Child Abuse and Neglect, 37*(12), 1091–1098.

Lerner, H.G. (1989). *The dance of intimacy.* New York: Harper & Row.

Lerner, J.V., & others (2013). Positive youth development: Processes, philosophies, and programs. In I.B. Weiner & others (Eds.), *Handbook of psychology* (2nd ed., Vol. 6). New York: Wiley.

Lerner, R.M., Boyd, M., & Du, D. (2008). Adolescent development. In I.B. Weiner & C.B. Craighead (Eds.), *Encyclopedia of psychology* (4th ed.). Hoboken, NJ: Wiley.

Lerner, R.M., Lerner, J.V., Bowers, E., & Geldhof, G.J. (2015). Positive youth development: A relational developmental systems model. In R.M. Lerner (Ed.), *Handbook of child psychology and developmental science* (7th ed.). New York: Wiley.

Lerner-Geva, L., Boyko, V., Blumstein, T., & Benyamini, Y. (2010). The impact of education, cultural background, and lifestyle on symptoms of the menopausal transition: The Women's Health at Midlife Study. *Journal of Women's Health, 19*(5), 975–985.

Lesaux, N.K., & Siegel, L.S. (2003). The development of reading in children who speak English as a second language. *Developmental Psychology, 39,* 1005–1019.

Leshikar, E.D., & Duarte, A. (2014). Medial prefrontal cortex supports source memory for self-referenced materials in young and older adults. *Cognitive, Affective, and Behavioral Neuroscience, 14,* 236–252.

Leslie, S.J., Cimpian, A., Meyer, M., & Freeland, E. (2015). Expectations of brilliance underlie gender distributions across academic disciplines. *Science, 347,* 262–265.

Lessow-Hurley, J. (2013). *The foundations of dual language instruction* (6th ed.). Upper Saddle River, NJ: Pearson.

Lester, B.M., & others (2002). The maternal lifestyle study: Effects of substance exposure during pregnancy on neurodevelopmental outcome in 1-month-old infants. *Pediatrics, 110,* 1182–1192.

Leung, C.Y., & others (2014). Surgency and negative affectivity, but not effortful control, are uniquely associated with obesogenic eating behaviors among low-income preschoolers. *Appetite, 78,* 139–146.

Leung, D.Y., & others (2015). The effect of a virtual ward program on emergency services utilization and quality of life in frail elderly patients after discharge: A pilot study. *Clinical Interventions in Aging, 10,* 413–420.

Levant, R.F. (2001). Men and masculinity. In J. Worell (Ed.), *Encyclopedia of women and gender.* San Diego: Academic Press.

Levasseur, M., & Couture, M. (2015). Coping strategies associated with participation and quality of life in older adults. *Canadian Journal of Occupational Therapy, 82,* 44–53.

Levelt, W.J.M. (1989). *Speaking: From intention to articulation.* Cambridge, MA: MIT Press.

Leventhal, T., & Brooks-Gunn, J. (2011). Changes in neighborhood poverty from 1990 to 2000 and youths' problem behaviors. *Developmental Psychology, 47,* 1680–1696.

Leventhal, T., Dupere, V., & Shuey, E. (2015). Children in neighborhoods. In R.M. Lerner (Ed.), *Handbook of child psychology and developmental science* (7th ed.). New York: Wiley.

Lever-Duffy, J., & McDonald, J. (2015). *Teaching and learning with technology* (5th ed.). Upper Saddle River, NJ: Pearson.

Levin, J.A., Fox, J.A., & Forde, D.R. (2014). *Elementary statistics in social research* (12th ed.). Upper Saddle River, NJ: Pearson.

Levine, T.P., & others (2008). Effects of prenatal cocaine exposure on special education in school-aged children. *Pediatrics, 122,* e83–e91.

Levinson, D.J. (1978). *The seasons of a man's life.* New York: Knopf.

Levinson, D.J. (1987, August). *The seasons of a woman's life.* Paper presented at the meeting of the American Psychological Association, New York.

Levinson, D.J. (1996). *Seasons of a woman's life.* New York: Knopf.

Levy, G.D., Sadovsky, A.L., & Troseth, G.L. (2000). Aspects of young children's perceptions of gender-typed occupations. *Sex Roles, 42,* 993–1006.

Levy, S., & others (2014). An electronic screen for triaging adolescent substance use by risk levels. *JAMA Pediatrics, 168,* 822–828.

Lewin, A., & others (2015, in press). Strengthening positive coparenting in teen parents: A cultural adaptation of an evidence-based intervention. *Journal of Primary Prevention.*

Lewis, A.C. (2007). Looking beyond NCLB. *Phi Delta Kappan, 88,* 483–484.

Lewis, G.J., Haworth, C.M.A., & Plomin, R. (2014). Identical genetic influences underpin behavior problems in adolescence and basic traits of personality. *Journal of Child Psychology and Psychiatry, 55,* 865–875.

Lewis, K.M., & others (2013). Problem behavior and urban, low-income youth: A randomized controlled trial of positive action in Chicago. *American Journal of Preventive Medicine, 44,* 622–630.

Lewis, M. (2005). Selfhood. In B. Hopkins (Ed.), *The Cambridge encyclopedia of child development.* Cambridge, UK: Cambridge University Press.

Lewis, M. (2007). Early emotional development. In A. Slater & M. Lewis (Eds.), *Introduction to infant development.* Malden, MA: Blackwell.

Lewis, M. (2008). The emergence of human emotions. In M. Lewis, J.M. Haviland Jones, & L. Feldman Barrett (Eds.), *Handbook of emotions* (3rd ed.). New York: Guilford.

Lewis, M. (2010). The emergence of consciousness and its role in human development. In W.F. Overton & R.M. Lerner (Eds.), *Handbook of life-span development.* New York: Wiley.

Lewis, M. (2015). Emotional development and consciousness. In R.M. Lerner (Ed.), *Handbook of child psychology and developmental science* (7th ed.). New York: Wiley.

Lewis, M., & Brooks-Gunn, J. (1979). *Social cognition and the acquisition of the self.* New York: Plenum.

Lewis, M., Feiring, C., & Rosenthal, S. (2000). Attachment over time. *Child Development, 71,* 707–720.

Lewis, R. (2015). *Human genetics* (11th ed.). New York: McGraw-Hill.

Lewis, T.L., & Maurer, D. (2005). Multiple sensitive periods in human visual development: Evidence from visually deprived children. *Developmental Psychobiology, 46,* 163–183.

Lewis, T.L., & Maurer, D. (2009). Effects of early pattern deprivation on visual development. *Optometry and Vision Science, 86,* 640–646.

Lewis-Morrarty, E., & others (2015). Infant attachment security and early childhood behavioral inhibition interact to predict adolescent social anxiety symptoms. *Child Development, 86,* 598–613.

Leyton, M., & Vezina, P. (2014). Dopamine ups and downs in vulnerability to addictions: A neurodevelopmental model. *Trends in Pharmacological Sciences, 35,* 268–276.

Li, C., Ford, E.S., McGuire, L.C., & Mokdad, A.H. (2007). Increasing trends in waist circumference and abdominal obesity among U.S. adults. *Obesity, 15,* 216–224.

Li, D., Zhang, W., Li, X., Li, N., & Ye, B. (2012). Gratitude and suicidal ideation and suicide attempts among Chinese adolescents: Direct, mediated, and moderated effects. *Journal of Adolescence, 35,* 55–66.

Li, F., & others (2014). Intrinsic brain abnormalities in attention deficit hyperactivity disorder: A resting-state functional MR imaging study. *Radiology, 272,* 514–523.

Li, F.J., Shen, L., & Ji, H.F. (2012). Dietary intakes of vitamin E, vitamin C, and b-carotene, and risk of Alzheimer's disease: A meta-analysis. *Journal of Alzheimer's Disease, 31*(2), 253–258.

Li, H., Ji, Y., & Chen, T. (2014). The roles of different sources of social support on emotional well-being among Chinese elderly. *PLoS One, 9*(3), e90051.

Li, J., Olsen, J., Vestergaard, M., & Obel, C. (2011). Low Apgar scores and risk of childhood attention deficit hyperactivity disorder. *Journal of Pediatrics, 158,* 775–779.

Li, J., & others (2015, in press). Global correlation analysis for microRNA and gene expression profiles in human obesity. *Pathology, Research, and Practice.*

Li, S., Callaghan, B.L., & Richardson, R. (2014). Infantile amnesia: Forgotten but not gone. *Learning and Memory, 21,* 135–139.

Li, T., & Chan, D. K-S. (2012). How anxious and avoidant attachment affect romantic relationship quality differently: A meta-analytic review, *42,* 406–419.

Li, T., & Zhang, Y. (2015). Social network types and the health of older adults: Exploring reciprocal associations. *Social Science & Medicine, 130,* 59–68.

Li, W., Farkas, G., Duncan, G.J., Burchinal, M.R., & Vandell, D.L. (2013). Timing of high-quality child care and cognitive, language, and preacademic development. *Developmental Psychology, 49*(8), 1440–1451.

Li, X., & others (2015). Sonographic markers of fetal a-thalassemia major. *Journal of Ultrasound Medicine, 34,* 197–206.

Li, X., & others (2015, in press). White matter changes in familial Alzheimer's disease.

Li, Y. (2007). Recovering from spousal bereavement in later life: Does volunteer participation play a role? *Journals of Gerontology B: Psychological Sciences and Social Sciences, 62,* S257–S266.

Li, Z., & others (2013). Maternal severe life events and risk of neural tube defects among rural Chinese. *Birth Defects Research A: Clinical and Molecular Teratology, 97,* 109–114.

Li, Z., Chang, S.H., Zhang, L.Y., Gao, L., & Wang, J. (2014). Molecular genetic studies of ADHD and its candidate genes: A review. *Psychiatry Research, 219,* 10–24.

Liben, L.S. (1995). Psychology meets geography: Exploring the gender gap on the national geography bee. *Psychological Science Agenda, 8,* 8–9.

Liben, L.S., Bigler, R.S., & Hilliard, L.J. (2014). Gender development. In E.T. Gershoff, R.S. Mistry, & D.A. Crosby (Eds.), *Societal contexts of child development.* New York: Oxford University Press.

Libertus, K., & Needham, A. (2010). Teach to reach: The effects of active vs. passive reaching experiences on action and perception. *Vision Research, 50,* 2750–2757.

Lickliter, R. (2013). Biological development: Theoretical approaches, techniques, and key findings. In P.D. Zelazo (Ed.), *Handbook of developmental psychology.* New York: Oxford University Press.

Lickliter, R., & Honeycutt, H. (2015). Biology, development, and human systems. In R.M. Lerner (Ed.), *Handbook of child psychology and developmental science* (7th ed.). New York: Wiley.

Liebenthal, J.A., & others (2015). Association of prone position with sudden unexpected death in epilepsy. *Neurology, 84,* 703–709.

Lieverse, R., & others (2013). Social support and social rhythm regularity in elderly patients with major depressive disorder. *American Journal of Geriatric Psychiatry, 21,* 1144–1153.

Lifton, R.J. (1977). The sense of immortality: On death and the continuity of life. In H. Feifel (Ed.), *New meanings of death.* New York: McGraw-Hill.

Li-Korotky, H.S. (2012). Age-related hearing loss: Quality of care for quality of life. *Gerontologist, 52,* 265–271.

Lillard, A. (2006). Pretend play in toddlers. In C.A. Brownell & C.B. Kopp (Eds.), *Socioemotional development in the toddler years.* New York: Oxford University Press.

Lillard, A. (2015). The development of play. In R.M. Lerner (Ed.), *Handbook of child psychology and developmental science* (7th ed.). New York: Wiley.

Lillard, A.S., & Kavanaugh, R.D. (2014). The contribution of symbolic skills to the development of explicit theory of mind. *Child Development, 85,* 1535–1551.

Lillard, A., Pinkham, A.M., & Smith, E. (2011). Pretend play and cognitive development. In U. Goswami (Ed.), *Wiley-Blackwell handbook of childhood cognitive development* (2nd ed.). New York: Wiley.

Lima, L.G., & others (2015, in press). Effect of aerobic training and aerobic and resistance training on the inflammatory status of hypertensive older adults. *Aging: Clinical and Experimental Research.*

Lin, C.C., & others (2013). In utero exposure to environmental lead and manganese and neurodevelopment at 2 years of age. *Environmental Research, 123,* 52–57.

Lin, F.R. (2011). Hearing loss and cognition among older adults in the United States, *66,* 1131–1136.

Lin, F.R., Thorpe, R., Gordon-Salant, S., & Ferrucci, L. (2011). Hearing loss prevalence and risk factors among older adults in the United States. *Journals of Gerontology A: Biological Sciences and Medical Sciences, 66A*(5), 582–590.

Lin, L.Y., & others (2015). Effects of television exposure on developmental skills of young children. *Infant Behavior and Development, 38,* 20–26.

Lindau, S.T., & others (2007). A study of sexuality and health among older adults in the United States. *New England Journal of Medicine, 357,* 762–774.

Lindberg, L.D., & Maddow-Zimet, I. (2012). Consequences of sex education on teen and young adult sexual behaviors and outcomes. *Journal of Adolescent Health, 51,* 332–338.

Lindberg, S.M., Hyde, S.S., Petersen, J.L., & Lin, M.C. (2010). New trends in gender and mathematics performance: A meta-analysis. *Psychological Bulletin, 136,* 1123–1135.

Lindholm, M.E., & others (2014). An integrative analysis reveals coordinated reprogramming of the epigenome and the transcriptome in human skeletal muscle after training. *Epigenetics, 9,* 1557–1569.

Lindwall, M., & others (2012). Dynamic associations of change in physical activity and change in cognitive function: Coordinated analyses across four studies with up to 21 years of longitudinal data. *Journal of Aging Research, 493598.*

Linn, S. (2008). *The case for make believe: Saving play in a commercialized world.* New York: The New Press.

Lipowski, M., Lipowska, M., Jochimek, M., & Krokosz, D. (2015, in press). Resilience as a factor protecting youths from risky behavior: Moderating effects of gender and sport. *European Journal of Sport Science.*

Lippa, R.A. (2005). *Gender, nature, and nurture* (2nd ed.). Mahwah, NJ: Erlbaum.

Lippman, L.A., & Keith, J.D. (2006). The demographics of spirituality among youth: International perspectives. In E. Roehlkepartain, P.E. King, L. Wagener, & P.L. Benson (Eds.), *The handbook of spirituality in childhood and adolescence.* Thousand Oaks, CA: Sage.

Lipton, J., & Sahin, M. (2013). Fragile X syndrome therapeutics: Translation, meet translational medicine. *Neuron, 77,* 212–213.

Lisiecka, D.M., & others (2015). Developmental white matter microstructure in autism phenotype and corresponding endophenotype during adolescence. *Translational Psychiatry, 5,* e529.

Lista, S., Dubois, B., & Hampel, H. (2015). Paths to Alzheimer's disease prevention: From modifiable risk factors to biomarker enrichment strategies. *Journal of Nutrition, Health, and Aging, 19,* 154–163.

Littleton, H. (2014). Interpersonal violence on college campuses: Understanding risk factors and working to find solutions. *Trauma, Violence, and Abuse, 15,* 297–303.

Liu, C.H., Murakami, J., Iap, S., & Nagayama Hall, G.C. (2009). Who are Asian Americans? An overview of history, immigration, and communities. In N. Tewari & A. Alvarez (Eds.), *Asian American psychology.* Clifton, NJ: Psychology Press.

Liu, D., Wellman, H.M., Tardif, T., & Sabbagh, M.A. (2008). Theory of mind development in Chinese children: A meta-analysis of false-belief understanding across cultures and languages. *Developmental Psychology, 44,* 523–531.

Liu, K., & others (2012). Advanced reproductive age and fertility. *International Journal of Gynecology and Obstetrics, 117*(1), 95–102.

Liu, X., & Liu, L. (2005). Sleep habits and insomnia in a sample of elderly persons in China. *Sleep, 28,* 1579–1587.

Livingston, G. (2014, June 5). *Growing number of dads home with the kids.* Washington, DC: Pew Research Center.

Lloyd, A.B., & others (2014). Maternal and paternal parenting practices and their influence on children's adiposity, screen-time, diet, and physical activity. *Appetite, 79,* 149–157.

Lloyd, J.W., & others (2015). *Evidence-based reading instruction for ALL learners.* Upper Saddle River, NJ: Pearson.

Lloyd-Fox, S., Wu, R., Richards, J.E., Elwell, C.E., & Johnson, M.H. (2015). Cortical activation to action perception is associated with action production abilities in young infants. *Cerebral Cortex, 25,* 289–297.

Lobstein, T., & others (2015, in press). Child and adolescent obesity: Part of a bigger picture. *Lancet.*

Lochlainn, M.N., & Kenny, R.A. (2013). Sexual activity and aging. *Journal of the American Medical Directors Association, 14,* 565–572.

Lock, M. (1998). Menopause: Lessons from anthropology. *Psychosomatic Medicine, 60,* 410–419.

Locke, A.E., & others (2015). Genetic studies of body mass index yield new insights for obesity biology. *Nature, 518,* 197–206.

Lockl, K., & Schneider, W. (2007). Knowledge about the mind: Links between theory of mind and later metamemory. *Child Development, 78,* 147–167.

Loeber, R., Burke, J., & Pardini, D. (2009). The etiology and development of antisocial and delinquent behavior. *Annual Review of Psychology* (Vol. 60). Palo Alto, CA: Annual Reviews.

Loeber, R., & Farrington, D.P. (Eds.). (2001). *Child delinquents: Development, intervention and service needs.* Thousand Oaks, CA: Sage.

Lonigan, C.J. (2015). Early literacy. In R.M. Lerner (Ed.), *Handbook of child psychology and developmental science* (7th ed.). New York: Wiley.

Lonner, W.J. (1988). *The introductory psychology text and cross-cultural psychology: A survey of cross-cultural psychologists.* Bellingham: Western Washington University, Center for Cross-Cultural Research.

Loosli, S.V., Buschkuehl, M., Perrig, W.J., & Jaeggi, S.M. (2012). Working memory training improves reading processes in typically developing children. *Child Neuropsychology, 18,* 62–78.

Lopes, V.P., Gabbard, C., & Rodriques, L.P. (2013). Physical activity in adolescence: Examining influence of the best friend dyad. *Journal of Adolescent Health, 52*(6), 752–756.

Lopez, A.B., Huynh, V.W., & Fuligni, A.J. (2011). A longitudinal study of religious identity and participation during adolescence. *Child Development, 82,* 1297–1309.

Lopez-Castroman, J., & others (2015, in press). The additive effect on suicidality of family history of suicidal behavior and early traumatic experiences. *Archives of Suicide Research.*

Lorenz, K.Z. (1965). *Evolution and the modification of behavior.* Chicago: University of Chicago Press.

Los, B. (2015). *A historical syntax of English.* New York: Oxford University Press.

Losel, F., & Bender, D. (2011). Emotional and antisocial outcomes of bullying and victimization at school: A follow-up from childhood to adolescence. *Journal of Aggression, Conflict, and Peace Research, 3,* 89–96.

Lovden, M., & Lindenberger, U. (2007). Intelligence. In J.E. Birren (Ed.), *Encyclopedia of gerontology* (2nd ed.). San Diego: Academic Press.

Lovden, M., Brehmer, Y., Li, S.C., & Lindenberger, U. (2012). Training-induced compensation versus magnification of individual differences in memory performance. *Frontiers in Human Neuroscience, 6,* 141.

Love, J.M., Chazan-Cohen, R., Raikes, H., & Brooks-Gunn, J. (2013). What makes a difference: Early Head Start evaluation findings in a developmental context. *Monographs of the Society for Research in Child Development, 78,* 1–173.

Low, S., & others (2014). Engagement matters: Lessons from assessing classroom implementation of Steps to Respect: A bullying prevention program over a one-year period. *Prevention Science, 15*(2), 165–176.

Lowdermilk, D.L., Cashion, M.C., & Perry, S.E. (2014). Maternity and women's health care: Text and simulation learning package (10th ed.). New York: Elsevier.

Lowe, G., & Costabile, R.A. (2012). 10-year analysis of adverse event reports to the Food and Drug Administration for phosphodiesterase type-5 inhibitors. *Journal of Sexual Medicine, 9*(1), 265–270.

Lowe, J., & others (2014). Associations between maternal scaffolding and executive functioning in 3- and 4-year-olds born very low birth weight and normal birth weight. *Early Human Development, 90,* 587–593.

Lowe, K., & Dotterer, A.M. (2013). Parental monitoring, parental warmth, and minority youths' academic outcomes: Exploring the integrative model of parenting. *Journal of Youth and Adolescence, 42,* 1413–1475.

Lu, C.J., Yu, J.J., & Deng, J.W. (2012). Disease-syndrome combination clinical study of psoriasis: Present status, advantages, and prospects. *China Journal of Integrative Medicine, 18,* 166–171.

Lu, P.H., & others (2011). Age-related slowing in cognitive processing speed is associated with myelin integrity in a very healthy elderly sample. *Journal of Clinical and Experimental Neuropsychology, 33,* 1059–1068.

Lu, X., & others (2013). Prevalence of hypertension in overweight and obese children from a large school-based population in Shanghai, China. *BMC Public Health, 13,* 24.

Lubart, T.I. (2003). In search of creative intelligence. In R.J. Sternberg, J. Lautrey, & T.I. Lubart (Eds.), *Models of intelligence: International perspectives.* Washington, DC: American Psychological Association.

Lubinski, D. (2000). Measures of intelligence: Intelligence tests. In A. Kazdin (Ed.), *Encyclopedia of psychology.* New York: Oxford University Press.

Lucas, R.E., & Donnellan, M.B. (2011). Personality development across the life span: Longitudinal analyses with a national sample in Germany. *Journal of Personality and Social Psychology, 101,* 847–861.

Lucchetti, G., Lucchetti, A.L., & Koenig, H.G. (2011). Impact of spirituality/religiosity on mortality: Comparison with other health interventions. *Explore, 7,* 234–238.

Luchetti, M., Terracciano, A., Stephan, Y., & Sutin, A.R. (2015, in press). Personality and cognitive decline in older adults: Data from a longitudinal sample and meta-analysis. *Journals of Gerontology B: Psychological Sciences and Social Sciences.*

Lucifero, D. (2010). Stem cells—Smi's second annual conference: Achieving success in science and commercialization. *IDrugs, 13,* 232–234.

Luders, E., Narr, K.L., Thompson, P.M., & Toga, A.W. (2009). Neuroanatomical correlates of intelligence. *Intelligence, 37,* 156–163.

Luders, E., & others (2004). Gender difference in cortical complexity. *Nature Neuroscience, 7,* 799–800.

Luhmann, M., Hofmann, W., Eid, M., & Lucas, R.E. (2012). Subjective well-being and adaptation to life events: A meta-analysis. *Journal of Personality and Social Psychology 102,* 592–615.

Luijk, M.P., & others (2011). Dopaminergic, serotonergic, and oxytonergic candidate genes associated with infant attachment security and disorganization? In search of main and interaction effects. *Journal of Child Psychology and Psychiatry, 52,* 1295–1307.

Lukowski, A.F., & Bauer, P.J. (2014). Long-term memory in infancy and early childhood. In P.J. Bauer & R. Fivush (Eds.), *Wiley-Blackwell handbook of children's memory.* New York: Wiley.

Lum, H.D., Sudore, R.L., & Bekelman, D.B. (2015). Advance care planning in the elderly. *Medical Clinics of North America, 99,* 391–403.

Lumpkin, A. (2014). *Introduction to physical education, exercise science, and sport studies* (9th ed.). New York: McGraw-Hill.

Luna, B., Marek, S.A., & Larsen, B. (2015). Development of cognitive control. *Annual Review of Neuroscience.* Palo Alto, CA: Annual Reviews.

Luna, B., Padmanabhan, A., & Geier, C. (2014). The adolescent sensation-seeking period: Development of reward processing and its effect on cognitive control. In V.F. Reyna & V. Zayas (Eds.), *Neuroscience of decision making.* Washington, DC: American Psychological Association.

Lund, D.A., Utz, R., Caserta, M.S., & De Vries, B. (2009). Humor, laughter, and happiness in the lives of recently bereaved spouses. *Omega, 58,* 87–105.

Lund, H.G., Reider, B.D., Whiting, A.B., & Prichard, J.R. (2010). Sleep patterns and predictors of disturbed sleep in a large population of college students. *Journal of Adolescent Health, 46,* 124–136.

Lundin, A., Falkstedt, D., Lundberg, I., & Hemmingsson, T. (2014). Unemployment and coronary heart disease among middle-aged men in Sweden: 39,243 men followed for 8 years. *Occupational and Environmental Medicine, 71,* 183–188.

Lunenfeld, B., & others (2015, in press). Recommendations on the diagnosis, treatment, and monitoring of hypogonadism in men. *Aging Male.*

Lunkenheimer, E.S., Shields, A.M., & Cortina, K.S. (2007). Parental emotion coaching and dismissing in family interaction. *Social Development, 16,* 232–248.

Luo, Y., Hawkley, L.C., Waite, L.J., & Caccioppo, J.T. (2012). Loneliness, health, and mortality in old age: A national longitudinal study. *Social Science and Medicine, 74,* 907–914.

Luo, Y., & Waite, L.J. (2014). Loneliness and mortality among older adults in China. *Journals of Gerontology B: Psychological Sciences and Social Sciences, 69,* 633–645.

Luong, G., Rauers, A., & Fingerman, K.L. (2015). The multi-faceted nature of late-life socialization: Older adults as agents and targets of socialization. In J.E. Grusec & P.D. Hastings (Eds.), *Handbook of socialization* (2nd ed.). New York: Guilford.

Luque-Contreras, D., & others (2014). Oxidative stress and metabolic syndrome: Cause or consequence of Alzheimer's disease? *Oxidative Medicine and Cellular Longevity, 2014:* 497802.

Luria, A., & Herzog, E. (1985, April). *Gender segregation across and within settings.* Paper presented at the biennial meeting of the Society for Research in Child Development, Toronto.

Lusby, C.M., Goodman, S.H., Bell, M.A., & Newport, D.J. (2014). Electroencephalogram patterns in infants of depressed mothers. *Developmental Psychobiology, 56*(3), 459–473.

Lushington, K., Pamula, Y., Martin, A.J., & Kennedy, J.D. (2014). Developmental changes in sleep. In A.R. Wolfson & H.E. Montgomery-Downs (Eds.), *Oxford handbook of infant, child, and adolescent sleep and behavior.* New York: Oxford University Press.

Luszcz, M. (2011). Executive functioning and cognitive aging. In K.W. Schaie & S.L. Willis (Eds.), *Handbook of the psychology of aging* (7th ed.). New York: Elsevier.

Luthar, S.S. (2006). Resilience in development: A synthesis of research across five decades. In D. Cicchetti & D.J. Cohen (Eds.), *Developmental psychopathology: Vol. 3. Risk, disorder, and adaptation* (2nd ed.). Hoboken, NJ: Wiley.

Luthar, S.S., Barkin, S.H., & Crossman, E.J. (2013). "I can, therefore I must": Fragility in the upper-middle classes. *Development and Psychopathology, 25,* 1529–1549.

Luthar, S.S., & Goldstein, A.S. (2008). Substance use and related behaviors among suburban late adolescents: The importance of perceived parent containment. *Development and Psychopathology, 20,* 591–614.

Luyckx, K., & Robitschek, C. (2014). Personal growth initiative and identity formation in adolescence through young adulthood: Mediating processes on the pathway to well-being. *Journal of Adolescence, 37,* 973–981.

Luyster, F.S., & others (2012). Sleep: A health imperative. *Sleep, 35,* 727–734.

Lyberg, A., Viken, B., Haruna, M., & Severinsson, E. (2012). Diversity and challenges in the management of maternity care for immigrant women. *Journal of Nursing Management, 20,* 287–295.

Lynch, A., Elmore, B., & Kotecki, J. (2015). *Choosing health* (2nd ed.). Upper Saddle River, NJ: Pearson.

Lynch, E., Dezen, T., & Brown, N. (2012). *U.S. preterm birth rate shows five-year improvement.* Retrieved February 17, 2013, from www.marchofdimes.com/news/10894.html

Lyndaker, C., & Hulton, L. (2004). The influence of age on symptoms of perimenopause. *Journal of Obstetric, Gynecological, and Neonatal Nursing, 33,* 340–347.

Lyon, G.J., & Wang, K. (2012). Identifying disease mutations in genomic medicine settings: Current challenges and how to accelerate the process. *Genome Medicine, 4,* 58.

Lyon, T.D., & Flavell, J.H. (1993). Young children's understanding of forgetting over time. *Child Development, 64,* 789–800.

Lyons, D.M., & others (2010). Stress coping stimulates hippocampal neurogenesis in adult monkeys. *Proceedings of the National Academy of Sciences U.S.A.*

Lyons, H., Manning, W.D., Longmore, M.A., & Girodano, P.C. (2015, in press). Gender and casual sexual activity from adolescence to emerging adulthood: Social and life course correlates. *Journal of Sex Research.*

M

Ma, J.K., Le Mare, L., & Gurd, B.J. (2015, in press). Four minutes of in-class high intensity interval activity improves selective attention in 9- to 11-year-olds. *Applied Physiology, Nutrition, and Metabolism.*

Ma, Y., & others (2015). Genetic variants modify the effect of age on APOE methylation in the Genetics of Lipid Lowering Drugs and Diet Network Study, *Aging Cell, 14,* 49–59.

Maccallum, F., & Bryant, R.A. (2013). A cognitive attachment model of prolonged grief: Integrating attachments, memory, and identity. *Clinical Psychology Review, 33,* 713–727.

Maccallum, F., Sawday, S., Rinck, M., & Bryant, R.A. (2015). The push and pull of grief: Approach and avoidance in bereavement. *Journal of Behavior Therapy and Experimental Psychiatry, 48,* 105–109.

Maccoby, E.E. (1998). *The two sexes: Growing up apart, coming together.* Cambridge, MA: Harvard University Press.

Maccoby, E.E. (2002). Gender and group process: A developmental perspective. *Current Directions in Psychological Science, 11,* 54–57.

Maccoby, E.E. (2007). Historical overview of socialization theory and research. In J.E. Grusec & P.D. Hastings (Eds.), *Handbook of socialization.* New York: Guilford.

Maccoby, E.E. (2015). Historical overview of socialization theory and research. In J.E. Grusec & P.D. Hastings (Eds.), *Handbook of socialization* (2nd ed.). New York: Guilford.

Maccoby, E.E., & Martin, J.A. (1983). Socialization in the context of the family: Parent-child interaction. In P.H. Mussen (Ed.), *Handbook of child psychology* (4th ed., Vol. 4). New York: Wiley.

MacDougall, B.J., Robinson, J.D., Kappus, L., Sudikoff, S.N., & Greer, D.M. (2014). Simulation-based training in brain death determination. *Neurocritical Care, 21,* 383–391.

MacFarlane, J.A. (1975). Olfaction in the development of social preferences in the human neonate. In *Parent–infant interaction.* Ciba Foundation Symposium No. 33. Amsterdam: Elsevier.

Machado, B., & others (2014). Risk factors and antecedent life events in the development of anorexia nervosa: A Portuguese case-control study. *European Eating Disorders Review, 22,* 243–251.

Machielse, A. (2015, in press). The heterogeneity of socially isolated older adults: A social isolation typology. *Journal of Gerontological Social Work.*

Maciejewski, P.K., Zhang, B., Block, S.D., & Prigerson, H.G. (2007). An empirical examination of the stage theory of grief. *Journal of the American Medical Association, 297,* 716–723.

Maciokas, J.B., & Crognale, M.A. (2003). Cognitive and attentional changes with age: Evidence from attentional blink deficits. *Experimental/Aging Research, 29,* 137–153.

Mackin, R.S., & others (2014). Association of age at depression onset with cognitive functioning in individuals with late-life depression and executive dysfunction. *American Journal of Geriatric Psychiatry, 22,* 1633–1641.

MacLean, P.C., & others (2014). Mother-infant mutual eye gaze supports emotion regulation in infancy during the still-face paradigm. *Infant Behavior and Development, 37,* 512–522.

Macleod, A.D. (2015). Euthanasia and physician-assisted dying: Editorial comment and reply to the Waikato GP survey findings by Dr. Havill. *New Zealand Medical Journal, 128,* 9–11.

MacWhinney, B. (2015). Language development. In R.M. Lerner (Ed.), *Handbook of child psychology and developmental science* (7th ed.). New York: Wiley. *Developmental Science.*

Macy, M.L., Cunningham, R.M., Resnicow, K., & Freed, G.L. (2014). Disparities in age-appropriate child passenger restraint use among children aged 1 to 12 years. *Pediatrics, 133,* 262–271.

Madden, D.J., & others (1999). Aging and recognition memory: Changes in regional cerebral blood flow associated with components of reaction time distributions. *Journal of Cognitive Neuroscience, 11,* 511–520.

Mader, S.S. (2014). *Inquiry into life* (14th ed.). New York: McGraw-Hill.

Mader, S.S., & Windelspecht, M. (2015). *Essentials of biology* (4th ed.). New York: McGraw-Hill.

Mader, S.S., & Windelspecht, M. (2016, in press). *Human biology* (14th ed.). New York: McGraw-Hill.

Madill, A. (2012). Interviews and interviewing techniques. In H. Cooper (Ed.), *APA handbook of research methods in psychology.* Washington, DC: American Psychological Association.

Madkour, A.S., Farhat, T., Halpern, C.T., Godeu, E., & Gabhainn, S.N. (2010). Early adolescent sexual initiation as a problem behavior: A comparative study of five nations. *Journal of Adolescent Health, 47*(4), 389–398.

Maercker, A., & Lalor, J. (2012). Diagnostic and clinical considerations in prolonged grief disorder. *Dialogues in Clinical Neuroscience, 14,* 167–176.

Magdon-Maksymowicz, M.S., & Maksymowicz, A.Z. (2015, in press). Epigenetic contribution to age distribution of mortality within the Penna model. *Theory in Biosciences.*

Magno, C. (2010). The role of metacognitive skills in developing critical thinking. *Metacognition and Learning, 5,* 137–156.

Mahn, H., & John-Steiner, V. (2013). Vygotsky and sociocultural approaches to teaching and learning. In I.B. Weiner & others (Eds.), *Handbook of psychology* (2nd ed., Vol. 7). New York: Wiley.

Mahoney, J.L., Larson, R.W., & Eccles, J.S. (Eds.). (2004). *Organized activities as contexts of development.* Mahwah, NJ: Erlbaum.

Mahoney, J.L., & Vest, A.E. (2012). The overscheduling hypothesis revisited: Intensity of organized activity participation during adolescence and young adult outcomes. *Journal of Research on Adolescence, 22,* 409–418.

Mahy, C.E., Moses, L.J., & Pfeifer, J.H. (2014). How and where: Theory-of-mind in the brain. *Developmental Cognitive Neuroscience, 9,* 66–81.

Malamitsi-Puchner, A., & Boutsikou, T. (2006). Adolescent pregnancy and perinatal outcome. *Pediatric Endocrinology Review, 3*(Suppl. 1), 170–171.

Malik, R., & others (2014). Multilocus genetic risk score associates with ischemic stroke in case-control and prospective cohort studies. *Stroke, 45,* 394–402.

Malinger, G., & Lerman-Sagie, T. (2015). Re: Additional value fetal magnetic resonance imaging in the prenatal diagnosis of central nervous system anomalies: A systematic review of the literature. *Ultrasound in Obstetrics and Gynecology, 45,* 236–237.

Malloy, L.C., La Rooy, D.J., Lamb, M.A., & Katz, C. (2012). Developmentally sensitive interviewing for legal purposes. In M.E. Lamb, D.J. La Rooy, L.C. Malloy, & C. Katz (Eds.), *Children's testimony* (2nd ed.). New York: Wiley.

Malti, T., & Buchmann, M. (2010). Socialization and individual antecedents of adolescents' and young adults' moral motivation. *Journal of Youth and Adolescence, 39,* 138–149.

Malti, T., & Ongley, S.F. (2014). The development of moral emotions and moral reasoning. In M. Killen & J.G. Smetana (Eds.), *Handbook of moral development* (2nd ed.). New York: Psychology Press.

Mandal, S., Abebe, F., & Chaudhary, J. (2014). −174G/C polymorphism in the interleukin-6 promoter is differently associated with prostate cancer incidence depending on race. *Genetics and Molecular Research, 13,* 139–151.

Mandelbrot, L., Duro, D., Belissa, E., & Peytavin, G. (2015, in press). Placental transfer or rilpivirine in an ex vivo human cotyledon perfusion model. *Antimicrobiological Agents and Chemotherapy*.

Mandler, J.M. (2000). Unpublished review of J.W. Santrock's *Life-span Development*, 8th ed. (New York: McGraw-Hill).

Mandler, J.M. (2004). *The functions of mind*. New York: Oxford University Press.

Mandler, J.M. (2006). *Jean Mandler*. Retrieved June 6, 2006, from http://cogsci.ucsd.edu/~jean/

Mandler, J.M. (2010). *Jean Mandler*. Retrieved May 26, 2010, from http://www.cogsci.ucsd.edu/~jean/

Mandler, J.M., & DeLoach, J. (2013). The beginnings of conceptual development. In S. Pauen & M. Bornstein (Eds.), *Early child development and later outcome*. New York: Cambridge University Press.

Mandler, J.M., & McDonough, L. (1993). Concept formation in infancy. *Cognitive Development, 8*, 291–318.

Manenti, R., Cotelli, M., & Miniussi, C. (2011). Successful physiological aging and episodic memory: A brain stimulation study. *Behavioral Brain Research, 216*(1), 153–158.

Mannell, R.C. (2000). Older adults, leisure, and wellness. *Journal of Leisurability, 26*, 3–10.

Manning, W.D., Smock, P.J., Dorius, C., & Cooksey, E. (2014). Cohabitation expectations among young adults in the United States: Do they match behavior? *Population Research and Policy Review, 33*, 287–305.

Manuck, S.B., & McCaffery, J.M. (2014). Gene-environment interaction. *Annual Review of Psychology* (Vol. 65). Palo Alto, CA: Annual Reviews.

Maramara, L.A., He, W., & Ming, X. (2014). Pre- and perinatal risk factors for autism spectrum disorder in a New Jersey cohort. *Journal of Child Neurology, 29*, 1645–1651.

Maras, D., & others (2015). Screen time is associated with depression and anxiety in Canadian youth. *Preventive Medicine, 73*, 133–138.

Marcdante, K., & Kliegman, R.M. (2014). *Nelson essentials of pediatrics* (7th ed.). New York: Elsevier.

March of Dimes (2014). *Premature birth report card*. White Plains, NY: March of Dimes.

Marcia, J.E. (1980). Ego identity development. In J. Adelson (Ed.), *Handbook of adolescent psychology*. New York: Wiley.

Marcia, J.E. (1987). The identity status approach to the study of ego identity development. In T. Honess & K. Yardley (Eds.), *Self and identity: Perspectives across the lifespan*. London: Routledge & Kegan Paul.

Marcia, J.E. (1994). The empirical study of ego identity. In H.A. Bosma, T.L.G. Graafsma, H.D. Grotevant, & D.J. De Levita (Eds.), *Identity and development*. Newbury Park, CA: Sage.

Marcia, J.E. (1996). Unpublished review of J.W. Santrock's *Adolescence*, 7th ed., for Brown & Benchmark, Dubuque, Iowa.

Marcia, J.E. (2002). Identity and psychosocial development in adulthood. *Identity, 2*, 7–28.

Marecek, J., Finn, S.E., & Cardell, M. (1988). Gender roles in the relationships of lesbians and gay men. In J.P. De Cecco (Ed.), *Gay relationships*. New York: Harrington Park Press.

Mares, M-L., & Pan, Z. (2013). Effects of *Sesame Street*: A meta-analysis of children's learning in 15 countries. *Journal of Applied Developmental Psychology, 34*, 140–151.

Margolis, A., & others (2013). Using IQ discrepancy scores to examine neural correlates of specific cognitive abilities. *Journal of Neuroscience, 33*, 14135–14145.

Margran, T.H., & Boulton, M. (2005). Sensory impairment. In M.L. Johnson (Ed.), *The Cambridge handbook of age and aging*. New York: Cambridge University Press.

Marinova, P. (2013, February 12). The upside of online dating: There's always a funny story to tell. *CNN Living*. Retrieved February 27, 2013, from www.cnn.com/2012/02/11/living/online-dating-irpt

Marioni, R.E., & others (2014). Molecular genetic contributions to socioeconomic status and intelligence. *Intelligence, 44*, 26–42.

Markant, J.C., & Thomas, K.M. (2013). Postnatal brain development. In P.D. Zelazo (Ed.), *Oxford handbook of developmental psychology*. New York: Wiley.

Markham, C.M., & others (2010). Neighborhood poverty, aspirations and expectations, and initiation of sex. *Journal of Adolescent Health, 47*, 399–406.

Markman, H.J., Rhoades, G.K., Stanley, S.M., & Peterson, K.M. (2013). A randomized clinical trial of the effectiveness of premarital intervention: Moderators of divorce outcomes. *Journal of Family Psychology, 27*, 165–172.

Marks, A.K., Ejesi, K., McCullough, M.B., & Garcia Coll, C. (2015). The implications of discrimination for child and adolescent development. In R.M. Lerner (Ed.), *Handbook of child psychology and developmental science* (7th ed.). New York: Wiley.

Markus, H.R., & Kitayama, S. (2010). Cultures and selves: A cycle of multiple constitution. *Perspectives on Psychological Science, 5*, 420–430.

Markus, H.R., & Kitayama, S. (2012). Culture and the self. In K. Vohs & R.F. Baumeister (Eds.), *Self and identity*. Thousand Oaks, CA: Sage.

Markus, H.R., & Nurius, P. (1986). Possible selves. *American Psychologist, 41*, 954–969.

Marques, L., & others (2013). Complicated grief symptoms in anxiety disorders: Prevalence and associated impairment. *Depression and Anxiety, 30*, 1211–1216.

Marshall, C., & others (2013). WIC participation and breastfeeding among White and Black mothers: Data from Mississippi. *Maternal and Child Health Journal, 17*, 1784–1792.

Marshall, P.J. (2015). Neuroscience, embodiment, and development. In R.M. Lerner (Ed.), *Handbook of child psychology and developmental science* (7th ed.). New York: Wiley.

Marshall, S.L., Parker, P.D., Ciarrochi, J., & Heaven, P.C.L. (2014). Is self-esteem a cause or consequence of social support? A 4-year longitudinal study. *Child Development, 85*, 1275–1291.

Martin, C.L. (1990). Attitudes and expectations about children with nontraditional and traditional gender roles. *Sex Roles, 22*, 151–165.

Martin, C.L., & Fabes, R.A. (2001). The stability and consequences of young children's same-sex peer interactions. *Developmental Psychology, 37*, 431–446.

Martin, C.L., & Ruble, D.N. (2010). Patterns of gender development. *Annual Review of Psychology* (Vol. 61). Palo Alto, CA: Annual Reviews.

Martin, C.L., Ruble, D.N., & Szkrybalo, J. (2002). Cognitive theories of early gender development. *Psychological Bulletin, 128*, 903–933.

Martin, C.L., & others (2013). The role of sex of peers and gender-typed activities in young children's peer affiliative networks: A longitudinal analysis of selection and influence. *Child Development, 84*(3), 921–937.

Martin, J.A., & others (2012). Births: Final data for 2010. *National Vital Statistics Reports, 61*(1), 1–72.

Martin, J.A., & others (2013). Births: Final data for 2011. *National Vital Statistics Reports, 62*(1), 1–70.

Martin, J.A., & others (2015). *Births: Final data for 2013*. Hyattsville, MD: National Center for Health Statistics.

Martin, L.R., Friedman, H.S., & Schwartz, J.E. (2007). Personality and mortality risk across the lifespan: The importance of conscientiousness as a biopsychosocial attribute. *Health Psychology, 26*, 428–436.

Martin, P., & others (2014). APOE e4, rated life experiences, and affect among centenarians. *Aging and Mental Health, 18*, 240–247.

Martin, P., & others (2015, in press). Defining successful aging: A tangible or elusive concept? *Gerontologist*.

Martin-Storey, A., & Crosnoe, R. (2012). Sexual minority status, peer harassment, and adolescent depression. *Journal of Adolescence, 35*, 1001–1011.

Martinez, Y.A., Schneider, B.H., Zambrana, A., Batista, G.S., & Soca, Z.S. (2015, in press). Does comorbid anger exacerbate the rejection of children with depression by their school peers? *Child Psychiatry and Human Development*.

Marx, A.M., & others (2015). Near-infrared spectroscopy (NIRS) neurofeedback as a treatment for children with attention deficit hyperactivity disorder (ADHD)—a pilot study. *Frontiers in Human Neuroscience, 8*, 1038.

Mary, A., & others (2015, in press). Executive and attentional contributions to theory of mind deficit in attention deficit/hyperactivity disorder (ADHD). *Child Neuropsychology*.

Masaki, S., & Asai, A. (2013). Seeing-off of dead bodies at death discharges in Japan. *Medical Humanities, 39*, 131–136.

Masapollo, M., Polka, L., & Ménard, L. (2015, in press). When infants talk, infants listen: Pre-babbling infants prefer listening to speech with infant vocal properties.

Mascolo, M.F., & Fischer, K. (2007). The co-development of self and socio-moral emotions during the toddler years. In C.A. Brownell & C.B. Kopp (Eds.), *Transitions in early development*. New York: Guilford.

Mascolo, M.F., & Fischer, K.W. (2010). The dynamic development of thinking, feeling, and acting over the life span. In W.F. Overton & R.M. Lerner (Eds.), *Handbook of life-span development* (Vol. 1). New York: Wiley.

Mash, E.J., & Wolfe, D.A. (2013). Disorders of childhood and adolescence. In I.B. Weiner & others (Eds.), *Handbook of psychology* (2nd ed., Vol. 8). New York: Wiley.

Mash, E.J., & Wolfe, D.A. (2016, in press). *Abnormal child psychology* (6th ed.). Boston: Cengage.

Mashburn, A.J., Justice, L.M., Downer, J.T., & Pianta, R.C. (2009). Peer effects on children's language achievement during pre-kindergarten. *Child Development, 80*, 686–702.

Mason, K.A., Johnson, G.B., Losos, J.B., & Singer, S. (2015). *Understanding biology*. New York: McGraw-Hill.

Mason, M.J., Mennis, J., Linker, J., Bares, C., & Zaharakis, N. (2014). Peer attitudes effects on adolescent substance use: The moderating role of race and gender. *Prevention Science, 15*, 56–64.

Mason, M.J., Zaharakis, N., & Benotsch, E.G. (2014). Social networks, substance use, and mental health in college students. *Journal of American College Health, 62*, 470–477.

Masten, A.S. (2001). Ordinary magic: Resilience processes in development. *American Psychologist, 56*(3), 227–238.

Masten, A.S. (2005). Peer relationships and psychopathology in developmental perspective: Reflections on progress and promise. *Journal of Clinical Child and Adolescent Psychology, 34*, 87–92.

Masten, A.S. (2006). Developmental psychopathology: Pathways to the future. *International Journal of Behavioral Development, 31*, 46–53.

Masten, A.S. (2009). Ordinary Magic: Lessons from research on resilience in human development. *Education Canada, 49*(3), 28–32.

Masten, A.S. (2011). Resilience in children threatened by extreme adversity: Frameworks for research, practice, and translational synergy. *Development and Psychopathology, 23,* 141–153.

Masten, A.S. (2012). Faculty profile: Ann Masten. *The Institute of Child Development further developments.* Minneapolis: School of Education.

Masten, A.S. (2013). Risk and resilience in development. In P.D. Zelazo (Ed.), *Oxford handbook of developmental psychology.* New York: Oxford University Press.

Masten, A.S. (2014a). *Ordinary magic.* New York: Guilford.

Masten, A.S. (2014b). Global perspectives on resilience in children and youth. *Child Development, 85,* 6–20.

Masten, A.S. (2014c). Resilience and positive youth development frameworks in developmental science: A commentary. *Journal of Youth and Adolescence, 43,* 1018–1024.

Masten, A.S. (2014d). Promoting capacity for peace in early childhood: Perspectives from research on resilience in families and children. In J.F. Leckman & others (Eds.), *Raising a peaceful world.* Cambridge, MA: Harvard University Press.

Masten, A.S., & Narayan, A.J. (2012). Child development in the context of disaster, war, and terrorism: Pathways of risk and resilience. *Annual Review of Psychology* (Vol. 63). Palo Alto, CA: Annual Reviews.

Masten, A.S., Narayan, A.J., Silverman, W.K., & Osofsky, J.D. (2015). Children in war and disaster. In R.M. Lerner (Eds.), *Handbook of child psychology and developmental science* (7th ed.). New York: Wiley.

Masten, A.S., & others (2008). School success in motion: Protective factors for academic achievement in homeless and highly mobile children in Minneapolis. *Center for Urban and Regional Affairs Reporter, 38,* 3–12.

Masters, N.T., Casey, E., Wells, E.A., & Morrison, D.M. (2013). Sexual scripts among young heterosexually active men and women: Continuity and change. *Journal of Sexual Research, 50,* 409–420.

Mastroeni, D., & others (2015, in press). Novel antioxidants protect mitochondria from the effects of oligomeric amyloid beta and contribute to the maintenance of epigenome function. *ACS Chemical Neuroscience.*

Match.com (2011). *The Match.com Single in America Study.* Retrieved February 7, 2011, from http://blog.match.com/singles-study

Match.com (2012). *Singles in America 2012.* Retrieved June 10, 2012, from http://blog.match.com/singles-in-america/

Mate, I., Madrid, J.A., & la Fuente, M.D. (2014). Chronobiology of the neuroimmunoendocrine system and aging. *Current Pharmaceutical Design, 20,* 4642–4655.

Mateus, C., & others (2013). Aging of low and high level vision: From chromatic to achromatic contrast sensitivity to local and 3D object motion perception. *PLoS One, 8*(1), e55348.

Mather, R., & others (2015). A reduced astrocyte response to *B*-amyloid plaques in the aging brain associates with cognitive impairment. *PLoS One, 10*(2), e18463.

Mathes, W.F., & others (2010). Dopaminergic dysregulation in mice selectively bred for excessive exercise or obesity. *Behavioral Brain Research, 210,* 155–163.

Matias, M., & Fontaine, M. (2015). Coping with work and family: How do dual-earners interact? *Scandinavian Journal of Psychology, 56,* 212–222.

Matlin, M.W. (2012). The *psychology of women* (7th ed.). Belmont, CA: Wadsworth.

Matlow, J.N., Jubetsky, A., Alesksa, K., Berger, H., & Koren, G. (2013). The transfer of ethyl glucuronide across the dually perfused human placenta. *Placenta, 34,* 369–373.

Matos, A.P., Ferreira, J.A., & Haase, R.F. (2012). Television and aggression: A test of a mediated model with a sample of Portuguese students. *Journal of Social Psychology, 152,* 75–91.

Matsuba, M.K., Murzyn, T., & Hart, D. (2014). Moral identity development and community. In M. Killen & J.G. Smetana (Eds.), *Handbook of moral development* (2nd ed.). New York: Psychology Press.

Matsuba, M.K., & Walker, L.J. (2004). Extraordinary moral commitment: Young adults involved in social organizations. *Journal of Personality, 72,* 413–436.

Matsumoto, D., & Juang, L. (2013). *Culture and psychology* (5th ed.). Boston: Cengage.

Matthews, C.E., & others (2007). Influence of exercise, walking, cycling, and overall nonexercise physical activity on mortality in Chinese women. *American Journal of Epidemiology, 165,* 1343–1350.

Matthiessen, C. (2015). *Overweight children: Tips for parents.* Retrieved February 25, 2015, from www.webmd.com/parenting/raising-fit-kids/mood/talking-kids...

Mattison, J.A., & others (2012). Impact of caloric restriction on health and survival in rhesus monkeys from the NIA study. *Nature, 489,* 318–321.

Maurer, D., & Lewis, T.L. (2013). Sensitive periods in visual development. In P.D. Zelazo (Ed.), *Oxford handbook of developmental psychology.* New York: Oxford University Press.

Maurer, D., Lewis, T.L., Brent, H.P., & Levin, A.V. (1999). Rapid improvement in the acuity of infants after visual input. *Science, 286,* 108–110.

Maurer, D., Mondloch, C.J., & Leis, T.L. (2007). Effects of early visual deprivation on perceptual and cognitive development. In C. von Hofsten & K. Rosander (Eds.), *Progress in Brain Research, 164,* 87–104.

Maxson, S.C. (2013). Behavioral genetics. In I.B. Weiner & others (Eds.), *Handbook of psychology* (2nd ed., Vol. 3). New York: Wiley.

Mayas, J., Parmentier, F.B., Andres, P., & Ballesteros, S. (2014). Plasticity of attentional functions in older adults after non-action video game training: A randomized controlled trial. *PLoS One, 9*(3), e92269.

Mayer, K.D., & Zhang, L. (2009). Short- and long-term effects of cocaine abuse during pregnancy on heart development. *Therapeutic Advances in Cardiovascular Disease, 3,* 7–16.

Mayer, R.E. (2008). *Curriculum and instruction* (2nd ed.). Upper Saddle River, NJ: Prentice Hall.

Maynard, M., Carabin, D., Jaspar, M., & Collette, F. (2014). Age-related decline in cognitive control: The role of fluid intelligence and processing speed. *BMC Neuroscience, 15*(1), 7.

Mayo Clinic (2014). *Male hypogonadism.* Rochester, MN: Mayo Clinic.

McAbee, S.T., & Oswald, F.L. (2013). The criterion-related validity of personality measures for predicting GPA: A meta-analytic validity comparison. *Psychological Assessment, 25,* 532–544.

McAdams, D.P. (2012). Personality, modernity, and the storied self. In K. Vohs & R.F. Baumeister (Eds.), *Self and identity.* Thousand Oaks, CA: Sage.

McAdams, D.P., & Cox, K.S. (2011). Self and identity across the life span. In A. Freund, M. Lambs, & R. Lerner (Eds.), *Handbook of life-span development* (Vol. 2). New York: Wiley.

McAdams, D.P., & McLean, K.C. (2013). Narrative identity. *Current Directions in Psychological Science, 22,* 233–238.

McAdams, D.P., & Olson, B.D. (2010). Personality development: Continuity and change over the life course. *Annual Review of Psychology* (Vol. 61). Palo Alto, CA: Annual Reviews.

McAdams, D.P., & Zapata-Gietl, C. (2015). Three strands of identity development across the human life course: Reading Erik Erikson in full. In K.C. McLean & M. Syed (Eds.), *Oxford handbook of identity development.* New York: Oxford University Press.

McAdams, D.P., Josselson, R., & Lieblich, A. (Eds.). (2006). *Identity and story: Creating self in narrative.* Washington, DC: American Psychological Association Press.

McAdams, T.A., & others (2014). Co-occurrence of antisocial behavior and substance use: Testing for sex differences in the impact of older male friends, low parental knowledge, and friends' delinquency. *Journal of Adolescence, 37,* 247–256.

McAlister, A.R., & Peterson, C.C. (2007). A longitudinal study of child siblings and theory of mind development. *Cognitive Development, 22,* 258–270.

McAlister, A.R., & Peterson, C.C. (2013). Siblings, theory of mind, and executive functioning in children aged 3–6 years: New longitudinal evidence. *Child Development, 84,* 1442–1458.

McAvoy, M., & others (2015, in press). Unmasking language lateralization in human brain intrinsic activity. *Cerebral Cortex.*

McBride, D.L. (2013). Like girls, boys are entering puberty earlier, new research finds. *Journal of Pediatric Nursing, 28*(2), 189–190.

McBride-Chang, C. (2004). *Children's literacy development* (Texts in Developmental Psychology Series). London: Edward Arnold/Oxford Press.

McBride-Chang, C., & others (2005). Changing models across cultures: Associations of phonological and morphological awareness to reading in Beijing, Hong Kong, Korea, and America. *Journal of Experimental Child Psychology, 92,* 140–160.

McBride Murry, V., Hill, N.E., Witherspoon, D., Berkel, C., & Bartz, D. (2015). Children in diverse social contexts. In R.M. Lerner (Ed.), *Handbook of child psychology and developmental science* (7th ed.). New York: Wiley.

McCall, R.B., Applebaum, M.I., & Hogarty, P.S. (1973). Developmental changes in mental performance. *Monographs of the Society for Research in Child Development, 38* (Serial No. 150).

McCardle, P., Miller, B., Lee, J.R., & Tzeng, O.J. (2011). *Dyslexia across languages.* Baltimore: Paul H. Brookes.

McCartney, K. (2003, July 16). Interview with Kathleen McCartney in A. Bucuvalas, "Child care and behavior," *HGSE News,* 1–4. Cambridge, MA: Harvard Graduate School of Education.

McCartney, K., & Yoshikawa, H. (Eds.) (2015). *Framing the future for America's children: In honor of 40 years of the Children's Defense Fund.* Cambridge, MA: Harvard University Press.

McClain, C.S., Rosenfeld, B., & Breitbart, W.S. (2003). *The influence of spirituality on end-of-life despair in cancer patients close to death.* Paper presented at the meeting of the American Psychosomatic Society, Phoenix.

McClelland, M.M., Geldhof, J., Cameron, C.E., & Wanless, S.B. (2015). Development and self-regulation. In R.M. Lerner (Ed.), *Handbook of child psychology and developmental science* (7th ed.). New York: Wiley.

McCombs, B.L. (2013). Educational psychology and educational transformation. In I.B. Weiner & others

(Eds.), *Handbook of psychology* (2nd ed., Vol. 7). New York: Wiley.

McCormack, S.E., & others (2014). Effects of exercise and lifestyle modification on fitness, insulin resistance, skeletal muscle oxidative phosphorylation and intramyocellular lipid content in obese children and adolescents. *Pediatric Obesity, 9,* 281–291.

McCormick, C.B., Dimmitt, C., & Sullivan, F.R. (2013). Metacognition, learning, and instruction. In I.B. Weiner & others (Eds.), *Handbook of psychology* (2nd ed., Vol. 7). New York: Wiley.

McCoy, D.C., & Raver, C.C. (2011). Caregiver emotional expressiveness, child emotion regulation, and child behavior problems among Head Start families. *Social Development, 20*(4), 741–761.

McCrae, R.R., & Costa, P.T. (1990). *Personality in adulthood.* New York: Guilford.

McCrae, R.R., & Costa, P.T. (2006). Cross-cultural perspectives on adult personality trait development. In D.K. Mroczek & T.D. Little (Eds.), *Handbook of personality development.* Mahwah, NJ: Erlbaum.

McCrae, R.R., & Sutin, A.R. (2009). Openness to experience. In M.R. Leary & R.H. Hoyle (Eds.), *Handbook of individual differences in social behavior.* New York: Guilford.

McCullough, M.E., & Willoughby, B.L. (2009). Religion, self-regulation, and self-control: Associations, explanations, and implications. *Psychological Bulletin, 135,* 69–93.

McDougall, S., & House, B. (2012). Brain training in older adults: Evidence of transfer to memory span performance and pseudo-Matthew effects. *Neuropsychology, Development, and Cognition B. Aging, Neuroscience, and Cognition, 19,* 195–221.

McDowell, D.J., & Parke, R.D. (2009). Parental correlates of children's peer relations: An empirical test of a tripartite model. *Developmental Psychology, 45,* 224–235.

McDuffie, A., Thurman, A.J., Hagerman, R.J., & Abbeduto, L. (2015, in press). Symptoms of autism in males with fragile X syndrome: A comparison to nonsyndromic ASD using current ADI-R scores. *Journal of Autism and Developmental Disorders.*

McElhaney, K.B., & Allen, J.P. (2012). Sociocultural perspectives on adolescent autonomy. In P.K. Kreig, M.S. Schulz, & S.T. Hauser (Eds.), *Adolescence and beyond.* New York: Oxford University Press.

McEwen, B.S. (1998). Protective and damaging effects of stress mediators. *New England Journal of Medicine, 338,* 171–180.

McEwen, B.S. (2013). Neuroscience, hormones and the social brain. *Science, 339,* 279–280.

McGarry, J., Kim, H., Sheng, X., Egger, M., & Baksh, L. (2009). Postpartum depression and help-seeking behavior. *Journal of Midwifery and Women's Health, 54,* 50–56.

McGarvey, C., McDonnell, M., Hamilton, K., O'Regan, M., & Matthews, T. (2006). An eight-year study of risk factors for SIDS: Bed-sharing versus non-sharing. *Archives of Disease in Childhood, 91,* 318–323.

McGue, M., Hirsch, B., & Lykken, D.T. (1993). Age and the self-perception of ability: A twin analysis. *Psychology and Aging, 8,* 72–80.

McHale, J.P., Salman-Engin, S., & Coovert, M.D. (2015, in press). Improvements in unmarried African American parents' rapport, communication, and problem-solving following a prenatal coparenting intervention. *Family Process.*

McHale, S.M., Updegraff, K.A., & Whiteman, S.D. (2013). Sibling relationships. In G.W. Peterson & K.R. Bush (Eds.), *Handbook of marriage and family* (3rd ed.). New York: Springer.

McIlfatrick, S., & Hasson, F. (2014). Evaluating an holistic assessment tool for palliative care practice. *Journal of Clinical Nursing, 23,* 1064–1075.

McInnis, C.M., & others (2015, in press). Response and habituation of pro- and anti-inflammatory gene expression to repeated acute stress. *Brain, Behavior, and Immunity.*

McKain, W.C. (1972). A new look at older marriages. *The Family Coordinator, 21,* 61–69.

McKay, A.S., & Kaufman, J.C. (2014). Literary geniuses: Their life, work, and death. In D.K. Simonton (Ed.), *Wiley-Blackwell handbook of genius.* New York: Wiley.

McKiernan, F., Spreadbury, J., Carr, T., & Waller, G. (2013). Psychological aspects of bereavement in adults: Preliminary development of the bereavement experiences index. *Journal of Social Work in End-of-Life & Palliative Care, 9,* 7–26.

McLaughlin, K. (2003, December 30). Commentary in K. Painter, "Nurse dispenses dignity for dying." *USA Today,* pp. D1–D2.

McLaughlin, K.A., & others (2014). Widespread reductions in cortical thickness following severe early-life deprivation: A neurodevelopmental pathway to attention-deficit/hyperactivity disorder. *Biological Psychiatry, 76,* 629–638.

McLean, I.A., Balding, V., & White, C. (2005). Further aspects of male-on-male rape and sexual assault in greater Manchester. *Medical Science and Law, 45,* 225–232.

McLean, K.C., & Breen, A.V. (2009). Processes and content of narrative identity development in adolescence: Gender and well-being. *Developmental Psychology, 45,* 702–710.

McLean, K.C., Breen, A.V., & Fournier, M.A. (2010). Constructing the self in early, middle, and late adolescent boys: Narrative identity, individuation, and well-being. *Journal of Research on Adolescence, 20,* 166–187.

McLean, K.C., & Jennings, L.E. (2012). Teens telling tall tales: How maternal and peer audiences support narrative identity development. *Journal of Adolescence, 35,* 1455–1469.

McLean, K.C., & Pratt, M.W. (2006). Life's little (and big) lessons: Identity statuses and meaning-making in the turning point narratives of emerging adults. *Developmental Psychology, 42,* 714–722.

McLean, K.C., & Syed, M. (2015). The field of identity development needs an identity: An introduction to the *Handbook of identity development.* In K.C. McLean & M. Syed (Eds.), *Oxford handbook of identity development.* New York: Oxford University Press.

McLean, K.C., Syed, M., Yoder, A., & Greenhoot, A.F. (2015, in press). The role of domain content in understanding identity developmental processes. *Journal of Research on Adolescence.*

McLean, K.C., & Thorne, A. (2006). Identity light: Entertainment stories as vehicle for self-development. In D.P. McAdams, R. Josselson, & A. Lieblich (Eds.), *Identity and story.* Washington, DC: American Psychological Association.

McLoyd, V.C. (1990). The impact of economic hardship on Black families and children: Psychological distress, parenting, and socioemotional development. *Child Development, 61,* 311–346.

McLoyd, V.C. (1998). Children in poverty: Development, public policy, and practice. In W. Damon (Ed.), *Handbook of child psychology* (5th ed., Vol. 4). New York: Wiley.

McLoyd, V.C., Kaplan, R., Purtell, K.M., & Huston, A.C. (2011). Assessing the effects of a work-based antipoverty program for parents on youths' future orientation and employment experiences. *Child Development, 82,* 113–132.

McLoyd, V.C., Mistry, R.S., & Hardaway, C.R. (2014). Poverty and children's development: Familial processes and mediating influences. In E.T. Gershoff, R.S. Mistry, & D.A. Crosby (Eds.), *Societal contexts of child development.* New York: Oxford University Press.

McLoyd, V.C., Purtell, K.M., & Hardaway, C.R. (2015). Race, class, and ethnicity as they affect emerging adulthood. In R.M. Lerner (Ed.), *Handbook of child psychology and developmental science* (7th ed.). New York: Wiley.

McMahon, C.G. (2014). Erectile dysfunction. *International Medical Journal, 44,* 18–26.

McMahon, D.M., Liu, J., Zhang, H., Torres, M.E., & Best, R.G. (2013). Maternal obesity, folate intake, and neural tube defects in offspring. *Birth Defects A: Clinical and Molecular Teratology, 97,* 115–122.

McMahon, M., & Stryjewski, G. (2011). *Pediatrics.* New York: Elsevier.

McMillan, C.T., & others (2014). The power of neuroimaging biomarkers for screening frontotemporal dementia. *Human Brain Mapping, 135,* 4827–4840.

McMillan, J.H. (2014). *Classroom assessment* (6th ed.). Upper Saddle River, NJ: Pearson.

McNamara, M., Batur, P., & DeSapri, K.T. (2015, in press). In the clinic. Perimenopause. *Annals in Internal Medicine.*

McNicholas, F., & others (2014). Medical, cognitive, and academic outcomes of very low birth weight infants at 10–14 years in Ireland. *Irish Journal of Medical Science, 183,* 525–532.

McWilliams, L.A., & Bailey, S.J. (2010). Association between adult attachment rating and health conditions: Evidence from the National Comorbidity Survey replication. *Health Psychology, 29,* 446–453.

Mead, M. (1978, Dec. 30–Jan. 5). The American family: An endangered species. *TV Guide,* 21–24.

Meade, C.S., Kershaw, T.S., & Ickovics, J.R. (2008). The intergenerational cycle of teenage motherhood: An ecological approach. *Health Psychology, 27,* 419–429.

Mechakra-Tahiri, S.D., Zunzunegui, M.V., Preville, M., & Dube, M. (2010). Gender, social relationships and depressive disorders in adults aged 65 and over in Quebec. *Chronic Diseases in Canada, 30,* 56–65.

Meeks, L., Heit, P., & Page, R. (2016, in press). *Concepts in health* (8th ed.). New York: McGraw-Hill.

Meerlo, P., Sgoifo, A., & Suchecki, D. (2008). Restricted and disrupted sleep: Effects on autonomic function, neuroendocrine stress systems, and stress responsivity. *Sleep Medicine Review, 12,* 197–210.

Meert, K.L., & others (2015). Meaning making during parent-physician bereavement meetings after a child's death. *Health Psychology, 34,* 453–461.

Meffert, C., Stobel, U., Korner, M., & Becker, G. (2015). Perceptions of a good death among German medical students. *Death Studies, 39,* 307–315.

Mehta, C.M., & Strough, J. (2009). Sex segregation in friendships and normative contexts across the life span. *Development Review, 29,* 201–220.

Mehta, C.M., & Strough, J. (2010). Gender segregation and gender-typing in adolescence. *Sex Roles, 63,* 251–263.

Meisel, V., Servera, M., Garcia-Banda, G., Cardo, E., & Moreno, I. (2013). Neurofeedback and standard pharmacological intervention in ADHD: A randomized controlled trial with six-month follow-up. *Biological Psychology, 94,* 12–21.

Melancon, M.O., Lorrain, D., & Dionne, I.J. (2015). Sleep depth and continuity before and after chronic exercise in older men: Electrophysiological evidence. *Physiology and Behavior, 140,* 203–208.

Meldrum, R.C., & Hay, C. (2012). Do peers matter in the development of self-control? Evidence from a longitudinal study of youth. *Journal of Youth and Adolescence, 41,* 691–703.

Meléndez, J.C., Fortuna, F.B., Sales, A., & Mayordomo, T. (2015). The effects of instrumental reminiscence on resilience and coping in elderly. *Archives of Gerontology and Geriatrics, 60,* 294–298.

Melendez-Moral, J.C., Charco-Ruiz, L., Mayordomo-Rodriguez, T., & Sales-Galan, A. (2013). Effects of a reminiscence program among institutionalized elderly adults. *Psicothema, 25,* 319–323.

Melia, K.M. (2014). When the body is past fixing: Caring for bodies, caring for people. *Journal of Clinical Nursing, 23,* 1616–1622.

Mella, N., Fagot, D., Lecerf, T., & de Ribaupierre, A. (2015, in press). Working memory and intraindividual variability in processing speed: A lifespan developmental and individual-differences study. *Memory and Cognition.*

Mendes, A. (2015). Nursing care to facilitate and support 'good' grieving. *British Journal of Nursing, 24,* 95.

Mendler, M., & others (2015, in press). Daf-16/FOXO and glod-4/glyoxalase-1 are required for the life-prolonging effect of human insulin under high glucose conditions in Caenorhabditis elegans. *Diabetologia.*

Mendoza, N., & others (2013). Position of the Spanish Menopause Society regarding the management of perimenopause. *Maturitas, 74,* 283–290.

Menec, V.H. (2003). The relation between everyday activities and successful aging: A 6-year longitudinal study. *Journals of Gerontology B: Psychological Sciences and Social Sciences, 58,* 574–582.

Meng, N.H., & others (2015, in press). Sarcopenia defined by combining height- and weight-adjusted skeletal muscle indices is closely associated with poor physical performance. *Journal of Aging and Physical Activity.*

Meng, X., & D'Arcy, C. (2014). Successful aging in Canada: Prevalence and predictors from a population-based sample of older adults. *Gerontology, 60,* 65–72.

Menn, L., & Stoel-Gammon, C. (2009). Phonological development: Learning sounds and sound patterns. In J. Berko Gleason (Ed.), *The development of language* (7th ed.). Boston: Allyn & Bacon.

Mennella, J.A. (2009). Taste and smell. In R.A. Shweder & others (Eds.), *The child: An encyclopedic companion.* Chicago: University of Chicago Press.

Menon, R., & others (2011). Cigarette smoking induces oxidative stress and atopsis in normal fetal membranes. *Placenta, 32,* 317–322.

Menon, R., & others (2014). Amniotic fluid metabolomic analysis in spontaneous preterm birth. *Reproductive Sciences, 21,* 791–803.

Menyuk, P., Liebergott, J., & Schultz, M. (1995). *Early language development in full-term and premature infants.* Hillsdale, NJ: Erlbaum.

Merad, M., & others (2014). Molecular interaction of acetylcholinesterase with carnosic acid derivatives: A neuroinformatics study. *CNS & Neurological Disorders, 13*(3), 440–446.

Meraz-Rios, M.A., & others (2014). Early onset Alzheimer's disease and oxidative stress. *Oxidative Medicine and Cellular Longevity, 2014:* 375968.

Mercer, N. (2008). Talk and the development of reasoning and understanding. *Human Development, 51,* 90–100.

Meredith, N.V. (1978). Research between 1960 and 1970 on the standing height of young children in different parts of the world. In H.W. Reece & L.P. Lipsitt (Eds.), *Advances in child development and behavior* (Vol. 12). New York: Academic Press.

Merrill, D.A., & others (2012). Self-reported memory impairment and brain PET of amyloid and tau in middle-aged and older adults without dementia. *International Psychogeriatrics, 24,* 1076–1084.

Merrill, D.M. (2009). Parent-child relationships: Later-life. In D. Carr (Ed.), *Encyclopedia of the life course and human development.* Boston: Gale Cengage.

Messiah, S.E., Miller, T.L., Lipshultz, S.E., & Bandstra, E.S. (2011). Potential latent effects of prenatal cocaine exposure on growth and the risk of cardiovascular and metabolic disease in childhood. *Progress in Pediatric Cardiology, 31,* 59–65.

Messinger, D. (2008). Smiling. In M.M. Haith & J.B. Benson (Eds.), *Encyclopedia of infant and early childhood development.* Oxford, UK: Elsevier.

Messinger, J.C. (1971). Sex and repression in an Irish folk community. In D.S. Marshall & R.C. Suggs (Eds.), *Human sexual behavior: Variations in the ethnic spectrum.* New York: Basic Books.

Mestre, T.A., & others (2014). Reluctance to start medication for Parkinson's disease: A mutual misunderstanding by patients and physicians. *Parkinsonism and Related Disorders, 20,* 608–612.

Metcalf, C.J., & Jones, J.H. (2015, in press). The evolutionary dynamics of timing of maternal immunity: Evaluating the role of age-specific mortality. *Journal of Evolutionary Biology.*

Metts, S., & Cupach, W.R. (2007). Responses to relational transgressions. In M. Tafoya & B.H. Spitzberg (Eds.), *The dark side of interpersonal communication.* Mahwah, NJ: Erlbaum.

Metz, E. C., & Youniss, J. (2005). Longitudinal gains in civic development through school-based required service. *Political Psychology, 26,* 413–437.

Meyer, M.H., & Parker, W.M. (2011). Gender, aging, and social policy. In R.H. Binstock & L.K. George (Eds.), *Handbook of aging and the social sciences* (7th ed.). New York: Elsevier.

Meyer, U., & others (2014). Long-term effect of a school-based physical activity program (KISS) on fitness and adiposity in chidren: A cluster-randomized controlled trial. *PLoS One, 9*(2), e87929.

Michael, R.T., Gagnon, J.H., Laumann, E.O., & Kolate, G. (1994). *Sex in America.* Boston: Little Brown.

Mike, A., Harris, K., Roberts, B.W., & Jackson, J.J. (2015). Conscientiousness: Lower-order structure, life course consequences, and development. In J. Wright (Ed.), *International encyclopedia of social and behavioral sciences* (2nd ed.). New York: Elsevier.

Mikulincer, M., & Shaver, P.R. (2014). The role of attachment security in adolescent and adult close relationships. In J.A. Simpson & L. Campbell (Eds.), *Oxford handbook of close relationships.* New York: Oxford University Press.

Mikulincer, M., & Shaver, P.R. (2015). Boosting attachment security in adulthood: The "broaden-and-build" effects of security-enhancing mental representations and interpersonal contexts. In J.A. Simpson & W.S. Rholes (Eds.), *Attachment theory and research.* New York: Guilford.

Milani, H.J., & others (2015). Fetal brain tumors: Prenatal diagnosis by ultrasound and magnetic resonance imaging. *World Journal of Radiology, 28,* 17–21.

Milesi, G., & others (2014). Assessment of human hippocampal developmental neuroanatomy by means of EX-VIVO 7T magnetic resonance imaging. *International Journal of Developmental Neuroscience. 34,* 33–41.

Milgrom, J., & others (2015, in press). Treatment of postnatal depression with cognitive behavioral therapy, sertraline, and combination therapy: A randomized controlled trial. *Australia and New Zealand Journal of Psychiatry.*

Miller, A.B., Esposito-Smythers, C., Weismoore, J.T., & Renshaw, K.D. (2013). The relation between child maltreatment and adolescent suicidal behavior: A systematic review and critical examination of the literature. *Clinical Child and Family Psychology Review, 16*(2), 146–172.

Miller, B.C., Benson, B., & Galbraith, K.A. (2001). Family relationships and adolescent pregnancy risk: A research synthesis. *Developmental Review, 21,* 1–38.

Miller, C.F., Lurye, L.E., Zosuls, K.M., & Ruble, D.N. (2009). Accessibility of gender stereotype domains: Developmental and gender differences in children. *Sex Roles, 60,* 870–881.

Miller, E.B, Farkas, G., Vandell, D.L., & Duncan, G.J. (2014). Do the effects of Head Start vary by parental preacademic stimulation? *Child Development, 85*(4), 1385–1400.

Miller, E.M., & others (2012). Theories of willpower affect sustained learning. *PLoS One, 7*(6), e38680.

Miller, J.B. (1986). *Toward a new psychology of women* (2nd ed.). Boston: Beacon Press.

Miller, J.G., & Bland, C.G. (2014). A cultural psychology perspective on moral development. In M. Killen & J.G. Smetana (Eds.), *Handbook of moral development* (2nd ed.). New York: Psychology Press.

Miller, J.W. (2013). Age-related macular degeneration revisited—piecing the puzzle: The LXIX Edward Jackson Memorial lecture. *American Journal of Ophthalmology, 155,* 1–35.

Miller, L.M., & Bell, R.A. (2012). Online health information seeking: The influence of age, information trustworthiness, and search challenges. *Journal of Aging and Health, 24,* 525–541.

Miller, M.A., & Cappuccio, F.P. (2007). Inflammation, sleep, obesity, and cardiovascular disease. *Current Vascular Pharmacology, 5,* 92–102.

Miller, P.H. (2010). *Theories of developmental psychology* (5th ed.). New York: Worth.

Miller, P.H. (2011). Piaget's theory: Past, present, and future. In U. Goswami (Ed.), *Wiley-Blackwell handbook of childhood cognitive development* (2nd ed.). New York: Wiley-Blackwell.

Miller, P.H. (2014). The history of memory development research: Remembering our roots. In P. Bauer & R. Fivush (Eds.), *Wiley handbook on the development of children's memory.* New York: Wiley.

Miller, R., Wankerl, M., Stalder, T., Kirschbaum, C., & Alexander, N. (2013). The serotonin transporter gene-linked polymorphic region (5-HTTLPR) and cortisol stress reactivity: A meta-analysis. *Molecular Psychiatry, 18,* 1018–1024.

Miller, S., Malone, P., Dodge, K.A., & The Conduct Problems Prevention Research Group (2011). Developmental trajectories of boys' and girls' delinquency: Sex differences and links to later adolescent outcomes. *Journal of Abnormal Child Psychology, 38*(7), 1021–1032.

Miller-Perrin, C.L., Perrin, R.D., & Kocur, J.L. (2009). Parental, physical, and psychological aggression: Psychological symptoms in young adults. *Child Abuse and Neglect, 33,* 1–11.

Mills, C.M. (2013). Knowing when to doubt: Developing a critical stance when learning from others. *Developmental Psychology, 114,* 63–76.

Mills, C.M., & Elashi, F.B. (2014). Children's skepticism: Developmental and individual differences in children's ability to detect and explain distorted claims. *Journal of Experimental Psychology, 124,* 1–17.

Mills, D., & Mills, C. (2000). *Hungarian kindergarten curriculum translation.* London: Mills Production.

Mills-Koonce, W.R., Propper, C.B., & Barnett, M. (2012). Poor infant soothability and later insecure-ambivalent attachment: Developmental change in phenotypic markers of risk or two measures of the same construct? *Infant Behavior and Development, 35,* 215–235.

Milne, E., & others (2012). Parental prenatal smoking and risk of childhood acute lymphoblastic leukemia. *American Journal of Epidemiology, 175,* 43–53.

Milner, A., & others (2014). The effects of involuntary job loss on suicide and suicide attempts among young adults: Evidence from a matched case-control study.

Australian and New Zealand Journal of Psychiatry, 48, 333–340.

Milte, C.M., & others (2014). How important is health status in defining quality of life in older people? An exploratory study of the views of older South Australians. *Applied Health Economics and Health Policy, 13,* 73–84.

Miner, M.M., Bhattacharya, R.K., Blick, G., Kushner, H., & Khera, M. (2013). 12-month observation of testosterone replacement effectiveness in a general population of men. *Postgraduate Medicine, 125,* 8–18.

Minkler, M., & Fuller-Thompson, E. (2005). African American grandparents raising grandchildren: A national study using the Census 2000 American Community Survey. *Journals of Gerontology B: Psychological Sciences and Social Sciences, 60,* S82–S92.

Minnes, S., & others (2010). The effects of prenatal cocaine exposure on problem behavior in children 4–10 years. *Neurotoxicology and Teratology, 32,* 443–451.

Minnesota Family Investment Program (2009). *Longitudinal study of early MFIP recipients.* Retrieved January 12, 2009, from www.dhs.state.mn.us/main/

Minsart, A.F., Buekens, P., De Spiegelaere, M., & Englert, Y. (2013). Neonatal outcomes in obese mothers: A population-based analysis. *BMC Pregnancy and Childbirth, 13,* 36.

Minuchin, P.O., & Shapiro, E.K. (1983). The school as a context for social development. In P.H. Mussen (Ed.), *Handbook of child psychology* (4th ed., Vol. 4). New York: Wiley.

Mioni, G., & others (2015, in press). Test-retest consistency of virtual week: A task to investigate prospective memory. *Neuropsychological Rehabilitation.*

Mirachi, F.L., & others (2015). TRIAD VII: Do prehospital providers understand Physician Orders for Life-Sustaining Treatment documents? *Journal of Patient Safety, 11,* 9–17.

Mireault, G.C., & others (2014). Social looking, social referencing, and humor perception in 6- and 12-month-old infants. *Infant Behavior and Development, 37,* 536–545.

Mirkovic, B., & others (2015). Coping skills among adolescent suicide attempters: Results of a multisite study. *Canadian Journal of Psychiatry, 60*(Suppl. 1), S37–S45.

Mischel, W. (1968). *Personality and assessment.* New York: Wiley.

Mischel, W. (1974). Process in delay of gratification. In L. Berkowitz (Ed.), *Advances in experimental social psychology* (Vol. 7). New York: Academic Press.

Mischel, W. (2004). Toward an integrative science of the person. *Annual Review of Psychology* (Vol. 55). Palo Alto, CA: Annual Reviews.

Mischel, W. (2014). *The marshmallow test: Mastering self-control.* New York: Little Brown.

Mischel, W., & Mischel, H. (1975, April). *A cognitive social-learning analysis of moral development.* Paper presented at the meeting of the Society for Research in Child Development, Denver.

Mischel, W., & Moore, B.S. (1980). The role of ideation in voluntary delay for symbolically presented rewards. *Cognitive Therapy and Research, 4,* 211–221.

Mischel, W., Cantor, N., & Feldman, S. (1996). Principles of self-regulation: The nature of will power and self-control. In E.T. Higgins & A.W. Kruglanski (Eds.), *Social psychology.* New York: Guilford.

Mischel, W., & others (2011). 'Willpower' over the life span: Decomposing self-regulation. *Social Cognitive and Affective Neuroscience, 6,* 252–256.

Mishra, G.D., Cooper, R., Tom, S.E., & Kuh, D. (2009). Early life circumstances and their impact on

menarche and menopause. *Women's Health, 5,* 175–190.

Mistry, J., & Dutta, R. (2015). Human development and culture: Conceptual and methodological issues. In R.M. Lerner (Ed.), *Handbook of child psychology and developmental science* (7th ed.). New York: Wiley.

Mistry, R.S., Vandewater, E.A., Huston, A.C., & McLoyd, V.C. (2002). Economic well-being and children's social adjustment: The role of family process in an ethnically diverse low-income sample. *Child Development, 3,* 935–951.

Mitchell, A.B., & Stewart, J.B. (2013). The efficacy of all-male academies: Insights from critical race theory (CRT). *Sex Roles, 69,* 382–392.

Mitchell, A.J., Yates, C., Williams, K., & Hall, R.W. (2013). Effects of daily kangaroo care on cardiorespiratory parameters in preterm infants. *Journal of Neonatal and Perinatal Medicine, 6,* 243–249.

Mitchell, E.A., & Krous, H.F. (2015). Sudden unexpected death in infancy: A historical perspective. *Journal of Pediatric and Child Health, 51,* 108–112.

Mitchell, J.A., Rodriguez, D., Schmitz, K.H., & Audrain-McGovern, J. (2013). Greater screen time is associated with adolescent obesity: A longitudinal study of the BMI distribution from ages 14 to 18. *Obesity, 21*(3), 572–575.

Mitchell, M.B., & others (2012). Cognitively stimulating activities: Effects on cognition across four studies with up to 21 years of longitudinal data. *Journal of Aging Research, 461592.*

Mitchell, M.B., & others (2013). Norms for the Georgia Centenarian Study: Measures of verbal abstract reasoning, fluency, memory, and motor function. *Neuropsychology, Development, and Cognition B: Aging, Neuropsychology, and Cognition, 20,* 620–637.

Mitchell, S., & Dale, S. (2015). Advance care planning in palliative care: A qualitative investigation into the perspective of pediatric intensive care unit staff. *Palliative Medicine, 29,* 371–379.

Miyagawa, S., Ojima, S., Berwick, R.C., & Okanoya, K. (2014). The integration hypothesis of human language evolution and the nature of contemporary languages. *Frontiers in Psychology, 5,* 564.

Miyake, K., Chen, S., & Campos, J. (1985). Infants' temperament, mothers' mode of interaction and attachment in Japan: An interim report. In I. Bretherton & F. Waters (Eds.), Growing points of attachment theory and research, *Monographs of the Society for Research in Child Development, 50*(1–2, Serial No. 109), 276–297.

Miyakoshi, K., & others (2013). Perinatal outcomes: Intravenous patient-controlled fentanyl versus no analgesia in labor. *Journal of Obstetrics and Gynecology Research, 39,* 783–789.

Mize, K.D., & Jones, N.A. (2012). Infant physiological and behavioral responses to loss of maternal attention to a social-rival. *International Journal of Psychophysiology, 83,* 16–23.

Mize, K.D., Pineda, M., Blau, A.K., Marsh, K., & Jones, N.A. (2014). Infant physiological and behavioral responses to a jealousy-provoking condition. *Infancy, 19,* 338–348.

Mlczoch, E., & others (2014). Fetal cardiac disease and fetal lung volume: An in utero MRI investigation. *Prenatal Diagnosis, 34,* 273–278.

Mock, S.E., & Eibach, R.P. (2012). Stability and change in sexual orientation identity over a 10-year period in adulthood. *Archives of Sexual Behavior, 41,* 641–648.

Modecki, K.L., & others (2014). Bullying prevalence across contexts: A meta-analysis measuring cyber and traditional bullying. *Journal of Adolescent Health, 55,* 602–611.

Moed, A., & others (2015, in press). Parent-adolescent conflict as sequences of reciprocal negative emotion: Links with conflict resolution and adolescents' behavior problems. *Journal of Youth and Adolescence.*

Moen, P. (1998). Recasting careers: Changing reference groups, risks and realities. *Generations, 22,* 40–45.

Moen, P. (2007). Unpublished review of J.W. Santrock's *Life-span development,* 12th ed. (New York: McGraw-Hill).

Moen, P. (2009a). Careers. In D. Carr (Ed.), *Encyclopedia of the life course and human development.* Boston: Gale Cengage.

Moen, P. (2009b). Dual-career couples. In D. Carr (Ed.), *Encyclopedia of the life course and human development.* Boston: Gale Cengage.

Moen, P., Kelly, E.L., & Magennis, R. (2008). Gender strategies: Social and institutional clocks, convoys, and cycles of control. In M.C. Smith and N. DeFrates-Densch (Eds.), *The handbook of research on adult development and learning.* New York: Routledge.

Moen, P., & Spencer, D. (2006). Converging divergences in age, gender, health, and well-being. In R.H. Binstock & L.K. George (Eds.), *Handbook of aging and the social sciences* (6th ed.). San Diego: Academic Press.

Moilanen, J.M., & others (2012). Effect of aerobic training on menopausal symptoms—a randomized controlled trial. *Menopause, 19,* 691–696.

Moise, K.J., & others (2015, in press). Circulating cell-free DNA for the detection of RHD status and sex using reflex fetal identifiers. *Prenatal Diagnosis.*

Molina, B.S., & Pelham, W.E. (2014). The attention deficit/hyperactivity disorder (ADHD) substance use connection. *Annual Review of Clinical Psychology* (Vol. 10). Palo Alto, CA: Annual Reviews.

Mollenkopf, H. (2007). Mobility and flexibility. In J.E. Birren (Ed.), *Encyclopedia of gerontology* (2nd ed.). San Diego: Academic Press.

Moller, J., Bjorkeenstam, E., Ljung, R., & Yngwe, M.A. (2011). Widowhood and the risk of psychiatric care, psychotropic medication, and all-cause mortality: A cohort of 658,022 elderly people in Sweden. *Aging and Mental Health, 15,* 259–266.

Molton, I.R., & Terrill, A.L. (2014). Overview of persistent pain in older adults. *American Psychologist, 69,* 197–207.

Momtaz, Y.A., Ibrahim, R., Hamid, T.A., & Yahaya, N. (2010). Mediating effects of social and personal religiosity on the psychological well-being of widowed elderly people. *Omega, 61,* 145–162.

Monahan, K., Guyer, A., Sil, J., Fitzwater, T., & Steinberg, L. (2015, in press). Integration of developmental neuroscience and contextual approaches to the study of adolescent psychopathology. In D. Cicchetti (Ed.), *Handbook of developmental psychology* (3rd ed.). New York: Wiley.

Monette, S., Bigras, M., & Guay, M.C. (2011). The role of executive functions in school achievement at the end of grade 1. *Journal of Experimental Child Psychology, 109,* 158–173.

Money, J. (1975). Ablatio penis: Normal male infant sex-reassigned as a girl. *Archives of Sexual Behavior, 4,* 65–71.

Moninger, J. (2015). *How to talk with your child about losing weight.* Retrieved February 25, 2015, from http://www.parents.com/kids/teens/weight-loss/how-to-talk-to-your-child-about-losing-weight/

Monserud, M.A. (2008). Intergenerational relationships and affectual solidarity between grandparents and young adults. *Journal of Marriage and the Family, 70,* 182–195.

Montagna, P., & Chokroverty, S. (2011). *Sleep disorders.* New York: Elsevier.

Montano, Z., & others (2015). Longitudinal relations between observed parenting behaviors and dietary quality of meals from ages 2 to 5. *Appetite, 87,* 324–329.

Montemayor, R. (1982). The relationship between parent-adolescent conflict and the amount of time adolescents spend with parents, peers, and alone. *Child Development, 53,* 1512–1519.

Monti, J.M., Hillman, C.H., & Cohen, N.J. (2012). Aerobic fitness enhances relational memory in preadolescent children: The FITKids randomized control trial. *Hippocampus, 22*(9), 1876–1882.

Montirosso, R., & others (2015). A categorical approach to infants' individual differences during the still-face paradigm. *Infant Behavior and Development, 38,* 67–76.

Moon, R.Y., & Fu, L. (2012). Sudden infant death syndrome: An update. *Pediatrics in Review, 33,* 314–320.

Moon, R.Y., & others (2012). Pacifier use and SIDS: Evidence for a consistently reduced risk. *Maternal and Child Health Journal, 16,* 609–614.

Moore, D. (2001). *The dependent gene.* New York: W.H. Freeman.

Moore, D. (2013). Behavioral genetics, genetics, and epigenetics. In P.D. Zelazo (Ed.), *Handbook of developmental psychology.* New York: Oxford University Press.

Moore, D. (2015). *The developing genome.* New York: Oxford University Press.

Moore, G.E., & others (2015). The role and interaction of imprinted genes in human fetal growth. *Philosophical Transactions of the Royal Society of London. Biological Sciences, 370,* 1663.

Moore, M. (2012). Behavioral sleep problems in children and adolescents. *Journal of Clinical Psychology in Medical Settings, 19,* 77–83.

Moore, M.W., Brendel, P.C., & Fiez, J.A. (2014). Reading faces: Investigating the use of a novel face-based orthography in acquired alexia. *Brain and Language, 129C,* 7–13.

Moore, R.M. (2015). Appreciating cultural dimensions and connections in hospice care. *Journal of Social Work in End-of-Life and Palliative Care, 11,* 6–10.

Moore, S.R., Harden, K.P., & Mendle, J. (2014). Pubertal timing and adolescent sexual behavior in girls. *Developmental Psychology, 50*(6), 1734–1745.

Morasch, K.C., & Bell, M.A. (2012). Self-regulation of negative affect at 5 and 10 months. *Developmental Psychobiology, 54,* 215–221.

Morasch, K.C., Raj, V.R., & Bell, M.A. (2013). The development of cognitive control from infancy through childhood. In D. Reisberg (Ed.), *Oxford handbook of cognitive psychology.* New York: Oxford University Press.

Morean, M.E., & others (2014). First drink to first drunk: Age of onset and delay to intoxication are associated with adolescent alcohol use and binge drinking. *Alcoholism, Clinical and Experimental Research, 38,* 2615–2621.

Morgentaler, A., Feibus, A., & Baum, N. (2015). Testosterone and cardiovascular disease—the controversy and the facts. *Postgraduate Medicine, 127,* 159–165.

Morita, T., & others (2015, in press). Palliative care physicians' attitudes toward patient autonomy and a good death in Asian countries. *Journal of Pain and Symptom Management.*

Morokuma, S., & others (2008). Developmental change in fetal response to repeated low-intensity sound. *Developmental Science, 11,* 47–52.

Morris, A., Cui, L., & Steinberg, L. (2012). Parenting research and themes: What we have learned and where to go next. In R.E. Larzelere, A.S. Morris, & A.W.

Harrist (Eds.), *Authoritative parenting.* Washington, DC: American Psychological Association.

Morris, A., Cui, L., & Steinberg, L. (2013). Arrested development: The effects of incarceration on the development of psychosocial maturity. *Development and Psychopathology, 24*(3), 1073–1090.

Morris, A.S., & others (2014). Effortful control, behavior problems, and peer relations: What predicts academic adjustment in kindergartners from low-income families? *Early Education and Development, 24,* 813–828.

Morris, R.J., Thompson, K.C., & Morris, Y.P. (2013). Child psychotherapy. In I.B. Weiner & others (Eds.), *Handbook of psychology* (2nd ed., Vol. 8). New York: Wiley.

Morrison, D.M., & others (2014). "He enjoys giving her pleasure": Diversity and complexity in young men's sexual scripts. *Archives of Sexual Behavior, 44,* 655–688.

Morrison, G.S. (2014). *Fundamentals of early childhood education* (7th ed.). Upper Saddle River, NJ: Pearson.

Morrison, G.S. (2015). *Early childhood education today* (13th ed.). Upper Saddle River, NJ: Pearson.

Morrison, R.S. (2013). Models of palliative care delivery in the United States. *Current Opinion in Supportive and Palliative Care, 7,* 201–206.

Morrissey, T.W. (2009). Multiple child-care arrangements and young children's behavioral outcomes. *Child Development, 80,* 59–76.

Morrow-Howell, N. (2010). Volunteering in later life: Research frontiers. *Journals of Gerontology B: Psychological Sciences and Social Sciences, 65,* 461–469.

Morrow-Howell, N., & others (2014). An investigation of activity profiles of older adults. *Journals of Gerontology B: Psychological Sciences and Social Sciences, 69,* 809–821.

Mortell, S. (2015). Assisting clients with disenfranchised grief: The role of a mental health nurse. *Journal of Psychosocial Nursing and Mental Health Services, 53,* 52–57.

Mortensen, O., Torsheim, T., Melkevik, O., & Thuen, F. (2012). Adding a baby to the equation. Married and cohabiting women's relationship satisfaction in the transition to parenthood. *Family Process, 51,* 122–139.

Moulson, M.C., & Nelson, C.A. (2008). Neurological development. In M.M. Haith & J.B. Benson (Eds.), *Encyclopedia of infant and early childhood development.* Oxford, UK: Elsevier.

Moulton, D. (2014). Midwifery to be offered in Newfoundland. *Canadian Medical Association Journal, 186*(8), E243.

Moyer, M.W. (2013). The myth of antioxidants. *Scientific American, 308,* 62–67.

Mparmpakas, D., & others (2013). Immune system function, stress, exercise, and nutrition profile can affect pregnancy outcome: Lessons from a Mediterranean cohort. *Experimental and Therapeutic Medicine, 5,* 411–418.

Mrkva, K., & Narváez, D. (2015). Moral psychology and the "cultural other": Cultivating openness to experience and the new. In B. Zizek & A. Escher (Eds.), *Ways of approaching the strange.* Dornach, Switzerland: Steiner Verlag.

Mroczek, B., & others (2013). Psychosexual needs and sexual behaviors of nursing care home residents. *Archives of Gerontology and Geriatrics, 57*(1), 32–38.

Mroczek, D.K., & Kolarz, C.M. (1998). The effect of age on positive and negative affect: A developmental perspective on happiness. *Journal of Personality and Social Psychology, 75,* 1333–1349.

Mroczek, D.K., & Spiro, A. (2007). Personality change influences mortality in older men. *Psychological Science, 18,* 371–376.

Mroczek, D.K., Spiro, A., & Griffin, P.W. (2006). Personality and aging. In J.E. Birren & K.W. Schaie (Eds.), *Handbook of the psychology of aging* (6th ed.). San Diego: Academic Press.

Mruk, C.J., & O'Brien, E.J. (2013). Changing self-esteem through competence and worthiness training: A positive therapy. In V. Zeigler-Hill (Ed.), *Self-esteem.* New York: Psychology Press.

Mullally, S.L., & Maguire, E.A. (2014). Learning to remember: The early ontogeny of episodic memory. *Developmental Cognitive Neuroscience, 9,* 12–29.

Muller, L., & Pawelec, G. (2015). As we age: Does slippage of quality control in the immune system lead to collateral damage? *Aging Research Reviews,* S1568–S1637.

Muller, U., & Kerns, K. (2015). Development of executive function. In R.M. Lerner (Ed.), *Handbook of child psychology and developmental science* (7th ed.). New York: Wiley.

Mullola, S., & others (2012). Gender differences in teachers' perceptions of students' temperament, educational competence, and teachability. *British Journal of Educational Psychology, 82*(2), 185–206.

Mundy, P., & others (2007). Individual differences and the development of joint attention in infancy. *Child Development, 78,* 938–954.

Mungas, D., & others (2014). A 2-process model for neuropathology and Alzheimer's disease. *Neurobiology of Aging, 35,* 301–308.

Munnell, A.H. (2011). *What is the average retirement age?* (Issue Brief No.11-11). Chestnut Hill, MA: Center for Retirement Research, Boston College.

Murase, T. (2014). Japanese mothers' utterances about agents and actions during joint picture-book reading. *Frontiers in Psychology, 5,* 357.

Murphy, D.A., Brecht, M.L., Huang, D., & Herbeck, D.M. (2012). Trajectories of delinquency from age 14 to 23 in the National Longitudinal Survey of Youth sample. *International Journal of Adolescence and Youth, 17,* 47–62.

Murphy, M.C., & Dweck, C.S. (2010). A culture of genius: How an organization's lay theory shapes people's cognition, affect, and behavior. *Personality and Social Psychology Bulletin, 36,* 283–296.

Murphy, R.A., & others (2014). Associations of BMI and adipose tissue area and density with incident mobility limitation and poor performance in older adults. *American Journal of Clinical Nutrition, 99,* 1059–1065.

Murphy, S.L., Xu, J., Kochanek, K.D. (2012, January 12). Deaths: Preliminary data for 2010. *National Vital Statistics Reports, 60*(4), 54–58.

Murr, J., Carmichael, P.H., Julien, P., & Laurin, D. (2014). Plasma oxidized low-density lipoprotein levels and risk of Alzheimer's disease. *Neurobiology of Aging, 35,* 1833–1838.

Murray, S.S., & McKinney, E.S. (2014). *Foundations of maternal-newborn and women's health. Women's health nursing* (5th Ed.).

Murry, V.M., Hill, N.E., Witherspoon, D., Berkel, C., & Bartz, D. (2015). Children in diverse social contexts. In R.M. Lerner (Ed.), *Handbook of child psychology and developmental science* (7th ed.). New York: Wiley.

Musameh, M.D., & others (2015). Analysis of gene-gene interactions among common variants in candidate cardiovascular genes in coronary artery disease. *PLoS One, 10*(2), e117684.

Mussen, P.H., Honzik, M., & Eichorn, D. (1982). Early adult antecedents of life satisfaction at age 70. *Journal of Gerontology, 37,* 316–322.

Muthusamy, V.R., & others (2012). Acute exercise stress activates Nrf2/ARE signaling and promotes antioxidant mechanisms in myocardium. *Free Radical Biology and Medicine, 52,* 366–372.

Myer, G.D., & others (2015, in press). Sixty minutes of what? A developing brain perspective for activating children with an integrative exercise approach. *British Journal of Sports Medicine.*

Myers, D.G. (2000). *The American paradox.* New Haven, CT: Yale University Press.

Myers, D.G. (2008, June 2). Commentary in S. Begley & Interlandi, The dumbest generation? Don't be dumb. Retrieved July 22, 2008, from www.newsweek.com/id/13856/

Myers, D.G. (2010). *Psychology* (9th ed.). New York: Worth.

Myerson, J., Rank, M.R., Raines, F.Q., & Schnitzler, M.A. (1998). Race and general cognitive ability: The myth of diminishing returns in education. *Psychological Science, 9,* 139–142.

N

Nabe-Nielsen, K., & others (2014). Demand-specific work ability, poor health, and working conditions in middle-aged full-time employees. *Applied Ergonomics, 45,* 1174–1180.

Nader, P.R., Bradley, R.H., Houts, R.M., McRitchie, S.L., & O'Brian, M. (2008). Moderate-to-vigorous physical activity from 9 to 15 years. *Journal of the American Medical Association, 300,* 295–305.

Nadimpalli, S.B., & others (2015, in press). The association between discrimination and depressive symptoms among older African Americans: The role of psychological and social factors. *Experimental Aging Research.*

Nadler, M., & others (2013). Osteoporosis knowledge, health beliefs, and healthy bone behaviors in patients on androgen-deprivation therapy (ADT) for prostate cancer. *BJU International, 111*(8), 1301–1309.

NAEYC (National Association for the Education of Young Children) (2009). *Developmentally appropriate practice in early childhood programs serving children from birth through age 8.* Washington, DC: Author.

Nagamatsu, L.S., & others (2014). Exercise in medicine for the body and brain. *British Journal of Sports Medicine, 48,* 943–944.

Nagel, B.J., & others (2011). Altered white matter microstructure in children with attention-deficit/hyperactivity disorder. *Journal of the American Academy of Child and Adolescent Psychiatry, 50,* 283–292.

Nagy, M. (1948). The child's theories concerning death. *Journal of Genetic Psychology, 73,* 3–27.

Nair-Collins, M., Northrup, J., & Olcese, J. (2015, in press). Hypothalamic-pituitary function in brain death: A review. *Journal of Intensive Care Medicine.*

Najman, J.M., & others (2009). The impact of episodic and chronic poverty on child cognitive development. *Journal of Pediatrics, 154,* 284–289.

Najman, J.M., & others (2010). Timing and chronicity of family poverty and development of unhealthy behaviors in children: A longitudinal study. *Journal of Adolescent Health, 46,* 538–544.

Nakajima, S., Masaya, I., Akemi, S., & Takako, K. (2012). Complicated grief in those bereaved by violent death: The effects of post-traumatic stress disorder on complicated grief. *Dialogues in Clinical Neuroscience, 14,* 210–214.

Nansel, T.R., & others (2001). Bullying behaviors among U.S. youth. *Journal of the American Medical Association, 285,* 2094–2100.

Narayan, A., Cicchetti, D., Rogosch, F.A., & Toth, S.L. (2015). Interrelations of maternal expressed emotion, maltreatment, and separation/divorce and links to family conflict and children's externalizing behavior. *Journal of Abnormal Child Psychology, 43,* 217–228.

Nardone, R., & others (2014). Dopamine differentially modulates central cholinergic circuits in patients with Alzheimer disease and CADASIL. *Journal of Neural Transmission, 121,* 267–274.

Narváez, D. (2006). Integrative moral education. In M. Killen & J. Smetana (Ed.), *Handbook of moral development.* Mahwah, NJ: Erlbaum.

Narváez, D. (2008). Four Component Model. In F.C. Power, R.J. Nuzzi, D. Narváez, D.K. Lapsley, & T.C. Hunt (Eds.), *Moral education: A handbook.* Westport, CT: Greenwood Publishing.

Narváez, D. (2010a). Building a sustaining classroom climate for purposeful ethical citizenship. In T. Lovat, R. Toomey, & N. Clement (Eds.), *International research handbook of values education and student well-being.* New York: Springer.

Narváez, D. (2010b). The embodied dynamism of moral becoming. *Perspectives on Psychological Science, 5*(2), 185–186.

Narváez, D. (2014). *The neurobiology and development of human morality.* New York: Norton.

Narváez, D. (2015). The neurobiology of moral sensitivity: Evolution, epigenetics, and early experience. In D. Mowrer & P. Vanderberg (Eds.), *The art of morality.* New York: Routledge.

Narváez, D. (2016, in press). The ontogenesis of moral becoming. In A. Fuentes & A. Visala (Eds.). *Verbs, bones, and brains.* Notre Dame, IN: University of Notre Dame Press.

Narváez, D., Bock, T., Endicott, L., & Lies, J. (2004). Minnesota's Community Voices and Character Education Project. *Journal of Research in Character Education, 2,* 89–112.

Narváez, D., & Gleason, T.R. (2013). Developmental optimism. In D. Narváez & others (2013). *Evolution, early experience, and human development.* New York: Oxford University Press.

Narváez, D., & Hill, P.L. (2010). The relation of multicultural experiences to moral judgment and mindsets. *Journal of Diversity in Higher Education, 3,* 43–55.

Narváez, D., Panksepp, J., Schore, A.N., & Gleason, T.R. (Eds.) (2013). *Evolution, early experience, and human development.* New York: Oxford University Press.

Nascimento Dda, C., & others (2014). Sustained effect of resistance training on blood pressure and hand grip strength following a detraining period in elderly hypertensive women: A pilot study. *Clinical Interventions in Aging, 9,* 219–225.

Nash, J.M. (1997, February 3). Fertile minds. *Time,* 50–54.

National Assessment of Educational Progress (2014). *Reading 4th and 8th grades.* Washington, DC: National Center for Educational Statistics.

National Association for Gifted Children (2009). *State of the states in gifted education: 2008–2009.* Washington, DC: Author.

National Association for Single Sex Public Education (NASSPE) (2012). *Single-sex schools/schools with single-sex classrooms/what's the difference.* Retrieved from www.singlesexschools.org/schools-schools.com

National Autism Association (2010). *All about autism.* Retrieved January 5, 2010, from www.nationalautismassociation.org/definitions.php

National Center for Education Statistics (2002). *Work during college.* Washington, DC: U.S. Department of Education.

National Center for Education Statistics (2010). *School dropouts.* Washington, DC: U.S. Department of Education.

National Center for Education Statistics (2012). Indicator A-33-3: Status Dropout Rates. *Digest of Education Statistics.* Washington, DC: U.S. Department of Education.

National Center for Education Statistics (2013, May). *Characteristics of postsecondary students.* Washington, DC: U.S. Department of Education.

National Center for Education Statistics (2014). *School dropouts.* Washington, DC: U.S. Department of Education.

National Center for Health Statistics (2000). *Health United States, 1999.* Atlanta: Centers for Disease Control and Prevention.

National Center for Health Statistics (2002). *Sexual behavior and selected health measures: Men and women 15–44 years of age, United States, 2002,* PHS 2003–1250. Atlanta: Centers for Disease Control and Prevention.

National Center for Health Statistics (2011, March). Adult obesity prevalence in the United States and Canada. *NCHS Data Brief, No. 56.*

National Center for Health Statistics (2014). Accidents and deaths. Atlanta: Centers for Disease Control and Prevention.

National Center for Health Statistics (2014). *Sexually transmitted diseases.* Atlanta: Centers for Disease Control.

National Center for Vital Statistics (2013). *Births, marriages, divorces, death: 2011.* Washington, DC: Author.

National Clearinghouse on Child Abuse and Neglect (2013, July). *What is child abuse and neglect?* Washington, DC: U.S. Department of Health and Human Services.

National Institute of Child Health and Development (2014). *SIDS.* Bethesda, MD: Author.

National Institute of Mental Health (2015). *Autism spectrum disorder.* Retrieved May 15, 2015, from www.nimh.nih.gov/health/topics/autism-spectrum-disorders-asd/index.shtml

National Marriage Project (2011). *Unmarried cohabitation.* Retrieved June 9, 2012, from www.stateofourunions.org/2011/social_indicators.php

National Sleep Foundation (2007). *Sleep in America poll 2007.* Washington, DC: Author.

National Sleep Foundation (2014). *Children's sleep habits.* Retrieved July 26, 2013, from http://www.sleepfoundation.org

Natsuaki, M.N., & others (2010). Early pubertal maturation and internalizing problems in adolescence: Sex differences in the role of cortical reactivity to impersonal stress. *Journal of Clinical Child and Adolescent Psychology, 38,* 513–524.

Neal, A.R. (2009). Autism. In D. Carr (Ed.), *Encyclopedia of the life course and human development.* Boston: Gale Cengage.

Neal, J.W., Neal, Z.P., & Cappella, E. (2014). I know who my friends are, but do you? Predictors of self-reported and peer-inferred relationships. *Child Development, 85,* 1366–1372.

Needham, A., Barrett, T., & Peterman, K. (2002). A pick-me-up for infants' exploratory skills: Early simulated experiences reaching for object using "sticky mittens" enhances young infants' object exploration skills. *Infant Behavior and Development, 25,* 279–295.

Neff, L.A., & Geers, A.L. (2013). Optimistic expectations in early marriage: A resource or vulnerability for adaptive relationship functioning? *Journal of Personality and Social Psychology, 105,* 38–60.

Negriff, S., Susman, E.J., & Trickett, P.K. (2011). The development pathway from pubertal timing to delinquency and sexual activity from early to late adolescence. *Journal of Youth and Adolescence, 40,* 1343–1356.

Neikrug, A.B., & Ancoli-Israel, S. (2010). Sleep disorders in the older adult: A mini-review. *Gerontology, 56,* 181–189.

Neisser, U., & others (1996). Intelligence: Knowns and unknowns. *American Psychologist, 51,* 77–101.

Nelson, C. (2006). Unpublished review of J.W. Santrock's *Topical approach to life-span development,* 4th ed. (New York: McGraw-Hill).

Nelson, C.A. (2003). Neural development and lifelong plasticity. In R.M. Lerner, R. Jacobs, & D. Wertlieb (Eds.), *Handbook of applied developmental science* (Vol. 1). Thousand Oaks, CA: Sage.

Nelson, C.A. (2007). A developmental cognitive neuroscience approach to the study of atypical development: A model system involving infants of diabetic mothers. In D. Coch, G. Dawson, & K.W. Fischer (Eds.), *Human behavior, learning, and the developing brain.* New York: Guilford.

Nelson, C.A. (2013). Brain development and behavior. In A.M. Rudolph, C. Rudolph, L. First, G. Lister, & A.A. Gershon (Eds.), *Rudolph's pediatrics* (22nd ed.). New York: McGraw-Hill.

Nelson, C.A., Fox, N.A., & Zeanah, C.H. (2014). *Romania's abandoned children.* Cambridge, MA : Harvard University Press.

Nelson, D.A., & others (2014). Parenting, relational aggression, and borderline personality features: Associations over time in a Russian longitudinal sample. *Development and Psychopathology, 26,* 773–787.

Nelson, J.A., Leerkes, E.M., O'Brien, M., Calkins, S.D., & Maracovitch, S. (2012). African American and European American mothers' beliefs about negative emotions and emotion socialization practices. *Parenting, 12,* 22–41.

Nelson, K. (2014). Sociocultural theories of memory development. In P. Bauer & R. Fivush (Eds.), *Wiley handbook of the development of children's memory.* New York: Wiley.

Nelson, S.K., Kushlev, K., English, T., Dunn, E.W., & Lyubomirsky, S. (2013). In defense of parenthood: Children associated with more joy than misery. *Psychological Science, 24,* 3–10.

Nelson, S.K., Kushlev, K., & Lyubomirsky, S. (2014). The pains and pleasures of parenting: When, why, and how is parenthood associated with more or less well-being? *Psychological Bulletin, 140,* 846–895.

Nelson, S.E., Van Ryzin, M.J., & Dishion, T.J. (2015, in press). Alcohol, marijuana, and tobacco use trajectories from age 12 to 24 years: Demographic correlates and young adult substance use problems. *Development and Psychopathology.*

Neugarten, B.L., Havighurst, R.J., & Tobin, S.S. (1968). Personality and patterns of aging. In B.L. Neugarten (Ed.), *Middle age and aging.* Chicago: University of Chicago Press.

Neugarten, B.L., & Weinstein, K.K. (1964). The changing American grandparent. *Journal of Marriage and the Family, 26,* 199–204.

Neupert, S.D., Ennis, G.E., Ramsey, J.L., & Gall, A.A. (2015, in press). Solving tomorrow's problems today? Daily anticipatory coping and reactivity to daily stressors. *Journals of Gerontology B: Psychological Sciences and Social Sciences.*

Nevarez, M.D., & others (2010). Associations of early life risk factors with infant sleep duration. *Academic Pediatrics, 10,* 187–193.

Neville, C., & others (2015). Literature review: Use of respite care by carers of people with dementia. *Health and Social Care in the Community, 23,* 51–53.

Neville, H.J. (2006). Different profiles of plasticity within human cognition. In Y. Munakata & M.H. Johnson (Eds.), *Attention and Performance XXI: Processes of change in brain and cognitive development.* Oxford, UK: Oxford University Press.

Nevo, E., & Breznitz, Z. (2013). The development of working memory from kindergarten to first grade in children with different decoding skills. *Journal of Experimental Child Psychology, 114,* 217–228.

Newell, K., Scully, D.M., McDonald, P.V., & Baillargeon, R. (1989). Task constraints and infant grip configurations. *Developmental Psychobiology, 22,* 817–832.

Newsom, R.S., Boelen, P.A., Hofman, A., & Tiemeier, H. (2011). The prevalence and characteristics of complicated grief in older adults. *Journal of Affective Disorders, 132,* 231–238.

Newton, N.J., & Stewart, A.J. (2012). Personality development in adulthood. In S.K. Whitbourne & M. Sliwinski (Eds.), *Wiley-Blackwell handbook of adult development and aging.* New York: Wiley.

Ng, F.F., Pomerantz, E.M., & Deng C. (2014). Why are Chinese parents more psychologically controlling than American parents? "My child is my report card." *Child Development, 85,* 355–369.

Ng, F.F., Pomerantz, E.M., & Lam, S. (2013). Mothers' beliefs about children's learning in Hong Kong and the United States: Implications for mothers' child-based self-worth. *International Journal of Behavioral Development, 37,* 387–394.

Nho, K., & others (2015, in press). Comprehensive gene- and pathway-based analysis of depressive symptoms in older adults. *Journal of Alzheimer's Disease.*

NICHD (2015). *SIDS.* Retrieved January 14, 2015, from www.nichd.nih.gov/publications/pubs/safe_sleep_gen.cfm

NICHD Early Child Care Research Network (2001). Nonmaternal care and family factors in early development: An overview of the NICHD study of Early Child Care. *Journal of Applied Developmental Psychology, 22,* 457–492.

NICHD Early Child Care Research Network (2002). Structure → Process → Outcome: Direct and indirect effects of child care quality on young children's development. *Psychological Science, 13,* 199–206.

NICHD Early Child Care Research Network (2003). Does amount of time spent in child care predict socioemotional adjustment during the transition to kindergarten? *Child Development, 74,* 976–1005.

NICHD Early Child Care Research Network (2004). Type of child care and children's development at 54 months. *Early Childhood Research Quarterly, 19,* 203–230.

NICHD Early Child Care Research Network (2005). *Child care and development.* New York: Guilford.

NICHD Early Child Care Research Network (2005). Duration and developmental timing of poverty and children's cognitive and social development from birth through third grade. *Child Development, 76,* 795–810.

NICHD Early Child Care Research Network (2006). Infant-mother attachment classification: Risk and protection in relation to changing maternal caregiving quality. *Developmental Psychology, 42,* 38–58.

NICHD Early Child Care Research Network (2010). Testing a series of causal propositions relating time spent in child care to children's externalizing behavior. *Developmental Psychology, 46*(1), 1–17.

Nickalls, S. (2012, March 9). Why college students shouldn't online date. *The Tower.* Philadelphia: Arcadia University. Retrieved February 27, 2013, from http://tower.arcadia.edu/?p=754.

Nicolaisen, M., & Thorsen, K. (2014). Loneliness among men and women—a five-year follow-up study. *Aging and Mental Health, 18,* 194–206.

Nicoteri, J.A., & Miskovsky, M.J. (2014). Revisiting the freshman "15": Assessing body mass index in the first college year and beyond. *Journal of the American Association of Nurse Practitioners, 126,* 220–224.

Nielsen, M.B., & Einarsen, S. (2012). Prospective relationships between workplace sexual harassment and psychological distress. *Occupational Medicine, 62,* 226–228.

Nieto, A.M., & Yoshikawa, H. (2014). Beyond families and schools: Future directions in practice and policy for children in immigrant families. In E.T. Gershoff, R.S. Mistry, & D.A. Crosby (Eds.), *Societal contexts of child development.* New York: Oxford University Press.

Nikmat, A.W., Al-Mashoor, S.H., & Hashim, N.A. (2015). Quality of life in people with cognitive impairment: Nursing homes versus home care. *International Psychogeriatrics, 27*(5), 815–824.

Nilsson, J., Thomas, A.J., O'Brien, J.T., & Gallagher, P. (2014). White matter and cognitive decline in aging: A focus on processing speed and variability. *Journal of the International Neuropsychology Society, 20*(3), 262–267.

Ning, L.F., & others (2015). Meta-analysis of differentially expressed genes in autism based on gene expression data. *Genetics and Molecular Research, 14,* 2146–2155.

Ninio, A. (2015, in press). Bids for joint attention by parent-child dyads and by dyads of young peers in interaction. *Journal of Child Language.*

Nisbett, R. (2003). *The geography of thought.* New York: Free Press.

Nisbett, R.E., & others (2012). Intelligence: New findings and theoretical developments. *American Psychologist, 67,* 130–159.

Niwa, A., & others (2015, in press). Voluntary exercise induces neurogenesis in the hypothalamus and ependymal lining of the third ventricle. *Brain Structure and Function.*

Nixon, S.A., Rubincam, C., Casale, M., & Flicker, S. (2011). Is 80% a passing grade? Meanings attached to condom use in an abstinence-plus HIV prevention programme in South Africa. *AIDS Care, 23,* 213–220.

Noddings, N. (2008). Caring and moral education. In L. Nucci & D. Narváez (Eds.), *Handbook of moral and character education.* Clifton, NJ: Psychology Press.

Noddings, N. (2014). Caring and moral education. In L. Nucci, T. Krettenauer, & D. Narváez (Eds.), *Handbook of moral and character education* (2nd ed.). New York: Routledge.

Nodine, P.M., & Hastings-Tolsma, M. (2012). Maternal obesity: Improving pregnancy outcomes. *MCN: American Journal of Maternal Child Nursing, 37,* 110–115.

Noel-Miller, C.M. (2011). Partner caregiving in older cohabiting couples. *Journals of Gerontology B: Psychological Sciences and Social Sciences, 66B,* 341–353.

Noftle, E.E., & Fleeson, W. (2010). Age differences in Big Five factor behavior averages and variabilities across the adult life span: Moving beyond retrospective, global summary accounts of personality. *Psychology and Aging, 25,* 95–107.

Noguchi, H., & others (2015, in press). Expression of DNMT1 in neural stem/precursor cells is critical for survival of newly generated neurons in the adult hippocampus. *Neuroscience Research.*

Nogueira, M., & others (2014). Early-age clinical and developmental features associated with substance use disorders in attention-deficit/hyperactivity disorder in adults. *Comprehensive Psychiatry, 55*(3), 639–649.

Nolen-Hoeksema, S. (2011) *Abnormal psychology* (5th ed.). New York: McGraw-Hill.

Nolen-Hoeksema, S. (2012). Emotion regulation and psychopathology: The role of gender. *Annual Review of Clinical Psychology* (Vol. 8). Palo Alto, CA: Annual Reviews.

Nomi, J.S., & Uddin, L.Q. (2015). Developmental changes in large-scale network connectivity in autism. *Neuroimage: Clinical, 7,* 732–741.

Norris, A.E., Hughes, C., Hecht, M., Peragallo, N., & Nickerson, D. (2013). Randomized trial of a peer resistance skill-building game for Hispanic early adolescent girls. *Nursing Research, 62,* 25–35.

North, M.S., & Fiske, S.T. (2013a). Act your (old) age: Prescriptive, ageist biases over succession, consumption, and identity. *Personality and Social Psychology Bulletin, 39,* 720–734.

North, M.S., & Fiske, S.T. (2013b). A prescriptive intergenerational-tension ageism scale: Succession, identity, and consumption. *Psychological Assessment, 25,* 706–713.

Nosraty, L., Jylha, M., Raittila, T., & Lumme-Sandt, K. (2015). Perceptions by the oldest old of successful aging, vitality 90+ study. *Journal of Aging Studies, 32,* 50–58.

Nottelmann, E.D., & others (1987). Gonadal and adrenal hormone correlates of adjustment in early adolescence. In R.M. Leiner & T.T. Foch (Eds.), *Biological psychological interactions in early adolescence.* Hillsdale, NJ: Erlbaum.

Nouchi, R., & others (2012). Brain training game improves executive functions and processing speed in the elderly: A randomized controlled trial. *PLoS One, 7*(1), e29676.

Nouchi, R., & others (2013). Brain training game boosts executive functions, working memory, and processing speed in young adults: A randomized controlled trial. *PLoS, 8*(2), e55518.

Nucci, L. (2006). Education for moral development. In M. Killen & J. Smetana (Eds.), *Handbook of moral development.* Mahwah, NJ: Erlbaum.

Nucci, L., Krettenauer, T., & Narváez, D. (Eds.) (2014). *Handbook of moral and character education* (2nd ed.). New York: Routledge.

Nutter, E., Meyer, S., Shaw-Battista, J., & Marowitz, A. (2014). Waterbirth: An integrative analysis of peer-reviewed literature. *Journal of Midwifery and Women's Health, 59,* 286–319.

Nyberg, L., & others (2012). Memory aging and brain maintenance. *Trends in Cognitive Science, 16,* 292–305.

Nye, C.D., & others (2015, in press). Personality trait differences between young and middle-aged adults: Measurement artifacts or actual trends? *Journal of Personality.*

Nygard, C-H. (2013). *The ability to work peaks in middle age.* Interview. Retrieved September 15, 2013, from http://researchandstudy.uta.fi/2013/09/12/the-ability-to-work-peaks-in-middle-age/

O

O'Brien, E.J., Bartoletti, M., & Leitzel, J.D. (2013). Self-esteem, psychopathology, and psychotherapy. In M.H. Kernis (Ed.), *Self-esteem issues and answers.* New York: Psychology Press.

O'Brien, J.L., & others (2013). Cognitive training and selective attention in the aging brain: An electrophysiological study. *Clinical Neurophysiology, 124,* 2198–2208.

O'Brien, M., & others (2014). Women's work and child care: Perspectives and prospects. In E.T. Gershoff, R.S. Mistry, & D.A. Crosby (Eds.), *Societal contexts of child development.* New York: Oxford University Press.

O'Callaghan, F.V., & others (2010). The link between sleep problems in infancy and early childhood and attention problems at 5 and 14 years: Evidence from a birth cohort study. *Early Human Development, 86,* 419–424.

O'Conner, E.E., Scott, M.A., McCormick, M.P., & Weinberg, S.L. (2014). Early mother-child attachment and behavior problems in middle childhood: The role of the subsequent caregiving environment. *Attachment and Human Development, 17,* 590–612.

O'Dell, C. (2013). *Centenarians' secrets. What you can learn from people who've lived 100-plus years.* Retrieved February 20, 2013, from www.caring.com/articles/centenarians-secrets

O'Donnell, L., O'Donnell, C., Wardlaw, D.M., & Stueve, A. (2004). Risk and resiliency factors influencing suicidality among urban African-American and Latino youth. *American Journal of Community Psychology, 33,* 37–49.

O'Grady, W. (2013). An emergent approach to syntax. In B. Heine & H. Narrog (Eds.), *Oxford handbook of linguistic analysis.* New York: Oxford University Press.

O'Hara, M., & others (2015, in press). Children neglected: Where cumulative risk theory fails. *Child Abuse and Neglect.*

O'Hara, M.W., & McCabe, F. (2013). Postpartum depression: Current status and future directions. *Annual Review of Clinical Psychology.* Palo Alto, CA: Annual Reviews.

O'Keefe, J.H., Bhatti, S.K., Baiwa, A., Dinicolantonio, J.J., & Lavie, C.J. (2014). Alcohol and cardiovascular health: The dose does make the poison . . . or the remedy. *Mayo Clinic Proceedings, 89,* 382–393.

O'Keefe, J.H., Schnohr, P., & Lavie, C.J. (2013). The dose of running that best confers longevity. *Heart, 99,* 588–590.

O'Keeffe, L.M., Greene, R.A., & Kearney, P.M. (2014). The effect of moderate gestational alcohol consumption during pregnancy on speech and language outcomes in children: A systematic review. *Systematic Reviews, 3,* 1.

O'Neill, J., & Csicsvari, J. (2014). Learning by example in the hippocampus. *Neuron, 83,* 8–10.

O'Neill, S., & others (2013). Cesarean section and subsequent ectopic pregnancy: A systematic review and meta-analysis. *BJOG, 13,* 165.

Oakes, L.M. (2012). Advances in eye-tracking in infancy research. *Infancy, 17,* 1–8.

Oates, J., & Abraham, S. (2010). *Llewellyn-Jones fundamentals of obstetrics and gynecology* (9th ed.). New York: Elsevier.

Obermann, M.L. (2011). Moral disengagement in self-reported and peer-nominated school bullying. *Aggressive Behavior, 37,* 133–144.

Obler, L.K. (2009). Developments in the adult years. In J. Berko Gleason & N.B. Ratner (Eds.), *The development of language* (7th ed.). Boston: Allyn & Bacon.

Occupational Outlook Handbook (2014–2015). Washington, DC: U.S. Department of Labor, Bureau of Labor Statistics.

Odom, S., Boyd, B., Hall, L.J., & Hume, K.A. (2014). Comprehensive treatment models for children and youth with autism. In F.R. Volkmar & others (Eds.), *Handbook of autism and pervasive developmental disorders.* New: York: Wiley.

OECD (2010). *Obesity and the economics of prevention—Fit or fat.* Paris: OECD.

OECD (2010). *Strong performers and successful reformers in education: Lessons from PISA for the United States.* Paris, France: OECD.

Offer, D., Ostrove, E., Howard, K.I., & Atkinson, R. (1988). *The teenage world: Adolescents' self-image in ten countries.* New York: Plenum Press.

Ogbu, J., & Stern, P. (2001). Caste status and intellectual development. In R.J. Sternberg & E.L. Grigorenko (Eds.), *Environmental effects on cognitive abilities.* Mahwah, NJ: Erlbaum.

Ogbuanu, I.U., & others (2014). Maternal, fetal, and neonatal outcomes associated with measles during pregnancy: Namibia, 2009–2010. *Clinical Infectious Diseases, 158,* 1086–1092.

Ogden, C.L., Carroll, M.D., Kit, B.K., & Flegal, K.M. (2012, January). Prevalence of obesity in the United States, 2009–2010. *NCHS Data Brief,* 1–9.

Ogden, C.L., Carroll, M.D., Kit, B.K., & Flegal, K.M. (2014). Prevalence of childhood obesity in the United States, 2011–2012. *Journal of the American Medical Association, 311,* 806–814.

Okada, H.C., Alleyne, B., Varghai, K., Kinder, K., & Guyuron, B. (2013). Facial changes caused by smoking: A comparison between smoking and non-smoking identical twins. *Plastic and Reconstructive Surgery, 132*(5), 1085–1092.

Okada, K., & others (2014). Comprehensive evaluation of androgen replacement therapy in aging Japanese men with late-onset hypogonadism. *Aging Male, 17,* 72–75.

Okado, Y., & Bierman, K.L. (2015, in press). Differential risk for late adolescent conduct problems and mood dysregulation among children with early externalizing behavior problems. *Journal of Abnormal Child Psychology.*

Okubo, Y., & others (2015, in press). Walking can be more effective than balance in fall prevention among community-dwelling older adults. *Geriatrics and Gerontology International.*

Okun, M.A., August, K.J., Rook, K.S., & Newsom, J.T. (2010). Does volunteering moderate the relation between functional limitations and mortality? *Social Science Medicine, 71,* 1662–1668.

Okun, N., & others (2014). Pregnancy outcomes after assisted human reproduction. *Journal of Obstetrics and Gynecology Canada, 36*(1), 64–83.

Olafsdottir, E., Andersson, D.K., & Stefansson, E. (2012). The prevalence of cataract in a population with and without type 2 diabetes mellitus. *Acta Ophthalmologica, 90,* 334–340.

Oldehinkel, A.J., Ormel, J., Veenstra, R., De Winter, A., & Verhulst, F.C. (2008). Parental divorce and offspring depressive symptoms: Dutch developmental trends during early adolescence. *Journal of Marriage and the Family, 70,* 284–293.

Oleksiewicz, U., & others (2015). Computational characterization of cancer molecular profiles derived using next-generation sequencing. *Contemporary Oncology, 19*(1A), A78–A91.

Olesen, K., Rugulies, R., Rod, N.H., & Bonde, J.P. (2014). Does retirement reduce the risk of myocardial infarction? A prospective registry linkage study of 617,511 Danish workers. *International Journal of Epidemiology, 43,* 160–167.

Oliveira, S.R., & others (2012). Child safety seat usage errors in under-4s. *Journal of Pediatrics, 88.*

Olmstead, S.B., Roberson, P.N., Pasley, K., & Fincham, F.D. (2015). Hooking up and risk behaviors among first-semester college men: What is the role of precollege experience? *Journal of Sexual Research, 52,* 186–198.

Olshansky, S.J., & others (2012). Differences in life-expectancy due to race and educational differences are widening, and many may not catch up. *Health Affairs, 31,* 373–377.

Olson, M.M., Trevino, D.B., Geske, J.A., & Vanderpool, H. (2012). Religious coping and mental health outcomes: An exploratory study of socioeconomically disadvantaged patients. *Explore, 8,* 172–176.

Olszewski-Kubilius, P., & Thomson, D. (2013). Gifted education programs and procedures. In I.B. Weiner & others (Eds.), *Handbook of psychology* (2nd ed., Vol. 7). New York: Wiley.

Olweus, D. (2003). Prevalence estimation of school bullying with the Olweus bully/victim questionnaire. *Aggressive Behavior, 29*(3), 239–269.

Olweus, D. (2013). School bullying: Development and some important changes. *Annual Review of Clinical Psychology* (Vol. 9). Palo Alto, CA: Annual Reviews.

Oman, D., & Thoresen, C.E. (2006). Do religion and spirituality influence health? In R.F. Paloutzian & C.L. Park (Eds.), *Handbook of the psychology of religion and spirituality.* New York: Guilford.

Ongley, S.F., & Malti, T. (2014). The role of moral emotions in the development of children's sharing behavior. *Developmental Psychology, 50,* 1148–1159.

Ongley, S.F., Nola, M., & Malti, T. (2014). Children's giving: Moral reasoning and moral emotions in the development of donation behaviors. *Frontiers in Psychology, 5,* 456.

Onwuteaka-Philipsen, B.D., Rurup, M.L., Pasman, H.R., & van der Heide, A. (2010). The last phase of life: Who requests and who receives euthanasia or physician-assisted suicide? *Medical Care, 48,* 596–603.

Opfer, J.E., & Gelman, S.A. (2011). Development of the animate-inanimate distinction. In U. Goswami (Ed.), *Wiley-Blackwell handbook of childhood cognitive development* (2nd ed.). New York: Wiley.

Ophir, E., Nass, C., & Wagner, A.D. (2009). Cognitive control in media multitaskers. *Proceedings of the National Academy of Sciences USA, 106,* 15583–15587.

Oppezo, M., & Schwartz, D.L. (2014). Give your ideas some legs: The positive effect of walking on creative thinking. *Journal of Experimental Psychology: Learning, Memory, and Cognition, 40,* 1142–1152.

Orbeta, R.L., Overpeck, M.D., Ramamcharran, D., Kogan, M.D., & Ledsky, R. (2006). High caffeine intake in adolescents: Associations with difficulty sleeping and feeling tired in the morning. *Adolescent Health, 38,* 451–453.

Ornstein, K., & others (2013). The differential impact of unique behavioral and psychological symptoms for the dementia caregiver: How and why do patients' individual symptom clusters impact caregiver depressive symptoms? *American Journal of Geriatric Psychiatry, 21,* 1277–1286.

Ornstein, P.A., Coffman, J.L., & Grammer, J.K. (2007, April). *Teachers' memory-relevant conversations and children's memory performance.* Paper presented at the biennial meeting of the Society for Research in Child Development, Boston.

Ornstein, P.A., Coffman, J.L., Grammer, J.K., San Souci, P.P., & McCall, L.E. (2010). Linking the classroom context and the development of children's memory skills. In J. Meece & J. Eccles (Eds.), *The handbook of research on schools, schooling, and human development.* New York: Routledge.

Ornstein, P.A., Gordon, B.N., & Larus, D. (1992). Children's memory for a personally experienced event: Implications for testimony. *Applied Cognition and Psychology, 6,* 49–60.

Ornstein, P.A., Grammer, J., & Coffman, J. (2010). Teacher's "mnemonic style" and the development of skilled memory. In H.S. Waters & W. Schneider (Eds.), *Metacognition, strategy use, and instruction.* New York: Guilford.

Ornstein, P.A., Haden, C.A., & Coffman, J.L. (2010). Learning to remember: Mothers and teachers talking with children. In N.L. Stein & S. Raudenbush (Eds.), *Development science goes to school.* New York: Taylor & Francis.

Ornstein, P.A., & Light, L.L. (2010). Memory development across the life span. In W.F. Overton & R.H. Lerner (Eds.), *Handbook of life-span development.* New York: Wiley.

Orpinas, P., McNicholas, C., & Nahapetyan, L. (2015, in press). Gender differences in trajectories of relational aggression perpetration and victimization from middle to high school. *Aggressive Behavior.*

Ortigosa Gomez, S., & others (2011). Use of illicit drugs over gestation and their neonatal impact. Comparison between periods 1982–1988 and 2002–2008. *Medicina Clinica, 136,* 423–430.

Ortigosa, S., & others (2012). Feto-placental morphological effects of prenatal exposure to drugs of abuse. *Reproductive Toxicology, 34,* 73–79.

Orzech, K.M., Acebo, C., Seifer, R., Barker, D., & Carskadon, M.A. (2014). Sleep patterns associated with common illness in adolescents. *Journal of Sleep Research, 23,* 133–142.

Osorio, R.S., & others (2014). Imaging and cerebrospinal fluid biomarkers in the search for Alzheimer's disease mechanisms. *Neurodegenerative Disease, 13,* 163–165.

Ossher, L., Flegal, K.E., & Lustig, C. (2013). Everyday memory errors in older adults. *Neuropsychology, Development, and Cognition, B: Aging, Neuroscience, and Cognition, 20,* 220–242.

Osterberg, E.C., Bernie, A.M., & Ramasamy, R. (2014). Risk of replacement testosterone therapy in men. *Indian Journal of Urology, 30,* 2–7.

Oswald, D.L., & Clark, E.M. (2003). Best friends forever? High school best friendships and the transition to college. *Personal Relationships, 10,* 187–196.

Otaegui-Arrazola, A., & others (2014). Diet, cognition, and Alzheimer's disease: Food for thought. *European Journal of Nutrition, 53,* 1–23.

Otte, R.A., Donkers, F.C., Braeken, M.A., & Van den Bergh, B.R. (2015). Multimodal processing of emotional information in 9-month-old infants I: Emotional faces and voices. *Brain and Cognition, 95,* 99–106.

Otto, H., & Keller, H. (Eds.) (2013). *Different faces of attachment.* New York: Cambridge University Press.

Owen, J., Fincham, F.D., & Manthos, M. (2013). Friendship after a friends with benefits relationship: Deception, psychological function, and social connectedness. *Archives of Sexual Behavior, 42,* 1443–1449.

Owen, J.J., Rhoades, G.K., Stanley, S.M., & Markman, H.J. (2011). The role of leaders' working alliance in premarital education. *Journal of Family Psychology, 25,* 49–57.

Owens, J.A. (2014). Insufficient sleep in adolescents and young adults: An update on causes and consequences. *Pediatrics, 134,* e921–e932.

Owens, J.A., Belon, K., & Moss, P. (2010). Impact of delaying school start time on adolescent sleep, mood, and behavior. *Archives of Pediatric and Adolescent Medicine, 164,* 608–614.

Owsley, C. (2011). Aging and vision. *Vision Research, 51,* 1610–1622.

Oxford, M.L., Gilchrist, L.D., Gillmore, M.R., & Lohr, M.J. (2006). Predicting variation in the life course of adolescent mothers as they enter adulthood. *Journal of Adolescent Health, 39,* 20–36.

Ozanne, A.O., Graneheim, U.H., & Strang, S. (2013). Finding meaning despite anxiety over life and death in amyotrophic lateral sclerosis patients. *Journal of Clinical Nursing, 22,* 2141–2149.

Ozturk, S. (2015, in press). Telomerase activity and telomere length in male germ cells. *Biology of Reproduction.*

P

Pabon, M., & others (2014). Estrogen replacement therapy for stroke. *Cell Medicine, 6,* 111–122.

Pacala, J.T., & Yeuh, B. (2012). Hearing defects in the older patient: "I didn't notice anything." *JAMA, 307,* 1185–1194.

Pace-Schott, E.F., & Spencer, R.M. (2015, in press). Sleep-dependent memory consolidation in healthy aging and mild cognitive impairment. *Current Topics in Behavioral Neuroscience.*

Padilla-Walker, L.M., Carlo, G., Christensen, K.J., & Yorgason, J.B. (2012). Bidirectional relations between authoritative parenting and adolescents' prosocial behaviors. *Journal of Research on Adolescence, 22,* 400–408.

Padilla-Walker, L.M., & Coyne, S.M. (2011). "Turn that thing off!" Parent and adolescent predictors of proactive media monitoring. *Journal of Youth and Adolescence, 34,* 705–715.

Padilla-Walker, L.M., & Nelson, L.J. (2012). Black hawk down?: Establishing helicopter parenting as distinct construct from other forms of parental control during emerging adulthood. *Journal of Adolescence, 35,* 1177–1190.

Padilla-Walker, L.M., Nelson, L.J., Carroll, J.S., & Jensen, A.C. (2010). More than just a game: Video game and Internet use during emerging adulthood. *Journal of Youth and Adolescence, 39,* 103–113.

Padmanabhanunni, A., & Edwards, D. (2015, in press). Rape survivors' experiences of the silent protest: Implications for promoting healing and resilience. *Qualitative Health Research.*

Paganinini-Hill, A., Kawas, C.H., & Corrada, M.M. (2015). Antioxidant vitamin intake and mortality: The Leisure World Cohort Study. *American Journal of Epidemiology, 181,* 120–126.

Pageon, H., & others (2014). Skin aging by glycation: Lessons from the reconstructed skin model. *Clinical Chemistry and Laboratory Medicine, 52*(1), 169–174.

Pahlke, E., Hyde, J.S., & Allison, C.M. (2014). The effects of single-sex compared with coeducational schooling on students' performance and attitudes: A meta-analysis. *Psychological Bulletin, 140,* 1042–1072.

Painter, K. (2008, June 16). Older, wiser, but less active. *USA Today,* p. 4D.

Pakhomov, S.V., & Hemmy, L.S. (2014). A computational linguistic measure of clustering behavior on semantic verbal fluency task predicts risk of future dementia in the Nun Study. *Cortex. 55,* 97–106.

Pallini, S., & others (2014). Early child-parent attachment and peer relations: A meta-analysis of recent research. *Journal of Family Psychology, 28,* 118–123.

Palmore, E.B. (2004). Research note: Ageism in Canada and the United States. *Journal of Cross Cultural Gerontology, 19,* 41–46.

Paloutzian, R.F. (2000). *Invitation to the psychology of religion* (3rd ed.). Needham Heights, MA: Allyn & Bacon.

Pals, J.L. (2006). Constructing the "springboard effect": Causal connections, self-making, and growth within the life story. In D.P. McAdams, R. Josselson, & A. Lieblich (Eds.), *Identity and story.* Washington, DC: American Psychological Association.

Pan, B.A., Rowe, M.L., Singer, J.D., & Snow, C.E. (2005). Maternal correlates of growth in toddler vocabulary production in low-income families. *Child Development, 76,* 763–782.

Pan, C.Y., & others (2015, in press). Effects of physical exercise intervention on motor skills and executive functions in children with ADHD: A pilot study. *Journal of Attention Disorders.*

Pan, Y., & others (2015, in press). Association of genetic variants of GRIN2B with autism. *Scientific Reports.*

Pan, Z., & Chang, C. (2012). Gender and the regulation of longevity: Implications for autoimmunity. *Autoimmunity Reviews, 11,* A393–A403.

Pandita, R.K., & others (2015, in press). Single-strand DNA-binding protein SSB1 facilitates TERT recruitment for telomeres and maintains telomere G-overhangs. *Cancer Research.*

Paneque, M., Sequeiros, J., & Skirton, H. (2015, in press). Quality issues concerning genetic counseling for presymptomatic testing: a European Delphi study. *European Journal of Human Genetics.*

Panizzon, M.S., & others (2014). Interaction of APOE genotype and testosterone on episodic memory in middle-aged men. *Neurobiology of Aging, 35,* e1–e8.

Pann, K.M., & Crosbie-Burnett, M. (2005). Remarriage and re-coupling: A stress perspective. In P.C. McKenry & S.J. Price (Eds.), *Families and change* (3rd ed.). Thousand Oaks, CA: Sage.

Papadopoulos, C., Foster, J., & Caldwell, K. (2013). "Individualism-collectivism" as an explanatory device for mental illness stigma. *Community Mental Health, 49,* 270–280.

Papastavrou, E., Charlalambous, A., Tsangari, H., & Karayiannis, G. (2012). The burdensome and depressive experience of caring: What cancer, schizophrenia, and Alzheimer's disease caregivers have in common. *Cancer Nursing, 35,* 187–194.

Parens, E., & Johnston, J. (2009). Facts, values, and attention-deficit hyperactivity disorder (ADHD): An update on the controversies. *Child and Adolescent Psychiatry and Mental Health, 3,* 1.

Parillo, V.N. (2014). *Strangers to these shores* (11th ed.). Upper Saddle River, NJ: Pearson.

Parish-Morris, J., Golinkoff, R.M., & Hirsh-Pasek, K. (2013). From coo to code: A brief story of language development. In P.D. Zelazo (Ed.), *Oxford handbook of developmental psychology.* New York: Oxford University Press.

Parisi, J.M., & others (2014). The association between lifestyle activities and late-life depressive symptoms. *Activities, Adaptation, and Aging, 38,* 1–10.

Park, C.J., Yelland, G.W., Taffe, J.R., & Gray, K.M. (2012). Morphological and syntactic skills in language samples of pre-school aged children with autism: Atypical development? *International Journal of Speech and Language Pathology, 14,* 95–108.

Park, C.L. (2005). Religion as a meaning-making system. *Psychology of Religion Newsletter, 30*(2), 1–9.

Park, C.L. (2007). Religiousness/spirituality and health: A meaning systems perspective. *Journal of Behavioral Medicine, 30,* 319–328.

Park, C.L. (2008). Estimated longevity and changes in spirituality in the context of advanced congestive heart failure. *Palliative and Supportive Care, 6,* 1–9.

Park, C.L. (2010). Making sense out of the meaning literature: An integrative review of meaning making and its effect on adjustment to stressful life events. *Psychological Bulletin, 136,* 257–301.

Park, C.L. (2012a). Meaning making in cancer survivorship. In P.T.P. Wong (Ed.), *Handbook of meaning* (2nd ed.). Mahwah, NJ: Sage.

Park, C.L. (2012b). Meaning, spirituality, and growth: Protective and resilience factors in health and illness. In A.S. Baum, T.A. Revenson, & J.E. Singer (Eds.), *Handbook of health psychology* (2nd ed.). New York: Sage.

Park, C.L. (2013). Religion and meaning. In R.F. Paloutzian & Park, C.L. (Eds.), *Handbook of the psychology of religion* (2nd ed.). New York: Guilford.

Park, C.L., & Iacocca, M.O. (2014). A stress and coping perspective on health behaviors: Theoretical and methodological considerations. *Anxiety, Stress, and Coping, 27,* 123–137.

Park, C.L., Malone, M.R., Suresh, D.P., Bliss, D., & Rosen, R.I. (2008). Coping, meaning in life, and quality of life in congestive heart failure patients. *Quality of Life Research, 17,* 21–26.

Park, D.C., & others (2014). The impact of sustained engagement on cognitive function in older adults: The Synapse Project. *Psychological Science, 25,* 103–112.

Park, D.C., & Reuter-Lorenz, P. (2009). The adaptive brain: Aging and neurocognitive scaffolding. *Annual Review of Psychology* (Vol. 60). Palo Alto, CA: Annual Reviews.

Park, K.M., & Park, H. (2015). Effects of self-esteem improvement program on self-esteem and peer attachment in elementary school children with observed problematic behaviors. *Asian Nursing Research, 9,* 53–59.

Park, M.J., Brindis, C.D., Chang, F., & Irwin, C.E. (2008). A midcourse review of the Healthy People 2010: 21 critical health objectives for adolescents and young adults. *Journal of Adolescent Health, 42,* 329–334.

Park, M.J., Mulye, T.P., Adams, S.H., Brindis, C.D., & Irwin, C.E. (2006). The health status of young adults in the United States. *Journal of Adolescent Health, 39,* 305–317.

Park, S.H., Han, K.S., & Kang, C.B. (2014). Effects of exercise programs on depressive symptoms, quality of life, and self-esteem in older people: A systematic review of randomized controlled trials. *Applied Nursing Research, 27,* 219–226.

Park, S.H., & others (2013). Sarcopenic obesity as an independent risk factor of hypertension. *Journal of the American Society of Hypertension, 7*(6), 420–425.

Park, W., & Epstein, N.B. (2013). The longitudinal causal directionality between body image distress and self-esteem among Korean adolescents: The moderating effect of relationships with parents. *Journal of Adolescence, 36*(2), 403–411.

Parkay, F.W. (2016, in press). *Becoming a teacher* (10th ed.). Upper Saddle River, NJ: Pearson.

Parke, R.D. (2013). *Future families: Diverse forms, rich possibilities.* New York: Wiley-Blackwell.

Parke, R.D., & Buriel, R. (1998). Socialization in the family. In N. Eisenberg (Ed.), *Handbook of child psychology* (5th ed., Vol. 3). New York: Wiley.

Parke, R.D., & Buriel, R. (2006). Socialization in the family: Ethnic and ecological perspectives. In W. Damon & R. Lerner (Eds.), *Handbook of child psychology* (6th ed.). New York: Wiley.

Parke, R.D., Coltrane, S., & Schofield, T. (2011). The bicultural advantage. In J. Marsh, R. Mendoza-Denton, & J.A. Smith (Eds.), *Are we born racist?* Boston: Beacon Press.

Parker, M.A. (2011). Biotechnology in the treatment of sensorineural hearing loss: Foundations and future of hair cell regeneration. *Journal of Speech, Language, and Hearing Research, 54*(6) 1709–1731.

Parker, S.K. (2014). Work design for our times: Going beyond intrinsic motivation. *Annual Review of Psychology* (Vol. 65). Palo Alto, CA: Annual Reviews.

Parkinson, P. (2010). Changing policies regarding separated fathers in Australia. In M.E. Lamb (Ed.), *The role of the father in child development* (5th ed.). New York: Wiley.

Parr, E.B., Coffey, V.G., & Hawley, J.A. (2013). 'Sarcobesity': A medical conundrum. *Maturitas, 74,* 109–113.

Parrott, A.C., & others (2014). MDMA and heightened cortisol: A neurohormonal perspective on the pregnancy outcomes of mothers who used 'Ecstasy' during pregnancy. *Human Psychopharmacology, 29,* 109–119.

Pasterski, V., Golombok, S., & Hines, M. (2011). Sex differences in social behavior. In P.K. Smith & C.H. Hart (Eds.), *Wiley-Blackwell handbook of childhood social development* (2nd ed.). New York: Wiley.

Pasupathi, M. (2015). Autobiographical reasoning and my discontent: Alternative paths to narrative identity. In K.C. McLean & M. Syed (Eds.), *Oxford handbook of identity development.* New York: Oxford University Press.

Pathman, T., Doydum, A., & Bauer, P.J. (2015, in press). Bringing order to life events: Memory for the temporal order of autobiographical events over an extended period in school-aged children and adults. *Journal of Experimental Child Psychology.*

Patrick, M.E., & Schulenberg, J.E. (2010). Alcohol use and heavy episodic drinking prevalence among national samples of American eighth- and tenth-grade students. *Journal of Studies on Alcohol and Drugs, 71,* 41–45.

Patterson, C., & D'Augelli, A.R. (Eds.) (2013). *The psychology of sexual orientation.* New York: Cambridge University Press.

Patterson, C.J. (2004). What differences does a civil union make? Changing public policies and the experiences of same-sex couples: Comment on Solomon, Rothblum, and Balsam (2004). *Journal of Family Psychology, 18,* 287–289.

Patterson, C.J. (2013). Family lives of gay and lesbian adults. In G.W. Peterson & K.R. Bush (Eds.), *Handbook of marriage and the family* (3rd ed.). New York: Springer.

Patterson, C.J. (2014). Sexual minority youth and youth with sexual minority parents. In A. Ben Areah & others (Eds.), *Handbook of child research.* Thousand Oaks, CA: Sage.

Patterson, C.J., & Farr, R.H. (2014). Children of lesbian and gay parents: Reflections on the research-policy interface. In H.R. Schaffer & K. Durkin (Eds.), *Blackwell handbook of developmental psychology in action.* New York: Wiley.

Patterson, C.J., Farr, R.H., & Hastings, P.D. (2015). Socialization in the context of family diversity. In J.E. Grusec & P.D. Hastings (Eds.), *Handbook of socialization* (2nd ed.). New York: Guilford.

Patti, G.J., & others (2014). Meta-analysis of global metabolomics data identifies metabolites associated with life-span extension. *Metabolomics, 10,* 737–743.

Patton, G.C., & others (2011). A prospective study of the effects of optimism on adolescent health risks. *Pediatrics, 127,* 308–316.

Paulhus, D.L. (2008). Birth order. In M.M. Haith & J.B. Benson (Eds.), *Encyclopedia of infant and early childhood development.* Oxford, UK: Elsevier.

Paulus, M. (2014). The early origins of human charity: Developmental changes in preschoolers' sharing with poor and wealthy individuals. *Frontiers in Psychology, 5,* 344.

Paunesku, D., & others (2015, in press). Mind-set interventions are a scaleable treatment for academic underachievement. *Psychological Science.*

Paus, T., & others (2008). Morphological properties of the action–observation cortical network in adolescents with low and high resistance to peer influence. *Social Neuroscience, 3,* 303–316.

Payer, L. (1991). The menopause in various cultures. In H. Burger & M. Boulet (Eds.), *A portrait of menopause.* Park Ridge, NJ: Parthenon.

Pea, R., & others (2012). Media use, face-to-face communication, media multitasking, and social well-being among 8- to 12-year-old girls. *Developmental Psychology, 48,* 327–336.

Pedersen, C.B., McGrath, J., Mortensen, P.B., & Pedersen, L. (2014). The importance of the father's age to schizophrenia risk. *Molecular Psychiatry, 19,* 530–531.

Pederson, D.R., & Moran, G. (1996). Expressions of the attachment relationship outside of the Strange Situation. *Child Development, 67,* 915–927.

Peek, L., & Stough, L.M. (2010). Children with disabilities in the context of disaster: A social vulnerability perspective. *Child Development, 81,* 1260–1270.

Peek, M.K. (2009). Marriage in later life. In D. Carr (Ed.), *Encyclopedia of the life course and human development.* Boston: Gale Cengage.

Peeters, G., Brown, W., & Burton, N. (2014). Physical activity context preferences in people with arthritis and osteoporosis. *Journal of Physical Activity and Health, 11,* 536–542.

Peets, K., Hodges, E.V., & Salmivalli, C. (2013). Forgiveness and its determinants depending on the interpersonal context of hurt. *Journal of Experimental Child Psychology, 114,* 131–145.

Pelaez, M., Virues-Ortega, J., & Gewirtz, J.L. (2012). Acquisition of social referencing via discrimination training in infants. *Journal of Applied Behavior Analysis, 45,* 23–36.

Pelton, S.I., & Leibovitz, E. (2009). Recent advances in otitis media. *Pediatric and Infectious Disease Journal, 28*(Suppl. 10), S133–S137.

Peltz, C.B., Gratton, G., & Fabiani, M. (2011). Age-related changes in electrophysiological and neuropsychological indices of working memory, attention control, and cognitive flexibility. *Frontiers in Psychology, 2,* 190.

Pena, E., & Bedore, J.A. (2009). Bilingualism. In R.G. Schwartz (Ed.), *Handbook of childhood language disorders.* New York: Psychology Press.

Penela, E.C., & others (2012). Maternal caregiving moderates the relation between temperamental fear and social behavior with peers. *Infancy, 17*(6), 715–730.

Peng, P., & Fuchs, D. (2015, in press). A meta-analysis of working memory deficits in children with learning difficulties: Is there a difference between the verbal domain and numerical domain? *Journal of Learning Disabilities.*

Peretto, P., & Bonfanti, L. (2014). Major unsolved points in adult neurogenesis: Doors open on a translational future? *Frontiers in Neuroscience, 8,* 154.

Perez-Alcala, I., Sievert, L.L., Obermeyer, C.M., & Reher, D.S. (2013). Cross-cultural analysis of determinants of hot flashes and night sweats: Latin-American immigrants to Madrid and their Spanish neighbors. *Menopause, 20,* 1111–1119.

Perez-Edgar, K.E., & Guyer, A.E. (2014). Behavioral inhibition: Temperament or prodrome? *Current Behavioral Neuroscience Reports, 1,* 182–190.

Perkins, D. (1994, September). Creativity by design. *Educational Leadership, 51,* 18–25.

Perkins, S.C., Finegood, E.D., & Swain, J.E. (2013). Poverty and language development: Roles of parenting and stress. *Innovations in Clinical Neuroscience, 10,* 10–19.

Perlman, L. (2008, July 22). Am I an I or We? *Twins,* pp.1–2.

Perlman, L. (2013). Twin psychological development. Retrieved February 14, 2013, from http://christinabaglivitinglof.com/twin-pregnancy/six-twin-experts-tell-all/

Perls, T.T. (2007). Centenarians. In J.E. Birren (Ed.), *Encyclopedia of gerontology* (2nd ed.). San Diego: Academic Press.

Perrig-Chiello, P., Spahni, S., Hopflinger, F., & Carr, D. (2015, in press). Cohort and gender differences in psychosocial adjustment to later-life widowhood. *Journals of Gerontology B: Psychological Sciences and Social Sciences.*

Perry, D.G. (2012, April). *The intrapsychics of gender.* Paper presented at the Gender Development Research conference, San Francisco.

Perry, D.G., & Pauletti, R.E. (2011). Gender and adolescent development. *Journal of Research in Adolescence, 21,* 61–74.

Perry, S.B., & Downey, P.A. (2012). Fracture risk and prevention: A multidimensional approach. *Physical Therapy, 92,* 164–178.

Perry, W.G. (1970). *Forms of intellectual and ethical development in the college years.* New York: Holt, Rinehart & Winston.

Persky, H.R., Dane, M.C., & Jin, Y. (2003). *The nation's report card: Writing 2002.* U.S. Department of Education.

Persson, K.E., Fridlund, B., Kvist, L.J., & Dykes, A.K. (2011). Mothers' sense of security in the first postnatal week: Interview study. *Journal of Advanced Nursing, 67,* 105–116.

Peskin, H. (1967). Pubertal onset ego functioning. *Journal of Abnormal Psychology, 72,* 1–15.

Petersen, A.C., Joseph, J., & Feit, M. (Eds.) (2014). *New directions in child abuse and neglect research.* Washington, DC: National Academies Press.

Petersen, I.T., & others (2012). Interaction between serotonin transporter polymorphism (5-HTTLPR) and stressful life events in adolescents' trajectories of anxious/depressed symptoms. *Developmental Psychology, 48*(5), 1463–1475.

Peterson, C.C. (2005). Mind and body: Concepts of human cognition, physiology and false belief in children with autism or typical development. *Journal of Autism and Developmental Disorders, 35,* 487–497.

Peterson, J.L., & Hyde, J.S. (2010). A meta-analytic review of research on gender differences in sexuality, 1973–2007. *Psychological Bulletin, 136,* 21–38.

Petrick-Steward, E. (2012). *Beginning writers in the zone of proximal development.* New York: Psychology Press.

Petts, R.J. (2014). Family, religious attendance, and trajectories of psychological well-being among youth. *Journal of Family Psychology, 28,* 759–768.

Pew Research Center (2008). *Pew forum on religion and public life: U.S. Religious Landscape Survey.* Washington, DC: Author.

Pew Research Center (2010). *Millennials: Confident, connected, open to change.* Washington, DC: Pew Research Center.

Pew Research Center (2010). *The decline of marriage and rise of new families.* Washington, DC: Author.

Pew Research Center (2011, December). *Barely half of U.S. adults are married—a record low.* Washington, DC: Pew Research Center.

Pew Research Center (2012). *Religion and Public Life Project.* Washington, DC: Pew Research Center.

Pew Research Center (2013). *Social & demographic trends.* Washington, DC: Pew Research Center.

Pew Research Center (2015). *For most highly educated women, motherhood doesn't start until the 30s.* Washington, DC: Pew Research Center.

Pfefferbaum, B., Newman, E., & Nelson, S.D. (2014). Mental health interventions for children exposed to disasters and terrorism. *Journal of Child and Adolescent Psychopharmacology, 24,* 24–31.

Pfluger, M., Winkler, C., Hummel, S., & Ziegler, A.G. (2010). Early infant diet in children at risk for type 1 diabetes. *Hormone and Metabolic Research, 42,* 143–148.

Phaniendra, A., Jestadi, D.B., & Periyasamy, L. (2015). Free radicals: Sources, targets, and their implication for various diseases. *Indian Journal of Clinical Biochemistry, 30,* 11–26.

Phillips, D.A., & Lowenstein, A.E. (2011). Early care, education, and child development. *Annual Review of Psychology* (Vol. 62). Palo Alto, CA: Annual Reviews.

Phillips, J.A., & Nugent, C.N. (2014). Suicide and the great recession of 2007–2009: The role of economic factors in the 50 U.S. states. *Social Science and Medicine, 116,* 22–31.

Phillips, S.A., Mahmoud, A.M., Brown, M.D., & Haus, J.M. (2015, in press). Exercise interventions and peripheral arterial function: Implications for cardio-metabolic disease. *Progress in Cardiovascular Diseases.*

Phinney, J.S. (1996). When we talk about American ethnic groups, what do we mean? *American Psychologist, 51,* 918–927.

Phinney, J.S. (2006, April). *Acculturation and adaptation of immigrant adolescents in thirteen countries.* Paper presented at the meeting of the Society for Research on Adolescence, San Francisco.

Phinney, J.S. (2008). Bridging identities and disciplines: Advances and challenges in understanding multiple identities. *New Directions for Child and Adolescent Development, 120,* 97–109.

Phinney, J.S., Berry, J.W., Sam, D.L., & Vedder, P. (2013a). Understanding immigrant youth: Conclusions and implications. In J.W. Berry & others (Eds.), *Immigrant youth in cultural transition.* New York: Psychology Press.

Phinney, J.S., Berry, J.W., Vedder, P., & Liebkind, K. (2013b). Acculturation experience: Attitudes, identities, and behaviors of immigrant youth. In J.W. Berry & others (Eds.), *Immigrant youth in cultural transition.* New York: Psychology Press.

Phinney, J.S., & Vedder, P. (2013). Family relationship values of adolescents and parents: Intergenerational discrepancies and adaptation. In J.W. Berry & others (Eds.), *Immigrant youth in cultural transition.* New York: Psychology Press.

Piaget, J. (1932). *The moral judgment of the child.* New York: Harcourt Brace Jovanovich.

Piaget, J. (1954). *The construction of reality in the child.* New York: Basic Books.

Piaget, J. (1962). *Play, dreams, and imitation in childhood.* New York: Norton.

Piaget, J., & Inhelder, B. (1969). *The child's conception of space* (F.J. Langdon & J.L. Lunger, Trans.). New York: Norton.

Piazza, J.R., Almeida, D.M., Dmitrieva, N.O., & Klein, L.C. (2010). Frontiers in the use of biomarkers of health in research on stress and aging. *Journals of Gerontology B: Psychological Sciences and Social Sciences, 65B,* 513–525.

Piazza, J.R., & Charles, S.T. (2012). Affective disorders and age: The view through a developmental lens. In S.K. Whitbourne & M.J. Sliwinski (Eds.), *Wiley-Blackwell handbook of adult development and aging.* New York: Wiley.

Picchioni, D., Reith, R.M., Nadel, J.L., & Smith, C.B. (2014). Sleep, plasticity, and the pathophysiology of neurodevelopmental disorders: The potential roles of protein synthesis and other cellular processes. *Brain Sciences, 4,* 150–201.

Pierce, J., Schmidt, C., & Stoddard, S.A. (2015). The role of feared possible selves in the relationship between peer influence and delinquency. *Journal of Adolescence, 38,* 17–26.

Pierce, R.S., & Andersen, G.J. (2014). The effects of age and workload on 3D spatial attention in dual-task driving. *Accident Analysis and Prevention, 67C,* 96–104.

Piko, B.F., & Balazs, M.A. (2012). Authoritative parenting style and adolescent smoking and drinking. *Addictive Behaviors, 37,* 353–356.

Pillas, D., Naicker, K., Colman, I., & Hertzman, C. (2014). Public health policy and practice: Implications of life course approaches to mental illness. In K.C. Koenen & others (Eds.), *A life course approach to mental disorders.* New York: Oxford University Press.

Pinette, M., Wax, J., & Wilson, E. (2004). The risks of underwater birth. *American Journal of Obstetrics & Gynecology, 190,* 1211–1215.

Ping, H., & Hagopian, W. (2006). Environmental factors in the development of type 1 diabetes. *Reviews in Endocrine and Metabolic Disorders, 7,* 149–162.

Pinker, S. (2015, in press). *Language, cognition, and human nature.* New York: Oxford University Press.

Pinquart, M., Feubner, C., & Ahnert, L. (2013). Meta-analytic evidence for stability of attachments from infancy to early adulthood. *Attachment and Human Development, 15,* 189–218.

Pinquart, M., & Forstmeier, S. (2012). Effects of reminiscence interventions on psychosocial outcomes: A meta-analysis. *Aging and Mental Health, 16,* 541–558.

Pinsker, J.E. (2012). Turner syndrome: Updating the paradigm of clinical care. *Journal of Clinical Endocrinology and Metabolism, 97*(6), E994–E1003.

Pitkanen, T., Lyyra, A.L., & Pulkkinen, L. (2005). Age of onset of drinking and the use of alcohol in adulthood: A follow-up study from age 8–42 for females and males. *Addiction, 100,* 652–661.

Pittman, J.F., Keiley, M.H., Kerpelman, J.L., & Vaughn, B.E. (2011). Attachment, identity, and intimacy: Parallels between Bowlby's and Erikson's paradigms. *Journal of Family Theory and Review, 3,* 32–46.

Planalp, E.M., & Braungart-Rieker, J.M. (2015). Trajectories of regulatory behaviors in early infancy: Determinants of infant self-distraction and self-comforting. *Infancy, 20,* 129–159.

Plassman, B.L., & Grafman, J. (2015). Traumatic brain injury and late-life dementia. *Handbook of Clinical Neurology, 128,* 711–722.

Platt, B., Kadosh, K.C., & Lau, J.Y. (2013). The role of peer rejection in adolescent depression. *Depression and Anxiety, 30,* 809–821.

Pleck, J.H. (1995). The gender-role strain paradigm. In R.F. Levant & W.S. Pollack (Eds.), *A new psychology of men.* New York: Basic Books.

Plener, P.L., Singer, H., & Goldbeck, L. (2011). Traumatic events and suicidality in a German adolescent community sample. *Journal of Traumatic Stress, 24,* 121–124.

Plomin, R. (1999). Genetics and general cognitive ability. *Nature, 402*(Suppl.), C25–C29.

Plomin, R. (2004). Genetics and developmental psychology. *Merrill-Palmer Quarterly, 50,* 341–352.

Plomin, R. (2011). Commentary: Why are children in the same family so different? Nonshared environment three decades later. *International Journal of Epidemiology, 40,* 582–592.

Plucker, J. (2010, July 10). Interview. In P. Bronson & A. Merryman, The creativity crisis. *Newsweek,* 42–48.

Pluess, M., & Belsky, J. (2009). Differential susceptibility to rearing experience: The case of childcare. *Journal of Child Psychology and Psychiatry, 50,* 396–404.

Polanczyk, G.V., & others (2015, in press). Annual research review: A meta-analysis of the worldwide prevalence of mental disorders in children and adolescents. *Journal of Child Psychology and Psychiatry.*

Polat, U., & others (2012). Training the brain to overcome the effect of aging on the human eye. *Scientific Reports, 2,* 278.

Pollack, W. (1999). *Real boys.* New York: Owl Books.

Pomerantz, E.M. (2013). *Center for Parent-Child Studies.* Retrieved July 20, 2013, from http://labs.psychology.illinois.edu/cpcs/

Pomerantz, E.M. (2014). *Six principles to motivate your child to do well in school.* Retrieved November 20, 2014, from http://i-parents.illinois.edu/research/pomerantz.html

Pomerantz, E.M., Cheung, C.S., & Qin, L. (2012). Relatedness between children and parents: Implications for motivation. In R. Ryan (Ed.), *Oxford handbook of motivation.* New York: Oxford University Press.

Pomerantz, E.M., & Kempner, S.G. (2013). Mothers' daily person and process praise: Implications for children's intelligence and motivation. *Developmental Psychology, 49,* 2040–2046.

Pomerantz, E.M., Kim, E.M., & Cheung, C.S. (2012). Parents' involvement in children's learning. In K.R. Harris & others (Eds.), *APA educational psychology handbook.* Washington, DC: American Psychological Association.

Pontifex, M.B., Saliba, B.J., Raine, L.B., Picchietti, D.L., & Hillman, C.H. (2013). Exercise improves behavioral, neurocognitive, and scholastic performance in children with attention-deficit/hyperactivity disorder. *Journal of Pediatrics, 162,* 543–551.

Pooler, A.M., Noble, W., & Hanger, D.P. (2014). A role for tau at the synapse in Alzheimer's disease pathogenesis. *Neuropharmacology, 76* (Pt. A), 1–8.

Poon, L.W., & others (2010). Understanding centenarians' psychosocial dynamics and their contributions to health and quality of life. *Current Gerontology and Geriatrics Research.* doi:10.1155/2010/680657

Poon, L.W., & others (2012). Understanding dementia prevalence among centenarians. *Journals of Gerontology A: Biological Sciences and Medical Sciences, 67,* 358–365.

Popenoe, D. (2008). *Cohabitation, marriage, and child wellbeing: A cross-national perspective.* Piscataway, NJ: The National Marriage Project, Rutgers University.

Popenoe, D. (2009). *The state of our unions 2008. Updates of social indicators: Tables and charts.* Piscataway, NJ: The National Marriage Project.

Popham, W.J. (2014). *Classroom assessment* (7th ed.). Upper Saddle River, NJ: Pearson.

Posada, G., & Kaloustian, G. (2011). Parent-infant interaction. In J.G. Bremner & T.D. Wachs (Eds.), *Wiley-Blackwell handbook of infant development* (2nd ed.). New York: Wiley.

Posada, G., & others (2002). Maternal caregiving and infant security in two cultures. *Developmental Psychology, 38,* 67–78.

Posner, M.I., & Rothbart, M.K. (2007a). *Educating the human brain.* Washington, DC: American Psychological Association.

Posner, M.I., & Rothbart, M.K. (2007b). Research on attention networks as a model for the integration of psychological sciences. *Annual Review of Psychology, 58,* 1–23.

Posner, M.I., Rothbart, M.K., Sheese, B.E., & Voelker, P. (2014). Developing attention: Behavioral and brain mechanisms. *Advances in Neuroscience, 2014,* 405094.

Potapova, N.V., Gartstein, M.A., & Bridgett, D.J. (2014). Paternal influences on infant temperament: Effects of father internalizing problems, parent-related stress, and temperament. *Infant Behavior and Development, 37,* 105–110.

Potard, C., Courtois, R., & Rusch, E. (2008). The influence of peers on risky behavior during adolescence. *European Journal of Contraception and Reproductive Health Care, 13,* 264–270.

Potter, J.D. (2014). The failure of cancer chemoprevention. *Carcinogenesis, 35,* 974–982.

Potthast, N., Neuner, F., & Catani, C. (2014). The contribution of emotional maltreatment to alcohol dependence in a treatment-seeking sample. *Addictive Behaviors 39,* 949–958.

Poulin, F., & Pedersen, S. (2007). Developmental changes in gender composition of friendship networks in adolescent girls and boys. *Developmental Psychology, 43,* 1484–1496.

Powell, S.D. (2015). *Your introduction to education* (3rd ed.). Upper Saddle River, NJ: Pearson.

Power, F.C., & Higgins-D'Alessandro, A. (2008). The Just Community approach to moral education and moral atmosphere of the school. In L. Nucci & D. Narváez (Eds.), *Handbook of moral and character education.* Clifton, NJ: Psychology Press.

Power, F.C., & Higgins-D'Alessandro, A. (2014). The Just Community approach to moral education and moral atmosphere of the school. In L. Nucci, T. Krettenauer, & D. Narváez (Eds.), *Handbook of moral and character education* (2nd ed.). New York: Routledge.

Power, S. (2011). Social play. In P.K. Smith & C.H. Hart (Eds.), *Wiley-Blackwell handbook of childhood social development* (2nd ed.). New York: Wiley.

Powers, C.J., & Bierman, K.L. (2013). The multifaceted impact of peer relations on aggressive-disruptive behavior in early elementary school. *Developmental Psychology, 49,* 1174–1186.

Powers, S., & Howley, E. (2015). *Exercise physiology* (9th ed.). New York: McGraw-Hill.

Powers, S.M., Bisconti, T.L., & Bergeman, C.S. (2014). Trajectories of social support and well-being across the first two years of widowhood. *Death Studies, 38,* 499–509.

Prakash, R.S., Voss, M.W., Erickson, K.I., & Kramer, A.F. (2015). Moving toward a healthier brain and mind. *Annual Review of Psychology* (Vol. 66). Palo Alto, CA: Annual Reviews.

Prameela, K.K. (2011). Breastfeeding—anti-viral potential and relevance to the influenza virus pandemic. *Medical Journal of Malaysia, 66,* 166–169.

Pratt, C., & Bryant, P.E. (1990). Young children understand that looking leads to knowing (so long as they are looking in a single barrel). *Child Development, 61,* 973–982.

Prendergast, C., & Gidding, S.S. (2014). Cardiovascular risk in children and adolescents with type 2 diabetes mellitus. *Current Diabetes Reports, 14,* 454.

Prenderville, J.A., Kennedy, P.J., Dinan, T.G., & Cryan, J.F. (2015). Adding fuel to the fire: The impact of stress on the aging brain. *Trends in Neuroscience, 38,* 13–25.

Pressley, M. (2003). Psychology of literacy and literacy instruction. In I.B. Weiner (Ed.), *Handbook of psychology* (Vol. 7). New York: Wiley.

Pressley, M. (2007). Achieving best practices. In L.B. Bambrell, L.M. Morrow, & M. Pressley (Eds.), *Best practices in literacy instruction.* New York: Guilford.

Pressley, M., Allington, R., Wharton-McDonald, R., Block, C.C., & Morrow, L.M. (2001). *Learning to read: Lessons from exemplary first grades.* New York: Guilford.

Pressley, M., Raphael, L., Gallagher, D., & DiBella, J. (2004). Providence–St. Mel School: How a school that works for African-American students works. *Journal of Educational Psychology, 96,* 216–235.

Pressley, M., & others (2003). *Motivating primary-grades teachers.* New York: Guilford.

Price, C.A., & Joo, E. (2005). Exploring the relationship between marital status and women's retirement satisfaction. *International Journal of Aging and Human Development, 61,* 37–55.

Priess, H.A., & Lindberg, S.M. (2011a). Gender intensification. In B.B. Brown & M. Prinstein (Eds.), *Encyclopedia of adolescence.* San Diego: Academic Press.

Priess, H.A., & Lindberg, S.M. (2011b). Gender roles. In B.B. Brown & M. Prinstein (Eds.), *Encyclopedia of adolescence.* San Diego: Academic Press.

Priess, H.A., Lindberg, S.M., & Hyde, J.S. (2009). Adolescent gender-role identity and mental health: Gender intensification revisited. *Child Development, 80,* 1531–1544.

Prigerson, H.G., & Maciejwski, P.K. (2014). Predicting prolonged grief disorder: Caregiver prodrome turns bereaved survivor syndrome. Commentary on Thomas et al. *Journal of Pain and Symptom Management, 47,* 516–517.

Prinstein, M.J., Brechwald, W.A., & Cohen, G.L. (2011). Susceptibility to peer influence: Using a performance-based measure to identify adolescent males at heightened risk for deviant peer socialization. *Developmental Psychology, 47,* 116–122.

Prinstein, M.J., & Dodge, K.A. (2008). Current issues in peer influence research. In M.J. Prinstein & K.A. Dodge (Eds.), *Understanding peer influence in children and adolescents.* New York: Guilford.

Prinstein, M.J., & Giletta, M. (2015). Peer relations and developmental psychopathology. In D. Cicchetti (Ed.), *Developmental psychopathology* (3rd ed.). New York: Wiley.

Prinstein, M.J., Rancourt, D., Guerry, J.D., & Browne, C.B. (2009). Peer reputations and psychological adjustment. In K.H. Rubin, W.M. Bukowksi, & B. Laursen (Eds.), *Handbook of peer interactions, relationships, and groups.* New York: Guilford.

Privitera, G.J., McGrath, H.K., Windus, B.A., & Doraiswamy, P.M. (2015). Eat now or later: Self-control as an overlapping cognitive mechanism of depression and obesity. *PLoS One, 10*(3), e0123136.

Prot, S., & others (2015). Media as agents of socialization. In J.E. Grusec & P.D. Hastings (Eds.), *Handbook of socialization* (2nd ed.). New York: Guilford.

Prouix, C.M., & Snyder-Rivas, L.A. (2013). The longitudinal associations between marital happiness, problems, and self-rated health. *Journal of Family Psychology, 27,* 194–202.

Provenzo, E.F. (2002). *Teaching, learning, and schooling in American culture: A critical perspective.* Boston: Allyn & Bacon.

Pryor, J.H., DeAngelo, L., & Blake, L.P. (2011). *The American freshman: National norms for fall 2011.* Los Angeles: Higher Education Research Institute, UCLA.

Psychster Inc (2010). *Psychology of social media.* Retrieved February 21, 2013, from www.psychster.com

Pudrovska, T. (2009). Midlife crises and transitions. In D. Carr (Ed.), *Encyclopedia of the life course and human development.* Boston: Gale Cengage.

Pulliam, C.L., & others (2015, in press). Motion sensor strategies for automated optimization of deep brain stimulation in Parkinson's Disease. *Parkinsonism and Related Disorders.*

Pulopulos, M.M., & others (2015, in press). Acute stress and working memory in older people. *Stress.*

Puma, M., & others (2010). *Head Start impact study: Final report.* Washington, DC: Administration for Children and Families.

Purcell, L.K., & others (2014). Sport-related concussion: Evaluation and management. *Pediatric Child Health, 19,* 153–165.

Putallaz, M., & others (2007). Overt and relational aggression and victimization: Multiple perspectives within the school setting. *Journal of School Psychology, 45,* 523–547.

Putnam Investments (2006). *Survey of the working retired.* Franklin, MA: Author.

Putnick, D.L., & others (2015, in press). Perceived mother and father acceptance-rejection predict four unique aspects of child adjustment across nine countries. *Journal of Child Psychology and Psychiatry.*

Puzzanchera, C., & Robson, C. (2014). *Delinquency cases in juvenile court, 2010.* Washington, DC: U.S. Department of Justice.

Q

Qazi, F., & others (2013). The degree of certainty in brain death: Probability in clinical and Islamic legal discourse. *Theoretical Medicine and Bioethics, 34*(2), 117–131.

Qin, J.B., & others (2014). Risk factors for congenital syphilis and adverse pregnancy outcomes in offspring of women with syphilis in Shenzhen, China: A prospective nested case-control study. *Sexually Transmitted Diseases, 41,* 13–23.

Qin, L., & Pomerantz, E.M. (2013). Reciprocal pathways between American and Chinese early adolescents' sense of responsibility and disclosure to parents. *Child Development, 84,* 1887–1895.

Qu, Y., & Pomerantz, E.M. (2015, in press). Divergent school trajectories in early adolescence in the United States and China: An examination of underlying mechanisms. *Journal of Youth and Adolescence.*

Qu, Y., Pomerantz, E.M., & Deng, C. (2015, in press). American and Chinese parents' goals for their early adolescents: Content and transmission. *Journal of Research on Adolescence.*

Quigley, C., & Muller, M.M. (2014). Feature-selective attention in healthy old age: A selective decline in selective attention. *Journal of Neuroscience, 34,* 2471–2476.

Quinn, N., & Mageo, J. (Eds.) (2013). *Cross-cultural challenges to attachment theory.* New York: Macmillan.

Quinn, P.C. (2015, in press). What do infants know about cats, dogs, and people? Development of a "like-people" representation for nonhuman animals. In L. Esposito & others (Eds.), *Social neuroscience of human-animal interaction.* New York: Elsevier.

R

Rachner, T.D., Khosla, S., & Hofbauer, L.C. (2011). Osteoporosis: Now and the future. *Lancet, 377,* 1276–1287.

Raffaelli, M., & Ontai, L. (2001). "She's sixteen years old and there's boys calling over to the house": An exploratory study of sexual socialization in Latino families. *Culture, Health, and Sexuality, 3,* 295–310.

Raffaelli, M., & Ontai, L.L. (2004). Gender socialization in Latino/a families: Results from two retrospective studies. *Sex Roles, 50,* 287–299.

Rahilly-Tierney, C.R., Spiro, A., Vokonas, P., & Gaziano, J.M. (2011). *American Journal of Cardiology, 107,* 1173–1177.

Rahnema, C.D., & others (2014). Anabolic steroid-induced hypogonadism: Diagnosis and treatment. *Fertility and Sterility, 101,* 1271–1279.

Raikes, H., & others (2006). Mother-child bookreading in low-income families: Correlates and outcomes during the first three years of life. *Child Development, 77,* 924–953.

Raikes, H.A., Virmani, E.A., Thompson, R.A., & Hatton, H. (2013). Declines in peer conflict from preschool through first grade: Influences from early attachment and social information processing. *Attachment and Human Development, 15,* 65–82.

Rajan, V., & Bell, M.A. (2015). Developmental changes in fact and source recall: Contributions from executive function and brain electrical activity. *Developmental Cognitive Neuroscience, 12,* 1–11.

Rakison, D.H., & Lawson, C.A. (2013). Categorization. In P.D. Zelazo (Ed.), *Oxford handbook of developmental psychology.* New York: Oxford University Press.

Rakoczy, H. (2012). Do infants have a theory of mind? *British Journal of Developmental Psychology, 30,* 59–74.

Ram, N., Morelli, S., Lindberg, C., & Carstensen, L.L. (2008). From static to dynamic: The ongoing dialectic about human development. In K.W. Schaie & R.P. Abeles (Eds.), *Social structures and aging individuals: Continuing challenges.* Mahwah, NJ: Erlbaum.

Ram, N., Shikyo, M., Lunkenheimer, E.S., Doerksen, S., & Conroy, D. (2014). Families as coordinated symbiotic systems: Making use nonlinear dynamic models. In S. McHale, P. Amato, & A. Booth (Eds.), *Emerging methods in family research.* New York: Springer.

Ramani, G.B., & Siegler, R.S. (2014). How informal learning activities can promote children's numerical knowledge. In R.C. Kadosh & A. Dowker (Eds.), *Oxford handbook of mathematical cognition.* New York: Oxford University Press.

Ramchandani, P.G., & others (2013). Do early father-infant interactions predict the onset of externalizing behaviors in young children? Findings from a longitudinal cohort study. *Journal of Child Psychology and Psychiatry, 54,* 56–64.

Ramey, C.T., & Campbell, F.A. (1984). Preventive education for high-risk children: Cognitive consequences of the Carolina Abecedarian Project. *American Journal of Mental Deficiency, 88,* 515–523.

Ramey, C.T., & Ramey, S.L. (1998). Early prevention and early experience. *American Psychologist, 53,* 109–120.

Ramey, C.T., Ramey, S.L., & Lanzi, R.G. (2001). Intelligence and experience. In R.J. Sternberg & E.L. Grigorenko (Eds.), *Environment effects on cognitive development.* Mahwah, NJ: Erlbaum.

Ramey, S.L. (2005). Human developmental science serving children and families: Contributions of the NICHD study of early child care. In NICHD Early Child Care Network (Eds.), *Child care and development.* New York: Guilford.

Ramirez-Esparza, N., Garcia-Sierra, A., & Kuhl, P.K. (2014). Look who's talking: Speech style and social context in language input to infants are linked to concurrent and future speech development. *Developmental Science, 17,* 880–891.

Ramirez-Rodriquez, G., & others (2014). Environmental enrichment induces neuroplastic changes in middle age female BalbC mice and increases the hippocampal levels of BDNF, p-Akt, and p-MAPK1/2. *Neuroscience, 260,* 158–170.

Ramsdell, H.L., Oller, D.K., Buder, E.H., Ethington, C.A., & Chorna, L. (2012). Identification of prelinguistic phonological categories. *Journal of Speech, Language, and Hearing Research, 55,* 1626–1639.

Ramus, F. (2014). Neuroimaging sheds new light on the phonological deficit in dyslexia. *Trends in Cognitive Science, 18,* 274–275.

Rancourt, D., Choukas-Bradley, S., Cohen, G.L., & Prinstein, M.J. (2014). An experimental examination of peers' influence on adolescent girls' intent to engage in maladaptive weight-related behaviors. *International Journal of Eating Disorders, 47,* 437–447.

Randall, W.L. (2013). The importance of being ironic: Narrative openness and personal resilience in later life. *Gerontologist, 53*(1), 9–16.

Rapee, R.M. (2014). Preschool environment and temperament as predictors of social and nonsocial anxiety disorders in middle adolescence. *Journal of the American Academy of Child and Adolescent Psychiatry, 53,* 320–328.

Rapp, S.R., & others (2013). Educational attainment, MRI changes, and cognitive function in older postmenopausal women from the Women's Health Initiative Memory Study. *International Journal of Psychiatry in Medicine, 46,* 121–143.

Rash, J.A., Campbell, T.S., Letourneau, N., & Giesbrecht, G.F. (2015). Maternal cortisol during pregnancy is related to infant cardiac vagal control. *Psychoneuroimmunology, 54C,* 78–89.

Rasulo, D., Christensen, K., & Tomassini, C. (2005). The influence of social relations on mortality in later life: A study on elderly Danish twins. *The Gerontologist, 45,* 601–608.

Rathunde, K., & Csikszentmihalyi, M. (2006). The developing person: An experiential perspective. In W. Damon & R. Lerner (Eds.), *Handbook of child psychology* (6th ed.). New York: Wiley.

Rauner, A., Mess, F., & Woll, A. (2013). The relationship between physical activity, physical fitness, and overweight in adolescents: A systematic review of studies published in or after 2000. *BMC Pediatrics, 13,* 19.

Raven, P.H., Johnson, G.B., Mason, K.A., Loscos, J., & Singer, S. (2014). *Biology* (10th ed.). New York: McGraw-Hill.

Raver, C.C., & others (2011). CSRP's impact on low-income preschoolers' preacademic skills: Self-regulation as a mediating mechanism. *Child Development, 82,* 362–378.

Raver, C.C., & others (2012). Testing models of children's self-regulation within educational contexts: Implications for measurement. *Advances in Child Development and Behavior, 42,* 245–270.

Raver, C.C., & others (2013). Predicting individual differences in low-income children's executive control from early to middle childhood. *Developmental Science, 16*(3), 394–408.

Rawlins, W.K. (2009). *The compass of friendship.* Thousand Oaks, CA: Sage.

Raznahan, A., & others (2014). Longitudinal four-dimensional mapping of subcortical anatomy in human development. *Proceedings of the National Academy of Sciences USA, 111,* 1592–1597.

Razza, R.A., Martin, A., & Brooks-Gunn, J. (2012). The implications of early attentional regulational for school success among low-income children. *Journal of Applied Developmental Psychology, 33,* 311–319.

Reale, M.A., & others (2014). Selective acetyl- and butyrylcholinesterase inhibitors reduce amyloid-B ex vivo activation of peripheral chemo-cytokines from Alzheimer's disease subjects: Exploring the cholinergic anti-inflammatory pathway. *Current Alzheimer Research, 11,* 608–612.

Realini, J.P., Buzi, R.S., Smith, P.B., & Martinez, M. (2010). Evaluation of "big decisions": An abstinence-plus sexuality. *Journal of Sex and Marital Therapy, 36,* 313–326.

Ream, G.L., & Savin-Williams, R. (2003). Religious development in adolescence. In G. Adams & M. Berzonksy (Eds.), *Blackwell handbook of adolescence.* Malden, MA: Blackwell.

Rebok, G.W., & others (2014). Ten-year effects of the advanced cognitive training for independent and vital elderly cognitive training trial on cognition and everyday functioning in older adults. *Journal of the American Geriatrics Society, 62,* 16–24.

Redick, T.S., & others (2013). No evidence of intelligence improvement after working memory training: A randomized, placebo-controlled design. *Journal of Experimental Psychology: General, 142,* 359–379.

Reed, I.C. (2005). Creativity: Self-perceptions over time. *International Journal of Aging & Development, 60,* 1–18.

Reed, S.D., & others (2014). Menopausal quality of life: RCT of yoga, exercise, and omega-3 supplements. *American Journal of Obstetrics and Gynecology, 210*(3), 244.e1–e11.

Reedy, M.N., Birren, J.E., & Schaie, K.W. (1981). Age and sex differences in satisfying relationships across the adult life span. *Human Development, 24,* 52–66.

Reese, B.M., Haydon, A.A., Herring, A.H., & Halpern, C.T. (2013). The association between sequences of sexual initiation and the likelihood of teenage pregnancy. *Journal of Adolescent Health, 52,* 228–233.

Regalado, M., Sareen, H., Inkelas, M., Wissow, L.S., & Halfon, N. (2004). Parents' discipline of young children: Results from the National Survey of Early Childhood Health. *Pediatrics, 113,* 1952–1958.

Regan, J.C., & Partridge, L. (2013). Gender and longevity: Why do men die earlier than women? Comparative and experimental evidence. *Best Practices in Research. Clinical Endocrinology and Metabolism, 27,* 467–479.

Regev, R.H., & others (2003). Excess mortality and morbidity among small-for-gestational-age premature infants: A population based study. *Journal of Pediatrics, 143,* 186–191.

Reichstadt, J., Depp, C.A., Palinkas, L.A., Folsom, D.P., & Jeste, D.V. (2007). Building blocks of successful aging: A focus group study of older adults' perceived contributors to successful aging. *American Journal of Geriatric Psychiatry, 15,* 194–201.

Reid, P.T., & Zalk, S.R. (2001). Academic environments: Gender and ethnicity in U.S. higher education. In J. Worell (Ed.), *Encyclopedia of women and gender.* San Diego: Academic Press.

Reijmerink, N.E., & others (2011). Toll-like receptors and microbial exposure: Gene-gene and gene-environment interaction in the development of atopy. *European Respiratory Journal, 38,* 833–840.

Reijntjes, A., & others (2013). Costs and benefits of bullying in the context of the peer group: A three-wave longitudinal analysis. *Journal of Abnormal Psychology, 41,* 1217–1219.

Reilly, D., & Neumann, D.L. (2013). Gender-role differences in spatial ability: A meta-analytic review. *Sex Roles, 68,* 521–535.

Reiner, W.G., & Gearhart, J.P. (2004). Discordant sexual identity in some genetic males with cloacal exstrophy assigned to female sex at birth. *New England Journal of Medicine, 350,* 333–341.

Reis, O., & Youniss, J. (2004). Patterns of identity change and development in relationships with mothers and friends. *Journal of Adolescent Research, 19,* 31–44.

Reis, S.M., & Renzulli, J.S. (2014). Challenging gifted and talented learners with a continuum of research-based intervention strategies. In M.A. Bray & T.J.

Kehle (Eds.), *Oxford handbook of school psychology.* New York: Oxford University Press.

Reiss, D.E., Eccles, J.S., & Nielsen, L. (2014). Conscientiousness and public health: Synthesizing current research to promote healthy aging. *Developmental Psychology, 50,* 1303–1314.

Rejeski, W.J., & others (2011). Translating weight loss and physical activity programs into the community to preserve mobility in older, obese adults in poor cardiovascular health. *Archives of Internal Medicine, 171*(10), 880–886.

Rendall, M.S., Weden, M.M., Faveault, M.M., & Waldron, H. (2011). The protective effect of marriage for survival: A review and update. *Demography, 48,* 481–506.

Rengasamy, M., & others (2013). The bi-directional relationship between parent-adolescent conflict and treatment outcome for treatment-resistant adolescent depression. *Journal of the American Academy of Child and Adolescent Psychiatry, 52,* 370–377.

Renju, J.R., & others (2011). Scaling up adolescent sexual and reproductive health interventions through existing government systems? A detailed process evaluation of a school-based intervention in the Mwanza region in the northwest of Tanzania. *Journal of Adolescent Health, 48,* 79–86.

Renzetti, C.M., & Kennedy-Bergen, R.M. (2015). *Understanding diversity.* Upper Saddle River, NJ: Pearson.

Repacholi, B.M., & Gopnik, A. (1997). Early reasoning about desires: Evidence from 14- and 18-month-olds. *Developmental Psychology, 33,* 12–21.

Rest, J.R. (1995). *Concerns for the social-psychological development of youth and educational strategies: Report for the Kaufmann Foundation.* Minneapolis: University of Minnesota, Department of Educational Psychology.

Reuter-Lorenz, P.A., & Park, D.C. (2014). How does it STAC up? Revisiting the scaffolding theory of aging and cognition. *Neuropsychology Review, 24,* 355–370.

Reuter-Lorenz, P.A., & others (2000). Age difference in the frontal lateralization of verbal and spatial working memory revealed by PET. *Journal of Cognitive Neuroscience, 12,* 174–187.

Reutzel, D.R., & Cooter, R.B. (2015). *Teaching children to read* (7th ed.). Upper Saddle River, NJ: Pearson.

Reville, B., & Foxwell, A.M. (2014). The global state of palliative care-progress and challenges in cancer care. *Annals of Palliative Medicine, 3,* 129–138.

Reyna, V., & Farley, F. (2006). Risk and rationality in adolescent decision-making: Implications of theory, practice, and public policy. *Psychological Science in the Public Interest, 7,* 1–44.

Reyna, V.F., & Brainerd, C.J. (2011). Dual processes in decision making and developmental neuroscience: A fuzzy-trace model. *Developmental Review, 31,* 180–206.

Reyna, V.F., & Rivers, S.E. (2008). Current theories of risk and rational decision making. *Developmental Review, 28,* 1–11.

Reyna, V.F., & Zayas, V. (Eds). (2014). *The neuroscience of risky decision making.* Washington, DC: American Psychological Association.

Reyna, V.F., & others (2010). Gist-based conceptions of risk in adolescent alcohol consumption: A fuzzy trace theory approach. *Annals of Behavioral Medicine, 39,* s196.

Reyna, V.F., & others (2011). Neurobiological and memory models of risky decision making in adolescents versus young adults. *Journal of Experimental Psychology: Learning, Memory, and Cognition, 37,* 1125–1142.

Reynolds, E.H. (2014). The neurology of folic acid deficiency. *Handbook of Clinical Neurology, 120,* 927–943.

Reznick, J.S. (2013). Research design and methods: Toward a cumulative developmental science. In P.D. Zelazo (Ed.), *Oxford handbook of developmental psychology.* New York: Oxford University Press.

Reznick, J.S. (2014). Working memory in infancy. In P. Bauer & R. Fivush (Eds.), *Handbook on the development of children's memory.* New York: Wiley.

Rhoades, G.K., & Stanley, S.M. (2014). *Before "I do": What do premarital experiences have to do with marital quality among today's young adults?* Charlottesville, VA: The National Marriage Project at the University of Virginia.

Rhoades, G.K., Stanley, S.M., & Markman, H.J. (2009). The pre-engagement cohabitation effect: A replication and extension of previous findings. *Journal of Family Psychology, 23,* 107–111.

Rhoades, G.K., Stanley, S.M., & Markman, H.J. (2012). The impact of transition to cohabitation on relationship functioning: Cross-sectional and longitudinal findings. *Journal of Family Psychology, 26,* 348–358.

Rhodes, M., & Brandone, A.C. (2014). Three-year-olds' theories of mind in actions and words. *Frontiers in Psychology, 5,* 263.

Rhodes, M., Hetherington, C., Brink, K., & Wellman, H.M. (2015, in press). Infants' use of social partnerships to predict behavior. *Developmental Science.*

Ricco, R.B. (2015). Development of reasoning. In R.M. Lerner (Ed.), *Handbook of child psychology and developmental science* (7th ed.). New York: Wiley.

Richards, J., & others (2015). Don't worry, be happy: Cross-sectional associations between physical activity and happiness in 15 European countries. *BMC Public Health, 15*(1), 53.

Richards, J.E. (2009). Attention to the brain in infancy. In S. Johnson (Ed.), *Neuroconstructivism: The new science of cognitive development.* New York: Oxford University Press.

Richards, J.E. (2010). Infant attention, arousal, and the brain. In L.M. Oakes, C.H. Cashon, M. Casasola, & D.H. Rakison (Eds.), *Infant perception and cognition.* New York: Oxford University Press.

Richards, J.E. (2013). Cortical sources of ERP in the prosaccade and antisaccade task using realistic source models. *Frontiers in Systems Neuroscience, 7,* 27.

Richards, J.E., Boswell, C., Stevens, M., & Vendemia, J.M. (2015). Evaluating methods for constructing average high-density electrode positions. *Brain Topography, 28,* 70–86.

Richards, J.E., Reynolds, G.D., & Courage, M.I. (2010). The neural bases of infant attention. *Current Directions in Psychological Science, 19,* 41–46.

Richardson, E.D., & Marottoli, R.A. (2003). Visual attention and driving behaviors among community-living older persons. *Journals of Gerontology A: Biological Sciences and Medical Sciences, 58,* M832–M836.

Richardson, G.A., Goldschmidt, L., Leech, S., & Williford, J. (2011). Prenatal cocaine exposure: Effects on mother- and teacher-rated behavior problems and growth in school-aged children. *Neurotoxicology and Teratology, 33,* 69–77.

Richardson, G.A., Goldschmidt, L., & Williford, J. (2008). The effects of prenatal cocaine use on infant development. *Neurotoxicology and Teratology, 30,* 96–106.

Richardson, M.S., & Schaeffer, C. (2013). From work and family to a dual model of working. In D.L. Blustein (Ed.), *Oxford handbook of the psychology of working.* New York: Oxford University Press.

Richardson, V.E. (2007). A dual process model of grief counseling: Findings from the Changing Lives of Older Couples (CLOC) study. *Journal of Gerontological Social Work, 48,* 311–329.

Richens, J.L., Morgan, K., & O'Shea, P. (2014). Reverse engineering of Alzheimer's disease based on biomarker pathways analysis. *Neurobiology of Aging, 35,* 2029–2038.

Richmond, E.J., & Rogol, A.D. (2007). Male pubertal development and the role of androgen therapy. *Nature Clinical Practice: Endocrinology and Metabolism, 3,* 338–344.

Rideout, V.J., Foehr, U.G., & Roberts, D.F. (2010). *Generation M: Media in the lives of 8- to 18-year-olds.* Menlo Park, CA: Kaiser Family Foundation.

Riesch, S.K., & others (2003). Conflict and conflict resolution: Parent and young teen perceptions. *Journal of Pediatric Health Care, 17,* 22–31.

Riggins, T. (2012). Building blocks of recollection. In S. Ghetti & P.J. Bauer (Eds.), *Origins of recollection.* New York: Oxford University Press.

Righi, G., & others (2014). Infants' experience-dependent processing of male and female faces: Insights from eye tracking and event-related potentials. *Developmental Cognitive Neuroscience, 8,* 144–152.

Riina, E.M., & McHale, S.M. (2014). Bidirectional influences between dimensions of coparenting and adolescent adjustment. *Journal of Youth and Adolescence, 43,* 257–269.

Ristic, J., & Enns, J.T. (2015). Attentional development: The past, the present, and the future. In R.M. Lerner (Ed.), *Handbook of child psychology and developmental science* (7th ed.). New York: Wiley.

Ritchie, S.J. (2014). Review of: *G is for genes* (K. Asbury and R. Plomin) and education, social background, and cognitive ability: The decline of the social. *Intelligence, 43,* 79–80.

Riva Crugnola, C., Ierardi, E., Gazzotti, S., & Albizzati, A. (2014). Motherhood in adolescent mothers: Maternal attachment, mother-infant styles of interaction, and emotion regulation at three months. *Infant Behavior and Development, 37,* 44–56.

Rivas-Drake, D., & others (2014). Feeling good, happy, and proud: A meta-analysis of positive ethnic-racial affect and adjustment. *Child Development, 85,* 77–102.

Rivera, R.G., Roberson, S.P., Whelan, M., & Rohan, A. (2015, in press). Concussion evaluation and management in pediatrics. *MCN American Journal of Maternal and Child Nursing.*

Rizvi, S., Raza, S.T., & Mahdi, F. (2015, in press). Telomere length variations in aging and age-related diseases. *Current Aging Science.*

Rizvi, S.J., & others (2015). Depression and employment status in primary and tertiary care settings. *Canadian Journal of Psychiatry, 60,* 14–22.

Rizzo, M.S. (1999, May 8). Genetic counseling combines science with a human touch. *Kansas City Star,* p. 3.

Robbers, S., & others (2012). Childhood problem behavior and parental divorce: Evidence for gene-environment interaction. *Social Psychiatry and Psychiatric Epidemiology, 47*(10), 1539–1548.

Roberson, P.N., Olmstead, S.B., & Fincham, F.D. (2015). Hooking up during the college years: Is there a pattern? *Culture, Health, and Sexuality, 17,* 576–591.

Robert, L., & Fulop, T. (2014). Longevity and its regulation: Centenarians and beyond. *Interdisciplinary Topics in Gerontology, 39,* 198–211.

Roberto, K.A., & Skoglund, R.R. (1996). Interactions with grandparents and great-grandparents: A comparison of activities, influences, and relationships. *International Journal of Aging and Human Development, 43,* 107–117.

Roberts, B.W., Donnellan, M.B., & Hill, P.L. (2013). Personality trait development in adulthood: Findings and implications. In I.B. Weiner & others (Eds.), *Handbook of psychology* (2nd ed., Vol. 5). New York: Wiley.

Roberts, B.W., Helson, R., & Klohnen, E.C. (2002). Personality development and growth in women across 30 years: Three perspectives. *Journal of Personality, 70,* 79–102.

Roberts, B.W., & Mroczek, D. (2008). Personality trait change in adulthood. *Current Directions in Psychological Science, 17,* 31–35.

Roberts, B.W., Walton, K.E., & Viechtbauer, W. (2006). Pattern of mean-level change in personality traits across the life course: A meta-analysis of longitudinal studies. *Psychological Bulletin, 132,* 1–25.

Roberts, B.W., & Wood, D. (2006). Personality development in the context of the Neo-Socioanalytic Model of personality. In D. Mroczek & T. Little (Eds.), *Handbook of personality development.* Mahwah, NJ: Erlbaum.

Roberts, B.W., & others (2014). What is conscientiousness and how can it be assessed? *Developmental Psychology, 50,* 1315–1330.

Roberts, D.F., & Foehr, U.G. (2008). Trends in media use. *Future of Children, 18*(1), 11–37.

Roberts, S.B., & Rosenberg, I. (2006). Nutrition and aging: Changes in the regulation of energy metabolism with aging. *Physiology Review, 86,* 651–667.

Robertson, L.T., & Mitchell, J.R. (2013). Benefits of short-term dietary restriction in mammals. *Experimental Gerontology, 48,* 1043–1048.

Robins, R.W., Trzesniewski, K.H., Tracev, J.L., Potter, J., & Gosling, S.D. (2002). Age differences in self-esteem from age 9 to 90. *Psychology and Aging, 17,* 423–434.

Robles, T.F. (2014). Marital quality and health: Implications for marriage in the 21st century. *Current Directions in Psychological Science, 23,* 427–432.

Roblyer, M.D., & Doering, A.H. (2013). *Integrating educational technology into teaching* (6th ed.). Upper Saddle River, NJ: Pearson.

Rocca, W.A., & others (2011). Trends in the incidence and prevalence of Alzheimer's disease, dementia, and cognitive impairment in the United States. *Alzheimer's and Dementia, 7,* 80–93.

Rochlen, A.B., McKelley, R.A., Suizzo, M-A., & Scaringi, V. (2008). Predictors of relationship satisfaction, psychological well-being, and life-satisfaction among stay-at-home fathers. *Psychology of Men and Masculinity, 9,* 17–28.

Rode, S.S., Chang, P., Fisch, R.O., & Sroufe, L.A. (1981). Attachment patterns of infants separated at birth. *Developmental Psychology, 17,* 188–191.

Rodgers, C. (2013). Why kangaroo care should be standard for all newborns. *Journal of Midwifery and Women's Health, 58,* 249–252.

Rodin, J., & Langer, E.J. (1977). Long-term effects of a control-relevant intervention with the institutionalized aged. *Journal of Personality and Social Psychology, 35,* 397–402.

Rodrique, K.M., & Kennedy, K.M. (2011). The cognitive consequences of structural changes to the aging brain. In K.W. Schaie & S.L.Willis (Eds.), *Handbook of the psychology of aging* (7th ed.). New York: Elsevier.

Rodriquez Villar, S., & others (2012). Prolonged grief disorder in the next of kin of adult patients who die during or after admission to intensive care. *Chest, 141,* 1635–1636.

Roese, N.J., & Summerville, A. (2005). What we regret most . . . and why. *Personality and Social Psychology Bulletin, 31,* 1273–1285.

Roeser, R.W., & Pinela, C. (2014). Mindfulness and compassion training in adolescence: A developmental contemplative science perspective. *New Directions in Youth Development, 142,* 9–30.

Roeser, R.W., & Zelazo, P.D. (2012). Contemplative science, education and child development. *Child Development Perspectives, 6,* 143–145.

Rognum, I.J., & others (2014). Serotonin metabolites in the cerebrospinal fluid in sudden infant death syndrome. *Journal of Neuropathology and Experimental Neurology, 73,* 115–122.

Rogoff, B., Moore, L.C., Correa-Dhavez, M., & Dexter, A.L. (2015). Children develop cultural repertoires through engaging in everyday routines and practices. In J.E. Grusec & P.D. Hastings (Eds.), *Handbook of socialization* (2nd ed.). New York: Guilford.

Rohde, C., & others (2014). Unrestricted fruits and vegetables in the PKU diet: A 1-year follow-up. *European Journal of Clinical Nutrition, 68,* 401–403.

Roisman, G.I., Aguilar, B., & Egeland, B. (2004). Antisocial behavior in the transition to adulthood: The independent and interactive roles of developmental history and emerging development tasks. *Development and Psychopathology, 16,* 857–872.

Roisman, G.I., & Fraley, R.C. (2012). A behavior-genetic study of the legacy of early caregiving experiences: Academic skills, social competence, and externalizing behavior in kindergarten. *Child Development, 83,* 728–742.

Roisman, G.I., & Groh, A.M. (2011). Attachment theory and research in developmental psychology: An overview and appreciative critique. In M.K. Underwood & L.H. Rosen (Eds.), *Social development.* New York: Wiley.

Rolland, Y., & others (2011). Treatment strategies for sarcopenia and frailty. *Medical Clinics of North America, 95,* 427–438.

Romano, A.D., Greco, E., Vendemiale, G., & Serviddio, G. (2014). Bioenergetics and mitochondrial dysfunction in aging: Recent insights for a therapeutical approach. *Current Pharmaceutical Design. 20,* 2978–2992.

Romero, M.M., Ott, C.H., & Kelber, S.T. (2014). Predictors of grief in bereaved family caregivers of persons with Alzheimer's disease. A prospective study. *Death Studies, 38,* 395–403.

Romo, L.F., Mireles-Rios, R., & Lopez-Tello, G. (2014). Latina mothers' and daughters' expectations for autonomy at age 15 (La Quinceañera). *Journal of Adolescent Research, 29*(2), 279–294.

Rönnlund, M., Nyberg, L., Bäckman, L., & Nilsson, L.-G. (2005). Stability, growth, and decline in adult life span development of declarative memory: Cross-sectional and longitudinal data from a population-based study. *Psychology and Aging, 20,* 3–18.

Rook, K.S., Mavandadi, S., Sorkin, D.H., & Zettel, L.A. (2007). Optimizing social relationships as a source for health and well-being in later life. In C.M. Aldwin, C.L. Park, & A. Spiro (Eds.), *Handbook of health psychology and aging.* New York: Guilford.

Root, B.L., & Exline, J.J. (2014). The role of continuing bonds in coping with grief: Overview and future directions. *Death Studies, 38,* 1–8.

Rosano, C., & others (2012). Slower gait, slower information processing, and smaller prefrontal area in older adults. *Age and Aging, 41,* 58–64.

Rose, A.J., Carlson, W., & Waller, E.M. (2007). Prospective associations of co-rumination with friendship and emotional adjustment: Considering the socioemotional trade-offs of co-rumination. *Developmental Psychology, 43,* 1019–1031.

Rose, A.J., & Rudolph, K.D. (2006). A review of sex differences in peer relationship processes: Potential tradeoffs for the emotional and behavioral development of girls and boys. *Psychological Bulletin, 132,* 98–131.

Rose, A.J., & others (2012). How girls and boys expect disclosure about problems will make them feel: Implications for friendship. *Child Development, 83,* 844–863.

Rose, S., Feldman, J.F., Jankowski, J.J., & Van Rossem, R. (2012). Information processing from infancy to 11 years: Continuities and prediction of IQ. *Intelligence, 40,* 445–457.

Roseberry, S., Hirsh-Pasek, K., & Golinkoff, R. (2014). Skype me! Socially contingent interactions help toddlers learn language. *Child Development, 85,* 956–970.

Roseberry, S., Hirsh-Pasek, K., Parish-Morris, J., & Golinkoff, R. (2009). Live action: Can young children learn verbs from video? *Child Development, 80,* 1360–1375.

Rose-Greenland, F., & Smock, P.J. (2013). Living together unmarried: What do we know about cohabiting families? In G.W. Peterson & K.R. Bush (Eds.), *Handbook of marriage and the family* (3rd ed.). New York: Springer.

Rosen, L., Cheever, N., & Carrier, L.M. (2008). The association of parenting style and age with parental limit setting and adolescent MySpace behavior. *Journal of Applied Developmental Psychology, 29,* 459–471.

Rosenblith, J.F. (1992). *In the beginning* (2nd ed.). Newbury Park, CA: Sage.

Rosenblum, G.D., & Lewis, M. (2003). Emotional development in adolescence. In G. Adams & M. Berzonsky (Eds.), *Blackwell handbook of adolescence.* Malden, MA: Blackwell.

Rosenfeld, A., & Stark, E. (1987, May). The prime of our lives. *Psychology Today,* pp. 62–72.

Rosenstein, D., & Oster, H. (1988). Differential facial responses to four basic tastes in newborns. *Child Development, 59,* 1555–1568.

Rosnow, R.L., & Rosenthal, R. (1996). *Beginning behavioral research* (2nd ed.). Upper Saddle River, NJ: Prentice Hall.

Rosnow, R.L., & Rosenthal, R. (2013). *Beginning psychological research* (7th ed.). Boston: Cengage.

Ross, A.H., & Juarez, C.A. (2014). A brief history of fatal child maltreatment and neglect. *Forensic Science, Medicine, and Pathology, 10,* 413–422.

Ross, J.L., & others (2012). Behavioral and social phenotypes in boys with 47, XYY syndrome or 47, XXY Klinefelter syndrome. *Pediatrics, 129,* 769–778.

Ross, K., Handal, P.J., Clark, E.M., & Vander Wal, J.S. (2009). The relationship between religion and religious coping: Religious coping as a moderator between coping and adjustment. *Journal of Religion and Health, 48,* 454–467.

Rossi, A.S. (1989). A life-course approach to gender, aging, and intergenerational relations. In K.W. Schaie & C. Schooler (Eds.), *Social structure and aging.* Hillsdale, NJ: Erlbaum.

Rossi, S., & others (2005). Age-related functional changes of prefrontal cortex in long-term memory: A repetitive transcranial magnetic stimulation study. *Journal of Neuroscience, 24,* 7939–7944.

Rote, W.M., Smetana, J.G., Campione-Barr, N., Villalobos, M., & Tasopoulos-Chan, M. (2012). Associations between observed mother-adolescent interactions and adolescent information management. *Journal of Research on Adolescence, 22,* 206–214.

Rothbart, M.K. (2004). Temperament and the pursuit of an integrated developmental psychology. *Merrill-Palmer Quarterly, 50,* 492–505.

Rothbart, M.K. (2011). *Becoming who we are.* New York: Guilford.

Rothbart, M.K., & Bates, J.E. (2006). Temperament. In W. Damon & R. Lerner (Eds.), *Handbook of child psychology* (6th ed.). New York: Wiley.

Rothbart, M.K., & Gartstein, M.A. (2008). Temperament. In M.M. Haith & J.B. Benson (Eds.), *Encyclopedia of infant and early childhood development.* Oxford, UK: Elsevier.

Rothbaum, F., Poll, M., Azuma, H., Miyake, K., & Weisz, J. (2000). The development of close relationships in Japan and the United States: Paths of symbiotic harmony and generative tension. *Child Development, 71,* 1121–1142.

Rothbaum, F., & Trommsdorff, G. (2007). Do roots and wings complement or oppose one another? The socialization of relatedness and autonomy in cultural context. In J.E. Grusec & P.D. Hastings (Eds.), *Handbook of socialization.* New York: Guilford.

Rothman, M.S., Miller, P.D., Lewiecki, E.M., & Bilezikian, J.P. (2014). Bone density testing: Science, the media, and patient care. *Current Osteoporosis Reports, 12,* 227–229.

Rothman, S.M., & Mattson, M.P. (2012). Sleep disturbances in Alzheimer's and Parkinson's diseases. *Neuromolecular Medicine, 14*(3), 194–204.

Roussotte, F.F., & others (2014). Combined effects of Alzheimer risk variants in the LU and ApoE genes on ventricular expansion patterns in the elderly. *Journal of Neuroscience, 34,* 6537–6545.

Rovee-Collier, C. (1987). Learning and memory in children. In J.D. Osofsky (Ed.), *Handbook of infant development* (2nd ed.). New York: Wiley.

Rovee-Collier, C. (2004). Infant learning and memory. In U. Goswami (Ed.), *Blackwell handbook of childhood cognitive development.* Malden, MA: Blackwell.

Rovee-Collier, C. (2007). The development of infant memory. In N. Cowan & M. Courage (Eds.), *The development of memory in childhood.* Philadelphia: Psychology Press.

Rovee-Collier, C., & Barr, R. (2010). Infant learning and memory. In J.G. Bremner & T.D. Wachs (Ed.), *Wiley-Blackwell handbook of infant development* (2nd ed.). New York: Wiley.

Rowe, J.W., & Kahn, R.L. (2015, in press). Successful aging 2.0: Conceptual expansions for the 21st century. *Journals of Gerontology B: Psychological Sciences and Social Sciences.*

Rowe, M.L., & Goldin-Meadow, S. (2009). Differences in early gesture explain SES disparities in child vocabulary size at school entry. *Science, 323,* 951–953.

Rowsell, H.C., Ciarrochi, J., Heaven, P.C., & Deane, F.P. (2014). The role of emotion identification skill in the formation of male and female friendships: A longitudinal study. *Journal of Adolescence, 37,* 103–111.

Royer-Pokora, B. (2013). Genetics of pediatric renal tumors. *Pediatric Nephrology, 28,* 113–123.

Rozzini, R., Ranhoff, A., & Trabucchi, M. (2007). Alcoholic beverage and long-term mortality in elderly people living at home. *Journals of Gerontology A: Biological Sciences and Medical Science, 62A,* M1313–M1314.

Rubie-Davies, C.M. (2007). Classroom interactions: Exploring the practices of high- and low-expectation teachers. *British Journal of Educational Psychology, 77,* 289–306.

Rubie-Davies, C.M. (Ed.). (2011). *Educational psychology.* New York: Routledge.

Rubin, K.H., Bowker, J.C., McDonald, K.L., & Menzer, M. (2013). Peer relationships in childhood. In P.D. Zelazo (Ed.), *Oxford handbook of developmental psychology.* New York: Oxford University Press.

Rubin, K.H., Bukowski, W.M., & Bowker, J. (2015). Children in peer groups. In R.E. Lerner (Ed.), *Handbook of child psychology and developmental science* (7th ed.). New York: Wiley.

Rubin, K.H., Bukowski, W., & Parker, J. (2006). Peer interactions, relationships, and groups. In W. Damon & R. Lerner (Eds.), *Handbook of child psychology* (6th ed.). New York: Wiley.

Rubinstein, R.L., & others (2015, in press). Extending the framework of generativity theory through research: A qualitative study. *Gerontologist.*

Rubio-Aurioles, E., & others (2012). A randomized open-label trial with a cross-over comparison of sexual self-confidence and other treatment outcomes following tadalafil once a day vs. tadalafil or sildenafil on-demand in men with erectile dysfunction. *Journal of Sexual Medicine, 9*(5), 1418–1429.

Rudang, R., Mellstrom, D., Clark, E., Ohlsson, C., & Lorentzon, M. (2012). Advancing maternal age is associated with lower bone mineral density in young adult male offspring. *Osteoporosis International, 23,* 475–482.

Rudman, L.A., Fetterolf, J.C., & Sanchez, D.T. (2013). What motivates the sexual double standard? More support for male versus female control theory. *Personality and Social Psychology Bulletin, 39,* 250–263.

Rueda, M.R., & Posner, M.I. (2013). Development of attentional networks. In P.D. Zelazo (Ed.), *Oxford handbook of developmental psychology.* New York: Oxford University Press.

Rueda, M.R., Posner, M.I., & Rothbart, M.K. (2005). The development of executive attention: Contributions to the emergence of self-regulation. *Developmental Neuropsychology, 28,* 573–594.

Ruffman, T. (2014). To belief or not belief: Children's theory of mind. *Developmental Review, 34,* 265–293.

Ruffman, T., Slade, L., & Crowe, B. (2002). The relation between children's and mothers' mental state language and theory-of-mind understanding. *Child Development, 73,* 734–751.

Ruitenberg, M.F., & others (2015). Sequential movement skill in Parkinson's disease: A state-of-the-art. *Cortex, 65C,* 102–112.

Ruiter, M., & others (2012, June 11). *Short sleep predicts stroke symptoms in persons of normal weight.* Paper presented at the annual meeting of the Associated Professional Sleep Societies (APSS), Boston.

Rulison, K.L., Kreager, D.A., & Osgood, D.W. (2014). Delinquency and peer acceptance in adolescence: A within-person test of Moffitt's hypotheses. *Developmental Psychology, 50,* 2437–2448.

Rumberger, R.W. (1995). Dropping out of middle school: A multilevel analysis of students and schools. *American Education Research Journal, 3,* 583–625.

Rupp, D.E., Vodanovich, S.J., & Crede, M. (2005). The multidimensional nature of ageism: Construct validity and group differences. *Journal of Social Psychology, 145,* 335–362.

Russ, S.A., Hanna, D., DesGeorges, J., & Forsman, I. (2010). Improving follow-up to newborn hearing screening: A learning-collaborative experience. *Pediatrics, 126*(Suppl. 1), S59–S69.

Russell, M., & Airasian, P.W. (2012). *Classroom assessment* (7th ed.). New York: McGraw-Hill.

Russell, S.T., Crockett, L.J., & Chao, R.K. (2010). *Asian American parenting and parent-adolescent relationships.* New York: Springer.

Russell, V.M., Baker, L.R., & McNulty, J.K. (2013). Attachment insecurity and infidelity in marriage: Do studies of dating relationships inform us about marriage? *Journal of Family Psychology, 27,* 242–251.

Rutter, J., & Thapar, A. (2014). Genetics of autism spectrum disorders. In F.R. Volkmar & others (Eds.), *Handbook of autism and pervasive developmental disorders.* New York: Wiley.

Ryan, A.S., & others (2014). Aerobic exercise and weight loss reduce vascular markers of inflammation and improve insulin sensitivity in obese women. *Journal of the American Geriatrics Society, 62,* 607–614.

Ryan, R.M., & Deci, E.L. (2009). Promoting self-determined school engagement: Motivation, learning, and well-being. In K. Wentzel & A. Wigfield (Eds.), *Handbook of motivation at school.* New York: Routledge.

Ryff, C.D. (1984). Personality development from the inside: The subjective experience of change in adulthood and aging. In P.B. Baltes & O.G. Brim (Eds.), *Life-span development and behavior.* New York: Academic Press.

S

Saarinen, S., & others (2015). Visuospatial working memory in 7- to 12-year-old children with disruptive behavior disorders. *Child Psychiatry and Human Development, 46,* 34–43.

Saarni, C. (1999). *The development of emotional competence.* New York: Guilford.

Saarni, C., Campos, J., Camras, L.A., & Witherington, D. (2006). Emotional development. In W. Damon & R. Lerner (Eds.), *Handbook of child psychology* (6th ed.). New York: Wiley.

Sabbagh, M.A., Xu, F., Carlson, S.M., Moses, L.J., & Lee, K. (2006). The development of executive functioning and theory of mind: A comparison of Chinese and U.S. preschoolers. *Psychological Science, 17,* 74–81.

Sabina, C., & Ho, L.Y. (2014). Campus and college victim responses to sexual assault and dating violence: Disclosure, service utilization, and service provision. *Trauma, Violence, and Abuse, 15,* 1201–1226.

Sabini, J. (1995). *Social psychology* (2nd ed.). New York: Norton.

Sabir, M., Henderson, C.R., Kang, S.Y., & Pillemer, K. (2015, in press). Attachment-focused integrative reminiscence with older African Americans: A randomized controlled intervention study. *Aging and Mental Health.*

Sacrey, L.A., Germani, T., Bryson, S.E., & Zwaigenbaum, L. (2014). Reaching and grasping in autism spectrum disorder: A review of recent literature. *Frontiers in Neurology, 5,* 6.

Sadeh, A. (2007). Consequences of sleep loss or sleep disruption in children. *Sleep Medicine, 2,* 513–520.

Sadeh, A. (2008). Sleep. In M.M. Haith & J.B. Benson (Eds.), *Encyclopedia of infant and early childhood development.* Oxford, UK: Elsevier.

Sadker, D.M., & Zittleman, K. (2012). *Teachers, schools, and society* (3rd ed.). New York: McGraw-Hill.

Sadker, M.P., & Sadker, D.M. (2005). *Teachers, schools, and society* (7th ed.). New York: McGraw-Hill.

Sadowski-Bartosz, I., & Bartosz, G. (2015, in press). Effect of antioxidants supplementation on aging and longevity. *Biomedical Research International.*

Saewyc, E.M. (2011). Research on adolescent sexual orientation: Development, health disparities, stigma, and resilience. *Journal of Research on Adolescence, 21,* 256–272.

Saffran, J.R., Werker, J.F., & Werner, L.A. (2006). The infant's auditory world: Hearing, speech, and the beginnings of language. In R.M. Lerner & W. Damon (Eds.), *Handbook of child psychology* (6th ed.). New York: Wiley.

Sagiv, S.K., Epstein, J.N., Bellinger, D.C., & Korrick, S.A. (2012). Pre- and postnatal risk factors for ADHD in a nonclinical pediatric population. *Journal of Attention Disorders, 166,* 1123–1131.

Saint Onge, J.M. (2009). Mortality. In D. Carr (Ed.), *Encyclopedia of the life course and human development.* Boston: Gale Cengage.

Sakaluk, J.K., & others (2014). Dominant heterosexual scripts in emerging adulthood: Conceptualization and measurement. *Journal of Sexual Research, 51,* 516–531.

Sakamoto, Y., & others (2009). Effect of exercise, aging, and functional capacity on acute secretory immunoglobulin: A response in elderly people over 75 years of age. *Geriatrics and Gerontology International, 9,* 81–88.

Sakuma, K., & Yamaguchi, A. (2010). Molecular mechanisms in aging and current strategies to counteract sarcopenia. *Current Aging Science, 3*(2), 90–101.

Sala, S., Agosta, F., Pagani, E., Copetti, M., Comi, G., & Filippi, M. (2012). Microstructural changes and atrophy in brain white matter tracts with aging. *Neurobiology of Aging, 33,* 488–498.

Salama, R.H., & others (2013). Clinical and biochemical effects of environmental tobacco smoking on pregnancy outcome. *Indian Journal of Clinical Biochemistry, 28,* 368–373.

Sale, A., Berardi, N., & Maffei, L. (2014). Environment and brain plasticity: Towards an endogenous pharmacotherapy. *Physiological Reviews, 94,* 189–234.

Salend, S.J. (2016, in press). *Creating inclusive classrooms* (8th ed.). Upper Saddle River, NJ: Pearson.

Saling, L.L., Laroo, N., & Saling, M.M. (2012). When more is less: Failure to compress discourse with re-telling in normal aging. *Acta Psychologica, 139,* 220–224.

Salmivalli, C., & Peets, K. (2009). Bullies, victims, and bully-victim relationships in middle childhood and adolescence. In K.H. Rubin, W.M. Bukowski, & B. Laursen (Eds.), *Handbook of peer interactions, relationships, and groups.* New York: Guilford.

Salovey, P., & Mayer, J.D. (1990). Emotional intelligence. *Imagination, Cognition, and Personality, 9,* 185–211.

Salthouse, T.A. (1991). *Theoretical perspectives on cognitive aging.* Hillsdale, NJ: Erlbaum.

Salthouse, T.A. (1994). The nature of influence of speed on adult age differences in cognition. *Developmental Psychology, 30,* 240–259.

Salthouse, T.A. (2007). Reaction time. In J.E. Birren (Ed.), *Encyclopedia of gerontology* (2nd ed.). San Diego: Academic Press.

Salthouse, T.A. (2009). When does age-related cognitive decline begin? *Neurobiology of Aging, 30,* 507–514.

Salthouse, T.A. (2012). Consequences of age-related cognitive decline. *Annual Review of Psychology* (Vol. 63). Palo Alto, CA: Annual Reviews.

Salthouse, T.A. (2013). Executive functioning. In D.C. Park & N. Schwartz (Eds.), *Cognitive aging* (2nd ed.). New York: Psychology Press.

Salthouse, T.A. (2015a, in press). Aging cognition unconfounded by prior test experience. *Journals of Gerontology B: Psychological Sciences and Social Sciences.*

Salthouse, T.A. (2015b, in press). Implications of the Flynn Effect for age-cognition relations. *Intelligence, 48,* 51–57.

Salthouse, T.A. (2015c, in press). Why are there different age relations in cross-sectional and longitudinal comparisons of cognitive functioning? *Current Directions in Psychological Science.*

Salthouse, T.A., & Mandell, A.R. (2013). Do age-related increases in tip-of-the-tongue experiences signify episodic memory deficits? *Psychological Science, 24,* 2489–2497.

Salvatore, J.E., Kuo, S.I., Steele, R.D., Simpson, J.A., & Collins, W.A. (2011). Recovering from conflict in romantic relationships: A developmental perspective. *Psychological Science, 22,* 376–383.

Samanez-Larkin, G.R., & Carstensen, L L. (2011). Socioemotional functioning and the aging brain. In J. Decety & J.T. Cacioppo (Eds.), *Handbook of social neuroscience.* New York: Oxford University Press.

Sameroff, A.J. (2009). The transactional model. In A.J. Sameroff (Ed.), *The transactional model of development: How children and contexts shape each other.* Washington, DC: American Psychological Association.

Samsonraj, R.M., & others (2013). Telomere length analysis of human mesenchymal stem cells by quantitative PCR. *Gene, 519*(2), 348–355.

Sanbonmatsu, D.M., Strayer, D.L., Medeiros-Ward, N., & Watson, J.M. (2013). Who multi-tasks and why? Multi-tasking ability, perceived multi-tasking ability, impulsivity, and sensation seeking. *PLoS One, 8*(1), e54402.

Sanchez, C.E., Richards, J.E., & Almi, C.R. (2012). Neurodevelopmental MRI brain templates from 2 weeks to 4 years of age. *Developmental Psychobiology, 54,* 77–91.

Sandin, S., & others (2014). The familial risk of autism. *JAMA, 311,* 1770–1777.

Sanger, M.N. (2008). What we need to prepare teachers for the moral nature of their work. *Journal of Curriculum Studies, 40,* 169–185.

Sangree, W.H. (1989). Age and power: Life-course trajectories and age structuring of power relations in East and West Africa. In D.I. Kertzer & K.W. Schaie (Eds.), *Age structuring in comparative perspective.* Hillsdale, NJ: Erlbaum.

Sanson, A., & Rothbart, M.K. (1995). Child temperament and parenting. In M.H. Bornstein (Ed.), *Handbook of parenting* (Vol. 4). Hillsdale, NJ: Erlbaum.

Santangeli, L., Satter, N., & Huda, S.S. (2015, in press). Impact of maternal obesity on perinatal and child outcomes: Best practices and research. *Clinical Obstetrics and Gynecology.*

Santarnecchi, E., Rossi, S., & Rossi, A. (2015). The smarter, the stronger: Intelligence level correlates with brain resilience to systematic insults. *Cortex, 64,* 293–309.

Santen, R.J., Stuenkel, C.A., Burger, H.G., & Manson, J.E. (2014). Competency in menopause management: Whither goest the internist? *Journal of Women's Health, 23,* 281–285.

Santiago, C.D., Etter, E.M., Wadsworth, M.E., & Raviv, T. (2012). Predictors of responses to stress among families coping with poverty-related stress. *Anxiety, Stress, and Coping, 25,* 239–258.

Santrock, J.W., & Halonen, J.A. (2013). *Your guide to college success* (7th ed.). Belmont, CA: Wadsworth.

Santrock, J.W., Sitterle, K.A., & Warshak, R.A. (1988). Parent-child relationship in stepfather families. In P. Bronstein & C.P. Cowan (Eds.), *Fatherhood today: Men's changing roles in the family.* New York: Wiley.

Sanz-Cortes, M., & others (2015, in press). Association of brain metabolism with sulcation and corpus callosum development assessed by MRI in late-onset small fetuses. *American Journal of Obstetrics and Gynecology.*

Sarchiapone, M., & others (2014). Hours of sleep in adolescents and its association with anxiety, emotional concerns, and suicidal ideation. *Sleep Medicine, 15,* 248–254.

Sarlak, G., & Vincent, B. (2015, in press). The roles of the stem cell-controlling Sox2 transcription factor: From neuroectoderm development to Alzheimer's disease? *Molecular Neurobiology.*

Sarlos, P., & others (2014). Susceptibility to ulcerative colitis in Hungarian patients determined by gene-gene interaction. *World Journal of Gastroenterology, 20*(1), 219–227.

Saroglou, V. (2013). Religion, spirituality, and altruism. In K.I. Pargament, J. Exline, & J. Jones (Eds.), *Handbook of psychology, religion, and spirituality.* Washington, DC: American Psychological Association.

Sarwar, S.R., Mangewala, V., & Baron, R. (2013). Helping the angels: A review of understanding and helping children. *Innovations in Clinical Neuroscience, 10,* 31–34.

Sasson, N.J., & Touchstone, E.W. (2014). Visual attention to competing social and object images by preschool children with autism spectrum disorder. *Journal of Autism and Developmental Disorders, 44,* 584–592.

Sauter, D., McDonald, N.M., Grangi, D., & Messinger, D.S. (2014). Nonverbal expressions of positive emotions. In M. Tugade, & others (Eds.), *Handbook of positive emotions.* New York: Guilford.

Savage, R.S., Abrami, P., Hipps, G., & Dealut, L. (2009). A randomized controlled trial study of the ABRACADABRA reading intervention program in grade 1. *Journal of Educational Psychology, 101,* 590–604.

Savin-Williams, R.C. (2015). The new sexual-minority teenager. In D.A. Powell & J.S. Kaufman (Eds.), *The meaning of sexual identity in the 21st century.* New York: Cambridge.

Savin-Williams, R.C., & Cohen, K. (2015). Gay, lesbian, and bisexual youth. In J.D. Wright (Ed.), *International encyclopedia of the social and behavioral sciences* (2nd ed.). New York: Oxford University Press.

Savolainen, J., & others (2012). Antisocial personality, adolescent school outcomes, and the risk of criminal conviction. *Journal of Research on Adolescence, 22,* 54–64.

Sawyer, R.K., & DeZutter, S. (2007). Improvisation: A lens for play and literacy research. In K.A. Roskos & J.F. Christie (Eds.), *Play and literacy in early childhood.* Mahwah, NJ: Erlbaum.

Sayer, A.A., & others (2013). New horizons in the pathogenesis, diagnosis, and management of sarcopenia. *Age and Aging, 42*(2), 145–150.

Sbarra, D.A. (2012). Marital dissolution and physical health outcomes: A review of mechanisms. In L. Campbell, J. LaGuardia, J.M. Olson, & M.P. Zanna (Eds.), *The science of the couple. The Ontario Symposium* (Vol. 12). New York: Psychology Press.

Scarr, S. (1993). Biological and cultural diversity: The legacy of Darwin for development. *Child Development, 64,* 1333–1353.

Scarr, S., & Weinberg, R.A. (1983). The Minnesota adoption studies: Genetic differences and malleability. *Child Development, 54,* 182–259.

Schaan, B. (2013). Widowhood and depression among older Europeans—the role of gender, caregiving, marital quality, and regional context. *Journals of Gerontology B: Psychological Sciences and Social Sciences, 68,* 431–442.

Schaefer, R.T. (2015). *Racial and ethnic groups* (14th ed.). Upper Saddle River, NJ: Pearson.

Schafer, A. (2013). Physician assisted suicide: The great Canadian euthanasia debate. *International Journal of Law and Psychiatry, 36,* 522–531.

Schaffer, H.R. (1996). *Social development.* Cambridge, MA: Blackwell.

Schaffer, M.A., Goodhue, A., Stennes, K., & Lanigan, C. (2012). Evaluation of a public health nurse visiting program for pregnant and parenting teens. *Public Health Nursing, 29,* 218–231.

Schaie, K.W. (1977). Toward a stage theory of adult cognitive development. *Aging and Human Development, 8,* 129–138.

Schaie, K.W. (1983). Consistency and changes in cognitive functioning of the young-old and old-old. In M. Bergner, U. Lehr, E. Lang, & R. Schmidt-Scherzer (Eds.), *Aging in the eighties and beyond.* New York: Springer.

Schaie, K.W. (1994). The life course of adult intellectual abilities. *American Psychologist, 49,* 304–313.

Schaie, K.W. (1996). *Intellectual development in adulthood: The Seattle Longitudinal Study.* New York: Cambridge University Press.

Schaie, K.W. (2000). The impact of longitudinal studies on understanding development from young adulthood to old age. *International Journal of Behavioral Development, 24,* 257–266.

Schaie, K.W. (2005). *Developmental influences on adult intelligence: The Seattle Longitudinal Study.* New York: Oxford University Press.

Schaie, K.W. (2007). Generational differences: The age-period cohort. In J.E. Birren (Ed.), *Encyclopedia of gerontology* (2nd ed.). New York: Elsevier.

Schaie, K.W. (2010). Adult intellectual abilities. *Corsini encyclopedia of psychology.* New York: Wiley.

Schaie, K.W. (2011). Historical influences on aging and behavior. In K.W. Schaie & S.L. Willis (Eds.), *Handbook of the psychology of aging* (7th ed.). New York: Elsevier.

Schaie, K.W. (2012). *Developmental influences on adult intelligence: The Seattle Longitudinal Study* (2nd ed.). New York: Oxford University Press.

Schaie, K.W. (2013). *The Seattle Longitudinal Study: Developmental influences on adult intellectual development* (2nd ed.). New York: Oxford University Press.

Schaie, K.W., & Zanjani, F.A.K. (2014). Intellectual development across adulthood. In C. Hoare (Ed.), *Handbook of adult development and learning.* New York: Oxford University Press.

Scheeringa, M.S., Cobham, V.E., & McDermott, B. (2014). Policy and administrative issues for large-scale clinical interventions following disasters. *Journal of Child and Adolescent Psychopharmacology, 24,* 39–46.

Scheibe, S., & Carstensen, L.L. (2010). Emotional aging: Recent and future trends. *Journal of Gerontology B: Psychological Sciences, 65,* 135–144.

Scher, A., & Harel, J. (2008). Separation and stranger anxiety. In M.M. Haith & J.B. Benson (Eds.), *Encyclopedia of infant and early childhood development.* Oxford, UK: Elsevier.

Schermer, J.A., Petrides, K.V., & Vernon, P.A. (2015, in press). On the genetic and environmental correlations between trait emotional intelligence and vocational interest factors. *Twin Research and Human Genetics.*

Schiff, W.J. (2015). *Nutrition essentials.* New York: McGraw-Hill.

Schiff, W.J. (2016, in press). *Nutrition for healthy living* (4th ed.). New York: McGraw-Hill.

Schiffman, S.S. (2007). Smell and taste. In J.E. Birren (Ed.,), *Encyclopedia of gerontology* (2nd ed.), San Diego: Academic Press.

Schlam, T.R., Wilson, N.L., Shoda, Y., Mischel, W., & Ayduk, O. (2013). Preschoolers' delay of gratification predicts their body mass 30 years later. *Journal of Pediatrics, 162*(1), 90–93.

Schlegel, M. (2000). All work and play. *Monitor on Psychology, 31*(11), 50–51.

Schmidt, L.I., Wahl, H.W., & Plischke, H. (2014). Older adults' performance in technology-based tasks: Cognitive ability and beyond. *Journal of Gerontological Nursing, 40,* 18–24.

Schmidt, M.E., & Vandewater, E.A. (2008). Media and attention, cognition, and school achievement. *Future of Children, 18*(1), 64–85.

Schmitt, D.P., & others (2012). A reexamination of sex differences in sexuality: New studies reveal old truths. *Psychological Science, 21,* 135–139.

Schneider, E., & others (2014). Widespread differences in cortex DNA methylation of the "language gene" CNTNAP2 between humans and chimpanzees. *Epigenetics, 9,* 533–545.

Schneider, W. (2011). Memory development in childhood. In U. Goswami (Ed.), *Wiley-Blackwell handbook of childhood cognitive development.* New York: Wiley.

Schnittker, J. (2007). Look (closely) at all the lonely people: Age and social psychology of school support. *Journal of Aging and Health, 19,* 659–682.

Schnohr, P., & others (2015). Dose of jogging and long-term mortality: The Copenhagen Heart Study. *Journal of the American College of Cardiology, 65,* 411–419.

Schoenfeld, T.J., & Gould, E. (2013). Differential effects of stress and glucocorticoids on adult neurogenesis. *Current Topics in Behavioral Neuroscience, 15,* 139–164.

Schoffstall, C.L., & Cohen, R. (2011). Cyber aggression: The relation between online offenders and offline social competence. *Social Development, 20*(3), 587–604.

Schofield, H.L., Bierman, K.L., Heinrichs, B., Nix, R.L., & The Conduct Problems Prevention Research Group (2008). Predicting early sexual activity with behavior problems exhibited at school entry and in early adolescence. *Journal of Abnormal Child Psychology, 36*(8), 1175–1188.

Schooler, C. (2007). Use it—and keep it longer, probably: A reply to Salthouse (2006). *Perspectives on Psychological Science, 2,* 24–29.

Schooler, C., Mulatu, S., & Oates, G. (1999). The continuing effects of substantively complex work on the intellectual functioning of older workers. *Psychology and Aging, 14,* 483–506.

Schoon, I., Jones, E., Cheng, H., & Maughan, B. (2012). Family hardship, family instability, and cognitive development. *Journal of Epidemiology and Community Health, 66*(8), 716–722.

Schreiber, L.R. (1990). *The parents' guide to kids' sports.* Boston: Little, Brown.

Schrijvers, D.L., Bollen, J., & Sabbe, B.G. (2012). The gender paradox in suicidal behavior and its impact on the suicidal process. *Journal of Affective Disorders, 138,* 19–26.

Schulenberg, J.E., & Zarrett, N.R. (2006). Mental health during emerging adulthood: Continuities and discontinuities in course, content, and meaning. In J.J. Arnett & J. Tanner (Eds.), *Advances in emerging adulthood.* Washington, DC: American Psychological Association.

Schultz, R., & Curnow, C. (1988). Peak performance and age among super athletes: Track and field, swimming, baseball, and golf. *Journal of Gerontology, 43,* P113–P120.

Schunk, D.H. (2012). *Learning theories: An educational perspective* (6th ed.). Upper Saddle River, NJ: Prentice Hall.

Schunk, D.H. (2016, in press). *Learning theories: An educational perspective* (7th ed.). Upper Saddle River, NJ: Prentice Hall.

Schunk, D.H., Meece, J.R., & Pintrich, P.R. (2014). *Motivation in education* (4th ed.). Upper Saddle River, NJ: Pearson.

Schunk, D.H., Pintrich, P.R., & Meece, J.L. (2008). *Motivation in education: Theory, research, and applications* (3rd ed.). Upper Saddle River, NJ: Prentice Hall.

Schunk, D.H., & Zimmerman, B.J. (2013). Self-regulation and learning. In I.B. Weiner & others (Eds.), *Handbook of psychology* (2nd ed.). New York: Wiley.

Schuurmans, C., & Kurrasch, D. (2013). Neurodevelopmental consequences of maternal distress: What do we really know? *Clinical Genetics, 83,* 108–117.

Schwalbe, C.S., Gearing, R.E., MacKenzie, M.J., Brewer, K.B., & Ibrahim, R. (2012). A meta-analysis of experimental studies of diversion programs for juvenile offenders. *Clinical Psychology Review, 32,* 26–33.

Schwartz, D., & others (2015). Peer victimization during middle childhood as a lead indicator of internalizing problems and diagnostic outcomes in late adolescence. *Journal of Clinical Child and Adolescent Psychology, 44,* 393–404.

Schwartz, M.A., & Scott, B.M. (2012). *Marriages and families, census update* (6th ed.). Upper Saddle River, NJ: Pearson.

Schwartz, S.J., Donnellan, M.B., Ravert, R.D., Luyckx, K., & Zamboanga, B.L. (2013). Identity development, personality, and well-being in adolescence and emerging adulthood: Theory, research, and recent advances. In I.B. Weiner & others (Eds.), *Handbook of psychology* (2nd ed., Vol. 6). New York: Wiley.

Schwartz, S.J., Vignoles, V.L., Brown, R., & Zagefka, H. (2015b). The identity dynamics of acculturation and multiculturalism: Situating acculturation in context. In V. Benet-Martinez & Y.Y. Hong (Eds.), *Oxford handbook of multicultural identity.* New York: Oxford University Press.

Schwartz, S.J., Zamboanga, B.L., Meca, A., & Ritchie, R.A. (2012). Identity around the world: An overview. *New Directions in Child and Adolescent Development, 138,* 1–14.

Schwartz, S.J., & others (2015). Identity. In J.J. Arnett (Ed.), *Oxford handbook of emerging adulthood.* New York: Oxford University Press.

Schwartz, S.J., & others (2015). The identity of acculturation and multiculturalism: Situational acculturation in context. In V. Benet-Martinez & Y.Y. Hong (Eds.), *Oxford handbook of multicultural identity.* New York: Oxford University Press.

Schwartz, S.J., & others (2015). Trajectories of cultural stressors and effects on mental health and substance use among Hispanic immigrant adolescents. *Journal of Adolescent Health, 56,* 433–439.

Schwartz, S.J., & others (2015). What have we learned since Schwartz (2001)? A reappraisal of the field In K. McLean & M. Syed (Eds.), *Oxford handbook of identity development.* New York: Oxford University Press.

Schwarzer, R., & Luszczynska, A. (2013). Stressful life events. In I.B. Weiner & others (Eds.), *Handbook of psychology* (2nd ed., Vol. 9). New York: Wiley.

Schweinhart, L.J., & others (2005). *Lifetime effects: The High/Scope Perry Preschool Study through age 40.* Ypsilanti, MI: High/Scope Press.

Scialfa, C.T., & Kline, D.W. (2007). Vision. In J.E. Birren (Ed.), *Encyclopedia of gerontology* (2nd ed.). San Diego: Academic Press.

Sciberras, E., Ukoumunne, O.C., & Efron, D. (2011). Predictors of parent-reported attention-deficit/hyperactivity disorder in children aged 6–7 years: A national longitudinal study. *Journal of Abnormal Child Psychology, 39,* 1125–1134.

Sclar, D.A., & others (2012). Attention deficit/hyperactivity disorder among children and adolescents in the United States: Trend in diagnosis and use of pharmacotherapy by gender. *Clinical Pediatrics, 51*(6), 584–589.

Scott, D., & others (2014). Sarcopenic obesity and dynamic obesity: 5-year associations with falls risk in middle-aged and older adults. *Obesity, 22,* 1568–1574.

Scott, J.A., Ng, S.Y., & Cobiac, L. (2012). The relationship between breastfeeding and weight status in a national sample of Australian children and adolescents. *BMC Public Health, 12,* 107.

Scott, R.M., & Baillargeon, R. (2013). Do infants really expect others to act efficiently? A critical test of the rationality principle. *Psychological Science, 24,* 466–474.

Scourfield, J., Van den Bree, M., Martin, N., & McGuffin, P. (2004). Conduct problems in children and adolescents: A twin study. *Archives of General Psychiatry, 61,* 489–496.

Scullin, M.K., Bugg, J.M., & McDaniel, M.A. (2012). Whoops, I did it again: Commission errors in prospective memory. *Psychology of Aging, 27,* 46–53.

Seay, G. (2011). Euthanasia and common sense: A reply to Garcia. *Journal of Medical Philosophy, 36,* 321–327.

Sebastiani, P., & Perls, T.T. (2012). The genetics of extreme longevity: Lessons from the New England Centenarian study. *Frontiers in Genetics, 30*(3), 277.

Seccombe, K. (2015). *Exploring marriages and families* (2nd ed.). Upper Saddle River, NJ: Pearson.

Sedgh, G., & others (2015). Adolescent pregnancy, birth, and abortion rates across countries: Levels and recent trends. *Journal of Adolescent Health, 56,* 223–230.

Segerberg, O. (1982). *Living to be 100: 200 who did and how they did it.* New York: Charles Scribner's Sons.

Seligman, M.E.P (2007). *The optimistic child.* New York: Mariner.

Selman, R.L. (1980). *The growth of interpersonal understanding.* New York: Academic Press.

Semanik, P.A., Chang, R.W., & Dunlop, D.D. (2012). Aerobic activity in prevention and symptom control of osteoarthritis. *PM & R, 4* (5 Suppl.), S37–S44.

Sen, B. (2010). The relationship between frequency of family dinner and adolescent problem behaviors after adjusting for other characteristics. *Journal of Adolescence, 33,* 187–196.

Sener, A., Terzioglu, R.G., & Karabulut, E. (2007). Life satisfaction and leisure activities during men's retirement: A Turkish sample. *Aging and Mental Health, 11,* 30–36.

Senter, L., Sackoff, J., Landi, K., & Boyd, L. (2010). Studying sudden and unexpected deaths in a time of changing death certification and investigation practices: Evaluating sleep-related risk factors for infant death in New York City. *Maternal and Child Health, 15*(2), 242–248.

Sepulcre, J., & others (2012). Stepwise connectivity of the model cerebral cortex reveals the multimodal organization of the human brain. *Journal of Neuroscience, 32,* 10649–10661.

Serhan, N., Eg, E., Ayranci, U., & Kosgeroglu, N. (2013). Prevalence of postpartum depression in mothers and fathers and its correlates. *Journal of Clinical Nursing, 22,* 279–284.

Sery, O., & others (2015). Diabetes, hypertension, and stroke—does Alzheimer protect you? *Neuro Endocrinology Letters, 35,* 691–696.

Sethna, V., Murray, L., & Ramchandani, P.G. (2012). Depressed fathers' speech to their 3-month-old infants: A study of cognitive and mentalizing features in paternal speech. *Psychological Medicine, 42*(11), 2361–2371.

Setta, S.M., & Shemie, S.D. (2015). An explanation and analysis of how world religions formulate their ethical decisions on withdrawing treatment and determining death. *Philosophy, Ethics, and Humanities in Medicine, 10*(1), 6.

Settersten, R.A., Furstenberg, F.F., & Rumbaut, R.G. (Eds.). (2005). *On the frontier of adulthood: Theory, research, and public policy.* Chicago: University of Chicago Press.

Shah, A., & Bhandarkar, R. (2011). Does adversity early in life affect general population suicide rates? A cross-sectional study. *Journal of Injury and Violence Research, 3,* 25–27.

Shaheen, S. (2014). How child's play impacts executive function-related behaviors. *Applied Neuropsychology: Child, 3,* 182–187.

Shahrokni, A., Mahmoudzadeh, S., Saeedi, R., & Ghasemzadeh, H. (2015, in press). Older people with access to hand-held devices: Who are they? *Telemedicine Journal and E-Health.*

Shallcross, A.J., Ford, B.Q., Floerke, V.A., & Mauss, I.B. (2013). Getting better with age: The relationship between age, acceptance, and negative affect. *Journal of Personality and Social Psychology, 104,* 734–749.

Shan, Z.Y., Liu, J.Z., Sahgal, V., Wang, B., & Yue, G.H. (2005). Selective atrophy of left hemisphere and frontal lobe of the brain in older men. *Journals of Gerontology A: Biological Sciences and Medical Sciences, 60,* A165–A174.

Shankar, A., Hamer, M., McMunn, A., & Steptoe, A. (2013). Social isolation and loneliness: Relationships with cognitive function during 4 years of follow-up in the English Longitudinal Study of Aging. *Psychosomatic Aging, 75,* 161–170.

Shankaran, S., & others (2010). Prenatal cocaine exposure and BMI and blood pressure at 9 years of age. *Journal of Hypertension, 28,* 1166–1175.

Shapiro, A.F., & Gottman, J.M. (2005). Effects on marriage of a psycho-education intervention with couples undergoing the transition to parenthood: Evaluation at 1-year post intervention. *Journal of Family Communication, 5,* 1–24.

Sharkey, W. (1993). Who embarrasses whom? Relational and sex differences in the use of intentional embarrassment. In P.J. Kalbfleisch (Ed.), *Interpersonal communication.* Mahwah, NJ: Erlbaum.

Sharp, E.S., Reynolds, C.A., Pedersen, N.L., & Gatz, M. (2010). Cognitive engagement and cognitive aging: Is openness protective? *Psychology and Aging, 25,* 60–73.

Shatz, M., & Gelman, R. (1973). The development of communication skills: Modifications in the speech of young children as a function of the listener. *Monographs of the Society for Research in Child Development, 38* (Serial No. 152).

Shavelle, D. (2014). *Coronary artery disease.* New York: Elsevier.

Shaw, D.S. (2013). Commentary: Early father-infant interaction and externalizing behaviors—a response to Ramchandani et al. (2013). *Journal of Child Psychology and Psychiatry, 54,* 65–66.

Shaw, P., & others (2007). Attention-deficit/hyperactivity disorder is characterized by a delay in cortical maturation. *Proceedings of the National Academy of Sciences, 104*(49), 19649–19654.

Shay, J.W., Reddel, R.R., & Wright, W.E. (2012). Cancer and telomeres—an ALTernative to telomerase. *Science, 336,* 1388–1390.

Shaywitz, B.A., Lyon, G.R., & Shaywitz, S.E. (2006). The role of functional magnetic resonance imaging in understanding reading and dyslexia. *Developmental Neuropsychology, 30,* 613–632.

Shaywitz, S.E., Gruen, J.R., & Shaywitz, B.A. (2007). Management of dyslexia, its rationale, and underlying neurobiology. *Pediatric Clinics of North America, 54,* 609–623.

Shear, M.K. (2015). Clinical practice: Complicated grief. *New England Journal of Medicine, 372,* 153–160.

Shear, M.K. (2012a). Getting straight about grief. *Depression and Anxiety, 29,* 461–464.

Shear, M.K. (2012b). Grief and mourning gone awry: Pathway and course of complicated grief. *Dialogues in Clinical Neuroscience, 14,* 119–128.

Shear, M.K., Ghesquiere, A., & Glickman, K. (2013). Bereavement and complicated grief. *Current Psychiatric Reports, 15*(11), 406.

Shebloski, B., Conger, K.J., & Widaman, K.F. (2005). Reciprocal links among differential parenting, perceived partiality, and self worth: A three-wave longitudinal study. *Journal of Family Psychology, 19,* 633–642.

Sheehan, M.J., & Watson, M.W. (2008). Reciprocal influences between maternal discipline and techniques and aggression in children and adolescents. *Aggressive Behavior, 34,* 245–255.

Sheftall, A.H., Mathias, C.W., Furr, R.M., & Dougherty, D.M. (2013). Adolescent attachment security, family functioning, and suicide attempts. *Attachment and Human Development, 15,* 368–383.

Sheftall, A.H., Schoppe-Sullivan, S.J., & Bridge, J.A. (2014). Insecure attachment and suicidal behavior in adolescents. *Crisis. 35,* 426–430.

Shenhav, A., & Greene, J.D. (2014). Integrative moral judgment: Dissociating the roles of the amygdala and the ventromedial prefrontal cortex. *Journal of Neuroscience, 34,* 4741–4749.

Sher-Censor, E., Parke, R.D., & Coltrane, S. (2010). Parents' promotion of psychological autonomy, psychological control, and Mexican-American adolescents' adjustment. *Journal of Youth and Adolescence, 40*(5), 620–632.

Sherwood, C.C., & others (2011). Aging of the cerebral cortex differs between humans and chimpanzees. *Proceedings of the National Academy of Sciences U.S.A., 108,* 13029–13034.

Shibata, Y., & others (2012). Extrachromosomal microDNAs and chromosomal microdeletions in normal tissues. *Science, 336,* 82–86.

Shields, S.A. (1998, August). *What Jerry Maguire can tell us about gender and emotion.* Paper presented at the meeting of the International Society for Research on Emotions, Würzburg, Germany.

Shimazu, A., & others (2014). Work-to-family conflict and family-to-work conflict among Japanese dual-earner couples with preschool children: A spillover-crossover perspective. *Journal of Occupational Health, 55,* 234–243.

Shimizu, S., & Ohno, Y. (2013). Improving the treatment of Parkinson's disease: A novel approach by modulating 5-HT(1A) receptors. *Aging and Disease, 4,* 1–13.

Shin, K.O., & others (2014). Exercise training improves cardiac autonomic nervous system activity in type 1 diabetic children. *Journal of Physical Therapy Science, 26,* 111–115.

Shin, M.S., & others (2013). Treadmill exercise ameliorates symptoms of methimazole-induced hypothyroidism through enhancing neurogenesis and suppressing apoptosis in the hippocampus of rat pups. *International Journal of Neuroscience, 31*(3), 214–223.

Shin, S.H., Lee, S., Jeon, S.M., & Wills, T.A. (2015, in press). Childhood emotional abuse, negative emotion-driven impulsivity, and alcohol use in young adulthood. *Child Abuse and Neglect.*

Shin, W., & Ismail, N. (2014). Exploring the role of parents and peers in young adolescents' risk taking on social networking sites. *Cyberpsychology, Behavior, and Social Networking, 17,* 578–583.

Shiner, R.L., & DeYoung, C.G. (2013). The structure of temperament and personality: A developmental approach. In P.D. Zelazo (Ed.), *Oxford handbook of developmental psychology.* New York: Oxford University Press.

Shirai, N., & Imura, T. (2014). Looking away before moving forward: Changes in optic-flow perception precede locomotor development. *Psychological Science, 25,* 485–493.

Shokhirev, M.N., & Johnson, A.A. (2014). Effects of extrinsic mortality on the evolution of aging: A stochastic modeling approach. *PLoS One, 9*(1), e86602.

Shor, E., Roelfs, D.J., Bugyi, P., & Schwartz, J.E. (2012). Meta-analysis of marital dissolution and mortality: Reevaluating the intersection of gender and age. *Social Science and Medicine, 75,* 46–59.

Shore, L.M., & Goldberg, C.B. (2005). Age discrimination in the workplace. In R.L. Dipobye & A. Colella (Eds.), *Discrimination at work.* Mahwah, NJ: Erlbaum.

Shors, T.J. (2009). Saving new brain cells. *Scientific American, 300,* 46–52.

Short, D. (2015, April 7). *Demographic trends in the 50-and-older work force.* Retrieved April 19, 2015, from www.advisorperspectives.com/dshort/commentaries/Aging-Labor-Force.php

Short, M.A., Gradisar, M., Lack, L.C., Wright, H.R., & Dohnt, H. (2012). The sleep patterns and well-being of Australian adolescents. *Journal of Adolescence, 36*(1), 103–110.

Shulman, E., & Steinberg, L. (2015). Human development and the juvenile justice system. In K. Heilbrun (Ed.), *Handbook of psychology and juvenile justice.* Washington, DC: APA Books.

Shwalb, D.W., Shwalb, B.J., & Lamb, M.E. (2013). *Fathers in cultural context.* New York: Routledge.

Sibley, M.H., & others (2012). Diagnosing ADHD in adolescence. *Journal of Consulting and Clinical Psychology, 80,* 139–150.

Siegel, D.H. (2013). Open adoption: Adoptive parents' reactions two decades later. *Social Work, 58,* 43–52.

Siegel, R.S., & Brandon, A.R. (2014). Adolescents, pregnancy, and mental health. *Journal of Pediatric and Adolescent Gynecology, 27,* 138–150.

Siegler, I.C., Bosworth, H.B., Davey, A., & Elias, M.F. (2013). Disease, health, and aging in the first decade of the 21st century. In I.B. Weiner & others (Eds.), *Handbook of psychology* (2nd ed., Vol. 6). New York: Wiley.

Siegler, I.C., Elias, M.F., Brummett, B.H., & Bosworth, H.B. (2013). Adult development and aging. In I.B. Weiner & others (Eds.), *Handbook of psychology* (2nd ed., Vol. 9). New York: Wiley.

Siegler, R.S. (2006). Microgenetic analysis of learning. In W. Damon & R. Lerner (Eds.), *Handbook of child psychology* (6th ed.). New York: Wiley.

Siegler, R.S. (2009). Improving preschoolers' number sense using information processing theory. In O.A. Barbarin & K. Miller (Eds.), *Handbook of child development and early education.* New York: Guilford.

Siegler, R.S. (2012). From theory to application and back: Following in the giant footsteps of David Klahr. In S.M. Carver & J. Shrager (Eds.), *The journey from child to scientist: Integrating cognitive development and the education sciences.* Thousand Oaks, CA: Sage.

Siegler, R.S. (2013). How do people become experts? In J. Staszewski (Ed.), *Experience and skill acquisition.* New York: Taylor & Francis.

Siegler, R.S. (2015, in press). Cognitive development in childhood. In E. Diener & R. Biswas-Diener (Eds.), *Noba textbook series: Psychology,* Champaign, IL: DEF Publishers.

Siegler, R.S., Fazio, L.K., Bailey, D.H., & Zhou, X. (2013). Fractions: The new frontier for theories of numerical development. *Trends in Cognitive Science, 17,* 13–19.

Siegler, R.S., & Lortie-Forgues, H. (2015, in press). An integrative theory of numerical development. *Child Developmental Perspectives.*

Siegler, R.S., & Mu, Y. (2008). Chinese children excel on novel mathematics problems even before elementary school. *Psychological Science, 19,* 759–763.

Siegler, R.S., & Thompson, C.A. (2014). Numerical landmarks are useful—except when they're not. *Journal of Experimental Child Psychology, 120,* 39–58.

Siegler, R.S., & others (2015, in press). The Center for Improving Learning of Fractions: A progress report. In S. Chinn (Ed.), *The international handbook for dyscalculia and mathematical difficulties.* New York: Guilford.

Siener, S., & Kerns, K.A. (2012). Emotion regulation and depressive symptoms in preadolescence. *Child Psychiatry and Human Development, 43,* 414–430.

Sievert, L.L., & Obermeyer, C.M. (2012). Symptom clusters at midlife: A four-country comparison of checklist and qualitative responses. *Menopause, 19,* 133–144.

Siller, M., Swanson, M.R., Serlin, G., & George, A. (2014). Internal state language in the storybook narratives of children with and without autism spectrum disorder: Investigating relations to theory of mind abilities. *Research in Autism Spectrum Disorders.*

Silva, C. (2005, October 31). When teen dynamo talks, city listens. *Boston Globe,* pp. 81–84.

Silveira, M.J., Witala, W., & Piette, J. (2014). Advance directive completion by elderly Americans: A decade of change. *Journal of the American Geriatrics Society, 162,* 706–710.

Silver, E.J., & Bauman, L.J. (2006). The association of sexual experience with attitudes, beliefs, and risk behaviors of inner-city adolescents. *Journal of Research on Adolescence, 16,* 29–45.

Silverstein, M. (2009). Caregiving. In D. Carr (Ed.), *Encyclopedia of the life course and human development.* Boston: Gale Cengage.

Silverstein, M., Conroy, S.J., Wang, H., Giarrusso, R., & Bengtson, V.L. (2002). Reciprocity in parent-child relations over the adult life course. *Journal of Gerontology B: Social Sciences, 57,* S3–S13.

Sim, M.P.Y., & Lamb, M.E. (2015, in press). Children's disclosure about sexual abuse: How motivational factors affect linguistic categories related to deception detection. *Psychology, Crime, and Law.*

Simkin, P., & Bolding, A. (2004). Update on nonpharmacological approaches to relieve labor pain and prevent suffering. *Journal of Midwifery and Women's Health, 49,* 489–504.

Simmons, E.S., Lanter, E., & Lyons, M. (2014). Supporting mainstream educational success. In F.R. Volkmer & others (Eds.), *Handbook of autism and pervasive developmental disorders.* New York: Wiley.

Simon, E.J. (2015). *Biology.* Upper Saddle River, NJ: Pearson.

Simon, E.J., Dickey, J.L., Reece, J.B., & Hogan, K.A. (2016, in press). *Campbell essential biology* (5th ed.). Upper Saddle River, NJ: Pearson.

Simonton, D.K. (1996). Creativity. In J.E. Birren (Ed.), *Encyclopedia of aging.* San Diego: Academic Press.

Simpkins, S.D., Delgado, M.Y., Price, C.D., Quach, A., & Starbuck, E. (2013). Socioeconomic status, ethnicity, culture, and immigration: Examining the potential mechanisms underlying Mexican-origin adolescents' organized activity participation. *Developmental Psychology, 49*(4), 706–721.

Simpson, H.B., & others (2013). Treatment of obsessive-compulsive disorder complicated by comorbid eating disorders. *Cognitive Behaviour Therapy, 42,* 64–76.

Simpson, J., & Belsky, J. (2016, in press). Attachment theory within a modern evolutionary framework. In J. Cassidy & P. Shaver (Eds.), *Handbook of attachment theory and research* (3rd ed.). New York: Guilford.

Simpson, R.J., & others (2012). Exercise and the aging immune system. *Aging Research and Reviews, 1,* 404–420.

Sims, T., Hogan, C., & Carstensen, L.L. (2015, in press). Selectivity as an emotion regulation strategy. Lessons from older adults. *Current Opinion in Psychology.*

Singer, D., Golinkoff, R.M., & Hirsh-Pasek, K. (Eds.) (2006). *Play = learning: How play motivates and enhances children's cognitive and social-emotional growth.* New York: Oxford University Press.

Singer, J.A., & Kasmark, A.M. (2015). A translational approach to narrative identity in psychotherapy. In K.C. McLean & M. Syed (Eds.), *Oxford handbook of identity development.* New York: Oxford University Press.

Singh, S., Wulf, D., Samara, R., & Cuca, Y.P. (2000). Gender differences in the timing of first intercourse: Data from 14 countries. *International Family Planning Perspectives, 26,* 21–28, 43.

Singh-Manoux, A., & others (2012). Timing and onset of cognitive decline: Results from Whitehall II prospective cohort study. *BMJ, 344,* d7622.

Sinha, J.W., Cnaan, R.A., & Gelles, R.J. (2007). Adolescent risk behaviors and religion: Findings from a national study. *Journal of Adolescence, 30,* 231–249.

Sinnott, J.D. (2003). Postformal thought and adult development: Living in balance. In J. Demick & C. Andreoletti (Eds.), *Handbook of adult development.* New York: Kluwer.

Sinnott, J.D., & Johnson, L. (1997). Brief report: Complex formal thought in skilled research administrators. *Journal of Adult Development, 4,* 45–53.

Sirsch, U., Dreher, E., Mayr, E., & Willinger, U. (2009). What does it take to be an adult in Austria? Views of adulthood in Austrian adolescents, emerging adults, and adults. *Journal of Adolescent Research, 24,* 275–292.

Siu, A.M., Shek, D.T., & Law, B. (2012). Prosocial norms as a positive youth development construct: A conceptual review. *Scientific World Journal, 2012,* 832026.

Skingley, A. (2013). Older people, isolation, and loneliness: Implications for community nursing. *British Journal of Community Nursing, 18,* 84–90.

Skinner, B.F. (1938). *The behavior of organisms: An experimental analysis.* New York: Appleton-Century-Crofts.

Skinner, B.F. (1957). *Verbal behavior.* New York: Appleton-Century-Crofts.

Skinner, S.R., & others (2015). Childhood behavior problems and age at first sexual intercourse: A prospective birth cohort study. *Pediatrics, 135,* 255–263.

Slater, A., Morison, V., & Somers, M. (1988). Orientation discrimination and cortical function in the human newborn. *Perception, 17,* 597–602.

Slater, A.M., Bremner, J.G., Johnson, S.P., & Hayes, R. (2011). The role of perceptual processes in infant addition/subtraction events. In L.M. Oakes, C.H. Cashon, M. Casasola, & D.H. Rakison (Eds.), *Early perceptual and cognitive development.* New York: Oxford University Press.

Slobin, D. (1972, July). Children and language: They learn the same way around the world. *Psychology Today,* pp. 71–76.

Slomkowski, C., Rende, R., Conger, K.J., Simons, R.L., & Conger, R.D. (2001). Sisters, brothers, and delinquency: Social influence during early and middle adolescence. *Child Development, 72,* 271–283.

Sloutsky, V. (2015). Conceptual development. In R.M. Lerner (Ed.), *Handbook of child psychology and developmental science* (7th ed.). New York: Wiley.

Smaldino, S.E., Lowther, D.L., Russell, J.W., & Mims, C. (2015). *Instructional technology and media for learning* (11th ed.). Upper Saddle River, NJ: Pearson.

Smaldone, A., Honig, J.C., & Byrne, M.W. (2007). Sleepless in America: Inadequate sleep and relationships to health and well-being of our nation's children. *Pediatrics, 119*(Suppl. 1), S29–S37.

Small, B.J., Rawson, K.S., Eisel, S., & McEvoy, C.L. (2012). Memory and aging. In S.K. Whitbourne & M. Sliwinski (Eds.), *Wiley-Blackwell handbook of adulthood and aging.* New York: Wiley.

Small, H. (2011). *Why not? My seventy-year plan for a college degree.* Franklin, TN: Carpenter's Son Publishing.

Small, S.A. (1990). *Preventive programs that support families with adolescents.* Washington, DC: Carnegie Council on Adolescent Development.

Smetana, J.G. (2008). "It's 10 o'clock: Do you know where your children are?" Recent advances in understanding parental monitoring and adolescents' information management. *Child Development Perspectives, 2,* 19–25.

Smetana, J.G. (2011a). *Adolescents, families, and social development: How adolescents construct their worlds.* West Sussex, England: Wiley-Blackwell, Inc.

Smetana, J.G. (2011b). Adolescents' social reasoning and relationships with parents: Conflicts and coordinations within and across domains. In E. Amsel & J. Smetana, (Eds.), *Adolescent vulnerabilities and opportunities: Constructivist and developmental perspectives.* New York: Cambridge University Press.

Smetana, J.G. (2013). Moral development: The social domain theory view. In P.D. Zelazo (Ed.), *Oxford handbook of developmental psychology.* New York: Oxford University Press.

Smetana, J.G., Jambon, M., & Ball, C. (2014). The social domain approach to children's moral and social judgments. In M. Killen & J.G. Smetana (Eds.), *Handbook of moral development* (2nd ed.). New York: Psychology Press.

Smetana, J.G., Robinson, J., & Rote, W.M. (2015). Socialization in adolescence. In J.E. Grusec & P.D. Hastings (Eds.), *Handbook of socialization* (2nd ed.). New York: Guilford.

Smith, A. (2014, April 3). *Older adults and technology use.* Washington, DC: Pew Research Center.

Smith, A., & Collene, A. (2016, in press). *Wardlaw's contemporary nutrition* (10th ed.). New York: McGraw-Hill.

Smith, A.J., Abeyta, A.A., Hughes, M., & Jones, R.T. (2015). Persistent grief in the aftermath of mass violence: The predictive roles of posttraumatic stress symptoms, self-efficacy, and disrupted worldview. *Psychological Trauma, 7,* 179–186.

Smith, A.J., Humphries, S.E., & Talmud, P.J. (2015, in press). Identifying functional noncoding variants from genome-wide association studies for cardiovascular disease and related traits. *Current Opinion in Lipidology.*

Smith, B.D., & Tyler, N.C. (2014). *Introduction to contemporary special education.* Upper Saddle River, NJ: Pearson.

Smith, C.A., Levett, K.M., Collins, C.T., & Jones, L. (2012). Massage, reflexology, and other manual methods for pain management. *Cochrane Database of Systematic Reviews, 15*(2), CD009290.

Smith, G.E., & others (2009). A cognitive training program based on principles of brain plasticity: Results from the improvement in memory with plasticity-based adaptive cognitive training (IMPACT) study. *Journal of the American Geriatrics Society, 57,* 594–603.

Smith, J. (2009). Self. In D. Carr (Ed.), *Encyclopedia of the life course and human development.* Boston: Gale Cengage.

Smith, L.E., & Howard, K.S. (2008). Continuity of paternal social support and depressive symptoms among new mothers. *Journal of Family Psychology, 22,* 763–773.

Smith, M.C., & Reio, T.G. (2007). *The handbook on adult development and learning.* Mahwah, NJ: Erlbaum.

Smith, P.K. (2007). Pretend play and children's cognitive and literacy development: Sources of evidence and some lessons from the past. In K.A. Roskos & J.F. Christie (Eds.), *Play and literacy in early childhood.* Mahwah, NJ: Erlbaum.

Smith, R.A., & Davis, S.F. (2013). *The psychologist as detective* (6th ed.). Upper Saddle River, NJ: Prentice Hall.

Smith, R.L. (2009). *Social perspective-taking in the friendships of adolescents: Implications for friendship quality and emotional adjustment.* Thesis, University of Missouri—Columbia.

Smith, R.L., & Rose, A.J. (2011). The "cost of caring" in youths' friendships: Considering associations among social perspective taking, co-rumination, and empathetic distress. *Developmental Psychology, 47,* 1792–1803.

Smith, R.L., Rose, A.J., & Schwartz-Mette, R.A. (2010). Relational and overt aggression in childhood and adolescence: Clarifying mean-level gender differences and associations with peer acceptance. *Social Development, 19,* 243–269.

Smith, T.B., McCullough, M.E., & Poll, J. (2003). Religiousness and depression: Evidence for a main effect and the moderating influences of stressful life events. *Psychological Bulletin, 129,* 614–636.

Smith, T.E., & others (2016, in press). *Teaching students with special needs in inclusive settings* (7th ed.). Upper Saddle River, NJ: Pearson.

Smock, P.J., & Gupta, S. (2013). Cohabitation in contemporary North America. In A. Booth, A.C. Crouter, & N.S. Landale (Eds.), *Just living together.* New York: Psychology Press.

Smokowski, P.R., Bacallao, M.L., Cotter, K.L., & Evans, C.B. (2015). The effects of positive and negative parenting practices on adolescent mental health outcomes in a multicultural sample of rural youth. *Child Psychiatry and Human Development, 46,* 333–345.

Smoreda, Z., & Licoppe, C. (2000). Gender-specific use of the domestic telephone. *Social Psychology Quarterly, 63,* 238–252.

Snarey, J. (1987, June). A question of morality. *Psychology Today,* pp. 6–8.

Snarey, J. (2014). Lawrence Kohlberg's revolutionary ideas: Moral education in the cognitive-developmental tradition. In L. Nucci, T. Krettenaur, & D. Narváez (Eds.), *Handbook of moral and character education* (2nd ed.). New York: Routledge.

Snow, C.E., Burns, M.S., & Griffin, P. (1998). *Preventing reading difficulties in young children.* Washington, DC: National Academies Press.

Snow, C.E., & Kang, J.Y. (2006). Becoming bilingual, biliterate, and bicultural. In W. Damon & R. Lerner (Eds.), *Handbook of child psychology* (6th ed.). New York: Wiley.

Snowdon, D.A. (1997). Aging and Alzheimer's disease: Lessons from the nun study. *Gerontologist, 37,* 150–156.

Snowdon, D.A. (2002). *Aging with grace: What the Nun Study teaches us about leading longer, healthier, and more meaningful lives.* New York: Bantam.

Snowdon, D.A. (2003). Healthy aging and dementia: Findings from the Nun Study. *Annals of Internal Medicine, 139,* 450–454.

Snyder, K.A., & Torrence, C.M. (2008). Habituation and novelty. In M.M. Haith & J.B. Benson (Eds.), *Encyclopedia of infant and early childhood development.* Oxford, UK: Elsevier.

Soares, N.S., & Patel, D.R. (2012). Office screening and early identification of children with autism. *Pediatric Clinics of North America, 59,* 89–102.

Soderstrom, M., & others (2012). Insufficient sleep predicts clinical burnout. *Journal of Occupational Health Psychology, 17,* 175–183.

Soerensen, M., & others (2010). Replication of an association of variation in the FOXO3A gene with human longevity using both case control and longitudinal data. *Aging Cell, 9,* 1010–1017.

Sokol, B.W., Snjezana, H., & Muller, U. (2010). Social understanding and self-regulation: From perspective-taking to theory of mind. In B. Sokol, U. Muller, J. Carpendale, A. Young, & G. Iarocci (Eds.), *Self- and social cognition.* New York: Oxford University Press.

Sokol, E.W. (2013). National plan to address Alzheimer's disease offers hope for new home care and hospice provisions. *Caring, 32,* 24–27.

Solberg, P.A., Halvari, H., Ommundsen, Y., & Hopkins, W.G. (2014). A one-year follow-up of effects of exercise programs on well-being in older adults. *Journal of Aging and Physical Activity, 22,* 52–64.

Soller, B. (2014). Caught in a bad romance: Adolescent romantic relationships and mental health. *Journal of Health and Social Behavior, 55,* 56–72.

Solomon, B.C., & Jackson, J.J. (2014). Why do personality traits predict divorce? Multiple pathways through satisfaction. *Journal of Personality and Social Psychology, 106,* 978–996.

Solomon, D., Watson, P., & Battistich, V.A. (2002). Teaching and school effects on moral/prosocial development. In V. Richardson (Ed.), *Handbook for research on teaching.* Washington, DC: American Educational Research Association.

Solomon, D., Watson, P., Schapes, E., Battistich, V., & Solomon, J. (1990). Cooperative learning as part of a comprehensive program designed to promote prosocial development. In S. Sharan (Ed.), *Cooperative learning.* New York: Praeger.

Soloski, K.L., Kale Monk, J., & Durtschi, J.A. (2015, in press). Trajectories of early binge drinking: A function of family cohesion and peer use. *Journal of Marital and Family Therapy.*

Song, A.V., & Halpern-Felsher, B.L. (2010). Predictive relationship between adolescent oral and vaginal sex: Results from a prospective, longitudinal study. *Archives of Pediatric and Adolescent Medicine, 165*(3), 243–249.

Song, L.J., & others (2010). The differential effects of general mental ability and emotional intelligence on academic performance and social interactions. *Intelligence, 38,* 137–143.

Sonuga-Barke, E.J. (2014). Editorial: Building global science capacity in child psychology and psychiatry— between etic and emic of cross-cultural enquiry. *Journal of Child Psychology and Psychiatry, 55,* 301–303.

Sophian, C. (1985). Perseveration and infants' search: A comparison of two- and three-location tasks. *Developmental Psychology, 21,* 187–194.

Sorbo, M.F., Grimstad, H., Bjorngaard, J.H., Schei, B., & Lukasse, M. (2013). Prevalence of sexual, physical, and emotional abuse in the Norwegian Mother and Child Cohort Study. *BMC Public Health, 13,* 186.

Sorensen, T.L., & Kemp, H. (2010). Ranibizumab treatment in patients with neovascular age-related macular degeneration and very low vision. *Acta Ophthalmologica, 89*(1), e97.

Sorte, J., Daeschel, I., & Amador, C. (2014). *Nutrition, health, and safety for young children* (2nd ed.). Upper Saddle River, NJ: Pearson.

Sosic-Vasic, Z., & others (2015). The impact of motivation and teachers' autonomy support on children's executive functions. *Frontiers in Psychology, 6,* 146.

Soska, K.S., Robinson, S.R., & Adolph, K.E. (2015). A new twist on old ideas: How sitting reorients crawlers. *Developmental Science, 18*(2), 206–218.

Soter, A.O. (2013). *Grammar, usage, and punctuation.* Boston: Allyn & Bacon.

Soto, C.J. (2015, in press). Is happiness good for your personality? Concurrent and prospective relations of the Big Five with subjective well-being. *Journal of Personality.*

Soto, C.J., John, O.P., Gosling, S.D., & Potter, J. (2011). Age differences in personality traits from 10 to 65: Big Five domains and facets in a large cross-sectional sample. *Journal of Personality and Social Psychology, 100,* 333–348.

Spandel, V. (2009). *Creating young writers* (3rd ed.). Boston: Allyn & Bacon.

Spangler, G., Johann, M., Ronai, Z., & Zimmermann, P. (2009). Genetic and environmental influence on attachment disorganization. *Journal of Child Psychology and Psychiatry, 50,* 952–961.

Specht, J., Egloff, B., & Schukle, S.C. (2011). Stability and change of personality across the life course: The impact of age and major life events on mean-level and rank-order stability of the Big Five. *Journal of Personality and Social Psychology, 101,* 862–882.

Spelke, E.S. (1979). Perceiving bimodally specified events in infancy. *Developmental Psychology, 5,* 626–636.

Spelke, E.S. (1991). Physical knowledge in infancy. Reflections on Piaget's theory. In S. Carey & R. Gelman (Eds.), *The epigenesis of mind: Essays on biology and cognition.* Hillsdale, NJ: Erlbaum.

Spelke, E.S. (2000). Core knowledge. *American Psychologist, 55,* 1233–1243.

Spelke, E.S. (2003). Developing knowledge of space: Core systems and new combinations. In S.M. Kosslyn & A. Galaburda (Eds.), *Languages of the brain.* Cambridge, MA: Harvard University Press.

Spelke, E.S. (2011). Natural number and natural geometry. In E. Brannon & S. Dehaene (Eds.), *Space, time, and number in the brain.* New York: Oxford University Press.

Spelke, E.S., Bernier, E.P., & Snedeker, J. (2013). Core social cognition. In M.R. Banaji & S.A. Gelman (Eds.), *Navigating the social world: What infants, children, and other species can teach us.* New York: Oxford University Press.

Spelke, E.S., Breinlinger, K., Macomber, J., & Jacobson, K. (1992). Origins of knowledge. *Psychological Review, 99,* 605–632.

Spelke, E.S., & Hespos. S.J. (2001). Continuity, competence, and the object concept. In E. Dupoux (Ed.), *Language, brain, and behavior.* Cambridge, MA: Bradford/MIT Press.

Spelke, E.S., & Owsley, C.J. (1979). Intermodal exploration and knowledge in infancy. *Infant Behavior and Development, 2,* 13–28.

Spence, A.P. (1989). *Biology of human aging.* Englewood Cliffs, NJ: Prentice Hall.

Spencer, M.B., Swanson, D.P., & Harpalani, V. (2015). Conceptualizing the self: Contributions of normative human processes, diverse contexts, and opportunity. In R.M. Lerner (Ed.), *Handbook of child psychology and developmental science* (7th ed.). New York: Wiley.

Spiegler, M.D. (2016, in press). *Contemporary behavior therapy* (6th ed.). Boston: Cengage.

Spilman, S.K., Neppl, T.K., Donnellan, M.B., Schofield, T.J., & Conger, R.D. (2013). Incorporating religiosity into a developmental model of positive family functioning across generations. *Developmental Psychology, 49*(4), 762–774.

Spira, D., & others (2015, in press). Association of low lean body mass with frailty and physical performance: A comparison between two operational definitions of sarcopenia-data from the Berlin Aging Study II (BASE-II). *Journals of Gerontology A: Biological Sciences and Medical Sciences.*

Sprecher, S., Treger, S., & Sakaluk, J.K. (2013). Premarital sexual standards and sociosexuality: Gender, ethnicity, and cohort differences. *Archives of Sexual Behavior, 42,* 1395–1405.

Sprei, J.E., & Courtois, C.A. (1988). The treatment of women's sexual dysfunctions arising from sexual assault. In R.A. Brown & J.R. Fields (Eds.), *Treatment of sexual problems in individual and group therapy.* Great Neck, NY: PMA.

Sroufe, L.A. (2000, Spring). The inside scoop on child development: Interview. *Cutting through the hype.* Minneapolis: College of Education and Human Development, University of Minnesota.

Sroufe, L.A., Coffino, B., & Carlson, E.A. (2010). Conceptualizing the role of early experience: Lessons from the Minnesota longitudinal study. *Developmental Review, 30,* 36–51.

Sroufe, L.A., Egeland, B., Carlson, E., & Collins, W.A. (2005). The place of early attachment in developmental context. In K.E. Grossman, K. Grossman, & E. Waters (Eds.), *The power of attachment research.* New York: Guilford.

Staff, J., Messersmith, E.E., & Schulenberg, J.E. (2009). Adolescents and the world of work. In R.M. Lerner & L. Steinberg (Eds.), *Handbook of adolescent psychology* (3rd ed.). New York: Wiley.

Stafford, A.C., Alswayan, M.S., & Tenni, P.C. (2010). Inappropriate prescribing in older residents of Australian care homes. *Journal of Clinical Pharmacy and Therapeutics, 36,* 33–44.

Stagg, S.D., Linnell, K.J., & Heaton, P. (2014). Investigating eye movement patterns, language, and social ability in children with autism spectrum disorder. *Development and Psychopathology, 26,* 529–537.

Staiano, A.E., Abraham, A., & Calvert, S.L. (2012). Competitive versus cooperative exergame play for African American adolescents' executive functioning skills. *Developmental Psychology, 48,* 337–342.

Stanford Center for Longevity (2011). *Experts' consensus on brain health.* Retrieved April 30, 2011, from http://longevity.stanford.edu/my mind/cognitiveagingstatement

Stangor, C. (2015). *Research methods for the behavioral sciences* (5th ed.). Boston: Cengage.

Stanley, S.M., Amato, P.R., Johnson, C.A., & Markman, H.J. (2006). Premarital education, marital quality, and marital stability: Findings from a large, household survey. *Journal of Family Psychology, 20,* 117–126.

Stanley, S.M., Rhoades, G.K., Amato, P.R., Markman, H.J., & Johnson, C.A. (2010). The timing of cohabitation and engagement: Impact on first and second marriages. *Journal of Marriage and the Family, 72,* 906–918.

Stanovich, K.E., West, R.F., & Toplak, M.E. (2012). Judgment and decision making in adolescence: Separating intelligence from rationality. In V.F. Reyna (Ed.), *The adolescent brain.* Washington, DC: American Psychological Association.

Staplin, L.K., Lococo, K., & Sim, J. (1993). *Traffic maneuver problems of older drivers: Final technical report.* McLean, VA: Federal Highway Administration.

Starr, C., Evers, C., & Starr, L. (2015). *Biology* (9th ed.). Boston: Cengage.

Starr, C., Evers, C., & Starr, L. (2016, in press). *Biology today and tomorrow* (5th ed.). Boston: Cengage.

Starr, C., Taggart, R., Evers, C., & Starr, L. (2016, in press). *Biology: The unity and diversity of life* (14th ed.). Boston: Cengage.

Starr, L.R., & others (2012). Love hurts (in more ways than one): Specificity of psychological symptoms as predictors and consequences of romantic activity among early adolescent girls. *Journal of Clinical Psychology, 68,* 403–420.

Staszewski, J. (Ed.) (2013). *Expertise and skill acquisition: The impact of William C. Chase.* New York: Taylor & Francis.

Staudinger, U.M. (1996). Psychologische produktivitat und delbstenfaltung im alter. In M.M. Baltes & L. Montada (Eds.), *Produktives leben im alter.* Frankfurt: Campus.

Staudinger, U.M., & Gluck, J. (2011). Intelligence and wisdom. In R.J. Sternberg & S.B. Kaufman (Eds.), *Cambridge handbook of intelligence.* New York: Cambridge University Press.

Staudinger, U.M., & Jacobs, C.B. (2010). Life-span perspectives on positive personality development in adulthood and old age. In R.M. Lerner, W.F. Overton, A.M. Freund, & M.E. Lamb (Eds.), *Handbook of life-span development.* New York: Wiley.

Stavrinos, D., & others (2013). Impact of distracted driving on safety and traffic flow. *Accident Analysis and Prevention, 61,* 63–70.

Steca, P., Bassi, M., Caprara, G.V., & Fave, A.D. (2011). Parents' self-efficacy beliefs and their children's psychosocial adaptation during adolescence. *Journal of Youth and Adolescence, 40*(3), 320–331.

Steck, N., & others (2013). Euthanasia and assisted suicide in selected European countries and U.S. states: Systematic literature review. *Medical Care, 51,* 938–944.

Steele, J., Waters, E., Crowell, J., & Treboux, D. (1998, June). *Self-report measures of attachment: Secure bonds to other attachment measures and attachment theory.* Paper presented at the meeting of the International Society for the Study of Personal Relationships, Saratoga Springs, NY.

Steele, L.G., & Lynch, S.M. (2013). The pursuit of happiness in China: Individualism, collectivism, and subjective well-being during China's economic and social transformation. *Social Indicators Research, 114*(2).

Steffener, J., Barulli, D., Habeck, C., & Stern, Y. (2014). Neuroimaging explanations of age-related differences in task performance. *Frontiers in Aging Neuroscience, 6,* 46.

Stegeman, S., & others (2015, in press). A large-scale analysis of genetic variants within putative miRNA binding sites in prostate cancer. *Cancer Discoveries.*

Steiger, A.E., Allemand, M., Robins, R.W., & Fend, H.A. (2014). Low and decreasing self-esteem during adolescence predict adult depression two decades later.

Journal of Personality and Social Psychology, 106, 325–338.

Stein, P.K., & others (2012). Caloric restriction may reverse age-related autonomic decline in humans. *Aging Cell, 11*(4), 644–650.

Steinberg, L. (2012, Spring). Should the science of adolescent brain development inform public policy? *Issues in Science and Technology,* 67–78.

Steinberg, L. (2015a). How should the science of adolescent brain pathology inform legal policy? In J. Bhabha (Ed.), *Coming of age.* Philadelphia: University of Pennsylvania Press.

Steinberg, L. (2015b). The neural underpinnings of adolescent risk-taking: The roles of reward-seeking, impulse control, and peers. In G. Oettigen & P. Gollwitzer (Eds.), *Self-regulation in adolescence.* New York: Cambridge University Press.

Steinberg, S. (2011, June 11). New dating site helps college students find love. *CNN Living.* Retrieved February 27, 2013, from www.cnn.com/2011/LIVING/06/22date.my.school/index.html

Steiner, J.E. (1979). Human facial expression in response to taste and smell stimulation. In H. Reese & L. Lipsitt (Eds.), *Advances in child development and behavior* (Vol. 13). New York: Academic Press.

Steiner, K.L., Pillemer, D.B., Thomsen, D.K., & Minigan, A.P. (2014). The reminiscence bump in older adults' life story transitions. *Memory, 22,* 1002–1009.

Steiner, N.J., & others (2014a). In-school neurofeedback traning for ADHD: Sustained improvements from a randomized controlled trial. *Pediatrics, 35,* 18–27.

Steiner, N.J., & others (2014b). Neurofeedback and cognitive attention training for children with attention deficit hyperactivity disorder in schools. *Journal of Developmental and Behavioral Pediatrics, 35,* 18–27.

Steinhilber, J., & others (2015). Next-generation sequencing identifies deregulation of microRNAs involved in both innate and adaptive immune response in ALK+ ALCL. *PLoS One, 10*(2), e0117780.

Stenholm, S., & others (2014). Age-related trajectories of physical functioning in work and retirement: The role of sociodemographic factors, lifestyles, and disease. *Journal of Epidemiology and Community Health, 68,* 503–509.

Stensvold, D., & others (2015). A randomized controlled study of the long-term effects of exercise training on mortality in elderly people: Study protocol for the Generation 100 Study. *BMJ Open, 5*(2), e007519.

Stephens, C., Breheny, M., & Mansvelt, J. (2015). Healthy aging from the perspective of older people: A capabilities approach to resilience. *Psychology and Health, 30,* 715–731.

Stephens, J.M. (2008). Cheating. In N.J. Salkind (Ed.), *Encyclopedia of educational psychology.* Thousand Oaks, CA: Sage.

Stephenson, T., & Schiff, W. (2016, in press). *Human nutrition: Science for healthy living.* New York: McGraw-Hill.

Steptoe, A., & Kivimaki, M. (2012). Stress and cardiovascular disease. *Nature Reviews. Cardiology, 9,* 360–370.

Steptoe, A., Shankar, A., Demakakos, P., & Wardle, J. (2013). Social isolation, loneliness, and all-cause mortality in older men and women. *Proceedings of the National Academy of Sciences, 110,* 5797–5801.

Sterin, J.C. (2014). *Mass media revolution* (2nd ed.). Upper Saddle River, NJ: Pearson.

Stern, D.N., Beebe, B., Jaffe, J., & Bennett, S.L. (1977). Infants' stimulus world during social interaction: A study of caregiver behaviors with particular reference to repetition and timing. In

H.R. Schaffer (Ed.), *Studies in mother-infant interaction.* London: Academic Press.

Stern, W. (1912). The psychological methods of testing intelligence. *Educational Psychology Monographs* (No. 13).

Sternberg, K., & Sternberg, R.J. (2013). Love. In H. Pasler (Eds.), *Encyclopedia of the mind.* Thousand Oaks, CA: Sage.

Sternberg, R.J. (1986). *Intelligence applied.* San Diego: Harcourt Brace Jovanovich.

Sternberg, R.J. (1988). *The triangle of love.* New York: Basic Books.

Sternberg, R.J. (2003). Contemporary theories of intelligence. In I.B. Weiner (Ed.), *Handbook of psychology* (Vol. 7). New York: Wiley.

Sternberg, R.J. (2004). Individual differences in cognitive development. In U. Goswami (Ed.), *Blackwell handbook of childhood cognitive development.* Malden, MA: Blackwell.

Sternberg, R.J. (2010). The triarchic theory of successful intelligence. In B. Kerr (Ed.), *Encyclopedia of giftedness, creativity, and talent.* Thousand Oaks, CA: Sage.

Sternberg, R.J. (2011). Individual differences in cognitive development. In U. Goswami (Ed.), *Blackwell handbook of childhood cognitive development.* Malden, MA: Blackwell.

Sternberg, R.J. (2012). Intelligence. *Dialogues in Clinical Neuroscience, 14,* 19–27.

Sternberg, R.J. (2013). Contemporary theories of intelligence. In I.B. Weiner & others (Eds.), *Handbook of psychology* (2nd ed., Vol. 7). New York: Wiley.

Sternberg, R.J. (2013). Searching for love. *The psychologist, 26*(Part 2), 98–101.

Sternberg, R.J. (2014a). Building wisdom and character. In S. Lynn (Ed.), *Health, happiness, and well-being.* Thousand Oaks, CA: Sage.

Sternberg, R.J. (2014b). Teaching about the nature of intelligence. *Intelligence, 42,* 176–179.

Sternberg, R.J. (2015a, in press). Competence versus performance models of people and tests. *Applied Developmental Psychology.*

Sternberg, R.J. (2015b). Human intelligence: Historical and conceptual perspectives. In J. Wright (Ed.), *Encyclopedia of social and behavioral sciences* (2nd ed.). New York: Elsevier.

Sternberg, R.J. (2015c). Multiple intelligences in the new age of thinking. In S. Goldstein, D. Princiotta, & J. Naglieri (Eds.), *Handbook of intelligence.* New York: Springer.

Sternberg, R.J., & Bridges, S.L. (2014). Varieties of genius. In D.K. Simonton (Ed.), *Wiley-Blackwell handbook of genius.* New York: Wiley.

Sternberg, R.J., Jarvin, L., & Grigorenko, E.L. (2011). *Explorations of the nature of giftedness.* New York: Cambridge University Press.

Sternberg, R.J., & Sternberg, K. (2012). *Cognitive psychology* (6th ed.). Boston: Cengage.

Sternberg, R.J., & Sternberg, K. (2016, in press). *Cognitive psychology* (7th ed.). Boston: Cengage.

Sternberg, R.J., & Williams, W.M. (1996). *How to develop student creativity.* Alexandria, VA: ASCD.

Sternberg, R.J., & others (2001). The relationship between academic and practical intelligence: A case study in Kenya. *Intelligence, 29,* 401–418.

Sterns, H.L., & Huyck, H. (2001). The role of work in midlife. In M.E. Lachman (Ed.), *Handbook of midlife development.* New York: John Wiley.

Sterns, H.L., & Sterns, A.A. (2013). Approaches to aging and working. In D.L. Blustein (Ed.), *Oxford handbook of the psychology of working.* New York: Oxford University Press.

Stessman, J., & others (2014). Loneliness, health, and longevity. *Journals of Gerontology B: Psychological Sciences and Social Sciences, 69,* 744–750.

Stevens, C., & Bavelier, D. (2012). The role of selective attention on academic foundations: A cognitive neuroscience perspective. *Developmental Cognitive Neurosience, 15*(Suppl. 1), S30–S48.

Stevenson, H.W. (1995). Mathematics achievement of American students: First in the world by the year 2000? In C.A. Nelson (Ed.), *Basic and applied perspectives on learning, cognition, and development.* Minneapolis: University of Minnesota Press.

Stevenson, H.W. (2000). Middle childhood: Education and schooling. In A. Kazdin (Ed.), *Encyclopedia of psychology.* Washington, DC, & New York: American Psychological Association and Oxford University Press.

Stevenson, H.W., Hofer, B.K., & Randel, B. (1999). *Middle childhood: Education and schooling.* Unpublished manuscript, Department of Psychology, University of Michigan, Ann Arbor.

Stevenson, H.W., Lee, S., & Stigler, J.W. (1986). Mathematics achievement of Chinese, Japanese, and American children. *Science, 231,* 693–699.

Stevenson, H.W., & Zusho, A. (2002). Adolescence in China and Japan: Adapting to a changing environment. In B.B. Brown, R.W. Larson, & T.S. Saraswathi (Eds.), *The world's youth.* New York: Cambridge University Press.

Stevenson, H.W., & others (1990). Contexts of achievement. *Monographs of the Society for Research in Child Development, 55*(Serial No. 221).

Stevenson, M., & others (2015, in press). Burden of disease variants in participants of the Long Life Family Study. *Aging.*

Stewart, A.D., & others (2012). Body image, shape, and volumetric assessments using 3D whole body laser scanning and 2D digital photography in females with a diagnosed eating disorder: Preliminary novel findings. *British Journal of Psychology, 103*(2), 183–202.

Stewart, A.J., Ostrove, J.M., & Helson, R. (2001). Middle aging in women: Patterns of personality change from the 30s to the 50s. *Journal of Adult Development, 8,* 23–37.

Stice, F., Presnell, K., & Spangler, D. (2002). Risk factors for binge eating onset in adolescent girls: A 2-year prospective investigation. *Health Psychology, 21,* 131–138.

Stiggins, R. (2008). *Introduction to student-involved assessment for learning* (5th ed.). Upper Saddle River, NJ: Prentice Hall.

Stikes, R., & Barbier, D. (2013). Applying the plan-do-study-act model to increase the use of kangaroo care. *Journal of Nursing Management, 21,* 70–78.

Stiles, J., Brown, T.T., Haist, F., & Jernigan, T.L. (2015). Brain and cognitive development. In R.M. Lerner (Ed.), *Handbook of child psychology and developmental science* (7th ed.). New York: Wiley.

Stipek, D.J. (2002). *Motivation to learn* (4th ed.). Boston: Allyn & Bacon.

Stipek, D.J. (2005, February 16). Commentary in *USA Today,* p. ID.

Stocker, C., & Dunn, J. (1990). Sibling relationships in childhood: Links with friendships and peer relationships. *British Journal of Developmental Psychology, 8,* 227–244.

Stoel-Gammon, C., & Sosa, A.V. (2010). Phonological development. In E. Hoff & M. Shatz (Eds.), *Blackwell handbook of language development* (2nd ed.). New York: Wiley.

Stokes, C.E., & Raley, R.K. (2009). Cohabitation. In D. Carr (Ed.), *Encyclopedia of the life course and human development.* Boston: Gale Cengage.

Stolp, H.B., & Molnar, Z. (2015). Neurogenic niches in the brain: help and hindrance of the barrier systems. *Frontiers in Neuroscience, 9,* 20.

Stone, A.A., Schwartz, J.E., Broderick, J.E., & Deaton, A. (2010). A snapshot of the age distribution of psychological well-being in the United States. *Proceedings of the National Academy of Sciences USA, 107,* 9985–9990.

Stoppa, T.M., & Lefkowitz, E.S. (2010). Longitudinal changes in religiosity among emerging adult college students. *Journal of Research on Adolescence, 20,* 23–38.

Stouthamer-Loeber, M., Loeber, R., Wei, E., Farrington, D.P., & Wikstrom, P.H. (2002). Risk and promotive effects in the explanation of persistent serious delinquency in boys. *Journal of Consulting and Clinical Psychology, 70,* 111–123.

Stouthamer-Loeber, M., Wei, E., Loeber, R., & Masten, A. (2004). Desistance from serious delinquency in the transition to adulthood. *Development and Psychopathology, 16,* 897–918.

Stracciolini, A., & others (2014). Pediatric sports injuries: A comparison of males and females. *American Journal of Sports Medicine, 42,* 965–972.

Strathearn, L. (2007). Exploring the neurobiology of attachment. In L.C. Mayes, P. Fonagy, & M. Target (Eds.), *Developmental science and psychoanalysis.* London: Karnac Press.

Strathearn, L. (2011). Maternal neglect: Oxytocin, dopamine, and the neurobiology of attachment. *Journal of Neuroendocrinology, 23,* 1054–1065.

Straubhaar, J., LaRose, R., & Davenport, L. (2014). *Media now* (8th ed.). Boston: Cengage.

Streib, H. (1999). Off-road religion? A narrative approach to fundamentalist and occult orientations of adolescents. *Journal of Adolescence, 22,* 255–267.

Strickland, A.D. (2014). Prevention of cerebral palsy, autism spectrum disorder, and attention deficit hyperactivity disorder. *Medical Hypotheses, 82,* 522–528.

Striegel-Moore, R.H., & Bulik, C.M. (2007). Risk factors for eating disorders. *American Psychologist, 62,* 181–198.

Stright, A.D., Herr, M.Y., & Neitzel, C. (2009). Maternal scaffolding of children's problem solving and children's adjustment in kindergarten: Hmong families in the United States. *Journal of Educational Psychology, 101,* 207–218.

Stroebe, M., Schut, H., & Stroebe, W. (2005). Attachment in coping with bereavement: A theoretical integration. *Review of General Psychology, 9,* 48–66.

Strohmeier, D., & Noam, G.G. (2012). Bullying in schools: What is the problem and how can educators solve it? *New Directions in Youth Development, 133,* 7–13.

Strough, J., Leszczynski, J.P., Neely, T.L., Flinn, J.A., & Margrett, J. (2007). From adolescence to later adulthood: Femininity, masculinity and androgyny in six age groups. *Sex Roles, 57,* 385–396.

Strout, K.A., & Howard, E. (2012). The six dimensions of wellness and cognition in aging adults. *Journal of Holistic Nursing, 30*(3), 195–204.

Stubbs, B., Brefka, S., & Denkinger, M.D. (2015, in press). What works to prevent falls in community-dwelling older adults? An umbrella review of meta-analyses of randomized controlled trials. *Physical Therapy.*

Stuebe, A.M., & Schwarz, E.G. (2010). The risks and benefits of infant feeding practices for women and their children. *Journal of Perinatology, 30,* 155–162.

Su, Y., & others (2013). Identification of novel human glioblastoma-specific transcripts by serial analysis of gene expression data mining. *Cancer Biomarkers, 13,* 367–375.

Subramaniam, P., & Woods, B. (2012). The impact of individual reminiscence therapy for people with dementia: Systematic review. *Expert Review of Neurotherapeutics, 12*, 545–555.

Substance Abuse and Mental Health Services Administration (2005). Substance use tables [online database]. Retrieved November 15, 2005, from http://www.icpsr.umich.edu/

Sudfeld, C.R., & others (2013). Herpes simplex virus type 2 cross-sectional seroprevalence and the estimated rate of neonatal infections among a cohort of rural Malawian female adolescents. *Sexually Transmitted Diseases, 89*, 561–567.

Suehs, B.T., & others (2014). Household members of persons with Alzheimer's disease: Health conditions, healthcare resource use, and healthcare costs. *Journal of the American Geriatrics Society, 62*, 435–441.

Sugimura, K., & Mizokami, S. (2012). Personal identity in Japan. *New Directions in Child and Adolescent Development, 138*, 123–143.

Sugita, Y. (2004). Experience in early infancy is indispensable for color perception. *Current Biology, 14*, 1267–1271.

Suleiman, A.B., & Deardorff, J. (2015). Multiple dimensions of peer influence in adolescent romantic and sexual relationships: A descriptive, qualitative study. *Archives of Sexual Behavior, 44*, 765–775.

Sullivan, A.R., & Fenelon, A. (2014). Patterns of widowhood mortality. *Journals of Gerontology B: Psychological Sciences and Social Sciences, 69*, 53–62.

Sullivan, H.S. (1953). *The interpersonal theory of psychiatry.* New York: W.W. Norton.

Sullivan, K., & Sullivan, A. (1980). Adolescent-parent separation. *Developmental Psychology, 16*, 93–99.

Sullivan, M.D., & others (2015, in press). Early stage second-language learning improves executive control: Evidence from ERP. *Brain and Language.*

Sumaroka, M., & Bornstein, M.H. (2008). Play. In M.M. Haith & J.B. Benson (Eds.), *Encyclopedia of infant and early childhood development.* Oxford, UK: Elsevier.

Sun, F., & others (2012). Predicting the trajectories of depressive symptoms among southern community-dwelling older adults: The role of religiosity. *Aging and Mental Health, 16*, 189–198.

Sun, R., Liu, M., Lu, L., Zheng, Y., & Zhang, P. (2015, in press). Congenital heart disease: Causes, diagnosis, symptoms, and treatment. *Cell Biochemistry and Biophysics.*

Sung, J., Lee, J., Noh, H.M., Park, Y.S., & Ahn, E.J. (2013). Associations between the risk of Internet addiction and problem behaviors among Korean adolescents. *Korean Journal of Family Medicine, 34*, 115–132.

Sung, S.C., & others (2011). Complicated grief among individuals with major depression: Prevalence, comorbidity, and associated features. *Journal of Affective Disorders, 134*, 453–458.

Super, C.M., & Harkness, S. (2010). Culture in infancy. In J.G. Bremner & T.D. Wachs (Eds.), *Wiley-Blackwell handbook of infant development* (2nd ed.). New York: Wiley.

Supiano, K.P., & Luptak, M. (2014). Complicated grief in older adults: A randomized controlled trial of complicated grief group therapy. *Gerontologist, 54*, 840–856.

Suri, G., & Gross, J.J. (2012). Emotion regulation and successful aging. *Trends in Cognitive Science, 16*, 409–410.

Susman, E.J., & Dorn, L.D. (2013). Puberty: Its role in development. In I.B. Weiner & others (Eds.), *Handbook of psychology* (2nd ed., Vol. 6). New York: Wiley.

Suter, M.A., Mastrobattista, J., Sachs, M., & Aagaard, K. (2015, in press). Is there evidence for potential harm of electronic cigarette use in pregnancy? *Birth Defects Research A. Clinical and Molecular Technology.*

Sveistrup, H., Schneiberg, S., McKinley, P.A., McGadyen, B.J., & Levin, M.F. (2008). Head, arm and trunk coordination during reaching in children. *Experimental Brain Research, 188*, 237–247.

Sviri, S., & others (2009). Contraindications in end-of-life decisions for self and others, expressed by relatives of chronically ventilated persons. *Journal of Critical Care, 24*, 293–301.

Swaab, D.F., Chung, W.C., Kruijver, F.P., Hofman, M.A., & Ishunina, T.A. (2001). Structural and functional sex differences in the human hypothalamus. *Hormones and Behavior, 40*, 93–98.

Swain, J.E., & others (2014). Approaching the biology of human parental attachment: Brain imaging, oxytocin, and coordinated assessments of mothers and fathers. *Brain Research, 1580*, 78–101.

Swain, S.O. (1992). Men's friendships with women. In P.M. Nardi (Ed.), *Gender in intimate relationships.* Belmont, CA: Wadsworth.

Swanson, H.L. (2014). Learning disabilities. In M.A. Bray & T.J. Kehle (Eds.), *Oxford handbook of school psychology.* New York: Oxford University Press.

Swanson, J.L. (2013). Traditional and emerging career development theory and the psychology of working. In D.L. Blustein (Ed.), *Oxford handbook of the psychology of working.* New York: Oxford University Press.

Swartz, T.T., Kim, M., Uno, M., Mortimer, J., & O'Brien, K.B. (2011). Safety nets and scaffolds: Parental support in the transition to adulthood. *Journal of Marriage and the Family, 73*, 414–429.

Sweeney, M.M. (2009). Remarriage. In D. Carr (Ed.), *Encyclopedia of the life course and human development.* Boston: Gale Cengage.

Sweeney, M.M. (2010). Remarriage and stepfamilies: Strategic sites for family scholarship in the 21st century. *Journal of Marriage and the Family, 72*(3), 667–684.

Swing, E.L., Gentile, D.A., Anderson, C.A., & Walsh, D.A. (2010). Television and video game exposure and the development of attention problems. *Pediatrics, 126*, 214–221.

Syed, M. (2013). Assessment of ethnic identity and acculturation. In K. Geisinger (Ed.), *APA handbook of testing and assessment in psychology.* Washington, DC: American Psychological Association.

Syed, M., & Juang, L.P. (2014). Ethnic identity, ethnic coherence, and psychological functioning: Testing basic assumptions of the developmental model. *Cultural Diversity and Ethnic Minority Psychology, 20*, 176–190.

Syeda, M.M., & Climie, E.A. (2014). Test review: Wechsler Preschool and Primary Scale of Intelligence. *Journal of Psychoeducational Assessment, 32*, 265–272.

Sykes, C.J. (1995). *Dumbing down our kids: Why America's children feel good about themselves but can't read, write, or add.* New York: St. Martin's Press.

Sylvain-Roy, S., Lungu, O., & Belleville, S. (2015, in press). Normal aging of the attentional control functions that underlie working memory. *Journals of Gerontology B: Psychological Sciences and Social Sciences.*

Sypniewska, G. (2015, in press). Laboratory assessment of cardiometabolic risk in overweight and obese children. *Clinical Biochemistry.*

Syvaoja, H.J., & others (2013). Physical activity, sedentary behavior, and academic performance in Finnish children. *Medicine and Science in Sports and Exercise, 45*, 2098–2104.

Szinovacz, M.E. (2009). Grandparenthood. In D. Carr (Ed.), *Encyclopedia of the life course and human development.* Boston: Gale Cengage.

Sztramko, R., & others (2013). Demographics, health-care utilization, and substance use profiles of older adults in Canada's lowest income neighbourhood. *Canadian Geriatrics Journal, 17*, 5–11.

Szwedo, D.E., Mikami, A.Y., & Allen, J.P. (2011). Qualities of peer relations on social networking websites: Predictions from negative mother-teen interactions. *Journal of Research on Adolescence, 21*, 595–607.

T

Tach, L.M., & Eads, A. (2015). Trends in the economic conseequences of marital and cohabitation dissolution in the United States. *Demography, 52*, 401–432.

Tahir, L., & Gruber, H.E. (2003). Developmental trajectories and creative work in late life. In J. Demick & C. Andreoletti (Eds.), *Handbook of adult development.* New York: Kluwer.

Tai, L.M., & others (2015, in press). APOE-modulated AB-induced neuroinflammation in Alzheimer's disease: Current landscape, novel data, and future perspective. *Journal of Neurochemistry.*

Taige, N.M., & others (2007). Antenatal maternal stress and long-term effects on child neurodevelopment: How and why? *Journal of Child Psychology and Psychiatry, 48*, 245–261.

Taler, S.J. (2009). Hypertensions in women. *Current Hypertensions Reports, 11*, 23–28.

Tallerman, M. (2013). *Understanding syntax.* New York: Oxford University Press.

Tam, H.M., Lam, C.L., Huang, H., Wang, B., & Lee, T.M. (2015). Age-related difference in relationships between cognitive processing speed and general cognitive status. *Applied Neuropsychology: Adult, 22*, 94–99.

Tamers, S.L., & others (2014). The impact of stressful life events on excessive alcohol consumption in the French population: Findings from the GAZEL cohort study. *PLoS One, 9*(1), e87653.

Tamis-LeMonda, C.S., & others (2008). Parents' goals for children: The dynamic coexistence of individualism and collectivism in cultures and individuals. *Social Development, 17*, 183–209.

Tan, P.Z., Armstrong, L.M., & Cole, P.M. (2013). Relations between temperament and anger regulation over early childhood. *Social Development, 22*, 755–772.

Tan, Q., Christiansen, L., Bornemann Hjelmborg, J., & Christiansen, K. (2015). Twin methodology in epigenetic studies. *Journal of Experimental Biology, 18*, 134–139.

Tando, T., & others (2014). Developmental changes in frontal lobe function during a verbal fluency task: A multi-channel near-infrared spectroscopy study, *36*, 844–852.

Tang, F., Choi, E., & Morrow-Howell, N. (2010). Organizational support and volunteering benefits older adults. *Gerontologist, 50*, 603–612.

Tang, M., & others (2014). GSK-3/CREB pathway involved in the gx-50's effect on Alzheimer's disease. *Neuropharmacology, 81C*, 256–266.

Tang, S., Davis-Kean, P.E., Chen, M., & Sexton, H.R. (2015, in press). Adolescent pregnancy's intergenerational effects: Does an adolescent mother's education have consequences for her children's achievement? *Journal of Research on Adolescence.*

Tannen, D. (1990). *You just don't understand: Women and men in conversation.* New York: Ballantine.

Tashiro, T., & Frazier, P. (2003). "I'll never be in a relationship like that again": Personal growth following romantic relationship breakups. *Personal Relationships, 10*, 113–128.

Tashiro, T., Frazier, P., & Berman, M. (2006). Stress-related growth following divorce and relationship dissolution. In M.A. Fine & J.H. Harvey (Eds.), *Handbook of divorce and relationship dissolution.* Mahwah, NJ: Erlbaum.

Tauman, R., & Gozal, D. (2006). Obesity and obstructive sleep apnea in children. *Pediatric Respiratory Reviews, 7*, 247–259.

Tavris, C., & Wade, C. (1984). *The longest war: Sex differences in perspective* (2nd ed.). San Diego: Harcourt Brace Jovanovich.

Taylor, C.A., Manganello, J.A., Lee, S.J., & Rice, J.C. (2010). Mother's spanking of 3-year-old children and subsequent risk of children's aggressive behavior. *Pediatrics, 125*, e1057–e1065.

Taylor, E.M., Jones, A.D., & Henagan, T.M. (2014). A review of mitochondrial-derived fatty acids in epigenetic regulation of obesity and type 2 diabetes. *Journal of Nutrition, Health, and Food Sciences, 2*(3), 1–4.

Taylor, S.E. (2011a). Affiliation and stress. In S.S. Folkman (Ed.), *Oxford handbook of stress, health, and coping.* New York: Oxford University Press.

Taylor, S.E. (2011b). *Health psychology* (8th ed.). New York: McGraw-Hill.

Taylor, S.E. (2011c). Tend and befriend theory. In A.M. van Lange, AW. Kruglanski, & E.T. Higgins (Eds.), *Handbook of theories of social psychology.* Thousand Oaks, CA: Sage.

Taylor, S.E. (2015). *Health psychology* (9th ed.). New York: McGraw-Hill.

Taylor, S.E., & others (2000). Biobehavioral responses to stress in females: Tend-and-befriend, not fight-or-flight. *Psychological Review, 107*, 411–429.

Taylor, T., & others (2014). Computerized tomography (CT) angiography for confirmation of the clinical diagnosis of brain death. *Cochrane Database of Systematic Reviews, 3*, CD009694.

te Nijenhuis, J., Jongeneel-Grimen, B., & Kirkegaard, E.O.W. (2014). Are Head Start gains on the g factor? A meta-analysis. *Intelligence, 46*, 209–215.

te Velde, S.J., & others (2012). Energy balance-related behaviors associated with overweight and obesity in preschool children: A systematic review of prospective studies. *Obesity Reviews, 13*(Suppl. 1), S56–S74.

Telzer, E.H., Fuligni, A.J., Lieberman, M.D., & Galvan, A. (2013). Meaningful family relationships: Neurocognitive buffers of adolescent risk taking. *Journal of Cognitive Neuroscience, 25*, 374–387.

Temple, C., Nathan, R., Temple, F., & Burris, N.A. (1993). *The beginnings of writing* (3rd ed.). Boston: Allyn & Bacon.

Temple, C.A., Nathan, R., & Temple, C. (2013) *Beginnings of writing* (4th ed.). Boston: Allyn & Bacon.

Templeton, J.L., & Eccles, J.S. (2006). The relation between spiritual development and identity processes. In E. Roehlkepartain, P.E. King, L. Wagener, & P.L. Benson (Eds.), *The handbook of spirituality in childhood and adolescence.* Thousand Oaks, CA: Sage.

Templeton, S., & Gehsmann, K. (2014). *Teaching reading and writing.* Upper Saddle River, NJ: Pearson.

Terman, L. (1925). *Genetic studies of genius. Vol. 1: Mental and physical traits of a thousand gifted children.* Stanford, CA: Stanford University Press.

Terry, D.F., Nolan, V.G., Andersen, S.L., Perls, T.T., & Cawthon, R. (2008). Association of longer telomeres with better health in centenarians. *Journals*

of Gerontology A: Biological Sciences and Medical Sciences, 63, 809–812.

Teti, D. (2001). Retrospect and prospect in the psychological study of sibling relationships. In J.P. McHale & W.S. Grolnick (Eds.), *Retrospect and prospect in the psychological study of families.* Mahwah, NJ: Erlbaum.

Teunissen, H.A., & others (2014). An experimental study of the effects of peer drinking norms on adolescents' drinker prototypes. *Addictive Behaviors, 39*, 85–93.

Thabet, A.A., Ibraheem, A.N., Shivram, R., Winter, E.A., & Vostanis, P. (2009). Parenting support and PTSD in children of a war zone. *International Journal of Social Psychiatry, 55*, 225–227.

Thapar, A., Collishaw, S., Pine, D.S., & Thapar, A.K. (2012). Depression in adolescence. *Lancet, 379*, 1056–1067.

Thelen, E. (2000). Perception and motor development. In A. Kazdin (Ed.), *Encyclopedia of psychology.* Washington, DC, & New York: American Psychological Association and Oxford University Press.

Thelen, E., & Smith, L.B. (2006). Dynamic development of action and thought. In W. Damon & R. Lerner (Eds.), *Handbook of child psychology* (6th ed.). New York: Wiley.

Thelen, E., & others (1993). The transition to reaching: Mapping intention and intrinsic dynamics. *Child Development, 64*, 1058–1098.

Theokas, C. (2009). Youth sports participation—A view of the issues: Introduction to the special section. *Developmental Psychology, 45*, 303–306.

Theunissen, M.H., Vogels, A.G., & Reijneveld, S.A. (2015). Punishment and reward in parental discipline for children aged 5 to 6 years: Prevalence and groups at risk. *Academic Pediatrics, 15*, 96–102.

Thio, A. (2010). *Deviant behavior* (10th ed.). Boston: Allyn & Bacon.

Thoma, S.J., & Bebeau, M. (2008). *Moral judgment competency is declining over time: Evidence from 20 years of defining issues test data.* Paper presented at the meeting of the American Educational Research meeting, New York, NY.

Thomas, A., & Chess, S. (1991). Temperament in adolescence and its functional significance. In R.M. Lerner, A.C. Petersen, & J. Brooks-Gunn (Eds.), *Encyclopedia of adolescence* (Vol. 2). New York: Garland.

Thomas, M.S.C., & Johnson, M.H. (2008). New advances in understanding sensitive periods in brain development. *Current Directions in Psychological Science, 17*, 1–5.

Thomas, S., & Kunzmann, U. (2014). Age differences in wisdom-related knowledge: Does the age relevance of the task matter? *Journals of Gerontology B: Psychological Sciences and Social Sciences, 69*, 897–905.

Thompson, A.E., & Voyer, D. (2014). Sex differences in the ability to recognize non-verbal displays of emotion: A meta-analysis. *Cognition and Emotion, 28*, 1164–1195.

Thompson, J., & Manore, M. (2015). *Nutrition* (4th ed.). Upper Saddle River, NJ: Pearson.

Thompson, M., Kuruwita, C., & Foster, E.M. (2009). Transitions in suicide risk in a nationally representative sample of adolescents. *Journal of Adolescent Health, 44*, 458–463.

Thompson, P.A., & others (2015, in press). Developmetal dyslexia: Predicting individual risk. *Journal of Child Psychology and Psychiatry.*

Thompson, R., & Murachver, T. (2001). Predicting gender from electronic discourse. *British Journal of Social Psychology, 40*, 193–201.

Thompson, R.A. (2006). The development of the person. In W. Damon & R. Lerner (Eds.), *Handbook of child psychology* (6th ed.). New York: Wiley.

Thompson, R.A. (2008). Unpublished review of J.W. Santrock's *Life-span development,* 12th ed. (New York: McGraw-Hill).

Thompson, R.A. (2009). Early foundations: Conscience and the development of moral character. In D. Narváez & D. Lapsley (Eds.), *Personality, identity, and character.* New York: Cambridge University Press.

Thompson, R.A. (2011). The emotionate child. In D. Cicchetti & G.I. Roisman (Eds.), The origins and organization of adaptation and maladaptation. *Minnesota Symposium on Child Psychology* (Vol. 36). New York: Wiley.

Thompson, R.A. (2012). Whither the preoperational child? Toward a life-span moral development theory. *Perspectives on Child Development, 6*, 423–429.

Thompson, R.A. (2014). Conscience development in early childhood. In M. Killen & J.G. Smetana (Eds.), *Handbook of moral development* (2nd ed.). New York: Guilford.

Thompson, R.A. (2014). Why are relationships important to children's well-being?. In A. Ben-Arieh, I. Frones, F. Cases, & J. Korbin (Eds.), *Handbook of child well-being.* New York: Springer.

Thompson, R.A. (2015). Relationships, regulation, and development. In R.M. Lerner (Ed.), *Handbook of child psychology and developmental science* (7th ed.). New York: Wiley.

Thompson, R.A. (2016, in press). Early attachment and later development: New questions. In J. Cassidy & P.R. Shaver (Eds.), *Handbook of attachment* (3rd ed.). New York: Guilford.

Thompson, R.A., & Goodvin, R. (2007). Taming the tempest in the teapot: Emotion regulation in toddlers. In C.A. Brownell & C.B. Kopp (Eds.), *Socioemotional development in toddlers.* New York: Guilford.

Thompson, R.A., McGinley, M., & Meyer, S. (2006). Understanding values in relationships. In M. Killen & J.G. Smetana (Eds.), *Handbook of moral development.* Mahwah, NJ: Erlbaum.

Thompson, R.A., & Newton, E.K. (2013). Baby altruists? Examining the complexity of prosocial motivation in young children. *Infancy, 18*, 120–133.

Thompson, R.A., Winer, A.C., & Goodvin, R. (2011). The individual child: Temperament, emotion, self, and personality. In M. Bornstein & M.E. Lamb (Eds.), *Developmental science: An advanced textbook* (6th ed.). New York: Psychology Press/Taylor & Francis.

Thornberg, R., & Jungert, T. (2014). School bullying and mechanisms of moral disengagement. *Aggressive Behavior, 40*, 99–108.

Thornton, R., & Light, L.L. (2006). Language comprehension and production in normal aging. In J.E. Birren & K.W. Schaie (Eds.), *Handbook of the psychology of aging* (6th ed.). San Diego: Academic Press.

Thornton, W.J.L., & Dumke, H.A. (2005). Age differences in everyday problem-solving and decision-making effectiveness: A meta-analytic review. *Psychology and Aging, 20*, 85–99.

Thorpe, R.J., Szanton, S.L., Bell, C.N., & Whitfield, K.E. (2013). Education, income, and disability in African Americans. *Ethnicity and Disease, 23*, 12–17.

Thorton, A., & Camburn, D. (1989). Religious participation and sexual behavior and attitudes. *Journal of Marriage and the Family, 49*, 117–128.

Tian, T., Zhang, B., Jia, Y., & Li, Z. (2014). Promise and challenge: The lens model as a biomarker for early diagnosis of Alzheimer's disease. *Disease Markers, 2014*, #826503.

Tikotzky, L., & Shaashua, L. (2012). Infant sleep and early parental sleep-related cognitions predict sleep in pre-school children. *Sleep Medicine, 13*, 185–192.

Tilton-Weaver, L.C., Burk, W.J., Kerr, M., & Stattin, H. (2013). Can parental monitoring and peer management reduce the selection or influence of delinquent peers? Testing the question using a dynamic social network approach. *Developmental Psychology, 49*, 2057–2070.

TIMMS (2008). *Trends in international mathematics and science study, 2007*. Washington, DC: National Center for Education Statistics.

Todd, A.S., & others (2015). Overweight and obese adolescent girls: The importance of promoting sensible eating and activity behaviors from the start of the adolescent period. *International Journal of Environmental Research and Public Health, 12*, 2306–2329.

Toepper, M., & others (2014). The impact of age on load-related dorsolateral prefrontal cortex. *Frontiers in Aging Neuoroscience, 6*, 9.

Tolani, N., & Brooks-Gunn, J. (2008). Family support, international trends. In M.M. Haith & J.B. Benson (Eds.), *Encyclopedia of infant and early childhood development*. Oxford, UK: Elsevier.

Tolman, D.L., & McClelland, S.I. (2011). Normative sexuality development in adolescence: A decade in review, 2000–2009. *Journal of Research on Adolescence, 21*, 242–255.

Tomasello, M. (2003). *Constructing a language: A usage-based theory of language acquisition*. Cambridge, MA: Harvard University Press.

Tomasello, M. (2006). Acquiring linguistic constructions. In W. Damon & R. Lerner (Eds.), *Handbook of child psychology* (6th ed.). New York: Wiley.

Tomasello, M. (2011). Language development. In U. Goswami (Ed.), *Wiley-Blackwell handbook of childhood cognitive development* (2nd ed.). New York: Wiley.

Tomasello, M. (2014). *A natural history of human thinking*. Cambridge, MA: Harvard University Press.

Tome-Carneiro, J., & others (2012). One-year consumption of a grape nutraceutical containing resveratrol improves the inflammatory and fibrinolytic status of patients in primary prevention of cardiovascular disease. *American Journal of Cardiology, 110*, 356–363.

Tomiyama, H., & others (2010). Continuous smoking and progression of arterial stiffening: A prospective study. *Journal of the American College of Cardiology, 55*, 1979–1987.

Tomlinson, E., Spector, A., Nurock, S., & Stott, J. (2015, in press). Euthanasia and physician-assisted suicide in dementia: A qualitative study of the views of former dementia carers. *Palliative Medicine*.

Tompkins, G.E. (2013). *Language arts* (8th ed.). Boston: Allyn & Bacon.

Tompkins, G.E. (2015). *Literacy in the early grades* (4th ed.). Upper Saddle River, NJ: Pearson.

Tong, X., Deacon, S.H., & Cain, K. (2014). Morphological and syntactic awareness in poor comprehenders: Another piece of the puzzle. *Journal of Learning Disabilities, 47*, 22–33.

Torres, J.M. (2013). Breast milk and labor support: Lactation consultants' and doulas' strategies for navigating the medical context of maternity care. *Sociology of Health and Illness, 35*, 924–938.

Totenhagen, C.J., Serido, J., Curran, M.A., & Butler, E.A. (2012). Daily hassles and uplifts: A diary study on understanding relationship quality. *Journal of Family Psychology, 26*(5), 719–728.

Trafimow, D., Triandis, H.C., & Goto, S.G. (1991). Some tests of the distinction between the prime and collective self. *Journal of Personality and Social Psychology, 60*, 649–655.

Trahan, L.H., Stuebing, K.K., Fletcher, J.M., & Hiscock, M. (2014). The Flynn effect: A meta-analysis. *Psychological Bulletin, 140*, 1332–1360.

Trainor, L.J., & He, C. (2013). Auditory and musical development. In P.D. Zelazo (Ed.), *Oxford handbook of developmental psychology*. New York: Oxford University Press.

Trehub, S.E., Schneider, B.A., Thorpe, L.A., & Judge, P. (1991). Observational measure of auditory sensitivity in early infancy. *Developmental Psychology, 27*, 40–49.

Tremblay, M.S., & others (2012). Canadian sedentary behavior guidelines for the early years (0–4 years). *Applied Physiology, Nutrition, and Metabolism, 37*, 370–380.

Triandis, H.C. (1994). *Culture and social behavior*. New York: McGraw-Hill.

Triandis, H.C. (2001). Individualism and collectivism. In D. Matsumoto (Eds.), *The handbook of culture and psychology*. New York: Oxford University Press.

Triandis, H.C. (2007). Culture and psychology: A history of their relationship. In S. Kitayama & D. Cohen (Eds.), *Handbook of cultural psychology*. New York: Guilford.

Trimble, J.E. (1988, August). *The enculturation of contemporary psychology*. Paper presented at the meeting of the American Psychological Association, New Orleans.

Trochim, W., Donnelly, J.P., & Arora, K. (2016, in press). *Research methods: The essential knowledge base* (2nd ed.). Boston: Cengage.

Troop-Gordon, W., & Ladd, G.W. (2015). Teachers' victimization-related beliefs and strategies: Associations with students' aggressive behavior and peer victimization. *Journal of Abnormal Child Psychology, 43*, 45–60.

Trucco, E.M., & others (2014). Early adolescent alcohol use in context: How neighborhoods, parents, and peers impact youth. *Development and Psychopathology, 26*, 425–436.

Trzaskowski, M., Yang, J., Visscher, P.M., & Plomin, R. (2014). DNA evidence for strong genetic stability and increasing heritability of intelligence from age 7 to 12. *Molecular Psychiatry, 19*, 380–384.

Trzesniewski, K.H., & others (2006). Low self-esteem during adolescence predicts poor health, criminal behavior, and limited economic prospects during adulthood. *Developmental Psychology, 42*, 381–390.

Trzesniewski, M., Donnellan, M.B., & Robins, R.W. (2013). Development of self-esteem. In V. Zeigler-Hill (Ed.), *Self-esteem*. New York: Psychology Press.

Tsang, A., & others (2008). Common persistent pain conditions in developed and developing countries: Gender and age differences and comorbidity with depression-anxiety disorders. *Journal of Pain, 9*, 883–891.

Tselepis, A.D. (2014). Cilostazol-based triple antiplatelet therapy in the era of generic clopidogrel and new potent antiplatelet agents. *Current Medical and Research Opinion, 30*, 51–54.

Tsitsika, A.K., & others (2014). Bullying behaviors in children and adolescents: "An ongoing story." *Frontiers in Public Health, 2*, 7.

Ttofi, M.M., Farrington, D.P., Losel, F., & Loeber, R. (2011). The predictive efficiency of school bullying versus later offending: A systematic/meta-analytic review of longitudinal studies. *Criminal Behavior and Mental Health, 21*, 80–89.

Tucker, C.J., McHale, S.M., & Crouter, A.C. (2003). Conflict resolution: Links with adolescents' family relationships and individual well-being. *Journal of Family Issues, 24*, 715–726.

Tucker, J.S., Ellickson, P.L., & Klein, M.S. (2003). Predictors of the transition to regular smoking during adolescence and young adulthood. *Journal of Adolescent Health, 32*, 314–324.

Tun, P.A., & Lachman, M.E. (2010). The association between computer use and cognition across adulthood: Use it so you won't lose it? *Psychology and Aging, 25*(3), 560–568.

Turchik, J.A., & Hassija, C.M. (2014). Female sexual victimization among college students: Assault severity, health risk behaviors, and sexual functioning. *Journal of Interpersonal Violence, 29*, 2439–2457.

Turiel, E. (2014). Morality: Epistemology, development, and social opposition. In M. Killen & J.G. Smetana (Eds.), *Handbook of moral development* (2nd ed.). New York: Psychology Press.

Turiel, E. (2015). Moral development. In R.M. Lerner (Ed.), *Handbook of child psychology and developmental science* (7th ed.). New York: Wiley.

Turnbull, A., & others (2016, in press). *Exceptional lives* (8th ed.). Upper Saddle River, NJ: Pearson.

Turner, B.F. (1982). Sex-related differences in aging. In B.B. Wolman (Ed.), *Handbook of developmental psychology*. Englewood Cliffs, NJ: Prentice Hall.

Tutone, M., Pantano, L., Lauria, A., & Almerico, A.M. (2014). Molecular dynamics, dynamic site mapping, and highthroughput virtual screening on leptin and the Ob receptor as anti-obesity target. *Journal of Molecular Medicine, 20*, 2247.

Tyas, S.L., & others (2007). Transitions to mild cognitive impairments, dementia, and death: Findings from the Nun Study. *American Journal of Epidemiology, 165*, 1231–1238.

Tzourio, C., Laurent, S., & Debette, S. (2014). Is hypertension associated with an accelerated aging in the brain? *Hypertension, 63*, 894–903.

U

U.S. Census Bureau (2008). *People*. Washington, DC: U.S. Department of Labor.

U.S. Census Bureau (2011). *People*. Washington, DC: U.S. Department of Labor.

U.S. Census Bureau (2011, March 23). Older Americans Month: May 2011. *U.S. Census Bureau News*. Washington, DC: U.S. Department of Commerce.

U.S. Census Bureau (2012). *Death statistics*. Washington, DC: Author.

U.S. Census Bureau (2012). *Families and living arrangements 2012*. Washington, DC: U.S. Department of Labor.

U.S. Census Bureau (2012). *Profile American: Facts for features. Father's Day, June 17, 2012*. Washington, DC: Author.

U.S. Census Bureau (2013). *Marriages, births, and deaths*. Washington, DC: U.S. Department of Labor.

U.S. Census Bureau (2013). *Poverty*. Washington, DC: Author.

U.S. Census Bureau (2014). *Marriages*. Washington, DC: U.S. Department of Labor.

U.S. Census Bureau (2014). *People*. Washington, DC: U.S. Department of Labor.

U.S. Census Bureau (2015). *Death statistics*. Washington, DC: Author.

U.S. Department of Energy (2001). *The human genome project*. Washington, DC: U.S. Department of Energy.

U.S. Department of Health and Human Services (2010). *Child maltreatment 2009*. Washington, DC: Author.

Uchino, B.N., & others (2012). Social relationships and health: Is feeling positive, negative, or both (ambivalent) about your social ties related to telomeres? *Health Psychology, 31*(6), 789–796.

Udry, J.R., & others (1985), Serum androgenic hormones motivate sexual behavior in adolescent boys. *Fertility and Sterility, 43,* 90–94.

Ueno, K., & McWilliams, S. (2010). Gender-typed behaviors and school adjustment. *Sex Roles, 63,* 580–591.

Ulbricht, J.A., & others (2013). Marital adjustment as a moderator for genetic and environmental influences on parenting. *Journal of Family Psychology, 27,* 42–52.

Ullah, M.I., Riche, D.M., & Koch, C.A. (2014). Transdermal testosterone replacement therapy in men. *Drug Design, Development, and Therapy, 8,* 101–112.

Umana-Taylor, A.J., & others (2014). Ethnic and racial identity in adolescence and into young adulthood: An integrated conceptualization. *Child Development, 85,* 21–39.

Umana-Taylor, A.J., & others (2014). Ethnic and racial identity revisited: An integrated conceptualization. *Child Development, 85,* 40–57.

Umemura, T., & Jacobvitz, D.B. (2014). Nonmaternal care hours and temperament predict proximity-seeking behavior and attachment subgroups. *Infant Behavior and Development, 37,* 352–365.

UNAIDS (2011). *AIDS at 30: Nations at a crossroads.* Geneva, Switzerland: United Nations.

Underhill, K., Montgomery, P., & Operario, D. (2007). Sexual abstinence programs to prevent HIV infection in high-income countries. *British Medical Journal, 335,* 248.

Underwood, M.K., & others (2012). The BlackBerry project: Capturing the content of adolescents' text messaging. *Developmental Psychology, 48,* 295–302.

Undheim, A.M. (2013). Involvement in bullying as predictor of suicidal ideation among 12- to 15-year-old Norwegian adolescents. *European Child and Adolescent Psychiatry, 22*(6), 357–365.

Ungar, M. (2015). Practitioner review: Diagnosing childhood resilience—a systematic approach to the diagnosis of adaptation in adverse social and physical ecologies. *Journal of Child Psychology and Psychiatry, 56,* 4–17.

UNICEF (2006). *The state of the world's children: 2006.* Geneva, Switzerland: Author.

UNICEF (2007). *The state of the world's children: 2007.* Geneva, Switzerland: Author.

UNICEF (2013). *The state of the world's children: 2013.* Geneva, Switzerland: Author.

UNICEF (2014). *The state of the world's children: 2014.* Geneva, Switzerland: Author.

UNICEF (2015). *The state of the world's children: 2014.* Geneva, Switzerland: Author.

UNSTAT (2011). *Marriages and crude marriage rates.* Retrieved September 4, 2013, from http://unstats.un.org/unsd/demographic/products/dyb/dyb2011/Table 23.pdf

Updegraff, K.A., Umana-Taylor, A.J., McHale, S.M., Wheeler, L.A., & Perez-Brena, J. (2012). Mexican-origin youths' cultural orientations and adjustment: Changes from early to late adolescence. *Child Development, 83,* 1655–1671.

Urbanos-Garrido, R.M., & Lopez-Valcárcel, B.G. (2015). The influence of the economic crisis on the association between unemployment and health: An empirical analysis for Spain. *European Journal of Health Economics, 16*(2), 175–184.

Urdan, T. (2012). Factors affecting the motivation and achievement of immigrant students. In K.R. Harris, S. Graham, & T. Urdan (Eds.), *APA educational psychology handbook.* Washington, DC: American Psychological Association.

Ursache, A., Blair, C., & Raver, C.C. (2012). The promotion of self-regulation as a means of enhancing school readiness and early achievement in children at risk for school failure. *Child Development Perspectives, 6,* 122–128.

Ursache, A., Blair, C., Stifter, C., & Voegtline, K. (2013). Emotional reactivity and regulation in infancy interact to predict executive functioning in early childhood. *Developmental Psychology, 49*(1), 127–137.

Utz, R.L., & others (2014). Feeling lonely versus being alone: Loneliness and social support among recently bereaved persons. *Journals of Gerontology B: Psychological Sciences and Social Sciences, 69,* 85–94.

V

Vacca, J.A., & others (2012). *Reading and learning to read* (8th ed.). Boston: Allyn & Bacon.

Vahia, I.V., & others (2011). Correlates of spirituality in older women. *Aging and Mental Health, 15*(1), 97–102.

Vaillant, G.E. (1977). *Adaptation to life.* Boston: Little Brown.

Vaillant, G.E. (2002). *Aging well.* Boston: Little Brown.

Vaish, A., Carpenter, M., & Tomasello, M. (2010). Young children selectively avoid helping people with harmful intentions. *Child Development, 81,* 1661–1669.

Valcarcel-Ares, M.N., & others (2014). Mitochondrial dysfunction promotes and aggravates the inflammatory response in normal human synoviocytes. *Rheumatology, 53,* 1332–1343.

Valentino, K., & others (2014). Mother-child reminiscing and autobiographical memory specificity among preschool-age children. *Developmental Psychology, 50,* 1197–1207.

Valenza, E., Franchin, L., & Bulf, H. (2014). How a face may affect object-based attention: Evidence from 8-month-old infants. *Frontiers in Integrative Neuroscience, 8,* 27.

Valenzuela, C.F., Morton, R.A., Diaz, M.R., & Topper, L. (2012). Does moderate drinking harm the fetal brain? Insights from animal models. *Trends in Neuroscience, 35,* 284–292.

Valero, S., & others (2014). Neuroticism and impulsivity: Their hierarchical organization in the personality characterization of drug-dependent patients from a decision tree learning perspective. *Comprehensive Psychiatry, 55,* 1227–1233.

Valkanova, V., & Ebmeier, K.P. (2014). Neuroimaging in dementia. *Maturitas, 79,* 202–208.

van Alphen, J.E., Donker, G.A., & Marquet, R.L. (2010). Requests for euthanasia in general practice before and after implementation of the Dutch Euthanasia Act. *British Journal of General Practice, 60,* 263–267.

Van Assche, L., & others (2013). Attachment in old age: Theoretical assumptions, empirical findings, and implications for clinical practice. *Clinical Psychology Review, 33*(1), 67–81.

Van Beveren, T.T. (2011, March). Personal conversation. Richardson, TX: Department of Psychology, University of Texas at Dallas.

van de Weijer-Bergsma, E., Formsma, A.R., de Bruin, E.I., & Bogels, S.M. (2012). The effectiveness of mindfulness training on behavioral problems and attentional functioning in adolescents with ADHD. *Journal of Child and Family Studies, 21,* 775–787.

van den Boom, D.C. (1989). Neonatal irritability and the development of attachment. In G.A. Kohnstamm, J.E. Bates, & M.K. Rothbart (Eds.), *Temperament in childhood.* New York: Wiley.

van der Stel, M., & Veenman, M.V.J. (2010). Development of metacognitive skillfulness: A longitudinal study. *Learning and Individual Differences, 20,* 220–224.

Van Eeden-Moorefield, B., & Pasley, B.K. (2013). Remarriage and stepfamily life. In G.W. Peterson & K.R. Bush (Eds.), *Handbook of marriage and the family* (3rd ed.). New York: Springer.

van Geel, M., Vedder, P., & Tanilon, J. (2014). Relationship between peer victimization, cyberbullying, and suicide in children and adolescents: A meta-analysis. *JAMA Pediatrics, 168,* 435–442.

van Goethem, A.A.J., & others (2012). The role of adolescents' morality and identity in volunteering: Age and gender differences in the process model. *Journal of Adolescence, 35,* 509–520.

Van Hecke, V., & others (2012). Infant responding to joint attention, executive processes, and self-regulation in preschool children. *Infant Development and Behavior, 35,* 303–311.

Van Hedel, K., & others (2015, in press). Marital status, labor force activity, and mortality: A study in the USA and six European countries. *Scandinavian Journal of Public Health.*

van Hooft, E.A. (2014). Motivating and hindering factors during the reemployment process: The added value of employment counselors' assessment. *Journal of Occupational Health Psychology, 19,* 1–17.

Van Hoorn, J.V., Nourot, P.M., Scales, B., & Alward, K.R. (2015). *Play at the center of the curriculum* (6th ed.). Upper Saddle River, NJ: Pearson.

Van Horn, M.L., Fagan, A.A., Hawkins, J.D., & Oesterle, S. (2014). Effects of the communities that care system on cross-sectional profiles of adolescence substance abuse and delinquency. *American Journal of Preventive Medicine, 47,*188–197.

van IJzendoorn, M.H., Kranenburg, M.J., Pannebakker, F., & Out, D. (2010). In defense of situational morality: Genetic, dispositional, and situational determinants of children's donating to charity. *Journal of Moral Education, 39,* 1–20.

van IJzendoorn, M.H., & Kroonenberg, P.M. (1988). Cross-cultural patterns of attachment: A meta-analysis of the Strange Situation. *Child Development, 59,* 147–156.

van IJzendoorn, M.H., & Sagi-Schwartz, A. (2008). Cross-cultural patterns of attachment: Universal and contextual dimensions. In J. Cassidy & P.R. Shaver (Eds.), *Handbook of attachment* (2nd ed.). New York: Guilford.

van Kesteren, M.T., & others (2014). Building on prior knowledge: Schema-dependent encoding processes relate to academic performance. *Journal of Cognitive Neuroscience, 26,* 2250–2261.

van Rijn, L.J., & others (2011). Prevalence of impairment of visual function in European drivers. *Acta Ophthalmologica, 89,* 124–131.

Van Ryzin, M.J., Carlson, E.A., & Sroufe, L.A. (2011). Attachment discontinuity in a high-risk sample. *Attachment and Human Development, 13,* 381–401.

Van Ryzin, M.J., & Dishion, T.J. (2012). The impact of a family-centered intervention on the ecology of adolescent antisocial behavior: Modeling developmental sequelae and trajectories during adolescence. *Development and Psychopathology, 24*(3), 1139–1155.

Van Ryzin, M.J., Johnson, A.B., Leve, L.D., & Kim, H.K. (2011). The number of sexual partners and health-risking sexual behavior: Prediction from high school entry to high school exit. *Archives of Sexual Behavior, 40*(5), 939–949.

Van Solinge, H., & Henkens, K. (2005). Couples' adjustment to retirement: A multi-actor panel study.

Journals of Gerontology B: Psychological Sciences and Social Sciences, 60, S11–S20.

Van Voorhees, B.W., & others (2008). Protective and vulnerability factors predicting new-onset depressive episode in a representative sample of U.S. adolescents. *Journal of Adolescent Health, 42,* 605–616.

Van Wesemael, Y., & others (2011). Process and outcomes of euthanasia requests under the Belgian Act on Euthanasia: A nationwide survey. *Journal of Pain and Symptom Management, 42,* 721–733.

Vandehey, M., Diekhoff, G., & LaBeff, E. (2007). College cheating: A 20-year follow-up and the addition of an honor code. *Journal of College Development, 48,* 468–480.

Vandell, D.L., & others (2010). Do effects of early childcare extend to age 15 years? From the NICHD Study of Early Child Care and Youth Development. *Child Development, 81,* 737–756.

Vandell, D.L., & others (2015). Children's organized activities. In R.M. Lerner (Ed.), *Handbook of child psychology and developmental science* (7th ed.). New York: Wiley.

Varner, M.W., & others (2014). Association between stillbirth and illicit drug use and smoking during pregnancy. *Obstetrics and Gynecology, 123,* 113–125.

Vasan, N. (2002). Commentary in "18-year-old inductees." Retrieved April 4, 2009, from http://thekidshalloffame.com/CustomPage19.html

Vasilenko, S.A., Kreager, D.A., & Lefkowitz, E.S. (2015). Gender, contraceptive attitudes, and condom use in adolescent romantic relationships: A dyadic approach. *Journal of Research on Adolescence, 25,* 51–62.

Vaughn, B.E., Elmore-Staton, L., Shin, N., & el-Sheikh, M. (2015, in press). Sleep as a support for social competence, peer relations, and cognitive functioning in preschool children. *Behavioral Sleep Medicine.*

Vaughn, S.R., & Bos, C.S. (2015). *Strategies for teaching students with learning and behavior problems* (9th ed.). Upper Saddle River, NJ: Pearson.

Vaughn, S.R., Bos, C.S., & Schumm, J.S. (2014). *Teaching students who are exceptional, diverse, and at risk in the general education classroom* (6th ed.). Upper Saddle River, NJ: Pearson.

Vazsonyi, A.T., & Huang, L. (2010). Where self-control comes from: On the development of self-control and its relationship to deviance over time. *Developmental Psychology, 46,* 245–257.

Veatch, R.M. (2015, in press). Killing by organ procurement: Brain-based death and legal fictions. *Journal of Medicine and Philosophy.*

Veenman, M.V.J. (2011). Learning to self-monitor and self-regulate. In P.A. Alexander & R.E. Mayer (Eds.), *Handbook of research on learning and instruction.* New York: Routledge.

Vela, R.M. (2014). The effect of severe stress on brain development, attachment, and emotions: A psychoanatomical formulation. *Psychiatric Clinics of North America, 37,* 519–534.

Velayudhan, L., & others (2014). Review of brief cognitive tests for patients with suspected dementia. *International Psychogeriatrics, 26,* 1247–1262.

Velez, C.E., Wolchik, S.A., Tein, J.Y., & Sandler, I. (2011). Protecting children from the consequences of divorce: A longitudinal study of the effects of parenting on children's coping responses. *Child Development, 82,* 244–257.

Vella, S.A., Cliff, D.P., Magee, C.A., & Okely, A.D. (2014). Sports participation and parent-reported health-related quality of life in children: Longitudinal associations. *Journal of Pediatrics, 164,* 1469–1474.

Venditti, P., Di Stefano, L., & Di Meo, S. (2013). Mitochondrial metabolism of reactive oxygen species. *Mitochondrion, 13*(2), 71–82.

Veness, C., Prior, M., Eadie, P., Bavin, E., & Reilly, S. (2014). Predicting autism diagnosis by 7 years of age using parent report of infant social communication skills. *Journal of Pediatrics and Child Health, 50,* 693–700.

Venners, S.A., & others (2004). Paternal smoking and pregnancy loss: A prospective study using a biomarker of pregnancy. *American Journal of Epidemiology, 159,* 993–1001.

Verhaeghen, P. (2013). *The elements of cognitive aging: Meta-analyses of age-related differences in processing speed and their consequences.* New York: Oxford University Press.

Verhoef, M., van den Eijnden, R.J., Koning, I.M., & Vollebergh, W.A. (2014). Age at menarche and adolescent alcohol use. *Journal of Youth and Adolelscence, 43*(8), 1333–1345.

Verly, M., & others (2014). Altered functional connectivity of the language network in ASD: Role of classical language areas and cerebellum. *Neuroimage Clinical, 4,* 374–382.

Verma, V., & others (2015, in press). Designed modulation of sex steroid signaling inhibits telomerase activity and proliferation of human prostate cancer cells. *Toxicology and Applied Pharmacology.*

Veronneau, M.H., Racer, K.H., Fosco, G.M., & Dishion, T.J. (2014). The contribution of adolescent effortful control to early adult educational attainment. *Journal of Educational Psychology, 106,* 730–743.

Vesco, K.K., & others (2012). Healthy Moms, a randomized trial to promote and evaluate weight maintenance among obese pregnant women: Study design and rationale. *Contemporary Clinical Trials, 33*(4), 777–785.

Vespa, J. (2012). Union formation in later life: Economic determinants of cohabitation and remarriage in later life. *Demography, 49,* 1103–1125.

Vest, A.E., & Simpkins, S.D. (2013). When is sport participation risky or protective for alcohol use? The role of teammates, friendships, and popularity. *New Directions in Child and Adolescent Development, 140,* 37–55.

Vetter, N.C., & others (2013). Ongoing development of social cognition in adolescence. *Child Neuropsychology, 19,* 615–629.

Vigorito, C., & Giallauria, F. (2014). Effects of exercise on cardiovascular performance in the elderly. *Frontiers in Physiology, 5,* 51.

Vihman, M.M. (2014). *Phonological development* (2nd ed.). New York: Wiley.

Villanueva, C.M., & Buriel, R. (2010). Speaking on behalf of others: A qualitative study of the perceptions and feelings of adolescent Latina language brokers. *Journal of Social Issues, 66,* 197–210.

Villaverde, C., & others (2012). Influence of exercise on mood in postmenopausal women. *Journal of Clinical Nursing, 21,* 923–928.

Villegas, R., & others (2008). Duration of breast-feeding and the incidence of type 2 diabetes mellitus in the Shanghai Women's Health Study. *Diabetologia, 51,* 258–266.

Villodas, M.T., Litrownik, A.J., Newton, R.R., & Davis, I.P. (2015, in press). Long-term placement trajectories of children who were maltreated and entered the child welfare system at an early age: Consequences for physical and behavioral well-being. *Journal of Pediatric Psychology.*

Vinters, H.V. (2015). Emerging concepts in Alzheimer disease. *Annual Review of Pathology: Mechanisms of Disease* (Vol. 10). Palo Alto, CA: Annual Reviews.

Virta, J.J., & others (2013). Midlife cardiovascular risk factors and late cognitive development. *European Journal of Epidemiology, 28,* 405–416.

Visher, E., & Visher, J. (1989). Parenting coalitions after remarriage: Dynamics and therapeutic guidelines. *Family Relations, 38,* 65–70.

Vitaro, F., Pedersen, S., & Brendgen, M. (2007). Children's disruptiveness, peer rejection, friends' deviancy, and delinquent behaviors: A process-oriented approach. *Development and Psychopathology, 19,* 433–453.

Vittrup, B., Holden, G.W., & Buck, M. (2006). Attitudes predict the use of physical punishment: A prospective study of the emergence of disciplinary practices. *Pediatrics, 117,* 2055–2064.

Vlatkovic, I.B., & others (2014). Prenatal diagnosis of sex chromosome aneuploidies and disorders of sex development—a retrospective analysis of 11-year data. *Journal of Perinatal Medicine, 42,* 529–534.

Vo, V.A., Li, R., Kornell, N., Pouget, A., & Cantlon, J.F. (2014). Young children bet on their numerical skills: Metacognition in the numerical domain. *Psychological Science, 25,* 1712–1721.

Volbrecht, M.M., & Goldsmith, H.H. (2010). Early temperamental and family predictors of shyness and anxiety. *Developmental Psychology, 46,* 1192–1205.

Volkmar, F.R., Riechow, B., Westphal, A., & Mandell, D.S. (2014). Autism and autism spectrum diagnostic concepts. In F.R. Volkmar & others (Eds.), *Handbook of autism and pervasive developmental disorders.* New York: Wiley.

Volpe, E.M., & others (2013). What's age got to do with it? Partner age difference, power, intimate partner violence, and sexual risk in urban adolescents. *Journal of Interpersonal Violence, 28,* 2068–2087.

von Bonsdorff, M.B., & others (2011). Work ability in midlife as a predictor of mortality and disability in later life: A 28-year prospective follow-up study. *Canadian Medical Association Journal, 183,* E235–E242.

von Bonsdorff, M.B., & others (2012). Work ability as a determinant of old age disability severity: Evidence from the 28-year Finnish longitudinal study on municipal employees. *Aging: Clinical and Experimental Research, 24,* 354–360.

von Ganzewinkel, C.J., Anand, K.J., Kramer, B.W., & Andrriessen, P. (2014). Chronic pain in the newborn: Toward a definition. *Clinical Journal of Pain, 30,* 970–977.

Voorpostel, M., & Blieszner, R. (2008). Intergenerational solidarity and support between adult siblings. *Journal of Marriage and the Family, 70,* 157–167.

Vorona, R.D., & others (2014). Adolescent crash rates and school start times in two central Virginia counties, 2009–2011: A follow-up study to a southeastern Virginia study, 2007–2008. *Journal of Clinical Sleep Medicine, 10,* 1169–1177.

Vos, S.J., & others (2015, in press). Prevalence and prognosis of Alzheimer's disease at the mild cognitive impairment stage. *Brain.*

Voss, M.W., & others (2013). Neurobiological markers of exercise-related brain plasticity in older adults. *Brain, Behavior, and Immunity, 28,* 90–99.

Votavova, H., & others (2012). Deregulation of gene expression induced by environmental tobacco smoke exposure in pregnancy. *Nicotine and Tobacco Research, 14*(9), 1073–1082.

Vrangalova, Z. (2015a, in press). Does casual sex harm college students' well-being? A longitudinal investigation of the role of motivation. *Archives of Sexual Behavior.*

Vrangalova, Z. (2015b, in press). Hooking up and psychological well-being in college students: Short-term prospective links across different hookup definitions. *Journal of Sex Research.*

Vrantsidis, F., & others (2014). Living Longer Living Stronger: A community-delivered strength training program improving function and quality of life. *Australasian Journal on Aging, 33,* 22–25.

Vreeman, R.C., & Carroll, A.E. (2007). A systematic review of school-based interventions to prevent bullying. *Archives of Pediatric and Adolescent Medicine, 161,* 78–88.

Vukelich, C., Christie, J.F., & Enz, B.J. (2012). *Helping children learn language and literacy* (3rd ed.). Boston: Allyn & Bacon.

Vurpillot, E. (1968). The development of scanning strategies and their relation to visual differentiation. *Journal of Experimental Child Psychology, 6,* 632–650.

Vygotsky, L.S. (1962). *Thought and language.* Cambridge, MA: MIT Press.

W

Waasdorp, T.E., & Bradshaw, C.P. (2015, in press). The overlap between cyberbullying and traditional bullying. *Journal of Adolescent Health.*

Wachs, T.D. (2000). *Necessary but not sufficient.* Washington, DC: American Psychological Association.

Wachs, T.D., & Bates, J.E. (2011). Temperament. In J.G. Bremner & T.D. Wachs (Eds.), *Wiley-Blackwell handbook of infant development* (2nd ed.). New York: Wiley.

Wai, J., Putallaz, M., & Makel, M.C. (2012). Studying intellectual outliers: Are there sex differences and are the smart getting smarter? *Current Directions in Psychological Science, 21,* 382–390.

Wainryb, C., & Recchia, H. (2014). Moral lives across cultures: Heterogeneity and conflict. In M. Killen & J.G. Smetana (Eds.), *Handbook of moral development* (2nd ed.). New York: Psychology Press.

Waite, L.J. (2009). Marriage. In D. Carr (Ed.), *Encyclopedia of the life course and human development.* Boston: Gale Cengage.

Waiter, G.D., & others (2009). Exploring possible neural mechanisms of intelligence differences using processing speed and working memory tasks. *Intelligence, 37,* 199–206.

Waldenstrom, U., & others (2014). Adverse pregnancy outcomes related to advanced maternal age compared with smoking and being overweight. *Obstetrics and Gynecology, 123,* 104–112.

Waldinger, R.J., & Schulz, M.C. (2010). What's love got to do with it? Social functioning, perceived health, and daily happiness in married octogenarians. *Psychology and Aging, 25,* 422–431.

Walfield, S.M. (2015, in press). When a cleared rape is not cleared: A multilevel study of arrest and exceptional clearance. *Journal of Interpersonal Violence.*

Walker, L.J. (1982). The sequentiality of Kohlberg's stages of moral development. *Child Development, 53,* 1130–1136.

Walker, L.J. (2002). Moral exemplarity. In W. Damon (Ed.), *Bringing in a new era of character education.* Stanford, CA: Hoover Press.

Walker, L.J. (2004). Progress and prospects in the psychology of moral development. *Merrill-Palmer Quarterly, 50,* 546–557.

Walker, L.J. (2006). Gender and morality. In M. Killen & J.G. Smetana (Eds.), *Handbook of moral development.* Mahwah, NJ: Erlbaum.

Walker, L.J. (2013). Exemplars' moral behavior is self-regarding. *New Directions in Child and Adolescent Development, 142,* 27–40.

Walker, L.J. (2014). Moral personality, motivation, and identity. In M. Killen & J.G. Smetana (Eds.), *Handbook of moral development* (2nd ed.). New York: Psychology Press.

Walker, L.J., Frimer, J.A., & Dunlop, W.L. (2011). Varieties of moral personality: Beyond the banality of heroism. *Journal of Personality, 78*(3), 907–942.

Walle, E.A., & Campos, J.J. (2014). Infant language development is related to the acquisition of walking. *Developmental Psychology, 50,* 336–348.

Wallenborg, K., & others (2009). Red wine triggers cell death and thiroredoxin reductase inhibition: Effects beyond resveratrol and SIRT 1. *Experimental Cell Research, 315*(8), 1360–1371.

Waller, E.M., & Rose, A.J. (2013). Brief report: Adolescents' co-rumination with mothers, co-rumination with friends, and internalizing symptoms. *Journal of Adolescence, 36,* 429–433.

Wallerstein, J.S. (2008). Divorce. In M.M. Haith & J.B. Benson (Eds.), *Encyclopedia of infant and early childhood development.* Oxford, UK: Elsevier.

Walsh, L.A. (2000, Spring). The inside scoop on child development: Interview. *Cutting through the hype.* Minneapolis: College of Education and Human Development, University of Minnesota.

Walsh, P., & others (2014). Using a pacifier to decrease sudden infant death syndrome: An emergency department educational intervention. *PeerJ, 2,* e309.

Walsh, R. (2011). Lifestyle and mental health. *American Psychologist, 66,* 79–92.

Walton, K.E., & Roberts, B.W. (2004). On the relationship between substance abuse and personality traits: Abstainers are not maladjusted. *Journal of Research in Personality, 38,* 515–535.

Wandell, P.E., Carlsson, A.C., & Theobald, H. (2009). The association between BMI value and long-term mortality. *International Journal of Obesity, 33,* 577–582.

Wang, B., & Jin, K. (2015). Current perspectives on the link between neuroinflammation and neurogenesis. *Metabolic Brain Disease, 30*(2), 355–365.

Wang, B., & others (2014). The impact of youth, family, peer, and neighborhood risk factors on developmental trajectories of risk involvement from early through middle adolescence. *Social Science Medicine, 106,* 43–52.

Wang, H.M., Chen, T.C., Jiang, S.Q., Liu, Y.J., & Tian, J.W. (2015). Association of conventional risk factors for cardiovascular disease with IMT in middle-aged and elderly Chinese. *International Journal of Cardiovascular Imaging, 30,* 759–768.

Wang, M. (2012). Retirement: An adult development perspective. In S.K. Whitbourne & M.J. Sliwinski (Eds.), *Wiley-Blackwell handbook of adult development and aging.* New York: Wiley.

Wang, M., & Shi, J. (2014). Psychological research on retirement. *Annual Review of Psychology* (Vol. 65). Palo Alto, CA: Annual Reviews.

Wang, Q., & Pomerantz, E.M. (2009). The motivational landscape of early adolescence in the United States and China: A longitudinal study. *Child Development, 80,* 1272–1287.

Wang, S.W., & Repetti, R.L. (2014). Psychological well-being and job stress predict marital support interactions: A naturalistic observational study of dual-earner couples in their homes. *Journal of Personality and Social Psychology, 107,* 864–878.

Ward, E.V., Berry, C.J., & Shanks, D.R. (2013). Age effects on explicit and implicit memory. *Frontiers in Psychology, 4,* 639.

Ward, M.C., & Edelstein, M.D. (2014). *World full of women* (6th ed.). Upper Saddle River, NJ: Pearson.

Ward, W.F., & others (2005). Effects of age and caloric restriction on lipid peroxidation: Measurement of oxidative stress by F2-isoprostane levels. *Journals of Gerontology A: Biological Sciences and Medical Sciences, 60,* 847–851.

Wardlaw, G.M., Smith, A.M., & Collene, A.L. (2015). *Contemporary nutrition* (4th ed.). New York: McGraw-Hill.

Ware, J.E., Kosinski, M., & Dewey, J.E. (2000). *How to score Version 2 of the SF-36 Health Survey.* Boston: Quality Metric.

Wariki, W.M., & others (2013). Risk factors associated with outcomes of very low birthweight infants in four Asian countries. *Journal of Pediatrics and Child Health, 49,* E23–E27.

Warneken, F., & Tomasello, M. (2006). Altruistic helping in human infants and young chimpanzees. *Science, 311,* 1301–1303.

Warr, P. (1994). Age and employment. In M. Dunnette, L. Hough, & H. Triandis (Eds.), *Handbook of industrial and organizational psychology* (Vol. 4). Palo Alto, CA: Consulting Psychologists Press.

Warrier, V., Baron-Cohen, S., & Chakrabarti, B. (2013). Genetic variation in GABRB3 is associated with Asperger syndrome and multiple endophenotypes relevant to autism. *Molecular Autism, 4,* 48.

Warshak, R.A. (2008, January). Personal communication. Department of Psychology, University of Texas at Dallas, Richardson.

Warshak, R.A. (2014). Social science and parenting plans for young children: A consensus report. *Psychology, Public Policy, and the Law, 20,* 46–67.

Waszczuk, M.A., & others (2015, in press). A multivariate twin study of trait mindfulness, depressive symptoms, and anxiety sensitivity. *Depression and Anxiety.*

Watamura, S.E., Phillips, D.A., Morrissey, D.A., McCartney, T.W., & Bub, K. (2011). Double jeopardy: Poorer social-emotional outcomes for children in the NICHD SECCYD who experience home and child-care environments that convey risk. *Child Development, 82,* 48–65.

Waterman, A.S. (1985). Identity in the context of adolescent psychology. In A.S. Waterman (Ed.), *Identity in adolescence: Processes and contents.* San Francisco: Jossey-Bass.

Waterman, A.S. (1992). Identity as an aspect of optimal psychological functioning. In G.R. Adams, T.P. Gulotta, & R. Montemayor (Eds.), *Adolescent identity formation.* Newbury Park, CA: Sage.

Waters, S.F., West, T.V., & Mendes, W.B. (2014). Stress contagion: Physiological covariation between mothers and infants. *Psychological Science, 25,* 934–942.

Watson, G.L., Arcona, A.P., Antonuccio, D.O., & Healy, D. (2014). Shooting the messenger: The case of ADHD. *Journal of Contemporary Psychotherapy, 44,* 43–52.

Watson, J.A., Randolph, S.M., & Lyons, J.L. (2005). African-American grandmothers as health educators in the family. *International Journal of Aging and Human Development, 60,* 343–356.

Watson, J.B. (1928). *Psychological care of infant and child.* New York: Norton.

Watt, H.M.G., & Eccles, J.S. (Eds.). (2008). *Gender and occupational outcomes.* Washington, DC: American Psychological Association.

Watts, C., & Zimmerman, C. (2002). Violence against women: Global scope and magnitude. *Lancet, 359,* 1232–1237.

Waugh, C.K., & Gronlund, N.E. (2013). *Assessment of student achievement* (10th ed.). Upper Saddle River, NJ: Pearson.

Waxman, S. (2013). Building a better bridge. In M. Banaji, S. Gelman, & S. Lehr (Eds.), *Navigating the social world: The early years.* New York: Oxford University Press.

Waxman, S., & Goswami, U. (2012). Acquiring language: Learning the spoken and written word.

In S. Pauen & M. Bornstein (Eds.), *Early child development and later outcome*. New York: Cambridge University Press.

Waxman, S., & others (2013). Are nouns learned before verbs? Infants provide insight into a longstanding debate. *Child Development Perspectives, 7,* 155–159.

Wayne, P.M., & others (2014). Effect of tai chi on cognitive performance in older adults: Systematic review and meta-analysis. *Journal of the American Geriatrics Society, 62,* 25–39.

Weakley, A., & Schmitter-Edgecombe, M. (2014). Analysis of verbal fluency ability in Alzheimer's disease: The role of clustering, switching, and semantic proximities. *Archives of Clinical Neuropsychology, 29,* 256–268.

Weaver. J.M., & Schofield, T.J. (2015). Mediation and moderation of divorce effects on children's behavior problems. *Journal of Family Psychology, 29,* 39–48.

Webb, J.A., Horton, J.R., & Johnson, K. (2015, in press). Update in hospice and palliative care. *Journal of Palliative Medicine.*

Webb, L.D., Metha, A., & Jordan, K.F. (2013). *Foundations of American education* (7th ed.). Upper Saddle River, NJ: Pearson.

Webb, M.S., Passmore, D., Cline, G., & Maguire, D. (2014). Ethical issues related to caring for low birth weight infants. *Nursing Ethics, 21,* 731–741.

Weber, S.R., & Pargament, K.I. (2014). The role of religion and spirituality in mental health. *Current Opinion in Psychiatry, 27,* 358–363.

Webster, N.S., & Worrell, F.C. (2008). Academically-talented adolescents' attitudes toward service in the community. *Gifted Child Quarterly, 52,* 170–179.

Wechsler, D. (1939). *The measurement of adult intelligence*. Baltimore: Williams & Wilkins.

Wechsler, H., Davenport, A., Sowdall, G., Moetykens, B., & Castillo, S. (1994). Health and behavioral consequences of binge drinking in college. *Journal of the American Medical Association, 272,* 1672–1677.

Wei, Y., & others (2014). Paternally induced transgenerational inheritance of susceptibility to diabetes in mammals. *Proceedings of the National Academy of Sciences U.S.A., 111,* 1873–1878.

Weikert, D.P. (1993). *Long-term positive effects in the Perry Preschool Head Start Program*. Unpublished data. High/Scope Foundation, Ypsilanti, MI.

Weinraub, M., & others (2012). Patterns of developmental change in infants' nighttime sleep awakenings from 6 through 36 months of age. *Developmental Psychology, 148,* 1511–1528.

Weinstein, R. S. (2004). *Reaching higher: The power of expectations in schooling*. Cambridge, MA: Harvard University Press.

Weisleder, A., & Fernald, A. (2013). Talking to children matters: Early language experience strengthens processing and builds vocabulary. *Psychological Science, 24,* 2143–2152.

Weisman, O., Zagoory-Sharon, O., & Feldman, R. (2014). Oxytocin administration, salivary testosterone, and father-infant social behavior. *Progress in Neuro-Psychopharmacology and Biological Psychiatry, 49,* 47–52.

Weisner, T.S., & Duncan, G.J. (2014). The world isn't linear or additive or decontextualized: Pluralism and mixed methods in understanding the effects of antipoverty programs on children and parenting. In E.T. Gershoff, R.S. Mistry, and D.A. Crosby (Eds.), *Societal contexts of child development*. New York: Oxford University Press.

Weiss, L.A., & others (2008). Association between microdeletion and microduplication at 16p 11.2

and autism. *New England Journal of Medicine, 358,* 667–675.

Weissman, P., & Hendrick, J. (2014). *The whole child: Developmental education for the early years* (10th ed.). Upper Saddle River, NJ: Pearson.

Welch, A.A., & Hardcastle, A.C. (2014). The effects of flavonoids on bone. *Current Osteoporosis Reports, 12,* 205–210.

Welch, K.J. (2011). *THINK human sexuality*. Upper Saddle River, NJ: Pearson.

Welch, K.J. (2015). *Family life now* (2nd ed.). Upper Saddle River, NJ: Pearson.

Wellman, H.M. (2011). Developing a theory of mind. In U. Goswami (Ed.), *The Blackwell handbook of childhood cognitive development* (2nd ed.). New York: Wiley.

Wellman, H.M., Cross, D., & Watson, J. (2001). Meta-analysis of theory-of-mind development: The truth about false belief. *Child Development, 72,* 655–684.

Wellman, H.M., & Woolley, J.D. (1990). From simple desires to ordinary beliefs: The early development of everyday psychology. *Cognition, 35,* 245–275.

Welmer, A.K., Rizzuto, D., Qiu, C., Caracciolo, B., & Laukka, E.J. (2014). Walking speed, processing speed, and dementia: A population-based longitudinal study. *Journals of Gerontology A: Biological Sciences and Medical Sciences, 69,* 1503–1510.

Wenestam, C.G., & Wass, H. (1987). Swedish and U.S. children's thinking about death: A qualitative study and cross-cultural comparison. *Death Studies, 11,* 99–121.

Wenger, N.K. (2014). Prevention of cardiovascular disease: Highlights for the clinician of the 2013 American College of Cardiology/American Heart Association guidelines. *Clinical Cardiology, 37,* 239–251.

Wenger, N.S., & others (2003). The quality of medical care provided to vulnerable community-dwelling older patients. *Annals of Internal Medicine, 139,* 740–747.

Wennergren, G., & others (2015, in press). Updated Swedish advice on reducing the risk of sudden infant death syndrome. *Acta Pediatrica.*

Wentzel, K. (1997). Student motivation in middle school: The role of perceived pedagogical caring. *Journal of Educational Psychology, 89,* 411–419.

Wentzel, K.R. (2013). School adjustment. In I.B. Weiner & others (Eds.), *Handbook of psychology* (2nd ed., Vol. 7). New York: Wiley.

Wentzel, K.R. (2015). Socialization and experiences with peers. In J.E. Grusec & P.D. Hastings (Eds.), *Handbook of socialization* (2nd ed.). New York: Guilford.

Wentzel, K.R., & Asher, S.R. (1995). The academic lives of neglected, rejected, popular, and controversial children. *Child Development, 66,* 754–763.

Werker, J.F., & Gervain, J. (2013). Speech perception in infancy: A foundation of language acquisition. In P.D. Zelazo (Ed.), *Handbook of developmental psychology*. New York: Oxford University Press.

Werner, N.E., & others (2014). Maternal social coaching quality interrupts the development of relational aggression during early childhood. *Social Development, 23,* 470–486.

West, S.K., & others (2010). Older drivers and failure to stop at red lights. *Journals of Gerontology A: Biological Sciences and Medical Sciences, 65A,* 179–183.

Westerhof, G.J., Whitbourne, S.K., & Freeman, G.P. (2012). The aging self in cultural context: The relation of conceptions of aging to identity processes and self-esteem in the United States and the Netherlands. *Journals of Gerontology B: Psychological Sciences and Social Sciences, 67,* 52–60.

Westermann, G., Thomas, M.S.C., & Karmiloff-Smith, A. (2011). Neuroconstructivism. In U. Goswami (Ed.), *Wiley-Blackwell handbook of childhood cognitive development* (2nd ed.). New York: Wiley.

Wethington, E., Kessler, R., & Pixley, J. (2004). Turning points in adulthood. In G. Brim, C.D. Ryff, & R. Kessler (Eds.), *How healthy we are: A national study of well-being in midlife*. Chicago: University of Chicago Press.

Whaley, L. (2013). Syntactic typology. In J.J. Song (Ed.), *Oxford handbook of linguistic typology*. New York: Oxford University Press.

Wheeler, J.J., Mayton, M.R., & Carter, S.L. (2015). *Methods of teaching students with autism spectrum disorders*. Upper Saddle River, NJ: Pearson.

Whetstone, L.M., Morrissey, S.L., & Cummings, D.M. (2007). Children at risk: The association between weight status and suicidal thoughts and attempts in middle school youth. *Journal of School Health, 77,* 59–66.

Whitbourne, S.K., & Meeks, S. (2011). Psychopathology, bereavement, and aging. In K.W. Schaie & S.L. Willis (Eds.), *Handbook of the psychology of aging* (7th ed.). New York: Elsevier.

White, D.K., & others (2015, in press). Can an intensive diet and exercise program prevent knee pain among overweight adults at high risk? *Arthritis Care and Research.*

White, E., Slane, J.D., Klump, K.L., Burt, S.A., & Pivarnik, J. (2014). Sex differences in genetic and environmental influences on percent body fatness and physical activity. *Journal of Physical Activity and Health, 11,* 1187–1193.

White, K., Yeager, V.A., Menachemi, N., & Scarinci, I.C. (2014). Impact of Alabama's immigration law on access to health care among Latina immigrants and children: Implications for national reform. *American Journal of Public Health, 104,* 397–405.

White, L. (1994). Stepfamilies over the life course: Social support. In A. Booth and J. Dunne (Eds.), *Stepfamilies: Who benefits and who does not*. Hillsdale, NJ: Lawrence Erlbaum.

White, R., & Kramer-Albers, E.M. (2014). Axon-glia interaction and membrane traffic in myelin formation. *Frontiers in Cellular Neuroscience, 7,* 284.

Whitton, S.W., Stanley, S.M., Markman, H.W., & Johnson, C.A. (2013). Attitudes toward divorce, commitment, and divorce proneness in first marriages and remarriages, *75,* 276–287.

Wickelgren, I. (1999). Nurture helps to mold able minds. *Science, 283,* 1832–1834.

Wickrama, K.A.S., Bryant, C.M., Conger, R.D., & Meehan, J.M. (2004). Change and continuity in marital relationships during the middle years. In R.D. Conger, F.O. Lorenz, & K.A.S. Wickrama (Eds.), *Continuity and change in family relations*. Mahwah, NJ: Erlbaum.

Widiger, T.A. (2009). Neuroticism. In M.R. Leary & R.H. Hoyle (Eds.), *Handbook of individual differences in social behavior*. New York: Guilford.

Widman, L., & McNulty, J.K. (2010). Sexual narcissism and the perpetration of sexual aggression. *Archives of Sexual Behavior, 39,* 926–939.

Widman, L., & others (2014). Sexual communication between early adolescents and their dating partners, parents, and best friends. *Journal of Sex Research, 51,* 731–741.

Widom, C.S., & Nikulina, V. (2012). Long-term consequences of child neglect in low-income families. In V. Maholmes & R.B. King (Eds.), *Oxford handbook of poverty and child development*. New York: Oxford University Press.

Widom, C.S., Czaja, S.J., Bentley, T., & Johnson, M.S. (2012). A prospective investigation of physical health outcomes in abused and neglected children: New findings from a 30-year follow-up. *American Journal of Public Health, 102*(6), 1135–1144.

Widom, C.S., Czaja, S.J., & DuMont, K.A. (2015). Intergenerational transmission of child abuse and neglect: Real or detection bias? *Science, 347,* 1480–1485.

Wigfield, A., & Cambria, J. (2010). Students' achievement values, goal orientations, and interest: Definitions, development, and relations to achievement outcomes. *Developmental Review, 30,* 1–35.

Wigfield, A., Eccles, J.S., Schiefele, U., Roeser, R., & Davis-Kean, P. (2006). Development of achievement motivation. In W. Damon & R. Lerner (Eds.), *Handbook of child psychology* (6th ed.). New York: Wiley.

Wigfield, A., Klauda, S.L., & Cambria, J. (2011). Motivational sources and outcomes of self-regulated learning and performance. In B.J. Zimmerman & D.H. Schunk (Eds.), *Handbook of self-regulation of learning and performance.* New York: Routledge.

Wigfield, A., & others (2015). Development of achievement motivation and engagement. In R.M. Lerner (Ed.), *Handbook of child psychology and developmental science* (7th ed.). New York: Wiley.

Wilcox, S., & others (2003). The effects of widowhood on physical and mental health, health behaviors, and health outcomes: The women's health initiative. *Health Psychology, 22,* 513–522.

Wilczynski, S.M., & others (2014). Evidence-based practice and autism spectrum disorders. In M.A. Bray & T.J. Kehle (Eds.), *Oxford handbook of school psychology.* New York: Oxford University Press.

Wilhelmsen, L., Dellborg, M., Welin, L., & Svardsudd, K. (2015, in press). Men born in 1913 followed to 100 years. *Scandinavian Cardiovascular Journal.*

Willcox, D.C., Scapagnini, G., & Willcox, B.J. (2014). Healthy aging diets other than Mediterranean: A focus on the Okinawan diet. *Mechanisms of Aging and Development, 136–137,* 148–162.

Willett, W. (2013). The current evidence on healthy eating. *Annual Review of Nutrition* (Vol. 34). Palo Alto, CA: Annual Reviews.

Willette, A.A., & others (2012). Calorie restriction reduces the influence of glucoregulatory dysfunction on regional brain volume in aged rhesus monkeys. *Diabetes, 61,* 1036–1042.

Williams, D.D., Yancher, S.C., Jensen, L.C., & Lewis, C. (2003). Character education in a public high school: A multi-year inquiry into unified studies. *Journal of Moral Education, 32,* 3–33.

Williams, D.R., & Sternthal, M.J. (2007). Spirituality, religion, and health: Evidence and research directions. *Medical Journal of Australia, 186*(Suppl.), S47–S50.

Williams, G.L., Keigher, S., & Williams, A.V. (2012). Spiritual well-being among older African Americans in a midwestern city. *Journal of Religion and Health, 51*(2), 355–370.

Williams, J., & others (2014). Is there a place for extended assessments in addressing child sexual abuse allegations? How sensitivity and specificity impact professional perspectives. *Journal of Child Sexual Abuse, 23,* 179–197.

Williams, K.M., Nathanson, C., & Paulhus, D.L. (2010). Identifying and profiling academic cheaters: Their personality, cognitive ability, and motivation. *Journal of Experimental Psychology: Applied, 16,* 293–307.

Williams, M.E. (1995). *The American Geriatric Society's complete guide to aging and health.* New York: Harmony Books.

Williams, M.E., Sando, L., & Soles, T.G. (2014). Cognitive tests in early childhood: Psychometric and cultural considerations. *Journal of Psychoeducational Assessment, 32,* 455–476.

Williamson, H.C., & others (2015, in press). Risk moderates the outcome of relationship education: A randomized controlled trial. *Journal of Consulting and Clinical Psychology.*

Williamson, J. (2011). The future of retirement security. In R.H. Binstock & L.K. George (Eds.), *Handbook of aging and the social sciences* (7th ed.). New York: Elsevier.

Williamson, R.A., Donohue, M.R., & Tully, E.C. (2013). Learning how to help others: Two-year-olds' social learning of a prosocial act. *Journal of Experimental Child Psychology, 114,* 543–550.

Willis, R. (2012). Individualism, collectivism, and ethnic identity: Cultural assumptions in accounting for caregiving behavior in Britain. *Journal of Cross-Cultural Gerontology, 27,* 201–216.

Willis, S.L. (2015, in press). Aging overview. In M.J. Aminoff & D. Daroff (Eds.), *Encyclopedia of neurological sciences* (2nd ed.). New York: Elsevier.

Willis, S.L., & Caskie, G. (2013). Reasoning training in the ACTIVE study: Who benefits. *Journal of Aging and Health, 25*(Suppl. 8), S43–S64.

Willits, J.A., Seidenberg, M.S., & Saffran, J.R. (2014). Distributional structure in language: Contributions of noun-verb difficulty in infant word recognition. *Cognition, 132,* 429–436.

Willoughby, M., & others (2015). The epidemiology of observed temperament: Factor structure and demographic differences. *Infant Behavior and Development, 39C,* 21–34.

Wilson, B.J. (2008). Media and children's aggression, fear, and altruism. *Future of Children, 18*(1), 87–118.

Wilson, B.J., & others (2014). Parental emotion coaching: Associations with self-regulation in aggressive/rejected and low aggressive/popular children. *Child and Family Behavior Therapy, 36,* 81–106.

Wilson, D.M., Cohen, J., Deliens, L., Hewitt, J.A., & Houttekier, D. (2013). The preferred place of last days: Results of a representative population-based survey. *Journal of Palliative Medicine, 16*(5), 502–508.

Wilson, L.C., & Miller, K.E. (2015, in press). Meta-analysis of the prevalence of unacknowledged rape. *Trauma, Violence, and Abuse.*

Wilson, R.S., Mendes de Leon, C.F., Bienas, J.L., Evans, D.A., & Bennett, D.A. (2004). Personality and mortality in old age. *Journals of Gerontology B: Psychological Sciences and Social Sciences, 59,* 110B–116B.

Wilson, R.S., & others (2002). Participation in cognitively stimulating activities and risk of incident Alzheimer disease. *Journal of the American Medical Association, 287,* 742–748.

Wilson, R.S., & others (2015). Conscientiousness, dementia-related pathology, and trajectories of cognitive aging. *Psychology and Aging, 30,* 74–82.

Windsor, T.D., Burns, R.A., & Byles, J.E. (2013). Age, physical functioning, and affect in midlife and older adulthood. *Journals of Gerontology B: Psychological Sciences and Social Sciences, 68,* 395–399.

Winerman, L. (2005, January). Leading the way. *Monitor on Psychology, 36*(1), 64–67.

Winett, R.A., & others (2014). Development of a new treatment paradigm for disease prevention and healthy aging. *Translational Behavior Medicine, 4,* 117–123.

Wink, P., & Dillon, M. (2002). Spiritual development across the adult life course: Findings from a longitudinal study. *Journal of Adult Development, 9,* 79–94.

Winne, P.H., & Nesbit, J.C. (2010). The psychology of academic achievement. *Annual Review of Psychology* (Vol. 61). Palo Alto, CA: Annual Reviews.

Winner, E. (1986, August). Where pelicans kiss seals. *Psychology Today,* pp. 24–35.

Winner, E. (1996). *Gifted children: Myths and realities.* New York: Basic Books.

Winner, E. (2000). The origins and ends of giftedness. *American Psychologist, 55,* 159–169.

Winner, E. (2006). Development in the arts: Drawing and music. In W. Damon & R. Lerner (Eds.), *Handbook of child psychology* (6th ed.). New York: Wiley.

Winsper, C., Lereya, T., Zanarini, M., & Wolke, D. (2012). Involvement in bullying and suicide-related behavior at 11 years: A prospective birth cohort study. *Journal of the Academy of Child and Adolescent Psychiatry, 51,* 271–282.

Winsvold Prang, I., & Jelsness-Jorgensen, L.P. (2014). Should I report? A qualitative study of barriers to incident reporting among nurses working in nursing homes. *Getriatric Nursing, 35,* 441–447.

Wintre, M.G., & Vallance, D.D. (1994). A developmental sequence in the comprehension of emotions: Intensity, multiple emotions, and valence. *Developmental Psychology, 30,* 509–514.

Wise, P.M. (2006). Aging of the female reproductive system. In E.J. Masor & S.N. Austad (Eds.), *Handbook of the biology of aging* (6th ed.). New York: Elsevier.

Wisniewski, T., & Goni, F. (2014). Immunotherapy for Alzheimer's disease. *Biochemical Pharmacology, 88,* 499–507.

Wit, J.M., Kiess, W., & Mullis, P. (2011). Genetic evaluation of short stature. *Best Practices & Research: Clinical Endocrinology and Metabolism, 25,* 1–17.

Witelson, S.F., Kigar, D.L., & Harvey, T. (1999). The exceptional brain of Albert Einstein. *The Lancet, 353,* 2149–2153.

Witherington, D.C., Campos, J.J., Harriger, J.A., Bryan, C., & Margett, T.E. (2011). Emotion and its development in infancy. In J.G. Bremner & T.D. Wachs (Eds.), *Wiley-Blackwell handbook of infant development* (2nd ed.). New York: Wiley.

Witkin, H.A., & others (1976). Criminality in XYY and XYY men. *Science, 193,* 547–555.

Witt, W.P., & others (2014). Maternal stressful life events prior to conception and the impact on infant birth in the United States. *American Journal of Public Health, 104*(Suppl. 1), S81–S89.

Witte, A.V., & others (2009). Caloric restriction improves memory in elderly humans. *Proceedings of the National Academy of Sciences, U.S.A., 106,* 1255–1260.

Witte, A.V., & others (2014). Long-chain omega-3 fatty acids improve brain function and structure in older adults. *Cerebral Cortex, 24,* 3059–3068.

Witte, R. (2012). *Classroom assessment for teachers.* New York: McGraw-Hill.

Woelders, L.C.S., Larsen, J.K., Scholte, R., Cillessen, T., & Engles, R.C.M.E. (2010). Friendship group influences on body dissatisfaction and dieting among adolescent girls: A prospective study. *Journal of Adolescent Health, 47*(5), 456–462.

Wolfinger, N.H. (2011). More evidence for trends in the intergenerational transmission of divorce: A completed cohort approach using data from the General Social Survey. *Demography, 48,* 581–592.

Wolinsky, F.D., Vander Weg, M.W., Howren, M.B., Jones, M.P., & Dotson, M.M. (2013). A randomized controlled trial of cognitive training using a visual speed of processing intervention in middle aged and older adults. *PLoS One,8*(5), e61624.

Wolitzky-Taylor, K.B., & others (2011). Reporting rape in a national sample of college women. *American Journal of College Health, 59,* 582–587.

Wolke, D., & Lereya, S.T. (2015, in press). Long-term effects of bullying. *Archives of Disease in Childhood.*

Women's Sports Foundation (2001). *The 10 commandments for parents and coaches in youth sports.* Eisenhower Park, NY: Author.

Wong, A.P., & others (2014). Estimating volume of the pituitary gland from T1-weighted magnetic-resonance images: Effects of age, puberty, testosterone, and estradiol. *Neuroimage, 94,* 216–221.

Wong, F., & others (2013). Cerebrovascular control is altered in healthy term infants when they sleep prone. *Sleep, 36,* 1911–1918.

Wong, M.D., & others (2014). Successful schools and risky behaviors among low-income adolescents. *Pediatrics, 134,* e389-e396.

Wong, M.M., Brower, K.J., Nigg, J.T., & Zucker, R.A. (2010). Childhood sleep problems, response inhibition, and alcohol and drug outcomes in adolescence and young adulthood. *Alcoholism, Clinical and Experimental Research, 34,* 10033–10044.

Wong, P.T.P., & Watt, L.M. (1991). What types of reminiscence are associated with successful aging? *Psychology and Aging, 6,* 272–279.

Wong, S.S., Sugimoto-Matsuda, J.J., Chang, J.Y., & Hishinuma, E.S. (2012). Ethnic differences in risk factors for suicide among American high school students, 2009: The vulnerability of multiracial and Pacific Islander adolescents. *Archives of Suicide Research, 16,* 159–173.

Wong Briggs, T. (2007, October 18). An early start for learning. *USA Today,* p. 6D.

Wood, D., Harms, P., & Vazire, S. (2010). Perceiver effects as projective tests: What your perceptions of others say about you. *Journal of Personality and Social Psychology, 99,* 174–190.

Wood, J., & others (2011). Risk of falls, injurious falls, and other injuries resulting from visual impairment among older adults with age-related macular degeneration. *Investigative Ophthalmology & Visual Science, 52*(8), 5088–5092.

Wood, J.T. (2011). *Communication mosaics* (6th ed.). Boston: Cengage.

Wood, J.T. (2012). *Communication in our lives* (6th ed.). Boston: Cengage.

Woodward, A., Markman, E., & Fitzsimmons, C. (1994). Rapid word learning in 13- and 18-month-olds. *Developmental Psychology, 30,* 553–556.

Woodward, A.L., & Markman, E.M. (1998). Early word learning. In D. Kuhn & R.S. Siegler (Eds.), *Handbook of child psychology* (5th ed., Vol. 2). New York: Wiley.

Woolgar, M., & Scott, S. (2013). The negative consequences of over-diagnosing attachment disorders in adopted children: The importance of comprehensive formulations. *Clinical Child Psychology and Psychiatry, 19,* 355–366.

World Health Organization (2000, February 2). *Adolescent health behavior in 28 countries.* Geneva, Switzerland: World Health Organization.

Worthington, E.L. (1989). Religious faith across the life span: Implications for counseling and research. *Counseling Psychologist, 17,* 555–612.

Wortmann, J.H., & Park, C.L. (2008). Religion and spirituality in adjustment following bereavement: An integrative review. *Death Studies, 32,* 703–736.

Wright, C.F., Wei, Y., Higgins, J.P., & Sagoo, G.S. (2012). Non-invasive prenatal diagnostic test accuracy for fetal sex using cell-free DNA: A review and meta-analysis. *BMC Research Notes, 5,* 476.

Wright, R.H., Mindel, C.H., Tran, T.V., & Habenstein, R.W. (2012). *Ethnic families in America* (5th ed.). Upper Saddle River, NJ: Pearson.

Wu, L.T., & Blazer, D.G. (2011). Illicit and nonmedical drug use among older adults: A review. *Journal of Aging and Health, 23,* 481–504.

Wu, T., Gao, X., Chen, M., & van Dam, R.M. (2009). Long-term effectiveness of diet-plus-exercise interventions vs. diet-only interventions for weight loss: A meta-analysis. *Obesity Reviews, 10,* 313–323.

Wu, T.W., & others (2014). Maintenance of whole-body therapeutic hypothermia during patient transport and magnetic resonance imaging. *Pediatric Radiology, 44,* 613–617.

Wu, Z., Schimmele, C.M., & Quellet, N. (2015, in press). Repartnering after widowhood. *Journals of Gerontology B: Psychological Sciences and Social Sciences.*

Wuest, D.A., & Fisette, J.L. (2015). *Foundations of physical education, exercise science, and sport* (18th ed.). New York: McGraw-Hill.

Wurm, S., & Benyamini, Y. (2014). Optimism buffers the detrimental effect of negative self-perceptions of aging on physical and mental health. *Psychology and Health, 29,* 832–848.

X

Xia, N. (2010). *Family factors and student outcomes.* Unpublished doctoral dissertation, RAND Corporation, Pardee RAND Graduate School, Pittsburgh.

Xiao, W.S., Quinn, P.C., Pascalis, O., & Lee, K. (2014). Own- and other-race face scanning in infants: Implications for perceptual narrowing. *Developmental Psychobiology, 56,* 262–273.

Xie, L., & others (2013). Sleep drives metabolite clearance from the adult brain. *Science, 342,* 373–377.

Xie, Q., & Young, M.E. (1999). Integrated child development in rural China. *Education: The World Bank.* Washington, DC: The World Bank.

Xu, C., & others (2015, in press). Calorie restriction prevents metabolic aging caused by abnormal SIRT 1 function in adipose tissues. *Diabetes.*

Xu, H., Wen, L.M., & Rissel, C. (2015, in press). Associations of parental influence with physical activity and screen time among young children: A systematic review. *Journal of Obesity.*

Y

Yakoboski, P.J. (2011). Worries and plans as individuals approach retirement. *Benefits Quarterly, 27,* 34–37.

Yan, L., Cheung, R., & Cummings, E.M. (2015, in press). Marital conflict and emotional insecurity among Chinese adolescents: Cultural value moderation. *Journal of Research on Adolescence.*

Yang, P., & others (2015, in press). Developmental profile of neurogenesis in prenatal human hippocampus: An immunohistochemical study. *International Journal of Developmental Science.*

Yang, Y. (2008). Social inequalities in happiness in the United States, 1972–2004: An age-period-cohort analysis. *American Sociological Review, 73,* 204–226.

Yang, Y., Bender, A.R., & Raz, N. (2015). Age related differences in reaction time components and diffusion properties of normal-appearing white matter in healthy adults. *Neuropsychologia, 66,* 246–258.

Yang, Y., & Kozloski, M. (2011). Sex differences in age trajectories of physiological dysregulation: Inflammation, metabolic syndrome, and allostatic load. *Journals of Gerontology A: Biological Sciences and Medical Sciences, 66A,* 493–500.

Yanof, J.A. (2013). Play technique in psychodynamic psychotherapy. *Child and Adolescent Psychiatric Clinics of North America, 22,* 261–282.

Yao, Y., Gu, X., Zhu, J., Yuan, D., & Song, Y. (2013). Hormone replacement therapy in females can decrease the risk of lung cancer: A meta-analysis. *PLoS One, 8*(8), e71236.

Yap, M.B., Pilkington, P.D., Ryan, S.M., & Jorm, A.F. (2014). Parental factors associated with depression and anxiety in young people: A systematic review and meta-analysis. *Journal of Affective Disorders, 156,* 8–23.

Yarber, W., Sayad, B., & Strong, B. (2013). *Human sexuality* (8th ed.). New York: McGraw-Hill.

Yassin, A.A., Akhras, F., El-Sakka, A.I., & Saad, F. (2011). Cardiovascular diseases and erectile dysfunction: The two faces of the coin on androgen deficiency. *Andrologia, 43,* 1–8.

Yates, L.B., Djuousse, L., Kurth, T., Buring, J.E., & Gaziano, J.M. (2008). Exceptional longevity in men: Modifiable factors associated with survival and function to age 90 years. *Archives of Internal Medicine, 168,* 284–290.

Ybarra, M.L., & Mitchell, K.J. (2014). "Sexting" and its relation to sexual activity and sexual risk behavior in a national survey of adolescents. *Journal of Adolescent Health, 55,* 757–764.

Yeh, D.C., & others (2015, in press). Adipose tissue derived stem cells in neural regenerative medicine. *Cell Transplantation.*

Yen, C.F., & others (2014). Association between school bullying levels/types and mental health problems among Taiwanese adolescents. *Comprehensive Psychiatry, 55*(3), 405–413.

Yen, S.C. (2008). Short-term memory. In N.J. Salkind (Ed.), *Encyclopedia of educational psychology.* Thousand Oaks, CA: Sage.

Yeung, W.J. (2012). Explaining the black-white achievement gap: An international stratification and developmental perspective. In K.R. Harris, S. Graham, & T. Urdan (Eds.), *APA handbook of educational psychology.* Washington, DC: American Psychological Association.

Yin, R.K. (2012). Case study methods. In H. Cooper (Ed.), *APA handbook of research methods in psychology.* Washington, DC: American Psychological Association.

Yochum, C., & others (2014). Prenatal cigarette smoke exposure causes hyperactivity and aggressive behavior: Role of catecholamines and BDNF. *Experimental Neurology, 254C,* 145–152.

Yokoya, T., Demura, S., & Sato, S. (2009). Three-year follow-up of the fall risk and physical function characteristics of the elderly participating in a community exercise class. *Journal of Physiological Anthropology, 28,* 55–62.

Yokoyama, A., & others (2013). Trends in gastrectomy and ADH1B and ALDH2 genotypes in Japanese alcoholic men and their gene-gastrectomy, gene-gene, and gene-age interactions. *Alcohol and Alcoholism, 48,* 146–152.

Yonker, J.E., Schnabelrauch, C.A., & DeHaan, L.G. (2012). The relationship between spirituality and religiosity on psychological outcomes in adolescents and emerging adults: A meta-analytic review. *Journal of Adolescence, 35,* 299–314.

Yoo, H., Feng, X., & Day, R.D. (2013). Adolescents' empathy and prosocial behavior in the family context: A longitudinal study. *Journal of Youth and Adolescence, 42,* 1858–1872.

Yoshida, S., Kozu, T., Gotoda, T., & Salto, D. (2006). Detection and treatment of early cancer in high-risk populations. *Best Practice and Research: Clinical Gastroenterology, 20,* 745–765.

Yoshikawa, H., Aber, J.L., & Beardslee, W.R. (2012). The effects of poverty on the mental, emotional, and behavioral health of children and youth. *American Psychologist, 67,* 272–284.

Young, B.J., Furman, W., & Laursen, B. (2014). Models of change and continuity in romantic experiences. In F.D. Fincham & M. Cui (Eds.), *Romantic relationships in emerging adulthood.* New York: Cambridge University Press.

Young, K.T. (1990). American conceptions of infant development from 1955 to 1984: What the experts are telling parents. *Child Development, 61,* 17–28.

Youniss, J., McLellan, J.A., & Yates, M. (1999). Religion, community service, and identity in American youth. *Journal of Adolescence, 22,* 243–253.

Yousefi, M., & others (2013). Relationships between age of puberty onset and height at age 18 years in girls and boys. *World Journal of Pediatrics, 9,* 230–238.

Youth Risk Behavior Survey (2011). *Trends in the prevalence of suicide-related behaviors National YRB: 1991–2011.* Retrieved June 6, 2012, from www.cdc.gov/yrbss

Ysseldyk, R., Haslam, S.A., & Haslam, C. (2013). Abide with me: Religious group identification among older adults promotes health and well-being by maintaining multiple group memberships. *Aging and Mental Health, 17,* 869–879.

Yu, C.Y., & others (2012). Prenatal predictors for father-infant attachment after childbirth. *Journal of Clinical Nursing, 21*(11–12), 1577–1583.

Yu, F., Ryan, L.H., Schaie, K.W., & Willis, S.L. (2014, in press). Using multi-level modeling to understand factors associated with cognition in older adults: The Seattle Longitudinal Study. *Journal of Nursing and Health.*

Yu, R., Branje, S., Keijsers, L., Koot, H.M., & Meeus, W. (2013). Pals, problems, and personality: The moderating role of personality in the longitudinal association between adolescents' and best friends' delinquency. *Journal of Personality, 89*(5), 499–509.

Yu, S.M., & Singh, G.K. (2012). High parenting aggravation among U.S. immigrant families. *American Journal of Public Health, 102,* 2102–2108.

Yuan, P., & Raz, N. (2014). Prefrontal cortex and executive functions in healthy adults: A meta-analysis of structural neuroimaging studies. *Neuroscience and Biobehavioral Reviews, 42C,* 180–192.

Yudkin, D., Hayward, B., Aladjem, M.I., Kumari, D., & Usdin, K. (2014). Chromosome fragility and the abnormal replication of the FMR1 locus in fragile X syndrome. *Human Molecular Genetics, 23,* 2940–2952.

Yuen, R., Chen, B., Blair, J.D., Robinson, W.P., & Nelson, D.M. (2013). Hypoxia alters the epigenetic profile in cultured human placental trophoblasts, *Epigenetics, 8,* 192–202.

Yun, K., & others (2014). Effects of maternal-child home visitation on pregnancy spacing for first-time Latina mothers. *American Journal of Public Health, 104*(Suppl. 1), S152–S158.

Z

Zachrisson, H.D., Lekhal, R., Dearing, E., & Toppelberg, C.O. (2013). Little evidence that time in child care causes externalizing problems during early childhood in Norway. *Child Development. 84,* 1152–1170.

Zack, S.E., & others (2015, in press). Attachment history as a moderator of the alliance outcome relationship in adolescents. *Psychotherapy.*

Zaff, J.F., Hart, D., Flanagan, C., Youniss, J., & Levine, P. (2010). Developing civic engagement within a civic context. In M.E. Lamb, A.M. Freund, & R.M. Lerner (Eds.), *Handbook of life-span development* (Vol. 2). New York: Wiley.

Zagorsky, J.L. (2007). Do you have to be smart to be rich? The impact of IQ on wealth, income, and financial distress. *Intelligence, 35,* 489–501.

Zagozdzon, P., Parszuto, J., Wrotkowska, M., & Dydjow-Bendek, D. (2014). Effect of unemployment on cardiovascular risk factors and mental health. *Occupational Medicine.*

Zalli, A., & others (2015). Shorter telomeres with high telomerase activity are associated with raised allostatic load and impoverished psychosocial resources. *Proceedings of the National Academy of Sciences U.S.A., 111,* 4519–4524.

Zamuner, T., Fais, L., & Werker, J.F. (2014). Infants track words in early word-object associations. *Developmental Science, 17*(4), 481–491.

Zanella, S., & others (2014). When norepinephrine becomes a driver of breathing irregularities: How intermittment hypoxia fundamentally alters the modulatory response of the respiratory network. *Journal of Neuroscience, 34,* 36–50.

Zannas, A.S., & others (2012). Stressful life events, perceived stress, and 12-month course of geriatric depression: Direct effects and moderation by the 5-HTTLPR and COMT Val158Met polymorphisms. *Stress, 15*(4), 425–434.

Zarit, S.H., & Knight, B.G. (Eds.). (1996). *A guide to psychotherapy and aging.* Washington, DC: American Psychological Association.

Zayas, V., & Hazan, C. (2014) (Eds.). *Bases of adult attachment.* New York: Springer.

Zayas, V., Mischel, W., & Pandey, G. (2014). Mind and brain in delay of gratification. In V.F. Reyna & V. Zayas (Eds.), *The neuroscience of risky decision making.* Washington, DC: American Psychological Association.

Zehe, J.M., & Colder, C.R. (2014). A latent growth curve analysis of alcohol-use specific parenting and parent alcohol use. *Addictive Behaviors, 39,* 1701–1705.

Zeifman, D., & Hazan, C. (2008). Pair bonds as attachments: Reevaluating the evidence. In J. Cassidy & P.R. Shaver (Eds.), *Handbook of attachment* (2nd ed.). New York: Guilford.

Zeigler-Hill, V. (2013). The current state of research concerning self-esteem. In V. Zeigler-Hill (Ed.), *Self-esteem.* New York: Psychology Press.

Zelazo, P.D. (2013). Developmental psychology: A new synthesis. In P.D. Zelazo (Ed.), *Oxford handbook of developmental psychology.* New York: Oxford University Press.

Zelazo, P.D., & Lyons, K.E. (2012). The potential benefits of mindfulness training in early childhood: A developmental social cognitive neuroscience perspective. *Child Development Perspectives, 6,* 154–160.

Zelazo, P.D., & Muller, U. (2011). Executive function in typical and atypical development. In U. Goswami (Ed.), *Wiley-Blackwell handbook of childhood cognitive development.* New York: Wiley.

Zelinksi, E.M., & Kennison, R.F. (2007). Not your parents' test scores: Cohort reduces psychometric aging effects. *Psychology and Aging, 22,* 546–557.

Zembal-Saul, C.L., McNeill, K.L., & Hershberger, K. (2013). *What's your evidence?* Upper Saddle River, NJ: Pearson.

Zeng, R., & Greenfield, P.M. (2015). Cultural evolution over the last 40 years in China: Using the Google Ngram viewer to study implications of social and political change for cultural values. *International Journal of Psychology, 50,* 47–55.

Zeng, Y., & Shen, K. (2010). Resilience significantly contributes to exceptional longevity. *Current Gerontology and Geriatrics Research.* doi:10.1155/2010/525693

Zeskind, P.S. (2007). Impact of the cry of the infant at risk on psychosocial development. In R.E. Tremblay, R. de V. Peters, M. Boivin, & R.G. Barr (Eds.), *Encyclopedia on early childhood development.* Montreal: Centre of Excellence for Early Childhood Development. Retrieved November 24, 2008, from www.child-encyclopedia.com/en-ca/list-of-topics.html

Zettel-Watson, L., & Rook, K.S. (2009). Friendship, later life. In D. Carr (Ed.), *Encyclopedia of the life course and human development.* Boston: Gale Cengage.

Zhai, F., Raver, C.C., & Jones, S. (2012). Quality of subsequent schools and impacts of early interventions: Evidence from a randomized controlled trial in Head Start settings. *Children and Youth Services Review, 34*(5), 946–954.

Zhang, F., & Jiang, L. (2015). Neuroinflammation in Alzheimer's disease. *Neuropsychiatric Disease and Treatment, 11,* 243–256.

Zhang, L-F., & Sternberg, R.J. (2012). Learning in cross-cultural perspective. In T. Husen & T.N. Postlethwaite (Eds.), *International encyclopedia of education* (3rd ed.). New York: Elsevier.

Zhang, M., & others (2015, in press). Cognitive function in older adults according to current socioeconomic status. *Neuropsychology, Development, and Cognition B: Aging, Neuropsychology, and Cognition.*

Zhang, T., & others (2015). Improved knee extensor strength with resistance training associated with muscle specific miRNAs in older adults. *Experimental Gerontology, 62,* 7–13.

Zhang, W.G., & others (2014). Select aging biomarkers based on telomere length and chronological age to build a biological age equation. *Age, 36*(3), 9639.

Zhang, Y.X., Zhang, Z.C., & Xie, L. (2014). Distribution curve of waist-to-height ratio and its association with blood pressure among children and adolescents: Study in a large population in an eastern coastal province, China. *European Journal of Pediatrics, 173,* 879–885.

Zhao, H., Seibert, S.E., & Lumpkin, G.T. (2010). The relationship of personality to entrepreneurial intentions and performance: A meta-analytic review. *Journal of Management, 36,* 381–404.

Zhao, M., Kong, L., & Qu, H. (2014). A systems biology approach to identify intelligence quotient score-related genomic regions, and pathways relevant to potential therapeutic targets. *Scientific Reports, 4,* 4176.

Zhao, P., & others (2014a). Solving the puzzle of Parkinson's disease using inducted pluripotent stem cells. *Experimental Biology and Medicine, 239,* 1421–1432.

Zhao, X., & others (2014). An obesity genetic risk score is associated with metabolic syndrome in Chinese children. *Gene, 535,* 299–302.

Zhao, Z., Pan, X., Liu, L., & Liu, N. (2014b). Telomere length maintenance, shortening, and lengthening. *Journal of Cellular Physiology, 229,* 1323–1329.

Zhou, Q. (2013). Commentary in S. Smith, "Children of 'tiger parents' develop more aggression and depression, research shows. Retrieved July 20, 2013, from http://www.cbsnews.com/news/children-of-tiger-parents-develop-more-aggression-and-depression-research-shows/

Zhou, Q., & others (2012). Asset and protective factors for Asian American children's mental health adjustment. *Child Development Perspectives, 6,* 312–319.

Zhu, S., Tse, S., Cheung, S.H., & Oyserman, D. (2014). Will I get there? Effects of parental support on children's possible selves. *British Journal of Educational Psychology, 84,* 435–453.

Ziegler, D.V., Wiley, C.D., & Velarde, M.C. (2015, in press). Mitochondrial effectors of cellular senescence: Beyond the free radical theory of aging. *Aging Cell.*

Zielinski, D.S. (2009). Child maltreatment and adult socioeconomic well-being. *Child Abuse and Neglect, 33,* 666–678.

Ziemer, C.J., Plumert, J.M., & Pick, A.D. (2012). To grasp or not to grasp: Infants' actions toward objects and pictures. *Infancy, 17*(5), 479–497.

Zigler, E.F., & Styfco, S.J. (1994). Head Start: Criticisms in a constructive context. *American Psychologist, 49,* 127–132.

Zigler, E.F., & Styfco, S.J. (2010). *The hidden history of Head Start.* New York: Oxford University Press.

Zimmerman, B.J. (2012). Motivational sources and outcomes of self-regulated learning and performance. In B.J. Zimmerman & D.H. Schunk (Eds.), *Handbook of self-regulation of learning and performance.* New York: Routledge.

Zimmerman, B.J., & Kitsantas, A. (1997). Developmental phases in self-regulation: Shifting from process goals to outcome goals. *Journal of Educational Psychology, 89,* 29–36.

Zimmerman, B.J., & Labuhn, A.S. (2012). Self-regulation of learning: Process approaches to personal development. In K.R. Harris & others (Eds.), *APA handbook of educational psychology.* Washington, DC: American Psychological Association.

Zimmerman, F.J., Christakis, D.A., & Meltzoff, A.N. (2007). Association between media viewing and language development in children under age 2 years. *Journal of Pediatrics, 151,* 364–368.

Ziol-Guest, K.M. (2009). Child custody and support. In D. Carr (Ed.), *Encyclopedia of the life course and human development.* Boston: Cengage.

Zirpoli, T.J. (2016, in press). *Behavior management* (7th ed.). Upper Saddle River, NJ: Pearson.

Zosuls, K.M., & others (2009). The acquisition of gender labels in infancy: Implications for gender-typed play. *Developmental Psychology, 45,* 688–701.

Zotter, H., & Pichler, G. (2012). Breast feeding is associated with decreased risk of sudden infant death syndrome. *Evidence Based Medicine, 17,* 126–127.

Zuberer, A., Brandeis, D., & Drechsler, R. (2015). Are treatments for neurofeedback training in children with ADHD related to successful regulation of brain activity? A review on the learning of regulation of brain activity and a contribution to the discussion on specificity. *Frontiers in Human Neuroscience, 9,* 135.

Zulauf, C.A., Sprich, S.E., Safren, S.A., & Wilens, T.E. (2014). The complicated relationship between attention-deficit/hyperactivity disorder and substance use disorders. *Current Psychiatry Reports, 16,* 436.

Name Index

Bauman, R. W., 49
Baumeister, R. F., 342, 345, 437, 440
Baumrind, D., 461, 469
Baur, K., 386–388, 456
Bavelier, D., 209
Bay-Cheng, L. Y., 394
Bayley, N., 254
Baysinger, C. L., 68
Beal, C. R., 380, 381
Beals, M., 556
Bean, D. S., 415
Beardslee, W. R., 346, 514
Beaty, J. J., 279, 290
Beauchamp, G., 166
Beaulieu, D. A., 15, 44
Bebeau, M., 411
Bechtold, A. G., 167
Bechtold, J., 429
Becker, M. W., 509
Beckmann, M. M., 72
Bedford, V. H., 478
Bedore, J. A., 283
Beduer, A., 123
Beebe, D. W., 107
Beech, A. R., 390
Beecher, H. W., 457
Beeghly, M., 65–66
Begley, T. H., 48
Begus, K., 274
Behrens, H., 280
Behrens, K. Y., 298
Behrens, R., 353
Bekelman, D. B., 568
Belansky, E. S., 381
Belk, C., 48
Bell, K. A., 205
Bell, M. A., 28, 94, 95, 209, 221, 295, 309–310
Bell, R. A., 513
Bell, R. D., 123
Bell, S. M., 300
Beller, A. H., 516
Belleville, S., 210
Belon, K., 107
Belsky, J., 307, 311, 347, 444
Benbow, C. P., 261
Bender, D., 491–492
Bendersky, M., 158, 159
Benenson, J. F., 493
Bengali, L., 533
Bengtson, V. L., 341, 345, 478
Bengtsson, H., 338
Benichov, J., 285
Benjamins, M. R., 435
Benka, J., 470
Benner, A. D., 532, 539
Bennett, C. I., 539, 540
Bennett, K. M., 454
Bennett, S. A., 64
Benokraitis, N., 446, 452
Benotsch, E. G., 487
Benowitz-Fredericks, C. A., 88, 133
Benson, B., 395
Benyamini, Y., 358
Ben-Zur, 2012, 583
Bera, A., 75

Berardi, N., 92
Berchicci, M., 506
Berenbaum, S. A., 370, 372, 376, 411
Berens, A. E., 94, 95–96
Berge, J. M., 132
Bergeman, C. S., 584
Bergen, D., 499–500
Berger, I., 536
Berger, S. E., 147–150, 169
Bergman, L. R., 556
Bergmuller, S., 508
Berk, L. E., 193
Berko, J., 277
Berko Gleason, J., 280, 281, 285, 288
Berlin, L. J., 463
Berlyne, D. E., 499
Berman, M., 454
Berman, M. G., 221
Berman, S. L., 354
Bernard, J. P., 62–63
Bernard, K., 318
Berndt, T. J., 495
Berner, J., 513
Bernie, A. M., 400
Bernier, A., 105
Bernier, E. P., 180, 181
Berninger, V., 535
Berninger, V. W., 277, 527
Bernstein, N., 395
Bernstsen, D., 218
Berntsen, D., 218
Berntsen, N., 218
Berookhim, B. M., 400
Berry, A., 100
Berry, C. J., 218
Berry, D. J., 460
Berry, J. W., 7
Berryman, N., 228
Bersamin, M. M., 392, 398
Berscheid, E., 327, 329
Bertenthal, B. I., 161
Bertoglio, K., 237
Bertorelle, R., 113
Bertrand, R., 89, 347, 356–357
Bertrand, R. M., 347
Berwid, O. G., 537
Best, J. R., 136
Betti, U., 335
Betts, D., 72
Betts, K. S., 67
Beuker, K. T., 209
Bevan, D., 78
Beyene, Y., 90, 399
Beyers, W., 12, 421
Bezilla, R., 436
Bhandarkar, R., 574
Bhat, M. A., 93
Bhullar, N., 247
Bialystok, E., 283, 286
Bian, Z., 163
Bibby, P. A., 362
Bick, J., 94
Biehle, S. N., 458
Bielak, A. A., 138
Bierman, K. L., 426, 495, 529
Bigham, S., 237

Bigler, R., 7
Bigler, R. S., 7
Bigras, M., 214
Bihlmeyer, N. A., 112
Billy, J. O. G., 497
Binet, A., 244, 267
Birch, L. L., 128
Birch, R., 161
Birch, S., 236
Birditt, K., 10, 15
Birditt, K. S., 480, 481, 505, 583
Birkeland, M. S., 342
Birman, B. F., 527
Birren, J. E., 90, 328–329, 559
Bischoff, K. E., 568
Bisconti, T. L., 584
Bjorklund, D. F., 44, 235
Bjorvatn, B., 77
Black, M. M., 65–66, 128
Blackford, J. U., 309
Blackwell, L. S., 544
Blaga, O. M., 255
Blair, C., 222, 301–302, 346, 460
Blair, S. N., 138
Blake, J. S., 120–121
Blake, L. P., 431
Blake, M., 341
Blake, W., 299
Blakemore, J. E. O., 376, 377, 379, 411
Blakemore, S-J., 95, 97–98
Blanchard-Fields, F., 227, 425
Blanck, H. M., 134
Bland, C. G., 410
Blankinship, L., 397
Blass, E., 148
Blazer, D. G., 143
Blieszner, R., 453, 478, 481
Bloodworth, M., 568
Bloodworth, N., 568
Bloom, B., 261, 262
Bloom, L., 275, 288
Bloom, P., 236
Bloomer, R. J., 134
Bloor, C., 137
Bluck, S., 218
Blumberg, J. H., 448
Blumberg, S. J., 448
Blumel, J. E., 90
Blustein, D. L., 552
Boccardi, V., 113
Boccia, M., 218
Boden, J. S., 452
Bodner, E., 327, 504
Bodrova, E., 193, 194, 222, 499
Boelen, P. A., 358, 580
Boer, D., 508
Boer, L. M., 580
Boerner, L. M., 452–453
Bogart, L. M., 491
Bohlin, G., 179
Boiter, C., 431
Bolding, A., 71
Bolea-Alamanac, B., 536
Bolkan, C., 340–341

Bollen, J., 574
Bonaccorso, C. M., 51
Bonanno, R. A., 492
Bond, B. J., 510
Bonfanti, L., 100
Boniel-Nissim, M., 446
Bono, G., 425
Bonvillian, J., 288
Booij, G. E., 272
Bookwala, J., 452
Boor, M. E., 102
Booth, A., 471
Boraska, V., 132
Borchert, J., 160
Borden Maier, V., 48
Borella, E., 217
Borges, E., 556
Borges, N. J., 552
Borges, S. M., 199
Borich, G. D., 526
Bornick, P., 66
Bornstein, M. H., 160, 175, 444, 500
Boron, J. B., 232
Borrell, L. N., 14
Borst, G., 191
Bos, C. S., 535, 539
Bosma, H. A., 354
Bosman, E. A., 165
Boss, L., 505
Bosworth, B., 557
Bosworth, H. B., 505
Botkin, D., 464
Bouchard, T. J., 261
Boucher, J., 237
Bould, H., 306
Boulton, M., 166
Bouman, W. P., 401
Bourassa, K. J., 455
Boutsikou, T., 396, 397
Bowen, C. E., 556
Bower, T. G. R., 161
Bowker, J., 296, 372, 486, 488
Bowlby, J., 22, 300, 313, 314, 317, 332, 572
Boyatzis, C. J., 431–433
Boyatzis, R. E., 247
Boyd, M., 99
Boyle, J., 106
Boyle, P. A., 228
Boynton-Jarrett, R., 87
Brabek, K. M., 382
Brabek, M. M., 382
Bradbury, T. N., 449
Braddick, O, 160, 162
Bradley, R. H., 516, 539
Bradshaw, C. P., 491
Brady, K. W., 278
Brainerd, C. J., 216, 226–227
Braithwaite, I., 132
Bramham, C. R., 103
Brand, J., 555–556
Brand, M., 228
Brandeis, D., 537
Brandes, N., 113
Brandon, A. R., 396
Brandone, A. C., 235
Brandstädter, J., 344, 347

Brann, J. H., 100
Brannon, L., 372
Brannstrom, L., 486
Bransford, J., 228, 527
Branson, S., 505
Branum, A. M., 61
Brassard, A., 326
Brassen, S., 304, 341
Braun-Courville, D. K., 392
Braungart-Rieker, J. M., 312
Braver, S. L., 453, 470–472
Bray, M. A., 243
Brechwald, W. A., 487–488, 493
Brecklin, L. R., 390
Bredekamp, S., 529, 530
Breen, A. V., 344, 351
Brefka, S., 154
Breheny, M., 395, 505
Breitbart, W. S., 577
Brekke, J. S., 343
Brember, I., 342
Bremner, J. G., 167
Brendel, P. C., 93
Brendgen, M., 429
Brent, R. L., 63, 64, 67, 68
Breslau, J., 453
Brewer, M. B., 507
Brez, C. C., 28, 207, 208
Breznitz, Z., 214
Bridge, J. A., 467
Bridgeland, J. M., 421
Bridges, J. S., 480, 481
Bridges, S. L., 260, 262
Bridgett, D. J., 298–299, 309
Brigham, M., 539
Briley, D. A., 357
Brim, O., 401, 434, 452
Brin, S., 528
Brinkman-Stoppelenburg, A., 568
Brion, M., 105
Brislin, R., 507
Brittian, A. S., 355
Broadie, K., 538
Broadus, I., 425
Brockie, J., 90, 399
Brockmeyer, S., 481
Brockmeyer, T., 343
Brockmole, J. R., 217
Brodaty, H., 122
Brody, D. J., 503
Brody, G. H., 516
Brody, L. R., 379
Brody, N., 245, 247–248, 252
Brody, S., 386
Brodzinsky, D. M., 474–475
Brondolo, E., 520
Bronfenbrenner, U., 23, 24, 35–36, 379, 443, 445, 482, 506
Broning, S., 142
Bronstein, P., 372
Brook, J. S., 469
Brooker, R. J., 15, 44, 46, 49
Brookhart, S. M., 527
Brooks, J. G., 222
Brooks, M. G., 222

Christie, J., 279
Christie, J. F., 280, 499
Christodoulidou, A., 113
Chua, A., 549
Chuang, Y. F., 27, 230
Chui, H., 15
Chumakina, M., 272
Chung, J. K., 163
Cicchetti, D., 6, 30, 57, 112, 317, 463–466
Cicirelli, V. G., 327, 477, 478
Cillessen, A. H. N., 489–490
Ciol, M. A., 520
Citkovitz, C., 72
Claes, H. I., 400
Clancy, S. M., 227
Clardy, C. E., 433
Clark, B., 262, 527
Clark, C. D., 499
Clark, E. M., 497
Clark, E. V., 272, 277, 280
Clark-Cotton, M. R., 285
Clarke-Stewart, A., 5
Clarke-Stewart, A. K., 319, 320, 446, 460, 470, 472
Clausen, J. A., 363, 434
Clauss, J. A., 309
Claxton, L. J., 221
Clay, O. J., 163
Clearfield, M. W., 179
Clements, J. M., 568
Clements, P., 381
Cleveland, M. J., 142
Cliffordson, C., 250
Clifton, R. K., 154, 167
Climer, R., 111
Climie, E. A., 245
Clinkinbeard, S. S., 107
Cluett, E. R., 72
Cnaan, R. A., 433
Cobham, V. E., 302
Cobiac, L., 128
Cochran, B. N., 456
Coe, N. B., 556, 558
Coehlo, D., 340–341
Coffey, V. G., 89
Coffino, B., 316, 318
Coffman, J., 217
Coffman, J. L., 217
Cohen, A., 7
Cohen, G. L., 487
Cohen, K., 387, 392–393
Cohen, N. J., 136
Cohen, O., 425
Cohen, R., 492
Cohen-Fridel, S., 327, 504
Cohen-Kadosh, K., 97
Cohen-Woods, S., 47
Cohler, B., 456
Coie, J., 490
Coie, J. D., 490
Colangelo, N. C., 262
Colapinto, J., 370
Colbert, B. J., 48
Colby, A., 409
Colcombe, S. J., 231, 233
Colder, C. R., 142
Cole, M., 195

Cole, M. W., 248
Cole, P. M., 7, 296, 301, 308, 309
Cole, W. G., 150
Coleman, A. M., 568
Coleman, M., 455, 472
Coleman, M. R., 538
Coleman, P. D., 101
Coleman-Phox, K., 105
Coleridge, S. T., 59
Coley, R. L., 320, 394
Collene, A., 133
Collene, A. L., 129, 130
Collins, C. E., 131
Collins, D., 421
Collins, M., 553
Collins, W. A., 467, 468, 497, 532
Collin-Vezina, D., 465
Colman, R. J., 134
Colom, R., 248
Coltrane, S., 467
Columbo, J., 28
Columbo, J., 207, 208
Comer, J., 541
Comings, J., 534
Commoner, B., 47
Commons, M. L., 198
Compton, W. M., 554
Comstock, G., 511–512
Conde-Agudelo, A., 75
Conel, J. L., 95
Cong, X., 75
Conger, K. J., 477
Conger, R. D., 357
Connell, N. M., 491
Connery, S., 89
Connolly, J., 323
Connolly, J. A., 323, 324
Connor-Smith, J., 357
Conry-Murray, C., 374
Consoli, A., 574
Constantine, N. A., 398
Contant, T. L., 224
Conti, E., 538
Converse, A. K., 537
Cook, M., 161
Cook, P. J., 531
Cook, R. F., 513
Cook, S. W., 330
Cooksey, E. C., 396
Coombs, N., 138
Coontz, S., 451
Cooper, C. R., 353, 354, 468, 519
Cooper, S., 136
Cooter, R. B., 281
Coovert, M. D., 464
Copeland, C., 557, 558
Copen, C. E., 447–449, 453
Copple, C., 528, 529
Corazzini, K., 126–127
Corbett, G. G., 272
Corbit, J., 182
Cordier, S., 68
Cordova, D., 394
Corna, D. R., 575
Cornelissen, K. K., 132

Cornelius, J. R., 394
Cornwell, B., 14, 425
Corpuz, R., 15, 44
Corrada, M. M., 135
Corso, J. F., 166
Cortes, E., 72
Cortina, K. S., 297, 498
Cosco, T. D., 505
Costa, P. T., 356, 359, 361, 362, 366
Costa, R. M., 386
Costabile, R. A., 401
Costley, K. C., 193
Coté, J. E., 350–352
Cotelli, M., 230
Cotten, S. R., 513
Coubart, A., 181
Courage, M. I., 94
Courage, M. L., 336
Court, F., 50
Courtois, C. A., 390
Courtois, R., 392
Couture, M., 347
Couwenbergs, C., 385
Cowan, C., 458
Cowan, C. P., 458
Cowan, M. K., 15, 46
Cowan, N., 214
Cowan, P., 458
Cowan, P. A., 458
Cowan, R., 535
Cox, K. S., 353, 361
Cox, M. J., 444
Coxon, J. P., 228
Coyne, S. M., 378, 513
Craft, C. S., 48
Craig, I. W., 47
Craik, F. I. M., 283
Crain, S., 272, 277, 281
Cramm, J. M., 505
Crane, J. D., 91
Craparo, G., 326
Crede, M., 504
Crick, N. R., 378
Crnic, K. A., 297
Crocco, P., 112
Crocetti, E., 354, 421
Crockenberg, S. B., 308
Crockett, L. J., 395, 462
Crognale, M. A., 211
Crone, E. A., 86
Crooks, R. L., 386–388, 456
Cropley, M., 106
Crosbie-Burnett, M., 455
Crosnoe, R., 387, 532, 539
Cross, C., 490
Cross, D., 235, 492
Cross, S., 341
Crossley, M., 286
Crossman, E. J., 515
Crouter, A. C., 467, 470, 476
Crowe, B., 237
Crowell, J. A., 481
Crowley, K., 26
Crowley, M., 380
Cruchaga, C., 52
Csicsvari, J., 212

Csikszentmihalyi, M., 6, 263, 266
Cuddy-Casey, M., 572
Cuenca-Garcia, M., 90, 121
Cuevas, K., 94, 205, 209, 221, 222, 295
Cui, L., 303, 461
Cui, X., 360
Cui, Y., 400
Culicover, P. W., 272
Cumming, E., 504
Cummings, D. M., 574
Cummings, E. M., 470, 471
Cummings, M., 46
Cunningham, M., 555
Cunningham, S. A., 130, 131
Cupach, W. R., 329
Cupito, S. H., 71
Curci, A., 247
Curnow, C., 152
Curran, K., 462
Currie, C., 87
Curtindale, L. M., 28, 207, 208
Cushner, K., 540
Cushner, K. H., 5
Cuzzolaro, M., 133
Cvencek, D., 378
Cvijetic, S., 54
Cybele Raver, C., 516
Czaja, S. J., 465

Dabholkar, A. S., 95
da Costa Souza, A., 48
da Cruz, A. C., 113
Daeschel, I., 119
Dahl, R. E., 98, 99
Dahlberg, L., 10
Dahlen, H. G., 72
Dale, B., 245, 253
Dale, S., 568
da Luz, M. H., 126
Daly, M., 554
Daly, M. C., 533
Damasio, A. R., 410
Damman, M., 558
Damon, W., 413, 414, 423, 424, 431, 439
Dan, B., 51
Dan, Z., 248
Dane, M. C., 282
Daniels, C. E., 447, 448, 453
Daniels, H., 192
Danielson, Y. S., 131
Danner, D., 102
D'Aoust, L. N., 47
D'Apolito, K., 129
Darcy, E., 132
D'Arcy, C., 505
Darling-Hammond, N., 527
da Rocha, A. F., 248
da Rosa, G., 111
Darwin, C., 43, 46, 79, 331
Das, A., 582
D'Augelli, A. R., 473
Davanzo, R., 75
Dave, D., 574
Davenport, L., 512
David, J., 472

Davidov, M., 298, 317
Davidson, B., 262
Davidson, D., 210
Davidson, J., 262
Davidson, M., 420
Davies, G., 249
Davies, J., 342
Davies, M., 390
Davies, P. T., 57, 112, 470
Davis, B. E., 150
Davis, C. L., 136
Davis, L., 460
Davis, M. C., 121, 122
Davis, S. F., 17
Davis, S. W., 101, 230
Davis-Unger, A. C., 21
Dawes, N. P., 502
Dawson, A. E., 323
Dawson-McClure, S., 426, 427
Day, N. L., 66
Day, R. D., 413, 418
Day, R. H., 161
Deacon, S. H., 281
DeAngelo, L., 431
Deardorff, J., 323
Deary, I., 248, 249
Deater-Deckard, K., 309–310, 444, 463
Debats, D. L., 437
Debette, S., 89
De Bolle, M., 356
DeCasper, A. J., 164
deCharms, R., 542
Deci, E. L., 542
DeClaire, J., 296
Dedon, P. C., 48
de Frias, C. M., 4, 230, 231
De Giovanni, N., 65
Degnan, K. A., 295
de Guzman, N. S., 88
DeHaan, L. G., 433
de Haan, M., 92, 318
DeJong, W., 142
de Jongh, B. E., 67
Dekovic, M., 476, 477
de la Cuesta-Benjumea, C., 125
Delahunt, P. B., 206
DeLamater, J. D., 370, 387, 398, 447–448, 474
de las Fuentes, C., 383
Del Campo, L., 272, 281, 535
De Leo, D., 575
Delgado Alves, J., 121
Del Giudice, M., 327
DeLisi, R., 499
DeLoache, J. S., 182, 221
Deloian, B., 130
de Looze, M., 394
Demanachick, S. P., 499
Demiray, B., 218
Demircin, S., 575
Dempster, F. N., 214
Demsky, C. A., 553
Demura, S., 154
Denard, P. J., 166
De Navas-Walt, C., 515
Deng, C., 549
Deng, J. W., 50

Deng C., 549
Denham, S. A., 295, 297, 301, 302
Denkinger, M. D., 154
Denmark, F. L., 32
Denney, N. W., 227
Dennis, M., 92, 93, 96
Dennis, N. A., 101, 230
DePaulo, B., 447
de Planell-Saguer, M., 63
Der Ananian, C., 138
Derebail, V. K., 52
DeRicco, B., 142
DeRosa, D. A., 224
DeSapri, K. T., 399
Destan, N., 234
de Toledo, S., 478
Deutsch, A. R., 495, 497
Deutsch, R., 471
Devaney, S. A., 63
de Villers-Sidani, E., 92
de Villiers, J., 277
de Villiers, P., 277
Devine, R. T., 235, 237
DeVos, J., 180
Devos, T., 355
de Vries, S. L., 429, 467
Dew, J., 458
DeWall, C. N., 510
Dewey, J., 419, 439
Dewey, J. E., 583
Dewey, K. G., 128
de Wind, A. W., 556
de Wit, L., 133
Deye, K., 465
DeYoung, C. G., 309
Dezen, T., 74
DeZolt, D. M., 373, 378
DeZutter, S., 500
Dharnidharka, V. R., 137
Diamond, A., 11, 97, 179, 194, 222, 225, 311, 346, 456
Diamond, A. D., 179
Diamond, L. M., 387, 392, 393
Diamond, M., 370
Diaz, A., 94
Diaz-Rossello, J. L., 75
Dickens, B. M., 63
Dickinson, D., 246
Dickinson, G. E., 571
Dickinson, W. J., 505
Diderich, H. M., 465
Diego, M., 76
Diego, M. A., 76
Diekelmann, S., 103
Diekhoff, G., 421
Diener, E., 14, 357, 534
Diener, R. M., 64
Dietz, E. L., 494
Di Florio, A., 78
DiLeonardo, M. J., 131
Dillon, J., 566
Dillon, M., 435
Dilulio, J. J., 421
Di Meo, S., 114
Dimitropoulos, G., 132
Dimmitt, C., 224, 234, 281, 282

Di Nardo, W., 165
Ding, X. P., 421
Ding, Y. H., 316
Ding, Z., 113
Dinges, D. F., 108
Dionne, G., 105
Dionne, I. J., 108
Dishion, T. J., 141, 378, 428, 458, 487
Di Stefano, L., 114
Dixon, L., 465
Dixon, R. A., 4, 45, 231, 238, 305
Doane, L. D., 106
Dobson, C. F., 71
Dodd, J. M., 61
Dodge, K. A., 426, 429, 489, 493, 495
Doering, A. H., 512
Dohnt, H., 106
Dolcos, S., 305
Doll, C. A., 538
Dollar, J., 301
Domiteaux, M., 357
Domsch, H., 254
Donaldson, G., 199, 255
Donatelle, R. J., 6, 133, 137
Donath, C., 574
Dondi, M., 299
Donegan, S., 129
Dong, M., 49
Dong, W., 460
Donker, G. A., 569
Donnellan, M. B., 343, 357, 361, 364
Donnelly, J. P., 25
Donnelly, N., 48
Donohue, M. R., 412
Doornwaard, S. M., 494
Dorey, E., 123
Dorffner, G., 108
Dorheim, S. K., 77
Dorn, L. D., 27, 85–88, 399
Dotterer, A. M., 458, 459
Doty, R. L., 166
Doub, A. E., 128
Doumen, S., 354
Dovis, S., 536
Dow, R. S., 281
Dowda, M., 135
Downey, P. A., 139
Doydum, A., 213, 214
Dozier, M., 466
Drabick, D. A., 487
Draghi-Lorenz, R., 298
Drake, B., 466
Drake, K., 347
Drake, K. M., 132
Drechsler, R., 537
Dregan, A., 107
Drollette, E. S., 136
Drummond, J., 414
Dryfoos, J. G., 398
Du, D., 99
Du, M., 139
Duan, X., 248
Duarte, A., 218, 230
Dublin, S., 124

Dubois, B., 124
Dubois, J., 61
Duck, S., 329
Dudley, R. L., 431
Dudova, I., 74
Duff, D., 272
Duggan, K. A., 261
Duggan, P. M., 187
Duke, J., 119
Duke, S. A., 87
Dulaney, A., 377
Dulas, M., 218
DuMont, K. A., 465
Duncan, D. T., 574
Duncan, G. J., 7–9, 251, 445, 514–516, 539
Dunifon, R., 478
Dunlop, D. D., 122
Dunlop, W. L., 415, 416
Dunlosky, J., 199, 217, 232
Dunn, D. W., 536
Dunn, E. C., 466
Dunn, J., 411, 418, 476–478, 489
Dunn, M., 535
Dunphy-Lelii, S., 208–209
Dupere, V., 9, 16, 445, 514, 539
Durham, R., 77
Durrant, R., 43
Durston, S., 97
Durtschi, J. A., 120
Dutta, R., 445, 507
Dvornyk, V., 87
Dweck, C., 561
Dweck, C. S., 543–544
Dworkin, S. L., 393
Dykas, M. J., 314
Dy-Liacco, G., 435
Dyson, J. C., 501

Eads, A., 447
Eagan, K., 430–431, 534
Eagly, A. H., 370, 371, 378–380
Eapen, V., 318
East, P., 476
Easterbrooks, M. A., 308, 346
Eaton, C. B., 121
Eaton, D. K., 106, 137, 390
Eaton, W. O., 150
Eberhard-Gran, M., 77
Ebmeier, K. P., 122
Ebstein, R. P., 318
Eccles, J., 531
Eccles, J. S., 347, 378, 432, 503, 531, 542, 543, 546
Echevarria, J. J., 34, 283
Eckert, G. P., 114
Edelman, M. W., 8
Edelstein, M. D., 516
Edelstein, R. S., 327
Edgington, C., 324
Edison, S. C., 336
Edison, T., 263, 265
Ednick, M., 105
Edwards, D., 390

Edwards, J. D., 206
Efron, D., 536
Egeland, B., 427, 532
Egeloff, B., 361
Eibach, R. P., 387
Eichbaum, Q., 508
Eichorn, D., 121
Eichorn, D. H., 362
Eidelman, A. I., 75
Einarsen, S., 391
Einstein, A., 17, 248
Eisdorfer, C., 558–559
Eisenberg, M. E., 398
Eisenberg, N., 345, 347, 411, 413, 414, 419, 420, 422–425
Eisler, I., 120, 132
Ekblad, A., 62
Ekin, A., 62
Eklund, K., 260–261
Elashi, F. B., 337, 339
Elbourne, P., 272
Elder, D., 105
Elder, G. H., 194–195, 445
El Haj, M., 218
Elias, M. F., 505
Eliasieh, K., 101
Elisa, C., 14
Elkind, D., 183, 187, 189
Ellickson, P. L., 141
Elliott, E., 543
Elliott, E. M., 217
Ellis, B. J., 43, 311
Ellis, L., 387
Ellis, M. A., 553
Ellison, A., 207
Elmes, D. G., 29
Elmore, B., 9, 131
Else-Quest, N., 371, 382
El-Sheikh, M., 106, 471
Ely, E. W., 568
Emeny, R. T., 327
Emerson, R. W., 271, 497
Emery, R. E., 472
Emes, R. D., 93
Emmons, R. A., 14, 357
Enfield, A., 421
Engberg, H., 358
Engler, B., 358
English, G. W., 8, 516
English, T., 14, 304, 305, 356–357, 362, 504, 506
Englund, M. M., 532, 546
Enns, J. T., 181, 204, 207, 221
Enomoto, H., 126
Enright, R., 424–425
Enright, R. D., 425
Ensor, R., 301
Enz, B. J., 280
Epstein, N. B., 87
Erickson, K. I., 100, 139, 206, 231
Ericsson, K. A., 261
Erikson, E., 293
Erikson, E. H., 18, 19, 24, 27, 35, 313, 314, 341, 349–352, 354, 361, 366, 427, 432

Erikson, J., 18
Ernst, M., 98
Escalante, Y., 136
Escobar-Chaves, S. L., 510
Espie, J., 120, 132
Estes, T. H., 526
Etaugh, C., 480, 481
Evans, G. W., 8, 515, 516
Evans, J. R., 162
Evans, S. Z., 486–487
Evers, A. W., 126
Evers, C., 43, 44
Eviatar, Z., 93
Exline, J. J., 580
Ezkurdia, L., 47

Fabes, R. A., 372
Fabiani, M., 228
Fabiano, G. A., 536
Fabricius, W. V., 471
Fagan, J., 464
Fagan, J. F., 254, 255
Fagundes, C. P., 126
Fahlberg, B., 568
Fairbairn, C. E., 356
Fairweather, A. K., 575
Fais, L., 275
Faja, S., 221
Fakhoury, M., 538
Falbe, J., 107, 511
Falbo, T., 477
Falci, C. D., 344
Falconier, M. K., 360
Falk, M. C., 233
Fandakova, Y., 230
Fantz, R. L., 158, 160
Farabaugh, A., 574
Farb, A. F., 396
Farioli-Vecchioli, S., 100–101
Farley, F., 226–227
Farr, R. H., 473, 475
Farrell, M. J., 166
Farrell, M. P., 359
Farrell, S. K., 556
Farrell, S. W., 138
Farrington, D., 427
Farrington, D. P., 426, 427
Fasig, L., 336
Fatusi, A. O., 120
Fava, N. M., 394
Fearon, R. P., 316
Fearon, R. M. P., 347
Federmeier, K. D., 286
Fedor, A., 139
Feeney, M. P., 165
Feeney, S., 528
Fei, J., 327
Feibus, A., 400
Feinberg, M., 458, 476
Feiring, C., 316, 324–325
Feit, M., 466
Feldhusen, J., 260
Feldman, H. M., 536
Feldman, R., 75, 318
Feldman, S., 221, 392
Feldman, S. S., 393, 394, 467
Fenelon, A., 582
Feng, L., 111

Feng, X., 413, 418
Feng, Z., 111
Fenning, R. M., 297
Fenton, A., 110
Ferencz, B., 123
Ferguson, C. J., 463, 510
Ferguson, E., 362
Fergusson, D. M., 6, 129, 470
Fernald, A., 279, 289
Fernyhough, C., 192, 193
Ferreira, J. A., 510
Ferrer, E., 205
Fetterman, A. K., 43
Fetterolf, J. C., 390
Feubner, C., 317
Field, D., 481
Field, N., 401
Field, T., 76
Field, T. M., 66, 76, 78
Fielder, R. L., 398
Fields, R., 140, 141
Fiez, J. A., 93
Finch, C. E., 114, 257
Fincham, F. D., 398, 425
Finegood, E. D., 279
Finer, L. B., 395
Finer, S., 67
Finger, B., 317
Fingerhut, A. W., 387, 456
Fingerman, K. L., 10, 16, 469, 479–481
Finion, K. J., 301
Finkelstein, E. A., 133
Finkelstein, L. M., 555, 556
Finlay, B. L., 44
Finlayson, M., 435
Finn, S. E., 456
Fiori, K. L., 498
Fiori, M., 247
Firestein, S. J., 100
Fischel, E., 352
Fischer, C. E., 286
Fischer, J. L., 452
Fischer, K., 335
Fischer, K. W., 197
Fischer, R., 508
Fischer-Baum, S., 535
Fischhoff, B., 572
Fischoff, B., 187
Fisette, J. L., 135, 136
Fisher, D., 390
Fisher, G. G., 229, 556
Fisher, K. R., 192
Fisher, P. A., 466, 474
Fiske, S. T., 504
Fitzgerald, A., 137
Fitzgerald, N., 137
Fitzpatrick, K. K., 132
Fitzsimmons, C., 278
Fivush, R., 213, 214–215, 221
Fizke, E., 237
Fjell, A. M., 100
Flaherty, E. G., 465
Flanagan, C., 421
Flanagan, J. C., 78
Flannery, D., 187
Flavell, E. R., 235, 236

Flavell, J. H., 205, 215, 234–236, 340
Fleeson, W., 362
Flegal, K. E., 218, 285
Fleming, A. S., 318
Fletcher, B. R., 257
Fletcher-Watson, S., 237
Flicek, P., 47
Flinck, A., 465
Flint, M. S., 48
Floel, A., 230, 231
Flom, R., 209
Flores, G., 396
Florsheim, P., 324, 458
Flouri, E., 346
Flynn, J. R., 250, 251
Foehr, U. G., 508–509
Follari, L., 251, 529, 530
Foltynie, T., 101
Fontaine, M., 555
Fontaine, R. G., 491
Fontana, L., 134
Ford, B. Q., 295, 296
Ford, D. Y., 260, 262
Forde, D. R., 28
Forgatch, M. S., 428
Forienza, O. V., 199
Forssman, L., 179
Forstmeier, S., 341
Forzano, L. B., 29
Foshee, V. A., 487
Foster, E. M., 574
Foster, G. A., 69
Foster, J., 508
Fournier, M. A., 351
Fowler-Brown, A., 132
Fox, B. J., 281
Fox, J., 510
Fox, J. A., 28
Fox, M. K., 130
Fox, N. A., 11, 94, 95–96, 295
Foxwell, A. M., 570
Fragala, M. S., 91
Fraiberg, S., 147
Fraley, C., 16
Fraley, R. C., 316, 317, 327
France, A., 526
Franchak, J. M., 147, 149, 159, 162
Franchin, L., 159
Francis, A. L., 222
Francis, J., 353
Frank, G. K. W., 133
Frankl, V., 437, 440
Frankland, P. W., 213
Franklin, A., 160
Franklin, B., 265
Franklin, N. C., 121
Franklin, S., 238
Fraser, G., 353
Fraser, S., 250
Frazier, L. D., 340–341
Frazier, P., 330, 454
Frazier, P. A., 316, 330
Freddy, G., 137
Frederick II (emperor), 273
Frederickson, B. L., 379
Frederikse, M., 377

Freeman, G. P., 344
Frenkel, T. I., 11, 295
Freud, S., 17–19, 35, 313, 371, 402, 413, 438, 503, 552
Freund, A. M., 344, 347, 348, 425, 506
Frey, B. S., 305
Frey, W. H., 557
Frick, J., 312
Fried, I., 245
Friedman, A. H., 529
Friedman, D., 217
Friedman, H. S., 15, 261, 347, 362
Friedman, J., 55
Friedman, S. L., 322
Friedman, W. J., 215
Friedrichs, A., 235
Friend, M., 536, 539
Friesen, W., 102
Frimer, J. A., 415, 416
Fritz, C., 553
Froh, J. J., 425
Froimson, J., 295, 296, 312, 324, 463
Fromm, E., 576
Frost, D. M., 456
Fry, P. S., 583
Frydenberg, E., 345
Fu, L., 571
Fu, R., 296
Fuchs, D., 214
Fuglset, T. S., 132–133
Fuhs, M. W., 222
Fujisawa, D., 580
Fujiwara, E., 341
Fukunaga, A., 166
Fulginiti, A., 343
Fuligni, A. J., 106, 107, 120, 432, 445, 468, 469
Fuller-Thompson, E., 478–479
Fulop, T., 112
Fung, Y. L., 575
Furman, E., 479
Furman, W., 323, 324, 493, 495, 496
Furstenberg, F. F., 120, 472, 552
Furth, H. G., 185
Furukawa, S., 72

Gabbard, C., 496
Gabor, M., 553
Gaffney, K. F., 105
Gage, F. H., 101
Gaias, L. M., 308
Gaillard, A., 78
Gaither, S. E., 160
Galambos, N. L., 108, 372, 377, 379, 381
Galbally, M., 318
Galbraith, K. A., 395
Gale, C. R., 357
Galinsky, A. M., 397–398
Galinsky, E., 225, 280, 290, 338, 472
Gallagher, J. J., 538

Galland, B. C., 104
Gallicchio, L., 399
Galliher, R. V., 354, 355
Galloway, J. C., 83
Gallup, G. W., 436
Galton, F., 267
Galupo, M. P., 198
Gambacciani, M., 399
Gamble, W. C., 519
Gander, M., 316
Gandhi, M., 27
Gandhi, S., 135
Ganguli, M., 230
Ganley, C. M., 377
Ganong, L., 455, 472
Ganzach, Y., 245
Gao, W., 92
Gao, X, 124
Garand, L., 575
Garbarino, J., 430, 514
Garcia, S., 139
Garcia, Y., 529, 530
Garcia-Hermoso, A., 136
Garcia-Mila, M., 224
Garcia-Sierra, A., 288–289
Gardner, G., 106
Gardner, H., 246, 247, 267
Gardner, M., 226
Gardner, M. K., 248, 250
Gardosi, J., 67
Garfield, C. F., 537
Garlow, S. J., 575
Garneau, C. L., 464
Garofalo, R., 128, 393
Gartland, N., 357
Gartner, J., 435
Gartstein, M. A., 209, 309
Gartzia, L., 371
Garvey, C., 500
Garvin, C. W., 450
Gaspar, A., 123
Gasser, L., 492
Gaston-Johansson, F. G., 520
Gates, B., 262
Gates, G. J., 387
Gatz, M., 347
Gauthier, A. H., 552
Gauvain, M., 20, 24, 191–195
Gavazzi, S., 444
Gawlik, S., 78
Gearhart, J. P., 370
Gee, C. C., 520
Geers, A. L., 449
Gehsmann, K., 535
Geier, C., 98
Gelles, R. J., 433
Gelman, R., 185, 191, 278
Gelman, S. A., 182–183, 277, 376
Gems, D., 110, 113, 114
Genesee, F., 283
Genie, 271, 289
Gennetian, L. A., 9, 517
Gentile, D. A., 510, 511
George, L. G., 363
George, L. K., 364
George, P., 121
Gerhardinger, L., 395

German, T. P., 236
Gerritsen, L., 123
Gershoff, E. T., 462, 463
Gerson, S. A., 147
Gervain, J., 275
Gesell, A., 147, 169
Gevensleben, H., 537
Gewirtz, J., 300
Gewirtz, J. L., 313
Ghesquiere, A., 580
Ghetti, S., 215
Ghosh, S., 68
Giagulli, V. A., 400
Gialamas, A., 320
Giallauria, F., 112, 138
Giallo, R., 78
Giandrea, M. D., 556
Giangregorio, L. M., 122
Giarrusso, R., 345
Gibbs, J. C., 410
Gibson, E. J., 157, 161, 162, 167–169, 171, 180
Gibson, J. J., 157, 167–169, 171
Gibson-Davis, C., 449
Gidding, S. S., 131
Giedd, J. N., 98, 377
Gielen, S., 139
Gilbert, G., 282
Gilbertson, S. L., 136
Gildengers, A. G., 231
Giletta, M., 487–488, 493, 495
Gill, P., 581
Gillen, M. M., 397
Gillen-O'Neel, C., 107
Gillespie, C., 134
Gilligan, C., 382, 411, 438
Gillum, R. F., 434, 435
Gilston, J., 390
Gilstrap, L. L., 250
Gimovsky, A., 62
Gino, F., 425
Glaser, R., 125, 126
Glass, L., 64–65
Glavind, J., 72
Glazebrook, K., 467
Gleason, T. R., 411
Glickman, K., 580
Gliga, T., 92, 97
Glover, V., 536
Gluck, J., 258
Godwin, J., 429
Goel, A., 400
Goethe, W. V., 265
Goga, A. E., 129
Gogtay, N., 95, 97
Gola, A. H., 511
Gold, D., 566
Gold, M. S., 536
Gold, S. J., 513
Goldbeck, L., 574
Goldberg, C. B., 556
Goldberg, J., 214
Goldberg, J. S., 464
Goldberg, W. A., 470
Goldfield, B. A., 288
Goldin-Meadow, S., 274
Goldschmidt, L., 65–66

Goldsmith, H. H., 308, 309
Goldstein, A. S., 515
Goldstein, M. H., 288
Goldston, D. B., 574
Goldstone, E., 84
Goleman, D., 247, 263
Golinkoff, R., 288
Golinkoff, R. M., 272, 275, 278, 288–290, 499–501
Golombok, S., 369, 372, 473–474
Gomes, R. S., 131
Gomez-Pinilla, F., 139
Goncu, A., 195
Goni, F., 122–123
Gonzales, M., 464
Gonzalez, A., 318
Gonzalez, E., 353, 354
Gonzalez, J., 341
Gonzalez, L., 48
Gonzalez, R., 370
Gonzalez-Echavarri, C., 63
Gonzalez Rey, F. L., 191, 192
Good, C., 543, 544
Good, M., 432
Goodkind, S., 374
Goodman, E., 7
Goodman, G. S., 215
Goodman, J. C., 278
Goodman, W. B., 470
Goodnight, J. A., 309
Goodnow, J. J., 191, 507
Goodvin, R., 301, 304, 335, 337
Gopinath, B., 165
Gopnik, A., 220, 235, 275
Goral, M., 285
Gorby, H. E., 233
Gorchoff, S. M., 479
Gordon, B. A., 210
Gordon, B. N., 215
Gordon, C., 341
Gordon, I., 318
Gordon, J., 391–392
Gordon, M., 566
Gordon, S., 391–392
Gormley-Fleming, L., 568
Gorrese, A., 467, 493
Gosden, R. G., 399
Goswami, U., 275
Gothe, N. P., 228
Goto, S. G., 508
Gottfried, A. E., 542
Gottlieb, G., 47, 48, 56
Gottman, J., 483
Gottman, J. M., 296, 451, 458, 495
Gottman, J. S., 451, 458
Gouin, K., 65
Gould, E., 100
Gove, W. R., 452
Govia, I. O., 384
Gowan, D. E., 566
Gozal, D., 131
Grabenhenrich, L. B., 65
Graber, J. A., 87, 88
Grace, F. M., 138–139
Gradisar, M., 106, 107

Grafman, J., 122
Graham, E. K., 89, 347, 356–357
Graham, G. M., 136
Graham, J. A., 519
Graham, J. H., 516
Graham, S., 282, 344, 546, 547
Grammas, P., 124
Grammer, J., 217
Grammer, J. K., 217
Graneheim, U. H., 577
Grant, A. M., 425
Grant, S. G. N., 93
Gratton, G., 228
Graven, S., 104
Graves, B. A., 136
Graves, C. R., 65
Gravetter, F. J., 29
Gray, D. L., 543
Gray, J., 379
Green, F. L., 236
Green, K. M., 396
Green, M. J., 108
Greenberger, E., 551
Greene, C., 465
Greene, J. D., 410
Greene, R. A., 65
Greene, S. M., 455
Greenfield, L. A., 426
Greenfield, P. M., 507–508
Greenhaus, J., 553
Greenough, W., 57
Greenwald, A. G., 378
Greer, F. R., 128
Greer, K. B., 477
Gregoire, C. A., 100
Gregorson, M., 264
Gregory, R. J., 27
Greif, M. L., 154
Griffin, I. J., 74
Griffin, P., 279
Griffin, P. W., 362, 364
Griffin, S., 14
Griffiths, J. D., 93
Grigorenko, E., 249, 262
Grivell, R. M., 61
Groh, A. M., 316, 317
Gronli, J., 103
Gronlund, N. E., 527
Gross, J. J., 304, 341, 379
Gross, M. U. M., 262
Grossi, L., 390
Grossman, I., 508
Grossman, K., 315
Grossmann, K., 317
Grossmann, T., 97
Grotevant, H., 474
Grotevant, H. D., 353, 475
Gruber, H. E., 265
Gruber, K. J., 71
Gruen, J. R., 535
Gruhn, D., 197
Grusec, J. E., 317, 411, 412, 418, 460, 463
Grych, J. H., 444
Grzywacz, J. G., 554
Gu, X., 124

Guan, S., 511
Guarente, L., 134
Guariglia, C., 218
Guay, M. C., 214
Gudmundson, J. A., 300
Guerra, N. G., 491
Guevara-Lopez, U., 570
Guilford, J. P., 263
Guimard-Brunault, M., 160
Guiney, H., 228
Guirado, G. N., 139
Gulgoz, S., 218
Gump, B., 503
Gunderson, E. A., 378
Gunnar, M. R., 27, 166, 296, 318, 466
Gunning, T. G., 499
Gunstad, J., 139
Guo, Q., 569
Gupta, S., 447, 448
Gur, R. C., 377
Gurd, B. J., 136
Gururaj, G., 119
Gurwitch, R. H., 303
Gustafsson, J-E., 250
Gutchess, A. H., 231
Guthery, A. M., 537
Gutmann, D. L., 383
Guttentag, C. L., 397, 444
Guttmannova, K., 141
Guyer, A. E., 307

Haase, R. F., 510
Habermas, T., 351
Hadani, H., 223
Haden, C. A., 214–215, 217
Hadfield, J. C., 478
Hadjimattheou, A., 247
Hagestad, G. O., 478
Hagman, J. O., 133
Hagopian, W., 128
Hahn, E. A., 347
Haidt, J., 410
Haier, R. J., 247, 248
Hakuta, K., 283–284
Hale, L., 511
Hale, N., 69
Hale, S., 205–206
Hale, W. J., 342
Haley, M. H., 34, 283
Hall, C. B., 231
Hall, C. M., 370
Hall, D. T., 554
Hall, G. S., 303
Hall, J. A., 357, 379
Hall, J. R., 124
Hall, S. S., 51
Hall, W. J., 110
Hallahan, D. P., 260, 538, 539
Halonen, J. A., 533–534
Halperin, J. M., 537
Halpern, D. F., 374, 377–378
Halpern, G. T., 324
Halpern-Felsher, B. L., 394
Halpern-Meekin, S., 397
Halpin, K. S., 164
Halt, K., 59
Haltigan, J. D., 316, 317

Hambrick, D. Z., 233
Hamilton, J. L., 88
Hamilton, M. A., 552
Hamilton, S. F., 552
Hamilton-Giachritsis, C., 465
Hamlin, J. K., 181, 423
Hamman, D., 340–341
Hammes, B. J., 568
Hammond, R., 427, 428
Hampel, H., 124
Hampl, S., 131
Hampson, S. E., 356–357, 362
Han, J. J., 215
Han, K. S., 137, 506
Han, W-J., 470
Hanger, D. P., 123
Hanish, L. D., 491
Hannah, D. G., 72
Hannon, E. E., 28
Hannon, E. H., 157, 161, 167, 168, 181, 190, 221
Hans, J., 455
Hansson, R., 571, 573
Hantman, S., 425
Haran, C., 77
Hardaway, C. R., 7–9, 445, 514, 518, 519
Hardcastle, A. C., 122
Harden, K. P., 88
Hardt, J., 574
Hardy, M., 557
Hardy, S. A., 415
Harel, J., 300
Harkins, S. W., 166
Harkness, S., 150, 317
Harlow, H. F., 313–314
Harmon, O. R., 421
Harms, P., 357
Harold, G. T., 444
Harpalani, V., 354
Harper, K. M., 64–65
Harrell, R., 557
Harrington, B. C., 133
Harris, G., 479
Harris, J., 275, 278
Harris, K. R., 282
Harris, P. L., 162, 235, 237
Harris, R. A., 496–497
Harris, Y. R., 519
Harrison, K., 113, 568
Harrist, A. W., 444
Hart, B., 250, 279
Hart, C. H., 461, 529
Hart, D., 336, 415, 420
Hart, S., 298, 299
Harter, S., 236, 335–340, 342–345, 542
Hartman, S., 311, 444
Hartshorne, H., 412, 415, 421
Hartup, W. W., 488, 490, 495
Harvey, T., 248
Hasher, L., 13, 218, 227, 228
Hashim, H. A., 137
Hashim, N. A., 127
Hasin, D. S., 453
Haslam, C., 434
Haslam, S. A., 434
Hassan, B., 327

Hassija, C. M., 390
Hasson, F., 569
Hastings, P. D., 473
Hastings-Tolsma, M., 67
Hattery, A. J., 518
Hatton, H., 488
Hatzenbuehler, M. L., 453, 574
Hatzfeld, J. J., 520
Haugrud, N., 286
Havighurst, R. J., 504
Hawi, Z., 47
Hawken, L. S., 282
Hawkes, C., 166
Hawking, S. J., 227
Hawkley, L. C., 505
Hawley, J. A., 89
Haworth, C. M. A., 57
Hay, C., 486
Hayashino, D., 519
Haydon, A., 324
Haydon, A. A., 393
Haydon, K. C., 325
Hayflick, L., 112, 113, 117
Hayslip, B., 571, 573
Hayutin, A., 556
Hayward, R. D., 435, 437
Hazan, C., 324–326
He, C., 164
He, K., 47
He, W., 74
Healey, M. K., 217, 228
Heard, E., 505
Heath, S. M., 279–280
Heaton, P., 160
Heberle, A. E., 515
Hecht, M. A., 379
Hegele, R. A., 47
Heiman, G. W., 28
Heimann, M., 208, 312
Hein, D., 465
Heine-Cohen, E., 453
Heir, T., 581
Heisel, M. J., 575
Heit, P., 121
Helles, A., 538
Helman, R., 557, 558
Helmuth, L., 13
Helson, R., 353, 361, 363, 366, 479
Hemmy, L. S., 102
Henagan, T. M., 48
Henderson, J., 71
Henderson, V. W., 399
Hendren, R. L., 237
Hendrick, J., 528
Hendricks-Munoz, K. D., 75
Heninger, M., 575
Henkens, K., 558
Henneberger, A. K., 428
Hennessey, B., 264, 265
Hennessey, B. A., 265
Henninger, D. E., 228
Henretta, J. C., 452
Henricks, T. S., 499
Henriquez, A., 456
Henry, W., 504
Hensel, D. J., 395

Juang, L. P., 354, 469
Juarez, C. A., 465
Judas, M., 61
Judd, F. K., 399
Jung, C., 11
Jung, W. P., 155
Jungert, T., 491
Jurkowski, J. M., 131
Jusczyk, P. W., 164
Jutengren, G., 491

Kadlecova, P., 30
Kadosh, K. C., 490, 496–497
Kaffashi, F., 75
Kagan, J., 91, 295, 298–300, 307–309, 317, 332
Kagan, S., 91
Kahana, B., 505
Kahana, E., 505
Kahn, R. L., 505
Kahrs, B. A., 155
Kahwati, L. C., 132
Kail, R. V., 206
Kaiser, L. L., 131
Kalak, N., 137
Kale Monk, J., 120
Kalish, C. W., 277
Kalish, R. A., 573, 576, 579
Kalmijn, M., 558
Kalomiris, A. E., 296
Kalousova, L., 554
Kaloustian, G., 318
Kamii, C., 189
Kamiya, M., 124
Kan, M. L., 458
Kan, P. F., 278
Kancherla, V., 63, 67
Kandler, C., 15
Kang, C. B., 137, 506
Kang, D. H., 505
Kang, H. K., 70–71
Kang, J. H., 435
Kang, J. Y., 284
Kann, L., 132, 393–395, 573
Kanoy, K., 463
Kantowitz, B. H., 29
Kao, T. A., 519
Kaplan, D. L., 394
Kappeler, E. M., 396
Kappes, C., 304
Karabulut, E., 559
Karantzas, G. C., 327
Karasik, L. B., 150–151
Karel, M. J., 347
Karelitz, T. M., 258
Karlamangia, A. S., 126
Karlsson, P., 5
Karmel, M. P., 336
Karmiloff-Smith, A., 93
Karnes, F. A., 262
Karney, B. R., 450
Karr, C., 536
Karreman, A., 464
Karsenti, T., 543
Kashdan, T. B., 425
Kask, K., 100
Kasmark, A. M., 351
Kastbom, A. A., 394

Kastenbaum, 586
Kastenbaum, R. J., 565, 566, 572, 576, 577
Kaszniak, A. W., 305
Kato, T., 330
Katsumi, Y., 305
Katz, L., 530
Katz, P. R., 126
Katzel, L. I., 138
Kauffman, J. M., 538, 539
Kaufman, J. C., 264–265
Kaufman, P., 263
Kaufmann, J. M., 260
Kaur, A., 51–52
Kaur, M., 399
Kavanaugh, R. D., 237
Kavsek, M., 208
Kawabata, Y., 378
Kawachi, I., 445
Kawagoe, T., 217
Kawai, M., 208
Kawamoto, K., 9
Kawas, C. H., 135
Kaynak, O., 459
Kazanis, I., 100
Keage, H. A., 108
Kearney, P. M., 65
Kearsley, R. B., 300
Keating, D. P., 196, 226, 227
Keen, R., 147, 154, 155, 160, 162
Keevern, E., 568
Kehle, T. J., 243
Keigher, S., 436
Keijsers, L., 459–460
Keith, J. D., 432
Kelber, S. T., 579
Kell, H. J., 261, 262
Kelleher, C. J., 72
Keller, H., 315
Keller, M., 492
Kelley, A. S., 570
Kelley, J., 139
Kellman, P. J., 161
Kelly, A. J., 219
Kelly, D. J., 160
Kelly, E. L., 557
Kelly, G. F., 390
Kelly, J., 454, 473
Kelly, J. P., 160
Kelly, J. R., 503
Kelly, Y., 65
Keltner, K. W., 549
Kemp, H., 163
Kempe, A., 119
Kempermann, G., 101
Kempner, S. G., 549
Kendler, K. S., 54
Kendrick, C., 477
Kendrick, K., 491
Kenko, Y., 295
Kennedy, K. M., 4, 27, 100, 219
Kennedy, P., 421
Kennedy, R., 457
Kennedy-Bergen, R. M., 7, 518
Kennell, H. H., 75

Kennell, J. H., 75
Kenney, R., 215
Kennis, E., 138
Kennison, R. F., 228–229
Kenny, A. M., 91
Kenny, R. A., 401
Kenny, S., 161
Kenyon, C., 49
Kerig, P. K., 323, 467
Kernis, M. H., 342
Kerns, K., 21, 190, 237
Kerns, K. A., 295, 322
Kerpelman, J. L., 354
Kershaw, K. N., 360
Kershaw, T. S., 396
Kessler, R., 360
Ketcham, C. J., 153
Kevorkian, J., 569
Keyes, C. L., 359
Keyes, K. M., 106, 453
Keyser, J., 460
Khairullah, A., 87
Khan, M. R., 142
Khera, M., 400
Khmelkov, V., 420
Khosia, S., 89
Khuc, K., 128
Khurana, A., 395
Khurana, S., 144
Kiang, L., 355
Kidd, C., 207
Kiecolt-Glaser, J. K., 125, 126
Kiel, E. J., 296
Kiess, W., 85
Kigar, D. L., 248
Kilbane, C. R., 526
Kilic, S., 65
Killen, M., 410, 416–417, 487
Kim, E., 400
Kim, E. M., 549
Kim, E. S., 358, 574
Kim, H. J., 126, 234
Kim, J., 435, 465, 558
Kim, J. M., 374
Kim, K., 10
Kim, K. H., 264
Kim, M. J., 491–492
Kim, O. M., 474
Kim, P., 8, 515, 516
Kim, S., 227, 316, 317
Kim, S. H., 581, 582
Kimble, M., 390
Kim-Fuchs, C., 126
King, A. P., 288
King, L. A., 341, 387
King, P. E., 431–433
King, V., 448
Kingston, E. R., 520
Kingstone, A., 510
Kins, E., 12
Kirby, D. B., 398
Kirchmaier, E., 110
Kirk, S. A., 538
Kirkegaard, E. O. W., 247
Kirkham, N. Z., 167
Kirkorian, H. L., 160, 511
Kirk-Sanchez, N. J., 139, 230, 231

Kisilevsky, B. S., 164
Kissoon, N., 465
Kitayama, S., 339, 340
Kitsantas, A., 545
Kitsantas, P., 105
Kiuhara, S. A., 282
Kivimaki, M., 114
Kiyak, H. A., 9, 578
Klahr, A. M., 54
Klatt, J., 424–425
Klauda, S. L., 545
Klaus, M., 75
Kleiman, E. M., 343
Klein, M. S., 141
Klein, S., 374
Kliegman, R. M., 84, 150
Klima, C., 69
Klimstra, T. A., 352
Kline, D. W., 163
Klinenberg, E., 446, 447
Kling, K. C., 344
Klohnen, E. C., 363
Knafo, A., 411, 414, 424
Knafo-Noam, A., 444
Knight, B. G., 559
Knight, C. P., 354–355
Knight, L. F., 387
Knox, M., 462, 463
Knuesel, I., 123
Knussmann, R., 385
Ko, S. H., 77
Ko, Y. L., 78
Kobak, R. R., 323, 467, 487
Kober, C., 351
Koch, C. A., 400
Kochanek, K. D., 121
Kochanska, G., 316, 317, 413, 418
Kocur, J. L., 466
Koeblinger, C., 62
Koenig, H. G., 431, 435, 436–437
Koenig, J. L., 413
Koenig, L. B., 432
Koestner, R., 542
Koh, H., 396, 398
Kohen, D. E., 539
Kohl, P. L., 466
Kohlberg, L., 406, 407–411, 415, 417, 418, 420, 422, 423, 438
Kohler, P. K., 398
Kohon, J., 517
Kok, R., 222
Kokkevi, A., 574
Kokotas, H., 163
Kolarz, C. M., 304
Kolialexi, A., 63
Kolkman, M. E., 214
Kollins, S. H., 536
Kolovou, G., 113
Kolter, J. D., 398
Komter, A. E., 481
Kong, A., 68, 129
Kong, L., 249
Konrath, S. H., 326
Koo, Y. J., 68
Koolhof, R., 429
Koolschijn, P. C., 86

Koorevaar, A. M., 357
Kopp, C. B., 300, 346
Kopp, F., 208
Koppel, J., 218
Koppelman, K., 539
Koppelman, K. L., 7
Koren, G., 63
Kornblum, J., 512
Koropeckyj-Cox, T., 505
Korosi, A., 100
Korte, J., 341
Korten, N. C., 230
Kosinski, M., 583
Koss, K. J., 471
Kostelnik, M. J., 499, 528
Kostovic, I., 61
Kotecki, J., 9, 131
Kotovsky, L., 180
Kotre, J., 361
Koulouglioti, C., 106
Kouros, C. D., 106, 471
Kowalski, R. M., 491, 492
Koziel, J. E., 113
Kozloski, M., 110
Kozol, J., 540
Kraft, J. M., 398
Krafft, C. E., 136
Krahe, B., 378
Krajnik, M., 383
Krakoff, L. R., 91
Kramer, A. F., 206, 211, 233
Kramer, C. K., 91
Kramer, L., 476
Kramer, M. R., 130, 131
Kramer-Albers, E. M., 93
Krampe, R., 261
Kranz, E., 359
Krause, N., 435–437
Krause, N., 437, 435
Kraybill, J. H., 94
Kreager, D. A., 395, 486
Krebs, C., 390
Kremen, W. S., 217
Kretch, K. S., 147, 149, 157, 159, 162, 170
Krettenauer, T., 419
Kreutzer, M. A., 235
Kriemler, S., 136
Kring, A. M., 379
Kristensen, P., 581
Kristjansson, A. L., 107
Kristjuhan, U., 229
Kroesbergen, E. H., 214
Kroger, J., 350–351
Kroger, J., 353, 432
Kronenberger, W. G., 536
Kroonenberg, P. M., 315–316
Krous, H. F., 105
Krowitz, A., 162
Krstic, D., 123
Krueger, P. M., 517
Kruger, J., 134
Kruger, N. N., 43
Kruse, A., 477
Krushkal, J., 54
Kubicek, B., 558
Kübler-Ross, E., 576–577, 587
Kuchel, G. A., 91

Luong, G., 16, 480, 481
Luptak, M., 580
Luque-Contreras, D., 123
Luria, A., 372
Lusby, C. M., 94
Lushington, K., 104, 106
Lussier, C. M., 214
Lustig, C., 218, 285
Luszcz, M., 228
Luszczynska, A., 360
Luthar, S. S., 515
Lutkenhaus, P., 336
Luyckx, K., 351, 352
Luyster, F. S., 108
Lyberg, A., 69
Lykken, D. T., 344
Lynch, A., 9, 131
Lynch, E., 74
Lynch, M. E., 381
Lynch, S. M., 508
Lyndaker, C., 399
Lyon, G. J., 47
Lyon, G. R., 535
Lyon, T. D., 234
Lyons, D. M., 100
Lyons, H., 398
Lyons, J. L., 478
Lyons, K. E., 222, 223
Lyons, M., 538
Lyubomirsky, S., 457
Lyyra, A. L., 141

Ma, J. K., 136
Ma, Y., 48
Ma, Y-Y., 262
Macari, S., 221
Maccallum, F., 580
Maccalum, F., 579
Maccoby, E. E., 372, 443, 461, 462, 493, 496
MacDougall, B. J., 567
MacFarlan, S. J., 319
MacFarlane, I. W., 255
MacFarlane, J. A., 166
Machado, B., 132
Machado, L., 228
Machielse, A., 10
Maciejewski, P. K., 580
Maciokas, J. B., 211
Mack, W. J., 399
Mackin, R. S., 230
MacLean, P. C., 312
Macleod, A. D., 568
Macneil, L. G., 91
MacWhinney, B., 271
Macy, M. L., 119
Madden, D. J., 101, 211, 218, 228
Maddow-Zimet, I., 398
Mader, S. S., 16, 43, 48
Madill, A., 26
Madkour, A. S., 394
Madrid, J. A., 114
Maercker, A., 581
Maffei, L., 92
Magdon-Maksymowicz, M. S., 16
Magee, C. A., 495

Magennis, R., 557
Mageo, J., 315
Maggs, J. L., 108
Magno, C., 234, 237
Magnuson, K., 7–9, 251, 445, 514, 539
Maguire, E. A., 213
Mahdi, F., 113
Mahn, H., 21, 192, 195, 526
Mahncke, H. W., 206
Mahoney, J. L., 503, 532
Mahy, C. E., 235
Makel, M. C., 250
Maksymowicz, A. Z., 16
Malamitsi-Puchner, A., 396, 397
Malcolm, K. T., 357
Malik, R., 47
Malinger, G., 62
Mallet, E., 105
Malloy, L. C., 215
Malmstrom, F. V., 421
Malouff, J. M., 247
Malti, T., 413, 414, 419, 424
Mandal, S., 50
Mandelbrot, L., 59
Mandell, A. R., 218
Mandler, J. M., 182, 213, 220, 221, 240
Manenti, R., 230
Mangels, J. A., 543
Mangewala, V., 571
Manhart, L. E., 398
Mann, N., 166
Mannell, R. C., 503
Manning, W. D., 447
Manore, M., 120, 130, 134, 137
Mansvelt, J., 505
Manthos, M., 398
Manuck, S. B., 56–57
Maramara, L. A., 74
Maras, D., 511
Marcdante, K., 84, 150
Marchetti, D., 65
Marchman, V. A., 279
Marcia, J. E., 351–353, 366, 415
Marecek, J., 456
Marek, S. A., 92
Mares, M. L., 510
Margolis, A., 248
Margraf, J., 536
Margran, T. H., 166
Marinova, P., 327
Marioni, R. E., 249
Markant, J. C., 97
Markham, C. M., 394, 395
Markman, E. M., 275, 278
Markman, H. J., 448, 451–452
Markowitsch, H. J., 228
Marks, A. K., 7, 519–520
Marks, N. F., 426
Markus, H., 341
Markus, H. R., 339, 340
Marottoli, R. A., 210
Marques, L., 580
Marquet, R. L., 569

Marrero, M. D., 460
Marshall, C., 129
Marshall, P. J., 182
Marshall, S. L., 343
Martin, A., 210
Martin, C. L., 372, 374, 376, 381
Martin, J. A., 70, 72, 74, 396, 461
Martin, L. R., 15, 362
Martin, P., 111, 347
Martinelli, M., 166
Martinez, Y. A., 489
Martin-Storey, A., 387
Martinussen, M., 353
Marx, A. M., 537
Mary, A., 536
Masaki, S., 566
Masapollo, M., 274
Mascalo, M. F., 197
Mascolo, M. F., 335
Mash, E. J., 302, 426, 537
Mashburn, A. J., 289
Mason, K. A., 46
Mason, M. J., 487, 495
Massad, E., 248
Masten, A. S., 8, 222, 302, 303, 445, 487
Master, A., 544
Mastergeorge, A. M., 529
Masters, C., 327
Masters, N. T., 385
Mastroeni, D., 114
Mata, J., 217
Mate, I., 114
Mateus, C., 163
Mather, M., 498
Mather, R., 122–123
Mathes, W. F., 134
Matias, M., 555
Matlin, M. W., 375, 382
Matlow, J. N., 59
Matos, A. P., 510
Matsuba, M. K., 415, 416, 420
Matsumoto, D., 507
Matthews, C. E., 138
Matthews, K., 503
Matthiessen, C., 131
Mattison, J. A., 134
Mattson, M. P., 108
Mattson, S. N., 64–65
Maurer, D., 168
Mauss, I. B., 296
Maxson, S. C., 54
May, M., 412
May, M. S., 415, 421
Mayas, J., 210, 232
Mayer, J. D., 247
Mayer, K. D., 66
Mayer, R. E., 282
Mayes, A., 237
Mayeux, L., 490
Maynard, M., 4
Mayton, M. R., 537, 538
McAbee, S. T., 357
McAdams, D. P., 351, 353, 361
McAdams, T. A., 142

McAlister, A. R., 237
McAvoy, M., 93
McBride, D. L., 87
McBride-Chang, C., 280
McBride Murry, V., 194–195
McCabe, F., 78
McCaffery, J. M., 56–57
McCall, R. B., 255
McCardle, P., 280
McCartney, K., 8, 9, 322
McClain, C. S., 577
McClelland, A., 5, 540
McClelland, M. M., 345
McClelland, S. I., 392
McCombs, B. L., 526
McCormack, S. E., 136
McCormick, C. B., 224, 234, 281, 282
McCourt, S. N., 426, 429
McCoy, D. C., 301–302
McCrae, R. R., 356, 357, 359, 361, 366
McCullough, B. M., 513
McCullough, M. E., 434, 577
McDaniel, M. A., 219
McDermott, B., 302
McDermott, J. M., 474
McDonald, J., 512
McDonald, K. L., 490
McDonough, L., 220
McDougall, S., 513
McDowell, D. J., 487
McDowell, M. A., 503
McDuffie, A., 51
McElhaney, K. B., 467
McEwen, B. S., 98, 114
McGarry, J., 78
McGarvey, C., 105
McGee, H., 568
McGee, K., 539
McGinley, M., 418, 419
McGough, E. L., 139, 230, 231
McGrath, S. K., 75
McGue, M., 344, 432
McGuffin, P., 47
McHale, J. P., 464
McHale, S., 470
McHale, S. M., 372, 464, 467, 476
McIlfatrick, S., 569
McInnis, C. M., 48
McKain, W. C., 456
McKay, A. S., 265
McKee, K. J., 10
McKenna, K. Y. A., 328
McKenzie, B. E., 161
McKiernan, F., 582
McKinney, E. S., 67
McLaughlin, K., 570
McLaughlin, K. A., 94
McLean, I. A., 390
McLean, K. C., 344, 351, 354
McLellan, J. A., 433
McLeod, G. F., 6, 470
McLoyd, V. C., 7–9, 445, 514, 516–519
McIsaac, C., 323, 324
McMahon, C. G., 400

McMahon, D. M., 61
McMahon, M., 84
McMillan, C. T., 122
McMillan, J. H., 526, 527
McNamara, M., 399
McNeill, K. L., 224
McNicholas, C., 378
McNicholas, F., 74
McNulty, J. K., 326, 390
McSwain, P., 15
McWilliams, L. A., 326
McWilliams, S., 381
Mead, M., 445, 446
Meade, C. S., 396
Mechakra-Tahiri, S. D., 583
Meece, J. L., 547
Meece, J. R., 345
Meeks, L., 121
Meeks, S., 573, 583
Meerlo, P., 77
Meert, K. L., 581
Meeus, W., 421
Meffert, C., 569
Mehta, C. M., 372
Mehta, J. S., 162
Meisel, V., 537
Melancon, M. O., 108
Meldrum, R. C., 486
Meléndez, J. C., 341–342
Melendez-Moral, J. C., 341
Melhuish, E., 322
Melia, K. M., 570
Mella, N., 214
Melnyk, L., 215
Meltzoff, A. N., 208–209, 378, 511
Ménard, L., 274
Menchola, M., 305
Mendes, A., 580
Mendes, W. B., 296
Mendle, J., 88
Mendler, M., 49
Mendoza, N., 399
Menec, V. H., 504
Meng, N. H., 89
Meng, X., 505
Menn, L., 159
Mennella, J. A., 166
Menon, R., 59, 62
Menyuk, P., 275
Merad, M., 100
Meraz-Rios, M. A., 123
Mercer, N., 193
Meredith, N. V., 84
Merrill, D. A., 257
Merrill, D. M., 481
Mess, F., 131
Messersmith, E. E., 551
Messiah, S. E., 66
Messinger, D., 299
Messinger, J. C., 385
Mestre, T. A., 126
Metcalf, C. J., 113
Metha, A., 526
Metts, S., 329
Metz, E. C., 421
Meyer, A. M., 286
Meyer, M. H., 384

Meyer, S., 418, 419
Meyer, U., 136
Mezzacappa, E., 346
Michael, R. T., 386, 387, 400
Michaels, S., 456
Miche, M., 498, 506
Mickelson, K. D., 458
Midouhas, E., 346
Miga, E. M., 323, 467
Mikami, A. Y., 513
Mike, A., 357
Mikels, J. A., 498
Mikulincer, M., 16, 326
Milani, H. J., 62
Milesi, G., 62
Milgrom, J., 78
Miller, A. B., 466
Miller, B. C., 395
Miller, C., 9, 517
Miller, C. F., 376
Miller, E. B., 529
Miller, E. M., 544
Miller, J. B., 382
Miller, J. G., 410
Miller, J. W., 163
Miller, K. E., 390
Miller, L. M., 471, 513
Miller, M. A., 108
Miller, P. H., 19, 21, 190, 205, 214, 215
Miller, R., 57
Miller, R. L., 63
Miller, S., 120, 215, 429
Miller-Perrin, C. L., 466
Mills, C., 209, 337, 339
Mills, C. M., 337
Mills, D., 209
Mills, K., 95, 97–98
Mills-Koonce, W. R., 300
Milman, N. B., 526
Milne, E., 68
Milner, A., 554
Milte, C. M., 9
Miner, J. L., 320, 470, 472
Miner, M., 400
Miner, M. M., 400
Ming, X., 74
Miniussi, C., 230
Minkler, M., 478–479
Minnes, S., 65–66
Minsart, A. F., 67
Mintz, S. L., 526
Minuchin, P. O., 540
Mioni, G., 219
Mirarchi, F. L., 568
Mireault, G. C., 313
Mireles-Rios, R., 467
Mirkovic, B., 574
Mirvis, P. H., 554
Misailidi, P., 247
Mischel, H., 412
Mischel, W., 206, 221, 358, 412, 415
Mishra, G. D., 399
Miskovsky, M. J., 121
Mistry, J., 445, 507
Mistry, R. S., 7–8, 514, 516
Mitchell, A. B., 374

Mitchell, A. J., 75
Mitchell, D., 390
Mitchell, E. A., 105
Mitchell, J. R., 134
Mitchell, K. J., 392
Mitchell, M. B., 111, 233, 511
Mitchell, S., 568
Mitchell, W., 321
Miyagawa, S., 286–287
Miyake, K., 315
Miyakoshi, K., 72
Mize, K. D., 298, 308
Mizokami, S., 508
Mlczoch, E., 62
Mock, S. E., 387
Modecki, K. L., 492
Modry-Mandell, K., 519
Moed, A., 467
Moen, P., 550, 555, 557–559
Mohamed, Z., 47, 133
Moilanen, J. M., 399–400
Moise, K. J., 63
Molina, B. S., 536, 537
Molina, K. M., 445
Mollenkopf, H., 153
Moller, J., 582
Molnar, Z., 100
Molton, I. R., 166
Momtaz, Y. A., 436
Monahan, K., 97–99
Monette, S., 214
Money, J., 370
Moninger, J., 131
Monserud, M. A., 482
Montagna, P., 105
Montano, Z., 128
Monteiro, M., 570
Montemayor, R., 469
Montessori, M., 528
Montgomery, P., 398
Monti, J. M., 136
Montirosso, R., 312
Moon, R. Y., 105, 571
Moore, B. S., 221
Moore, D., 47, 48, 50, 56, 57, 324, 444, 570
Moore, G. E., 50
Moore, M., 106, 225
Moore, M. W., 93
Moore, S. R., 88
Morales Hope, D. A., 387
Moran, G., 316
Morasch, K. C., 94, 295
Moravcik, E., 528
Morean, M. E., 141
Morgentaler, A., 400
Morison, V., 158, 159
Morita, T., 566
Morokuma, S., 164
Morris, A., 166, 303, 461
Morris, A. S., 308, 413, 414, 419, 420, 423–425
Morris, P., 23, 24, 443, 445
Morris, R. G., 491
Morris, R. J., 302
Morris, Y. P., 302
Morrison, D. M., 386

Morrison, G. S., 6, 499, 528, 530
Morrison, R. S., 570
Morrissey, S. L., 574
Morrissey, T. W., 320
Morrow-Howell, N., 138, 425
Mortell, S., 581
Mortensen, O., 458
Moses, L. J., 221, 235
Mosher, W. D., 447, 448, 453
Moss, P., 107
Moulson, M. C., 94
Moulton, D., 70
Moyer, A., 448
Moyer, M. W., 135
Mozart, W. A., 265
Mparmpakas, D., 67
Mrkva, K., 410
Mroczek, B., 401
Mroczek, D., 304, 361, 362, 364
Mruk, C. J., 345
Mu, Y., 549
Mulatu, S., 229
Mullally, S. L., 213
Muller, L., 114
Muller, M. M., 211
Muller, U., 21, 190, 221, 237, 337
Muller, W. E., 114
Mullis, P., 85
Mullola, S., 373
Mundy, P., 288
Mungas, D., 122–123
Munnell, A. H., 557
Murachver, T., 382
Murase, T., 289
Murdock, T. B., 421
Murphy, D. A., 428
Murphy, M. C., 543
Murphy, R. A., 91, 153
Murphy, S. L., 121
Murr, J., 124
Murray, L., 319
Murray, S. S., 67
Murry, V. M., 7, 9, 354, 445, 515, 518, 519–520, 540
Murzyn, T., 415
Musameh, M. D., 50
Mussen, P. H., 121
Mutchler, J. E., 505
Muthusamy, V. R., 113
Myer, G. D., 136
Myers, D. G., 58, 210, 434
Myerson, J., 253

Nabe-Nielsen, K., 555
Nader, P. R., 136–137
Nadimpalli, S. B., 520
Nadler, M., 122
Nagamatsu, L. S., 137, 139, 506
Nagel, B. J., 536
Nagy, M., 572
Nahapetyan, L., 378
Nair-Collins, M., 567
Najman, J. M., 427–428, 539
Nakajima, S., 581

Nansel, T. R., 491
Narayan, A., 471
Narayan, A. J., 303
Narayan, K. M., 130, 131
Nardone, R., 122
Narváez, D., 95–96, 410, 411, 414, 415, 419, 420, 422
Nascimento Dda, C., 138
Nash, J. M., 97
Nass, C., 509
Nathan, R., 282
Nathanson, C., 421
Natsuaki, M. N., 88
Neal, A. R., 537
Neal, J. W., 495
Neal, Z. P., 495
Nechita, A., 261
Needham, A., 154, 155
Neff, L. A., 449
Negriff, S., 88
Neikrug, A. B., 108
Neisser, U., 249
Neitzel, C., 444
Nelson, C., 100
Nelson, C. A., 61, 92, 94, 95–96, 98, 181, 213
Nelson, D. A., 378–379
Nelson, J. A., 301
Nelson, K., 215
Nelson, L. J., 480
Nelson, S. D., 302
Nelson, S. E., 141
Nelson, S. K., 457
Nesbit, J. C., 346
Neugarten, B. L., 478, 504
Neukam, K. A., 558
Neumann, D. L., 378
Neuner, F., 465
Neupert, S. D., 15
Nevarez, M. D., 104
Nevill, S., 552
Neville, C., 125
Neville, H. J., 282
Nevo, E., 214
Newell, K., 154
Newman, E., 302
Newman, H., 431
Newport, E. L., 282
Newsom, R. S., 580
Newton, E. K., 423
Newton, I., 260
Newton, N. J., 361, 478
Ng, F. F., 549
Ng, S. Y., 128
Nguyen, S. P., 376
Nho, K., 47
Nicholson, J., 364
Nickalls, S., 328
Nickel, L. B., 356
Nicolaisen, M., 455, 505
Nicoteri, J. A., 121
Nieboer, A. P., 505
Niehuis, S., 452
Nielsen, L., 347
Nielsen, M. B., 391
Nieto, A. M., 445
Nikitin, J., 347, 348, 506
Nikmat, A. W., 127

Nikulina, V., 516
Nilsson, J., 217
Nimrod, G., 348
Ning, L. F., 538
Ninio, A., 487
Nisbett, R., 252
Nisbett, R. E., 250, 253
Nishina, A., 88
Nitko, A. J., 527
Niwa, A., 100
Nixon, S. A., 398
Noack, M. G., 556
Noam, G. G., 493
Noble, W., 123
Noddings, N., 420
Nodine, P. M., 67
Noel-Miller, C. M., 448
Noftle, E. E., 362
Noguchi, H., 100–101
Nogueira, M., 537
Nola, M., 424
Nolan, V. G., 113
Nolen-Hoeksema, S., 303, 379
Nolte, S., 528
Nomi, J. S., 538
Nordeng, H., 63
Nordone, Y., 61
Norman, K., 187
Norris, A. E., 493–494
North, M. S., 504
Northrup, J., 567
Nosraty, L., 506
Nottelmann, E. D., 87
Nouchi, R., 233, 513
Nucci, L., 419, 420
Nugent, C. N., 554
Nurius, P., 339
Nutter, E., 72
Nyberg, L., 217, 233
Nye, C. D., 364
Nygard, C-H., 555

Oakes, L. M., 159
Oakley, G. P., 63, 67
Oates, G., 229
Oates, J., 71
Obermann, M. L., 492
Obermeyer, C. M., 90
Obler, L. K., 285, 286
O'Brien, E. J., 342, 345
O'Brien, J. L., 206
O'Brien, M., 470
O'Callaghan, F. V., 106
O'Conner, E. E., 316
O'Connor, M. F., 580
O'Dell, C., 111
Odom, S., 538
O'Donnell, L., 574
Odouli, R., 105
Offer, D., 344
Ogbu, J., 253
Ogbuanu, I. U., 66
Ogden, C. L., 130, 131
O'Grady, W., 277
O'Hara, M., 465
O'Hara, M. W., 78
Ohno, Y., 126
Okada, H. C., 89

Subject Index

death system, 565–566
debriefing, 32
deception, 32
decision making
    in adolescents, 226–227
    in adults, 228
declarative memory. *See*
    explicit memory
deep brain stimulation
    (DBS), 126
dementia. *See also* Alzheimer
    disease
    Alzheimer disease as form
        of, 122–125
    explanation of, 122, 123
    Parkinson disease as form
        of, 125–126
dendrites, 93, 95, 101
denial and isolation stage of
    dying, 576
depression
    in adolescents, 396
    bullying and, 491
    in college students, 534
    physical exercise and, 139
    postpartum, 77–78
    during pregnancy, 67
    self-esteem and, 342–343
    suicide and, 574, 575
depression stage of dying, 577
depth perception
    in infants, 161–162
    in older adults, 163
descriptive research, 28
development. *See also* life-
    span development;
    physical development
    biological, cognitive, and
        socioemotional
        processes of, 10–11
    characteristics of, 3–6
    as co-construction of
        biology, culture, and
        individual, 6
    contextuality of, 5–6
    continuity-discontinuity
        issue and, 16
    evaluating issues in, 16
    explanation of, 3
    growth, maintenance, and
        regulation of loss in, 6
    as lifelong process, 4
    multidimensionality of, 4
    nature-nurture issue and,
        15–16, 167–168, 181
    periods of, 11–14
    plasticity of, 4
    processes of, 175–176
    stability-change issue
        and, 16
developmental cascade
    model, 316, 317
developmental cognitive
    neuroscience, 11, 230
developmentally appropriate
    practice (DAP), 529
developmental period, 11

developmental science, 4–5
developmental social
    neuroscience, 11, 98, 318
development psychologists, 33
development theories
    behavioral and social
        cognitive, 21–22
    cognitive, 19–21
    comparison of, 24
    eclectic theoretical
        orientation and, 24–25
    ecological, 23–24
    ethological, 22–23
    psychoanalytic, 17–19
diabetes, 128, 129
dialects, 285
dialogue, 192
diet. *See also* nutrition
    gene behavior and, 48
    during pregnancy, 66–67
dieting
    calorie restriction, 134
    eating disorders and,
        132–133
differential susceptibility
    model, 311
difficult child, 307
direct instruction approach to
    education, 526–527
disabilities. *See* children with
    disabilities
disasters, coping with, 302–303
discontinuity. *See* continuity-
    discontinuity issue
disease. *See also* specific
    diseases
    breastfeeding and, 128
    obesity and, 133
    stress and, 126
disenfranchised grief, 581
disengagement theory, 504
disequilibrium, 176
dishabituation, 158, 160, 208
divergent thinking, 263
diversity. *See* cultural
    differences
divided attention, 207, 210
divorce
    children and, 470–472
    cohabitation and, 448
    communication with
        children about, 472
    coping with, 453, 454
    in middle and late
        adulthood, 454–455
    outcomes of, 454–455
    personality and, 453
    statistics related to, 453
DNA, 46–49, 56–57
dominant genes, 50
dopamine, 126, 318, 319
doulas, 70–71
Down syndrome, 51, 259
drug counselors, 39
drug use. *See* alcohol use/
    abuse; substance use/
    abuse

dual-career couples, 554–555
dual-language approach,
    283–284
dual-process model, of decision
    making, 226–227
*Dumbing Down Our Kids:
    Why American Children
    Feel Good About
    Themselves But Can't
    Read, Write, or Add*
    (Sykes), 344
dynamic systems theory,
    147–148
dyscalculia, 535
dysgraphia, 535
dyslexia, 535

early adulthood. *See* emerging
    adulthood/early
    adulthood
early childhood. *See also*
    children; infants/
    infancy; toddlers
    attention in, 209, 210
    brain development in, 97
    emotional development
        in, 296
    emotional expression in,
        301–302
    executive function in, 221
    explanation of, 11
    height and weight in, 84–85
    language development in,
        276–280
    media use and, 511
    self-regulation in, 346
    self-understanding in,
        336–338
early childhood education
    controversy over
        curriculum in, 530
    for students who are
        disadvantaged, 529–530
    variations in, 528–529
early childhood educators,
    37–38
Early Head Start, 529
easy child, 306, 307
eating behavior. *See* nutrition
eating disorders, 132–133
eclectic theoretical
    orientation, 24–25
ecological theory, 23–24
ecological view of sensory and
    perceptive development,
    157, 167–168
ectoderm, 59
education. *See also* schools
    for adolescents, 531–533
    adult, 534
    character, 420
    child development and, 191
    for children with
        disabilities, 538–539
    cognitive functioning and,
        228–229
    cognitive moral, 420

college, 533–534
    constructivist approach to,
        526 527
    creativity and, 264–265
    direct instruction approach
        to, 526–527
    early childhood, 528–530
    elementary, 530–531
    ethnicity and, 540–541
    for gifted children, 262
    intelligence and, 250
    in life-span perspective, 6
    moral development and,
        419–422
    Piaget's theory and, 189–190
    premarital, 451–452
    sex, 397, 398
    single-sex, 374
    socioeconomic status and,
        539–540
    value of college, 533
    Vygotsky's theory in,
        193–194
educational achievement
    children of adolescent
        mothers and, 396
    cohabitation among parents
        and, 449
    delinquency and, 429
    early intervention and, 251
    ethnicity and culture and,
        546–548
    extracurricular activities
        and, 532
    extrinsic and intrinsic
        motivation and, 542, 543
    goal setting, planning and
        self-monitoring and,
        545–546
    intelligence tests and, 245
    poverty and, 517
    sleep and, 107–108
    television viewing and,
        510, 511–512
    work and, 551–552
educational psychologists,
    33, 38
Education for All
    Handicapped Children
    Act (Public Law
    94-142), 538
effortful control. *See* self-
    regulation
effortful control (self-
    regulation), 308, 348
eggs, 48
egocentrism
    in adolescents, 182, 187, 188
    in preschoolers, 182
    social awareness and,
        337, 338
ego ideal, 413
elaboration, 216
electroencephalography
    (EEG), 27–28, 75, 94
electronic media. *See* media/
    media use

elementary schools, 530–531.
    See also schools
elementary school teachers, 37
embryonic period, 59
embryos, 59, 370
emerging adulthood/early
    adulthood. *See also*
    adolescents/adolescence;
    adults; college students
    attention in, 210
    characteristics of, 12–13
    explanation of, 12
    friendship in, 497
    health in, 120–121
    identity in, 351–353
    physical development in, 88
    relationship with parents
        during, 469
    religion and, 431–432
    sexuality in, 397–398
    sleep in, 108
    substance use in, 142–143
    work and, 552
emotional abuse, 465
emotional competence, 297
emotional intelligence, 247
emotion-coaching approach,
    296–297
emotion-dismissing
    approach, 296
emotions/emotional
    expression
    in adolescents, 303–304
    in adults, 304–305
    developmental changes
        in, 302
    in early childhood,
        301–302
    explanation of, 295–296
    in infants, 298–301
    in middle and late
        childhood, 302–303
    moral development and,
        410, 412, 414–415
    peer relations and, 489
    positive and negative,
        304–305
    during pregnancy, 67
    regulation of, 295–297,
        301–302
empathy
    in children, 413–414
    explanation of, 413
    moral development and,
        413–414
    moral feeling and, 413–414
empiricists, 167
empty nest syndrome, 479–480
encoding, 204–205
endoderm, 59
English language learners
    (ELLs), 283–284
environment
    intelligence and, 250–252
    language development and,
        287–289
    obesity and, 134

environmental systems, 23, 24, 443
epigenetic view, 56–57, 112, 444
episodic memory, 126, 217–218
equality, 424
equilibration, 176
erectile dysfunction (ED), 400, 401
Erikson's psychosocial theory, 18–19, 349, 350
estradiol, 86, 87
estrogen, 90, 369, 399
ethics, in research, 31–32
ethnic bias, 32–34, 541
ethnic gloss, 32–33
ethnic identity, 354–355
ethnicity. *See also* cultural differences
  aging and, 520
  educational achievement and, 546–548
  explanation of, 7
  families and, 518–520
  gifted programs and, 262
  identity development and, 354–355
  immigration and, 518
  intelligence tests and, 252–253
  life expectancy and, 109–110
  parenting styles and, 462
  poverty and, 515
  role of older individuals and, 384
  school dropout rate and, 532
  in schools, 540–541
  sexual activity and, 394
  suicide rates and, 574, 575
ethnocentrism, 507
ethological theory, 22–23
ethology, 22
euthanasia, 568–569
evocative genotype-environment correlations, 54, 55
evolution, life-span development and, 44–45
evolutionary developmental psychology, 44
evolutionary psychology
  evaluation of, 45
  explanation of, 43
  gender in, 370–371
evolutionary theory of aging, 113
exceptional children teachers, 37
executive attention, 207, 209, 221
executive function
  in adults, 228
  in children, 221–222
  explanation of, 221, 222

exercise. *See* aerobic exercise; physical exercise
exosystem, 24, 443
expanding, 289
expectations
  educational achievement and, 546
  perceptual development and, 180–181
experimental research, 28–29
expertise, 227–228
explicit memory, 213, 217–218
extracurricular activities, 531, 532
extraversion, 357
extraversion/surgency, 307
extreme binge drinking, 142
extremely preterm infants, 74
extrinsic motivation, 542–543
eye contact, 443
eye diseases, 163
eye movement, 28
eye-tracking equipment, 159–160
eyewitness testimony, 215

Facebook, 512
face-to-face play, 312
Fagan Test of Infant Intelligence, 254–255
families. *See also* adult lifestyles; marriage; parents/parenting
  child care and influence of, 322
  child maltreatment and, 465, 466
  children in divorced, 470–472
  dual-career, 554–555
  identity formation and, 353
  moral development and, 411
  one-child, 457–458
  poverty and, 516–517
  reciprocal socialization and, 443–444
  single-parent, 515, 518–519
  sociocultural and historical influences on, 445–446
  socioeconomic variations in, 514–515
  stepfamilies, 455, 472–473
  as system, 444
  transnational, 445–446
family and consumer science educators, 38, 397
family policy, 9
family therapy, delinquency and, 428–429
fast mapping, 278
Fast Track, 429
fathers. *See also* parents/parenting
  as caregivers, 319
  gender development and, 372

in postpartum period, 78
prenatal issues related to, 68
fear, in infants, 299–300
females. *See also* gender differences
  adult education and, 534
  divorce and, 453
  emotional expression and, 380
  friendship and, 372, 496, 497
  gender development in, 380–384
  in intergenerational relationships, 481–482
  life expectancy for, 109, 110
  peer relations and, 493
  poverty among, 516–518
  puberty in, 86–88
  retirement adjustment in, 558
  in same-sex relationships, 387
  school dropout rate and, 532
  sexuality and, 385–386
femininity, 376, 383
feminization of poverty, 516–518
fertility
  female, 399
  male, 90
fertilization, 48
fetal alcohol spectrum disorders (FASD), 64–65
fetal MRI, 62
fetal period, 59–61
fetus
  brain development in, 61
  development of, 58–61
  hazards to, 63–68
  hearing in, 164
  sex of, 63
  transition to newborn, 72–73
fight or flight, 304
fine motor skills
  in adults, 155–156
  in children and adolescents, 155
  explanation of, 154
  in infants, 154–155
first habits and primary circular reactions substage (Piaget), 177
Fitting In, Standing Out (Crosnoe), 532
fluid intelligence, 199, 255–256
folic acid, 67
forgiveness, 424–425
formal operational stage (Piaget)
  abstract, idealistic, and logical thinking in, 186–187

adolescent egocentrism and, 187
  explanation of, 20, 186
fragile X syndrome, 51
free-radical theory, 113
Freud's psychoanalytical theory, 17–18
friendship. *See also* peer relations
  in adolescence, 495–497
  in adults, 497–498
  in childhood, 495
  cross-gender, 498
  in emerging adulthood, 497
  functions of, 495
  gender differences in, 372, 496–498
  identity and, 354
  intimacy in, 495
  in late adulthood, 498
  strategies to develop, 496
frontal lobes, 93, 95, 100, 248
functional magnetic resonance imaging (fMRI), 27, 230
funerals, 584–585
fuzzy trace theory, 216

games, 500–501
gametes, 48–49
gays/lesbians
  adolescent, 393
  as couples, 456
  as parents, 473–474
  sexual attitudes and behaviors of, 386
gaze following, 208
gender
  adult education and, 534
  categorization and, 221
  explanation of, 7, 369
  life expectancy and, 110, 377
  psychoanalytic theory of, 371
  social cognitive theory of, 371–372
gender bias, 32, 411
gender development
  in adolescence, 381
  in adulthood, 382–383
  aging and, 383–384
  in childhood, 380–381
  media and peers and, 372
  observations of adults and, 372
  parents and, 372
  schools and teachers and, 373–374
  socialization and, 372
gender differences. *See also* sexuality
  in adolescent autonomy-granting, 467
  autism spectrum disorders and, 537–538

biological influences on, 369–371
  body image and, 88
  care perspective and, 411
  chronic disorders and, 121, 122
  cognitive, 374, 377–378
  communication and, 382
  conscience development and, 413
  in context, 379–380
  controversy over, 379
  in divorce outcomes, 453
  emotions and, 303
  explanation of, 7
  friendship and, 372, 496–498
  in intergenerational relationships, 481–482
  juvenile delinquency and, 427
  life expectancy and, 109–110
  peer relations and, 493
  physical, 377
  physical exercise and, 137
  prosocial behavior and, 425
  school dropout rate and, 532
  self-esteem and, 343
  sexuality and, 385–386
  social influences on, 371–374
  socioemotional, 378–379
  stress and, 304
  in suicide rates, 574
  temperament and, 308
gender identity, 369
gender-intensification hypothesis, 381
gender roles
  explanation of, 369
  same-sex relationships and, 456
gender schemas, 374
gender schema theory, 374
gender stereotypes, 376
gender-typing, 369
gene-gene interaction, 50
generativity versus stagnation (Erikson), 19, 361
genes
  abnormalities linked to, 52–53
  collaborative, 47–48
  dominant, 50
  explanation of, 46–47
  heredity and, 57–58
  longevity, 49, 112
  mitosis, meiosis, and fertilization and, 48
  mutated, 49
  polygenic inheritance and, 50
  recessive, 50
  sex-linked, 50
  susceptibility, 49, 112
  variability and, 48–49
gene therapy, 126

overweight. *See also* obesity
in adolescence, 131–132
breast feeding and, 128
in childhood, 130–131
during pregnancy, 67
oxidative stress, 123
oxytocin, 318

pain, perception of,
165–166
pain cry, 299
palliative care, 570
parental leave, 319–320
parent educators, 460
parenting styles
Baumrind's, 461
child maltreatment and,
464–466
in context, 461–462
coparenting, 464
overview of, 460
punishment and, 462–463
parents/parenting. *See also*
caregivers; families
adolescent relationships
and, 466–469
adolescent substance abuse
and, 142
of adopted children, 475
adopted children and,
473–474
attachment to, 311–322,
467–469 (*See also*
attachment)
authoritarian, 461, 462
authoritative, 461
child care and influence
of, 322
child maltreatment and,
465, 466
child's temperament and,
309–310
contemporary issues related
to, 6
conversational dialogue
with, 418–419
in divorced families,
470–472
educational achievement
and, 547–549
emerging adults and, 469
emotional regulation and,
295–297
gay and lesbian, 473–474
gender development
and, 372
goodness of fit and,
310–311
identity formation and, 353
indulgent, 461
influence on children
of, 444
juvenile delinquency and,
428–429
language development and,
288–290
in life-span perspective, 6

literacy development
and, 280
as managers, 458–460
marriage satisfaction
and, 444
as monitors, 459–460
moral development and,
418–419
neglectful, 461
peer relations and, 487
proactive strategies of, 418
relationship quality and, 418
in stepfamilies, 472–473
timing of having children
and, 457–458
transition to, 458
working, 469–470
parietal lobe, 93
Parkinson disease, 125–126
passion, 329
passive euthanasia, 568, 569
passive genotype-environment
correlations, 54, 55
*The Path to Purpose: Helping
Children Find Their
Calling in Life*
(Damon), 431
pediatricians, 39
pediatric nurses, 39, 129, 130
peer pressure, 493–494
peer relations. *See also*
friendship
in adolescence, 493–496
bullying and, 491–493
contexts of, 487–488
developmental changes
and, 488–489
emotions and, 489
functions of, 486–487
gender and, 493
gender development
and, 372
identity and, 354
juvenile delinquency and,
486–487
parent-child relations
and, 487
sexual risk taking and, 395
social cognition and, 489
statuses of, 489–491
peers
explanation of, 486
health promotion and, 120
individual differences
among, 488
influences of, 486, 493–494
interactions with, 487–488
pelvic field defect, 370
penis, 370
perceived control, death and,
577–578
perception. *See also* sensory
and perceptual
development
depth, 161–162
expectations and, 180–181
explanation of, 157

in infants, 157–162
intermodal, 167
nature/nurture view and,
167–168
of occluded objects, 161
visual, 157–163
perceptual categorization, 220
perceptual constancy,
160–161
perceptual-motor coupling,
154, 169–170
performance orientation, 543
perimenopause, 399
perinatal nurses, 73
personal fable, 186, 187
personality/personality
development
in adults, 358–360
Big Five factors of,
356–357, 361
cheating and, 421
child's temperament and
adult, 309–310
explanation of, 335
life-events approach to, 360
longevity and, 362
moral, 415–416
optimism and, 357–358
stage-crisis view of,
358–360
trait theories of, 356–358
personal life investments,
348, 349
perspective taking, 338, 413
phenotype, 49
phenylketonuria (PKU), 52
phonics approach, 281
phonology
in early childhood, 276–277
explanation of, 271–272
physical abuse, 465
physical appearance
body image and, 88–89
in late adulthood, 91
in middle adulthood, 89
self-esteem and, 342
physical development
in early adulthood, 88
gender differences in, 377
in infants and children,
83–85, 136
in late adulthood, 91–92
in middle adulthood, 89–90
patterns of, 83
during puberty, 85–88
physical exercise
in adolescents, 136–137
in adults, 90, 137–138
aerobic, 91, 108, 136,
137, 400
aging and, 138–139
in children, 135–136
cognitive functioning
and, 233
disease prevention and,
138–139
gender and, 137

in late adulthood, 91
menopause and, 400
positive effects of, 136–139
physical therapists, 39
Physician Orders for Life-
Sustaining Treatment
(POLST), 568
physiological measures, for
research, 27–28
Piaget's theory of cognitive
development
concrete operational stage
of, 20, 185–186
education and, 189–190
evaluation of, 179–182,
190–191
explanation of, 19
formal operational stage of,
20, 186–187
moral thought and,
406–407
preoperational stage of,
19–20, 182–185
processes in, 175–176
sensorimotor stage in, 19,
20, 176–182
stages in, 19–20, 196
Vygotsky's theories vs., 195
pincer grip, 154
pitch, 164
Pittsburgh Youth Study, 427
pituitary gland, 86, 87
placenta, 59, 70
plasticity, 4
play
explanation of, 499
face-to-face, 312
functions of, 499
sex, 391
trends in, 501
types of, 499–501
play therapy, 499
pointing, 274
polygenic inheritance, 50
popular children, 490
positive emotions, 304–305
possible selves, 339–341
postconventional
reasoning, 409
postformal thought, 197–198
postpartum depression, 77–78
postpartum period, 77–78
poverty. *See also*
socioeconomic
status (SES)
among children, 8, 9,
119–120, 144, 515
among older adults,
517–518
children with disabilities
living in, 303
educational achievement
and, 517
education for young
children living in,
529–530
ethnicity and, 515

families and, 516–617
feminization of, 516
health and, 119–120
intelligence and, 251
overview of, 515
psychological ramifications
of, 516
statistics related to, 8, 515
practical intelligence, 246
practice play, 500
pragmatics
in early childhood, 278
explanation of, 272–273
in middle and late
childhood, 281
pragmatic thinking,
196–197
preconventional reasoning,
408–409
prefrontal cortex, 98, 100,
230, 248
pregaming, 142
pregnancy. *See also* prenatal
development
adolescent, 67–68,
396–398
depression during, 67
premarital education,
451–452
prenatal care, 68–69
prenatal development
brain and, 61, 94
conception and, 58
course of, 58–61
hazards to, 63–68
prenatal care and, 68–69
trimesters of, 60–61
prenatal diagnostic tests,
62–63
prenatal hazards
emotional states and stress
as, 67
environmental hazards
as, 68
general principles of, 63
maternal age as, 67–68
maternal diet and nutrition
and, 66–67
maternal diseases as, 66
paternal factors as, 68
prescription and
nonprescription drugs
as, 63–64
psychoactive drugs as,
64–66
teratogens as, 63
prenatal period, 11
preoperational stage of
cognitive development
(Piaget)
centration and limits of,
184–185
explanation of, 19–20, 182
intuitive thought substage
of, 183
symbolic function substage
of, 182–183

preoperational thought, 182–185
prepared childbirth, 71
preschoolers. *See* early childhood; toddlers
preschool teachers, 38
prescription drugs, 63–64. *See also* medication
pretense/symbolic play, 500
preterm infants, 74–75
primary circular reactions (Piaget), 177
primary emotions, 298
principle of persistence, 180
problem solving
  in adults, 227–228
  in children, 224–225
Project Head Start, 529–530
prolonged grief, 580
prosocial behavior
  altruism and reciprocity and, 423
  explanation of, 423
  gender and, 425
  infants and, 423
  in older adults, 425–426
  sharing and fairness and, 423–425
prospective memory, 219
proximodistal pattern, 83
psychiatrists, 38
psychoactive drugs, 64–66. *See also* substance use/abuse
psychoanalytic theories
  Erikson's theory, 18–19
  evaluation of, 19
  explanation of, 17
  Freud's theory, 17–18
  of gender, 371
  of moral development, 413
psychological age, 15
psychosocial moratorium, 350
puberty. *See also* adolescents/adolescence
  explanation of, 85
  hormonal changes during, 86–87
  psychological accompaniments of, 87–88
  sexual maturation, height, and weight in, 85
  timing and variations in, 87
punishment, 462–463

rape, 389–390
rapport talk, 382
reading skills
  gender differences in, 378
  in middle and late childhood, 281
realistic thinking, 196–197
reasoning
  conventional, 409
  hypothetical-deductive, 186

moral, 407, 410–411
postconventional, 409
preconventional, 408–409
scientific, 224
social conventional, 417
recasting, 289
recessive genes, 50
reciprocal socialization, 443–444, 462
reciprocity, 423
reflective thinking, 197
reflexes, 148–149, 176
reflexive smile, 299
regrets, 341
rehabilitation counselors, 38
rejected children, 490–491
relational aggression, 378–379
relaxation. *See* leisure activities; play
religion. *See also* spirituality
  adults and, 433–435
  children, adolescents, and young adults and, 431–432
  cognitive development and, 432
  coping and, 435, 436
  explanation of, 431
  health and, 434–435
  identity development and, 432
  marital preferences and, 450
  meaning in life and, 436, 437
  older adults and, 435–437
  sexual activity and, 393
religiousness, 431
remarried adults, 455–456
reminiscence therapy, 341–342
REM sleep, 104–105
repetition, memory and, 214
report talk, 382
research
  best time of day to conduct, 13
  bias in, 32–34
  cohort effects in, 30–31
  correlational, 28
  cross-sectional approach to, 30, 255–356
  data collection and, 25–28
  descriptive, 28
  ethical, 31–32
  experimental, 28–29
  longitudinal approach to, 30
  scientific method for, 17
researchers, 37
resilience, in children, 8
retina, 156, 163
retirement
  adjustment to, 558–559
  facts about, 556–557
  global studies of, 557–558

risk taking
  in adolescents, 99, 120
  creativity and, 263, 265
  sexual, 394–395
Ritalin, 536, 537
role-strain view, 382–383
romantic love, 327–328
romantic relationships. *See also* love
  in adolescents, 323–324
  identity and, 354
romantic scripts, 385
rooming-in hospital arrangements, 77
rooting reflex, 148

same-sex relationships. *See also* gays/lesbians
  attitudes and behaviors within, 387
  biological basis of, 387
  children with parents in, 473–474
sarcopenia, 89
satire, 284
scaffolding, 194, 444
schemas, 212, 374, 375
schema theory of memory, 212
schemes, 175
school counselors, 38
school dropout rate, 532
school psychologists, 38
school readiness, executive function and, 222
schools. *See also* education; educational achievement
  accountability in, 527–528
  constructivist approach in, 526–527
  controversy over curriculum in, 530
  creativity in, 264–265
  direct instruction approach in, 526–527
  elementary schools, 530–531
  ethnicity in, 540–541
  gender development and, 373–374
  high schools, 531–533
  middle or junior high schools, 531
  moral development and, 419–422
  students with disadvantages in, 529–530
scientific method, 17
scientific reasoning, 224
scientific thinking, 223–224
Seattle Longitudinal Study, 256–257
secondary circular reactions (Piaget), 177
secondary school teachers, 37
second-language learning, 282–284

secure attachment style, 326
securely attached children, 314, 315
selective attention, 207, 211
selective optimization with compensation theory (SOC), 347–348
self
  contradictions within, 339
  development of, 337, 338
  explanation of, 335
  fluctuating, 339
  possible, 339–341
  real and ideal, 338
self-awareness, 336
self-concept, 342
self-conceptions, 508
self-conscious emotions, 298
self-consciousness, 339
self-control, 346, 412
self-determination, 542
self-efficacy, 226, 544–545
self-esteem
  developmental changes in, 343–345
  explanation of, 342
  issues in, 342–343
  strategies to increase, 345
self-integration, 340
self-modification, 205
self-regulation
  achievement and, 345, 545
  in adulthood, 347–348
  explanation of, 345
  in infancy and early childhood, 346
  in middle/late childhood and adolescence, 346–347
self-talk, 193
self-understanding
  in adolescence, 339–340
  in adulthood, 340–342
  in early childhood, 336–338
  explanation of, 335
  in infancy, 335–336
  in middle and late childhood, 338–339
semantic memory, 218
semantics
  in early childhood, 277–278
  explanation of, 272
sensation, 156
sensitive period, 23
sensorimotor play, 500
sensorimotor stage of cognitive development (Piaget)
  A-not-B error and, 179
  evaluation of, 179–182
  explanation of, 19, 20, 176
  object permanence and, 178–179
  substages of, 176–178

sensory and perceptual development, 15–16, 167–168, 181
sensory receptors, 156
separation protest, 300, 301
seriation, 185–186
service learning, 420–421
sex education, 397, 398
sex glands, 86, 369, 370
sex hormones, 369, 370
Sex in America survey (1994), 386, 387, 400–401
sexism, 384
sex-linked chromosomal abnormalities, 51–52
sex-linked genes, 50
sexting, 392
sexual abuse, 87, 465
sexual activity
  in adolescence, 88, 393–397
  cross-cultural studies of, 396
  in emerging adulthood, 397–398
  in late adulthood, 401
  in middle adulthood, 400–401
  risk taking and, 394–395
  statistics related to, 386
sexual harassment, 390–391
sexual identity, 392–393
sexuality. *See also* gender differences
  in adolescence, 392–397
  biological factors and, 385
  in childhood, 391–392
  cultural factors and, 385–386
  in emerging adulthood, 397–398
  in late adulthood, 401
  in middle adulthood, 90, 399–401
sexually transmitted infections (STIs). *See also* HIV/AIDS
  in adolescents, 395–396
  explanation of, 387–388
  strategies to protect against, 389
  types and descriptions of, 388
sexual maturation. *See* puberty
sexual orientation, 386–387
sexual reassignment, 370
sexual scripts, 385
shape constancy, 160, 161
shared environmental experiences, 56
sharing, 419, 423
short-term memory, 213–214
sibling relationships
  in adulthood, 478
  birth order and, 477–478
  characteristics of, 476–477

tracking, 159
traditional religious
    scripts, 385
trait-situation interaction, 358
trait theories, 356–358
transactional interchanges, 443
transitions
    to becoming college
        students, 142, 533–534
    to becoming parents, 458
    from fetus to newborn,
        72–73
    to middle or junior high
        school, 531
    from school to work, 552
transitivity, 186
transnational families,
    445–446
triangular theory of
    love, 329
triarchic theory of intelligence
    (Sternberg), 246
trimesters, 60–61
triple screen test, 63
trophoblast, 59
trust versus mistrust
    (Erikson), 18, 19, 314
tuberculosis, 129

Turner syndrome, 51–52
twins, 55
twin studies, on behavioral
    similarities, 54
two-word utterances, 276

ultrasound sonography, 62
umbilical cord, 59, 70, 72
unemployment
    of college graduates, 553
    ethnicity and, 519
    retirement and, 557
    stress related to, 554
universal ethical
    principles, 409
university professors, 37
use it or lose it concept, 231

values, 430–431
values clarification, 420
verbal intelligence, 246
very preterm infants, 74
video games, 510
vision, color, 160, 163
visual acuity
    in adults, 162–163
    in infants, 157, 160
visual attention, 210

visual perception
    in adults, 162–163
    in children, 162
    in infants, 157–162, 168
visual preference method,
    158, 160
visuospatial skills,
    377–378
vitamin supplements, aging
    and, 135
vocabulary. See also
    language/language
    development; literacy
    in infants and young
        children, 275–278
    in middle and late
        childhood, 280–281
volunteerism, 423,
    425–426, 583
Vygotsky's theory of
    cognitive development
    evaluation of, 194–195
    explanation of, 20–21,
        191–192
    language and thought and,
        192–193
    Piaget's theories vs., 195
    scaffolding and, 192

teaching strategies and,
    193–194
zone of proximal
    development and, 192

walking, 149–150
waterbirth, 71–72
Wechsler Scales, 245
weight
    in early childhood, 84
    in infants, 83, 84
    in late adulthood, 91
    in middle adulthood, 89
    in middle and late
        childhood, 85
    during puberty, 85
    in puberty, 85
well-being, 6, 14
Wernicke's area,
    286, 287
whole-language approach, 281
widowhood, 582–584
wisdom, 258–259
women. See females; gender
    differences
Women's Health Initiative, 583
words, 275–276. See also
    vocabulary

work. See also careers
    in adolescence, 551–552
    in adulthood, 552–555
    cognitive functioning
        and, 229
    dual-career couples and,
        554–555
    in emerging adulthood,
        552, 553
    in late adulthood, 556
    in middle adulthood,
        555–556
    role of, 550
    transition from school to, 552
working memory, 214, 217
working parents, 469–470
work performance, intelligence
    tests and, 245
writing skills
    gender differences in, 378
    in middle and late
        childhood, 281–282

XYY syndrome, 52

zone of proximal development
    (ZPD), 192
zygote, 48, 58